LITERARY TYPES and THEMES

MAURICE B. McNAMEE
Saint Louis University

JAMES E. CRONIN
Wesleyan University

JOSEPH A. ROGERS
Saint Louis University

LITERARY TYPES and THEMES
second edition

HOLT, RINEHART AND WINSTON, INC.
*New York   Chicago   San Francisco
Atlanta   Dallas   Montreal   Toronto*

Copyright © 1971 by Holt, Rinehart and Winston, Inc.
Copyright © 1960 by Maurice B. McNamee, James E. Cronin,
and Joseph A. Rogers
All Rights Reserved
Library of Congress Catalog Card Number: 72–133046
SBN: 03–078675–4
Printed in the United States of America
1 2 3 4   074   9 8 7 6 5 4 3 2 1

PREFACE

Of the several roots that have nurtured this anthology the most important is the editors' belief that for many students the historical survey has hindered rather than helped in achieving the goal of introductory courses in literature: the development of intelligent and perceptive readers, competent cocreators of the literary experience who find in it such satisfactions that they extend the experience far beyond the introductory course. In the historical survey course some prospective readers do survive; a few even flourish. Yet the majority appear to find little relevance between Early and Middle English literature and their own lives and interests. For them the beginning often marks the end.

A more viable experience with literature for these students lies along a pathway marked by types rather than by centuries. Such an approach introduces the student, through the short story and the novel, into a world and time with which he is already reasonably familiar. Moreover, these introductions may be made in a leisurely way, for the teacher is under no compulsion to spur the student past Dryden by January and past Tennyson by May. When the student has gained a sense of confidence and critical self-sufficiency in reading a piece of literature, he can move back to the literature of earlier periods. The arrangement by type also permits him to move beyond the confines of British literature into American and Continental realms—an extended itinerary desirable in an age when the development of all the arts transcends national boundaries.

The book begins with the short story, the type that is most characteristically modern, and moves through the short novel and drama, to a selection of humorous and satirical works in both prose and poetry. The balance of the book is made up of units of narrative, lyric, and dramatic poetry.

Preceding each type, there are some provocative general essays by well-known critics on the type of literature anthologized in the unit. In addition to this, the editors themselves have written brief essays to introduce some of the technical and philosophical notions helpful for understanding the type. It was not our intention to make the individual units illustrate the development of history of the type, although in some few instances (as in some of the units of lyric poetry) the selections are arranged chronologically.

In the selection of material, we have considered theme even more important than type. We are strongly convinced that one of the most educative of all devices in teaching both the techniques and the content of literature is the juxtaposition of works that are somewhat related in theme. Literary works so studied comment on one another. It is much easier to see the specifically personal element, in both fundamental attitudes and in external form and expression, that goes into any successful literary creation, when it is closely compared with a work on a similar theme by another author. To facilitate that kind of comparative study, selections are grouped thematically as well as by type throughout the anthology.

In addition, the editors have tried to select works that singly and together make a worthwhile assertion about some facet of modern life. This does not mean that we are necessarily in agreement with all the assertions made in the selections. As a matter of fact, in the grouping of the novels listed in the *Instructor's Manual,* an effort has been made to include novels that express different and often contradictory attitudes. This is to encourage dealing tolerantly and understandingly with people, in life and in literature, who have different attitudes and notions than ours. The novel and the play provide ample opportunity for experiencing some of these diverse and sometimes even contradictory points of view. But for the most part the selections in the anthology itself rest upon this important postulate: They presuppose an image of man as a free and responsible being, capable of great heights and tragic depths, inhabiting a world neither entirely good nor entirely evil, a world in which man is, in a significant measure, the shaper of his own destiny, a world that is not an unintelligible chaos.

The anthology is not meant to be self-sufficient. Since the advent of the paperback, no anthology should be. In studying some of the types, particularly the novel and the play, heavy reliance will have to be placed on paperback supplements—a desirable procedure because it makes possible flexible choice of material from semester to semester in these important areas. Far more poetry has been included than could be used by any one class, and here again this amplitude of material provides a great range of choice for individual classes.

The glossary provided for many selections is not meant to eliminate the use of a dictionary. Only that material has been glossed that might be either hard to find or difficult to interpret even if found. Some sample analyses have been provided in the Appendixes, as well as in "Some Notes on Poetry." In the Index, following the authors' names, are the dates of their lives so that they can be easily placed in time.

In preparing this second edition of the anthology, the editors have intentionally included more contemporary material, in order to make sure that the reader is aware of the creative activity that is going forward in the categories of the short story, the novel, the play, and modern poetry.

St. Louis, Missouri M.B.M.
October 1970 J.E.C.
　　　　　　　　　　　　　　　　　　　　　　　　　　　　　　J.A.R.

CONTENTS

Preface v

Unit 1 FICTION: CRITICAL ESSAYS

On Fiction 3
    Robert Gorham Davis   *At the Heart of the Story Is Man* 6
    Frank O'Connor   *And It's a Lonely, Personal Art* 8

Unit 2 SHORT STORIES

On the Short Story 13
Love 16
    Fyodor Dostoevsky   *The Peasant Marey* 17
    Willa Cather   *Neighbour Rosicky* 20
    F. Scott Fitzgerald   *Babylon Revisited* 37
Courage 48
    Katherine Anne Porter   *The Jilting of Granny Weatherall* 48
    Ernest Hemingway   *The Killers* 53
    Harry Mark Petrakis   *Pericles on 31st Street* 58
The Complexity of Life 65
    Shirley Jackson   *After You, My Dear Alphonse* 65

x   CONTENTS

    Frank O'Connor   *The Majesty of the Law* 67
    Graham Greene   *The Destructors* 72
    Flannery O'Connor   *A Good Man Is Hard to Find* 80
The Quest for Meaning 89
    William Faulkner   *The Bear* 89
    John Steinbeck   *Breakfast* 97
    Joseph Carroll   *At Mrs. Farrelly's* 99
    Katherine Mansfield   *The Garden-Party* 105
The Deprived 112
    Anton Chekhov   *The Lament* 113
    James Joyce   *Clay* 116
    Wilbur Daniel Steele   *How Beautiful with Shoes* 119
    Ernest J. Gaines   *The Sky Is Gray* 130
    D. H. Lawrence   *The Rocking-Horse Winner* 145
Beyond Categories 153
    Franz Kafka   *An Old Manuscript* 153
    Ray Bradbury   *There Will Come Soft Rains* 154
    Caroline Gordon   *Old Red* 157
    Eudora Welty   *A Visit of Charity* 167

Unit 3 THE SHORT NOVEL

On the Short Novel 173
    Fyodor Dostoevsky   *The Dream of a Ridiculous Man* 174
    James Joyce   *The Dead* 184

Unit 4 DRAMA: CRITICAL ESSAYS

On Drama 209
    Henry Alonzo Myers   Romeo and Juliet *and* A Midsummer Night's Dream: *Tragedy and Comedy* 212
    Louis I. Bredvold   *The Modern Temper and Tragic Drama* 219
    Thornton Wilder   *"A Platform and a Passion or Two"* 225
    William I. Oliver   *Between Absurdity and the Playwright* 229

Unit 5 A SELECTION OF MODERN PLAYS

On This Selection of Plays 239
    Tennessee Williams   *The Glass Menagerie* 239
    Arthur Miller   *Death of a Salesman* 274
    Thornton Wilder   *Pullman Car Hiawatha* 323
    Luigi Pirandello   *Six Characters in Search of an Author* 331
    Edward Albee   *The American Dream* 360

Unit 6 HUMOR AND SATIRE

On Humor and Satire 381
Prose 384
    Ellen Douglass Leyburn   *Animal Stories* 384
    John Steinbeck   *My War with the Ospreys* 393
    E. B. White   *Walden* 398
    Art Buchwald   *New York, C'est Formidable!* 402

CONTENTS xi

Susan Lardner   *A Wonderful Time*   404
Richard Steele   *The Spectator Club* (The Spectator, No. 2)   406
Joseph Addison   *Sir Roger at Church* (The Spectator, No. 112)   409
Jonathan Swift   *A Modest Proposal*   410

Poetry   415

Edward Lear   *The Jumblies*   415
Ogden Nash   *Kind of an Ode to Duty*   417
Emily Dickinson   *Two Butterflies Went Out at Noon*   417
John Clare   *Little Trotty Wagtail*   418
Arthur Guiterman   *The Singletrack Mind*   418
                Strictly Germ-proof   418
Robert Frost   *Departmental*   419
Geoffrey Chaucer   *Portraits from the Prologue to the Canterbury Tales*   420
              Portrait of the Prioress   420
              Portrait of the Monk   421
              Portrait of the Friar   422
              Portrait of the Clerk   424
              Portrait of the Parson   425
              Portrait of the Pardoner   426
              The Nun's Priest's Tale (Nevill Coghill translation)   428
Alexander Pope   from *The Epistle to Dr. Arbuthnot*   437
              Character of Atticus—Joseph Addison   437
              Character of Sporus—Lord Hervey   438
              The Rape of the Lock   438
Jonathan Swift   *A Satirical Elegy on the Death of a Late Famous General*   454
Thomas Hardy   *Ah, Are You Digging on My Grave?*   454
A. E. Housman   *Hell Gate*   455
W. H. Auden   *In Schrafft's*   456
              The Unknown Citizen   457
John Betjeman   *In Westminister Abbey*   458
Kenneth Fearing   *Portrait*   458
              Confession Overheard in a Subway   459
James Stephens   *A Glass of Beer*   461
Karl Shapiro   *Haircut*   461
Howard Nemerov   *Boom!*   462

Unit 7   POETRY: CRITICAL ESSAYS

Donald A. Stauffer   *The Nature of Poetry*   467
John Ciardi   *Robert Frost: The Way to the Poem*   473
Dylan Thomas   *Notes on the Art of Poetry*   479

Unit 8   BALLADS, AND OTHER FORMS OF NARRATIVE POETRY

On the Ballad   485
  Edward   489
  The Twa Corbies   490

xii CONTENTS

    The Twa Sisters   491
    Lord Randal   492
    Sweet William's Ghost   493
    Sir Patrick Spens   494
    The Wife of Usher's Well   495
    Robin Hood and Little John   495
    Get Up and Bar the Door   498
    The Cherry-Tree Carol   499

On the Romance   500
    Sir Gawain and the Green Knight   502

On Other Types of Medieval Narrative Poetry   565

On Narrative Poetry   565
    Robert Frost   "*Out, Out—*"   566
    William Wordsworth   *Michael*   567

Unit 9 LYRIC POEMS ARRANGED BY TYPE

On Lyric Poetry   579

On the Sonnet   584
    William Wordsworth   *Nuns Fret Not at Their Convent's Narrow Room*   585
    Karl Shapiro   *I Swore to Stab the Sonnet with My Pen*   586
    William Shakespeare   *Sonnets*   586
        33. Full many a glorious morning have I seen   586
        65. Since brass, nor stone, nor earth, nor boundless sea   586
        73. That time of year thou mayst in me behold   587
        129. Th' expense of spirit in a waste of shame   587
    John Donne   *Batter My Heart*   587
        At the Round Earth's Imagined Corners   588
    John Milton   *When I Consider How My Light Is Spent*   588
    William Wordsworth   *Composed upon Westminster Bridge*   588
        The World Is Too Much with Us   589
    Percy Bysshe Shelley   *Ozymandias*   589
    John Keats   *In First Looking into Chapman's Homer*   590
    George Meredith   *Lucifer in Starlight*   590
    Gerard Manley Hopkins   *Spring*   590
        Harrahing in Harvest   591
        The Caged Skylark   591
        The Windhover   592
    Archibald MacLeish   *The End of the World*   593
    Robert Frost   *The Silken Tent*   593

On the Ode   593
    Robert Herrick   *Corinna's Going A-Maying*   594
    John Dryden   *A Song for St. Cecelia's Day*   595
    John Keats   *Ode to the Nightingale*   596
    Gerard Manley Hopkins   *The Leaden Echo and the Golden Echo*   598
    Percy Bysshe Shelley   *Ode to the West Wind*   600
    Walt Whitman   *Out of the Cradle Endlessly Rocking*   601
    Allen Ginsberg   from *Howl, part I*   606

On the Elegy   609
    John Milton   *Lycidas*   610
    Edna St. Vincent Millay   *Memorial to D. C.*   614
    Song of a Second April   614
    Walt Whitman   *When Lilacs Last in the Dooryard Bloom'd*   615
    Gerard Manley Hopkins   *Felix Randal*   621
    John Crowe Ransom   *Bells for John Whiteside's Daughter*   622
    Dead Boy   622
    Kenneth Fearing   *Dirge*   623
    Theodore Roethke   *Elegy for Jane: My Student Thrown by a Horse*   624
    Wendell Berry   *Elegy*   624
    Dorothy Rosenberg   *Bringing Mother Home*   626

Unit 10   LYRIC POEMS ARRANGED BY TOPIC

A Selection of Poems about Poetry   631
    Gerard Manley Hopkins   *To R. B.*   631
    Marianne Moore   *Poetry*   631
    Archibald MacLeish   *Ars Poetica*   632
    W. H. Auden   *In Memory of W. B. Yeats*   633

Nature   634
    George Herbert   *The Pulley*   634
    Robert Herrick   *To Daffodils*   635
    Robert Burns   *To a Mouse*   635
    John Keats   *To Autumn*   636
    William Wordsworth   *I Wandered Lonely as a Cloud*   637
    Lines Composed a Few Miles above Tintern Abbey   637
    Alfred, Lord Tennyson   *The Lotos Eaters*   640
    A. E. Housman   *Loveliest of Trees*   643
    White in the Moon the Long Road Lies   644
    Thomas Hardy   *The Darkling Thrush*   644
    Matthew Arnold   *In Harmony with Nature*   645
    Robert Browning   *Home-Thoughts, from Abroad*   645
    Gerard Manley Hopkins   *God's Grandeur*   646
    Francis Thompson   *To a Snowflake*   646

John Masefield	*Sea-Fever*	647
Stephen Spender	*The Landscape Near an Aerodrome*	647
Dylan Thomas	*Fern Hill*	648
William Carlos Williams	*Pastoral*	649
e. e. cummings	*when serpents bargain for the right to squirm*	649
John Wain	*Reason for Not Writing Orthodox Nature Poetry*	650
Sylvia Plath	*Black Rook in Rainy Weather*	650
Robert Frost	*Dust of Snow*	651
Robinson Jeffers	*The Eye*	651
George Starbuck	*Bone Thoughts on a Dry Day*	652
Robert Bly	*Surprised by Evening*	653
Donald Finkel	*Spring Song*	653
Galway Kinnell	*Cells Breathe in the Emptiness*	654

War 654

Richard Lovelace	*To Lucasta, Going to the Wars*	655
George Gordon, Lord Byron	*The Destruction of Sennacherib*	655
Thomas Hardy	*Channel Firing*	656
	The Man He Killed	656
Gerard Manley Hopkins	*The Soldier*	657
A. E. Housman	*1887*	657
Wilfred Owen	*Arms and the Boy*	658
	Anthem for Doomed Youth	658
Stephen Spender	*Ultima Ratio Regum*	659
Randall Jarrell	*The Death of the Ball Turret Gunner*	659
	Losses	660
Richard Eberhart	*The Fury of Aerial Bombardment*	660
e. e. cummings	*the season 'tis, my lovely lambs*	661
	next to of course god america i	662
William Stafford	*Watching the Jet Planes Dive*	662
David Etter	*The Hometown Hero Comes Home*	663

Love 663

Edmund Spenser	*My Love Is Like to Ice*	654
William Shakespeare	*Sonnets*	664
	116. *Let me not to the marriage of true minds*	664
	130. *My mistress' eyes are nothing like the sun*	664
Sir Philip Sidney	*A Litany*	665
John Donne	*A Valediction: Forbidding Mourning*	665
	Love's Diet	666
George Herbert	*Love*	666
Edmund Waller	*On a Girdle*	667
Robert Burns	*John Anderson, My Jo*	667
	A Red, Red Rose	667
William Wordsworth	*She Dwelt among the Untrodden Ways*	668
Elizabeth Barrett Browning	*How Do I Love Thee?*	668

William Butler Yeats   *A Prayer for My Daughter*   668
Down by the Salley Garden   670
Edna St. Vincent Millay   *Love Is Not All*   670
e. e. cummings   *if everything happens that can't be done*   670
Richard Wilbur   *Love Calls Us to the Things of This World*   671
Karl Shapiro   *Love, It Is Time I Memorized Your Phone*   672
Theodore Roethke   *I Knew a Woman Lovely in Her Bones*   672
Vassar Miller   *Defense Rests*   673
Mona Van Duyn   *Notes from a Suburban Heart*   673

Death   674

William Shakespeare   *Sonnet*   674
    146. *Poor soul, the center of my sinful earth*   674
Francis Beaumont   *On the Tombs in Westminster Abbey*   675
John Donne   *Death*   675
Robert Browning   *Prospice*   675
Alfred, Lord Tennyson   *Crossing the Bar*   676
Robert Frost   *After Apple-Picking*   676
Emily Dickinson   *Because I Could Not Stop for Death*   677
I Heard a Fly Buzz When I Died   678
William Butler Yeats   *Sailing to Byzantium*   678
Karl Shapiro   *Auto Wreck*   679
William Carlos Williams   *Tract*   679
James Dickey   *Sled Burial, Dream Ceremony*   680
James Wright   *Old Age Compensation*   681

Anxiety   682

Matthew Arnold   *Dover Beach*   682
Gerard Manley Hopkins   *I Wake and Feel the Fell of Dark, Not Day*   683
Carrion Comfort   683
T. S. Eliot   *Preludes*   684
David Ignatow   *About Money*   685
John Logan   *Song on the Dread of a Chill Spring*   685
John Knoepfle   *North on one-eleven*   685
Delmore Schwartz   *The Heavy Bear Who Goes with Me*   686
Countee Cullen   *Incident*   686
James Wright   *At the Slackening of the Tide*   687

In Quest of Meaning   687

William Butler Yeats   *Lapis Lazuli*   688
Robert Frost   *Birches*   689
William Carlos Williams   *To a Dog Injured in the Street*   690
Marianne Moore   *The Steeple-Jack*   691

xvi CONTENTS

    Rupert Brooke   *Heaven* 692
    Richard Wilbur   *A Baroque Wall-Fountain in the Villa Sciarra* 692
    T. S. Eliot   *Journey of the Magi* 693
The Jet and Urban Setting 694
    Walt Whitman   *To a Locomotive in Winter* 694
    Allen Ginsberg   *A Supermarket in California* 695
    Louis MacNeice   *Morning Sun* 696
    Denise Levertov   *Merrit Parkway* 697
    Yvor Winters   *At the San Francisco Airport* 697
    Siegfried Sassoon   *Storm on Fifth Avenue* 698
    Louis Simpson   *Hot Night on Water Street* 698
    Samuel Hazo   *The Day I Schooled Myself in Stone* 699
    Marge Piercy   *The skyscrapers of the financial district dance with Gasman* 700
    David Ray   *Committee* 700
    James Dickey   *For the First Manned Moon Orbit* 701

Unit 11 IMPRESSIONISTIC AND EXPRESSIONISTIC POETRY

On Impressionistic and Expressionistic Poetry 705
    Carl Sandburg   *Fog* 705
        The Harbor 706
    James Stephens   *The Main Deep* 706
    H. D.   *Oread* 706
        Heat 707
        Pear Tree 707
    Amy Lowell   *Night Clouds* 707
        A Tulip Garden 708
    Walter de la Mare   *Silver* 708
    Emily Dickinson   *The Train* 709
    Stephen Spender   *The Express* 709
    Alfred, Lord Tennyson   *The Eagle* 710
    Emily Dickinson   *A Bird Came Down the Walk* 710
    Walt Whitman   *A Noiseless Patient Spider* 710
    Emily Dickinson   *The Snake* 711
    Roy Campbell   *To a Pet Cobra* 711
    D. H. Lawrence   *Snake* 712
    Ted Robins   *The Dive* 714
    Robert Farren   *The Cyclist* 714
    John Gillespie Magee, Jr.   *High Flight* 715
    John Masefield   *Cargoes* 715
    Richard LeGallienne   *Brooklyn Bridge at Dawn* 716
    Carl Sandburg   *Chicago* 716
    Karl Shapiro   *Hollywood* 717

Unit 12 DRAMATIC POETRY

On Dramatic Poetry 721
- William Shakespeare   *Soliloquies from* Hamlet 722
- *Soliloquy from* Richard III 723
- Alfred, Lord Tennyson   *Ulysses* 724
- Robert Browning   *My Last Duchess* 726
- Robert Frost   *The Death of the Hired Man* 727
- Edwin Arlington Robinson   *Mr. Flood's Party* 730
- T. S. Eliot   *The Love Song of J. Alfred Prufrock* 731

APPENDIXES

Appendix One
Sample Analyses of Short Stories 737
- Fyodor Dostoevsky   *The Peasant Marey* 737
- Harry Mark Petrakis   *Pericles on 31st Street* 739

Appendix Two
Sample Analysis of a Short Novel 741
- James Joyce   *The Dead* 741

Appendix Three
Some Notes on Poetry 743
- The Words of Poetry   *Diction in Poetry* 743
- *Imagery in Poetry* 744
- The Sounds of Poetry   *Rhythm in Life* 745
- *Nonmetrical Rhythm in Poetry* 747
- *Metrical Rhythm in Poetry* 752

Appendix Four
Sample Analyses of Poems 756
- William Shakespeare   *Since Brass, Nor Stone, Nor Earth* 756
- John Donne   *At the Round Earth's Imagined Corners* 758
- Eileen Duggan   *Pilgrimage* 760

INDEX 765

Unit **1**

FICTION:
CRITICAL ESSAYS

ON FICTION

Once upon a time about two thousand years ago a somber-faced social commentator sat in the top row of an ancient Greek theater. Counting the members of the audience as they strolled in, he made a quick computation. If this sort of thing kept on, if the drama really "caught hold," as he told his friends later, there would soon be scarcely a reading Greek remaining. Centuries later one of his lineal descendants checked the gate at a Roman amphitheater. Shouting to make himself heard above the screams of the crowd and the roaring of hungry lions, he prophesied that, if the supply of Christians held out, there would soon be not a dozen good Romans left who either could or would read a manuscript.

Within the past fifty years similar pronunciamentos about the decline in reading have come to us on three separate occasions: with the development of motion pictures as a form of mass entertainment, with the invention of radio, and, finally, with the phenomenal growth of television. And what has happened? Far more books—good books—are being published and read than ever before. The mob has always liked spectacles, games, "productions" of any kind; it always will. Intelligent men, while sharing in a highly selective way this fondness for spectacle, have always been interested in the written word.

The great advantage of a book as compared to a dramatic presentation of any kind is, of course, that the book is always at hand. The reader can set his own pace. He can skim the dull part, he can linger over a superb description or a humorous scene, he can ponder the meaning of a difficult passage. When he chooses he can read the book again—all of it, or any favorite section. It would seem to follow, then, that the important superiority of the printed word over other forms of entertainment lies in good books—those worth reading more than once—rather than in the ephemeral trash that crowds the bookracks in many stores.

All of the short stories, short novels, and novels presented or discussed in the following pages have been chosen because the editors believe them to be interesting, amusing, exciting, or thought-provoking, not only on first reading, but for a second and third. Each illustrates one or more of the "values" discussed by Robert Gorham Davis in "At the Heart of the Story Is Man." The idea behind our choices is simply this: if, as a more or less captive audience, you can be helped to read these pieces with fuller understanding and enjoyment of them both in themselves and as examples of literary types, you will find good reason to read a great many more books during the remainder of your lives. A hunger, never to be fully appeased, will be created in you; this hunger, more than its partial satisfaction in the text, is the significant goal. Most important, you will be helped to read more skillfully.

The word "skill" should be emphasized. For genuine enjoyment, it is just as important to know precisely how to get the most out of a piece of fiction as it is necessary to know how to hit a ball correctly in order to enjoy golf or tennis. You may have already developed this literary skill. If so, you will probably find material here to please you from the start and to further develop your appreciation. If, on the other hand, despite a sincere and wholly admirable determination to improve yourself, you have for some time been reading "good" things and disliking them thoroughly, you can learn in these pages to equip yourself to receive genuine rather than simulated pleasure from great literature. If you choose, you can begin now.

The first requisite for progress is an open mind—open, not blank; not passively acquiescent to suggestion or dogmatic assertion, but cooperatively active and selective. If everything in this text were familiar and therefore easy to understand, there would be no reason for reading it. Real progress comes principally from the investigation of values to be found in the new and unfamiliar. It may be assumed that you have or are willing to develop an open mind.

A second requisite is an understanding of the nature of fiction. Occasionally a student will take pride in asserting, "I'm serious about education. I can't waste my time reading about made-up situations or make-believe people. I want the truth." What he does not understand is that good fiction *is* truth, or at any rate an attempt at it—truth distilled, concentrated, intensified. The serious writer is always making a comment on life. Through a character true to type, but at the same time possessed of individuality, set against a background also true to type, but with unusual characteristics, the writer works out his truth. Usually the reader's experience is wide enough for him to recognize the validity of the character type and the authenticity of the background. He nods in agreement. What holds him to the story, then, is the way in which the author has looked penetratingly into the lives of characters closely resembling people the reader knows, or the person he himself is, and found there things of which the reader has scarcely dreamed. Thus his appreciation of his own life and his relation to society is sharpened and deepened. As Davis says:

> The reader shares the characters, the events, the particular vision of the novel, not only with the author but with all his readers, past and present. Novels and their characters exist both inside and outside history as objective references in our common attempt to understand and evaluate and control our experience.

It is this truth of fiction that caused Jessamyn West to describe a short story as an "unveiling" or a "revelation." It is to the enduring existence of such truth—which the author finds, refines, and presents rather than invents—that a sculptor referred when he replied half-humorously to a lady who inquired how he had managed to carve such a beautiful figure, "Madam, the girl was already there in the block of marble, and I knew it. All I did was cut away the extra pieces, and there she is!" Any artist or writer cuts away those extra pieces, clears the ground around a scene, discards the accidental and incidental. That is the essence of the selection which gives impact and value to his art. An unexpected verification of the truth which the writer finds when he has completed this work is suggested by the frequency with which psychologists refer to characters from great novels as near-perfect examples of human behavior patterns, both normal and abnormal, although many of these portraits were drawn a century or more before psychology existed as a science.

In a similar way, the great fiction writer attempts to see life in proportion and balance—in Matthew Arnold's words, to "see life steadily and see it whole." No one can be unaware of the overwhelming preoccupation with sex and violence and the cult of ugliness and barbarism in cheap literature. Often, one suspects, the immature and unsophisticated reader is drawn to such shoddy writing under the mistaken assumption that here are writers truly brave and honest, whereas the so-called great writers are timid old maids pussyfooting carefully around "the real truth." The real truth is that the interest in sex and violence shown by the hack writers has all the characteristics of a maniacal obsession. They can see, think of, and portray nothing else; or, if they can, they find it unprofitable and avoid doing so. Even writers of considerable stature are not immune when a particular obsession becomes widespread. But whatever the direction or misdirection of their efforts, genuinely fine writers may be credited with a sincere attempt to show, as writer Frank O'Connor maintains, "stories of real people in real situations."

With this emphasis on the truth of fiction should go a warning, perhaps unnecessary, that no reader is free to presume that anything and everything he finds in fiction, even by the most famous writers, is gospel. The serious writer presents truth as he sees it. Usually the philosophical basis for his conclusions will be shared by a large number of people in his generation, but it is not necessarily the truth as the individual reader knows it. The author, through his long apprenticeship, must learn to select. The reader, through his long but less arduous apprenticeship in reading, must learn to select also; good reading, like good writing, is something of an art.

Even when a reader knows that he can never agree with the major premises of a particular writer, there may nevertheless remain for him great values in the author's work. He need not share with Kafka the existentialist belief that life is utter chaos in order to marvel at the force and impact of "An Old Manuscript" and the truth it manifests about a particular kind of person; neither is it necessary to share Faulkner's conclusions about the relationships existing between courage and truth, beauty and ugliness, to find "The Bear" engrossing and revealing. As Davis points out, one of the contributions of a great writer to our development is his sharing with us his awareness of and sensitivity to spiritual values. And because a writer reacts more strongly to stimuli of any kind than do most of us, he often finds our placidity unbearable. He will do his best to make us feel, to pull us beyond an emotional range lying between a slight smile and a light sigh, to make us rage with him, laugh with him, and perhaps weep with him for the pity of it all.

Every age shares many of the characteristics of preceding ages, but always with some differences. To interpret these differences for us we have the historian, the sociologist, and, to some extent, the psychologist and the philosopher. Working as a fusing or synthesizing force for the findings of all of them is the writer of fiction, selecting, concentrating, explaining the changing time spirit and the curiously unchanging nature of man. Few of us know so much that we have no need for his help. Most of us have far to go before we can say, "I have read enough!"

At the Heart of the Story Is Man*
by ROBERT GORHAM DAVIS

In recent criticism it has become a commonplace to blame the low estate of literature in general and the novel in particular on society's failure to provide young writers with a "stable order of values" or "common assumptions of value." These phrases appear in recent books on the novel by John W. Aldridge and Edward Wagenknecht.

The more enthusiastically critics use the term "values," however, the less need they seem to feel of defining it, though the word has given philosophers great trouble for centuries. Critics attribute the decline of the novel in the last twenty years to the absence or instability of values. But they do not test this thesis by seeing how it works when applied to the novel in the past—before Hemingway, before Henry James, before Jane Austen.

If we leave out Petronius, who wrote his "Satyricon" in Nero's time, when values were debased, indeed, Boccaccio is the first major author of realistic fiction. Writing nearly six centuries ago, before the Middle Ages were officially over, Boccaccio described a world in which clergy and the middle classes alike were becoming highly materialistic in their values, and ingeniously unscrupulous in achieving their ends.

The novel proper began in Spain when travel, trade, colonial enterprises and the rise of great cities were destroying medieval stability, apparently forever. "Don Quixote" is Exhibit A. The heroes of Spanish and French picaresque novels were ill-born or disinherited men, a succession of lost generations, living by their wits, creating their own values in a complex world of ambition and deceit.

When Richardson, Fielding, Smollett and Sterne created the English novel in the third quarter of the eighteenth century, the need for a "return to values" was as urgent as it is today. Political corruption, bribery and place-buying were far worse. The cities abounded in poverty, filth, crime and sexual license. Among the squirearchy, the brutal Westerns of Fielding's "Tom Jones" were more common than the benevolent Allworthys. The universities and established church were in a state of torpor.

In this society—with little dependence on absolutes—these four novelists, the "great quaternity," as they were called, not only created the English novel but also created or extended values as well. They taught their readers generosity, sympathy, humor, moral and esthetic sensibility. They stimulated a desire to reform institutions, to improve social conditions. Yet they did not hold common assumptions of value. Though both were moralists, Fielding and Richardson had little use for each other's morality. Laurence Sterne, a clergyman, the most sensitive and witty of the four, the most brilliant formal experimenter, was also the most indecent by nineteenth-century standards.

Nor in the nineteenth century, in the novels, say, of Jane Austen, Emily Brontë, George Eliot, George Meredith, Thomas Hardy and George Moore, do we find so much agreement on basic or ultimate values as we might expect. If non-English writers are included, like Henry James, Mark Twain, Flaubert, Zola and Dostoevsky, the divergences become only more striking. What they had in common was an intense interest in people, in human variety, in the consequences of certain kinds of action, consequences that differ little from generation to generation.

Yet if the human situation remains basically the same, novelists' perspectives on it vary greatly. Point of view is so important in fiction because values are, as Nietzsche said, "perspectival." They depend on how you look at things, and that depends, in turn, on what you are. When life seems to have lost its meaning or value, it is because something has happened to the valuer, not to life. Values result from valuing, and different men in dif-

---

* From *Highlights of Modern Literature: A Permanent Collection of Memorable Essays from The New York Times Book Review*, edited by Francis Brown (New York: The New American Library, 1954). Reprinted by permission of Mr. Davis.

ferent social circumstances value different things.

In the difficult choices which life is constantly offering, men show their order of values by what they are willing to pay or sacrifice for what they consider the greater good. As long as men are capable of any desires and satisfactions, life has potential value for them. As long as a novel communicates or extends appreciation of any of life's goods, it is wrong to speak of its author as having no values, even though the reader does not hold them to be adequate.

The contrast between Graham Greene's "The End of the Affair" and Hemingway's "The Sun Also Rises" illustrates this. Greene's novel is based on absolute values, on the return to religious orthodoxy, so important at the present time. "The Sun Also Rises," published in 1926, took its title from Ecclesiastes, and was the most influential expression of the disillusionment among the Lost Generation after World War I.

And yet in one perfectly legitimate sense of the word, "The Sun Also Rises" has more values than "The End of the Affair." Though they have their bitterly unhappy moments, Hemingway's characters are great appreciators. They appreciate Paris, Spain, peasants, wine, fishing, bullfights, wit, courage and each other. Moreover, these appreciations are effectively communicated, if in somewhat simple language.

In Greene's novel everything is as drab and dreary as possible. London is bomb-damaged; it rains all the time; the heroine has a bad cough; the meals are indigestible and made to sound so; the people are boring or nerve-racking; love is described largely in physical terms, and those repellent ones. The characters turn to the church because they find life intolerable. The heroine catches faith, "like a disease," and God's mercy, when it is manifested, seems more like punishment.

Ultimately, of course, it is a question of awareness, and Greene's awareness of spiritual realities is undoubtedly finer than Hemingway's. Henry James said of the characters in novels, "their being finely aware—as Hamlet and Lear, say, are finely aware—makes absolute the intensity of their adventure, gives the maximum of sense to what befalls them." But awareness can be of many things. The great religions and philosophies, like the great novels, have widely disagreed on what they affirmed and denied in life.

Despite "The End of the Affair," faith is not necessarily incompatible with joy in the created world and in human love. Seeing Montana or bullfights through Hemingway's eyes, or Navajo dances and Etruscan places through D. H. Lawrence's, increases the reader's values, but does not require him to accept some of the more dubious notions expounded in "Death in the Afternoon" or "Fantasia of the Unconscious." Above all it is important to remember, in talking of the relation of literature to values, that imaginative literature is itself a value, an end in itself, with its own immediate satisfactions for both writer and reader.

A democracy is organized to permit as free a play of personal choice as possible, to enable men with very different values to pursue their own ends freely and still make the greatest possible contribution to society. The novel helps in this by letting us see things from very different points of view, by increasing sympathy, tolerance and a sense of individual responsibility. Historically the novel originated along with democratic individualism, flourished with it in the nineteenth century, and seemed doomed along with it in the twentieth century.

However, there are no known laws of literary development, nothing in the flexible form of the novel itself, to make its prospects any darker now than they might have seemed in the year of Sterne's "Tristram Shandy" or Hardy's "Jude the Obscure." "Tristram Shandy" might have seemed the final dissolution of the form. "Jude the Obscure" might have seemed to write a gloomy finis to that individualism which the earlier novel had celebrated.

Now, in the course of the struggle against Communist totalitarianism, politics, religion and philosophy are all hard at work rediscovering the individual, reasserting his uniqueness, his capacity for moral responsibility, his ability to influence both his own destiny and the destiny of his nation. This should create a very favorable atmosphere for novel-writing. The novelist, in an individualist society, has an advantage over social scientists who tend to treat individuals as members of groups. The very nature of the novelist's art requires him to test every generalization, every value, every form of action according to its meaning for the individual.

The difficulty with individualism lies in the sense of human isolation, of alienation, it is likely to create. Through a use of "point of view," a reflecting consciousness, which is not possible to dramatist or biographer, the novelist helps overcome this separation. By seeing life through another's eyes, feeling what he feels, thinking what he thinks, we share the meaning and value that experience has for him. The characters of novels, moreover, are not simply the real individuals known in actual life, transferred to the printed page, but still seen from the outside. Larger than life, "more true than real," as Hardy said, they are seen through the mind of the author, with whom the reader is conscious of sharing and judging them. Nor is the author outside them, either. Their life, their individuality derive directly from him. "Bovary, c'est moi," Flaubert declared.

The reader shares the characters, the events, the particular vision of a novel, not only with the author but with all his readers, past and present. Novels and their characters exist both inside and outside history as objective references in our common attempt to understand and evaluate and control our experience.

"My lawyer," Fielding said, "is not only alive, but hath been so these four thousand years." Novels show both the persistence and modification of types of character and types of experience in changing social circumstances. They relate the individual to the group without requiring him to sacrifice his individuality. They are one of the chief means of getting beyond the limits of individual experience and knowing what it is like to be human.

Critics of every period have complained of the people and actions about which realistic novelists chose to write. But it is only as the novel includes the eccentrics, the outcasts, the brutalized, the publicans and sinners, that imaginative sympathy becomes complete in its humanity or Christianity, and recognizes the grounds of social responsibility in a common human nature.

It is because they have such a conception, conscious or unconscious, of the novel's importance that so many people are publicly worried about the novel's present state and future prospects. This is a good sign. But nothing in the history of the novel gives reason for pessimism about its future so long as the freedom and responsibility and dignity of the individual remain primary concerns in our society, and so long as writers know that they themselves have the power to create values. On the contrary, there is every reason to suppose that young novelists, sensing the spirit of the times, and with reawakened excitement over the possibilities of their art, will find new ways of showing us both what it means to be human under the aspect of eternity and to be Americans in the Nineteen Fifties, a knowledge which only the novel, perhaps, can properly give us.

And It's a Lonely, Personal Art*
by FRANK O'CONNOR

Definitions are a nuisance, but they prevent misunderstandings. When E. M. Forster wrote a book on the novel, he accepted a French definition of it as "a prose fiction of a certain length" which was incontrovertible, like saying it was written on paper, but not very helpful, as it implied that practically everything "of a certain length" was a novel and consequently that there was nothing useful to be said about it. Anthologies of short stories also suggest that everything "of a certain length" is a short story—squibs by Dorothy Parker or Saki, articles, essays, and plain

---

* From *Highlights of Modern Literature: A Permanent Collection of Memorable Essays from The New York Times Book Review*, edited by Francis Brown (New York: The New American Library, 1954). Copyright 1953 by Frank O'Connor. Reprinted by permission of Harold Matson Company, Inc.

shockers, and that nothing useful can be said about that, either. I don't share either view. I admit I am not at all clear what I mean by a short story, or else I should have much less trouble in writing it, but I am passionately clear about what I do *not* mean, and for me, anthologies are full of negative definitions.

A yarn, for instance, is not a short story, as—begging Mr. Forster's pardon—a medieval saga or romance is not a novel. Every literary form is, to a certain extent, a convention; it is what people generally mean when they use the word that defines it, exactly as when a man says, "I'll meet you with the car," you expect to be met with an automobile, not a perambulator. A novel is *Tom Jones, Sense and Sensibility, Vanity Fair, War and Peace*, and *The Charterhouse of Parma*, and *not*—Mr. Forster's pardon again—*The Pilgrim's Progress, Marius the Epicurean,* or *Zuleika Dobson*. (When Mr. Forster launches into a discussion of *Zuleika Dobson*, I feel exactly as I should if the man who was to meet me with the car appeared with the perambulator.) By convention, the novel and the short story have both come to mean stories of real people in real situations, rather than what I call "The Cat's Whisker," the sort of yarn, so popular with magazine editors, which ends, usually in italics *"The face was the face of Minkie, the cat, but the whiskers were the whiskers of Colonel Claude Combpyne."* If we must have a word for the thing, let us call it a "tale," and not mix it up with Chekhov's "Lady with the Toy Dog," with which it has nothing whatever in common but the fact that it is "a prose fiction of a certain length."

For me, what makes the short story what it is, is its attitude to Time. In any novel the principal character is Time—*Ulysses, The Informer,* and *Mrs. Dalloway* notwithstanding. Even in inferior novels and in books which are strictly creative literature, the chronological ordering of events establishes a rhythm, which is the rhythm of life itself, and I have known novelists who sometimes wrote hundreds of pages until the novel proper began. But what to the novelist is the most precious element in his work is a nightmare to the short-story writer. He is all the while trying to get round the necessity for describing events in sequence; the rhythm is too slow, and when novelists like Henry James and Hardy turn storytellers and use the rhythms of the novel, he finds the result disastrous. Hardy will cheerfully waste three pages getting his hero up the hill before he even begins to reveal what his story is about. Time the collaborator has become Time the gasbag.

Every great short story represents a struggle with Time—the novelist's Time—a refusal to allow it to establish its majestic rhythms (Chapter I, "A Walk on the Heath"). It attempts to reach some point of vantage, some glowing center of action from which past and future will be equally visible. The crisis of a short story *is* the short story, and not, as in the novel, the logical, inescapable result of everything preceding it, the mere flowering of events. I should almost say that in the story what precedes the crisis becomes a consequence of the crisis.

It is one of the weaknesses of the story writer that, because of his awareness of the importance of the crisis, he tends to inflate it, to give it artificial, symbolic significance. In teaching the short story, I have had to warn students that anyone using symbolism would be instantly expelled from the class. Joyce, who was fascinated by the problem, did use symbolism, but being Joyce, used it in such a remote form that he manages to conceal it from most readers. In "Ivy-Day in the Committee Room," a satirical comment on Ireland after Parnell, we meet a few political figures consumed with rancor for the want of a drink. Then some bottles of stout appear, and the tone of their sentiment at once becomes nobler, till, in a mock-heroic parody of a Hero's funeral, a sentimental poem takes the place of a Dead March and three bottles of stout, placed before the fire to open, that of the three volleys fired over the Hero's grave.

The device of the muted symbol is superbly used in "The Dead." The events of the story have already long taken place, and were never very significant. A tubercular young man who sang a song called "The Lass of Aughrin" fell in love with a West of Ireland girl called Gretta. One night, she found him outside her window, wet and shivering, and soon after, he died. The story proper opens years later with the arrival of Gretta and her husband at a musical party given by two old music teachers in Dublin. As Gabriel Conroy, the husband, enters, he scrapes snow from his galoshes and cracks a joke with the maid about getting married. She retorts bitterly that "the men that does be there nowadays are nothing but old palaver and all they can get out of you." These two things—the snow and the maid's retort—form the theme of the story, and they are repeated in varied and more menacing forms until the climax.

"The men that does be there nowadays" cannot be great lovers; it is only the dead who can be perfect. The young Gaelic League girl with whom Gabriel chats about the West of Ireland—the subject, like the dead themselves, rising—may be charming, but she cannot have the courtesy and grace of the old music teachers who are passing into the shadow; Caruso—a subtle touch, this—may, for all we know, be a good singer, but he cannot be as great as Parkinson, the obscure English tenor, whom one of the old ladies once heard. And in the tremendous cadenza we realize that Gabriel, good husband though he may be, can never mean to his wife what the dead boy who once stood shivering beneath her window means—till he too has been buried under the snow which is Death's symbol.

This, of course, is only a way of saying that the short story is lyrical, not epic; that it springs from the heart of a situation rather than mounts up to and explains it. There is yet another way of expressing the same thing in relation to the novel. The novel, it is generally agreed, is the typical art of the middle classes which reached its highest development in the century of the middle classes, the nineteenth. The nineteenth-century novel in Europe had a peculiar geographical distribution. It is at its greatest in England, France, and Russia.

The distribution of the short story is quite different. Here, the Russians have the field to themselves; the French with Maupassant are barely in sight; while the English are still hovering round the starting post, eagerly searching for the whiskers of Colonel Claude Combpyne. It is true that the great period of the short story didn't come until the decline of the novel, about 1880, but long before that Turgenev had done things with the short story which have never been bettered. This hints at a basic difference in approach between novel and story.

It is even more peculiar in our own times. Now, it is America which takes the place of Imperial Russia and produces both novels and short stories of the first rank. But Ireland, which has never produced a novel, has produced short stories of remarkable quality, and, in spite of Coppard and Pritchett, far superior to English short stories which still mainly investigate whiskers in italics. This suggests that the difference has something to do with the attitude that the two art forms impose on their writers. I have small doubt that the difference is in the attitude to society.

The thing which makes the Irish novel impossible is that the subject of a novel is almost invariably the relation of the individual to society, and Ireland does not have a society which can absorb the individual; as an American critic has put it, every good Irish novel ends on a ship to England or America. But the emotion of Gabriel Conroy in "The Dead" is not conditioned by society, and the loneliness of the people in Winesburg, Ohio, is not likely to be changed by any change in their social condition. Their troubles "are from eternity and shall not fail."

In fact, the short story, compared with the novel, is a lonely, personal art; the lyric cry in face of human destiny, it does not deal as the novel must do with types or with problems of moment, but with what Synge calls "the profound and common interests of life"; the little servant girl so weary of her nursing that she smothers the baby; the cabman so obsessed by his son's death that when one of his busy customers will not listen to his grief, he tells it to his old cab horse. It is not for nothing that some of the great storytellers like Gorki have been tramps. The story writer is not a soldier in the field, but a guerrilla fighter, fighting the obscure duels of a great campaign. He stands always somewhere on the outskirts of society, less interested in its famous and typical figures than in the lonely and gnarled and obscure individuals of Winesburg, Ohio, and Dublin, Ireland.

Unit 2

SHORT STORIES

ON THE SHORT STORY

Short-story reading can be a pleasure and an enlargement and enrichment of life. The finer the story, the more deeply and perceptively it helps us to see into life, the greater the pleasure. The happiest reaction we can have is a recognition, based on our own experience, of the fundamental truth of the incident recorded and a realization that somehow the author has given us an increased appreciation or new material for understanding ourselves or our associates. Again and again the reading of a fine story will bring this kind of response, "You know, I knew a man almost exactly like that once, and he was in the same kind of trouble. But who would have thought that it could make such a wonderful story?"

The stories in the following section have been carefully selected to interest, amuse, and delight you—not all of them will please every reader but the majority should do so. In addition, the stories have been selected for the second purpose mentioned above, for the enlargement and enrichment of your life. In many instances you will like stories so much that you will want to read others that these authors have written. When you do that, you are really beginning to get an education for yourself, for you are demonstrating that you understand what a course in literature actually is—a framework, an outline, a series of suggestions, a presentation of certain techniques which you yourself then take up, use, make part of your culture. And so the pleasure you get from reading, understanding, and appreciating these few stories is no more than a brief introduction and a promise of much more pleasure to come.

One thing might be remembered: reading, at any level, is an acquired and developed taste. Some readers may try a few of these stories only to find so little in them that they wonder why on earth these particular stories were selected. At that point such readers may decide that trying to find anything of value in "quality" stories is useless, or they may realize that what they need for a genuine understanding of good fiction is greater control of the techniques of reading and interpretation.

Fiction involves an active partnership between writer and reader. The writer has initiated the process: he has set down, necessarily in cold, inert symbols, the outline of an experience that may be built into a living experience only in the mind and heart of a living person. The reader animates the outline intellectually, imaginatively, and emotionally. Like creative writing, creative reading demands training and practice. Fortunately, the apprenticeship of a reader need not be as arduous or extended as that of a writer, but it must be undertaken intelligently and pursued intensively. Any college student is aware that his reading ability and interests are far beyond those of a first-grader. He may not be aware, however, that his reading ability may have reached a plateau some months or years back, perhaps in his high school years. Frequently when this happens the reader looks for the causes of his boredom with "good" stories in the presumed shortcomings of the writers rather than where he should look, in his own lack of skill in reading.

Such a reader is likely to ask, "If the writer has something to say, why doesn't he say it so that I can understand it?" A good writer, particularly a contemporary writer, almost never imposes a moral on his story; neither is he likely to say anywhere in his story that it means precisely this or that. With some justice, he feels that the meaning of the story is to be found in the whole story—if he could have given the full richness of meaning in shorter space, he would have done so.

It is not necessarily true that if a story is well written its meaning will be clear to any reasonably intelligent person. The reader, whatever his intelligence, must bring to a story some knowledge of a rather specialized nature. He should understand, for example, the meaning and possible ramifications of *irony*. He should know that in addition to *denotation* words also have *connotation* and that the whole meaning of a passage or story may hang on that fact. An understanding of *symbolism* is of central importance for many of the best stories of the past fifty years. *Implication, understatement, distortion* must be recognized and taken account of.

These are niceties, of course, but what game or serious pursuit in life does not demand control of such things by those who would get the most from experience? Even so relatively unimportant a thing as baseball can furnish an example. Consider two people watching a superbly played game, a pitchers' battle. One is a former professional player. The other is his maiden aunt from Europe, who is seeing her first game. The maiden aunt is a highly intelligent individual, much more so than her nephew—but which one will get the most out of the game, the subtle shifts, the reason the shortstop is playing three feet out of his usual position, the situations of tension? Even here, knowledge carries its rewards; how much more so in the things that a great story can offer to the mind and spirit of man.

So far, the term "short story" has been used as though it had a precise meaning. In practice, almost any literate individual can identify a short story at a glance; it is a little surprising, therefore, that the term is so difficult to define. One reason is that the short story, in one form or another, has been a part of man's literary experience almost from the beginning of writing. Enough time has elapsed for it to have taken an extraordinarily wide variety of forms and to have embraced and treated almost every known attitude, idea, fancy, or hope.

Short stories appear as incidents in the epics and as chapters in the Bible. They are found in Greek and Roman myths, in Arthurian legends, and in the Arabian Nights. Bede, Boccaccio, and Chaucer told them; Chaucer's were frequently in verse. The ballads give us short stories in song, and there are even examples of short stories told with no words at all in series of drawings or cartoons. Historically, there is nothing intrinsic in the short story that would require it to be a prose form, nor is there any definable limit on the variety of material it may contain. In despair of arriving at anything more specific, one critic defined it this way, "A short story is a story that is short."

But even that won't do. Some short stories, it is true, are no more than eight hundred words, but others may extend to ten or fifteen thousand. Those with fewer than one thousand words are usually catalogued as ancedotes or prose lyrics; those longer than fifteen thousand are frequently labelled "novelettes." Generally speaking, a short story will be concerned with one major problem or situation. It will have a single plot and a small cast of characters. Older stories, like those of Washington Irving, in which the author begins at the beginning and carries the narrative straight through to the end, with more emphasis on sequential than on consequential development, are now often called "tales." The term "story" is usually reserved for a more tightly organized, more economical narrative, with greater emphasis on plot and much freer handling of time sequences. However, even this cautious attempt at nomenclature is of little value. Modern Irish writers habitually use a form very like but subtly different from the old tale, and many pieces of writing today are called stories although they are devoid of plot and sometimes devoid of characterization.

Many writers would accept this definition: "A short story is a brief, concentrated illumination or revelation of some facet of life." Elizabeth Bowen says that it is a narrative in which there is a psychological change. A familiar attempt to limit it describes it as a narrative in which a character passes through a situation, and either the character or the situation changes. It has been defined as a "time fight," a narrative in which the character has a limited time to accomplish his objective; in a sense, most stories are of this group.

What you as a reader might profitably notice is that the philosophy of the writer will condition not only the material and resolution of a story, but the form as well. If, for example, the writer is a Christian who believes that man is a creature possessing a body and a soul, that he is the adopted son of God and gifted with a free will, then his stories will usually make that plain, and, in addition, they are likely to be plotted stories. The reason for this is simple. The writer can show us man as he believes him to be, capable of making a rational decision or acting on it. The man faces a problem and he acts; to that action there is a reaction; etc. But to a full-blown naturalist such a story is impossible. For him, influenced by Darwin, Freud, and Zola, man is a creature almost completely determined by environment and heredity and the sex drive—any variations are due to chance. Such a man cannot act; he is acted upon. As a result, the naturalist's story will usually present a helpless, befuddled social animal who is shown in a situation that frightens him. He dabbles at his problem, but he has no real chance. He is defeated; or if he does happen to win, it is an accident and he is amazed.

Although there is no particular philosophical connection, the naturalist will usually limit himself to two types of characters: the normal (usually defeated) and the neurotic (always defeated), and either or both will be cowards. What he is reluctant or unable to realize is that man is frequently heroic. It is astonishing how firmly fixed in the minds of "serious" writers is the conviction that all men are cowards—and yet it is simply not true. If courage is taken to mean the ability to act sturdily and forthrightly even in the face of the overwhelming risk of death, then courage not only exists, it is all around us. Any day the front page of almost any newspaper will confirm the fact. On occasion a writer who wishes to be taken seriously will have the courage himself to present us with a courageous character, but even the thoroughly Christian writer seems to have been too often frightened into conformity through the influence of the naturalists.

As an intelligent reader you should try to avoid stories that embody any kind of character or situation clichés. If it is true that most slick paper magazines concentrate on the happy ending until it becomes a cliché, it is no less true that several highly sophisticated publications are quite as insistent that no story can end happily even if the editor has to drown the hero himself. One type is quite as sterotyped as the other.

The good story will present a situation that has dimension and significance. With insight and usually with compassion, the good writer will show us a character involved in the situation and the details of his efforts—physical, intellectual, and moral—to resolve it. The conclusion should satisfy the reader's sense of the fitness of things, his belief that for this particular character in this particular situation no other ending could have quite so much truth.

Love

One of the salient facts about human life is that it is surrounded by mystery. And nothing in it is more likely to stir wonder than that strange element called love. In "Neighbour Rosicky," Polly is touched by the wonderment of love:

> She had a sudden feeling that nobody in the world, not her mother, not Rudolph, or anyone, really loved her as much as old Rosicky did. It perplexed her. She sat frowning and trying to puzzle it out. It was as if Rosicky had a special gift for loving people, something that was like an ear for music or an eye for color. It was quiet, unobstrusive; it was merely there.

In part, at least, Rosicky's ability to relate positively to others derives from his ability to relate positively to the earth and sky that give context to all human relationships. Like the man in Frost's poem who stopped by the woods on a snowy evening, Rosicky sometimes pauses to look with pleasure at the countryside around him. One night he hesitates outside the door of his farmhouse; ". . . that kitchen with the shining windows was dear to him; but the sleeping fields and bright stars and the noble darkness were dearer still." In "The Peasant Marey" the Russian prisoner, when he remembers the gentle affection with which a seemingly crude serf calmed a frightened boy, experiences much the same wonderment that love stirred in Polly. In both stories there is implication that love grows best when it has roots deeply planted in the good earth. Dostoevsky, author of "The Peasant Marey," wrote in his masterpiece *The Brothers Karamazov*:

> Love all God's creations, the whole and every grain of sand in it. Love every leaf, every ray of God's light. Love the animals, love the plants, love everything. If you love everything, you will perceive the divine mystery in things. Once you perceive it, you will begin to comprehend it better every day. And you will come at last to love the whole world with an all-embracing love.

The Peasant Marey*
by FYODOR DOSTOEVSKY

It was Easter Monday. The air was warm, the sky blue, the sun high, "warm" and bright, but I was plunged in gloom. I wandered aimlessly behind the barracks in the prison yard, looked at the palings of the strong prison fence, counting them mechanically, though I did not particularly want to count them, but doing it more out of habit than anything else. It was the second day of "holidays" in prison. The convicts were not taken out to work, lots of them were drunk, cursing and quarrelling broke out every minute in different corners of the prison. Disgusting, coarse songs; groups of convicts playing cards under the bunks; several convicts who had run amok and had been dealt with summarily by their own comrades, were lying half dead on the bunks, covered with sheepskins, until they should recover consciousness; the knives that had already been drawn several times—all this had so harrowing an effect on me during the two days of holidays that it made me ill. I could never bear without disgust the wild orgies of the common people, and here in this place this was specially true. On such days even the officials never looked into the prison, carried out no searches, did not look for drinks, realising that once a year even these outcasts had to be given a chance of enjoying themselves and that otherwise things would be much worse. At last blind fury blazed up in my heart. I met the Pole, M—ski, one of the political prisoners. He gave me a black look, with flashing eyes and trembling lips. "*Je hais ces brigands!*" he hissed at me in an undertone and walked past me. I went back to the barracks, although I had rushed out of them like a madman only a quarter of an hour before, when six strong peasants had hurled themselves on the drunken Tartar Gazin in an attempt to quieten him and had begun beating him. They beat him senselessly —a camel might have been killed by such blows. But they knew that it was not easy to kill this Hercules, and they beat him therefore without any qualms. Now, on my return, I noticed Gazin lying unconscious and without any sign of life on a bunk in a corner at the other end of the barracks; he lay covered with a sheepskin, and they all passed by him in silence, knowing very well that if the man was unlucky he might die from a beating like that. I made my way to my place opposite the window with the iron bars and lay on my back with my eyes closed and my hands behind my head. I liked to lie like that: no one would bother a sleeping man, and meanwhile one could dream and think. But I found it difficult to dream: my heart was beating uneasily and M—ski's words were still echoing in my ears: "*Je hais ces brigands!*" However, why dwell on these scenes; I sometimes even now dream of those times at night, and none of my dreams is more agonising. Perhaps it will be noticed that to this day I have hardly ever spoken in print of my life in prison; *The House of the Dead* I wrote fifteen years ago in the person of a fictitious character who was supposed to have killed his wife. I may add, incidentally, just as an interesting detail, that many people have thought and have been maintaining ever since the publication of that book of mine, that I was sent to Siberia for the murder of my wife.

By and by I did forget my surroundings and became imperceptibly lost in memories. During the four years of my imprisonment I was continually recalling my past and seemed in my memories to live my former life all over again. These memories cropped up by themselves; I seldom evoked them consciously. It would begin from some point, some imperceptible feature, which then grew little by little into a complete picture, into some clear-cut and vivid impression. I used to analyse those impressions, adding new touches to an event

---
* From *The Best Short Stories of Fyodor Dostoevsky*. Reprinted by permission of Random House, Inc. All rights reserved.

that had happened long ago, and, above all, correcting it, correcting it incessantly, and that constituted my chief amusement. This time I for some reason suddenly remembered one fleeting instant in my early childhood when I was only nine years old—an instant that I seemed to have completely forgotten; but at that time I was particularly fond of memories of my early childhood. I remembered an August day in our village; a dry, bright day, though rather cold and windy; summer was drawing to a close, and we should soon have to leave for Moscow and again have to spend all winter over the boring French lessons, and I was so sorry to leave the country. I walked past the threshing floors and, going down a ravine, climbed up into the dense thicket of bushes which stretched from the other side of the ravine to the wood. I got amongst the bushes, and I could hear not very far away, about thirty yards perhaps, a peasant ploughing by himself on a clearing. I knew he was ploughing up the steep slope of a hill. The horse must have found it very hard going, for from time to time I heard the peasant's call from a distance: "Gee up! Gee up!" I knew almost all our peasants, but I did not know which of them was ploughing now, nor did it really matter to me who it was because I was occupied with my own affairs—I too was busy, breaking off a switch from a hazel-tree to strike frogs with; hazel twigs are very lovely, but they are also very brittle, much more brittle than birch twigs. I was also interested in beetles and other insects, and I was collecting them: some of them were very beautiful. I also liked the small quick red and yellow lizards with black spots, but I was afraid of snakes. However, there were many fewer snakes than lizards. There were not many mushrooms there; to get mushrooms one had to go to the birch wood, and I was about to go there. And there was nothing in the world I loved so much as the wood with its mushrooms and wild berries, its beetles and its birds, its hedgehogs and squirrels, and its damp smell of rotted leaves. And even as I write this I can smell the fragrance of our birch wood: these impressions remain with you for your whole life. Suddenly amid the dead silence I heard clearly and distinctly the shout, "Wolf! Wolf!" I uttered a shriek and, panic-stricken, screamed at the top of my voice and rushed out to the clearing straight to the ploughing peasant.

It was our peasant Marey. I do not know if there is such a name, but everybody called him Marey. He was a peasant of about fifty, thick-set and over medium height, with a large, grizzled, dark-brown beard. I knew him, but till that day I had scarcely ever spoken to him. When he heard my cry, he even stopped his old mare, and when, unable to stop myself I clutched at his wooden plough with one hand and at his sleeve with the other, he saw how terrified I was.

"There's a wolf there!" I cried, breathless.

He threw up his head and looked round involuntarily, for a moment almost believing me.

"Where's the wolf?"

"Someone shouted—shouted just now 'Wolf! Wolf!'" I stammered.

"There, there! There are no wolves hereabouts," he murmured, trying to calm me. "You've been dreaming, sonny. Who ever heard of wolves in these parts?"

But I was trembling all over and I was still clutching at his smock, and I suppose I must have been very pale. He looked at me with a worried smile, evidently anxious and troubled about me.

"Dear, dear, how frightened you are," he said, shaking his head. "Don't be frightened, sonny. Oh, you poor thing, you! There, there."

He stretched out his hand and suddenly stroked my cheek.

"There now! Christ be with you, cross yourself, there's a good lad!"

But I did not cross myself; the corners of my mouth were still twitching, and that seemed to strike him particularly. He quietly stretched out his thick finger with its black nail, smeared with earth, and gently touched my trembling lips.

"Dear, oh dear," he smiled at me with a slow motherly sort of smile, "Lord, how frightened he is, the poor lad!"

I realised at last that there was no wolf and that I had imagined the shout, "Wolf!

Wolf!" The shout, though, was very clear and distinct, but such shouts (and not only about wolves) I had imagined once or twice before, and I knew it. (I grew out of these hallucinations a few years later.)

"Well, I'll go now," I said, looking up at him, questioningly and shyly.

"Run along, run along, son, I'll be awatching you," he said, adding, "Don't you worry, I shan't let the wolf get you!" and he smiled at me with the same motherly smile. "Well, Christ be with you. Run along, run along, sonny," and he made the sign of the cross over me, and then crossed himself too.

I walked away, looking back anxiously every few yards. While I was walking away, Marey stood still with his mare and looked after me, nodding his head at me every time I looked around. As a matter of fact, I was a little ashamed of myself for having let him see how frightened I was, but I was still very much afraid of the wolf as I was walking away till I climbed up the steep side of the ravine and came to the first threshing barn. There my terror left me completely, and our watch-dog Volchok suddenly appeared out of nowhere and rushed at me. With Volchok at my side I completely recovered my spirits and turned around to Marey for the last time. I could no longer see his face clearly, but I felt that he was still nodding and smiling tenderly at me. I waved to him and he waved back to me and started his mare.

"Gee-up!" I heard his call in the distance again, and the mare pulled at the wooden plough once more.

All this came back to me all at once, I don't know why, but with an amazing accuracy of detail. I suddenly came to and sat up on my bunk and, I remember, I could still feel the gentle smile of memory on my lips. For another minute I went on recalling that incident from my childhood.

When I returned home from Marey that day I did not tell anybody about my "adventure." It was not much of an adventure, anyway. And, besides, I soon forgot all about Marey. Whenever I happened to come across him now and then, I never spoke to him either about the wolf or anything else, and now twenty years later in Siberia I suddenly remembered this meeting so distinctly that not a single detail of it was lost, which means of course that it must have been hidden in my mind without my knowing it, of itself and without any effort on my part, and came back to me suddenly when it was wanted. I remembered the tender, motherly smile of that serf, the way he made the sign of the cross over me and crossed himself, the way he nodded at me. "Lord, how afeered he is, the poor lad!" And particularly that thick finger of his, smeared with earth, with which he touched my twitching lips so gently and with such shy tenderness. No doubt, anyone would have done his best to calm a child, but something quite different seemed to have happened during that solitary meeting; and if I had been his own son, he could not have looked at me with eyes shining with brighter love. And who compelled him to look like that? He was one of our serfs, a peasant who was our property, and after all I was the son of his master. No one would have known that he had been so good to me, and no one would have rewarded him for it. Did he really love little children as much as that? There are such people, no doubt. Our meeting took place in a secluded spot, in a deserted field, and only God perhaps saw from above with what profound and enlightened human feeling, and with what delicate, almost womanly, tenderness the heart of a coarse, savagely ignorant Russian serf was filled, a serf who at the time neither expected nor dreamt of his emancipation.

Tell me, was not this what Konstantin Akaskov perhaps meant when he spoke of the high degree of culture of our people?

And so when I got off the bunk and looked round, I suddenly felt I remember, that I could look at these unhappy creatures with quite different eyes, and that suddenly by some miracle all hatred and anger had vanished from my heart. I walked round the prison peering into the faces I came across. That rascal of a peasant with his shaven head and branded face, yelling his hoarse drunken song at the top of his voice—why, he, too, may be the same sort of peasant as Marey:

I cannot possibly look into his heart, can I? That evening I again met M—ski. Poor man! He could have no memories about Marey or peasants like him and he could have no other opinion of these people except, *"Je hais ces brigands!"* Yes, it was much harder for those Poles than for us!

Neighbour Rosicky*
by WILLA CATHER

I

When Doctor Burleigh told neighbour Rosicky he had a bad heart, Rosicky protested.

"So? No, I guess my heart was always pretty good. I got a little asthma, maybe. Just a awful short breath when I was pitchin' hay last summer, dat's all."

"Well now, Rosicky, if you know more about it than I do, what did you come to me for? It's your heart that makes you short of breath. I tell you. You're sixty-five years old, and you've always worked hard, and your heart's tired. You've got to be careful from now on, and you can't do heavy work any more. You've got five boys at home to do it for you."

The old farmer looked up at the Doctor with a gleam of amusement in his queer triangular-shaped eyes. His eyes were large and lively, but the lids were caught up in the middle in a curious way, so that they formed a triangle. He did not look like a sick man. His brown face was creased but not wrinkled, he had a ruddy colour in his smooth-shaven cheeks and in his lips, under his long brown moustache. His hair was thin and ragged around his ears, but very little grey. His forehead, naturally high and crossed by deep parallel lines, now ran all the way up to his pointed crown. Rosicky's face had the habit of looking interested,—suggested a contented disposition and a reflective quality that was gay rather than grave. This gave him a certain detachment, the easy manner of an onlooker and observer.

"Well, I guess you ain't got no pills fur a bad heart, Doctor Ed. I guess the only thing is fur me to git me a new one."

Doctor Burleigh swung round in his desk-chair and frowned at the old farmer. "I think if I were you I'd take a little care of the old one, Rosicky."

Rosicky shrugged. "Maybe I don't know how. I expect you mean fur me not to drink my coffee no more."

"I wouldn't, in your place. But you'll do as you choose about that. I've never yet been able to separate a Bohemian from his coffee or his pipe. I've quit trying. But the sure thing is you've got to cut out farm work. You can feed the stock and do chores about the barn, but you can't do anything in the fields that makes you short of breath."

"How about shelling corn?"

"Of course not!"

Rosicky considered with puckered brows.

"I can't make my heart go no longer'n it wants to, can I, Doctor Ed?"

"I think it's good for five or six years yet, maybe more, if you'll take the strain off it. Sit around the house and help Mary. If I had a good wife like yours, I'd want to stay around the house."

His patient chuckled. "It ain't no place fur a man. I don't like no old man hanging round the kitchen too much. An' my wife, she's a awful hard worker her own self."

"That's it; you can help her a little. My Lord, Rosicky, you are one of the few men

---

* Copyright 1930 by The Crowell Publishing Co. and renewed 1958 by Executors of the Estate of Willa Cather. Reprinted from *Obscure Destinies*, by Willa Cather, by permission of Alfred A. Knopf, Inc.

I know who has a family he can get some comfort out of; happy dispositions, never quarrel among themselves, and they treat you right. I want to see you live a few years and enjoy them."

"Oh, they're good kids, all right," Rosicky assented.

The Doctor wrote him a prescription and asked him how his oldest son, Rudolph, who had married in the spring, was getting on. Rudolph had struck out for himself, on rented land. "And how's Polly? I was afraid Mary mightn't like an American daughter-in-law, but it seems to be working out all right."

"Yes, she's a fine girl. Dat widder woman bring her daughters up very nice. Polly got lots of spunk, an' she got some style, too. Da's nice, for young folks to have some style." Rosicky inclined his head gallantly. His voice and his twinkly smile were an affectionate compliment to his daughter-in-law.

"It looks like a storm, and you'd better be getting home before it comes. In town in the car?" Doctor Burleigh rose.

"No, I'm in de wagon. When you got five boys, you ain't got much chance to ride around in de Ford. I ain't much for cars, noway."

"Well, it's a good road out to your place; but I don't want you bumping around in a wagon much. And never again on a hay-rake, remember!"

Rosicky placed the Doctor's fee delicately behind the desk-telephone, looking the other way, as if this were an absent-minded gesture. He put on his plush cap and his corduroy jacket with a sheepskin collar, and went out.

The Doctor picked up his stethoscope and frowned at it as if he were seriously annoyed with the instrument. He wished it had been telling tales about some other man's heart, some old man who didn't look the Doctor in the eye so knowingly, or hold out such a warm brown hand when he said good-bye. Doctor Burleigh had been a poor boy in the country before he went away to medical school; he had known Rosicky almost ever since he could remember, and he had a deep affection for Mrs. Rosicky.

Only last winter he had had such a good breakfast at Rosicky's, and that when he needed it. He had been out all night on a long, hard confinement case at Tom Marshall's,—a big rich farm where there was plenty of stock and plenty of feed and a great deal of expensive farm machinery of the newest model, and no comfort whatever. The woman had too many children and too much work, and she was no manager. When the baby was born at last, and handed over to the assisting neighbour woman, and the mother was properly attended to, Burleigh refused any breakfast in that slovenly house, and drove his buggy—the snow was too deep for a car— eight miles to Anton Rosicky's place. He didn't know another farm-house where a man could get such a warm welcome, and such good strong coffee with rich cream. No wonder the old chap didn't want to give up his coffee!

He had driven in just when the boys had come back from the barn and were washing up for breakfast. The long table, covered with a bright oilcloth, was set out with dishes waiting for them, and the warm kitchen was full of the smell of coffee and hot biscuit and sausage. Five big handsome boys, running from twenty to twelve, all with what Burleigh called natural good manners,—they hadn't a bit of the painful self-consciousness he himself had to struggle with when he was a lad. One ran to put his horse away, another helped him off with his fur coat and hung it up, and Josephine, the youngest child and the only daughter, quickly set another place under her mother's direction.

With Mary, to feed creatures was the natural expression of affection,—her chickens, the calves, her big hungry boys. It was a rare pleasure to feed a young man whom she seldom saw and of whom she was as proud as if he belonged to her. Some country housekeepers would have stopped to spread a white cloth over the oilcloth, to change the thick cups and plates for their best china, and the wooden-handled knives for plated ones. But not Mary.

"You must take us as you find us, Doctor Ed. I'd be glad to put out my good things for you if you was expected, but I'm glad to get you any way at all."

He knew she was glad,—she threw back

her head and spoke out as if she were announcing him to the whole prairie. Rosicky hadn't said anything at all; he merely smiled his twinkling smile, put some more coal on the fire, and went into his own room to pour the Doctor a little drink in a medicine glass. When they were all seated, he watched his wife's face from his end of the table and spoke to her in Czech. Then, with the instinct of politeness which seldom failed him, he turned to the Doctor and said slyly; "I was just tellin' her not to ask you no questions about Mrs. Marshall till you eat some breakfast. My wife, she's terrible fur to ask questions."

The boys laughed, and so did Mary. She watched the Doctor devour her biscuit and sausage, too much excited to eat anything herself. She drank her coffee and sat taking in everything about her visitor. She had known him when he was a poor country boy, and was boastfully proud of his success, always saying: "What do people go to Omaha for, to see a doctor, when we got the best one in the State right here?" If Mary liked people at all, she felt physical pleasure in the sight of them, personal exultation in any good fortune that came to them. Burleigh didn't know many women like that, but he knew she was like that.

When his hunger was satisfied, he did, of course, have to tell them about Mrs. Marshall, and he noticed what a friendly interest the boys took in the matter.

Rudolph, the oldest one (he was still living at home then), said: "The last time I was over there, she was lifting them big heavy milk-cans, and I knew she oughtn't to be doing it."

"Yes, Rudolph told me about that when he come home, and I said it wasn't right," Mary put in warmly. "It was all right for me to do them things up to the last, for I was terrible strong, but that woman's weakly. And do you think she'll be able to nurse it, Ed?" She sometimes forgot to give him the title she was so proud of. "And to think of your being up all night and then not able to get a decent breakfast! I don't know what's the matter with such people."

"Why, Mother," said one of the boys, "if Doctor Ed had got breakfast there, we wouldn't have him here. So you ought to be glad."

"He knows I'm glad to have him, John, any time. But I'm sorry for that poor woman, how bad she'll feel the Doctor had to go away in the cold without his breakfast."

"I wish I'd been in practice when these were getting born." The doctor looked down the row of close-clipped heads. "I missed some good breakfasts by not being."

The boys began to laugh at their mother because she flushed so red, but she stood her ground and threw up her head. "I don't care, you wouldn't have got away from this house without breakfast. No doctor ever did. I'd have had something ready fixed that Anton could warm up for you."

The boys laughed harder than ever, and exclaimed at her: "I'll bet you would!" "She would, that!"

"Father, did you get breakfast for the doctor when we were born?"

"Yes, and he used to bring me my breakfast, too, mighty nice. I was always awful hungry!" Mary admitted with a guilty laugh.

While the boys were getting the Doctor's horse, he went to the window to examine the house plants. "What do you do to your geraniums to keep them blooming all winter, Mary? I never pass this house that from the road I don't see your windows full of flowers."

She snapped off a dark red one, and a ruffled new green leaf, and put them in his buttonhole. "There, that looks better. You look too solemn for a young man, Ed. Why don't you git married? I'm worried about you. Settin' at breakfast, I looked at you real hard, and I seen you've got some grey hairs already."

"Oh, yes! They're coming. Maybe they'd come faster if I married."

"Don't talk so. You'll ruin your health eating at the hotel. I could send your wife a nice loaf of nut bread, if you only had one. I don't like to see a young man getting grey. I'll tell you something, Ed; you make some strong black tea and keep it handy in a bowl, and every morning just brush it into your hair, an' it'll keep the grey from showin' much. That's the way I do!"

Sometimes the Doctor heard the gossipers in the drug-store wondering why Rosicky didn't get on faster. He was industrious, and so were his boys, but they were rather free and easy, weren't pushers, and they didn't always show good judgment. They were comfortable, they were out of debt, but they didn't get much ahead. Maybe, Doctor Burleigh reflected, people as generous and warm-hearted and affectionate as the Rosickys never got ahead much; maybe you couldn't enjoy your life and put it into the bank, too.

II

When Rosicky left Doctor Burleigh's office he went into the farm-implement store to light his pipe and put on his glasses and read over the list Mary had given him. Then he went into the general merchandise place next door and stood about until the pretty girl with the plucked eyebrows, who always waited on him, was free. Those eyebrows, two thin India-ink strokes, amused him, because he remembered how they used to be. Rosicky always prolonged his shopping by a little joking; the girl knew the old fellow admired her, and she liked to chaff with him.

"Seems to me about every other week you buy ticking, Mr. Rosicky, and always the best quality," she remarked as she measured off the heavy bolt with red stripes.

"You see, my wife is always makin' goose-fedder pillows, an' de thin stuff don't hold in dem little down-fedders."

"You must have lots of pillows at your house."

"Sure. She makes quilts of dem, too. We sleeps easy. Now she's makin' a fedder quilt for my son's wife. You know Polly, that married my Rudolph. How much my bill, Miss Pearl?"

"Eight eighty-five."

"Chust make it nine, and put in some candy fur de women."

"As usual. I never did see a man buy so much candy for his wife. First thing you know, she'll be getting too fat."

"I'd like dat. I ain't much fur all dem slim women like what de style is now."

"That's one for me, I suppose, Mr. Bohunk!" Pearl sniffed and elevated her India-ink strokes.

When Rosicky went out to his wagon, it was beginning to snow,—the first snow of the season, and he was glad to see it. He rattled out of town and along the highway through a wonderfully rich stretch of country, the finest farms in the county. He admired this High Prairie, as it was called, and always liked to drive through it. His own place lay in a rougher territory, where there was some clay in the soil and it was not so productive. When he bought his land, he hadn't the money to buy on High Prairie; so he told his boys, when they grumbled, that if their land hadn't some clay in it, they wouldn't own it at all. All the same, he enjoyed looking at these fine farms, as he enjoyed looking at a prize bull.

After he had gone eight miles, he came to the graveyard, which lay just at the edge of his own hay-land. There he stopped his horses and sat still on his wagon seat, looking about at the snowfall. Over yonder on the hill he could see his own house, crouching low, with the clump of orchard behind and the windmill before, and all down the gentle hill-slope the rows of pale gold cornstalks stood out against the white field. The snow was falling over the cornfield and the pasture and the hay-land, steadily, with very little wind,—a nice dry snow. The graveyard had only a light wire fence about it and was all overgrown with long red grass. The fine snow, settling into this red grass and upon the few little evergreens and the headstones, looked very pretty.

It was a nice graveyard, Rosicky reflected, sort of snug and homelike, not cramped or mournful,—a big sweep all around it. A man could lie down in the long grass and see the complete arch of the sky over him, hear the wagons go by; in summer the mowing-machine rattled right up to the wire fence. And it was so near home. Over there across the cornstalks his own roof and windmill looked so good to him that he promised himself to mind the Doctor and take care of himself. He was awful fond of his place, he admitted. He wasn't anxious to leave it. And it was a comfort to think that he would never have to go farther than the edge of his own hayfield. The snow, falling over his barnyard and the graveyard, seemed to draw things together like. And they were all old neighbours in the graveyard, most of them friends; there was nothing to feel awkward or embarrassed about. Embarrassment was the most disagreeable feeling Rosicky knew. He didn't often have it,—only with certain people whom he didn't understand at all.

Well, it was a nice snowstorm; a fine sight to see the snow falling so quietly and graciously over so much open country. On his cap and shoulders, on the horses' backs and manes, light, delicate, mysterious it fell; and with it a dry cool fragrance was released into the air. It meant rest for vegetation and men and beasts, for the ground itself; a season of long nights for sleep, leisurely breakfasts, peace by the fire. This and much more went through Rosicky's mind, but he merely told himself that winter was coming, clucked to his horses, and drove on.

When he reached home, John, the youngest boy, ran out to put away his team for him, and he met Mary coming up from the outside cellar with her apron full of carrots. They went into the house together. On the table, covered with oilcloth figured with clusters of blue grapes, a place was set, and he smelled hot coffee-cake of some kind. Anton never lunched in town; he thought that extravagant, and anyhow he didn't like the food. So Mary always had something ready for him when he got home.

After he was settled in his chair, stirring his coffee in a big cup, Mary took out of the oven a pan of *kolache* stuffed with apricots, examined them anxiously to see whether they had got too dry, put them beside his plate, and then sat down opposite him.

Rosicky asked her in Czech if she wasn't going to have any coffee.

She replied in English, as being somehow the right language for transacting business: "Now what did Doctor Ed say, Anton? You tell me just what."

"He said I was to tell you some compliments, but I forgot 'em." Rosicky's eyes twinkled.

"About you, I mean. What did he say about your asthma?"

"He says I ain't got no asthma." Rosicky took one of the little rolls in his broad brown fingers. The thickened nail of his right thumb told the story of his past.

"Well, what is the matter? And don't try to put me off."

"He don't say nothing much, only I'm a little older, and my heart ain't so good like it used to be."

Mary started and brushed her hair back from her temples with both hands as if she were a little out of her mind. From the way she glared, she might have been in a rage with him.

"He says there's something the matter with your heart? Doctor Ed says so?"

"Now don't yell at me like I was a hog in de garden, Mary. You know I always did like to hear a woman talk soft. He didn't say anything de matter wid my heart, only it ain't so young like it used to be, an' he tell me not to pitch hay or run de corn-sheller."

Mary wanted to jump up, but she sat still. She admired the way he never under any circumstances raised his voice or spoke roughly. He was city-bred, and she was country-bred; she often said she wanted her boys to have their papa's nice ways.

"You never have no pain there, do you? It's your breathing and your stomach that's been wrong. I wouldn't believe nobody but Doctor Ed about it. I guess I'll go see him myself. Didn't he give you no advice?"

"Chust to take it easy like, an' stay round de house dis winter. I guess you got some carpenter work for me to do. I kin make some new shelves for you, and I want dis long time to build a closet in de boys' room and make dem two little fellers keep dere clo'es hung up."

Rosicky drank his coffee from time to time, while he considered. His moustache was of the soft long variety and came down over his mouth like the teeth of a buggy-rake over a bundle of hay. Each time he put down his cup, he ran his blue handkerchief over his lips. When he took a drink of water, he managed very neatly with the back of his hand.

Mary sat watching him intently, trying to find any change in his face. It is hard to see anyone who has become like your own body to you. Yes, his hair had got thin, and his high forehead had deep lines running from left to right. But his neck, always clean shaved except in the busiest seasons, was not loose or baggy. It was burned a dark reddish brown, and there were deep creases in it, but it looked firm and full of blood. His cheeks had a good colour. On either side of his mouth there was a half-moon down the length of his cheek, not wrinkles, but two lines that had come there from his habitual expression. He was shorter and broader than when she married him; his back had grown broad and curved, a good deal like the shell of an old turtle, and his arms and legs were short.

He was fifteen years older than Mary, but she had hardly ever thought about it before. He was her man, and the kind of man she liked. She was rough, and he was gentle,—city-bred, as she always said. They had been shipmates on a rough voyage and had stood by each other in trying times. Life had gone well with them because, at bottom, they had the same ideas about life. They agreed, without discussion, as to what was most important and what was secondary. They didn't often exchange opinions, even in Czech,—it was as if they had thought the same thought together. A good deal had to be sacrificed and thrown overboard in a hard life like theirs, and they had never disagreed as to the things that could go. It had been a hard life, and a soft life, too. There wasn't anything brutal in the short, broad-backed man with the three-cornered eyes and the forehead that went on to the top of his skull. He was a city man, a gentle man, and though he had married a rough farm girl, he had never touched her without gentleness.

They had been at one accord not to hurry through life, not to be always skimping and saving. They saw their neighbours buy more land and feed more stock than they did, without discontent. Once when the creamery agent came to the Rosickys to persuade them to sell him their cream, he told them how much money the Fasslers, their nearest neighbours, had made on their cream last year.

"Yes," said Mary, "and look at them Fassler children! Pale, pinched little things, they look like skimmed milk. I'd rather put some colour into my children's faces than put money into the bank."

The agent shrugged and turned to Anton.

"I guess we'll do like she says," said Rosicky.

III

Mary very soon got into town to see Doctor Ed, and then she had a talk with her boys and set a guard over Rosicky. Even John, the youngest, had his father on his mind. If Rosicky went to throw hay down from the loft, one of the boys ran up the ladder and took the fork from him. He sometimes complained that though he was getting to be an old man, he wasn't an old woman yet.

That winter he stayed in the house in the afternoons and carpentered, or sat in the chair between the window full of plants and the wooden bench where the two pails of drinking-water stood. This spot was called "Father's corner," though it was not a corner at all. He had a shelf there, where he kept his Bohemian papers and his pipes and tobacco, and his shears and needles and thread and tailor's thimble. Having been a tailor in his youth, he couldn't bear to see a woman patching at his clothes, or at the boys'. He liked tailoring, and always patched all the overalls and jackets and work shirts. Occasionally he made a pair of pants one of the older boys had outgrown, for the little fellow.

While he sewed, he let his mind run back over his life. He had a good deal to remember, really; life in three countries. The only part of his youth he didn't like to remember was the two years he had spent in London, in Cheapside, working for a German tailor who was wretchedly poor. Those days, when he was nearly always hungry, when his clothes were dropping off him for dirt, and the sound of a strange language kept him in continual bewilderment, had left a sore spot in his mind that wouldn't bear touching.

He was twenty when he landed at Castle Garden in New York, and he had a protector who got him work in a tailor shop in Vesey Street, down near the Washington Market. He looked upon that part of his life as very happy. He became a good workman, he was industrious, and his wages were increased from time to time. He minded his own business and envied nobody's good fortune. He went to night school and learned to read English. He often did overtime work and was well paid for it, but somehow he never saved anything. He couldn't refuse a loan to a friend, and he was self-indulgent. He liked a good dinner, and a little went for beer, a little for tobacco; a good deal went to the girls. He often stood through an opera on Saturday nights; he could get standing-room for a dollar. Those were the great days of opera in New York, and it gave a fellow something to think about for the rest of the week. Rosicky had a quick ear, and a childish love of all the stage splendour; the scenery, the costumes, the ballet. He usually went with a chum, and after the performance they had beer and maybe some oysters somewhere. It was a fine life; for the first five years or so it satisfied him completely. He was never hungry or cold or dirty, and everything amused him: a fire, a dog fight, a parade, a storm, a ferry ride. He thought New York the finest, richest, friendliest city in the world.

Moreover, he had what he called a happy home life. Very near the tailor shop was a small furniture-factory, where an old Austrian, Loeffler, employed a few skilled men and made unusual furniture, most of it to order, for the rich German housewives uptown. The top floor of Loeffler's five-storey factory was a loft, where he kept his choice lumber and stored the odd pieces of furniture left on his hands. One of the young workmen he employed was a Czech, and he and Rosicky became fast friends. They persuaded Loeffler to let them have a sleeping-room in one corner of the loft. They bought goods, beds and bedding and had their pick of the furniture kept up there. The loft was low-pitched, but light and airy, full of windows, and good-smelling by reason of the fine lumber put up there to season. Old Loeffler used to go down to the docks and buy wood from South America and the East from the sea captains. The young men were as foolish about their house as a bridal pair. Zichec, the young cabinet-maker, devised every sort of convenience, and Rosicky kept their clothes in order. At night and on Sundays, when the quiver of machinery underneath was still, it was the quietest place in the world, and on summer nights all the sea winds blew in. Zichec often practised on his flute in the evening. They were both fond of music and went to the opera together. Rosicky thought he wanted to live like that for ever.

But as the years passed, all alike, he began to get a little restless. When spring came round, he would begin to feel fretted, and he got to drinking. He was likely to drink too much of a Saturday night. On Sunday he was languid and heavy, getting over his spree. On Monday he plunged into work again. So he never had time to figure out what ailed him, though he knew something did. When the grass turned green in Park Place, and the lilac hedge at the back of Trinity churchyard put out its blossoms, he was tormented by a longing to run away. That was why he drank too much; to get a temporary illusion of freedom and wide horizons.

Rosicky, the old Rosicky, could remember as if it were yesterday the day when the young Rosicky found out what was the matter with him. It was on a Fourth of July afternoon, and he was sitting in Park Place in the sun. The lower part of New York was empty. Wall Street, Liberty Street, Broadway, all empty. So much stone and asphalt with nothing going on, so many empty windows. The emptiness was intense, like the stillness in a great factory when the machinery stops and the belts and bands cease running. It was too great a change, it took all the strength out of one. Those blank buildings, without the stream of life pouring through them, were like empty jails. It struck young Rosicky that this was the trouble with big cities; they built you in from the earth itself, cemented you away from any contact with the ground. You lived in an unnatural world, like the fish in an aquarium, who were probably much more comfortable than they ever were in the sea.

On that very day he began to think seriously about the articles he had read in the Bohemian papers, describing prosperous Czech farming communities in the West. He believed he would like to go out there as a farm hand; it was hardly possible that he could ever have land of his own. His people had always been workmen; his father and grandfather had worked in shops. His mother's parents had lived in the country, but they rented their farm and had a hard time to get along. Nobody in his family had ever owned any land, —that belonged to a different station of life altogether. Anton's mother died when he was little, and he was sent into the country to her parents. He stayed with them until he was twelve, and formed those ties with the earth and the farm animals and growing things which are never made at all unless they are made early. After his grandfather died, he went back to live with his father and stepmother, but she was very hard on him, and his father helped him to get passage to London.

After that Fourth of July day in Park Place, the desire to return to the country never left him. To work on another man's farm would be all he asked; to see the sun rise and set and to plant things and watch them grow. He was a very simple man. He was like a tree that has not many roots, but one taproot that goes down deep. He subscribed for a Bohemian paper printed in Chicago, then for one printed in Omaha. His mind got farther and farther west. He began to save a little money to buy his liberty. When he was thirty-five, there was a great meeting in New York of Bohemian athletic societies, and Rosicky left the tailor shop and went home with the Omaha delegates to try his fortune in another part of the world.

IV

Perhaps the fact that his own youth was well over before he began to have a family was one reason why Rosicky was so fond of his boys. He had almost a grandfather's indulgence for them. He had never had to worry about any of them—except, just now, a little about Rudolph.

On Saturday night the boys always piled into the Ford, took little Josephine, and went to town to the moving-picture show. One Saturday morning they were talking at the breakfast table about starting early that evening, so that they would have an hour or so to see the Christmas things in the stores before the show began. Rosicky looked down the table.

"I hope you boys ain't disappointed, but I want you to let me have de car tonight. Maybe some of you can go in with de neighbours."

Their faces fell. They worked hard all week, and they were still like children. A new jack-knife or a box of candy pleased the older ones as much as the little fellow.

"If you and Mother are going to town," Frank said, "maybe you could take a couple of us along with you, anyway."

"No, I want to take de car down to Rudolph's, and let him an' Polly go in to de show. She don't git into town enough, an' I'm afraid she's gettin' lonesome, an' he can't afford no car yet."

That settled it. The boys were a good deal dashed. Their father took another piece of applecake and went on: "Maybe next Saturday night de two little fellers can go along wid dem."

"Oh, is Rudolph going to have the car every Saturday night?"

Rosicky did not reply at once; then he began to speak seriously: "Listen, boys: Polly ain't lookin' so good. I don't like to see nobody lookin' sad. It comes hard fur a town girl to be a farmer's wife. I don't want no trouble to start in Rudolph's family. When it starts, it ain't so easy to stop. An American girl don't git used to our ways all at once. I like to tell Polly she and Rudolph can have the car every Saturday night till after New Year's, if it's all right with you boys."

"Sure it's all right, Papa," Mary cut in. "And it's good you thought about that. Town girls is used to more than country girls. I lay awake nights, scared she'll make Rudolph discontented with the farm."

The boys put as good a face on it as

they could. They surely looked forward to their Saturday nights in town. That evening Rosicky drove the car the half-mile down to Rudolph's new, bare little house.

Polly was in a short-sleeved gingham dress, clearing away the supper dishes. She was a trim, slim little thing, with blue eyes and shingled yellow hair, and her eyebrows were reduced to a mere brush-stroke, like Miss Pearl's.

"Good evening, Mr. Rosicky. Rudolph's at the barn, I guess." She never called him father, or Mary mother. She was sensitive about having married a foreigner. She never in the world would have done it if Rudolph hadn't been such a handsome, persuasive fellow and such a gallant lover. He had graduated in her class in the high school in town, and their friendship began in the ninth grade.

Rosicky went in, though he wasn't exactly asked. "My boys ain't goin' to town tonight, an' I brought de car over fur you two to go in to de picture show."

Polly, carrying dishes to the sink, looked over her shoulder at him. "Thank you. But I'm late with my work tonight, and pretty tired. Maybe Rudolph would like to go in with you."

"Oh, I don't go to de shows! I'm too old-fashioned. You won't feel so tired after you ride in de air a ways. It's a nice clear night, an' it ain't cold. You go an' fix yourself up, Polly, an' I'll wash de dishes an' leave everything nice fur you."

Polly blushed and tossed her bob. "I couldn't let you do that, Mr. Rosicky. I wouldn't think of it."

Rosicky said nothing. He found a bib apron on a nail behind the kitchen door. He slipped it over his head and then took Polly by her two elbows and pushed her gently toward the door of her own room. "I washed up de kitchen many times for my wife, when de babies was sick or somethin'. You go an' make yourself look nice. I like you to look prettier'n any of dem town girls when you go in. De young folks must have some fun, an' I'm goin' to look out fur you, Polly."

That kind, reassuring grip on her elbows, the old man's funny bright eyes, made Polly want to drop her head on his shoulder for a second. She restrained herself, but she lingered in his grasp at the door of her room, murmuring tearfully: "You always lived in the city when you were young, didn't you? Don't you ever get lonesome out here?"

As she turned round to him, her hand fell naturally into his, and he stood holding it and smiling into her face with his peculiar, knowing, indulgent smile without a shadow of reproach in it. "Dem big cities is all right fur de rich, but dey is terrible hard fur de poor."

"I don't know. Sometimes I think I'd like to take a chance. You lived in New York, didn't you?"

"An' London. Da's bigger still. I learned my trade dere. Here's Rudolph comin', you better hurry."

"Will you tell me about London some time?"

"Maybe. Only I ain't no talker, Polly. Run an' dress yourself up."

The bedroom door closed behind her, and Rudolph came in from the outside, looking anxious. He had seen the car and was sorry any of his family should come just then. Supper hadn't been a very pleasant occasion. Halting in the doorway, he saw his father in a kitchen apron, carrying dishes to the sink. He flushed crimson and something flashed in his eye. Rosicky held up a warning finger.

"I brought de car over fur you an' Polly to go to de picture show, an' I made her let me finish here so you won't be late. You go put on a clean shirt, quick!"

"But don't the boys want the car, Father?"

"Not tonight dey don't." Rosicky fumbled under his apron and found his pants pocket. He took out a silver dollar and said in a hurried whisper: "You go an' buy dat girl some ice cream an' candy tonight, like you was courtin'. She's awful good friends wid me."

Rudolph was very short of cash, but he took the money as if it hurt him. There had been a crop failure all over the country. He had more than once been sorry he'd married this year.

In a few minutes the young people came out, looking clean and a little stiff. Rosicky hurried them off, and then he took his own time with the dishes. He scoured the pots and pans and put away the milk and swept the kitchen. He put some coal in the stove and shut off the draughts, so the place would be warm for them when they got home late at night. Then he sat down and had a pipe and listened to the clock tick.

Generally speaking, marrying an American girl was certainly a risk. A Czech should marry a Czech. It was lucky that Polly was the daughter of a poor widow woman; Rudolph was proud, and if she had a prosperous family to throw up at him, they could never make it go. Polly was one of four sisters, and they all worked; one was book-keeper in the bank, one taught music, and Polly and her younger sister had been clerks, like Miss Pearl. All four of them were musical, had pretty voices, and sang in the Methodist choir, which the eldest sister directed.

Polly missed the sociability of a store position. She missed the choir, and the company of her sisters. She didn't dislike housework, but she disliked so much of it. Rosicky was a little anxious about this pair. He was afraid Polly would grow so discontented that Rudy would quit the farm and take a factory job in Omaha. He had worked for a winter up there, two years ago, to get money to marry on. He had done very well, and they would always take him back at the stockyards. But to Rosicky that meant the end of everything for his son. To be a landless man was to be a wage-earner, a slave, all your life; to have nothing, to be nothing.

Rosicky thought he would come over and do a little carpentering for Polly after the New Year. He guessed she needed jollying. Rudolph was a serious sort of chap, serious in love and serious about his work.

Rosicky shook out his pipe and walked home across the fields. Ahead of him the lamplight shone from his kitchen windows. Suppose he were still in a tailor shop on Vesey Street, with a bunch of pale, narrow-chested sons working on machines, all coming home tired and sullen to eat supper in a kitchen that was a parlour also; with another crowded, angry family quarrelling just across the dumbwaiter shaft, and squeaking pulleys at the windows where dirty washings hung on dirty lines above a court full of old brooms and mops and ashcans....

He stopped by the windmill to look up at the frosty winter stars and draw a long breath before he went inside. That kitchen with the shining windows was dear to him; but the sleeping fields and bright stars and the noble darkness were dearer still.

V

On the day before Christmas the weather set in very cold; no snow, but a bitter, biting wind that whistled and sang over the flat land and lashed one's face like fine wires. There was baking going on in the Rosicky kitchen all day, and Rosicky sat inside, making over a coat that Albert had outgrown into an overcoat for John. Mary had a big red geranium in bloom for Christmas, and a row of Jerusalem cherry trees, full of berries. It was the first year she had ever grown these; Doctor Ed brought her the seeds from Omaha when he went to some medical convention. They reminded Rosicky of plants he had seen in England; and all afternoon, as he stitched, he sat thinking about those two years in London, which his mind usually shrank from even after all this while.

He was a lad of eighteen when he dropped down into London, with no money and no connexions except the address of a cousin who was supposed to be working at a confectioner's. When he went to the pastry shop, however, he found that the cousin had gone to America. Anton tramped the streets for several days, sleeping in doorways and on the Embankment, until he was in utter despair. He knew no English, and the sound of the strange language all about him confused him. By chance he met a poor German tailor who had learned his trade in Vienna, and could speak a little Czech. This tailor, Lifschnitz, kept a repair shop in a Cheapside basement, underneath a cobbler. He didn't much need an apprentice, but he was sorry for the boy and took him in for no wages but his keep and what he could pick up. The pickings were supposed to be coppers given you when you took work home to a customer. But most of the customers called for their clothes themselves, and the coppers that came Anton's way were very few. He had, however, a place to sleep. The tailor's family lived upstairs in three rooms; a kitchen, a bedroom, where Lifschnitz and his wife and five children slept, and a living-room. Two corners of this living-room were curtained off for lodgers; in one Rosicky slept on an old horsehair sofa, with a feather quilt to wrap himself in. The other corner was rented to a wretched, dirty boy, who was studying the violin. He actually practised there. Rosicky was dirty, too. There was no way to be anything else. Mrs. Lifschnitz got the water she cooked and washed with from a pump in a brick court, four flights down. There were bugs in the place, and multitudes of fleas, though the poor woman did the best she could. Rosicky knew she often went empty to give another potato or a spoonful of dripping to the two hungry, sad-eyed boys who lodged with her. He used to think he would never get out of there, never get a clean shirt to his back again. What would he do, he wondered, when his clothes actually dropped to pieces and the worn cloth wouldn't hold patches any longer?

It was still early when the old farmer put aside his sewing and his recollections. The sky had been a dark grey all day, with not a gleam of sun, and the light failed at four o'clock. He went to shave and change his shirt while the turkey was roasting. Rudolph and Polly were coming over for supper.

After supper they sat round in the kitchen, and the younger boys were saying how sorry they were it hadn't snowed. Everybody was sorry. They wanted a deep snow that would lie long and keep the wheat warm, and leave the ground soaked when it melted.

"Yes, sir!" Rudolph broke out fiercely; "if we have another dry year like last year, there's going to be hard times in this country."

Rosicky filled his pipe. "You boys don't know what hard times is. You don't owe nobody, you got plenty to eat an' keep warm, an' plenty water to keep clean. When you got them, you can't have it very hard."

Rudolph frowned, opened and shut his big right hand, and dropped it clenched upon his knee. "I've got to have a good deal more than that, Father, or I'll quit this farming gamble. I can always make good wages railroading, or at the packing house, and be sure of my money."

"Maybe so," his father answered dryly.

Mary, who had just come in from the pantry and was wiping her hands on the roller towel, thought Rudy and his father were getting too serious. She brought her darning-basket and sat down in the middle of the group.

"I ain't much afraid of hard times, Rudy," she said heartily. "We've had a plenty, but we've always come through. Your father wouldn't never take nothing very hard, not even hard times. I got a mind to tell you a story on him. Maybe you boys can't hardly remember the year we had that terrible hot wind, that burned everything up on the Fourth of July? All the corn an' the gardens. An' that was in the days when we didn't have alfalfa yet,—I guess it wasn't invented.

"Well, that very day your father was out cultivatin' corn, and I was here in the kitchen makin' plum preserves. We had bushels of plums that year. I noticed it was terrible hot, but it's always hot in the kitchen when you're preservin', an' I was too busy with my plums to mind. Anton come in from the field about three o'clock, an' I asked him what was the matter.

"'Nothin', he says, 'but it's pretty hot, an' I think I won't work no more today.' He stood round for a few minutes, an' then he says: 'Ain't you near through? I want you should git up a nice supper for us tonight. It's Fourth of July.'

"I told him to git along, that I was right in the middle of preservin', but the plums would taste good on hot biscuit. 'I'm goin' to have fried chicken, too,' he says, and he went off an' killed a couple. You three oldest boys was little fellers, playin' round outside, real hot an' sweaty, an' your father took you to the horse tank down by the windmill an' took off your clothes an' put you in. Them two box-elder trees was little then, but they made shade over the tank. Then he took off all his own clothes, an' got in with you. While he was playin' in the water with you, the Methodist preacher drove into our place to say how all the neighbours was goin' to meet at the schoolhouse that night, to pray for rain. He drove right to the windmill, of course, and there was your father and you three with no clothes on. I was in the kitchen door, an' I had to laugh, for the preacher acted like he ain't never seen a naked man before. He surely was embarrassed, an' your father couldn't git to his clothes; they was all hangin' up on the windmill to let the sweat dry out of 'em. So he laid in the tank where he was, an' put one of you boys on top of him to cover him up a little, an' talked to the preacher.

"When you got through playin' in the water, he put clean clothes on you and a clean shirt on himself, an' by that time I'd begun to get supper. He says: 'It's too hot in here to eat comfortable. Let's have a picnic in the orchard. We'll eat our supper behind the mulberry hedge, under them linden trees.'

"So he carried our supper down, an' a bottle of my wild-grape wine, an' everything tasted good, I can tell you. The wind got cooler as the sun was goin' down, and it turned out pleasant, only I noticed how the leaves was curled up on the linden trees. That made me think, an' I asked your father if that hot wind all day hadn't been terrible hard on the gardens an' the corn.

"'Corn,' he says, 'there ain't no corn.'

"'What you talkin' about?' I said. 'Ain't we got forty acres?'

"'We ain't got an ear,' he says, 'nor nobody else ain't got none. All the corn in this country was cooked by three o'clock today, like you'd roasted it in an oven.'

"'You mean you won't get no crop at all?' I asked him. I couldn't believe it, after he'd worked so hard.

"'No crop this year,' he says. 'That's why we're havin' a picnc. We might as well enjoy what we got.'

"An' that's how your father behaved, when all the neighbours was so discouraged they couldn't look you in the face. An' we enjoyed ourselves that year, poor as we was, an' our neighbours wasn't a bit better off for bein' miserable. Some of 'em grieved till they got poor digestions and couldn't relish what they did have."

The younger boys said they thought their father had the best of it. But Rudolph was thinking that, all the same, the neighbours had managed to get ahead more, in the fifteen years since that time. There must be something wrong about his father's way of doing things. He wished he knew what was going on in the back of Polly's mind. He knew she liked his father, but he knew, too, that she was afraid of something. When his mother sent over coffee-cake or prune tarts or a loaf of fresh bread, Polly seemed to regard them with a certain suspicion. When she observed to him that his brothers had nice manners, her tone implied that it was remarkable they should have. With his mother she was stiff and on her guard. Mary's hearty frankness and gusts of good humour irritated her. Polly was afraid of being unusual or conspicuous in any way, of being "ordinary," as she said!

When Mary had finished her story, Rosicky laid aside his pipe.

"You boys like me to tell you about some of dem hard times I been through in London?" Warmly encouraged, he sat rubbing his forehead along the deep creases. It was bothersome to tell a long story in English (he nearly always talked to the boys in Czech), but he wanted Polly to hear this one.

"Well, you know about dat tailor shop I worked in in London? I had one Christmas dere I ain't never forgot. Times was awful bad before Christmas; de boss ain't got much work, an' have it awful hard to pay his rent. It ain't so much fun, bein' poor in a big city like London, I'll say! All de windows is full of good t'ings to eat, an' all de pushcarts in de streets is full, an' you smell 'em all de time, an' you ain't got no money,—not a damn bit. I didn't mind de cold so much, though I didn't have no overcoat, chust a short jacket I'd outgrowed so it wouldn't meet on me, an' my hands was chapped raw. But I always had a good appetite, like you all know, an' de sight of dem pork pies in de windows was awful fur me!

"Day before Christmas was terrible foggy dat year, an' dat fog gits into your bones and makes you all damp like. Mrs. Lifschnitz didn't give us nothin' but a little bread an' drippin' for supper, because she was savin' to try for to give us a good dinner on Christmas Day. After supper de boss say I can go an' enjoy myself, so I went into de streets to listen to de Christmas singers. Dey sing old songs an' make very nice music, an' I run round after dem a good ways, till I got awful hungry. I t'ink maybe if I go home, I can sleep till morning an' forget my belly.

"I went into my corner real quiet, and roll up in my fedder quilt. But I ain't got my head down, till I smell somet'ing good. Seem like it git stronger an' stronger, an' I can't git to sleep noway. I can't understand dat smell. Dere was a gas light in a hall across de court, dat always shine in at my window a little. I got up an' look round. I got a little wooden box in my corner fur a stool, 'cause I ain't got no chair. I picks up dat box, and under it dere is a roast goose on a platter! I can't believe my eyes. I carry it to de window where de light comes in, an' touch it and smell it to find out, an' den I taste it to be sure. I say, I will eat chust one little bite of dat goose, so I can go to sleep, and tomorrow I won't eat none at all. But I tell you, boys, when I stop, one half of dat goose was gone!"

The narrator bowed his head, and the boys shouted. But little Josephine slipped behind his chair and kissed him on the neck beneath his ear.

"Poor little Papa, I don't want him to be hungry!"

"Da's long ago, child. I ain't never been hungry since I had your mudder to cook fur me."

"Go on and tell us the rest, please," said Polly.

"Well, when I come to realize what I done, of course, I felt terrible. I felt better in de stomach, but very bad in de heart. I sat on my bed wid dat platter on my knees, an' it all come to me; how hard dat poor woman save to buy dat goose, and how she get some neighbour to cook it dat got more fire, an' how she put it in my corner to keep it away from dem hungry children. Dey was a old carpet hung up to shut my corner off, an' de children wasn't allowed to go in dere. An' I know she put it in my corner because she trust me more'n she did de violin boy. I can't stand it to face her after I spoil de Christmas. So I put on my shoes and go out into de city. I tell myself I better throw myself in de river; but I guess I ain't dat kind of a boy.

"It was after twelve o'clock, an' terrible cold, an' I start out to walk about London all night. I walk along de river awhile, but dey was lots of drunks all along; men, and women too. I chust move along to keep away from de police. I git on to de Strand, an' den over to New Oxford Street where dere was a big German restaurant on de ground floor, wid big windows all fixed up fine, an' I could see de people havin' parties inside. While I was lookin' in, two men and two ladies come out, laughin' and talkin' and feelin' happy about all dey been eatin' an' drinkin', and dey was speakin' Czech,—not like de Austrians, but like de home folks talk it.

"I guess I went crazy, an' I done what I ain't never done before nor since. I went right up to dem gay people an' begun to beg dem: 'Fellow-countrymen, for God's sake give me money enough to buy a goose!'

"Dey laugh, of course, but de ladies speak awful kind to me, an' dey take me back into de restaurant and give me hot coffee and cakes, an' make me tell all about how I happened to come to London, an' what I was doin' dere. Dey take my name and where I work down on paper, an' both of dem ladies give me ten shillings.

"De big market at Covent Garden ain't very far away, an' dat time it was open. I go dere an' buy a big goose an' some pork pies, an' potatoes and onions, an' cakes an' oranges fur de children,—all I could carry! When I git home, everybody is still asleep. I pile all I bought on de kitchen table, an' go in an' lay down on my bed, an' I ain't waken up till

I hear dat woman scream when she come out into her kitchen. My goodness, but she was surprise! She laugh an' cry at de same time, an' hug me and waken all de children. She ain't stop fur no breakfast; she git de Christmas dinner ready dat morning, and we all sit down an' eat all we can hold. I ain't never seen dat violin boy have all he can hold before.

"Two tree days after dat, de two men come to hunt me up, an' dey ask my boss, and he give me a good report an' tell dem I was a steady boy all right. One of dem Bohemians was very smart an' run a Bohemian newspaper in New York, an' de odder was a rich man, in de importing business, an' dey been travelling togedder. Dey told me how t'ings was easier in New York, an' offered to pay my passage when dey was goin' home soon on a boat. My boss say to me: 'You go. You ain't got no chance here, an' I like to see you git ahead, fur you always been a good boy to my woman, and fur dat fine Christmas dinner you give us all.' An' da's how I got to New York."

That night when Rudolph and Polly, arm in arm, were running home across the fields with the bitter wind at their backs, his heart leaped for joy when she said she thought they might have his family come over for supper on New Year's Eve. "Let's get up a nice supper, and not let your mother help at all; make her be company for once."

"That would be lovely of you, Polly," he said humbly. He was a very simple, modest boy, and he, too, felt vaguely that Polly and her sisters were more experienced and worldly than his people.

VI

The winter turned out badly for farmers. It was bitterly cold, and after the first light snows before Christmas there was no snow at all,—and no rain. March was as bitter as February. On those days when the wind fairly punished the country, Rosicky sat by his window. In the fall he and the boys had put in a big wheat planting, and now the seed had frozen in the ground. All that land would have to be ploughed up and planted over again, planted in corn. It had happened before, but he was younger then, and he never worried about what had to be. He was sure of himself and of Mary; he knew they could bear what they had to bear, that they would always pull through somehow. But he was not so sure about the young ones, and he felt troubled because Rudolph and Polly were having such a hard start.

Sitting beside his flowering window while the panes rattled and the wind blew in under the door, Rosicky gave himself to reflection as he had not done since those Sundays in the loft of the furniture-factory in New York, long ago. Then he was trying to find what he wanted in life for himself; now he was trying to find what he wanted for his boys, and why it was he so hungered to feel sure they would be here, working this very land, after he was gone.

They would have to work hard on the farm, and probably they would never do much more than make a living. But if he could think of them as staying here on the land, he wouldn't have to fear any great unkindness for them. Hardships, certainly; it was a hardship to have the wheat freeze in the ground when seed was so high; and to have to sell your stock because you had no feed. But there would be other years when everything came along right, and you caught up. And what you had was your own. You didn't have to choose between bosses and strikers, and go wrong either way. You didn't have to do with dishonest and cruel people. They were the only things in his experience he had found terrifying and horrible; the look in the eyes of a dishonest and crafty man, of a scheming and rapacious woman.

In the country, if you had a mean neighbour, you could keep off his land and make him keep off yours. But in the city, all the foulness and misery and brutality of your neighbours was part of your life. The worst things he had come upon in his journey through the world were human,—depraved and poisonous specimens of man. To this day he could recall certain terrible faces in the London streets. There were mean people everywhere, to be sure, even in their own country town here. But they weren't tempered, hardened, sharpened, like the treacherous people in cities who live by grinding or cheating or poisoning their fellow-men. He had helped to bury two of his fellow-workmen in the tailoring trade, and he was distrustful of the organized industries that see one out of the world in big cities. Here, if you were sick, you had Doctor Ed to look after you; and if you died, fat Mr. Haycock, the kindest man in the world, buried you.

It seemed to Rosicky that for good, honest boys like his, the worst thing they could do on the farm was better than the best they would be likely to do in the city. If he'd had a mean boy now, one who was crooked and sharp and tried to put anything over on his brothers, then town would be the place for him. But he had no such boy. As for Rudolph, the discontented one, he would give the shirt off his back to anyone who touched his heart. What Rosicky really hoped for his boys was that they could get through the world without ever knowing much about the cruelty of human beings. "Their mother and me ain't prepared them for that," he sometimes said to himself.

These thoughts brought him back to a grateful consideration of his own case. What an escape he had had, to be sure! He, too, in his time, had had to take money for repair work from the hand of a hungry child who let it go so wistfully; because it was money due his boss. And now, in all these years, he had never had to take a cent from anyone in bitter need,—never had to look at the face of a woman become like a wolf's from struggle and famine. When he thought of these things, Rosicky would put on his cap and jacket and slip down to the barn and give his workhorses a little extra oats, letting them eat it out of his hand in their slobbery fashion. It was his way of expressing what he felt, and made him chuckle with pleasure.

The spring came warm, with blue skies,— but dry, dry as a bone. The boys began ploughing up the wheat-fields to plant them over in corn. Rosicky would stand at the fence corner and watch them, and the earth was so dry it blew up in clouds of brown dust that hid the horses and the sulky plough and the driver. It was a bad outlook.

The big alfalfa-field that lay between the home place and Rudolph's came up green, but Rosicky was worried because during that open windy winter a great many Russian thistle plants had blown in there and lodged. He kept asking the boys to rake them out; he was afraid their seed would root and "take the alfalfa." Rudolph said that was nonsense. The boys were working so hard planting corn, their father felt he couldn't insist about the thistles, but he set great store by that big alfalfa field. It was a feed you could depend on,—and there was some deeper reason, vague, but strong. The peculiar green of that clover woke early memories in old Rosicky, went back to something in his childhood in the old world. When he was a little boy, he had played in fields of that strong blue-green colour.

One morning, when Rudolph had gone to town in the car, leaving a work-team idle in his barn, Rosicky went over to his son's place, put the horses to the buggy-rake, and set about quietly raking up those thistles. He behaved with guilty caution, and rather enjoyed stealing a march on Doctor Ed, who was just then taking his first vacation in seven years of practice and was attending a clinic in Chicago. Rosicky got the thistles raked up, but did not stop to burn them. That would take some time, and his breath was pretty short, so he thought he had better get the horses back to the barn.

He got them into the barn and to their stalls, but the pain had come on so sharp in his chest that he didn't try to take the harness off. He started for the house, bending lower with every step. The cramp in his chest was shutting him up like a jack-knife. When he reached the windmill, he swayed and caught at the ladder. He saw Polly coming down the hill, running with the swiftness of a slim greyhound. In a flash she had her shoulder under his armpit.

"Lean on me, Father, hard! Don't be afraid. We can get to the house all right."

Somehow they did, though Rosicky became blind with pain; he could keep on his legs, but he couldn't steer his course. The next thing he was conscious of was lying on Polly's bed, and Polly bending over him wringing out bath towels in hot water and putting them on his chest. She stopped only to throw coal into the stove, and she kept the tea-kettle and the black pot going. She put these hot applications on him for nearly an hour, she told him afterwards, and all that time he was drawn up stiff and blue, with the sweat pouring off him.

As the pain gradually loosed its grip, the stiffness went out of his jaws, the black circles around his eyes disappeared, and a little of his natural colour came back. When his daughter-in-law buttoned his shirt over his chest at last, he sighed.

"Da's fine, de way I feel now, Polly. It was a awful bad spell, an' I was so sorry it all come on you like it did."

Polly was flushed and excited. "Is the pain really gone? Can I leave you long enough to telephone over to your place?"

Rosicky's eyelids fluttered. "Don't telephone, Polly. It ain't no use to scare my wife. It's nice and quiet here, an' if I ain't too much trouble to you, just let me lay still till I feel like myself. I ain't got no pain now. It's nice here."

Polly bent over him and wiped the moisture from his face. "Oh, I'm so glad it's over!" she broke out impulsively. "It just broke my heart to see you suffer so, Father."

Rosicky motioned her to sit down on the chair where the tea-kettle had been, and looked up at her with that lively affectionate gleam in his eyes. "You was awful good to me, I won't never forget dat. I hate it to be sick on you like dis. Down at de barn I say to myself, dat young girl ain't had much experience in sickness, I don't want to scare her, an' maybe she's got a baby comin' or somet'ing."

Polly took his hand. He was looking at her so intently and affectionately and confidingly; his eyes seemed to caress her face, to regard it with pleasure. She frowned with her funny streaks of eyebrows, and then smiled back at him.

"I guess maybe there is something of that kind going to happen. But I haven't told anyone yet, not my mother or Rudolph. You'll be the first to know."

His hand pressed hers. She noticed that it was warm again. The twinkle in his yellow-brown eyes seemed to come nearer.

"I like mighty well to see dat little child, Polly," was all he said. Then he closed his eyes and lay half-smiling. But Polly sat still, thinking hard. She had a sudden feeling that nobody in the world, not her mother, not Rudolph, or anyone, really loved her as much as old Rosicky did. It perplexed her. She sat frowning and trying to puzzle it out. It was as if Rosicky had a special gift for loving people, something that was like an ear for music or an eye for colour. It was quiet, unobtrusive; it was merely there. You saw it in his eyes,— perhaps that was why they were merry. You felt it in his hands, too. After he dropped off to sleep, she sat holding his warm, broad, flexible brown hand. She had never seen another in the least like it. She wondered if it wasn't a kind of gypsy hand, it was so alive and quick and light in its communications,— very strange in a farmer. Nearly all the farmers she knew had huge lumps of fists, like mauls, or they were knotty and bony and uncomfortable-looking, with stiff fingers. But Rosicky's was like quick-silver, flexible, muscular, about the colour of a pale cigar, with deep, deep creases across the palm. It wasn't nervous, it wasn't a stupid lump; it was a warm brown human hand, with some cleverness in it, a great deal of generosity, and something else which Polly could only call "gypsy-like,"— something nimble and lively and sure, in the way that animals are.

Polly remembered that hour long afterwards; it had been like an awakening to her. It seemed to her that she had never learned so much about life from anything as from old Rosicky's hand. It brought her to herself; it communicated some direct and untranslatable message.

When she heard Rudolph coming in the car she ran out to meet him.

"Oh, Rudy, your father's been awful

sick! He raked up those thistles he's been worrying about, and afterwards he could hardly get to the house. He suffered so I was afraid he was going to die."

Rudolph jumped to the ground. "Where is he now?"

"On the bed. He's asleep. I was terribly scared, because, you know, I'm so fond of your father." She slipped her arm through his and they went into the house. That afternoon they took Rosicky home and put him to bed, though he protested that he was quite well again.

The next morning he got up and dressed and sat down to breakfast with his family. He told Mary that his coffee tasted better than usual to him, and he warned the boys not to bear any tales to Doctor Ed when he got home. After breakfast he sat down by his window to do some patching and asked Mary to thread several needles for him before she went to feed her chickens,—her eyes were better than his, and her hands steadier. He lit his pipe and took up John's overalls. Mary had been watching him anxiously all morning, and as she went out of the door with her bucket of scraps, she saw that he was smiling. He was thinking, indeed, about Polly, and how he might never have known what a tender heart she had if he hadn't got sick over there. Girls nowadays didn't wear their heart on their sleeves. But now he knew Polly would make a fine woman after the foolishness wore off. Either a woman had that sweetness at her heart or she hadn't. You couldn't always tell by the look of them; but if they had that, everything came out right in the end.

After he had taken a few stitches, the cramp began in his chest, like yesterday. He put his pipe cautiously down on the window-sill and bent over to ease the pull. No use,—he had better try to get to his bed if he could. He rose and groped his way across the familiar floor, which was rising and falling like the deck of a ship. At the door he fell. When Mary came in, she found him lying there, and the moment she touched him she knew that he was gone.

Doctor Ed was away when Rosicky died, and for the first few weeks after he got home he was hard driven. Every day he said to himself that he must get out to see that family that had lost their father. One soft, warm moonlight night in early summer he started for the farm. His mind was on other things, and not until his road ran by the graveyard did he realize that Rosick wasn't over there on the hill where the red lamplight shone, but here, in the moonlight. He stopped his car, shut off the engine, and sat there for a while.

A sudden hush had fallen on his soul. Everything here seemed strangely moving and significant, though signifying what, he did not know. Close by the wire fence stood Rosicky's mowing-machine, where one of the boys had been cutting hay that afternoon; his own workhorses had been going up and down there. The new-cut hay perfumed all the night air. The moonlight silvered the long, billowy grass that grew over the graves and hid the fence; the few little evergreens stood out black in it, like shadows in a pool. The sky was very blue and soft, the stars rather faint because the moon was full.

For the first time it struck Doctor Ed that this was really a beautiful graveyard. He thought of city cemeteries; acres of shrubbery and heavy stone, so arranged and lonely and unlike anything in the living world. Cities of the dead, indeed; cities of the forgotten, of the "put away." But this was open and free, this little square of long grass which the wind for ever stirred. Nothing but the sky overhead, and the many-coloured fields running on until they met that sky. The horses worked here in summer; the neighbours passed on their way to town; and over yonder, in the cornfield, Rosicky's own cattle would be eating fodder as winter came on. Nothing could be more undeathlike than this place; nothing could be more right for a man who had helped to do the work of great cities and had always longed for the open country and had got to it at last. Rosicky's life seemed to him complete and beautiful.

Babylon Revisited*
by F. SCOTT FITZGERALD

"And where's Mr. Campbell?" Charlie asked.

"Gone to Switzerland. Mr. Campbell's a pretty sick man, Mr. Wales."

"I'm sorry to hear that. And George Hardt?" Charlie inquired.

"Back in America, gone to work."

"And where is the Snow Bird?"

"He was in here last week. Anyway, his friend, Mr. Schaeffer, is in Paris."

Two familiar names from the long list of a year and a half ago. Charlie scribbled an address in his notebook and tore out the page.

"If you see Mr. Schaeffer, give him this," he said. "It's my brother-in-law's address. I haven't settled on a hotel yet."

He was not really disappointed to find Paris was so empty. But the stillness in the Ritz bar was strange and portentous. It was not an American bar any more—he felt polite in it, and not as if he owned it. It had gone back into France. He felt the stillness from the moment he got out of the taxi and saw the doorman, usually in a frenzy of activity at this hour, gossiping with a *chasseur*[1] by the servants' entrance.

Passing through the corridor, he heard only a single, bored voice in the once-clamorous women's room. When he turned into the bar he traveled the twenty feet of green carpet with his eyes fixed straight ahead by old habit; and then, with his foot firmly on the rail, he turned and surveyed the room, encountering only a single pair of eyes that fluttered up from a newspaper in the corner. Charlie asked for the head barman, Paul, who in the latter days of the bull market had come to work in his own custom-built car—disembarking, however, with due nicety at the nearest corner. But Paul was at his country house today and Alix giving him information.

"No, no more," Charlie said. "I'm going slow these days."

Alix congratulated him: "You were going pretty strong a couple of years ago."

"I'll stick to it all right," Charlie assured him. "I've stuck to it for over a year and a half now."

"How do you find conditions in America?"

"I haven't been to America for months. I'm in business in Prague, representing a couple of concerns there. They don't know about me down there."

Alix smiled.

"Remember the night of George Hardt's bachelor dinner here?" said Charlie. "By the way, what's become of Claude Fessenden?"

Alix lowered his voice confidentially: "He's in Paris, but he doesn't come here any more. Paul doesn't allow it. He ran up a bill of thirty thousand francs, charging all his drinks and his lunches, and usually his dinner, for more than a year. And when Paul finally told him he had to pay, he gave him a bad check."

Alix shook his head sadly.

"I don't understand it, such a dandy fellow. Now he's all bloated up—" He made a plump apple of his hands.

Charlie watched a group of strident queens installing themselves in a corner.

"Nothing affects them," he thought. "Stocks rise and fall, people loaf or work, but they go on forever." The place oppressed him. He called for the dice and shook with Alix for the drink.

"Here for long, Mr. Wales?"

"I'm here for four or five days to see my little girl."

"Oh-h! You have a little girl?"

Outside, the fire-red, gas-blue, ghost-green signs shone smokily through the tranquil rain.

---

* "Babylon Revisited" (Copyright 1931 The Curtis Publishing Company; renewal copyright © 1959 Frances S. F. Lanahan) is reprinted with the permission of Charles Scribner's Sons from *Taps at Reveille* by F. Scott Fitzgerald.

[1] *chasseur* footman or bellboy.

It was late afternoon and the streets were in movement; the *bistros* gleamed. At the corner of the Boulevard des Capucines he took a taxi. The Place de la Concorde moved by in pink majesty; they crossed the logical Seine, and Charlie felt the sudden provincial quality of the left bank.

Charlie directed his taxi to the Avenue de l'Opera, which was out of his way. But he wanted to see the blue hour spread over the magnificent façade, and imagine that the cab horns, playing endlessly the first few bars of *Le Plus que Lent*, were the trumpets of the Second Empire. They were closing the iron grill in front of Brentano's Book-store, and people were already at dinner behind the trim little bourgeois hedge of Duval's. He had never eaten at a really cheap restaurant in Paris. Five-course dinner, four francs fifty, eighteen cents, wine included. For some odd reason he wished that he had.

As they rolled on to the Left Bank and he felt its sudden provincialism, he thought, "I spoiled this city for myself. I didn't realize it, but the days came along one after another, and then two years were gone, and everything was gone, and I was gone."

He was thirty-five, and good to look at. The Irish mobility of his face was sobered by a deep wrinkle between his eyes. As he rang his brother-in-law's bell in the Rue Palatine, the wrinkle deepened till it pulled down his brows; he felt a cramping sensation in his belly. From behind the maid who opened the door darted a lovely little girl of nine who shrieked "Daddy!" and flew up, struggling like a fish, into his arms. She pulled his head around by one ear and set her cheek against his.

"My old pie," he said.

"Oh, daddy, daddy, daddy, daddy, dads, dads, dads!"

She drew him into the salon, where the family waited, a boy and a girl his daughter's age, his sister-in-law and her husband. He greeted Marion with his voice pitched carefully to avoid either feigned enthusiasm or dislike, but her response was more frankly tepid, though she minimized her expression of unalterable distrust by directing her regard toward his child. The two men clasped hands in a friendly way and Lincoln Peters rested his for a moment on Charlie's shoulder.

The room was warm and comfortably American. The three children moved intimately about, playing through the yellow oblongs that led to other rooms; the cheer of six o'clock spoke in the eager smacks of the fire and the sounds of French activity in the kitchen. But Charlie did not relax; his heart sat up rigidly in his body and he drew confidence from his daughter, who from time to time came close to him, holding in her arms the doll he had brought.

"Really extremely well," he declared in answer to Lincoln's question. "There's a lot of business there that isn't moving at all, but we're doing even better than ever. In fact, damn well. I'm bringing my sister over from America next month to keep house for me. My income last year was bigger than it was when I had money. You see, the Czechs—"

His boasting was for a specific purpose; but after a moment, seeing a faint restiveness in Lincoln's eye, he changed the subject:

"Those are fine children of yours, well brought up, good manners."

"We think Honoria's a great little girl too."

Marion Peters came back from the kitchen. She was a tall woman with worried eyes, who had once possessed a fresh American loveliness. Charlie had never been sensitive to it and was always suprised when people spoke of how pretty she had been. From the first there had been an instinctive antipathy between them.

"Well, how do you find Honoria?" she asked.

"Wonderful. I was astonished how much she's grown in ten months. All the children are looking well."

"We haven't had a doctor for a year. How do you like being back in Paris?"

"It seems very funny to see so few Americans around."

"I'm delighted," Marion said vehemently. "Now at least you can go into a store without their assuming you're a millionaire. We've suffered like everybody, but on the whole it's a good deal pleasanter."

"But it was nice while it lasted," Charlie said. "We were a sort of royalty, almost infallible, with a sort of magic around us. In the bar this afternoon"—he stumbled, seeing his mistake—"there wasn't a man I knew."

She looked at him keenly. "I should think you'd have had enough of bars."

"I only stayed a minute. I take one drink every afternoon, and no more."

"Don't you want a cocktail before dinner?" Lincoln asked.

"I take only one drink every afternoon, and I've had that."

"I hope you keep to it," said Marion.

Her dislike was evident in the coldness with which she spoke, but Charlie only smiled; he had larger plans. Her very aggressiveness gave him an advantage, and he knew enough to wait. He wanted them to initiate the discussion of what they knew had brought him to Paris.

At dinner he couldn't decide whether Honoria was most like him or her mother. Fortunate if she didn't combine the traits of both that had brought them to disaster. A great wave of protectiveness went over him. He thought he knew what to do for her. He believed in character; he wanted to jump back a whole generation and trust in character again as the eternally valuable element. Everything else wore out.

He left soon after dinner, but not to go home. He was curious to see Paris by night with clearer and more judicious eyes than those of other days. He bought a *strapontin*[2] for the Casino and watched Josephine Baker go through her chocolate arabesques.

After an hour he left and strolled toward Montmartre, up the Rue Pigalle into the Place Blanche. The rain had stopped and there were a few people in evening clothes disembarking from taxis in front of cabarets, and *cocottes*[3] prowling singly or in pairs, and many Negroes. He passed a lighted door from which issued music, and stopped with the sense of familiarity; it was Bricktop's, where he had parted with so many hours and so much money. A few doors farther on he found another ancient rendezvous and incautiously put his head inside. Immediately an eager orchestra burst into sound, a pair of professional dancers leaped to their feet and a maître d'hôtel swooped toward him, crying, "Crowd just arriving, sir!" But he withdrew quickly.

"You have to be damn drunk," he thought.

Zelli's was closed, the bleak and sinister cheap hotels surrounding it were dark; up in the Rue Blanche there was more light and a local, colloquial French crowd. The Poet's Cave had disappeared, but the two great mouths of the Café of Heaven and the Café of Hell still yawned—even devoured, as he watched, the meager contents of a tourist bus—a German, a Japanese, and an American couple who glanced at him with frightened eyes.

So much for the effort and ingenuity of Montmartre. All the catering to vice and waste was on an utterly childish scale, and he suddenly realized the meaning of the word "dissipate"—to dissipate into thin air; to make nothing out of something. In the little hours of the night every move from place to place was an enormous human jump, an increase of paying for the privilege of slower and slower motion.

He remembered thousand-franc notes given to an orchestra for playing a single number, hundred-franc notes tossed to a doorman for calling a cab.

But it hadn't been given for nothing.

It had been given, even the most wildly squandered sum, as an offering to destiny that he might not remember the things most worth remembering, the things that now he would always remember—his child taken from his control, his wife escaped to a grave in Vermont.

In the glare of a *brasserie*[4] a woman spoke to him. He bought her some eggs and coffee,

---

[2] *strapontin* seat in a carriage.
[3] *cocottes* streetwalkers.

[4] *brasserie* tavern or beer hall.

and then, eluding her encouraging stare, gave her a twenty-franc note and took a taxi to his hotel.

II

He woke upon a fine fall day—football weather. The depression of yesterday was gone and he liked the people on the streets. At noon he sat opposite Honoria at Le Grand Vatel, the only restaurant he could think of not reminiscent of champagne dinners and long luncheons that began at two and ended in a blurred and vague twilight.

"Now, how about vegetables? Oughtn't you to have some vegetables?"

"Well, yes."

"Here's *épinards* and *chou-fleur* and carrots and *haricots*."[5]

"I'd like *chou-fleur*."

"Wouldn't you like to have two vegetables?"

"I usually only have one at lunch."

The waiter was pretending to be inordinately fond of children. "*Qu'elle est mignonne la petite! Elle parle exactement comme une Française.*"[6]

"How about dessert? Shall we wait and see?"

The waiter disappeared. Honoria looked at her father expectantly.

"What are we going to do?"

"First, we're going to that toy store in the Rue Saint-Honoré and buy you anything you like. And then we're going to the vaudeville at the Empire."

She hesitated. "I like it about the vaudeville, but not the toy store."

"Why not?"

"Well, you brought me this doll." She had it with her. "And I've got lots of things. And we're not rich any more, are we?"

"We never were. But today you are to have anything you want."

"All right," she agreed resignedly.

When there had been her mother and a French nurse he had been inclined to be strict; now he extended himself, reached out for a new tolerance; he must be both parents to her and not shut any of her out of communication.

"I want to get to know you," he said gravely. "First let me introduce myself. My name is Charles J. Wales, of Prague."

"Oh, daddy!" her voice cracked with laughter.

"And who are you, please?" he persisted, and she accepted a rôle immediately: Honoria Wales, Rue Palatine, Paris."

"Married or single?"

"No, not married. Single."

He indicated the doll. "But I see you have a child, madame."

Unwilling to disinherit it, she took it to her heart and thought quickly: "Yes, I've been married, but I'm not married now. My husband is dead."

He went on quickly, "And the child's name?"

"Simone. That's after my best friend at school."

"I'm very pleased that you're doing so well at school."

"I'm third this month," she boasted. "Elsie"—that was her cousin—"is only about eighteenth, and Richard is about at the bottom."

"You like Richard and Elsie, don't you?"

"Oh, yes. I like Richard quite well and I like her all right."

Cautiously and casually he asked: "And Aunt Marion and Uncle Lincoln—which do you like best?"

"Oh, Uncle Lincoln, I guess."

He was increasingly aware of her presence. As they came in, a murmur of ". . . adorable" followed them, and now the people at the next table bent all their silences upon her, staring as if she were something no more conscious than a flower.

"Why don't I live with you?" she asked suddenly. "Because mamma's dead?"

"You must stay here and learn more French. It would have been hard for daddy to take care of you so well."

---

[5] *épinards* spinach *chou-fleur* cauliflower *haricots* kidney beans.
[6] *Qu'elle est mignonne*, etc. What a darling little girl! She speaks exactly like a Frenchman.

"I don't really need much taking care of any more. I do everything for myself."

Going out of the restaurant, a man and a woman unexpectedly hailed him.

"Well, the old Wales!"

"Hello there, Lorraine. . . . Dunc."

Sudden ghosts out of the past: Duncan Schaeffer, a friend from college. Lorraine Quarrles, a lovely, pale blonde of thirty; one of a crowd who had helped them make months into days in the lavish times of three years ago.

"My husband couldn't come this year," she said, in answer to his question. "We're poor as hell. So he gave me two hundred a month and told me I could do my worst on that. . . . This your little girl?"

"What about coming back and sitting down?" Duncan asked.

"Can't do it." He was glad for an excuse. As always, he felt Lorraine's passionate, provocative attraction, but his own rhythm was different now.

"Well, how about dinner?" she asked.

"I'm not free. Give me your address and let me call you."

"Charlie, I believe you're sober," she said judicially. "I honestly believe he's sober, Dunc. Pinch him and see if he's sober."

Charlie indicated Honoria with his head. They both laughed.

"What's your address?" said Duncan skeptically.

He hesitated, unwilling to give the name of his hotel.

"I'm not settled yet. I'd better call you. We're going to see the vaudeville at the Empire."

"There! That's what I want to do," Lorraine said. "I want to see some clowns and acrobats and jugglers. That's just what we'll do, Dunc."

"We've got to do an errand first," said Charlie. "Perhaps we'll see you there."

"All right, you snob. . . . Good-by, beautiful little girl."

"Good-by."

Honoria bobbed politely.

Somehow, an unwelcome encounter. They liked him because he was functioning, because he was serious; they wanted to see him, because he was stronger than they were now, because they wanted to draw a certain sustenance from his strength.

At the Empire, Honoria proudly refused to sit upon her father's folded coat. She was already an individual with a code of her own, and Charlie was more and more absorbed by the desire of putting a little of himself into her before she crystallized utterly. It was hopeless to try to know her in so short a time.

Between the acts they came upon Duncan and Lorraine in the lobby where the band was playing.

"Have a drink?"

"All right, but not up at the bar. We'll take a table."

"The perfect father."

Listening abstractedly to Lorraine, Charlie watched Honoria's eyes leave their table, and he followed them wistfully about the room, wondering what they saw. He met her glance and she smiled.

"I liked that lemonade," she said.

What had she said? What had he expected? Going home in a taxi afterward, he pulled her over until her head rested against his chest.

"Darling, do you ever think about your mother?"

"Yes, sometimes," she answered vaguely.

"I don't want you to forget her. Have you got a picture of her?"

"Yes, I think so. Anyhow, Aunt Marion has. Why don't you want me to forget her?"

"She loved you very much."

"I loved her too."

They were silent for a moment.

"Daddy, I want to come and live with you," she said suddenly.

His heart leaped; he had wanted it to come like this.

"Aren't you perfectly happy?"

"Yes, but I love you better than anybody. And you love me better than anybody, don't you, now that mummy's dead?"

"Of course I do. But you won't always like me best, honey. You'll grow up and meet somebody your own age and go marry him and forget you ever had a daddy."

"Yes, that's true," she agreed tranquilly.

He didn't go in. He was coming back at nine o'clock and he wanted to keep himself fresh and new for the thing he must say then.

"When you're safe inside, just show yourself in that window."

"All right. Good-by, dads, dads, dads, dads."

He waited in the dark street until she appeared, all warm and glowing, in the window above and kissed her fingers out into the night.

III

They were waiting. Marion sat behind the coffee service in a dignified black dinner dress that just faintly suggested mourning. Lincoln was walking up and down with the animation of one who had already been talking. They were as anxious as he was to get into the question. He opened it almost immediately:

"I suppose you know what I want to see you about—why I really came to Paris."

Marion played with the black stars on her necklace and frowned.

"I'm awfully anxious to have a home," he continued. "And I'm awfully anxious to have Honoria in it. I appreciate your taking in Honoria for her mother's sake, but things have changed now"—he hesitated and then continued more forcibly—"changed radically with me, and I want to ask you to reconsider the matter. It would be silly for me to deny that about three years ago I was acting badly——"

Marion looked up at him with hard eyes.

"—but all that's over. As I told you, I haven't had more than a drink a day for over a year, and I take that drink deliberately, so that the idea of alcohol won't get too big in my imagination. You see the idea?"

"No," said Marion succinctly.

"It's a sort of stunt I set myself. It keeps the matter in proportion."

"I get you," said Lincoln. "You don't want to admit it's got any attraction for you."

"Something like that. Sometimes I forget and don't take it. But I try to take it. Anyhow, I couldn't afford to drink in my position. The people I represent are more than satisfied with what I've done, and I'm bringing my sister over from Burlington to keep house for me, and I want awfully to have Honoria too. You know that even when her mother and I weren't getting along well we never let anything that happened touch Honoria. I know she's fond of me and I know I'm able to take care of her and—well, there you are. How do you feel about it?"

He knew that now he would have to take a beating. It would last an hour or two hours, and it would be difficult, but if he modulated his inevitable resentment to the chastened attitude of the reformed sinner, he might win his point in the end.

Keep your temper, he told himself. You don't want to be justified. You want Honoria.

Lincoln spoke first: "We've been talking it over since we got your letter last month. We're happy to have Honoria here. She's a dear little thing, and we're glad to be able to help her, but of course that isn't the question——"

Marion interrupted suddenly. "How long are you going to stay sober, Charlie?" she asked.

"Permanently, I hope."

"How can anybody count on that?"

"You know I never did drink heavily until I gave up business and came over here with nothing to do. Then Helen and I began to run around with——"

"Please leave Helen out of it. I can't bear to hear you talk about her like that."

He stared at her grimly; he had never been certain how fond of each other the sisters were in life.

"My drinking only lasted about a year and a half—from the time we came over until I—collapsed."

"It was time enough."

"It was time enough," he agreed.

"My duty is entirely to Helen," she said. "I try to think what she would have wanted me to do. Frankly, from the night you did that terrible thing you haven't really existed for me. I can't help that. She was my sister."

"Yes."

"When she was dying she asked me to look out for Honoria. If you hadn't been in a sanitarium then, it might have helped matters."

He had no answer.

"I'll never in my life be able to forget the morning when Helen knocked at my door, soaked to the skin and shivering and said you'd locked her out."

Charlie gripped the sides of the chair. This was more difficult than he expected; he wanted to launch out into a long expostulation and explanation, but he only said: "The night I locked her out—" and she interrupted, "I don't feel up to going over that again."

After a moment's silence Lincoln said: "We're getting off the subject. You want Marion to set aside her legal guardianship and give you Honoria. I think the main point for her is whether she has confidence in you or not."

"I don't blame Marion," Charlie said slowly, "but I think she can have entire confidence in me. I had a good record up to three years ago. Of course, it's within human possibilities I might go wrong any time. But if we wait much longer I'll lose Honoria's childhood and my chance for a home." He shook his head, "I'll simply lose her, don't you see?"

"Yes, I see," said Lincoln.

"Why didn't you think of all this before?" Marion asked.

"I suppose I did, from time to time, but Helen and I were getting along badly. When I consented to the guardianship, I was flat on my back in a sanitarium and the market had cleaned me out. I knew I'd acted badly, and I thought if it would bring any peace to Helen, I'd agree to anything. But now it's different. I'm functioning, I'm behaving damn well, so far as——"

"Please don't swear at me," Marion said.

He looked at her, startled. With each remark the force of her dislike became more and more apparent. She had built up all her fear of life into one wall and faced it toward him. This trivial reproof was possibly the result of some trouble with the cook several hours before. Charlie became increasingly alarmed at leaving Honoria in this atmosphere of hostility against himself; sooner or later it would come out, in a word here, a shake of the head there, and some of that distrust would be irrevocably implanted in Honoria. But he pulled his temper down out of his face and shut it up inside him; he had won a point, for Lincoln realized the absurdity of Marion's remark and asked her lightly since when she had objected to the word "damn."

"Another thing," Charlie said: "I'm able to give her certain advantages now. I'm going to take a French governess to Prague with me. I've got a lease on a new apartment——"

He stopped, realizing that he was blundering. They couldn't be expected to accept with equanimity the fact that his income was again twice as large as their own.

"I suppose you can give her more luxuries than we can," said Marion. "When you were throwing away money we were living along watching every ten francs. . . . I suppose you'll start doing it again."

"Oh, no," he said. "I've learned. I worked hard for ten years, you know—until I got lucky in the market, like so many people. Terribly lucky. It won't happen again."

There was a long silence. All of them felt their nerves straining, and for the first time in a year Charlie wanted a drink. He was sure now that Lincoln Peters wanted him to have his child.

Marion shuddered suddenly; part of her saw that Charlie's feet were planted on the earth now, and her own maternal feeling recognized the naturalness of his desire; but she had lived for a long time with a prejudice—a prejudice founded on a curious disbelief in her sister's happiness, and which, in the shock of one terrible night, had turned to hatred for him. It had all happened at a point in her life where the discouragement of ill health and adverse circumstances made it necessary for her to believe in tangible villainy and a tangible villain.

"I can't help what I think!" she cried out suddenly. "How much you were responsible for Helen's death, I don't know. It's something you'll have to square with your own conscience."

An electric current of agony surged through him; for a moment he was almost on his feet, an unuttered sound echoing in his throat. He hung on to himself for a moment, another moment.

"Hold on there," said Lincoln uncomfortably. "I never thought you were responsible for that."

"Helen died of heart trouble," Charlie said dully.

"Yes, heart trouble." Marion spoke as if the phrase had another meaning for her.

Then, in the flatness that followed her outburst, she saw him plainly and she knew he had somehow arrived at control over the situation. Glancing at her husband, she found no help from him, and as abruptly as if it were a matter of no importance, she threw up the sponge.

"Do what you like!" she cried, springing up from her chair. "She's your child. I'm not the person to stand in your way. I think if it were my child I'd rather see her—" She managed to check herself. "You two decide it. I can't stand this. I'm sick. I'm going to bed."

She hurried from the room; after a moment Lincoln said:

"This has been a hard day for her. You know how strongly she feels—" His voice was almost apologetic: "When a woman gets an idea in her head."

"Of course."

"It's going to be all right. I think she sees now that you—can provide for the child, and so we can't very well stand in your way or Honoria's way."

"Thank you, Lincoln."

"I'd better go along and see how she is."

"I'm going."

He was still trembling when he reached the street, but a walk down the Rue Bonaparte to the *quais* set him up, and as he crossed the Seine, fresh and new by the *quai* lamps, he felt exultant. But back in his room he couldn't sleep. The image of Helen haunted him. Helen whom he had loved so until they had senselessly begun to abuse each other's love, tear it into shreds. On that terrible February night that Marion remembered so vividly, a slow quarrel had gone on for hours. There was a scene at the Florida, and then he attempted to take her home, and then she kissed young Webb at a table; after that there was what she had hysterically said. When he arrived home alone he turned the key in the lock in wild anger. How could he know she would arrive an hour later alone, that there would be a snowstorm in which she wandered about in slippers, too confused to find a taxi? Then the aftermath, her escaping pneumonia by a miracle, and all the attendant horror. They were "reconciled," but that was the beginning of the end, and Marion, who had seen with her own eyes and who imagined it to be one of many scenes from her sister's martyrdom, never forgot.

Going over it again brought Helen nearer, and in the white, soft light that steals upon half sleep near morning he found himself talking to her again. She said that he was perfectly right about Honoria and that she wanted Honoria to be with him. She said she was glad he was being good and doing better. She said a lot of other things—very friendly things—but she was in a swing in a white dress, and swinging faster and faster all the time, so that at the end he could not hear clearly all that she said.

IV

He woke up feeling happy. The door of the world was open again. He made plans, vistas, futures for Honoria and himself, but suddenly he grew sad, remembering all the plans he and Helen had made. She had not planned to die. The present was the thing—work to do and someone to love. But not to love too much, for he knew the injury that a father can do to a daughter or a mother to a son by attaching them too closely: afterward, out in the world, the child would seek in the marriage partner the same blind tenderness and, failing probably to find it, turn against love and life.

It was another bright, crisp day. He called Lincoln Peters at the bank where he worked and asked if he could count on taking Honoria when he left for Prague. Lincoln agreed that there was no reason for delay. One thing—the legal guardianship. Marion wanted to retain that a while longer. She was upset by the whole matter, and it would oil things if she felt that the situation was still in her control for another year. Charlie agreed, wanting only the tangible, visible child.

Then the question of a governess. Charles sat in a gloomy agency and talked to a cross Béarnaise and to a buxom Breton peasant, neither of whom he could have endured. There were others whom he would see tomorrow.

He lunched with Lincoln Peters at Griffons, trying to keep down his exultation.

"There's nothing quite like your own child," Lincoln said. "But you understand how Marion feels too."

"She's forgotten how hard I worked for seven years there," Charlie said. "She just remembers one night."

"There's another thing." Lincoln hesitated. "While you and Helen were tearing around Europe throwing money away, we were just getting along. I didn't touch any of the prosperity because I never got ahead enough to carry anything but my insurance. I think Marion felt there was some kind of injustice in it—you not even working toward the end, and getting richer and richer."

"It went just as quick as it came," said Charlie.

"Yes, a lot of it stayed in the hands of *chasseurs* and saxophone players and *maîtres d'hôtel*—well, the big party's over now. I just said that to explain Marion's feeling about those crazy years. If you drop in about six o'clock tonight before Marion's too tired, we'll settle the details on the spot."

Back at his hotel, Charlie found a *pneumatique*[7] that had been redirected from the Ritz bar where Charlie had left his address for the purpose of finding a certain man.

"DEAR CHARLIE: You were so strange when we saw you the other day that I wondered if I did something to offend you. If so, I'm not conscious of it. In fact, I have thought about you too much for the last year, and it's always been in the back of my mind that I might see you if I came over here. We *did* have such good times that crazy spring, like the night you and I stole the butcher's tricycle, and the time we tried to call on the president and you had the old derby rim and the wire cane. Everybody seems so old lately, but I don't feel old a bit. Couldn't we get together some time today for old time's sake? I've got a vile hang-over for the moment, but will be feeling better this afternoon and will look for you about five in the sweatshop at the Ritz.

"Always devotedly,
"LORRAINE."

His first feeling was one of awe that he had actually, in his mature years, stolen a tricycle and pedaled Lorraine all over the Étoile between the small hours and dawn. In retrospect it was a nightmare. Locking out Helen didn't fit in with any other act of his life, but the tricycle incident did—it was one of many. How many weeks or months of dissipation to arrive at that condition of utter irresponsibility?

He tried to picture how Lorraine had appeared to him then—very attractive; Helen was unhappy about it, though she said nothing. Yesterday, in the restaurant, Lorraine had seemed trite, blurred, worn away. He emphatically did not want to see her, and he was glad Alix had not given away his hotel address. It was a relief to think, instead, of Honoria, to think of Sundays spent with her and of saying good morning to her and of knowing she was there in his house at night, drawing her breath in the darkness.

At five he took a taxi and bought presents for all the Peters—a piquant cloth doll, a box of Roman soldiers, flowers for Marion, big linen handkerchiefs for Lincoln.

He saw, when he arrived in the apartment, that Marion had accepted the inevitable. She greeted him now as though he were a recalcitrant member of the family, rather than a menacing outsider. Honoria had been told she was going; Charlie was glad to see that

---

[7] *pneumatique* a letter sent by the pneumatic tube system in Paris.

her tact made her conceal her excessive happiness. Only on his lap did she whisper her delight and the question "When?" before she slipped away with the other children.

He and Marion were alone for a minute in the room, and on an impulse he spoke out boldly:

"Family quarrels are bitter things. They don't go according to any rules. They're not like aches or wounds; they're more like splits in the skin that won't heal because there's not enough material. I wish you and I could be on better terms."

"Some things are hard to forget," she answered. "It's a question of confidence." There was no answer to this and presently she asked, "When do you propose to take her?"

"As soon as I can get a governess. I hoped the day after tomorrow."

"That's impossible. I've got to get her things in shape. Not before Saturday."

He yielded. Coming back into the room, Lincoln offered him a drink.

"I'll take my daily whisky," he said.

It was warm here, it was a home, people together by a fire. The children felt very safe and important; the mother and father were serious, watchful. They had things to do for the children more important than his visit here. A spoonful of medicine was, after all, more important than the strained relations between Marion and himself. They were not dull people, but they were very much in the grip of life and circumstances. He wondered if he couldn't do something to get Lincoln out of his rut at the bank.

A long peal at the door-bell; the *bonne à tout faire*[8] passed through and went down the corridor. The door opened upon another long ring, and then voices, and the three in the salon looked up expectantly; Richard moved to bring the corridor within his range of vision, and Marion rose. Then the maid came back along the corridor, closely followed by the voices, which developed under the light into Duncan Schaeffer and Lorraine Quarrles.

They were gay, they were hilarious, they were roaring with laughter. For a moment

---

[8] *bonne à tout faire*   maid or general servant.

Charlie was astounded; unable to understand how they ferreted out the Peters' address.

"Ah-h-h!" Duncan wagged his finger roguishly at Charlie. "Ah-h-h!"

They both slid down another cascade of laughter. Anxious and at a loss, Charlie shook hands with them quickly and presented them to Lincoln and Marion. Marion nodded, scarcely speaking. She had drawn back a step toward the fire; her little girl stood beside her, and Marion put an arm about her shoulder.

With growing annoyance at the intrusion, Charlie waited for them to explain themselves. After some concentration Duncan said:

"We came to invite you out to dinner. Lorraine and I insist that all this shishi, cagy business 'bout your address got to stop."

Charlie came closer to them, as if to force them backward down the corridor.

"Sorry, but I can't. Tell me where you'll be and I'll phone you in half an hour."

This made no impression. Lorraine sat down suddenly on the side of a chair, and focusing her eyes on Richard, cried, "Oh, what a nice little boy! Come here, little boy." Richard glanced at his mother, but did not move. With a perceptible shrug of her shoulders, Lorraine turned back to Charlie:

"Come and dine. Sure your cousins won' mine. See you so sel'om. Or solemn."

"I can't," said Charlie sharply. "You two have dinner and I'll phone you."

Her voice became suddenly unpleasant. "All right, we'll go. But I remember once when you hammered on my door at four A.M. I was enough of a good sport to give you a drink. Come on, Dunc."

Still in slow motion, with blurred, angry faces, with uncertain feet, they retired along the corridor.

"Good night," Charlie said.

"Good night!" responded Lorraine emphatically.

When he went back into the salon Marion had not moved, only now her son was standing in the circle of her other arm. Lincoln was still swinging Honoria back and forth like a pendulum from side to side.

"What an outrage!" Charlie broke out. "What an absolute outrage!"

Neither of them answered. Charlie dropped into an armchair, picked up his drink, set it down again and said:

"People I haven't seen for two years having the colossal nerve——"

He broke off. Marion had made the sound "Oh!" in one swift, furious breath, turned her body from him with a jerk and left the room.

Lincoln set down Honoria carefully.

"You children go in and start your soup," he said, and when they obeyed, he said to Charlie:

"Marion's not well and she can't stand shocks. That kind of people make her really physically sick."

"I didn't tell them to come here. They wormed your name out of somebody. They deliberately——"

"Well, it's too bad. It doesn't help matters. Excuse me a minute."

Left alone, Charlie sat tense in his chair. In the next room he could hear the children eating, talking in monosyllables, already oblivious to the scene between their elders. He heard a murmur of conversation from a farther room and then the ticking bell of a telephone receiver picked up, and in a panic he moved to the other side of the room and out of earshot.

In a minute Lincoln came back. "Look here. Charlie. I think we'd better call off dinner for tonight. Marion's in bad shape."

"Is she angry with me?"

"Sort of," he said, almost roughly. "She's not strong and——"

"You mean she's changed her mind about Honoria?"

"She's pretty bitter right now. I don't know. You phone me at the bank tomorrow."

"I wish you'd explain to her I never dreamed these people would come here. I'm just as sore as you are."

"I couldn't explain anything to her now."

Charlie got up. He took his coat and hat and started down the corridor. Then he opened the door of the dining room and said in a strange voice, "Good night, children."

Honoria rose and ran around the table to hug him.

"Good night, sweetheart," he said vaguely, and then trying to make his voice more tender, trying to conciliate something, "Good night, dear children."

V

Charlie went directly to the Ritz bar with the furious idea of finding Lorraine and Duncan, but they were not there, and he realized that in any case there was nothing he could do. He had not touched his drink at the Peters, and now he ordered a whisky-and-soda. Paul came over to say hello.

"It's a great change," he said sadly. "We do about half the business we did. So many fellows I hear about back in the States lost everything, maybe not in the first crash, but then in the second. Your friend George Hardt lost every cent, I hear. Are you back in the States?"

"No, I'm in business in Prague."

"I heard that you lost a lot in the crash."

"I did," and he added grimly, "but I lost everything I wanted in the boom."

"Selling short."

"Something like that."

Again the memory of those days swept over him like a nightmare—the people they had met travelling; then people who couldn't add a row of figures or speak a coherent sentence. The little man Helen had consented to dance with at the ship's party, who had insulted her ten feet from the table; the women and girls carried screaming with drink or drugs out of public places——

—The men who locked their wives out in the snow, because the snow of twenty-nine wasn't real snow. If you didn't want it to be snow, you just paid some money.

He went to the phone and called the Peters' apartment; Lincoln answered.

"I called up because this thing is on my mind. Has Marion said anything definite?"

"Marion's sick," Lincoln answered shortly. "I know this thing isn't altogether your fault, but I can't have her go to pieces about it. I'm afraid we'll have to let it slide for six months; I can't take the chance of working her up to this state again."

"I see."

"I'm sorry, Charlie."

He went back to his table. His whisky glass was empty, but he shook his head when Alix looked at it questioningly. There wasn't much he could do now except send Honoria some things; he would send her a lot of things tomorrow. He thought rather angrily that this was just money—he had given so many people money. . . .

"No, no more," he said to another waiter. "What do I owe you?"

He would come back some day; they couldn't make him pay forever. But he wanted his child, and nothing was much good now, beside that fact. He wasn't young any more, with a lot of nice thoughts and dreams to have by himself. He was absolutely sure Helen wouldn't have wanted him to be so alone.

Courage

Too often our imagination requires a spectacular backdrop—a battlefield or a sinking ship—to envision a display of courage. Easily we forget that people sometimes manifest extraordinary courage in meeting the trials of ordinary life. At three points the courage of Granny Weathcrall is tested: at her jilting, at her widowhood, and in the moments just before death. Deeply committed to life and its unfolding processes, she surmounts the first two crises only to find that the isolation of life's last moments poses a challenge even more severe. Anguished by the terrible loneliness of death, she cries out in protest—Katherine Anne Porter is describing a woman, not a paragon—but she endures this trial as bravely as she has met the others and dies as she has lived, a valiant, self-possessed woman. "She stretched herself with a deep breath and blew out the light."

The Jilting of Granny Weatherall*
by KATHERINE ANNE PORTER

She flicked her wrist neatly out of Doctor Harry's pudgy careful fingers and pulled the sheet up to her chin. The brat ought to be in knee breeches. Doctoring around the country with spectacles on his nose! "Get along now, take your schoolbooks and go. There's nothing wrong with me."

Doctor Harry spread a warm paw like a cushion on her forehead where the forked green vein danced and made her eyelids twitch. "Now, now, be a good girl, and we'll have you up in no time."

"That's no way to speak to a woman nearly eighty years old just because she's down. I'd have you respect your elders, young man."

"Well, Missy, excuse me." Doctor Harry patted her cheek. "But I've got to warn you, haven't I? You're a marvel, but you must be careful or you're going to be good and sorry."

"Don't tell me what I'm going to be. I'm on my feet now, morally speaking. It's Cornelia. I had to go to bed to get rid of her."

Her bones felt loose, and floated around in her skin, and Doctor Harry floated like a balloon around the foot of the bed. He floated and pulled down his waistcoat and swung his glasses on a cord. "Well, stay where you are, it certainly can't hurt you."

---

* Copyright, 1930, 1958, by Katherine Anne Porter. Reprinted from her volume, *Flowering Judas and Other Stories*, by permission of Harcourt, Brace & World, Inc.

"Get along and doctor your sick," said Granny Weatherall. "Leave a well woman alone. I'll call for you when I want you.... Where were you forty years ago when I pulled through milk-leg and double pneumonia? You weren't even born. Don't let Cornelia lead you on," she shouted, because Doctor Harry appeared to float up to the ceiling and out "I pay my own bills, and I don't throw my money away on nonsense!"

She meant to wave good-by, but it was too much trouble. Her eyes closed of themselves, it was like a dark curtain drawn around the bed. The pillow rose and floated under her, pleasant as a hammock in a light wind. She listened to the leaves rustling outside the window. No, somebody was swishing newspapers: no, Cornelia and Doctor Harry were whispering together. She leaped broad awake, thinking they whispered in her ear.

"She was never like this, *never* like this!" "Well, what can we expect?" "Yes, eighty years old...."

Well, and what if she was? She still had ears. It was like Cornelia to whisper around doors. She always kept things secret in such a public way. She was always being tactful and kind. Cornelia was dutiful; that was the trouble with her. Dutiful and good: "So good and dutiful," said Granny, "that I'd like to spank her." She saw herself spanking Cornelia and making a fine job of it.

"What'd you say, Mother?"

Granny felt her face tying up in hard knots.

"Can't a body think, I'd like to know?"

"I thought you might want something."

"I do. I want a lot of things. First off, go away and don't whisper."

She lay and drowsed, hoping in her sleep that the children would keep out and let her rest a minute. It had been a long day. Not that she was tired. It was always pleasant to snatch a minute now and then. There was always so much to be done, let me see: tomorrow.

Tomorrow was far away and there was nothing to trouble about. Things were finished somehow when the time came; thank God there was always a little margin over for peace: then a person could spread out the plan of life and tuck in the edges orderly. It was good to have everything clean and folded away, with the hair brushes and tonic bottles sitting straight on the white embroidered linen: the day started without fuss and the pantry shelves laid out with rows of jelly glasses and brown jugs and white stone-china jars with blue whirligigs and words painted on them: coffee, tea, sugar, ginger, cinnamon, allspice: and the bronze clock with the lion on top nicely dusted off. The dust that lion could collect in twenty-four hours! The box in the attic with all those letters tied up, well, she'd have to go through that tomorrow. All those letters—George's letters and John's letters and her letters to them both—lying around for the children to find afterwards made her uneasy. Yes, that would be tomorrow's business. No use to let them know how silly she had been once.

While she was rummaging around she found death in her mind and it felt clammy and unfamiliar. She had spent so much time preparing for death there was no need for bringing it up again. Let it take care of itself now. When she was sixty she had felt very old, finished, and went around making farewell trips to see her children and grandchildren, with a secret in her mind: This is the very last of your mother, children! Then she made her will and came down with a long fever. That was all just a notion like a lot of other things, but it was lucky too, for she had once for all got over the idea of dying for a long time. Now she couldn't be worried. She hoped she had better sense now. Her father had lived to be one hundred and two years old and had drunk a noggin of strong hot toddy on his last birthday. He told the reporters it was his daily habit, and he owed his long life to that. He had made quite a scandal and was very pleased about it. She believed she'd just plague Cornelia a little.

"Cornelia! Cornelia!" No footsteps, but a sudden hand on her cheek. "Bless you, where have you been?"

"Here, Mother."

"Well, Cornelia, I want a noggin of hot toddy."

"Are you cold darling?"

"I'm chilly, Cornelia. Lying in bed stops

the circulation. I must have told you that a thousand times."

Well, she could just hear Cornelia telling her husband that Mother was getting a little childish and they'd have to humor her. The thing that most annoyed her was that Cornelia thought she was deaf, dumb, and blind. Little hasty glances and tiny gestures tossed around her and over her head saying, "Don't cross her, let her have her way, she's eighty years old," and she sitting there as if she lived in a thin glass cage. Sometimes Granny almost made up her mind to pack up and move back to her own house where nobody could remind her every minute that she was old. Wait, wait, Cornelia, till your own children whisper behind your back!

In her day she had kept a better house and had got more work done. She wasn't too old yet for Lydia to be driving eighty miles for advice when one of the children jumped the track, and Jimmy still dropped in and talked things over: "Now, Mammy, you've a good business head, I want to know what you think of this? . . ." Old. Cornelia couldn't change the furniture around without asking. Little things, little things! They had been so sweet when they were little. Granny wished the old days were back again with the children young and everything to be done over. It had been a hard pull, but not too much for her. When she thought of all the food she had cooked, and all the clothes she had cut and sewed, and all the gardens she had made—well, the children showed it. There they were, made out of her, and they couldn't get away from that. Sometimes she wanted to see John again and point to them and say, Well, I didn't do so badly, did I? But that would have to wait. That was for tomorrow. She used to think of him as a man, but now all the children were older than their father, and he would be a child beside her if she saw him now. It seemed strange and there was something wrong in the idea. Why, he couldn't possibly recognize her. She had fenced in a hundred acres once, digging the post holes herself and clamping the wires with just a Negro boy to help. That changed a woman. John would be looking for a young woman with the peaked Spanish comb in her hair and the painted fan. Digging post holes changed a woman. Riding country roads in the winter when women had their babies was another thing: sitting up nights with sick horses and sick Negroes and sick children and hardly ever losing one. John, I hardly ever lost one of them! John would see that in a minute, that would be something he could understand, she wouldn't have to explain anything!

It made her feel like rolling up her sleeves and putting the whole place to rights again. No matter if Cornelia was determined to be everywhere at once, there were a great many things left undone on this place. She would start tomorrow and do them. It was good to be strong enough for everything, even if all you made melted and changed and slipped under your hands, so that by the time you finished you almost forgot what you were working for. What was it I set out to do? she asked herself intently, but she could not remember. A fog rose over the valley, she saw it marching across the creek swallowing the trees and moving up the hill like an army of ghosts. Soon it would be at the near edge of the orchard, and then it was time to go in and light the lamps. Come in, children, don't stay out in the night air.

Lighting the lamps had been beautiful. The children huddled up to her and breathed like little calves waiting at the bars in the twilight. Their eyes followed the match and watched the flames rise and settle in a blue curve, then they moved away from her. The lamp was lit, they didn't have to be scared and hang on to mother any more. Never, never, never more. God, for all my life I thank Thee. Without Thee, my God, I could never have done it. Hail, Mary, full of grace.

I want you to pick all the fruit this year and see that nothing is wasted. There's always someone who can use it. Don't let good things rot for want of using. You waste life when you waste good food. Don't let things get lost. It's bitter to lose things. Now, don't let me get to thinking, not when I am tired and taking a little nap before supper. . . .

The pillow rose about her shoulders and pressed against her heart and the memory was being squeezed out of it: oh, push down the pillow, somebody: it would smother her if she tried to hold it. Such a fresh breeze blowing and such a green day with no threats in it. But he had not come, just the same. What does a woman do when she has put on the white veil and set out the white cake for a man and he doesn't come? She tried to remember. No, I swear he never harmed me but in that. He never harmed me but in that . . . and what if he did? There was the day, the day, but a whirl of dark smoke rose and covered it, crept up and over into the bright field where everything was planted so carefully in orderly rows. That was hell, she knew hell when she saw it. For sixty years she had prayed against remembering him and against losing her soul in the deep pit of hell, and now the two things were mingled in one and the thought of him was a smoky cloud from hell that moved and crept in her head when she had just got rid of Doctor Harry and was trying to rest a minute. Wounded vanity, Ellen, said a sharp voice in the top of her mind. Don't let your wounded vanity get the upper hand of you. Plenty of girls get jilted. You were jilted, weren't you? Then stand up to it. Her eyelids wavered and let in streamers of blue-gray light like tissue paper over her eyes. She must get up and pull the shades down or she'd never sleep. She was in bed again and the shades were not down. How could that happen? Better turn over, hide from the light, sleeping in the light gave you nightmares. "Mother, how do you feel now?" and a stinging wetness on her forehead. But I don't like having my face washed in cold water!

Hapsy? George? Lydia? Jimmy? No, Cornelia, and her features were swollen and full of little puddles. "They're coming, darling, they'll all be here soon." Go wash your face, child, you look funny.

Instead of obeying, Cornelia knelt down and put her head on the pillow. She seemed to be talking but there was no sound. "Well, are you tongue-tied? Whose birthday is it? Are you going to give a party?"

Cornelia's mouth moved urgently in strange shapes. "Don't do that, you bother me, daughter."

"Oh, no, Mother. Oh, no. . . ."

Nonsense. It was strange about children. They disputed your every word. "No what, Cornelia?"

"Here's Doctor Harry."

"I won't see that boy again. He just left five minutes ago."

"That was this morning, Mother. It's night now. Here's the nurse."

"This is Doctor Harry, Mrs. Weatherall. I never saw you look so young and happy!"

"Ah, I'll never be young again—but I'd be happy if they'd let me lie in peace and get rested."

She thought she spoke up loudly, but no one answered. A warm weight on her forehead, a warm bracelet on her wrist, and a breeze went on whispering, trying to tell her something. A shuffle of leaves in the everlasting hand of God, He blew on them and they danced and rattled. "Mother, don't mind, we're going to give you a little hypodermic." "Look here, daughter, how do ants get in this bed? I saw sugar ants yesterday." Did you send for Hapsy too?

It was Hapsy she really wanted. She had to go a long way back through a great many rooms to find Hapsy standing with a baby on her arm. She seemed to herself to be Hapsy also, and the baby on Hapsy's arm was Hapsy and himself and herself, all at once, and there was no surprise in the meeting. Then Hapsy melted from within and turned flimsy as gray gauze and the baby was a gauzy shadow, and Hapsy came up close and said, "I thought you'd never come," and looked at her very searchingly and said, "You haven't changed a bit!" They leaned forward to kiss, when Cornelia began whispering from a long way off, "Oh, is there anything you want to tell me? Is there anything I can do for you?"

Yes, she had changed her mind after sixty years and she would like to see George. I want you to find George. Find him and be sure to tell him I forgot him. I want him to know I had my husband just the same and my children and my house like any other woman. A good house too and a good husband that I loved and fine children out of him. Better than I hoped for even. Tell him I was given back everything he took away and more. Oh, no, oh, God, no, there was something else besides the house and the man and the children. Oh, surely they were not all? What was it? Something not given back.... Her breath crowded down under her ribs and grew into a monstrous frightening shape with cutting edges; it bored up into her head, and the agony was unbelievable: Yes, John, get the Doctor now, no more talk, my time has come.

When this one was born it should be the last. The last. It should have been born first, for it was the one she had truly wanted. Everything came in good time. Nothing left out, left over. She was strong, in three days she would be as well as ever. Better. A woman needed milk in her to have her full health.

"Mother, do you hear me?"

"I've been telling you—"

"Mother, Father Connolly's here."

"I went to Holy Communion only last week. Tell him I'm not so sinful as all that."

"Father just wants to speak to you."

He could speak as much as he pleased. It was like him to drop in and inquire about her soul as if it were a teething baby, and then stay on for a cup of tea and a round of cards and gossip. He always had a funny story of some sort, usually about an Irishman who made his little mistakes and confessed them, and the point lay in some absurd thing he would blurt out in the confessional showing his struggles between native piety and original sin. Granny felt easy about her soul. Cornelia, where are your manners? Give Father Connolly a chair. She had her secret comfortable understanding with a few favorite saints who cleared a straight road to God for her. All as surely signed and sealed as the papers for the new Forty Acres. Forever . . . heirs and assigns forever. Since the day the wedding cake was not cut, but thrown out and wasted. The whole bottom dropped out of the world, and there she was blind and sweating with nothing under her feet and the walls falling away. His hand had caught her under the breast, she had not fallen, there was the freshly polished floor with the green rug on it, just as before. He had cursed like a sailor's parrot and said, "I'll kill him for you." Don't lay a hand on him, for my sake leave something to God. "Now, Ellen, you must believe what I tell you...."

So there was nothing, nothing to worry about any more, except sometimes in the night one of the children screamed in a nightmare, and they both hustled out shaking and hunting for the matches and calling, "There, wait a minute, here we are!" John, get the doctor now, Hapsy's time has come. But there was Hapsy standing by the bed in a white cap. "Cornelia, tell Hapsy to take off her cap. I can't see her plain."

Her eyes opened very wide and the room stood out like a picture she had seen somewhere. Dark colors with the shadows rising toward the ceiling in long angles. The tall black dresser gleamed with nothing on it but John's picture, enlarged from a little one, with John's eyes very black when they should have been blue. You never saw him, so how do you know how he looked? But the man insisted the copy was perfect, it was very rich and handsome. For a picture, yes, but it's not my husband. The table by the bed had a linen cover and a candle and a crucifix. The light was blue from Cornelia's silk lampshades. No sort of light at all, just frippery. You had to live forty years with kerosene lamps to appreciate honest electricity. She felt very strong and she saw Doctor Harry with a rosy nimbus around him.

"You look like a saint, Doctor Harry, and I vow that's as near as you'll ever come to it."

"She's saying something."

"I heard you, Cornelia. What's all this carrying-on?"

"Father Connolly's saying—"

Cornelia's voice staggered and bumped like a cart in a bad road. It rounded corners and turned back again and arrived nowhere. Granny stepped up in the cart very lightly and reached for the reins, but a man sat beside her and she knew him by his hands, driving the cart. She did not look in his face, for she knew without seeing, but looked instead down the road where the trees leaned over and bowed to each other and a thousand birds were singing a Mass. She felt like singing too, but she put her hand in the bosom of her dress and pulled out a rosary, and Father Connolly murmured Latin in a very solemn voice and tickled her feet. My God, will you stop that nonsense? I'm a married woman. What if he did run away and leave me to face the priest by myself? I found another a whole world better. I wouldn't have exchanged my husband for anybody except St. Michael himself, and you may tell him that for me with a thank you in the bargain.

Light flashed on her closed eyelids, and a deep roaring shook her. Cornelia, is that lightning? I hear thunder. There's going to be a storm. Close all the windows. Call the children in. . . . "Mother, here we are, all of us." "Is that you, Hapsy?" "Oh, no, I'm Lydia. We drove as fast as we could." Their faces drifted above her, drifted away. The rosary fell out of her hands and Lydia put it back. Jimmy tried to help, their hands fumbled together, and Granny closed two fingers around Jimmy's thumb. Beads wouldn't do, it must be something alive. She was so amazed her thoughts ran round and round. So, my dear Lord, this is my death and I wasn't even thinking about it. My children have come to see me die. But I can't, it's not time. Oh, I always hated surprises. I wanted to give Cornelia the amethyst set—Cornelia, you're to have the amethyst set, but Hapsy's to wear it when she wants, and, Doctor Harry, do shut up. Nobody sent for you. Oh, my dear Lord, do wait a minute. I meant to do something about the Forty Acres, Jimmy doesn't need it and Lydia will later on, with that worthless husband of hers. I meant to finish the altar cloth and send six bottles of wine to Sister Borgia for her dyspepsia. I want to send six bottles of wine to Sister Borgia, Father Connolly, now don't let me forget.

Cornelia's voice made short turns and titled over and crashed. "Oh, Mother, oh, Mother, oh, Mother. . . ."

"I'm not going, Cornelia. I'm taken by surprise. I can't go."

You'll see Hapsy again. What about her? "I thought you'd never come." Granny made a long journey outward, looking for Hapsy. What if I don't find her? What then? Her heart sank down and down, there was no bottom to death, she couldn't come to the end of it. The blue light from Cornelia's lampshade drew into a tiny point in the center of her brain, it flickered and winked like an eye, quietly it fluttered and dwindled. Granny lay curled down within herself, amazed and watchful, staring at the point of light that was herself; her body was now only a deeper mass of shadow in an endless darkness and this darkness would curl around the light and swallow it up. God, give a sign!

For the second time there was no sign. Again no bridegroom and the priest in the house. She could not remember any other sorrow because this grief wiped them all away. Oh, no, there's nothing more cruel than this— I'll never forgive it. She stretched herself with a deep breath and blew out the light.

The Killers*

by ERNEST HEMINGWAY

The door of Henry's lunch-room opened and two men came in. They sat down at the counter.

---

* "The Killers" (Copyright 1927 Charles Scribner's Sons; renewal copyright © 1955) is reprinted with the permission of Charles Scribner's Sons from *Men without Women* by Ernest Hemingway.

"What's yours?" George asked them.

"I don't know," one of the men said. "What do you want to eat, Al?"

"I don't know," said Al. "I don't know what I want to eat."

Outside it was getting dark. The street-light came on outside the window. The two men at the counter read the menu. From the other end of the counter Nick Adams watched them. He had been talking to George when they came in.

"I'll have a roast pork tenderloin with apple sauce and mashed potatoes," the first man said.

"It isn't ready yet."

"What the hell do you put it on the card for?"

"That's the dinner," George explained. "You can get that at six o'clock."

George looked at the clock on the wall behind the counter.

"It's five o'clock."

"The clock says twenty minutes past five," the second man said.

"It's twenty minutes fast."

"Oh, to hell with the clock," the first man said. "What have you got to eat?"

"I can give you any kind of sandwiches," George said. "You can have ham and eggs, bacon and eggs, liver and bacon, or a steak."

"Give me chicken croquettes with green peas and cream sauce and mashed potatoes."

"That's the dinner."

"Everything we want's the dinner, eh? That's the way you work it."

"I can give you ham and eggs, bacon and eggs, liver——"

"I'll take ham and eggs," the man called Al said. He wore a derby hat and a black overcoat buttoned across the chest. His face was small and white and he had tight lips. He wore a silk muffler and gloves.

"Give me bacon and eggs," said the other man. He was about the same size as Al. Their faces were different, but they were dressed like twins. Both wore overcoats too tight for them. They sat leaning forward, their elbows on the counter.

"Got anything to drink?" Al asked.

"Silver beer, bevo, ginger-ale," George said.

"I mean you got anything to *drink*?"

"Just those I said."

"This is a hot town," said the other. "What do they call it?"

"Summit."

"Ever hear of it?" Al asked his friend.

"No," said the friend.

"What do you do here nights?" Al asked.

"They eat the dinner," his friend said. "They all come here and eat the big dinner."

"That's right," George said.

"So you think that's right?" Al asked George.

"Sure."

"You're a pretty bright boy, aren't you?"

"Sure," said George.

"Well, you're not," said the other little man. "Is he, Al?"

"He's dumb," said Al. He turned to Nick. "What's your name?"

"Adams."

"Another bright boy," Al said. "Ain't he a bright boy, Max?"

"The town's full of bright boys," Max said.

George put the two platters, one of ham and eggs, the other of bacon and eggs, on the counter. He set down two side-dishes of fried potatoes and closed the wicket into the kitchen.

"Which is yours?" he asked Al.

"Don't you remember?"

"Ham and eggs."

"Just a bright boy," Max said. He leaned forward and took the ham and eggs. Both men ate with their gloves on. George watched them eat.

"What are *you* looking at?" Max looked at George.

"Nothing."

"The hell you were. You were looking at me."

"Maybe the boy meant it for a joke, Max," Al said.

George laughed.

"*You* don't have to laugh," Max said to him. "*You* don't have to laugh at all, see?"

"All right," said George.

"So he thinks it's all right." Max turned to Al. "He thinks it's all right. That's a good one."

"Oh, he's a thinker," Al said. They went on eating.

"What's the bright boy's name down the counter?" Al asked Max.

"Hey, bright boy," Max said to Nick. "You go around on the other side of the counter with your boy friend."

"What's the idea?" Nick asked.

"There isn't any idea."

"You better go around, bright boy," Al said. Nick went around behind the counter.

"What's the idea?" George asked.

"None of your damn business," Al said. "Who's out in the kitchen?"

"The nigger."

"What do you mean the nigger?"

"The nigger that cooks."

"Tell him to come in."

"What's the idea?"

"Tell him to come in."

"Where do you think you are?"

"We know danm well where we are," the man called Max said. "Do we look silly?"

"You talk silly," Al said to him. "What the hell do you argue with this kid for? Listen," he said to George, "tell the nigger to come out here."

"What are you going to do to him?"

"Nothing. Use your head, bright boy. What would we do to a nigger?"

George opened the slit that opened back into the kitchen. "Sam," he called. "Come in here a minute."

The door to the kitchen opened and the nigger came in. "What was it?" he asked. The two men at the counter took a look at him.

"All right, nigger. You stand right there," Al said.

Sam, the nigger, standing in his apron, looked at the two men sitting at the counter. "Yes, sir," he said. Al got down from his stool.

"I'm going back to the kitchen with the nigger and bright boy," he said. "Go on back to the kitchen, nigger. You go with him, bright boy." The little man walked after Nick and Sam, the cook, back into the kitchen. The door shut after them. The man called Max sat at the counter opposite George. He didn't look at George but looked in the mirror that ran along back of the counter. Henry's had been made over from a saloon into a lunch-counter.

"Well, bright boy," Max said looking into the mirror, "why don't you say something?"

"What's it all about?"

"Hey, Al," Max called, "bright boy wants to know what it's all about."

"Why don't you tell him?" Al's voice came from the kitchen.

"What do you think it's all about?"

"I don't know."

"What do you think?"

Max looked into the mirror all the time he was talking.

"I wouldn't say."

"Hey, Al, bright boy says he wouldn't say what he thinks it's all about."

"I can hear you, all right," Al said from the kitchen. He had propped open the slit that dishes passed through into the kitchen with a catsup bottle. "Listen, bright boy," he said from the kitchen to George. "Stand a little further along the bar. You move a little to the left, Max." He was like a photographer arranging for a group picture.

"Talk to me, bright boy," Max said. "What do you think's going to happen?"

George did not say anything.

"I'll tell you," Max said. "We're going to kill a Swede. Do you know a big Swede named Ole Anderson?"

"Yes."

"He comes here to eat every night, don't he?"

"Sometimes he comes here."

"He comes here at six o'clock, don't he?"

"If he comes."

"We know all that, bright boy," Max said. "Talk about something else. Ever go to the movies?"

"Once in a while."

"You ought to go to the movies more. The movies are fine for a bright boy like you."

"What are you going to kill Ole Anderson for? What did he ever do to you?"

"He never had a chance to do anything to us. He never even seen us."

"And he's only going to see us once," Al said from the kitchen.

"What are you going to kill him for, then?" George asked.

"We're killing him for a friend. Just to oblige a friend, bright boy."

"Shut up," said Al from the kitchen. "You talk too goddam much."

"Well, I got to keep bright boy amused. Don't I, bright boy?"

"You talk too damn much," Al said. "The nigger and my bright boy are amused by themselves. I got them tied up like a couple of girls friends in the convent."

"I suppose you were in a convent."

"You never know."

"You were in a kosher convent. That's where you were."

George looked up at the clock.

"If anybody comes in you tell them the cook is off, and if they keep after it, you tell them you'll go back and cook yourself. Do you get that, bright boy?"

"All right," George said. "What you going to do with us afterward?"

"That'll depend," Max said. "That's one of those things you never know at the time."

George looked up at the clock. It was a quarter past six. The door from the street opened. A streetcar motorman came in."

"Hello, George," he said. "Can I get supper?"

"Sam's gone out," George said. "He'll be back in about half an hour."

"I'd better go up the street," the motorman said. George looked at the clock. It was twenty minutes past six.

"That was nice, bright boy," Max said. "You're a regular little gentleman."

"He knew I'd blow his head off," Al said from the kitchen.

"No," said Max. "It ain't that. Bright boy is nice. He's a nice boy. I like him."

At six-fifty-five George said: "He's not coming."

Two other people had been in the lunch-room. Once George had gone out to the kitchen and made a ham-and-egg sandwich "to go" that a man wanted to take with him. Inside the kitchen he saw Al, his derby hat tipped back, sitting on a stool beside the wicket with the muzzle of a sawed-off shotgun resting on the ledge. Nick and the cook were back to back in the corner, a towel tied in each of their mouths. George had cooked the sandwich, wrapped it up in oiled paper, put it in a bag, brought it in, and the man had paid for it and gone out.

"Bright boy can do everything," Max said. "He can cook and everything. You'd make some girl a nice wife, bright boy."

"Yes?" George said. "Your friend, Ole Anderson, isn't going to come."

"We'll give him ten minutes," Max said.

Max watched the mirror and the clock. The hands of the clock marked seven o'clock, and then five minutes past seven.

"Come on, Al," said Max. "We better go. He's not coming."

"Better give him five minutes," Al said from the kitchen.

In the five minutes a man came in, and George explained that the cook was sick.

"Why the hell don't you get another cook?" the man asked. "Aren't you running a lunch-counter?" He went out.

"Come on, Al" Max said.

"What about the two bright boys and the nigger?"

"They're all right."

"You think so?"

"Sure. We're through with it."

"I don't like it," said Al. "It's sloppy. You talk too much."

"Oh, what the hell," said Max. "We got to keep amused, haven't we?"

"You talk too much, all the same," Al said. He came out from the kitchen. The cut-off barrels of the shotgun made a slight bulge under the waist of his too tight-fitting overcoat. He straightened his coat with his gloved hands.

"So long, bright boy," he said to George. "You got a lot of luck."

"That's the truth," Max said. "You ought to play the races, bright boy."

The two of them went out the door. George watched them, through the window, pass under the arc-light and cross the street. In their tight overcoats and derby hats they looked like a vaudeville team. George went back through the swinging-door into the kitchen and untied Nick and the cook.

"I don't want any more of that," said

Sam, the cook. "I don't want any more of that."

Nick stood up. He had never had a towel in his mouth before.

"Say," he said. "What the hell?" He was trying to swagger it off.

"They were going to kill Ole Anderson," George said. "They were going to shoot him when he came in to eat."

"Ole Anderson?"

"Sure."

The cook felt the corners of his mouth with his thumbs.

"They all gone?" he asked.

"Yeah," said George. "They're gone now."

"I don't like it," said the cook. "I don't like any of it at all."

"Listen," George said to Nick. "You better go see Ole Anderson."

"All right."

"You better not have anything to do with it at all," Sam, the cook said. "You better stay way out of it."

"Don't go if you don't want to," George said.

"Mixing up in this ain't going to get you anywhere," the cook said. "You stay out of it."

"I'll go see him," Nick said to George. "Where does he live?"

The cook turned away.

"Little boys always know what they want to do," he said.

"He lives up at Hirsch's rooming-house," George said to Nick.

"I'll go up there."

Outside the arc-light shone through the bare branches of a tree. Nick walked up the street beside the car-tracks and turned at the next arc-light down a side-street. Three houses up the street was Hirsch's rooming-house. Nick walked up the two steps and pushed the bell. A woman came to the door.

"Is Ole Anderson here?"

"Do you want to see him?"

"Yes, if he's in."

Nick followed the woman up a flight of stairs and back to the end of a corridor. She knocked on the door.

"Who is it?"

"It's somebody to see you, Mr. Anderson," the woman said.

"It's Nick Adams."

"Come in."

Nick opened the door and went into the room. Ole Anderson was lying on the bed with all his clothes on. He had been a heavy-weight prizefighter and he was too long for the bed. He lay with his head on two pillows. He did not look at Nick.

"What was it?" he asked.

"I was up at Henry's," Nick said, "and two fellows came in and tied up me and the cook, and they said they were going to kill you."

It sounded silly when he said it. Ole Anderson said nothing.

"They put us out in the kitchen," Nick went on. "They were going to shoot you when you came in to supper."

Ole Anderson looked at the wall and did not say anything.

"George thought I better come and tell you about it."

"There isn't anything I can do about it," Ole Anderson said.

"I'll tell you what they were like."

"I don't want to know what they were like," Ole Anderson said. He looked at the wall. "Thanks for coming to tell me about it."

"That's all right."

Nick looked at the big man lying on the bed.

"Don't you want me to go and see the police?"

"No," Ole Anderson said. "That wouldn't do any good."

"Isn't there something I could do?"

"No. There ain't anything to do."

"Maybe it was just a bluff."

"No. It ain't just a bluff."

Ole Anderson rolled over toward the wall.

"The only thing is," he said, talking toward the wall, "I just can't make up my mind to go out. I been in here all day."

"Couldn't you get out of town?"

"No," Ole Anderson said. "I'm through with all that running around."

He looked at the wall.

"There ain't anything to do now."

"Couldn't you fix it up some way?"

"No. I got in wrong." He talked in the same flat voice. "There ain't anything to do. After a while I'll make up my mind to go out."

"I better go back and see George," Nick said.

"So long," said Ole Anderson. He did not look toward Nick. "Thanks for coming around."

Nick went out. As he shut the door he saw Ole Anderson with all his clothes on, lying on the bed looking at the wall.

"He's been in his room all day," the landlady said downstairs. "I guess he don't feel well. I said to him: 'Mr. Anderson, you ought to go out and take a walk on a nice fall day like this,' but he didn't feel like it."

"He doesn't want to go out."

"I'm sorry he don't feel well," the woman said. "He's an awfully nice man. He was in the ring, you know."

"I know it."

"You'd never know it except from the way his face is," the woman said. They stood talking just inside the street door. "He's just as gentle."

"Well, good night, Mrs. Hirsch," Nick said.

"I'm not Mrs. Hirsch," the woman said. "She owns the place. I just look after it for her. I'm Mrs. Bell."

"Well, good night, Mrs. Bell," Nick said.

"Good night," the woman said.

Nick walked up the dark street to the corner under the arc-light, and then along the car-tracks to Henry's eating-house. George was inside, back of the counter.

"Did you see Ole?"

"Yes," said Nick. "He's in his room and he won't go out."

The cook opened the door from the kitchen when he heard Nick's voice.

"I don't even listen to it," he said and shut the door.

"Did you tell him about it?" George asked.

"Sure. I told him but he knows what it's all about."

"What's he going to do?"

"Nothing."

"They'll kill him."

"I guess they will."

"He must have got mixed up in something in Chicago."

"I guess so," said Nick.

"It's a hell of a thing."

"It's an awful thing," Nick said.

They did not say anything. George reached down for a towel and wiped the counter.

"I wonder what he did?" Nick said.

"Double-crossed somebody. That's what they kill them for."

"I'm going to get out of this town," Nick said.

"Yes," said George. "That's a good thing to do."

"I can't stand to think about him waiting in the room and knowing he's going to get it. It's too damned awful."

"Well," said George, "you better not think about it."

Pericles on 31st Street[*]

by HARRY MARK PETRAKIS

Louie Debella's bar was located on the corner of 31st Street and Dart Avenue, the last store in a group of five stores owned by Leonard Barsevick, who besides being a landlord operated the Lark Wholesale Clothing Company across the street.

My name is George. My last name is not important. I'm Louie Debella's night bartender and I count myself a good bartender. I might mention a few of the quality places I have

---

[*] Reprinted by permission of Quadrangle Books, Inc., from *Pericles on 31st Street* by Harry Mark Petrakis, copyright © 1965 by Harry Mark Petrakis.

tended bar, but that has nothing to do with this story.

If I have learned anything from fifteen years of tending bar it is that a bartender cannot takes sides with anything that goes on across the bar. He has got to be strictly nonpartisan. A cousin of mine in South Bend, also in the business, once tried to mediate an argument about Calvin Coolidge. Somebody hit him in the back of the head with a bottle of beer that was not yet empty, and besides needing stitches he got wet. Now when I am on the job I never take sides. That is, I never did until the episode of Pericles.

As I understand it this fellow Pericles was a Greek general and statesman who lived back in those Greek golden years you read about in the school history books. From all reports he was a pretty complete sort of guy who laid down a set of rules and was tough on everybody who did not read them right.

If you are wondering what a Greek who lived a couple of thousand years ago has got to do with this story, I guess it all started because the store keepers in our row of stores gathered in the bar in the evening after they locked their doors for a glass of beer.

The first man in was usually Dan Ryan, who had the butcher shop. Ryan was a heavy beer man and needed the head start on the others. A little later Olaf Johnson, who ran the Sunlight lunchroom, came in with Sol Reidman the tailor. Olaf had a huge belly that was impossible to keep under a coat. Sol liked nothing better than to tease Olaf about when the triplets were expected.

The last man in was Bernard Klioris, who had a little grocery next to Sol's tailor shop. Bernard usually got lost in the arguments, and swung back and forth like a kitchen door in a restaurant. He had a sad thin face and was not so bright, but among our patrons you could hardly tell.

Last Tuesday night after I had served Ryan his fourth beer, Olaf and Sol and Bernard came in together, with Olaf and Sol arguing as usual.

"She told me she was a Republican," Olaf said. "They want some lunk for Congress. I told her to come by you and get her petition signed."

Sol waggled his bald head indignantly. "Who gave you leave to advertise my business?" he said. "A man's politics is a sacred trust that belongs to him alone."

"She only had a petition, not a gun," Olaf said. "I knew you was a Republican so I sent her."

"How can anyone," Ryan said from the bar, "be in his right mind and still be a Republican?"

Sol waved a warning finger. "Be careful," he said. "You are stepping on the Constitution when you ridicule a man's politics."

"I read about the Constitution," Bernard said.

They lined up at the bar. I poured them beer. All they ever drank was beer.

The door opened and Nick Simonakis came in. He was the vendor who took his stand at night on the corner of 31st and Dart. He had a glassed-in wagon that he pushed into place under the street lamp, and from the wagon he sold hot dogs and tamales and peanuts. Several times during the evening he locked up the wagon and came into the bar for a glass of wine. He would sit alone at a table to the side of the room, his dark eyes in his hollow-cheeked face glaring at the room from above the white handle-bar mustache. Every now and then he would sip his wine and shake his head, making his thick white hair hang more disordered over his forehead.

Other men might have thought he was a little crazy because sometimes he sat there alone talking to himself, but like I said, I do not take sides. At other times he gave up muttering and loudly berated the drinkers of beer. "Only Turks would drink beer," he said, "when they could drink wine. One for the belly and the other for wisdom." He would sip his wine slowly, mocking their guzzling of beer, and the storekeepers would try to ignore him.

"The sun-ripened grapes," Simonakis said, "hanging until they become sweet. Then the trampling by the young maidens to extract the lovely juices. A ceremony of the earth."

"Beer don't just grow in barrels," Olaf said. "Good beer takes a lot of making."

The old man laughed softly as if he was amused. "You are a Turk," he said. "I excuse you because you think and talk like a Turk."

"Say, old man," Sol said. "Someone wants a bag of peanuts. You are losing business."

Simonakis looked at Sol with bright piercing eyes. "I will lose business," he said. "I am drinking my wine."

"He must be rich," Ryan said, "and pushing business away. I wish I had gone into peddling peanuts myself."

"It is not a case of wealth," Simonakis said. "There is a time for labor and a time for leisure. A man must have time to sit and think. This made Greece great."

"Made who what?" Olaf asked with sarcasm.

The old man swept him with contempt. "In ancient Greece," he said coldly, "an elephant like you would have been packed on a mountaintop as bait for buzzards."

"Watch the language," Olaf said. "I don't have to take that stuff from an old goat like you."

"A land of ruined temples," Sol said, and he moved from the bar and carried his beer to a near-by table. "A land of philosophers without shoes."

"A land of men!" Simonakis spit out. "We gave the world learning and courage. We taught men how to live and how to die."

Ryan and Bernard and Olaf had followed Sol to the table, drawing their chairs.

"Would you mind, old man," Ryan said as he sat down, "leaving a little bit of credit to the Irish?"

"I give them credit," Simonakis said, "for inventing the wheelbarrow, and giving the world men to push it."

"Did you hear that!" Ryan said indignantly and looked fiercely at the old man.

The old man went on as if he had not heard. "A model of courage for the world," he said. "Leonidas with three hundred men holding the pass at Thermopylae against the Persian hordes. Themistocles destroying the great fleet of Xerxes at Salamis."

"That's history," Olaf said. "What have they done lately?"

Simonakis ignored him. He motioned to me and I took him the bottle of port. He raised the full glass and held it up and spoke in Greek to the wine as if performing some kind of ceremony. The men watched him and somebody laughed. Simonakis glared at them. "Laugh, barbarians," he said. "Laugh and forget your debt to Greece. Forget the golden age and the men like lions. Hide in your smoking cities and drown in your stinking beer."

"What a goat," Olaf said.

Sol shook his head sadly. "It is a pity to see a man ruined by drink," he said. "That wine he waves has soaked his head."

"Wheelbarrow indeed," Ryan said, and he glared back at the old man.

2

At that moment the front door opened and Leonard Barsevick, the landlord, walked in. He carried an air of elegance into the bar. Maybe because of his Homburg and the black chesterfield coat he wore.

The storekeepers greeted him in a respectful chorus. He waved his hand around like a politician at a beer rally and smiled broadly. "Evening, boys," he said. "Only got a minute but I couldn't pass by without stopping to buy a few of my tenants a beer. George, set up the drinks and mark it on my tab."

"Thank you, Mr. Barsevick," Olaf said. "You sure look like a million bucks tonight."

Barsevick laughed and looked pleased. "Got to keep up a front, Olaf," he said. "If a man in my position gets a spot on his suit he might as well give up."

"That's right, Mr. Barsevick," Ryan said. "A man in your position has got to keep up with the best and you sure do."

"Say, Mr. Barsevick," Bernard said. "You know the leak in the roof at my store I spoke to you about last month. It hasn't been fixed yet and that rain the other night . . ."

"Wait a minute, Bernie," Barsevick laughed. Not tonight. If I promised to fix it, I'm going to have it fixed. Leonard Barsevick is a man of his word. Ain't that right, boys?"

They all nodded and Olaf said, "Yes, sir," emphatically.

"But not tonight," Barsevick said. "Tonight I'm out for a little relaxation with a baby doll that looks like Marilyn Monroe." He made a suggestive noise with his mouth.

"You're sure a lucky man, Mr. Barsevick," Olaf said admiringly.

"Not luck at all, Olaf," Barsevick said, and his voice took on a tone of serious confidence. "It's perseverance and the ability to get along with people. I always say if I didn't know how to get along with people I wouldn't be where I am today."

"That's sure right, Mr. Barsevick," Ryan said. The others nodded agreement.

"Fine," Barsevick beamed. "All right, boys, drink up, and pass your best wishes to Leonard Barsevick for a successful evening." He winked broadly.

The storekeepers laughed and raised their glasses. Everybody toasted Barsevick but Simonakis. He sat scowling at the landlord from beneath his shaggy brows. Barsevick noticed him.

"You didn't give this gentleman a drink, George," he said. "What are you drinking, sir?"

"He ain't no gentleman," Olaf said. "He is a peanut peddler."

"An authority on wheelbarrows," Ryan said.

Simonakis cocked a thumb at Barsevick. "Hurry, landlord," he said, "your Monroe is waiting."

Barsevick gave him a cool glance, but the old man just looked bored. Finally the landlord gave up and turned away pulling on his suede gloves. He strode to the door cutting a fancy figure and waved grandly. "Good night, boys," he said.

The boys wished him good night. Simonakis belched.

3

On the following Thursday the notices came from Barsevick's bookkeeper announcing a fifteen per cent rent increase all along the block. All the storekeepers got a notice of the raise becoming effective with the expiration of their leases about a month away. Louie was so disturbed he called me down in the middle of the afternoon and took off early.

That night the storekeepers were a sad bunch. They sat around the table over their beer, looking like their visas had expired.

"I don't understand," Ryan said. "Mr. Barsevick knows that business has not been good. Fifteen per cent at this time makes for an awful load."

"With license fees and the rest," Olaf said, "a lunchroom ain't hardly worth while. I was not making nothing before. With this increase it ain't going to get no better."

"Two hands to sew pants will not be enough," Sol said. "I must sew with four hands, all my own."

Bernard looked distressed from one to the other. "Mr. Barsevick must have a good reason," he said.

"He's got expenses," Olaf said.

"He should have mine," Ryan said. "Beef is up six cents a pound again."

Simonakis came into the bar pulling off his gloves. He ignored the men as he walked by them to his table against the wall and signaled to me for his bottle of wine.

"I am going to buy a wagon," Olaf said loudly, "and sell peanuts and hot dogs on the street."

"You must first," Simonakis said, "have the wisdom to tell them apart."

Olaf flushed and started to get up. Sol shook him down. "No time for games with crazy men tonight," Sol said. "This matter is serious. We must organize a delegation to speak to Mr. Barsevick. It must be explained that this increase imposes a terrible burden on us at this time. Perhaps a little later."

"Shoot him," Simonakis said. He waved the glass I had just filled with dark wine.

"You mind your own business, peddler," Ryan said. "Nobody is talking to you."

"A Greek would shoot him," Simonakis said. "But you are toads."

"I get my rent raised," Olaf said, "and now I got to sit here and be insulted by a peanut peddler."

The front door opened and the room went quiet.

Barsevick closed the door softly behind

him and walked over to the storekeepers' table and pulled up a chair and sat down like a sympathetic friend coming to share their grief.

I guess they were all as surprised as I was and for a long moment no one spoke and Barsevick looked solemnly from one to the other. "I hope you do not mind my butting in, boys," he said and he motioned to me. "George, bring the boys a round on me."

"Mr. Barsevick," Ryan said, "the boys and me were just discussing . . ."

Barsevick raised his hand gravely. "I know, Danny," he said. "I know what you are going to say. I want to go on record first as saying there is nobody any sorrier than Leonard Barsevick about this. That is why I am here. My bookkeeper said I did not have to come over tonight and talk to you. I told him I would not stand for that, that you boys were not just tenants, you were friends of mine."

"It is a lot of money, Mr. Barsevick," Olaf said "I mean if we were making more, things might be different."

"I know that, Olaf," Barsevick said. "Believe me, if there was any other way I would jump at the chance. I said to Jack, my bookkeeper, 'Isn't there any other way?' I swear to you boys he said, 'Mr. Barsevick, if that rent is not increased it will be charity.'" I brought the tray of fresh beer and set the glasses around the table. "Not that I mind a little help to my friends," Barsevick said, "but it is not good business. I would be shamed before my competitors. 'There's Barsevick,' they would laugh, 'too soft to raise his tenants' rent.' They would put the screws on me and in no time at all I might be out of business."

Everybody was silent for a moment, probably examining the prospect of Leonard Barsevick put out of business because of his soft heart.

"We know you got expenses," Ryan said.

Barsevick shook his head mournfully. "You got no idea," he said. "I mean you boys got no idea. I am afraid sometimes for the whole economy. Costs cannot keep rising and still keep the country sound. Everything is going up. Believe me, boys, being a landlord and a businessman is hell."

"Shoot him," Simonakis said loudly.

Barsevick stopped talking and looked across the tables at the old man.

"He is a crazy man," Sol said. "That wine he drinks makes him talk to himself."

Barsevick turned back to the men but he was disturbed. He looked over at the old man once more like he was trying to understand and then started to get up. "I got to go now, boys," he said. "I'm working late tonight with my bookkeeper. If we see any other way to cut costs I will be glad to reconsider the matter of the increase. That is my promise to you boys as friends."

"We sure appreciate you stopping by, Mr. Barsevick," Ryan said. "We know there is many a landlord would not have bothered."

Barsevick shook his head vigorously. "Not Leonard Barsevick," he said. "Not even his worst enemy will say that Barsevick does not cut a straight corner when it comes to his friends."

"We know that, Mr. Barsevick," Olaf said.

"We sure do," Bernard said.

"Shoot him," Simonakis said. "Shoot him before he gets away."

4

Barsevick whirled around and stared in some kind of shock at the old man. I guess he was trying very fast to figure out if the old man was serious.

"Don't pay him no mind, Mr. Barsevick," Olaf said. "He has been out in the rain too long."

"You are a demagogue." Simonakis spoke loudly to the landlord. "You wave your greedy fingers and tell them you are a friend. Aaaaaaaaa!" The old man smiled craftily. "I know your kind. In Athens they would tie you under a bull."

Barsevick stood there like rocks were being bounced off his head, his face turning a bright shade of red.

Sol motioned angrily at the old man. "Somebody wants a hot dog," he said. "You are losing business."

Simonakis looked at Sol for a moment with his mustache bristling, then looked at the others. "I have lost business," he said slowly. "You have lost courage."

A sound of hissing came from Barsevick, his red cheeks shaking off heat like a capped kettle trying to let off steam. "You goddam pig," he said huskily. "You unwashed old bum. You damn peddler of peanuts."

The old man would not give an inch. "You are a hypocrite," he said. "A hypocrite and a libertine. You live on the sweat of better men."

Barsevick's jaw was working furiously like he was trying to chew up the right words.

"Let me tell you," Simonakis said, and his voice took on a more moderate tone as if he were pleased to be able to pass information on to the landlord, "let me tell you how the hypocrite goes in the end. One day the people wake up. They know he is a liar and a thief. They pick up stones. They aim for his head." He pointed a big long finger at Barsevick and made a rattling sound rise from his throat. "What a mess a big head like yours would make."

Barsevick gasped and whirled to the men at the table. "He's threatening me," he shouted. "Did you hear him? Throw the old bastard out."

No one moved. I kept wiping glasses. A good bartender learns to keep working.

"Did you hear me!" Barsevick yelled. "Somebody throw him out."

"He is a crazy old man," Sol said. "He talks without meaning."

"Shut up!" Barsevick said. "You stick with him because you are no damn good either."

"I do not stick with him," Sol said, and he drew himself up hurt. "I am trying to be fair."

Barsevick turned to me. "George, throw him out."

I kept wiping the glasses. "I am underpaid, Mr. Barsevick," I said. "My salary barely covers my work. Any extra service would be charity."

The old man took after him again. "Who likes you, landlord?" he said. "Be honest and speak truth before your tenants. Who likes you?"

"You shut up!" Barsevick shouted.

"I mean really likes you," Simonakis said. "I do not mean the poor girls you buy with your tainted money."

"I'll shut the old bastard up!" Barsevick hollered and started for the table against the wall.

Simonakis stood up and Barsevick stopped. The old man looked tall and menacing with his big hands and bright eyes and his white mustache standing out like a joyous challenge to battle. "You cannot shut up truth," Simonakis said. "And the truth is that you are a leech feeding on the labor of better men. You wish to become richer by making them poorer."

Barsevick stood there a couple of tables away from the old man with his back bent a little waiting for a word to be raised in his defense. No one spoke and the old man stared at him with eyes like knives.

"You old bastard . . ." Barsevick said weakly.

Ryan made a sound clearing his throat. He wore a stern and studied look on his face. "Fifteen per cent is a steep raise," he said. "Right at this time when it is tough to make ends meet."

Barsevick whirled on him. "You keep out of this," he said. "You just mind your own business."

"I would say," Ryan said slowly, "fifteen per cent more rent to pay each month is my business."

"I'll make it twenty-five per cent," Barsevick shouted. "If you don't like it you can get out!"

"I have a lease," Ryan said quietly. He was looking at the landlord like he was seeing him for the first time.

"I will break it," Barsevick said. He looked angrily around at the other storekeepers. "I will break all your leases."

"I did not say nothing!" Bernard protested.

"The way of tyrants and thieves," Simonakis said. "All who oppose them suffer." He raised his head and fixed his eyes upon the ceiling. "O Pericles, lend us a stick so we may drive the tyrant from the market place."

"Stop calling me a tyrant," Barsevick fumed.

Simonakis still had his head raised praying to that guy Pericles.

"I'm going to put every one of you into the street," Barsevick said. "I'm going to teach you all not to be so damn smart."

Sol shook his head with measured contempt for the landlord on his face. "You will not put us out," he said. "First, you are too greedy for the rent. Second, you would not rent those leaking barns again without major repairs, and third . . ." He paused. "Third, I do not admire your personality."

"Amen," Bernard said. "My roof keeps leaking."

"O Pericles!" Simonakis suddenly cried out and everybody looked at him. "They are barbarians and not of Athens but they are honest men and need your help. Give them strength to destroy the common enemy. Lend them your courage to sweep out the tyrant."

"You are all crazy," Barsevick said and he looked driven and disordered. His tie was outside his coat and the Homburg perched lopsided over one ear.

"You are a tiger," Sol said. "Tell me what circus you live in and I will rent a cage to take you home."

"Do not be insulting," Ryan said to Sol. "You will hurt the landlord's feelings. He cannot help he has got a head like a loin of pork."

"You ignorant bastards!" Barsevick shouted.

Ryan got up and came over to the bar. He stepped behind and pulled out the little sawed-off bat Louie kept under the counter. He winked at me. "I am just borrowing it," he said. "I want to put a new crease in the landlord's hat."

Simonakis came back from calling on Pericles. "Do not strike him," he said. "Stone him. Stone him as they stone tyrants in Athens." He looked at the floor and around the room as if excitedly searching for stones.

Barsevick in full retreat began to edge toward the door. He opened his mouth to try and speak some final word of defiance but one look at the bat in Ryan's hands must have choked off his wind.

"Tyrant!" Simonakis shouted.

"Vulture," Olaf said. "Stop and eat on me, and I'll grind some glass for your salad."

"Greedy pig," Ryan said, and he waved the bat. "You try and collect that rent and we all move out."

"Judas," Sol said. "Come to me only to sew your shroud."

"Fix my leaking roof," Bernard said.

With one last helpless wail, Barsevick stumbled out through the door.

For a long moment after the door closed nobody moved. Then Ryan handed me back the bat. I put it under the counter. Olaf started to the bar with his glass. Bernard came after him. Soon all were lined up at the bar. All except Simonakis, who had gone back to sit down at his table staring moodily into his glass of wine.

Ryan turned his back to the bar and looked across the tables at Simonakis. He looked at him for a long time and no one spoke. The old man kept staring at his wine. Ryan looked back helplessly at Olaf and Sol and they watched him struggling. Bernard looked dazed. I held a wet towel in my hands and forgot to wipe the bar. When Ryan finally turned back to Simonakis, you could see he had made up his mind. He spoke slowly and carefully.

"Mr. Simonakis," he said.

The old man raised his head scowling.

"Mr. Simonakis," Ryan said. "Will you be kind enough to join my friends and me in a drink?"

The old man stopped scowling. He nodded gravely and stood up tall and straight, his mustache curved in dignity, and came to the bar. Ryan moved aside to make a place for him.

I began to pour the beer.

"No, George," Ryan said. "We will have wine this trip."

"Yes, sir," I said.

I took down the bottle of port and filled a row of small glasses.

Ryan raised his glass and looked belligerently at the others. "To the glory of Greece," he said.

The rest of them raised their glasses.

"To Athens," Sol said.

"To Mr. Simonakis," Olaf said.

"Ditto," Bernard said.

I took down another wineglass. I poured myself some wine. They all looked at me. I did not care I was abandoning a professional tradition of neutrality.

"To Pericles," I said.

Simonakis stroked his mustache and sipped of his wine. The rest of us sipped right with him.

The Complexity of Life

One characteristic of superior fiction is that it reflects an awareness that good and evil are often so intermingled in the human situation that characters are not easily classified nor issues readily resolved. Mrs. Wilson, the central figure in "After You, My Dear Alphonse," is an admirable woman in several ways; the vein of meanness that appears in her is the more disturbing because it arises from a charitable impulse. But if man is sometimes defeated by contradictions within himself or within his society, other times, as in "The Majesty of the Law," he gains heartening triumphs. In this story the Sergeant does arrest his friend Dan, but both men handle the awkward situation with such tact, diplomacy, and verbal grace that we witness a victory of personalism over institutionalism. But if men are free to become very good human beings, they are equally free to become very bad persons—even as men sometimes express themselves by detroying beauty. If, in Graham Greene's story, we tend to see the senseless vandalism of Blackie as a manifestation of twentieth-century alienation, we would do well to remember that it is a portion of the problem of evil that vexed Sophocles in the fifth century B.C. It is another aspect of the same problem that concerns Flannery O'Connor in her inquiry into why a good man is hard to find. When we examine Grandma closely, Miss O'Connor suggests we can find a large part of the reason. Grandma has, to be sure, at least a few virtues, but her influence on her progeny has not been for good, and when she claims a share in shaping The Misfit, who is filled with self-hatred, she deserves at least part of the response that she provokes.

After You, My Dear Alphonse*
by SHIRLEY JACKSON

Mrs. Wilson was just taking the gingerbread out of the oven when she heard Johnny outside talking to someone.

"Johnny," she called, "you're late. Come in and get your lunch."

"Just a minute, Mother," Johnny said. "After you, my dear Alphonse."

"After *you*, my dear Alphonse," another voice said.

"No, after *you*, my dear Alphonse," Johnny said.

Mrs. Wilson opened the door. "Johnny," she said, "you come in this minute and get your lunch. You can play after you've eaten."

---

* Reprinted with the permission of Farrar, Straus & Giroux, Inc., from *The Lottery* by Shirley Jackson, copyright 1943, 1949 by Shirley Jackson.

Johnny came in after her, slowly. "Mother," he said, "I brought Boyd home for lunch with me."

"Boyd?" Mrs. Wilson thought for a moment. "I don't believe I've met Boyd. Bring him in, dear, since you've invited him. Lunch is ready."

"Boyd!" Johnny yelled. "Hey, Boyd, come on in!"

"I'm coming. Just got to unload this stuff."

"Well, hurry, or my mother'll be sore."

"Johnny, that's not very polite to either your friend or your mother," Mrs. Wilson said. "Come sit down, Boyd."

As she turned to show Boyd where to sit, she saw he was a Negro boy, smaller than Johnny but about the same age. His arms were loaded with split kindling wood. "Where'll I put this stuff, Johnny?" he asked.

Mrs. Wilson turned to Johnny. "Johnny," she said, "what did you make Boyd do? What is that wood?"

"Dead Japanese," Johnny said mildly. "We stand them in the ground and run over them with tanks."

"How do you do, Mrs. Wilson?" Boyd said.

"How do you do, Boyd? You shouldn't let Johnny make you carry all that wood. Sit down now and eat lunch, both of you."

"Why shouldn't he carry the wood, Mother? It's his wood. We got it at his place."

"Johnny," Mrs. Wilson said, "go on and eat your lunch."

"Sure," Johnny said. He held out the dish of scrambled eggs to Boyd. "After you, my dear Alphonse."

"After *you,* my dear Alphonse," Boyd said.

"After *you,* my dear Alphonse," Johnny said. They began to giggle.

"Are you hungry, Boyd?" Mrs. Wilson asked.

"Yes, Mrs. Wilson."

"Well, don't you let Johnny stop you. He always fusses about eating, so you just see that you get a good lunch. There's plenty of food here for you to have all you want."

"Thank you, Mrs. Wilson."

"Come on, Alphonse," Johnny said. He pushed half the scrambled eggs on to Boyd's plate. Boyd watched while Mrs. Wilson put a dish of stewed tomatoes beside his plate.

"Boyd don't eat tomatoes, do you, Boyd?" Johnny said.

"*Doesn't* eat tomatoes, Johnny. And just because you don't like them, don't say that about Boyd. Boyd will eat *anything.*"

"Bet he won't," Johnny said, attacking his scrambled eggs.

"Boyd wants to grow up and be a big strong man so he can work hard," Mrs. Wilson said. "I'll bet Boyd's father eats stewed tomatoes."

"My father eats anything he wants to," Boyd said.

"So does mine," Johnny said. "Sometimes he doesn't eat hardly anything. He's a little guy, though. Wouldn't hurt a flea."

"Mine's a little guy, too," Boyd said.

"I'll bet he's strong, though," Mrs. Wilson said. She hesitated. "Does he . . . work?"

"Sure," Johnny said. "Boyd's father works in a factory."

"There, you see?" Mrs. Wilson said. "And he certainly has to be strong to do that—all that lifting and carrying at a factory."

"Boyd's father doesn't have to," Johnny said. "He a foreman."

Mrs. Wilson felt defeated. "What does your mother do, Boyd?"

"My mother?" Boyd was surprised. "She takes care of us kids."

"Oh. She doesn't work, then?"

"Why should she?" Johnny said through a mouthful of eggs. "You don't work."

"You really don't want any stewed tomatoes, Boyd?"

"No, thank you, Mrs. Wilson," Boyd said.

"No, thank you, Mrs. Wilson, no, thank you, Mrs. Wilson, no, thank you, Mrs. Wilson," Johnny said. "Boyd's sister's going to work, though. She's going to be a teacher."

"That's a very fine attitude for her to have, Boyd." Mrs. Wilson restrained an impulse to pat Boyd on the head. "I imagine you're all very proud of her?"

"I guess so," Boyd said.

"What about all your other brothers and sisters? I guess all of you want to make just as much of yourselves as you can."

"There's only me and Jean," Boyd said.

"I don't know yet what I want to be when I grow up."

"We're going to be tank drivers, Boyd and me," Johnny said. "Zoom." Mrs. Wilson caught Boyd's glass of milk as Johnny's napkin ring, suddenly transformed into a tank plowed heavily across the table.

"Look, Johnny," Boyd said. "Here's a foxhole. I'm shooting at you."

Mrs. Wilson, with the speed born of long experience, took the gingerbread off the shelf and placed it carefully between the tank and the foxhole.

"Now eat as much as you want to, Boyd," she said. "I want to see you get filled up."

"Boyd eats a lot, but not as much as I do," Johnny said. "I'm bigger than he is."

"You're not much bigger," Boyd said. "I can beat you running."

Mrs. Wilson took a deep breath. "Boyd," she said. Both boys turned to her. "Boyd, Johnny has some suits that are a little too small for him, and a winter coat. It's not new, of course, but there's lots of wear in it still. And I have a few dresses that your mother or sister could probably use. Your mother can make them over into lots of things for all of you, and I'd be very happy to give them to you. Suppose before you leave I make up a big bundle and then you and Johnny can take it over to your mother right away . . ." Her voice trailed off as she saw Boyd's puzzled expression.

"But I have plenty of clothes, thank you," he said. "And I don't think my mother knows how to sew very well, and anyway I guess we buy about everything we need. Thank you very much, though."

"We don't have time to carry that old stuff around, Mother," Johnny said. "We got to play tanks with the kids today."

Mrs. Wilson lifted the plate of gingerbread off the table as Boyd was about to take another piece. "There are many little boys like you, Boyd, who would be very grateful for the clothes someone was kind enough to give them."

"Boyd will take them if you want him to, Mother," Johnny said.

"I didn't mean to make you mad, Mrs. Wilson," Boyd said.

"Don't think I'm angry, Boyd. I'm just disappointed in you, that's all. Now let's not say anything more about it."

She began clearing the plates off the table, and Johnny took Boyd's hand and pulled him to the door. " 'Bye, Mother," Johnny said. Boyd stood for a minute, staring at Mrs. Wilson's back.

"After you, my dear Alphonse," Johnny said, holding the door open.

"Is your mother still mad?" Mrs. Wilson heard Boyd ask in a low voice.

"I don't know," Johnny said. "She's screwy sometimes."

"So's mine," Boyd said. He hesitated. "After *you*, my dear Alphonse."

The Majesty of the Law*

by FRANK O'CONNOR

Old Dan Bride was breaking brosna for the fire when he heard a step up the path. He paused, a bundle of saplings on his knee.

Dan had looked after his mother while the spark of life was in her, and after her death no other woman had crossed the threshold. Signs on it, his house had that look. Almost everything in it he had made with his own hands in his own way. The seats of the chairs were only slices of log, rough and round and thick as the saw had left them, and with the rings still plainly visible through the grime and polish that coarse trouser bottoms had in the course of long years imparted. Into these Dan had rammed stout knotted ash boughs which served

---

* From *The Stories of Frank O'Connor.* Copyright 1952 by Frank O'Connor. Reprinted by permission of Alfred A. Knopf, Inc., and A. D. Peters & Company.

alike for legs and back. The deal table, bought in a shop, was an inheritance from his mother, and a great pride and joy to him, though it rocked forward and back whenever he touched it. On the wall, unglazed and flyspotted, hung in mysterious isolation a Marcus Stone print and beside the door was a calendar representing a racehorse. Over the door hung a gun, old but good and in excellent condition, and before the fire was stretched an old setter who raised his head expectantly whenever Dan rose or even stirred.

He raised it now as the steps came nearer, and when Dan, laying down the bundle of saplings, cleaned his hands thoughtfully in the seat of his trousers, he gave a loud bark, but this expressed no more than a desire to display his own watchfulness. He was half human and knew that people thought he was old and past his prime.

A man's shadow fell across the oblong of dusty light thrown over the half door before Dan looked round.

"Are you alone, Dan?" asked an apologetic voice.

"Oh, come in, come in, sergeant, come in and welcome," exclaimed the old man, hurrying on rather uncertain feet to the door, which the tall policeman opened and pushed in. He stood there, half in sunlight, half in shadow, and seeing him so, you would have realised how dark was the interior of Dan's house. One side of his red face was turned so as to catch the light, and behind it an ash tree raised its boughs of airy green against the sky. Green fields, broken here and there by clumps of redbrown rock, flowed downhill, and beyond them, stretched all across the horizon was the sea, flooded and almost transparent with light. The sergeant's face was fat and fresh, the old man's face, emerging from the twilight of the kitchen, had the colour of wind and sun, while the features had been so shaped by the struggle with time and the elements that they might as easily have been found impressed upon the surface of a rock.

"Begor, Dan," said the sergeant, " 'tis younger you're getting."

"Middling I am, sergeant, middling," agreed the old man in a voice which seemed to accept the remark as a compliment of which politeness would not allow him to take too much advantage. "No complaints."

"Faix, and 'tis as well. No wan but a born idiot would believe them. And th' ould dog don't look a day older."

The dog gave a low growl as though to show the sergeant that he would remember this unmannerly reference to his age, but indeed he growled every time he was mentioned, under the impression that people could have nothing but ill to say of him.

"And how's yourself, sergeant?"

"Well, now, like that in the story, Dan, neither on the pig's back or at the horse's tail. We have our own little worries, but, thanks be to God, we have our compensations."

"And the wife and care?"

"Good, glory and praise be to God, good. They were away from me with a month, the lot of them, at the mother-in-law's place in Clare."

"Ah, do you tell me so?"

"I had a fine, quiet time."

The old man looked about him, and then retired to the near-by bedroom from which he emerged a moment later with an old shirt. With this he solemnly wiped the seat and back of the log-chair nearest the fire.

"Take your ease, now, take your ease. 'Tis tired you must be after the journey. How did you come?"

"Teigue Leary it was that gave me a lift. Wisha, now Dan, don't you be putting yourself about. I won't be stopping. I promised them I'd be back inside an hour."

"What hurry is on you?" asked the old man. "Look now, your foot was on the path when I rose from putting kindling on the fire."

"Now! Now! You're not making tea for me."

"I am not then, but for myself, and very bad I'll take it if you won't join me."

"Dan, Dan, that I mightn't stir, but 'tisn't an hour since I had a cup at the barracks."

"Ah, *Dhe*, whisht, now! Whisht, will you! I have something that'll put an appetite on you."

The old man swung the heavy kettle on to the chain over the open fire, and the dog sat up, shaking his ears with an expression of the deepest interest. The policeman unbuttoned his tunic, opened his belt, took a pipe and a plug of tobacco from his breast-pocket, and crossing his legs in easy posture, began to cut the tobacco slowly and carefully with his pocket-knife. The old man went to the dresser, and took down two handsomely decorated cups, the only cups he had, which, though chipped and handleless, were used at all only on very rare occasions: for himself, he preferred tea from a basin. Happening to glance into them, he noticed that they bore the trace of disuse and had collected a substantial share of the fine white dust which was constantly circulating within the little smoky cottage. Again he thought of the shirt, and, rolling up his sleeves with a stately gesture, he wiped them inside and out till they shone. Then he bent and opened the cupboard. Inside was a quart bottle of pale liquid, obviously untouched. He removed the cork and smelt the contents, pausing for a moment in the act as though to recollect where exactly he had noticed that particular smoky odour before. Then, reassured, he rose and poured out with a liberal hand.

"Try that now, sergeant," he said.

The sergeant, concealing whatever qualms he might have felt at the thought of imbibing illegal whiskey, looked carefully into the cup, sniffed, and glanced up at old Dan.

"It looks good," he commented.

"It should be."

"It tastes good, too," he added.

"Ah, sha," said Dan, clearly not wishing to praise his own hospitality in his own house, "'tis of no great excellence."

"You're a good judge, I'd say," said the sergeant without irony.

"Ever since things became what they are," said Dan, carefully guarding himself from a too direct reference to the peculiarities of the law administered by his guest, "liquor is not what it used to be."

"I have heard that remark made before now," said the sergeant thoughtfully. "I have often heard it said by men of wide experience that liquor used to be better in the old days."

"Liquor," said the old man, "is a thing that takes time. There was never a good job done in a hurry."

"'Tis an art in itself."

"Just so."

"And an art takes time."

"And knowledge," added Dan with emphasis. "Every art has its secrets, and the secrets of distilling are being lost the way the old songs were lost. When I was a boy there wasn't a man in the barony but had a hundred songs in his head, but with people running here, there and everywhere, the songs were lost. . . . Ever since things became what they are," he repeated on the same guarded note, "there's so much running about the secrets are lost."

"There must have been a power of them."

"There was. Ask any man to-day that makes liquor do he know how to make it of heather."

"And was it made of heather?" asked the policeman.

"It was."

"Did you ever drink it yourself?"

"I did not; but I knew men that drank it. And a purer, sweeter, wholesomer drink never tickled a man's gullet. Babies they used to give it to and growing children."

"Musha, Dan, I think sometimes 'twas a great mistake of the law to set its hand against it."

Dan shook his head. His eyes answered for him, but it was not in nature that in his own house a man should criticise the occupation of his guest.

"Maybe so, maybe not," he said in a noncommittal tone.

"But sure, what else have the poor people?"

"Them that makes the laws have their own good reasons."

"All the same, Dan, all the same, 'tis a hard law."

The sergeant would not be outdone in generosity. Politeness required him not to yield to the old man's defence of his superiors and their mysterious ways.

"It is the secrets I would be sorry for," said Dan, summing up. "Men die, and men are born, and where one man drained another will plough, but a secret lost is lost for ever."

"True," said the sergeant mournfully. "Lost for ever."

Dan took the policeman's cup, rinsed it in a bucket of clear water beside the door and cleaned it anew with the aid of the shirt. Then he placed it carefully at the sergeant's elbow. From the dresser he took a jug of milk and a blue bag containing sugar: this he followed up with a slab of country butter and—a sign that his visitor was not altogether unexpected —a round cake of home-made bread, fresh and uncut. The kettle sang and spat, and the dog, shaking his ears, barked at it angrily.

"Go 'way, you brute!" growled Dan, kicking him out of his way.

He made the tea and filled the two cups. The sergeant cut himself a large slice of bread and buttered it thickly.

"It is just like medicines," said the old man, resuming his theme with the imperturbability of age. "Every secret there was is lost. And leave no one tell me a doctor is the measure of one that has secrets from old times."

"How could he?" asked the sergeant with his mouth full.

"The proof of that was seen when there were doctors and wise people there together."

"It wasn't to the doctors the people went, I'll engage."

"It was not. And why?" . . . With a sweeping gesture the old man took in the whole world outside his cabin. "Out there on the hillsides is the sure cure for every disease. Because it is written"—he tapped the table with his thumb—"it is written by the poets *'an galar 'san leigheas go bhfaghair le ceile'* ('wherever you find the disease you will find the cure'). But people walk up the hills and down the hills and all they see is flowers. Flowers! As if God Almighty—honour and praise to Him!—had nothing better to do with His time than be making ould flowers!"

"Things no doctor could cure the wise people cured."

"Ah musha, 'tis I know it," said Dan bitterly, " 'tis I know it, not in my mind but in my own four bones."

"Do you tell me the rheumatics do be at you always?"

"They do. . . . Ah, if you were living, Kitty O'Hara, or you, Nora Malley of the Glen, 'tisn't I would be dreading the mountain wind or the sea wind; 'tisn't I'd be creeping down with me misfortunate red ticket for the blue and pink and yellow dribble-drabble of their ignorant dispensary!"

"Why then, indeed," said the sergeant with sudden determination, "I'll get you a bottle for that."

"Ah, there's no bottle ever made will cure me!"

"There is, there is. Don't talk now till you try it. My own mother's brother, it cured him when he was that bad he wanted the carpenter to cut the two legs off him with a hand-saw."

"I'd give fifty pounds to be rid of it," said Dan. "I would and five hundred!"

The sergeant finished his tea in a gulp, blessed himself and struck a match which he then allowed to go out as he answered some question of the old man's. He did the same with a second and third, as though titillating his appetite with delay. At last he succeeded in getting it alight, and then the two men pulled round their chairs, placed their toes side by side in the ashes, and in deep puffs, lively bursts of conversation and long long silences, enjoyed their pipes.

"I hope I'm not keeping you," said the sergeant, as though struck by the length of his visit.

"Erra, what keep?"

"Tell me if I am. The last thing I'd like to do is to waste a man's time."

"Och, I'd ask nothing better than to have you here all night."

"I like a little talk myself," admitted the policeman.

And again they became lost in conversation. The light grew thick and coloured, and wheeling about the kitchen before it disappeared became tinged with gold; the kitchen itself sank into a cool greyness with cold light upon the cups and the basins and plates upon the dresser. From the ash tree a thrush began to sing. The open hearth gathered brightness till its light was a warm, even splash of crimson in the twilight.

Twilight was also descending without when the sergeant rose to go. He fastened his belt and tunic and carefully brushed his clothes. Then he put on his cap, tilted a little to side and back.

"Well," he said, "that was a great talk."

"It's a pleasure," said Dan, "a real pleasure, that's what it is."

"And I won't forget the bottle."

"Heavy handling from God to you!"

"Good-bye now, Dan."

"Good-bye and good luck."

Dan did not offer to accompany the sergeant beyond the door. Then he sat down in his old place by the fire. He took out his pipe once more, blew through it thoughtfully, and just as he leaned forward for a twig to kindle it he heard steps returning to the house. It was the sergeant. He put his head a little way over the half door.

"Oh, Dan," he called softly.

"Ay, sergeant," replied Dan, looking round, but with one hand still reaching for the twig. He could not see the sergeant's face, only hear his voice.

"I suppose you're not thinking of paying that little fine, Dan?"

There was a brief silence. Dan pulled out the lighted twig, rose slowly and shambled towards the door, stuffing it down into the almost empty bowl of the pipe. He leaned over the half door, while the sergeant with hands in the pockets of his trousers gazed rather in the direction of the laneway, yet taking in a considerable portion of the sea-line.

"The way it is with me, sergeant," replied Dan unemotionally, "I am not."

"I was thinking that, Dan. I was thinking you wouldn't."

There was a long silence during which the voice of the thrush grew shriller and merrier. The sunken sun lit up islands of purple cloud moored high above the wind.

"In a way," said the sergeant, "that was what brought me."

"I was just thinking so, sergeant, it struck me and you going out the door."

"If 'twas only the money, I'm sure there's many would be glad to oblige you."

"I know that, sergeant. No, 'tisn't the money so much as giving that fellow the satisfaction of paying. Because he angered me, sergeant."

The sergeant made no comment upon this and another long silence ensued.

"They gave me the warrant," he said at last in a tone which dissociated him from all connection with the document.

"Ay, begod!" said Dan, without interest.

"So whenever 'twould be convenient to you——"

"Well, now you mention it," said Dan, by way of throwing out a suggestion for debate, "I could go with you now."

"Oh, tut, tut!" protested the sergeant with a wave of his hand, dismissing the idea as the tone required.

"Or I could go to-morrow," added Dan, warming up to the issue.

"Just as you like now," replied the sergeant, scaling up his voice accordingly.

"But as a matter of fact," said the old man emphatically, "the day that would be most convenient to me would be Friday after dinner, seeing that I have some messages to do in town, and I wouldn't have me jaunt for nothing."

"Friday will do grand," said the sergeant with relief that this delicate matter was now practically disposed of. "You could just walk in yourself and tell them I told you."

"I'd rather have yourself, if 'twould be no inconvenience, sergeant. As it is, I'd feel a bit shy."

"You needn't then. There's a man from my own parish there, a warder; one Whelan. You could say you wanted him, and I'll guarantee when he knows you're a friend of mine he'll make you as comfortable as if you were at home by your own fire."

"I'd like that fine," said Dan with satisfaction.

"Well, good-bye again now, Dan. I'll have to hurry."

"Wait now, wait, till I see you to the road!"

Together the two men strolled down the laneway while Dan explained how it was that he, a respectable old man, had had the grave misfortune to open the head of another old man in such a way as to necessitate his being removed to hospital, and why it was that he could not give the old man in question the satisfaction of paying in cash for an injury brought about through the victim's own unmannerly method of argument.

"You see, sergeant," he said, "the way

it is, he's there now, and he's looking at us as sure as there's a glimmer of sight in his wake, wandering, watery eyes, and nothing would give him more gratification than for me to pay. But I'll punish him. I'll lie on bare boards for him. I'll suffer for him, sergeant, till he won't be able to rise his head, nor any of his children after him, for the suffering he put on me."

On the following Friday he made ready his donkey and butt and set out. On his way he collected a number of neighbours who wished to bid him farewell. At the top of the hill he stopped to send them back. An old man, sitting in the sunlight, hastily made his way within doors, and a moment later the door of his cottage was quietly closed.

Having shaken all his friends by the hand, Dan lashed the old donkey, shouted "hup, there!" and set out alone along the road to prison.

The Destructors*

by GRAHAM GREENE

1

It was on the eve of August Bank Holiday that the latest recruit became the leader of the Wormsley Common Gang. No one was surprised except Mike, but Mike at the age of nine was surprised by everything. "If you don't shut your mouth," somebody once said to him, "you'll get a frog down it." After that Mike had kept his teeth tightly clamped except when the surprise was too great.

The new recruit had been with the gang since the beginning of the summer holidays, and there were possibilities about his brooding silence that all recognized. He never wasted a word even to tell his name until that was required of him by the rules. When he said "Trevor" it was a statement of fact, not as it would have been with the others a statement of shame or defiance. Nor did anyone laugh except Mike, who finding himself without support and meeting the dark gaze of the newcomer opened his mouth and was quiet again. There was every reason why T., as he was afterwards referred to, should have been an object of mockery—there was his name (and they substituted the initial because otherwise they had no excuse not to laugh at it), the fact that his father, a former architect and present clerk, had "come down in the world" and that his mother considered herself better than the neighbours. What but an odd quality of danger, of the unpredictable, established him in the gang without any ignoble ceremony of initiation?

The gang met every morning in an impromptu car-park, the site of the last bomb of the first blitz. The leader, who was known as Blackie, claimed to have heard it fall, and no one was precise enough in his dates to point out that he would have been one year old and fast asleep on the down platform of Wormsley Common Underground Station. On one side of the car-park leant the first occupied house, number 3, of the shattered Northwood Terrace—literally leant, for it had suffered from the blast of the bomb and the side walls were supported on wooden struts. A smaller bomb and some incendiaries had fallen beyond, so that the house stuck up like a jagged tooth and carried on the further wall relics of its neighbour, a dado, the remains of a fireplace. T., whose words were almost confined to voting "Yes" or "No" to the plan of operations proposed each day by Blackie, once startled the whole gang by saying broodingly, "Wren built that house, father says."

"Who's Wren?"

"The man who built St. Paul's."

---

* From 21 *Stories* by Graham Greene. Copyright 1954 by Graham Greene. Reprinted by permission of The Viking Press, Inc., and William Heinemann Limited.

"Who cares?" Blackie said. "It's only old Misery's."

Old Misery—whose real name was Thomas—had once been a builder and decorator. He lived alone in the crippled house, doing for himself: once a week you could see him coming back across the common with bread and vegetables, and once as the boys played in the car-park he put his head over the smashed wall of his garden and looked at them.

"Been to the loo," one of the boys said, for it was common knowledge that since the bombs fell something had gone wrong with the pipes of the house and Old Misery was too mean to spend money on the property. He could do the redecorating himself at cost price, but he had never learnt plumbing. The loo was a wooden shed at the bottom of the narrow garden with a star-shaped hole in the door: it had escaped the blast which had smashed the house next door and sucked out the window-frames of No. 3.

The next time the gang became aware of Mr. Thomas was more surprising. Blackie, Mike, and a thin yellow boy, who for some reason was called by his surname Summers, met him on the common coming back from the market. Mr. Thomas stopped them. He said glumly, "You belong to the lot that play in the car-park?"

Mike was about to answer when Blackie stopped him. As the leader he had responsibilities. "Suppose we are?" he said ambiguously.

"I got some chocolates," Mr. Thomas said. "Don't like 'em myself. Here you are. Not enough to go round, I don't suppose. There never is," he added with sombre conviction. He handed over three packets of Smarties.

The gang were puzzled and perturbed by this action and tried to explain it away. "Bet someone dropped them and he picked 'em up," somebody suggested.

"Pinched 'em and then got in a bleeding funk," another thought aloud.

"It's a bribe," Summers said. "He wants us to stop bouncing balls on his wall."

"We'll show him we don't take bribes," Blackie said, and they sacrificed the whole morning to the game of bouncing that only Mike was young enough to enjoy. There was no sign from Mr. Thomas.

Next day T. astonished them all. He was late at the rendezvous, and the voting for that day's exploit took place without him. At Blackie's suggestion the gang was to disperse in pairs, take buses at random, and see how many free rides could be snatched from unwary conductors (the operation was to be carried out in pairs to avoid cheating). They were drawing lots for their companions when T. arrived.

"Where you been, T.?" Blackie asked. "You can't vote now. You know the rules."

"I've been *there*," T. said. He looked at the ground, as though he had thoughts to hide.

"Where?"

"At Old Misery's." Mike's mouth opened and then hurriedly closed again with a click. He had remembered the frog.

"At Old Misery's?" Blackie said. There was nothing in the rules against it, but he had a sensation that T. was treading on dangerous ground. He asked hopefully, "Did you break in?"

"No. I rang the bell."

"And what did you say?"

"I said I wanted to see his house."

"What did he do?"

"He showed it me."

"Pinch anything?"

"No."

"What did you do it for then?"

The gang had gathered round: it was as though an impromptu court were about to form and try some case of deviation. T. said, "It's a beautiful house," and still watching the ground, meeting no one's eyes, he licked his lips first one way, then the other.

"What do you mean, a beautiful house?" Blackie asked with scorn.

"It's got a staircase two hundred years old like a corkscrew. Nothing holds it up."

"What do you mean, nothing holds it up. Does it float?"

"It's to do with opposite forces, Old Misery said."

"What else?"

"There's panelling."

"Like in the Blue Boar?"

"Two hundred years old."

"Is Old Misery two hundred years old?"

Mike laughed suddenly and then was quiet again. The meeting was in a serious mood. For the first time since T. had strolled into the car-park on the first day of the holidays his position was in danger. It only needed a single use of his real name and the gang would be at his heels.

"What did you do it for?" Blackie asked. He was just, he had no jealousy, he was anxious to retain T. in the gang if he could. It was the word "beautiful" that worried him—that belonged to a class world that you could still see parodied at the Wormsley Common Empire by a man wearing a top hat and a monocle, with a haw-haw accent. He was tempted to say, "My dear Trevor, old chap," and unleash his hell hounds. "If you'd broken in," he said sadly—that indeed would have been an exploit worthy of the gang.

"This was better," T. said. "I found out things." He continued to stare at his feet, not meeting anybody's eye, as though he were absorbed in some dream he was unwilling—or ashamed—to share.

"What things?"

"Old Misery's going to be away all tomorrow and Bank Holiday."

Blackie said with relief, "You mean we could break in?"

"And pinch things?" somebody asked.

Blackie said, "Nobody's going to pinch things. Breaking in—that's good enough, isn't it? We don't want any court stuff."

"I don't want to pinch anything," T. said. "I've got a better idea."

"What is it?"

T. raised eyes, as grey and disturbed as the drab August day. "We'll pull it down," he said. "We'll destroy it."

Blackie gave a single hoot of laughter and then, like Mike, fell quiet, daunted by the serious implacable gaze. "What'd the police be doing all the time?" he said.

"They'd never know. We'd do it from inside. I've found a way in." He said with a sort of intensity, "We'd be like worms, don't you see, in an apple. When we came out again there'd be nothing there, no staircase, no panels, nothing but just walls, and then we'd make the walls fall down—somehow."

"We'd go to jug," Blackie said.

"Who's to prove? And anyway we wouldn't have pinched anything." He added without the smallest flicker of glee, "There wouldn't be anything to pinch after we'd finished."

"I've never heard of going to prison for breaking things," Summers said.

"There wouldn't be time," Blackie said. "I've seen housebreakers at work."

"There are twelve of us," T. said. "We'd organize."

"None of us know how—"

"I know," T. said. He looked across at Blackie, "Have you got a better plan?"

"Today," Mike said tactlessly, "we're pinching free rides—"

"Free rides," T. said. "You can stand down, Blackie, if you'd rather...."

"The gang's got to vote."

"Put it up then."

Blackie said uneasily, "It's proposed that tomorrow and Monday we destroy Old Misery's house."

"Here, here," said a fat boy called Joe.

"Who's in favour?"

T. said, "It's carried."

"How do we start?" Summers asked.

"He'll tell you," Blackie said. It was the end of his leadership. He went away to the back of the car-park and began to kick a stone, dribbling it this way and that. There was only one old Morris in the park, for few cars were left there except lorries: without an attendant there was no safety. He took a flying kick at the car and scraped a little paint off the rear mudguard. Beyond, paying no more attention to him than to a stranger, the gang had gathered round T.; Blackie was dimly aware of the fickleness of favour. He thought of going home, of never returning, of letting them all discover the hollowness of T.'s leadership, but suppose after all what T. proposed was possible—nothing like it had ever been done before. The fame of the Wormsley Common car-park gang would surely reach around London. There would be headlines in the papers. Even the grown-up gangs who ran the betting at the all-in wrestling and the barrow-boys would hear with respect of how Old Misery's house had been destroyed. Driven by the pure, simple, and altruistic ambition of fame for the gang, Blackie came back to where T. stood in the shadow of Misery's wall.

T. was giving his orders with decision: it was as though this plan had been with him all his life, pondered through the seasons, now in his fifteenth year crystallized with the pain of puberty. "You," he said to Mike, "bring some big nails, the biggest you can find, and a hammer. Anyone else who can better bring a hammer and a screwdriver. We'll need plenty of them. Chisels too. We can't have too many chisels. Can anybody bring a saw?"

"I can," Mike said.

"Not a child's saw," T. said. "A real saw."

Blackie realized he had raised his hand like any ordinary member of the gang.

"Right, you bring one, Blackie. But now there's a difficulty. We want a hacksaw."

"What's a hacksaw?" someone asked.

"You can get 'em at Woolworth's," Summers said.

The fat boy called Joe said gloomily, "I knew it would end in a collection."

"I'll get one myself," T. said. "I don't want your money. But I can't buy a sledgehammer."

Blackie said, "They are working on number fifteen. I know where they'll leave their stuff for Bank Holiday."

"Then that's all," T. said. "We meet here at nine sharp."

"I've got to go to church," Mike said.

"Come over the wall and whistle. We'll let you in."

2

On Sunday morning all were punctual except Blackie, even Mike. Mike had had a stroke of luck. His mother felt ill, his father was tired after Saturday night, and he was told to go to church alone with many warnings of what would happen if he strayed. Blackie had had difficulty in smuggling out the saw, and then in finding the sledge-hammer at the back of number 15. He approached the house from a lane at the rear of the garden, for fear of the policeman's beat along the main road. The tired evergreens kept off a stormy sun: another wet Bank Holiday was being prepared over the Atlantic, beginning in swirls of dust under the trees. Blackie climbed the wall into Misery's garden.

There was no sign of anybody anywhere. The loo stood like a tomb in a neglected graveyard. The curtains were drawn. The house slept. Blackie lumbered nearer with the saw and the sledge-hammer. Perhaps after all nobody had turned up: the plan had been a wild invention: they had woken wiser. But when he came close to the back door he could hear a confusion of sound, hardly louder than a hive in swarm: a clickety-clack, a bang bang bang, a scraping, a creaking, a sudden painful crack. He thought, It's true, and whistled.

They opened the back door to him and he came in. He had at once the impression of organization, very different from the old happy-go-lucky ways under his leadership. For a while he wandered up and down stairs looking for T. Nobody addressed him: he had a sense of great urgency, and already he could begin to see the plan. The interior of the house was being carefully demolished without touching the outer walls. Summers with hammer and chisel was ripping out the skirting-boards in the ground floor dining-room: he had already smashed the panels of the door. In the same room Joe was heaving up the parquet blocks, exposing the soft wood floor-boards over the cellar. Coils of wire came out of the damaged skirting and Mike sat happily on the floor, clipping the wires.

On the curved stairs two of the gang were working hard with an inadequate child's saw on the banisters—when they saw Blackie's big saw they signalled for it wordlessly. When he next saw them a quarter of the banisters had been dropped into the hall. He found T. at last in the bathroom—he sat moodily in the least cared-for room in the house, listening to the sounds coming up from below.

"You've really done it," Blackie said with awe. "What's going to happen?"

"We've only just begun," T. said. He

looked at the sledge-hammer and gave his instructions. "You stay here and break the bath and the wash-basin. Don't bother about the pipes. They come later."

Mike appeared at the door. "I've finished the wire, T.," he said.

"Good. You've just got to go wandering round now. The kitchen's in the basement. Smash all the china and glass and bottles you can lay hold of. Don't turn on the taps—we don't want a flood—yet. Then go into all the rooms and turn out drawers. If they are locked get one of the others to break them open. Tear up any papers you find and smash all the ornaments. Better take a carving-knife with you from the kitchen. The bedroom's opposite here. Open the pillows and tear up the sheets. That's enough for the moment. And you, Blackie, when you've finished in here crack the plaster in the passage up with your sledge-hammer."

"What are you going to do?" Blackie asked.

"I'm looking for something special," T. said.

It was nearly lunch-time before Blackie had finished and went in search of T. Chaos had advanced. The kitchen was a shambles of broken glass and china. The dining-room was stripped of parquet, the skirting was up, the door had been taken off its hinges, and the destroyers had moved up a floor. Streaks of light came in through the closed shutters where they worked with the seriousness of creators—and destruction after all is a form of creation. A kind of imagination had seen this house as it had now become.

Mike said, "I've got to go home for dinner."

"Who else?" T. asked, but all the others on one excuse or another had brought provisions with them.

They squatted in the ruins of the room and swapped unwanted sandwiches. Half an hour for lunch and they were at work again. By the time Mike returned, they were on the top floor, and by six the superficial damage was completed. The doors were all off, all the skirtings raised, the furniture pillaged and ripped and smashed—no one could have slept in the house except on a bed of broken plaster. T. gave his orders—eight o'clock next morning —and to escape notice they climbed singly over the garden wall, into the car-park. Only Blackie and T. were left; the light had nearly gone, and when they touched a switch, nothing worked—Mike had done his job thoroughly.

"Did you find anything special?" Blackie asked.

T. nodded. "Come over here," he said, "and look." Out of both pockets he drew bundles of pound notes. "Old Misery's savings," he said. "Mike ripped out the mattress, but he missed them."

"What are you going to do? Share them?"

"We aren't thieves," T. said. "Nobody's going to steal anything from this house. I kept these for you and me—a celebration." He knelt down on the floor and counted them out—there were seventy in all. "We'll burn them," he said, "one by one," and taking it in turns they held a note upwards and lit the top corner, so that the flame burnt slowly towards their fingers. The grey ash floated above them and fell on their heads like age. "I'd like to see Old Misery's face when we are through," T. said.

"You hate him a lot?" Blackie asked.

"Of course I don't hate him," T. said. "There'd be no fun if I hated him." The last burning note illuminated his brooding face. "All this hate and love," he said, "it's soft, it's hooey. There's only things, Blackie," and he looked round the room crowded with the unfamiliar shadows of half things, broken things, former things. "I'll race you home, Blackie," he said.

3

Next morning the serious destruction started. Two were missing—Mike and another boy whose parents were off to Southend and Brighton in spite of the slow warm drops that had begun to fall and the rumble of thunder in the estuary like the first guns of the old blitz. "We've got to hurry," T. said.

Summers was restive. "Haven't we done enough?" he said. "I've been given a bob for slot machines. This is like work."

"We've hardly started," T. said. "Why, there's all the floors left, and the stairs. We haven't taken out a single window. You voted like the others. We are going to *destroy* this house. There won't be anything left when we've finished."

They began again on the first floor picking up the top floor-boards next the outer wall, leaving the joists exposed. Then they sawed through the joists and retreated into the hall, as what was left of the floor heeled and sank. They had learnt with practise, and the second floor collapsed more easily. By the evening an odd exhilaration seized them as they looked down the great hollow of the house. They ran risks and made mistakes: when they thought of the windows it was too late to reach them. "Cor," Joe said, and dropped a penny down into the dry rubble-filled well. It cracked and span among the broken glass.

"Why did we start this?" Summers asked with astonishment; T. was already on the ground, digging at the rubble, clearing a space along the outer wall. "Turn on the taps," he said. "It's too dark for anyone to see now, and in the morning it won't matter." The water overtook them on the stairs and fell through the floorless rooms.

It was then they heard Mike's whistle at the back. "Something's wrong," Blackie said. They could hear his urgent breathing as they unlocked the door.

"The bogies?" Summers asked.

"Old Misery," Mike said. "He's on his way." He put his head between his knees and retched. "Ran all the way," he said with pride.

"But why?" T. said. "He told me . . ." He protested with the fury of the child he had never been, "It isn't fair."

"He was down at Southend," Mike said, "and he was on the train coming back. Said it was too cold and wet." He paused and gazed at the water. "My, you've had a storm here. Is the roof leaking?"

"How long will he be?"

"Five minutes. I gave Ma the slip and ran."

"We better clear," Summers said. "We've done enough, anyway."

"Oh, no, we haven't. Anybody could do this—" "this" was the shattered hollowed house with nothing left but the walls. Yet walls could be preserved. Façades were valuable. They could build inside again more beautifully than before. This could again be a home. He said angrily, "We've got to finish. Don't move. Let me think."

"There's no time," a boy said.

"There's got to be a way," T. said. "We couldn't have got thus far . . ."

"We've done a lot," Blackie said.

"No. No, we haven't. Somebody watch the front."

"We can't do any more."

"He may come in at the back."

"Watch the back too." T. began to plead. "Just give me a minute and I'll fix it. I swear I'll fix it." But his authority had gone with his ambiguity. He was only one of the gang. "Please," he said.

"Please," Summers mimicked him, and then suddenly struck home with the fatal name. "Run along home, Trevor."

T. stood with his back to the rubble like a boxer knocked groggy against the ropes. He had no words as his dreams shook and slid. Then Blackie acted before the gang had time to laugh, pushing Summers backward. "I'll watch the front, T.," he said, and cautiously he opened the shutters of the hall. The grey wet common stretched ahead, and the lamps gleamed in the puddles. "Someone's coming, T. No, it's not him. What's your plan, T.?"

"Tell Mike to go out to the loo and hide close beside it. When he hears me whistle he's got to count ten and start to shout."

"Shout what?"

"Oh, 'Help,' anything."

"You hear, Mike," Blackie said. He was the leader again. He took a quick look between the shutters. "He's coming, T."

"Quick, Mike. The loo. Stay here, Blackie, all of you till I yell."

"Where are you going, T.?"

"Don't worry. I'll see to this. I said I would, didn't I?"

Old Misery came limping off the common. He had mud on his shoes and he stopped to scrape them on the pavement's edge. He didn't want to soil his house, which stood jagged and dark between the bomb-sites, saved so narrowly, as he believed, from destruction. Even the fanlight had been left unbroken by the bomb's blast. Somewhere somebody whistled. Old Misery looked sharply round. He didn't trust whistles. A child was shouting: it seemed to come from his own garden. Then a boy ran into the road from the car-park. "Mr. Thomas," he called, "Mr. Thomas."

"What is it?"

"I'm terribly sorry, Mr. Thomas. One of us got taken short, and we thought you wouldn't mind, and now he can't get out."

"What do you mean, boy?"

"He's got stuck in your loo."

"He'd no business—Haven't I seen you before?"

"You showed me your house."

"So I did. So I did. That doesn't give you the right to—"

"Do hurry, Mr. Thomas. He'll suffocate."

"Nonsense. He can't suffocate. Wait till I put my bag in."

"I'll carry your bag."

"Oh, no, you don't. I carry my own."

"This way, Mr. Thomas."

"I can't get in the garden that way. I've got to go through the house."

"But you *can* get in the garden this way, Mr. Thomas. We often do."

"You often do?" He followed the boy with a scandalized fascination. "When? What right . . ."

"Do you see . . . ? The wall's low."

"I'm not going to climb walls into my own garden. It's absurd."

"This is how we do it. One foot here, one foot there, and over." The boy's face peered down, an arm shot out, and Mr. Thomas found his bag taken and deposited on the other side of the wall.

"Give me back my bag." Mr. Thomas said. From the loo a boy yelled and yelled. "I'll call the police."

"Your bag's all right, Mr. Thomas. Look. One foot there. On your right. Now just above. To your left." Mr. Thomas climbed over his own garden wall. "Here's your bag, Mr. Thomas."

"I'll have the wall built up," Mr. Thomas said, "I'll not have you boys coming over here, using my loo." He stumbled on the path, but the boy caught his elbow and supported him. "Thank you, thank you, my boy," he murmured automatically. Somebody shouted again through the dark. "I'm coming, I'm coming," Mr. Thomas called. He said to the boy beside him, "I'm not unreasonable. Been a boy myself. As long as things are done regular. I don't mind you playing round the place Saturday morning. Sometimes I like company. Only it's got to be regular. One of you asks leave and I say Yes. Sometimes I'll say No. Won't feel like it. And you come in at the front door and out at the back. No garden walls."

"Do get him out, Mr. Thomas."

"He won't come to any harm in my loo," Mr. Thomas said, stumbling slowly down the garden. "Oh, my rheumatics," he said. "Always get 'em on Bank Holiday. I've got to go careful. There's loose stones here. Give me your hand. Do you know what my horoscope said yesterday? 'Abstain from any dealings in first half of week. Danger of serious crash.' That might be on this path," Mr. Thomas said. "They speak in parables and double meanings." He paused at the door of the loo. "What's the matter in there?" he called. There was no reply.

"Perhaps he's fainted," the boy said.

"Not in my loo. Here, you, come out," Mr. Thomas said, and giving a great jerk at the door he nearly fell on his back when it swung easily open. A hand first supported him and then pushed him hard. His head hit the opposite wall and he sat heavily down. His bag hit his feet. A hand whipped the key out of the lock and the door slammed. "Let me out," he called, and heard the key turn in the lock. "A serious crash," he thought, and felt dithery and confused and old.

A voice spoke to him softly through the star-shaped hole in the door. "Don't worry, Mr. Thomas," it said, "we won't hurt you, not if you stay quiet."

Mr. Thomas put his head between his hands and pondered. He had noticed that there was only one lorry in the car-park, and he felt certain that the driver would not come in for it before the morning. Nobody could hear him from the road in front, and the lane at the back was seldom used. Anyone who passed there would be hurrying home and would not pause for what they would certainly take to be drunken cries. And if he did call "Help," who, on a lonely Bank Holiday evening, would have the courage to investigate? Mr. Thomas sat on the loo and pondered with the wisdom of age.

After a while it seemed to him that there were sounds in the silence—they were faint and came from the direction of his house. He stood up and peered through the ventilation-hole—between the cracks in one of the shutters he saw a light, not the light of a lamp, but the wavering light that a candle might give. Then he thought he heard the sound of hammering and scraping and chipping. He thought of burglars—perhaps they had employed the boy as a scout, but why should burglars engage in what sounded more and more like a stealthy form of carpentry? Mr. Thomas let out an experimental yell, but nobody answered. The noise could not even have reached his enemies.

4

Mike had gone home to bed, but the rest stayed. The question of leadership no longer concerned the gang. With nails, chisels, screwdrivers, anything that was sharp and penetrating they moved around the inner walls worrying at the mortar between the bricks. They started too high, and it was Blackie who hit on the damp course and realized the work could be halved if they weakened the joints immediately above. It was a long, tiring, unamusing job, but at last it was finished. The gutted house stood there balanced on a few inches of mortar between the damp course and the bricks.

There remained the most dangerous task of all, out in the open at the edge of the bomb-site. Summers was sent to watch the road for passers-by, and Mr. Thomas, sitting on the loo, heard clearly now the sound of sawing. It no longer came from his house, and that a little reassured him. He felt less concerned. Perhaps the other noises too had no significance.

A voice spoke to him through the hole. "Mr. Thomas."

"Let me out," Mr. Thomas said sternly.

"Here's a blanket," the voice said, and a long grey sausage was worked through the hole and fell in swathes over Mr. Thomas's head.

"There's nothing personal," the voice said. "We want you to be comfortable tonight."

"Tonight," Mr. Thomas repeated incredulously.

"Catch," the voice said. "Penny buns—we've buttered them, and sausage-rolls. We don't want you to starve, Mr. Thomas."

Mr. Thomas pleaded desperately. "A joke's a joke, boy. Let me out and I won't say a thing. I've got rheumatics. I got to sleep comfortable."

"You wouldn't be comfortable, not in your house, you wouldn't. Not now."

"What do you mean, boy?" but the footsteps receded. There was only the silence of night: no sound of sawing. Mr. Thomas tried one more yell, but he was daunted and rebuked by the silence—a long way off an owl hooted and made away again on its muffled flight through the soundless world.

At seven next morning the driver came to fetch his lorry. He climbed into the seat and tried to start the engine. He was vaguely aware of a voice shouting, but it didn't concern him. At last the engine responded and he backed the lorry until it touched the great wooden shore that supported Mr. Thomas's house. That way he could drive right out and down the street without reversing. The lorry moved forward, was momentarily checked as though something were pulling it from behind, and then went on to the sound of a long rumbling crash. The driver was astonished to see bricks bouncing ahead of him, while stones hit the roof of his cab. He put on his brakes. When he climbed out the whole landscape had suddenly altered. There was no house beside the carpark, only a hill of rubble. He went round and examined the back of his car for damage, and found a rope tied there that was still twisted at the other end round part of a wooden strut.

The driver again become aware of somebody shouting. It came from the wooden erection which was the nearest thing to a house in that desolation of broken brick. The driver climbed the smashed wall and unlocked the door. Mr. Thomas came out of the loo. He was wearing a grey blanket to which flakes of pastry adhered. He gave a sobbing cry. "My house," he said. "Where's my house?"

"Search me," the driver said. His eye lit on the remains of a bath and what had once been a dresser and he began to laugh. There wasn't anything left anywhere.

"How dare you laugh," Mr. Thomas said. "It was my house. My house."

"I'm sorry," the driver said, making heroic efforts, but when he remembered the sudden check to his lorry, the crash of bricks falling, he became convulsed again. One moment the house had stood there with such dignity between the bomb-sites like a man in a top hat, and then, bang, crash, there wasn't anything left—not anything. He said, "I'm sorry. I can't help it, Mr. Thomas. There's nothing personal, but you got to admit it's funny."

A Good Man Is Hard to Find*

by FLANNERY O'CONNOR

The grandmother didn't want to go to Florida. She wanted to visit some of her connections in east Tennessee and she was seizing at every chance to change Bailey's mind. Bailey was the son she lived with, her only boy. He was sitting on the edge of his chair at the table, bent over the orange sports section of the *Journal*. "Now look here, Bailey," she said, "see here, read this," and she stood with one hand on her thin hip and the other rattling the newspaper at his bald head. "Here this fellow that calls himself The Misfit is aloose from the Federal Pen and headed toward Florida and you read here what it says he did to these people. Just you read it. I wouldn't take my children in any direction with a criminal like that aloose in it. I couldn't answer to my conscience if I did."

Bailey didn't look up from his reading so she wheeled around then and faced the children's mother, a young woman in slacks, whose face was as broad and innocent as a cabbage and was tied around with a green head-kerchief that had two points on the top like rabbit's ears. She was sitting on the sofa, feeding the baby his apricots out of a jar. "The children have been to Florida before," the old lady said. "You all ought to take them somewhere else for a change so they would see different parts of the world and be broad. They never have been to east Tennessee."

The children's mother didn't seem to hear her but the eight-year-old boy, John Wesley, a stocky child with glasses, said, "If you don't want to go to Florida, why dontcha stay at home?" He and the little girl, June Star, were reading the funny papers on the floor.

"She wouldn't stay at home to be queen for a day," June Star said without raising her yellow head.

"Yes and what would you do if this fellow, The Misfit, caught you?" the grandmother asked.

"I'd smack his face," John Wesley said.

"She wouldn't stay at home for a million bucks," June Star said. "Afraid she'd miss something. She has to go everywhere we go."

"All right, Miss," the grandmother said. "Just remember that the next time you want me to curl your hair."

June Star said her hair was naturally curly.

The next morning the grandmother was the first one in the car, ready to go. She had her big black valise that looked like the head of a hippopotamus in one corner, and underneath it she was hiding a basket with Pitty Sing, the cat, in it. She didn't intend for the cat to be left alone in the house for three days because he would miss her too

---

* Copyright, 1953, by Flannery O'Connor. Reprinted from her volume *A Good Man Is Hard to Find and Other Stories* by permission of Harcourt Brace Jovanovich, Inc.

much and she was afraid he might brush against one of the gas burners and accidentally asphyxiate himself. Her son, Bailey, didn't like to arrive at a motel with a cat.

She sat in the middle of the back seat with John Wesley and June Star on either side of her. Bailey and the children's mother and the baby sat in front and they left Atlanta at eight forty-five with the mileage on the car at 55890. The grandmother wrote this down because she thought it would be interesting to say how many miles they had been when they got back. It took them twenty minutes to reach the outskirts of the city.

The old lady settled herself comfortably, removing her white cotton gloves and putting them up with her purse on the shelf in front of the back window. The children's mother still had on slacks and still had her head tied up in a green kerchief, but the grandmother had on a navy blue straw sailor hat with a bunch of white violets on the brim and a navy blue dress with a small white dot in the print. Her collars and cuffs were white organdy trimmed with lace and at her neckline she had pinned a purple spray of cloth violets containing a sachet. In case of an accident, anyone seeing her dead on the highway would know at once that she was a lady.

She said she thought it was going to be a good day for driving, neither too hot nor too cold, and she cautioned Bailey that the speed limit was fifty-five miles an hour and that the patrolmen hid themselves behind billboards and small clumps of trees and sped out after you before you had a chance to slow down. She pointed out interesting details of the scenery: Stone Mountain; the blue granite that in some places came up to both sides of the highway; the brilliant red clay banks slightly streaked with purple; and the various crops that made rows of green lace-work on the ground. The trees were full of silver-white sunlight and the meanest of them sparkled. The children were reading comic magazines and their mother had gone back to sleep.

"Let's go through Georgia fast so we won't have to look at it much," John Wesley said.

"If I were a little boy," said the grandmother, "I wouldn't talk about my native state that way. Tennessee has the mountains and Georgia has the hills."

"Tennessee is just a hillbilly dumping ground," John Wesley said, "and Georgia is a lousy state too."

"You said it," June Star said.

"In my time," said the grandmother, folding her thin veined fingers, "children were more respectful of their native states and their parents and everything else. People did right then. Oh look at the cute little pickaninny!" she said and pointed to a Negro child standing in the door of a shack. "Wouldn't that make a picture, now?" she asked and they all turned and looked at the little Negro out of the back window. He waved.

"He didn't have any britches on," June Star said.

"He probably didn't have any," the grandmother explained. "Little niggers in the country don't have things like we do. If I could paint, I'd paint that picture," she said.

The children exchanged comic books.

The grandmother offered to hold the baby and the children's mother passed him over the front seat to her. She set him on her knee and bounced him and told him about the things they were passing. She rolled her eyes and screwed up her mouth and stuck her leathery thin face into his smooth bland one. Occasionally he gave her a faraway smile. They passed a large cotton field with five or six graves fenced in the middle of it, like a small island. "Look at the graveyard!" the grandmother said, pointing it out. "That was the old family burying ground. That belonged to the plantation."

"Where's the plantation?" John Wesley asked.

"Gone With the Wind," said the grandmother. "Ha. Ha."

When the children finished all the comic books they had brought, they opened the lunch and ate it. The grandmother ate a peanut butter sandwich and an olive and would not let the children throw the box and the paper napkins out the window. When there was nothing else to do they played a game by choosing a cloud and making the other two guess what shape it suggested. John Wesley took one the shape of a cow and June Star guessed a cow and John Wesley said, no, an automobile, and June Star said he didn't play fair, and they began to slap each other over the grandmother.

The grandmother said she would tell them a story if they would keep quiet. When she told a story, she rolled her eyes and waved her head and was very dramatic. She said once when she was a maiden lady she had been courted by a Mr. Edgar Atkins Teagarden from Jasper, Georgia. She said he was a very good-looking man and a gentleman and that he brought her a watermelon every Saturday afternoon with his initials cut in it, E. A. T. Well, one Saturday, she said, Mr. Teagarden brought the watermelon and there was nobody at home and he left it on the front porch and returned in his buggy to Jasper, but she never got the watermelon, she said, because a nigger boy ate it when he saw the initials, E. A. T.! This story tickled John Wesley's funny bone and he giggled and giggled but June Star didn't think it was any good. She said she wouldn't marry a man that just brought her a watermelon on Saturday. The grandmother said she would have done well to marry Mr. Teagarden because he was a gentleman and had bought Coca-Cola stock when it first came out and that he had died only a few years ago, a very wealthy man.

They stopped at The Tower for barbecued sandwiches. The Tower was a part stucco and part wood filling station and dance hall set in a clearing outside of Timothy. A fat man named Red Sammy Butts ran it and there were signs stuck here and there on the building and for miles up and down the highway saying, TRY RED SAMMY'S FAMOUS BARBECUE. NONE LIKE FAMOUS RED SAMMY'S! RED SAM! THE FAT BOY WITH THE HAPPY LAUGH. A VETERAN! RED SAMMY'S YOUR MAN!

Red Sammy was lying on the bare ground outside The Tower with his head under a truck while a gray monkey about a foot high, chained to a small chinaberry tree, chattered nearby. The monkey sprang back into the tree and got on the highest limb as soon as he saw the children jump out of the car and run toward him.

Inside, The Tower was a long dark room with a counter at one end and tables at the other and dancing space in the middle. They all sat down at a board table next to the nickelodeon and Red Sam's wife, a tall burnt-brown woman with hair and eyes lighter than her skin, came and took their order. The children's mother put a dime in the machine and played "The Tennessee Waltz," and the grandmother said that tune always made her want to dance. She asked Bailey if he would like to dance but he only glared at her. He didn't have a naturally sunny disposition like she did and trips made him nervous. The grandmother's brown eyes were very bright. She swayed her head from side to side and pretended she was dancing in her chair. June Star said play something she could tap to so the children's mother put in another dime and played a fast number and June Star stepped out onto the dance floor and did her tap routine.

"Ain't she cute?" Red Sam's wife said, leaning over the counter. "Would you like to come be my little girl?"

"No I certainly wouldn't," June Star said. "I wouldn't live in a broken-down place like this for a million bucks!" and she ran back to the table.

"Ain't she cute?" the woman repeated, stretching her mouth politely.

"Arn't you ashamed?" hissed the grandmother.

Red Sam came in and told his wife to quit lounging on the counter and hurry up with these people's order. His khaki trousers reached just to his hip bones and his stomach hung over them like a sack of meal swaying under his shirt. He came over and sat down at a table nearby and let out a combination sigh and yodel. "You can't win," he said. "You can't win," and he wiped his sweating red face off with a gray handkerchief. "These days you don't know who to trust," he said. "Ain't that the truth?"

"People are certainly not nice like they used to be," said the grandmother.

"Two fellers come in here last week,"

Red Sammy said, "driving a Chrysler. It was a old beat-up car but it was a good one and these boys looked all right to me. Said they worked at the mill and you know I let them fellers charge the gas they bought? Now why did I do that?"

"Because you're a good man!" the grandmother said at once.

"Yes'm, I suppose so," Red Sam said as if he were struck with this answer.

His wife brought the orders, carrying the five plates all at once without a tray, two in each hand and one balanced on her arm. "It isn't a soul in this green world of God's that you can trust," she said. "And I don't count nobody out of that, not nobody," she repeated, looking at Red Sammy.

"Did you read about the criminal, The Misfit, that's escaped?" asked the grandmother.

"I wouldn't be a bit surprised if he didn't attact this place right here," said the woman. "If he hears about it being here, I wouldn't be none surprised to see him. If he hears it's two cent in the cash register, I wouldn't be a tall surprised if he . . ."

"That'll do," Red Sam said. "Go bring these people their Co'-Colas," and the woman went off to get the rest of the order.

"A good man is hard to find," Red Sammy said. "Everything is getting terrible. I remember the day you could go off and leave your screen door unlatched. Not no more."

He and the grandmother discussed better times. The old lady said that in her opinion Europe was entirely to blame for the way things were now. She said the way Europe acted you would think we were made of money and Red Sam said it was no use talking about it, she was exactly right. The children ran outside in the white sunlight and looked at the monkey in the lacy chinaberry tree. He was busy catching fleas on himself and biting each one carefully between his teeth as if it were a delicacy.

They drove off again into the hot afternoon. The grandmother took cat naps and woke up every few minutes with her own snoring. Outside of Toombsboro she woke up and recalled an old plantation that she had visited in this neighborhood once when she was a young lady. She said the house had six white columns across the front and that there was an avenue of oaks leading up to it and two little wooden trellis arbors on either side in front where you sat down with your suitor after a stroll in the garden. She recalled exactly which road to turn off to get to it. She knew that Bailey would not be willing to lose any time looking at an old house, but the more she talked about it, the more she wanted to see it once again and find out if the little twin arbors were still standing. "There was a secret panel in this house," she said craftily, not telling the truth but wishing that she were, "and the story went that all the family silver was hidden in it when Sherman came through but it was never found. . . ."

"Hey!" John Wesley said. "Let's go see it! We'll find it! We'll poke all the woodwork and find it! Who lives there? Where do you turn off at? Hey Pop, can't we turn off there?"

"We never have seen a house with a secret panel!" June Star shrieked. "Let's go to the house with the secret panel! Hey Pop, can't we go see the house with the secret panel!"

"It's not far from here, I know," the grandmother said. "It wouldn't take over twenty minutes."

Bailey was looking straight ahead. His jaw was as rigid as a horseshoe. "No," he said.

The children began to yell and scream that they wanted to see the house with the secret panel. John Wesley kicked the back of the front seat and June Star hung over her mother's shoulder and whined desperately into her ear that they never had any fun even on their vacation, that they could never do what THEY wanted to do. The baby began to scream and John Wesley kicked the back of the seat so hard that his father could feel the blows in his kidney.

"All right!" he shouted and drew the car to a stop at the side of the road. "Will you all shut up? Will you all just shut up for one second? If you don't shut up, we won't go anywhere."

"It would be very educational for them," the grandmother murmured.

"All right," Bailey said, "but get this: this is the only time we're going to stop for anything like this. This is the one and only time."

"The dirt road that you have to turn down is about a mile back," the grandmother directed. "I marked it when we passed."

"A dirt road," Bailey groaned.

After they had turned around and were headed toward the dirt road, the grandmother recalled other points about the house, the beautiful glass over the front doorway and the candle-lamp in the hall. John Wesley said that the secret panel was probably in the fireplace.

"You can't go inside this house," Bailey said. "You don't know who lives there."

"While you all talk to the people in front, I'll run around behind and get in a window," John Wesley suggested.

"We'll all stay in the car," his mother said.

They turned onto the dirt road and the car raced roughly along in a swirl of pink dust. The grandmother recalled the times when there were no paved roads and thirty miles was a day's journey. The dirt road was hilly and there were sudden washes in it and sharp curves on dangerous embankments. All at once they would be on a hill, looking down over the blue tops of trees for miles around, then the next minute, they would be in a red depression with the dust-coated trees looking down on them.

"This place had better turn up in a minute," Bailey said, "or I'm going to turn around."

The road looked as if no one had traveled on it in months.

"It's not much farther," the grandmother said and just as she said it, a horrible thought came to her. The thought was so embarrassing that she turned red in the face and her eyes dilated and her feet jumped up, upsetting her valise in the corner. The instant the valise moved, the newspaper top she had over the basket under it rose with a snarl and Pitty Sing, the cat, sprang onto Bailey's shoulder.

The children were thrown to the floor and out the door onto the ground; the old lady was thrown into the front seat. The car turned over once and landed right-side-up in a gulch off the side of the road. Bailey remained in the driver's seat with the cat—gray-striped with a broad white face and an orange nose—clinging to his neck like a caterpillar.

As soon as the children saw they could move their arms and legs, they scrambled out of the car, shouting, "We've had an ACCIDENT!" The grandmother was curled up under the dashboard, hoping she was injured so that Bailey's wrath would not come down on her all at once. The horrible thought she had had before the accident was that the house she had remembered so vividly was not in Georgia but in Tennessee.

Bailey removed the cat from his neck with both hands and flung it out the window against the side of a pine tree. Then he got out of the car and started looking for the children's mother. She was sitting against the side of the red gutted ditch, holding the screaming baby, but she only had a cut down her face and a broken shoulder. "We've had an ACCIDENT!" the children screamed in a frenzy of delight.

"But nobody's killed," June Star said with disappointment as the grandmother limped out of the car, her hat still pinned to her head but the broken front brim standing up at a jaunty angle and the violet spray hanging off the side. They all sat down in the ditch, except the children, to recover from the shock. They were all shaking.

"Maybe a car will come along," said the children's mother hoarsely.

"I believe I have injured an organ," said the grandmother, pressing her side, but no one answered her. Bailey's teeth were clattering. He had on a yellow sport shirt with bright blue parrots designed in it and his face was as yellow as the shirt. The grandmother decided that she would not mention that the house was in Tennessee.

The road was about ten feet above and they could see only the tops of the trees on the other side of it. Behind the ditch they were sitting in there were more woods, tall and dark and deep. In a few minutes they saw a car some distance away on top of a hill, coming slowly as if the occupants were watching them. The grandmother stood up and waved both arms dramatically to attract their attention. The car continued to come on slowly, disappeared around a bend and appeared again, moving even slower, on top of the hill they had gone over. It was a big black battered hearse-like automobile. There were three men in it.

It came to a stop just over them and for some minutes, the driver looked down with a steady expressionless gaze to where they were sitting, and didn't speak. Then he turned his head and muttered something to the other two and they got out. One was a fat boy in black trousers and a red sweat shirt with a silver stallion embossed on the front of it. He moved around on the right side of them and stood staring, his mouth partly open in a kind of loose grin. The other had on khaki pants and a blue striped coat and a gray hat pulled down very low, hiding most of his face. He came around slowly on the left side. Neither spoke.

The driver got out of the car and stood by the side of it, looking down at them. He was an older man than the other two. His hair was just beginning to gray and he wore silver-rimmed spectacles that gave him a scholarly look. He had a long creased face and didn't have on any shirt or undershirt. He had on blue jeans that were too tight for him and was holding a black hat and a gun. The two boys also had guns.

"We've had an ACCIDENT!" the children screamed.

The grandmother had the peculiar feeling that the bespectacled man was someone she knew. His face was as familiar to her as if she had known him all her life but she could not recall who he was. He moved away from the car and began to come down the embankment, placing his feet carefully so that he wouldn't slip. He had on tan and white shoes and no socks, and his ankles were red and thin. "Good afternoon," he said "I see you all had you a little spill."

"We turned over twice!" said the grandmother.

"Oncet," he corrected. "We seen it happen. Try their car and see will it run, Hiram," he said quietly to the boy with the gray hat.

"What you got that gun for?" John Wesley asked. "Whatcha gonna do with that gun?"

"Lady," the man said to the children's mother, "would you mind calling them children to sit down by you? Children make me nervous. I want all you all to sit down right together there where you're at."

"What are you telling US what to do for?" June Star asked.

Behind them the line of woods gaped like a dark open mouth. "Come here," said their mother.

"Look here now," Bailey began suddenly, "we're in a predicament! We're in . . ."

The grandmother shrieked. She scrambled to her feet and stood staring. "You're The Misfit!" she said. "I recognized you at once!"

"Yes'm," the man said, smiling slightly as if he were pleased in spite of himself to be known, "but it would have been better for all of you, lady, if you hadn't reckernized me."

Bailey turned his head sharply and said something to his mother that shocked even the children. The old lady began to cry and The Misfit reddened.

"Lady," he said, "don't you get upset. Sometimes a man says things he don't mean. I don't reckon he meant to talk to you thataway."

"You wouldn't shoot a lady, would you?" the grandmother said and removed a clean handkerchief from her cuff and began to slap at her eyes with it.

The Misfit pointed the toe of his shoe into the ground and made a little hole and then covered it up again. "I would hate to have to," he said.

"Listen," the grandmother almost screamed, "I know you're a good man. You don't look a bit like you have common blood. I know you must come from nice people!"

"Yes mam," he said, "finest people in the world." When he smiled he showed a row of strong white teeth. "God never made a finer woman than my mother and my daddy's heart was pure gold," he said. The boy with the red sweat shirt had come around behind them and was standing with his gun at his hip. The Misfit squatted down on the ground. "Watch them children, Bobby Lee," he said. "You know they make me nervous." He looked at the six of them huddled together in front of him and he seemed to be embarrassed as if he couldn't think of anything to say. "Ain't a cloud in the sky," he remarked, looking up at it. "Don't see no sun but don't see no cloud neither."

"Yes, it's a beautiful day," said the grandmother. "Listen," she said, "you shouldn't call yourself The Misfit because I know you're a good man at heart. I can just look at you and tell."

"Hush!" Bailey yelled. "Hush! Everybody shut up and let me handle this!" He was squatting in the position of a runner about to sprint forward but he didn't move.

"I pre-chate that, lady," The Misfit said and drew a little circle in the ground with the butt of his gun.

"It'll take a half a hour to fix this here car," Hiram called, looking over the raised hood of it.

"Well, first you and Bobby Lee get him and that little boy to step over yonder with you," the Misfit said, pointing to Bailey and John Wesley. "The boys want to ast you something," he said to Bailey. "Would you mind stepping back in them woods there with them?"

"Listen," Bailey began, "we're in a terrible predicament! Nobody realizes what this is," and his voice cracked. His eyes were as blue and intense as the parrots in his shirt and he remained perfectly still.

The grandmother reached up to adjust her hat brim as if she were going to the woods with him but it came off in her hand. She stood staring at it and after a second she let it fall on the ground. Hiram pulled Bailey up by the arm as if he were assisting an old man. John Wesley caught hold of his father's hand and Bobby Lee followed. They went off toward the woods and just as they reached the dark edge, Bailey turned and supporting himself against a gray naked pine trunk, he shouted, "I'll be back in a minute, Mamma, wait on me!"

"Come back this instant!" his mother shrilled but they all disappeared into the woods.

"Bailey Boy!" the grandmother called in a tragic voice but she found she was looking at The Misfit squatting on the ground in front of her. "I just know you're a good man," she said desperately. "You're not a bit common!"

"Nome, I ain't a good man," The Misfit said after a second as if he had considered her statement carefully, "but I ain't the worst in the world neither. My daddy said I was a different breed of dog from my brothers and sisters. 'You know,' Daddy said, 'it's some that can live their whole life out without asking about it and it's others has to know why it is, and this boy is one of the latters. He's going to be into everything!'" He put on his black hat and looked up suddenly and then away deep into the woods as if he were embarrassed again. "I'm sorry I don't have on a shirt before you ladies," he said, hunching his shoulders slightly. "We buried our clothes that we had on when we escaped and we're just making do until we can get better. We borrowed these from some folks we met," he explained.

"That's perfectly all right," the grandmother said. "Maybe Bailey has an extra shirt in his suitcase."

"I'll look and see terrectly," The Misfit said.

"Where are they taking him?" the children's mother screamed.

"Daddy was a card himself," The Misfit said. "You couldn't put anything over on him. He never got in trouble with the Authorities though. Just had the knack of handling them."

"You could be honest too if you'd only try," said the grandmother. "Think how wonderful it would be to settle down and live a comfortable life and not have to think about somebody chasing you all the time."

The Misfit kept scratching in the ground with the butt of his gun as if he were thinking about it. "Yes'm, somebody is always after you," he murmured.

The grandmother noticed how thin his shoulder blades were just behind his hat because she was standing up looking down on him. "Do you ever pray?" she asked.

He shook his head. All she saw was the black hat wiggle between his shoulder blades. "Nome," he said.

There was a pistol shot from the woods, followed closely by another. Then silence. The old lady's head jerked around. She could hear the wind move through the tree tops like a long satisfied insuck of breath. "Bailey Boy!" she called.

"I was a gospel singer for a while," The Misfit said. "I been most everything. Been in the arm service, both land and sea, at home and abroad, been twict married, been an undertaker, been with the railroads, plowed Mother Earth, been in a tornado, seen a man burnt alive oncet," and he looked up at the children's mother and the little girl who were sitting close together, their faces white and their eyes glassy; "I even seen a woman flogged," he said.

"Pray, pray," the grandmother began, "pray, pray . . ."

"I never was a bad boy that I remember of," The Misfit said in an almost dreamy voice, "but somewheres along the line I done something wrong and got sent to the penitentiary. I was buried alive," and he looked up and held her attention to him by a steady stare.

"That's when you should have started to pray," she said. "What did you do to get sent to the penitentiary that first time?"

"Turn to the right, it was a wall," The Misfit said, looking up again at the cloudless sky. "Turn to the left, it was a wall. Look up it was a ceiling look down it was a floor. I forget what I done, lady. I set there and set there, trying to remember what it was I done and I ain't recalled it to this day. Oncet in a while, I would think it was coming to me, but it never come."

"Maybe they put you in by mistake," the old lady said vaguely.

"Nome," he said. "It wasn't no mistake. They had the papers on me."

"You must have stolen something," she said.

The Misfit sneered slightly. "Nobody had nothing I wanted," he said. "It was a head-doctor at the penitentiary said what I had done was kill my daddy but I known that for a lie. My daddy died in nineteen ought nineteen of the epidemic flu and I never had a thing to do with it. He was buried in the Mount Hopewell Baptist churchyard and you can go there and see for yourself."

"If you would pray," the old lady said, "Jesus would help you."

"That's right," The Misfit said.

"Well then, why don't you pray?" she asked trembling with delight suddenly.

"I don't want no hep," he said. "I'm doing all right by myself."

Bobby Lee and Hiram came ambling back from the woods. Bobby Lee was dragging a yellow shirt with bright blue parrots in it.

"Thow me that shirt, Bobby Lee," The Misfit said. The shirt came flying at him and landed on his shoulder and he put it on. The grandmother couldn't name what the shirt reminded her of. "No, lady," The Misfit said while he was buttoning it up, "I found out the crime don't matter. You can do one thing or you can do another, kill a man or take a tire off his car, because sooner or later you're going to forget what it was you done and just be punished for it."

The children's mother had begun to make heaving noises as if she couldn't get her breath. "Lady," he asked, "would you and that little girl like to step off yonder with Bobby Lee and Hiram and join your husband?"

"Yes, thank you," the mother said faintly. Her left arm dangled helplessly and she was holding the baby, who had gone to sleep, in the other. "Hep that lady up, Hiram," The Misfit said as she struggled to climb out of the ditch, "and Bobby Lee, you hold onto that little girl's hand."

"I don't want to hold hands with him," June Star said. "He reminds me of a pig."

The fat boy blushed and laughed and caught her by the arm and pulled her off into the woods after Hiram and her mother.

Alone with The Misfit, the grandmother found that she had lost her voice. There was not a cloud in the sky nor any sun. There was nothing around her but woods. She wanted to tell him that he must pray. She opened and closed her mouth several times before anything came out. Finally she found herself saying, "Jesus. Jesus," meaning, Jesus will help you, but the way she was saying it, it sounded as if she might be cursing.

"Yes'm," The Misfit said as if he agreed. "Jesus thown everything off balance. It was the same case with Him as with me except He hadn't committed any crime and they could prove I had committed one because they had the papers on me. Of course," he said, "they never shown me my papers. That's why I sign myself now. I said long ago, you get you a signature and sign everything you do and keep a copy of it. Then you'll know what you done and you can hold up the crime to the punishment and see do they match and in the end you'll have something to prove you ain't been treated right. I call myself The Misfit," he said, "because I can't make what all I done wrong fit what all I gone through in punishment."

There was a piercing scream from the woods, followed closely by a pistol report. "Does it seem right to you, lady, that one is punished a heap and another ain't punished at all?"

"Jesus!" the old lady cried. "You've got good blood! I know you wouldn't shoot a lady! I know you come from nice people! Pray! Jesus, you ought not to shoot a lady. I'll give you all the money I've got!"

"Lady," The Misfit said, looking beyond her far into the woods, "there never was a body that give the undertaker a tip."

There were two more pistol reports and the grandmother raised her head like a parched old turkey hen crying for water and called, "Bailey Boy, Bailey Boy!" as if her heart would break.

"Jesus was the only One that ever raised the dead," The Misfit continued, "and He shouldn't have done it. He thown everything off balance. If He did what He said, then it's nothing for you to do but thow away everything and follow Him, and if He didn't, then it's nothing for you to do but enjoy the few minutes you got left the best way you can—by killing somebody or burning down his house or doing some other meanness to him. No pleasure but meanness," he said and his voice had become almost a snarl.

"Maybe He didn't raise the dead," the old lady mumbled, not knowing what she was saying and feeling so dizzy that she sank down in the ditch with her legs twisted under her.

"I wasn't there so I can't say He didn't," The Misfit said. "I wish I had of been there," he said, hitting the ground with his fist. "It ain't right I wasn't there because if I had of been there I would of known. Listen lady," he said in a high voice, "if I had of been there I would of known and I wouldn't be like I am now." His voice seemed about to crack and the grandmother's head cleared for an instant. She saw the man's face twisted close to her own as if he were going to cry and she murmured, "Why you're one of my babies. You're one of my own children!" She reached out and touched him on the shoulder. The Misfit sprang back as if a snake had bitten him and shot her three times through the chest. Then he put his gun down on the ground and took off his glasses and began to clean them.

Hiram and Bobby Lee returned from the woods and stood over the ditch, looking down at the grandmother who half sat and half lay in a puddle of blood with her legs crossed under her like a child's and her face smiling up at the cloudless sky.

Without his glasses, The Misfit's eyes were red-rimmed and pale and defenseless-looking. "Take her off and thow her where you thown the others," he said, picking up the cat that was rubbing itself against his leg.

"She was a talker, wasn't she?" Bobby Lee said, sliding down the ditch with a yodel.

"She would of been a good woman," The Misfit said, "if it had been somebody there to shoot her every minute of her life."

"Some fun!" Bobby Lee said.

"Shut up, Bobby Lee," The Misfit said. "It's no real pleasure in life."

The Quest for Meaning

At its best, fiction does something more than lead us through an experience. A good short story has significance; it answers in at least a small measure the ancient question: "What abides?"

In one of their confrontations in Faulkner's story, the boy and the bear "pledged something, affirmed something more lasting than the frail web of bones and flesh which any accident could obliterate." In the discipline of the wilderness, his "college," the boy learns poise, self-control, alertness, endurance—in brief, he develops into a superior human being. To realize his best self he needs the bear, because both are linked in a pattern and a process, good and unfolding toward good. When his father tries to help him to define his experience in the woods, the boy finds that experience lies beyond the word system; but he is at least vaguely aware that the bear, his alma mater, helped him to become what he ought to become.

In "The Garden Party" we are, as in "The Bear," witness to a venture ending in affirmation. Shielded and protected within the circle of a wholesome family, Laura moves a few steps outside that circle in a pleasant encounter with the workingmen who come to install the marquee for the party. Later in the day, however, she ventures far beyond the limits intended by her parents when she confronts and comes to positive terms with the outermost ring of human experience, death.

The Bear*

by WILLIAM FAULKNER

He was ten. But it had already begun, long before that day when at last he wrote his age in two figures and he saw for the first time the camp where his father and Major de Spain and old General Compson and the others spent two weeks each November and two weeks again each June. He had already inherited then, without ever having seen it, the tremendous bear with one trap-ruined foot which, in an area almost a hundred miles deep, had earned itself a name, a definite designation like a living man.

He had listened to it for years: the long legend of corncribs rifled, of shotes and grown pigs and even calves carried bodily into the woods and devoured, of traps and deadfalls overthrown and dogs mangled and slain, and shotgun and even rifle charges delivered at point-blank range and with no more effect than so many peas blown through a tube by a boy—a corridor of wreckage and destruction beginning back before he was born, through which sped, not fast but rather with the ruthless and irresistible deliberation of a locomotive, the shaggy tremendous shape.

It ran in his knowledge before he ever saw it. It looked and towered in his dreams before he even saw the unaxed woods where it left its crooked print, shaggy, huge, red-eyed, not malevolent but just big—too big for the dogs which tried to bay it, for the horses which tried to ride it down, for the men and bullets they fired into it, too big for the very

---

* Copyright 1942 by The Curtis Publishing Co. Reprinted by permission of Random House, Inc. An expanded version of this story appears in *Go Down Moses*, by William Faulkner.

country which was its constricting scope. He seemed to see it entire with a child's complete divination before he ever laid eyes on either—the doomed wilderness whose edges were being constantly and punily gnawed at by men with axes and plows who feared it because it was wilderness, men myriad and nameless even to one another in the land where the old bear had earned a name, through which ran not even a mortal animal but an anachronism, indomitable and invincible, out of an old dead time, a phantom, epitome and apotheosis of the old wild life at which the puny humans swarmed and hacked in a fury of abhorrence and fear, like pygmies about the ankles of a drowsing elephant: the old bear solitary, indomitable and alone, widowered, childless, and absolved of mortality—old Priam reft of his old wife and having outlived all his sons.

Until he was ten, each November he would watch the wagon containing the dogs and the bedding and food and guns and his father and Tennie's Jim, the Negro, and Sam Fathers, the Indian, son of a slave woman and a Chickasaw chief, depart on the road to town, to Jefferson, where Major de Spain and the others would join them. To the boy, at seven, eight, and nine, they were not going into the Big Bottom to hunt bear and deer, but to keep yearly rendezvous with the bear which they did not even intend to kill. Two weeks later they would return, with no trophy, no head and skin. He had not expected it. He had not even been afraid it would be in the wagon. He believed that even after he was ten and his father would let him go too, for those two weeks in November, he would merely make another one, along with his father and Major de Spain and General Compson and the others, the dogs which feared to bay at it and the rifles and shotguns which failed even to bleed it, in the yearly pageant of the old bear's furious immortality.

Then he heard the dogs. It was in the second week of his first time in the camp. He stood with Sam Fathers against a big oak beside the faint crossing where they had stood each dawn for nine days now, hearing the dogs. He had heard them once before, one morning last week—a murmur, sourceless, echoing through the wet woods, swelling presently into separate voices which he could recognize and call by name. He had raised and cocked the gun as Sam told him and stood motionless again while the uproar, the invisible course, swept up and past and faded; it seemed to him that he could actually see the deer, the buck, blond, smoke-colored, elongated with speed, fleeing, vanishing, the woods, the gray solitude, still ringing even when the cries of the dogs had died away.

"Now let the hammers down," Sam said.

"You knew they were not coming here too," he said.

"Yes," Sam said. "I want you to learn how to do when you didn't shoot. It's after the chance for the bear or the deer has done already come and gone that men and dogs get killed."

"Anyway," he said, "it was just a deer."

Then on the tenth morning he heard the dogs again. And he readied the too-long, too-heavy gun as Sam had taught him, before Sam even spoke. But this time it was no deer, no ringing chorus of dogs running strong on a free scent, but a moiling yapping an octave too high, with something more than indecision and even abjectness in it, not even moving very fast, taking a long time to pass completely out of hearing, leaving then somewhere in the air that echo, thin, slightly hysterical, abject, almost grieving, with no sense of a fleeing, unseen, smoke-colored, grass-eating shape ahead of it, and Sam, who had taught him first of all to cock the gun and take position where he could see everywhere and then never move again, had himself moved up beside him; he could hear Sam breathing at his shoulder, and he could see the arched curve of the old man's inhaling nostrils.

"Hah," Sam said. "Not even running. Walking."

"Old Ben!" the boy said. "But up here!" he cried. "Way up here!"

"He do it every year," Sam said. "Once. Maybe to see who in camp this time, if he can shoot or not. Whether we got the dog yet that can bay and hold him. He'll take them to the river, and then he'll send them back home. We may as well go back too; see how they look when they come back to camp."

When they reached the camp the hounds were already there, ten of them crouching back under the kitchen, the boy and Sam squatting to peer back into the obscurity where they had huddled, quiet, the eyes luminous glowing at them and vanishing, and no sound, only that effluvium of something more than dog, stronger than dog and not just animal, just beast, because still there had been nothing in front of that abject and almost painful yapping save the solitude, the wilderness, so that when the eleventh hound came in at noon and with all the others watching—even old Uncle Ash, who called himself first a cook—Sam daubed the tattered ear and the raked shoulder with turpentine and axle grease, to the boy it was still no living creature, but the wilderness which, leaning for the moment down, had patted lightly once the hound's temerity.

"Just like a man," Sam said. "Just like folks. Put off as long as she could having to be brave, knowing all the time that sooner or later she would have to be brave to keep on living with herself, and knowing all the time before hand what was going to happen to her when she done it."

That afternoon, himself on the one-eyed wagon mule which did not mind the smell of blood nor, as they told him, of bear, and with Sam on the other one, they rode for more than three hours through the rapid, shortening winter day. They followed no path, no trail even that he could see; almost at once they were in a country which he had never seen before. Then he knew why Sam had made him ride the mule which would not spook. The sound one stopped short and tried to whirl and bolt even as Sam got down, blowing its breath, jerking and wrenching at the rein, while Sam held it, coaxing it forward with his voice, since he could not risk tying it, drawing it forward while the boy got down from the marred one.

Then, standing beside Sam in the gloom of the dying afternoon, he looked down at the routed over-turned log, gutted and scored with claw marks and, in the wet earth beside it, the print of the enormous warped two-toed foot. He knew now what he had smelled when he peered under the kitchen where the dogs huddled. He realized for the first time that the bear which had run in his listening and loomed in his dreams since before he could remember to the contrary, and which, therefore, must have existed in the listening and dreams of his father and Major de Spain and even old General Compson, too, before they began to remember in their turn, was a mortal animal, and that if they had departed for the camp each November without any actual hope of bringing its trophy back, it was not because it could not be slain, but because so far they had had no actual hope to.

"Tomorrow," he said.

"We'll try tomorrow," Sam said. "We ain't got the dog yet."

"We've got eleven. They ran him this morning."

"It won't need but one," Sam said. "He ain't here. Maybe he ain't nowhere. The only other way will be for him to run by accident over somebody that has a gun."

"That wouldn't be me," the boy said. "It will be Walter or Major or—"

"It might," Sam said. "You watch close in the morning. Because he's smart. That's how come he has lived this long. If he gets hemmed up and has to pick out somebody to run over, he will pick out you."

"How?" the boy said. "How will he know—" He ceased. "You mean he already knows me, that I ain't never been here before, ain't had time to find out yet whether I—" He ceased again, looking at Sam, the old man whose face revealed nothing until it smiled. He said humbly, not even amazed, "It was me he was watching. I don't reckon he did need to come but once."

The next morning they left the camp three hours before daylight. They rode this time because it was too far to walk, even the dogs in the wagon; again the first gray light found him in a place which he had never seen before, where Sam had placed him and told him to stay and then departed. With the gun which was too big for him, which did not even belong to him, but to Major de Spain, and which he had fired only once—at a stump on the first day, to learn the recoil and how to reload it—he stood against a gun tree beside a little bayou whose black still water crept without movement out of a canebrake and crossed a small clearing and into cane again, where, invisible, a bird—the big woodpecker called Lord-to-God by Negroes—clattered at a dead limb.

It was a stand like any other, dissimilar only in incidentals to the one where he had stood each morning for ten days; a territory new to him, yet no less familiar than that other one which, after almost two weeks, he had come to believe he knew a little—the same solitude, the same loneliness through which human beings had merely passed without altering it, leaving no mark, no scar, which looked exactly as it must have looked when the first ancestor of Sam Fathers' Chickasaw predecessors crept into it and looked about, club or stone ax or bone arrow drawn and poised; different only because, squatting at the edge of the kitchen, he smelled the hounds huddled and cringing beneath it and saw the raked ear and shoulder of the one who, Sam said, had had to be brave once in order to live with herself, and saw yesterday in the earth beside the gutted log the print of the living foot.

He heard no dogs at all. He never did hear them. He only heard the drumming of the woodpecker stop short off and knew that the bear was looking at him. He never saw it. He did not know whether it was in front of him or behind him. He did not move, holding the useless gun, which he had not even had warning to cock and which even now he did not cock, tasting in his saliva that taint as of brass which he knew now because he had smelled it when he peered under the kitchen at the huddled dogs.

Then it was gone. As abruptly as it had ceased, the woodpecker's dry, monotonous clatter set up again, and after a while he even believed he could hear the dogs—a murmur, scarce a sound even, which he had probably been hearing for some time before he even remarked it, drifting into hearing and then out again, dying away. They came nowhere near him. If it was a bear they ran, it was another bear. It was Sam himself who came out of the cane and crossed the bayou, followed by the injured bitch of yesterday. She was almost at heel, like a bird dog, making no sound. She came and crouched against his leg, trembling, staring off into the cane.

"I didn't see him," he said. "I didn't, Sam!"

"I know it," Sam said. "He done the looking. You didn't hear him neither, did you?"

"No," the boy said. "I—"

"He's smart," Sam said. "Too smart." He looked down at the hound, trembling faintly and steadily against the boy's knee. From the raked shoulder a few drops of fresh blood oozed and clung. "Too big. We ain't got the dog yet. But maybe someday. Maybe not next time. But someday."

So I must see him, he thought. *I must look at him*. Otherwise, it seemed to him that it would go on like this forever, as it had gone on with his father and Major de Spain, who was older than his father, and even with old General Compson, who had been old enough to be a brigade commander in 1865. Otherwise, it would go on so forever, next time and next time, after and after and after. It seemed to him that he could never see the two of them, himself and the bear, shadowy in the limbo from which time emerged, becoming time; the old bear absolved of mortality and himself partaking, sharing a little of it, enough of it. And he knew now what he had smelled in the huddled dogs and tasted in his saliva. He recognized fear. *So I will have to see him*, he thought, without dread or even hope. *I will have to look at him*.

It was June of the next year. He was eleven. They were in camp again, celebrating Major de Spain's and General Compson's birthdays. Although the one had been born in September and the other in the depth of winter and in another decade, they had met for two weeks to fish and shoot squirrels and turkey and run coons and wildcats with the dogs at night. That is, he and Boon Hoggenbeck and the Negroes fished and shot squirrels and ran the coons and cats, because the proved hunters, not only Major de Spain and old General

Compson, who spent those two weeks sitting in a rocking chair before a tremendous iron pot of Brunswick stew, stirring and tasting, with old Ash to quarrel with about how he was making it and Tennie's Jim to pour whiskey from the demijohn into the tin dipper from which he drank it, but even the boy's father and Walter Ewell, who were still young enough, scorned such, other than shooting the wild gobblers with pistols for wagers on their marksmanship.

Or, that is, his father and the others believed he was hunting squirrels. Until the third day, he thought that Sam Fathers believed that too. Each morning he would leave the camp right after breakfast. He had his own gun now, a Christmas present. He went back to the tree beside the bayou where he had stood that morning. Using the compass which old General Compson had given him, he ranged from that point; he was teaching himself to be a better-than-fair woodsman without knowing he was doing it. On the second day he even found the gutted log where he had first seen the crooked print. It was almost completely crumbled now, healing with unbelievable speed, a passionate and almost visible relinquishment, back into the earth from which the tree had grown.

He ranged the summer woods now, green with gloom; if anything, actually dimmer than in November's gray dissolution, where, even at noon, the sun fell only in intermittent dappling upon the earth, which never completely dried out and which crawled with snakes—moccasins and water snakes and rattlers, themselves the color of the dappling gloom, so that he would not always see them until they moved, returning later and later, first day, second day, passing in the twilight of the third evening the little log pen enclosing the log stable where Sam was putting up the horses for the night.

"You ain't looked right yet," Sam said.

He stopped. For a moment he didn't answer. Then he said peacefully, in a peaceful rushing burst as when a boy's miniature dam in a little brook gives way, "All right. But how? I went to the bayou. I even found that log again. I—"

"I reckon that was all right. Likely he's been watching you. You never saw his foot?"

"I," the boy said—"I didn't—I never thought—"

"It's the gun," Sam said. He stood beside the fence motionless—the old man, the Indian, in the battered faded overalls and the five-cent straw hat which in the Negro's race had been the badge of its enslavement and was now the regalia of his freedom. The camp—the clearing, the house, the barn and its tiny lot with which Major de Spain in his turn had scratched punily and evanescently at the wilderness—faded in the dusk, back into the immemorial darkness of the woods. *The gun,* the boy thought. *The gun.*

"Be scared," Sam said. "You can't help that. But don't be afraid. Ain't nothing in the woods going to hurt you unless you corner it, or it smells that you are afraid. A bear or a deer, too, has got to be scared of a coward the same as a brave man has got to be."

The gun, the boy thought.

"You will have to choose," Sam said.

He left the camp before daylight, long before Uncle Ash would wake in his quilts on the kitchen floor and start the fire for breakfast. He had only the compass and a stick for snakes. He could go almost a mile before he would begin to need the compass. He sat on a log, the invisible compass in his invisible hand, while the secret night sounds, fallen still at his movements, scurried again and then ceased for good, and the owls ceased and gave over to the waking of day birds, and he could see the compass. Then he went fast yet still quietly; he was becoming better and better as a woodsman, still without having yet realized it.

He jumped a doe and a fawn at sunrise, walked them out of the bed, close enough to see them—the crash of undergrowth, the white scut, the fawn scudding behind her faster than he had believed it could run. He was hunting right, upwind, as Sam had taught him; not that it mattered now. He had left the gun; of his own will and relinquishment he had accepted not a gambit, not a choice, but a condition in which not only the bear's heretofore inviolable anonymity but all the old rules and balances of hunter and hunted had been abrogated. He would not even be afraid, not even in the moment when the fear would take him completely—blood, skin, bowels, bones, memory from the long time before it became his memory—all save that thin, clear, immortal lucidity which alone differed him from this bear and from all the other bear and deer he would ever kill in the humility and pride of his skill and endurance, to which Sam had spoken when he leaned in the twilight on the lot fence yesterday.

By noon he was far beyond the little bayou, farther into the new and alien country than he had ever been. He was traveling now not only by the old, heavy, biscuit-thick silver watch which had belonged to his grandfather. When he stopped at last, it was for the first time since he had risen from the log at dawn when he could see the compass. It was far enough. He had left the camp nine hours ago; nine hours from now, dark would have already been an hour old. But he didn't think that. He thought, *All right. Yes. But what?* and stood for a moment, alien and small in the green and topless solitude, answering his own question before it had formed and ceased. It was the watch, the compass, the stick—the three lifeless mechanicals with which for nine hours he had fended the wilderness off; he hung the watch and compass carefully on a bush and leaned the stick beside them and relinquished completely to it.

He had not been going very fast for the last two or three hours. He went no faster now, since distance would not matter even if he could have gone fast. And he was trying to keep a bearing on the tree where he had left the compass, trying to complete a circle which would bring him back to it or at least intersect itself, since direction would not matter now either. But the tree was not there, and he did as Sam had schooled him—made the next circle in the opposite direction, so that the two patterns would bisect somewhere, but crossing no print of his own feet, finding the tree at last, but in the wrong place—no bush, no compass, no watch—and the tree not even the tree, because there was a down log beside it and he did what Sam Fathers had told him was the next thing and the last.

As he sat down on the log he saw the crooked print—the warped, tremendous, two-toed indentation which, even as he watched it, filled with water. As he looked up, the wilderness coalesced, solidified—the glade, the tree he sought, the bush, the watch and the compass glinting where a ray of sunshine touched them. Then he saw the bear. It did not emerge, appear; it was just there, immobile, solid, fixed in the hot dappling of the green and windless noon, not as big as he had dreamed it, but as big as he had expected it, bigger, dimensionless, against the dappled obscurity, looking at him where he sat quietly on the log and looked back at it.

Then it moved. It made no sound. It did not hurry. It crossed the glade, walking for an instant into the full glare of the sun; when it reached the other side it stopped again and looked back at him across one shoulder while his quiet breathing inhaled and exhaled three times.

Then it was gone. It didn't walk into the woods, the under-growth. It faded, sank back into the wilderness as he had watched a fish, a huge old bass, sink and vanish into the dark depths of its pool without even any movement of its fins.

He thought, *It will be next fall.* But it was not next fall, nor the next nor the next. He was fourteen then. He had killed his buck, and Sam Fathers had marked his face with the hot blood, and in the next year he killed a bear. But even before that accolade he had become as competent in the woods as many grown men with the same experience; by his fourteenth year he was a better woodsman than most grown men with more. There was no territory within thirty miles of the camp that he did not know—bayou, ridge, brake, landmark, tree and path. He could have led anyone to any point in it without deviation, and brought them out again. He knew the game trails that even Sam Fathers did not know; in his thirteenth year he found a buck's bedding place, and unbeknown to his father he borrowed Walter Ewell's rifle and lay in wait at dawn and killed the buck when it walked back to the bed, as Sam had told him how the old Chickasaw fathers did.

But not the old bear, although by now he

knew its footprints better than he did his own, and not only the crooked one. He could see any one of the three sound ones and distinguish it from any other, and not only by its size. There were other bears within these thirty miles which left tracks almost as large, but this was more than that. If Sam Fathers had been his mentor and the back-yard rabbits and squirrels at home his kindergarten, then the wilderness the old bear ran was his college, the old male bear itself, so long unwifed and childless as to have become its own ungendered progenitor, was his alma mater. But he never saw it.

He could find the crooked print now almost whenever he liked, fifteen or ten or five miles, or sometimes nearer the camp than that. Twice while on stand during the three years he heard the dogs strike its trail by accident; on the second time they jumped it seemingly, the voices high, abject, almost human in hysteria, as on that first morning two years ago. But not the bear itself. He would remember that noon three years ago, the glade, himself and the bear fixed during that moment in the windless and dappled blaze, and it would seem to him that it had never happened, that he had dreamed that too. But it had happened. They had looked at each other, they had emerged from the wilderness old as earth, synchronized to the instant by something more than the blood that moved the flesh and bones which bore them, and touched, pledged something, affirmed, something more lasting than the frail web of bones and flesh which any accident could obliterate.

Then he saw it again. Because of the very fact that he thought of nothing else, he had forgotten to look for it. He was still hunting with Walter Ewell's rifle. He saw it cross the end of a long blow-down, a corridor where a tornado had swept, rushing through rather than over the tangle of trunks and branches as a locomotive would have, faster than he had ever believed it could move, almost as fast as a deer even, because a deer would have spent most of that time in the air, faster than he could bring the rifle sights up with it. And now he knew what had been wrong during all the three years. He sat on a log, shaking and trembling as if he had never seen the woods before nor anything that ran them, wondering with incredulous amazement how he could have forgotten the very thing which Sam Fathers had told him and which the bear itself had proved the next day and had now returned after three years to reaffirm.

And now he knew what Sam Fathers had meant about the right dog, a dog in which size would mean less than nothing. So when he returned alone in April—school was out then, so that the sons of farmers could help with the land's planting, and at last his father had granted him permission, on his promise to be back in four days—he had the dog. It was his own, a mongrel of the sort called by Negroes a fyce, a ratter, itself not much bigger than a rat and possessing that bravery which had long since stopped being courage and had become foolhardiness.

It did not take four days. Alone again, he found the trail on the first morning. It was not a stalk; it was an ambush. He timed the meeting almost as if it were an appointment with a human being. Himself holding the fyce muffled in a feed sack and Sam Fathers with two of the hounds on a piece of a plow-line rope, they lay down wind of the trail at dawn of the second morning. They were so close that the bear turned without even running, as if in surprised amazement at the shrill and frantic uproar of the released fyce, turning at bay against the trunk of a tree, on its hind feet; it seemed to the boy that it would never stop rising, taller and taller, and even the two hounds seemed to take a desperate and despairing courage from the fyce, following it as it went in.

Then he realized that the fyce was actually not going to stop. He flung, threw the gun away, and ran; when he overtook and grasped the frantically pin-wheeling little dog, it seemed to him that he was directly under the bear.

He could smell it, strong and hot and rank. Sprawling, he looked up to where it loomed and towered over him like a cloudburst and colored like a thunderclap, quite familiar, peacefully and even lucidly familiar, until he remembered: This was the way he had used to dream about it. Then it was gone. He didn't see it go. He knelt, holding the frantic fyce with both hands, hearing the abashed wailing of the hounds drawing farther and farther away, until Sam came up. He carried the gun. He laid it down quietly beside the boy and stood looking down at him.

"You've done seed him twice now with a gun in your hands," he said. "This time you couldn't have missed him."

The boy rose. He still held the fyce. Even in his arms and clear of the ground, it yapped frantically, straining and surging after the fading uproar of the two hounds like a tangle of wire springs. He was panting a little, but he was neither shaking nor trembling now.

"Neither could you!" he said. "You had the gun! Neither did you!"

"And you didn't shoot," his father said. "How close were you?"

"I don't know, sir," he said. "There was a big wood tick inside his right hind leg. I saw that. But I didn't have the gun then."

"But you didn't shoot when you had the gun," his father said. "Why?"

But he didn't answer, and his father didn't wait for him to, rising and crossing the room, across the pelt of the bear which the boy had killed two years ago and the larger one which his father had killed before he was born, to the bookcase beneath the mounted head of the boy's first buck. It was the room which his father called the office, from which all the plantation business was transacted; in it for the fourteen years of his life he had heard the best of all talking. Major de Spain would be there and sometimes old General Compson, and Walter Ewell and Boon Hoggenbeck and Sam Fathers and Tennie's Jim, too, were hunters, knew the woods and what ran them.

He would hear it, not talking himself but listening—the wilderness, the big woods, bigger and older than any recorded document of white man fatuous enough to believe he had bought any fragment of it or Indian ruthless enough to pretend that any fragment of it had been his to convey. It was of the men, not white nor black nor red, but men, hunters with the will and hardihood to endure and the humility and skill to survive, and the dogs and the bear and deer juxtaposed and reliefed against it, ordered and compelled by and within the wilderness in the ancient and unremitting contest by the ancient and immitigable rules which voided all regrets and brooked no quarter, the voices quiet and weighty and deliberate for retrospection and recollection and exact remembering, while he squatted in the blazing firelight as Tennie's Jim squatted, who stirred only to put more wood on the fire and to pass the bottle from one glass to another. Because the bottle was always present, so that after a while it seemed to him that those fierce instants of heart and brain and courage and wiliness and speed were concentrated and distilled into that brown liquor which not women, not boys and children, but only hunters drank, drinking not of the blood they had spilled but some condensation of the wild immortal spirit, drinking it moderately, humbly even, not with the pagan's base hope of acquiring the virtues of cunning and strength and speed, but in salute to them.

His father returned with the book and sat down again and opened it: "Listen," he said. He read the five stanzas aloud, his voice quiet and deliberate in the room where there was no fire now because it was already spring. Then he looked up. The boy watched him. "All right," his father said. "Listen." He read again, but only the second stanza this time, to the end of it, the last two lines, and closed the book and put it on the table beside him. "She cannot fade, though thou hast not thy bliss, forever wilt thou love, and she be fair," he said.

"He's talking about a girl," the boy said.

"He had to talk about something," his father said. Then he said, "He was talking about truth. Truth doesn't change. Truth is one thing. It covers all things which touch the heart—honor and pride and pity and justice and courage and love. Do you see now?"

He didn't know. Somehow it was simpler than that. There was an old bear, fierce and ruthless, not merely just to stay alive, but with the fierce pride of liberty and freedom, proud enough of the liberty and freedom to see it threatened without fear or even alarm; nay, who at times even seemed deliberately to put that freedom and liberty in jeopardy in order to savor them, to remind his old strong bones and flesh to keep supple and quick to defend and preserve them. There was an old man, son of a Negro slave and an Indian king, inheritor on the one side of the long chronicle of a people who had learned humility through suffering, and pride through the endurance which survived the suffering and injustice, and on the other side, the chronicle of a people even longer in the land than the first, yet who no longer existed in the land at all save in the solitary brotherhood of an old Negro's alien blood and the wild and invincible spirit of an old bear. There was a boy who wished to learn humility and pride in order to become skillful and worthy in the woods, who suddenly found himself becoming so skillful so rapidly that he feared he would never become worthy because he had not learned humility and pride, although he had tried to, until one day and as suddenly he discovered that an old man who could not have defined either had led him, as though by the hand, to that point where an old bear and a little mongrel of a dog showed him that, by possessing one thing other, he would possess them both.

And a little dog, nameless and mongrel and many-fathered, grown, yet weighing less than six pounds, saying as if to itself, "I can't be dangerous, because there's nothing much smaller than I am; I can't be fierce, because they would call it just a noise; I can't be humble, because I'm already too close to the ground to genuflect; I can't be proud, because I wouldn't be near enough to it for anyone to know who was casting the shadow, and I don't even know that I'm not going to heaven, because they have already decided that I don't possess an immortal soul. So all I can be is brave. But it's all right. I can be that, even if they still call it just noise."

That was all. It was simple, much simpler than somebody talking in a book about youth and a girl he would never need to grieve over, because he could never approach any nearer her and would never have to get any farther away. He had heard about a bear, and finally got big enough to trail it, and he trailed it four years and at last met it with a gun in his hands and he didn't shoot. Because a little dog—But he could have shot long before the little dog covered the twenty yards to where the bear waited, and Sam Fathers could have shot at any time during that interminable minute while Old Ben stood on his hind feet over them. He stopped. His father was watching him gravely across the spring-rife twilight of the room; when he spoke, his words were as quiet as the twilight, too, not loud, because they did not need to be because they would last. "Courage, and honor, and pride," his father said, "and pity, and love of justice and of liberty. They all touch the heart, and what the heart holds to becomes truth, as far as we know the truth. Do you see now?"

Sam, and Old Ben, and Nip, he thought. And himself too. He had been all right too. His father had said so. "Yes, sir," he said.

Breakfast*

by JOHN STEINBECK

This thing fills me with pleasure. I don't know why, I can see it in the smallest detail. I find myself recalling it again and again, each time bringing more detail out of a sunken memory, remembering brings the curious warm pleasure.

It was very early in the morning. The eastern mountains were black-blue, but behind them the light stood up faintly colored at the mountain rims with a washed red, growing colder, greyer and darker as it went up and overhead until, at a place near the west, it merged with pure night.

---

* From *The Long Valley*, by John Steinbeck. Copyright 1938, copyright © renewed 1966 by John Steinbeck. Reprinted by permission of The Viking Press, Inc., New York.

And it was cold, not painfully so, but cold enough so that I rubbed my hands and shoved them deep into my pockets, and I hunched my shoulders up and scuffled my feet on the ground. Down in the valley where I was, the earth was that lavender grey of dawn. I walked along a country road and ahead of me I saw a tent that was only a little lighter grey than the ground. Beside the tent there was a flash of orange fire seeping out of cracks of an old rusty iron stove. Grey smoke spurted up out of the stubby stovepipe, spurted up a long way before it spread out and dissipated.

I saw a young woman beside the stove, really a girl. She was dressed in a faded cotton skirt and waist. As I came close I saw that she carried a baby in a crooked arm and the baby was nursing, its head under her waist out of the cold. The mother moved about, poking the fire, shifting the rusty lids of the stove to make a greater draft, opening the oven door; and all the time the baby was nursing, but that didn't interfere with the mother's work, nor with the light quick gracefulness of her movements. There was something very precise and practiced in her movements. The orange fire flicked out of the cracks in the stove and threw dancing reflections on the tent.

I was close now and I could smell frying bacon and baking bread, the warmest, pleasantest odors I know. From the east the light grew swiftly. I came near to the stove and stretched my hands out to it and shivered all over when the warmth struck me. Then the tent flap jerked up and a young man came out and an older man followed him. They were dressed in new blue dungarees and in new dungaree coats with the brass buttons shining. They were sharp-faced men, and they looked much alike.

The younger had a dark stubble beard and the older had a grey stubble beard. Their heads and faces were wet, their hair dripped with water, and water stood out on their stiff beards and their cheeks shone with water. Together they stood looking quietly at the lightening east; they yawned together and looked at the light on the hill rims. They turned and saw me.

"Morning," said the older man. His face was neither friendly nor unfriendly.

"Morning, sir" I said.

"Morning," said the young man.

The water was slowly drying on their faces. They came to the stove and warmed their hands at it.

The girl kept to her work, her face averted and her eyes on what she was doing. Her hair was tied back out of her eyes with a string and it hung down her back and swayed as she worked. She set tin cups on a big packing box, set tin plates and knives and forks out too. Then she scooped fried bacon out of the deep grease and laid it on a big tin platter, and the bacon cricked and rustled as it grew crisp. She opened the rusty oven door and took out a square pan full of high big biscuits.

When the smell of that hot bread came out, both of the men inhaled deeply. The young man said softly, "Keerist!"

The elder man turned to me, "Had your breakfast?"

"No."

"Well, sit down with us, then."

That was the signal. We went to the packing case and squatted on the ground about it. The young man asked, "Picking cotton?"

"No."

"We had twelve days' work so far," the young man said.

The girl spoke from the stove. "They even got new clothes."

The two men looked down at their new dungarees and they both smiled a little.

The girl set out the platter of bacon, the brown high biscuits, a bowl of bacon gravy and a pot of coffee, and then she squatted down by the box too. The baby was still nursing, its head up under her waist out of the cold. I could hear the sucking noises it made.

We filled our plates, poured bacon gravy over our biscuits and sugared our coffee. The older man filled his mouth full and he chewed and chewed and swallowed. Then he said, "God Almighty, it's good," and he filled his mouth again.

The young man said, "We been eating good for twelve days."

We all ate quickly, frantically, and refilled our plates and ate quickly again until we were full and warm. The hot bitter coffee scalded our throats. We threw the last little bit with the grounds in it on the earth and refilled our cups.

There was color in the light now, a reddish gleam that made the air seem colder. The two men faced the east and their faces were lighted by the dawn, and I looked up for a moment and saw the image of the mountain and the light coming over it reflected in the older man's eyes.

Then the two men threw the grounds from their cups on the earth and they stood up together. "Got to get going," the older man said.

The younger man turned to me. "'Fyou want to pick cotton, we could maybe get you on."

"No. I got to go along. Thanks for breakfast."

The older man waved his hand in a negative. "O.K. Glad to have you." They walked away together. The air was blazing with light at the eastern skyline. And I walked away down the country road.

That's all. I know, of course, some of the reasons why it was pleasant. But there was some element of great beauty there that makes the rush of warmth when I think of it.

At Mrs. Farrelly's*
by JOSEPH CARROLL

Brennan always stayed at Mrs. Farrelly's rooming house when he was between voyages and when he was on the beach altogether, waiting for a berth. The house was one of a grimy red-brick row fronting the North River docks on a downtown street; it was within easy walking distance of the union hall on Seventeenth Street and close to Greenwich Village with its opportunities for companionship and carousal. Brennan had no family except a married sister in Ohio, with whom he exchanged perfunctorily dutiful letters once a year; and insofar as he had a home at all, it was Mrs. Farrelly's.

The first time he stayed there, Mrs. Farrelly took an immediate liking to him and he to her. He had been shipping out for more than a year, and he was sick of blowing his pay on hotels; there were better things to blow it on. Brennan never saved any money but he liked to get value for what he spent, even if it was only a howling hangover and the memory of brief luxuries to take back to sea with him. A shipmate steered him to Mrs. Farrelly's when they shipped in from South America, and when she opened the door to him, Brennan could tell he was making an impression.

He was used to being liked by women and wasn't conceited about it: he figured they liked him not for his looks, which were average pleasant, but because he was a nice guy. He knew he was a nice guy and couldn't imagine being anything else. Brennan was only twenty-two, but he'd been kicking around more or less on his own since he was a kid, and he had decided a long time ago that you had an easier time of it if you were a nice guy though it didn't necessarily put money in your pocket. He liked women, too, most of them, so long as they didn't embarrass him with importunities. Brennan liked to do the importuning himself— it was half the fun.

He liked Mrs. Farrelly right away, and

---

* Copyright March 1952 by *The Atlantic Monthly*. Reprinted by permission of Littauer and Wilkinson on behalf of the author.

not for her looks. She was in her late forties and wouldn't have been a beauty even in her prime. The attempt to dye her hair had clearly been a mistake, for the natural mousy brown showed through under strands of the most startling magenta. Her figure was nothing much, and she had the chalky pallor of so many women who live their lives within the curious limits that a great city, no less than a prairie village, can impose; Mrs. Farrelly was a New Yorker born and bred, but she rarely traveled above Fourteenth Street or below Houston.

But her pale face was kind, and Brennan liked her smile. It was still early forenoon when he arrived with his gear, and Mrs. Farrelly was wearing a frayed robe of faded pink. "Excuse my being in my penorr," she said, "but honest to God if I'm ever awake till noon. I just can't seem to get *started* in the morning." Every vowel came out flat and long, as if someone had been at it with a rolling pin.

She led Brennan up a flight of stairs and into his room. It was a narrow room, with a bed and small table, a chest of drawers, two chairs, and very little else; but it was clean and prettified with various five-and-dime touches, such as the blue ribbons that looped back the gray-white window curtains. On the wall over the chest was a picture in an ornate frame, whose gilt was peeling; the picture, in blurry blues and greens and yellows, showed a child crossing a narrow bridge over an angry stream, and behind him a girlish angel with wings outspread protectively.

Mrs. Farrelly said: "The you-know is down the hall—second door. Two other roomers on this floor and they use it too, but it is all right if everybody just coöperates. If someone's in there too long, keep hammering loud. Nesbitt—he's in the room across the hall—he goes in there with the *Daily News* sometimes. And he'll stay until he's got his horoscope worked out unless you make a racket. Honest, some people don't have the least consideration."

Brennan nodded, but Mrs. Farrelly showed no disposition to go; she wanted to talk. "It'd be a real nice view," she said, pointing to the window, "except the pier fronts are in the way and you can't see the river. I always say what's the use of having a river that you can't see it. Blocks and blocks and you can't see it, unless you go up to the market by Little West Twelfth Street, where they fish off the pier. Honest, isn't that some name? Little West Twelfth, how I love thee! You can see the river from the roof, but it's too cold to go up there now. Summertimes, we go up—Farrelly and me. Farrelly's my husband. It's real pretty at night, all the lights over to Jersey and like on the boats. Some people they just never notice things like that, but Farrelly's different. He's a poet. He *writes* poetry."

Brennan was interested. "You mean for a living?" he asked.

She looked doubtful. "Well, he writes it all the time, but I wouldn't say he made a living out of it. There's not much money in poetry. Farrelly says things are slow for poets these times. People just don't have the money."

Brennan started to laugh, and changed his mind: Mrs. Farrelly wasn't being funny.

"You like poetry?" Mrs. Farrelly said.

"Yeah," Brennan said. "I like it. I'd like to see Far—your husband's."

She shook her head. "He's so *funny*. He won't show it to anybody—except me. He's afraid somebody'll steal it off him. He says poets are clickish—a little bunch of them have it all their own way and without you're in the click you can't have your poems printed up in books. Honest, I guess it's the same in every line. Like the longshoremen—that's what Nesbitt is, a longshoreman—unless they know the boss and slip him a little something once and a while they just don't get through the shape-up. Nesbitt hasn't had a day's work in three weeks."

Brennan had an odd vision of poets going through a shape-up and started to laugh again; again he changed his mind. "Yeah," he said, "it's the same in everything. It's not what you know, it's who you know."

Mrs. Farrelly clasped her hands together appreciatively. "I'll have to remember that to tell Farrelly. He likes things that are said neat. It's not what you know, it's who you know," she repeated. She went to the door but then turned; Brennan had started to sit down on the bed. "Sit right down," she said, "I'll be going in a minute. You must be tired. Where was your ship? South America? My! I never been but to Hoboken. You sound educated."

Brennan sat down, shaking his head. "Uh-uh. Grammar school. My old man died and I went to work as soon as it was legal. I tried a lot of things, but I like shipping best. You get time to read."

Mrs. Farrelly sighed. "You don't know how lucky you are," she said. "I never get time to read, running this place like I do. Honest, if it isn't this it's that, in a rooming house. Keeping the place clean and going to the stores. I hardly even get to read the papers. Farrelly is a great reader—always was. And of course, he has his poetry to keep up on. He can't do no writing here. Too noisy—trucks going by all the time, and sirens on the river, and the kids yelling out in the street. He goes over to the library up near Eighth Avenue every morning and stays there all day and writes. Honest, he has just pages and pages covered with it, and he won't let me do a thing with it."

She looked at Brennan pensively. "You seem like a real nice boy. I'd like for you to meet Farrelly. When do you ship out?"

"Next week," Brennan said. "I'd like the room until Sunday night."

She looked pleased. "You could eat with us Sunday. We take our big meal in the afternoon and have just cold stuff for supper."

Brennan was touched, and embarrassed. "Wouldn't want to put you to any trouble," he said.

She laughed. "Trouble? Why, all the trouble is putting out another plate. Farrelly and me never had a kid, isn't that funny? We been married long enough to have them older than you. I used to kid him about it. It must be you just simply don't have it, I told him once. And honest, it made him so mad I was scared. He hardly ever gets mad. But he hates anything *vulgar*."

Brennan was blushing a little. "I guess you do, too," she said. "But I don't mean anything by it. It's just my way. I grew up around here— this house was my father's, rest his soul. I had a brother was killed in an accident on the docks. He was older than me, and he talked real rough. This is a rough neighborhood. But Farrelly's different."

Brennan couldn't think of anything to say, but she didn't expect an answer. "You eat with us Sunday," she said, and started out the door. Then she turned again. "Another thing," she said diffidently. "I hope you'll excuse me mentioning it. If you want to bring—uh— anybody up here nights—"

Brennan was now blushing all over, the rough redness at his cheekbones spreading throughout his olive face.

"—it's all right if you aren't too noisy about it. It's just we don't want the police on us. Lots of seamen stay here, and I know how it is. A person has their passions."

Brennan was looking at the floor.

She coughed, artificially. "I hope you won't take what I'm saying wrong. You're so kind of young. Watch out for them hustling girls in the bar and grills. They're no good— and you never know what you can pick up off them."

She closed the door after her, and Brennan lay back on the bed, wondering why he liked the damn woman so much.

II

He met Farrelly at the Sunday meal. It was a good meal: baked ham and mashed potatoes and green vegetables and a bakery pie for dessert; but Brennan, who had spent too much time in Bleecker Street bars the night before, was in no condition to enjoy it.

"You need a drink," Farrelly said, watching him nibble at the food; and he brought out a bottle of whisky. Mrs. Farrelly poured a hooker for each of them, but didn't take any herself. She whisked back and forth between the kitchen and the dining room, which was brightly papered in a pattern of some yellow flower that made it look as though someone had been throwing eggs at the wall.

After the drink, Brennan felt better and could eat. He didn't think Farrelly looked much like a poet, though you never could tell about poets. Farrelly's hair was all white, which made his face look young. It was a coarse face in its surfaces: configurations of veins threaded his cheeks with an unhealthy blue over glittering crimson. Guiltily, Brennan reflected that his face might come to look like that if he spent the next five years as strenuously as he had spent it in Bleecker Street and environs the night before. Farrelly's dissipations had not marred the odd juvenility of his features; his eyes were large and pale, and—white hair and all—he looked like an altar boy who had been on one hell of a toot.

If Mrs. Farrelly was disturbed by these evidences of intemperance, or even aware of them, she didn't show it. She left the bottle close to Farrelly's hand and looked at him dotingly whenever he spoke.

Farrelly was most courteous in his manner toward Brennan. "So you follow the sea?" he said bookishly.

"Yeah," Brennan said. "It gives me something to do."

"Do you admire Conrad?" asked Farrelly.

Brennan thought that was quite a leap, but he answered politely: "Some of him."

"Do you find him true to life?"

Yes, and no, Brennan said; he didn't think seamen talked like that, even when Conrad was writing, but he guessed that if anyone ever wrote the way seamen really talked he wouldn't be able to get it printed.

"I like Melville better," Farrelly said. "I read him all the time." Brennan thought to himself that he couldn't have read Melville very carefully because he kept talking about Moby Dick as though it were a man; he said he had once seen John Barrymore in the title role.

All of Farrelly's literary knowledge seemed fragmentary, and some of it was mistaken, Brennan knew. He tried to change the conversation, so as to work Mrs. Farrelly into it. She looked from one to another of them admiringly, and Brennan felt like a phony. He read books when he felt like it, the same way he drank or chased girls, when he felt like that. Unhappily, he told Farrelly that, no, he didn't plan to write a book: he went to sea because it was a living, better than some other ways of making money, at least for him. If he ever got married, he thought he would want a shoreside job.

Farrelly didn't listen to his answers; every question was a topic sentence for himself; and after the meal was over, when he had a lot more drinks, he didn't even bother asking questions: he just talked. At Mrs. Farrelly's urging, he recited a lot of poetry in a declamatory voice.

Brennan didn't think he recited very well, though it might have been the liquor; he stopped at the end of every line, and, unless you knew the poem he was reciting, you wouldn't have been able to make any sense out of it at all. Mrs. Farrelly did not seem to mind this: her rapt face showed that she was having a very good time.

In one of the pauses, she asked Farrelly to bring out his own poetry or recite it to Brennan. Farrelly, whose eyes were pretty glassy by this time, turned to her coldly. "The time hasn't come," he said. "You know that. This is a fine young man"—he pointed to Brennan—"but what do we *know* about him?"

And then he went upstairs, walking rigidly and holding to the banister as he walked.

Mrs. Farrelly hoped Brennan's feelings weren't hurt. "He has to be so careful," she said enigmatically. Brennan said not at all and it was time for him to be going anyway.

The next few times he hit port, Brennan saw a lot of Mrs. Farrelly but very little of her husband. Brennan stayed out till all hours, and it was always late when he got up. Mrs. Farrelly took to asking him down to the kitchen for coffee and talked to him confidentially about Farrelly, who still spent his days at the library.

"He's failing," Mrs. Farrelly said one morning. "All you have to do is look at him to see he's failing. And it isn't as if he was old: he's only fifty-three. He's sick, that's what he is, and is it any wonder with the way he's treated when all he wants is to put in a fair day's work at his poetry? My sisters won't even talk to him—and the way they talk about him would make you sick to your stomach. Nell's the worst. She never married and she's never *been* with anyone. You know the way women like that are?"

Brennan drank his coffee unquiveringly; he had got over blushing at Mrs. Farrelly's occasional physiological allusions, and this one was only mildly blunt. He told her he knew what she meant.

"Nell's got scabs on her knees from going to church every day of her life but all she ever thinks about is the one thing. She's always going on about the Porto Ricans and the colored in the neighborhood, and she like to of died when I had a colored for a roomer. I didn't see there was anything wrong about it, being he was a lot cleaner than most that stay here. But you bust Nell's head open and you'd find only the one thing. Every time she looks at Farrelly I know she's thinking dirty. I know he takes his drop, but I never heard him say a dirty word.

"The other sister—Hattie—has her own man and four kids, but she's never got over it that Pa left this place to me. Farrelly moved in here right after we were married—he was working over to the market then, but he never liked it because he got no time to work on his poetry at all. So after Pa died, he quit and ever since it's been the poetry."

Flickeringly, her eyes looked wistful, Brennan thought.

"So the two of them are all the time chewing about Farrelly," she went on. "They're the only family I got now but I sent the pair of them flying out of this kitchen only last week for having their foul mouths on Farrelly. It was 'why don't he work?' and 'why do you give him money for drink?' until I told the both of them to kiss the left cheek of my behind and threw them out."

She poured more coffee for Brennan and herself. "He's failing, though. I can see it every day goes by. He don't read out what he's wrote during the day to me any more, like he always used to—and he bites my head off if I ask him about it. He just sits and don't say anything, only to himself, stuff I can't even understand, over and over and over. And you know something? He *cries*. All by himself in the bedroom, he cries. I found him like that last night and I told him, 'What's the matter lovey?' And he just said to go away, and kept on crying."

Brennan stood up quickly. "I have to meet a fellow," he said.

She followed him to the front door. "You think—you think maybe I shouldn't let him have money for the drink, like Hattie says? It's the only thing he takes any pleasure in, except the poetry."

Brennan said awkwardly, "I don't know, Mrs. Farrelly. Maybe better call a doctor to look at him."

"He hates doctors," Mrs. Farrelly said. "I might call one, if he gets worse."

Brennan went out.

III

Brennan shipped out on the longest trip he had ever made, and what with layovers for repairs and weather delays, it was more than three months before he saw Mrs. Farrelly again. His ship docked late on a summer afternoon but after he was paid off he stopped in a saloon on South Street where he met the union delegate from his ship and got in an argument about the handling of a beef on the trip. Other crew members were there, and the argument wasn't very parliamentary; Brennan was too tired for a fight, so he slipped out and walked to Mrs. Farrelly's. The walk cleared his head, which badly needed clearing.

It was almost midnight when he rang the doorbell. He saw the light go on behind the glass panels that flanked the door; then the door opened and Mrs. Farrelly stood blinking at him. She was fully dressed, in a black dress. As soon as she saw Brennan she started to cry, and he knew what must have happened.

He stepped inside and put an arm around her shoulder, waiting until the sobbing stopped. She leaned her head against him. "You were the only one," she said. "You were the only one was ever nice about his poetry."

Brennan kept his arm around her. "Would you make me some coffee?" he asked.

"Honest to God," she said, stepping away from him, "I forgot all about it. I got some on."

He followed her through the dark hallway

and into the lighted kitchen. The coffee had boiled over and the lid of the pot was rattling over the bubbling sounds.

Brennan sat down at the table and waited. She wiped off the smeared sides of the pot, brought cups from the pantry, and poured. Brennan lighted a cigarette, waiting for his coffee to cool.

"I buried Farrelly yesterday," she said.

She sat down, her chair close to Brennan. "The end came suddenly," she said, relishing the formal obituary phrase, "though, like I told you, I seen it coming. He fell over in the street coming from the library and they took him to Bellevue. He didn't even know me when they let me see him. He just cried and stared up at the ceiling. And then he screamed a lot— and then he didn't do anything. He just passed away."

She was quite dry-eyed now, and enjoying telling him about it. Brennan said how sorry he was.

"I know," she said. "I told my sister Hattie and Nell and all them snotnoses came to the wake about you. I told them you *know* about poetry. We waked him here, and I like to screamed listening to Hattie blabbering about it was a blessed release, and Nell with her 'it's the will of God and he's at peace at last.' And I wouldn't give them the satisfaction of crying or taking on or anything. I just sat in there in the front room the whole three days and looked at him. He was laid out nice, in his good blue serge. And he looked so young. He was a fine-looking man, Farrelly was."

She waited for Brennan to agree. "A fine-looking man," he echoed.

"And I'd look at Farrelly, and then I'd look at that big bruiser Hattie's married to, with the black hairs sticking out from his collar, and no gentleness to him at all and no brains in his thick head to understand poetry. And when I'd look at Farrelly again, I'd almost cry, thinking: it may be the will of God, but I hope He knows what He's doing—taking away a man that never did anyone a day's harm and could make up poetry right in the middle of the dirty streets and never take his mind off it for anything else, only his glass of whisky now and again—taking away a man like that and leaving only the slobs of men that laugh at poetry.

She pushed back her chair and stood up. "He's gone now and it can't hurt him if I show it to you. I don't care if it never gets printed up in books. The hell with the clicks. You been nice. I'll show it to you."

She went out and Brennan could hear her footsteps on the stairs. He stared into the grounds in his coffee cup. When she came back she was carrying a cardboard carton, which she placed on the table. She raised the covers, and Brennan saw that the box was filled with paper, tied in bundles. "This is only some of it," Mrs. Farrelly told him, lifting out a bundle and undoing the ribbon that bound it. She handed it to Brennan and her hand shook.

He glanced at the topsheet of lined tablet paper such as school children use. The handwriting was large and legible, not beautiful but painstakingly neat, as though it were an exercise in penmanship.

Brennan read the opening lines on the top sheet:—

Yet once more, O ye Laurels, and once more
Ye Myrtles brown, with Ivy never-sear,
I come to pluck your Berries harsh and crude,
And with forc'd fingers rude,
Shatter your leaves before the mellowing year.

He riffled the sheets, glancing at the titles carefully written in block capitals at the top of the pages: Kubla Khan, Lines Composed a Few Miles Above Tintern Abbey, Lines Written Among the Euganean Hills, On First Looking into Chapman's Homer, The Lotus-Eaters, The Blessed Damozel, Chorus from Atalanta in Calydon, The Hound of Heaven. . . .

He looked up at Mrs. Farrelly. "I can't read them all now," he said smiling.

She smiled back. "Sure you can't. You take all the time you want." She put her hand on Brennan's arm. "You read some of the first one. I seen you. Is it good poetry?"

Brennan lifted his free hand and touched her cheek gently. "The best," he said.

The Garden-Party*
by KATHERINE MANSFIELD

And after all the weather was ideal. They could not have had a more perfect day for a garden-party if they had ordered it. Windless, warm, the sky without a cloud. Only the blue was veiled with a haze of light gold, as it is sometimes in early summer. The gardener had been up since dawn, mowing the lawns and sweeping them, until the grass and the dark flat rosettes where the daisy plants had been seemed to shine. As for the roses, you could not help feeling they understood that roses are the only flowers that impress people at garden-parties; the only flowers that everybody is certain of knowing. Hundreds, yes, literally hundreds, had come out in a single night; the green bushes bowed down as though they had been visited by archangels.

Breakfast was not yet over before the men came to put up the marquee.

"Where do you want the marquee put, mother?"

"My dear child, it's no use asking me. I'm determined to leave everything to you children this year. Forget I am your mother. Treat me as an honoured guest."

But Meg could not possibly go and supervise the men. She had washed her hair before breakfast, and she sat drinking her coffee in a green turban, with a dark wet curl stamped on each cheek. Jose, the butterfly, always came down in a silk petticoat and a kimono jacket.

"You'll have to go, Laura; you're the artistic one."

Away Laura flew, still holding her piece of bread-and-butter. It's so delicious to have an excuse for eating out of doors, and besides, she loved having to arrange things; she always felt she could do it so much better than anybody else.

Four men in their shirt-sleeves stood grouped together on the garden path. They carried staves covered with rolls of canvas, and they had big toolbags slung on their backs. They looked impressive. Laura wished now that she had not got the bread-and-butter, but there was nowhere to put it, and she couldn't possibly throw it away. She blushed and tried to look severe and even a little bit short-sighted as she came up to them.

"Good morning," she said, copying her mother's voice. But that sounded so fearfully affected that she was ashamed, and stammered like a little girl, "Oh—er—have you come—is it about the marquee?"

"That's right, miss," said the tallest of the men, a lanky, freckled fellow, and he shifted his tool-bag, knocked back his straw hat and smiled down at her. "That's about it."

His smile was so easy, so friendly that Laura recovered. What nice eyes he had, small, but such a dark blue! And now she looked at the others, they were smiling too. "Cheer up, we won't bite," their smile seemed to say. How very nice workmen were! And what a beautiful morning! She mustn't mention the morning; she must be businesslike. The marquee.

"Well, what about the lily-lawn? Would that do?"

And she pointed to the lily-lawn with the hand that didn't hold the bread-and-butter. They turned, they stared in the direction. A little fat chap thrust out his under-lip, and the tall fellow frowned.

"I don't fancy it," said he. "Not conspicuous enough. You see, with a thing like a marquee," and he turned to Laura in his easy way, "you want to put it somewhere where it'll give you a bang slap in the eye, if you follow me."

Laura's upbringing made her wonder for a moment whether it was quite respectful of a workman to talk to her of bangs slap in the eye. But she did quite follow him.

"A corner of the tennis-court," she sug-

---

* Copyright 1922 by Alfred A. Knopf, Inc., and renewed 1950 by J. Middleton Murry. Reprinted from *The Short Stories of Katherine Mansfield* by permission of the publishers, and The Society of Authors as the literary representative of the Estate of Katherine Mansfield.

gested. "But the band's going to be in one corner."

"H'm, going to have a band, are you?" said another of the workmen. He was pale. He had a haggard look as his dark eyes scanned the tennis-court. What was he thinking?

"Only a very small band," said Laura gently. Perhaps he wouldn't mind so much if the band was quite small. But the tall fellow interrupted.

"Look here, miss, that's the place. Against those trees. Over there. That'll do fine."

Against the karakas. Then the karaka-trees would be hidden. And they were so lovely, with their broad, gleaming leaves, and their clusters of yellow fruit. They were like trees you imagined growing on a desert island, proud, solitary, lifting their leaves and fruits to the sun in a kind of silent splendour. Must they be hidden by a marquee?

They must. Already the men had shouldered their staves and were making for the place. Only the tall fellow was left. He bent down, pinched a sprig of lavender, put his thumb and forefinger to his nose and snuffed up the smell. When Laura saw that gesture she forgot all about the karakas in her wonder at him caring for things like that—caring for the smell of lavender. How many men that she knew would have done such a thing? Oh, how extraordinarily nice workmen were, she thought. Why couldn't she have workmen for friends rather than the silly boys she danced with and who came to Sunday night supper? She would get on much better with men like these.

It's all the fault, she decided, as the tall fellow drew something on the back of an envelope, something that was to be looped up or left to hang, of these absurd class distinctions. Well, for her part, she didn't feel them. Not a bit, not an atom. . . . And now there came the chock-chock of wooden hammers. Some one whistled, some one sang out, "Are you right there, matey?" "Matey!" The friendliness of it, the—the—— Just to prove how happy she was, just to show the tall fellow how at home she felt, and how she despised stupid conventions, Laura took a big bite of her bread-and-butter as she stared at the little drawing. She felt just like a work-girl.

"Laura, Laura, where are you? Telephone, Laura!" a voice cried from the house.

"Coming!" Away she skimmed, over the lawn, up the path, up the steps, across the veranda, and into the porch. In the hall her father and Laurie were brushing their hats ready to go to the office.

"I say, Laura," said Laurie very fast, "you might just give a squiz at my coat before this afternoon. See if it wants pressing."

"I will," said she. Suddenly she couldn't stop herself. She ran at Laurie and gave him a small, quick squeeze. "Oh, I do love parties, don't you?" gasped Laura.

"Ra-ther," said Laurie's warm, boyish voice, and he squeezed his sister too, and gave her a gentle push. "Dash off to the telephone, old girl."

The telephone. "Yes, yes; oh yes. Kitty? Good morning, dear. Come to lunch? Do, dear. Delighted of course. It will only be a very scratch meal—just the sandwich crusts and broken meringue-shells and what's left over. Yes, isn't it a perfect morning? Your white? Oh, I certainly should. One moment—hold the line. Mother's calling." And Laura sat back. "What, mother? Can't hear."

Mrs. Sheridan's voice floated down the stairs. "Tell her to wear that sweet hat she had on last Sunday."

"Mother says you're to wear that *sweet* hat you had on last Sunday. Good. One o'clock. Bye-bye."

Laura put back the receiver, flung her arms over her head, took a deep breath, stretched and let them fall. "Huh," she sighed, and the moment after the sigh she sat up quickly. She was still, listening. All the doors in the house seemed to be open. The house was alive with soft, quick steps and running voices. The green baize door that led to the kitchen regions swung open and shut with a muffled thud. And now there came a long, chuckling absurd sound. It was the heavy piano being moved on its stiff castors. But the air! If you stopped to notice, was the air always like this? Little faint winds were playing chase, in at the tops of the windows, out at the doors. And there were two tiny spots of sun, one on the inkpot, one on a silver photograph frame, playing too. Darling little spots. Especially the one on the inkpot lid. It was quite warm. A warm little silver star. She could have kissed it.

The front door bell pealed, and there sounded the rustle of Sadie's print skirt on the stairs. A man's voice murmured; Sadie answered, careless, "I'm sure I don't know. Wait. I'll ask Mrs. Sheridan."

"What is it, Sadie?" Laura came into the hall.

"It's the florist, Miss Laura."

It was, indeed. There, just inside the door, stood a wide, shallow tray full of pots of pink lilies. No other kind. Nothing but lilies—canna lilies, big pink flowers, wide open, radiant, almost frighteningly alive on bright crimson stems.

"O-oh, Sadie!" said Laura, and the sound was like a little moan. She crouched down as if to warm herself at that blaze of lilies; she felt they were in her fingers, on her lips, growing in her breast.

"It's some mistake," she said faintly. "Nobody ever ordered so many. Sadie, go and find mother."

But at that moment Mrs. Sheridan joined them.

"It's quite right," she said calmly. "Yes, I ordered them. Aren't they lovely?" She pressed Laura's arm. "I was passing the shop yesterday, and I saw them in the window. And I suddenly thought for once in my life I shall have enough canna lilies. The garden-party will be a good excuse."

"But I thought you said you didn't mean to interfere," said Laura. Sadie had gone. The florist's man was still outside at his van. She put her arm round her mother's neck and gently, very gently, she bit her mother's ear.

"My darling child, you wouldn't like a logical mother, would you? Don't do that. Here's the man."

He carried more lilies still, another whole tray.

"Bank them up, just inside the door, on both sides of the porch, please," said Mrs. Sheridan. "Don't you agree, Laura?"

"Oh, I *do*, mother."

In the drawing-room Meg, Jose and good little Hans had at last succeeded in moving the piano.

"Now, if we put this chesterfield against the wall and move everything out of the room except the chairs, don't you think?"

"Quite."

"Hans, move these tables into the smoking-room, and bring a sweeper to take these marks off the carpet and—one moment, Hans——" Jose loved giving orders to the servants, and they loved obeying her. She always made them feel they were taking part in some drama. "Tell mother and Miss Laura to come here at once."

"Very good, Miss Jose."

She turned to Meg. "I want to hear what the piano sounds like, just in case I'm asked to sing this afternoon. Let's try over 'This life is Weary.'"

Pom! Ta-ta-ta Tee-ta! The piano burst out so passionately that Jose's face changed. She clasped her hands. She looked mournfully and enigmatically at her mother and Laura as they came in.

This Life is W*ee*-ary,
A Tear—a Sigh.
A Love that *Chan*-ges,
This Life is W*ee*-a1y,
A Tear—a Sigh.
A Love that *Chan*-ges,
And then . . . Good-bye!

But at the word "Good-bye," and although the piano sounded more desperate than ever, her face broke into a brilliant, dreadfully unsympathetic smile.

"Aren't I in good voice, mummy?" she beamed.

This Life is W*ee*-ary,
Hope comes to Die.
A Dream—a W*a*-kening.

But now Sadie interrupted them. "What is it, Sadie?"

"If you please, m'm, cook says have you got the flags for the sandwiches?"

"The flags for the sandwiches, Sadie?" echoed Mrs. Sheridan dreamily. And the children knew by her face that she hadn't got them. "Let me see." And she said to Sadie firmly, "Tell cook I'll let her have them in ten minutes."

Sadie went.

"Now, Laura," said her mother quickly. "Come with me into the smoking-room. I've got the names somewhere on the back of an envelope. You'll have to write them out for me. Meg, go upstairs this minute and take that wet thing off your head. Jose, run and finish dressing this instant. Do you hear me, children, or shall I have to tell your father when he comes home to-night? And—and, Jose, pacify cook if you do go into the kitchen, will you? I'm terrified of her this morning."

The envelope was found at last behind the dining-room clock, though how it had got there Mrs. Sheridan could not imagine.

"One of you children must have stolen it out of my bag, because I remember vividly—cream cheese and lemon-curd. Have you done that?"

"Yes."

"Egg and——" Mrs. Sheridan held the envelope away from her. "It looks like mice. It can't be mice, can it?"

"Olive, pet," said Laura, looking over her shoulder.

"Yes, of course, olive. What a horrible combination it sounds. Egg and olive."

They were finished at last, and Laura took them off to the kitchen. She found Jose there pacifying the cook, who did not look at all terrifying.

"I have never seen such exquisite sandwiches," said Jose's rapturous voice. "How many kinds did you say there were, cook? Fifteen?"

"Fifteen, Miss Jose."

"Well, cook, I congratulate you."

Cook swept up crusts with the long sandwich knife, and smiled broadly.

"Godber's has come," announced Sadie, issuing out of the pantry. She had seen the man pass the window.

That meant the cream puffs had come. Godber's were famous for their cream puffs. Nobody ever thought of making them at home.

"Bring them in and put them on the table, my girl," ordered cook.

Sadie brought them in and went back to the door. Of course Laura and Jose were far too grown-up to really care about such things. All the same, they couldn't help agreeing that the puffs looked very attractive. Very. Cook began arranging them, shaking off the extra icing sugar.

"Don't they carry one back to all one's parties?" said Laura.

"I suppose they do," said practical Jose, who never liked to be carried back. "They look beautifully light and feathery, I must say."

"Have one each, my dears," said cook in her comfortable voice. "Yer ma won't know."

Oh, impossible. Fancy cream puffs so soon after breakfast. The very idea made one shudder. All the same, two minutes later Jose and Laura were licking their fingers with that absorbed inward look that only comes from whipped cream.

"Let's go into the garden, out by the back way," suggested Laura. "I want to see how the men are getting on with the marquee. They're such awfully nice men."

But the back door was blocked by cook, Sadie, Godber's man and Hans.

Something had happened.

"Tuk-tuk-tuk," clucked cook like an agitated hen. Sadie had her hand clapped to her cheek as though she had toothache. Hans's face was screwed up in the effort to understand. Only Godber's man seemed to be enjoying himself; it was his story.

"What's the matter? What's happened?"

"There's been a horrible accident," said Cook. "A man killed."

"A man killed! Where? How? When?"

But Godber's man wasn't going to have his story snatched from under his very nose.

"Know those little cottages just below here, miss?" Know them? Of course, she knew them. "Well, there's a young chap living there, name of Scott, a carter. His horse shied at a traction-engine, corner of Hawke Street this morning, and he was thrown out on the back of his head. Killed."

"Dead!" Laura stared at Godber's man.

"Dead when they picked him up," said Godber's man with relish. "They were taking the body home as I come up here." And he said to the cook, "He's left a wife and five little ones."

"Jose, come here." Laura caught hold of her sister's sleeve and dragged her through the kitchen to the other side of the green baize door. There she paused and leaned against it. "Jose!" she said, horrified, "however are we going to stop everything?"

"Stop everything, Laura!" cried Jose in astonishment. "What do you mean?"

"Stop the garden-party, of course." Why did Jose pretend?

But Jose was still more amazed. "Stop the garden-party? My dear Laura, don't be so absurd. Of course we can't do anything of the kind. Nobody expects us to. Don't be so extravagant."

"But we can't possibly have a garden-party with a man dead just outside the front gate."

That really was extravagant, for the little cottages were in a lane to themselves at the very bottom of a steep rise that led up to the house. A broad road ran between. True, they were far too near. They were the greatest possible eyesore, and they had no right to be in that neighbourhood at all. They were little mean dwellings painted a chocolate brown. In the garden patches there was nothing but cabbage stalks, sick hens and tomato cans. The very smoke coming out of their chimneys was poverty-stricken. Little rags and shreds of smoke, so unlike the great silvery plumes that uncurled from the Sheridans' chimneys. Washerwomen lived in the lane and sweeps and a cobbler, and a man whose house-front was studded all over with minute bird-cages. Children swarmed. When the Sheridans were little they were forbidden to set foot there because of the revolting language and of what they might catch. But since they were grown up, Laura and Laurie on their prowls sometimes walked through. It was disgusting and sordid. They came out with a shudder. But still one must go everywhere; one must see everything. So through they went.

"And just think of what the band would sound like to that poor woman," said Laura.

"Oh, Laura!" Jose began to be seriously annoyed. "If you're going to stop a band playing every time some one has an accident, you'll lead a very strenuous life. I'm every bit as sorry about it as you. I feel just as sympathetic." Her eyes hardened. She looked at her sister just as she used to when they were little and fighting together. "You won't bring a drunken workman back to life by being sentimental," she said softly.

"Drunk! Who said he was drunk?" Laura turned furiously on Jose. She said, just as they had used to say on those occasions, "I'm going straight up to tell mother."

"Do, dear," cooed Jose.

"Mother, can I come into your room?" Laura turned the big glass door-knob.

"Of course, child. Why, what's the matter? What's given you such a colour?" And Mrs. Sheridan turned round from her dressing-table. She was trying on a new hat.

"Mother, a man's been killed," began Laura.

"*Not* in the garden?" interrupted her mother.

"No, no!"

"Oh, what a fright you gave me!" Mrs. Sheridan sighed with relief, and took off the big hat and held it on her knees.

"But listen, mother," said Laura. Breathless, half-choking, she told the dreadful story. "Of course, we can't have our party, can we?" she pleaded. "The band and everybody arriving. They'd hear us, mother; they're nearly neighbours!"

To Laura's astonishment her mother behaved just like Jose; it was harder to bear because she seemed amused. She refused to take Laura seriously.

"But, my dear child, use your common sense. It's only by accident we've heard of it. If some one had died there normally—and I can't understand how they keep alive in those poky little holes—we should still be having our party, shouldn't we?"

Laura had to say "yes" to that, but she felt it was all wrong. She sat down on her mother's sofa and pinched the cushion frill.

"Mother, isn't it really terribly heartless of us?" she asked.

"Darling!" Mrs. Sheridan got up and came over to her, carrying the hat. Before Laura could stop her she had popped it on. "My child!" said her mother, "the hat is yours. It's made for you. It's much too young for me. I have never seen you look such a picture. Look at yourself!" And she held up her hand-mirror.

"But, mother," Laura began again. She couldn't look at herself; she turned aside.

This time Mrs. Sheridan lost patience just as Jose had done.

"You are being very absurd, Laura," she said coldly. "People like that don't expect sacrifices from us. And it's not very sympathetic to spoil everybody's enjoyment as you're doing now."

"I don't understand," said Laura, and she walked quickly out of the room into her own bedroom. There, quite by chance, the first thing she saw was this charming girl in the mirror, in her black hat trimmed with gold daisies, and a long black velvet ribbon. Never had she imagined she could look like that. Is mother right? she thought. And now she hoped her mother was right. Am I being extravagant? Perhaps it was extravagant. Just for a moment she had another glimpse of that poor woman and those little children, and the body being carried into the house. But it all seemed blurred, unreal, like a picture in the newspaper. I'll remember it again after the party's over, she decided. And somehow that seemed quite the best plan. . . .

Lunch was over by half-past one. By half-past two they were all ready for the fray. The green-coated band had arrived and was established in a corner of the tennis-court.

"My dear!" trilled Kitty Maitland, "aren't they too like frogs for words? You ought to have arranged them round the pond with the conductor in the middle on a leaf."

Laurie arrived and hailed them on his way to dress. At the sight of him Laura remembered the accident again. She wanted to tell him. If Laurie agreed with the others, then it was bound to be all right. And she followed him into the hall.

"Laurie!"

"Hallo!" He was half-way upstairs, but when he turned round and saw Laura he suddenly puffed out his cheeks and goggled his eyes at her. "My word, Laura! You do look stunning," said Laurie. "What an absolutely topping hat!"

Laura said faintly "Is it?" and smiled up at Laurie, and didn't tell him after all.

Soon after that people began coming in streams. The band struck up; the hired waiters ran from the house to the marquee. Wherever you looked there were couples strolling, bending to the flowers, greeting, moving on over the lawn. They were like bright birds that had alighted in the Sheridans' garden for this one afternoon, on their way to—where? Ah, what happiness it is to be with people who all are happy, to press hands, press cheeks, smile into eyes.

"Darling Laura, how well you look!"

"What a becoming hat, child!"

"Laura, you look quite Spanish. I've never seen you look so striking."

And Laura, glowing, answered softly, "Have you had tea? Won't you have an ice? The passion-fruit ices really are rather special." She ran to her father and begged him. "Daddy darling, can't the band have something to drink?"

And the perfect afternoon slowly ripened, slowly faded, slowly its petals closed.

"Never a more delightful garden-party . . ." "The greatest success . . ." "Quite the most . . ."

Laura helped her mother with the good-byes. They stood side by side in the porch till it was all over.

"All over, all over, thank heaven," said Mrs. Sheridan. "Round up the others, Laura. Let's go and have some fresh coffee. I'm exhausted. Yes, it's been very successful. But oh, these parties, these parties! Why will you children insist on giving parties!" And they all of them sat down in the deserted marquee.

"Have a sandwich, daddy dear. I wrote the flag."

"Thanks." Mr. Sheridan took a bite and the sandwich was gone. He took another. "I suppose you didn't hear of a beastly accident that happened to-day?" he said.

"My dear," said Mrs. Sheridan, holding up her hand, "we did. It nearly ruined the party. Laura insisted we should put it off."

"Oh, mother!" Laura didn't want to be teased about it.

"It was a horrible affair all the same," said Mr. Sheridan. "The chap was married too. Lived just below in the lane, and leaves a wife and half a dozen kiddies, so they say."

An awkward little silence fell. Mrs. Sheridan fidgeted with her cup. Really, it was very tactless of father . . .

Suddenly she looked up. There on the table were all those sandwiches, cakes, puffs, all uneaten, all going to be wasted. She had one of her brilliant ideas.

"I know," she said. "Let's make up a basket. Let's send that poor creature some of this perfectly good food. At any rate, it will be the greatest treat for the children. Don't you agree? And she's sure to have neighbours calling in and so on. What a point to have it all ready prepared. Laura!" She jumped up. "Get me the big basket out of the stairs cupboard."

"But, mother, do you really think it's a good idea?" said Laura.

Again, how curious, she seemed to be different from them all. To take scraps from their party. Would the poor woman really like that?

"Of course! What's the matter with you to-day? An hour or two ago you were insisting on us being sympathetic, and now——"

Oh, well! Laura ran for the basket. It was filled, it was heaped by her mother.

"Take it yourself, darling," said she. "Run down just as you are. No, wait, take the arum lilies too. People of that class are so impressed by arum lilies."

"The stems will ruin her lace frock," said practical Jose.

So they would. Just in time. "Only the basket, then. And, Laura!"—her mother followed her out of the marquee—"don't on any account——"

"What, mother?"

No, better not put such ideas into the child's head! "Nothing! Run along."

It was just growing dusky as Laura shut their garden gates. A big dog ran by like a shadow. The road gleamed white, and down below in the hollow the little cottages were in deep shade. How quiet it seemed after the afternoon. Here she was going down the hill to somewhere where a man lay dead, and she couldn't realize it. Why couldn't she? She stopped a minute. And it seemed to her that kisses, voices, tinkling spoons, laughter, the smell of crushed grass were somehow inside her. She had no room for anything else. How strange! She looked up at the pale sky, and all she thought was, "Yes, it was the most successful party."

Now the broad road was crossed. The lane began, smoky and dark. Women in shawls and men's tweed caps hurried by. Men hung over the palings; the children played in the doorways. A low hum came from the mean little cottages. In some of them there was a flicker of light, and a shadow, crab-like, moved across the window. Laura bent her head and hurried on. She wished now she had put on a coat. How her frock shone! And the big hat with the velvet streamer—if only it was another hat! Were the people looking at her? They must be. It was a mistake to have come; she knew all along it was a mistake. Should she go back even now?

No, too late. This was the house. It must be. A dark knot of people stood outside. Beside the gate an old, old woman with a crutch sat in a chair, watching. She had her feet on a newspaper. The voices stopped as Laura drew near. The group parted. It was as though she was expected, as though they had known she was coming here.

Laura was terribly nervous. Tossing the velvet ribbon over her shoulder, she said to a woman standing by, "Is this Mrs. Scott's house?" and the woman, smiling queerly, said, "It is, my lass."

Oh, to be away from this! She actually said, "Help me, God," as she walked up the tiny path and knocked. To be away from those staring eyes, or to be covered up in anything, one of those women's shawls even. I'll just leave the basket and go, she decided. I shan't even wait for it to be emptied.

Then the door opened. A little woman in black showed in the gloom.

Laura said, "Are you Mrs. Scott?" But to her horror the woman answered, "Walk in please, miss," and she was shut in the passage.

"No," said Laura, "I don't want to come in. I only want to leave this basket. Mother sent——"

The little woman in the gloomy passage seemed not to have heard her. "Step this way, please, miss," she said in an oily voice, and Laura followed her.

She found herself in a wretched little low kitchen, lighted by a smoky lamp. There was a woman sitting before the fire.

"Em," said the little creature who had let her in. "Em! It's a young lady." She turned to Laura. She said meaningly, "I'm 'er sister, Miss. You'll excuse 'er, won't you?"

"Oh, but of course!" said Laura. "Please, please don't disturb her. I—I only want to leave——"

But at that moment the woman at the fire turned round. Her face, puffed up, red, with swollen eyes and swollen lips, looked terrible. She seemed as though she couldn't understand why Laura was there. What did it mean? Why was this stranger standing in the kitchen with a basket? What was it all about? And the poor face puckered up again.

"All right, my dear," said the other. "I'll thank the young lady."

And again she began, "You'll excuse her, miss, I'm sure," and her face, swollen too, tried an oily smile.

Laura only wanted to get out, to get away. She was back in the passage. The door opened. She walked straight through into the bedroom, where the dead man was lying.

"You'd like a look at 'im, wouldn't you?" said Em's sister, and she brushed past Laura over to the bed. "Don't be afraid, my lass,—" and now her voice sounded fond and sly, and fondly she drew down the sheet—" 'e looks a picture. There's nothing to show. Come along, my dear."

Laura came.

There lay a young man, fast asleep—sleeping so soundly, so deeply, that he was far, far away from them both. Oh, so remote, so peaceful. He was dreaming. Never wake him up again. His head was sunk in the pillow, his eyes were closed; they were blind under the closed eyelids. He was given up to his dream. What did garden-parties and baskets and lace frocks matter to him? He was far from all those things. He was wonderful, beautiful. While they were laughing and while the band was playing, this marvel had come to the lane. Happy . . . happy. . . . All is well, said that sleeping face. This is just as it should be. I am content.

But all the same you had to cry, and she couldn't go out of the room without saying something to him. Laura gave a loud childish sob.

"Forgive my hat," she said.

And this time she didn't wait for Em's sister. She found her way out of the door, down the path, past all those dark people. At the corner of the lane she met Laurie.

He stepped out of the shadow. "Is that you, Laura?"

"Yes."

"Mother was getting anxious. Was it all right?"

"Yes, quite. Oh, Laurie!" She took his arm, she pressed up against him.

"I say, you're not crying, are you?" asked her brother.

Laura shook her head. She was.

Laurie put his arm round her shoulder. "Don't cry," he said in his warm, loving voice. "Was it awful?"

"No," sobbed Laura. "It was simply marvellous. But, Laurie——" She stopped, she looked at her brother. "Isn't life," she stammered, "isn't life——" But what life was she couldn't explain. No matter. He quite understood.

"*Isn't* it, darling?" said Laurie.

The Deprived

When we hear poverty mentioned we are likely to think of a lack of money and of the manner in which such a lack can blight life. As several of the following stories may remind us, deprivation sometimes takes forms other than financial. In Maria, the central figure of "Clay," we are meeting with a woman so devoid of intellectual, volitional, imaginative, emotional, familial, and social resources that our eyes, like Joe's, should be misted as we contemplate her pathetic situation. In "How Beautiful with Shoes" we meet with a girl so starved for beauty that she clings to the memory of a dangerous encounter with a homicidal maniac because in it were the only strands of poetry she has ever known. In "The Sky Is Gray" we witness what Edith Wharton has called "the hard compulsions of the poor," but at the story's end we are not depressed, perhaps because we are confident that in the child's memory the love and courage of his mother will outlive the hardships of one gray day.

The Lament

by ANTON CHEKHOV

It is twilight. A thick wet snow is slowly twirling around the newly lighted street lamps, and lying in soft thin layers on roofs, on horses' backs, on people's shoulders and hats. The cabdriver Iona Potapov is quite white, and looks like a phantom; he is bent double as far as a human body can bend double; he is seated on his box; he never makes a move. If a whole snowdrift fell on him, it seems as if he would not find it necessary to shake it off. His little horse is also quite white, and remains motionless; its immobility, its angularity, and its straight wooden-looking legs, even close by, give it the appearance of a gingerbread horse worth a *kopek*. It is, no doubt, plunged in deep thought. If you were snatched from the plow, from your usual gray surroundings, and were thrown into this slough full of monstrous lights, unceasing noise, and hurrying people, you too would find it difficult not to think.

Iona and his little horse have not moved from their place for a long while. They left their yard before dinner, and up to now, not a fare. The evening mist is descending over the town, the white lights of the lamps replacing brighter rays, and the hubbub of the street getting louder. "Cabby for Viborg way!" suddenly hears Iona. "Cabby!"

Iona jumps, and through his snow-covered eyelashes sees an officer in a greatcoat, with his hood over he head.

"Viborg way!" the officer repeats. "Are you asleep, eh? Viborg way!"

With a nod of assent Iona picks up the reins, in consequence of which layers of snow slip off the horse's back and neck. The officer seats himself in the sleigh, the cabdriver smacks his lips to encourage his horse, stretches out his neck like a swan, sits up, and, more from habit than necessity, brandishes his whip. The little horse also stretches its neck, bends its wooden-looking legs, and makes a move undecidedly.

"What are you doing, werewolf!" is the exclamation Iona hears from the dark mass moving to and fro, as soon as they have started.

"Where the devil are you going? To the r-r-right!"

"You do not know how to drive. Keep to the right!" calls the officer angrily.

A coachman from a private carriage swears at him; a passerby, who has run across the road and rubbed his shoulder against the horse's nose, looks at him furiously as he sweeps the snow from his sleeve. Iona shifts about on his seat as if he were on needles, moves his elbows as if he were trying to keep his equilibrium, and gapes about like someone suffocating, who does not understand why and wherefore he is there.

"What scoundrels they all are!" jokes the officer; "one would think they had all entered into an agreement to jostle you or fall under your horse."

Iona looks round at the officer, and moves his lips. He evidently wants to say something, but the only sound that issues is a snuffle.

"What?" asks the officer.

Iona twists his mouth into a smile, and with an effort says hoarsely:

"My son, *barin*, died this week."

"Hm! What did he die of?"

Iona turns with his whole body toward his fare, and says:

"And who knows! They say high fever. He was three days in the hospital, and then died. . . . God's will be done."

"Turn round! The devil!" sounds from the darkness. "Have you popped off, old doggie, eh? Use your eyes!"

"Go on, go on," says the officer, "otherwise we shall not get there by tomorrow. Hurry up a bit!"

The cabdriver again stretches his neck, sits up, and, with a bad grace, brandishes his whip. Several times again he turns to look at his fare, but the latter has closed his eyes, and apparently is not disposed to listen. Having deposited the officer in the Viborg, he stops by the tavern, doubles himself up on his seat, and again remains motionless, while the snow once more begins to cover him and his horse. An hour, and another. . . . Then, along the footpath, with a squeak of galoshes, and quarreling, come three young men, two of them tall and lanky, the third one short and humpbacked.

"Cabby, to the Police Bridge!" in a cracked voice calls the humpback. "The three of us for two *griveniks!*"

Iona picks up his reins, and smacks his lips. Two *griveniks* is not a fair price, but he does not mind whether it is a *rouble* or five *kopeks*—to him it is all the same now, so long as they are fares. The young men, jostling each other and using bad language, approach the sleigh, and all three at once try to get onto the seat; then begins a discussion as to which two shall sit and who shall be the one to stand. After wrangling, abusing each other, and much petulance, it is at last decided that the humpback shall stand, as he is the smallest.

"Now then, hurry up!" says humpback in a twanging voice, as he takes his place and breathes in Iona's neck. "Old furry! Here, mate, what a cap you have! There is not a worse one to be found in all Petersburg! . . ."

"He-he!—he-he!" giggles Iona. "Such a . . ."

"Now you, 'such a,' hurry up, are you going the whole way at this pace? Are you? . . . Do you want it in the neck?"

"My head feels like bursting," says one of the lanky ones. "Last night at the Donkmasovs, Vaska and I drank the whole of four bottles of cognac."

"I don't understand what you lie for," says the other lanky one angrily; "you lie like a brute."

"God strike me, it's the truth!"

"It's as much the truth as that a louse coughs!"

"He, he," grins Iona, "what gay young gentlemen"

"Pshaw, go to the devil!" says the humpback indignantly.

"Are you going to get on or not, you old pest? Is that the way to drive? Use the whip a bit! Go on, devil, go on, give it to him well!"

Iona feels at his back the little man wriggling, and the tremble in his voice. He listens to the insults hurled at him, sees the people, and little by little the feeling of loneliness leaves him. The humpback goes on swearing until he gets mixed up in some elaborate six-foot oath, or chokes with coughing. The lankies begin to talk about a certain Nadejda Petrovna. Iona looks round at them several times; he waits for a temporary silence, then, turning round again, he murmurs:

"My son . . . died this week."

"We must all die," sighs the humpback, wiping his lips after an attack of coughing. "Now, hurry up, hurry up! Gentlemen, I really cannot go any farther like this! When will he get us there?"

"Well, just you stimulate him a little in the neck!"

"You old pest, do you hear, I'll bone your neck for you! If one treated the like of you with ceremony one would have to go on foot! Do you hear, old serpent Gorinytch! Or do you not care a spit?"

Iona hears rather than feels the blows they deal him.

"He, he," he laughs. "They are gay young gentlemen, God bless 'em!"

"Cabby, are you married?" asks a lanky one.

"I? He, he, gay young gentlemen! Now I have only a wife and the moist ground. . . . He, ho, ho . . . that is to say, the grave. My son has died, and I am alive. . . . A wonderful thing, death mistook the door . . . instead of coming to me, it went to my son. . . ."

Iona turns round to tell them how his son died, but at this moment, the humpback, giving a little sigh, announces, "Thank God, we have at last reached our destination," and Iona watches them disappear through the dark entrance. Once more he is alone, and again surrounded by silence. . . . His grief, which has abated for a short while, returns and rends his heart with greater force. With an anxious and hurried look, he searches among the crowds passing on either side of the street to find whether there may be just one person who will listen to him. But the crowds hurry by without noticing him or his trouble. Yet it is such an immense, illimitable grief. Should his heart break and the grief pour out, it would flow over the whole earth, so it seems, and yet no one sees it. It has managed to conceal itself in such an insignificant shell that no one can see it even by day and with a light.

Iona sees a hall porter with some sacking, and decides to talk to him.

"Friend, what sort of time is it?" he asks.

"Past nine. What are you standing here for? Move on."

Iona moves on a few steps, doubles himself up, and abandons himself to his grief. He sees it is useless to turn to people for help. In less than five minutes he straightens himself, holds up his head as if he felt some sharp pain, and gives a tug at the reins; he can bear it no longer. "The stables," he thinks, and the little horse, as if it understood, starts off at a trot.

About an hour and a half later Iona is seated by a large dirty stove. Around the stove, on the floor, on the benches, people are snoring; the air is thick and suffocatingly hot. Iona looks at the sleepers, scratches himself, and regrets having returned so early.

"I have not even earned my fodder," he thinks. "That's what's my trouble. A man who knows his job, who has had enough to eat, and his horse too, can always sleep peacefully."

A young cabdriver in one of the corners half gets up, grunts sleepily, and stretches towards a bucket of water.

"Do you want a drink?" Iona asks him.

"Don't I want a drink!"

"That's so? Your good health! But listen, mate—you know, my son is dead. . . . Did you hear? This week, in the hospital. . . . It's a long story."

Iona looks to see what effect his words have, but sees none—the young man has hidden his face and is fast asleep again. The old man sighs, and scratches his head. Just as much as the young one wants to drink, the old man wants to talk. It will soon be a week since his son died, and he has not been able to speak about it properly to anyone. One must tell it slowly and carefully; how his son fell ill, how he suffered, what he said before he died, how he died. One must describe every detail of the funeral, and the journey to the hospital to fetch the dead son's clothes. His daughter Anissia has remained in the village—one must talk about her too. Is it nothing he has to tell? Surely the listener would gasp and sigh, and sympathize with him? It is better, too, to talk to women; although they are stupid, two words are enough to make them sob.

"I'll go and look after my horse," thinks Iona; "there's always time to sleep. No fear of that!"

He puts on his coat, and goes to the stables to his horse; he thinks of the corn, the hay, the weather. When he is alone, he dares not think of his son; he can speak about him to anyone, but to think of him, and picture him to himself, is unbearably painful.

"Are you tucking in?" Iona asks his horse, looking at its bright eyes; "go on, tuck in, though we've not earned our corn, we can eat hay. Yes! I am too old to drive—my son could have, not I. He was a first-rate cabdriver. If only he had lived!"

Iona is silent for a moment, then continues:

"That's how it is, my old horse. There's no more Kuzma Ionitch. He has left us to live and he went off pop. Now let's say, you had a foal, you were the foal's mother, and suddenly let's say, that foal went and left you to live after him. It would be sad, wouldn't it?"

The little horse munches, listens, and breathes over its master's hand. . . .

Iona's feelings are too much for him, and he tells the little horse the whole story.

Clay*

by JAMES JOYCE

The matron had given her leave to go out as soon as the women's tea was over, and Maria looked forward to her evening out. The kitchen was spick and span: the cook said you could see yourself in the big copper boilers. The fire was nice and bright and on one of the side-tables were four very big barmbracks. These barmbracks seemed uncut; but if you went closer you would see that they had been cut into long thick even slices and were ready to be handed round at tea. Maria had cut them herself.

Maria was a very, very small person indeed, but she had a very long nose and a very long chin. She talked a little through her nose, always soothingly: *Yes, my dear*, and *No, my dear*. She was always sent for when the women quarrelled over their tubs and always succeeded in making peace. One day the matron had said to her:

—Maria, you are a veritable peace-maker!

And the sub-matron and two of the Board ladies had heard the compliment. And Ginger Mooney was always saying what she wouldn't do to the dummy who had charge of the irons if it wasn't for Maria. Every one was so fond of Maria.

The women would have their tea at six o'clock and she would be able to get away before seven. From Ballsbridge to the Pillar, twenty minutes; from the Pillar to Drumcondra, twenty minutes; and twenty minutes to buy the things. She would be there before eight. She took out her purse with the silver clasps and read again the words *A Present from Belfast*. She was very fond of that purse because Joe had brought it to her five years before when he and Alphy had gone to Belfast on a Whit-Monday trip. In the purse were two half-crowns and some coppers. She would have five shillings clear after paying tram fare. What a nice evening they would have, all the children singing! Only she hoped that Joe wouldn't come in drunk. He was so different when he took any drink.

Often he had wanted her to go and live with them; but she would have felt herself in the way (though Joe's wife was ever so nice with her) and she had become accustomed to the life of the laundry. Joe was a good fellow. She had nursed him and Alphy too; and Joe used often to say:

—Mamma is mamma, but Maria is my proper mother.

After the break-up at home the boys had got her that position in the *Dublin by Lamplight* laundry, and she liked it. She used to have such a bad opinion of Protestants, but now she thought they were very nice people, a little quiet and serious, but still very nice people to live with. Then she had her plants in the conservatory and she liked looking after them. She had lovely ferns and wax-plants and, whenever anyone came to visit her, she always gave the visitor one or two slips from her conservatory. There was one thing she didn't like and that was the tracts on the walls; but the matron was such a nice person to deal with, so genteel.

When the cook told her everything was ready she went into the women's room and began to pull the big bell. In a few minutes the women began to come in by twos and threes, wiping their steaming hands in their petticoats and pulling down the sleeves of their blouses over their red steaming arms. They settled down before their huge mugs which the cook and the dummy filled up with hot tea, already mixed with milk and sugar in huge tin cans. Maria superintended the distribution of the barmbrack and saw that every woman got her four slices. There was a great deal of laughing and joking during the meal. Lizzie Fleming said Maria was sure to get the ring and, though Fleming had said that for so many Hallow

---

* From *Dubliners* by James Joyce. Originally published by B. W. Huebsch, Inc., in 1916. Copyright © 1967 by the Estate of James Joyce. All rights reserved. Reprinted by permission of The Viking Press, Inc.

Eves, Maria had to laugh and say she didn't want any ring or man either; and when she laughed her grey-green eyes sparkled with disappointed shyness and the tip of her nose nearly met the tip of her chin. Then Ginger Mooney lifted up her mug of tea and proposed Maria's health, while all the other women clattered with their mugs on the table, and said she was sorry she hadn't a sup of porter to drink it in. And Maria laughed again till the tip of her nose nearly met the tip of her chin and till her minute body nearly shook itself asunder, because she knew that Mooney meant well, though of course she had the notions of a common woman.

But wasn't Maria glad when the women had finished their tea and the cook and the dummy had begun to clear away the tea-things! She went into her little bedroom and, remembering that the next morning was a mass morning, changed the hand of the alarm from seven to six. Then she took off her working skirt and her house-boots and laid her best skirt out on the bed and her tiny dress-boots beside the foot of the bed. She changed her blouse too and, as she stood before the mirror, she thought of how she used to dress for mass on Sunday morning when she was a young girl; and she looked with quaint affection at the diminutive body which she had so often adorned. In spite of its years she found it a nice tidy little body.

When she got outside the streets were shining with rain and she was glad of her old brown raincloak. The tram was full and she had to sit on the little stool at the end of the car, facing all the people, with her toes barely touching the floor. She arranged in her mind all she was going to do, and thought how much better it was to be independent and to have your own money in your pocket. She hoped they would have a nice evening. She was sure they would, but she could not help thinking what a pity it was Alphy and Joe were not speaking. They were always falling out now, but when they were boys together they used to be the best of friends; but such was life.

She got out of her tram at the Pillar and ferreted her way quickly among the crowds. She went into Downes's cake-shop but the shop was so full of people that it was a long time before she could get herself attended to. She bought a dozen of mixed penny cakes, and at last came out of the shop laden with a big bag. Then she thought what else would she buy: she wanted to buy something really nice. They would be sure to have plenty of apples and nuts. It was hard to know what to buy and all she could think of was cake. She decided to buy some plumcake, but Downes's plumcake had not enough almond icing on top of it, so she went over to a shop in Henry Street. Here she was a long time in suiting herself, and the stylish young lady behind the counter, who was evidently a little annoyed by her, asked her was it wedding-cake she wanted to buy. That made Maria blush and smile at the young lady; but the young lady took it all very seriously and finally cut a thick slice of plumcake, parcelled it up and said:

—Two-and-four, please.

She thought she would have to stand in the Drumcondra tram because none of the young men seemed to notice her, but an elderly gentleman made room for her. He was a stout gentleman and he wore a brown hard hat; he had a square red face and a greyish moustache. Maria thought he was a colonel-looking gentleman and she reflected how much more polite he was than the young men who simply stared straight before them. The gentleman began to chat with her about Hallow Eve and the rainy weather. He supposed the bag was full of good things for the little ones and said it was only right that the youngsters should enjoy themselves while they were young. Maria agreed with him and favoured him with demure nods and hems. He was very nice with her, and when she was getting out at the Canal Bridge she thanked him and bowed, and he bowed to her and raised his hat and smiled agreeably; and while she was going up along the terrace, bending her tiny head under the rain, she thought how easy it was to know a gentleman even when he has a drop taken.

Everybody said: O, *here's Maria!* when she came to Joe's house. Joe was there, having come home from business, and all the children had their Sunday dresses on. There were two big girls in from next door and games were going on. Maria gave the bag of cakes to the eldest boy, Alphy, to divide, and Mrs Donnelly said it was too good of her to bring such a big bag of cakes, and made all the children say:

—Thanks, Maria.

But Maria said she had brought something special for papa and mamma, something they would be sure to like, and she began to look for her plumcake. She tried in Downes's bag and then in the pockets of her raincloak and then on the hallstand, but nowhere could she find it. Then she asked all the children had any of them eaten it—by mistake, of course—but the children all said no and looked as if they did not like to eat cakes if they were to be accused of stealing. Everybody had a solution for the mystery and Mrs Donnelly said it was plain that Maria had left it behind her in the tram. Maria, remembering how confused the gentleman with the greyish moustache had made her, coloured with shame and vexation and disappointment. At the thought of the failure of her little surprise and of the two and fourpence she had thrown away for nothing she nearly cried outright.

But Joe said it didn't matter and made her sit down by the fire. He was very nice with her. He told her all that went on in his office, repeating for her a smart answer which he had made to the manager. Maria did not understand why Joe laughed so much over the answer he had made, but she said that the manager must have been a very overbearing person to deal with. Joe said he wasn't so bad when you knew how to take him, that he was a decent sort so long as you didn't rub him the wrong way. Mrs Donnelly played the piano for the children and they danced and sang. Then the two next-door girls handed round the nuts. Nobody could find the nutcrackers, and Joe was nearly getting cross over it and asked how did they expect Maria to crack nuts without a nutcracker. But Maria said she didn't like nuts and that they weren't to bother about her. Then Joe asked would she take a bottle of stout, and Mrs Donnelly said there was port wine too in the house if she would prefer that. Maria said she would rather they didn't ask her to take anything: but Joe insisted.

So Maria let him have his way and they sat by the fire talking over old times and Maria thought she would put in a good word for Alphy. But Joe cried that God might strike him stone dead if ever he spoke a word to his brother again and Maria said she was sorry she had menitoned the matter. Mrs Donnelly told her husband it was a great shame for him to speak that way of his own flesh and blood, but Joe said that Alphy was no brother of his and there was nearly being a row on the head of it. But Joe said he would not lose his temper on account of the night it was, and asked his wife to open some more stout. The two next-door girls had arranged some Hallow Eve games and soon everything was merry again. Maria was delighted to see the children so merry and Joe and his wife in such good spirits. The next-door girls put some saucers on the table and then led the children up to the table, blindfold. One got the prayer-book and the other three got the water; and when one of the next-door girls got the ring Mrs Donnelly shook her finger at the blushing girl as much as to say: *O, I know all about it!* They insisted then on blindfolding Maria and leading her up to the table to see what she would get; and, while they were putting on the bandage, Maria laughed and laughed again till the tip of her nose nearly met the tip of her chin.

They led her up to the table amid laughing and joking, and she put her hand out in the air as she was told to do. She moved her hand about here and there in the air and descended on one of the saucers. She felt a soft wet substance with her fingers and was surprised that nobody spoke or took off her bandage. There was a pause for a few seconds; and then a great deal of scuffing and whispering. Somebody said something about the garden, and at last Mrs Donnelly said something very cross to one of the next-door girls and told her to throw it out at once: that was no play. Maria understood that it was wrong that time and so she had to do it over again: and this time she got the prayer-book.

After that Mrs Donnelly played Miss McCloud's Reel for the children, and Joe made Maria take a glass of wine. Soon they were all quite merry again, and Mrs Donnelly said Maria would enter a convent before the year was out because she had got the prayer-book. Maria had never seen Joe so nice to her as he was that night, so full of pleasant talk and reminiscences. She said they were all very good to her.

At last the children grew tired and sleepy and Joe asked Maria would she not sing some little song before she went, one of the old songs. Mrs Donnelly said *Do, please, Maria!* and so Maria had to get up and stand beside the piano. Mrs Donnelly bade the children be quiet and listen to Maria's song. Then she played the prelude and said *Now, Maria!* and Maria, blushing very much, began to sing in a tiny quavering voice. She sang *I Dreamt that I Dwelt*, and when she came to the second verse she sang again:

"I dreamt that I dwelt in marble halls
  With vassals and serfs at my side,
And of all who assembled within those walls
  That I was the hope and the pride.
"I had riches too great to count, could boast
  Of a high ancestral name,
But I also dreamt, which pleased me most,
  That you loved me still the same."

But no one tried to show her her mistake; and when she had ended her song Joe was very much moved. He said that there was no time like the long ago and no music for him like poor old Balfe, whatever other people might say; and his eyes filled up so much with tears that he could not find what he was looking for and in the end he had to ask his wife to tell him where the corkscrew was.

How Beautiful with Shoes*
by WILBUR DANIEL STEELE

By the time the milking was finished, the sow, which had farrowed the past week, was making such a row that the girl spilled a pint of the warm milk down the trough-lead to quiet the animal before taking the pail to the well-house. Then in the quiet she heard a sound of hoofs on the bridge, where the road crossed the creek a hundred yards below the house, and she set the pail down on the ground beside her bare, barn-soiled feet. She picked it up again. She set it down. It was as if she calculated its weight.

That was what she was doing, as a matter of fact, setting off against its pull toward the well-house the pull of that wagon team in the road, with little more of personal will or wish in the matter than has a wooden weather-vane between two currents in the wind. And as with the vane, so with the wooden girl—the added behest of a whip-lash cracking in the distance was enough; leaving the pail at the barn door; she set off in a deliberate, docile beeline through the cow-yard, over the fence, and down in a diagonal across the farm's one tilled field toward the willow brake that walled the road at the dip. And once under way, though her mother came to the kitchen door and called in her high, flat voice, "Amarantha, where you goin', Amarantha?" the girl went on apparently unmoved, as though she had been as deaf as the woman in the doorway; indeed, if there was emotion in her it was the purely sensuous one of feeling the clods of the furrows breaking softly between her toes. It was spring time in the mountains.

"Amarantha, why don't you answer me, Amarantha?"

For moments after the girl had disappeared beyond the willows the widow continued to call, unaware through long habit of how absurd it sounded, the name which that strange man her husband had put upon their

---

* Copyright 1932, 1959 by Wilbur Daniel Steele. Reprinted by permission of Harold Matson Company, Inc.

daughter in one of his moods. Mrs. Doggett had been deaf so long she did not realize that nobody else ever thought of it for the broad-fleshed, slow-minded girl, but called her Mary or, even more simply, Mare.

Ruby Herter had stopped his team this side of the bridge, the mules' heads turned into the lane to his father's farm beyond the road. A big-barrelled, heavy-limbed fellow with a square, sallow, not unhandsome face, he took out youth in ponderous gestures of masterfulness; it was like him to have cracked his whip above his animals' ears the moment before he pulled them to a halt. When he saw the girl getting over the fence under the willows he tongued the wad of tobacco out of his mouth into his palm, threw it away beyond the road, and drew a sleeve of his jumper across his lips.

"Don't run youself out o' breath, Mare; I got all night."

"I was comin'." It sounded sullen only because it was matter of fact.

"Well, keep a-comin' and give us a smack." Hunched on the wagon seat, he remained motionless for some time after she had arrived at the hub, and when he stirred it was but to cut a fresh bit of tobacco, as if already he had forgotten why he threw the old one away. Having satisfied his humor, he unbent, climbed down, kissed her passive mouth, and hugged her up to him, roughly and loosely, his hands careless of contours. It was not out of the way; they were used to handling animals, both of them; and it was spring. A slow warmth pervaded the girl, formless, nameless, almost impersonal.

Her betrothed pulled her head back by the braid of her yellow hair. He studied her face, his brows gathered and his chin out.

"Listen, Mare, you wouldn't leave nobody else hug and kiss you, dang you!"

She shook her head, without vehemence or anxiety.

"Who's that?" She hearkened up the road. "Pull your team out," she added, as a Ford came in sight around the bend above the house, driven at speed. "Geddap!" she said to the mules herself.

But the car came to a halt near them, and one of the five men crowded in it called,
"Come on, Ruby, climb in. They's a loony loose out o' Dayville Asylum, and they got him trailed over somewheres on Split Ridge and Judge North phoned up to Slosson's store for ever'body come help circle him—come on, hop the runnin'-board!"

Ruby hesitated, an eye on his team.

"Scared, Ruby?" The driver raced his engine. "They say this boy's a killer."

"Mare, take the team in and tell pa." The car was already moving when Ruby jumped in. A moment after it had sounded on the bridge it was out of sight.

"Amarantha, Amarantha, why don't you come, Amarantha?"

Returning from her errand, fifteen minutes later, Mare heard the plaint lifted in the twilight. The sun had dipped behind the back ridge, and though the sky was still bright with day, the dusk began to smoke up out of the plowed field like a ground-fog. The girl had returned through it, got the milk, and started toward the well-house before the widow saw her.

"Daughter, seems to me you might!" she expostulated without change of key. "Here's some young man friend o' yourn stopped to say howdy, and I been rackin' my lungs out after you.... Put that milk in the cool and come!"

Some young man friend? But there was no good to be got from puzzling. Mare poured the milk in the pan in the dark of the low house over the well, and as she came out, stooping, she saw a figure waiting for her, black in silhouette against the yellowing sky.

"Who are you?" she asked, a native timidity making her sound sulky.

"Amarantha!" the fellow mused. "That's poetry." And she knew then that she did not know him.

She walked past, her arms straight down and her eyes front. Strangers always affected her with a kind of muscular terror simply by being strangers. So she gained the kitchen steps, aware by his tread that he followed. There, taking courage at sight of her mother in the doorway, she turned on him, her eyes down at the level of his knees.

"Who are you and what d' y' want?"

He still mused. "Amarantha! Amarantha in Carolina! That makes me happy!"

Mare hazarded one upward look. She saw that he had red hair, brown eyes, and hollows under his cheekbones, and though the green sweater he wore on top of a gray overall was plainly not meant for him, sizes too large as far as girth went, yet he was built so long of limb that his wrists came inches out of the sleeves and made his big hands look even bigger.

Mrs. Doggett complained. "Why don't you introduce us, daughter?"

The girl opened her mouth and closed it again. Her mother, unaware that no sound had come out of it, smiled and nodded, evidently taking to the tall, homely fellow and tickled by the way he could not seem to get his eyes off her daughter. But the daughter saw none of it, all her attention centered upon the stranger's hands.

Restless, hard-fleshed, and chap-bitten, they were like a countryman's hands; but the fingers were longer than the ordinary, and slightly spatulate at their ends, and these ends were slowly and continuously at play among themselves.

The girl could not have explained how it came to her to be frightened and at the same time to be calm, for she was inept with words. It was simply that in an animal way she knew animals, knew them in health and ailing, and when they were ailing she knew by instinct, as her father had known, how to move so as not to fret them.

Her mother had gone in to light up; from beside the lampshelf she called back, "If he's aimin' to stay to supper you should've told me, Amarantha, though I guess there's plenty of the side-meat to go 'round, if you'll bring me in a few more turnips and potatoes, though it is late."

At the words the man's cheeks moved in and out. "I'm very hungry," he said.

Mare nodded deliberately. Deliberately, as if her mother could hear her, she said over her shoulder, "I'll go get the potatoes and turnips, ma." While she spoke she was moving, slowly, softly, at first, toward the right of the yard, where the fence gave over into the field. Unluckily her mother spied her through the window.

"Amarantha, where *are* you goin'?"

"I'm goin' to get the potatoes and turnips." She neither raised her voice nor glanced back, but lengthened her stride. "He won't hurt her," she said to herself. "He won't hurt her; it's me, not her," she kept repeating, while she got over the fence and down into the shadow that lay more than ever like a fog on the field.

The desire to believe that it actually did hide her, the temptation to break from her rapid but orderly walk grew till she could no longer fight it. She saw the road willows only a dash ahead of her. She ran, her feet floundering among the furrows.

She neither heard nor saw him, but when she realized he was with her she knew he had been with her all the while. She stopped, and he stopped, and so they stood, with the dark open of the field all around. Glancing sidewise presently, she saw he was no longer looking at her with those strangely importunate brown eyes of his, but had raised them to the crest of the wooded ridge behind her.

By and by, "What does it make you think of?" he asked. And when she made no move to see, "Turn around and look!" he said, and though it was low and almost tender in its tone, she knew enough to turn.

A ray of the sunset hidden in the west struck through the tops of the topmost trees, far and small up there, a thin, bright hem.

"What does it make you think of, Amarantha? . . . Answer!"

"Fire," she made herself say.

"Or blood."

"Or blood, yeh. That's right, or blood." She had heard a Ford going up the road beyond the willows, and her attention was not on what she said.

The man soliloquized. "Fire and blood, both; spare one or the other, and where is beauty, the way the world is? It's an awful thing to have to carry, but Christ had it. Christ came with a sword. I love beauty, Amarantha. . . . I say, I love beauty!"

"Yeh, that's right, I hear." What she heard was the car stopping at the house.

"Not prettiness. Prettiness'll have to go with ugliness, because it's only ugliness trigged up. But beauty!" Now again he was looking at her. "Do you know how beautiful you are, Amarantha, 'Amarantha sweet and fair'?" Of a sudden, reaching behind her, he began to unravel the meshes of her hairbraid, the long, flat-tipped fingers at once impatient and infinitely gentle. " 'Braid no more that shining hair!' "

Flat-faced Mare Doggett tried to see around those glowing eyes so near to hers, but wise in her instinct, did not try too hard, "Yeh," she temporized. "I mean, no, I mean."

"Amarantha, I've come a long, long way for you. Will you come away with me now?"

"Yeh—that is—in a minute I will, mister —yeh . . ."

"Because you want to, Amarantha? Because you love me as I love you? Answer!"

"Yeh—sure uh . . . *Ruby!*"

The man tried to run, but there were six against him, coming up out of the dark that lay in the plowed ground. Mare stood where she was while they knocked him down and got a rope around him; after that she walked back toward the house with Ruby and Older Haskins, her father's cousin.

Ruby wiped his brow and felt of his muscles. "Gees, you're lucky we come, Mare. We're no more'n past the town, when they come hollerin' he'd broke over this way."

When they came to the fence the girl sat on the rail for a moment and rebraided her hair before she went into the house, where they were making her mother smell ammonia.

Lots of cars were coming. Judge North was coming, somebody said. When Mare heard this she went into her bedroom off the kitchen and got her shoes and put them on. They were brand new two-dollar shoes with cloth tops, and she had only begun to break them in last Sunday; she wished afterwards she had put her stockings on too, for they would have eased the seams. Or else that she had put on the old button pair, even though the soles were worn through.

Judge North arrived. He thought first of taking the loony straight through to Dayville that night, but then decided to keep him in the lock-up at the courthouse till morning and make the drive by day. Older Haskins stayed in, gentling Mrs. Doggett, while Ruby went out to help get the man into the Judge's sedan. Now that she had them on, Mare didn't like to take the shoes off till Older went; it might make him feel small, she thought.

Older Haskins had a lot of facts about the loony.

"His name's Humble Jewett," he told them. "They belong back in Breed County, all them Jewetts, and I don't reckon there's none on 'em that's not a mite unbalanced. He went to college though, worked his way, and he taught somethin' 'rother in some academy-school a spell, till he went off his head all of a sudden and took after folks with an axe. I remember it in the paper at the time. They give out one while how the Principal wasn't goin' to live, and there was others—there was a girl he tried to strangle. That was four-five year back."

Ruby came in guffawing. "Know the only thing they can get 'im to say, Mare? Only thing he'll say is, 'Amarantha, she's goin' with me.' . . . Mare!"

"Yeh, I know."

The cover of the kettle the girl was handling slid off on the stove with a clatter. A sudden sick wave passed over her. She went out to the back, out into the air. It was not till now she knew how frightened she had been.

Ruby went home, but Older Haskins stayed to supper with them, and helped Mare do the dishes afterward; it was nearly nine when he left. The mother was already in bed, and Mare was about to sit down to get those shoes off her wretched feet at last, when she heard the cow carrying on up at the barn, lowing and kicking, and next minute the sow was in it with a horning note. It might be a fox passing by to get at the henhouse, or a weasel. Mare forgot her feet, took a broom-handle they used in boiling clothes, opened the back door, and stepped out. Blinking the lamplight from her eyes, she peered up toward the outbuildings, and saw the gable end of the barn standing like a red arrow in the dark, and the top of a butternut tree beyond it drawn in skeleton traceries, and just then a cock crowed.

She went to the right corner of the house and saw where the light came from, ruddy above the woods down the valley. Returning into the house, she bent close to her mother's ear and shouted, "Somethin's a-fire down to the town, look like," then went out again and up to the barn. "Soh! Soh!" she called to the animals. She climbed up and stood on the top rail of the cow-pen fence, only to find she could not locate the flame even there.

Ten rods behind the buildings a mass of rock mounted higher than their ridgepoles, a chopped-off buttress of the back ridge, covered with oak scrub and wild grapes and blackberries, whose thorny ropes the girl beat away from her skirt with the broom-handle as she scrambled up in the wine-colored dark. Once at the top, and the brush held aside, she could see the tongue-tip of the conflagration half a mile away at the town. And she knew by the bearing of the two church steeples that it was the building where the lock-up was that was burning.

There is a horror in knowing animals trapped in a fire, no matter what the animals.

"Oh, my God!" Mare said.

A car went down the road. Then there was a horse galloping. That would be Older Haskins probably. People were out at Ruby's father's farm; she could hear their voices raised. There must have been another car up from the other way, for lights wheeled and shouts were exchanged in the neighborhood of the bridge. Next thing she knew, Ruby was at the house below, looking for her probably.

He was telling her mother. Mrs. Doggett was not used to him, so he had to shout even louder than Mare had to.

"What y' reckon he done, the hellion! he broke the door and killed Lew Fyke and set the courthouse afire! . . . Where's Mare?"

Her mother would not know. Mare called "Here, up the rock here."

She had better go down. Ruby would likely break his bones if he tried to climb the rock in the dark, not knowing the way. But the sight of the fire fascinated her simple spirit, the fearful element, more fearful than ever now, with the news. "Yes, I'm comin'," she called sulkily, hearing feet in the brush. "You wait; I'm comin'."

When she turned and saw it was Humble Jewett, right behind her among the branches, she opened her mouth to screech. She was not quick enough. Before a sound came out he got one hand over her face and the other arm around her body.

Mare had always thought she was strong, and the loony looked gangling, yet she was so easy for him that he need not hurt her. He made no haste and little noise as he carried her deeper into the undergrowth. Where the hill began to mount it was harder though. Presently he set her on her feet. He let the hand that had been over her mouth slip down to her throat, where the broad-tipped fingers wound, tender as yearning, weightless as caress.

"I was afraid you'd scream before you knew who 'twas, Amarantha. But I didn't want to hurt your lips, dear heart, your lovely, quiet lips."

It was so dark under the trees she could hardly see him, but she felt his breath on her mouth, near to. But then, instead of kissing her, he said, "No! No!" took from her throat an instant the hand that had held her mouth, kissed its palm, and put it back softly against her skin.

She stood stock still. Her mother's voice was to be heard in the distance, strident and meaningless. More cars were on the road. Nearer, around the rock, there were sounds of tramping and thrashing. Ruby fussed and cursed. He shouted, "Mare, dang you, where are you, Mare?" his voice harsh with uneasy anger. Now, if she aimed to do anything, was the time to do it. But there was neither breath nor power in her windpipe. It was as if those yearning fingers had paralyzed the muscles.

"Come!" The arm he put around her shivered against her shoulder blades. It was anger. "I hate killing. It's a dirty, ugly thing. It makes me sick." He gagged, judging by the sound. But then he ground his teeth. "Come away, my love!"

She found herself moving. Once when she broke a branch underfoot with an instinctive awkwardness he chided her. "Quiet, my heart, else they'll hear!" She made herself heavy. He thought she grew tired and bore more of her weight till he was breathing hard.

Men came up the hill. There must have been a dozen spread out, by the angle of their voices as they kept touch. Always Humble Jewett kept caressing Mare's throat with one hand; all she could do was hang back.

"You're tired and you're frightened," he said at last. "Get down here."

There were twigs in the dark, the overhang of a thicket of some sort. He thrust her in under this, and lay beside her on the bed of groundpine. The hand that was not in love with her throat reached across her; she felt the weight of its forearm on her shoulder and its fingers among the strands of her hair, eagerly, but tenderly, busy. Not once did he stop speaking, no louder than breathing, his lips to her ear.

" 'Amarantha sweet and fair—Ah, braid no more that shining hair . . .' "

Mare had never heard of Lovelace, the poet; she thought the loony was just going on, hardly listened, got little sense. But the cadence of it added to the lethargy of all her flesh.

" 'Like a clew of golden thread—Most excellently ravelled . . .' "

Voices loudened; feet came tramping; a pair went past not two rods away.

" '. . . Do not then wind up the light—In ribbands, and o'ercloud in night . . .' "

The search went on up the woods, men shouting to one another and beating the brush.

" '. . . But shake your head and scatter day!' I've never loved, Amarantha. They've tried me with prettiness, but prettiness is too cheap, yes, it's too cheap."

Mare was cold, and the coldness made her lazy. All she knew was that he talked on.

"But dogwood blowing in the spring isn't cheap. The earth on a field isn't cheap. Lots of times I've laid down and kissed the earth of a field, Amarantha. That's beauty, and a kiss for beauty." His breath moved up her cheek. He trembled violently. "No, no, not yet!" He got to his knees and pulled her by an arm. "We can go now."

They went back down the slope, but at an angle, so that when they came to the level they passed two hundred yards to the north of the house, and crossed the road there. More and more, her walking was like sleepwalking, the feet numb in their shoes. Even where he had to let go of her, crossing the creek on stones, she stepped where he stepped with an obtuse docility. The voices of the searchers on the back ridge were small in distance when they began to climb the face of Coward Hill, on the opposite side of the valley.

There is an old farm on top of Coward Hill, big hayfields as flat as tables. It had been half-past nine when Mare stood on the rock above the barn; it was toward midnight when Humble Jewett put aside the last branches of the woods and led her out on the height, and half a moon had risen. And a wind blew there, tossing the withered tops of last year's grasses, and mists ran with the wind, and ragged shadows with the mists, and mares'-tails of clear moonlight among the shadows, so that now the boles of birches on the forest's edge beyond the fences were but opal blurs and now cut alabaster. It struck so cold against the girl's cold flesh, this wind, that another wind of shivers blew through her, and she put her hands over her face and eyes. But the madman stood with his eyes wide open and his mouth open, drinking the moonlight and the wet wind.

His voice, when he spoke at last, was thick in his throat.

"Get down on your knees." He got down on his and pulled her after. "And pray!"

Once in England a poet sang four lines. Four hundred years have forgotten his name, but they have remembered his lines. The daft man knelt upright, his face raised to the wild scud, his long wrists hanging to the dead grass. He began simply:

" 'O western wind, when wilt thou blow
That the small rain down can rain?' "

The Adam's-apple was big in his bent throat. As simply he finished.

" 'Christ, that my love were in my arms
And I in my bed again!' "

Mare got up and ran. She ran without aim or feeling in the power of the wind. She told herself again that the mists would hide her from him, as she had done at dusk. And again, seeing that he ran at her shoulder, she knew he had been there all the while, making a race of it, flailing the air with his long arms for joy of play in the cloud of spring, throwing his knees high, leaping the moon-blue waves of the brown grass, shaking his bright hair; and her own hair was a weight behind her, lying level on the wind. Once a shape went bounding ahead of them for instants; she did not realize it was a fox till it was gone.

She never thought of stopping; she never thought anything, except once, "Oh, my God, I wish I had my shoes off!" And what would have been the good in stopping or in turning another way, when it was only play? The man's ecstasy magnified his strength. When a snake-fence came at them he took the top rail in flight, like a college hurdler, and, seeing the girl hesitate and half turn as if to flee, he would have releaped it without touching a hand. But then she got a loom of buildings, climbed over quickly, before he should jump, and ran along the lane that ran with the fence.

Mare had never been up there, but she knew that the farm and the house belonged to a man named Wyker, a kind of cousin of Rudy Herter's, a violent, bearded old fellow who lived by himself. She could not believe her luck. When she had run half the distance and Jewett had not grabbed her, doubt grabbed her instead. "Oh, my God, go careful!" she told herself. "Go slow!" she implored herself, and stopped running, to walk.

Here was a misgiving the deeper in that it touched her special knowledge. She had never known an animal so far gone that its instincts failed it; a starving rat will scent the trap sooner than a fed one. Yet, after one glance at the house they approached, Jewett paid it no further attention, but walked with his eyes to the right, where the cloud had blown away, and wooded ridges, like black waves rimmed with silver, ran down away toward the Valley of Virginia.

"I've never lived!" In his single cry there were two things, beatitude and pain.

Between the bigness of the falling world and his eyes the flag of her hair blew. He reached out and let it whip between his fingers. Mare was afraid it would break the spell then, and he would stop looking away and look at the house again. So she did something almost incredible; she spoke.

"It's a pretty—I mean a beautiful view down that-away."

"God Almighty beautiful, to take your breath away. I knew I'd never loved, Belovéd—" He caught a foot under the long end of one of the boards that covered the well and went down heavily on his hand and knees. It seemed to make no difference. "But I never knew I'd never lived," he finished in the same tone of strong rapture, quadruped in the grass, while Mare ran for the door and grabbed the latch.

When the latch would not give, she lost what little sense she had. She pounded with her fists. She cried with all her might: "Oh—hey—in there—hey—in there!" Then Jewett came and took her gently between his hands and drew her away, and then, though she was free, she stood in something like an awful embarrassment while he tried shouting.

"Hey! Friend! whoever you are, wake up and let my love and me come in!"

"No!" wailed the girl.

He grew peremptory. "Hey, wake up!" He tried the latch. He passed to full fury in a wink's time; he cursed, he kicked, he beat the door till Mare thought he would break his hands. Withdrawing, he ran at it with his shoulder; it burst at the latch, went slamming in, and left a black emptiness. His anger dissolved in a big laugh. Turning in time to catch her by a wrist, he cried joyously, "Come, my Sweet One!"

"No! No! Please—aw—listen. There ain't nobody there. He ain't to home. It wouldn't be right to go in anybody's house if they wasn't to home, you know that."

His laugh was blither than ever. He caught her high in his arms.

"I'd do the same by his love and him if 'twas my house, I would." At the threshold he paused and thought, "That is, if she was the true love of his heart forever."

The room was the parlor. Moonlight slanted in at the door, and another shaft came through a window and fell across a sofa, its covering dilapidated, showing its wadding in places. The air was sour, but both of them were farm-bred.

"Don't, Amarantha!" His words were pleading in her ear. "Don't be so frightened."

He set her down on the sofa. As his hands let go of her they were shaking.

"But look, I'm frightened too." He knelt on the floor before her, reached out his hands, withdrew them. "See, I'm afraid to touch you." He mused, his eyes rounded. "Of all the ugly things there are, fear is the ugliest. And yet, see, it can be the very beautifulest. That's a strange queer thing."

The wind blew in and out of the room, bringing the thin, little bitter sweetness of new April at night. The moonlight that came across Mare's shoulders fell full upon his face, but hers it left dark, ringed by the aureole of her disordered hair.

"Why do you wear a halo, Love?" He thought about it. "Because you're an angel, is that why?" The swift, untempered logic of the mad led him to dismay. His hands came flying to hers, to make sure they were earth; and he touched her breast, her shoulders, and her hair. Peace returned to his eyes as his fingers twined among the strands.

" '*Thy hair is a flock of goats that appear from Gilead . . .*' " He spoke like a man dreaming. " '*Thy temples are like a piece of pomegranate within thy locks.*' "

Mare never knew that he could not see her for the moonlight.

"Do you remember, Love?"

She dared not shake her head under his hand. "Yeh, I reckon," she temporized.

"You remember how I sat at your feet, long ago, like this, and made up a song? And all the poets in all the world have never made one to touch it, have they, Love?"

"Ugh-ugh—never."

" '*How beautiful are thy feet with shoes . . .*' Remember?"

"Oh, my God, what's he sayin' now?" she wailed to herself.

" '*How beautiful are thy feet with shoes, O prince's daughter! the joints of thy thighs are like jewels, the work of the hands of a cunning workman.*

Thy navel is like a round goblet, which wanteth not liquor; thy belly is like an heap of wheat set about with lilies.

Thy two breasts are like two young roes that are twins.' "

Mare had not been to church since she was a little girl, when her mother's black dress wore out. "No, no!" she wailed under her breath. "You're awful to say such awful things." She might have shouted it; nothing could have shaken the man now, rapt in the immortal, passionate periods of Solomon's song.

" '*. . . now also thy breasts shall be as clusters of the vine, and the smell of thy nose like apples.*' "

Hotness touched Mare's face for the first time. "Aw, no, don't talk so!"

" '*And the roof of thy mouth like the best wine for my belovèd . . . causing the lips of them that are asleep to speak.*' "

He had ended. His expression changed. Ecstasy gave place to anger, love to hate. And Mare felt the change in the weight of the fingers in her hair.

"What do you mean, I mustn't say it like that?" But it was not to her his fury spoke for he answered himself straight-away. "Like poetry, Mr. Jewett; I won't have blasphemy around my school."

"Poetry! My God! if that isn't poetry—if that isn't music—" . . . "It's Bible, Jewett. What you're paid to teach here is *literature*."

"Doctor Ryeworth, you're the blasphemer and you're an ignorant man." . . . "And your Principal. And I won't have you going around reading sacred allegory like earthly love."

"Ryeworth, you're an old man, a dull man, a dirty man, and you'd be better dead."

Jewett's hand had slid down from Mare's head. "Then I went to put my fingers around his throat, so. But my stomach turned, and I didn't do it. I went to my room. I laughed all the way to my room. I sat in my room at my table and I laughed. I laughed all afternoon and long after dark came. And then, about ten, somebody came and stood beside me in my room."

" '*Wherefore dost thou laugh, son?*'

"Then I knew who He was, He was Christ.

" '*I was laughing about that dirty, ignorant, crazy old fool, Lord.*'

" '*Wherefore dost thou laugh?*'

"I didn't laugh any more. He didn't say any more. I kneeled down, bowed my head.

" 'Thy will be done! Where is he, Lord?'"

" 'Over at the girls' dormitory, waiting for Blossom Sinckley.'"

"Brassy Blossom, dirty Blossom . . ."

It had come so suddenly it was nearly too late. Mare tore at his hands with hers, tried with all her strength to pull her neck away.

"Filthy Blossom! and him an old filthy man, Blossom! and you'll find him in Hell when you reach there, Blossom . . ."

It was more the nearness of his face than the hurt of his hands that gave her power of fright to choke out three words.

"I—ain't—Blossom!"

Light ran in crooked veins. Through the veins she saw his face bewildered. His hands loosened. One fell down and hung; the other he lifted and put over his eyes, took away again and looked at her.

"Amarantha!" His remorse was fearful to see. "What have I done!" His hands returned to hover over the hurts, ravening with pity, grief and tenderness. Tears fell down his cheeks. And with that, dammed desire broke its dam.

"Amarantha, my love, my dove, my beautiful love—"

"And I ain't Amarantha neither, I'm Mary! Mary, that's my name!"

She had no notion what she had done. He was like a crystal crucible that a chemist watches, changing hue in a wink with one adeptly added drop; but hers was not the chemist's eye. All she knew was that she felt light and free of him; all she could see of his face as he stood away above the moonlight were the whites of his eyes.

"Mary!" he muttered. A slight paroxysm shook his frame. So in the transparent crucible desire changed its hue. He retreated farther, stood in the dark by some tall piece of furniture. And still she could see the whites of his eyes.

"Mary! Mary Adorable!" A wonder was in him. "Mother of God!"

Mare held her breath. She eyed the door, but it was too far. And already he came back to go on his knees before her, his shoulders so bowed and his face so lifted that it must have cracked his neck, she thought; all she could see on the face was pain.

"Mary Mother, I'm sick to my death. I'm so tired."

She had seen a dog like that, one she had loosed from a trap after it had been there three days, its caught leg half gnawed free. Something about the eyes.

"Mary Mother, take me in your arms . . ."

Once again her muscles tightened. But he made no move.

". . . and give me sleep."

No, they were worse than the dog's eyes.

"Sleep, sleep! why won't they let me sleep? Haven't I done it all yet, Mother? Haven't I washed them yet of all their sins? I've drunk the cup that was given me; is there another? They've mocked me and reviled me, broken my brow with thorns and my hands with nails, and I've forgiven them, for they knew not what they did. Can't I go to sleep now, Mother?"

Mare could not have said why, but now she was more frightened than she had ever been. Her hands lay heavy on her knees, side by side, and she could not take them away when he bowed his head and rested his face upon them.

After a moment he said one thing more. "Take me down gently when you take me from the Tree."

Gradually the weight of his body came against her shins, and he slept.

The moon streak that entered by the eastern window crept north across the floor, thinner and thinner; the one that fell through the southern doorway traveled east and grew fat. For a while Mare's feet pained her terribly and her legs too. She dared not move them, though, and by and by they did not hurt so much.

A dozen times, moving her head slowly on her neck, she canvassed the shadows of the room for a weapon. Each time her eyes came back to a heavy earthenware pitcher on a stand some feet to the left of the sofa. It would have had flowers in it when Wyker's wife was alive; probably it had not been moved from its dust-ring since she died. It would be a long grab, perhaps too long; still, it might be done if she had her hands.

To get her hands from under the sleeper's head was the task she set herself. She pulled first one, then the other, infinitesimally. She waited. Again she tugged a very, very little. The order of his breathing was not disturbed. But at the third trial he stirred.

"Gently! gently!" His own muttering waked him more. With some drowsy instinct of possession he threw one hand across her wrists, pinning them together between thumb and fingers. She kept dead quiet, shut her eyes, lengthened her breathing, as if she too slept.

There came a time when what was pretense grew to be a peril; strange as it was, she had to fight to keep her eyes open. She never knew whether or not she really napped. But something changed in the air, and she was wide awake again. The moonlight was fading on the doorsill, and the light that runs before dawn waxed in the window behind her head.

And then she heard a voice in the distance, lifted in maundering song. It was old man Wyker coming home after a night, and it was plain he had had some whisky.

Now a new terror laid hold of Mare.

"Shut up, you fool you!" she wanted to shout. "Come quiet, quiet!" She might have chanced it now to throw the sleeper away from her and scramble and run, had his powers of strength and quickness not taken her simple imagination utterly in thrall.

Happily the singing stopped. What had occurred was that the farmer has espied the open door and, even befuddled as he was, wanted to know more about it quietly. He was so quiet that Mare began to fear he had gone away. He had the squirrel-hunter's foot, and the first she knew of him was when she looked and saw his head in the doorway, his hard, soiled, whiskery face half-up-side-down with craning.

He had been to the town. Between drinks he had wondered in and out of the night's excitement; had even gone a short distance with one search party himself. Now he took in the situation in the room. He used his forefinger. First he held it to his lips. Next he pointed it with a jabbing motion at the sleeper. Then he tapped his own forehead and described wheels. Lastly, with his whole hand, he made pushing gestures, for Mare to wait. Then he vanished as silently as he had appeared.

The minutes dragged. The light in the east strengthened and turned rosy. Once she thought she heard a board creaking in another part of the house, and looked down sharply to see if the loony stirred. All she could see of his face was a temple with freckles on it and the sharp ridge of a cheekbone, but even from so little she knew how deeply and peacefully he slept. The door darkened. Wyker was there again. In one hand he carried something heavy; with the other he beckoned.

"Come jumpin'!" he said out loud.

Mare went jumping, but her cramped legs threw her down half way to the sill; the rest of the distance she rolled and crawled. Just as she tumbled through the door it seemed as if the world had come to an end above her; two barrels of a shotgun discharged into a room make a noise. Afterwards all she could hear in there was something twisting and bumping on the floor-boards. She got up and ran.

Mare's mother had gone to pieces; neighbor women put her to bed when Mare came home. They wanted to put Mare to bed, but she would not let them. She sat on the edge of her bed in her lean-to bedroom off the kitchen, just as she was, her hair down all over her shoulders and her shoes on, and stared away from them, at a place in the wallpaper.

"Yeh, I'll go myself. Lea' me be!"

The women exchanged quick glances, thinned their lips, and left her be. "God knows," was all they would answer to the questionings of those that had not gone in, "but she's gettin' herself to bed."

When the doctor came through he found her sitting just as she had been, still dressed, her hair down on her shoulders and her shoes on.

"What d' y' want?" she muttered and stared at the place in the wallpaper.

How could Doc Paradise say, when he did not know himself?

"I didn't know if you might be—might be feeling very smart, Mary."

"I'm all right. Lea' me be."

It was a heavy responsibility. Doc shouldered it. "No, it's all right," he said to the men in the road. Ruby Herter stood a little apart, chewing sullenly and looking another way. Doc raised his voice to make certain it carried. "Nope, nothing."

Ruby's ears got red, and he clamped his jaws. He knew he ought to go in and see Mare, but he was not going to do it while everybody hung around waiting to see if he would. A mule tied near him reached out and mouthed his sleeve in idle innocence; he wheeled and banged a fist against the side of the animal's head.

"Well, what d' y' aim to do 'bout it?" he challenged its owner.

He looked at the sun then. It was ten in the morning. "Hell, I got work!" he flared, and set off down the road for home. Doc looked at Judge North, and the Judge started after Ruby. But Ruby shook his head angrily. "Lea' me be!" He went on, and the Judge came back.

It got to be eleven and then noon. People began to say, "Like enough she'd be as thankful if the whole neighborhood wasn't camped here." But none went away.

As a matter of fact they were no bother to the girl. She never saw them. The only move she made was to bend her ankles over and rest her feet on edge, her shoes hurt terribly and her feet knew it, though she did not. She sat all the while staring at that one figure in the wallpaper, and she never saw the figure.

Strange as the night had been, this day was stranger. Fright and physical pain are perishable things once they are gone. But while pain merely dulls and telescopes in memory and remains diluted pain, terror looked back upon has nothing of terror left. A gambling chance taken, at no matter what odds, and won was a sure thing since the world's beginning; perils come through safely were never perilous. But what fright does do in retrospect is this—it heightens each sensuous recollection, like a hard, clear lacquer laid on wood, bringing out the color and grain of it vividly.

Last night Mare had lain stupid with fear on groundpine beneath a bush, loud foot-falls and light whispers confused in her ear. Only now, in her room, did she smell the groundpine.

Only now did the conscious part of her brain begin to make words of the whispering.

"*Amarantha*," she remembered, "*Amarantha sweet and fair*." That was as far as she could go for the moment, except that the rhyme with "fair" was "hair." But then a puzzle, held in abeyance, brought other words. She wondered what "ravel Ed" could mean. "*Most excellently ravelled.*" It was left to her mother to bring the end.

They gave up trying to keep her mother out at last. The poor woman's prostration took the form of fussiness.

"Good gracious, daughter, you look a sight. Them new shoes, half ruined; ain't your feet *dead?* And look at your hair, all tangled like a wild one!"

She got a comb.

"Be quiet, daughter; what's ailin' you. Don't shake your head!"

"'*But shake your head and scatter day.*'"

"What you say, Amarantha?" Mrs. Doggett held an ear down.

"Go 'way! Lea' me be!"

Her mother was hurt and left. And Mare ran, as she stared at the wallpaper.

"*Christ, that my love were in my arms . . .*"

Mare ran. She ran through a wind white with moonlight and wet with "the small rain." And the wind she ran through, it ran through her, and made her shiver as she ran. And the man beside her leaped high over the waves of the dead grasses and gathered the wind in his arms, and her hair was heavy and his was tossing, and a little fox ran before them across the top of the world. And the world spread down around in waves of black and silver, more immense than she had ever known the world could be, and more beautiful.

"*God Almighty beautiful, to take your breath away!*"

Mare wondered, and she was not used to wondering. "Is it only crazy folks ever run like that and talk that way?"

She no longer ran; she walked; for her breath was gone. And there was some other reason, some other reason. Oh, yes, it was because her feet were hurting her. So, at last, and roundabout, her shoes had made contact with her brain.

Bending over the side of the bed, she loosened one of them mechanically. She pulled it half off. But then she looked down at it sharply, and she pulled it on again.

"*How beautiful . . .*"

Color overspread her face in a slow wave.

"*How beautiful are thy feet with shoes . . .*"

"Is it only crazy folks ever say such things?"

"O *prince's daughter!*"

"Or call you that?"

By and by there was a knock at the door. It opened, and Ruby Herter came in.

"Hello, Mare old girl!" His face was red. He scowled and kicked at the floor. "I'd 'a' been over sooner, except we got a mule down sick." He looked at his dumb betrothed. "Come on, cheer up, forget it! He won't scare you no more, not that boy, not what's left o' him. What you lookin' at, sourface? Ain't you glad to see me?"

Mare quit looking at the wallpaper and looked at the floor.

"Yeh," she said.

"That's more like it, babe." He came and sat beside her; reached down behind her and gave her a spank. "Come on, give us a kiss, babe!" He wiped his mouth on his jumper sleeve, a good farmer's sleeve, spotted with milking. He put his hands on her; he was used to handling animals. "Hey, you, warm up a little, reckon I'm goin' to do all the lovin'?"

"Ruby, lea' me be!"

"What!"

She was up, twisting. He was up, purple.

"What's ailin' you, Mare? What you bawlin' about?"

"Nothin'—only go 'way!"

She pushed him to the door and through it with all her strength, and closed it in his face, and stood with her weight against it, crying "Go 'way! Go 'way! Lea' me be!"

The Sky Is Gray*

by ERNEST J. GAINES

Go'n be coming in a few minutes. Coming 'round that bend down there full speed. And I'm go'n get out my hankercher and I'm go'n wave it down, and us go'n get on it and go.

I keep on looking for it, but Mama don't look that way no more. She looking down the road where us jest come from. It's a long old road, and far's you can see you don't see nothing but gravel. You got dry weeds on both sides, and you got trees on both sides, and fences on both sides, too. And you got cows in the pastures and they standing close together. And when us was coming out yer to catch the bus I seen the smoke coming out o' the cow's nose.

I look at my mama and I know what she thinking. I been with Mama so much, jest me and her, I know what she thinking all the time. Right now it's home—Auntie and them. She thinking if they got 'nough wood—if she left 'nough there to keep 'em warm till us get back. She thinking if it go'n rain and if any of 'em go'n have to go out in the rain. She thinking 'bout the hog—if he go'n get out, and if Ty and Val be able to get him back in. She always worry like that when she leave the house. She don't worry too much if she leave me there with the smaller ones 'cause she know I'm go'n look after 'em and look after Auntie and everything else. I'm the oldest and she say I'm the man.

I look at my mama and I love my mama. She wearing that black coat and that black hat and she looking sad. I love my mama and I want put my arm 'round her and tell her. But I'm not s'pose to do that. She say that's weakness and that's cry-baby stuff, and she don't want no cry-baby 'round her. She don't want you to be scared neither. 'Cause Ty scared of ghosts and she always whipping him. I'm scared of the dark, too. But I make 'tend I ain't. I make 'tend I ain't 'cause I'm the oldest, and I got to set a good sample for the rest. I can't ever be scared and I can't ever cry. And

---

* Reprinted from *Bloodline* by Ernest J. Gaines. Copyright © 1963, 1964, 1968 by Ernest J. Gaines and used by permission of the publisher, The Dial Press, Inc.

that's the reason I didn't never say nothing 'bout my teef. It been hurting me and hurting me close to a month now. But I didn't say it. I didn't say it 'cause I didn't want act like no cry-baby, and 'cause I know us didn't have 'nough money to have it pulled. But, Lord, it been hurting me. And look like it won't start till at night when you trying to get little sleep. Then soon's you shet your eyes—umm-umm, Lord, Look like it go right down to your heart string.

"Hurting, hanh?" Ty'd say.

I'd shake my head, but I wouldn't open my mouth for nothing. You open your mouth and let that wind in, and it almost kill you.

I'd just lay there and listen to 'em snore. Ty, there, right 'side me, and Auntie and Val over by the fireplace. Val younger 'an me and Ty, and he sleep with Auntie. Mama sleep 'round the other side with Louis and Walker.

I'd just lay there and listen to 'em, and listen to that wind out there, and listen to that fire in the fireplace. Sometime it'd stop long enough to let me get little rest. Sometime it just hurt, hurt, hurt. Lord, have mercy.

II

Auntie knowed it was hurting me. I didn't tell nobody but Ty, 'cause us buddies and he ain't go'n tell nobody. But some kind o' way Auntie found out. When she asked me, I told her no, nothing was wrong. But she knowed it all the time. She told me to mesh up a piece o' aspirin and wrap it in some cotton and jugg it down in that hole. I did it, but it didn't do no good. It stopped for a little while, and started right back again. She wanted to tell Mama, but I told her Uh-uh. 'Cause I knowed it didn't have no money, and it jest was go'n make her mad again. So she told Monsieur Bayonne, and Monsieur Bayonne came to the house and told me to kneel down 'side him on the fireplace. He put his finger in his mouth and made the Sign of the Cross on my jaw. The tip of Monsieur Bayonne finger is some hard, 'cause he always playing on that guitar. If us sit outside at night us can always hear Monsieur Bayonne playing on his guitar. Sometime us leave him out there playing on the guitar.

He made the Sign of the Cross over and over on my jaw, but that didn't do no good. Even when he prayed and told me to pray some, too, that teef still hurt.

"How you feeling?" he say.

"Same," I say.

He kept on praying and making the Sign of the Cross and I kept on praying, too.

"Still hurting?" he say.

"Yes, sir."

Monsieur Bayonne mashed harder and harder on my jaw. He mashed so hard he almost pushed me on Ty. But then he stopped.

"What kind o' prayers you praying, boy?" he say.

"Baptist," I say.

"Well, I'll be—no wonder that teef still killing him. I'm going one way and he going the other. Boy, don't you know any Catholic prayers?"

"Hail Mary," I say.

"Then you better start saying it."

"Yes, sir."

He started mashing again, and I could hear him praying at the same time. And, sure 'nough, afterwhile it stopped.

Me and Ty went outside where Monsieur Bayonne two hounds was, and us started playing with 'em. "Let's go hunting," Ty say. "All right," I say; and us went on back in the pasture. Soon the hounds got on a trail, and me and Ty followed 'em all cross the pasture and then back in the woods, too. And then they cornered this little old rabbit and killed him, and me and Ty made 'em get back, and us picked up the rabbit and started on back home. But it had started hurting me again. It was hurting me plenty now, but I wouldn't tell Monsieur Bayonne. That night I didn't sleep a bit, and first thing in the morning Auntie told me go back and let Monsieur Bayonne pray over me some more. Monsieur Bayonne was in his kitchen making coffee when I got there. Soon's he seen me, he knowed what was wrong.

"All right, kneel down there 'side that stove," he say. "And this time pray Catholic. I don't know nothing 'bout Baptist, and don't want know nothing 'bout him."

III

Last night Mama say: "Tomorrow us going to town."

"It ain't hurting me no more," I say. "I can eat anything on it."

"Tomorrow us going to town," she say.

And after she finished eating, she got up and went to bed. She always go to bed early now. 'Fore Daddy went in the Army, she used to stay up late. All o' us sitting out on the gallery or 'round the fire. But now, look like soon's she finish eating she go to bed.

This morning when I woke up, her and Auntie was standing 'fore the fireplace. She say: " 'Nough to get there and back. Dollar and a half to have it pulled. Twenty-five for me to go, twenty-five for him. Twenty-five for me to come back, twenty-five for him. Fifty cents left. Guess I get a little piece o' salt meat with that."

"Sure can use a piece," Auntie say. "White beans and no salt meat ain't white beans."

"I do the best I can," Mama say.

They was quiet after that, and I made 'tend I was still sleep.

"James, hit the floor," Auntie say.

I still made 'tend I was sleep. I didn't want 'em to know I was listening.

"All right," Auntie say, shaking me by the shoulder. "Come on. Today's the day."

I pushed the cover down to get out, and Ty grabbed it and pulled back.

"You, too, Ty," Auntie say.

"I ain't getting no teef pulled," Ty say.

"Don't mean it ain't time to get up," Auntie say. "Hit it, Ty."

Ty got up grumbling.

"James, you hurry up and get in your clothes and eat your food," Auntie say. "What time y'all coming back?" she say to Mama.

"That 'leven o'clock bus," Mama say. "Got to get back in that field this evening."

"Get a move on you, James," Auntie say.

I went in the kitchen and washed my face, then I ate my breakfast. I was having bread and syrup. The bread was warm and hard and tasted good. And I tried to make it last a long time.

Ty came back there, grumbling and mad at me.

"Got to get up," he say. "I ain't having no teef pulled. What I got to be getting up for."

Ty poured some sryup in his pan and got a piece of bread. He didn't wash his hands, neither his face, and I could see that white stuff in his eyes.

"You the one getting a teef pulled," he say. "What I got to get up for. I bet you if I was getting a teef pulled, you wouldn't be getting up. Shucks; syrup again. I'm getting tired of this old syrup. Syrup, syrup, syrup. I want me some bacon sometime."

"Go out in the field and work and you can have bacon," Auntie say. She stood in the middle door looking at Ty. "You better be glad you got syrup. Some people ain't got that—hard's time is."

"Shucks," Ty say. "How can I be strong."

"I don't know too much 'bout your strength," Auntie say; "but I know where you go'n be hot, you keep that grumbling up. James, get a move on you; your mama waiting."

I ate my last piece of bread and went in the front room. Mama was standing 'fore the fireplace warming her hands. I put on my coat and my cap, and us left the house.

IV

I look down there again, but it still ain't coming. I almost say, "It ain't coming, yet," but I keep my mouth shet. 'Cause that's something else she don't like. She don't like for you to say something just for nothing. She can see it ain't coming, I can see it ain't coming, so why say it ain't coming. I don't say it, and I turn and look at the river tha's back o' us. It so cold the smoke just raising up from the water. I see a bunch of pull-doos not too far out—jest on the other side the lilies. I'm wondering if you can eat pull-doos. I ain't too sure, 'cause I ain't never ate none. But I done ate owls and black birds, and I done ate red birds, too. I didn't want kill the red birds, but she made me kill 'em. They had two of 'em back there. One in my trap, one in Ty trap. Me and Ty was go'n play with 'em and let 'em go. But she made me kill 'em 'cause us needed the food.

"I can't," I say. "I can't."

"Here," she say. "Take it."

"I can't," I say. "I can't. I can't kill him, Mama. Please."

"Here," she say. "Take this fork, James."

"Please, Mama, I can't kill him," I say.

I could tell she was go'n hit me. And I jecked back, but I didn't jeck back soon enough.

"Take it," she say.

I took it and reached in for him, but he kept hopping to the back.

"I can't, Mama," I say. The water just kept running down my face. "I can't."

"Get him out o' there," she say.

I reached in for him and he kept hopping to the back. Then I reached in farther, and he pecked me on the hand.

"I can't, Mama," I say.

She slapped me again.

I reached in again, but he kept hopping out my way. Then he hopped to one side, and I reached there. The fork got him on the leg and I heard his leg pop. I pulled my hand out 'cause I had hurt him.

"Give it here," she say, and jecked the fork out my hand.

She reached and got the little bird right in the neck. I heard the fork go in his neck, and I heard it go in the ground. She brought him out and helt him right in front o' me.

"That's one," she say. She shook him off and gived me the fork. "Get the other one."

"I can't, Mama. I do anything. But I can't do that."

She went to the corner o' the fence and broke the biggest switch over there. I knelt 'side the trap crying.

"Get him out o' there," she say.

"I can't, Mama."

She started hitting me cross the back. I went down on the ground crying.

"Get him," she say.

"Octavia," Auntie say.

'Cause she had come out o' the house and she was standing by the tree looking at us.

"Get him out o' there," Mama say.

"Octavia," Auntie say; "explain to him. Explain to him. Jest don't beat him. Explain to him."

But she hit me and hit me and hit me.

I'm still young. I ain't no more'an eight. But I know now. I know why I had to. (They was so little, though. They was so little. I 'member how I picked the feathers off 'em and cleaned 'em and helt 'em over the fire. Then us all ate 'em. Ain't had but little bitty piece, but us all had little bitty piece, and ever'body jest looked at me, 'cause they was so proud.) S'pose she had to go away? That's why I had to do it. S'pose she had to go away like Daddy went away? Then who was go'n look after us? They had to be somebody left to carry on. I didn't know it then, but I know it now. Auntie and Monsieur Bayonne talked to me and made me see.

V

Time I see it, I get out my hankercher and start waving. It still 'way down there, but I keep waving anyhow. Then it come closer and stop and me and Mama get on. Mama tell me go sit in the back while she pay. I do like she say, and the people look at me. When I pass the little sign that say White and Colored, I start looking for a seat. I jest see one of 'em back there, but I don't take it, 'cause I want my mama to sit down herself. She come in the back and sit down, and I lean on the seat. They got seats in the front, but I know I can't sit there, 'cause I have to sit back o' the sign. Anyhow, I don't want sit there if my mama go'n sit back here.

They got a lady sitting 'side my mama and she look at me and grin little bit. I grin back, but I don't open my mouth, 'cause the wind'll get in and make that teef hurt. The lady take out a pack o' gum and reach me a slice, but I shake my head. She reach Mama a slice, and Mama shake her head. The lady jest can't understand why a little boy'll turn down gum, and she reached me a slice again. This time I point to my jaw. The lady understand and grin little bit, and I grin little bit, but I don't open my mouth, though.

They got a girl sitting 'cross from me. She got on a red overcoat, and her hair plaited in one big plait. First, I make 'tend I don't even see her. But then I start looking at her little bit. She make 'tend she don't see me neither, but I catch her looking that way. She got a cold, and ever' now and then she hist that little hankercher to her nose. She ought to blow it, but she don't. Must think she too much a lady or something.

Ever' time she hist that little hankercher, the lady 'side her say something in her yer. She shake her head and lay her hands in her lap again. Then I catch her kind o' looking where I'm at. I grin at her. But think she'll grin back? No. She turn up her little old nose like I got some snot on my face or something. Well, I show her both o' us can turn us head. I turn mine, too, and look out at the river.

The river is gray. The sky is gray. They have pull-doos on the water. The water is wavey, and the pull-doos go up and down. The bus go 'round a turn, and you got plenty trees hiding the river. Then the bus go 'round another turn, and I can see the river again.

I look to the front where all the white people sitting. Then I look at that little old gal again. I don't look right at her, 'cause I don't want all them people to know I love her. I jest look at her little bit, like I'm looking out that window over there. But she know I'm looking that way, and she kind o' look at me, too. The lady sitting 'side her catch her this time, and she lean over and say something in her yer.

"I don't love him nothing," that little old gal say out loud.

Ever'body back there yer her mouth, and all of 'em look at us and laugh.

"I don't love you, neither," I say. "So you don't have to turn up your nose, Miss."

"You the one looking," she say.

"I wasn't looking at you," I say. "I was looking out that window, there."

"Out that window, my foot," she say. "I seen you. Ever' time I turn 'round you look at me."

"You must o' been looking yourself if you seen me all them times," I say.

"Shucks," she say. "I got me all kind o' boyfriends."

"I got girlfriends, too," I say.

"Well, I just don't want you to get your hopes up," she say.

I don't say no more to that little old gal, 'cause I don't want have to bust her in the mouth. I lean on the seat where Mama sitting, and I don't even look that way no more. When us get to Bayonne, she jugg her little old tongue out at me. I make 'tend I'm go'n hit her, and she duck down side her mama. And all the people laugh at us again.

VI

Me and Mama get off and start walking in town. Bayonne is a little bitty town. Baton Rouge is a hundred times bigger 'an Bayonne. I went to Baton Rouge once—me, Ty, Mama, and Daddy. But that was 'way back yonder—'fore he went in the Army. I wonder when us go'n see him again. I wonder when. Look like he ain't ever coming home. . . . Even the pavement all cracked in Bayonne. Got grass shooting right out the sidewalk. Got weeds in the ditch, too; just like they got home.

It some cold in Bayonne. Look like it colder 'an it is home. The wind blow in my face, and I feel that stuff running down my nose. I sniff. Mama say use that hankercher. I blow my nose and put it back.

Us pass a school and I see them white children playing in the yard. Big old red school, and them children jest running and playing. Then us pass a café, and I see a bunch of 'em in there eating. I wish I was in there 'cause I'm cold. Mama tell me keep my eyes in front where they blonks.

Us pass stores that got dummies, and us pass another café, and then us pass a shoe shop, and that bald head man in there fixing on a shoe. I look at him and I butt into that white lady, and Mama jeck me in front and tell me stay there.

Us come to the courthouse, and I see the flag waving there. This one yer ain't like the one us got at school. This one yer ain't got but a handful of stars. One at school got a big pile of stars—one for ever' state. Us pass it and us turn and there it is—the dentist office. Me and Mama go in, and they got people sitting ever' where you look. They even got a little boy in there younger 'an me.

Me and Mama sit on that bench, and a white lady come in there and ask me what my name. Mama tell her, and the white lady go back. Then I yer somebody hollering in there. And soons that little boy hear him hollering, he start hollering, too. His mama pat him and pat him, trying to make him hush up, but he ain't thinking 'bout her.

The man that was hollering in there come out holding his jaw.

"Got it, hanh?" another man say.

The man shake his head.

"Man, I thought they was killing you in there," the other man say. "Hollering like a pig under a gate."

The man don't say nothing. He jest head for the door, and the other man follow him.

"John Lee," the white lady say. "John Lee Williams."

The little boy jugg his head down in his mama lap and holler more now. His mamma tell go with the nurse, but he ain't thinking 'bout her. His mama tell him again, but he don't even yer. His mama pick him up and take him in there, and even when the white lady shet the door I can still hear him hollering.

"I often wonder why the Lord let a child like that suffer," a lady say to my mama. The lady's sitting right in front o' us on another bench. She got on a white dress and a black sweater. She must be a nurse or something herself, I reckoned.

"Not us to question," a man say.

"Sometimes I don't know if we shouldn't," the lady say.

"I know definitely we shouldn't," the man say. The man look like a preacher. He big and fat and he got on a black suit. He got a gold chain, too.

"Why?" the lady say.

"Why anything?" the preacher say.

"Yes," the lady say. "Why anything?"

"Not us to question," the preacher say.

The lady look at the preacher a little while and look at Mama again.

"And look like it's the poor who do most the suffering," she say. "I don't understand it."

"Best not to even try," the preacher say. "He works in mysterious ways. Wonders to perform."

Right then Little John Lee bust out hollering, and ever'body turn they head.

"He's not a good dentist," the lady say. "Dr. Robillard is much better. But more expensive. That's why most of the colored people come here. The white people go to Dr. Robillard. Y'all from Bayonne?"

"Down the river," my mama say. And that's all she go'n say, 'cause she don't talk much. But the lady keep on looking at her, and so she say: "Near Morgan."

"I see," the lady say.

VII

"That's the trouble with the black people in this country today," somebody else say. This one yer sitting on the same side me and Mama sitting, and he kind o'sitting in front of that preacher. He look like a teacher or somebody that go to college. He got on a suit, and he got a book that he been reading. "We don't question is exactly the trouble," he say. "We should question and question and question. Question everything."

The preacher jest look at him a long time. He done put a toothpick or something in his mouth, and he jest keep turning it and turning it. You can see he don't like that boy with that book.

"Maybe you can explain what you mean," he say.

"I said what I meant," the boy say. "Question everything. Every stripe, every star, every word spoken. Everything."

"It 'pears to me this young lady and I was talking 'bout God, young man," the preacher say.

"Question Him, too," the boy say.

"Wait," the preacher say. "Wait now."

"You heard me right," the boy say. "His existence as well as everything else. Everything."

The preacher jest look cross the room at the boy. You can see he getting madder and madder. But mad or no mad, the boy ain't thinking 'bout him. He look at the preacher jest's hard's the preacher look at him.

"Is this what they coming to?" the preacher say. "Is this what we educating them for?"

"You're not educating me," the boy say. "I wash dishes at night to go to school in the day. So even the words you spoke need questioning."

The preacher jest look at him and shake his head.

"When I come in this room and seen you there with your book, I said to myself, There's an intelligent man. How wrong a person can be."

"Show me one reason to believe in the existence of a God," the boy say.

"My heart tell me," the preacher say.

"My heart tells me," the boy say. "My heart tells me. Sure, my heart tells me. And as long as you listen to what your heart tells you, you will have only what the white man gives you and nothing more. Me, I don't listen to my heart. The purpose of the heart is to pump blood throughout the body, and nothing else."

"Who's your paw, boy?" the preacher say.

"Why?"

"Who is he?"

"He's dead."

"And your mom?"

"She's in Charity Hospital with pneumonia. Half killed herself working for nothing."

"And 'cause he's dead and she sick, you mad at the world?"

"I'm not mad at the world. I'm questioning the world. I'm questioning it with cold logic, sir. What do words like Freedom, Liberty, God, White, Colored mean? I want to know. That's why *you* are sending us to school, to read and to ask questions. And because we ask these questions, you call us mad. No, sir, it is not us who are mad."

"You keep saying 'us'?"

" 'Us' . . . why not? I'm not alone."

The preacher jest shake his head. Then he look at ever'body in the room—ever'body. Some of the people look down at the floor, keep from looking at him. I kind o' look 'way myself, but soon's I know he done turn his head, I look that way again.

"I'm sorry for you," he say.

"Why?" the boy say. "Why not be sorry for yourself? Why are you so much better off than I am? Why aren't you sorry for these other people in here? Why not be sorry for the lady who had to drag her child into the dentist's office? Why not be sorry for the lady sitting on that bench over there? Be sorry for them. Not for me. Some way or other I'm going to make it."

"No, I'm sorry for you," the preacher say.

"Of course. Of course," the boy say, shaking his head. "You're sorry for me because I rock that pillar you're leaning on."

"You can't ever rock the pillar I'm leaning on, young man. It's stronger than anything man can ever do."

"You believe in God because a man told you to believe in God. A white man told you to believe in God. And why? To keep you ignorant, so he can keep you under his feet."

"So now, we the ignorant?"

"Yes," the boy say. "Yes." And he open his book again.

The preacher jest look at him there. The boy done forgot all about him. Ever'body else made 'tend they done forgot 'bout the squabble, too.

Then I see that preacher getting up real slow. Preacher a great big old man, and he got to brace hisself to get up. He come 'cross the room where the boy is. He jest stand there looking at him, but the boy don't raise his head.

"Stand up, boy," preacher say.

The boy look up at him, then he shet his book real slow and stand up. Preacher jest draw back and hit him in the face. The boy fall 'gainst the wall, but he straighten hisself up and look right back at that preacher.

"You forgot the other cheek," he say.

The preacher hit him again on the other side. But this time the boy don't fall.

"That hasn't changed a thing," he say.

The preacher jest look at the boy. The preacher breathing real hard like he jest run up a hill. The boy sit down and open his book again.

"I feel sorry for you," the preacher say. "I never felt so sorry for a man before."

The boy make 'tend he don't even hear that preacher. He keep on reading his book. The preacher go back and get his hat off the chair.

"Excuse me," he say to us. "I'll come back some other time. Y'all, please excuse me."

And he look at the boy and go out the room. The boy hist his hand up to his mouth one time, to wipe 'way some blood. All the rest o' the time he keep on reading.

VIII

The lady and her little boy come out the dentist, and the nurse call somebody else in. Then little bit later they come out, and the nurse call another name. But fast's she call somebody in there, somebody else come in the place where we at, and the room stay full.

The people coming in now, all of 'em wearing big coats. One of 'em say something 'bout sleeting, and another one say he hope not. Another one say he think it ain't nothing but rain. 'Cause, he say, rain can get awful cold this time o' year.

All 'cross the room they talking. Some of 'em talking to people right by 'em, some of 'em talking to people clare 'cross the room, some of 'em talking to anybody'll listen. It's a little bitty room, no bigger 'an us kitchen, and I can see ever'body in there. The little old room 's full of smoke, 'cause you got two old men smoking pipes. I think I feel my teef thumping me some, and I hold my breath and wait. I wait and wait, but it don't thump me no more. Thank God for that.

I feel like going to sleep, and I lean back 'gainst the wall. But I'm scared to go to sleep: Scared 'cause the nurse might call my name and I won't hear her. And Mama might go to sleep, too, and she be mad if neither us heard the nurse.

I look up at Mama. I love my mama. I love my mama. And when cotton come I'm go'n get her a newer coat. And I ain't go'n get a black one neither. I think I'm go'n get her a red one.

"They got some books over there," I say. "Want read one of 'em?"

Mama look at the books, but she don't answer me.

"You got yourself a little man there," the lady say.

Mama don't say nothing to the lady, but she must 'a' grin a little bit, 'cause I seen the lady grinning back. The lady look at me a little while, like she feeling sorry for me.

"You sure got that preacher out here in a hurry," she say to that other boy.

The boy look up at her and look in his book again. When I grow up I want be jest like him. I want clothes like that and I want keep a book with me, too.

"You really don't believe in God?" the lady say.

"No," he say.

"But why?" the lady say.

"Because the wind is pink," he say.

"What?" the lady say.

The boy don't answer her no more. He jest read in his book.

"Talking 'bout the wind is pink," that old lady say. She sitting on the same bench with the boy, and she trying to look in his face. The boy make 'tend the old lady ain't even there. He jest keep reading. "Wind is pink," she say again. "Eh, Lord, what children go'n be saying next?"

The lady 'cross from us bust out laughing.

"That's a good one," she say. "The wind is pink. Yes, sir, that's a good one."

"Don't you believe the wind is pink?" the boy say. He keep his head down in the book.

"Course I believe it, Honey," the lady say. "Course I do." She look at us and wink her eye. "And what color is grass, Honey?"

"Grass? Grass is black."

She bust out laughing again. The boy look at her.

"Don't you believe grass is black?" he say.

The lady quit laughing and look at him. Ever'body else look at him now. The place quiet, quiet.

"Grass is green, Honey," the lady say.

"It was green yesterday, it's green today, and it's go'n be green tomorrow."

"How do you know it's green?"

"I know because I know."

"You don't know it's green. You believe it's green because someone told you it was green. If someone had told you it was black you'd believe it was black."

"It's green," the lady say. "I know green when I see green."

"Prove it's green."

"Surely, now," the lady say. "Don't tell me it's coming to that?"

"It's coming to just that," the boy say. "Words mean nothing. One means no more than the other."

"That's what it all coming to?" that old lady say. That old lady got on a turban and she got on two sweaters. She got on a green sweater under a black sweater. I can see the green sweater 'cause some of the buttons on the other sweater missing.

"Yes, ma'am," the boy say. "Words mean nothing. Action is the only thing. Doing. That's the only thing."

"Other words, you want the Lord to come down here and show Hisself to you?" she say.

"Exactly, ma'am."

"You don't mean that, I'm sure?"

"I do, ma'am."

"Done, Jesus," the old lady say, shaking her head.

"I didn't go 'long with that preacher at first," the other lady say; "but now—I don't know. When a person say the grass is black, he's either a lunatic or something wrong."

"Prove to me that it's green."

"It's green because the people say it's green."

"Those same people say we're citizens of the United States."

"I think I'm a citizen."

"Citizens have certain rights. Name me one right that you have. One right, granted by the Constitution, that you can exercise in Bayonne."

The lady don't answer him. She jest look at him like she don't know what he talking 'bout. I know I don't.

"Things changing," she say.

"Things are changing because some black men have begun to follow their brains instead of their hearts."

"You trying to say these people don't believe in God?"

"I'm sure some of them do. Maybe most of them do. But they don't believe that God is going to touch these white people's hearts and change them tomorrow. Things change through action. By no other way."

Ever'body sit quiet and look at the boy. Nobody say a thing. Then the lady 'cross from me and Mama jest shake her head.

"Let's hope that not all your generation feel the same way you do," she say.

"Think what you please, it doesn't matter," the boy say. "But it will be men who listen to their heads and not their hearts who will see that your children have a better chance than you had."

"Let's hope they ain't all like you, though," the old lady say. "Done forgot the heart absolutely."

"Yes, ma'am, I hope they aren't all like me," the boy say. "Unfortunately I was born too late to believe in your God. Let's hope that the ones who come after will have your faith—if not in your God, then in something else, something definitely that they can lean on. I haven't anything. For me, the wind is pink; the grass is black."

IX

The nurse come in the room where us all sitting and waiting and say the doctor won't take no more patients till one o'clock this evening. My mama jump up off the bench and go up to the white lady.

"Nurse, I have to go back in the field this evening," she say.

"The doctor is treating his last patient now," the nurse say. "One o'clock this evening."

"Can I at least speak to the doctor?" my mama say.

"I'm his nurse," the lady say.

"My little boy sick," my mama say. "Right now his teef almost killing him."

The nurse look at me. She trying to make

up her mind if to let me come in. I look at her real pitiful. The teef ain't hurting me a tall, but Mama say it is, so I make 'tend for her sake.

"This evening," the nurse say, and go back in the office.

"Don't feel 'jected, Honey," the lady say to Mama. "I been 'round 'em a long time—they take you when they want to. If you was white, that's something else; but you the wrong shade."

Mama don't say nothing to the lady, and me and her go outside and stand 'gainst the wall. It's cold out there. I can feel that wind going through my coat. Some of the other people come out of the room and go up the street. Me and Mama stand there a little while and start to walking. I don't know where us going. When us come to the other street us jest stand there.

"You don't have to make water, do you?" Mama say.

"No, ma'am," I say.

Us go up the street. Walking real slow. I can tell Mama don't know where she going. When us come to a store us stand there and look at the dummies. I look at a little boy with a brown overcoat. He got on brown shoes, too. I look at my old shoes and look at his'n again. You wait till summer, I say.

Me and Mama walk away. Us come up to another store and us stop and look at them dummies, too. Then us go again. Us pass a café where the white people in there eating. Mama tell me keep my eyes in front where they blonks, but I can't help from seeing them people eat. My stomach start to growling 'cause I'm hungry. When I see people eating, I get hungry; when I see a coat, I get cold.

A man whistle at my mama when us go by a filling station. She make 'tend she don't even see him. I look back and I feel like hitting him in the mouth. If I was bigger, I say. If I was bigger, you see.

Us keep on going. I'm getting colder and colder, but I don't say nothing. I feel that stuff running down my nose and I sniff.

"That rag," she say.

I git it out and wipe my nose. I'm getting cold all over now—my face, my hands, my feet, ever'thing. Us pass another little café, but this'n for white people, too, and us can't go in there neither. So us jest walk. I'm so cold now, I'm 'bout ready to say it. If I knowed where us was going, I wouldn't be so cold, but I don't know where us going. Us go, us go, us go. Us walk clean out o' Bayonne. Then us cross the street and us come back. Same thing I seen when I got off the bus. Same old trees, same old walk, same old weeds, same old cracked pave—same old ever'thing.

I sniff again.

"That rag," she say.

I wipe my nose real fast and jugg that hankercher back in my pocket 'fore my hand get too cold. I raise my head and I can see David hardware store. When us come up to it, us go in. I don't know why, but I'm glad.

It warm in there. It so warm in there you don't want ever leave. I look for the heater, and I see it over by them ba'ls. Three white men standing 'round the heater talking in Creole. One of 'em come to see what Mama want.

"Got any ax handle?" she say.

Me, Mama, and the white man start to the back, but Mama stop me when us come to the heater. Her and the white man go on. I hold my hand over the heater and look at 'em. They go all the way in the back, and I see the white man point to the ax handle 'gainst the wall. Mama take one of 'em and shake it like she trying to figure how much it weigh. Then she rub her hand over it from one end to the other end. She turn it over and look at the other side, then she shake it again, and shake her head and put it back. She get another one and she do it jest like she did the first one, then she shake her head. Then she get a brown one and do it that, too. But she don't like this one neither. Then she get another one, but 'fore she shake it or anything, she look at me. Look like she trying to say something to me, but I don't know what it is. All I know is I done got warm now and I'm feeling right smart better. Mama shake this ax handle jest like she done the others, and shake her head and say something to the white man. The white man jest look at his pile of ax handle, and when Mama pass by him to come to the front, the white man jest scratch his head and follow her. She tell me come on, and us go on out and start walking again.

Us walk and walk, and no time at all I'm cold again. Look like I'm colder now 'cause I can still remember how good it was back there. My stomach growl and I suck it in to keep Mama from yering it. She walking right 'side me, and it growl so loud you can yer it a mile. But Mama don't say a word.

X

When us come up to the courthouse, I look at the clock. It got quarter to twelve. Mean us got another hour and a quarter to be out yer in the cold. Us go and stand side a building. Something hit my cap and I look up at the sky. Sleet falling.

I look at Mama standing there. I want stand close 'side her, but she don't like that. She say that's cry-baby stuff. She say you got to stand for yourself, by yourself.

"Let's go back to that office," she say.

Us cross the street. When us get to the dentist I try to open the door, but I can't. Mama push me on the side and she twist the knob. But she can't open it neither. She twist is some more, harder, but she can't open it. She turn 'way from the door. I look at her, but I don't move and I don't say nothing. I done seen her like this before and I'm scared.

"You hungry?" she say. She say it like she mad at me, like I'm the one cause of ever'thing.

"No, ma'am," I say.

"You want eat and walk back, or you rather don't eat and ride?"

"I ain't hungry," I say.

I ain't jest hungry, but I'm cold, too. I'm so hungry and I'm so cold I want cry. And look like I'm getting colder and colder. My feet done got numb. I try to work my toes, but I can't. Look like I'm go'n die. Look like I'm go'n stand right here and freeze to death. I think about home. I think about Val and Auntie and Ty and Louis and Walker. It 'bout twelve o'clock and I know they eating dinner. I can hear Ty making jokes. That's Ty. Always trying to make some kind o' joke. I wish I was right there listening to him. Give anything in the world if I was home 'round the fire.

"Come on," Mama say.

Us start walking again. My feet so numb I can't hardly feel 'em. Us turn the corner and go back up the street. The clock start hitting for twelve.

The sleet's coming down plenty now. They hit the pave and bounce like rice. Oh, Lord; oh, Lord, I pray. Don't let me die. Don't let me die. Don't let me die, Lord.

XI

Now I know where us going. Us going back o' town where the colored people eat. I don't care if I don't eat. I been hungry before. I can stand it. But I can't stand the cold.

I can see us go'n have a long walk. It 'bout a mile down there. But I don't mind. I know when I get there I'm go'n warm myself. I think I can hold out. My hands numb in my pockets and my feet numb, too, but if I keep moving I can hold out. Jest don't stop no more, that's all.

The sky's gray. The sleet keep falling. Falling like rain now—plenty, plenty. You can hear it hitting the pave. You can see it bouncing. Sometime it bounce two times 'fore it settle.

Us keep going. Us don't say nothing. Us jest keep going, keep going.

I wonder what Mama thinking. I hope she ain't mad with me. When summer come I'm go'n pick plenty cotton and get her a coat. I'm go'n get her a red one.

I hope they make it summer all the time. I be glad if it was summer all the time—but it ain't. Us got to have winter, too. Lord, I hate the winter. I guess ever'body hate the winter.

I don't sniff this time. I get out my hankercher and wipe my nose. My hand so cold I can hardly hold the hankercher.

I think us getting close, but us ain't there yet. I wonder where ever'body is. Can't see nobody but us. Look like us the only two people moving 'round today. Must be too cold for the rest of the people to move 'round.

I can hear my teefes. I hope they don't knock together too hard and make that bad one hurt. Lord, that's all I need, for that bad one to start off.

I hear a church bell somewhere. But today ain't Sunday. They must be ringing for a funeral or something.

I wonder what they doing at home. They must be eating. Monsieur Bayonne might be there with his guitar. One day Ty played with Monsieur Bayonne guitar and broke one o' the string. Monsieur Bayonne got some mad with Ty. He say Ty ain't go'n never 'mount to nothing. Ty can go just like him when he ain't there. Ty can make ever'body laugh mocking Monsieur Bayonne.

I used to like to be with Mama and Daddy. Us used to be happy. But they took him in the Army. Now, nobody happy no more. . . . I be glad when he come back.

Monsieur Bayonne say it wasn't fair for 'em to take Daddy and give Mama nothing and give us nothing. Auntie say, Shhh, Etienne. Don't let 'em yer you talk like that. Monsieur Bayonne say, It's God truth. What they giving his children? They have to walk three and a half mile to school hot or cold. That's anything to give for a paw? She got to work in the field rain or shine jest to make ends meet. That's anything to give for a husband? Auntie say, Shhh, Etienne, shhh. Yes, you right, Monsieur Bayonne say. Best don't say it in front of 'em now. But one day they go'n find out. One day. Yes, s'pose so, Auntie say. Then what, Rose Mary? Monsieur Bayonne say. I don't know, Etienne, Auntie say. All us can do is us job, and leave ever'thing else in His hand. . . .

Us getting closer, now. Us getting closer. I can see the railroad tracks.

Us cross the tracks, and now I see the café. Jest to get in there, I say. Jest to get in there. Already I'm starting to feel little better.

XII

Us go in. Ahh, it good. I look for the heater; there 'gainst the wall. One of them little brown ones. I jest stand there and hold my hand over it. I can't open my hands too wide 'cause they almost froze.

Mama standing right 'side me. She done unbuttoned her coat. Smoke rise out the coat, and the coat smell like a wet dog.

I move to the side so Mama can have more room. She open out her hands and rub 'em together. I rub mine together, too, 'cause this keep 'em from hurting. If you let 'em warm too fast, they hurt you sure. But if you let 'em warm jest little bit at a time, and you keep rubbing 'em, they be all right ever' time.

They got jest two more people in the café. A lady back o' the counter, and a man on this side the counter. They been watching us ever since us come in.

Mama get out the hankercher and count the money. Both o' us know how much money she got there. Three dollars. No, she ain't got three dollars. 'Cause she had to pay us way up here. She ain't got but two dollars and a half left. Dollar and a half to get my teef pulled, and fifty cents for us to go back on, and fifty cents worse o' salt meat.

She stir the money 'round with her finger. Most o' the money is change 'cause I can hear it rubbing together. She stir it and stir it. Then she look at the door. It still sleeting. I can yer it hitting 'gainst the wall like rice.

"I ain't hungry, Mama," I say.

"Got to pay 'em something for they heat," she say.

She take a quarter out the hankercher and tie the hankercher up again. She look over her shoulder at the people, but she still don't move. I hope she don't spend the money. I don't want her spend it on me. I'm hungry, I'm almost starving I'm so hungry, but I don't want her spending the money on me.

She flip the quarter over like she thinking. She must be thinking 'bout us walking back home. Lord, I sure don't want walk home. If I thought it done any good to say something, I say it. But my mama make up her own mind.

She turn way from the heater right fast, like she better hurry up and do it 'fore she change her mind. I turn to look at her go to the counter. The man and the lady look at her, too. She tell the lady something and the lady walk away. The man keep on looking at her. Her back to the man, and Mama don't even know he standing there.

The lady put some cakes and a glass o' milk on the counter. Then she pour up a cup o' coffee and set it side the other stuff. Mama pay her for the things and come back where I'm at. She tell me sit down at that table 'gainst the wall.

The milk and the cakes for me. The coffee for my mama. I eat slow, and I look at her. She looking outside at the sleet. She looking real sad. I say to myself, I'm go'n make all this up one day. You see, one day, I'm go'n make all this up. I want to say it now. I want to tell how I feel right now. But Mama don't like for us to talk like that.

"I can't eat all this," I say.

They got just three little cakes there. And I'm so hungry right now, the Lord know I can eat a hundred times three. But I want her to have one.

She don't even look my way. She know I'm hungry. She know I want it. I let it stay there a while, then I get it and eat it. I eat jest on my front teefes, 'cause if it tech that back teef I know what'll happen. Thank God it ain't hurt me a tall today.

After I finish eating I see the man go to the juke box. He drop a nickel in it, then he jest stand there looking at the record. Mama tell me keep my eyes in front where they blonks. I turn my head like she say, but then I yer the man coming towards us.

"Dance, Pretty?" he say.

Mama get up to dance with him. But 'fore you know it, she done grabbed the little man and done throwed him 'side the wall. He hit the wall so hard he stop the juke box from playing.

"Some pimp," the lady back o' the counter say. "Some pimp."

The little man jump up off the floor and start towards my mama. 'Fore you know it, Mama done sprung open her knife and she waiting for him.

"Come on," she say. "Come on. I'll cut you from your neighbo to your throat. Come on."

I go up to the little man to hit him, but Mama make me come and stand 'side her. The little man look at me and Mama and go back to the counter.

"Some pimp," the lady back o' the counter say. "Some pimp." She start laughing and pointing at the little man. "Yes, sir, you a pimp, all right. Yes, sir."

XIII

"Fasten that coat. Let's go," Mama say.

"You don't have to leave," the lady say.

Mama don't answer the lady, and us right out in the cold again. I'm warm right now—my hands, my yers, my feet—but I know this ain't go'n last too long. It done sleet so much now you got ice ever'where.

Us cross the railroad tracks, and soon's us do, I get cold. That wind go through this little old coat like it ain't nothing. I got a shirt and a sweater under it, but that wind don't pay 'em no mind. I look up and I can see us got a long way to go. I wonder if us go'n make it 'fore I get too cold.

Us cross over to walk on the sidewalk. They got jest one sidewalk back here. It's over there.

After us go jest a little piece, I smell bread cooking. I look, then I see a baker shop. When us get closer, I can smell it more better. I shet my eyes and make 'tend I'm eating. But I keep 'em shet too long and I butt up 'gainst a telephone post. Mama grab me and see if I'm hurt. I ain't bleeding or nothing and she turn me loose.

I can feel I'm getting colder and colder, and I look up to see how far us still got to go. Uptown is 'way up yonder. A half mile, I reckoned. I try to think of something. They say think and you won't get cold. I think of that poem, *Annabel Lee*. I ain't been to school in so long—this bad weather—I reckoned they done passed *Annabel Lee*. But passed it or not, I'm sure Miss Walker go'n make me recite it when I get there. That woman don't never forget nothing. I ain't never seen nobody like that.

I'm still getting cold. *Annabel Lee* or no *Annabel Lee*, I'm still getting cold. But I can see us getting closer. Us getting there gradually.

Soon's us turn the corner, I see a little old white lady up in front o' us. She the only lady on the street. She all in black and she got a long black rag over her head.

"Stop," she say.

Me and Mama stop and look at her. She must be crazy to be out in all this sleet. Ain't got but a few other people out there, and all of 'em men.

"Yall done ate?" she say.

"Jest finished," Mama say.

"Yall must be cold then?" she say.

"Us headed for the dentist," Mama say. "Us'll warm up when us get there."

"What dentist?" the old lady say. "Mr. Bassett?"

"Yes, ma'am," Mama say.

"Come on in," the old lady say. "I'll telephone him and tell him yall coming."

Me and Mama follow the old lady in the store. It's a little bitty store, and it don't have much in there. The old lady take off her head piece and fold it up.

"Helena?" somebody call from the back.

"Yes, Alnest?" the old lady say.

"Did you see them?"

"They're here. Standing beside me."

"Good. Now you can stay inside."

The old lady look at Mama. Mama waiting to hear what she brought us in here for. I'm waiting for that, too.

"I saw yall each time you went by," she say. "I came out to catch you, but you were gone."

"Us went back o' town," Mama say.

"Did you eat?"

"Yes, ma'am."

The old lady look at Mama a long time, like she thinking Mama might be jest saying that. Mama look right back at her. The old lady look at me to see what I got to say. I don't say nothing. I sure ain't going 'gainst my mama.

"There's food in the kitchen," she say to Mama. "I've been keeping it warm."

Mama turn right around and start for the door.

"Just a minute," the old lady say. Mama stop. "The boy'll have to work for it. It isn't free."

"Us don't take no handout," Mama say.

"I'm not handing out anything," the old lady say. "I need my garbage moved to the front. Ernest has a bad cold and can't go out there."

"James'll move it for you," Mama say.

"Not unless you eat," the old lady say. "I'm old, but I have my pride, too, you know."

Mama can see she ain't go'n beat this old lady down, so she jest shake her head.

"All right," the old lady say. "Come into the kitchen."

She lead the way with that rag in her hand. The kitchen is a little bitty little thing, too. The table and the stove jest about fill it up. They got a little room to the side. Somebody in there laying cross the bed. Must be the person she was talking with: Alnest or Ernest— I forget what she call him.

"Sit down," the old lady say to Mama. "Not you," she say to me. "You have to move the cans."

"Helena?" somebody say in the other room.

"Yes, Alnest?" the old lady say.

"Are you going out there again?"

"I must show the boy where the garbage is," the old lady say.

"Keep that shawl over your head," the old man say.

"You don't have to remind me. Come, boy," the old lady say.

Us go out in the yard. Little old back yard ain't no bigger 'an the store or the kitchen. But it can sleet here jest like it can sleet in any big back yard. And 'fore you know it I'm trembling.

"There," the old lady say, pointing to the cans. I pick up one of the cans. The can so light I put it back down to look inside o' it.

"Here," the old lady say. "Leave that cap alone."

I look at her in the door. She got that black rag wrapped 'round her shoulders, and she pointing one of her fingers at me.

"Pick it up and carry it to the front," she say. I go by her with the can. I'm sure the thing 's empty. She could 'a' carried the thing by herself, I'm sure. "Set it on the sidewalk by the door and come back for the other one," she say.

I go and come back, Mama look at me

when I pass her. I get the other can and take it to the front. It don't feel no heavier 'an the other one. I tell myself to look inside and see just what I been hauling. First, I look up and down the street. Nobody coming. Then I look over my shoulder. Little old lady done slipped there jest 's quiet 's mouse, watching me. Look like she knowed I was go'n try that.

"Ehh, Lord," she say. "Children, children. Come in here, boy, and go wash your hands."

I follow her into the kitchen, and she point, and I go to the bathroom. When I come out, the old lady done dished up the food. Rice, gravy, meat, and she even got some lettuce and tomato in a saucer. She even got a glass o' milk and a piece o' cake there, too. It look so good. I almost start eating 'fore I say my blessing.

"Helena?" the old man say.

"Yes, Alnest?" she say.

"Are they eating?"

"Yes," she say.

"Good," he say. "Now you'll stay inside."

The old lady go in there where he is and I can hear 'em talking. I look at Mama. She eating slow like she thinking. I wonder what's the matter now. I reckoned she think 'bout home.

The old lady come back in the kitchen.

"I talked to Dr. Bassett's nurse," she say. "Dr. Bassett will take you as soon as you get there."

"Thank you, ma'am," Mama say.

"Perfectly all right," the old lady say. "Which one is it?"

Mama nod towards me. The old lady look at me real sad. I look sad, too.

"You're not afraid, are you?" she say.

"No'm," I say.

"That's a good boy," the old lady say. "Nothing to be afraid of."

When me and Mama get through eating, us thank the old lady again.

"Helena, are they leaving?" the old man say.

"Yes, Alnest."

"Tell them I say good-by."

"They can hear you, Alnest."

"Good-by both mother and son," the old man say. "And may God be with you."

Me and Mama tell the old man good-by, and us follow the old lady in the front. Mama open the door to go out, but she stop and come back in the store.

"You sell salt meat?" she say.

"Yes."

"Give me two bits worse."

"That isn't very much salt meat," the old lady say.

"That's all I have," Mama say.

The old lady go back o' the counter and cut a big piece off the chunk. Then she wrap it and put in a paper bag.

"Two bits," she say.

"That look like awful lot of meat for a quarter," Mama say.

"Two bits," the old lady say. "I've been selling salt meat behind this counter twenty-five years. I think I know what I'm doing."

"You got a scale there," Mama say.

"What?" the old lady say.

"Weigh it," Mama say.

"What?" the old lady say. "Are you telling me how to run my business?"

"Thanks very much for the food," Mama say.

"Just a minute," the old lady say.

"James," Mama say to me. I move towards the door.

"Just one minute, I said," the old lady say.

Me and Mama stop again and look at her. The old lady take the meat out the bag and unwrap it and cut 'bout half o' it off. Then she wrap it up again and jugg it back in the bag and give it to Mama. Mama lay the quarter on the counter.

"Your kindness will never be forgotten," she say. "James," she say to me.

Us go out, and the old lady come to the door to look at us. After us go a little piece I look back, and she still there watching us.

The sleet 's coming down heavy, heavy now, and I turn up my collar to keep my neck warm. My mama tell me turn it right back down.

"You not a bum," she say. "You a man."

The Rocking-Horse Winner*
by D. H. LAWRENCE

There was a woman who was beautiful, who started with all the advantages, yet she had no luck. She married for love, and the love turned to dust. She had bonny children, yet she felt they had been thrust upon her, and she could not love them. They looked at her coldly, as if they were finding fault with her. And hurriedly she felt she must cover up some fault in herself. Yet what it was that she must cover up she never knew. Nevertheless, when her children were present, she always felt the centre of her heart go hard. This troubled her, and in her manner she was all the more gentle and anxious for her children, as if she loved them very much. Only she herself knew that at the centre of her heart was a hard little place that could not feel love, no, not for anybody. Everybody else said of her: "She is such a good mother. She adores her children." Only she herself, and her children themselves, knew it was not so. They read it in each other's eyes.

There were a boy and two little girls. They lived in a pleasant house, with a garden, and they had discreet servants, and felt themselves superior to anyone in the neighbourhood.

Although they lived in style, they felt always an anxiety in the house. There was never enough money. The mother had a small income, and the father had a small income, but not nearly enough for the social position which they had to keep up. The father went into town to some office. But though he had good prospects, these prospects never materialized. There was always the grinding sense of the shortage of money, though the style was always kept up.

At last the mother said: "I will see if I can't make something." But she did not know where to begin. She racked her brains, and tried this thing and the other, but could not find anything successful. The failure made deep lines come into her face. Her children were growing up, they would have to go to school. There must be more money, there must be more money. The father, who was always very handsome and expensive in his tastes, seemed as if he never would be able to do anything worth doing. And the mother, who had a great belief in herself, did not succeed any better, and her tastes were just as expensive.

And so the house came to be haunted by the unspoken phrase: There must be more money! There must be more money! The children could hear it all the time, though nobody said it aloud. They heard it at Christmas, when the expensive and splendid toys filled the nursery. Behind the shining modern rocking-horse, behind the smart doll's-house, a voice would start whispering: "There must be more money! There must be more money!" And the children would stop playing, to listen for a moment. They would look at each other's eyes, to see if they had all heard. And each one saw in the eyes of the other two that they too had heard. "There must be more money! There must be more money!"

It came whispering from the springs of the still-swaying rocking-horse, and even the horse, bending his wooden, champing head, heard it. The big doll, sitting so pink and smirking in her new pram, could hear it quite plainly, and seemed to be smirking all the more self-consciously because of it. The foolish puppy, too, that took the place of the teddy-bear, he was looking so extraordinarily foolish for no other reason but that he heard the secret whisper all over the house: "There must be more money!"

Yet nobody ever said it aloud. The whisper was everywhere, and therefore no one spoke it. Just as no one ever says: "We are breathing!" in spite of the fact that breath is coming and going all the time.

---

* From *The Complete Short Stories of D. H. Lawrence*, Vol. III. Copyright 1933 by The Estate of D. H. Lawrence, copyright © renewed 1961 by Angelo Ravagli and C. Montague Weekley, Executors of The Estate of Frieda Lawrence Ravagli. Reprinted by permission of The Viking Press, Inc.

"Mother," said the boy Paul one day, "why don't we keep a car of our own? Why do we always use uncle's, or else a taxi?"

"Because we're the poor members of the family," said the mother.

"But why are we, mother?"

"Well—I suppose," she said slowly and bitterly, "it's because your father has no luck."

The boy was silent for some time.

"Is luck money, mother?" he asked, rather timidly.

"No, Paul. Not quite. It's what causes you to have money."

"Oh!" said Paul vaguely. "I thought when Uncle Oscar said filthy lucker, it meant money."

"Filthy lucre does mean money," said the mother. "But it's lucre, not luck."

"Oh!" said the boy. "Then what is luck, mother?"

"It's what causes you to have money. If you're lucky you have money. That's why it's better to be born lucky than rich. If you're rich, you may lose your money. But if you're lucky, you will always get more money."

"Oh! Will you? And is father not lucky?"

"Very unlucky, I should say," she said bitterly.

The boy watched her with unsure eyes.

"Why?" he asked.

"I don't know. Nobody ever knows why one person is lucky and another unlucky."

"Don't they? Nobody at all? Does nobody know?"

"Perhaps God. But He never tells."

"He ought to, then. And aren't you lucky either, mother?"

"I can't be, if I married an unlucky husband."

"But by yourself, aren't you?"

"I used to think I was, before I married. Now I think I am very unlucky indeed."

"Why?"

"Well—never mind! Perhaps I'm not really," she said.

The child looked at her, to see if she meant it. But he saw, by the lines of her mouth, that she was only trying to hide something from him.

"Well, anyhow," he said stoutly, "I'm a lucky person."

"Why?" said his mother, with a sudden laugh.

He stared at her. He didn't even know why he had said it.

"God told me," he asserted, brazening it out.

"I hope He did, dear!" she said, again with a laugh, but rather bitter.

"He did, mother!"

"Excellent!" said the mother, using one of her husband's exclamations.

The boy saw she did not believe him; or, rather that she paid no attention to his assertion. This angered him somewhat, and made him want to compel her attention.

He went off by himself, vaguely, in a childish way, seeking for the clue to "luck." Absorbed, taking no heed of other people, he went about with a sort of stealth, seeking inwardly for luck. He wanted luck, he wanted it, he wanted it. When the two girls were playing dolls in the nursery, he would sit on his big rocking-horse, charging madly into space, with a frenzy that made the little girls peer at him uneasily. Wildly the horse careered, the waving dark hair of the boy tossed, his eyes had a strange glare in them. The little girls dared not speak to him.

When he had ridden to the end of his mad little journey, he climbed down and stood in front of his rocking-horse, staring fixedly into its lowered face. Its red mouth was slightly open, its big eye was wide and glassy-bright.

"Now!" he would silently command the snorting steed. "Now, take me to where there is luck! Now take me!"

And he would slash the horse on the neck with the little whip he had asked Uncle Oscar for. He knew the horse could take him to where there was luck, if only he forced it. So he would mount again, and start on his furious ride, hoping at last to get there. He knew he could get there.

"You'll break your horse, Paul!" said the nurse.

"He's always riding like that! I wish he'd leave off!" said his elder sister Joan.

But he only glared down on them in silence. Nurse gave him up. She could make nothing of him. Anyhow he was growing beyond her.

One day his mother and his Uncle Oscar came in when he was on one of his furious rides. He did not speak to them.

"Hallo, you young jockey! Riding a winner?" said his uncle.

"Aren't you growing too big for a rocking-horse? You're not a very little boy any longer, you know," said his mother.

But Paul only gave a blue glare from his big, rather close-set eyes. He would speak to nobody when he was in full tilt. His mother watched him with an anxious expression on her face.

At last he suddenly stopped forcing his horse into the mechanical gallop, and slid down.

"Well, I got there!" he announced fiercely, his blue eyes still flaring, and his sturdy long legs straddling apart.

"Where did you get to?" asked his mother.

"Where I wanted to go," he flared back at her.

"That's right, son!" said Uncle Oscar. "Don't you stop till you get there. What's the horse's name?"

"He doesn't have a name," said the boy.

"Gets on without all right?" asked the uncle.

"Well, he has different names. He was called Sansovino last week."

"Sansovino, eh? Won the Ascot. How did you know his name?"

"He always talks about horse-races with Bassett," said Joan.

The uncle was delighted to find that his small nephew was posted with all the racing news. Bassett, the young gardener, who had been wounded in the left foot in the war and had got his present job through Oscar Cresswell, whose batman he had been, was a perfect blade of the "turf." He lived in the racing events, and the small boy lived with him.

Oscar Cresswell got it all from Bassett.

"Master Paul comes and asks me, so I can't do more than tell him, sir," said Bassett, his face terribly serious, as if he were speaking of religious matters.

"And does he ever put anything on a horse he fancies?"

"Well—I don't want to give him away—he's a young sport, a fine sport, sir. Would you mind asking him yourself? He sort of takes a pleasure in it, and perhaps he'd feel I was giving him away, sir, if you don't mind."

Bassett was serious as a church.

The uncle went back to his nephew, and took him off for a ride in the car.

"Say, Paul, old man, do you ever put anything on a horse?" the uncle asked.

The boy watched the handsome man closely.

"Why, do you think I oughtn't to?" he parried.

"Not a bit of it! I thought perhaps you might give me a tip for the Lincoln."

The car sped on into the country, going down to Uncle Oscar's place in Hampshire.

"Honour bright?" said the nephew.

"Honour bright, son!" said the uncle.

"Well, then, Daffodil."

"Daffodil! I doubt it, sonny. What about Mirza?"

"I only know the winner," said the boy. "That's Daffodil."

"Daffodil, eh?"

There was a pause. Daffodil was an obscure horse comparatively.

"Uncle!"

"Yes, son?"

"You won't let it go any further, will you? I promised Bassett."

"Bassett be damned, old man! What's he got to do with it?"

"We're partners. We've been partners from the first. Uncle, he lent me my first five shillings, which I lost. I promised him, honour bright, it was only between me and him; only you gave me that ten-shilling note I started winning with, so I thought you were lucky. You won't let it go any further, will you?"

The boy gazed at his uncle from those big, hot, blue eyes, set rather close together. The uncle stirred and laughed uneasily.

"Right you are, son! I'll keep your tip private. Daffodil, eh? How much are you putting on him?"

"All except twenty pounds," said the boy. "I keep that in reserve."

The uncle thought it a good joke.

"You keep twenty pounds in reserve, do you, you young romancer? What are you betting, then?"

"I'm betting three hundred," said the boy gravely. "But it's between you and me, Uncle Oscar! Honour bright?"

The uncle burst into a roar of laughter.

"It's between you and me all right, you young Nat Gould," he said, laughing. "But where's your three hundred?"

"Bassett keeps it for me. We're partners."

"You are, are you? And what is Bassett putting on Daffodil?"

"He won't go quite as high as I do, I expect. Perhaps he'll go a hundred and fifty."

"What, pennies?" laughed the uncle.

"Pounds," said the child, with a surprised look at his uncle. "Bassett keeps a bigger reserve than I do."

Between wonder and amusement Uncle Oscar was silent. He pursued the matter no further, but he determined to take his nephew with him to the Lincoln races.

"Now, son," he said, "I'm putting twenty on Mirza, and I'll put five for you on any horse you fancy. What's your pick?"

"Daffodil, uncle."

"No, not the fiver on Daffodil!"

"I should if it was my own fiver," said the child.

"Good! Good! Right you are! A fiver for me and a fiver for you on Daffodil."

The child had never been to a race-meeting before, and his eyes were blue fire. He pursed his mouth tight, and watched. A Frenchman just in front had put his money on Lancelot. Wild with excitement, he flayed his arms up and down, yelling "Lancelot! Lancelot!" in his French accent.

Daffodil came in first, Lancelot second, Mirza third. The child, flushed and with eyes blazing, was curiously serene. His uncle brought him four five-pound notes, four to one.

"What am I to do with these?" he cried, waving them before the boy's eyes.

"I suppose we'll talk to Bassett," said the boy. "I expect I have fifteen hundred now; and twenty in reserve; and this twenty."

His uncle studied him for some moments.

"Look here, son!" he said. "You're not serious about Bassett and that fifteen hundred, are you?"

"Yes, I am. But it's between you and me, uncle. Honour bright!"

"Honour bright all right, son! But I must talk to Bassett."

"If you'd like to be a partner, uncle, with Bassett and me, we could all be partners. Only, you'd have to promise, honour bright, uncle, not to let it go beyond us three. Bassett and I are lucky, and you must be lucky, because it was your ten shillings I started winning with. . . ."

Uncle Oscar took both Bassett and Paul into Richmond Park for an afternoon, and there they talked

"It's like this, you see, sir," Bassett said. "Master Paul would get me talking about racing events, spinning yarns, you know, sir. And he was always keen on knowing if I'd made or if I'd lost. It's about a year since, now, that I put five shillings on Blush of Dawn for him—and we lost. Then the luck turned, with that ten shillings he had from you, that we put on Singhalese. And since that time, it's been pretty steady, all things considering. What do you say, Master Paul?"

"We're all right when we're sure," said Paul. "It's when we're not quite sure that we go down."

"Oh, but we're careful then," said Bassett.

"But when are you sure?" smiled Uncle Oscar.

"It's Master Paul, sir," said Bassett, in a secret, religious voice. "It's as if he had it from heaven. Like Daffodil, now, for the Lincoln. That was as sure as eggs."

"Did you put anything on Daffodil?" asked Oscar Cresswell.

"Yes, sir. I made my bit."

"And my nephew?"

Bassett was obstinately silent, looking at Paul.

"I made twelve hundred, didn't I, Bassett? I told uncle I was putting three hundred on Daffodil."

"That's right," said Bassett, nodding.

"But where's the money?" asked the uncle.

"I keep it safe locked up, sir. Master Paul he can have it any minute he likes to ask for it."

"What, fifteen hundred pounds?"

"And twenty! And forty, that is, with the twenty he made on the course."

"It's amazing!" said the uncle.

"If Master Paul offers you to be partners, sir, I would, if I were you; if you'll excuse me," said Bassett.

Oscar Cresswell thought about it.

"I'll see the money," he said.

They drove home again, and sure enough, Bassett came round to the garden-house with fifteen hundred pounds in notes. The twenty pounds reserve was left with Joe Glee, in the Turf Commission deposit.

"You see, it's all right, uncle, when I'm sure! Then we go strong, for all we're worth. Don't we, Bassett?"

"We do that, Master Paul."

"And when are you sure?" said the uncle, laughing.

"Oh, well, sometimes I'm absolutely sure, like about Daffodil," said the boy; "and sometimes I have an idea; and sometimes I haven't even an idea, have I, Bassett? Then we're careful, because we mostly go down."

"You do, do you! And when you're sure, like about Daffodil, what makes you sure, sonny?"

"Oh, well, I don't know," said the boy uneasily. "I'm sure, you know, uncle; that's all."

"It's as if he had it from heaven, sir," Bassett reiterated.

"I should say so!" said the uncle.

But he became a partner. And when the Leger was coming on, Paul was "sure" about Lively Spark, which was a quite inconsiderable horse. The boy insisted on putting a thousand on the horse, Bassett went for five hundred, and Oscar Cresswell two hundred. Lively Spark came in first, and the betting had been ten to one against him. Paul had made ten thousand.

"You see," he said. "I was absolutely sure of him."

Even Oscar Cresswell had cleared two thousand.

"Look here, son," he said, "this sort of thing makes me nervous."

"It needn't, uncle! Perhaps I shan't be sure again for a long time."

"But what are you going to do with your money?" asked the uncle.

"Of course," said the boy, "I started it for mother. She said she had no luck, because father is unlucky, so I thought if I was lucky, it might stop whispering."

"What might stop whispering?"

"Our house. I hate our house for whispering."

"What does it whisper?"

"Why—why"—the boy fidgeted—"Why, I don't know. But it's always short of money, you know, uncle."

"I know it, son, I know it."

"You know people send mother writs, don't you, uncle?"

"I'm afraid I do," said the uncle.

"And then the house whispers, like people laughing at you behind your back. It's awful, that is! I thought if I was lucky . . ."

"You might stop it," added the uncle.

The boy watched him with big blue eyes that had an uncanny cold fire in them, and he said never a word.

"Well, then!" said the uncle. "What are we doing?"

"I shouldn't like mother to know I was lucky," said the boy.

"Why not, son?"

"She'd stop me."

"I don't think she would."

"Oh!"—and the boy writhed in an odd way—"I don't want her to know, uncle."

"All right, son! We'll manage it without her knowing."

They managed it very easily. Paul, at the other's suggestion, handed over five thousand pounds to his uncle, who deposited it with the family lawyer, who was then to inform Paul's mother that a relative had put five thousand pounds into his hands, which sum was to be paid out a thousand pounds at a time, on the mother's birthday, for the next five years.

"So she'll have a birthday present of a thousand pounds for five successive years," said Uncle Oscar. "I hope it won't make it all the harder for her later."

Paul's mother had her birthday in November. The house had been "whispering" worse than ever lately, and, even in spite of his luck, Paul could not bear up against it. He was very anxious to see the effect of the birthday letter, telling his mother about the thousand pounds.

When there were no visitors, Paul now took his meals with his parents, as he was beyond the nursery control. His mother went into town nearly every day. She had discovered that she had an odd knack of sketching furs and dress materials, so she worked secretly in the studio of a friend who was the chief "artist" for the leading drapers. She drew the figures of ladies in furs and ladies in silk and sequins for the newspaper advertisements. This young woman artist earned several thousand pounds a year, but Paul's mother only made several hundred, and she was again dissatisfied. She so wanted to be first in something, and she did not succeed, even in making sketches for drapery advertisements.

She was down to breakfast on the morning of her birthday. Paul watched her face as she read her letters. He knew the lawyer's letter. As his mother read it, her face hardened and became more expressionless. Then a cold, determined look came on her mouth. She hid the letter under the pile of others, and said not a word about it.

"Didn't you have anything nice in the post for your birthday, mother?" said Paul.

"Quite moderately nice," she said, her voice cold and absent.

She went away to town without saying more.

But in the afternoon Uncle Oscar appeared. He said Paul's mother had had a long interview with the lawyer, asking if the whole five thousand could be advanced at once, as she was in debt.

"What do you think, uncle?" said the boy.

"I leave it to you, son."

"Oh, let her have it, then! We can get some more with the other," said the boy.

"A bird in the hand is worth two in the bush, laddie!" said Uncle Oscar.

"But I'm sure to know for the Grand National; or the Lincolnshire; or else the Derby. I'm sure to know for one of them," said Paul.

So Uncle Oscar signed the agreement, and Paul's mother touched the whole five thousand. Then something very curious happened. The voices in the house suddenly went mad, like a chorus of frogs on a spring evening. There were certain new furnishings, and Paul had a tutor. He was really going to Eton, his father's school, in the following autumn. There were flowers in the winter, and a blossoming of the luxury Paul's mother had been used to. And yet the voices in the house, behind the sprays of mimosa and almond blossom, and from under the piles of iridescent cushions, simply trilled and screamed in a sort of ecstasy: "There must be more money! Oh-h-h, there must be more money. Oh, now, now-w! Now-w-w—there must be more money!—more than ever! More than ever!"

It frightened Paul terribly. He studied away at his Latin and Greek with his tutors. But his intense hours were spent with Bassett. The Grand National had gone by: he had not "known," and had lost a hundred pounds. Summer was at hand. He was in agony for the Lincoln. But even for the Lincoln he didn't "know" and he lost fifty pounds. He became wild-eyed and strange, as if something were going to explode in him.

"Let it alone, son! Don't you bother about it!" urged Uncle Oscar. But it was as if the boy couldn't really hear what his uncle was saying

"I've got to know for the Derby! I've got to know for the Derby!" the child reiterated, his big blue eyes blazing with a sort of madness.

His mother noticed how overwrought he was.

"You'd better go to the seaside. Wouldn't you like to go now to the seaside, instead of waiting? I think you'd better," she said, looking down at him anxiously, her heart curiously heavy because of him.

But the child lifted his uncanny blue eyes.

"I couldn't possibly go before the Derby, mother!" he said. "I couldn't possibly!"

"Why not?" she said, her voice becoming heavy when she was opposed. "Why not? You can still go from the seaside to see the Derby with your Uncle Oscar, if that's what you wish. No need for you to wait here. Besides, I think you care too much about these races. It's a bad sign. My family has been a gambling family, and you won't know till you grow up how much damage it has done. But it has done damage. I shall have to send Bassett away, and ask Uncle Oscar not to talk racing to you, unless you promise to be reasonable about it; go away to the seaside and forget it. You're all nerves!"

"I'll do what you like, mother, so long as you don't send me away till after the Derby," the boy said.

"Send you away from where? Just from this house?"

"Yes," he said, gazing at her.

"Why, you curious child, what makes you care about this house so much, suddenly? I never knew you loved it."

He gazed at her without speaking. He had a secret within a secret, something he had not divulged, even to Bassett or to his Uncle Oscar.

But his mother, after standing undecided and a little bit sullen for some moments, said:

"Very well, then! Don't go to the seaside till after the Derby, if you don't wish it. But promise me you won't let your nerves go to pieces. Promise you won't think so much about horse-racing and events, as you call them!"

"Oh, no," said the boy casually. "I won't think much about them, mother. You needn't worry. I wouldn't worry, mother, if I were you."

"If you were me and I were you," said his mother, "I wonder what we should do!"

"But you know you needn't worry, mother, don't you?" the boy repeated.

"I should be awfully glad to know it," she said wearily.

"Oh, well, you can, you know. I mean, you ought to know you needn't worry," he insisted.

"Ought I? Then I'll see about it," she said.

Paul's secret of secrets was his wooden horse, that which had no name. Since he was emancipated from a nurse and a nursery-governess, he had had his rocking-horse removed to his own bedroom at the top of the house.

"Surely, you're too big for a rocking-horse!" his mother had remonstrated.

"Well, you see, mother, till I can have a real horse, I like to have some sort of animal about," had been his quaint answer.

"Do you feel he keeps you company?" she laughed.

"Oh, yes! He's very good, he always keeps me company, when I'm there," said Paul.

So the horse, rather shabby, stood in an arrested prance in the boy's bedroom.

The Derby was drawing near, and the boy grew more and more tense. He hardly heard what was spoken to him, he was very frail, and his eyes were really uncanny. His mother had sudden seizures of uneasiness about him. Sometimes, for half-an-hour, she would feel a sudden anxiety about him that was almost anguish. She wanted to rush to him at once, and know he was safe.

Two nights before the Derby, she was at a big party in town, when one of her rushes of anxiety about her boy, her first-born, gripped her heart till she could hardly speak. She fought with the feeling, might and main, for she believed in common sense. But it was too strong. She had to leave the dance and go downstairs to telephone to the country. The children's nursery-governess was terribly surprised and startled at being rung up in the night.

"Are the children all right, Miss Wilmot?"

"Oh, yes they are quite all right."

"Master Paul? Is he all right?"

"He went to bed as right as a trivet. Shall I run up and look at him?"

"No," said Paul's mother reluctantly. "No! Don't trouble. It's all right. Don't sit up. We shall be home fairly soon." She did not want her son's privacy intruded upon.

"Very good," said the governess.

It was about one o'clock when Paul's mother and father drove up to their house. All was still. Paul's mother went to her room and slipped off her white fur cloak. She had told her maid not to wait up for her. She heard her husband downstairs, mixing a whisky-and-soda.

And then, because of the strange anxiety at her heart, she stole upstairs to her son's room. Noiselessly she went along the upper corridor. Was there a faint noise? What was it?

She stood, with arrested muscles, outside his door, listening. There was a strange, heavy, and yet not loud noise. Her heart stood still. It was a soundless noise, yet rushing and powerful. Something huge, in violent, hushed motion. What was it? What in God's name was it? She ought to know. She felt that she knew the noise. She knew what it was.

Yet she could not place it. She couldn't say what it was. And on and on it went, like a madness.

Softly, frozen with anxiety and fear, she turned the door-handle.

The room was dark. Yet in the space near the window, she heard and saw something plunging to and fro. She gazed in fear and amazement.

Then suddenly she switched on the light, and saw her son, in his green pyjamas, madly surging on the rocking-horse. The blaze of light suddenly lit him up, as he urged the wooden horse, and lit her up, as she stood, blonde, in her dress of pale green and crystal, in the doorway.

"Paul!" she cried. "Whatever are you doing?"

"It's Malabar!" he screamed, in a powerful, strange voice. "It's Malabar."

His eyes blazed at her for one strange and senseless second, as he ceased urging his wooden horse. Then he fell with a crash to the ground, and she, all her tormented motherhood flooding upon her, rushed to gather him up.

But he was unconscious, and unconscious he remained, with some brain-fever. He talked and tossed, and his mother sat stonily by his side.

"Malabar! It's Malabar! Bassett, Bassett, I know! It's Malabar!"

So the child tried, trying to get up and urge the rocking-horse that gave him his inspiration.

"What does he mean by Malabar?" asked the heart-frozen mother.

"I don't know," said the father stonily.

"What does he mean by Malabar?" she asked her brother Oscar.

"It's one of the horses running for the Derby," was the answer.

And, in spite of himself, Oscar Cresswell spoke to Bassett, and himself put a thousand on Malabar: at fourteen to one.

The third day of the illness was critical: they were waiting for a change. The boy, with his rather long, curly hair, was tossing ceaselessly on the pillow. He neither slept nor regained consciousness, and his eyes were like blue stones. His mother sat, feeling her heart had gone, turned actually into a stone.

In the evening, Oscar Cresswell did not come, but Bassett sent a message, saying could he come up for one moment, just one moment? Paul's mother was very angry at the intrusion, but on second thought she agreed. The boy was the same. Perhaps Bassett might bring him to consciousness.

The gardener, a shortish fellow with a little brown moustache, and sharp little brown eyes, tiptoed into the room, touched his imaginary cap to Paul's mother, and stole to the bedside, staring with glittering, smallish eyes, at the tossing, dying child.

"Master Paul!" he whispered. "Master Paul! Malabar come in first all right, a clean win. I did as you told me. You've made over seventy thousand pounds, you have; you've got over eighty thousand. Malabar came in all right, Master Paul!"

"Malabar! Malabar! Did I say Malabar, mother? Did I say Malabar? Do you think I'm lucky, mother? I knew Malabar, didn't I? Over eighty thousand pounds! I call that lucky, don't you, mother? Over eighty thousand pounds! I knew, didn't I know I knew? Malabar came in all right. If I ride my horse till I'm sure, then I tell you, Bassett, you can go as high as you like. Did you go for all you were worth, Bassett?"

"I went a thousand on it, Master Paul."

"I never told you, mother, that if I can ride my horse, and get there, then I'm absolutely sure—oh, absolutely! Mother, did I ever tell you? I am lucky."

"No, you never did," said the mother.

But the boy died in the night.

And even as he lay dead, his mother heard her brother's voice saying to her: "My God, Hester, you're eighty-odd thousand to the good and a poor devil of a son to the bad. But, poor devil, poor devil, he's best gone out of a life where he rides his rocking-horse to find a winner."

Beyond Categories

As real life is more multifaceted than any literary representation of it, so are the varieties of the short story more numerous than the classifications that we contrive. The following stories differ in many respects from those we have met earlier in the book and they differ from each other.

Kafka's story is freighted with symbolism. Various interpretations of the symbols are possible, but in one coherent view the story describes the demise of Western civilization. If we see the palace as the church, its guards as the theologians and artists who developed its value system, and the shoemaker and the butcher as its merchants, we can ascertain who the nomads are and how these predators destroyed the most promising venture ever undertaken by the human race. An equally grim, perhaps a grimmer, prognosis is given by Ray Bradbury in a science-fiction story called "There Will Come Soft Rains." In "Old Red" Caroline Gordon asks us to consider again the perennial question of balancing the rights of the individual against those of the group. Because her sympathies lean toward individualism, she exults in wily old Maury's victory over the forces that would make him into something other than what he is.

An Old Manuscript*
by FRANZ KAFKA

It looks as if much had been neglected in our country's system of defense. We have not concerned ourselves with it until now and have gone about our daily work; but things that have been happening recently begin to trouble us.

I have a cobbler's workshop in the square that lies before the Emperor's palace. Scarcely have I taken my shutters down, at the first glimmer of dawn, when I see armed soldiers already posted in the mouth of every street opening on the square. But these soldiers are not ours, they are obviously nomads from the North. In some way that is incomprehensible to me they have pushed right into the capital, although it is a long way from the frontier. At any rate, here they are; it seems that every morning there are more of them.

As is their nature, they camp under the open sky, for they abominate dwelling houses. They busy themselves sharpening swords, whittling arrows and practicing horsemanship. This peaceful square, which was always kept so scrupulously clean, they have made literally into a stable. We do try every now and then to run out of our shops and clear away at least the worst of the filth, but this happens less and less often, for the labor is in vain and brings us besides into danger of falling under the hoofs of the wild horses or of being crippled with lashes from the whips.

Speech with the nomads is impossible. They do not know our language, indeed they hardly have a language of their own. They communicate with each other much as jackdaws do. A screeching as of jackdaws is always in our ears. Our way of living and our

---

* From *The Penal Colony*, by Franz Kafka, translated by Willa and Edwin Muir (New York: Schocken Books, 1948). Reprinted by permission of Schocken Books and Secker & Warburg, Ltd.

institutions they neither understand nor care to understand. And so they are unwilling to make sense even out of our sign language. You can gesture at them till you dislocate your jaws and your wrists and still they will not have understood you and will never understand. They often make grimaces; then the whites of their eyes turn up and foam gathers on their lips, but they do not mean anything by that, not even a threat; they do it because it is their nature to do it. Whatever they need, they take. You cannot call it taking by force. They grab at something and you simply stand aside and leave them to it.

From my stock, too, they have taken many good articles. But I cannot complain when I see how the butcher, for instance, suffers across the street. As soon as he brings in any meat the nomads snatch it all from him and gobble it up. Even their horses devour flesh; often enough a horseman and his horse are lying side by side, both of them gnawing at the same joint, one at either end. The butcher is nervous and does not dare to stop his deliveries of meat. We understand that, however, and subscribe money to keep him going. If the nomads got no meat, who knows what they might think of doing; who knows anyhow what they may think of, even though they get meat every day.

Not long ago the butcher thought he might at least spare himself the trouble of slaughtering, and so one morning he brought along a live ox. But he will never dare to do that again. I lay for a whole hour flat on the floor at the back of my workshop with my head muffled in all the clothes and rugs and pillows I had, simply to keep from hearing the bellowing of that ox, which the nomads were leaping on from all sides, tearing morsels out of its living flesh with their teeth. It had been quiet for a long time before I risked coming out; they were lying overcome round the remains of the carcass like drunkards round a wine cask.

This was the occasion when I fancied I actually saw the Emperor himself at a window of the palace; usually he never enters these outer rooms but spends all his time in the innermost garden; yet on this occasion he was standing, or so at least it seemed to me, at one of the windows, watching with bent head the ongoings before his residence.

"What is going to happen?" we all ask ourselves. "How long can we endure this burden and torment? The Emperor's palace has drawn the nomads here but does not know how to drive them away again. The gate stays shut; the guards, who used to be always marching out and in with ceremony, keep close behind barred windows. It is left to us artisans and tradesmen to save our country; but we are not equal to such a task; nor have we ever claimed to be capable of it. This is a misunderstanding of some kind; and it will be the ruin of us."

There Will Come Soft Rains*

by RAY BRADBURY

The house was a good house and had been planned and built by the people who were to live in it, in the year 1980. The house was like many another house in that year; it fed and slept and entertained its inhabitants, and made a good life for them. The man and wife and their two children lived at ease there, and lived happily, even while the world trembled. All of the fine things of living, the warm things, music and poetry, books that talked, beds that warmed and made themselves, fires that built themselves in the fireplaces of evenings, were in this house, and living there was a contentment.

And then one day the world shook and there was an explosion followed by ten thousand explosions and red fire in the sky and a rain of ashes and radioactivity, and the happy time was over.

---

* Copyright 1950 by Ray Bradbury. Reprinted by permission of Harold Matson Company, Inc.

In the living room the voice-clock sang, *Tick-tock, seven A.M. o'clock, time to get up!* as if it were afraid nobody would. The house lay empty. The clock talked on into the empty morning.

The kitchen stove sighed and ejected from its warm interior eight eggs, sunny side up, twelve bacon slices, two coffees, and two cups of hot cocoa. *Seven nine, breakfast time, seven nine.*

"Today is April 28th, 1985," said a phonograph voice in the kitchen ceiling. "Today, remember, is Mr. Featherstone's birthday. Insurance, gas, light and water bills are due."

Somewhere in the walls, relays clicked, memory tapes glided under electric eyes. Recorded voices moved beneath steel needles:

Eight one, run, run, off to school, off to work, run, run, ticktock, eight one o'clock!

But no doors slammed, no carpets took the quick tread of rubber heels. Outside, it was raining. The voice of the weather box on the front door sang quietly: "Rain, rain, go away, rubbers, raincoats for today." And the rain tapped on the roof.

At eight thirty the eggs were shriveled. An aluminum wedge scraped them into the sink, where hot water whirled them down a metal throat which digested and flushed them away to the distant sea.

Nine fifteen, sang the clock, *time to clean.*

Out of warrens in the wall, tiny mechanical mice darted. The rooms were acrawl with the small cleaning animals, all rubber and metal. They sucked up the hidden dust, and popped back in their burrows.

Ten o'clock. The sun came out from behind the rain. The house stood alone on a street where all the other houses were rubble and ashes. At night, the ruined town gave off a radioactive glow which could be seen for miles.

Ten fifteen. The garden sprinkler filled the soft morning air with golden fountains. The water tinkled over the charred west side of the house where it had been scorched evenly free of its white paint. The entire face of the house was black, save for five places. Here, the silhouette, in paint, of a man mowing a lawn. Here, a woman bent to pick flowers. Still farther over, their images burned on wood in one titanic instant, a small boy, hands flung in the air—higher up, the image of a thrown ball —and opposite him a girl, her hands raised to catch a ball which never came down.

The five spots of paint—the man, the woman, the boy, the girl, the ball—remained. The rest was a thin layer of charcoal.

The gentle rain of the sprinkler filled the garden with falling light.

Until this day, how well the house had kept its peace. How carefully it had asked, "Who goes there?" and getting no reply from rains and lonely foxes and whining cats, it had shut up its windows and drawn the shades. If a sparrow brushed a window, the shade snapped up. The bird, startled, flew off! No, not even an evil bird must touch the house.

And inside, the house was like an altar with nine thousand robot attendants, big and small, servicing, attending, singing in choirs, even though the gods had gone away and the ritual was meaningless.

A dog whined, shivering, on the front porch.

The front door recognized the dog voice and opened. The dog padded in wearily, thinned to the bone, covered with sores. It tracked mud on the carpet. Behind it whirred the angry robot mice, angry at having to pick up mud and maple leaves, which, carried to the burrows, were dropped down cellar tubes into an incinerator which sat like an evil Baal in a dark corner.

The dog ran upstairs, hysterically yelping at each door. It pawed the kitchen door wildly.

Behind the door, the stove was making pancakes which filled the whole house with their odor.

The dog frothed, ran insanely, spun in a circle, biting its tail, and died.

It lay in the living room for an hour.

One o'clock.

Delicately sensing decay, the regiments of mice hummed out of the walls, soft as blown leaves, their electric eyes blowing.

One fifteen.

The dog was gone.

The cellar incinerator glowed suddenly and a whirl of sparks leaped up the flue.

Two thirty-five.

Bridge tables sprouted from the patio walls. Playing cards fluttered onto pads in a shower of pips. Martinis appeared on an oaken bench.

But the tables were silent, the cards untouched.

At four thirty the tables folded back into the walls.

Five o'clock. The bathtubs filled with clear hot water. A safety razor dropped into a wall-mold, ready.

Six, seven, eight, nine o'clock

Dinner made, ignored, and flushed away; dishes washed; and in the study, the tobacco stand produced a cigar, half an inch of gray ash on it, smoking, waiting. The hearth fire bloomed up all by itself, out of nothing.

Nine o'clock. The beds began to warm their hidden circuits, for the night was cool.

A gentle click in the study wall. A voice spoke from above the crackling fireplace:

"Mrs. McClellan, what poem would you like to hear this evening?"

The house was silent.

The voice said, "Since you express no preference, I'll pick a poem at random." Quiet music rose behind the voice. "Sara Teasdale. A favorite of yours, as I recall."

> *"There will come soft rains and the smell of the ground,*
> *And swallows circling with their shimmering sound;*
>
> *And frogs in the pools singing at night,*
> *And wild plum-trees in tremulous white.*
>
> *Robins will wear their feathery fire*
> *Whistling their whims on a low fence-wire;*
>
> *And not one will know of the war, not one*
> *Will care at last when it is done.*
>
> *Not one would mind, neither bird nor tree,*
> *If mankind perished utterly;*
>
> *And Spring herself, when she woke at dawn,*
> *Would scarcely know that we were gone."*[1]

---

[1] Reprinted by permission of The Macmillan Company from *Flame and Shadow* by Sara Teasdale. Copyright 1920 by The Macmillan Company, renewed 1948 by Mamie T. Wheless.

The voice finished the poem. The empty chairs faced each other between the silent walls, and the music played.

At ten o'clock, the house began to die.

The wind blew. The bough of a falling tree smashed the kitchen window. Cleaning solvent, bottled, crashed on the stove.

"Fire!" screamed voices. "Fire!" Water pumps shot down water from the ceilings. But the solvent spread under the doors, making fire as it went, while other voices took up the alarm in chorus.

The windows broke with heat and the wind blew in to help the fire. Scurrying water rats, their copper wheels spinning, squeaked from the walls, squirted their water, ran for more.

Too late! Somewhere, a pump stopped. The ceiling sprays stopped raining. The reserve water supply, which had filled baths and washed dishes for many silent days, was gone.

The fire crackled upstairs, ate paintings, lay hungrily in the beds! It devoured every room.

The house was shuddering, oak bone on bone, the bared skeleton cringing from the heat, all the wires revealed as if a surgeon had torn the skin off to let the red veins quiver in scalded air. Voices screamed, *"Help, help, fire, run!"* Windows snapped open and shut, like mouths, undecided. *Fire, run!* the voices wailed a tragic nursery rhyme, and the silly Greek chorus faded as the sound-wires popped their sheathings. Ten dozen high, shrieking voices died, as emergency batteries melted.

In other parts of the house, in the last instant under the fire avalanche, other choruses could be heard announcing the time, the weather, appointments, diets; playing music, reading poetry in the fiery study, while doors opened and slammed and umbrellas appeared at the doors and put themselves away—a thousand things happening, like the interior of a clock shop at midnight, all clocks striking, a merry-go-round of squeaking, whispering, rushing, until all the film spools were burned and fell, and all the wires withered and the circuits cracked.

In the kitchen, an instant before the final

collapse, the stove, hysterically hissing, could be seen making breakfast at a psychopathic rate, ten dozen pancakes, six dozen loaves of toast.

The crash! The attic smashing kitchen down into cellar and subcellar. Deep freeze, armchairs, filmtapes, beds, were thrown in a cluttered mound deep under.

Smoke and silence.

Dawn shone faintly in the east. In the ruins, one wall stood alone. Within the wall, a voice said, over and over again and again, even as the sun rose to shine upon the heaped rubble and steam:

"Today is April 29th, 1985. Today is April 29th, 1985. Today is . . . ."

Old Red*

by CAROLINE GORDON

When the door had closed behind his daughter, Mister Maury went to the window and stood a few moments looking out. The roses that had grown in a riot all along that side of the fence had died or been cleared away, but the sun lay across the garden in the same level lances of light that he remembered. He turned back into the room. The shadows had gathered until it was nearly all in gloom. The top of his minnow bucket just emerging from the duffel bag glinted in the last rays of the sun. He stood looking down at his traps all gathered neatly in a heap at the foot of the bed. He would leave them like that. Even if they came in here sweeping and cleaning up—it was only in hotels that a man was master of his own room—even if they came in here cleaning up, he would tell them to leave all his things exactly as they were. It was reassuring to see them all there together, ready to be taken up in the hand, to be carried down and put into a car, to be driven off to some railroad station at a moment's notice.

As he moved toward the door, he spoke aloud, a habit that was growing on him:

"Anyhow, I won't stay but a week. . . . I ain't going to stay but a week, no matter what they say. . . ."

Downstairs in the dining room they were already gathered at the supper table, his white-haired, shrunken mother-in-law, his tall sister-in-law who had the proud carriage of the head, the aquiline nose, but not the spirit of his dead wife, his lean, blond new son-in-law, his black-eyed daughter who, but that she was thin, looked so much like him, all of them gathered there waiting for him, Alexander Maury. It occurred to him that this was the first time he had sat down in the bosom of the family for some years. They were always writing saying that he must make a visit this summer or certainly next fall. ". . . all had a happy Christmas together but missed you. . . ." They had even made the pretext that he ought to come up to inspect his new son-in-law. As if he hadn't always known exactly the kind of young man Sarah would marry! What was the boy's name? Stephen, yes, Stephen. He must be sure and remember that.

He sat down, and shaking out his napkin spread it over his capacious paunch and tucked it well up under his chin in the way his wife had never allowed him to do. He let his eyes rove over the table and released a long sigh.

"Hot batter bread," he said, "and ham. Merry Point ham. I sure am glad to taste them one more time before I die."

The old lady was sending the little Negro girl scurrying back to the kitchen for a hot plate of batter bread. He pushed aside the cold plate and waited. She had bridled when he spoke of the batter bread and a faint flush had dawned on her withered cheeks. Vain she had always been as a peacock, of her housekeeping,

---

* "Old Red" (Copyright 1933 Charles Scribner's Sons; renewal copyright © 1960 Caroline Gordon) is reprinted with the permission of Charles Scribner's Sons from *The Forest of the South* by Caroline Gordon.

her children, the animals on her place, anything that belonged to her. And she went on, even at her advanced age, making her batter bread, smoking her hams according to that old recipe she was so proud of; but who came here now to this old house to eat or to praise?

He helped himself to a generous slice of batter bread, buttered it, took the first mouthful and chewed it slowly. He shook his head.

"There ain't anything like it," he said. "There ain't anything else like it in this world."

His dark eye roving the table fell on his son-in-law. "You like batter bread?" he inquired.

Stephen nodded, smiling. Mister Maury, still masticating slowly, regarded his face, measured the space between the eyes—his favorite test for man, horse, or dog. Yes, there was room enough for sense between the eyes. But how young the boy looked! And infected already with the fatal germ, the *cacoëthes scribendi*. Well, their children would probably escape. It was like certain diseases of the eye, skipped every other generation. His own father had had it badly all his life. He could see him now sitting at the head of the table spouting his own poetry—or Shakespeare's—while the children watched the preserve dish to see if it was going around. He, Aleck Maury, had been lucky to be born in the generation he had. He had escaped that at least. A few translations from Heine in his courting days, a few fragments from the Greek, but no, he had kept clear of that on the whole. . . .

The eyes of his sister-in-law were fixed on him. She was smiling faintly. "You don't look much like dying, Aleck. Florida must agree with you."

The old lady spoke from the head of the table. "I can't see what you do with yourself all winter long. Doesn't time hang heavy on your hands?"

Time, he thought, time! They were always mouthing the word and what did they know about it? Nothing in God's world! He saw time suddenly, a dull, leaden-colored fabric depending from the old lady's hands, from the hands of all of them, a blanket that they pulled about, now this way, now that, trying to cover up their nakedness. Or they would cast it on the ground and creep in among the folds, finding one day a little more tightly rolled than another, but all of it everywhere the same dull gray substance. But time was a banner that whipped before him always in the wind. He stood on tiptoe to catch at the bright folds, to strain them to his bosom. They were bright and glittering. But they whipped by so fast and were whipping always ever faster. The tears came into his eyes. Where, for instance, had this year gone? He could swear he had not wasted a minute of it, for no man living, he thought, knew better how to make each day a pleasure to him. Not a minute wasted and yet here it was already May! If he lived to the Biblical three score and ten, which was all he ever allowed himself in his calculations, he had before him only nine more Mays. Only nine more Mays out of all eternity, and they wanted him to waste one of them sitting on the front porch at Merry Point!

The butter plate which had seemed to swim in a glittering mist was coming solidly to rest upon the white tablecloth. He winked his eyes rapidly and laying down his knife and fork squared himself about in his chair to address his mother-in-law:

"Well, ma'am, you know I'm a man that always likes to be learning something. Now this year I learned how to smell out fish." He glanced around the table, holding his head high and allowing his well-cut nostrils to flutter slightly with his indrawn breaths. "Yes, sir," he said, "I'm probably the only white man in this country knows how to smell out feesh."

There was a discreet smile on the faces of the others. Sarah was laughing outright. "Did you have to learn how or did it just come to you?" she asked.

"I learned it from an old nigger woman," her father said. He shook his head reminiscently. "It's wonderful how much you can learn from niggers. But you have to know how to handle them. I was half the winter wooing that old Fanny. . . ."

He waited until their laughter had died down. "We used to start off every morning from the same little cove and we'd drift in there together at night. I noticed how she always brought in a good string, so I says to her, 'Fanny, you just lemme go 'long with you.' But she wouldn't have nothing to do with me. I saw she was going to be a hard nut to crack, but kept right on. Finally I began giving her presents. . . ."

Laura was regarding him fixedly, a queer look on her face.

"What sort of presents did you give her, Aleck?"

He made his tones hearty in answer. "I gave her a fine string of fish one day and I gave her fifty cents. And finally I made her a present of a Barlow knife. That was when she broke down. She took me with her that morning. . . ."

"Could she really smell fish?" the old lady asked curiously.

"You ought to 'a' seen her," Mister Maury said. "She'd sail over that lake like a hound on the scent. She'd row right along and then all of a sudden she'd stop rowing." He bent over, wrinkling his nose and peering into the depths of imaginary water. " 'Thar they are, White Folks, thar they are. Cain't you smell 'em?' "

Stephen was leaning forward, eyeing his father-in-law intently. "Could you?" he asked.

"I got so I could smell feesh," Mister Maury told him. "I could smell out the feesh, but I couldn't tell which kind they were. Now Fanny could row over a bed and tell just by the smell whether it was bass or bream. But she'd been at it all her life." He paused, sighing. "You can't just pick these things up. You have to give yourself to them. Who was it said 'Gennius is an infinite capacity for taking pains'?"

Sarah was rising briskly. Her eyes sought her husband's across the table. She was still laughing. "Sir Izaak Walton," she said, "we'd better go in the other room. Mandy wants to clear the table."

The two older ladies remained in the dining room. Mister Maury walked across the hall to the sitting room, accompanied by Steve and Sarah. He lowered himself cautiously into the most solid-looking of the rocking chairs that were drawn up around the fire. Steve was standing on the hearthrug, back to the fire, gazing abstractedly off across the room.

Mister Maury glanced up at him curiously. "What are you thinking about, feller?" he asked.

Steve looked down. He smiled, but his gaze was still contemplative. "I was thinking about the sonnet," he said, "in the form in which it first came to England."

Mister Maury shook his head, "Wyatt and Surrey," he said. "Hey, nonny, nonny. . . . You'll have hardening of the liver long before you're my age." He looked past Steve's shoulder at the picture that hung over the mantel shelf: Cupid and Psyche holding between them a fluttering veil and running along a rocky path toward the beholder. "Old Merry Point," he said; "it don't change much, does it?"

He settled himself more solidly in his chair. His mind veered from the old house to his own wanderings in brighter places. He regarded his daughter and son-in-law affably.

"Yes, sir," he said, "this winter in Florida was valuable to me just for the acquaintances I made. Take my friend, Jim Barbee. Just to live in the same hotel with that man is an education." He paused, smiling reminiscently into the fire. "I'll never forget the first time I saw him. He came up to me there in the lobby of the hotel. 'Professor Maury!' he says, 'You been hearin' about me for twenty years and I been hearin' about you for twenty years. And now we've done met!' "

Sarah had sat down in the little rocking chair by the fire. She leaned toward him now, laughing. "They ought to have put down a cloth of gold for the meeting," she said.

Mister Maury shook his head. "Nature does that in Florida," he said. "I knew right off the reel it was him. There were half a dozen men standing around. I made 'em witness. 'Jim Barbee,' I says, 'Jim Barbee of Maysville or I'll eat my hat!' "

"Why is he so famous?" Sarah asked.

Mister Maury took out his knife and cut a slice from a plug of tobacco. When he had offered a slice to his son-in-law and it had been refused, he put the plug back in his pocket. "He's a man of imagination," he said slowly. "There ain't many in this world."

He took a small tin box out of his pocket and set it on the little table that held the lamp.

Removing the top he tilted the box so that they could see its contents: an artificial lure, a bug with a dark body and a red, bulbous head, a hook protruding from what might be considered its vitals.

"Look at her," he said, "ain't she a killer?"

Sarah leaned forward to look and Steve, still standing on the hearthrug, bent above them. The three heads ringed the light.

Mister Maury disregarded Sarah and addressed himself to Steve. "She takes nine strips of rind," he said, "nine strips just thick enough." He marked off the width of the strips with his two fingers on the table, then picking up the lure and cupping it in his palm he moved it back and forth quickly so that the painted eyes caught the light.

"Look at her," he said, "look at the wicked way she sets forward."

Sarah was poking at the lure with the tip of her finger.

"Wanton," she said, "simply wanton. What does he call her?"

"This is his Devil Bug," Mister Maury said. "He's the only man in this country makes it. I myself had the idea thirty years ago and let it slip by me the way I do with so many of my ideas." He sighed, then elevating his tremendous bulk slightly above the table level and continuing to hold Steve with his gaze he produced from his coat pocket the oilskin book that held his flies. He spread it open on the table and began to turn the pages. His eyes sought his son-in-law's as his hand paused before a gray, rather draggled-looking lure.

"Old Speck," he said. "I've had that fly for twenty years. I reckon she's taken five hundred pounds of fish in her day. . . ."

The fire burned lower. A fiery coal rolled from the grate and fell onto the hearthrug. Sarah scooped it up with a shovel and threw it among the ashes. In the circle of the lamplight the two men still bent over the table looking at the flies. Steve was absorbed in them but he spoke seldom. It was her father's voice that rising and falling filled the room. He talked a great deal, but he had a beautiful speaking voice. He was telling Steve now about Little West Fork, the first stream ever he put a fly in.

"My first love," he kept calling it. It sounded rather pretty, she thought, in his mellow voice. "My first love . . ."

II

When Mister Maury came downstairs the next morning the dining room was empty except for his daughter, Sarah, who sat dawdling over a cup of coffee and a cigarette. Mister Maury sat down opposite her. To the little Negro girl who presented herself at his elbow he outlined his wants briefly. "A cup of coffee and some hot batter bread just like we had last night." He turned to his daughter. "Where's Steve?"

"He's working," she said, "he was up at eight and he's been working ever since."

Mister Maury accepted the cup of coffee from the little girl, poured half of it into his saucer, set it aside to cool. "Ain't it wonderful," he said, "the way a man can sit down and work day after day? When I think of all the work I've done in my time. . . . Can he work *every* morning?"

"He sits down at his desk every morning," she said, "but of course he gets more done some mornings than others."

Mister Maury picked up the saucer, found the coffee cool enough for his taste. He sipped it slowly, looking out of the window. His mind was already busy with his day's program. No water—no running water—nearer than West Fork three miles away. He couldn't drive a car and Steve was going to be busy writing all morning. There was nothing for it but a pond. The Willow Sink. It was not much but it was better than nothing. He pushed his chair back and rose.

"Well," he said, "I'd better be starting."

When he came downstairs with his rod a few minutes later the hall was still full of the sound of measured typing. Sarah sat in the dining room in the same position in which he had left her, smoking. Mister Maury paused in the doorway while he slung his canvas bag over his shoulders. "How you ever going to get anything done if you don't take advantage of the morning hours?" he asked. He glanced at the door opposite as if it had been the entrance to a sick chamber.

"What's he writing about?" he inquired in a whisper.

"It's an essay on John Skelton."

Mister Maury looked out at the new green leaves framed in the doorway. "John Skelton," he said. "God Almighty!"

He went through the hall and stepped down off the porch onto the ground that was still moist with spring rains. As he crossed the lower yard he looked up into the branches of the maples. Yes, the leaves were full grown already even on the late trees. The year, how swiftly, how steadily it advanced! He had come to the far corner of the yard. Grown up it was in pokeberry shoots and honeysuckle, but there was a place to get through. The top strand of wire had been pulled down and fastened to the others with a ragged piece of rope. He rested his weight on his good leg and swung himself over onto the game one. It gave him a good, sharp twinge when he came down on it. It was getting worse all the time, that leg, but on the other hand he was learning better all the time how to handle it. His mind flew back to a dark, startled moment, that day when the cramp first came on him. He had been sitting still in the boat all day long and that evening when he had stood up to get out his leg had failed him utterly. He had pitched forward among the reeds, had lain there a second, face downwards, before it came to him what had happened. With the realization came a sharp picture of his faraway youth: Uncle Quent lowering himself ponderously out of the saddle after a hard day's hunting had fallen forward in exactly the same way, into a knot of yowling little Negroes. He had got up and cursed them all out of the lot. It had scared the old boy to death, coming down like that. The black dog he had had on his shoulder all that fall. But he himself had never lost one day's fishing on account of his leg. He had known from the start how to handle it. It meant simply that he was slowed down that much. It hadn't really made much difference in fishing. He didn't do as much wading but he got around just about as well on the whole. Hunting, of course, had had to go. You couldn't walk all day shooting birds, dragging a game leg. He had just given it up right off the reel, though it was a shame when a man was as good a shot as he was. That day he was out with Tom Kensington last November, the only day he got out during the season. Nine shots he'd had and he'd bagged nine birds. Yes, it was a shame. But a man couldn't do everything. He had to limit himself. . . .

He was up over the little rise now. The field slanted straight down before him to where the pond lay, silver in the morning sun. A Negro cabin was perched halfway up the opposite slope. A woman was hanging out washing on a line stretched between two trees. From the open doorway little Negroes spilled down the path toward the pond. Mister Maury surveyed the scene, spoke aloud:

"Ain't it funny now? Niggers always live in the good places."

He stopped under a wild cherry tree to light his pipe. It had been hot crossing the field, but the sunlight here was agreeably tempered by the branches. And that pond down there was fringed with willows. His eyes sought the bright disk of the water, then rose to where the smoke from the cabin chimney lay in a soft plume along the crest of the hill.

When he stooped to pick up his rod again it was with a feeling of sudden, keen elation. An image had risen in his memory, an image that was familiar but came to him infrequently of late and that only in moments of elation: the wide field in front of his uncle's old house in Albemarle, on one side the dark line of undergrowth that marked the Rivanna River, on the other the blue of Peters' Mountain. They would be waiting there in that broad plain when they had the first sight of the fox. On that little rise by the river, loping steadily, not yet alarmed. The sun would glint on his bright coat, on his quick-turning head as he dove into the dark of the woods. There would be hullabaloo after that and shouting and riding. Sometimes there was the tailing of the fox— that time old Whisky was brought home on a mattress! All of that to come afterward, but none of it ever like that first sight of the fox there on the broad plain between the river and the mountain.

There was one fox, they grew to know him in time, to call him affectionately by name. Old Red it was who showed himself always like that there on the crest of the hill. "There he goes, the damn' impudent scoundrel!" . . . Uncle Quent would shout and slap his thigh and yell himself hoarse at Whisky and Mag and the pups, but they would have already settled to their work. They knew his course, every turn of it by heart. Through the woods and then down across the fields again to the river. Their hope was always to cut him off before he could circle back to the mountain. If he got in there among those old field pines it was all up. But he always made it. Lost 'em every time and then dodged through to his hole in Pinnacle Rock. . . . A smart fox, Old Red. . . .

He descended the slope and paused in the shade of a clump of willows. The little Negroes who squatted, dabbling in the water, watched him out of round eyes as he unslung his canvas bag and laid it on a stump. He looked down at them gravely.

"D'you ever see a white man that could conjure?" he asked.

The oldest boy laid the brick he was fashioning out of mud down on a plank. He ran the tip of his tongue over his lower lip to moisten it before he spoke. "Naw suh."

"I'm the man," Mister Maury told him. "You chillun better quit that playin' and dig me some worms."

He drew his rod out of the case, jointed it up and laid it down on a stump. Taking out his book of flies he turned the pages, considering. "Silver Spinner," he said aloud. "They ought to take that . . . in May. Naw, I'll just give Old Speck a chance. It's a long time now since we had her out."

The little Negroes had risen and were stepping quietly off along the path toward the cabin, the two little boys hand in hand, the little girl following, the baby astride her hip. They were pausing now before a dilapidated building that might long ago have been a hen-house. Mister Maury shouted at them. "Look under them old boards. That's the place for worms." The biggest boy was turning around. His treble "Yassuh" quavered over the water. Then their voices died away. There was no sound except the light turning of the willow boughs in the wind.

Mister Maury walked along the bank, rod in hand, humming: "Bangum's gone to the wild boar's den . . . *Bangum's* gone to the wild boar's den . . ." He stopped where a white, peeled log protruded six or seven feet into the water. The pond made a little turn here. Two lines of willows curving in framed the whole surface of the water. He stepped out squarely upon the log, still humming. The line rose smoothly, soared against the blue and curved sweetly back upon the still water. His quick ear caught the little whish that the fly made when it clove the surface, his eye followed the tiny ripples of its flight. He cast again, leaning a little backward as he did sometimes when the mood was on him. Again and again his line soared out over the water. His eye rested now and then on his wrist. He noted with detachment the expert play of the muscles, admired each time the accuracy of his aim. It occurred to him that it was four days now since he had wet a line. Four days. One whole day packing up, parts of two days on the train and yesterday wasted sitting there on that front porch with the family. But the abstinence had done him good. He had never cast better than he was casting this morning.

There was a rustling along the bank, a glimpse of blue through the trees. Mister Maury leaned forward and peered around the clump of willows. A hundred yards away Steve, hatless, in an old blue shirt and khaki pants, stood jointing up a rod.

Mister Maury backed off his log and advanced along the path. He called out cheerfully, "Well, feller, do any good?"

Steve looked up. His face had lightened for a moment, but the abstracted expression stole over it again when he spoke. "Oh, I fiddled with it," he said, "all morning, but I didn't do much good."

Mister Maury nodded sympathetically. "*Minerva invita erat*," he said; "you can do nothing unless Minerva perches on the roof-tree. Why, I been castin' here all morning and not a strike. But there's a boat tied up over on the other side. What say we get in it and just drift around?" He paused, looked at the rod Steve had finished jointing up. "I brought another rod along," he said. "You want to use it?"

Steve shook his head. "I'm used to this one."

An expression of relief came over Mister Maury's face. "That's right," he said, "a man always does better with his own rod."

The boat was only a quarter full of water. They heaved her over and dumped it out, then dragged her down to the bank. The little Negroes had come up, bringing a can of worms. Mister Maury threw them each a nickel and set the can in the bottom of the boat. "I always like to have a few worms handy," he told Steve, "ever since I was a boy." He lowered himself ponderously into the bow and Steve pushed off and dropped down behind him.

The little Negroes still stood on the bank staring. When the boat was a little distance out on the water the boldest of them spoke: "Yo reckon 'at ole jawnboat going to hold you up, Cap'm?"

Mister Maury turned his head to call over his shoulder. "Go 'way, boy, ain't I done tole you I's a conjure?"

The boat dipped ominously. Steve changed his position a little and she settled to the water. Sitting well forward Mister Maury made graceful casts, now to this side, now to that. Steve, in the stern, made occasional casts, but he laid his rod down every now and then to paddle, though there was really no use in it. The boat drifted well enough with the wind. At the end of half an hour seven sizable bass lay on the bottom of the boat. Mister Maury had caught five of them. He reflected that perhaps he really ought to change places with Steve. The man in the bow certainly had the best chance at the fish. "But no," he thought, "it don't make any difference. He don't hardly know where he is now."

He stole a glance over his shoulder at the young man's serious, abstracted face. It was like that of a person submerged. Steve seemed to float up to the surface every now and then, his expression would lighten, he would make some observation that showed he knew where he was, then he would sink again. If you asked him a question he answered punctiliously, two minutes later. Poor boy, dead to the world and would probably be that way the rest of his life! A pang of pity shot through Mister Maury, and on the heels of it a gust of that black fear that occasionally shook him. It was he, not Steve, that was the queer one! The world was full of people like this boy, all of them walking around with their heads so full of this and that they hardly knew where they were going. There was hardly anybody—there was *nobody* really in the whole world like him. . . .

Steve, coming out of his abstraction, spoke politely. He had heard that Mister Maury was a fine shot. Did he like to fish better than hunt?

Mister Maury reflected. "Well," he said, "they's something about a covey of birds rising up in front of you . . . they's something. And a good dog. Now they ain't anything in this world that I like better than a good bird dog." He stopped and sighed. "A man has got to come to himself early in life if he's going to amount to anything. Now I was smart, even as a boy. I could look around me and see all the men of my family, Uncle Jeems, Uncle Quent, my father, every one of 'em weighed two hundred by the time he was fifty. You get as heavy on your feet as all that and you can't do any good shooting. But a man can fish as long as he lives. . . . Why, one place I stayed last summer there was an old man ninety years old had himself carried down to the river every morning. . . . Yes, sir, a man can fish as long as he can get down to the water's edge. . . ."

There was a little plop to the right. He turned just in time to see the fish flash out of the water. He watched Steve take it off the hook and drop it on top of the pile in the bottom of the boat. Eight bass that made and two bream. The old lady would be pleased. "Aleck always catches me fish," she'd say.

The boat glided on over the still water. There was no wind at all now. The willows that fringed the bank might have been cut out of paper. The plume of smoke hung perfectly horizontal over the roof of the Negro cabin. Mister Maury watched it stream out in little eddies and disappear into the bright blue.

He spoke softly: "Ain't it wonderful . . . ain't it wonderful now that a man of my gifts can content himself a whole morning on this here little old pond?"

III

Mister Maury woke with a start. He realized that he had been sleeping on his left side again. A bad idea. It always gave him palpitations of the heart. It must be that that had waked him up. He had gone to sleep almost immediately after his head hit the pillow. He rolled over, cautiously, as he always did since that bed in Leesburg had given down with him, and lying flat on his back stared at the opposite wall.

The moon rose late. It must be at its height now. That patch of light was so brilliant he could almost discern the pattern of the wall paper. It hung there, wavering, bitten by the shadows into a semblance of a human figure, a man striding with bent head and swinging arms. All the shadows in the room seemed to be moving toward him. The protruding corner of the washstand was an arrow aimed at his heart, the clumsy old-fashioned dresser was a giant towering above him.

They had put him to sleep in this same room the night after his wife died. In the summer it had been, too, in June, and there must have been a full moon, for the same giant shadows had struggled there with the same towering monsters. It would be like that here on this wall every full moon, for the pieces of furniture would never change their position, had never been changed, probably, since the house was built.

He turned back on his side. The wall before him was dark, but he knew every flower in the pattern of the wall paper, interlacing pink roses with thrusting up between every third cluster the enormous, spreading fronds of ferns. The wall paper in the room across the hall was like that too. The old lady slept there, and in the room next to his own, Laura, his sister-in-law, and in the east bedroom downstairs the young couple. He and Mary had slept there when they were first married, when they were the young couple in the house.

He tried to remember Mary as she must have looked the day he first saw her, the day he arrived from Virginia to open his school in the old office that used to stand there in the corner of the yard. He could see Mister Allard plainly, sitting there under the sugar tree with his chair tilted back, could discern the old lady—young she had been then!—hospitably poised in the doorway, could hear her voice: "Well, here are two of your pupils to start with. . . ." He remembered Laura, a shy child of nine hiding her face in her mother's skirts, but Mary was only a shadow in the dark hall. He could not even remember how her voice had sounded. "Professor Maury," she would have said and her mother would have corrected her with "Cousin Aleck. . . ."

That day a year later when she was getting off her horse at the stile blocks. . . . She had turned as she walked across the lawn to look back at him. Her white sunbonnet had fallen back on her shoulders, her eyes meeting his had been wide and startled. He had gone on and had hitched both the horses before he leaped over the stile to join her. But he had known in that moment that she was the woman he was going to have. He could not remember all the rest of it, only that moment stood out. He had won her. She had become his wife, but the woman he had won was not the woman he had sought. It was as if he had had her only in that moment there on the lawn. As if she had paused there only for that one moment, and was ever after retreating before him down a devious, a dark way that he would never have chosen.

The death of the first baby had been the start of it, of course. It had been a relief when she took so definitely to religion. Before that there had been those sudden, unaccountable forays out of some dark lurking place that she had. Guerrilla warfare and trying to the nerves, but that had been only at the first. For many years they had been two enemies contending in the open. . . . Toward the last she had taken mightily to prayer. He would wake often to find her kneeling by the side of the bed in the dark. It had gone on for years. She had never given up hope. . . .

Ah, a stout-hearted one, Mary! She had never given up hope of changing him, of making him over into the man she thought he ought to be. Time and again she almost had him. And there were long periods, of course, during which he had been worn down by the conflict, one spring when he himself said, when she had told all the neighbors that he was too old now to go fishing anymore. . . . But he had made a comeback. She had had to resort to stratagem. His lips curved in a smile, remembering the trick.

It had come over him suddenly, a general lassitude, an odd faintness in the mornings, the time when his spirits ordinarily were always at their highest. He had sat there looking out of the window at the woods glistening with spring rain; he had not even taken his gun down to shoot a squirrel.

Remembering Uncle Quent's last days, he had been alarmed, had decided finally that he must tell her so that they might begin preparations for the future—he had shuddered at the thought of eventual confinement, perhaps in some institution. She had looked up from her sewing, unable to repress a smile.

"You think it's your mind, Aleck. . . . It's coffee. . . . I've been giving you a coffee substitute every morning. . . ."

They had laughed together over her cleverness. He had not gone back to coffee, but the lassitude had worn off. She had gone back to the attack with redoubled vigor. In the afternoons she would stand on the porch calling after him as he slipped down to the creek, "Now, don't stay long enough to get that cramp. You remember how you suffered last time. . . ." He would have forgotten all about the cramp until that moment, but it would hang over him then through the whole afternoon's sport, and it would descend upon him inevitably when he left the river and started for the house.

Yes, he thought with pride. She was wearing him down—he didn't believe there was a man living who could withstand her a lifetime! —she was wearing him down and would have had him in another few months, another year certainly. But she had been struck down just as victory was in her grasp. The paralysis had come on her in the night. It was as if a curtain had descended, dividing their life sharply into two parts. In the bewildered year and a half that followed he had found himself forlornly trying to reconstruct the Mary he had known. The pressure she had so constantly exerted upon him had become for him a part of her personality. This new, calm Mary was not the woman he had loved all these years. She had lain there—heroically they all said—waiting for death. And lying there, waiting, all her faculties engaged now in defensive warfare, she had raised as it were her lifelong siege; she had lost interest in his comings and goings, had once even encouraged him to go out for an afternoon's sport. He felt a rush of warm pity. Poor Mary! She must have realized toward the last that she had wasted herself in conflict; she had spent her arms and her strength against an inglorious foe when all the time the real, the invincible adversary waited. . . .

He turned over on his back again. The moonlight was waning, the contending shadows paler now and retreating toward the door. From across the hall came the sound of long, sibilant breaths, ending each one on a little upward groan. The old lady . . . she would maintain till her dying day that she did not snore. He fancied that he could hear from the next room Laura's light, regular breathing, and downstairs were the young couple asleep in each other's arms. . . .

All of them quiet and relaxed now, but they had been lively enough at dinner time! It had started with the talk about Aunt Sally Crenfew's funeral Tuesday. Living as he had for some years away from women of his family he had forgotten the need to be cautious. He had spoken up before he thought:

"But that's the day Steve and I were going to Barker's Mill. . . ."

Sarah had cried out at the idea. "Barker's Mill!" she had said, "right on the Crenfew land . . . well, if not on the very farm in the very next field." It would be a scandal if he, Professor Maury, known by everybody to be in the neighborhood, could not spare one afternoon, one insignificant summer afternoon from his fishing long enough to attend the funeral of his cousin, the cousin of all of them, the oldest lady in the whole family connection. . . .

She had got him rattled; he had fallen back upon technicalities:

"I'm not a Crenfew. I'm a Maury. Aunt Sally Crenfew is no more kin to me than a catfish. . . ."

An unlucky crack, that about the catfish. Glancing around the table he had caught the same look in every eye. He had felt a gust of the same fright that had shaken him there on the pond. That look! Sooner or later you met it in every human eye. The thing was to be up and ready, ready to run for your life at a moment's notice. Yes, it had always been like that. It always would be. His fear of them was shot through suddenly with contempt. It was as if Mary was there laughing at them with him. *She* knew that none of them could have survived what he had survived, could have paid the price for freedom that he had paid. . . .

Sarah had come to a full stop. He had to say something. He shook his head:

"You think we just go fishing to have a good time. The boy and I hold high converse on that pond. . . . I'm starved for intellectual companionship, I tell you. In Florida I never see anybody but niggers. . . ."

They had all laughed out at that. "As if you didn't *prefer* the society of niggers," Sarah said scornfully.

The old lady had been moved to anecdote:

"I remember when Aleck first came out here from Virginia, Cousin Sophy said: 'Professor Maury is so well educated. Now Cousin Cave Maynor is dead, who is there in this neighborhood for him to associate with?' 'Well,' I said, 'I don't know about that. He seems perfectly satisfied now with Ben Hooser. They're off to the creek together every evening soon as school is out.'"

Ben Hooser. . . . He could see now the wrinkled face, overlaid with that ashy pallor of the aged Negro, the shrewd, smiling eyes, the pendulous lower lip that dropping away showed always some of the rotten teeth. A fine nigger, Ben, and on to a lot of tricks, the only man really that he'd ever cared to take fishing with him. . . .

But the first real friend of his bosom had been old Uncle Teague, back in Virginia. Once a week, or more likely every ten days, he fed the hounds on the carcass of a calf that had had time to get pretty high. They would drive the spring wagon out into the lot, he, a boy of ten, beside Uncle Teague on the driver's seat. The hounds would come in a great rush and rear their slobbering jowls against the wagon wheels. Uncle Teague would wield his whip, chuckling while he threw the first hunk of meat to Old Mag, his favorite.

"Dey goin' run on dis," he'd say, "dey goin' run like a shadow. . . ."

He shifted his position again, cautiously. People, he thought . . . people . . . so bone ignorant, all of them. Not one person in a thousand realized that a fox hound remains at heart a wild beast and must kill and gorge, and then when he is ravenous kill and gorge again. . . . Or that the channel cat is a night feeder. . . . Or . . . his daughter had told him once that he ought to set all his knowledges down in a book. "Why?" he had asked. "So everybody else can know as much as I do?"

If he allowed his mind to get active, really active, he would never get any sleep. He was fighting an inclination now to get up and find a cigarette. He relaxed again upon his pillows, deliberately summoned pictures up before his mind's eye. Landscapes—and streams. He observed their outlines, watched one flow into another. The Black River into West Fork, that in turn into Spring Creek and Spring Creek into the Withlicoochee. Then they were all flowing together, merging into one broad plain. He watched it take form slowly: the wide field in front of Hawkwood, the Rivanna River on one side, on the other Peters' Mountain. They would be waiting there till the fox showed himself on that little rise by the river. The young men would hold back till Uncle Quent had wheeled Old Filly, then they would all be off pell-mell across the plain. He himself would be mounted on Jonesboro. Blind as a bat, but she would take anything you put her at. That first thicket on the edge of the woods. They would break there, one half of them going around, the other half streaking it through the woods. He was always of those going around to try to cut the fox off on the other side. No, he was down off his horse. He was coursing with the fox. He could hear the sharp, pointed feet padding on the dead leaves, see the quick head turned now and then over the shoulder.

The trees kept flashing by, one black trunk after another. And now it was a ragged mountain field and the sage grass running before them in waves to where a narrow stream curved in between the ridges. The fox's feet were light in the water. He ran steadily, head down. The hounds' baying was louder now.

Old Mag knew the trick. She had stopped to give tongue by the big rock, and now they had all leaped the gulch and were scrambling up through the pines. But the fox's feet were already hard on the mountain path. He ran slowly now, past the big boulder, past the blasted pine to where the shadow of the Pinnacle Rock was black across the path. He ran on and the shadow rose and swayed to meet him. Its cool touch was on his hot tongue, his heaving flanks. He had slipped in under it. He was sinking down, panting, in black dark, on moist earth while the hounds' baying filled the bowl of the valley and reverberated from the mountainside.

A Visit of Charity*

by EUDORA WELTY

It was mid-morning—a very cold, bright day. Holding a potted plant before her, a girl of fourteen jumped off the bus in front of the Old Ladies' Home, on the outskirts of town. She wore a red coat, and her straight yellow hair was hanging down loose from the pointed white cap all the little girls were wearing that year. She stopped for a moment beside one of the prickly dark shrubs with which the city had beautified the Home, and then proceeded slowly toward the building, which was of whitewashed brick and reflected the winter sunlight like a block of ice. As she walked vaguely up the steps she shifted the small pot from hand to hand; then she had to set it down and remove her mittens before she could open the heavy door.

"I'm a Campfire Girl. . . . I have to pay a visit to some old lady," she told the nurse at the desk. This was a woman in a white uniform who looked as if she were cold; she had close-cut hair which stood up on the very top of her head exactly like a sea wave. Marian, the little girl, did not tell her that this visit would give her a minimum of only three points in her score.

"Acquainted with any of our residents?" asked the nurse. She lifted one eyebrow and spoke like a man.

"With any old ladies? No—but—that is, any of them will do," Marian stammered. With her free hand she pushed her hair behind her ears, as she did when it was time to study Science.

The nurse shrugged and rose. "You have a nice *multiflora cineraria* there," she remarked as she walked ahead down the hall of closed doors to pick out an old lady.

There was loose, bulging linoleum on the floor. Marian felt as if she were walking on the waves, but the nurse paid no attention to it. There was a smell in the hall like the interior of a clock. Everything was silent until, behind one of the doors, an old lady of some kind cleared her throat like a sheep bleating. This decided the nurse. Stopping in her tracks, she first extended her arm, bent her elbow, and leaned forward from the hips—all to examine the watch strapped to her wrist; then she gave a loud double-rap on the door.

"There are two in each room," the nurse remarked over her shoulder.

---

* From *A Curtain of Green and Other Stories*, copyright, 1941, 1969, by Eudora Welty. Reprinted by permission of Harcourt Brace Jovanovich, Inc.

"Two what?" asked Marian without thinking. The sound like a sheep's bleating almost made her turn around and run back.

One old woman was pulling the door open in short, gradual jerks, and when she saw the nurse a strange smile forced her old face dangerously awry. Marian, suddenly propelled by the strong, impatient arm of the nurse, saw next the side-face of another old woman, even older, who was lying flat in bed with a cap on and a counterpane drawn up to her chin.

"Visitor," said the nurse, and after one more shove she was off up the hall.

Marian stood tongue-tied; both hands held the potted plant. The old woman, still with that terrible, square smile (which was a smile of welcome) stamped on her bony face, was waiting. . . . Perhaps she said something. The old woman in bed said nothing at all, and she did not look around.

Suddenly Marian saw a hand, quick as a bird claw, reach up in the air and pluck the white cap off her head. At the same time, another claw to match drew her all the way into the room, and the next moment the door closed behind her.

"My, my, my," said the old lady at her side.

Marian stood enclosed by a bed, a washstand and a chair; the tiny room had altogether too much funiture. Everything smelled wet—even the bare floor. She held onto the back of the chair, which was wicker and felt soft and damp. Her heart beat more and more slowly, her hands got colder and colder, and she could not hear whether the old women were saying anything or not. She could not see them very clearly. How dark it was! The window shade was down, and the only door was shut. Marian looked at the ceiling. . . . It was like being caught in a robbers' cave, just before one was murdered.

"Did you come to be our little girl for a while?" the first robber asked.

Then something was snatched from Marian's hand—the little potted plant.

"Flowers!" screamed the old woman. She stood holding the pot in an undecided way. "Pretty flowers," she added.

Then the old woman in bed cleared her throat and spoke. "They are not pretty," she said, still without looking around, but very distinctly.

Marian suddenly pitched against the chair and sat down in it.

"Pretty flowers," the first old woman insisted. "Pretty—pretty . . ."

Marian wished she had the little pot back for just a moment—she had forgotten to look at the plant herself before giving it away. What did it look like?

"Stinkweeds," said the other old woman sharply. She had a bunchy white forehead and red eyes like a sheep. Now she turned them toward Marian. The fogginess seemed to rise in her throat again, and she bleated, "Who—are—you?"

To her surprise, Marian could not remember her name. "I'm a Campfire Girl," she said finally.

"Watch out for the germs," said the old woman like a sheep, not addressing anyone.

"One came out last month to see us," said the first old woman.

A sheep or a germ? wondered Marian dreamily, holding onto the chair.

"Did not!" cried the other old woman.

"Did so! Read to us out of the Bible, and we enjoyed it!" screamed the first.

"Who enjoyed it!" said the woman in bed. Her mouth was unexpectedly small and sorrowful, like a pet's.

"We enjoyed it," insisted the other. "You enjoyed it—I enjoyed it."

"We all enjoyed it," said Marian, without realizing that she had said a word.

The first old woman had just finished putting the potted plant high, high on the top of the wardrobe, where it could hardly be seen from below. Marian wondered how she had ever succeeded in placing it there, how she could ever have reached so high.

"You mustn't pay attention to old Addie," she now said to the little girl. "She's ailing today."

"Will you shut your mouth?" said the woman in bed. "I am not."

"You're a story."

"I can't stay but a minute—really, I can't," said Marian suddenly. She looked down at the wet floor and thought that if she were sick in here they would have to let her go.

With much to-do the first old woman sat down in a rocking chair—still another piece of furniture!—and began to rock. With the fingers of one hand she touched a very dirty cameo pin on her chest. "What do you do at school?" she asked.

"I don't know . . ." said Marian. She tried to think but she could not.

"Oh, but the flowers are beautiful," the old woman whispered. She seemed to rock faster and faster; Marian did not see how anyone could rock so fast.

"Ugly," said the woman in bed.

"If we bring flowers—" Marian began, and then fell silent. She had almost said that if Campfire Girls brought flowers to the Old Ladies' Home, the visit would count one extra point, and if they took a Bible with them on the bus and read it to the old ladies, it counted double. But the old woman had not listened, anyway; she was rocking and watching the other one, who watched back from the bed.

"Poor Addie is ailing. She has to take medicine—see?" she said, pointing a horny finger at a row of bottles on the table, and rocking so high that her black comfort shoes lifted off the floor like a little child's.

"I am no more sick than you are," said the woman in bed.

"Oh, yes you are!"

"I just got more sense than you have, that's all," said the other old woman, nodding her head.

"That's only the contrary way she talks when *you all* come," said the first old lady with sudden intimacy. She stopped the rocker with a neat pat of her feet and leaned toward Marian. Her hand reached over—it felt like a petunia leaf, clinging just a little sticky.

"Will you hush! Will you hush!" cried the other one.

Marian leaned back rigidly in her chair.

"When I was a little girl like you, I went to school and all," said the old woman in the same intimate, menacing voice. "Not here—another town. . . ."

"Hush!" said the sick woman. "You never went to school. You never came and you never went. You never were anything—only here. You never were born! You don't know anything. Your head is empty, your heart and hands and your old black purse are all empty, even that little old box that you brought with you you brought empty—you showed it to me. And yet you talk, talk, talk, talk, talk all the time until I think I'm losing my mind! Who are you? You're a stranger—a perfect stranger! Don't you know you're a stranger? Is it possible that they have actually done a thing like this to anyone—sent them in a stranger to talk, and rock, and tell away her whole long rigmarole? Do they seriously suppose that I'll be able to keep it up, day in, day out, night in, night out, living in the same room with a terrible old woman—forever?"

Marian saw the old woman's eyes grow bright and turn toward her. This old woman was looking at her with despair and calculation in her face. Her small lips suddenly dropped apart, and exposed a half circle of false teeth with tan gums.

"Come here, I want to tell you something," she whispered. "Come here!"

Marian was trembling, and her heart nearly stopped beating altogether for a moment.

"Now, now, Addie," said the first old woman. "That's not polite. Do you know what's really the matter with old Addie today?" She, too, looked at Marian; one of her eyelids drooped low.

"The matter?" the child repeated stupidly. "What's the matter with her?"

"Why, shes mad because it's her birthday!" said the first old woman, beginning to rock again and giving a little crow as though she had answered her own riddle.

"It is not, it is not!" screamed the old woman in bed. "It is not my birthday, no one knows when that is but myself, and will you please be quiet and say nothing more, or I'll go straight out of my mind!" She turned her eyes toward Marian again, and presently she said in the soft, foggy voice, "When the worst comes to the worst, I ring this bell, and the nurse comes." One of her hands was drawn out from under the patched counterpane—a thin little hand with enormous black freckles. With a finger which would not hold still she pointed to a little bell on the table among the bottles.

"How old are you?" Marian breathed. Now she could see the old woman in bed very closely and plainly, and very abruptly, from all sides, as in dreams. She wondered about her—she wondered for a moment as though there was nothing else in the world to wonder about. It was the first time such a thing had happened to Marian.

"I won't tell!"

The old face on the pillow, where Marian was bending over it, slowly gathered and collapsed. Soft whimpers came out of the small open mouth. It was a sheep that she sounded like—a little lamb. Marian's face drew very close, the yellow hair hung forward.

"She's crying!" She turned a bright, burning face up to the first old woman.

"That's Addie for you," the old woman said spitefully.

Marian jumped up and moved toward the door. For the second time, the claw almost touched her hair, but it was not quick enough. The little girl put her cap on.

"Well, it was a real visit," said the old woman, following Marian through the doorway and all the way out into the hall. Then from behind she suddenly clutched the child with her sharp little fingers. In an affected, high-pitched whine she cried, "Oh, little girl, have you a penny to spare for a poor old woman that's not got anything of her own? We don't have a thing in the world—not a penny for candy—not a thing! Little girl, just a nickel—a penny—"

Marian pulled violently against the old hands for a moment before she was free. Then she ran down the hall, without looking behind her and without looking at the nurse, who was reading *Field & Stream* at her desk. The nurse, after another triple motion to consult her wrist watch, asked automatically the question put to visitors in all institutions: "Won't you stay and have dinner with *us*?"

Marian never replied. She pushed the heavy door open into the cold air and ran down the steps.

Under the prickly shrub she stooped and quickly, without being seen, retrieved a red apple she had hidden there.

Her yellow hair under the white cap, her scarlet coat, her bare knees all flashed in the sunlight as she ran to meet the big bus rocketing through the street.

"Wait for me!" she shouted. As though at an imperial command, the bus ground to a stop.

She jumped on and took a big bite out of the apple.

Unit 3

THE SHORT NOVEL

ON THE SHORT NOVEL

At the heart of good fiction is revelation: a good writer enlightens as well as entertains us. Sometimes the predication at the core of the experience through which he is leading us is too complex to be worked out within the confines of a short story. For such predications a writer is likely to use the somewhat more extended form of the short novel, which has a length intermediate between that of a short story and a novel.

The theme of *The Dead* centers upon Gabriel Conroy and upon the change that takes place in his outlook between, say, 10 P.M. and 3 A.M. on a December night. Gabriel is not a bad man; he is concerned as well as puzzled that his encounters with other human beings somehow go awry. His meeting with Lily and his conversation with Miss Ivors both take disagreeable turns; at a more important level, his relationship with his lively wife, Gretta, has not lived up to its early promise. But the events at the party and at the hotel to which Gabriel and his wife repair lead Gabriel to an insight likely to help him become a better husband, a better nephew, a better friend, a better guest, and a better man. Preoccupied with self, concerned with things that separate him from other people, he had quite overlooked that which he shares with his fellow creatures: a vulnerability to the passage of time and to death. In the dim light of a Dublin hotel room he becomes aware of the pathos that surrounds all human beings; for the first time he discerns the mutability, the transiency of human life. As he looks at the form of his sleeping wife, remembering the beauty she no longer has, "a strange, friendly pity for her entered his soul." As he falls asleep he is filled with the compassion that, like the snow falling "all over Ireland," ought to surround, to soften, and to beautify every encounter between transitory, vulnerable human beings.

Consilient with Joyce's revelation in *The Dead* is that of Dostoevsky in *The Dream of a Ridiculous Man*. Like Gabriel Conroy, Dostoevsky's protagonist is isolated, alienated, ultrasubjective, imprisoned in the circle of self. When a wretched little girl asks his help, he spurns her because he intends to kill himself and is convinced that both child and world will disappear with his consciousness. In a dream of a strange planet, however, he encounters people who are neither alienated nor ultrasubjective, but who live intimately with "the earth, the sea, and the woods." The vision of their harmonious living, keyed not to ideology but rooted in the earth, impels the dreamer to forsake his suicide plans and to proclaim the doctrine that man is not his brother's keeper but his brother's brother. But before he preaches he finds and helps the little girl he once spurned.

The Dream of a Ridiculous Man*

by FYODOR DOSTOEVSKY

I

I am a ridiculous person. Now they call me a madman. That would be a promotion if it were not that I remain as ridiculous in their eyes as before. But now I do not resent it, they are all dear to me now, even when they laugh at me—and, indeed, it is just then that they are particularly dear to me. I could join in their laughter—not exactly at myself, but through affection for them, if I did not feel so sad as I look at them. Sad because they do not know the truth and I do know it. Oh, how hard it is to be the only one who knows the truth! But they won't understand that. No, they won't understand it.

In old days I used to be miserable at seeming ridiculous. Not seeming, but being. I have always been ridiculous, and I have known it, perhaps, from the hour I was born. Perhaps from the time I was seven years old I knew I was ridiculous. Afterwards I went to school, studied at the university, and, do you know, the more I learned, the more thoroughly I understood that I was ridiculous. So that it seemed in the end as though all the sciences I studied at the university existed only to prove and make evident to me as I went more deeply into them that I was ridiculous. It was the same with life as it was with science. With every year the same consciousness of the ridiculous figure I cut in every relation grew and strengthened. Every one always laughed at me. But not one of them knew or guessed that if there were one man on earth who knew better than anybody else that I was absurd, it was myself, and what I resented most of all was that they did not know that. But that was my own fault; I was so proud that nothing would have ever induced me to tell it to any one. This pride grew in me with the years; and if it had happened that I allowed myself to confess to any one that I was ridiculous, I believe that I should have blown out my brains the same evening. Oh, how I suffered in my early youth from the fear that I might give way and confess it to my schoolfellows. But since I grew to manhood, I have for some unknown reason become calmer, though I realised my awful characteristic more fully every year. I say "unknown," for to this day I cannot tell why it was. Perhaps it was owing to the terrible misery that was growing in my soul through something which was of more consequence than anything else about me: that something was the conviction that had come upon me that *nothing in the world mattered*. I had long had an inkling of it, but the full realisation came last year almost suddenly. I suddenly felt that it was all the same to me whether the world existed or whether there had never been anything at all: I began to feel with all my being that there was *nothing existing*. At first I fancied that many things had existed in the past, but afterwards I guessed that there never had been anything in the past either, but that it had only seemed so for some reason. Little by little I guessed that there would be nothing in the future either. Then I left off being angry with people and almost ceased to notice them. Indeed this showed itself even in the pettiest trifles: I used, for instance, to knock against people in the street. And not so much from being lost in thought: what had I to think about? I had almost given up thinking by that time; nothing mattered to me. If at least I had solved my problems! Oh, I had not settled one of them, and how many they were! But I gave up caring about anything, and all the problems disappeared.

And it was after that that I found out the truth. I learnt the truth last November—on the third of November, to be precise—and I remember every instant since. It was a gloomy

---

* Reprinted with permission of The Macmillan Company from *An Honest Thief and Other Stories* by Fyodor Dostoevsky, translated from the Russian by Constance Garnett. Also with permission of William Heinemann Limited. Printed in Great Britain.

evening, one of the gloomiest possible evenings. I was going home at about eleven o'clock, and I remember that I thought that the evening could not be gloomier. Even physically. Rain had been falling all day, and it had been a cold, gloomy, almost menacing rain, with, I remember, an unmistakable spite against mankind. Suddenly between ten and eleven it had stopped, and was followed by a horrible dampness, colder and damper than the rain, and a sort of steam was rising from everything, from every stone in the street, and from every by-lane if one looked down it as far as one could. A thought suddenly occurred to me, that if all the street lamps had been put out it would have been less cheerless, that the gas made one's heart sadder because it lighted it all up. I had had scarcely any dinner that day, and had been spending the evening with an engineer, and two other friends had been there also. I sat silent—I fancy I bored them. They talked of something rousing and suddenly they got excited over it. But they did not really care, I could see that, and only made a show of being excited. I suddenly said as much to them. "My friends," I said, "you really do not care one way or the other." They were not offended, but they all laughed at me. That was because I spoke without any note of reproach, simply because it did not matter to me. They saw it did not, and it amused them.

As I was thinking about the gas lamps in the street I looked up at the sky. The sky was horribly dark, but one could distinctly see tattered clouds, and between them fathomless black patches. Suddenly I noticed in one of these patches a star, and began watching it intently. That was because that star gave me an idea: I decided to kill myself that night. I had firmly determined to do so two months before, and poor as I was, I bought a splendid revolver that very day, and loaded it. But two months had passed and it was still lying in my drawer; I was so utterly indifferent that I wanted to seize a moment when I would not be so indifferent—why, I don't know. And so for two months every night that I came home I thought I would shoot myself. I kept waiting for the right moment. And so now this star gave me a thought. I made up my mind that it should certainly be that night. And why the star gave me the thought I don't know.

And just as I was looking at the sky, this little girl took me by the elbow. The street was empty, and there was scarcely any one to be seen. A cabman was sleeping in the distance in his cab. It was a child of eight with a kerchief on her head, wearing nothing but a wretched little dress all soaked with rain, but I noticed particularly her wet broken shoes and I recall them now. They caught my eye particularly. She suddenly pulled me by the elbow and called me. She was not weeping, but was spasmodically crying out some words which she could not utter properly, because she was shivering and shuddering all over. She was in terror about something, and kept crying, "Mammy, mammy!" I turned facing her, I did not say a word and went on; but she ran, pulling at me, and there was that note in her voice which in frightened children means despair. I know that sound. Though she did not articulate the words, I understood that her mother was dying, or that something of the sort was happening to them, and that she had run out to call some one, to find something to help her mother. I did not go with her; on the contrary, I had an impulse to drive her away. I told her first to go to a policeman. But clasping her hands, she ran beside me sobbing and gasping, and would not leave me. Then I stamped my foot, and shouted at her. She called out "Sir! sir! . . ." but suddenly abandoned me and rushed headlong across the road. Some other passer-by appeared there, and she evidently flew from me to him.

I mounted up to my fifth storey. I have a room in a flat where there are other lodgers. My room is small and poor, with a garret window in the shape of a semicircle. I have a sofa covered with American leather, a table with books on it, two chairs and a comfortable arm-chair, as old as old can be, but of the good old-fashioned shape. I sat down, lighted the candle, and began thinking. In the room next to mine, through the partition wall, a perfect Bedlam was going on. It had been going on for the last three days. A retired captain lived there, and he had half a dozen visitors, gentlemen of doubtful reputation, drinking vodka and playing *stoss* with old cards. The night before there had been a fight, and I know that two of them had been for a long time engaged in dragging each other about by the hair. The landlady wanted to complain, but she was in abject terror of the captain. There was only one other lodger in the flat, a thin little regimental lady, on a visit to Petersburg, with three little children who had been taken ill since they came into the lodgings. Both she and her children were in mortal fear of the captain, and lay trembling and crossing themselves all night, and the youngest child had a sort of fit from fright. That captain, I know for a fact, sometimes stops people in the Nevsky Prospect and begs. They won't take him into the service, but strange to say (that's why I am telling this), all this month that the captain has been here his behavior has caused me no annoyance. I have, of course, tried to avoid his acquaintance from the very beginning, and he, too, was bored with me from the first; but I never care how much they shout the other side of the partition nor how many of them there are in there: I sit up all night and forget them so completely that I do not even hear them. I stay awake till daybreak, and have been going on like that for the last year. I sit up all night in my arm-chair at the table, doing nothing. I only read by day. I sit—don't even think; ideas of a sort wander through my mind and I let them come and go as they will. A whole candle is burnt every night. I sat down quietly at the table, took out the revolver and put it down before me. When I had put it down I asked myself, I remember, "Is that so?" and answered with complete conviction, "It is." That is, I shall shoot myself. I knew that I should shoot myself that night for certain, but how much longer I should go on sitting at the table I did not know. And no doubt I should have shot myself if it had not been for that little girl.

II

You see, though nothing mattered to me, I could feel pain, for instance. If any one had struck me it would have hurt me. It was the same morally: if anything very pathetic happened, I should have felt pity just as I used to do in old days when there were things in life that did matter to me. I had felt pity that evening. I should have certainly helped a child. Why, then, had I not helped the little girl? Because of an idea that occurred to me at the time: when she was calling and pulling at me, a question suddenly arose before me and I could not settle it. The question was an idle one, but I was vexed. I was vexed at the reflection that if I were going to make an end of myself that night, nothing in life ought to have mattered to me. Why was it that all at once I did not feel that nothing mattered and was sorry for the little girl? I remember that I was very sorry for her, so much so that I felt a strange pang, quite incongruous in my position. Really I do not know better how to convey my fleeting sensation at the moment, but the sensation persisted at home when I was sitting at the table, and I was very much irritated as I had not been for a long time past. One reflection followed another. I saw clearly that so long as I was still a human being and not nothingness, I was alive and so could suffer, be angry and feel shame at my actions. So be it. But if I am going to kill myself, in two hours, say, what is the little girl to me and what have I to do with shame or with anything else in the world? I shall turn into nothing, absolutely nothing. And can it really be true that the consciousness that shall *completely* cease to exist immediately and so everything else will cease to exist, does not in the least affect my feeling of pity for the child nor the feeling of shame after a contemptible action? I stamped and shouted at the unhappy child as though to say not only I feel no pity, but even if I behave inhumanly and contemptibly, I am free to, for in another two hours everything will be extinguished. Do you believe that that was why I shouted that? I am almost convinced of it now. It seemed clear to me that life and the world somehow depended upon me now. I may almost say that the world now seemed created for me alone: if I shot myself the world would cease to be at least for me. I say nothing of its being likely that nothing will exist for any one when I am gone, and that as soon as my consciousness is extinguished the whole world will vanish too and become void like a phantom, as a mere appurtenance of my consciousness, for possibly all this world and all these people are only me myself. I remember that as I sat and reflected, I turned all these new questions that swarmed one after another quite the other way, and thought of something quite new. For instance, a strange reflection suddenly occurred to me, that if I had lived before on the moon or on Mars and there had committed the most disgraceful and dishonourable action and had there been put to such shame and ignominy as one can only conceive and realise in dreams, in nightmares, and if, finding myself afterwards on earth, I were able to retain the memory of what I had done on the other planet and at the same time knew that I should never, under any circumstances, return there, then looking from the earth to the moon—*should I care or not?* Should I feel shame for that action or not? These were idle and superfluous questions for the revolver was already lying before me, and I knew in every fibre of my being that *it* would happen for certain, but they excited me and I raged. I could not die now without having first settled something. In short, the child had saved me, for I put off my pistol shot for the sake of these questions. Meanwhile the clamour had begun to subside in the captain's room: they had finished their game, were settling down to sleep, and meanwhile were grumbling and languidly winding up their quarrels. At that point I suddenly fell asleep in my chair at the table—a thing which had never happened to me before. I dropped asleep quite unawares.

Dreams, as we all know, are very queer things: some parts are presented with appalling vividness, with details worked up with the elaborate finish of jewellery, while others one gallops through, as it were, without noticing them at all, as, for instance, through space and time. Dreams seem to be spurred on not by reason but by desire, not by the head but by the heart, and yet what complicated tricks my reason has played sometimes in dreams, what utterly incomprehensible things happen to it! My brother died five years ago, for instance. I sometimes dream of him; he takes part in my affairs, we are very much interested, and yet all through my dream I quite know and remember that my brother is dead and buried. How is it that I am not surprised that, though he is dead, he is here beside me and working with me? Why is it that my reason fully accepts it? But enough. I will begin about my dream. Yes, I dreamed a dream, my dream of the third of November. They tease me now, telling me it was only a dream. But does it matter whether it was a dream or reality, if the dream made known to me the truth? If once one has recognised the truth and seen it, you know that it is the truth and that there is no other and there cannot be, whether you are asleep or awake. Let it be a dream, so be it, but that real life of which you make so much I had meant to extinguish by suicide, and my dream, my dream—oh, it revealed to me a different life, renewed, grand and full of power!

Listen.

III

I have mentioned that I dropped asleep unawares and even seemed to be still reflecting on the same subjects. I suddenly dreamt that I picked up the revolver and aimed it straight at my heart—my heart, and not my head; and I had determined beforehand to fire at my head, at my right temple. After aiming at my chest I waited a second or two, and suddenly my candle, my table, and the wall in front of me began moving and heaving. I made haste to pull the trigger.

In dreams you sometimes fall from a height, or are stabbed, or beaten, but you never feel pain unless, perhaps, you really bruise yourself against the bedstead, then you feel pain and almost always wake up from it. It was the same in my dream. I did not feel any pain, but it seemed as though with my shot everything within me was shaken and everything was suddenly dimmed, and it grew horribly black around me. I seemed to be blinded and benumbed, and I was lying on something hard, stretched on my back; I saw nothing, and could not make the slightest movement. People were walking and shouting around me, the captain bawled, the landlady shrieked—and suddenly another break and I was being carried in a closed coffin. And I felt how the coffin was shaking and reflected upon it, and for the first time the idea struck me that I was dead, utterly dead, I knew it and had no doubt of it, I could neither see nor move and yet I was feeling and reflecting. But I was soon reconciled to the position, and as one usually does in a dream, accepted the facts without disputing them.

And now I was buried in the earth. They all went away, I was left alone, utterly alone. I did not move. Whenever before I had imagined being buried the one sensation I associated with the grave was that of damp and cold. So now I felt that I was very cold, especially the tips of my toes, but I felt nothing else.

I lay still, strange to say I expected nothing, accepting without dispute that a dead man had nothing to expect. But it was damp. I don't know how long a time passed—whether an hour, or several days, or many days. But all at once a drop of water fell on my closed left eye, making its way through a coffin lid; it was followed a minute later by a second, then a minute later by a third—and so on, regularly every minute. There was a sudden glow of profound indignation in my heart, and I suddenly felt in it a pang of physical pain. "That's my wound," I thought; "that's the bullet...." And drop after drop every minute kept falling on my closed eyelid. And all at once, not with my voice, but with my whole being, I called upon the power that was responsible for all that was happening to me:

"Whoever you may be, if you exist, and if anything more rational than what is happening here is possible, suffer it to be here now. But if you are revenging yourself upon me for my senseless suicide by the hideousness and absurdity of this subsequent existence, then let me tell you that no torture could ever equal the contempt which I shall go on dumbly feeling, though my martyrdom may last a million years!"

I made this appeal and held my peace. There was a full minute of unbroken silence and again another drop fell, but I knew with infinite unshakable certainty that everything would change immediately. And behold my grave suddenly was rent asunder, that is, I don't know whether it was opened or dug up, but I was caught up by some dark and unknown being and we found ourselves in space. I suddenly regained my sight. It was the dead of night, and never, never had there been such darkness. We were flying through space far away from the earth. I did not question the being who was taking me; I was proud and waited. I assured myself that I was not afraid, and was thrilled with ecstasy at the thought that I was not afraid. I do not know how long we were flying, I cannot imagine; it happened as it always does in dreams when you skip over space and time, and the laws of thought and existence, and only pause upon the points for which the heart yearns. I remember that I suddenly saw in the darkness a star. "Is that Sirius?" I asked impulsively, though I had not meant to ask any questions.

"No, that is the star you saw between the clouds when you were coming home," the being who was carrying me replied.

I knew that it had something like a human face. Strange to say, I did not like that being, in fact I felt an intense aversion for it. I had expected complete non-existence, and that was why I had put a bullet through my heart. And here I was in the hands of a creature not human, of course, but yet living, existing. "And so there is life beyond the grave," I thought with the strange frivolity one has in dreams. But in its inmost depth my heart remained unchanged. "And if I have got to exist again," I thought, "and live once more under the control of some irresistible power, I won't be vanquished and humiliated."

"You know that I am afraid of you and despise me for that," I said suddenly to my companion, unable to refrain from the humiliating question which implied a confession, and feeling my humiliation stab my heart as with a pin. He did not answer my question, but all at once I felt that he was not even despising me, but was laughing at me and had no compassion for me, and that our journey had an unknown and mysterious object that concerned me only. Fear was growing in my heart. Something was mutely and painfully communicated to me from my silent companion, and permeated my whole being. We were flying through dark, unknown space. I had for some time lost sight of the constellations familiar to my eyes. I knew that there were stars in the heavenly spaces the light of which took thousands or millions of years to reach the earth. Perhaps we were already flying through those spaces. I expected something with a terrible anguish that tortured my heart. And suddenly I was thrilled by a familiar feeling that stirred me to the depths: I suddenly caught sight of our sun! I knew that it could not be *our* sun, that gave life to *our* earth, and that we were an infinite distance from our sun, but for some reason I knew in my whole being that it was a sun exactly like ours, a duplicate of it. A sweet, thrilling feeling resounded with ecstasy in my heart: the kindred power of the same light which had given me light stirred an echo in my heart and awakened it, and I had a sensation of life, the old life of the past for the first time since I had been in the grave.

"But if that is the sun, if that is exactly the same as our sun," I cried, "where is the earth?"

And my companion pointed to a star twinkling in the distance with an emerald light. We were flying straight towards it.

"And are such repetitions possible in the universe? Can that be the law of Nature? . . . And if that is an earth there, can it be just the same earth as ours . . . just the same, as poor, as unhappy, but precious and beloved for ever, arousing in the most ungrateful of her children the same poignant love for her that we feel for our earth?" I cried out, shaken by irresistible, ecstatic love for the old familiar earth which I had left. The image of the poor child whom I had repulsed flashed through my mind.

"You shall see it all," answered my companion, and there was a note of sorrow in his voice.

But we were rapidly approaching the planet. It was growing before my eyes; I could already distinguish the ocean, the outline of Europe; and suddenly a feeling of a great and holy jealousy glowed in my heart.

"How can it be repeated and what for? I love and can love only that earth which I have left, stained with my blood, when, in my ingratitude, I quenched my life with a bullet in my heart. But I have never, never ceased to love that earth, and perhaps on the very night I parted from it I loved it more than ever. Is there suffering upon this new earth? On our earth we can only love with suffering and through suffering. We cannot love otherwise, and we know of no other sort of love. I want suffering in order to love. I long, I thirst, this very instant, to kiss with tears the earth that I have left, and I don't want, I won't accept life on any other!"

But my companion had already left me. I suddenly, quite without noticing how, found myself on this other earth, in the bright light of a sunny day, fair as paradise. I believe I was standing on one of the islands that make up on our globe the Greek archipelago, or on the coast of the mainland facing that archipelago. Oh, everything was exactly as it is with us, only everything seemed to have a festive radiance, the splendour of some great, holy triumph attained at last. The caressing sea, green as emerald, splashed softly upon the shore and kissed it with manifest, almost conscious love. The tall, lovely trees stood in all the glory of their blossom, and their innumerable leaves greeted me, I am certain, with their soft, caressing rustle and seemed to articulate words of love. The grass glowed with bright and fragrant flowers. Birds were flying in flocks in the air, and perched fearlessly on my shoulders and arms and joyfully struck me with their darling, fluttering wings. And at last I saw and knew the people of this happy land. They came to me of themselves, they surrounded me, kissed me. The children of the sun, the children of their sun—oh, how beautiful they were! Never had I seen on our own earth such beauty in mankind. Only perhaps in our children, in their earliest years, one might find some remote, faint reflection of this beauty. The eyes of these happy people shone with a clear brightness. Their faces were radiant with the light of reason and fulness of a serenity that comes of perfect understanding, but those faces were gay; in their words and voices there was a note of childlike joy. Oh, from the first moment, from the first glance at them, I understood it all! It was the earth untarnished by the Fall; on it lived people who had not sinned. They lived just in such a paradise as that in which, according to all the legends of mankind, our first parents lived before they sinned; the only difference was that all this earth was the same paradise. These people, laughing joyfully, thronged round me and caressed me; they took me home with them, and each of them tried to reassure me. Oh, they asked me no questions, but they seemed, I fancied, to know everything without asking, and they wanted to make haste and smooth away the signs of suffering from my face.

IV

And do you know what? Well, granted that it was only a dream, yet the sensation of the love of those innocent and beautiful people has remained with me for ever, and I feel as though their love is still flowing out to me from over there. I have seen them myself, have known them and been convinced; I loved them, I suffered for them afterwards. Oh, I understood at once even at the time that in many things I could not understand them at all; as an up-to-date Russian progressive and contemptible Petersburger, it struck me as inexplicable that, knowing so much, they had, for instance, no science like ours. But I soon realised that their knowledge was gained and fostered by intuitions different from those of us on earth, and that their aspirations, too, were quite different. They desired nothing and were at peace; they did not aspire to knowledge of life as we aspire to understand it, because their lives were full. But their knowledge was higher and deeper than ours; for our science seeks to explain what life is, aspires to understand it in order to teach others how to live, while they without science knew how to live; and that I understood, but I could not understand their knowledge. They showed me their trees, and I could not understand the intense love with which they looked at them; it was as though they were talking with creatures like themselves. And perhaps I shall not be mistaken if I say that they conversed with them. Yes, they had found their language, and I am convinced that the trees understood them. They looked at all Nature like that—at the animals who lived in peace with them and did not attack them, but loved them, conquered by their love. They pointed to the stars and told me something about them which I could not understand, but I am convinced that they were somehow in touch with the stars, not only in thought, but by some living channel. Oh, these people did not persist in trying to make me understand them, they loved me without that, but I knew that they would never understand me, and so I hardly spoke to them about our earth. I only kissed in their presence the earth on which they lived and mutely worshipped them themselves. And they saw that and let me worship them without being abashed at my adoration, for they themselves loved much. They were not unhappy on my account when at times I kissed their feet with tears, joyfully conscious of the love with which they would respond to mine. At times I asked myself with wonder how it was they were able never to offend a creature like me, and never once to arouse a feeling of jealousy or envy in me? Often I wondered how it could be that, boastful and untruthful as I was, I never talked to them of what I knew—of which, of course, they had no notion—that I was never tempted to do so by a desire to astonish or even to benefit them.

They were as gay and sportive as children. They wandered about their lovely woods and copses, they sang their lovely songs; their fare was light—the fruits of their trees, the honey from their woods, and the milk of the animals who loved them. The work they did for food and raiment was brief and not laborious. They loved and begot children, but I never noticed in them the impulse of that *cruel* sensuality which overcomes almost every man on this earth, all and each, and is the source of almost every sin of mankind on earth. They rejoiced at the arrival of children as new beings to share their happiness. There was no quarrelling, no jealousy among them, and they did not even know what the words meant. Their children were the children of all, for they all made up one family. There was scarcely any illness among them, though there was death; but their old people died peacefully, as though falling asleep, giving blessings and smiles to those who surrounded them to take their last farewell with bright and loving smiles. I never saw grief or tears on those occasions, but only love, which reached the point of ecstasy, but a calm ecstasy, made perfect and contemplative. One might think that they were still in contact with the departed after death, and that their earthly union was not cut short by death. They scarcely understood me when I questioned them about immortality, but evidently they were so convinced of it without reasoning that it was not for them a question at all. They had no temples, but they had a real living and uninterrupted sense of oneness with the whole of the universe; they had no creed, but they had a certain knowledge that when their earthly joy had reached the limits of earthly nature, then there would come for them, for the living and for the dead, a still greater fulness of contact with the whole of the universe. They looked forward to that moment with joy, but without haste, not pining for it, but seeming to have a foretaste of it in their hearts, of which they talked to one another.

In the evening before going to sleep they liked singing in musical and harmonious chorus. In those songs they expressed all the sensations that the parting day had given them, sang its glories and took leave of it. They sang the praises of nature, of the sea, of the woods. They liked making songs about one another, and praised each other like children; they were the simplest songs, but they sprang from their hearts and went to one's heart. And not only in their songs but in all their lives they seemed to do nothing but admire one another. It was like being in love with each other, but an all-embracing, universal feeling.

Some of their songs, solemn and rapturous, I scarcely understood at all. Though I understood the words I could never fathom their full significance. It remained, as it were, beyond the grasp of my mind, yet my heart unconsciously absorbed it more and more. I often told them that I had had a presentiment of it long before, that this joy and glory had come to me on our earth in the form of a yearning melancholy that at times approached insufferable sorrow; that I had had a foreknowledge of them all and of their glory in the dreams of my heart and the visions of my mind; that often on our earth I could not look at the setting sun without tears . . . that in my hatred for the men of our earth there was always a yearning anguish: why could I not hate them without loving them? why could I not help forgiving them? and in my love for them there was a yearning grief: why could I not love them without hating them? They listened to me, and I saw they could not conceive what I was saying, but I did not regret that I had spoken to them of it: I knew that they understood the intensity of my yearning anguish over those whom I had left. But when they looked at me with their sweet eyes full of love, when I felt that in their presence my heart, too, became as innocent and just as theirs, the feeling of the fulness of life took my breath away, and I worshipped them in silence.

Oh, every one laughs in my face now, and assures me that one cannot dream of such details as I am telling now, that I only dreamed or felt one sensation that arose in my heart in delirium and made up the details myself when I woke up. And when I told them that perhaps it really was so, my God, how they shouted with laughter in my face, and what mirth I caused! Oh, yes, of course I was overcome by the mere sensation of my dream, and that was all that was preserved in my cruelly wounded heart; but the actual forms and images of my dream, that is, the very ones I really saw at the very time of my dream, were filled with such harmony, were so lovely and enchanting and were so actual, that on awakening I was, of course, incapable of clothing them in our poor language, so that they were bound to become blurred in my mind; and so perhaps I really was forced afterwards to make up the details, and so of course to distort them in my passionate desire to convey some at least of them as quickly as I could. But on the other hand, how can I help believing that it was all true? It was perhaps a thousand times brighter, happier and more joyful than I describe it. Granted that I dreamed it, yet it must have been real. You know, I will tell you a secret: perhaps it was not a dream at all! For then something happened so awful, something so horribly true, that it could not have been imagined in a dream. My heart may have originated the dream, but would my heart alone have been capable of originating the awful event which happened to me afterwards? How could I alone have invented it or imagined it in my dream? Could my petty heart and my fickle, trivial mind have risen to such a revelation of truth? Oh, judge for yourselves: hitherto I have concealed it, but now I will tell the truth. The fact is that I . . . corrupted them all!

V

Yes, yes, it ended in my corrupting them all! How it could come to pass I do not know, but I remember it clearly. The dream embraced thousands of years and left in me only a sense of the whole. I only know that I was the cause of their sin and downfall. Like a vile trichina, like a germ of the plague infecting whole kingdoms, so I contaminated all this earth, so happy and sinless before my coming. They learnt to lie, grew fond of lying, and discovered the charm of falsehood. Oh, at first perhaps it began innocently, with a jest, coquetry, with amorous play, perhaps indeed with a germ, but that germ of falsity made its way into their hearts and pleased them. Then sensuality was soon begotten, sensuality begot jealousy, jealousy—cruelty. . . . Oh, I don't know, I don't remember; but soon, very soon the first blood was shed. They marvelled and were horrified, and began to be split up and divided. They formed into unions, but it was against one another. Reproaches, upbraidings followed. They came to know shame, and shame brought them to virtue. The conception of honor sprang up, and every union began waving its flags. They began torturing animals, and the animals withdrew from them into the forests and became hostile to them. They began to struggle for separation, for isolation, for individuality, for mine and thine. They began to talk in different languages. They became acquainted with sorrow and loved sorrow; they thirsted for suffering, and said that truth could only be attained through suffering. Then science appeared. As they became wicked they began talking of brotherhood and humanitarianism, and understood those ideas. As they became criminal, they invented justice and drew up whole legal codes in order to observe it, and to ensure their being kept, set up a guillotine. They hardly remembered what they had lost, in fact refused to believe that they had ever been happy and innocent. They even laughed at the possibility of this happiness in the past, and called it a dream. They could not even imagine it in definite form and shape, but, strange and wonderful to relate, though they lost all faith in their past happiness and called it a legend, they so longed to be happy and innocent once more that they succumbed to this desire like children, made an idol of it, set up temples and worshipped their own idea, their own desire; though at the same time they fully believed that it was unattainable and could not be realised, yet they bowed down to it and adored it with tears! Nevertheless, if it could have happened that they had returned to the innocent and happy condition which they had lost, and if some one had shown it to them again and had asked them whether they wanted to go back to it, they would certainly have refused. They answered me:

"We may be deceitful, wicked and unjust, we *know* it and weep over it, we grieve over it; we torment and punish ourselves more perhaps than that merciful Judge Who will judge us and whose Name we know not. But we have science, and by means of it we shall find the truth and we shall arrive at it consciously. Knowledge is higher than feeling, the consciousness of life is higher than life. Science will give us wisdom, wisdom will reveal the laws, and the knowledge of the laws of happiness is higher than happiness."

That is what they said, and after saying such things every one began to love himself better than any one else, and indeed they could not do otherwise. All became so jealous of the rights of their own personality that they did their very utmost to curtail and destroy them in others, and made that the chief thing in their lives. Slavery followed, even voluntary slavery; the weak eagerly submitted to the strong, on condition that the latter aided them to subdue the still weaker. Then there were saints who came to these people, weeping, and talked to them of their pride, of their loss of harmony and due proportion, of their loss of shame. They were laughed at or pelted with stones. Holy blood was shed on the threshold of the temples. Then there arose men who began to think how to bring all people together again, so that everybody, while still loving himself best of all, might not interfere with others, and all might live together in something like a harmonious society. Regular wars sprang up over this idea. All the combatants at the same time firmly believed that science, wisdom and the instinct of self-preservation would force men at last to unite into a harmonious and rational society; and so, meanwhile, to hasten matters, "the wise" endeavored to exterminate as rapidly as possible all who were "not wise" and did not understand their idea, that the latter might not hinder its triumph. But the instinct of self-preservation grew rapidly weaker; there arose men, haughty and sensual, who demanded all or nothing. In order to obtain everything they resorted to crime, and if they did not succeed—to suicide. There arose religions with a cult of non-existence and self-destruction for the sake of the everlasting peace of annihilation. At last these people grew weary of their meaningless toil, and signs of suffering came into their faces, and then they proclaimed that suffering was a beauty, for in suffering alone was there meaning. They glorified suffering in their songs. I moved about among them, wringing my hands and weeping over them, but I loved them perhaps more than in old days when there was no suffering in their faces and when they were innocent and so lovely. I loved the earth they had polluted even more than when it had been a paradise, if only because sorrow had come to it. Alas! I always loved sorrow and tribulation, but only for myself, for myself; but I wept over them, pitying them. I stretched out my hands to them in despair, blaming, cursing and despising myself. I told them that all this was my doing, mine alone; that it was I had brought them corruption, contamination and falsity. I besought them to crucify me, I taught them how to make a cross. I could not kill myself, I had not the strength, but I wanted to suffer at their hands. I yearned for suffering, I longed that my blood should be drained to the last drop in these agonies. But they only laughed at me, and began at last to look upon me as crazy.

They justified me, they declared that they had only got what they wanted themselves, and that all that now was could not have been otherwise. At last they declared to me that I was becoming dangerous and that they should lock me up in a madhouse if I did not hold my tongue. Then such grief took possession of my soul that my heart was wrung, and I felt as though I were dying; and then . . . then I awoke.

It was morning, that is, it was not yet daylight, but about six o'clock. I woke up in the same arm-chair; my candle had burnt out; every one was asleep in the captain's room, and there was a stillness all round, rare in our flat. First of all I leapt up in great amazement: nothing like this had ever happened to me before, not even in the most trivial detail; I had never, for instance, fallen asleep like this in my arm-chair. While I was standing and coming to myself I suddenly caught sight of my revolver lying loaded, ready—but instantly I thrust it away! Oh, now, life, life! I lifted up my hands and called upon eternal truth, not with words but with tears; ecstasy, immeasurable ecstasy flooded my soul. Yes, life and spreading the good tidings! Oh, I at that moment resolved to spread the tidings, and resolved it, of course, for my whole life. I go to spread the tidings, I want to spread the tidings —of what? Of the truth, for I have seen it, have seen it with my own eyes, have seen it in all its glory.

And since then I have been preaching! Moreover I love all those who laugh at me more than any of the rest. Why that is so I do not know and cannot explain, but so be it. I am told that I am vague and confused, and if I am vague and confused now, what shall I be later on? It is true indeed: I am vague and confused, and perhaps as time goes on I shall be more so. And of course I shall make many blunders before I find out how to preach, that is, find out what words to say, what things to do, for it is a very difficult task. I see all that as clear as daylight, but, listen, who does not make mistakes? And yet, you know, all are making for the same goal, all are striving in the same direction anyway, from the sage to the lowest robber, only by different roads. It is an old truth, but this is what is new: I cannot go far wrong. For I have seen the truth; I have seen and I know that people can be beautiful and happy without losing the power of living on earth. I will not and cannot believe that evil is the normal condition of mankind. And it is just this faith of mine that they laugh at. But how can I help believing it? I have seen the truth—it is not as though I had invented it with my mind, I have seen it, seen it, and *the living image* of it has filled my soul for ever. I have seen it in such full perfection that I cannot believe that it is impossible for people to have it. And so how can I go wrong? I shall make some slips no doubt, and shall perhaps talk in second-hand language, but not for long: the living image of what I saw will always be with me and will always correct and guide me. Oh, I am full of courage and freshness, and I will go on and on if it were for a thousand years! Do you know, at first I meant to conceal the fact that I corrupted them, but that was a mistake—that was my first mistake! But truth whispered to me that I was *lying*, and preserved me and corrected me. But how establish paradise—I don't know, because I do not know how to put it into words. After my dream I lost command of words. All the chief words, anyway, the most necessary ones. But never mind, I shall go and I shall keep talking, I won't leave off, for anyway I have seen it with my own eyes, though I cannot describe what I saw. But the scoffers do not understand that. It was a dream, they say, delirium, hallucination. Oh! As though that meant so much! And they are so proud! A dream! What is a dream? And is not our life a dream? I will say more. Suppose that this paradise will never come to pass (that I understand), yet I shall go on preaching it. And yet how simple it is: in one day, *in one hour* everything could be arranged at once! The chief thing is to love others like yourself, that's the great thing, and that's everything; nothing else is wanted—you will find out at once how to arrange it all. And yet it's an old truth which has been told and retold a billion times—but it has not formed part of our lives! The consciousness of life is higher than life, the knowledge of the laws of happiness is higher than happiness—that is what one must contend against. And I shall. If only every one wants it, it can all be arranged at once.

And I tracked out that little girl . . . and I shall go on and on!

The Dead*

by JAMES JOYCE

Lily, the caretaker's daughter, was literally run off her feet. Hardly had she brought one gentleman into the little pantry behind the office on the ground floor and helped him off with his overcoat than the wheezy hall-door bell clanged again and she had to scamper along the bare hallway to let in another guest. It was well for her she had not to attend to the ladies also. But Miss Kate and Miss Julia had thought of that and had converted the bathroom upstairs into a ladies' dressing-room. Miss Kate and Miss Julia were there, gossiping and laughing and fussing, walking after each other to the head of the stairs, peering down over the banisters and calling down to Lily to ask her who had come.

It was always a great affair, the Misses Morkan's annual dance. Everybody who knew them came to it, members of the family, old friends of the family, the members of Julia's choir, any of Kate's pupils that were grown up enough and even some of Mary Jane's pupils too. Never once had it fallen flat. For years and years it had gone off in splendid style as long

---

* From *Dubliners* by James Joyce. Originally published by B. W. Huebsch, Inc., in 1916. Copyright © 1967 by the Estate of James Joyce. All rights reserved. Reprinted by permission of The Viking Press, Inc.

as anyone could remember; ever since Kate and Julia, after the death of their brother Pat, had left the house in Stoney Batter and taken Mary Jane, their only niece, to live with them in the dark gaunt house on Usher's Island, the upper part of which they had rented from Mr. Fulham, the cornfactor on the ground floor. That was a good thirty years ago if it was a day. Mary Jane, who was then a little girl in short clothes, was now the main prop of the household for she had the organ in Haddington Road. She had been through the Academy and gave a pupils' concert every year in the upper room of the Antient Concert Rooms. Many of her pupils belonged to better-class families on the Kingstown and Dalkey line. Old as they were, her aunts also did their share. Julia, though she was quite grey, was still the leading soprano in Adam and Eve's, and Kate, being too feeble to go about much, gave music lessons to beginners on the old square piano in the back room. Lily, the caretaker's daughter, did housemaid's work for them. Though their life was modest they believed in eating well; the best of everything: diamond-bone sirloins, three-shilling tea and the best bottled stout. But Lily seldom made a mistake in the orders so that she got on well with her three mistresses. They were fussy, that was all. But the only thing they would not stand was back answers.

Of course they had good reason to be fussy on such a night. And then it was long after ten o'clock and yet there was no sign of Gabriel and his wife. Besides they were dreadfully afraid that Freddy Malins might turn up screwed. They would not wish for worlds that any of Mary Jane's pupils should see him under the influence; and when he was like that it was sometimes very hard to manage him. Freddy Malins always came late but they wondered what could be keeping Gabriel: and that was what brought them every two minutes to the banisters to ask Lily had Gabriel or Freddy come.

—O, Mr Conroy, said Lily to Gabriel when she opened the door for him, Miss Kate and Miss Julia thought you were never coming. Good-night, Mrs Conroy.

—I'll engage they did, said Gabriel, but they forget that my wife here takes three mortal hours to dress herself.

He stood on the mat, scraping the snow from his goloshes, while Lily led his wife to the foot of the stairs and called out:

—Miss Kate, here's Mrs Conroy.

Kate and Julia came toddling down the dark stairs at once. Both of them kissed Gabriel's wife, said she must be perished alive and asked was Gabriel with her.

—Here I am as right as the mail, Aunt Kate! Go on up. I'll follow, called out Gabriel from the dark.

He continued scraping his feet vigorously while the three women went upstairs, laughing, to the ladies' dressing-room. A light fringe of snow lay like a cape on the shoulders of his overcoat and like toecaps on the toes of his goloshes; and, as the buttons of his overcoat slipped with a squeaking noise through the snow-stiffened frieze, a cold fragrant air from out-of-doors escaped from crevices and folds.

—Is it snowing again, Mr Conroy? asked Lily.

She had preceded him into the pantry to help him off with his overcoat. Gabriel smiled at the three syllables she had given his surname and glanced at her. She was a slim, growing girl, pale in complexion and with hay-coloured hair. The gas in the pantry made her look still paler. Gabriel had known her when she was a child and used to sit on the lowest step nursing a rag doll.

—Yes, Lily, he answered, and I think we're in for a night of it.

He looked up at the pantry ceiling, which was shaking with the stamping and shuffling of feet on the floor above, listened for a moment to the piano and then glanced at the girl, who was folding his overcoat carefully at the end of a shelf.

—Tell me, Lily, he said in a friendly tone, do you still go to school?

—O no, sir, she answered. I'm done schooling this year and more.

—O, then, said Gabriel gaily, I suppose we'll be going to your wedding one of these fine days with your young man, eh?

The girl glanced back at him over her shoulder and said with great bitterness:

—The men that is now is only all palaver and what they can get out of you.

Gabriel coloured as if he felt he had made a mistake and, without looking at her, kicked off his goloshes and flicked actively with his muffler at his patent-leather shoes.

He was a stout tallish young man. The high colour of his cheeks pushed upwards even to his forehead where it scattered itself in a few formless patches of pale red; and on his hairless face there scintillated restlessly the polished lenses and the bright gilt rims of the glasses which screened his delicate and restless eyes. His glossy black hair was parted in the middle and brushed in a long curve behind his ears where it curled slightly beneath the groove left by his hat.

When he had flicked lustre into his shoes he stood up and pulled his waistcoat down more tightly on his plump body. Then he took a coin rapidly from his pocket.

—O Lily, he said, thrusting it into her hands, it's Christmas-time, isn't it? Just . . . here's a little. . . .

He walked rapidly towards the door.

—O no, sir! cried the girl, following him. Really, sir, I wouldn't take it.

—Christmas-time! Christmas-time! said Gabriel, almost trotting to the stairs and waving his hand to her in deprecation.

The girl, seeing that he had gained the stairs, called out after him:

—Well, thank you, sir.

He waited outside the drawing-room door until the waltz should finish, listening to the skirts that swept against it and to the shuffling of feet. He was still discomposed by the girl's bitter and sudden retort. It had cast a gloom over him which he tried to dispel by arranging his cuffs and the bows of his tie. Then he took from his waistcoat pocket a little paper and glanced at the headings he had made for his speech. He was undecided about the lines from Robert Browning for he feared they would be above the heads of his hearers. Some quotation that they could recognize from Shakespeare or from the Melodies would be better. The indelicate clacking of the men's heels and the shuffling of their soles reminded him that their grade of culture differed from his. He would only make himself ridiculous by quoting poetry to them which they could not understand. They would think that he was airing his superior education. He would fail with them just as he had failed with the girl in the pantry. He had taken up a wrong tone. His whole speech was a mistake from first to last, an utter failure.

Just then his aunts and his wife came out of the ladies' dressing-room. His aunts were two small plainly dressed old women. Aunt Julia was an inch or so the taller. Her hair, drawn low over the tops of her ears, was grey; and grey also, with darker shadows, was her large flaccid face. Though she was stout in build and stood erect her slow eyes and parted lips gave her the appearance of a woman who did not know where she was or where she was going. Aunt Kate was more vivacious. Her face, healthier than her sister's, was all puckers and creases, like a shrivelled red apple, and her hair, braided in the same old-fashioned way, had not lost its ripe nut colour.

They both kissed Gabriel frankly. He was their favourite nephew, the son of their dead elder sister, Ellen, who had married T. J. Conroy of the Port and Docks.

—Gretta tells me you're not going to take a cab back to Monkstown to-night, Gabriel, said Aunt Kate.

—No, said Gabriel, turning to his wife, we had quite enough of that last year, hadn't we. Don't you remember, Aunt Kate, what a cold Gretta got out of it? Cab windows rattling all the way, and the east wind blowing in after we passed Merrion. Very jolly it was. Gretta caught a dreadful cold.

Aunt Kate frowned severely and nodded her head at every word.

—Quite right, Gabriel, quite right, she said. You can't be too careful.

—But as for Gretta there, said Gabriel, she'd walk home in the snow if she were let.

Mrs Conroy laughed.

—Don't mind him, Aunt Kate, she said. He's really an awful bother, what with green shades for Tom's eyes at night and making him do the dumb-bells, and forcing Eva to eat the stirabout. The poor child! And she simply hates the sight of it! . . . O, but you'll never guess what he makes me wear now!

She broke out into a peal of laughter and glanced at her husband, whose admiring and happy eyes had been wandering from her dress to her face and hair. The two aunts laughed heartily too, for Gabriel's solicitude was a standing joke with them.

—Goloshes! said Mrs Conroy. That's the latest. Whenever it's wet underfoot I must put on my goloshes. To-night even he wanted me to put them on, but I wouldn't. The next thing he'll buy me will be a diving suit.

Gabriel laughed nervously and patted his tie reassuringly while Aunt Kate nearly doubled herself, so heartily did she enjoy the joke. The smile soon faded from Aunt Julia's face and her mirthless eyes were directed towards her nephew's face. After a pause she asked:

—And what are goloshes, Gabriel?

—Goloshes, Julia! exclaimed her sister. Goodness me, don't you know what goloshes are? You wear them over your . . . over your boots, Gretta, isn't it?

—Yes, said Mrs Conroy. Guttapercha things. We both have a pair now. Gabriel says everyone wears them on the continent.

—O, on the continent, murmured Aunt Julia, nodding her head slowly.

Gabriel knitted his brows and said, as if he were slightly angered:

—It's nothing very wonderful but Gretta thinks it very funny because she says the word reminds her of Christy Minstrels.

—But tell me, Gabriel, said Aunt Kate, with brisk tact. Of course, you've seen about the room. Gretta was saying . . .

—O, the room is all right, replied Gabriel. I've taken one in the Gresham.

—To be sure, said Aunt Kate, by far the best thing to do. And the children, Gretta, you're not anxious about them?

—O, for one night, said Mrs. Conroy. Besides, Bessie will look after them.

—To be sure, said Aunt Kate again. What a comfort it is to have a girl like that, one you can depend on! There's that Lily, I'm sure I don't know what has come over her lately. She's not the girl she was at all.

Gabriel was about to ask his aunt some questions on this point but she broke off suddenly to gaze after her sister who had wandered down the stairs and was craning her neck over the banisters.

—Now, I ask you, she said, almost testily, where is Julia going? Julia! Julia! Where are you going?

Julia, who had gone halfway down one flight, came back and announced blandly:

—Here's Freddy.

At the same moment a clapping of hands and a final flourish of the pianist told that the waltz had ended. The drawing-room door was opened from within and some couples came out. Aunt Kate drew Gabriel aside hurriedly and whispered into his ear:

—Slip down, Gabriel, like a good fellow and see if he's all right, and don't let him up if he's screwed. I'm sure he's screwed. I'm sure he is.

Gabriel went to the stairs and listened over the banisters. He could hear two persons talking in the pantry. Then he recognized Freddy Malins' laugh. He went down the stairs noisily.

—It's such a relief, said Aunt Kate to Mrs Conroy, that Gabriel is here. I always feel easier in my mind when he's here. . . . Julia, there's Miss Daly and Miss Power will take some refreshment. Thanks for your beautiful waltz, Miss Daly. It made lovely time.

A tall wizen-faced man, with a stiff grizzled moustache and swarthy skin, who was passing out with his partner said:

—And may we have some refreshment, too, Miss Morkan?

—Julia, said Aunt Kate summarily, and here's Mr Browne and Miss Furlong. Take them in, Julia, with Miss Daly and Miss Power.

—I'm the man for the ladies, said Mr Browne, pursing his lips until his moustache bristled and smiling in all his wrinkles. You know, Miss Morkan, the reason they are so fond of me is—

He did not finish his sentence, but, seeing that Aunt Kate was out of earshot, at once led the three young ladies into the back room. The middle of the room was occupied by two square tables placed end to end, and on these Aunt Julia and the caretaker were straightening and smoothing a large cloth. On the sideboard were arrayed dishes and plates, and glasses and bundles of knives and forks and spoons. The top of the closed square piano served also as a sideboard for viands and sweets. At a smaller sideboard in one corner two young men were standing, drinking hop-bitters.

Mr Browne led his charges thither and invited them all, in jest, to some ladies' punch, hot, strong and sweet. As they said they never took anything strong he opened three bottles of lemonade for them. Then he asked one of the young men to move aside, and, taking hold of the decanter, filled out for himself a goodly measure of whisky. The young men eyed him respectfully while he took a trial sip.

—God help me, he said, smiling, it's the doctor's orders.

His wizened face broke into a broader smile, and the three young ladies laughed in musical echo to his pleasantry, swaying their bodies to and fro, with nervous jerks of their shoulders. The boldest said:

—O, now, Mr Browne, I'm sure the doctor never ordered anything of the kind.

Mr Browne took another sip of his whisky and said, with sidling mimicry:

—Well, you see, I'm like the famous Mrs Cassidy, who is reported to have said: *Now, Mary Grimes, if I don't take it, make me take it, for I feel I want it.*

His hot face had leaned forward a little too confidentially and he had assumed a very low Dublin accent so that the young ladies, with one instinct, received his speech in silence. Miss Furlong, who was one of Mary Jane's pupils, asked Miss Daly what was the name of the pretty waltz she had played; and Mr Browne, seeing that he was ignored, turned promptly to the two young men who were more appreciative.

A red-faced young woman, dressed in pansy, came into the room, excitedly clapping her hands and crying:

—Quadrilles! Quadrilles!

Close on her heels came Aunt Kate, crying:

—Two gentlemen and three ladies, Mary Jane!

—O, here's Mr Bergin and Mr Kerrigan, said Mary Jane. Mr Kerrigan, will you take Miss Power? Miss Furlong, may I get you a partner, Mr Bergin. O, that'll just do now.

—Three ladies, Mary Jane, said Aunt Kate.

The two young gentlemen asked the ladies if they might have the pleasure, and Mary Jane turned to Miss Daly.

—O, Miss Daly, you're really awfully good, after playing for the last two dances, but really we're so short of ladies to-night.

—I don't mind in the least, Miss Morkan.

—But I've a nice partner for you, Mr Bartell D'Arcy, the tenor. I'll get him to sing later on. All Dublin is raving about him.

—Lovely voice, lovely voice! said Aunt Kate.

As the piano had twice begun the prelude to the first figure Mary Jane led her recruits quickly from the room. They had hardly gone when Aunt Julia wandered slowly into the room, looking behind her at something.

—What is the matter, Julia? asked Aunt Kate anxiously. Who is it?

Julia, who was carrying in a column of table-napkins, turned to her sister and said, simply, as if the question had surprised her:

—It's only Freddy, Kate, and Gabriel with him.

In fact right behind her Gabriel could be seen piloting Freddy Malins across the landing. The latter, a young man of about forty, was of Gabriel's size and build, with very round shoulders. His face was fleshy and pallid, touched with colour only at the thick hanging lobes of his ears and at the wide wings of his nose. He had coarse features, a blunt nose, a convex and receding brow, tumid and protruded lips. His heavy-lidded eyes and the disorder of his scanty hair made him look sleepy. He was laughing heartily in a high key at a story which he had been telling Gabriel on the stairs and at the same time rubbing the knuckles of his left fist backwards and forwards into his left eye.

—Good-evening, Freddy, said Aunt Julia.

Freddy Malins bade the Misses Morkan good-evening in what seemed an offhand fashion by reason of the habitual catch in his voice and then, seeing that Mr Browne was grinning at him from the sideboard, crossed the room on rather shaky legs and began to repeat in an undertone the story he had just told to Gabriel.

—He's not so bad, is he? said Aunt Kate to Gabriel.

Gabriel's brows were dark but he raised them quickly and answered:

—O no, hardly noticeable.

—Now, isn't he a terrible fellow! she said. And his poor mother made him take the pledge on New Year's Eve. But come on, Gabriel, into the drawing-room.

Before leaving the room with Gabriel she signalled to Mr Browne by frowning and shaking her forefinger in warning to and fro. Mr Browne nodded in answer and, when she had gone, said to Freddy Malins:

—Now, then, Teddy, I'm going to fill you out a good glass of lemonade just to buck you up.

Freddy Malins, who was nearing the climax of his story, waved the offer aside impatiently but Mr Browne, having first called Freddy Malins' attention to a disarray in his dress, filled out and handed him a full glass of lemonade. Freddy Malins' left hand accepted the glass mechanically, his right hand being engaged in the mechanical readjustment of his dress. Mr Browne, whose face was once more wrinkling with mirth, poured out for himself a glass of whisky while Freddy Malins exploded, before he had well reached the climax of his story, in a kink of high-pitched bronchitic laughter and, setting down his untasted and overflowing glass, began to rub the knuckles of his left fist backwards and forwards into his left eye, repeating words of his last phrase as well as his fit of laughter would allow him.

. . . .

Gabriel could not listen while Mary Jane was playing her Academy piece, full of runs and difficult passages, to the hushed drawing-room. He liked music but the piece she was playing had no melody for him and he doubted whether it had any melody for the other listeners, though they had begged Mary Jane to play something. Four young men, who had come from the refreshment-room to stand in the doorway at the sound of the piano, had gone away quietly in couples after a few minutes. The only persons who seemed to follow the music were Mary Jane herself, her hands racing along the key-board or lifted from it at the pauses like those of a priestess in momentary imprecation, and Aunt Kate standing at her elbow to turn the page.

Gabriel's eyes, irritated by the floor, which glittered with beeswax under the heavy chandelier, wandered to the wall above the piano. A picture of the balcony scene in *Romeo and Juliet* hung there and beside it was a picture of the two murdered princes in the Tower which Aunt Julia had worked in red, blue and brown wools when she was a girl. Probably in the school they had gone to as girls that kind of work had been taught, for one year his mother had worked for him as a birthday present a waistcoat of purple tabinet, with little foxes' heads upon it, lined with brown satin and having round mulberry buttons. It was strange that his mother had had no musical talent though Aunt Kate used to call her the brains carrier of the Morkan family. Both she and Julia had always seemed a little proud of their serious and matronly sister. Her photograph stood before the pierglass. She held an open book on her knees and was pointing out something in it to Constantine who, dressed in a man-o'-war suit, lay at her feet. It was she who had chosen the names for her sons for she was very sensible of the dignity of family life. Thanks to her, Constantine was now senior curate in Balbriggan and, thanks to her, Gabriel himself had taken his degree in the Royal University. A shadow passed over his face as he remembered her sullen opposition to his marriage. Some slighting phrases she had used still rankled in his memory; she had once spoken of Gretta as being country cute and that was not true of Gretta at all. It was Gretta who had nursed her during all her last long illness in their house at Monkstown.

He knew that Mary Jane must be near the end of her piece for she was playing again the opening melody with runs of scales after every bar and while he waited for the end the resentment died down in his heart. The piece ended with a trill of octaves in the treble and a final deep octave in the bass. Great applause greeted Mary Jane as, blushing and rolling up her music nervously, she escaped from the room. The most vigorous clapping came from the four young men in the doorway who had gone away to the refreshment-room at the beginning of the piece but had come back when the piano had stopped.

Lancers were arranged. Gabriel found himself partnered with Miss Ivors. She was a frank-mannered talkative young lady, with a freckled face and prominent brown eyes. She did not wear a low-cut bodice and the large brooch which was fixed in the front of her collar bore on it an Irish device.

When they had taken their places she said abruptly:

—I have a crow to pluck with you.

—With me? said Gabriel.

She nodded her head gravely.

—What is it? asked Gabriel, smiling at her solemn manner.

—Who is G. C.? answered Miss Ivors, turning her eyes upon him.

Gabriel coloured and was about to knit his brows, as if he did not understand, when she said bluntly:

—O, innocent Amy! I have found out that you write for *The Daily Express*. Now, aren't you ashamed of yourself?

—Why should I be ashamed of myself? asked Gabriel, blinking his eyes and trying to smile.

—Well, I'm ashamed of you, said Miss Ivors frankly. To say you'd write for a rag like that. I didn't think you were a West Briton.

A look of perplexity appeared on Gabriel's face. It was true that he wrote a literary column every Wednesday in *The Daily Express*, for which he was paid fifteen shillings. But that did not make him a West Briton surely. The books he received for review were almost more welcome than the paltry cheque. He loved to feel the covers and turn over the pages of newly printed books. Nearly every day when his teaching in the college was ended he used to wander down the quays to the second-hand booksellers, to Hickey's on Bachelor's Walk, to Webbs' or Massey's on Aston's Quay, or to O'Clohissey's in the by-street. He did not know how to meet her charge. He wanted to say that literature was above politics. But they were friends of many years' standing and their careers had been parallel, first at the University and then as teachers: he could not risk a grandiose phrase with her. He continued blinking his eyes and trying to smile and murmured lamely that he saw nothing political in writing reviews of books.

When their turn to cross had come he was still perplexed and inattentive. Miss Ivors promptly took his hand in a warm grasp and said in a soft friendly tone:

—Of course, I was only joking. Come, we cross now.

When they were together again she spoke of the University question and Gabriel felt more at ease. A friend of hers had shown her his review of Browning's poems. That was how she had found out the secret: but she liked the review immensely. Then she said suddenly:

—O, Mr Conroy, will you come for an excursion to the Aran Isles this summer? We're going to stay there a whole month. It will be splendid out in the Atlantic. You ought to come. Mr Clancy is coming, and Mr Kilkelly and Kathleen Kearney. It would be splendid for Gretta too if she'd come. She's from Connacht, isn't she?

—Her people are, said Gabriel shortly.

—But you will come, won't you? said Miss Ivors, laying her warm hand eagerly on his arm.

—The fact is, said Gabriel, I have already arranged to go—

—Go where? asked Miss Ivors.

—Well, you know, every year I go for a cycling tour with some fellows and so—

—But where? asked Miss Ivors.

—Well, we usually go to France or Belgium or perhaps Germany, said Gabriel awkwardly.

—And why do you go to France and Belgium, said Miss Ivors, instead of visiting your own land?

—Well, said Gabriel, it's partly to keep in touch with the languages and partly for a change.

—And haven't you your own language to keep in touch with—Irish? asked Miss Ivors.

—Well, said Gabriel, if it comes to that, you know, Irish is not my language.

Their neighbours had turned to listen to the cross-examination. Gabriel glanced right and left nervously and tried to keep his good humour under the ordeal which was making a blush invade his forehead.

—And haven't you your own land to visit, continued Miss Ivors, that you know nothing of, your own people, and your own country?

—O, to tell you the truth, retorted Gabriel suddenly, I'm sick of my own country, sick of it!

—Why? asked Miss Ivors.

Gabriel did not answer for his retort had heated him.

—Why? repeated Miss Ivors.

They had to go visiting together and, as he had not answered her, Miss Ivors said warmly:

—Of course, you've no answer.

Gabriel tried to cover his agitation by taking part in the dance with great energy. He avoided her eyes for he had seen a sour expression on her face. But when they met in the long chain he was surprised to feel his hand firmly pressed. She looked at him from under her brows for a moment quizzically until he smiled. Then, just as the chain was about to start again, she stood on tiptoe and whispered into his ear:

—West Briton!

When the lancers were over Gabriel went away to a remote corner of the room where Freddy Malins' mother was sitting. She was a stout feeble old woman with white hair. Her voice had a catch in it like her son's and she stuttered slightly. She had been told that Freddy had come and that he was nearly all right. Gabriel asked her whether she had had a good crossing. She lived with her married daughter in Glasgow and came to Dublin on a visit once a year. She answered placidly that she had had a beautiful crossing and that the captain had been most attentive to her. She spoke also of the beautiful house her daughter kept in Glasgow, and of all the nice friends they had there. While her tongue rambled on Gabriel tried to banish from his mind all memory of the unpleasant incident with Miss Ivors. Of course the girl or woman, or whatever she was, was an enthusiast but there was a time for all things. Perhaps he ought not to have answered her like that. But she had no right to call him a West Briton before people even in joke. She had tried to make him ridiculous before people, heckling him and staring at him with her rabbit's eyes.

He saw his wife making her way towards him through the waltzing couples. When she reached him she said into his ear:

—Gabriel, Aunt Kate wants to know won't you carve the goose as usual. Miss Daly will carve the ham and I'll do the pudding.

—All right, said Gabriel.

—She's sending in the younger ones first as soon as this waltz is over so that we'll have the table to ourselves.

—Were you dancing? asked Gabriel.

—Of course I was. Didn't you see me? What words had you with Molly Ivors?

—No words. Why? Did she say so?

—Something like that. I'm trying to get that Mr D'Arcy to sing. He's full of conceit, I think.

—There were no words, said Gabriel moodily, only she wanted me to go for a trip to the west of Ireland and I said I wouldn't.

His wife clasped her hands excitedly and gave a little jump.

—O, do go, Gabriel, she cried. I'd love to see Galway again.

—You can go if you like, said Gabriel coldly.

She looked at him for a moment, then turned to Mrs Malins and said:

—There's a nice husband for you, Mrs Malins.

While she was threading her way back across the room Mrs Malins, without adverting to the interruption, went on to tell Gabriel what beautiful places there were in Scotland and beautiful scenery. Her son-in-law brought them every year to the lakes and they used to go fishing. Her son-in-law was a splendid fisher. One day he caught a fish, a beautiful big big fish, and the man in the hotel boiled it for their dinner.

Gabriel hardly heard what she said. Now that supper was coming near he began to think again about his speech and about the quotation. When he saw Freddy Malins coming across the room to visit his mother Gabriel left the chair free for him and retired into the embrasure of the window. The room had already cleared and from the back room came the clatter of plates and knives. Those who still remained in the drawing-room seemed tired of dancing and were conversing quietly in little groups. Gabriel's warm trembling fingers tapped the cold pane of the window. How cool it must be outside! How pleasant it would be to walk out alone, first along by the river and then through the park! The snow would be lying on the branches of the trees and forming a bright cap on the top of the Wellington Monument. How much more pleasant it would be there than at the supper-table!

He ran over the headings of his speech: Irish hospitality, sad memories, the Three Graces, Paris, the quotation from Browning. He repeated to himself a phrase he had written in his review: *One feels that one is listening to a thought-tormented music.* Miss Ivors had praised the review. Was she sincere? Had she really any life of her own behind all her propagandism? There had never been any ill-feeling between them until that night. It unnerved him to think that she would be at the supper-table, looking up at him while he spoke with her critical quizzing eyes. Perhaps she would not be sorry to see him fail in his speech. An idea came into his mind and gave him courage. He would say, alluding to Aunt Kate and Aunt Julia: *Ladies and Gentlemen, the generation which is now on the wane among us may have had its faults but for my part I think it had certain qualities of hospitality, of humour, of humanity, which the new and very serious and hypereducated generation that is growing up around us seems to me to lack.* Very good: that was one for Miss Ivors. What did he care that his aunts were only two ignorant old women?

A murmur in the room attracted his attention. Mr Browne was advancing from the door, gallantly escorting Aunt Julia, who leaned upon his arm, smiling and hanging her head. An irregular musketry of applause escorted her also as far as the piano and then, as Mary Jane seated herself on the stool, and Aunt Julia, no longer smiling, half turned so as to pitch her voice fairly into the room, gradually ceased. Gabriel recognized the prelude. It was that of an old song of Aunt Julia's—*Arrayed for the Bridal.* Her voice, strong and clear in tone, attacked with great spirit the runs which embellish the air and though she sang very rapidly she did not miss even the smallest of the grace notes. To follow the voice, without looking at the singer's face, was to feel and share the excitement of swift and secure flight. Gabriel applauded loudly with all the others at the close of the song and loud applause was borne in from the invisible supper-table. It sounded so genuine that a little colour struggled into Aunt Julia's face as she bent to replace in the music-stand the old leather-bound song-book that had her initials on the cover. Freddy Malins, who had listened with his head perched sideways to hear her better, was still applauding when every one else had ceased and talking animatedly to his mother who nodded her head gravely and slowly in acquiescence. At last, when he could clap no more, he stood up suddenly and hurried across the room to Aunt Julia whose hand he seized and held in both his hands, shaking it when words failed him or the catch in his voice proved too much for him.

—I was just telling my mother, he said, I never heard you sing so well, never. No, I never heard your voice so good as it is to-night. Now! Would you believe that now? That's the truth. Upon my word and honour that's the truth. I never heard your voice sound so fresh and so . . . so clear and fresh, never.

Aunt Julia smiled broadly and murmured something about compliments as she released her hand from his grasp. Mr. Browne extended his open hand towards her and said to those who were near him in the manner of a showman introducing a prodigy to an audience:

—Miss Julia Morkan, my latest discovery!

He was laughing very heartily at this himself when Freddy Malins turned to him and said:

—Well, Browne, if you're serious you might make a worse discovery. All I can say is I never heard her sing half so well as long as I am coming here. And that's the honest truth.

—Neither did I, said Mr Browne. I think her voice has greatly improved.

Aunt Julia shrugged her shoulders and said with meek pride:

—Thirty years ago I hadn't a bad voice as voices go.

—I often told Julia, said Aunt Kate

emphatically, that she was simply thrown away in that choir. But she never would be said by me.

She turned as if to appeal to the good sense of the others against a refractory child where Aunt Julia gazed in front of her, a vague smile of reminiscence playing on her face.

—No, continued Aunt Kate, she wouldn't be said or led by anyone, slaving there in that choir night and day, night and day. Six o'clock on Christmas morning! And all for what?

—Well, isn't it for the honour of God, Aunt Kate? asked Mary Jane, twisting round on the piano-stool and smiling.

Aunt Kate turned fiercely on her niece and said:

—I know all about the honour of God, Mary Jane, but I think it's not at all honourable for the pope to turn out the women out of the choirs that have slaved there all their lives and put little whipper-snappers of boys over their heads. I suppose it is for the good of the Church if the pope does it. But it's not just, Mary Jane, and it's not right.

She had worked herself into a passion and would have continued in defence of her sister for it was a sore subject with her but Mary Jane, seeing that all the dancers had come back, intervened pacifically:

—Now, Aunt Kate, you're giving scandal to Mr Browne who is of the other persuasion.

Aunt Kate turned to Mr Browne, who was grinning at this allusion to his religion, and said hastily:

—O, I don't question the pope's being right. I'm only a stupid old woman and I wouldn't presume to do such a thing. But there's such a thing as common everyday politeness and gratitude. And if I were in Julia's place I'd tell that Father Healy straight up to his face . . .

—And besides, Aunt Kate, said Mary Jane, we really are all hungry and when we are hungry we are all very quarrelsome.

—And when we are thirsty we are also quarrelsome, added Mr Browne.

—So that we had better go to supper, said Mary Jane, and finish the discussion afterwards.

On the landing outside the drawing-room Gabriel found his wife and Mary Jane trying to persuade Miss Ivors to stay for supper. But Miss Ivors, who had put on her hat and was buttoning her cloak, would not stay. She did not feel in the least hungry and she had already overstayed her time.

—But only for ten minutes, Molly, said Mrs Conroy. That won't delay you.

—To take a pick itself, said Mary Jane, after all your dancing.

—I really couldn't, said Miss Ivors.

—I am afraid you didn't enjoy yourself at all, said Mary Jane hopelessly.

—Ever so much, I assure you, said Miss Ivors, but you really must let me run off now.

—But how can you get home? asked Mrs Conroy.

—O, it's only two steps up the quay.

Gabriel hesitated a moment and said:

—If you will allow me, Miss Ivors, I'll see you home if you really are obliged to go.

But Miss Ivors broke away from them.

—I won't hear of it, she cried. For goodness sake go in to your suppers and don't mind me. I'm quite well able to take care of myself.

—Well, you're the comical girl, Molly, said Mrs Conroy frankly.

—*Beannacht libh*, cried Miss Ivors, with a laugh, as she ran down the staircase.

Mary Jane gazed after her, a moody puzzled expression on her face, while Mrs. Conroy leaned over the banisters to listen for the hall-door. Gabriel asked himself was he the cause of her abrupt departure. But she did not seem to be in ill humour: she had gone away laughing. He stared blankly down the staircase.

At that moment Aunt Kate came toddling out of the supper-room, almost wringing her hands in despair.

—Where is Gabriel? she cried. Where on earth is Gabriel? There's everyone waiting in there, stage to let, and nobody to carve the goose!

—Here I am, Aunt Kate! cried Gabriel, with sudden animation, ready to carve a flock of geese, if necessary.

A fat brown goose lay at one end of the table and at the other end, on a bed of creased paper strewn with sprigs of parsley, lay a great ham, stripped of its outer skin and peppered over with crust crumbs, a neat paper frill round its shin and beside this was a round of spiced beef. Between these rival ends ran parallel lines of side-dishes: two little minsters of jelly, red and yellow; a shallow dish full of blocks of blancmange and red jam, a large green leaf-shaped dish with a stalk-shaped handle, on which lay bunches of purple raisins and peeled almonds, a companion dish on which lay a solid rectangle of Smyrna figs, a dish of custard topped with grated nutmeg, a small bowl full of chocolates and sweets wrapped in gold and silver papers and a glass vase in which stood some tall celery stalks. In the centre of the table there stood, as sentries to a fruit-stand which upheld a pyramid of oranges and American apples, two squat old-fashioned decanters of cut glass, one containing port and the other dark sherry. On the closed square piano a pudding in a huge yellow dish lay in waiting and behind it were three squads of bottles of stout and ale and minerals, drawn up according to the colours of their uniforms, the first two black, with brown and red labels, the third and smallest squad white, with transverse green sashes.

Gabriel took his seat boldly at the head of the table and, having looked to the edge of the carver, plunged his fork firmly into the goose. He felt quite at ease now for he was an expert carver and liked nothing better than to find himself at the head of a well-laden table.

—Miss Furlong, what shall I send you? he asked. A wing or a slice of the breast?

—Just a small slice of the breast.

—Miss Higgins, what for you?

—O, anything at all, Mr Conroy.

While Gabriel and Miss Daly exchanged plates of goose and plates of ham and spiced beef Lily went from guest to guest with a dish of hot floury potatoes wrapped in a white napkin. This was Mary Jane's idea and she had also suggested apple sauce for the goose but Aunt Kate had said that plain roast goose without apple sauce had always been good enough for her and she hoped she might never eat worse. Mary Jane waited on her pupils and saw that they got the best slices and Aunt Kate and Aunt Julia opened and carried across from the piano bottles of stout and ale for the gentlemen and bottles of minerals for the ladies. There was a great deal of confusion and laughter and noise, the noise of orders and counter-orders, of knives and forks, of corks and glass-stoppers. Gabriel began to carve second helpings as soon as he had finished the first round without serving himself. Everyone protested loudly so that he compromised by taking a long draught of stout for he had found the carving hot work. Mary Jane settled down quietly to her supper but Aunt Kate and Aunt Julia were still toddling round the table, walking on each other's heels, getting in each other's way and giving each other unheeded orders. Mr Browne begged of them to sit down and eat their suppers and so did Gabriel but they said there was time enough so that, at last, Freddy Malins stood up and, capturing Aunt Kate, plumped her down on her chair amid general laughter.

When everyone had been well served Gabriel said, smiling:

—Now, if anyone wants a little more of what vulgar people call stuffing let him or her speak.

A chorus of voices invited him to begin his own supper and Lily came forward with three potatoes which she had reserved for him.

—Very well, said Gabriel amiably, as he took another preparatory draught, kindly forget my existence, ladies and gentlemen, for a few minutes.

He set to his supper and took no part in the conversation with which the table covered Lily's removal of the plates. The subject of talk was the opera company which was then at the Theatre Royal. Mr Bartell D'Arcy, the tenor, a dark-complexioned young man with a smart moustache, praised very highly the leading contralto of the company but Miss Furlong thought she had a rather vulgar style of production. Freddy Malins said there was a negro chieftain singing in the second part of the Gaiety pantomime who had one of the finest tenor voices he had ever heard.

—Have you heard him? he asked Mr Bartell D'Arcy across the table.

—No, answered Mr Bartell D'Arcy carelessly.

—Because, Freddy Malins explained, now I'd be curious to hear your opinion of him. I think he has a grand voice.

—It takes Teddy to find out the really good things, said Mr Browne familiarly to the table.

—And why couldn't he have a voice too? asked Freddy Malins sharply. Is it because he's only a black?

Nobody answered this question and Mary Jane led the table back to the legitimate opera. One of her pupils had given her a pass for *Mignon*. Of course it was very fine, she said, but it made her think of poor Georgina Burns. Mr Browne could go back farther still, to the old Italian companies that used to come to Dublin —Tietjens, Ilma de Murzka, Campanini, the great Trebelli, Giuglini, Ravelli, Aramburo. Those were the days, he said, when there was something like singing to be heard in Dublin. He told too of how the top gallery of the old Royal used to be packed night after night, of how one night an Italian tenor had sung five encores to *Let Me Like a Soldier Fall*, introducing a high C every time, and of how the gallery boys would sometimes in their enthusiasm unyoke the horses from the carriage of some great *prima donna* and pull her themselves through the streets to her hotel. Why did they never play the grand old operas now, he asked, *Dinorah, Lucrezia Borgia?* Because they could not get the voices to sing them: that was why.

—O, well, said Mr Bartell D'Arcy, I presume there are as good singers to-day as there were then.

—Where are they? asked Mr Browne defiantly.

—In London, Paris, Milan, said Mr Bartell D'Arcy warmly. I suppose Caruso, for example, is quite as good, if not better than any of the men you have mentioned.

—Maybe so, said Mr. Browne. But I may tell you I doubt it strongly.

—O, I'd give anything to hear Caruso sing, said Mary Jane.

—For me, said Aunt Kate, who had been picking a bone, there was only one tenor. To please me, I mean. But I suppose none of you ever heard of him.

—Who was he, Miss Morkan? asked Mr Bartell D'Arcy politely.

His name, said Aunt Kate, was Parkinson. I heard him when he was in his prime and I think he had then the purest tenor voice that was ever put into a man's throat.

—Strange, said Mr Bartell D'Arcy. I never even heard of him.

—Yes, yes, Miss Morkan is right, said Mr Browne. I remember hearing of old Parkinson but he's too far back for me.

—A beautiful pure sweet mellow English tenor, said Aunt Kate with enthusiasm.

Gabriel having finished, the huge pudding was transferred to the table. The clatter of forks and spoons began again. Gabriel's wife served out spoonfuls of the pudding and passed the plates down the table. Midway down they were held up by Mary Jane, who replenished them with raspberry or orange jelly or with blancmange and jam. The pudding was of Aunt Julia's making and she received praises for it from all quarters. She herself said that it was not quite brown enough.

—Well, I hope, Miss Morkan, said Mr Browne, that I'm brown enough for you because, you know, I'm all brown.

All the gentlemen, except Gabriel, ate some of the pudding out of compliment to Aunt Julia. As Gabriel never ate sweets the celery had been left for him. Freddy Malins also took a stalk of celery and ate it with his pudding. He had been told that celery was a capital thing for the blood and he was just then under doctor's care. Mrs Malins, who had been silent all through the supper, said that her son was going down to Mount Melleray in a week or so. The table then spoke of Mount Melleray, how bracing the air was down there, how hospitable the monks were and how they never asked for a penny-piece from their guests.

—And do you mean to say, asked Mr Browne incredulously, that a chap can go down there and put up there as if it were a hotel and live on the fat of the land and then come away without paying a farthing?

—O, most people give some donation to the monastery when they leave, said Mary Jane.

—I wish we had an institution like that in our Church, said Mr Browne candidly.

He was astonished to hear that the monks never spoke, got up at two in the morning and slept in their coffins. He asked what they did it for.

—That's the rule of the order, said Aunt Kate firmly.

—Yes, but why? asked Mr Browne.

Aunt Kate repeated that it was the rule, that was all. Mr Browne still seemed not to understand. Freddy Malins explained to him, as best he could, that the monks were trying to make up for the sins committed by all the sinners in the outside world. The explanation was not very clear for Mr Browne grinned and said:

—I like that idea very much but wouldn't a comfortable spring bed do them as well as a coffin?

—The coffin, said Mary Jane, is to remind them of their last end.

As the subject had grown lugubrious it was buried in a silence of the table during which Mrs Malins could be heard saying to her neighbour in an indistinct undertone:

—They are very good men, the monks, very pious men.

The raisins and almonds and figs and apples and oranges and chocolates and sweets were now passed about the table and Aunt Julia invited all the guests to have either port or sherry. At first Mr Bartell D'Arcy refused to take either but one of his neighbours nudged him and whispered something to him upon which he allowed his glass to be filled. Gradually as the last glasses were being filled the conversation ceased. A pause followed, broken only by the noise of the wine and by unsettlings of chairs. The Misses Morkan, all three, looked down at the tablecloth. Some one coughed once or twice and then a few gentlemen patted the table gently as a signal for silence. The silence came and Gabriel pushed back his chair and stood up.

The patting at once grew louder in encouragement and then ceased altogether. Gabriel leaned his ten trembling fingers on the tablecloth and smiled nervously at the company. Meeting a row of upturned faces he raised his eyes to the chandelier. The piano was playing a waltz tune and he could hear the skirts sweeping against the drawing-room door. People, perhaps, were standing in the snow on the quay outside, gazing up at the lighted windows and listening to the waltz music. The air was pure there. In the distance lay the park where the trees were weighted with snow. The Wellington Monument wore a gleaming cap of snow that flashed westward over the white field of Fifteen Acres.

He began:

—Ladies and Gentlemen.

It has fallen to my lot this evening, as in years past, to perform a very pleasing task but a task for which I am afraid my poor powers as a speaker are all too inadequate.

—No, no! said Mr Browne.

—But, however that may be, I can only ask you to-night to take the will for the deed and to lend me your attention for a few moments while I endeavour to express to you in words what my feelings are on this occasion.

—Ladies and Gentlemen. It is not the first time that we have gathered together under this hospitable roof, around this hospitable board. It is not the first time that we have been the recipients—or perhaps, I had better say, the victims—of the hospitality of certain good ladies.

He made a circle in the air with his arm and paused. Every one laughed or smiled at Aunt Kate and Aunt Julia and Mary Jane who all turned crimson with pleasure. Gabriel went on more boldly:

—I feel more strongly with every recurring year that our country has no tradition which does it so much honour and which it should guard so jealously as that of its hospitality. It is a tradition that is unique as far as my experience goes (and I have visited not a few places abroad) among the modern nations. Some would say, perhaps, that with us it is rather a failing than anything to be boasted of. But granted even that, it is, to my mind, a princely failing, and one that I trust will long be cultivated among us. Of one thing, at least, I am sure. As long as this one roof shelters the good ladies aforesaid—and I wish from my heart it may do so for many and many a long year to come—the tradition of genuine warm-hearted courteous Irish hospitality, which our forefathers have handed down to us and which we in turn must hand down to our descendants, is still alive among us.

A hearty murmur of assent ran round the table. It shot through Gabriel's mind that Miss Ivors was not there and that she had gone away discourteously: and he said with confidence in himself:

—Ladies and Gentlemen.

—A new generation is growing up in our midst, a generation actuated by new ideas and new principles. It is serious and enthusiastic for these new ideas and its enthusiasm, even when it is misdirected, is, I believe, in the main sincere. But we are living in a sceptical and, if I may use the phrase, a thought-tormented age: and sometimes I fear that this new generation, educated or hypereducated as it is, will lack those qualities of humanity, of hospitality, of kindly humour which belonged to an older day. Listening to-night to the names of all those great singers of the past it seemed to me, I must confess, that we were living in a less spacious age. Those days might, without exaggeration, be called spacious days: and if they are gone beyond recall let us hope, at least, that in gatherings such as this we shall still speak of them with pride and affection, still cherish in our hearts the memory of those dead and gone great ones whose fame the world will not willingly let die.

—Hear, hear! said Mr Browne loudly.

—But yet, continued Gabriel, his voice falling into a softer inflection, there are always in gatherings such as this sadder thoughts that will recur to our minds: thoughts of the past, of youth, of changes, of absent faces that we miss here to-night. Our path through life is strewn with many such sad memories: and were we to brood upon them always we could not find the heart to go on bravely with our work among the living. We have all of us living duties and living affections which claim, and rightly claim, our strenuous endeavours.

—Therefore, I will not linger on the past. I will not let any gloomy moralizing intrude upon us here to-night. Here we are gathered together for a brief moment from the bustle and rush of our everyday routine. We are met here as friends, in the spirit of good-fellowship, as colleagues, also to a certain extent, in the true spirit of *camaraderie*, and as the guests of —what shall I call them?—the Three Graces of the Dublin musical world.

The table burst into applause and laughter at this sally. Aunt Julia vainly asked each of her neighbours in turn to tell her what Gabriel had said.

—He says we are the Three Graces, Aunt Julia, said Mary Jane.

Aunt Julia did not understand but she looked up, smiling, at Gabriel, who continued in the same vein:

—Ladies and Gentlemen.

—I will not attempt to play to-night the part that Paris played on another occasion. I will not attempt to choose between them. The task would be an invidious one and one beyond my poor powers. For when I view them in turn, whether it be our chief hostess herself, whose good heart, whose too good heart, has become a byword with all who know her, or her sister, who seems to be gifted with perennial youth and whose singing must have been a surprise and a revelation to us all to-night, or, last but not least, when I consider our youngest hostess, talented, cheerful, hard-working and the best of nieces, I confess, Ladies and Gentlemen, that I do not know to which of them I should award the prize.

Gabriel glanced down at his aunts and, seeing the large smile on Aunt Julia's face and the tears which had risen to Aunt Kate's eyes, hastened to his close. He raised his glass of port gallantly, while every member of the company fingered a glass expectantly, and said loudly:

—Let us toast them all three together. Let us drink to their health, wealth, long life, happiness and prosperity and may they long continue to hold the proud and self-won position which they hold in their profession and the position of honour and affection which they hold in our hearts.

All the guests stood up, glass in hand, and, turning towards the three seated ladies, sang in unison, with Mr Browne as leader:

For they are jolly gay fellows,
For they are jolly gay fellows,
For they are jolly gay fellows,
Which nobody can deny.

Aunt Kate was making frank use of her handkerchief and even Aunt Julia seemed moved. Freddy Malins beat time with his pudding-fork and the singers turned towards one another, as if in melodious conference, while they sang, with emphasis:

Unless he tells a lie,
Unless he tells a lie.

Then, turning once more towards their hostess, they sang:

For they are jolly gay fellows,
For they are jolly gay fellows,
For they are jolly gay fellows,
Which nobody can deny.

The acclamation which followed was taken up beyond the door of the supper-room by many of the other guests and renewed time after time, Freddy Malins acting as officer with his fork on high.

. . . .

The piercing morning air came into the hall where they were standing so that Aunt Kate said:

—Close the door, somebody. Mrs Malins will get her death of cold.

—Browne is out there, Aunt Kate, said Mary Jane.

—Browne is everywhere, said Aunt Kate, lowering her voice.

Mary Jane laughed at her tone.

—Really, she said archly, he is very attentive.

—He has been laid on here like the gas, said Aunt Kate in the same tone, all during the Christmas.

She laughed herself this time good-humouredly and then added quickly:

—But tell him to come in, Mary Jane, and close the door. I hope to goodness he didn't hear me.

At that moment the hall-door was opened and Mr Browne came in from the doorstep, laughing as if his heart would break. He was dressed in a long green overcoat with mock astrakhan cuffs and collar and wore on his head an oval fur cap. He pointed down the snow-covered quay from where the sound of shrill prolonged whistling was borne in.

—Teddy will have all the cabs in Dublin out, he said.

Gabriel advanced from the little pantry behind the office, struggling into his overcoat and, looking round the hall, said:

—Gretta not down yet?

—She's getting on her things, Gabriel, said Aunt Kate.

—Who's playing up there? asked Gabriel.

—Nobody. They're all gone.

—O no, Aunt Kate, said Mary Jane. Bartell D'Arcy and Miss O'Callaghan aren't gone yet.

—Someone is strumming at the piano, anyhow, said Gabriel.

Mary Jane glanced at Gabriel and Mr Browne and said with a shiver:

—It makes me feel cold to look at you two gentlemen muffled up like that. I wouldn't like to face your journey home at this hour.

—I'd like nothing better this minute, said Mr Browne stoutly, than a rattling fine walk in the country or a fast drive with a good spanking goer between the shafts.

—We used to have a very good horse and trap at home, said Aunt Julia sadly.

—The never-to-be-forgotten Johnny, said Mary Jane, laughing.

Aunt Kate and Gabriel laughed too.

—Why, what was wonderful about Johnny? asked Mr Browne.

—The late lamented Patrick Morkan, our grandfather, that is, explained Gabriel, commonly known in his later years as the old gentleman, was a glue-boiler.

—O, now, Gabriel, said Aunt Kate, laughing, he had a starch mill.

—Well, glue or starch, said Gabriel, the old gentleman had a horse by the name of Johnny. And Johnny used to work in the old gentleman's mill, walking round and round in order to drive the mill. That was all very well; but now comes the tragic part about Johnny. One fine day the old gentleman thought he'd like to drive out with the quality to a military review in the park.

—The Lord have mercy on his soul, said Aunt Kate compassionately.

—Amen, said Gabriel. So the old gentleman, as I said, harnessed Johnny and put on his very best tall hat and his very best stock collar and drove out in grand style from his ancestral mansion somewhere near Back Lane, I think.

Every one laughed, even Mrs Malins, at Gabriel's manner and Aunt Kate said:

—O now, Gabriel, he didn't live in Back Lane, really. Only the mill was there.

—Out from the mansion of his forefathers, continued Gabriel, he drove with Johnny. And everything went on beautifully until Johnny came in sight of King Billy's statue: and whether he fell in love with the horse King Billy sits on or whether he thought he was back again in the mill, anyhow he began to walk round the statue.

Gabriel paced in a circle round the hall in his goloshes amid the laughter of the others.

—Round and round he went, said Gabriel, and the old gentleman, who was a very pompous old gentleman, was highly indignant. *Go on, sir! What do you mean, sir? Johnny! Johnny! Most extraordinary conduct! Can't understand the horse!*

The peals of laughter which followed Gabriel's imitation of the incident were interrupted by a resounding knock at the hall-door. Mary Jane ran to open it and let in Freddy Malins. Freddy Malins, with his hat well back on his head and his shoulders humped with cold, was puffing and steaming after his exertions.

—I could only get one cab, he said.

—O, we'll find another along the quay, said Gabriel.

—Yes, said Aunt Kate. Better not keep Mrs Malins standing in the draught.

Mrs Malins was helped down the front steps by her son and Mr Browne and, after many manoeuvers, hoisted into the cab. Freddy Malins clambered in after her and spent a long time settling her on the seat, Mr Browne helping him with advice. At last she was settled comfortably and Freddy Malins invited Mr Browne into the cab. There was a good deal of confused talk, and then Mr Browne got into the cab. The cabman settled his rug over his knees, and bent down for the address. The confusion grew greater and the cabman was directed differently by Freddy Malins and Mr Browne, each of whom had his head out through a window of the cab. The difficulty was to know where to drop Mr Browne along the route and Aunt Kate, Aunt Julia and Mary Jane helped the discussion from the doorstep with cross-directions and contradictions and abundance of laughter. As for Freddy Malins he was speechless with laughter. He popped his head in and out of the window every moment, to the great danger of his hat, and told his mother how the discussion was progressing till at last Mr Browne shouted to the bewildered cabman above the din of everybody's laughter:

—Do you know Trinity College?

—Yes, sir, said the cabman.

—Well, drive bang up against Trinity College gates, said Mr Browne, and then we'll tell you where to go. You understand now?

—Yes, sir, said the cabman.

—Make like a bird for Trinity College.

—Right, sir, cried the cabman.

The horse was whipped up and the cab rattled off along the quay amid a chorus of laughter and adieus.

Gabriel had not gone to the door with the others. He was in a dark part of the hall gazing up the staircase. A woman was standing near the top of the first flight, in the shadow also. He could not see her face but he could see the terracotta and salmonpink panels of her skirt which the shadow made appear black and white. It was his wife. She was leaning on the banisters, listening to something. Gabriel was surprised at her stillness and strained his ear to listen also. But he could hear little save the noise of laughter and dispute on the front steps, a few chords struck on the piano and a few notes of a man's voice singing.

He stood still in the gloom of the hall, trying to catch the air that the voice was singing and gazing up at his wife. There was grace and mystery in her attitude as if she were a symbol of something. He asked himself what is a woman standing on the stairs in the shadow, listening to distant music, a symbol of. If he were a painter he would paint her in that attitude. Her blue felt hat would show off the bronze of her hair against the darkness and the dark panels of her skirt would show off the light ones. *Distant Music* he would call the picture if he were a painter.

The hall-door was closed; and Aunt Kate, Aunt Julia and Mary Jane came down the hall, still laughing.

—Well, isn't Freddy terrible? said Mary Jane. He's really terrible.

Gabriel said nothing but pointed up the stairs towards where his wife was standing. Now that the hall-door was closed the voice and the piano could be heard more clearly. Gabriel held up his hand for them to be silent. The song seemed to be in the old Irish tonality and the singer seemed uncertain both of his words and of his voice. The voice, made plaintive by distance and by the singer's hoarseness, faintly illuminated the cadence of the air with words expressing grief:

> O, the rain falls on my heavy locks
> And the dew wets my skin,
> My babe lies cold . . .

—O, exclaimed Mary Jane. It's Bartell D'Arcy singing and he wouldn't sing all the night. O, I'll get him to sing a song before he goes.

—O do, Mary Jane, said Aunt Kate.

Mary Jane brushed past the others and ran to the staircase but before she reached it the singing stopped and the piano was closed abruptly.

—O, what a pity! she cried. Is he coming down, Gretta?

Gabriel heard his wife answer yes and saw her come down towards them. A few steps behind her were Mr Bartell D'Arcy and Miss O'Callaghan.

—O, Mr D'Arcy, cried Mary Jane, it's downright mean of you to break off like that when we were all in raptures listening to you.

—I have been at him all the evening, said Miss O'Callaghan, and Mrs Conroy too and he told us he had a dreadful cold and couldn't sing.

—O, Mr. D'Arcy, said Aunt Kate, now that was a great fib to tell.

—Can't you see that I'm as hoarse as a crow? said Mr D'Arcy roughly.

He went into the pantry hastily and put on his overcoat. The others, taken aback by his rude speech, could find nothing to say. Aunt Kate wrinkled her brows and made signs to the others to drop the subject. Mr D'Arcy stood swathing his neck carefully and frowning.

—It's the weather, said Aunt Julia, after a pause.

—Yes, everybody has colds, said Aunt Kate readily, everybody.

—They say, said Mary Jane, we haven't had snow like it for thirty years; and I read this morning in the newspapers that the snow is general all over Ireland.

—I love the look of snow, said Aunt Julia sadly.

—So do I, said Miss O'Callaghan. I think Christmas is never really Christmas unless we have the snow on the ground.

—But poor Mr D'Arcy doesn't like the snow, said Aunt Kate, smiling.

Mr D'Arcy came from the pantry, fully swathed and buttoned, and in a repentant tone told them the history of his cold. Everyone gave him advice and said it was a great pity and urged him to be very careful of his throat in the night air. Gabriel watched his wife who did not join in the conversation. She was standing right under the dusty fanlight and the flame of the gas lit up the rich bronze of her hair which he had seen her drying at the fire a few days before. She was in the same attitude and seemed unaware of the talk about her. At last she turned towards them and Gabriel saw that there was colour on her cheeks and that her eyes were shining. A sudden tide of joy went leaping out of his heart.

—Mr D'Arcy, she said, what is the name of that song you were singing?

—It's called *The Lass of Aughrim*, said Mr D'Arcy, but I couldn't remember it properly. Why? Do you know it?

—*The Lass of Aughrim*, she repeated. I couldn't think of the name.

—It's a very nice air, said Mary Jane. I'm sorry you were not in voice to-night.

—Now, Mary Jane, said Aunt Kate, don't annoy Mr D'Arcy. I won't have him annoyed.

Seeing that all were ready to start she shepherded them to the door where good-night was said:

—Well, good-night, Aunt Kate, and thanks for the pleasant evening.

—Good-night, Gabriel. Good-night, Gretta!

—Good-night, Aunt Kate, and thanks ever so much. Good-night, Aunt Julia.

—O, good-night, Gretta, I didn't see you.

—Good-night, Mr D'Arcy. Good-night, Miss O'Callaghan.

—Good-night, Miss Morkan.

—Good-night, again.

—Good-night, all. Safe home.

—Good-night. Good-night.

The morning was still dark. A dull yellow light brooded over the houses and the river; and the sky seemed to be descending. It was slushy underfoot; and only streaks and patches of snow lay on the roofs, on the parapets of the quay and on the area railings. The lamps were still burning redly in the murky air and, across the river, the palace of the Four Courts stood out menacingly against the heavy sky.

She was walking on before him with Mr Bartell D'Arcy, her shoes in a brown parcel tucked under one arm and her hands holding her skirt up from the slush. She had no longer any grace of attitude but Gabriel's eyes were still bright with happiness. The blood went bounding along his veins; and the thoughts went rioting through his brain, proud, joyful, tender, valorous.

She was walking on before him so lightly and so erect that he longed to run after her noiselessly, catch her by the shoulders and say something foolish and affectionate into her ear. She seemed to him so frail that he longed to defend her against something and then to be alone with her. Moments of their secret life together burst like stars upon his memory. A heliotrope envelope was lying beside his breakfast-cup and he was caressing it with his hand. Birds were twittering in the ivy and the sunny web of the curtain was shimmering along the floor: he could not eat for happiness. They were standing on the crowded platform and he was placing a ticket inside the warm palm of her glove. He was standing with her in the cold, looking in through a grated window at a man making bottles in a roaring furnace. It was very cold. Her face, fragrant in the cold air, was quite close to his; and suddenly she called out to the man at the furnace:

—Is the fire hot, sir?

But the man could not hear her with the noise of the furnace. It was just as well. He might have answered rudely.

A wave of yet more tender joy escaped from his heart and went coursing in warm flood along his arteries. Like the tender fires of stars moments of their life together, that no one knew of or would ever know of, broke upon and illumined his memory. He longed to recall to her those moments, to make her forget the years of their dull existence together and remember only their moments of ecstasy. For the years, he felt, had not quenched his soul or hers. Their children, his writing, her household cares had not quenched all their souls' tender fire. In one letter that he had written to her then he had said: *Why is it that words like these seem to me so dull and cold? Is it because there is no word tender enough to be your name?*

Like distant music these words that he had written years before were borne towards him from the past. He longed to be alone with her. When the others had gone away, when he and she were in their room in the hotel, then they would be alone together. He would call her softly:

—Gretta!

Perhaps she would not hear at once: she would be undressing. Then something in his voice would strike her. She would turn and look at him. . . .

At the corner of Winetavern Street they met a cab. He was glad of its rattling noise as it saved him from conversation. She was looking out of the window and seemed tired. The others spoke only a few words, pointing out some building or street. The horse galloped along wearily under the murky morning sky, dragging his old rattling box after his heels, and Gabriel was again in a cab with her, galloping to catch the boat, galloping to their honeymoon.

As the cab drove across O'Connell Bridge Miss O'Callaghan said:

—They say you never cross O'Connell Bridge without seeing a white horse.

—I see a white man this time, said Gabriel.

—Where? asked Mr Bartell D'Arcy.

Gabriel pointed to the statue, on which lay patches of snow. Then he nodded familiarly to it and waved his hand.

—Good-night, Dan, he said gaily.

When the cab drew up before the hotel Gabriel jumped out and, in spite of Mr Bartell D'Arcy's protest, paid the driver. He gave the man a shilling over his fare. The man saluted and said:

—A prosperous New Year to you, sir.

—The same to you, said Gabriel cordially.

She leaned for a moment on his arm in getting out of the cab and while standing at the curbstone, bidding the others good-night. She leaned lightly on his arm, as lightly as when she had danced with him a few hours before. He had felt proud and happy then, happy that she was his, proud of her grace and wifely carriage. But now, after the kindling again of so many memories, the first touch of her body, musical and strange and perfumed, sent through him a keen pang of lust. Under cover of her silence he pressed her arm closely to his side; and, as they stood at the hotel door, he felt that they had escaped from their lives and duties, escaped from home and friends and run away together with wild and radiant hearts to a new adventure.

An old man was dozing in a great hooded chair in the hall. He lit a candle in the office and went before them to the stairs. They followed him in silence, their feet falling in soft thuds on the thickly carpeted stairs. She mounted the stairs behind the porter, her head bowed in the ascent, her frail shoulders curved as with a burden, her skirt girt tightly about her. He could have flung his arms about her hips and held her still for his arms were trembling with desire to seize her and only the stress of his nails against the palms of his hands held the wild impulse of his body in check. The porter halted on the stairs to settle his guttering candle. They halted too on the steps below him. In the silence Gabriel could hear the falling of the molten wax into the tray and the thumping of his own heart against his ribs.

The porter led them along a corridor and opened a door. Then he set his unstable candle down on a toilet-table and asked at what hour they were to be called in the morning.

—Eight, said Gabriel.

The porter pointed to the tap of the electric-light and began a muttered apology but Gabriel cut him short.

—We don't want any light. We have light enough from the street. And I say, he added, pointing to the candle, you might remove that handsome article, like a good man.

The porter took up his candle again, but slowly for he was surprised by such a novel idea. Then he mumbled good-night and went out. Gabriel shot the lock to.

A ghostly light from the street lamp lay in a long shaft from one window to the door. Gabriel threw his overcoat and hat on a couch and crossed the room towards the window. He looked down into the street in order that his emotion might calm a little. Then he turned and leaned against a chest of drawers with his back to the light. She had taken off her hat and cloak and was standing before a large swinging mirror, unhooking her waist. Gabriel paused for a few moments, watching her, and then said:

—Gretta!

She turned away from the mirror slowly and walked along the shaft of light towards him. Her face looked so serious and weary that the words would not pass Gabriel's lips. No, it was not the moment yet.

—You looked tired, he said.

—I am a little, she answered.

—You don't feel ill or weak?

—No, tired: that's all.

She went on to the window and stood there, looking out. Gabriel waited again and then, fearing that diffidence was about to conquer him, he said abruptly:

—By the way, Gretta!

—What is it?

—You know that poor fellow Malins? he said quickly.

—Yes. What about him?

—Well, poor fellow, he's a decent sort of chap after all, continued Gabriel in a false voice. He gave me back that sovereign I lent him and I didn't expect it really. It's a pity he wouldn't keep away from that Browne, because he's not a bad fellow at heart.

He was trembling now with annoyance.

Why did she seem so abstracted? He did not know how he could begin. Was she annoyed, too, about something? If she would only turn to him or come to him of her own accord! To take her as she was would be brutal. No, he must see some ardour in her eyes first. He longed to be master of her strange mood.

—When did you lend him the pound? she asked, after a pause.

Gabriel strove to restrain himself from breaking out into brutal language about the sottish Malins and his pound. He longed to cry to her from his soul, to crush her body against his, to overmaster her. But he said:

—O, at Christmas, when he opened that little Christmas-card shop in Henry Street.

He was in such a fever of rage and desire that he did not hear her come from the window. She stood before him for an instant, looking at him strangely. Then, suddenly raising herself on tiptoe and resting her hands lightly on his shoulders, she kissed him.

—You are a very generous person, Gabriel, she said.

Gabriel, trembling with delight at her sudden kiss and at the quaintness of her phrase, put his hands on her hair and began smoothing it back, scarcely touching it with his fingers. The washing had made it fine and brilliant. His heart was brimming over with happiness. Just when he was wishing for it she had come to him of her own accord. Perhaps her thoughts had been running with his. Perhaps she had felt the impetuous desire that was in him and then the yielding mood had come upon her. Now that she had fallen to him so easily he wondered why he had been so diffident.

He stood, holding her head between his hands. Then, slipping one arm swiftly about her body and drawing her towards him, he said softly:

—Gretta dear, what are you thinking about?

She did not answer nor yield wholly to his arm. He said again, softly:

—Tell me what it is, Gretta. I think I know what is the matter. Do I know?

She did not answer at once. Then she said in an outburst of tears.

—O, I am thinking about that song, *The Lass of Aughrim*.

She broke loose from him and ran to the bed and, throwing her arms across the bed-rail, hid her face. Gabriel stood stock-still for a moment in astonishment and then followed her. As he passed in the way of the cheval-glass he caught sight of himself in full length, his broad, well-filled shirt-front, the face whose expression always puzzled him when he saw it in a mirror and his glimmering gilt-rimmed eyeglasses. He halted a few paces from her and said:

—What about the song? Why does that make you cry?

She raised her head from her arms and dried her eyes with the back of her hand like a child. A kinder note than he had intended went into his voice.

—Why, Gretta? he asked.

—I am thinking about a person long ago who used to sing that song.

—And who was the person long ago? asked Gabriel, smiling.

—It was a person I used to know in Galway when I was living with my grandmother, she said.

The smile passed away from Gabriel's face. A dull anger began to gather again at the back of his mind and the dull fires of his lust began to glow angrily in his veins.

—Someone you were in love with? he asked ironically.

—It was a young boy I used to know, she answered, named Michael Furey. He used to sing that song, *The Lass of Aughrim*. He was very delicate.

Gabriel was silent. He did not wish her to think that he was interested in this delicate boy.

—I can see him so plainly, she said after a moment. Such eyes as he had: big dark eyes! And such an expression in them—an expression!

—O then, you were in love with him? said Gabriel.

—I used to go out walking with him, she said, when I was in Galway.

A thought flew across Gabriel's mind.

—Perhaps that was why you wanted to go to Galway with that Ivors girl? he said coldly.

She looked at him and asked in surprise:

—What for?

Her eyes made Gabriel feel awkward. He shrugged his shoulders and said:

—How do I know? To see him perhaps.

She looked away from him along the shaft of light towards the window in silence.

—He is dead, she said at length. He died when he was only seventeen. Isn't it a terrible thing to die so young as that?

—What was he? asked Gabriel, still ironically.

—He was in the gasworks, she said.

Gabriel felt humiliated by the failure of his irony and by the evocation of this figure from the dead, a boy in the gasworks. While he had been full of memories of their secret life together, full of tenderness and joy and desire, she had been comparing him in her mind with another. A shameful consciousness of his own person assailed him. He saw himself as a ludicrous figure, acting as a pennyboy for his aunts, a nervous well-meaning sentimentalist, orating to vulgarians and idealizing his own clownish lusts, the pitiable fatuous fellow he had caught a glimpse of in the mirror. Instinctively he turned his back more to the light lest she might see the shame that burned upon his forehead.

He tried to keep up his tone of cold interrogation but his voice when he spoke was humble and indifferent.

—I suppose you were in love with this Michael Furey, Gretta, he said.

—I was great with him at that time, she said.

Her voice was veiled and sad. Gabriel, feeling now how vain it would be to try to lead her whither he had purposed, caressed one of her hands and said, also sadly:

—And what did he die of so young, Gretta? Consumption, was it?

—I think he died for me, she answered.

A vague terror seized Gabriel at this answer as if, at that hour when he had hoped to triumph, some impalpable and vindictive being was coming against him, gathering forces against him in its vague world. But he shook himself free of it with an effort of reason and continued to caress her hand. He did not question her again for he felt that she would tell him of herself. Her hand was warm and moist: it did not respond to his touch but he continued to caress it just as he had caressed her first letter to him that spring morning.

—It was in the winter, she said, about the beginning of the winter when I was going to leave my grandmother's and come up here to the convent. And he was ill at the time in his lodgings in Galway and wouldn't be let out and his people in Oughterard were written to. He was in decline, they said, or something like that. I never knew rightly.

She paused for a moment and sighed.

—Poor fellow, she said. He was very fond of me and he was such a gentle boy. We used to go out together, walking, you know, Gabriel, like the way they do in the country. He was going to study singing only for his health. He had a very good voice, poor Michael Furey.

—Well; and then? asked Gabriel.

—And then when it came to the time for me to leave Galway and come up to the convent he was much worse and I wouldn't be let see him so I wrote a letter saying I was going up to Dublin and would be back in the summer and hoping he would be better then.

She paused for a moment to get her voice under control and then went on:

—Then the night before I left I was in my grandmother's house in Nuns' Island, packing up, and I heard gravel thrown up against the window. The window was so wet I couldn't see so I ran downstairs as I was and slipped out the back into the garden and there was the poor fellow at the end of the garden, shivering.

—And did you not tell him to go back? asked Gabriel.

—I implored of him to go home at once and told him he would get his death in the rain. But he said he did not want to live. I can see his eyes as well as well! He was standing at the end of the wall where there was a tree.

—And did he go home? asked Gabriel.

—Yes, he went home. And when I was only a week in the convent he died and he was buried in Oughterard where his people came from. O, the day I heard that, that he was dead!

She stopped, choking with sobs, and, overcome by emotion, flung herself face downward on the bed, sobbing in the quilt. Gabriel held her hand for a moment longer, irresolutely, and then, shy of intruding on her grief, let it fall gently and walked quietly to the window.

She was fast asleep.

Gabriel, leaning on his elbow, looked for a few moments unresentfully on her tangled hair and half-open mouth, listening to her deep-drawn breath. So she had had that romance in her life: a man had died for her sake. It hardly pained him now to think how poor a part he, her husband, had played in her life. He watched her while she slept as though he and she had never lived together as man and wife. His curious eyes rested long upon her face and on her hair: and, as he thought of what she must have been then, in that time of her first girlish beauty, a strange friendly pity for her entered his soul. He did not like to say even to himself that her face was no longer beautiful but he knew that it was no longer the face for which Michael Furey had braved death.

Perhaps she had not told him all the story. His eyes moved to the chair over which she had thrown some of her clothes. A petticoat string dangled to the floor. One boot stood upright, its limp upper fallen down: the fellow of it lay upon its side. He wondered at his riot of emotions of an hour before. From what had it proceeded? From his aunt's supper, from his own foolish speech, from the wine and dancing, the merry-making when saying good-night in the hall, the pleasure of the walk along the river in the snow. Poor Aunt Julia! She, too, would soon be a shade with the shade of Patrick Morkan and his horse. He had caught that haggard look upon her face for a moment when she was singing *Arrayed for the Bridal*. Soon, perhaps, he would be sitting in that same drawing-room, dressed in black, his silk hat on his knees. The blinds would be drawn down and Aunt Kate would be sitting beside him, crying and blowing her nose and telling him how Julia had died. He would cast about in his mind for some words that might console her, and would find only lame and useless ones. Yes, yes: that would happen very soon.

The air of the room chilled his shoulders. He stretched himself cautiously along under the sheets and lay down beside his wife. One by one they were all becoming shades. Better pass boldly into that other world, in the full glory of some passion, than fade and wither dismally with age. He thought of how she who lay beside him had locked in her heart for so many years that image of her lover's eyes when he had told her that he did not wish to live.

Generous tears filled Gabriel's eyes. He had never felt like that himself towards any woman but he knew that such a feeling must be love. The tears gathered more thickly in his eyes and in the partial darkness he imagined he saw the form of a young man standing under a dripping tree. Other forms were near. His soul had approached that region where dwell the vast hosts of the dead. He was conscious of, but could not apprehend, their wayward and flickering existence. His own identity was fading out into a grey impalpable world: the solid world itself which these dead had one time reared and lived in was dissolving and dwindling.

A few light taps upon the pane made him turn to the window. It had begun to snow again. He watched sleepily the flakes, silver and dark, falling obliquely against the lamplight. The time had come for him to set out on his journey westward. Yes, the newspapers were right: snow was general all over Ireland. It was falling on every part of the dark central plain, on the treeless hills, falling softly upon the Bog of Allen and, farther westward, softly falling into the dark mutinous Shannon waves. It was falling, too, upon every part of the lonely churchyard on the hill where Michael Furey lay buried. It lay thickly drifted on the crooked crosses and headstones, on the spears of the little gate, on the barren thorns. His soul swooned slowly as he heard the snow falling faintly through the universe and faintly falling, like the descent of their last end, upon all the living and the dead.

Unit **4**

DRAMA:
CRITICAL ESSAYS

ON DRAMA

Drama has always been one of the most vital forms of literary expression because its medium is the dialogue and action of living people on a stage. In order to be fully experienced, plays must be seen and not merely read, but even as reading they provide some of the deepest insights into the human situation that literature has to offer. Because of their concentrated dramatic action they achieve their specific effects with far greater emotional intensity than any other literary form, and their effects are also more easily discernible.

All drama is built on congruities or incongruities. When we go to the theatre, we sometimes enjoy the spectacle of some characters who, in spite of the ups and downs of life common to us all, are doing the things they ought to do, and who win our *admiration* for lives that run congruous to our own and their ideals. Thomas More in A Man for All Seasons is such a character.

But the vast majority of plays are built, not on any such congruity, but rather on the exact opposite. *Comedy* and *tragedy* have this in common, that they both grow out of radical human incongruities. Both the comic character and the tragic character have departed from the normal. In the one instance the character is seen to be laughable and ridiculous for having done so, and in the other he is deeply pitiable. If we can clarify some of the reasons for our reacting in these opposite ways to human actions that are departures from normal and expected actions, we will better understand the difference between the *comic* and the *tragic* in both life and literature.

At what kind of persons and situations are we apt to laugh? It is the sudden departure from the normal, the usual, the expected, that evokes laughter. Why is it that we are apt instinctively to laugh at the sight of a man slipping on a banana peel and sprawling gracelessly on the sidewalk? The sudden apprehension of this very unusual position and movement of the human form strikes us as funny. Incongruity lies at the heart of the comic. If the same person were suddenly struck by an automobile and sent sprawling before us just as gracelessly, we would not be apt to laugh; we would more probably be shocked because of the more obvious likelihood of injury to the person in this kind of accident. In other words, it is the relatively painless aberration from the normal that is laughable. At the same time, the situation must be one from which we ourselves are relatively detached. If one were walking down the street with his mother and she slipped on a banana peel, the situation would again be shocking rather than laughable. This suggests the thin partition that separates laughter from tears, the comic from the tragic in human experience. It also illustrates the fact that we are always somehow separate and aloof from the person or thing at which we laugh.

There is a criticism implicit in every laugh. A laugh is an instinctive way of ridiculing the aberration, the abnormality that invites the laugh. That is why animals don't laugh; only rational man sees a joke. And we consider ourselves in some way superior to the person at whom we laugh, at least in the aspect in which we find him laughable. When the aberration at which we are laughing is moral, the laugh is a judgment on the essential irrationality of all immorality. But the aberration, even the moral aberration that is seen to be laughable, is not usually catastrophically serious. Like Puck in *A Midsummer Night's Dream,* for a moment we are separate, apart, and above offending man, and saying "What fools these mortals be." If we examine carefully our own feelings toward the character or the situation at which we laugh in the theatre or in life, we always find something of this distance between ourselves and it. We do not identify ourselves with the comic character at the moment in which we find him funny.

With the tragic character the exact opposite is true. What we are looking at in a tragic spectacle is also an incongruity, a departure from the normal and usual, but more often than not, it is a moral aberration for which the tragic character is at least partly responsible, and the consequence of which is more or less catastrophic to himself and to others. Unlike the comic situation, tragedy is fraught with pain and evokes, not laughter, but tears. It invites our deepest sympathy and commiseration. We are not at all aloof and separate from the tragic spectacle but identify ourselves most closely with the tragic hero. And it is the business of the tragedian to build his characters with such convincing humanity that we can see ourselves in them. We do not feel superior to the tragic character but very much one with him. We sympathize with him, and feel that there, but for the grace of God, go I. Unlike comedy, it is not our critical sensitivity that is primarily evoked in the experience of tragedy, but our emotional sensitivity to what it is like to be human. Horace Walpole has said somewhere that life is a comedy to those who think and a tragedy to those who feel. This is not to say that we suspend our judicious powers when we experience a tragic spectacle nor that we entirely outlaw our power of sympathy at human failure when we experience a comic spectacle, but it does point up a fundamental contrast between the two types of experience. And sometimes it is a matter of a point of view: what is comic to one person may be tragic to another. The same irrational, stubborn, and self-willed King Lear who is an object of ridicule and mockery to the fool is at the same time the object of the most heartfelt pity to Kent and Cordelia. Thus close, in spite of their great differences, are the comic and the tragic. We react to the comic, however, with emotional detachment, but we are always vitally concerned with the tragic.

In reading comedies or tragedies, ancient or modern, much of the pleasure comes from discovering how the dramatist controls our reactions to the main characters, by the development and action of the characters themselves, by the reactions of other characters in the play toward them, and by the manipulation of the plot.

Much of the depth and dramatic intensity of tragic spectacle particularly is achieved through an expert use of *dramatic irony*. Irony of situation in general consists in the fact that the real situation is the exact opposite to what it appears to be on the surface. In drama, irony of situation arises from the fact that the audience and sometimes some of the characters within the play itself are possessed of a knowledge of facts about the past, present, or even the future of the main characters that they do not know themselves. In the play *Oedipus,* for instance, the audience knows from the outset and everybody in the cast soon learns all about the King's whole situation long before he discovers the terrible truth himself. This makes for endless ironies of both statement and situation—contrasts between what the King thinks he is saying and doing, and what his words and actions really mean to other characters in the play and to the audience from the perspective of their fuller knowledge. The pity that we feel for a tragic character is immeasurably deepened and intensified by this ignorance on the part of the hero himself of the tragic implications to himself and others of his choices and actions. Often enough, the tragic hero, does, in the end, learn to know himself and to see his tragic mistakes— but too late to remedy the catastrophe that has resulted from them. This has sometimes been called *reminiscent irony*. In it the tragic protagonist finally sees himself as the audience and other characters in the play have seen him all along. This reminiscent irony provides some of the most moving passages in all literature, such as that moment at the end of *Antigone* when Creon looks back upon his stubborn choices that have resulted in the tragic deaths of Antigone, of his own son, Haeman, and of his wife and finally realizes his responsibility for their deaths, or when Lear looks back and sees the havoc that his foolish decisions have wrought in his kingdom and his family—but again too late to remedy the chaos.

It is through the omniscient point of view and dramatic irony that what Aristotle calls the cathartic effect of tragedy is at least partly achieved. The emotions of pity and fear which the tragic spectacle arouses are really painful experiences, and yet we know that the end result of witnessing a genuine tragedy is a unique kind of pleasure. We leave the theatre, not wrought up emotionally by the painful emotions of pity and fear, but with a strange sense of peace and calm. It is interesting to speculate why this is so and how the dramatist achieves this effect. It would seem that one very large part of the explanation lies in the fact that the dramatist has put us in possession of a knowledge about the characters, their inmost mental and moral bents, which we seldom have about people, even about ourselves, in real life. We know the main characters so well that we know ahead of time what they will do, what choices they are apt to make; and when the catastrophe comes we see that it is inevitable—partly the consequence of the free but mistaken choices of the main protagonist and partly the result of outside forces that have played upon his will. In real life the spectacle of a catastrophe is apt either to shock us or tear our hearts out in agonizing pity. We seldom have a knowledge of the character and background of events that lead up to the catastrophe; it is these things that the omniscient dramatist provides us that make the catastrophe more understandable. In real life we seldom have the kind of knowledge of character and motivation, even about ourselves, that the dramatist provides about the characters of his play. We patronize the psychiatrist sometimes to try to discover the hidden motives of our own choices; a good dramatist uncovers some of the deep motivations of human decisions and their consequences that we do recognize as essentially true. This recognition the audience always experiences in a good tragedy, and the dramatist sometimes allows his tragic hero himself to experience it at the end of the play, in such reminiscent ironic flashbacks as we listen to from Oedipus and Lear in the final scenes of their plays. It is this momentary glimpse into the sources of the tragic catastrophe that creates a deepened understanding and a feeling of calm at the end of a successful tragedy.

To create this nice balance between pity and understanding at the end of the play the dramatist has to be careful about the kind of character he puts at the center of his drama. A complete villain would invite only scorn and win no sympathy at all. The catastrophe would merely look like what the character deserved by his villainy. A completely good character suffering a catastrophe which he in no way deserved would not serve either. Such a character would be simply pathetic, not genuinely tragic. We would certainly pity him, but when the catastrophe came upon him we would be merely outraged at the injustice of it all. To provide some insight into the whole problem of evil, the tragedy must be built around a character that is in part, at least, responsible for his own downfall, and not a mere victim of circumstances and environment. Great tragedy is built on the premise that man is a free and responsible agent. If you deny man's freedom, you may still be able to write a tremendously moving play, one that simply wrings the heart of the spectator at the sight of man's pitiable situation in the universe. You may even be able to evoke some admiration for a man gesturing in defiance against a universe that he does not understand and over which he has no control. What you will never be able to create is a play that gives the insight into the human situation that *King Lear* provides, in which, with Lear himself, you recognize the essential truth of the whole human situation—the tremendous potentialities for good and the terrible possibilities for evil that inhere in man's freedom, and with it all the tragic waste that is involved in the abuse of freedom.

Romeo and Juliet and A Midsummer Night's Dream:

*Tragedy and Comedy**

by HENRY ALONZO MYERS

At the end of Plato's *Symposium* we find an amusing picture of a great philosopher putting Agathon, the tragic poet, and Aristophanes, the greatest comic poet of Athens, to sleep with his discourse on the nature of tragedy and comedy. As Plato tells the story, it happened in the early hours of the morning, after a night spent in feasting and singing the praises of love:

> There remained [of the company] only Socrates, Aristophanes, and Agathon, who were drinking out of a large goblet which they passed round, and Socrates was discoursing to them. Aristodemus was only half awake, and he did not hear the beginning of the discourse; the chief thing which he remembered was Socrates compelling the other two to acknowledge that the genius of comedy was the same with that of tragedy, and that the true artist in tragedy was an artist in comedy also. To this they were constrained to assent, being drowsy, and not quite following the argument. And first of all Aristophanes dropped off, then, when the day was already dawning, Agathon. Socrates, having laid them to sleep, rose to depart. [Jowett translation]

Like all good comedy, this scene is entertaining as well as instructive. It is entertaining because it presents the opposite of the order we naturally expect: a tragic poet and a comic poet, whom we expect to be interested in a discourse on the nature of tragedy and comedy, fall

---

* Reprinted from Henry Alonzo Myers, *Tragedy: A View of Life.* © 1956 by Cornell University. Used by permission of Cornell University Press.

asleep; it is instructive because it makes the point, evident elsewhere in literary history, that tragic and comic poets do not need explicitly formulated theories of tragedy and comedy, that they are often indifferent to such abstract speculations.

The distinctive form and significance of tragedies and comedies indicate, however, that the successful poets have had an adequate sense of the tragic and the comic. Apparently the appreciative reader or spectator also possess this mysterious but adequate sense of the nature of tragedy and comedy, for as the artist can create without an explicitly formulated theory, so the reader can appreciate and enjoy the specific work of art without the benefit of definitions and generalizations. But although speculation about the nature of tragedy and comedy is not indispensable to either creation or appreciation, it is, nevertheless, a natural and, indeed, inevitable result of our curiosity as rational beings. If it did not begin before, dramatic theory began as the first spectators were leaving the first performance in the first theatre. When we have had an intensely interesting experience, we are eager to know its nature and its causes. Why do we enjoy the spectacle of a man who falls from prosperity to adversity? Why do we laugh at fools? As long as we are interested in drama and in its sources in life, we shall be asking these questions and trying to answer them.

The assertion that the genius of tragedy is the same as that of comedy and that the true artist in tragedy is an artist in comedy also is the kind of provocative conundrum or apparent paradox which Socrates loved to discuss. It was a bold speculative assertion rather than a description of known facts, for the Greek dramatic poets, as we know them, kept tragedy and comedy apart and excelled in one or the other, not in both. Plato, who recorded the assertion, supported it in practice by displaying a sharp comic sense in the *Symposium* and a deep tragic sense in the dialogues which describe the trial and death of Socrates. But its support in drama did not come until the 1590's, when Shakespeare wrote *Romeo and Juliet* and *A Midsummer Night's Dream*, displaying genius in both tragedy and comedy.

What did Socrates have in mind? If the genius of tragedy is the same as that of comedy, what is the difference between the two? Certainly, he rejected the popular choice of the distinction between an unhappy and a happy ending as the difference between tragedy and comedy: in Plato's *Philebus* he maintains that we view both forms of drama with mingled pleasure and pain, smiling through our tears at tragedy and responding to the ridiculous in others with laughter, which is pleasant, tinged with envy, which is unpleasant. But this view, although it supports the assertion that tragedy and comedy are similar, leaves us, if both have the same effect, with no way of distinguishing one from the other. It can hardly be all that Socrates had in mind.

After years of wondering what he had in mind when his audience at the symposium failed him, I do not know the answer, but I have reached the point where I know what I should have said if I had been Socrates and if I had been more fortunate than he in holding my audience.

Man, I should have said, is a rational animal: he is always looking for meaning in his experience. He looks for meaning and order everywhere, but since the desire to find some significant pattern in his joys and sorrows, some just relation between good and evil, is closest to his heart, surpassing even his desire to grasp the order of the physical world, he looks most intently for meaning in the realm of values. That is why tragedy, which is an artistic demonstration that justice governs our joys and sorrows, has always seemed to most critics to be the highest form of art.

Since man has only a finite intelligence, he cannot always find the order he craves, either in the inner world of values or in the outer world of science and external description. In his search for order he is everywhere confronted by disorder, absurdity, nonsense, and incongruity. Fortunately, however, he finds in laughter, at least in his relaxed moments, an enjoyable emotional reaction to these disappointments to his reason. We rightly honor the comic poet, who by presenting nonsense in contrast to sense points up the difference between the two and who through laughter reconciles us to those experiences which frustrate the effort of reason to find meaningful patterns in all experience.

Order and disorder, the congruous and the incongruous, sense and nonsense, profundity and absurdity are pairs of opposites; each member of each pair throws light on the other so that whoever has a keen sense of order, congruity, sense, and profundity must also have a keen sense of disorder, incongruity, nonsense, and absurdity. Clearly, then, if the discovery of order in the realm of good and evil is the glory of tragedy, which finds intelligibility and justice in our seemingly chance joys and sorrows, and if the glory of comedy lies in its transformation of the frustrations of reason into soothing laughter, the artist in tragedy may also be an artist in comedy, and vice versa; and it may also be said that the genius of tragedy is similar to that of comedy.

Socrates, who was a rationalist, might well have expounded his apparent paradox in this fashion; very probably, however, the rivalry between philosophers and poets in his time would have made it difficult for him to recognize the tragic poets as the discoverers of justice in our joys and sorrows and the comic poets as the teachers of the difference between sense and nonsense. Since we can never know what Socrates had in mind, the final episode of the *Symposium* must remain, as Plato intended, a frustration of reason made pleasant by laughter at the absurdity of the ideal audience falling asleep in the presence of the right speaker on the right subject. This pleasant frustration does not prevent us, however, from determining for ourselves whether the great teacher's provocative conundrum will serve as a key to the meaning of tragedy and comedy.

The hypothesis which I have offered as a substitute for the slumber-stifled discussion needs amplification and verification by specific examples. What better test can be found than the first test afforded by the history of dramatic literature—the appearance of *Romeo and Juliet* and *A Midsummer Night's Dream* as the works of one author? These plays prove that Shakespeare, at least, was an artist in both tragedy and comedy. Do they indicate also that the genius of tragedy is similar to that of comedy? Do they indicate that the two are related as order is related to disorder—that the function of tragedy is to reveal a just order in our joys and sorrows and the function of comedy to turn disorder into soothing laughter?

II

The answers to two questions lead us directly to the heart of the tragic meaning of *Romeo and Juliet*. The first question is, What causes the downfall of the hero and of the heroine who shares his fate? The second question is, In what sense does the play have universality: does the fate of Romeo and Juliet represent the fate of all lovers?

Shakespeare himself could not have correctly answered the first question—What causes the downfull of the hero and heroine?—before he finished the play. *Romeo and Juliet* is Shakespeare's first true tragedy; as he wrote it, he was developing his own sense of the tragic. He started the play with a view which he found unsatisfactory as he went on writing and ended with a view which he upheld in all his later tragedies. He started with the view that something outside the hero is the cause of his downfall, that something outside man is the cause of the individual's particular fate.

His first view is stressed in the Prologue, which announces that "a pair of star-cross'd lovers take their life." This forecast points ahead to Romeo's exclamation, when he hears and believes the report of Juliet's death:

Is it even so? then I defy you, stars!

From this point on, every step he takes leads to his downfall. He buys poison from the apothecary, goes to Juliet's tomb, drinks the poison, and dies—while Juliet still lives. The stars are triumphant. Romeo's defiance of his fate hastens its fulfillment.

The stars are symbolic of the elements of bad luck and chance in the action of the play, of the bad luck which involves Romeo in a renewal of the feud and of the chance delay of the messenger who would have told him that Juliet lived. But do the stars, do chance and bad luck, determine the particular fate of the individual? Bad luck and chance are facts of life, but is there a deeper fact than chance and bad luck, a truer cause of the individual's fate? Like Romeo, we all suffer at times from bad luck. Like Romeo, we all hear rumors and alarms and false warnings and reports of danger and disaster. We know from experience that our response to these chance and unlucky events is more important than the events themselves; and our responses depend upon our characters. Character is a deeper and more important influence in human affairs than luck or chance.

Some time ago a radio program presented, as a remarkable illustration of chance and bad luck, the story of a man from Pennsylvania who had been hit by a train three times at the same crossing. When we reflect upon his story, we are likely to conclude that it is a revelation of character rather than an illustration of chance. If we had been in his place, most of us, after the first accident, would have taken all possible precautionary measures to see that it did not happen again; and if by chance we were struck again by an unscheduled train on a day when the crossing signals were not working, it seems likely that we would never again cross the tracks at that point. It is difficult for us to avoid the conclusion that the man from Pennsylvania was the kind of man who gets hit by trains.

Examples of "chance" and "bad luck" are common in the news. The following is representative of many: "A year to the day after he broke his left leg in a fall caused by a loose plank in his doorstep, John Jones, 47, of . . ., broke his right leg when he tripped over the same plank." Obviously, this is another revelation of character: Jones is the kind of man who will risk another leg rather than fix the plank.

While writing his first tragedy, Shakespeare discovered that the individual's fate is determined from within, by character, and not from without, by chance or bad luck. Although the character of Romeo is not as clearly revealed as the characters of Lear, Hamlet, Macbeth, and Othello, it is nevertheless certain from a point early in the play that Romeo is the kind of person who is inclined to accept bad news at its face value and who is inclined, when he is confronted by apparent disaster, toward some despairing deed. In his despair when the feud broke out—at a time when he knew that Juliet lived—he would have killed himself if the Nurse and Friar Laurence had not prevented him from so doing. Since the Nurse and Friar Laurence could not always be present in his despairing moments and since the temptations to dispair are all too common in life, it was with Romeo only a matter of time.

The stars remain in *Romeo and Juliet*, as well as the chance and bad luck of which they are symbols, but the play also offers a better explanation for the downfall of Romeo. It suggests that "a man's character is his fate," as Heraclitus said—a dictum which sums up one pattern of tragic meaning, one aspect of the tragic poet's vision of order in the universe.

In all his later plays, Shakespeare looked within to character, and not to the stars or to chance or luck, for the causes of individual fates:

> The fault, dear Brutus, is not in our stars,
> But in ourselves, that we are underlings.

We come now to the second question: How is the fate of Romeo and Juliet representative of the fate of all lovers: in what sense does the play have universality?

In looking for the answer to this question, we should first notice how neatly balanced are the feelings of the principals in the play. Taking love as a representative emotional experience, Shakespeare stresses both sides of the experience—the joy and exaltation of the lovers when they are united and their anxiety and unhappiness when they are separated. We see the lovers at both extremes of feeling. The balanced pyramidal form of the play, the five-act structure with the turn at the middle following the rise and fall of the fortunes of the principals, parallels the balance between joy and sorrow which Shakespeare's insight finds in human experience. The artistic structure of the play is an outward show of its inner meaning.

In *Romeo and Juliet* the ending is a dramatic summing up of the whole action: the death of the lovers is symbolical of their lives.

Each realizes at the end the extremes of good and evil. In one sense they are united forever, as they wished to be; in another sense they are separated forever in death. Here we see not a happy ending, as in a fairy story, and not an unhappy ending, as in some grim naturalistic tale, in which the worm finally is stilled after wriggling on the hook, but a truly tragic ending, in which joy and sorrow are inevitably joined together—a victory in defeat, a victory of the human spirit accompanied by the inevitable defeat of finite human beings.

Shakespearean tragedy is an artistic vision and revelation of a kind of divine justice which regulates the lives of men and women. Through poetic insight, Shakespeare finds a pattern, an order, in the realm of values; through insight he measures the extremes of feeling, which cannot be measured in any other way. Whoever sees in Shakespearean tragedy only a spectacle of suffering, only an unhappy ending, is seeing only half the story, only one side of life. The artist has done his best to present the whole story and both sides of life. For in the relation between the poles of experience, good and evil, he finds order in the universe. First, he finds that the individual fate of the hero is determined by character, not by chance. Second, he finds that the universality of the hero rests on the fact that, like all of us, the hero is fated to experience the extremes of feeling; and, in accordance with his capacity for feeling, in something like balanced and equal measures, when we follow the rise and fall of the hero's fortunes, we feel ourselves joined to him and to all mankind in the justice of a common fate: this is the secret of the reconciliation to suffering which we find in tragedy.

III

At the time of writing *Romeo and Juliet* and *A Midsummer Night's Dream*, Shakespeare must have been deeply impressed by the thought that the same material—the theme of love, for example, or life itself—may be treated as either tragic or comic. At the beginning of *A Midsummer Night's Dream*, the Athenian lovers, Hermia and Lysander, are in a predicament as serious as the plight of Romeo and Juliet; well may Lysander say, "The course of true love never did run smooth." But the roughness in the course of their love turns out to be the laughable ups and down of comedy while the roughness in the course of Romeo's love turns into a profoundly tragic change of fortune. The story of Pyramus and Thisbe, the play within a play in *A Midsummer Night's Dream* is, in its main outlines, the same as the story of Romeo and Juliet, yet it becomes in production, as Hippolyta says, "the silliest stuff that ever I heard," while the story of Romeo and Juliet becomes in production a great demonstration that order and justice prevail.

What difference in treatment of the same material—what difference in point of view toward the same material—makes possible the difference between comedy and tragedy?

A Midsummer Night's Dream presents the theme of love on three levels: the level of common sense; the level of nonsense, incongruity, and absurdity; and the level of fantasy. The level of common sense is represented by the love and marriage of Theseus and Hippolyta, who provide the necessary contrast to nonsense. The level of nonsense is represented by the Athenian lovers, Lysander, Demetrius, Helena, and Hermia, and by the workmen, Quince, Snug, Bottom, Flute, Snout, and Starveling, who turn the tragic story of Pyramus and Thisbe into a comic revelation of their own inadequacies. The level of fantasy is represented by the loves of Titania and Oberon, and by the juice of the flower called love-in-idleness, which here serves Shakespeare as an explanation of the influence of chance, caprice, and propinquity on love between the sexes. Since two of these levels, sense and nonsense, are always represented in all comedies, they deserve a few words of comment and definition.

The world of sense is the world of orderly and meaningful patterns, both rational and conventional. Its first law is the law of identity, namely, A is A, which "simply expresses the fact that every term and idea which we use in our reasonings" and practical calculations "must remain what it is." Shakespeare, for example, can make "sense" of the world of human values and find a just order in it only if the law of identity holds true. A is A; and if Romeo is Romeo—that is, if we can be sure that Romeo's character does not change or will not change, then we can understand his fate or even in a general way predict it. Similarly, if for Romeo good is to-be-united-with-Juliet and evil is to-be-separated-from-her—if his values do not change—then we can see in the rise and fall of his fortunes a just balance between good and evil.

The world of nonsense is, in contrast, governed by a law which is the exact opposite of the law of identity. A is not always A; A is sometimes B, or C, or D; and for this reason the world of nonsense is a world of disorder and incongruities. The laughable absurdities and incongruities in A Midsummer Night's Dream are for the most part direct consequences of this law of change of identity. Every change of identity leads to incongruities or comic ups and downs. Lysander, for example, is first presented to us as the lover of Hermia; later, touched by the juice of the magic flower, he becomes the lover of Helena; still later through magic he becomes the lover of Hermia again: A becomes B, and then becomes A again. Helena, we are told, was once the object of Demetrius' love; she is first presented to us as an unloved maiden; later through magic she is the object of Lysander's love, later still the object of the love of both Lysander and Demetrius; and finally the object of Demetrius' love only. A becomes B, and then becomes C, and then becomes D, and finally becomes A again. And so on with the Athenian lovers.

In contrast, Theseus and Hippolyta, who represent sense, remain what they are throughout the play.

Bottom, that king of the world of nonsense, undergoes a series of "translations." An ass in the eyes of the audience from the beginning, but a man of parts to his fellows, he later becomes through magic an ass in appearance, later the object of Titania's doting, later still the object of her loathing, and later still Bottom once more. Meanwhile, to complicate the scheme, he wishes to become Pyramus in the play, and also Thisbe, and also Lion. (I'll spare you the working out of his "translations" in ABC's.)

The most effective comedy in A Midsummer Night's Dream comes from the subtle use of change of identity in the production of the play within the play, "Pyramus and Thisbe." In the world of sense we accept the convention whereby the actor assumes the identity of the part he plays. In the theatre Brian Aherne is Romeo, Katharine Cornell is Juliet. Not so in "Pyramus and Thisbe": Shakespeare reverses the convention and changes order into disorder and incongruity, so that the production excites in us uproarious laughter rather than tragic sympathy and insight. Following the convention of the theatre, we would accept Lion and forget the actor, but Lion insists on telling us that he is not Lion but Snug the joiner. Similarly, by every device at his command, Shakespeare makes certain that we cannot see Pyramus, Thisbe, Wall, Moonshine, and Lion because we must see Snug, Bottom, Flute, Snout, and Starveling. By such devices, based on change of identity, first principle in the world of nonsense and incongruity, what might be seen as tragedy must be seen as comedy.

If tragedy reveals significant patterns in experience, demonstrating that character is fate and that men are united in the justice which apportions equal measures of joy and sorrow to each individual, and if comedy reconciles us through laughter to the disorder, the nonsense, the incongruities and absurdities which we meet everywhere in experience, how does the artist, working with the same material, with love or with life itself, make the choice between comedy and tragedy and determine whether we shall respond to his work of art with laughter or with tragic insight? Shakespeare must have thought of the question in some form while he was writing *Romeo and Juliet* and *A Midsummer Night's Dream*; and possibly his answer is to be found in the reply of Theseus to Hippolyta's verdict on the workers' production of "Pyramus and Thisbe": Hippolyta exclaimed, "This is the silliest stuff that ever I heard." And Theseus replied, "The best in this kind are but shadows, and the worst are no worse, if imagination amend them." If there exists anywhere a wiser comment on drama and the theatre, I have not read or heard it.

Undoubtedly Shakespeare must have been thinking as he wrote the reply of Theseus to Hippolyta, that the same imagination which willingly accepts actors as Romeo, or Hamlet, or Macbeth, or Lear, that accepts the past as the present, the stage as a series of faraway places, and fiction as life itself, could also accept, if it were permitted to do so, his "Pyramus and Thisbe." He knew that his "Pyramus and Thisbe," with the incongruities in the diction removed, and with competent actors losing themselves in their parts (including Lion, Moonshine, and Wall), could be successfully presented as tragedy. For he knew that the chief difference between "silly stuff" and profound art is caused by the artist's power to enlist the spectator's imagination. We can be sure that he knew this because in "Pyramus and Thisbe," as we see it, he has deliberately frustrated, for the sake of laughter, our imagination and prevented us at every point from amending the inherent limitations of drama.

Perhaps he was thinking also of the wider question of what difference in the artist's point of view determines whether we shall focus our attention on the underlying order in experience or on its superficial disorder and incongruities. Can the answer be found in imagination understood as sympathetic insight?

In "Pyramus and Thisbe" we are never permitted to see the story from the point of view of the lovers themselves; we see it only from the outside, as detached and unsympathetic observers. Indeed, we are not permitted to see the lovers at all: we see only the incongruity of the workers presuming to play the parts of a highborn couple. Again, we see the Athenian lovers only from the outside. Hermia, Lysander, Demetrius, and Helena—each is identified for us only as the object of another's affection. They have no inwards for us, and since this is so, how can we possibly tell, from watching them, whether character is fate or whether each suffers and enjoys in equal measures?

Our experience in witnessing *Romeo and Juliet* is altogether different. Soon after the beginning, we follow the action with sympathetic insight from within, from the point of view of the lovers themselves. Inwardness—where character and values may be found and measured by insight—becomes for us the only reality. We live with Romeo and Juliet, seeing the world with their eyes, and as we rise and fall with their fortunes, we are carried finally beyond envy and pity and filled with a sense that all men share a common fate.

IV

Can we say, then, that life is comic if we view it chiefly from the outside, as detached observers whose attention is focused mainly on the disorder and incongruities of the surface? And can we say that life is tragic when we view it from within, from the point of view of an individual—our own point of view or that of someone with whom we identify ourselves by sympathetic insight, as we do with Romeo and Juliet?

Walpole's famous dictum that "the world is a comedy to those that think, a tragedy to those who feel" on first consideration may seem to sum up satisfactorily at this point, for the detached, outer view of man, which permits us to smile at nonsense and incongruity, is at least partially the kind of objectivity which we associate with thought. And sympathetic insight, indispensable in the appreciation of tragedy, obviously involves us in the world of feelings and values. But Walpole's equation of the difference between comedy and tragedy with the difference between thought and feeling does not take into account that, in the first place, laughter is itself an emotion and that, therefore, our response even to "pure" comedy is emotional. Secondly, the emotion of laughter mixes freely with other emotions, and this fact explains the existence of various kinds of comedy.

When the comic poet is amused by someone or something that he dislikes, the result is satire; when he is amused by someone or something that he likes, the result is humor. The spirit of *A Midsummer Night's Dream*, for example, is one of good humor rather than of satire. Shakespeare, we feel, likes human beings even while he laughs at them and is not motivated by a desire to change their ways. Their ways, especially the ways of lovers, are often absurd and nonsensical, but Shakespeare does not view these absurdities as a stern moralist or a cynic might.

A Midsummer Night's Dream is saved from cynicism by the third level of the comedy—the level of fantasy, the imaginative level which softens the sharp distinctions between the world of sense and the world of nonsense. If all the changes of identity on the part of the lovers were attributed to caprice and propinquity, the result would be cynicism, but most of them are attributed to magic in the world of fantasy, and the result is a softer, kindlier humor, which transforms our rational distress at chance and disorder into soothing laughter. There is insight in the background of *A Midsummer Night's Dream*, as in all great comedy. The magic juice of the flower called love-in-idleness seems to tell us that if only we knew the true causes of what seems to be mere chance and caprice in affairs of the heart, then even these apparent absurdities would make sense to us. The fact that it is a creature from fairyland, not a man, who exclaims: "Lord, what fools these mortals be!" takes the poison out of the comment.

Nor can tragedy be satisfactorily explained as the view of a man who is only a man of feeling—if such a man exists. Tragedy can best be explained by its appeal to our rational craving for order, for patterns of meaning; it satisfies this craving at the important point where our reason and our feelings unite. Tragedy offers a vision of order in the universe, which we grasp with sympathetic insight and respond to emotionally as we rise and fall, or fall and rise, with the hero's fortunes. Furthermore, tragedy requires artistic objectivity as well as insight. Sympathetic insight alone might tempt Shakespeare—who as artist enjoys the omnipotence of a creator—to save Romeo from the fate which inevitably flows from his character, but artistic objectivity will not permit him to do so. Even Zeus must bow to necessity.

The spectator also views serious drama with a combination of insight and artistic objectivity, and he applauds the tragic artist who offers both as greater than the writer who is tempted by sympathy to sacrifice objectivity and provide us with a happy ending. We readily recognize such writings as one-sided, as untrue to life, as appeals to our weakness.

Thought and feeling are involved in the creation and appreciation of both comedy and tragedy. In seeing each, we experience an intellectual awareness accompanied by appropriate emotional responses. The main difference is that in tragedy our intelligence is directed toward order in the universe; in comedy, toward disorder and incongruity. Without sympathetic insight, we cannot behold the tragic vision of the fate common to all men. Without detachment, we cannot realize the effect of comedy, which transforms the frustrations of reason into laughter. But there is objectivity as well as insight in the tragic vision, and there is always insight in the background of great comedy. The difference between the point of view of tragedy and that of comedy cannot, therefore, be equated simply with the difference between insight and detachment, but rather is to be found in a subtler proportion whereby insight is stressed in tragedy and detachment is stressed in comedy.

The Modern Temper and Tragic Drama*
by LOUIS I. BREDVOLD

Just twenty-five years ago Mr. Joseph Wood Krutch published a volume of essays on *The Modern Temper*, a devastating analysis which has enjoyed enormous prestige and influence among thoughtful people, young and old. It continues even now to find readers who regard it as a sort of classic for our times, and who cannot but admire the courage and candor with which Mr. Krutch has exposed our mod-

---

* Reprinted by permission of Louis I. Bredvold. This article first appeared in the *Quarterly Review*.

ern disillusionment. It is still read by college students, who, recognizing the brilliance and the persuasiveness of the writing, defer to it as to an unquestionable authority. The unequal battle between the unprepared college student and *The Modern Temper* has for years been one of the major crises facing undergraduates.

One of the essays, on "The Tragic Fallacy," is particularly troublesome to students of literature. It is a pitiless explanation of why "we read but we do not write tragedies." It admits that "when we turn the pages of a Sophoclean or a Shakespearean tragedy we participate faintly in the experience which created it," but the truth is, we learn, that even when we are most moved by such tragedy "we perceive a Sophocles or a Shakespeare soaring in an air which we can never hope to breathe." The great tragic dramas of the past have faded for us; "we no longer live in the world which they represent, but we can half imagine it, and we can measure the distance which we have moved away." As moderns we would be incapable of even forming by ourselves any conception of "the tragic spirit," and we can think about it only as we find it exemplified in these half-comprehended dramas left us from earlier ages.

The difficulty, says Mr. Krutch, is not a problem of art, but of two worlds, of a mind in the modern world trying to understand a mind from another world. We are separated from Shakespeare and Sophocles by our discovery of "the meanness of human life." A tragedy must have a hero, but "from the universe, as we see it, both the Glory of God and the Glory of Man have departed. Our cosmos may be farcical or it may be pathetic, but it has not the dignity of tragedy and we cannot accept it as such." We have lost the faith that makes possible the tragic vision; we can never recapture that faith because we live in the modern world. For that faith, says Mr. Krutch, was born "out of an instinctive confidence in life which is nearer to the animal's unquestioning allegiance to the scheme of nature than it is to that critical intelligence characteristic of a fully developed humanism." The modern reader of tragic drama is therefore in a dilemma: either he enjoys the drama and gives up his critical intelligence, or he gives up the drama as naive and adolescent.

All this argument is sweeping in its generality. But one may gather from the essay some more specific statements as to how the great tragedy of the past was generated by a view of the world and of man no longer tenable by the modern critical intelligence. First, the moderns have learned that the cosmos is indifferent to them. "They cannot believe that the universe trembles when their love is, like Romeo's, cut off, or when the place where they, small as they are, have gathered up their trivial treasure is, like Othello's sanctuary, defiled." But the man contemporary with Sophocles or Shakespeare, believing that he occupied "the exact centre of the universe which would have no meaning except for him," could naturally assume that "each of his acts reverberates through the universe." Such cosmic importance imparts dignity to the tragic hero. In the second place, "the tragic spirit is in reality the product of a religious faith," whether it be in "God, Nature, or that still vaguer thing called a Moral Order," and because this faith is an "assumption" and not valid for us, we cannot feel that the struggles of the tragic hero are important. It is more modern to conceive of the catastrophe of the tragic hero as not differing essentially from the destruction of bacteria in a test tube. Finally, the modern world has turned from the hero to the common man, as is so evident in our novels as well as in drama. "We can no longer tell tales of the fall of noble men, because we do not believe that noble men exist. The best that we can achieve is pathos, and the most that we can do is to feel sorry for ourselves. Man has put off his royal robes, and it is only in sceptred pomp that tragedy can come sweeping by." We may summarize the argument thus: modern science has destroyed the old illusions regarding the cosmos; consequently, as the older tragedy was written in this obsolete "world," we can no longer be moved by its representation of human life and destiny.

Such observations and sentiments are of course not peculiar to Mr. Krutch. They are the common property of the Modern Mind; we hear them constantly and sometimes utter them ourselves. They seem as indisputable as axioms and circulate among us with as little exercise of the critical intelligence as other clichés. It may be worth while to pause over them and scrutinize them more carefully. It is of course not to the point to reject them just because they are depressing, to accept fiction as truth because it is pleasant. The inquiry should be into the soundness of these generalizations. Are they true to facts? Are they truthful interpretations of tragedy and of human nature? Are they distorted in emphasis?

To illustrate the last point first: Mr. Krutch is certainly safe in saying that we read tragedies now-a-days, but we do not write them. Stated in that way the observation carries the implication that our failure to produce tragedy is a norm by which we may conclude that our reading of older tragedy is fatuous. But it is possible to turn the statement around and say that, although our modern dramatists are not writing any great tragedies, the public nevertheless insists on reading and seeing the great tragedies of the past. Thus the shoe of explanation is put on the other foot. One cannot dismiss lightly the fact that even modern people have some inner necessity for returning to Sophoclean and Shakespearean tragedy, that they find there some deep human satisfaction not given by modern drama. Does this signify that the product of our modern dramatists falls short of what the modern audience craves? If so, the supposedly uniform Modern Mind is only a generalized construct of the critic and fails to take account of the complexities of our contemporary experience.

Mr. Krutch argues ingeniously that we participate only faintly in the experience which the great tragedy of the past evoked when it was written, and that as it gradually fades with time, this tragedy will become "completely meaningless." This argument is not a brilliant example of scientific caution. The comparison it involves is not susceptible of any proof, as we obviously cannot find out the intensity of the emotional reactions of the audience of Shakespeare's day. As for our contemporary experience with these tragedies, a sufficient number of people could easily be produced who can assert with competence that their participation in the greatness of these plays is neither so faint nor so faded as the argument insists. Indeed, Mr. Krutch himself says as much. If we put the old tragedies alongside of a *Ghosts* or a *Weavers*, he says, "we shrink as from the impulse to commit some folly"; the new tragedy will not bear the comparison. Granted. But we would not shrink from the folly of comparison if our experience with Shakespeare were really so faint and superficial.

If the argument about the experience of the modern audience is thus highly dubious, the assumptions regarding the nature of tragic drama are even more so. Mr. Krutch is of course a distinguished critic, and his comments on tragic drama, even in this essay, are often so admirable and illuminating that it would be manifest injustice to say that his own experience of the old drama is either faded or faint. But his doctrinal argument is less felicitous than his appreciations. It is part of his doctrine that our modern enlightened view of the cosmos has made the old tragedy obsolete. We can no longer feel that the tragedies of man are important because we know that the cosmos is indifferent to them. We do not, like Romeo and Othello, believe that the universe will tremble when calamity strikes us. However, if we search the plays we do not find that Othello and Romeo ever express any expectation of such trembling. In fact, Shakespeare was too great a dramatist to need to rely on any cosmic demonstration of sympathy in order to build up the tragic stature and dignity of his heroes. It is likewise futile to search for places in Shakespeare where dignity is imputed to man because he occupies "the exact centre of the universe." Such astronomical ideas are completely irrelevant in the sphere of Shakespearan tragedy, as they are indeed also in our own modern daily life. The archangel Raphael explained to Adam in *Paradise Lost* that his problems in the conduct of life will in no way depend on whether the earth or the sun is the centre of our astronomical system. Raphael's prediction has been justified. We continue obstinately to say that the sun goes down. And when Shakespeare represented on the stage the tragic frustration of a noble romance, or the agony of Othello, victim of Iago's villainy and his own weakness, who threw away a pearl richer than all his tribe, he did not go outside of his story to borrow any cosmic significance. He found all that he needed in human life, even as we also may perchance know it and live it.

All this discussion about the divergent views of the cosmos amounts to an attempt to lay down such a prerequisite for the tragic vision of Shakespeare as no intelligent modern could subscribe to. But it does not inquire first whether the tragic vision does in fact depend on any such a prerequisite. It will be observed that it is a kind of deductive argument evolving out of an assumption, rather than an inductive examination of the tragedy we all agree to call great. We find a similar mode of reasoning in Mr. Krutch's other observations. He says that "the tragic spirit is in reality the product of religious faith," and the word "product" again lays down a prerequisite for tragedy. By "religious faith" we must understand such a faith as was held by a majority, at least, of the theatre audiences of sixteenth-century England, but not to be relied on in addressing audiences of our day. The modern reader must therefore hypothesize in some way this religious faith before he begins a Shakespearean tragedy, for the tragic spirit is derivative from it. This argument, presumably, is not to be taken as a trivial one, implying, let us say, that to appreciate *Macbeth* we must believe in witches, or that *Hamlet* is a sealed book unless we believe in ghosts, and also in Purgatory (the doctrine of which was to Shakespeare's Protestant audience a rank heresy). The issue is surely much more important and reaches to the profound depths of the tragic vision. There can be no doubt that the tragic experience is closely associated with religious feeling, but the sequence of cause and effect seems to be exactly the reverse of the way Mr. Krutch would have it.

Such prologues in Heaven as we find in Goethe's *Faust* and the Book of Job are not standard in tragedy. Like comedy, tragedy deals with human life here on earth, and it can exert no power over us unless we acknowledge it as a truthful representation of human experience. It is an exploration of human destiny which begins *in medias res* and has no theoretical prerequisites. It is not derivative from any doctrines which might conceivably be delivered to the audience by means of a prologue at the opening of the play. The effect of tragedy is not dependent on any insights other than those developed in the course of the action of the play. Even the common belief in the immortality of the soul does not enter into the tragic experience in Shakespeare's plays, any more than in Greek tragedy. Hamlet speaks of it only doubtfully, as he meditates suicide. But when death comes to one of Shakespeare's tragic heroes, destiny has reached, for the purposes of the drama, its completion without anything being said about what may come thereafter.

Those who would penetrate behind the play and formulate the religion of Shakespeare usually succeed only in exposing their own personal convictions. A Roman Catholic scholar once demonstrated to his own satisfaction that Shakespeare was a Catholic; a Protestant scholar that he was a Protestant; an agnostic that he was an agnostic. The great experience of the tragedy they probably all shared in common. Shakespeare eluded all of them, as he eludes all of us, putting between himself and us the action of the play, and that is all he gives us. We must read it and interpret it as we can. We must understand his characters in terms of our common humanity; he has left us no marginal commentary. When Mr. Krutch says that a Shakespearean hero perishes with dignity because "a God leans out from infinity to strike him down," he speaks strangely and apparently in momentary forgetfulness of the plays. Those grand figures perished because they struck themselves down, not without more or less assistance, it is true, from those around them. The moving forces in their destinies were in the human, not a superhuman, sphere and therefore universally understandable as experiences that are possible, alas, to us all.

As has been often observed, there is something strikingly pagan about Shakespeare, precisely because he does not rely on external buttressing for his tragic effects. The idea of divinity is remarkably unimportant dramatically, in no play more strikingly so than in *King*

Lear, which many readers think his greatest. This tragedy belongs to legendary Britain, and a Christian God would have been an anachronism; but we need not suppose that Shakespeare was handicapped by chronological difficulties. He produced the effect he wanted, by vague references to "the heavens," oftener "the gods," who are alluded to from time to time as remote existences, too remote, unfortunately, to rescue agonizing mankind from its accumulating woe. They appear to be more wished for than believed in.

> If that the heavens do not their visible spirits
> Send quickly down to tame these vile offences,
> It will come,
> Humanity must perforce prey on itself,
> Like monsters of the deep.

That is all the consolation Albany derives from his faith, as he contemplates the vileness of the daughters of Lear. A revealing turn comes a moment later when he learns that a servant had killed Cornwall, his brother-in-law, just as he was brutally putting out the eyes of Gloucester. Albany can now speak out more certainly, with a touch of triumph:

> This shows you are above,
> You justicers, that these our nether crimes
> So speedily can venge.

No "justicer" leaned out from infinity or sent his visible spirit down to punish Cornwall or protect Gloucester; only a humble but heroic servant meted out punishment and thus vindicated the "justicers"; and Albany could again believe that some kind of Moral Order was operative in the world of man. Albany needs no messenger from heaven, no divine judgment from Mt. Sinai, to make clear to him that Goneril and Regan are "tigers, not daughters," and that if humanity continues to develop in that direction it "must perforce prey on itself like monsters of the deep." If Cornwall's fate were not evident justice, it could not *show* that there are "justicers" above. Great tragedy, let it be repeated, presents an essentially human story, told in human terms, and providing such insights of its own as our common humanity can share. It can be understood by all the varieties of people who drift in from the streets through the doors of the theatre.

It is also true, however, that the story that unfolds in a great tragedy, rooted though it must be in human nature, presents a view of human destiny that raises issues beyond the power of a stage play to resolve. There are emotional upheavals, insights adumbrating into mystery, awesome revelations, that have the power to shake the complacency, one might think, of even the most hardened materialist, who might well leave the theatre in a momentary mood to say with Hamlet, "for mine own poor part, look you, I'll go pray." For the great theme of tragedy is the problem of evil, from which even the materialist is not immune, the greatest problem mankind has to face, and the inspiration of the greatest literature mankind has so far produced. The tragedian raises metaphysical and religious issues which pass beyond the limits of his art, and on which it is impossible for him as a playwright to commit himself. As has been pointed out, he can not resolve the problem of evil by assuming an existence after death in which rewards and punishments will balance the accounts of justice. Even if scenes of that sort were feasible in the theatre, they would have to be rejected as inharmonious with the tragic experience. No one wants an afterpiece showing Othello and Desdemona united happily in heaven. Tragedy must limit itself to showing heaven and hell as extreme possibilities of our destiny here on earth. The tragic hero is great, not because of any extraterrestrial relationships, but in himself. It is the depths of human nature, not the cosmos, that the dramatist must explore. He must have the creative power to plummet those depths and the dramatic technique to convey his tragic vision to his audience. The essential requirement for reading and writing great tragedy is therefore not a prescribed view of the universe, but a profound, imaginative, and sympathetic insight into human nature.

This, it seems, is where the modern dramatist falls short. He is unable to find in man the dignity and greatness necessary to true tragedy. He is unable, as Mr. Krutch says, to "tell the tales of the fall of noble men, because we do not believe that noble men exist." Against this proposition it must be permissible to expostulate. Are we to receive this universal negative as a scientific finding of the modern sociologist or the modern psychologist? Is this desperate generalization now become an obligatory creed? Is it the truth that "all contemporary minds" feel "that man is relatively trivial"? Our dramatists themselves might possibly have seen not so long ago some commonplace sewing-machine salesman (let us say) descend from the skies over Normandy and with his fellow troopers do heroic battle like the heroes of old. They have greater opportunity, if they can use it, to observe nobility and heroism in other commonplace people less spectacularly employed. It seems a very heavy ideology, indeed, that so dehumanizes a creative artist as to blind him to the very humanity which it is his mission to interpret. Mr. Krutch, like others afflicted with the "modern temper," falls back upon the cosmos as the explanation. "Our cosmos," he says, "may be farcical or it may be pathetic, but it has not the dignity of tragedy and we cannot accept it as such." If the humanity of man can be validly dismissed on such a priori grounds, the modern dramatist has of course only one problem to solve: how to utilize the highly developed technical expertness of the modern theatre to exploit the meanness and triviality of human life into a box-office success.

Because he chooses such limited contacts with human nature the modern dramatist produces a monotony of effect, tense though his play may be with suspense, which contrasts with the rich and variegated patterns of Shakespeare. As a matter of fact, it could be argued plausibly that Shakespeare was master of all the stock in trade of the modern dramatist, but used it in such a way as to justify Dryden's remark that of all ancients and moderns he had the most comprehensive mind. The tragic street battles in *Romeo and Juliet* take their rise in each case in trivial buffoonery by servants; in such a complex pattern even farce may suddenly take on a serious significance. In *Hamlet* Shakespeare created an atmosphere as depressing as can be found in any modern play; Hamlet speaks of Denmark as a prison, or as an "unweeded garden, things rank and gross infest it merely"; a moral miasma has settled over it, more death-dealing and blinding than a smog. And Hamlet is not incapable of some quite "modern" utterances about the farcical aspects of man. He can observe, for instance, that "we fat all creatures else to fat us, and we fat ourselves for maggots." What modern dramatist wouldn't envy Shakespeare that pitiless cynicism! But in *Hamlet* such moods are passing, mere aspects of a complex personality, falling into their proper place in a larger and nobler view of life. And the modern lament about the indifference of the cosmos to the destinies of men is in fact not something new; on that point the older tragedy anticipated the moderns. What Prossor Hall Frye has observed about Greek tragedy is equally applicable to Shakespeare's: "the tragic qualm is perhaps nothing more or less than a sudden and appalling recognition of our desperate plight in a universe apparently indiscriminate of good and evil as of happiness and misery."

It is because he cherishes so dearly a pinched and starved view of human nature that the modern dramatist finds himself incapable of rising above sordid misery and achieving the truly tragic vision. Mr. Krutch himself gives us a good statement of what is lacking in the moderns. We rise from reading the old tragedy, he says, with a feeling of "elation"; more specifically, the old tragedians understood that "it is only in calamity that the human spirit has the opportunity to reveal itself triumphant over the outward universe which fails to conquer it." The statement needs some minor qualification: the triumph of Othello or King Lear was not primarily over "the outward universe." But some sort of triumph there is in great tragedy, and the audience shares in it. For if the tragic vision is to impress us with a sense of profound loss, it must at the same time bring home to us an equally profound sense of the values without which the loss would not be real. As we participate sympathetically in the tragic role of the hero, we clutch more and more firmly certain values which the action of the play reveals to us as infinitely precious to us as human beings. These values appear concretely in the nobility of the characters, especially in the erring hero, and in a Lear, an Othello, an Oedipus they operate as a redemptive power. Matthew Arnold praised Sophocles for seeing life steadily and seeing it whole. This steady vision led Sophocles to a tragic self-knowledge; and, in the words of Werner Jaeger, "to know oneself is for Sophocles to know man's powerlessness; but it is also to know the indestructible and conquering majesty of suffering humanity." Perhaps no Greek drama impresses a modern reader more profoundly and powerfully than Sophocles' treatment of the Oedipus story, in spite of its oracle and sphinx and gods. Oedipus found himself unwittingly guilty of patricide and incest. When he is forced to acknowledge his guilt, he begins his expiation; he blinds himself, wanders many years as an outcast old man, in the deepest misery and agony, his one loyal daughter his only friend and support. But the strength and nobility of his character help him through his long ordeal, and as he ages he grows into a venerable figure. Like Lear, he reaches wisdom through suffering; his nobility is tested by his agony. And therefore even we, moderns as we are, agree that it is right that the gods themselves should at last give Oedipus mysterious release and sepulture. "No mortal eye," says Jaeger, a modern interpreter, "may see the mystery; only he who is consecrated by suffering may take part in it. Hallowed by pain, Oedipus is in some mysterious way brought near to divinity: his agonies have set him apart from other men. Now he rests on the hill of Colonus, in the poet's own dear homeland, in the eternally green grove of the Kind Spirits where the nightingale sings from the branches. No human foot may tread in that place, but from it there goes out a blessing over all the land of Attica."

Is it possible for the modern world to produce great tragic drama? No doubt it is, if dramatists with sufficient ability will give up their a priori inhibitions and see human nature steadily and see it whole. If they can do that, they will find a large and receptive audience awaiting them.

"A Platform and a Passion or Two"*
by THORNTON WILDER

Toward the end of the 'twenties I began to lose pleasure in going to the theatre. I ceased to believe in the stories I saw presented there. When I did go it was to admire some secondary aspect of the play, the work of a great actor or director or designer. Yet at the same time the conviction was growing in me that the theatre was the greatest of all the arts. I felt that something had gone wrong with it in my time and that it was fulfilling only a small part of its potentialities. I was filled with admiration for presentations of classical works by Max Reinhardt and Louis Jouvet and the Old Vic, as I was by the best plays of my time, like "Desire Under the Elms" and "The Front Page"; but it was with a grudging admiration, for at heart *I didn't believe a word of them.* I was like a schoolmaster grading a paper; to each of these offerings I gave an A +, but the condition of mind of one grading a paper is not that of one being overwhelmed by an artistic creation. The response we make when we "believe" a work of the imagination is that of saying: "This is the way things are. I have always known it without being fully aware that I knew it. Now in the presence of this play or novel or poem (or picture or piece of music) I know that I know it." It is this form of knowledge which Plato called "recollection." We have all murdered, in thought; and been murdered. We have all seen the ridiculous in estimable persons and in ourselves. We have all known terror as well as enchantment. Imaginative literature has nothing to say to those who

---

* Preface to *Three Plays* by Thornton Wilder. Copyright © 1957 by Thornton Wilder. Reprinted by permission of Harper & Row, Publishers.

do not recognize—who cannot be *reminded*—of such conditions. Of all the arts the theatre is best endowed to awaken this recollection within us—to believe is to say "yes"; but in the theatres of my time I did not feel myself prompted to any such grateful and self-forgetting acquiescence.

This dissatisfaction worried me. I was not ready to condemn myself as blasé and over-fastidious, for I knew that I was still capable of belief. I believed every word of *Ulysses* and of Proust and of *The Magic Mountain,* as I did of hundreds of plays when I read them. It was on the stage that imaginative narration became false. Finally, my dissatisfaction passed into resentment. I began to feel that the theatre was not only inadequate, it was evasive; it did not wish to draw upon its deeper potentialities. I found the word for it: it aimed to be *soothing*. The tragic had no heat; the comic had no bite; the social criticism failed to indict us with responsibility.

I began to search for the point where the theatre had run off the track, where it had chosen—and been permitted—to become a minor art and an inconsequential diversion.

The trouble began in the nineteenth century and was connected with the rise of the middle classes—they wanted their theatre soothing. There's nothing wrong with the middle classes in themselves. We know that now. The United States and Scandinavia and Germany are middle-class countries, so completely so that they have lost the very memory of their once despised and ludicrous inferiority (they had been inferior not only to the aristocracy but, in human dignity, to the peasantry). When a middle class is new, however, there is much that is wrong with it. When it is emerging under the shadow of an aristocracy, from the myth and prestige of those well-born Higher-ups, it is alternately insecure and aggressively complacent. It must find its justification and reassurance in making money and displaying it. To this day, members of the middle classes in England, France, and Italy feel themselves to be a little ridiculous and humiliated.

The prestige of aristocracies is based upon a dreary untruth: that moral superiority and the qualifications for leadership are transmittable through the chromosomes, and the secondary lie, that the environment afforded by privilege and leisure tends to nurture the flowers of the spirit. An aristocracy, defending and fostering its lie, extracts from the arts only such elements as can further its interests, the aroma and not the sap, the grace and not the trenchancy.

Equally harmful to culture is the newly arrived middle class. In the English-speaking world the middle classes came into power early in the nineteenth century and gained control over the theatre. They were pious, law-abiding, and industrious. They were assured of eternal life in the next world and, in this, they were squarely seated on Property and the privileges that accompany it. They were attended by devoted servants who knew their place. They were benevolent within certain limits, but chose to ignore wide tracts of injustice and stupidity in the world about them; and they shrank from contemplating those elements within themselves that were ridiculous, shallow, and harmful. They distrusted the passions and tried to deny them. Their questions about the nature of life seemed to be sufficiently answered by the demonstration of financial status and by conformity to some clearly established rules of decorum. These were precarious positions; abysses yawned on either side. The air was loud with questions that must not be asked.

These middle-class audiences fashioned a theatre which could not disturb them. They thronged to melodrama (which deals with tragic possibilities in such a way that you know from the beginning that all will end happily) and to sentimental drama (which accords a total license to the supposition that the wish is father to the thought) and to comedies in which the characters were so represented that they always resembled someone else and not oneself. Between the plays that Sheridan wrote in his twenties and the first works of Wilde and Shaw there was no play of even moderate interest written in the English language. (Unless you happen to admire and except Shelley's *The Cenci.*) These audiences, however, also thronged to Shakespeare. How did they shield themselves against his probing? How did they smother the theatre—and with such effect that it smothers us still? The box-set was already there, the curtain, the proscenium, but not taken "seriously"—it was a convenience in view of the weather in northern countries. They took it seriously and emphasized and enhanced everything that thus removed, cut off, and boxed the action; they increasingly shut the play up into a museum showcase.

Let us examine why the box-set stage stifles the life in drama and why and how it militates against belief.

JUGGLING WITH TIME

Every action which has ever taken place —every thought, every emotion—has taken place only once, at one moment in time and place. "I love you," "I rejoice," "I suffer," have been said and felt many billions of times, and never twice the same. Every person who has ever lived has lived an unbroken succession of unique occasions. Yet the more one is aware of this individuality in experience (innumerable! innumerable!) the more one becomes attentive to what these disparate moments have in common, to repetitive patterns. As an artist (or listener or beholder) which "truth" do you prefer—that of the isolated occasion, or that which includes and resumes the innumerable? Which truth is more worth telling? Every age differs in this. Is the Venus de Milo "one woman"? Is the play *Macbeth* the story of "one destiny"? The theatre is admirably fitted to tell both truths. It has one foot planted firmly in the particular, since each actor before us (even when he wears a mask!) is indubitably a living breathing "one"; yet it tends and strains to exhibit a general truth since its relation to a specific "realistic" truth is confused and undermined by the fact that it is an accumulation of untruths, pretenses, and fiction.

All the arts depend on preposterous fictions, but the theatre is the most proposterous of all. Imagine asking us to believe that we are in Venice in the sixteenth century, and that Mr. Billington is a moor, and that he is about to stifle the much-admired Miss Huckaby with a pillow; and imagine trying to make us believe that people ever talked in blank verse— more than that: that people were ever so marvelously articulate. The theatre is a lily that inexplicably arises from a jungle of weedy falsities. Yet it is precisely from the tension produced by all this absurdity, "contrary to fact," that it is able to create such poetry, power, enchantment, and truth.

The novel is pre-eminently the vehicle of the unique occasion, the theatre of the generalized one. It is through the theatre's power to raise the exhibited individual action into the realm of idea and type and universal that it is able to evoke our belief. But power is precisely what those nineteenth-century audiences did not—dared not—confront. They tamed it and drew its teeth; squeezed it into that removed showcase. They loaded the stage with specific objects, because every concrete object on the stage fixes and narrows the action to one moment in time and place. (Have you ever noticed that in the plays of Shakespeare no one— except occasionally a ruler—ever sits down? There were not even chairs on the English or Spanish stages in the time of Elizabeth I.) So it was by a jugglery with time that the middle classes devitalized the theatre. When you emphasize *place* in the theatre, you drag down and limit and harness time to it. You thrust the action back into past time, whereas it is precisely the glory of the stage that it is always "now" there. Under such production methods the characters are all dead before the action starts. You don't have to pay deeply from your heart's participation. No great age in the theatre ever attempted to capture the audience's belief through this kind of specification and localization. I became dissatisfied with the theatre because I was unable to lend credence to such childish attempts to be "real."

THE TORCH RACE

I began writing one-act plays that tried to capture not verisimilitude but reality. In *The Happy Journey to Trenton and Camden* four kitchen chairs represent an automobile and a family travels seventy miles in twenty minutes. Ninety years go by in *The Long Christmas Dinner*. In *Pullman Car Hiawatha* some more plain chairs serve as berths and we hear the very vital statistics of the towns and fields that passengers are traversing; we hear their thoughts; we even hear the planets over their heads. In Chinese drama a character, by straddling a stick, conveys to us that he is on horseback. In almost every No play of the Japanese an actor makes a tour of the stage and we know that he is making a long journey. Think of the ubiquity that Shakespeare's stage afforded for the battle scenes at the close of *Julius Caesar* and *Antony and Cleopatra*. As we see them today what a cutting and hacking of the text takes place—what condescension, what contempt for his dramaturgy.

Our Town is not offered as a picture of life in a New Hampshire village; or as a speculation about the conditions of life after death (that element I merely took from Dante's *Purgatory*). It is an attempt to find a value above all price for the smallest events in our daily life. I have made the claim as preposterous as possible, for I have set the village against the largest dimensions of time and place. The recurrent words in this play (few have noticed it) are "hundreds," "thousands," and "millions." Emily's joys and griefs, her algebra lessons and her birthday presents—what are they when we consider all the billions of girls who have lived, who are living, and who will live? Each individual's assertion to an absolute reality can only be inner, very inner. And here the method of staging finds its justification—in the first two acts there are at least a few chairs and tables; but when she revisits the earth and the kitchen to which she descended on her twelfth birthday, the very chairs and table are gone. Our claim, our hope, our despair are in the mind—not in things, not in "scenery." Molière said that for the theatre all he needed was a platform and a passion or two. The climax of this play needs only five square feet of boarding and the passion to know what life means to us.

The Matchmaker is an only slightly modified version of *The Merchant of Yonkers* which I wrote in the year after I had written *Our Town*. One way to shake off the nonsense of the nineteenth-century staging is to make fun of it. This play parodies the stock company plays that I used to see at Ye Liberty Theatre, Oakland, California, when I was a boy. I have already read small theses in German comparing it with the great Austrian original on which it is based. The scholars are very bewildered. There's most of the plot (except that our friend Dolly Levi is not in Nestroy's play); there are some of the tags; but it's all "about" quite different matters. Nestroy's wonderful and sardonic plays are—like most of Molière's and Goldoni's—"about" the havoc that people create in their own lives and in those about them through the wrong-headed illusions they cherish. My play is about the aspirations of the young (and not only of the young) for a fuller, freer participation in life. Imagine an Austrian pharmacist going to the shelf to draw from a bottle which he knows to contain a stinging corrosive liquid, guaranteed to remove warts and wens; and imagine his surprise when he discovers that it has been filled with very American birch-bark beer.

The Skin of Our Teeth begins, also, by making fun of old-fashioned playwriting; but the audience soon perceives that he is seeing "two times at once." The Antrobus family is living both in prehistoric times and in a New Jersey commuter's suburb today. Again the events of our homely daily life—this time the family life—are depicted against the vast dimensions of time and place. It was written on the eve of our entrance into the war and under strong emotion, and I think it mostly comes alive under conditions of crisis. It has been often charged with being a bookish fantasia about history, full of rather bloodless schoolmasterish jokes. But to have seen it in Germany soon after the war, in the shattered churches and beer halls that were serving as theatres, with audiences whose price of admission meant the loss of a meal and for whom it was of absorbing interest that there was a "recipe for grass soup that did not cause the diarrhea," was an experience that was not so cool. I am very proud that this year it has received a first and overwhelming reception in Warsaw.

The play is deeply indebted to James Joyce's *Finnegans Wake*. I should be very happy if, in the future, some author should feel similarly indebted to any work of mine. Literature has always more resembled a torch race than a furious dispute among heirs.

The theatre has lagged behind the other arts in finding the "new ways" to express how men and women think and feel in our time. I am not one of the dramatists we are looking for. I wish I were. I hope I have played a part in preparing the way for them. I am not an innovator but a rediscoverer of forgotten goods and I hope a remover of obtrusive bric-a-brac. And as I view the work of my contemporaries I seem to feel that I am exceptional in one thing —I give (don't I?) the impression of having enormously enjoyed it?

Between Absurdity and the Playwright*
by WILLIAM I. OLIVER

Few spectacles in the history of theatre have been more amusing than the current Babel raised upon the grounds of absurdist drama. The voices that cry out in many tongues issue from all walks of life (from expert and amateur, critic and playwright) and the appalling humor of it is that in all but a few instances—a very few instances—what they tell us is incomplete, opinionated, or downright balderdash. Clear and lucid thought on the subject of absurdist drama is indeed rare, and even then, as in the case of Esslin or Coe, it is marred by excessive sympathy or partisanship.

No one can write about absurdist playwrights and their craft without first defining in some way the nature of their subject: absurdity. It is their subject and not their craft that effectively distinguishes them and, at the same time, relates them to the stream of world drama. It is precisely because so many critics have attempted to define the absurdists from the point of view of craftsmanship that we have created the situation I have called a critical Babel. Perhaps the most serious critical limitation of Mr. Esslin's otherwise excellent work, *The Theatre of the Absurd*, is precisely this tendency to focus too quickly and exclusively on the stylistic breed without stressing the philosophical genus.

The absurdist playwrights believe that our existence is absurd because we are born without asking to be born, we die without seeking death, we live between birth and death trapped within our body and our reason, unable to conceive of a time in which we were not, or a time in which we will not be—for *nothingness* is very much like the concept of infinity: something we perceive only in so far as we cannot experience it. Thrust into life, armed with our senses, will and reason, we feel ourselves to be potent beings. Yet our senses give the lie to our thought and our thought defies our senses. We never perceive anything completely. We are permitted to entertain committedly only one perspective of any object, fact, or situation: our own. We labor to achieve distinction and permanence only to find that our assessments are perspectively incomplete and therefore never wholly effective. All of our creations are doomed to decay as we ourselves are doomed to death. We create in order to identify ourselves in some semblance of permanence, but our creations become autonomous facts the instant we have created them and do not identify us except in so far as we pretend that they do. Therefore, the more we strive for definition and permanent distinction, the more absurd we are. Yet, the only value we can affirm with certainty is a self-defeating complex that we do not understand: our life. If we despair of definition, of ever achieving a sense of permanence, and we contemplate suicide, we are put in the absurd situation of sacrificing our only concrete value, life, for a dream of power and

---

* This essay first appeared in the *Educational Theatre Journal*, Vol. XV, No. 3 (October 1963); it is reprinted by permission of the author and the *Journal*.

permanence that no man on this earth has ever experienced. On the other hand, if in despair we turn to religion or illusion of *any sort* we betray and deny our only means of preception: our reason. If, in a transport of ecstasy, be it mystical or sensuous, we feel at one with power and permanence . . . we are forced to admit the illusionistic aspect of this transport and we must confess that our sense of power, permanence and definition is achieved at the sacrifice of our reason. If it is impossible for us to act with complete efficacy, to perceive with complete accuracy, to create anything definite and lasting that expresses exactly our intentions, we must also remember that it is impossible for us to cease acting as long as we live. This then is the condition of man that we of the twentieth century call "absurd." It is the same state of being that Aristotle labeled as "ignorance." It is this complex of self-defeating paradoxes, this even check and balance of power and impotence, knowledge and ignorance, attunement and alienation that is the subject of the absurdist playwrights of all ages, no matter what form or style they may have chosen to express it.

If we begin our definition of absurdist drama with an examination of its subject matter rather than its style, we create an instantaneous bond between all manner of writers such as Beckett, Ionesco, Genet, Adamov, Miller, O'Neill, Brecht, Pirandello, Unamuno, Sartre, and Camus. Furthermore, we find no difficulty in making comparisons between the works of the current generation of absurdists and their historical ancestors: the Greek tragedians and farceurs as well as the great dramatists of the English Renaissance (including Shakespeare). What more explicit statements of man coming to terms with the absurdity of his condition than that of Oedipus, Hamlet, Lear, Vendice, D'Amville, Phaedra, Oreon, Hippolytus, Orestes, and Prospero?

It is possible that there are some who object to such a broad and inclusive definition. However, it must seem clear that if absurdity has any worth at all as a concept, it is precisely because it embraces anagogically the whole of human existence . . . it defines the condition of man, today, in the past, and into the future.

Within this circle of absurdity man may change his conventions of behavior and belief but he will not break out of the encompassing definition. Any writer who attempts to define the nature of man and proceeds reasonably and empirically will take an existential posture that in some way expresses man's confrontation with absurdity. It is precisely because of the accuracy and soundness of its postulates that absurdity can be used as a means to distinguish between those assertions about the nature of man that are dogmatically entertained and those that are the result of empirical assessments. Critico-philosophical tools such as the concept of absurdity which help us correlate diversity of artistic expression, are every bit as essential as those which help to establish the distinctions that isolate these expressions. The style of absurdist drama will change many times but the content will remain very much the same until man ceases to be man by becoming God, or by losing his power of reflection and becoming a beast. Absurdist drama then, is not new; it is as old as tragedy, as old as farce—for farce and tragedy are indeed the double mask of absurdity.

The absurdists of today write in such diverse styles that one hesitates to compare them in anything but their philosophical categories. However, some generalizations can be made. The modern absurdists, almost to a man, determinedly resist the traditional separation of farce and tragedy. The subject of farce is the same as that of tragedy: the terrible or comic discovery of man's absurdity, ignorance and impotence. The essential difference between the two forms is one of quality: farce arouses laughter and tragedy draws our tears—tragedy awakens our sympathy, while farce dispels our sympathy and frees our cruelty. The absurdists of today, as Euripides once did, commingle the qualities of farce and tragedy, making us laugh at that which hurts us most, making us weep at that which is most foolish in our nature. They are all, in the best sense of the word, ironists.

Of necessity, an absurdist playwright is one who is predominantly thematic in his dramaturgy. That is to say, these are dramatists of a philosophical bent who place the greatest value on their thematic statement. Consequently, their plays are constructed and polished in such a fashion as to call attention to their intellectual content, and this in spite of the fact that their thought refuses to be narrowly systematized. This tends to make their works more presentational than the works of authors less concerned with universals and more inclined to create a drama of sensuous experience, of realism. Now, the drama has had many authors of a philosophical bent, of an intellectual disposition, but they have never produced plays quite like these. What one must emphasize is the degree to which these modern absurdists mean to be intellectual, ideological, objective, and cerebral; and, concomitantly, the extent to which they want their audiences to accompany them on their cerebration. Only the authors of Medieval allegory have called attention to their thought as noisily as do the absurdists of today.

The tendency toward presentational drama is another pattern which identifies the creative posture of the absurdist. If there is one quality that marks the major trends of modern art and certainly the art which burgeons out of Paris, it is the movement toward pure art, or "de-humanized art" as Ortega y Gasset puts it. Modern artists and absurd playwrights in particular seem concerned with creating works that proclaim their independence from the traditional neo-Aristotelian strictures of imitation or representationalism. These playwrights want a drama that proclaims, "This is not life! It is my work of art about life!" or even, "This is life itself that I've created . . . man-made life . . . ersatz life." In order to achieve a level of abstraction sufficiently pronounced to evince such a response from their audiences, the absurdists have resorted to various devices, none of which are new to the theatre. They have taken up every conceivable symbolical device employed in allegory and dramatic expressionism. Furthermore, several of them have discarded psychology as a control of action. The action of these plays is intended to demonstrate symbolically the ideas of the playwright and to create the dramatic temperature necessary to maintain the interest of the audience. At first glance some of their plays appear to be utterly illogical until we realize that the logic of the author's thought is not directly expressed but rather symbolically stated in action. One might well question this procedure on grounds of deliberate obscurantism—"Why not come out and say what you mean?" The answer is simple and didactically sound. If one has an important body of thought to purvey one must beware of presenting it too facilely, lest the "student audience" simply *recognize* it and fail to *learn* it. Finally, the absurdists are not afraid of obscurity in art since they employ it as a direct symbol of the obscurity they find in life.

The tendency to dehumanize their art has another rather interesting application in the absurdists' understanding of the function of the actor. The founding fathers of absurd drama (Beckett, Ionesco, and Adamov) were not theatre people. It is significant that none of these men had any marked respect for the practice of theatre as they found it. They objected to the realistic drama of their youth on grounds that realism was an irritating, if not inferior, form of art that enslaved the artist in a photographic relationship to life. Ionesco, the most out spoken of the absurdist elders on technical matters, felt that realism reduced the actor to a puppet. When these men finally brought themselves to write their new drama, they had a revolutionary motivation that was not entirely philosophical: they were out to liberate the theatre and emancipate the actor from the bonds of naïve imitation. Their revolution has not been entirely effective. The more naïve and bold their allegorical expressionism, the less imaginative room they afford the actor. Only when the playwright is capable, as are Beckett and Genet, of creating plays which are microcosms in and of themselves, with their own peculiar behavioral rules and emotional responses, only then is the actor permitted some imaginative freedom and given an opportunity to speak through his emotional-intellectual attitudes and his states of being. Plays such as Ionesco's *A Maid to Marry* reduce the actor to absolute puppetry and enslave him interpretatively to the author's ideas in a way that he was never bound in realism to the imitation of life.

The question of intelligibility referred to

earlier is one which is further complicated by a popular concern amongst the absurdist playwrights: their distrust of language. Believing as they do that man's powers of perception, expression, and self-identification are pathetically limited by the fact of his individualistic perspective of anything and everything, it is only natural that they should question our means of communication. They are not inspecting semantic phenomena as semanticists. Rather, they are defining the gulf of misunderstanding that exists between our desire and our definition of it, between our expression of ourselves and its apprehension by others. This certainly is a dramatic concern, but the absurdist expresses the problem by forcing his language to nonsense. This device when added to the absurdist's general tendency to express himself in allegorical and expressionistic symbols, simply increases the difficulty of understanding their plays. The number of people who have difficulty catching secondary dialogue in the works of Chekhov is surprising; one can well imagine their difficulty when confronted by something like *The Bald Soprano*.

There is another important generalization that can be made about the absurdists: they are, almost without exception, ironic proselytizers. Their picture of the human condition, reasonable though it is, is not a very popular view. If it was clearly put in readily identifiable language, the majority of their audience would find the absurdist's view to be nihilistic. They would simply say, "Oh no! How dreary! That's all wrong!" and then make a mental note never to see another play by that horrible author! Yet a confrontation with the absurdity of one's condition is an inescapable prerequisite if one hopes to live sanely, that is to say, reasonably. How then to administer this view to an audience optimistically rooted in the certainty of faith—be it in God, or culture, or even in the potency of their own individuality? The answer is simple: pretend to give them something else. Make the play as amusing and sensational and surprising as possible *but* bury the message in symbols. Get the audience to swallow the comedy-coated pill of absurdity by letting them believe it as all harmless comedy or sensationalism This ironic approach to life and dramatic action is justified rhetorically since most of the audience find it difficult to equate the farcical cavorting with anything as disturbing as absurdity. Furthermore, this approach is also justified thematically since the absurdist thinks of life in the light of a tragic joke or comic tragedy.

On the negative side of the critical ledger of absurdist drama we find that these plays are no longer thought of as the drama of the future. Absurdist drama is, in fact, dated. It is now *the* fad across the country and is imitated by an alarming number of young student playwrights in our colleges. Somewhat like boogie woogie, absurdist drama has become the vogue with the neophyte at precisely the moment when its creators indicate that they are beginning to tire of their creation. Adamov now writes quite conventional social realism à la Brecht. Ionesco has moved steadily toward longer, more psychological plays. Only the slow-writing Beckett has remained more or less faithful to his original pattern . . . perhaps because his works, more than any other absurdist's, were rich intellectually and experientially to begin with. It is no accident that some of the young writers in the absurdist camp, such as Pinter and Albee, have chosen to write in a far more realistic vein than did the first masters of the form. It is quite easy to write a realistic allegory of the absurdist statement, and furthermore it accomplishes some, if not all, of the intents of the original absurdists without resorting to tedious expressionistic symbols. Audiences who have the thematic key to the play can understand it as readily as they understood the earlier works. Audiences who don't have the key to the absurdist code are nonetheless given greater opportunity for empathic or emotional response to the drama.

One of the so-called advantages of the expressionistic control in absurdist drama is its power to alienate the audience, keeping it alive to the ideological byplay of the symbols. Esslin, correctly enough, says that the absurdists have succeeded in achieving this alienation effect more completely than its so-called inventor, Bertolt Brecht. Beholding an action that is symbolic, the sequence of which is determined ideologically rather than psychologically and representationally, the spectator is supposed to have no recourse but to remain objective and analytical. But I have watched audiences ignorant of Mr. Esslin's assertion sit delightedly through *Waiting for Godot,* laughing as uncritically as though they were watching the Keystone Cops. The alienation-effect works beautifully in Brecht's plays where it is needed: a representational action is interrupted or qualified by all manner of presentational devices in order to draw the audience's attention to the ideological issues of the play. Alienation in absurdist drama is often, though not always, an effect incompatible with the play itself. If, for example, the author has rejected a linear approach to his plot, as well as psychological reality, the sequential structure of his theme—if, in effect, he is asking us to do a line-by-line, gesture-by-gesture analysis of his play in the manner of modern or new criticism—then the theatre is not the place for him. He should be content with the printed page. The cerebration demanded by such plays, and Beckett is the worst offender, is no longer a question of theatrical response, but of scholarly industry. The alienation-effect is justified when you provide the audience with an abundance of emotional representational action to be distanced, as it were, in order more clearly to perceive its meaning. It seems cruel, if nothing else, to confuse an audience to such an extent that the only way they have of saving face is to laugh uproariously at what they mistakenly presume to be sheer nonsense.

Working with allegorico-expressionistic devices, the absurdists demand of their audiences a skill in symbolic thought that they do not possess. In fact, if there is one major deficiency in our ability to perceive drama on the stage (as opposed to drama on the printed page) it is a lack of skill in interpreting symbolic action. We must commend any effort to strengthen our ability in this interpretative function. On the other hand, this predisposition toward a totally symbolic drama demands of the absurdists that they themselves be masters of the symbol. Some of them are not. The most notable example of symbolic bungling in the canon of absurdist masterworks is the end of *The Chairs.* Why, having gone to great lengths to establish the emptiness of the illusion of the oldsters, must Ionesco bring on that claptrap figure of the Orator? Why not let the old couple introduce a nonexistent orator, and allow the audience to sit facing the empty chairs until they realize the play is finished and that the emptiness of the stage is a symbol, an idea made concrete? The Orator completely negates the allégorical frame of the play. Not long ago I had occasion to meet Arrabal and I questioned him about his *Automobile Graveyard.* I wondered why the figures of the mother and her athlete son so clearly established in the first part of the play emerge in the last portion of the play as policemen. I had several explanations, none of which completely satisfied me. Arrabal shrugged and answered succinctly enough, "Because I needed policemen." I suggest that this is puerile writing.

Another danger that grows out of this density of symbols is that it makes it difficult to identify a sound work from a fraudulent one, the serious play from the spoof. If I'm not mistaken, Mr. Kopit meant *Oh Dad; Poor Dad, Mamma's Hung You in the Closet and I'm Feelin' So Sad* to be something of a parody of absurdist drama. Upon close inspection I find this play every bit as sound as many seriously recognized pieces in the absurdist field. Like jazz, or any other extreme artistic expression, absurdist drama will not bear parody, for the parodies often appear as good as the work parodied. I have also been amused by the ease with which my beginning playwriting students can ingeniously concoct plots that would pass for a good absurdist action. The plain truth of the matter is that writing an acceptable absurdist play is not difficult at all.

One of the dilemmas most frequently encountered by the absurdist is the problem of overcoming the boredom of depicting monotony. *This is really a new problem to the theatre.* Even in the works of Chekhov the problem depicted is boredom, not monotony. Any playwright of moderate sensitivity can make boredom dramatic if he focuses upon the agony and irritation of the person who endures it. Monotony, on the other hand, is altogether a different problem. As used by the absurdists, it is not a term which connotes an emotional response; it is, rather, a philosophical assessment, the absurdist assessment of the value of all action. All value in life must logically be predicated from the point of view of the individual and is, therefore, more a question of individualistic bias imperfectly formed than it is a question of abstract truth. This assessment *does not deny absolute truths*—it simply states that no human being's vital response to a truth is utterly comparable to another's. From a reasonable point of view—that is to say, from the vantage point of abstract thought that allows one to compare the values of the individual against the standards of the absolute truth—all action, all value, all hope is absurd because it is imperfect, transitory, or illusory. This absurd pronouncement reduces all actions to a hypothetical monotony of value. Running for president and running to the bathroom, loving and hating, killing and curing, striving and drifting, believing and not believing—when assessed from an individualistic and experiential view, are all reduced to the same plane, since no single action is worth more than the next, except in so far as that imperfect, perishable, and only partly reasonable figure, man, chooses to believe that it is. The rational hierarchy of ideals is leveled flat by the subjectivity of their employment in the life of the individual. This then is the monotony so crucial to the absurdist's statement. He must define the ignorance and impotence that undermine all our choices while at the same time he must point out the ironic distance that exists between our subjective opinion and our assessments of absolute truth. In order to do this he writes from a totally empirical and amoral vantage point. Unfortunately, this concept creates a technical problem in the drama which is singularly difficult, for the absurdist must make his statement comprehensive and, at the same time, demonstrate it in terms of action. The result is the destruction of plot and the boredom of the audience. One tires of the non-dramatic reduction of plot to the level of a dreary catalogue of equivalent actions. Yet if the playwright doesn't demonstrate *an exhaustive variety* of values in the light of absurdity, the audience may justifiably think that the playwright means to attack only one set of values and this, of course, could be interpreted as a non-absurdist affirmation of absolute value. The absurdist is therefore always in dramatic danger of foundering his play on one of the crucial tenets of his theme: the monotony of value. This danger increases as the structure of the play becomes more simple and shallow. For these reasons Ionesco always appears to write plays that are half again as long as they should be. Monotony of the sort described is often expressed by repetition of gestures and situations, time and time and time again within the course of one play (note the shoe and hat business of *Waiting for Godot*.) This creates a terrible problem for the actors and directors of the plays, for too bald a representation of this repetition is a sure way of being thematically clear, yet dramatically boring.

Again the most important thing that can be said against the practice of the absurdists is not primarily technical in its nature. One can accuse a good number of these playwrights of failing to extend their role of philosopher-playwright beyond the initial confrontation and definition of absurdity. If, as Kierkegaard says, "Authorship is and ought to be a serious calling implying an appropriate mode of personal existence. . . ." and, if I am just in describing the absurdists as ironic proselytizers, then I am free to criticize their didactic intentions. Time and time again absurdist plays carp at us that the human condition is absurd, as though the confrontation of absurdity were some sort of agonizing process that paralyzed our ability to act, that corroded our will, destroyed our hope, and sapped our imagination of all vigor. Granted, one's realization of absurdity is a terrible thing, but if this realization doesn't shock us into suicide we do go on living. We write plays, we build bridges, we run for public office, we fall in love, we raise families, we may even become religious! *Granted, no action we take after this confrontation or realization will be enacted with naïve and implicit faith in its existential rewards of definition and permanence.* The realization of absurdity makes ironists of all of us who undergo it and continue to live in action—but note that it is enlightened action in the sense that the action of Oepidus is enlightened once he has blinded himself to the optimistic vanities of man. One may even love God through disillusion! It was Unamuno who believed that the true saint was the man tortured by his inability to believe in God.

Generally, absurdist writers with the notable exception of Beckett and a few of the younger hybrid absurdists such as Mortimer, fail to give us a picture of man living beyond his confrontation with the abyss of ignorance and impotence. Even Beckett has a way of presenting his action in a particularly depressing and dreary light, as though all life after the confrontation suffered from a spiritual and emotional leukemia. Most of the absurdist writers limit their plays to dramatic definitions of absurdity or to depicting the plight of the immediate or naïve man who entertains illusions of power and definition without knowing that he is absurd. Having written one or two such plays, an author should at least begin to prepare himself to write about the engaged man who has sought to live actively in the knowledge of his own absurdity. Failing to develop in this direction casts the playwright in the unsavory role of a gloating harpy that delights in the misery of others—*for notice that the absurdist playwright is already engaged in the game of value by the very fact of his playwriting.* This strain of sentimentality and sadism is evident in the absurdists' fondness for images of man's impotent degradation. There was a time when I found these images startling and sensational but I have now wearied of them. I have developed an aesthetic allergy to men who gobble bananas, men who vomit, figures who have difficulty excreting or urinating, bums, perverts, human beings who are phenomenally unclean, bloody handkerchiefs, smelly feet, and climactic scenes of castration. I am so irritated with this sentimental ghoulishness that I have begun to make ironic parodies of it within the context of my own plays.

As I suggested earlier it is virtually impossible to generalize effectively about the absurdists of today because of the divergence of technique and contrast of interest that exist between one author and the next. Obviously no one virtue or flaw that I have alluded to is applicable to all absurdists. I have tried to cull out the main values in the thought and practice of those absurdists that write a more or less allegorical and expressionistic drama. It is my conviction that absurdity is best expressed in representational drama. Absurdity is a significant fact of life as we live it. It loses its impact in a "world" where women have three noses and people live buried in the sand or in garbage pails. Absurdity is something which is inextricably fused to our process of living! Absurdity as a theme is best served then, by the representational playwright. However, the title of *absurdist* has fallen not upon the men who state it best but upon those who have chosen to express it through the allegorical-expressionistic mode. I have avoided, therefore, reference to the plays of writers who have retained an allegiance to the conventions of representational drama such as O'Neill, Sartre, Brecht, Camus, Ghelderode, etc.

It was my original intention simply to state some of the significant virtues and flaws of that rather controversial group of playwrights founded by the awesome three. However, I now find my initial intent somewhat unsatisfactory. If there is any value to an aesthetic approach in the instance of absurdist drama, it lies in the freedom afforded me to correlate the artistic practice of the absurdist with the content of his plays, and, in turn, with the impact of these plays upon the mind of the beholder. I know of no better way to do this and, as it happens, to conclude this essay, than to give you what I consider to be a definition of the ideal absurdist playwright of the allegorical-expressionistic inclination.

The absurdist as a thinker: This man is convinced of the absurdity of the human condition. He is, therefore, certain of his own absurdity. He believes that a recognition of absurdity is essential in order for one to live a life of reasonable expectation and vital responsibility. He believes that without this recognition man is a puppet dangled on the strings of dogma and illusion. He knows that absurdity is a bitter discovery for all men, but believes that it is the only assessment which will accurately define man's power of perception, action, and accomplishment. Absurdity is, ironically enough, the only ground upon which man's reason can stand secure.

The absurdist as a social force: This man tries to awaken his audience to the logical conclusion of absurdity. He does this, not to attract notoriety, but for the good of his audience. Knowing that the greater portion of his audience is not in sympathy with his assessment of the human condition, he cannot assault their convictions with jeremiads. Such an approach would prompt his audience to brand him as a nihilistic crank. He knows that their illusion of optimistic attunement can never be destroyed directly, that only by indirect means can he successfully dispel this illusion. A direct assault only strengthens his audience in their optimistic conviction. He must know, as Kierkegaard knew, that in order to help his audience effectively, he must understand more than they—yet first of all, surely, he must understand what they understand. He must present his audience with the need to confront the absurdity of their own existence in order that they may no longer be unnecessarily vulnerable to the vicissitudes of life. He must eventually show them the reasonable advantages of absurd living in order that they may be induced to leave their nests of dogma, illusion and superstition. In short, he illustrates for the audience the unbreakable relationship of reason to courage in the face of ignorance.

The absurdist as a technician: This playwright has one major technical criterion: he will choose those devices that allow him to express his ideas and his intent indirectly. Until his audience becomes an absurdist one he must continue to use the devices of indirect communication, be they those of expressionism, allegory or irony. If he discards these three modes of expression, he will no longer be an absurdist, in our conventional use of the word; he will simply become a tragedian or a farceur. He may write representationally only if he maintains a strong allegorical or ironic control over his material. His major dilemma will be one of maintaining the dramatic temperature of his plays. He must never let the symbols or the thematic density of his play dampen his philosophical and social purposes. His drama must *induce* or *shock* a philosophical response from the audience—it must never openly demand such a response. In the light of these statements, we can say that the absurdist playwright will seek a form and style which, first of all, act as a disguise of his assertions rather than a direct and compatible expression of them. Yet this stylistic and structural disguise must never be so complete as to make it unnecessarily difficult for the audience to chance upon the proper perspective of interpretation that will reveal the true contour of the playwright's thought. Finally, the ideal absurdist will never present his views in symbols and action which connote that the confrontation with absurdity is a nihilistic experience. If he does this he becomes guilty of entrenching the uninitiated in their conviction that absurdists are nothing more or less than a pack of exhibitionistic misanthropes. A playwright guilty of this error will have defeated aesthetically his philosophical posture as an absurdist, by unwittingly revealing to his audience the fact that he is unable to accept and espouse the irony of the view he advocates.

Unit 5

A SELECTION OF MODERN PLAYS

ON THIS SELECTION OF PLAYS

Certainly any study of drama should put one in touch with some major examples of ancient Greek, Elizabethan, and modern plays. The essay by Myers on *Romeo and Juliet* and *A Midsummer Night's Dream*, exemplifying a tragic and a comic treatment of similar subject matter, might suggest one basis for a selection of plays to be studied. We might include *Antigone* as an example of Greek tragedy; a study of *Romeo and Juliet* as an early example of Shakespearean tragedy in which chance still plays a large part; *A Midsummer Night's Dream* for a humorous treatment of the same theme; and then one of Shakespeare's mature tragedies, such as *King Lear*, in which human responsibility as the source of the tragic catastrophe is very much more emphasized. This group might be followed by a study of such a play as Ibsen's *Ghosts*, which centers on heredity and environment as the determining factors in the human situation. In this sequence Arthur Miller's *Death of a Salesman* will take on special significance as a modern attempt to restore balance between environment and personal responsibility in the tragic situation. Luigi Pirandello did much to free drama from the cramping effects of the boxed-in realistic stage. His *Six Characters in Search of an Author* reveals some of the expressive nuances that this new freedom brought to the theatre. Both Thornton Wilder and Tennessee Williams were admittedly much influenced by Pirandello's innovations, as is obvious here in their *Pullman Car Hiawatha* and *The Glass Menagerie*. Perhaps the most distinctive development in modern drama is the Theatre of the Absurd—which can be illustrated from the plays of Ionesco, Beckett, Albee, or Pinter. All their plays are readily available in paperbacks.

The Glass Menagerie*

by TENNESSEE WILLIAMS

THE CHARACTERS

AMANDA WINGFIELD *the mother*

A little woman of great but confused vitality clinging frantically to another time and place. Her characterization must be carefully created, not copied from type. She is not paranoiac, but her life is paranoia. There is much to admire in Amanda, and as much to love and pity as there is to laugh at. Certainly she has endurance and a kind of heroism, and though her foolishness makes her unwittingly cruel at times, there is tenderness in her slight person.

LAURA WINGFIELD *her daughter*

Amanda, having failed to establish contact with reality, continues to live vitally in her illusions, but Laura's situation is even graver. A childhood illness has left her crippled, one leg slightly shorter than the other, and held in a brace. This defect need not be more than suggested on the stage. Stemming from this, Laura's separation increases till she is like a piece of her own glass collection, too exquisitely fragile to move from the shelf.

---

* Copyright 1945 by Tennessee Williams and Edwina D. Williams. Reprinted by permission of Random House, Inc. All rights reserved, including the right of reproduction in whole or in part in any form.

TOM WINGFIELD *her son*
   The narrator of the play. A poet with a job in a warehouse. His nature is not remorseless, but to escape from a trap he has to act without pity.

JIM O'CONNOR *the gentleman caller*
   A nice, ordinary, young man.

SCENE   An Alley in St. Louis.
PART I   Preparation for a Gentleman Caller.
PART II   The Gentleman calls.
TIME   Now and Past.

PRODUCTION NOTES

Being a "memory play," *The Glass Menagerie* can be presented with unusual freedom of convention. Because of its considerably delicate or tenuous material, atmospheric touches and subtleties of direction play a particularly important part. Expressionism and all other unconventional techniques in drama have only one valid aim, and that is a closer approach to truth. When a play employs unconventional techniques, it is not, or certainly shouldn't be trying to escape its responsibility of dealing with reality, or interpreting experience, but is actually or should be attempting to find a closer approach, a more penetrating and vivid expression of things as they are. The straight realistic play with its genuine frigidaire and authentic ice-cubes, its characters that speak exactly as its audience speaks, corresponds to the academic landscape and has the same virtue of a photographic likeness. Everyone should know nowadays the unimportance of the photographic in art: that truth, life, or reality is an organic thing which the poetic imagination can represent or suggest, in essence, only through transformation, through changing into other forms than those which were merely present in appearance.

These remarks are not meant as comments only on this particular play. They have to do with a conception of a new, plastic theatre which must take the place of the exhausted theatre of realistic conventions if the theatre is to resume vitality as a part of our culture.

The Screen Device

There is *only one important difference between the original and acting version of the play* and that is the *omission* in the latter of the device which I tentatively included in my *original* script. This device was the use of a screen on which were projected magic-lantern slides bearing images or titles. I do not regret the omission of this device from the present Broadway production. The extraordinary power of Miss Taylor's performance made it suitable to have the utmost simplicity in the physical production. But I think it may be interesting to some readers to see how this device was conceived. So I am putting it into the published manuscript. These images and legends, projected from behind, were cast on a section of wall between the front-room and dining-room areas, which should be indistinguishable from the rest when not in use.

The purpose of this will probably be apparent. It is to give accent to certain values in each scene. Each scene contains a particular point (or several) which is structurally the most important. In an episodic play, such as this, the basic structure or narrative line may be obscured from the audience; the effect may seem fragmentary rather than architectural. This may not be the fault of the play so much as a lack of attention in the audience. The legend or image upon the screen will strengthen the effect of what is merely allusion in the writing and allow the primary point to be made more simply and lightly than if the entire responsibility were on the spoken lines. Aside from this structural value, I think the screen will have a definite emotional appeal, less definable but just as important. An imaginative producer or director may invent many other uses for this device than those indicated in the present script. In fact the possibilities of the device seem much larger to me than the instance of this play can possibly utilize.

The Music

Another extra-literary accent in this play is provided by the use of music. A single recurring tune, "The Glass Menagerie," is used to give emotional emphasis to suitable passages. This tune is like circus music, not when you are on the grounds or in the immediate vicinity of the parade, but when you are at some distance and very likely thinking of something else. It seems under those circumstances to continue almost interminably and it weaves in and out of your preoccupied consciousness; then it is the lightest, most delicate music in the world and perhaps the saddest. It expresses the surface vivacity of life with the underlying strain of immutable and inexpressible sorrow. When you look at a piece of delicately spun glass you think of two things: how beautiful it is and how easily it can be broken. Both of those ideas should be woven into the recurring tune, which dips in and out of the play as if it were carried on a wind that changes. It serves as a thread of connection and allusion between the narrator with his separate point in time and space and the subject of his story. Between each episode it returns as reference to the emotion, nostalgia, which is the first condition of the play. It is primarily Laura's music and therefore comes out most clearly when the play focuses upon her and the lovely fragility of glass which is her image.

The Lighting

The lighting in the play is not realistic. In keeping with the atmosphere of memory, the stage is dim. Shafts of light are focused on selected areas or actors, sometimes in contradistinction to what is the apparent center. For instance, in the quarrel scene between Tom and Amanda, in which Laura has no active part, the clearest pool of light is on her figure. This is also true of the supper scene, when her silent figure on the sofa should remain the visual center. The light upon Laura should be distinct from the others, having a peculiar pristine clarity such as light used in early religious portraits of female saints or madonnas. A certain correspondence to light in religious paintings, such as El Greco's, where the figures are radiant in atmosphere that is relatively dusky, could be effectively used throughout the play. (It will also permit a more effective use of the screen.) A free, imaginative use of light can be of enormous value in giving a mobile, plastic quality to plays of a more or less static nature.   T.W.

SCENE ONE

The Wingfield apartment is in the rear of the building, one of those vast hive-like conglomerations of cellular living-units that flower as warty growths in overcrowded urban centers of lower middle-class population and are symptomatic of the impulse of this largest and fundamentally enslaved section of American society to avoid fluidity and differentiation and to exist and function as one interfused mass of automatism.

The apartment faces an alley and is entered by a fire-escape, a structure whose name is a touch of accidental poetic truth, for all of these huge buildings are always burning with the slow and implacable fires of human desperation. The fire-escape is included in the set—that is, the landing of it and steps descending from it.

The scene is memory and is therefore nonrealistic. Memory takes a lot of poetic license. It omits some details; others are exaggerated, according to the emotional value of the articles it touches, for memory is seated predominantly in the heart. The interior is therefore rather dim and poetic.

At the rise of the curtain, the audience is faced with the dark, grim rear wall of the Wingfield tenement. This building, which runs parallel to the footlights, is flanked on both sides by dark, narrow alleys which run into murky canyons of tangled clothes-lines, garbage cans and the sinister lattice-work of neighboring fire-escapes. It is up and down these side alleys that exterior entrances and exits are made, during the play. At the end of TOM's *opening commentary, the dark tenement wall slowly reveals (by means of a transparency) the interior of the ground floor Wingfield apartment.*

Downstage is the living room, which also serves as a sleeping room for LAURA, *the sofa unfolding to make her bed. Upstage, center, and divided by a wide arch or second proscenium with transparent faded portieres (or second curtain), is the dining room. In an old-fashioned what-not in the living room are seen scores of transparent glass animals. A blown-up photograph of the father hangs on the wall of the living room, facing the audience, to the left of the archway. It is the face of a very handsome young man in a doughboy's First World War cap. He is gallantly smiling, ineluctably smiling, as if to say, "I will be smiling forever."*

The audience hears and sees the opening scene in the dining room through both the transparent fourth wall of the building and the transparent gauze portieres of the dining-room arch. It is during this revealing scene that the fourth wall slowly ascends, out of sight. This transparent exterior wall is not brought down again until the very end of the play, during TOM's *final speech.*

The narrator is an undisguised convention of the play. He takes whatever license with dramatic convention as is convenient to his purposes.

TOM *enters dressed as a merchant sailor from alley, stage left, and strolls across the front of the stage to the fire-escape. There he stops and lights a cigarette. He addresses the audience.*

TOM   Yes, I have tricks in my pocket, I have things up my sleeve. But I am the opposite of a stage magician. He gives you illusion that has the appearance of truth. I give you truth in the pleasant disguise of illusion. To begin with, I turn back time. I reverse it to that quaint period, the thirties, when the huge middle class of America was matriculating in a school for the blind. Their eyes had failed them, or they had failed their eyes, and so they were having their fingers pressed forcibly down on the fiery Braille alphabet of a dissolving economy. In Spain there was revolution. Here there was only shouting and confusion. In Spain there was Guernica. Here there was disturbances of labor, sometimes pretty violent, in otherwise peaceful cities such as Chicago, Cleveland, Saint Louis . . . This is the social background of the play.

[MUSIC]

The play is memory. Being a memory play, it is dimly lighted, it is sentimental, it is not realistic. In memory everything seems to happen to music. That explains the fiddle in the wings. I am the narrator of the play, and also a character in it. The other characters are my mother, Amanda, my sister, Laura, and a gentleman caller who appears in the final scenes. He is the most realistic character in the play, being an emissary from a world of reality that we were somehow set apart from. But since I have a poet's weakness for symbols, I am using this character also as a symbol; he is the long delayed but always expected something that we live for. There is a fifth character in the play who doesn't appear except in this larger-than-life photograph over the mantel. This is our father who left us a long time ago. He was a telephone man who fell in love with long distances; he gave up his job with the telephone company and skipped the light fantastic out of town . . . The last we heard of him was a picture postcard from Mazatlan, on the Pacific coast of Mexico, containing a message of two words—"Hello—Goodbye!" and no address. I think the rest of the play will explain itself. . . .

[*Amanda's voice becomes audible through the portieres.*]

[LEGEND ON SCREEN: "OÙ SONT LES NEIGES."]

[*He divides the portieres and enters the upstage area.*]

[AMANDA *and* LAURA *are seated at a drop-leaf table. Eating is indicated by gestures without food or utensils.* AMANDA *faces the audience.* TOM *and* LAURA *are seated in profile.*]

[*The interior has lit up softly and through the scrim we see* AMANDA *and* LAURA *seated at the table in the upstage area.*]

AMANDA [*calling*]   Tom?
TOM   Yes, Mother.

AMANDA We can't say grace until you come to the table!

TOM Coming, Mother. [*He bows slightly and withdraws, reappearing a few moments later in his place at the table.*]

AMANDA [*to her son*] Honey, don't *push* with your *fingers*. If you have to push with something, the thing to push with is a crust of bread. And chew—chew! Animals have sections in their stomachs which enable them to digest food without mastication, but human beings are supposed to chew their food before they swallow it down. Eat food leisurely, son, and really enjoy it. A well-cooked meal has lots of delicate flavors that have to be held in the mouth for appreciation. So chew your food and give your salivary glands a chance to function!

[TOM *deliberately lays his imaginary fork down and pushes his chair back from the table.*]

TOM I haven't enjoyed one bite of this dinner because of your constant directions on how to eat it. It's you that makes me rush through meals with your hawk-like attention to every bite I take. Sickening—spoils my appetite—all this discussion of—animals' secretion—salivary glands—mastication!

AMANDA [*lightly*] Temperament like a Metropolitan star! [*He rises and crosses downstage.*] You're not excused from the table.

TOM I'm getting a cigarette.

AMANDA You smoke too much.

[LAURA RISES]

LAURA I'll bring in the blanc mange.

[*He remains standing with his cigarette by the portieres during the following.*]

AMANDA [*rising*] No, sister, no, sister—you be the lady this time and I'll be the darky.

LAURA I'm already up.

AMANDA Resume your seat, little sister—I want you to stay fresh and pretty—for gentleman callers!

LAURA I'm not expecting any gentleman callers.

AMANDA [*crossing out to kitchenette. Airily*] Sometimes they come when they are least expected! Why, I remember one Sunday afternoon in Blue Mountain—[*Enters kitchenette.*]

TOM I know what's coming!

LAURA Yes. But let her tell it.

TOM Again?

LAURA She loves to tell it.

[AMANDA *returns with bowl of dessert.*]

AMANDA One Sunday afternoon in Blue Mountain—your mother received—*seventeen!*—gentlemen callers! Why, sometimes there weren't chairs enough to accommodate them all. We had to send the nigger over to bring in folding chairs from the parish house.

TOM [*remaining at portieres*] How did you entertain those gentleman callers?

AMANDA I understood the art of conversation!

TOM I bet you could talk.

AMANDA Girls in those days *knew* how to talk, I can tell you.

TOM Yes?

[IMAGE: AMANDA AS A GIRL ON A PORCH, GREETING CALLERS.]

AMANDA They knew how to entertain their gentleman callers. It wasn't enough for a girl to be possessed of a pretty face and a graceful figure—although I wasn't slighted in either respect. She also needed to have a nimble wit and a tongue to meet all occasions.

TOM What did you talk about?

AMANDA Things of importance going on in the world! Never anything coarse or common or vulgar. [*She addresses* TOM *as though he were seated in the vacant chair at the table though he remains by portieres. He plays this scene as though he held the book.*] My callers were gentlemen—all! Among my callers were some of the most prominent young planters of the Mississippi Delta—planters and sons of planters!

[TOM *motions for music and a spot of light on* AMANDA. *Her eyes lift, her face glows, her voice becomes rich and elegiac.*]

[SCREEN LEGEND: "OÙ SONT LES NEIGES."]

There was young Champ Laughlin who later became vice-persident of the Delta Planters Bank. Hadley Stevenson who was drowned in Moon Lake and left his widow one hundred and fifty thousand in Government bonds. There were the Cutrere brothers, Wesley and Bates. Bates was one of my bright particular beaux! He got in a quarrel with that wild Wainwright boy. They shot it out on the floor of Moon Lake Casino. Bates was shot through the stomach. Died in the ambulance on his way to Memphis. His widow was also well-provided for, came into eight or ten thousand acres, that's all. She married him on the rebound—never loved her—carried my picture on him the night he died! And there was that boy that every girl in the Delta had set her cap for! That beautiful, brilliant young Fitzhugh boy from Greene County!

TOM What did he leave his widow?

AMANDA He never married! Gracious, you talk as though all of my old admirers had turned up their toes to the daisies!

TOM Isn't this the first you've mentioned that still survives?

AMANDA That Fitzhugh boy went North and made a fortune—came to be known as the Wolf of Wall Street! He had the Midas touch, whatever he touched turned to gold! And I could have been Mrs. Duncan J. Fitzhugh, mind you! But—I picked your father!

LAURA [*rising*] Mother, let me clear the table.

AMANDA No, dear, you go in front and study your typewriter chart. Or practice your shorthand a little. Stay fresh and pretty!—It's almost time for our gentlemen callers to start arriving. [*She flounces girlishly toward the kitchenette.*] How many do you suppose we're going to entertain this afternoon?

[*Tom throws down the paper and jumps up with a groan.*]

LAURA [*alone in the dining room*] I don't believe we're going to receive any, Mother.

AMANDA [*reappearing, airily*] What? No one—not one? You must be joking! [LAURA *nervously echoes her laugh. She slips in a fugitive manner though the half-open portieres and draws them gently behind her. A shaft of very clear light is thrown on her face against the faded tapestry of the curtains.* MUSIC: "THE GLASS MENAGERIE" UNDER FAINTLY. *Lightly:*] Not one gentleman caller? It can't be true! There must be a flood, there must have been a tornado!

LAURA It isn't a flood, it's not a tornado, Mother. I'm just not popular like you were in Blue Mountain.... [TOM *utters another groan.* LAURA *glances at him with a faint, apologetic smile. Her voice catching a little.*] Mother's afraid I'm going to be an old maid.

THE SCENE DIMS OUT WITH "GLASS MENAGERIE" MUSIC.

SCENE TWO

["*Laura, Haven't You Ever Liked Some Boy?*"]

On the dark stage the screen is lighted with the image of blue roses.

Gradually LAURA'*s figure becomes apparent and the screen goes out.*

The music subsides.

LAURA *is seated in the delicate ivory chair at the small claw-foot table.*

She wears a dress of soft violet material for a kimono—her hair tied back from her forehead with a ribbon.

She is washing and polishing her collection of glass. AMANDA *appears on the fire-escape steps. At the sound of her ascent,* LAURA *catches her breath, thrusts the bowl of ornaments away and seats herself stiffly before the diagram of the typewriter keyboard as though it held her spellbound. Something has happened to* AMANDA. *It is written in her face as she climbs to the landing: a look that is grim and hopeless and a little absurd.*

She has on one of those cheap or imitation velvety-looking cloth coats with imitation fur collar. Her hat is five or six years old, one of those dreadful cloche hats that were worn in the late twenties and she is clasping an enormous black patent-leather pocketbook with nickel clasps and initials. This is her full-dress outfit, the one she usually wears to the D.A.R.

Before entering she looks through the door.

She purses her lips, opens her eyes wide, rolls them upward and shakes her head.

Then she slowly lets herself in the door. Seeing her mother's expression, LAURA *touches her lips with a nervous gesture.*]

LAURA Hello, Mother, I was—[*She makes a nervous gesture toward the chart on the wall.* AMANDA *leans against the shut door and stares at* LAURA *with a martyred look.*]

AMANDA Deception? Deception? [*She slowly removes her hat and gloves, continuing the sweet suffering stare. She lets the hat and gloves fall on the floor—a bit of acting.*]

LAURA [*shakily*] How was the D.A.R. meeting? [AMANDA *slowly opens her purse and removes a dainty white handkerchief which she shakes out delicately and delicately touches to her lips and nostrils.*] Didn't you go to the D.A.R. meeting, Mother?

AMANDA [*faintly, almost inaudibly*] —No.— No. [*Then more forcibly:*] I did not have the strength—to go to the D.A.R. In fact, I did not have the courage! I wanted to find a hole in the ground and hide myself in it forever! [*She crosses slowly to the wall and removes the diagram of the typewriter keyboard. She holds it in front of her for a second, staring at it sweetly and sorrowfully —then bites her lips and tears it in two pieces.*]

LAURA [*faintly*] Why did you do that, Mother? [AMANDA *repeats the same procedure with the chart of the Gregg Alphabet.*] Why are you—

AMANDA Why? Why? How old are you, Laura?

LAURA Mother, you know my age.

AMANDA I thought that you were an adult; it seems that I was mistaken. [*She crosses slowly to the sofa and sinks down and stares at* LAURA.]

LAURA Please don't stare at me, Mother.

[AMANDA *closes her eyes and lowers her head. Count ten.*]

AMANDA What are we going to do, what is going to become of us, what is the future?

[*Count ten.*]

LAURA Has something happened, Mother? [AMANDA *draws a long breath and takes out the handkerchief again. Dabbing process.*] Mother, has—something happened?

AMANDA I'll be all right in a minute. I'm just bewildered—[*Count five*]—by life. . . .

LAURA Mother, I wish that you would tell me what's happened!

AMANDA As you know, I was supposed to be inducted into my office at the D.A.R. this afternoon. [IMAGE: A SWARM OF TYPEWRITERS.] But I stopped off at Rubicam's Business College to speak to your teachers about your having a cold and ask them what progress they thought you were making down there.

LAURA Oh. . . .

AMANDA I went to the typing instructor and introduced myself as your mother. She didn't know who you were. Wingfield, she said. We don't have any such student enrolled at the school! I assured her she did, that you had been going to classes since early in January. "I wonder," she said, "if you could be talking about that terribly shy little girl who dropped out of school after only a few days' attendance?" "No," I said. "Laura, my daughter has been going to school every day for the past six weeks!" "Excuse me," she said. She took the attendance book out and there was your name, unmistakably printed, and all the dates you were absent until they decided that you had dropped out of school. I still said, "No, there must have been some mistake! There must have been some mix-up in the records!" And she said, "No—I remember her perfectly now. Her hands shook so that she couldn't hit the right keys! The first time we gave a speed-test, she broke down completely—was sick at the stomach and almost had to be carried into the wash-room! After that morning she never showed up any more. We phoned the house but never got any answer—while I was working at Famous and Barr, I suppose, demonstrating those—Oh!" I felt so weak I could barely keep on my feet! I had to sit down while they got me a glass of water! Fifty dollars' tuition, all of our plans—my hopes and ambitions for you—just gone up the spout, just gone up the spout like that. [LAURA *draws a long breath and gets awkwardly to her feet. She crosses to the victrola and winds it up.*] What are you doing?

LAURA Oh! [*She releases the handle and returns to her seat.*]

AMANDA Laura, where have you been going when you've gone out pretending that you were going to business college?

LAURA I've just been going out walking.

AMANDA That's not true.

LAURA It is. I just went walking.

AMANDA Walking? Walking? In winter? Deliberately courting pneumonia in that light coat? Where did you walk to, Laura?

LAURA All sorts of places—mostly in the park.

AMANDA Even after you'd started catching that cold?

LAURA It was the lesser of two evils, Mother. [IMAGE: WINTER SCENE IN PARK.] I couldn't go back up. I—threw up—on the floor!

AMANDA From half past seven till after five every day you mean to tell me you walked around in the park, because you wanted to make me think that you were still going to Rubicam's Business College?

LAURA It wasn't as bad as it sounds. I went inside places to get warmed up.

AMANDA Inside where?

LAURA I went in the art museum and the birdhouses at the Zoo. I visited the penguins every day! Sometimes I did without lunch and went to the movies. Lately I've been spending most of my afternoons in the Jewelbox, that big glass house where they raise the tropical flowers.

AMANDA You did all this to deceive me, just for deception? [LAURA *looks down.*] Why?

LAURA Mother, when you're disappointed, you get that awful suffering look on your face, like the picture of Jesus' mother in the museum!

AMANDA Hush!

LAURA I couldn't face it.

[*Pause. A whisper of strings.*]

[LEGEND: "THE CRUST OF HUMILITY."]

AMANDA [*hopelessly fingering the huge pocketbook*] So what are we going to do the rest of our lives? Stay home and watch the parades go by? Amuse ourselves with the glass menagerie, darling? Eternally play those worn-out phonograph records your father left as a painful reminder of him? We won't have a business career—we've given that up because it gave us nervous indigestion! [*Laughs wearily.*] What is there left but dependency all our lives? I know so well what becomes of unmarried women who aren't prepared to occupy a position. I've seen such pitiful cases in the South—barely tolerated spinsters living upon the grudging patronage of sister's husband or brother's wife!—stuck away in some little mouse-trap of a room—encouraged by one in-law to visit another—little birdlike women without any nest—eating the crust of humility all their life! Is that the future that we've mapped out for ourselves? I swear it's the only alternative I can think of! It isn't a very pleasant alternative, is it? Of course—some girls *do marry.* [*Laura twists her hands nervously.*] Haven't you ever liked some boy?

LAURA Yes. I liked one once. [*Rises.*] I came across his picture a while ago.

AMANDA [*with some interest*] He gave you his picture?

LAURA No, it's in the year-book.

AMANDA [*disappointed*] Oh—a high-school boy.

[SCREEN IMAGE: JIM AS HIGH-SCHOOL HERO BEARING A SILVER CUP.]

LAURA Yes. His name was Jim. [LAURA *lifts the heavy annual from the claw-foot table.*] Here he is in *The Pirates of Penzance.*

AMANDA [*absently*] The what?

LAURA The operetta the senior class put on. He had a wonderful voice and we sat across the aisle from each other Mondays, Wednesdays and Fridays in the Aud. Here he is with the silver cup for debating! See his grin?

AMANDA [*absently*] He must have had a jolly disposition.

LAURA He used to call me—Blue Roses.

[IMAGE: BLUE ROSES.]

AMANDA Why did he call you such a name as that?

LAURA When I had that attack of pleurosis—he asked me what was the matter when I came back. I said pleurosis—he thought that I said Blue Roses! So that's what he always called me after that. Whenever he saw me, he'd holler, "Hello, Blue Roses!" I didn't care for the girl that he went out with. Emily Meisenbach. Emily was the best-dressed girl at Soldan. She never struck me, though, as being sincere . . . It says in the Personal Section—they're engaged. That's—six years ago! They must be married by now.

AMANDA Girls that aren't cut out for business careers usually wind up married to some nice man. [*Gets up with a spark of revival.*] Sister, that's what you'll do!

[LAURA *utters a startled, doubtful laugh. She reaches quickly for a piece of glass.*]

LAURA But, Mother—
AMANDA Yes? [*Crossing to the photograph.*]
LAURA [*in a tone of frightened apology*] I'm —crippled!

[IMAGE: SCREEN.]

AMANDA Nonsense! Laura, I've told you never, never to use that word. Why, you're not crippled, you just have a little defect—hardly noticeable, even! When people have some slight disadvantage like that, they cultivate other things to make up for it—develop charm—and vivacity—and—*charm!* That's all you have to do! [*She turns again to the photograph.*] One thing your father had plenty of—was *charm!*

[TOM *motions to the fiddle in the wings.*]

THE SCENE FADES OUT WITH MUSIC.

SCENE THREE

[LEGEND ON SCREEN: "AFTER THE FIASCO—"]

[TOM *speaks from the fire-escape landing.*]

TOM After the fiasco at Rubicam's Business College, the idea of getting a gentleman caller for Laura began to play a more important part in Mother's calculations. It became an obsession. Like some archetype of the universal unconscious, the image of the gentleman caller haunted our small apartment. . . . [IMAGE: YOUNG MAN AT DOOR WITH FLOWERS.] An evening at home rarely passed without some allusion to this image, this spectre, this hope. . . . Even when he wasn't mentioned, his presence hung in Mother's preoccupied look and in my sister's frightened, apologetic manner—hung like a sentence passed upon the Wingfields! Mother was a woman of action as well as words. She began to take logical steps in the planned direction. Late that winter and in the early spring—realizing that extra money would be needed to properly feather the nest and plume the bird—she conducted a vigorous campaign on the telephone, roping in subscribers to one of those magazines for matrons called *The Home-maker's Companion,* the type of journal that features the serialized sublimations of ladies of letters who think in terms of delicate cup-like breasts, slim, tapering waists, rich, creamy thighs, eyes like wood-smoke in autumn, fingers that soothe and caress like strains of music, bodies as powerful as Etruscan sculpture.

[SCREEN IMAGE: GLAMOR MAGAZINE COVER.]

[AMANDA *enters with phone on long extension cord. She is spotted in the dim stage.*]

AMANDA Ida Scott? This is Amanda Wingfield! We *missed* you at the D.A.R. last Monday! I said to myself: She's probably suffering with that sinus condition! How is that sinus condition? Horrors! Heaven have mercy!—You're a Christian martyr, yes, that's what you are, a Christian martyr! Well, I just now happened to notice that your subscription to the *Companion's* about to expire! Yes, it expires with the next issue, honey!—just when that wonderful new serial by Bessie Mae Hopper is getting off to such an exciting start. Oh, honey, it's something that you can't miss! You remember how *Gone With the Wind* took everybody by storm? You simply couldn't go out if you hadn't read it. All everybody *talked* was Scarlett O'Hara. Well, this is a book that critics already compare to *Gone With the Wind.* It's the *Gone With the Wind* of the post–World War generation!—What?—Burning?—Oh, honey, don't let them burn, go take a look in the oven and I'll hold the wire! Heavens—I think she's hung up!

DIM OUT

[LEGEND ON SCREEN: "YOU THINK I'M IN LOVE WITH CONTINENTAL SHOEMAKERS?"]

[*Before the stage is lighted, the violent voices of* TOM *and* AMANDA *are heard.*

They are quarreling behind the portieres. In front of them stands LAURA *with clenched hands and panicky expression.*

A clear pool of light on her figure throughout this scene.]

TOM   What in Christ's name am I—
AMANDA [*shrilly*]   Don't you use that—
TOM   Supposed to do!
AMANDA   Expression! Not in my—
TOM   Ohhh!
AMANDA   Presence! Have you gone out of your senses?
TOM   I have, that's true, *driven* out!
AMANDA   What is the matter with you, you—big—big—IDIOT!
TOM   Look—I've got *no thing*, no single thing—
AMANDA   Lower your voice!
TOM   In my life here that I can call my OWN! Everything is—
AMANDA   Stop that shouting!
TOM   Yesterday you confiscated my books! You had the nerve to—
AMANDA   I took that horrible novel back to the library—yes! That hideous book by that insane Mr. Lawrence. [TOM *laughs wildly.*] I cannot control the output of diseased minds or people who cater to them— [TOM *laughs still more wildly.*] BUT I WON'T ALLOW SUCH FILTH BROUGHT INTO MY HOUSE! No, no, no, no, no!
TOM   House, house! Who pays rent on it, who makes a slave of himself to—
AMANDA [*fairly screeching*]   Don't you DARE to—
TOM   No, no, *I* mustn't say things! *I've* got to just—

AMANDA   Let me tell you—
TOM   I don't want to hear any more! [*He tears the portieres open. The upstage area is lit with a turgid smoky red glow.*]

[AMANDA's *hair is in metal curlers and she wears a very old bathrobe, much too large for her slight figure, a relic of the faithless* MR. WINGFIELD.

An upright typewriter and a wild disarray of manuscripts is on the drop-leaf table. The quarrel was probably precipitated by AMANDA's *interruption of his creative labor. A chair lying overthrown on the floor.*

Their gesticulating shadows are cast on the ceiling by the fiery glow.]

AMANDA   You *will* hear more, you—
TOM   No, I won't hear more, I'm going out!
AMANDA   You come right back in—
TOM   Out, out, out! Because I'm—
AMANDA   Come back here, Tom Wingfield! I'm not through talking to you!
TOM   Oh, go—
LAURA [*desperately*]   —Tom!
AMANDA   You're going to listen, and no more insolence from you! I'm at the end of my patience! [*He comes back toward her.*]
TOM   What do you think I'm at? Aren't I supposed to have any patience to reach the end of Mother? I know, I know. It seems unimportant to you, what I'm *doing*—what I *want* to do—having a little *difference* between them! You don't think that—
AMANDA   I think you've been doing things that you're ashamed of. That's why you act like this. I don't believe that you go every night to the movies. Nobody goes to the movies night after night. Nobody in their right minds goes to the movies as often as you pretend to. People don't go to the movies at nearly midnight, and movies don't let out at two A.M. Come in stumbling. Muttering to yourself like a maniac! You get three hours' sleep and then go to work. Oh, I can picture the way you're doing down there. Moping, doping, because you're in no condition.
TOM [*wildly*]   No, I'm in no condition!
AMANDA   What right have you got to jeopardize your job? Jeopardize the security of us

all? How do you think we'd manage if you were—

TOM Listen! You think I'm crazy *about* the *warehouse?* [*He bends fiercely toward her slight figure.*] You think I'm in love with the Continental Shoemakers? You think I want to spend fifty-five *years* down there in that—*celotex interior!* with—*fluorescent—tubes!* Look! I'd rather somebody picked up a crowbar and battered out my brains—than go back mornings! I *go!* Every time you come in yelling that God damn *"Rise and Shine!" "Rise and Shine!"* I say to myself, "How *lucky dead* people are!" But I get up. I *go!* For sixty-five dollars a month I give up all that I dream of doing and being *ever!* And you say *self—self's* all I ever think of. Why, listen, if self is what I thought of, Mother, I'd be where he is—GONE! [*Pointing to father's picture.*] As far as the system of transportation reaches! [*He starts past her. She grabs his arm.*] Don't grab at me, Mother!

AMANDA Where are you going?

TOM I'm going to the *movies.*

AMANDA I don't believe that lie!

TOM [*crouching toward her, overtowering her tiny figure. She backs away, gasping*] I'm going to opium dens! Yes, opium dens, dens of vice and criminals' hang-outs, Mother. I've joined the Hogan gang, I'm a hired assassin, I carry a tommy-gun in a violin case! I run a string of cat-houses in the Valley! They call me Killer, Killer Wingfield, I'm leading a double-life, a simple, honest warehouse worker by day, by night, a dynamic *czar* of the *underworld,* Mother. I go to gambling casinos, I spin away fortunes on the roulette table! I wear a patch over one eye and a false mustache, sometimes I put on green whiskers. On those occasions they call me—*El Diablo!* Oh, I could tell you things to make you sleepless! My enemies plan to dynamite this place. They're going to blow us all sky-high some night! I'll be glad, very happy, and so will you! You'll go up, up on a broomstick, over Blue Mountain with seventeen gentlemen callers! You ugly—babbling old—*witch.* . . . [*He goes through a series of violent, clumsy movements, seizing his overcoat, lunging to the door, pulling it fiercely open. The women watch him, aghast. His arm catches in the sleeve of the coat as he struggles to pull it on. For a moment he is pinioned by the bulky garment. With an outraged groan he tears the coat off again, splitting the shoulder of it, and hurls it across the room. It strikes against the shelf of* LAURA's *glass collection, there is a tinkle of shattering glass.* LAURA *cries out as if wounded.*]

[MUSIC LEGEND: "THE GLASS MENAGERIE."]

LAURA [*shrilly*] My glass!—menagerie. . . . [*She covers her face and turns away.*]

[*But* AMANDA *is still stunned and stupefied by the "ugly witch" so that she barely notices this occurrence. Now she recovers her speech.*]

AMANDA [*in an awful voice*] I won't speak to you—until you apologize! [*She crosses through portieres and draws them together behind her.* TOM *is left with* LAURA. LAURA *clings weakly to the mantel with her face averted.* TOM *stares at her stupidly for a moment. Then he crosses to shelf. Drops awkwardly on his knees to collect the fallen glass, glancing at* LAURA *as if he would speak but couldn't.*]

"THE GLASS MENAGERIE" STEALS IN AS THE SCENE DIMS OUT.

SCENE FOUR

The interior is dark. Faint light in the alley.

A deep-voiced bell in a church is tolling the hour of five as the scene commences.

TOM *appears at the top of the alley. After each solemn boom of the bell in the tower, he shakes a little noise-maker or rattle as if to express the tiny spasm of man in contrast to the sustained power and dignity of the Almighty. This and the unsteadiness of his advance make it evident that he has been drinking.*

As he climbs the few steps to the fire-escape landing light steals up inside. LAURA *appears in nightdress, observing* TOM's *empty bed in the front room.*

TOM *fishes in his pockets for door-key, removing a motley assortment of articles in the search, including a perfect shower of movie-ticket stubs and an empty bottle. At last he finds the key, but just as he is about to insert it, it slips from his fingers. He strikes a match and crouches below the door.*

TOM [*bitterly*] One crack—and it falls through!

[LAURA *opens the door.*]

LAURA   Tom! Tom, what are you doing?
TOM   Looking for a door-key.
LAURA   Where have you been all this time?
TOM   I have been to the movies.
LAURA   All this time at the movies?
TOM   There was a very long program. There was a Garbo picture and a Micky Mouse and a travelogue and a newsreel and a preview of coming attractions. And there was an organ solo and a collection for the milk-fund—simultaneously—which ended up in a terrible fight between a fat lady and an usher!
LAURA [*innocently*] Did you have to stay through everything?
TOM   Of course! And, oh, I forgot! There was a big stage show! The headliner on this stage show was Malvolio the Magician. He performed wonderful tricks, many of them, such as pouring water back and forth between pitchers. First it turned to wine and then it turned to beer and then it turned to whiskey. I know it was whiskey it finally turned into because he needed somebody to come up out of the audience to help him, and I came up —both shows! It was Kentucky Straight Bourbon. A very generous fellow, he gave souvenirs. [*He pulls from his back pocket a shimmering rainbow-colored scarf.*] He gave me this. This is his magic scarf. You can have it, Laura. You wave it over a canary cage and you get a bowl of gold-fish. You wave it over the gold-fish bowl and they fly away canaries. . . . But the wonderfullest trick of all was the coffin trick. We nailed him into a coffin and he got out of the coffin without removing one nail. [*He has come inside.*] There is a trick that would come in handy for me—get out of this 2 by 4 situation! [*Flops onto bed and starts removing shoes.*]
LAURA   Tom—Shhh!
TOM   What're you shushing me for?
LAURA   You'll wake up Mother.
TOM   Goody, goody! Pay 'er back for all those "Rise an' Shines." [*Lies down, groaning.*] You know it don't take much intelligence to get yourself into a nailed-up coffin, Laura. But who in hell ever got himself out of one without removing one nail?

[As *if in answer, the father's grinning photograph lights up.*]

SCENE DIMS OUT

[*Immediately following: The church bell is heard striking six. At the sixth stroke the alarm clock goes off in* AMANDA's *room, and after a few moments we hear her calling:* "Rise and Shine! Rise and Shine! LAURA, *go tell your brother to rise and shine!*"]

TOM [*Sitting up slowly*]   I'll rise—but I won't shine.

[*The light increases.*]

AMANDA   Laura, tell your brother his coffee is ready.

[LAURA *slips into front room.*]

LAURA   Tom! it's nearly seven. Don't make Mother nervous. [*He stares at her stupidly. Beseechingly.*] Tom, speak to Mother this morning. Make up with her, apologize, speak to her!
TOM   She won't to me. It's her that started not speaking.
LAURA   If you just say you're sorry she'll start speaking.
TOM   Her not speaking—is that such a tragedy?
LAURA   Please—please!
AMANDA [*calling from kitchenette*]   Laura, are you going to do what I asked you to do, or do I have to get dressed and go out myself?
LAURA   Going, going—soon as I get on my coat! [*She pulls on a shapeless felt hat with nervous, jerky movement, pleadingly glanc-*

ing at TOM. *Rushes awkwardly for coat. The coat is one of* AMANDA's, *inaccurately made-over, the sleeves too short for* LAURA.] Butter and what else?

AMANDA [*entering upstage*] Just butter. Tell them to charge it.

LAURA Mother, they make such faces when I do that.

AMANDA Sticks and stones can break our bones, but the expression on Mr. Garfinkel's face won't harm us! Tell your brother his coffee is getting cold.

LAURA [*at door*] Do what I asked you, will you, will you, Tom?

[*He looks sullenly away.*]

AMANDA Laura, go now or just don't go at all!

LAURA [*rushing out*] Going—going! [*A second later she cries out.* TOM *springs up and crosses to door.* AMANDA *rushes anxiously in.* TOM *opens the door.*]

TOM Laura?

LAURA I'm all right. I slipped, but I'm all right.

AMANDA [*peering anxiously after her*] If anyone breaks a leg on those fire-escape steps, the landlord ought to be sued for every cent he possesses!

[*She shuts door. Remembers she isn't speaking and returns to other room.*

As TOM *enters listlessly for his coffee, she turns her back to him and stands rigidly facing the window on the gloomy gray vault of the areaway. Its light on her face with its aged but childish features is cruelly sharp, satirical as a Daumier print.*]

[MUSIC UNDER: "AVE MARIA."]

[*Tom glances sheepishly but sullenly at her averted figure and slumps at the table. The coffee is scalding hot; he sips it and gasps and spits it back in the cup. At his gasp,* AMANDA *catches her breath and half turns. Then catches herself and turns back to window.*

TOM *blows on his coffee, glancing sidewise at his mother. She clears her throat.* TOM *clears his. He starts to rise. Sinks back down again, scratches his head, clears his throat again.* AMANDA *coughs.* TOM *raises his cup in both hands to blow on it, his eyes staring over the rim of it at his mother for several moments. Then he slowly sets the cup down and awkwardly and hesitantly rises from the chair.*]

TOM [*hoarsely*] Mother. I—I apologize. Mother. [AMANDA *draws a quick, shuddering breath. Her face works grotesquely. She breaks into childlike tears.*] I'm sorry for what I said, for everything that I said, I didn't mean it.

AMANDA [*sobbingly*] My devotion has made me a witch and so I make myself hateful to my children!

TOM No, you *don't*.

AMANDA I worry so much, don't sleep, it makes me nervous!

TOM [*gently*] I understand that.

AMANDA I've had to put up a solitary battle all these years. But you're my right-hand bower! Don't fall down, don't fail!

TOM [*gently*] I try, Mother.

AMANDA [*with great enthusiasm*] Try and you will SUCCEED! [*The notion makes her breathless.*] Why, you—you're just *full* of natural endowments! Both of my children—they're *unusual* children! Don't you think I know it? I'm so—*proud!* Happy and—feel I've—so much to be thankful for but—Promise me one thing, son!

TOM What, Mother?

AMANDA Promise, son, you'll—never be a drunkard!

TOM [*turns to her grinning*] I will never be a drunkard, Mother.

AMANDA That's what frightened me so, that you'd be drinking! Eat a bowl of Purina!

TOM Just coffee, Mother.

AMANDA Shredded wheat biscuit?

TOM No. No, Mother, just coffee.

AMANDA You can't put in a day's work on an empty stomach. You've got ten minutes—don't gulp! Drinking too-hot liquids makes cancer of the stomach. . . . Put cream in.

TOM No, thank you.

AMANDA To cool it.

TOM No! No, thank you, I want it black.

AMANDA I know, but it's not good for you. We have to do all that we can to build ourselves up. In these trying times we live in, all that we have to cling to is—each other.... That's why it's so important to—Tom, I—I sent out your sister so I could discuss something with you. If you hadn't spoken I would have spoken to you. [*Sits down.*]

TOM [*gently*] What is it, Mother, that you want to discuss?

AMANDA Laura!

[*Tom puts his cup down slowly.*]

[LEGEND ON SCREEN: "LAURA."]

[MUSIC: "THE GLASS MENAGERIE."]

TOM —Oh.—Laura . . .

AMANDA [*touching his sleeve*] You know how Laura is. So quiet but—still water runs deep! She notices things and I think she—broods about them. [TOM *looks up.*] A few days ago I came in and she was crying.

TOM What about?

AMANDA You.

TOM Me?

AMANDA She has an idea that you're not happy here.

TOM What gave her that idea?

AMANDA What gives her any idea? However, you do act strangely. I—I'm not criticizing, understand *that*! I know your ambitions do not lie in the warehouse, that like everybody in the whole wide world—you've had to—make sacrifices, but—Tom—Tom—life's not easy, it calls for—Spartan endurance! There's so many things in my heart that I cannot describe to you! I've never told you but I —*loved* your father. . . .

TOM [*gently*] I know that, Mother.

AMANDA And you—when I see you taking after his ways! Staying out late—and—well, you *had* been drinking the night you were in that—terrifying condition! Laura says that you hate the apartment and that you go out nights to get away from it! Is that true, Tom?

TOM No. You say there's so much in your heart you can't describe to me. That's true of me, too. There's so much in my heart that I can't describe to *you*! So let's respect each other's—

AMANDA But, why—*why*, Tom—are you always so *restless*? Where do you *go* to, nights?

TOM I—go to the movies.

AMANDA Why do you go to the movies so much, Tom?

TOM I got to the movies because—I like adventure. Adventure is something I don't have much of at work, so I go to the movies.

AMANDA But, Tom, you go to the movies *entirely* too *much*!

TOM I like a lot of adventure.

[AMANDA *looks baffled, then hurt. As the familiar inquisition resumes he becomes hard and impatient again.* AMANDA *slips back into her querulous attitude toward him.*]

[IMAGE ON SCREEN: SAILING VESSEL WITH JOLLY ROGER.]

AMANDA Most young men find adventure in their careers.

TOM Then most young men are not employed in a warehouse.

AMANDA The world is full of young men employed in warehouses and offices and factories.

TOM Do all of them find adventure in their careers?

AMANDA They do or they do without it! Not everybody has a craze for adventure.

TOM Man is by instinct a lover, a hunter, a fighter, and none of those instincts are given much play at the warehouse!

AMANDA Man is by instinct! Don't quote instinct to me! Instinct is something that people have got away from! It belongs to animals! Christian adults don't want it!

TOM What do Christian adults want, then, Mother?

AMANDA Superior things! Things of the mind and the spirit! Only animals have to satisfy instincts! Surely your aims are somewhat higher than theirs! Than monkeys—pigs—

TOM I reckon they're not.

AMANDA You're joking. However, that isn't what I wanted to discuss.

TOM [*rising*] I haven't much time.

AMANDA [*pushing his shoulders*] Sit down.

TOM You want me to punch in red at the warehouse, Mother?

AMANDA You have five minutes. I want to talk about Laura.

[LEGEND: "PLANS AND PROVISIONS."]

TOM   All right! What about Laura?

AMANDA   We have to be making plans and provisions for her. She's older than you, two years, and nothing has happened. She just drifts along doing nothing. It frightens me terribly how she just drifts along.

TOM   I guess she's the type that people call home girls.

AMANDA   There's no such type, and if there is, it's a pity! That is unless the home is hers, with a husband!

TOM   What?

AMANDA   Oh, I can see the handwriting on the wall as plain as I see the nose in front of my face! It's terrifying! More and more you remind me of your father! He was out all hours without explanation—Then *left!* Good-bye! And me with the bag to hold. I saw that letter you got from the Merchant Marine. I know what you're dreaming of. I'm not standing here blindfolded. Very well, then. Then *do* it! But not till there's somebody to take your place.

TOM   What do you mean?

AMANDA   I mean that as soon as Laura has got somebody to take care of her, married, a home of her own, independent—why, then you'll be free to go wherever you please, on land, on sea, whichever way the wind blows you! But until that time you've got to look out for your sister. I don't say me because I'm old and don't matter! I say for your sister because she's young and dependent. I put her in business college—a dismal failure! Frightened her so it made her sick at the stomach. I took her over to the Young People's League at the church. Another fiasco. She spoke to nobody, nobody spoke to her. Now all she does is fool with those pieces of glass and play those worn-out records. What kind of a life is that for a girl to lead?

TOM   What can I do about it?

AMANDA   Overcome selfishness! Self, self, self is all that you ever think of! [TOM *springs up and crosses to get his coat. It is ugly and bulky. He pulls on a cap with earmuffs.*] Where is your muffler? Put your wool muffler on! [*He snatches it angrily from the closet and tosses it around his neck and pulls both ends tight.*] Tom! I haven't said what I had in mind to ask you.

TOM   I'm too late to—

AMANDA   [*catching his arm—very importantely. Then shyly*]   Down at the warehouse, aren't there some—nice young men?

TOM   No!

AMANDA   There *must* be—*some* . . .

TOM   Mother— [*Gesture.*]

AMANDA   Find out one that's clean-living—doesn't drink and—ask him out for sister!

TOM   What?

AMANDA   For *sister!* To *meet!* Get *acquainted!*

TOM [*stamping to door*]   Oh, my go-osh!

AMANDA   Will you? [*He opens door. Imploringly.*] Will you? [*He starts down.*] Will you? *Will* you, dear?

TOM [*calling back*]   Yes!

[AMANDA *closes the door hesitantly and with a troubled but faintly hopeful expression.*]

[SCREEN IMAGE: GLAMOR MAGAZINE COVER.]

[*Spot* AMANDA *at phone.*]

AMANDA   Ella Cartwright? This is Amanda Wingfield! How are you, honey? How is that kidney condition? [*Count five.*] Horrors! [*Count five.*] You're a Christian martyr, yes, honey, that's what you are, a Christian martyr! Well, I just happened to notice in my little red book that your subscription to the *Companion* has just run out! I knew that you wouldn't want to miss out on the wonderful serial starting in this new issue. It's by Bessie Mae Hopper, the first thing she's written since *Honeymoon for Three.* Wasn't that a strange and interesting story? Well, this one is even lovelier, I believe. It has a sophisticated, society background. It's all about the horsey set on Long Island!

FADE OUT

SCENE FIVE

[LEGEND ON SCREEN: "ANNUNCIATION." *Fade with music.*]

[*It is early dusk of a spring evening. Supper has just been finished in the Wingfield apartment.* AMANDA *and* LAURA *in light colored dresses are removing dishes from the table, in the upstage area, which is shadowy, their movements formalized almost as a dance or ritual, their moving forms as pale and silent as moths.*

TOM *in white shirt and trousers, rises from the table and crosses toward the fire-escape.*]

AMANDA [*as he passes her*] Son, will you do me a favor?

TOM What?

AMANDA Comb your hair! You look so pretty when your hair is combed! [TOM *slouches on sofa with evening paper. Enormous caption "Franco Triumphs."*] There is only one respect in which I would like you to emulate your father.

TOM What respect is that?

AMANDA The care he always took of his appearance. He never allowed himself to look untidy. [*He throws down the paper and crosses to fire-escape.*] Where are you going?

TOM I'm going out to smoke.

AMANDA You smoke too much. A pack a day at fifteen cents a pack. How much would that amount to in a month? Thirty times fifteen is how much. Tom? Figure it out and you will be astounded at what you could save. Enough to give you a night-school course in accounting at Washington U! Just think what a wonderful thing that would be for you, son!

[*Tom is unmoved by the thought.*]

TOM I'd rather smoke. [*He steps out on landing, letting the screen door slam.*]

AMANDA [*sharply*] I know! That's the tragedy of it.... [*Alone, she turns to look at her husband's picture.*]

[DANCE MUSIC: "ALL THE WORLD IS WAITING FOR THE SUNRISE!"]

TOM [*to the audience*] Across the alley from us was the Paradise Dance Hall. On evenings in spring the windows and doors were open and the music came outdoors. Sometimes the lights were turned out except for a large glass sphere that hung from the ceiling. It would turn slowly about and filter the dusk with delicate rainbow colors. Then the orchestra played a waltz or a tango, something that had a slow and sensuous rhythm. Couples would come outside, to the relative privacy of the alley. You could see them kissing behind ash-pits and telephone poles. This was the compensation for lives that passed like mine, without any change or adventure. Adventure and change were imminent in this year. They were waiting around the corner for all these kids. Suspended in the mist over Berchtesgaden, caught in the folds of Chamberlain's umbrella— In Spain there was Guernica! But here there was only hot swing music and liquor, dance halls, bars, and movies, and sex that hung in the gloom like a chandelier and flooded the world with brief, deceptive rainbows.... All the world was waiting for bombardments!

[AMANDA *turns from the picture and comes outside.*]

AMANDA [*sighing*] A fire-escape landing's a poor excuse for a porch. [*She spreads a newspaper on a step and sits down, gracefully and demurely as if she were settling into a swing on a Mississippi veranda.*] What are you looking at?

TOM The moon.

AMANDA Is there a moon this evening?

TOM It's rising over Garfinkel's Delicatessen.

AMANDA So it is! A little silver slipper of a moon. Have you made a wish on it yet?

TOM Um-hum.

AMANDA What did you wish for?

TOM That's a secret.

AMANDA A secret, huh? Well, I won't tell mine either. I will be just as mysterious as you.

TOM I bet I can guess what yours is.

AMANDA Is my head so transparent?

TOM You're not a sphinx.

AMANDA No, I don't have secrets. I'll tell you what I wished for on the moon. Success and happiness for my precious children! I wish for that whenever there's a moon, and when there isn't a moon, I wish for it, too.

TOM I thought perhaps you wished for a gentleman caller.

AMANDA Why do you say that?

TOM Don't you remember asking me to fetch one?

AMANDA I remember suggesting that it would be nice for your sister if you brought home some nice young man from the warehouse. I think that I've made that suggestion more than once.

TOM Yes, you have made it repeatedly.

AMANDA Well?

TOM We are going to have one.

AMANDA *What?*

TOM A gentleman caller!

[THE ANNUNCIATION IS CELEBRATED WITH MUSIC.]

[AMANDA *rises*.]

[IMAGE ON SCREEN: CALLER WITH BOUQUET.]

AMANDA You mean you have asked some nice young man to come over?

TOM Yep. I've asked him to dinner.

AMANDA You really did?

TOM I did!

AMANDA You did, and did he—*accept?*

TOM He did!

AMANDA Well, well—well, well! That's—lovely!

TOM I thought that you would be pleased.

AMANDA It's definite, then?

TOM Very definite.

AMANDA Soon?

TOM Very soon.

AMANDA For heaven's sake, stop putting on and tell me some things, will you?

TOM What things do you want me to tell you?

AMANDA *Naturally* I would like to know when he's *coming!*

TOM He's coming tomorrow.

AMANDA *Tomorrow?*

TOM Yep. Tomorrow.

AMANDA But, Tom!

TOM Yes, Mother?

AMANDA Tomorrow gives me no time!

TOM Time for what?

AMANDA Preparations! Why didn't you phone me at once, as soon as you asked him, the minute that he accepted? Then, don't you see, I could have been getting ready!

TOM You don't have to make any fuss.

AMANDA Oh, Tom, Tom, Tom, of course I have to make a fuss! I want things nice, not sloppy! Not thrown together. I'll certainly have to do some fast thinking, won't I?

TOM I don't see why you have to think at all.

AMANDA You just don't know. We can't have a gentleman caller in a pig-sty! All my wedding silver has to be polished, the monogrammed table linen ought to be laundered! The windows have to be washed and fresh curtains put up. And how about clothes? We have to *wear* something, don't we?

TOM Mother, this boy is no one to make a fuss over!

AMANDA Do you realize he's the first young man we've introduced to your sister? It's terrible, dreadful, disgraceful that poor little sister has never received a single gentleman caller! Tom, come inside! [*She opens the screen door.*]

TOM What for?

AMANDA I want to ask you some things.

TOM If you're going to make such a fuss, I'll call it off, I'll tell him not to come!

AMANDA You certainly won't do anything of the kind. Nothing offends people worse than broken engagements. It simply means I'll have to work like a Turk! We won't be brilliant, but we will pass inspection. Come on inside. [TOM *follows, groaning.*] Sit down.

TOM Any particular place you would like me to sit?

AMANDA Thank heavens I've got that new sofa! I'm also making payments on a floor lamp I'll have sent out! And put the chintz covers on, they'll brighten things up! Of course I'd hoped to have these walls re-papered. . . . What is the young man's name?

TOM His name is O'Connor.

AMANDA That, of course, means fish—tomorrow is Friday! I'll have that salmon loaf—with Durkee's dressing! What does he do? He works at the warehouse?

TOM Of course! How else would I—

AMANDA Tom, he—doesn't drink?

TOM Why do you ask me that?

AMANDA Your father *did!*

TOM Don't get started on that!

AMANDA He *does* drink, then?

TOM Not that I know of!

AMANDA Make sure, be certain! The last thing I want for my daughter's a boy who drinks!

TOM Aren't you being a little bit premature? Mr. O'Connor has not yet appeared on the scene!

AMANDA But will tomorrow. To meet your sister, and what do I know about his character? Nothing! Old maids are better off than wives of drunkards!

TOM Oh, my God!

AMANDA Be still!

TOM [*leaning forward to whisper*] Lots of fellows meet girls whom they don't marry!

AMANDA Oh, talk sensibly, Tom—and don't be sarcastic! [*She has gotten a hairbrush.*]

TOM What are you doing?

AMANDA I'm brushing that cow-lick down! What is this young man's position at the warehouse?

TOM [*submitting grimly to the brush and the interrogation*] This young man's position is that of a shipping clerk, Mother.

AMANDA Sounds to me like a fairly responsible job, the sort of a job *you* would be in if you just had more *get-up*. What is his salary? Have you any idea?

TOM I would judge it to be approximately eighty-five dollars a month.

AMANDA Well—not princely, but—

TOM Twenty more than I make.

AMANDA Yes, how well I know! But for a family man, eighty-five dollars a month is not much more than you can just get by on. . . .

TOM Yes, but Mr. O'Connor is not a family man.

AMANDA He might be, mightn't he? Some time in the future?

TOM I see. Plans and provisions.

AMANDA You are the only young man I know of who ignores the fact that the future becomes the present, the present the past, and the past turns into everlasting regret if you don't plan for it!

TOM I will think that over and see what I can make of it.

AMANDA Don't be supercilious with your mother. Tell me some more about this—what do you call him?

TOM James D. O'Connor. The D. is for Delaney.

AMANDA Irish on *both* sides! *Gracious!* And doesn't drink?

TOM Shall I call him up and ask him right this minute?

AMANDA The only way to find out about those things is to make discreet inquiries at the proper moment. When I was a girl in Blue Mountain and it was suspected that a young man drank, the girl whose attentions he had been receiving, if any girl *was*, would sometimes speak to the minister of his church, or rather her father would if her father was living, and sort of feel him out on the young man's character. That is the way such things are discreetly handled to keep a young woman from making a tragic mistake!

TOM Then how did you happen to make a tragic mistake?

AMANDA That innocent look of your father's had everyone fooled! He *smiled*—the world was *enchanted*! No girl can do worse than put herself at the mercy of a handsome appearance! I hope that Mr. O'Connor is not too good-looking.

TOM No, he's not too good-looking. He's covered with freckles and hasn't too much of a nose.

AMANDA He's not right-down homely, though?

TOM Not right-down homely. Just medium homely, I'd say.

AMANDA Character's what to look for in a man.

TOM That's what I've always said, Mother.

AMANDA You've never said anything of the kind and I suspect you would never give it a thought.

TOM Don't be so suspicious of me.

AMANDA At least I hope he's the type that's up and coming.

TOM I think he really goes in for self-improvement.

AMANDA What reason have you to think so?

TOM He goes to night school.

AMANDA [*beaming*] Splendid! What does he do, I mean study?

TOM Radio engineering and public speaking!

AMANDA Then he has visions of being advanced in the world! Any young man who studies public speaking is aiming to have an executive job some day! And radio engineering? A thing for the future! Both of these facts are very illuminating. Those are the sort of things that a mother should know concerning any young man who comes to call on her daughter. Seriously or—not.

TOM One little warning. He doesn't know about Laura. I didn't let on that we had dark ulterior motives. I just said, why don't you come and have dinner with us? He said okay and that was the whole conversation.

AMANDA I bet it was! You're eloquent as an oyster. However, he'll know about Laura when he gets here. When he sees how lovely and sweet and pretty she is, he'll thank his lucky stars he was asked to dinner.

TOM Mother, you mustn't expect too much of Laura.

AMANDA What do you mean?

TOM Laura seems all those things to you and me because she's ours and we love her. We don't even notice she's crippled any more.

AMANDA Don't say crippled! You know that I never allow that word to be used!

TOM But face facts, Mother. She is and— that's not all—

AMANDA What do you mean "not all"?

TOM Laura is very different from other girls.

AMANDA I think the difference is all to her advantage.

TOM Not quite all—in the eyes of others—strangers—she's terribly shy and lives in a world of her own and those things make her seem a little peculiar to people outside the house.

AMANDA Don't say peculiar.

TOM Face the facts. She is.

[THE DANCE-HALL MUSIC CHANGES TO A TANGO THAT HAS A MINOR AND SOMEWHAT OMINOUS TONE.]

AMANDA. In what way is she peculiar—may I ask?

TOM [*gently*] She lives in a world of her own—a world of—little glass ornaments, Mother.... [*Gets up.* AMANDA *remains holding brush, looking at him, troubled.*] She plays old phonograph records and—that's about all— [*He glances at himself in the mirror and crosses to door.*]

AMANDA [*sharply*] Where are you going?

TOM I'm going to the movies. [*Out screen door.*]

AMANDA Not to the movies, every night to the movies! [*Follows quickly to screen door.*] I don't believe you always go to the movies! [*He is gone.* AMANDA *looks worriedly after him for a moment. Then vitality and optimism return and she turns from the door. Crossing to portieres.*] Laura! Laura! [LAURA *answers from kitchenette.*]

LAURA Yes, Mother.

AMANDA Let those dishes go and come in front! [LAURA *appears with dish towel. Gaily.*] Laura, come here and make a wish on the moon!

[SCREEN IMAGE: MOON.]

LAURA [*entering*] Moon—moon?

AMANDA A little silver slipper of a moon. Look over your left shoulder, Laura, and make a wish! [LAURA *looks faintly puzzled as if called out of sleep.* AMANDA *seizes her shoulders and turns her at an angle by the door.*] Now! Now, darling, *wish*!

LAURA What shall I wish for, Mother?

AMANDA [*her voice trembling and her eyes suddenly filling with tears.*] Happiness! Good Fortune!

[*The violin rises and the stage dims out.*]

CURTAIN

SCENE SIX

[IMAGE: HIGH-SCHOOL HERO.]

TOM And so the following evening I brought Jim home to dinner. I had known Jim slightly in high school. In high school Jim was a hero. He had tremendous Irish good nature and vitality with the scrubbed and polished look of white chinaware. He seemed to move in a continual spotlight. He was a star in basketball, captain of the debating club, president of the senior class and the glee club and he sang the male lead in the annual light operas. He was always running or bounding, never just walking. He seemed always at the point of defeating the law of gravity. He was shooting with such velocity through his adolescence that you would logically expect him to arrive at nothing short of the White House by the time he was thirty. But Jim apparently ran into more interference after his graduation from Soldan. His speed had definitely slowed. Six years after he left high school he was holding a job that wasn't much better than mine.

[IMAGE: CLERK.]

He was the only one at the warehouse with whom I was on friendly terms. I was valuable to him as someone who could remember his former glory, who had seen him win basketball games and the silver cup in debating. He knew of my secret practice of retiring to a cabinet of the washroom to work on poems when business was slack in the warehouse. He called me Shakespeare. And while the other boys in the warehouse regarded me with suspicious hostility, Jim took a humorous attitude toward me. Gradually his attitude affected the others, their hostility wore off and they also began to smile at me as people smile at an oddly fashioned dog who trots across their path at some distance.

I knew that Jim and Laura had known each other at Soldan, and I had heard Laura speak admiringly of his voice. I didn't know if Jim remembered her or not. In high school Laura had been as unobtrusive as Jim had been astonishing. If he did remember Laura, it was not as my sister, for when I asked him to dinner, he grinned and said, "You know, Shakespeare, I never thought of you as having folks!"

He was about to discover that I did. . . .

[*Light upstage.*]

[LEGEND ON SRCEEN: "THE ACCENT OF A COMING FOOT."]

[*Friday evening. It is about five o'clock of a late spring evening which comes "scattering poems in the sky." A delicate lemony light is in the Wingfield apartment.*

AMANDA *has worked like a Turk in preparation for the gentleman caller. The results are astonishing. The new floor lamp with its rose-silk shade is in place, a colored paper lantern conceals the broken light fixture in the ceiling, new billowing white curtains are at the windows, chintz covers are on chairs and sofa, a pair of new sofa pillows make their initial appearance.*

Open boxes and tissue paper are scattered on the floor.

LAURA *stands in the middle with lifted arms while* AMANDA *crouches before her, adjusting the hem of the new dress, devout and ritualistic. The dress is colored and designed by memory. The arrangement of* LAURA's *hair is changed; it is softer and more becoming. A fragile, unearthly prettiness has come out in* LAURA: *she is like a piece of translucent glass touched by light, given a momentary radiance, not actual, not lasting.*]

AMANDA [*impatiently*] Why are you trembling?
LAURA Mother, you've made me so nervous!
AMANDA How have I made you nervous?
LAURA By all this fuss! You make it seem so important!
AMANDA I don't understand you, Laura. You couldn't be satisfied with just sitting home, and yet whenever I try to arrange something for you, you seem to resist it. [*She gets up.*] Now take a look at yourself. No, wait! Wait just a moment—I have an idea!
LAURA What is it now?

[AMANDA *produces two powder puffs which she wraps in handkerchiefs and stuffs in* LAURA's *bosom.*]

LAURA Mother, what are you doing?
AMANDA They call them "Gay Deceivers"!
LAURA I won't wear them!
AMANDA You will!
LAURA Why should I?
AMANDA Because, to be painfully honest, your chest is flat.
LAURA You make it seem like we were setting a trap.

AMANDA All pretty girls are a trap, a pretty trap, and men expect them to be. [LEGEND: "A PRETTY TRAP."] Now look at yourself, young lady. This is the prettiest you will ever be! I've got to fix myself now! You're going to be surprised by your mother's appearance! [*She crosses through portieres, humming gaily.*]

[LAURA *moves slowly to the long mirror and stares solemnly at herself.*

A wind blows the white curtains inward in a slow, graceful motion and with a faint, sorrowful sighing.]

AMANDA [*off stage*] It isn't dark enough yet. [*She turns slowly before the mirror with a troubled look.*]

[LEGEND ON SCREEN: "THIS IS MY SISTER: CELEBRATE HER WITH STRINGS!" MUSIC.]

AMANDA [*laughing, off*] I'm going to show you something. I'm going to make a spectacular appearance!

LAURA What is it, Mother?

AMANDA Possess your soul in patience—you will see! Something I've resurrected from that old trunk! Styles haven't changed so terribly much after all.... [*She parts the portieres.*] Now just look at your mother! [*She wears a girlish frock of yellow voile with a blue silk sash. She carries a bunch of jonquils—the legend of her yotuh is nearly revived. Feverishly.*] This is the dress in which I led the cotillion. Won the cakewalk twice at Sunset Hill, wore one spring to the Governor's ball in Jackson! See how I sashayed around the ballroom, Laura? [*She raises her skirt and does a mincing step around the room.*] I wore it on Sundays for my gentleman callers! I had it on the day I met your father—I had malaria fever all that spring. The change of climate from East Tennessee to the Delta—weakened resistance—I had a little temperature all the time—not enough to be serious—just enough to make me restless and giddy! Invitations poured in—parties all over the Delta!—"Stay in bed," said Mother, "you have fever!"—but I just wouldn't.—I took quinine but kept on going, going!—Evenings, dances!—Afternoons, long, long rides! Picnics—lovely!—So lovely, that country in May—All lacy with dogwood, literally flooded with jonquils!—That was the spring I had the craze for jonquils. Jonquils became an absolute obsession. Mother said, "Honey, there's no more room for jonquils." And still I kept on bringing in more jonquils. Whenever, wherever I saw them, I'd say, "Stop! Stop! I see jonquils!" I made the young men help me gather the jonquils! It was a joke, Amanda and her jonquils! Finally there were no more vases to hold them, every available space was filled with jonquils. No vases to hold them? All right, I'll hold them myself! And then I—[*She stops in front of the picture.* MUSIC] met your father! Malaria fever and jonquils and then—this—boy.... [*She switches on the rose-colored lamp.*] I hope they get here before it starts to rain. [*She crosses upstage and places the jonquils in bowl on table.*] I gave your brother a little extra change so he and Mr. O'Connor could take the service car home.

LAURA [*with altered look*] What did you say his name was?

AMANDA O'Connor.

LAURA What is his first name?

AMANDA I don't remember. Oh, yes, I do. It was—Jim!

[LAURA *sways slightly and catches hold of a chair.*]

[LEGEND ON SCREEN: "NOT JIM!"]

LAURA [*faintly*] Not—Jim!

AMANDA Yes, that was it, it was Jim! I've never known a Jim that wasn't nice!

[MUSIC: OMINOUS.]

LAURA Are you sure his name is Jim O'Connor?

AMANDA Yes. Why?

LAURA Is he the one that Tom used to know in high school?

AMANDA He didn't say so. I think he just got to know him at the warehouse.

LAURA There was a Jim O'Connor we both knew in high school— [*Then, with effort.*] If that is the one that Tom is bringing to dinner—you'll have to excuse me, I won't come to the table.

AMANDA   What sort of nonsense is this?

LAURA   You asked me once if I'd ever liked a boy. Don't you remember I showed you this boy's picture?

AMANDA   You mean the boy you showed me in the year book?

LAURA   Yes, that boy.

AMANDA   Laura, Laura, were you in love with that boy?

LAURA   I don't know, Mother. All I know is I couldn't sit at the table if it was him!

AMANDA   It won't be him! It isn't the least bit likely. But whether it is or not, you will come to the table. You will not be excused.

LAURA   I'll have to be, Mother.

AMANDA   I don't intend to humor your silliness, Laura, I've had too much from you and your brother, both! So just sit down and compose yourself till they come. Tom has forgotten his key so you'll have to let them in, when they arrive.

LAURA   [*panicky*]   Oh, Mother—*you* answer the door!

AMANDA   [*lightly*]   I'll be in the kitchen—busy!

LAURA   Oh, Mother, please answer the door, don't make me do it!

AMANDA   [*crossing into kitchenette*]   I've got to fix the dressing for the salmon. Fuss, fuss—silliness!—over a gentleman caller!

[*Door swings shut.* LAURA *is left alone.*]

[LEGEND: "TERROR!"]

[*She utters a low moan and turns off the lamp—sits stiffly on the edge of the sofa, knotting her fingers together.*]

[LEGEND ON SCREEN: "THE OPENING OF A DOOR!"]

[TOM *and* JIM *appear on the fire-escape steps and climb to landing. Hearing their approach,* LAURA *rises with a panicky gesture. She retreats to the portieres.*
 The doorbell. LAURA *catches her breath and touches her throat. Low drums.*]

AMANDA   [*calling*]   Laura, sweetheart! The door!

[LAURA *stares at it without moving.*]

TOM   Uh-huh. [*He rings again, nervously.* JIM *whistles and fishes for a cigarette.*]

AMANDA   [*very very gaily*]   Laura, that is your brother and Mr. O'Connor! Will you let them in, darling?

[LAURA *crosses toward kitchenette door.*]

LAURA   [*breathlessly*]   Mother—you go to the door!

[AMANDA *steps out of kitchenette and stares furiously at* LAURA. *She points imperiously at the door.*]

LAURA   Please, please!

AMANDA   [*in a fierce whisper*]   What is the matter with you, you silly thing?

LAURA   [*desperately*]   Please, you answer it, *please!*

AMANDA   I told you I wasn't going to humor you, Laura. Why have you chosen this moment to lose your mind?

LAURA   Please, please, please, you go!

AMANDA   You'll have to go to the door because I can't!

LAURA   [*despairingly*]   I can't either!

AMANDA   *Why?*

LAURA   I'm *sick!*

AMANDA   I'm sick, too—of your nonsense! Why can't you and your brother be normal people? Fantastic whims and behavior! [TOM *gives a long ring.*] Preposterous goings on! Can you give me one reason— [*Calls out lyrically:*] COMING! JUST ONE SECOND!—why you should be afraid to open a door? Now you answer it, Laura!

LAURA   Oh, oh, oh . . . [*She returns through the portieres. Darts to the victrola and winds it frantically and turns it on.*]

AMANDA   Laura Wingfield, you march right to that door!

LAURA   Yes—yes, Mother!

[*A faraway, scratchy rendition of "Dardanella" softens the air and gives her strength to move through it. She slips to the door and draws it cautiously open.*]

[TOM *enters with the caller,* JIM O'CONNOR.]

TOM Laura, this is Jim. Jim, this is my sister, Laura.
JIM [*stepping inside*] I didn't know that Shakespeare had a sister!
LAURA [*retreating stiff and trembling from the door*] How—how do you do?
JIM [*heartily extending his hand*] Okay!

[LAURA *touches it hesitantly with hers.*]

JIM Your hand's *cold*, Laura!
LAURA Yes, well—I've been playing the victrola....
JIM Must have been playing classical music on it! You ought to play a little hot swing music to warm you up!
LAURA Excuse me—I haven't finished playing the victrola....

[*She turns awkwardly and hurries into the front room. She pauses a second by the victrola. Then catches her breath and darts through the portieres like a frightened deer.*]

JIM [*grinning*] What was the matter?
TOM Oh—with Laura? Laura is—terribly shy.
JIM Shy, huh? It's unusual to meet a shy girl nowadays. I don't believe you ever mentioned you had a sister.
TOM Well, now you know. I have one. Here is the *Post Dispatch*. You want a piece of it?
JIM Uh-huh.
TOM What piece? The comics?
JIM Sports! [*Glances at it.*] Ole Dizzy Dean is on his bad behavior.
TOM [*disinterested*] Yeah? [*Lights cigarette and crosses back to fire-escape door.*]
JIM Where are *you* going?
TOM I'm going out on the terrace.
JIM [*goes after him*] You know, Shakespeare—I'm going to sell you a bill of goods!
TOM What goods?
JIM A course I'm taking.
TOM Huh?
JIM In public speaking! You and me, we're not the warehouse type.
TOM Thanks—that's good news. But what has public speaking got to do with it?
JIM It fits you for—executive positions!
TOM Awww.
JIM I tell you it's done a helluva lot for me.

[IMAGE: EXECUTIVE AT DESK.]

TOM In what respect?
JIM In every! Ask yourself what is the difference between you an' me and men in the office down front? Brains—No!—Ability?—No! Then what? Just one little thing—
TOM What is that one little thing?
JIM Primarily it amounts to—social poise! Being able to square up to people and hold your own on any social level!
AMANDA [*off stage*] Tom?
TOM Yes, Mother?
AMANDA Is that you and Mr. O'Connor?
TOM Yes, Mother.
AMANDA Ask Mr. O'Connor if he would like to wash his hands.
JIM Aw, no—no—thank you—I took care of that at the warehouse. Tom—
TOM Yes?
JIM Mr. Mendoza was speaking to me about you.
TOM Favorably?
JIM What do you think?
TOM Well—
JIM You're going to be out of a job if you don't wake up.
TOM I am waking up—
JIM You show no signs.
TOM The signs are interior.

[IMAGE ON SCREEN: THE SAILING VESSEL WITH JOLLY ROGER AGAIN.]

TOM I'm planning to change. [*He leans over the rail speaking with quiet exhilaration. The incandescent marquees and signs of the first-run movie houses light his face from across the alley. He looks like a voyager.*] I'm right at the point of committing myself to a future that doesn't include the warehouse and Mr. Mendoza or even a night-school course in public speaking.
JIM What are you gassing about?
TOM I'm tired of the movies.
JIM Movies!
TOM Yes, movies! Look at them— [*A wave toward the marvels of Grand Avenue.*] All of those glamorous people—having adventures—hogging it all, gobbling the whole thing up! You know what happens? People go to

the *movies* instead of *moving!* Hollywood characters are supposed to have all the adventures for everybody in America, while everybody in America sits in a dark room and watches them have them! Yes, until there's a war. That's when adventure becomes available to the masses! *Everyone's* dish, not only Gable's! Then the people in the dark room come out of the dark room to have some adventures themselves—Goody, goody!—It's our turn now, to go to the South Sea Islands—to make a safari—to be exotic, far-off!—But I'm not patient. I don't want to wait till then. I'm tired of the *movies* and I am *about to move!*

JIM [*incredulously*]   Move?
TOM   Yes.
JIM   When?
TOM   Soon!
JIM   Where? Where?

[*Theme three music seems to answer the question while Tom thinks it over. He searches among his pockets.*]

TOM   I'm starting to boil inside. I know I seem dreamy, but inside—well, I'm boiling! Whenever I pick up a shoe, I shudder a little thinking how short life is and what I am doing!—Whatever that means, I know it doesn't mean shoes—except as something to wear on a traveler's feet! [*Finds paper.*] Look—
JIM   What?
TOM   I'm a member.
JIM [*reading*]   The Union of Merchant Seamen.
TOM   I paid my dues this month, instead of the light bill.
JIM   You will regret it when they turn the lights off.
TOM   I won't be here.
JIM   How about your mother?
TOM   I'm like my father. The bastard son of a bastard! See how he grins? And he's been absent going on sixteen years!
JIM   You're just talking, you drip. How does your mother feel about it?
TOM   Shhh!—Here comes Mother! Mother is not acquainted with my plans!

AMANDA [*enters portieres*]   Where are you all?
TOM   On the terrace, Mother.

[*They start inside. She advances to them.* TOM *is distinctly shocked at her appearance. Even* JIM *blinks a little. He is making his first contact with girlish Southern vivacity and in spite of the night-school course in public speaking is somewhat thrown off the beam by the unexpected outlay of social charm.*

Certain responses are attempted by JIM *but are swept aside by* AMANDA's *gay laughter and chatter.* TOM *is embarrassed but after the first shock* JIM *reacts very warmly. Grins and chuckles, is altogether won over.*]

[IMAGE: AMANDA AS A GIRL.]

AMANDA [*coyly smiling, shaking her girlish ringlets*]   Well, well, well, so this is Mr. O'Connor. Introductions entirely unnecessary. I've heard so much about you from my boy. I finally said to him, Tom—good gracious!—why don't you bring this paragon to supper? I'd like to meet this nice young man at the warehouse!—Instead of just hearing him sing your praises so much! I don't know why my son is so standoffish—that's not Southern behavior! Let's sit down and—I think we could stand a little more air in here! Tom, leave the door open. I felt a nice fresh breeze a moment ago. Where has it gone to? Mmm, so warm already! And not quite summer, even. We're going to burn up when summer really gets started. However, we're having—we're having a very light supper. I think light things are better fo' this time of year. The same as light clothes are. Light clothes an' light food are what warm weather calls fo'. You know our blood gets so thick during th' winter—it takes a while fo' us to *adjust* ou'selves!—when the season changes . . . It's come so quick this year. I wasn't prepared. All of a sudden—heavens! Already summer!—I ran to the trunk an' pulled out this light dress—Terribly old! Historical almost! But feels so good—so good an' co-ol, y'know. . . .
TOM   Mother—
AMANDA   Yes, honey?
TOM   How about—supper?

AMANDA Honey, you go ask Sister if supper is ready! You know that Sister is in full charge of supper! Tell her you hungry boys are waiting for it. [*To* JIM.] Have you met Laura?

JIM She—

AMANDA Let you in? Oh, good, you've met already! It's rare for a girl as sweet an' pretty as Laura to be domestic! But Laura is, thank heavens, not only pretty but also very domestic. I'm not at all. I never was a bit. I never could make a thing but angel-food cake. Well, in the South we had so many servants. Gone, gone, gone. All vestige of gracious living! Gone completely! I wasn't prepared for what the future brought me. All of my gentleman callers were sons of planters and so of course I assumed that I would be married to one and raise my family on a large piece of land with plenty of servants. But man proposes—and woman accepts the proposal!—To vary that old, old saying a little bit—I married no planter! I married a man who worked for the telephone company!—That gallantly smiling gentleman over there! [*Points to the picture.*] A telephone man who—fell in love with long-distance— Now he travels and I don't even know where!— But what am I going on for about my tribulations? Tell me yours—I hope you don't have any! Tom?

TOM [*returning*] Yes, Mother?

AMANDA Is supper nearly ready?

TOM It looks to me like supper is on the table.

AMANDA Let me look— [*She rises prettily and looks through portieres.*] Oh, lovely!—But where is Sister?

TOM Laura is not feeling well and she says that she thinks she'd better not come to the table.

AMANDA What?—Nonsense!—Laura? Oh, Laura!

LAURA [*off stage, faintly*] Yes, Mother.

AMANDA You really must come to the table. We won't be seated until you come to the table! Come in, Mr. O'Connor. You sit over there, and I'll—Laura? Laura Wingfield! You're keeping us waiting, honey! We can't say grace until you come to the table!

[*The back door is pushed weakly open and* LAURA *comes in. She is obviously quite faint, her lips trembling, her eyes wide and staring. She moves unsteadily toward the table.*]

[LEGEND: "TERROR!"]

[*Outside a summer storm is coming abruptly. The white curtains billow inward at the windows and there is a sorrowful murmur and deep blue dusk.*

LAURA *suddenly stumbles—she catches at a chair with a faint moan.*]

TOM Laura!

AMANDA Laura! [*There is a clap of thunder.*] [LEGEND: "AH!" DESPAIRINGLY.] Why, Laura, you *are* sick, 'darling! Tom, help your sister into the living room, dear! Sit in the living room, Laura—rest on the sofa. Well! [*To the gentleman caller.*] Standing over the hot stove made her ill! I told her that it was just too warm this evening, but—[TOM *comes back in.* LAURA *is on the sofa.*] Is Laura all right now?

TOM Yes.

AMANDA What *is* that? Rain? A nice cool rain has come up! [*She gives the gentleman caller a frightened look.*] I think we may—have grace—now . . . [TOM *looks at her stupidly.*] Tom, honey—you say grace!

TOM Oh . . . "For these and all thy mercies—" [*They bow their heads,* AMANDA *stealing a nervous glance at* JIM. *In the living room* LAURA, *stretched on the sofa, clenches her hand to her lips, to hold back a shuddering sob.*] God's Holy Name be praised—

THE SCENE DIMS OUT

SCENE SEVEN

[*A Souvenir.*]

[*Half an hour later. Dinner is just being finished in the upstage area which is concealed by the drawn portieres.*

As the curtain rises LAURA *is still huddled upon the sofa, her feet drawn under her, her head resting on a pale blue pillow, her eyes wide and mysteriously watchful. The new floor lamp with its shade of rose-colored silk gives a soft, becoming light to her face, bringing out the fragile, unearthly prettiness which usually escapes attention. There is a steady murmur of rain, but it is slackening and stops soon after the scene begins; the air outside becomes pale and luminous as the moon breaks out.*

A moment after the curtain rises, the lights in both rooms flicker and go out.]

JIM Hey, there, Mr. Light Bulb!

[AMANDA *laughs nervously.*]

[LEGEND: "SUSPENSION OF A PUBLIC SERVICE."]

AMANDA Where was Moses when the lights went out? Ha-ha. Do you know the answer to that one, Mr. O'Connor?

JIM No, Ma'am, what's the answer?

AMANDA In the dark! [JIM *laughs appreciably.*] Everybody sit still. I'll light the candles. Isn't it lucky we have them on the table? Where's a match? Which of you gentlemen can provide a match?

JIM Here.

AMANDA Thank you, sir.

JIM Not at all, Ma'am!

AMANDA I guess the fuse has burnt out. Mr. O'Connor, can you tell a burnt-out fuse? I know I can't and Tom is a total loss when it comes to mechanics. [*Sound: Getting up: voices recede a little to kitchenette.*] Oh, be careful you don't bump into something. We don't want our gentleman caller to break his neck. Now wouldn't that be a fine howdy-do?

JIM Ha-ha! Where is the fuse-box?

AMANDA Right here next to the stove. Can you see anything?

JIM Just a minute.

AMANDA Isn't electricity a mysterious thing? Wasn't it Benjamin Franklin who tied a key to a kite? We live in such a mysterious universe, don't we? Some people say that science clears up all the mysteries for us. In my opinion it only creates more! Have you found it yet?

JIM No, Ma'am. All these fuses look okay to me.

AMANDA Tom!

TOM Yes, Mother?

AMANDA That light bill I gave you several days ago. The one I told you we got the notices about?

TOM Oh.—Yeah.

[LEGEND: "HA!"]

AMANDA You didn't neglect to pay it by any chance?

TOM Why, I—

AMANDA Didn't! I might have known it!

JIM Shakespeare probably wrote a poem on that light bill, Mrs. Wingfield.

AMANDA I might have known better than to trust him with it! There's such a high price for negligence in this world!

JIM Maybe the poem will win a ten-dollar prize.

AMANDA We'll just have to spend the remainder of the evening in the nineteenth century, before Mr. Edison made the Mazda lamp!

JIM Candlelight is my favorite kind of light.

AMANDA That shows you're romantic! But that's no excuse for Tom. Well, we got through dinner. Very considerate of them to let us get through dinner before they plunged us into everlasting darkness, wasn't it, Mr. O'Connor?

JIM Ha-ha!

AMANDA Tom, as a penalty for your carelessness you can help me with the dishes.

JIM Let me give you a hand.

AMANDA Indeed you will not!

JIM I ought to be good for something.

AMANDA Good for something? [*Her tone is rhapsodic.*] You? Why, Mr. O'Connor, nobody, *nobody's* given me this much entertainment in years—as you have!

JIM Aw, now, Mrs. Wingfield!

AMANDA I'm not exaggerating, not one bit! But Sister is all by her lonesome. You go keep her company in the parlor! I'll give you this lovely old candelabrum that used to be on the altar at the church of the Heavenly Rest. It was melted a little out of shape when the church burnt down. Lightning struck it one spring. Gypsy Jones was holding a revival at the time and he intimated that the church was destroyed because the Epicopalians gave card parties.

JIM Ha-ha.
AMANDA And how about you coaxing Sister to drink a little wine? I think it would be good for her! Can you carry both at once?
JIM Sure. I'm Superman!
AMANDA Now, Thomas, get into this apron!

[*The door of kitchenette swings closed on* AMANDA'S *gay laughter; the flickering light approaches the portieres.*

LAURA *sits up nervously as he enters. Her speech at first is low and breathless from the almost intolerable strain of being alone with a stranger.*]

[LEGEND: "I DON'T SUPPOSE YOU REMEMBER ME AT ALL!"]

[*In her first speeches in this scene, before* JIM'S *warmth overcomes her paralyzing shyness,* LAURA'S *voice is thin and breathless as though she has just run up a steep flight of stairs.*

JIM'S *attitude is gently humorous. In playing this scene it should be stressed that while the incident is apparently unimportant, it is to* LAURA *the climax of her secret life.*]

JIM Hello, there, Laura.
LAURA [*faintly*] Hello. [*She clears her throat.*]
JIM How are you feeling now? Better?
LAURA Yes. Yes, thank you.
JIM This is for you. A little dandelion wine. [*He extends it toward her with extravagant gallantry.*]
LAURA Thank you.
JIM Drink it—but don't get drunk! [*He laughs heartily.* LAURA *takes the glass uncertainly; laughs shyly.*] Where shall I set the candles?
LAURA Oh—oh, anywhere . . .
JIM How about here on the floor? Any objections?
LAURA No.
JIM I'll spread a newspaper under to catch the drippings. I like to sit on the floor. Mind if I do?
LAURA Oh, no.
JIM Give me a pillow?
LAURA What?
JIM A pillow!

LAURA Oh . . . [*Hands him one quickly.*]
JIM How about you? Don't you like to sit on the floor?
LAURA Oh—yes.
JIM Why don't you, then?
LAURA I—will.
JIM Take a pillow! [LAURA *does. Sits on the other side of the candelabrum. Jim crosses his legs and smiles engagingly at her.*] I can't hardly see you sitting way over there.
LAURA I can—see you.
JIM I know, but that's not fair, I'm in the limelight. [LAURA *moves her pillow closer.*] Good! Now I can see you! Comfortable?
LAURA Yes.
JIM So am I. Comfortable as a cow! Will you have some gum?
LAURA No, thank you.
JIM I think that I will indulge, with your pemission. [*Musingly unwraps it and holds it up.*] Think of the fortune made by the guy that invented the first piece of chewing gum. Amazing, huh? The Wrigley Building is one of the sights of Chicago—I saw it summer before last when I went up to the Century of Progress. Did you take in the Century of Progress?
LAURA No, I didn't.
JIM Well, it was quite a wonderful exposition. What impressed me most was the Hall of Science. Gives you an idea of what the future will be in America, even more wonderful than the present time is! [*Pause. Smiling at her.*] Your brother tells me you're shy. Is that right, Laura?
LAURA I—don't know.
JIM I judge you to be an old-fashioned type of girl. Well, I think that's a pretty good type to be. Hope you don't think I'm being too personal—do you?
LAURA [*hastily, out of embarrassment*] I believe I *will* take a piece of gum, if you—don't mind. [*Clearing her throat.*] Mr. O'Connor, have you—kept up with your singing?
JIM Singing? Me?
LAURA Yes. I remember what a beautiful voice you had.
JIM When did you hear me sing?

[*Voice off stage in the pause.*]

VOICE [*off stage*]
> O blow, ye winds, heigh-ho,
> A-roving I will go!
> I'm off to my love
> With a boxing glove—
> Ten thousand miles away!

JIM You say you've heard me sing?

LAURA Oh, yes! Yes, very often . . . I—don't suppose—you remember me—at all?

JIM [*smiling doubtfully*] You know I have an idea I've seen you before. I had that idea as soon as you opened the door. It seemed almost like I was about to remember your name. But the name that I started to call you—wasn't a name! And so I stopped myself before I said it.

LAURA Wasn't it—Blue Roses?

JIM [*springs up. Grinning*] Blue Roses! My gosh, yes—Blue Roses! That's what I had on my tongue when you opened the door! Isn't it funny what tricks your memory plays? I didn't connect you with high school somehow or other. But that's where it was; it was high school. I didn't even know you were Shakespeare's sister! Gosh, I'm sorry.

LAURA I didn't expect you to. You—barely knew me!

JIM But we did have a speaking acquaintance, huh?

LAURA Yes, we—spoke to each other.

JIM When did you recognize me?

LAURA Oh, right away!

JIM Soon as I came in the door?

LAURA When I heard your name I thought it was probably you. I knew that Tom used to know you a little in high school. So when you came in the door— Well, then I was—sure.

JIM Why didn't you *say* something, then?

LAURA [*breathlessly*] I didn't know what to say, I was—too surprised!

JIM For goodness' sakes! You know, this sure is funny!

LAURA Yes! Yes, isn't it, though . . .

JIM Didn't we have a class in something together?

LAURA Yes, we did.

JIM What class was that?

LAURA It was—singing—Chorus!

JIM Aw!

LAURA I sat across the aisle from you in the Aud.

JIM Aw.

LAURA Mondays, Wednesdays and Fridays.

JIM Now I remember—you always came in late.

LAURA Yes, it was so hard for me, getting upstairs. I had that brace on my leg—it clumped so loud!

JIM I never heard any clumping.

LAURA [*wincing at the recollection*] To me it sounded like—thunder!

JIM Well, well, well, I never even noticed.

LAURA And everybody was seated before I came in. I had to walk in front of all those people. My seat was in the back row. I had to go clumping all the way up the aisle with everyone watching!

JIM You shouldn't have been self-conscious.

LAURA I know, but I was. It was always such a relief when the singing started.

JIM Aw, yes, I've placed you now! I used to call you Blue Roses. How was it that I got started calling you that?

LAURA I was out of school a little while with pleurosis. When I came back you asked me what was the matter. I said I had pleurosis—you thought I said Blue Roses. That's what you always called me after that!

JIM I hope you didn't mind.

LAURA Oh, no—I liked it. You see, I wasn't acquainted with many people. . . .

JIM As I remember you sort of stuck by yourself.

LAURA I—I—never have had much luck at—making friends.

JIM I don't see why you wouldn't.

LAURA Well, I—started out badly.

JIM You mean being—

LAURA Yes, it sort of—stood between me—

JIM You shouldn't have let it!

LAURA I know, but it did, and—

JIM You were shy with people!

LAURA I tried not to be but never could—

JIM Overcome it?

LAURA No, I—I never could!

JIM I guess being shy is something you have to work out of kind of gradually.

LAURA [*sorrowfully*] Yes—I guess it—

JIM Takes time!

LAURA Yes—

JIM People are not so dreadful when you know them. That's what you have to remember! And everybody has problems, not just you, but practically everybody has got some problems. You think of yourself as having the only problems, as being the only one who is disappointed. But just look around you and you will see lots of people as disappointed as you are. For instance, I hoped when I was going to high school that I would be further along at this time, six years later, than I am now— You remember that wonderful write-up I had in *The Torch?*

LAURA Yes! [*She rises and crosses to table.*]

JIM It said I was bound to succeed in anything I went into! [LAURA *returns with the annual.*] Holy Jeez! [*The Torch! He accepts it reverently. They smile across it with mutual wonder.* LAURA *crouches beside him and they begin to turn through it.* LAURA's *shyness is dissolving in his warmth.*]

LAURA Here you are in *Pirates of Penzance!*

JIM [*wistfully*] I sang the baritone lead in that operetta.

LAURA [*rapidly*] So—*beautifully!*

JIM [*protesting*] Aw—

LAURA Yes, yes—beautifully—beautifully!

JIM You heard me?

LAURA All three times!

JIM No!

LAURA Yes!

JIM All three performances?

LAURA [*looking down*] Yes.

JIM Why?

LAURA I—wanted to ask you to—autograph my program.

JIM Why didn't you ask me to?

LAURA You were always surrounded by your own friends so much that I never had a chance to.

JIM You should have just—

LAURA Well, I—thought you might think I was—

JIM Thought I might think you was—what?

LAURA Oh—

JIM [*with reflective relish*] I was beleaguered by females in those days.

LAURA You were terribly popular!

JIM Yeah—

LAURA You had such a—friendly way—

JIM I was spoiled in high school.

LAURA Everybody—liked you!

JIM Including you?

LAURA I—yes, I—I did, too— [*She gently closes the book in her lap.*]

JIM Well, well, well!—Give me that program, Laura. [*She hands it to him. He signs it with a flourish.*] There you are—better late than never!

LAURA Oh, I—what a—surprise!

JIM My signature isn't worth very much right now. But some day—maybe—it will increase in value! Being disappointed is one thing and being discouraged is something else. I am disappointed but I am not discouraged. I'm twenty-three years old. How old are you?

LAURA I'll be twenty-four in June.

JIM That's not old age!

LAURA No, but—

JIM You finished high school?

LAURA [*with difficulty*] I didn't go back.

JIM You mean you dropped out?

LAURA I made bad grades in my final examinations. [*She rises and replaces the book and the program. Her voice strained.*] How is—Emily Meisenbach getting along?

JIM Oh, that kraut-head!

LAURA Why do you call her that?

JIM That's what she was.

LAURA You're not still—going with her?

JIM I never see her.

LAURA It said in the Personal Section that you were—engaged!

JIM I know, but I wasn't impressed by that—propaganda!

LAURA It wasn't—the truth?

JIM Only in Emily's optimistic opinion!

LAURA Oh—

[LEGEND: "WHAT HAVE YOU DONE SINCE HIGH-SCHOOL?"]

[JIM *lights a cigarette and leans indolently back on his elbows smiling at* LAURA *with a warmth and charm which lights her inwardly with altar candles. She remains by the table and turns in her hands a piece of glass to cover her tumult.*]

JIM [*after several reflective puffs on a cigarette*] What have you done since high school? [*She seems not to hear him.*] Huh? [LAURA *looks up.*] I said what have you done since high school, Laura?

LAURA Nothing much.

JIM You must have been doing something these six long years.

LAURA Yes.

JIM Well, then, such as what?

LAURA I took a business course at business college—

JIM How did that work out?

LAURA Well, not very—well—I had to drop out, it gave me—indigestion—

[JIM *laughs gently.*]

JIM What are you doing now?

LAURA. I don't do anything—much. Oh, please don't think I sit around doing nothing! My glass collection takes up a good deal of time. Glass is something you have to take good care of.

JIM What did you say—about glass?

LAURA Collection I said—I have one— [*She clears her throat and turns away again, acutely shy.*]

JIM [*abruptly*] You know what I judge to be the trouble with you? Inferiority complex! Know what that is? That's what they call it when someone low-rates himself! I understand it because I had it, too. Although my case was not so aggravated as yours seems to be. I had it until I took up public speaking, developed my voice, and learned that I had an aptitude for science. Before that time I never thought of myself as being outstanding in any way whatsoever! Now I've never made a regular study of it, but I have a friend who says I can analyze people better than doctors that make a profession of it. I don't claim that to be necessarily true, but I can sure guess a person's psychology, Laura! [*Takes out his gum.*] Excuse me, Laura. I always take it out when the flavor is gone. I'll use this scrap of paper to wrap it in. I know how it is to get it stuck on a shoe. Yep—that's what I judge to be your principle trouble. A lack of confidence in yourself as a person. You don't have the proper amount of faith in yourself. I'm basing that fact on a number of your remarks and also on certain observations I've made. For instance that clumping you thought was so awful in high school. You say that you even dreaded to walk into class. You see what you did? You dropped out of school, you gave up an education because of a clump, which as far as I know was practically non-existent! A little physical defect is what you have. Hardly noticeable even! Magnified thousands of times by imagination! You know what my strong advice to you is? Think of yourself as *superior* in some way!

LAURA In what way would I think?

JIM Why, man alive Laura! Just look about you a little. What do you see? A world full of common people! All of 'em born and all of 'em going to die! Which of them has one-tenth of your good points! Or mine! Or anyone else's, as far as that goes— Gosh! Everybody excels in some one thing. Some in many! [*Unconsciously glances at himself in the mirror.*] All you've got to do is discover in *what*! Take me, for instance. [*He adjusts his tie at the mirror.*] My interest happens to lie in electro-dynamics. I'm taking a course in radio engineering at night school, Laura, on top of a fairly responsible job at the warehouse. I'm taking that course and studying public speaking.

LAURA Ohhhh.

JIM Because I believe in the future of television! [*Turning back to her.*] I wish to be ready to go up right along with it. Therefore I'm planning to get in on the ground floor. In fact I've already made the right connections and all that remains is for the industry to get under way! Full steam—[*His eyes are starry.*] Knowledge—Zzzzzp! Money—Zzzzzp! —Power! That's the cycle democracy is built on! [*His attitude is convincingly dynamic.* LAURA *stares at him, even her shyness eclipsed in her absolute wonder. He suddenly grins.*] I guess you think I think a lot of myself!

LAURA No—o-o-o, I—

JIM Now how about you? Isn't there something you take more interest in than anything else?

LAURA Well, I do—as I said—have my—glass collection—

[A *peal of girlish laughter from the kitchen.*]

JIM I'm not right sure I know what you're talking about. What kind of glass is it?

LAURA Little articles of it, they're ornaments mostly! Most of them are little animals made out of glass, the tiniest little animals in the world. Mother calls them a glass menagerie! Here's an example of one, if you'd like to see it! This one is one of the oldest. It's nearly thirteen. [MUSIC: "THE GLASS MENAGERIE." HE STRETCHES OUT HIS HAND.] Oh, be careful—if you breathe, it breaks!

JIM I'd better not take it. I'm pretty clumsy with things.

LAURA Go on, I trust you with him! [*Places it in his palm.*] There now—you're holding him gently! Hold him over the light, he loves the light! You see how the light shines through him?

JIM It sure does shine!

LAURA I shouldn't be partial, but he is my favorite one.

JIM What kind of a thing is this one supposed to be?

LAURA Haven't you noticed the single horn on his forehead?

JIM A unicorn, huh?

LAURA Mmm-hmmm!

JIM Unicorns, aren't they extinct in the modern world?

LAURA I know!

JIM Poor little fellow, he must feel sort of lonesome.

LAURA [*smiling*] Well, if he does he doesn't complain about it. He stays on a shelf with some horses that don't have horns and all of them seem to get along nicely together.

JIM How do you know?

LAURA [*lightly*] I haven't heard any arguments among them!

JIM [*grinning*] No arguments, huh? Well, that's a pretty good sign! Where shall I set him?

LAURA Put him on the table. They all like a change of scenery once in a while!

JIM [*stretching*] Well, well, well, well— Look how big my shadow is when I stretch!

LAURA Oh, oh, yes—it stretches across the ceiling!

JIM [*crossing to door*] I think it's stopped raining. [*Opens fire-escape door.*] Where does the music come from?

LAURA From the Paradise Dance Hall across the alley.

JIM How about cutting the rug a little, Miss Wingfield?

LAURA Oh, I—

JIM Or is your program filled up? Let me have a look at it. [*Grasps imaginary card.*] Why, every dance is taken! I'll just have to scratch some out. [WALTZ MUSIC: "LA GOLONDRINA"] Ahhh, a waltz! [*He executes some sweeping turns by himself then holds his arms toward* LAURA.]

LAURA [*breathlessly*] I—can't dance!

JIM There you go, that inferiority stuff!

LAURA I've never danced in my life!

JIM Come on, try!

LAURA Oh, but I'd step on you!

JIM I'm not made out of glass.

LAURA How—how—how do we start?

JIM Just leave it to me. You hold your arms out a little.

LAURA Like this?

JIM A little bit higher. Right. Now don't tighten up, that's the main thing about it—relax.

LAURA [*laughing breathlessly*] It's hard not to.

JIM Okay.

LAURA I'm afraid you can't budge me.

JIM What do you bet I can't? [*He swings her into motion.*]

LAURA Goodness, yes, you can!

JIM Let yourself go, now, Laura, just let yourself go.

LAURA I'm—

JIM Come on!

LAURA Trying!

JIM Not so stiff— Easy does it!

LAURA I know but I'm—

JIM Loosen th' backbone! There now, that's a lot better.

LAURA Am I?

JIM Lots, lots better! [*He moves her about the room in a clumsy waltz.*]

LAURA Oh, my!

JIM Ha-ha!

LAURA Oh, my goodness!

JIM Ha-ha-ha! [*They suddenly bump into the table. Jim stops.*] What did we hit on?

LAURA Table.

JIM Did something fall off it? I think—

LAURA Yes.

JIM I hope that it wasn't the little glass horse with the horn!

LAURA Yes.

JIM Aw, aw, aw. Is it broken?

LAURA Now it is just like all the other horses.

JIM It's lost its—

LAURA Horn! It doesn't matter. Maybe it's a blessing in disguise.

JIM You'll never forgive me. I bet that was your favorite piece of glass.

LAURA I don't have favorites much. It's no tragedy, Freckles. Glass breaks so easily. No matter how careful you are. The traffic jars the shelves and things fall off them.

JIM Still I'm awfully sorry that I was the cause.

LAURA [*smiling*] I'll just imagine he had an operation. The horn was removed to make him feel less—freakish! [*They both laugh.*] Now he will feel more at home with the other horses, the ones that don't have horns. . . .

JIM Ha-ha, that's very funny! [*Suddenly serious.*] I'm glad to see that you have a sense of humor. You know—you're well—very different! Surprisingly different from anyone else I know! [*His voices becomes soft and hesitant with a genuine feeling.*] Do you mind me telling you that? [LAURA *is abashed beyond speech.*] I mean it in a nice way . . . [LAURA *nods shyly, looking away.*] You make me feel sort of—I don't know how to put it! I'm usually pretty good at expressing things, but— This is something that I don't know how to say! [LAURA *touches her throat and clears it—turns the broken unicorn in her hands. Even softer.*] Has anyone ever told you that you were pretty? [*Pause: Music.* LAURA *looks up slowly, with wonder, and shakes her head.*] Well, you are! In a very different way from anyone else. And all the nicer because of the difference, too. [*His voice becomes low and husky.* LAURA *turns away, nearly faint with the novelty of her emotions.*]

I wish that you were my sister. I'd teach you to have some confidence in yourself. The different people are not like other people, but being different is nothing to be ashamed of. Because other people are not such wonderful people. They're one hundred times one thousand. You're one times one! They walk all over the earth. You just stay here. They're common as—weeds, but—you—well, you're—*Blue Roses!*

[IMAGE ON SCREEN: BLUE ROSES.]

[MUSIC CHANGES.]

LAURA But blue is wrong for—roses . . .

JIM It's right for you— You're—pretty!

LAURA In what respect am I pretty?

JIM In all respects—believe me! Your eyes—your hair—are pretty! Your hands are pretty! [*He catches hold of her hand.*] You think I'm making this up because I'm invited to dinner and have to be nice. Oh, I could do that! I could put on an act for you, Laura, and say lots of things without being very sincere. But this time I am. I'm talking to you sincerely. I happened to notice you had this inferiority complex that keeps you from feeling comfortable with people. Somebody needs to build your confidence up and make you proud instead of shy and turning away and—blushing— Somebody ought to— Ought to—*kiss* you, Laura! [*His hand slips slowly up her arm to her shoulder.* MUSIC SWELLS TUMULTUOUSLY. *He suddenly turns her about and kisses her on the lips. When he releases her* LAURA *sinks on the sofa with a bright, dazed look.* JIM *backs away and fishes in his pocket for a cigarette.*] [LEGEND ON SCREEN: "SOUVENIR."] Stumble-john! [*He lights the cigarette, avoiding her look. There is a peal of girlish laughter from* AMANDA *in the kitchen.* LAURA *slowly rises and opens her hand. It still contains the little broken glass animal. She looks at it with a tender, bewildered expression.*] Stumble-john! I shouldn't have done that— That was way off beam. You don't smoke, do you? [*She looks up, smiling, not hearing the question. He sits beside her a little gingerly. She looks at him speechlessly—waiting. He coughs decorously and moves a little farther aside as he considers the situation and senses her feelings, dimly, with perturbation. Gently.*] Would you—care for a—mint? [*She doesn't seem to hear him but her look grows brighter even.*] Peppermint—Life Saver? My pocket's a regular drug store—wherever I go . . . [*He pops a mint in his mouth. Then gulps and decides to make a clean breast of it. He speaks slowly and gingerly.*] Laura, you know, if I had a sister like you, I'd do the same thing as Tom. I'd bring out fellows and—introduce her to them. The right type of boys of a type to—appreciate her. Only—well—he made a mistake about me. Maybe I've got no call to be saying this. That may not have been the idea in having me over. But what if it was? There's nothing wrong about that. The only trouble is that in my case—I'm not in a situation to—do the right thing. I can't take down your number and say I'll phone. I can't call up next week and—ask for a date. I thought I had better explain the situation in case you misunderstood it and—hurt your feelings. . . . [*Pause. Slowly, very slowly, LAURA's look changes, her eyes returning slowly from his to the ornament in her palm.*]

[AMANDA *utters another gay laugh in the kitchen.*]

LAURA [*faintly*] You—won't—call again?

JIM No, Laura, I can't. [*He rises from the sofa.*] As I was just explaining, I've—got strings on me, Laura, I've—been going steady! I go out all the time with a girl named Betty. She's a home-girl like you, and Catholic, and Irish, and in a great many ways we—get along fine. I met her last summer on a moonlight boat trip up the river to Alton, on the *Majestic*. Well—right away from the start it was—love! [LEGEND: "LOVE!"] [LAURA *sways slightly forward and grips the arm of the sofa. He fails to notice, now enrapt in his own comfortable being.*] Being in love has made a new man of me! [*Leaning stiffly forward, clutching the arm of the sofa, LAURA struggles visibly with her storm. But JIM is oblivious, she is a long way off.*] The power of love is really pretty tremendous! Love is something that—changes the whole world, Laura! [*The storm abates a little and* LAURA *leans back. He notices her again.*] It happened that Betty's aunt took sick, she got a wire and had to go to Centralia. So Tom—when he asked me to dinner—I naturally just accepted the invitation, not knowing that you—that he—that I— [*He stops awkwardly.*] Huh—I'm a stumble-john! [*He flops back on the sofa. The holy candles in the altar of* LAURA's *face have been snuffed out. There is a look of almost infinite desolation.* JIM *glances at her uneasily.*] I wish that you would—say something. [*She bites her lip which was trembling and then bravely smiles. She opens her hand again on the broken glass ornament. Then she gently takes his hand and raises it level with her own. She carefully places the unicorn in the palm of his hand, then pushes his fingers closed upon it.*] What are you—doing that for? You want me to have him?—Laura? [*She nods.*] What for?

LAURA A—souvenir . . .

[*She rises unsteadily and crouches beside the victrola to wind it up.*]

[LEGEND ON SCREEN: "THINGS HAVE A WAY OF TURNING OUT SO BADLY!"]

[OR IMAGE: "GENTLEMAN CALLER WAVING GOOD-BYE!—GAILY."]

[*At this moment* AMANDA *rushes brightly back in the front room. She bears a pitcher of fruit punch in an old-fashioned cut-glass pitcher and a plate of macaroons. The plate has a gold border and poppies painted on it.*]

AMANDA Well, well, well! Isn't the air delightful after the shower? I've made you children a little liquid refreshment. [*Turns gaily to the gentleman caller.*] Jim, do you know that song about lemonade?

"Lemonade, lemonade
   Made in the shade and stirred with a spade—
Good enough for any old maid!"

JIM [*uneasily*] Ha-ha! No—I never heard it.

AMANDA Why, Laura! You look so serious!

JIM We were having a serious conversation.

AMANDA Good! Now you're better acqauinted!

JIM [*uncertainly*] Ha-ha! Yes.

AMANDA You modern young people are much more serious-minded than my generation. I was so gay as a girl!

JIM You haven't changed, Mrs. Wingfield.

AMANDA Tonight I'm rejuvenated! The gaiety of the occasion, Mr. O'Connor! [*She tosses her head with a peal of laughter. Spills lemonade.*] Oooo! I'm baptizing myself!

JIM Here—let me—

AMANDA [*setting the pitcher down*] There now. I discovered we had some maraschino cherries. I dumped them in, juice and all!

JIM You shouldn't have gone to that trouble, Mrs. Wingfield.

AMANDA Trouble, trouble? Why it was loads of fun! Didn't you hear me cutting up in the kitchen? I bet your ears were burning! I told Tom how outdone with him I was for keeping you to himself so long a time! He should have brought you over much, much sooner! Well, now that you've found your way, I want you to be a very frequent caller! Not just occasional but all the time. Oh, we're going to have a lot of gay times together! I see them coming! Mmm, just breathe that air! So fresh, and the moon's so pretty! I'll skip back out—I know where my place is when young folks are having a—serious conversation!

JIM Oh, don't go out, Mrs. Wingfield. The fact of the matter is I've got to be going.

AMANDA Going now? You're joking! Why, it's only the shank of the evening, Mr. O'Connor!

JIM Well, you know how it is.

AMANDA You mean you're a young workingman and have to keep workingmen's hours. We'll let you off early tonight. But only on the condition that next time you stay later. What's the best night for you? Isn't Saturday night the best night for you workingmen?

JIM I have a couple of time-clocks to punch, Mrs. Wingfield. One at morning, another one at night!

AMANDA My, but you *are* ambitious! You work at night, too?

JIM No, Ma'am, not work but—Betty! [*He crosses deliberately to pick up his hat. The band at the Paradise Dance Hall goes into a tender waltz.*]

AMANDA Betty? Betty? Who's—Betty! [*There is an ominous cracking sound in the sky.*]

JIM Oh, just a girl. The girl I go steady with! [*He smiles charmingly. The sky falls.*]

[LEGEND: "THE SKY FALLS."]

AMANDA [*a long-drawn exhalation*] Ohhhh . . . Is it a serious romance, Mr. O'Connor?

JIM We're going to be married the second Sunday in June.

AMANDA Ohhhh—how nice! Tom didn't mention that you were engaged to be married.

JIM The cat's not out of the bag at the warehouse yet. You know how they are. They call you Romeo and stuff like that. [*He stops at the oval mirror to put on his hat. He carefully shapes the brim and the crown to give a discreetly dashing effect.*] It's been a wonderful evening, Mrs. Wingfield. I guess this is what they mean by Southern hospitality.

AMANDA It really wasn't anything at all.

JIM I hope it don't seem like I'm rushing off. But I promised Betty I'd pick her up at the Wabash depot, an' by the time I get my jalopy down there her train'll be in. Some women are pretty upset if you keep 'em waiting.

AMANDA Yes, I know— The tyranny of women! [*Extends her hand.*] Good-bye, Mr. O'Connor. I wish you luck—and happiness—and success! All three of them, and so does Laura!—Don't you, Laura?

LAURA Yes!

JIM [*taking her hand*] Good-bye, Laura. I'm certainly going to treasure that souvenir. And don't you forget the good advice I gave you. [*Raises his voice to a cheery shout.*] So long, Shakespeare! Thanks again, ladies— Good night!

[*He grins and ducks jauntily out.*
Still bravely grimacing, AMANDA *closes the door on the gentleman caller. Then she turns back to the room with a puzzled expression. She and* LAURA *don't dare to face each other.* [LAURA *crouches beside the victrola to wind it.*]

AMANDA [*faintly*] Things have a way of turning out so badly. I don't believe that I would play the victrola. Well, well—well— Our gentleman caller was engaged to be married! Tom!

TOM [*from back*] Yes, Mother?

AMANDA Come in here a minute. I want to tell you something awfully funny.

TOM [*enters with macaroon and a glass of the lemonade*] Has the gentleman caller gotten away already?

AMANDA The gentleman caller has made an early departure. What a wonderful joke you played on us!

TOM How do you mean?

AMANDA You didn't mention that he was engaged to be married!

TOM Jim? Engaged?

AMANDA That's what he just informed us.

TOM I'll be jiggered! I didn't know about that.

AMANDA That seems very peculiar.

TOM What's peculiar about it?

AMANDA Didn't you call him your best friend down at the warehouse?

TOM He is, but how did I know?

AMANDA It seems extremely peculiar that you wouldn't know your best friend was going to be married!

TOM The warehouse is where I work, not where I know things about people!

AMANDA You don't know things anywhere! You live in a dream; you manufacture illusions! [*He crosses to door.*] Where are you going?

TOM I'm going to the movies.

AMANDA That's right, now that you've had us make such fools of ourselves. The effort, the preparation, all the expense! The new floor lamp, the rug, the clothes for Laura! All for what? To entertain some other girl's fiancé! Go to the movies, go! Don't think about us, a mother deserted, an unmarried sister who's crippled and has no job! Don't let anything interfere with your selfish pleasure! Just go, go, go—to the movies!

TOM All right, I will! The more you shout about my selfishness to me the quicker I'll go, and I won't go to the movies!

AMANDA Go, then! Then go to the moon—you selfish dreamer!

[TOM *smashes his glass on the floor. He plunges out on the fire-escape, slamming the door.* LAURA *screams—cut by door.*

Dance-hall music up. Tom *goes to the rail and grips it desperately, lifting his face in the chill white moonlight penetrating the narrow abyss of the alley.*]

[LEGEND ON SCREEN: "AND SO GOOD-BYE . . ."]

[*Tom's closing speech is timed with the interior pantomime. The interior scene is played as though viewed through soundproof glass.* AMANDA *appears to be making a comforting speech to* LAURA *who is huddled upon the sofa. Now that we cannot hear the mother's speech, her silliness is gone and she has dignity and tragic beauty.* LAURA's *dark hair hides her face until at the end of the speech she lifts it to smile at her mother.* AMANDA's *gestures are slow and graceful, almost dancelike, as she comforts the daughter. At the end of her speech she glances a moment at the father's picture—then withdraws through the portieres. At close of* TOM's *speech,* LAURA *blows out the candles, ending the play.*]

TOM I didn't go to the moon, I went much further—for time is the longest distance between two places— Not long after that I was fired for writing a poem on the lid of a shoe-box. I left Saint Louis. I descended the steps of this fire-escape for a last time and followed, from then on, in my father's footsteps, attempting to find in motion what was lost in space— I traveled around a great deal. The cities swept about me like dead leaves, leaves that were brightly colored but torn away from the branches. I would have stopped, but I was pursued by something. It always came upon me unawares, taking me altogether by surprise. Perhaps it was a familiar bit of music. Perhaps it was only a piece of transparent glass— Perhaps I am walking along a street at night, in some strange city, before I have found companions. I pass the lighted window of a shop where perfume is sold. The window is filled with pieces of colored glass, tiny transparent bottles in delicate colors, like bits of a shattered rainbow.

Then all at once my sister touches my shoulder. I turn around and look into her eyes . . . Oh, Laura, Laura, I tried to leave you behind me, but I am more faithful than I intended to be! I reach for a cigarette, I cross the street, I run into the movies or a bar, I buy a drink, I speak to the nearest stranger— anything that can blow your candles out! [LAURA *bends over the candles.*]—for nowadays the world is lit by lightning! Blow out your candles, Laura—and so good-bye. . . .

[*She blows the candles out.*]

THE SCENE DISSOLVES

Death of a Salesman*

Certain Private Conversations in Two Acts and a Requiem

by ARTHUR MILLER

The Characters

WILLY LOMAN
LINDA
BIFF
HAPPY
BERNARD
THE WOMAN
CHARLEY
UNCLE BEN
HOWARD WAGNER
JENNY
STANLEY
MISS FORSYTHE
LETTA

The action takes place in Willy Loman's house and yard and in various places he visits in the New York and Boston of today.

ACT ONE

A melody is heard, played upon a flute. It is small and fine, telling of grass and trees and the horizon. The curtain rises.

---

* Copyright 1949 by Arthur Miller. Reprinted by permission of The Viking Press, Inc. All rights reserved: no public or private performances of the play, professional or amateur, may be given, no film, radio or television use or public reading, without authorization from the author's representative, MCA Management, Ltd., 598 Madison Avenue, New York, N.Y. 10022. For permission to reprint excerpts from the play, address The Viking Press, Inc., 625 Madison Avenue, New York, N.Y. 10022.

Before us is the Salesman's house. We are aware of towering, angular shapes behind it, surrounding it on all sides. Only the blue light of the sky falls upon the house and forestage; the surrounding area shows an angry glow of orange. As more light appears, we see a solid vault of apartment houses around the small, fragile-seeming home. An air of the dream clings to the place, a dream rising out of reality. The kitchen at center seems actual enough, for there is a kitchen table with three chairs, and a refrigerator. But no other fixtures are seen. At the back of the kitchen there is a draped entrance, which leads to the livingroom. To the right of the kitchen, on a level raised two feet, is a bedroom furnished only with a brass bedstead and a straight chair. On a shelf over the bed a silver athletic trophy stands. A window opens onto the apartment house at the side.

Behind the kitchen, on a level raised six and a half feet, is the boys' bedroom, at present barely visible. Two beds are dimly seen, and at the back of the room a dormer window. (This bedroom is above the unseen livingroom.) At the left a stairway curves up to it from the kitchen.

The entire setting is wholly or, in some places, partially transparent. The roof-line of the house is one-dimensional; under and over it we see the apartment buildings. Before the house lies an apron, curving beyond the forestage into the orchestra. This forward area serves as the back yard as well as the locale of all Willy's imaginings and of his city scenes. Whenever the action is in the present the actors observe the imaginary wall-lines, entering the house only through its door at the left. But in the scenes of the past these boundaries are broken, and characters enter or leave a room by skipping "through" a wall onto the forestage.

From the right, Willy Loman, the Salesman, enters, carrying two large sample cases. The flute plays on. He hears but is not aware of it. He is past sixty years of age, dressed quietly. Even as he crosses the stage to the doorway of the house, his exhaustion is apparent. He unlocks the door, comes into the kitchen, and thankfully lets his burden down, feeling the soreness of his palms. A word-sigh escapes his lips—it might be "Oh, boy, oh, boy." He closes the door, then carries his cases out into the livingroom, through the draped kitchen doorway.

Linda, his wife, has stirred in her bed at the right. She gets out and puts on a robe, listening. Most often jovial, she has developed an iron repression of her exceptions to Willy's behavior—she more than loves him, she admires him, as though his mercurial nature, his temper, his massive dreams and little cruelties, served her only as sharp reminders of the turbulent longings within him, longings which she shares but lacks the temperament to utter and follow to their end.

LINDA, *hearing Willy outside the bedroom, calls with some trepidation* Willy!

WILLY It's all right. I came back.

LINDA Why? What happened? *Slight pause.* Did something happen, Willy?

WILLY No, nothing happened.

LINDA You didn't smash the car, did you?

WILLY, *with casual irritation* I said nothing happened. Didn't you hear me?

LINDA Don't you feel well?

WILLY I'm tired to the death. *The flute has faded away. He sits on the bed beside her, a little numb.* I couldn't make it. I just couldn't make it, Linda.

LINDA, *very carefully, delicately* Where were you all day? You look terrible.

WILLY I got as far as a little above Yonkers. I stopped for a cup of coffee. Maybe it was the coffee.

LINDA What?

WILLY, *after a pause* I suddenly couldn't drive any more. The car kept going off onto the shoulder, y'know?

LINDA, *helpfully* Oh. Maybe it was the steering again. I don't think Angelo knows the Studebaker.

WILLY No, it's me, it's me. Suddenly I realize I'm going sixty miles an hour and I don't remember the last five minutes. I'm—I can't seem to—keep my mind to it.

LINDA Maybe it's your glasses. You never went for your new glasses.

WILLY No, I see everything. I came back ten miles an hour. It took me nearly four hours from Yonkers.

LINDA, *resigned* Well, you'll just have to take a rest, Willy, you can't continue this way.

WILLY I just got back from Florida.

LINDA But you didn't rest your mind. Your mind is overactive, and the mind is what counts, dear.

WILLY I'll start out in the morning. Maybe I'll feel better in the morning. *She is taking off his shoes.* These goddam arch supports are killing me.

LINDA Take an aspirin. Should I get you an aspirin? It'll soothe you.

WILLY, *with wonder* I was driving along, you understand? And I was fine. I was even observing the scenery. You can imagine, me looking at scenery, on the road every week of my life. But it's so beautiful up there, Linda, the trees are so thick, and the sun is warm. I opened the windshield and just let the warm air bathe over me. And then all of a sudden I'm goin' off the road! I'm tellin' ya, I absolutely forgot I was driving. If I'd've gone the other way over the white line I might've killed somebody. So I went on again —and five minutes later I'm dreamin' again, and I nearly— *He presses two fingers against his eyes.* I have such thoughts, I have such strange thoughts.

LINDA Willy, dear. Talk to them again. There's no reason why you can't work in New York.

WILLY They don't need me in New York. I'm the New England man. I'm vital in New England.

LINDA But you're sixty years old. They can't expect you to keep traveling every week.

WILLY I'll have to send a wire to Portland. I'm supposed to see Brown and Morrison tomorrow morning at ten o'clock to show the line. Goddammit, I could sell them! *He starts putting on his jacket.*

LINDA, *taking the jacket from him* Why don't you go down to the place tomorrow and tell Howard you've simply got to work in New York? You're too accommodating, dear.

WILLY If old man Wagner was alive I'd a been in charge of New York now! That man was a prince, he was a masterful man. But that boy of his, that Howard, he don't appreciate. When I went north the first time, the Wagner Company didn't know where New England was!

LINDA Why don't you tell those things to Howard, dear?

WILLY, *encouraged* I will, I definitely will. Is there any cheese?

LINDA I'll make you a sandwich.

WILLY No, go to sleep. I'll take some milk. I'll be up right away. The boys in?

LINDA They're sleeping. Happy took Biff on a date tonight.

WILLY, *interested* That so?

LINDA It was so nice to see them shaving together, one behind the other, in the bathroom. And going out together. You notice? The whole house smells of shaving lotion.

WILLY Figure it out. Work a lifetime to pay off a house. You finally own it, and there's nobody to live in it.

LINDA Well, dear, life is a casting off. It's always that way.

WILLY No, no, some people—some people accomplish something. Did Biff say anything after I went this morning?

LINDA You shouldn't have criticized him, Willy, especially after he just got off the train. You mustn't lose your temper with him.

WILLY When the hell did I lose my temper? I simply asked him if he was making any money. Is that a criticism?

LINDA But, dear, how could he make any money?

WILLY, *worried and angered* There's such an undercurrent in him. He became a moody man. Did he apologize when I left this morning?

LINDA He was crestfallen, Willy. You know how he admires you. I think if he finds himself, then you'll both be happier and not fight any more.

WILLY How can he find himself on a farm? Is that life? A farmhand? In the beginning, when he was young, I thought, well, a young man, it's good for him to tramp around, take a lot of different jobs. But it's more than ten years now and he has yet to make thirty-five dollars a week!

LINDA He's finding himself, Willy.

WILLY Not finding yourself at the age of thirty-four is a disgrace!

LINDA Shh!

WILLY The trouble is he's lazy, goddammit!

LINDA Willy, please!

WILLY Biff is a lazy bum!

LINDA They're sleeping. Get something to eat. Go on down.

WILLY Why did he come home? I would like to know what brought him home.

LINDA I don't know. I think he's still lost, Willy. I think he's very lost.

WILLY Biff Loman is lost. In the greatest country in the world a young man with such —personal attractiveness, gets lost. And such a hard worker. There's one thing about Biff— he's not lazy.

LINDA Never.

WILL, *with pity and resolve* I'll see him in the morning; I'll have a nice talk with him. I'll get him a job selling. He could be big in no time. My God! Remember how they used to follow him around in high school? When he smiled at one of them their faces lit up. When he walked down the street . . . *He loses himself in reminiscences.*

LINDA, *trying to bring him out of it* Willy, dear, I got a new kind of American-type cheese today. It's whipped.

WILLY Why do you get American when I like Swiss?

LINDA I just thought you'd like a change—

WILLY I don't want a change! I want Swiss cheese. Why am I always being contradicted?

LINDA, *with a covering laugh* I thought it would be a surprise.

WILLY Why don't you open a window in here, for God's sake?

LINDA, *with infinite patience* They're all open, dear.

WILLY The way they boxed us in here. Bricks and windows, windows and bricks.

LINDA We should've bought the land next door.

WILLY The street is lined with cars. There's not a breath of fresh air in the neighborhood. The grass don't grow any more, you can't raise a carrot in the back yard. They should've had a law against apartment houses. Remember those two beautiful elm trees out there? When I and Biff hung the swing between them?

LINDA Yeah, like being a million miles from the city.

WILLY They should've arrested the builder for cutting those down. They massacred the neighborhood. *Lost:* More and more I think of those days, Linda. This time of year it was lilac and wisteria. And then the peonies would come out, and the daffodils. What fragrance in this room!

LINDA Well, after all, people had to move somewhere.

WILLY No, there's more people now.

LINDA I don't think there's more people. I think—

WILLY There's more people! That's what's ruining this country! Population is getting out of control. The competition is maddening! Smell the stink from that apartment house! And another one on the other side . . . How can they whip cheese?

On Willy's last line, Biff and Happy raise themselves up in their beds, listening.

LINDA Go down, try it. And be quiet.

WILLY, *turning to Linda, guiltily* You're not worried about me, are you, sweetheart?

BIFF What's the matter?

HAPPY Listen!

LINDA You've got too much on the ball to worry about.

WILLY You're my foundation and my support, Linda.

LINDA Just try to relax, dear. You make mountains out of molehills.

WILLY I won't fight with him any more. If he wants to go back to Texas, let him go.

LINDA He'll find his way.

WILLY Sure. Certain men just don't get started till later in life. Like Thomas Edison, I think. Or B. F. Goodrich. One of them was deaf. *He starts for the bedroom doorway.* I'll put my money on Biff.

LINDA And Willy—if it's warm Sunday we'll drive in the country. And we'll open the windshield, and take lunch.

WILLY No, the windshields don't open on the new cars.

LINDA But you opened it today.

WILLY Me? I didn't. *He stops.* Now isn't that peculiar! Isn't that a remarkable— *He breaks off in amazement and fright as the flute is heard distantly.*

LINDA What, darling?

WILLY That is the most remarkable thing.

LINDA What, dear?

WILLY I was thinking of the Chevvy. *Slight pause.* Nineteen twenty-eight . . . when I had that red Chevvy— *Breaks off.* That funny? I coulda sworn I was driving that Chevvy today.

LINDA Well, that's nothing. Something must've reminded you.

WILLY Remarkable. Ts. Remember those days? The way Biff used to simonize that car? The dealer refused to believe there was eighty thousand miles on it. *He shakes his head.* Heh! To Linda: Close your eyes, I'll be right up. *He walks out of the bedroom.*

HAPPY, *to Biff* Jesus, maybe he smashed up the car again!

LINDA, *calling after Willy* Be careful on the stairs, dear! The cheese is on the middle shelf! *She turns, goes over to the bed, takes his jacket, and goes out of the bedroom.*

Light has risen on the boys' room. Unseen, Willy is heard talking to himself, "Eighty thousand miles," and a little laugh. Biff gets out of bed, comes downstage a bit, and stands attentively. Biff is two years older than his brother Happy, well built, but in these days bears a worn air and seems less self-assured. He has succeeded less, and his dreams are stronger and less acceptable than Happy's. Happy is tall, powerfully made. Sexuality is like a visible color on him, or a scent that many women have discovered. He, like his brother, is lost, but in a different way, for he has never allowed himself to turn his face toward defeat and is thus more confused and hard-skinned, although seemingly more content.

HAPPY, *getting out of bed* He's going to get his license taken away if he keeps that up. I'm getting nervous about him, y'know, Biff?
BIFF His eyes are going.
HAPPY No, I've driven with him. He sees all right. He just doesn't keep his mind on it. I drove into the city with him last week. He stops at a green light and then it turns red and he goes. *He laughs.*
BIFF Maybe he's color-blind.
HAPPY Pop? Why he's got the finest eye for color in the business. You know that.
BIFF, *sitting down on his bed* I'm going to sleep.
HAPPY You're not still sour on Dad, are you, Biff?
BIFF He's all right, I guess.
WILLY, *underneath them, in the livingroom* Yes, sir, eighty thousand miles—eighty-two thousand!
BIFF You smoking?
HAPPY, *holding out a pack of cigarettes* Want one?
BIFF, *taking a cigarette* I can never sleep when I smell it.
WILLY What a simonizing job, heh!
HAPPY, *with deep sentiment* Funny, Biff, y'know? Us sleeping in here again? The old beds. *He pats his bed affectionately.* All the talk that went across those two beds, huh? Our whole lives.
BIFF Yeah. Lotta dreams and plans.
HAPPY, *with a deep and masculine laugh* About five hundred women would like to know what was said in this room.

They share a soft laugh.

BIFF Remember that big Betsy something—what the hell was her name—over on Bushwick Avenue?
HAPPY, *combing his hair* With the collie dog!
BIFF That's the one. I got you in there, remember?
HAPPY Yeah, that was my first time—I think. Boy, there was a pig! *They laugh, almost crudely.* You taught me everything I know about women. Don't forget that.
BIFF I bet you forget how bashful you used to be. Especially with girls.
HAPPY Oh, I still am, Biff.
BIFF Oh, go on.
HAPPY I just control it, that's all. I think I got less bashful and you got more so. What happened, Biff? Where's the old humor, the old confidence? *He shakes Biff's knee. Biff gets up and moves restlessly about the room.* What's the matter?
BIFF Why does Dad mock me all the time?
HAPPY He's not mocking you, he—
BIFF Everything I say there's a twist of mockery on his face. I can't get near him.
HAPPY He just wants you to make good, that's all. I wanted to talk to you about Dad for a long time, Biff. Something's—happening to him. He—talks to himself.
BIFF I noticed that this morning. But he always mumbled.
HAPPY But not so noticeable. It got so embarrassing I sent him to Florida. And you know something? Most of the time he's talking to you.
BIFF What's he say about me?
HAPPY I can't make it out.
BIFF What's he say about me?
HAPPY I think the fact that you're not settled, that you're still kind of up in the air . . .
BIFF There's one or two other things depressing him, Happy.
HAPPY What do you mean?
BIFF Never mind. Just don't lay it all to me.
HAPPY But I think if you just got started—I mean—is there any future for you out there?
BIFF I tell ya, Hap, I don't know what the future is. I don't know—what I'm supposed to want.

HAPPY What do you mean?

BIFF Well, I spent six or seven years after high school trying to work myself up. Shipping clerk, salesman, business of one kind or another. And it's a measly manner of existence. To get on that subway on the hot mornings in summer. To devote your whole life to keeping stock, or making phone calls, or selling or buying. To suffer fifty weeks of the year for the sake of a two-week vacation, when all you really desire is to be outdoors, with your shirt off. And always to have to get ahead of the next fella. And still—that's how you build a future.

HAPPY Well, you really enjoy it on a farm? Are you content out there?

BIFF, *with rising agitation* Hap, I've had twenty or thirty different kinds of jobs since I left home before the war, and it always turns out the same. I just realized it lately. In Nebraska when I herded cattle, and the Dakotas, and Arizona, and now in Texas. It's why I came home now, I guess, because I realized it. This farm I work on, it's spring there now, see? And they've got about fifteen new colts. There's nothing more inspiring or —beautiful than the sight of a mare and a new colt. And it's cool there now, see? Texas is cool now, and it's spring. And whenever spring comes to where I am, I suddenly get the feeling, my God, I'm not gettin' anywhere! What the hell am I doing, playing around with horses, twenty-eight dollars a week! I'm thirty-four years old, I oughta be makin' my future. That's when I come running home. And now, I get here, and I don't know what to do with myself. *After a pause:* I've always made a point of not wasting my life, and everytime I come back here I know that all I've done is to waste my life.

HAPPY You're a poet, you know that, Biff? You're a—you're an idealist!

BIFF No, I'm mixed up very bad. Maybe I oughta get married. Maybe I oughta get stuck into something. Maybe that's my trouble. I'm like a boy. I'm not married, I'm not in business, I just—I'm like a boy. Are you content, Hap? You're a success, aren't you? Are you content?

HAPPY Hell, no!

BIFF Why? You're making money, aren't you?

HAPPY, *moving about with energy, expressiveness* All I can do now is wait for the merchandise manager to die. And suppose I get to be merchandise manager? He's a good friend of mine, and he just built a terrific estate on Long Island. And he lived there about two months and sold it, and now he's building another one. He can't enjoy it once it's finished. And I know that's just what I would do. I don't know what the hell I'm workin' for. Sometimes I sit in my apartment —all alone. And I think of the rent I'm paying. And it's crazy. But then, it's what I always wanted. My own apartment, a car, and plenty of women. And still, goddammit, I'm lonely.

BIFF, *with enthusiasm* Listen, why don't you come out West with me?

HAPPY You and I, heh?

BIFF Sure, maybe we could buy a ranch. Raise cattle, use our muscles. Men built like we are should be working out in the open.

HAPPY, *avidly* The Loman Brothers, heh?

BIFF, *with vast affection* Sure, we'd be known all over the counties!

HAPPY, *enthralled* That's what I dream about, Biff. Sometimes I want to just rip my clothes off in the middle of the store and outbox that goddam merchandise manager. I mean I can outbox, outrun, and outlift anybody in that store, and I have to take orders from those common, petty sons-of-bitches till I can't stand it any more.

BIFF I'm tellin' you, kid, if you were with me I'd be happy out there.

HAPPY, *enthused* See, Biff, everybody around me is so false that I'm constantly lowering my ideals . . .

BIFF Baby, together we'd stand up for one another, we'd have someone to trust.

HAPPY If I were around you—

BIFF Hap, the trouble is we weren't brought up to grub for money. I don't know how to do it.

HAPPY Neither can I!

BIFF Then let's go!

HAPPY The only thing is—what can you make out there?

BIFF But look at your friend. Builds an estate and then hasn't the peace of mind to live in it.

HAPPY Yeah, but when he walks into the store the waves part in front of him. That's fifty-two thousand dollars a year coming through the revolving door, and I got more in my pinky finger than he's got in his head.

BIFF Yeah, but you just said—

HAPPY I gotta show some of those pompous, self-important executives over there that Hap Loman can make the grade. I want to walk into the store the way he walks in. Then I'll go with you, Biff. We'll be together yet, I swear. But take those two we had tonight. Now weren't they gorgeous creatures?

BIFF Yeah, yeah, most gorgeous I've had in years.

HAPPY I get that any time I want, Biff. Whenever I feel disgusted. The only trouble is, it gets like bowling or something. I just keep knockin' them over and it doesn't mean anything. You still run around a lot?

BIFF Naa. I'd like to find a girl—steady, somebody with substance.

HAPPY That's what I long for.

BIFF Go on! You'd never come home.

HAPPY I would! Somebody with character, with resistance! Like Mom, y'know? You're gonna call me a bastard when I tell you this. That girl Charlotte I was with tonight is engaged to be married in five weeks. *He tries on his new hat.*

BIFF No kiddin'!

HAPPY Sure, the guy's in line for the vice-presidency of the store. I don't know what gets into me, maybe I just have an overdeveloped sense of competition or something, but I went and ruined her, and furthermore I can't get rid of her. And he's the third executive I've done that to. Isn't that a crummy characteristic? And to top it all, I go to their weddings! *Indignantly, but laughing:* Like I'm not supposed to take bribes. Manufacturers offer me a hundred-dollar bill now and then to throw an order their way. You know how honest I am, but it's like this girl, see. I hate myself for it. Because I don't want the girl, and, still, I take it and—I love it!

BIFF Let's go to sleep.

HAPPY I guess we didn't settle anything, heh?

BIFF I just got one idea that I think I'm going to try.

HAPPY What's that?

BIFF Remember Bill Oliver?

HAPPY Sure, Oliver is very big now. You want to work for him again?

BIFF No, but when I quit he said something to me. He put his arm on my shoulder, and he said, "Biff, if you ever need anything, come to me."

HAPPY I remember that. That sounds good.

BIFF I think I'll go to see him. If I could get ten thousand or even seven or eight thousand dollars I could buy a beautiful ranch.

HAPPY I bet he'd back you. 'Cause he thought highly of you, Biff. I mean, they all do. You're well liked, Biff. That's why I say to come back here, and we both have the apartment. And I'm tellin' you, Biff, any babe you want...

BIFF No, with a ranch I could do the work I like and still be something. I just wonder though. I wonder if Oliver still thinks I stole that carton of basketballs.

HAPPY Oh, he probably forgot that long ago. It's almost ten years. You're too sensitive. Anyway, he didn't really fire you.

BIFF Well, I think he was going to. I think that's why I quit. I was never sure whether he knew or not. I know he thought the world of me, though. I was the only one he'd let lock up the place.

WILLY, *below* You gonna wash the engine, Biff?

HAPPY Shh!

Biff looks at Happy, who is gazing down, listening. Willy is mumbling in the parlor.

HAPPY You hear that?

They listen. Willy laughs warmly.

BIFF, *growing angry* Doesn't he know Mom can hear that?

WILLY Don't get your sweater dirty, Biff!

A look of pain crosses Biff's face.

HAPPY Isn't that terrible? Don't leave again, will you? You'll find a job here. You gotta stick around. I don't know what to do about him, it's getting embarrassing.
WILLY What a simonizing job!
BIFF Mom's hearing that!
WILLY No kiddin', Biff, you got a date? Wonderful!
HAPPY Go to sleep. But talk to him in the morning, will you?
BIFF, *reluctantly getting into bed* With her in the house. Brother!
HAPPY, *getting into bed* I wish you'd have a good talk with him.

The light on their room begins to fade.

BIFF, *to himself in bed* That selfish, stupid . . .
HAPPY Sh . . . Sleep, Biff.

Their light is out. Well before they have finished speaking, Willy's form is dimly seen below in the darkened kitchen. He opens the refrigerator, searches in there, and takes out a bottle of milk. The apartment houses are fading out, and the entire house and surroundings become covered with leaves. Music insinuates itself as the leaves appear.

WILLY Just wanna be careful wtih those girls, Biff, that's all. Don't make any promises. No promises of any kind. Because a girl, y'know, they always believe what you tell 'em, and you're very young, Biff, you're too young to be talking seriously to girls.

Light rises on the kitchen. Willy, talking, shuts the refrigerator door and comes downstage to the kitchen table. He pours milk into a glass. He is totally immersed in himself, smiling faintly.

WILLY Too young entirely, Biff. You want to watch your schooling first. Then when you're all set, there'll be plenty of girls for a boy like you. *He smiles broadly at a kitchen chair.* That so? The girls pay for you? *He laughs.* Boy, you must really be makin' a hit.

Willy is gradually addressing—physically —a point offstage, speaking through the wall of the kitchen, and his voice has been rising in volume to that of a normal conversation.

WILLY I been wondering why you polish the car so careful. Ha. Don't leave the hubcaps, boys. Get the chamois to the hubcaps. Happy, use newspapers on the windows, it's the easiest thing. Show him how to do it, Biff! You see, Happy? Pad it up, use it like a pad. That's it, that's it, good work. You're doin' it all right, Hap. *He pauses, then nods in approbation for a few seconds, then looks upward.* Biff, first thing we gotta do when we get time is clip that big branch over the house. Afraid it's gonna fall in a storm and hit the roof. Tell you what. We get a rope and sling her around, and then we climb up there with a couple of saws and take her down. Soon as you finish the car, boys, I wanna see ya. I got a surprise for you, boys.
BIFF, *offstage* Whatta ya got, Dad?
WILLY No, you finish first. Never leave a job till you're finished—remember that. *Looking toward the "big trees":* Biff, up in Albany I saw a beautiful hammock. I think I'll buy it next trip, and we'll hang it right between those two elms. Wouldn't that be something? Just swingin' there under those branches. Boy, that would be . . .

Young Biff and Young Happy appear from the direction Willy was addressing. Happy carries rags and a pail of water. Biff, wearing a sweater with a block "S," carries a football.

BIFF, *pointing in the direction of the car offstage* How's that, Pop, professional?
WILLY Terrific. Terrific job, boys. Good work, Biff.
HAPPY Where's the surprise, Pop?
WILLY In the back seat of the car.
HAPPY Boy! *He runs off.*
BIFF What is it, Dad? Tell me, what'd you buy?
WILLY, *laughing, cuffs him* Never mind, something I want you to have.
BIFF, *turns and starts off* What is it, Hap?
HAPPY, *offstage* It's a punching bag!
BIFF Oh, Pop!
WILLY It's got Gene Tunney's signature on it!

Happy runs onstage with a punching bag.

BIFF Gee, how'd you know we wanted a punching bag?

WILLY Well, it's the finest thing for the timing.

HAPPY, *lies down on his back and pedals with his feet* I'm losing weight, you notice, Pop?

WILLY, *to Happy* Jumping rope is good too.

BIFF Did you see the new football I got?

WILLY, *examining the ball* Where'd you get a new ball?

BIFF The coach told me to practice my passing.

WILLY That so? And he gave you the ball, heh?

BIFF Well, I borrowed it from the locker room. *He laughs confidentially.*

WILLY, *laughing with him at the theft* I want you to return that.

HAPPY I told you he wouldn't like it!

BIFF, *angrily* Well, I'm bringing it back!

WILLY, *stopping the incipient argument, to Happy* Sure, he's gotta practice with a regulation ball, doesn't he? *To Biff*: Coach'll probably congratulate you on your initiative!

BIFF Oh, he keeps congratulating my initiative all the time, Pop.

WILLY That's because he likes you. If somebody else took that ball there'd be an uproar. So what's the report, boys, what's the report?

BIFF Where'd you go this time, Dad? Gee we were lonesome for you.

WILLY, *pleased, puts an arm around each boy and they come down to the apron* Lonesome, heh?

BIFF Missed you every minute.

WILLY Don't say? Tell you a secret, boys. Don't breathe it to a soul. Someday I'll have my own business, and I'll never have to leave home any more.

HAPPY Like Uncle Charley, heh?

WILLY Bigger than Uncle Charley! Because Charley is not—liked. He's liked, but he's not—well liked.

BIFF Where'd you go this time, Dad?

WILLY Well, I got on the road, and I went north to Providence. Met the Mayor.

BIFF The Mayor of Providence!

WILLY He was sitting in the hotel lobby.

BIFF Wha'd he say?

WILLY He said, "Morning!" And I said, "You got a fine city here, Mayor." And then he had coffee with me. And then I went to Waterbury. Waterbury is a fine city. Big clock city, the famous Waterbury clock. Sold a nice bill there. And then Boston—Boston is the cradle of the Revolution. A fine city. And a couple of other towns in Mass., and on to Portland and Bangor and straight home!

BIFF Gee, I'd love to go with you sometime, Dad.

WILLY Soon as summer comes.

HAPPY Promise?

WILLY You and Hap and I, and I'll show you all the towns. America is full of beautiful towns and fine, upstanding people. And they know me, boys, they know me up and down New England. The finest people. And when I bring you fellas up, there'll be open sesame for all of us, 'cause one thing, boys: I have friends. I can park my car in any street in New England, and the cops protect it like their own. This summer, heh?

BIFF and HAPPY, *together* Yeah! You bet!

WILLY We'll take our bathing suits.

HAPPY We'll carry your bags, Pop!

WILLY Oh, won't that be something! Me comin' into the Boston stores with you boys carryin' my bags. What a sensation!

Biff is prancing around, practicing passing the ball.

WILLY You nervous, Biff, about the game?

BIFF Not if you're gonna be there.

WILLY What do they say about you in school, now that they made you captain?

HAPPY There's a crowd of girls behind him every time the classes change.

BIFF, *taking Willy's hand* This Saturday, Pop, this Saturday—just for you, I'm going to break through for a touchdown.

HAPPY You're supposed to pass.

BIFF I'm takin' one play for Pop. You watch me, Pop, and when I take off my helmet, that means I'm breakin' out. Then you watch me crash through that line!

WILLY, *kisses Biff* Oh, wait'll I tell this in Boston!

Bernard enters in knickers. He is younger than Biff, earnest and loyal, a worried boy.

BERNARD Biff, where are you? You're supposed to study with me today.
WILLY Hey, looka Bernard. What're you lookin' so anemic about, Bernard?
BERNARD He's gotta study, Uncle Willy. He's got Regents next week.
HAPPY, *tauntingly, spinning Bernard around* Let's box, Bernard!
BERNARD Biff! *He gets away from Happy.* Listen, Biff, I heard Mr. Birnbaum say that if you don't start studyin' math he's gonna flunk you, and you won't graduate. I heard him!
WILLY You better study with him, Biff. Go ahead now.
BERNARD I heard him!
BIFF Oh, Pop, you didn't see my sneakers! *He holds up a foot for Willy to look at.*
WILLY Hey, that's a beautiful job of printing!
BERNARD, *wiping his glasses* Just because he printed University of Virginia on his sneakers doesn't mean they've got to graduate him, Uncle Willy!
WILLY, *angrily* What're you talking about? With scholarships to three universities they're gonna flunk him?
BERNARD But I heard Mr. Birnbaum say—
WILLY Don't be a pest, Bernard! *To his boys:* What an anemic!
BERNARD Okay, I'm waiting for you in my house, Biff.

Bernard goes off. The Lomans laugh.

WILLY Bernard is not well liked, is he?
BIFF He's liked, but he's not well liked.
HAPPY That's right, Pop.
WILLY That's just what I mean. Bernard can get the best marks in school, y'understand, but when he gets out in the business world, y'understand, you are going to be five times ahead of him. That's why I thank Almighty God you're both built like Adonises. Because the man who makes an appearance in the business world, the man who creates personal interest, is the man who gets ahead. Be liked and you will never want. You take me, for instance. I never have to wait in line to see a buyer. "Willy Loman is here!" That's all they have to know, and I go right through.
BIFF Did you knock them dead, Pop?
WILLY Knocked 'em cold in Providence, slaughtered 'em in Boston.
HAPPY, *on his back, pedaling again* I'm losing weight, you notice, Pop?

Linda enters, as of old, a ribbon in her hair, carrying a basket of washing.

LINDA, *with youthful energy* Hello, dear!
WILLY Sweetheart!
LINDA How'd the Chevvy run?
WILLY Chevrolet, Linda, is the greatest car ever built. *To the boys:* Since when do you let your mother carry wash up the stairs?
BIFF Grab hold there, boy!
HAPPY Where to, Mom?
LINDA Hang them up on the line. And you better go down to your friends, Biff. The cellar is full of boys. They don't know what to do with themselves.
BIFF Ah, when Pop comes home they can wait!
WILLY, *laughs appreciatively* You better go down and tell them what to do, Biff.
BIFF I think I'll have them sweep out the furnace room.
WILLY Good work, Biff.
BIFF, *goes through wall-line of kitchen to doorway at back and calls down* Fellas! Everybody sweep out the furnace room! I'll be right down!
VOICES All right! Okay, Biff.
BIFF George and Sam and Frank, come out back! We're hangin' up the wash! Come on, Hap, on the double! *He and Happy carry out the basket.*
LINDA The way they obey him!
WILLY Well, that's training, the training. I'm tellin' you, I was sellin' thousands and thousands, but I had to come home.
LINDA Oh, the whole block'll be at that game. Did you sell anything?
WILLY I did five hundred gross in Providence and seven hundred gross in Boston.
LINDA No! Wait a minute, I've got a pencil. *She pulls pencil and paper out of her apron pocket.* That makes your commission . . .

Two hundred—my God! Two hundred and twelve dollars!

WILLY Well, I didn't figure it yet, but . . .

LINDA How much did you do?

WILLY Well, I—I did—about a hundred and eighty gross in Providence. Well, no—it came to—roughly two hundred gross on the whole trip.

LINDA, *without hesitation* Two hundred gross. That's . . . *She figures.*

WILLY The trouble was that three of the stores were half closed for inventory in Boston. Otherwise I woulda broke records.

LINDA Well, it makes seventy dollars and some pennies. That's very good.

WILLY What do we owe?

LINDA Well, on the first there's sixteen dollars on the refrigerator—

WILLY Why sixteen?

LINDA Well, the fan belt broke, so it was a dollar eighty.

WILLY But it's brand new.

LINDA Well, the man said that's the way it is. Till they work themselves in, y'know.

They move through the wall-line into the kitchen.

WILLY I hope we didn't get stuck on that machine.

LINDA They got the biggest ads of any of them!

WILLY I know, it's a fine machine. What else?

LINDA Well, there's nine-sixty for the washing machine. And for the vacuum cleaner there's three and a half due on the fifteenth. Then the roof, you got twenty-one dollars remaining.

WILLY It don't leak, does it?

LINDA No, they did a wonderful job. Then you owe Frank for the carburetor.

WILLY I'm not going to pay that man! That goddam Chevrolet, they ought to prohibit the manufacture of that car!

LINDA Well, you owe him three and a half. And odds and ends, comes to around a hundred and twenty dollars by the fifteenth.

WILLY A hundred and twenty dollars! My God, if business don't pick up I don't know what I'm gonna do!

LINDA Well, next week you'll do better.

WILLY Oh, I'll knock 'em dead next week. I'll go to Hartford. I'm very well liked in Hartford. You know, the trouble is, Linda, people don't seem to take to me.

They move onto the forestage.

LINDA Oh, don't be foolish.

WILLY I know it when I walk in. They seem to laugh at me.

LINDA Why? Why would they laugh at you? Don't talk that way, Willy.

Willy moves to the edge of the stage. Linda goes into the kitchen and starts to darn stockings.

WILLY I don't know the reason for it, but they just pass me by. I'm not noticed.

LINDA But you're doing wonderful, dear. You're making seventy to a hundred dollars a week.

WILLY But I gotta be at it ten, twelve hours a day. Other men—I don't know—they do it easier. I don't know why—I can't stop myself—I talk too much. A man oughta come in with a few words. One thing about Charley. He's a man of few words, and they respect him.

LINDA You don't talk too much, you're just lively.

WILLY, *smiling* Well, I figure, what the hell, life is short, a couple of jokes. *To himself:* I joke too much! *The smile goes.*

LINDA Why? You're—

WILLY I'm fat. I'm very—foolish to look at, Linda. I didn't tell you, but Christmas time I happened to be calling on F. H. Stewarts, and a salesman I know, as I was going in to see the buyer I heard him say something about—walrus. And I—I cracked him right across the face. I won't take that. I simply will not take that. But they do laugh at me. I know that.

LINDA Darling . . .

WILLY I gotta overcome it. I know I gotta overcome it. I'm not dressing to advantage, maybe.

LINDA Willy, darling, you're the handsomest man in the world—

WILLY Oh, no, Linda.
LINDA To me you are. *Slight pause.* The handsomest.

From the darkness is heard the laughter of a woman. Willy doesn't turn to it, but it continues through Linda's lines.

LINDA And the boys, Willy. Few men are idolized by their children the way you are.

Music is heard as behind a scrim, to the left of the house, The Woman, dimly seen, is dressing.

WILLY, *with great feeling* You're the best there is, Linda, you're a pal, you know that? On the road—on the road I want to grab you sometimes and just kiss the life outa you.

The laughter is loud now, and he moves into a brightening area at the left, where The Woman has come from behind the scrim and is standing, putting on her hat, looking into a "mirror" and laughing.

WILLY 'Cause I get so lonely—especially when business is bad and there's nobody to talk to. I get the feeling that I'll never sell anything again, that I won't make a living for you, or a business, a business for the boys. *He talks through The Woman's subsiding laughter! The Woman primps at the "mirror."* There's so much I want to make for—

THE WOMAN Me? You didn't make me, Willy. I picked you.

WILLY, *pleased* You picked me?

THE WOMAN, *who is quite proper-looking, Willy's age* I did. I've been sitting at that desk watching all the salesmen go by, day in, day out. But you've got such a sense of humor, and we do have such a good time together, don't we?

WILLY Sure, sure. *He takes her in his arms.* Why do you have to go now?

THE WOMAN It's two o'clock . . .

WILLY No, come on in! *He pulls her.*

THE WOMAN . . . my sisters'll be scandalized. When'll you be back?

WILLY Oh, two weeks about. Will you come up again?

THE WOMAN Sure thing. You do make me laugh. It's good for me. *She squeezes his arm, kisses him.* And I think you're a wonderful man.

WILLY You picked me, heh?

THE WOMAN Sure. Because you're so sweet. And such a kidder.

WILLY Well, I'll see you next time I'm in Boston.

THE WOMAN I'll put you right through to the buyers.

WILLY, *slapping her bottom* Right. Well, bottoms up!

THE WOMAN, *slaps him gently and laughs* You just kill me, Willy. *He suddenly grabs her and kisses her roughly.* You kill me. And thanks for the stockings. I love a lot of stockings. Well, good night.

WILLY Good night. And keep your pores open!

THE WOMAN Oh, Willy!

The Woman bursts out laughing, and Linda's laughter blends in. The Woman disappears into the dark. Now the area at the kitchen table brightens. Linda is sitting where she was at the kitchen table, but now is mending a pair of her silk stockings.

LINDA You are, Willy. The handsomest man. You've got no reason to feel that—

WILLY, *coming out of The Woman's dimming area and going over to Linda* I'll make it all up to you, Linda, I'll—

LINDA There's nothing to make up, dear. You're doing fine, better than—

WILLY, *noticing her mending* What's that?

LINDA Just mending my stockings. They're so expensive—

WILLY, *angrily, taking them from her* I won't have you mending stockings in this house! Now throw them out!

Linda puts the stockings in her pocket.

BERNARD, *entering on the run* Where is he? If he doesn't study!

WILLY, *moving to the forestage, with great agitation* You'll give him the answers!

BERNARD I do, but I can't on a Regents! That's a state exam! They're liable to arrest me!

WILLY Where is he? I'll whip him, I'll whip him!

LINDA And he'd better give back that football, Willy, it's not nice.
WILLY Biff! Where is he? Why is he taking everything?
LINDA He's too rough with the girls, Willy. All the mothers are afraid of him!
WILLY I'll whip him!
BERNARD He's driving the car without a license!

The Woman's laugh is heard.

WILLY Shut up!
LINDA All the mothers—
WILLY Shut up!
BERNARD, *backing quietly away and out* Mr. Birnbaum says he's stuck up.
WILLY Get outa here!
BERNARD If he doesn't buckle down he'll flunk math! *He goes off.*
LINDA He's right, Willy, you've gotta—
WILLY, *exploding at her* There's nothing the matter with him! You want him to be a worm like Bernard? He's got spirit, personality . . .

As he speaks, Linda, almost in tears, exits into the livingroom. Willy is alone in the kitchen, wilting and staring. The leaves are gone. It is night again, and the apartment houses look down from behind.

WILLY Loaded with it. Loaded! What is he stealing? He's giving it back, isn't he? Why is he stealing? What did I tell him? I never in my life told him anything but decent things.

Happy in pajamas has come down the stairs; Willy suddenly becomes aware of Happy's presence.

HAPPY Let's go now, come on.
WILLY, *sitting down at the kitchen table* Huh! Why did she have to wax the floors herself? Every time she waxes the floors she keels over. She knows that!
HAPPY Shh! Take it easy. What brought you back tonight?
WILLY I got an awful scare. Nearly hit a kid in Yonkers. God! Why didn't I go to Alaska with my brother Ben that time! Ben! That man was a genius, that man was success incarnate! What a mistake! He begged me to go.
HAPPY Well, there's no use in—
WILLY You guys! There was a man started with the clothes on his back and ended up with diamond mines!
HAPPY Boy, some day I'd like to know how he did it.
WILLY What's the mystery? The man knew what he wanted and went out and got it! Walked into a jungle, and comes out, the age of twenty-one, and he's rich! The world is an oyster, but you don't crack it open on a mattress!
HAPPY Pop, I told you I'm gonna retire you for life.
WILLY You'll retire me for life on seventy goddam dollars a week? And your women and your car and your apartment, and you'll retire me for life! Christ's sake, I couldn't get past Yonkers today! What are you guys, where are you? The woods are burning! I can't drive a car!

Charley has appeared in the doorway. He is a large man, slow of speech, laconic, immovable. In all he says, despite what he says, there is pity, and, now, trepidation. He has a robe over pajamas, slippers on his feet. He enters the kitchen.

CHARLEY Everything all right?
HAPPY Yeah, Charley, everything's . . .
WILLY What's the matter?
CHARLEY I heard some noise. I thought something happened. Can't we do something about the walls? You sneeze in here, and in my house hats blow off.
HAPPY Let's go to bed, Dad. Come on.

Charley signals to Happy to go.

WILLY You go ahead, I'm not tired at the moment.
HAPPY, *to Willy* Take it easy, huh? *He exits.*
WILLY What're you doin' up?
CHARLEY, *sitting down at the kitchen table opposite Willy* Couldn't sleep good. I had a heartburn.

WILLY Well, you don't know how to eat.
CHARLEY I eat with my mouth.
WILLY No, you're ignorant. You gotta know about vitamins and things like that.
CHARLEY Come on, let's shoot. Tire you out a little.
WILLY, *hesitantly* All right. You got cards?
CHARLEY, *taking a deck from his pocket* Yeah, I got them. Some place. What is it with those vitamins?
WILLY, *dealing* They build up your bones. Chemistry.
CHARLEY Yeah, but there's no bones in a heartburn.
WILLY What are you talkin' about? Do you know the first thing about it?
CHARLEY Don't get insulted.
WILLY Don't talk about something you don't know anything about.

They are playing. Pause.

CHARLEY What're you doin' home?
WILLY A little trouble with the car.
CHARLEY Oh. *Pause.* I'd like to take a trip to California.
WILLY Don't say.
CHARLEY You want a job?
WILLY I got a job, I told you that. *After a slight pause:* What the hell are you offering me a job for?
CHARLEY Don't get insulted.
WILLY Don't insult me.
CHARLEY I don't see no sense in it. You don't have to go on this way.
WILLY I got a good job. *Slight pause.* What do you keep comin' in here for?
CHARLEY You want me to go?
WILLY, *after a pause, withering* I can't understand it. He's going back to Texas again. What the hell is that?
CHARLEY Let him go.
WILLY I got nothin' to give him, Charley, I'm clean, I'm clean.
CHARLEY He won't starve. None a them starve. Forget about him.
WILLY Then what have I got to remember?
CHARLEY You take it too hard. To hell with it. When a deposit bottle is broken you don't get your nickel back.
WILLY That's easy enough for you to say.
CHARLEY That ain't easy for me to say.
WILLY Did you see the ceiling I put up in the living room?
CHARLEY Yeah, that's a piece of work. To put up a ceiling is a mystery to me. How do you do it?
WILLY What's the difference?
CHARLEY Well, talk about it.
WILLY You gonna put up a ceiling?
CHARLEY How could I put up a ceiling?
WILLY Then what the hell are you bothering me for?
CHARLEY You're insulted again.
WILLY A man who can't handle tools is not a man. You're disgusting.
CHARLEY Don't call me disgusting, Willy.

Uncle Ben, carrying a valise and an umbrella, enters the forestage from around the right corner of the house. He is a stolid man, in his sixties, with a mustache and an authoritative air. He is utterly certain of his destiny, and there is an aura of far places about him. He enters exactly as Willy speaks.

WILLY I'm getting awfully tired, Ben.

Ben's music is heard. Ben looks around at everything.

CHARLEY Good, keep playing; you'll sleep better. Did you call me Ben?

Ben looks at his watch.

WILLY That's funny. For a second there you reminded me of my brother Ben.
BEN I only have a few minutes. *He strolls, inspecting the place. Willy and Charley continued playing.*
CHARLEY You never heard from him again, heh? Since that time?
WILLY Didn't Linda tell you? Couple of weeks ago we got a letter from his wife in Africa. He died.
CHARLEY That so.
BEN, *chuckling* So this is Brooklyn, eh?
CHARLEY Maybe you're in for some of his money.
WILLY Naa, he had seven sons. There's just one opportunity I had with that man . . .

BEN I must make a train, William. There are several properties I'm looking at in Alaska.
WILLY Sure, sure! If I'd gone with him to Alaska that time, everything would've been totally different.
CHARLEY Go on, you'd froze to death up there.
WILLY What're you talking about?
BEN Opportunity is tremendous in Alaska, William. Surprised you're not up there.
WILLY Sure, tremendous.
CHARLEY Heh?
WILLY There was the only man I ever met who knew the answers.
CHARLEY Who?
BEN How are you all?
WILLY, *taking a pot, smiling* Fine, fine.
CHARLEY Pretty sharp tonight.
BEN Is Mother living with you?
WILLY No, she died a long time ago.
CHARLEY Who?
BEN That's too bad. Fine specimen of a lady, Mother.
WILLY, *to Charley* Heh?
BEN I'd hoped to see the old girl.
CHARLEY Who died?
BEN Heard anything from Father, have you?
WILLY, *unnerved* What do you mean, who died?
CHARLEY, *taking a pot* What're you talkin' about?
BEN, *looking at his watch* William, it's half-past eight!
WILLY, *as though to dispel his confusion he angrily stops Charley's hand* That's my build!
CHARLEY I put the ace—
WILLY If you don't know how to play the game I'm not gonna throw my money away on you!
CHARLEY, *rising* It was my ace, for God's sake!
WILLY I'm through, I'm through!
BEN When did Mother die?
WILLY Long ago. Since the beginning you never knew how to play cards.
CHARLEY, *picks up the cards and goes to the door* All right! Next time I'll bring a deck with five aces.
WILLY I don't play that kind of game!

CHARLEY, *turning to him* You ought to be ashamed of yourself!
WILLY Yeah?
CHARLEY Yeah! *He goes out.*
WILLY, *slamming the door after him* Ignoramus!
BEN, *as Willy comes toward him through the wall-line of the kitchen* So you're William.
WILLY, *shaking Ben's hand* Ben! I've been waiting for you so long! What's the answer? How did you do it?
BEN Oh, there's a story in that.

Linda enters the forestage, as of old, carrying the wash basket.

LINDA Is this Ben?
BEN, *gallantly* How do you do, my dear.
LINDA Where've you been all these years? Willy's always wondered why you—
WILLY, *pulling Ben away from her impatiently* Where is Dad? Didn't you follow him? How did you get started?
BEN Well, I don't know how much you remember.
WILLY Well, I was just a baby, of course, only three or four years old—
BEN Three years and eleven months.
WILLY What a memory, Ben!
BEN I have many enterprises, William, and I have never kept books.
WILLY I remember I was sitting under the wagon in—was it Nebraska?
BEN It was South Dakota, and I gave you a bunch of wild flowers.
WILLY I remember you walking away down some open road.
BEN, *laughing* I was going to find Father in Alaska.
WILLY Where is he?
BEN At that age I had a very faulty view of geography, William. I discovered after a few days that I was heading due south, so instead of Alaska, I ended up in Africa.
LINDA Africa!
WILLY The Gold Coast!
BEN Principally diamond mines.
LINDA Diamond mines!
BEN Yes, my dear. But I've only a few minutes—

WILLY No! Boys! Boys! *Young Biff and Happy appear.* Listen to this. This is your Uncle Ben, a great man! Tell my boys, Ben!

BEN Why, boys, when I was seventeen I walked into the jungle, and when I was twenty-one I walked out. *He laughs.* And by God I was rich.

WILLY, *to the boys* You see what I been talking about? The greatest things can happen!

BEN, *glancing at his watch* I have an appointment in Ketchikan Tuesday week.

WILLY No, Ben! Please tell about Dad. I want my boys to hear. I want them to know the kind of stock they spring from. All I remember is a man with a big beard, and I was in Mamma's lap, sitting around a fire, and some kind of high music.

BEN His flute. He played the flute.

WILLY Sure, the flute, that's right!

New music is heard, a high, rollicking tune.

BEN Father was a very great and very wild-hearted man. We would start in Boston, and he'd toss the whole family into the wagon, and then he'd drive the team right across the country; through Ohio, and Indiana, Michigan, Illinois, and all the Western states. And we'd stop in the towns and sell the flutes that he'd made on the way. Great inventor, Father. With one gadget he made more in a week than a man like you could make in a lifetime.

WILLY That's just the way I'm bringing them up, Ben—rugged, well liked, all-around.

BEN Yeah? *To Biff:* Hit that, boy—hard as you can. *He pounds his stomach.*

BIFF Oh, no, sir!

BEN, *taking boxing stance* Come on, get to me! *He laughs.*

WILLY Go to it, Biff! Go ahead, show him!

BIFF Okay! *He cocks his fists and starts in.*

LINDA, *to Willy* Why must he fight, dear?

BEN, *sparring with Biff* Good boy! Good boy!

WILLY How's that, Ben, heh?

HAPPY Give him the left, Biff!

LINDA Why are you fighting?

BEN Good boy! *Suddenly comes in, trips Biff, and stands over him, the point of his umbrella poised over Biff's eye.*

LINDA Look out, Biff!

BIFF Gee!

BEN, *patting Biff's knee* Never fight fair with a stranger, boy. You'll never get out of the jungle that way. *Taking Linda's hand and bowing:* It was an honor and a pleasure to meet you, Linda.

LINDA, *withdrawing her hand coldly, frightened* Have a nice—trip.

BEN, *to Willy* And good luck with your—what do you do?

WILLY Selling.

BEN Yes. Well . . . *He raises his hand in farewell to all.*

WILLY No, Ben, I don't want you to think . . . *He takes Ben's arm to show him.* It's Brooklyn, I know, but we hunt too.

BEN Really, now.

WILLY Oh, sure, there's snakes and rabbits and—that's why I moved out here. Why, Biff can fell any one of these trees in no time! Boys! Go right over to where they're building the apartment house and get some sand. We're gonna rebuild the entire front stoop right now! Watch this, Ben!

BIFF Yes, sir! On the double, Hap!

HAPPY, *as he and Biff run off* I lost weight, Pop, you notice?

Charley enters in knickers, even before the boys are gone.

CHARLEY Listen, if they steal any more from that building the watchman'll put the cops on them!

LINDA, *to Willy* Don't let Biff . . .

Ben laughs lustily.

WILLY You shoulda seen the lumber they brought home last week. At least a dozen six-by-tens worth all kinds a money.

CHARLEY Listen, if that watchman—

WILLY I gave them hell, understand. But I got a couple of fearless characters there.

CHARLEY Willy, the jails are full of fearless characters.

BEN, *clapping Willy on the back, with a laugh at Charley* And the stock exchange, friend!

WILLY, *joining in Ben's laughter* Where are the rest of your pants?

CHARLEY My wife bought them.
WILLY Now all you need is a golf club and you can go upstairs and go to sleep. *To Ben:* Great athlete! Between him and his son Bernard they can't hammer a nail!
BERNARD, *rushing in* The watchman's chasing Biff!
WILLY, *angrily* Shut up! He's not stealing anything!
LINDA, *alarmed, hurrying off left* Where is he? Biff, dear!

She exits.

WILLY, *moving toward the left, away from Ben* There's nothing wrong. What's the matter with you?
BEN Nervy boy. Good!
WILLY, *laughing* Oh, nerves of iron, that Biff!
CHARLEY Don't know what it is. My New England man comes back and he's bleedin', they murdered him up there.
WILLY It's contacts, Charley, I got important contacts!
CHARLEY, *sarcastically* Glad to hear it, Willy. Come in later, we'll shoot a little casino. I'll take some of your Portland money. *He laughs at Willy and exits.*
WILLY, *turning to Ben* Business is bad, it's murderous. But not for me, of course.
BEN I'll stop by on my way back to Africa.
WILLY, *longingly* Can't you stay a few days? You're just what I need, Ben, because I—I have a fine position here, but I—well, Dad left when I was such a baby and I never had a chance to talk to him and I still feel—kind of temporary about myself.
BEN I'll be late for my train.

They are at opposite ends of the stage.

WILLY Ben, my boys—can't we talk? They'd go into the jaws of hell for me, see, but I—
BEN William, you're being first-rate with your boys. Outstanding, manly chaps!
WILLY, *hanging on to his words* Oh, Ben, that's good to hear! Because sometimes I'm afraid that I'm not teaching them the right kind of—Ben, how should I teach them?
BEN, *giving great weight to each word, and with a certain vicious audacity* William, when I walked into the jungle, I was seventeen. When I walked out I was twenty-one. And, by God, I was rich! *He goes off into darkness around the right corner of the house.*
WILLY . . . was rich! That's just the spirit I want to imbue them with! To walk into a jungle! I was right! I was right! I was right!

Ben is gone, but Willy is still speaking to him as Linda, in nightgown and robe, enters the kitchen, glances around for Willy, then goes to the door of the house, looks out and sees him. Comes down to his left. He looks at her.

LINDA Willy, dear? Willy?
WILLY I was right!
LINDA Did you have some cheese? *He can't answer.* It's very late, darling. Come to bed, heh?
WILLY, *looking straight up* Gotta break your neck to see a star in this yard.
LINDA You coming in?
WILLY Whatever happened to that diamond watch fob? Remember? When Ben came from Africa that time? Didn't he give me a watch fob with a diamond in it?
LINDA You pawned it, dear. Twelve, thirteen years ago. For Biff's radio correspondence course.
WILLY Gee, that was a beautiful thing. I'll take a walk.
LINDA But you're in your slippers.
WILLY, *starting to go around the house at the left* I was right! I was! *Half to Linda, as he goes, shaking his head:* What a man! There was a man worth talking to. I was right!
LINDA, *calling after Willy* But in your slippers, Willy!

Willy is almost gone when Biff, in his pajamas, comes down the stairs and enters the kitchen.

BIFF What is he doing out there?
LINDA Sh!
BIFF God Almighty, Mom, how long has he been doing this?
LINDA Don't, he'll hear you.
BIFF What the hell is the matter with him?

LINDA It'll pass by morning.
BIFF Shouldn't we do anything?
LINDA Oh, my dear, you should do a lot of things, but there's nothing to do, so go to sleep.

Happy comes down the stairs and sits on the steps.

HAPPY I never heard him so loud, Mom.
LINDA Well, come around more often; you'll hear him. *She sits down at the table and mends the lining of Willy's jacket.*
BIFF Why didn't you ever write me about this, Mom?
LINDA How would I write to you? For over three months you had no address.
BIFF I was on the move. But you know I thought of you all the time. You know that, don't you, pal?
LINDA I know, dear, I know. But he likes to have a letter. Just to know that there's still a possibility for better things.
BIFF He's not like this all the time, is he?
LINDA It's when you come home he's always the worst.
BIFF When I come home?
LINDA When you write you're coming, he's all smiles, and talks about the future, and—he's just wonderful. And then the closer you seem to come, the more shaky he gets, and then, by the time you get here, he's arguing, and he seems angry at you. I think it's just that maybe he can't bring himself to—open up to you. Why are you so hateful to each other? Why is that?
BIFF, *evasively* I'm not hateful, Mom.
LINDA But you no sooner come in the door than you're fighting!
BIFF I don't know why. I mean to change. I'm tryin', Mom, you understand?
LINDA Are you home to stay now?
BIFF I don't know. I want to look around, see what's doin'.
LINDA Biff, you can't look around all your life, can you?
BIFF I just can't take hold, Mom. I can't take hold of some kind of a life.
LINDA Biff, a man is not a bird, to come and go with the springtime.
BIFF Your hair . . . *He touches her hair.* Your hair got so gray.
LINDA Oh, it's been gray since you were in high school. I just stopped dyeing it, that's all.
BIFF Dye it again, will ya? I don't want my pal looking old. *He smiles.*
LINDA You're such a boy! You think you can go away for a year and . . . You've got to get it into your head now that one day you'll knock on this door and there'll be strange people here—
BIFF What are you talking about? You're not even sixty, Mom.
LINDA But what about your father?
BIFF, *lamely* Well, I meant him too.
HAPPY He admires Pop.
LINDA Biff, dear, if you don't have any feeling for him, then you can't have any feeling for me.
BIFF Sure I can, Mom.
LINDA No. You can't just come to see me, because I love him. *With a threat, but only a threat, of tears:* He's the dearest man in the world to me, and I won't have anyone making him feel unwanted and low and blue. You've got to make up your mind now, darling, there's no leeway any more. Either he's your father and you pay him that respect, or else you're not to come here. I know he's not easy to get along with—nobody knows that better than me—but . . .
WILLY, *from the left, with a laugh* Hey, hey, Biffo!
BIFF, *starting to go out after Willy* What the hell is the matter with him? *Happy stops him.*
LINDA Don't—don't go near him!
BIFF Stop making excuses for him! He always, always wiped the floor with you. Never had an ounce of respect for you.
HAPPY He's always had respect for—
BIFF What the hell do you know about it?
HAPPY, *surlily* Just don't call him crazy!
BIFF He's got no character—Charley wouldn't do this. Not in his own house—spewing out that vomit from his mind.
HAPPY Charley never had to cope with what he's got to.
BIFF People are worse off than Willy Loman. Believe me, I've seen them!

LINDA Then make Charley your father, Biff. You can't do that, can you? I don't say he's a great man. Willy Loman never made a lot of money. His name was never in the paper. He's not the finest character that ever lived. But he's a human being, and a terrible thing is happening to him. So attention must be paid. He's not to be allowed to fall into his grave like an old dog. Attention, attention must be finally paid to such a person. You called him crazy—

BIFF I didn't mean—

LINDA No, a lot of people think he's lost his —balance. But you don't have to be very smart to know what his trouble is. The man is exhausted.

HAPPY Sure!

LINDA A small man can be just as exhausted as a great man. He works for a company thirty-six years this March, opens up unheard-of territories to their trademark, and now in his old age they take his salary away.

HAPPY, *indignantly* I didn't know that, Mom.

LINDA You never asked, my dear! Now that you get your spending money someplace else you don't trouble your mind with him.

HAPPY But I gave you money last—

LINDA Christmas time, fifty dollars! To fix the hot water it cost ninety-seven fifty! For five weeks he's been on straight commission, like a beginner, an unknown!

BIFF Those ungrateful bastards!

LINDA Are they any worse than his sons? When he brought them business, when he was young, they were glad to see him. But now his old friends, the old buyers that loved him so and always found some order to hand him in a pinch—they're all dead, retired. He used to be able to make six, seven calls a day in Boston. Now he takes his valises out of the car and puts them back and takes them out again and he's exhausted. Instead of walking he talks now. He drives seven hundred miles, and when he gets there no one knows him any more, no one welcomes him. And what goes through a man's mind, driving seven hundred miles home without having earned a cent? Why shouldn't he talk to himself? Why? When he has to go to Charley and borrow fifty dollars a week and pretend to me that it's his pay? How long can that go on? How long? You see what I'm sitting here and waiting for? And you tell me he has no character? The man who never worked a day but for your benefit? When does he get the medal for that? Is this his reward—to turn around at the age of sixty-three and find his sons, who he loved better than his life, one a philandering bum—

HAPPY Mom!

LINDA That's all you are, my baby! *To Biff*: And you! What happened to the love you had for him? You were such pals! How you used to talk to him on the phone every night! How lonely he was till he could come home to you!

BIFF All right, Mom. I'll live here in my room, and I'll get a job. I'll keep away from him, that's all.

LINDA No, Biff. You can't stay here and fight all the time.

BIFF He threw me out of this house, remember that.

LINDA Why did he do that? I never knew why.

BIFF Because I know he's a fake and he doesn't like anybody around who knows!

LINDA Why a fake? In what way? What do you mean?

BIFF Just don't lay it all at my feet. It's between me and him—that's all I have to say. I'll chip in from now on. He'll settle for half my pay check. He'll be all right. I'm going to bed. *He starts for the stairs.*

LINDA He won't be all right.

BIFF, *turning on the stairs, furiously* I hate this city and I'll stay here. Now what do you want?

LINDA He's dying, Biff.

Happy turns quickly to her, shocked.

BIFF, *after a pause* Why is he dying?

LINDA He's been trying to kill himself.

BIFF, *with great horror* How?

LINDA I live from day to day.

BIFF What're you talking about?

LINDA Remember I wrote you that he smashed up the car again? In February?

BIFF Well?

LINDA The insurance inspector came. He said that they have evidence. That all these accidents in the last year—weren't—weren't—accidents.

HAPPY How can they tell that? That's a lie.

LINDA It seems there's a woman . . . *She takes a breath as*

BIFF, *sharply but contained* What woman?

LINDA, *simultaneously* . . . and this woman

LINDA What?

BIFF Nothing. Go ahead.

LINDA What did you say?

BIFF Nothing. I just said what woman?

HAPPY What about her?

LINDA Well, it seems she was walking down the road and saw his car. She says that he wasn't driving fast at all, and that he didn't skid. She says he came to that little bridge, and then deliberately smashed into the railing, and it was only the shallowness of the water that saved him.

BIFF Oh, no, he probably just fell asleep again.

LINDA I don't think he fell asleep.

BIFF Why not?

LINDA Last month . . . *With great difficulty:* Oh, boys, it's so hard to say a thing like this! He's just a big stupid man to you, but I tell you there's more good in him than in many other people. *She chokes, wipes her eyes.* I was looking for a fuse. The lights blew out, and I went down the cellar. And behind the fuse box—it happened to fall out—was a length of rubber pipe—just short.

HAPPY No kidding?

LINDA There's a little attachment on the end of it. I knew right away. And sure enough, on the bottom of the water heater there's a new little nipple on the gas pipe.

HAPPY, *angrily* That—jerk.

BIFF Did you have it taken off?

LINDA I'm—I'm ashamed to. How can I mention it to him? Every day I go down and take away that little rubber pipe. But, when he comes home, I put it back where it was. How can I insult him that way? I don't know what to do. I live from day to day, boys. I tell you, I know every thought in his mind. It sounds so old-fashioned and silly, but I tell you he put his whole life into you and you've turned your backs on him. *She is bent over in the chair, weeping, her face in her hands.* Biff, I swear to God! Biff, his life is in your hands!

HAPPY, *to Biff* How do you like that damned fool!

BIFF, *kissing her* All right, pal, all right. It's all settled now. I've been remiss. I know that, Mom. But now I'll stay, and I swear to you, I'll apply myself. *Kneeling in front of her, in a fever of self-reproach:* It's just—you see, Mom, I don't fit in business. Not that I won't try. I'll try, and I'll make good.

HAPPY Sure you will. The trouble with you in business was you never tried to please people.

BIFF I know, I—

HAPPY Like when you worked for Harrison's. Bob Harrison said you were tops, and then you go and do some damn fool thing like whistling whole songs in the elevator like a comedian.

BIFF, *against Happy* So what? I like to whistle sometimes.

HAPPY You don't raise a guy to a responsible job who whistles in the elevator!

LINDA Well, don't argue about it now.

HAPPY Like when you'd go off and swim in the middle of the day instead of taking the line around.

BIFF, *his resentment rising* Well, don't you run off? You take off sometimes, don't you? On a nice summer day?

HAPPY Yeah, but I cover myself!

LINDA Boys!

HAPPY If I'm going to take a fade the boss can call any number where I'm supposed to be and they'll swear to him that I just left. I'll tell you something that I hate to say, Biff, but in the business world some of them think you're crazy.

BIFF, *angered* Screw the business world!

HAPPY All right, screw it! Great, but cover yourself!

LINDA Hap, Hap!

BIFF I don't care what they think! They've laughed at Dad for years, and you know why?

Because we don't belong in this nuthouse of a city! We should be mixing cement on some open plain, or—or carpenters. A carpenter is allowed to whistle!

Willy walks in from the entrance of the house, at left.

WILLY Even your grandfather was better than a carpenter. *Pause. They watch him.* You never grew up. Bernard does not whistle in the elevator, I assure you.
BIFF, *as though to laugh Willy out of it* Yeah, but you do, Pop.
WILLY I never in my life whistled in an elevator! And who in the business world thinks I'm crazy?
BIFF I didn't mean it like that, Pop. Now don't make a whole thing out of it, will ya?
WILLY Go back to the West! Be a carpenter, a cowboy, enjoy yourself!
LINDA Willy, he was just saying—
WILLY I heard what he said!
HAPPY, *trying to quiet Willy* Hey, Pop, come on now . . .
WILLY, *continuing over Happy's line* They laugh at me, heh? Go to Filene's, go to the Hub, go to Slattery's, Boston. Call out the name Willy Loman and see what happens! Big shot!
BIFF All right, Pop.
WILLY Big!
BIFF All right!
WILLY Why do you always insult me?
BIFF I didn't say a word. *To Linda:* Did I say a word?
LINDA He didn't say anything, Willy.
WILLY, *going to the doorway of the livingroom* All right, good night, good night.
LINDA Willy, dear, he just decided . . .
WILLY, *to Biff* If you get tired hanging around tomorrow, paint the ceiling I put up in the livingroom.
BIFF I'm leaving early tomorrow.
HAPPY He's going to see Bill Oliver, Pop.
WILLY, *interestedly* Oliver? For what?
BIFF, *with reserve, but trying, trying* He always said he'd stake me. I'd like to go into business, so maybe I can take him up on it.
LINDA Isn't that wonderful?

WILLY Don't interrupt. What's wonderful about it? There's fifty men in the City of New York who'd stake him. *To Biff:* Sporting goods?
BIFF I guess so. I know something about it and—
WILLY He knows something about it! You know sporting goods better than Spalding, for God's sake! How much is he giving you?
BIFF I don't know, I didn't even see him yet, but—
WILLY Then what're you talkin' about?
BIFF, *getting angry* Well, all I said was I'm gonna see him, that's all!
WILLY, *turning away* Ah, you're counting your chickens again.
BIFF, *starting left for the stairs* Oh, Jesus, I'm going to sleep!
WILLY, *calling after him* Don't curse in this house!
BIFF, *turning* Since when did you get so clean?
HAPPY, *trying to stop them* Wait a . . .
WILLY Don't use that language to me! I won't have it!
HAPPY, *grabbing Biff, shouts:* Wait a minute! I got an idea. I got a feasible idea. Come here, Biff, let's talk this over now, let's talk some sense here. When I was down in Florida last time, I thought of a great idea to sell sporting goods. It just came back to me. You and I, Biff—we have a line, the Loman line. We train a couple of weeks, and put on a couple of exhibitions, see?
WILLY That's an idea!
HAPPY Wait! We form two basketball teams, see? Two water-pool teams. We play each other. It's a million dollars' worth of publicity. Two brothers, see? The Loman Brothers. Displays in the Royal Palms—all the hotels. And banners over the ring and the basketball court: "Loman Brothers." Baby, we could sell sporting goods!
WILLY That is a one-million-dollar idea!
LINDA Marvelous!
BIFF I'm in great shape as far as that's concerned.
HAPPY And the beauty of it is, Biff, it wouldn't be like a business. We'd be out playin' ball again . . .

BIFF, *enthused* Yeah, that's . . .

WILLY Million-dollar . . .

HAPPY And you wouldn't get fed up with it, Biff. It'd be the family again. There'd be the old honor, and comradeship, and if you wanted to go off for a swim or something'—well, you'd do it! Without some smart cooky gettin' up ahead of you!

WILLY Lick the world! You guys together could absolutely lick the civilized world.

BIFF I'll see Oliver tomorrow. Hap, if we could work that out . . .

LINDA Maybe things are beginning to—

WILLY, *wildly enthused, to Linda* Stop interrupting! *To Biff:* But don't wear sport jacket and slacks when you see Oliver.

BIFF No, I'll—

WILLY A business suit, and talk as little as possible, and don't crack any jokes.

BIFF He did like me. Always liked me.

LINDA He loved you!

WILLY, *to Linda* Will you stop! *To Biff:* Walk in very serious. You are not applying for a boy's job. Money is to pass. Be quiet, fine, and serious. Everybody likes a kidder, but nobody lends him money.

HAPPY I'll try to get some myself, Biff. I'm sure I can.

WILLY I see great things for you kids, I think your troubles are over. But remember, start big and you'll end big. Ask for fifteen. How much you gonna ask for?

BIFF Gee, I don't know—

WILLY And don't say "Gee." "Gee" is a boy's word. A man walking in for fifteen thousand dollars does not say "Gee!"

BIFF Ten, I think, would be top though.

WILLY Don't be so modest. You always started too low. Walk in with a big laugh. Don't look worried. Start off with a couple of your good stories to lighten things up. It's not what you say, it's how you say it—because personality always wins the day.

LINDA Oliver always thought the highest of him—

WILLY Will you let me talk?

BIFF Don't yell at her, Pop, will ya?

WILLY, *angrily* I was talking, wasn't I?

BIFF I don't like you yelling at her all the time, and I'm tellin' you, that's all.

WILLY What're you, takin' over this house?

LINDA Willy—

WILLY, *turning on her* Don't take his side all the time, goddammit!

BIFF, *furiously* Stop yelling at her!

WILLY, *suddenly pulling on his cheek, beaten down, guilt ridden:* Give my best to Bill Oliver—he may remember me. *He exits through the livingroom doorway.*

LINDA, *her voice subdued* What'd you have to start that for? *Biff turns away.* You see how sweet he was as soon as you talked hopefully? *She goes over to Biff.* Come up and say good night to him. Don't let him go to bed that way.

HAPPY Come on, Biff, let's buck him up.

LINDA Please, dear. Just say good night. It takes so little to make him happy. Come. *She goes through the livingroom doorway, calling upstairs from within the livingroom:* Your pajamas are hanging in the bathroom, Willy!

HAPPY, *looking toward where Linda went out* What a woman! They broke the mold when they made her. You know that, Biff?

BIFF He's off salary. My God, working on commission!

HAPPY Well, let's face it: He's no hot-shot selling man. Except that sometimes, you have to admit, he's a sweet personality.

BIFF, *deciding* Lend me ten bucks, will ya? I want to buy some new ties.

HAPPY I'll take you to a place I know. Beautiful stuff. Wear one of my striped shirts tomorrow.

BIFF She got gray. Mom got awful old. Gee, I'm gonna go in to Oliver tomorrow and knock him for a—

HAPPY Come on up. Tell that to Dad. Let's give him a whirl. Come on.

BIFF, *steamed up* You know, with ten thousand bucks, boy!

HAPPY, *as they go into the livingroom* That's the talk, Biff, that's the first time I've heard the old confidence out of you! *From within the livingroom, fading off:* You're gonna live with me, kid, and any babe you want just say the word . . . *The last lines are hardly heard. They are mounting the stairs to their parents' bedroom.*

LINDA, *entering her bedroom and addressing Willy, who is in the bathroom. She is straightening the bed for him* Can you do anything about the shower? It drips.

WILLY, *from the bathroom* All of a sudden everything falls to pieces! Goddam plumbing, oughta be sued, those people. I hardly finished putting it in and the thing . . . *His words rumble off.*

LINDA I'm just wondering if Oliver will remember him. You think he might?

WILLY, *coming out of the bathroom in his pajamas:* Remember him? What's the matter with you, you crazy? If he'd've stayed with Oliver he'd be on top by now! Wait'll Oliver gets a look at him. You don't know the average caliber any more. The average young man today—*he is getting into bed*—is got a caliber of zero. Greatest thing in the world for him was to bum around.

Biff and Happy enter the bedroom. Slight pause.

WILLY, *stops short, looking at Biff* Glad to hear it, boy.

HAPPY He wanted to say good night to you, sport.

WILLY, *to Biff* Yeah. Knock him dead, boy. What'd you want to tell me?

BIFF Just take it easy, Pop. Good night. *He turns to go.*

WILLY, *unable to resist* And if anything falls off the desk while you're talking to him—like a package or something—don't pick it up. They have office boys for that.

LINDA I'll make a big breakfast—

WILLY Will you let me finish? *To Biff:* Tell him you were in the business in the West. Not farm work.

BIFF All right, Dad.

LINDA I think everything—

WILLY, *going right through her speech* And don't undersell yourself. No less than fifteen thousand dollars.

BIFF, *unable to bear him* Okay. Good night, Mom. *He starts moving.*

WILLY Because you got a greatness in you, Biff, remember that. You got all kinds a greatness . . . *He lies back, exhausted. Biff walks out.*

LINDA, *calling after Biff* Sleep well, darling!

HAPPY I'm gonna get married, Mom. I wanted to tell you.

LINDA Go to sleep, dear.

HAPPY, *going* I just wanted to tell you.

WILLY Keep up the good work. *Happy exits.* God . . . remember that Ebbets Field game? The championship of the city?

LINDA Just rest. Should I sing to you?

WILLY Yeah. Sing to me. *Linda hums a soft lullaby.* When that team came out—he was the tallest, remember?

LINDA Oh, yes. And in gold.

Biff enters the darkened kitchen, takes a cigarette, and leaves the house. He comes downstage into a golden pool of light. He smokes, staring at the night.

WILLY Like a young god. Hercules—something like that. And the sun, the sun all around him. Remember how he waved to me? Right up from the field, with the representatives of three colleges standing by? And the buyers I brought, and the cheers when he came out—Loman, Loman, Loman! God Almighty, he'll be great yet. A star like that, magnificent, can never really fade away!

The light on Willy is fading. The gas heater begins to glow through the kitchen wall, near the stairs, a blue flame beneath red coils.

LINDA, *timidly* Willy dear, what has he got against you?

WILLY I'm so tired. Don't talk any more.

Biff slowly returns to the kitchen. He stops, stares toward the heater.

LINDA Will you ask Howard to let you work in New York?

WILLY First thing in the morning. Everything'll be all right.

Biff reaches behind the heater and draws out a length of rubber tubing. He is horrified and turns his head toward Willy's room, still dimly lit, from which the strains of Linda's desperate but monotonous humming rise.

WILLY, *staring through the window into the moonlight.* Gee, look at the moon moving between the buildings!

Biff wraps the tubing around his hand and quickly goes up the stairs.

Curtain.

ACT TWO

Music is heard, gay and bright. The curtain rises as the music fades away. Willy, in shirt sleeves, is sitting at the kitchen table, sipping coffee, his hat in his lap. Linda is filling his cup when she can.

WILLY Wonderful coffee. Meal in itself.

LINDA Can I make you some eggs?

WILLY No. Take a breath.

LINDA You look so rested, dear.

WILLY I slept like a dead one. First time in months. Imagine, sleeping till ten on a Tuesday morning. Boys left nice and early, heh?

LINDA They were out of here by eight o'clock.

WILLY Good work!

LINDA It was so thrilling to see them leave together. I can't get over the shaving lotion in this house!

WILLY, *smiling* Mmm—

LINDA Biff was very changed this morning. His whole attitude seemed to be hopeful. He couldn't wait to get downtown to see Oliver.

WILLY He's heading for a change. There's no question, there simply are certain men that take longer to get—solidified. How did he dress?

LINDA His blue suit. He's so handsome in that suit. He could be a—anything in that suit!

Willy gets up from the table. Linda holds his jacket for him.

WILLY There's no question, no question at all. Gee, on the way home tonight I'd like to buy some seeds.

LINDA, *laughing* That'd be wonderful. But not enough sun gets back there. Nothing'll grow any more.

WILLY You wait, kid, before it's all over we're gonna get a little place out in the country, and I'll raise some vegetables, a couple of chickens . . .

LINDA You'll do it yet, dear.

Willy walks out of his jacket. Linda follows him.

WILLY And they'll get married, and come for a weekend. I'd build a little guest house. 'Cause I got so many fine tools, all I'd need would be a little lumber and some peace of mind.

LINDA, *joyfully* I sewed the lining . . .

WILLY I could build two guest houses, so they'd both come. Did he decide how much he's going to ask Oliver for?

LINDA, *getting him into the jacket* He didn't mention it, but I imagine ten or fifteen thousand. You going to talk to Howard today?

WILLY Yeah. I'll put it to him straight and simple. He'll just have to take me off the road.

LINDA And Willy, don't forget to ask for a little advance, because we've got the insurance premium. It's the grace period now.

WILLY That's a hundred . . . ?

LINDA A hundred and eight, sixty-eight. Because we're a little short again.

WILLY Why are we short?

LINDA Well, you had the motor job on the car . . .

WILLY That goddam Studebaker!

LINDA And you got one more payment on the refrigerator . . .

WILLY But it just broke again!

LINDA Well, it's old, dear.

WILLY I told you we should've bought a well-advertised machine. Charley bought a General Electric and it's twenty years old and it's still good, that son-of-a-bitch.

LINDA But, Willy—

WILLY Who ever heard of a Hastings refrigerator? Once in my life I would like to own something outright before it's broken! I'm always in a race with the junkyard! I just finished paying for the car and it's on its last legs. The refrigerator consumes belts like a goddam maniac. They time those things. They time them so when you finally paid for them, they're used.

LINDA, *buttoning up his jacket as he unbuttons it* All told, about two hundred dollars would carry us, dear. But that includes the last payment on the mortgage. After this payment, Willy, the house belongs to us.

WILLY It's twenty-five years!

LINDA Biff was nine years old when we bought it.

WILLY Well, that's a great thing. To weather a twenty-five year mortgage is—

LINDA It's an accomplishment.

WILLY All the cement, the lumber, the reconstruction I put in this house. There ain't a crack to be found in it any more.

LINDA Well, it served its purpose.

WILLY What purpose? Some stranger'll come along, move in, and that's that. If only Biff would take this house, and raise a family . . . *He starts to go.* Good-by, I'm late.

LINDA, *suddenly remembering* Oh, I forgot! You're supposed to meet them for dinner.

WILLY Me?

LINDA At Frank's Chop House on Forty-eighth near Sixth Avenue.

WILLY Is that so! How about you?

LINDA No, just the three of you. They're gonna blow you to a big meal!

WILLY Don't say! Who thought of that?

LINDA Biff came to me this morning, Willy, and he said, "Tell Dad, we want to blow him to a big meal." Be there six o'clock. You and your two boys are going to have dinner.

WILLY Gee whiz! That's really somethin'. I'm gonna knock Howard for a loop, kid. I'll get an advance, and I'll come home with a New York job. Goddammit, now I'm gonna do it!

LINDA Oh, that's the spirit, Willy!

WILLY I will never get behind a wheel the rest of my life!

LINDA It's changing, Willy, I can feel it changing!

WILLY Beyond a question. G'by, I'm late. *He starts to go again.*

LINDA, *calling after him as she runs to the kitchen table for a handkerchief* You got your glasses?

WILLY, *feels for them, then comes back in* Yeah, yeah, got my glasses.

LINDA, *giving him the handkerchief* And a handkerchief.

WILLY Yeah, handkerchief.

LINDA And your saccharine?

WILLY Yeah, my saccharine.

LINDA Be careful on the subway stairs.

She kisses him, and a silk stocking is seen hanging from her hand. Willy notices it.

WILLY Will you stop mending stockings? At least while I'm in the house. It gets me nervous. I can't tell you. Please.

Linda hides the stocking in her hand as she follows Willy across the forestage in front of the house.

LINDA Remember, Frank's Chop House.

WILLY, *passing the apron* Maybe beets would grow out there.

LINDA, *laughing* But you tried so many times.

WILLY Yeah. Well, don't work hard today. *He disappears around the right corner of the house.*

LINDA Be careful!

As Willy vanishes, Linda waves to him. Suddenly the phone rings. She runs across the stage and into the kitchen and lifts it.

LINDA Hello? Oh, Biff! I'm so glad you called, I just . . . Yes, sure, I just told him. Yes, he'll be there for dinner at six o'clock, I didn't forget. Listen, I was just dying to tell you. You know that little rubber pipe I told you about? That he connected to the gas heater? I finally decided to go down cellar and destroy it. But it's gone! Imagine? He took it away himself, it isn't there! *She listens.* When? Oh, then you took it. Oh—nothing, it's just that I'd hoped he'd taken it away himself. Oh, I'm not worried, darling, because this morning he left in such high spirits, it was like the old days! I'm not afraid any more. Did Mr. Oliver see you? . . . Well, you wait there then. And make a nice impression on him, darling. Just don't perspire too much before you see him. And have a nice time with Dad. He may have big news too! . . . That's right, a New York job. And be sweet to him tonight, dear. Be loving to him. Because he's only a little boat looking for a harbor. *She is trembling with sorrow and joy.* Oh, that's wonderful, Biff, you'll save his life. Thanks, darling. Just put your arm around him when he comes into the restaurant. Give him a smile. That's the boy . . . Good-by, dear. . . . You got your comb? . . . That's fine. Good-bye, Biff dear.

In the middle of her speech, Howard Wagner, thirty-six, wheels on a small typewriter table on which is a wire-recording machine and proceeds to plug it in. This is on the left forestage. Light slowly fades on Linda as it rises on Howard. Howard is intent on threading the machine and only glances over his shoulder as Willy appears.

WILLY   Pst! Pst!
HOWARD   Hello, Willy, come in.
WILLY   Like to have a little talk with you, Howard.
HOWARD   Sorry to keep you waiting. I'll be with you in a minute.
WILLY   What's that, Howard?
HOWARD   Didn't you ever see one of these? Wire recorder.
WILLY   Oh. Can we talk a minute?
HOWARD   Records things. Just got delivery yesterday. Been driving me crazy, the most terrific machine I ever saw in my life. I was up all night with it.
WILLY   What do you do with it?
HOWARD   I bought it for dictation, but you can do anything with it. Listen to this. I had it home last night. Listen to what I picked up. The first one is my daughter. Get this. *He flicks the switch and "Roll Out the Barrel" is heard being whistled.* Listen to that kid whistle.
WILLY   That is lifelike, isn't it?
HOWARD   Seven years old. Get that tone.
WILLY   Ts, ts. Like to ask a little favor if you . . .

The whistling breaks off, and the voice of Howard's daughter is heard.

HIS DAUGHTER   "Now you, Daddy."
HOWARD   She's crazy for me! *Again the same song is whistled.* That's me! Ha! *He winks.*
WILLY   You're very good!

The whistling breaks off again. The machine runs silent for a moment.

HOWARD   Sh! Get this now, this is my son.
HIS SON   "The capital of Alabama is Montgomery; the capital of Arizona is Phoenix; the capital of Arkansas is Little Rock; the capital of California is Sacramento . . ." *and on, and on.*
HOWARD, *holding up five fingers*   Five years old, Willy!
WILLY   He'll make an announcer some day!
HIS SON, *continuing*   "The capital . . ."
HOWARD   Get that—alphabetical order! *The machine breaks off suddenly.* Wait a minute. The maid kicked the plug out.
WILLY   It certainly is a—
HOWARD   Sh, for God's sake!
HIS SON   "It's nine o'clock, Bulova watch time. So I have to go to sleep."
WILLY   That really is—
HOWARD   Wait a minute! The next is my wife.

They wait.

HOWARD'S VOICE   "Go on, say something." *Pause.* "Well, you gonna talk?"
HIS WIFE   "I can't think of anything."
HOWARD'S VOICE   "Well, talk—it's turning."
HIS WIFE, *shyly, beaten*   "Hello." *Silence.* "Oh, Howard, I can't talk into this . . ."
HOWARD, *snapping the machine off*   That was my wife.
WILLY   That is a wonderful machine. Can we—
HOWARD   I tell you, Willy, I'm gonna take my camera, and my bandsaw, and all my hobbies, and out they go. This is the most fascinating relaxation I ever found.
WILLY   I think I'll get one myself.
HOWARD   Sure, they're only a hundred and a half. You can't do without it. Suppose you wanna hear Jack Benny, see? But you can't be at home at that hour. So you tell the maid to turn the radio on when Jack Benny comes on, and this automatically goes on with the radio . . .
WILLY   And when you come home you . . .
HOWARD   You can come home twelve o'clock, one o'clock, any time you like, and you get yourself a Coke and sit yourself down, throw the switch, and there's Jack Benny's program in the middle of the night!

WILLY I'm definitely going to get one. Because lots of times I'm on the road, and I think to myself, what I must be missing on the radio!
HOWARD Don't you have a radio in the car?
WILLY Well, yeah, but who ever thinks of turning it on?
HOWARD Say, aren't you supposed to be in Boston?
WILLY That's what I want to talk to you about, Howard. You got a minute? *He draws a chair in from the wing.*
HOWARD What happened? What're you doing here?
WILLY Well . . .
HOWARD You didn't crack up again, did you?
WILLY Oh, no. No . . .
HOWARD Geez, you had me worried there for a minute. What's the trouble?
WILLY Well, tell you the truth, Howard. I've come to the decision that I'd rather not travel any more.
HOWARD Not travel! Well, what'll you do?
WILLY Remember, Christmas time, when you had the party here? You said you'd try to think of some spot for me here in town.
HOWARD With us?
WILLY Well, sure.
HOWARD Oh, yeah, yeah. I remember. Well, I couldn't think of anything for you, Willy.
WILLY I tell ya, Howard. The kids are all grown up, y'know. I don't need much any more. If I could take home—well, sixty-five dollars a week, I could swing it.
HOWARD Yeah, but Willy, see I—
WILLY I tell ya why, Howard. Speaking frankly and between the two of us, y'know—I'm just a little tired.
HOWARD Oh, I could understand that, Willy. But you're a road man, Willy, and we do a road business. We've only got a half-dozen salesmen on the floor here.
WILLY God knows, Howard, I never asked a favor of any man. But I was with the firm when your father used to carry you in here in his arms.
HOWARD I know that, Willy, but—
WILLY Your father came to me the day you were born and asked me what I thought of the name of Howard, may he rest in peace.
HOWARD I appreciate that, Willy, but there just is no spot here for you. If I had a spot I'd slam you right in, but I just don't have a single solitary spot.

He looks for his lighter. Willy has picked it up and gives it to him. Pause.

WILLY, *with increasing anger* Howard, all I need to set my table is fifty dollars a week.
HOWARD But where am I going to put you, kid?
WILLY Look, it isn't a question of whether I can sell merchandise, is it?
HOWARD No, but it's a business, kid, and everybody's gotta pull his own weight.
WILLY, *desperately* Just let me tell you a story, Howard—
HOWARD 'Cause you gotta admit, business is business.
WILLY, *angrily* Business is definitely business, but just listen for a minute. You don't understand this. When I was a boy—eighteen, nineteen—I was already on the road. And there was a question in my mind as to whether selling had a future for me. Because in those days I had a yearning to go to Alaska. See, there were three gold strikes in one month in Alaska, and I felt like going out. Just for the ride, you might say.
HOWARD, *barely interested* Don't say.
WILLY Oh, yeah, my father lived many years in Alaska. He was an adventurous man. We've got quite a little streak of self-reliance in our family. I thought I'd go out with my older brother and try to locate him, and maybe settle in the North with the old man. And I was almost decided to go, when I met a salesman in the Parker House. His name was Dave Singleman. And he was eighty-four years old, and he'd drummed merchandise in thirty-one states. And old Dave, he'd go up to his room, y'understand, put on his green velvet slippers—I'll never forget—and pick up his phone and call the buyers, and without ever leaving his room, at the age of eighty-four, he made his living. And when I saw that, I realized that selling was the greatest career a man could want. 'Cause what could be more satisfying than to be

able to go, at the age of eighty-four, into twenty or thirty different cities, and pick up a phone, and be remembered and loved and helped by so many different people? Do you know? when he died—and by the way he died the death of a salesman, in his green velvet slippers in the smoker of the New York, New Haven and Hartford, going into Boston—when he died, hundreds of salesmen and buyers were at his funeral. Things were sad on a lotta trains for months after that. *He stands up. Howard has not looked at him.* In those days there was personality in it, Howard. There was respect, and comradeship, and gratitude in it. Today, it's all cut and dried, and there's no chance for bringing friendship to bear—or personality. You see what I mean? They don't know me any more.

HOWARD, *moving away, to the right* That's just the thing, Willy.

WILLY If I had forty dollars a week—that's all I'd need. Forty dollars, Howard.

HOWARD Kid, I can't take blood from a stone, I—

WILLY, *desperation is on him now* Howard, the year Al Smith was nominated, your father came to me and—

HOWARD, *starting to go off* I've got to see some people, kid.

WILLY, *stopping him* I'm talking about your father! There were promises made across this desk! You mustn't tell me you've got people to see—I put thirty-four years into this firm, Howard, and now I can't pay my insurance! You can't eat the orange and throw the peel away—a man is not a piece of fruit! *After a pause:* Now pay attention. Your father—in 1928 I had a big year. I averaged a hundred and seventy dollars a week in commissions.

HOWARD, *impatiently* Now, Willy, you never averaged—

WILLY, *banging his hand on the desk* I averaged a hundred and seventy dollars a week in the year of 1928! And your father came to me—or rather, I was in the office here—it was right over this desk—and he put his hand on my shoulder—

HOWARD, *getting up* You'll have to excuse us, Willy, I gotta see some people. Pull yourself together. *Going out:* I'll be back in a little while.

On Howard's exit, the light on his chair grows very bright and strange.

WILLY Pull myself together! What the hell did I say to him? My God, I was yelling at him! How could I! *Willy breaks off, staring at the light, which occupies the chair, animating it. He approaches this chair, standing across the desk from it.* Frank, Frank, don't you remember what you told me that time? How you put your hand on my shoulder, and Frank . . . *He leans on the desk and as he speaks the dead man's name he accidentally switches on the recorder, and instantly.*

HOWARD'S SON ". . . of New York is Albany. The capital of Ohio is Cincinnati, the capital of Rhode Island is . . ." *The recitation continues.*

WILLY, *leaping away with fright, shouting* Ha! Howard! Howard! Howard!

HOWARD, *rushing in* What happened?

WILLY, *pointing at the machine, which continues nasally, childishly, with the capital cities* Shut it off! Shut it off!

HOWARD, *pulling the plug out* Look, Willy . . .

WILLY, *pressing his hands to his eyes* I gotta get myself some coffee. I'll get some coffee . . .

Willy starts to walk out. Howard stops him.

HOWARD, *rolling up the cord* Willy, look . . .
WILLY I'll go to Boston.
HOWARD Willy, you can't go to Boston for us.
WILLY Why can't I go?
HOWARD I don't want you to represent us. I've been meaning to tell you for a long time now.
WILLY Howard, are you firing me?
HOWARD I think you need a good long rest, Willy.
WILLY Howard—
HOWARD And when you feel better, come back, and we'll see if we can work something out.

WILLY But I gotta earn money, Howard. I'm in no position to—

HOWARD Where are your sons? Why don't your sons give you a hand?

WILLY They're working on a very big deal.

HOWARD This is no time for false pride, Willy. You go to your sons and you tell them that you're tired. You've got two great boys, haven't you?

WILLY Oh, no question, no question, but in the meantime . . .

HOWARD Then that's that, heh?

WILLY All right, I'll go to Boston tomorrow.

HOWARD No, no.

WILLY I can't throw myself on my sons. I'm not a cripple!

HOWARD Look, kid, I'm busy this morning.

WILLY, *grasping Howard's arm* Howard, you've got to let me go to Boston!

HOWARD, *hard, keeping himself under control* I've got a line of people to see this morning. Sit down, take five minutes, and pull yourself together, and then go home, will ya? I need the office, Willy. *He starts to go, turns, remembering the recorder, starts to push off the table holding the recorder.* Oh, yeah. Whenever you can this week, stop by and drop off the samples. You'll feel better, Willy, and then come back and we'll talk. Pull yourself together, kid, there's people outside.

Howard exits, pushing the table off left. Willy stares into space, exhausted. Now the music is heard—Ben's music—first distantly, then closer, closer. As Willy speaks, Ben enters from the right. He carries valise and umbrella.

WILLY Oh, Ben, how did you do it? What is the answer? Did you wind up the Alaska deal already?

BEN Doesn't take much time if you know what you're doing. Just a short business trip. Boarding ship in an hour. Wanted to say good-by.

WILLY Ben, I've got to talk to you.

BEN, *glancing at his watch* Haven't the time, William.

WILLY, *crossing the apron to Ben* Ben, nothing's working out. I don't know what to do.

BEN Now, look here, William. I've bought timberland in Alaska and I need a man to look after things for me.

WILLY God, timberland! Me and my boys in those grand outdoors!

BEN You've a new continent at your doorstep, William. Get out of these cities, they're full of talk and time payments and courts of law. Screw on your fists and you can fight for a fortune up there.

WILLY Yes, yes! Linda, Linda!

Linda enters as of old, with the wash.

LINDA Oh, you're back?

BEN I haven't much time.

WILLY No, wait! Linda, he's got a proposition for me in Alaska.

LINDA But you've got— *To Ben:* He's got a beautiful job here.

WILLY But in Alaska, kid, I could—

LINDA You're doing well enough, Willy!

BEN, *to Linda* Enough for what, my dear?

LINDA, *frightened of Ben and angry at him* Don't say those things to him! Enough to be happy right here, right now. *To Willy, while Ben laughs:* Why must everybody conquer the world? You're well liked, and the boys love you, and someday—*to Ben*—why, old man Wagner told him just the other day that if he keeps it up he'll be a member of the firm, didn't he, Willy?

WILLY Sure, sure. I am building something with this firm, Ben, and if a man is building something he must be on the right track, mustn't he?

BEN What are you building? Lay your hand on it. Where is it?

WILLY, *hesitantly* That's true, Linda, there's nothing.

LINDA Why? *To Ben:* There's a man eighty-four years old—

WILLY That's right, Ben, that's right. When I look at that man I say, what is there to worry about?

BEN Bah!

WILLY It's true, Ben. All he has to do is go into any city, pick up the phone, and he's making his living and you know why?

BEN, *picking up his valise* I've got to go.

WILLY, *holding Ben back* Look at this boy!

Biff, in his high school sweater, enters carrying suitcase. Happy carries Biff's shoulder guards, gold helmet, and football pants.

WILLY Without a penny to his name, three great universities are begging for him, and from there the sky's the limit, because it's not what you do, Ben. It's who you know and the smile on your face! It's contacts, Ben, contacts! The whole wealth of Alaska passes over the lunch table at the Commodore Hotel, and that's the wonder, the wonder of this country, that a man can end with diamonds here on the basis of being liked. *He turns to Biff.* And that's why when you get out on that field today it's important. Because thousands of people will be rooting for you and loving you. *To Ben, who has again begun to leave:* And Ben! when he walks into a business office his name will sound out like a bell and all the doors will open to him! I've seen it, Ben, I've seen it a thousand times! You can't feel it with your hand like timber, but it's there!

BEN Good-by, William.

WILLY Ben, am I right? Don't you think I'm right? I value your advice.

BEN There's a new continent at your doorstep, William. You could walk out rich. Rich! *He is gone.*

WILLY We'll do it here, Ben! You hear me? We're gonna do it here!

Young Bernard rushes in. The gay music of the Boys is heard.

BERNARD Oh, gee, I was afraid you left already!

WILLY Why? What time is it?

BERNARD It's half-past one!

WILLY Well, come on, everybody! Ebbets Field next stop! Where's the pennants? *He rushes through the wall-line of the kitchen and out into the livingroom.*

LINDA, *to Biff* Did you pack fresh underwear?

BIFF, *who has been limbering up* I want to go!

BERNARD Biff, I'm carrying your helmet, ain't I?

HAPPY No, I'm carrying the helmet.

BERNARD Oh, Biff, you promised me.

HAPPY I'm carrying the helmet.

BERNARD How am I going to get in the locker room?

LINDA Let him carry the shoulder guards. *She puts her coat and hat on in the kitchen.*

BERNARD Can I, Biff? 'Cause I told everybody I'm going to be in the locker room.

HAPPY In Ebbets Field it's the clubhouse.

BERNARD I meant the clubhouse. Biff!

HAPPY Biff!

BIFF, *grandly, after a slight pause* Let him carry the shoulder guards.

HAPPY, *as he gives Bernard the shoulder guards* Stay close to us now.

Willy rushes in with the pennants.

WILLY, *handing them out* Everybody wave when Biff comes out on the field. *Happy and Bernard run off.* You set now, boy?

The music has died away.

BIFF Ready to go, Pop. Every muscle is ready.

WILLY, *at the edge of the apron* You realize what this means?

BIFF That's right, Pop.

WILLY, *feeling Biff's muscles* You're comin' home this afternoon captain of the All-Scholastic Championship Team of the City of New York.

BIFF I got it, Pop. And remember, pal, when I take off my helmet, that touchdown is for you.

WILLY Let's go! *He is starting out, with his arm around Biff, when Charley enters, as of old, in knickers.* I got no room for you, Charley.

CHARLEY Room? For what?

WILLY In the car.

CHARLEY You goin' for a ride? I wanted to shoot some casino.

WILLY, *furiously* Casino! *Incredulously:* Don't you realize what today is?

LINDA Oh, he knows, Willy. He's just kidding you.

WILLY That's nothing to kid about!

CHARLEY No, Linda, what's goin' on?

LINDA He's playing in Ebbets Field.

CHARLEY Baseball in this weather?

WILLY Don't talk to him. Come on, come on! *He is pushing them out.*

CHARLEY Wait a minute, didn't you hear the news?

WILLY What?

CHARLEY Don't you listen to the radio? Ebbets Field just blew up.

WILLY You go to hell! *Charley laughs. Pushing them out:* Come on, come on! We're late.

CHARLEY, *as they go* Knock a homer, Biff, knock a homer!

WILLY, *the last to leave, turning to Charley* I don't think that was funny, Charley. This is the greatest day of his life.

CHARLEY Willy, when are you going to grow up?

WILLY Yeah, heh? When this game is over, Charley, you'll be laughing out of the other side of your face. They'll be calling him another Red Grange. Twenty-five thousand a year.

CHARLEY, *kidding* Is that so?

WILLY Yeah, that's so.

CHARLEY Well, then, I'm sorry, Willy. But tell me something.

WILLY What?

CHARLEY Who is Red Grange?

WILLY Put up your hands. Goddam you, put up your hands!

Charley, chuckling, shakes his head and walks away, around the left corner of the stage. Willy follows him. The music rises to a mocking frenzy.

WILLY Who the hell do you think you are, better than everybody else? You don't know everything, you big, ignorant, stupid . . . Put up your hands!

Light rises, on the right side of the forestage, on a small table in the reception room of Charley's office. Traffic sounds are heard. Bernard, now mature, sits whistling to himself. A pair of tennis rackets and an overnight bag are on the floor beside him.

WILLY, *offstage* What are you walking away for? Don't walk away! If you're going to say something say it to my face! I know you laugh at me behind my back. You'll laugh out of the other side of your goddam face after this game. Touchdown! Touchdown! Eighty thousand people! Touchdown! Right between the goal posts.

Bernard is a quiet, earnest, but self-assured young man. Willy's voice is coming from right upstage now. Bernard lowers his feet off the table and listens. Jenny, his father's secretary, enters.

JENNY, *distressed* Say, Bernard, will you go out in the hall?

BERNARD What is that noise? Who is it?

JENNY Mr. Loman. He just got off the elevator.

BERNARD, *getting up* Who's he arguing with?

JENNY Nobody. There's nobody with him. I can't deal with him any more, and your father gets all upset everytime he comes. I've got a lot of typing to do, and your father's waiting to sign it. Will you see him?

WILLY, *entering* Touchdown! Touch— *He sees Jenny.* Jenny, Jenny, good to see you. How're ya? Workin'? Or still honest?

JENNY Fine. How've you been feeling?

WILLY Not much any more, Jenny. Ha, ha! *He is surprised to see the rackets.*

BERNARD Hello, Uncle Willy.

WILLY, *almost shocked* Bernard! Well, look who's here! *He comes quickly, guiltily, to Bernard and warmly shakes his hand.*

BERNARD How are you? Good to see you.

WILLY What are you doing here?

BERNARD Oh, just stopped by to see Pop. Get off my feet till my train leaves. I'm going to Washington in a few minutes.

WILLY Is he in?

BERNARD Yes, he's in his office with the accountant. Sit down.

WILLY, *sitting down* What're you going to do in Washington?

BERNARD Oh, just a case I've got there, Willy.

WILLY That so? *Indicating the rackets:* You going to play tennis there?

BERNARD I'm staying with a friend who's got a court.

WILLY Don't say. His own tennis court. Must be fine people, I bet.

BERNARD They are, very nice. Dad tells me Biff's in town.

WILLY, *with a big smile* Yeah, Biff's in. Working on a very big deal, Bernard.

BERNARD What's Biff doing?

WILLY Well, he's been doing very big things in the West. But he decided to establish himself here. Very big. We're having dinner. Did I hear your wife had a boy?

BERNARD That's right. Our second.

WILLY Two boys! What do you know!

BERNARD What kind of a deal has Biff got?

WILLY Well, Bill Oliver—very big sporting-goods man—he wants Biff very badly. Called him in from the West. Long distance, carte blanche, special deliveries. Your friends have their own private tennis court?

BERNARD You still with the old firm, Willy?

WILLY, *after a pause* I'm—I'm overjoyed to see how you made the grade, Bernard, overjoyed. It's an encouraging thing to see a young man really—really— Looks very good for Biff—very— *He breaks off, then:* Bernard— *He is so full of emotion, he breaks off again.*

BERNARD What is it, Willy?

WILLY, *small and alone* What—what's the secret?

BERNARD What secret?

WILLY How—how did you? Why didn't he ever catch on?

BERNARD I wouldn't know that, Willy.

WILLY, *confidentially, desperately* You were his friend, his boyhood friend. There's something I don't understand about it. His life ended after that Ebbets Field game. From the age of seventeen nothing good ever happened to him.

BERNARD He never trained himself for anything.

WILLY But he did, he did. After high school he took so many correspondence courses. Radio mechanics; television; God knows what, and never made the slightest mark.

BERNARD, *taking off his glasses* Willy, do you want to talk candidly?

WILLY, *rising, faces Bernard* I regard you as a very brilliant man, Bernard. I value your advice.

BERNARD Oh, the hell with the advice, Willy. I couldn't advise you. There's just one thing I've always wanted to ask you. When he was supposed to graduate, and the math teacher flunked him—

WILLY Oh, that son-of-a-bitch ruined his life.

BERNARD Yeah, but, Willy, all he had to do was go to summer school and make up that subject.

WILLY That's right, that's right.

BERNARD Did you tell him not to go to summer school?

WILLY Me? I begged him to go. I ordered him to go!

BERNARD Then why wouldn't he go?

WILLY Why? Why? Bernard, that question has been trailing me like a ghost for the last fifteen years. He flunked the subject, and laid down and died like a hammer hit him!

BERNARD Take it easy, kid.

WILLY Let me talk to you—I got nobody to talk to. Bernard, Bernard, was it my fault? Y'see? It keeps going around in my mind, maybe I did something to him. I got nothing to give him.

BERNARD Don't take it so hard.

WILLY Why did he lay down? What is the story there? You were his friend!

BERNARD Willy, I remember, it was June, and our grades came out. And he'd flunked math.

WILLY That son-of-a-bitch!

BERNARD No, it wasn't right then. Biff just got very angry, I remember, and he was ready to enroll in summer school.

WILLY, *surprised* He was?

BERNARD He wasn't beaten by it at all. But then, Willy, he disappeared from the block for almost a month. And I got the idea that he'd gone up to New England to see you. Did he have a talk with you then?

Willy stares in silence.

BERNARD Willy?

WILLY, *with a strong edge of resentment in his voice* Yeah, he came to Boston. What about it?

BERNARD Well, just that when he came back—I'll never forget this, it always mystifies me. Because I'd thought so well of Biff, even though he'd always taken advantage of me. I loved him, Willy, y'know? And he came back after that month and took his sneakers—remember those sneakers with "University of Virginia" printed on them? He was so proud of those, wore them every day. And he took them down in the cellar, and burned them up in the furnace. We had a fist fight. It lasted at least half an hour. Just the two of us, punching each other down the cellar, and crying right through it. I've often thought of how strange it was that I knew he'd given up his life. What happened in Boston, Willy?

Willy looks at him as at an intruder.

BERNARD I just bring it up because you asked me.
WILLY, *angrily* Nothing. What do you mean, "What happened?" What's that got to do with anything?
BERNARD Well, don't get sore.
WILLY What are you trying to do, blame it on me? If a boy lays down is that my fault?
BERNARD Now, Willy, don't get—
WILLY Well, don't—don't talk to me that way! What does that mean, "What happened?"

Charley enters. He is in his vest, and he carries a bottle of bourbon.

CHARLEY Hey, you're going to miss that train. *He waves the bottle.*
BERNARD Yeah, I'm going. *He takes the bottle.* Thanks, Pop. *He picks up his rackets and bag.* Good-by, Willy, and don't worry about it. You know, "If at first you don't succeed . . ."
WILLY Yes, I believe in that.
BERNARD But sometimes, Willy, it's better for a man just to walk away.
WILLY Walk away?
BERNARD That's right.
WILLY But if you can't walk away?
BERNARD, *after a slight pause* I guess that's when it's tough. *Extending his hand:* Good-by, Willy.
WILLY, *shaking Bernard's hand* Good-by, boy.
CHARLEY, *an arm on Bernard's shoulder* How do you like this kid? Gonna argue a case in front of the Supreme Court.
BERNARD, *protesting* Pop!
WILLY, *genuinely shocked, pained, and happy* No! The Supreme Court!
BERNARD I gotta run. 'By, Dad!
CHARLEY Knock 'em dead, Bernard!

Bernard goes off.

WILLY, *as Charley takes out his wallet* The Supreme Court! And he didn't even mention it!
CHARLEY, *counting out money on the desk* He don't have to—he's gonna do it.
WILLY And you never told him what to do, did you? You never took any interest in him.
CHARLEY My salvation is that I never took any interest in anything. There's some money—fifty dollars. I got an accountant inside.
WILLY Charley, look . . . *With difficulty:* I got my insurance to pay. If you can manage it—I need a hundred and ten dollars.

Charley doesn't reply for a moment; merely stops moving.

WILLY I'd draw it from my bank but Linda would know, and I . . .
CHARLEY Sit down, Willy.
WILLY, *moving toward the chair* I'm keeping an account of everything, remember. I'll pay every penny back. *He sits.*
CHARLEY Now listen to me, Willy.
WILLY I want you to know I appreciate . . .
CHARLEY, *sitting down on the table* Willy, what're you doin'? What the hell is goin' on in your head?
WILLY Why? I'm simply . . .
CHARLEY I offered you a job. You can make fifty dollars a week. And I won't send you on the road.
WILLY I've got a job.
CHARLEY Without pay? What kind of a job is a job without pay? *He rises.* Now, look, kid, enough is enough. I'm no genius but I know when I'm being insulted.
WILLY Insulted!
CHARLEY Why don't you want to work for me?
WILLY What's the matter with you? I've got a job.
CHARLEY Then what're you walkin' in here every week for?
WILLY, *getting up* Well, if you don't want me to walk in here—
CHARLEY I am offering you a job.
WILLY I don't want your goddam job!
CHARLEY When the hell are you going to grow up?
WILLY, *furiously* You big ignoramus, if you say that to me again I'll rap you one! I don't care how big you are! *He's ready to fight.*

Pause.

CHARLEY, *kindly, going to him* How much do you need, Willy?
WILLY Charley, I'm strapped, I'm strapped. I don't know what to do. I was just fired.
CHARLEY Howard fired you?
WILLY That snotnose. Imagine that? I named him. I named him Howard.
CHARLEY Willy, when're you gonna realize that them things don't mean anything? You named him Howard, but you can't sell that. The only thing you got in this world is what you can sell. And the funny thing is that you're a salesman, and you don't know that.
WILLY I've always tried to think otherwise, I guess. I always felt that if a man was impressive, and well liked, that nothing—
CHARLEY Why must everybody like you? Who liked J. P. Morgan? Was he impressive? In a Turkish bath he'd look like a butcher. But with his pockets on he was very well liked. Now listen, Willy, I know you don't like me, and nobody can say I'm in love with you, but I'll give you a job because—just for the hell of it, put it that way. Now what do you say?
WILLY I—I just can't work for you, Charley.
CHARLEY What're you, jealous of me?
WILLY I can't work for you, that's all, don't ask me why.
CHARLEY, *angered, takes out more bills* You been jealous of me all your life, you damned fool! Here, pay your insurance. *He puts the money in Willy's hand.*
WILLY I'm keeping strict accounts.
CHARLEY I've got some work to do. Take care of yourself. And pay your insurance.
WILLY, *moving to the right* Funny, y'know? After all the highways, and the trains, and the appointments, and the years, you end up worth more dead than alive.
CHARLEY Willy, nobody's worth nothin' dead. *After a slight pause:* Did you hear what I said?

Willy stands still, dreaming.

CHARLEY Willy!
WILLY Apologize to Bernard for me when you see him. I didn't mean to argue with him. He's a fine boy. They're all fine boys, and they'll end up big—all of them. Someday they'll all play tennis together. Wish me luck, Charley. He saw Bill Oliver today.
CHARLEY Good luck.
WILLY, *on the verge of tears* Charley, you're the only friend I got. Isn't that a remarkable thing? *He goes out.*
CHARLEY Jesus!

Charley stares after him a moment and follows. All light blacks out. Suddenly raucous music is heard, and a red glow rises behind the screen at right. Stanley, a young waiter, appears, carrying a table, followed by Happy, who is carrying two chairs.

STANLEY, *putting the table down* That's all right, Mr. Loman, I can handle it myself. *He turns and takes the chairs from Happy and places them at the table.*
HAPPY, *glancing around* Oh, this is better.
STANLEY Sure, in the front there you're in the middle of all kinds a noise. Whenever you got a party, Mr. Loman, you just tell me and I'll put you back here. Y'know, there's a lotta people they don't like it private, because when they go out they like to see a lotta action around them because they're sick and tired to stay in the house by theirself. But I know you, you ain't from Hackensack. You know what I mean?
HAPPY, *sitting down* So how's it coming, Stanley?
STANLEY Ah, it's a dog's life. I only wish during the war they'd a took me in the Army. I coulda been dead by now.
HAPPY My brother's back, Stanley.
STANLEY Oh, he come back, heh? From the Far West.
HAPPY Yeah, big cattle man, my brother, so treat him right. And my father's coming too.
STANLEY Oh, your father too!
HAPPY You got a couple of nice lobsters?
STANLEY Hundred per cent, big.
HAPPY I want them with the claws.
STANLEY Don't worry, I don't give you no mice. *Happy laughs.* How about some wine? It'll put a head on the meal.
HAPPY No. You remember, Stanley, that recipe I brought you from overseas? With the champagne in it?

STANLEY Oh, yeah, sure. I still got it tacked up yet in the kitchen. But that'll have to cost a buck apiece anyways.

HAPPY That's all right.

STANLEY What'd you, hit a number or somethin'?

HAPPY No, it's a little celebration. My brother is—I think he pulled off a big deal today. I think we're going into business together.

STANLEY Great! That's the best for you. Because a family business, you know what I mean?—that's the best.

HAPPY That's what I think.

STANLEY 'Cause what's the difference? Somebody steals? It's in the family. Know what I mean? *Sotto voce:* Like this bartender here. The boss is goin' crazy what kinda leak he's got in the cash register. You put it in but it don't come out.

HAPPY, *raising his head* Sh!

STANLEY What?

HAPPY You notice I wasn't lookin' right or left, was I?

STANLEY No.

HAPPY And my eyes are closed.

STANLEY So what's the—?

HAPPY Strudel's comin'.

STANLEY, *catching on, looks around* Ah, no, there's no— *He breaks off as a furred, lavishly dressed girl enters and sits at the next table. Both follow her with their eyes.*

STANLEY Geez, how'd ya know?

HAPPY I got radar or something. *Staring directly at her profile:* Oooooooo . . . Stanley.

STANLEY I think that's for you, Mr. Loman.

HAPPY Look at that mouth. Oh, God. And the binoculars.

STANLEY Geez, you got a life, Mr. Loman.

HAPPY Wait on her.

STANLEY, *going to the girl's table* Would you like a menu, ma'am?

GIRL I'm expecting someone, but I'd like a—

HAPPY Why don't you bring her—excuse me, miss, do you mind? I sell champagne, and I'd like you to try my brand. Bring her a champagne, Stanley.

GIRL That's awfully nice of you.

HAPPY Don't mention it. It's all company money.

He laughs.

GIRL That's a charming product to be selling, isn't it?

HAPPY Oh, gets to be like everything else. Selling is selling, y'know.

GIRL I suppose.

HAPPY You don't happen to sell, do you?

GIRL No, I don't sell.

HAPPY Would you object to a compliment from a stranger? You ought to be on a magazine cover.

GIRL, *looking at him a little archly* I have been.

Stanley comes in with a glass of champagne.

HAPPY What'd I say before, Stanley? You see? She's a cover girl.

STANLEY Oh, I could see, I could see.

HAPPY, *to the Girl* What magazine?

GIRL Oh, a lot of them. *She takes the drink.* Thank you.

HAPPY You know what they say in France, don't you? "Champagne is the drink of the complexion"—Hya, Biff!

Biff has entered and sits with Happy.

BIFF Hello, kid. Sorry I'm late.

HAPPY I just got here. Uh, Miss—?

GIRL Forsythe.

HAPPY Miss Forsythe, this is my brother.

BIFF Is Dad here?

HAPPY His name is Biff. You might've heard of him. Great football player.

GIRL Really? What team?

HAPPY Are you familiar with football?

GIRL No, I'm afraid I'm not.

HAPPY Biff is quarterback with the New York Giants.

GIRL Well, that is nice, isn't it? *She drinks.*

HAPPY Good health.

GIRL I'm happy to meet you.

HAPPY That's my name. Hap. It's really Harold, but at West Point they called me Happy.

GIRL, *now really impressed* Oh, I see. How do you do? *She turns her profile.*

BIFF Isn't Dad coming?

HAPPY You want her?

BIFF Oh, I could never make that.

HAPPY I remembered the time that idea would never come into your head. Where's the old confidence, Biff?

BIFF I just saw Oliver—

HAPPY Wait a minute. I've got to see that old confidence again. Do you want her? She's on call.

BIFF Oh, no. *He turns to look at the Girl.*

HAPPY I'm telling you. Watch this. *Turning to the Girl:* Honey? *She turns to him.* Are you busy?

GIRL Well, I am . . . but I could make a phone call.

HAPPY Do that, will you, honey? And see if you can get a friend. We'll be here for a while. Biff is one of the greatest football players in the country.

GIRL, *standing up* Well, I'm certainly happy to meet you.

HAPPY Come back soon.

GIRL I'll try.

HAPPY Don't try, honey, try hard.

The Girl exits. Stanley follows, shaking his head in bewildered admiration.

HAPPY Isn't that a shame now? A beautiful girl like that? That's why I can't get married. There's not a good woman in a thousand. New York is loaded with them, kid!

BIFF Hap, look—

HAPPY I told you she was on call!

BIFF, *strangely unnerved* Cut it out, will ya? I want to say something to you.

HAPPY Did you see Oliver?

BIFF I saw him all right. Now look, I want to tell Dad a couple of things and I want you to help me.

HAPPY What? Is he going to back you?

BIFF Are you crazy? You're out of your goddam head, you know that?

HAPPY Why? What happened?

BIFF, *breathlessly* I did a terrible thing today, Hap. It's been the strangest day I ever went through. I'm all numb, I swear.

HAPPY You mean he wouldn't see you?

BIFF Well, I waited six hours for him, see? All day. Kept sending my name in. Even tried to date his secretary so she'd get me to him, but no soap.

HAPPY Because you're not showin' the old confidence, Biff. He remembered you, didn't he?

BIFF, *stopping Happy with a gesture* Finally, about five o'clock, he comes out. Didn't remember who I was or anything. I felt like such an idiot, Hap.

HAPPY Did you tell him my Florida idea?

BIFF He walked away. I saw him for one minute. I got so mad I could've torn the walls down! How the hell did I ever get the idea I was a salesman there? I even believed myself that I'd been a salesman for him! And then he gave me one look and—I realized what a ridiculous lie my whole life has been! We've been talking in a dream for fifteen years. I was a shipping clerk.

HAPPY What'd you do?

BIFF, *with great tension and wonder* Well, he left, see. And the secretary went out. I was all alone in the waiting-room. I don't know what came over me, Hap. The next thing I know I'm in his office—paneled walls, everything. I can't explain it. I—Hap, I took his fountain pen.

HAPPY Geez, did he catch you?

BIFF I ran out. I ran down all eleven flights. I ran and ran and ran.

HAPPY That was an awful dumb—what'd you do that for?

BIFF, *agonized* I don't know, I just—wanted to take something, I don't know. You gotta help me, Hap, I'm gonna tell Pop.

HAPPY You crazy? What for?

BIFF Hap, he's got to understand that I'm not the man somebody lends that kind of money to. He thinks I've been spiting him all these years and it's eating him up.

HAPPY That's just it. You tell him something nice.

BIFF I can't.

HAPPY Say you got a lunch date with Oliver tomorrow.

BIFF So what do I do tomorrow?

HAPPY You leave the house tomorrow and come back at night and say Oliver is thinking it over. And he thinks it over for a couple of weeks, and gradually it fades away and nobody's the worse.

BIFF But it'll go on forever!

HAPPY Dad is never so happy as when he's looking forward to something!

Willy enters.

HAPPY Hello, scout!
WILLY Gee, I haven't been here in years!

Stanley has followed Willy in and sets a chair for him. Stanley starts off but Happy stops him.

HAPPY Stanley!

Stanley stands by, waiting for an order.

BIFF, *going to Willy with guilt, as to an invalid* Sit down, Pop. You want a drink?
WILLY Sure, I don't mind.
BIFF Let's get a load on.
WILLY You look worried.
BIFF N-no. *To Stanley:* Scotch all around. Make it doubles.
STANLEY Doubles, right. *He goes.*
WILLY You had a couple already, didn't you?
BIFF Just a couple, yeah.
WILLY Well, what happened, boy? *Nodding affirmatively, with a smile:* Everything go all right?
BIFF, *takes a breath, then reaches out and grasps Willy's hand* Pal . . . *He is smiling bravely, and Willy is smiling too.* I had an experience today.
HAPPY Terrific, Pop.
WILLY That so? What happened?
BIFF, *high, slightly alcoholic, above the earth* I'm going to tell you everything from first to last. It's been a strange day. *Silence. He looks around, composes himself as best he can, but his breath keeps breaking the rhythm of his voice.* I had to wait quite a while for him, and—
WILLY Oliver?
BIFF Yeah, Oliver. All day, as a matter of cold fact. And a lot of—instances—facts, Pop, facts about my life came back to me. Who was it, Pop? Who ever said I was a salesman with Oliver?
WILLY Well, you were.
BIFF No, Dad, I was a shipping clerk.
WILLY But you were practically—

BIFF, *with determination* Dad, I don't know who said it first, but I never was a salesman for Bill Oliver.
WILLY What're you talking about?
BIFF Let's hold on to the facts tonight, Pop. We're not going to get anywhere bullin' around. I was a shipping clerk.
WILLY, *angrily* All right, now listen to me—
BIFF Why don't you let me finish?
WILLY I'm not interested in stories about the past or any crap of that kind because the woods are burning, boys, you understand? There's a big blaze going on all around. I was fired today.
BIFF, *shocked* How could you be?
WILLY I was fired, and I'm looking for a little good news to tell your mother, because the woman has waited and the woman has suffered. The gist of it is that I haven't got a story left in my head, Biff. So don't give me a lecture about facts and aspects. I am not interested. Now what've you got to say to me?

Stanley enters with three drinks. They wait until he leaves.

WILLY Did you see Oliver?
BIFF Jesus, Dad!
WILLY You mean you didn't go up there?
HAPPY Sure he went up there.
BIFF I did. I—saw him. How could they fire you?
WILLY, *on the edge of his chair* What kind of a welcome did he give you?
BIFF He won't even let you work on commission?
WILLY I'm out! *Driving:* So tell me, he gave you a warm welcome?
HAPPY Sure, Pop, sure!
BIFF, *driven* Well, it was kind of—
WILLY I was wondering if he'd remember you. *To Happy:* Imagine, man doesn't see him for ten, twelve years and gives him that kind of a welcome!
HAPPY Damn right!
BIFF, *trying to return to the offensive* Pop, look—
WILLY You know why he remembered you, don't you? Because you impressed him in those days.

BIFF Let's talk quietly and get this down to the facts, huh?
WILLY, *as though Biff had been interrupting* Well, what happened? It's great news, Biff. Did he take you into his office or'd you talk in the waiting-room?
BIFF Well, he came in, see, and—
WILLY, *with a big smile* What'd he say? Betcha he threw his arm around you.
BIFF Well, he kinda—
WILLY He's a fine man. *To Happy:* Very hard man to see, y'know.
HAPPY, *agreeing* Oh, I know.
WILLY, *to Biff* Is that where you had the drinks?
BIFF Yeah, he gave me a couple of—no, no!
HAPPY, *cutting in* He told him my Florida idea.
WILLY Don't interrupt. *To Biff:* How'd he react to the Florida idea?
BIFF Dad, will you give me a minute to explain?
WILLY I've been waiting for you to explain since I sat down here! What happened? He took you into his office and what?
BIFF Well—I talked. And—and he listened, see.
WILLY Famous for the way he listens, y'know. What was his answer?
BIFF His answer was— *He breaks off, suddenly angry.* Dad, you're not letting me tell you what I want to tell you!
WILLY, *accusing, angered* You didn't see him, did you?
BIFF I did see him!
WILLY What'd you insult him or something? You insulted him, didn't you?
BIFF Listen, will you let me out of it, will you just let me out of it!
HAPPY What the hell!
WILLY Tell me what happened!
BIFF, *to Happy* I can't talk to him!

A single trumpet note jars the ear. The light of green leaves stains the house, which holds the air of night and a dream. Young Bernard enters and knocks on the door of the house.

YOUNG BERNARD, *frantically* Mrs. Loman, Mrs. Loman!
HAPPY Tell him what happened!
BIFF, *to Happy* Shut up and leave me alone!
WILLY No, no! You had to go and flunk math!
BIFF What math? What're you talking about?
YOUNG BERNARD Mrs. Loman, Mrs. Loman!

Linda appears in the house, as of old.

WILLY, *wildly* Math, math, math!
BIFF Take it easy, Pop!
YOUNG BERNARD Mrs. Loman!
WILLY, *furiously* If you hadn't flunked you'd've been set by now!
BIFF Now, look, I'm gonna tell you what happened, and you're going to listen to me.
YOUNG BERNARD Mrs. Loman!
BIFF I waited six hours—
HAPPY What the hell are you saying?
BIFF I kept sending in my name but he wouldn't see me. So finally he . . . *He continues unheard as light fades low on the restaurant.*
YOUNG BERNARD Biff flunked math!
LINDA No!
YOUNG BERNARD Birnbaum flunked him! They won't graduate him!
LINDA But they have to. He's gotta go to the university. Where is he? Biff! Biff!
YOUNG BERNARD No, he left. He went to Grand Central.
LINDA Grand— You mean he went to Boston!
YOUNG BERNARD Is Uncle Willy in Boston?
LINDA Oh, maybe Willy can talk to the teacher. Oh, the poor, poor boy!

Light on house area snaps out.

BIFF, *at the table, now audible, holding up a gold fountain pen* . . . so I'm washed up with Oliver, you understand? Are you listening to me?
WILLY, *at loss* Yeah, sure. If you hadn't flunked—
BIFF Flunked what? What're you talking about?
WILLY Don't blame everything on me! I didn't flunk math—you did! What pen?
HAPPY That was awful dumb, Biff, a pen like that is worth—

WILLY, *seeing the pen for the first time* You took Oliver's pen?

BIFF, *weakening* Dad, I just explained it to you.

WILLY You stole Bill Oliver's fountain pen!

BIFF I didn't exactly steal it! That's just what I've been explaining to you!

HAPPY He had it in his hand and just then Oliver walked in, so he got nervous and stuck it in his pocket!

WILLY My God, Biff!

BIFF I never intended to do it, Dad!

OPERATOR'S VOICE Standish Arms, Good evening!

WILLY, *shouting* I'm not in my room!

BIFF, *frightened* Dad, what's the matter? *He and Happy stand up.*

OPERATOR Ringing Mr. Loman for you!

WILLY I'm not there, stop it!

BIFF, *horrified, gets down on one knee before Willy* Dad, I'll make good, I'll make good. *Willy tries to get to his feet. Biff holds him down.* Sit down now.

WILLY No, you're no good, you're no good for anything.

BIFF I am, Dad, I'll find something else, you understand? Now don't worry about anything. *He holds up Willy's face:* Talk to me, Dad.

OPERATOR Mr. Loman does not answer. Shall I page him?

WILLY, *attempting to stand, as though to rush and silence the Operator* No, no, no!

HAPPY He'll strike something. Pop!

WILLY No, no . . .

BIFF, *desperately, standing over Willy* Pop, listen! Listen to me! I'm telling you something good. Oliver talked to his partner about the Florida idea. You listening? He—he talked to his partner, and he came to me . . . I'm going to be all right, you hear? Dad, listen to me, he said it was just a question of the amount!

WILLY Then you . . . got it?

HAPPY He's gonna be terrific, Pop!

WILLY, *trying to stand* Then you got it, haven't you? You got it! You got it!

BIFF, *agonized, holds Willy down* No, no. Look, Pop. I'm supposed to have lunch with them tomorrow. I'm just telling you this so you'll know that I can still make an impression, Pop. And I'll make good somewhere, but I can't go tomorrow, see?

WILLY Why not? You simply—

BIFF But the pen, Pop!

WILLY You give it to him and tell him it was an oversight!

HAPPY Sure, have lunch tomorrow!

BIFF I can't say that—

WILLY You were doing a crossword puzzle and accidentally used his pen!

BIFF Listen, kid, I took those balls years ago, now I walk in with his fountain pen? That clinches it, don't you see? I can't face him like that! I'll try elsewhere.

PAGE'S VOICE Paging Mr. Loman!

WILLY Don't you want to be anything?

BIFF Pop, how can I go back?

WILLY You don't want to be anything, is that what's behind it?

BIFF, *now angry at Willy for not crediting his sympathy* Don't take it that way! You think it was easy walking into that office after what I'd done to him? A team of horses couldn't have dragged me back to Bill Oliver!

WILLY Then why'd you go?

BIFF Why did I go? Why did I go! Look at you! Look at what's become of you!

Off left, The Woman laughs.

WILLY Biff, you're going to go to that lunch tomorrow, or—

BIFF I can't go. I've got no appointment!

HAPPY Biff, for . . . !

WILLY Are you spiting me?

BIFF Don't take it that way! Goddammit!

WILLY, *strikes Biff and falters away from the table* You rotten little louse! Are you spiting me?

THE WOMAN Someone's at the door, Willy!

BIFF I'm no good, can't you see what I am.

HAPPY, *separating them* Hey, you're in a restaurant! Now cut it out, both of you? *The girls enter.* Hello, girls, sit down.

The Woman laughs, off left.

MISS FORSYTHE I guess we might as well. This is Letta.

THE WOMAN Willy, are you going to wake up?

BIFF, *ignoring* Willy How're ya, miss, sit down. What do you drink?
MISS FORSYTHE Letta might not be able to stay long.
LETTA I gotta get up very early tomorrow. I got jury duty. I'm so excited! Were you fellows ever on a jury?
BIFF No, but I been in front of them! *The girls laugh.* This is my father.
LETTA Isn't he cute? Sit down with us, Pop.
HAPPY Sit him down, Biff!
BIFF, *going to him* Come on, slugger, drink us under the table. To hell with it! Come on, sit down, pal.

On Biff's last insistence, Willy is about to sit.

THE WOMAN, *now urgently* Willy, are you going to answer the door!

The Woman's call pulls Willy back. He starts right, befuddled.

BIFF Hey, where are you going?
WILLY Open the door.
BIFF The door?
WILLY The washroom . . . the door . . . where's the door?
BIFF, *leading Willy to the left* Just go straight down.

Willy moves left.

THE WOMAN Willy, Willy, are you going to get up, get up, get up, get up?

Willy exits left.

LETTA I think it's sweet you bring your daddy along.
MISS FORSYTHE Oh, he isn't really your father!
BIFF, *at left, turning to her resentfully* Miss Forsythe, you've just seen a prince walk by. A fine, troubled prince. A hard-working, unappreciated prince. A pal, you understand? A good companion. Always for his boys.
LETTA That's so sweet.
HAPPY Well, girls, what's the program? We're wasting time. Come on, Biff. Gather round. Where would you like to go?
BIFF Why don't you do something for him?

HAPPY Me!
BIFF Don't you give a damn for him, Hap?
HAPPY What're you talking about? I'm the one who—
BIFF I sense it, you don't give a good goddam about him. *He takes the rolled-up hose from his pocket and puts it on the table in front of Happy.* Look what I found in the cellar, for Christ's sake. How can you bear to let it go on?
HAPPY Me? Who goes away? Who runs off and—
BIFF Yeah, but he doesn't mean anything to you. You could help him—I can't! Don't you understand what I'm talking about? He's going to kill himself, don't you know that?
HAPPY Don't I know it! Me!
BIFF Hap, help him! Jesus . . . help him . . . Help me, help me, I can't bear to look at his face! *Ready to weep, he hurries out, up right.*
HAPPY, *starting after him* Where are you going?
MISS FORSYTHE What's he so mad about?
HAPPY Come on, girls, we'll catch up with him.
MISS FORSYTHE, *as Happy pushes her out* Say, I don't like that temper of his!
HAPPY He's just a little overstrung, he'll be all right!
WILLY, *off left, as The Woman laughs* Don't answer! Don't answer!
LETTA Don't you want to tell your father—
HAPPY No, that's not my father. He's just a guy. Come on, we'll catch Biff, and, honey, we're going to paint this town! Stanley, where's the check! Hey, Stanley!

They exit. Stanley looks toward left.

STANLEY, *calling to Happy indignantly* Mr. Loman! Mr. Loman!

Stanley picks up a chair and follows them off. Knocking is heard off left. The Woman enters, laughing. Willy follows her. She is in a black slip; he is buttoning his shirt. Raw, sensuous music accompanies their speech.

WILLY Will you stop laughing? Will you stop?
THE WOMAN Aren't you going to answer the door? He'll wake the whole hotel.

WILLY I'm not expecting anybody.
THE WOMAN Whyn't you have another drink, honey, and stop being so damn self-centered?
WILLY I'm so lonely.
THE WOMAN You know you ruined me, Willy? From now on, whenever you come to the office, I'll see that you go right through to the buyers. No waiting at my desk any more, Willy. You ruined me.
WILLY That's nice of you to say that.
THE WOMAN Gee, you are self-centered! Why so sad? You are the saddest, self-centerdest soul I ever did see-saw. *She laughs. He kisses her.* Come on inside, drummer boy. It's silly to be dressing in the middle of the night. *As knocking is heard:* Aren't you going to answer the door?
WILLY They're knocking on the wrong door.
THE WOMAN But I felt the knocking. And he heard us talking in here. Maybe the hotel's on fire!
WILLY, *his terror rising* It's a mistake.
THE WOMAN Then tell him to go away!
WILLY There's nobody there.
THE WOMAN It's getting on my nerves, Willy. There's somebody standing out there and it's getting on my nerves!
WILLY, *pushing her away from him* All right, stay in the bathroom here, and don't come out. I think there's a law in Massachusetts about it, so don't come out. It may be that new room clerk. He looked very mean. So don't come out. It's a mistake, there's no fire.

The knocking is heard again. He takes a few steps away from her, and she vanishes into the wing. The light follows him, and now he is facing Young Biff, who carries a suitcase. Biff steps toward him. The music is gone.

BIFF Why didn't you answer?
WILLY Biff! What are you doing in Boston?
BIFF Why didn't you answer? I've been knocking for five minutes, I called you on the phone—
WILLY I just heard you. I was in the bathroom and had the door shut. Did anything happen home?
BIFF Dad—I let you down.
WILLY What do you mean?
BIFF Dad . . .
WILLY Biffo, what's this about? *Putting his arm around Biff:* Come on, let's go downstairs and get you a malted.
BIFF Dad, I flunked math.
WILLY Not for the term?
BIFF The term. I haven't got enough credits to graduate.
WILLY You mean to say Bernard wouldn't give you the answers?
BIFF He did, he tried, but I only got a sixty-one.
WILLY And they wouldn't give you four points?
BIFF Birnbaum refused absolutely. I begged him, Pop, but he won't give me those points. You gotta talk to him before they close the school. Because if he saw the kind of man you are, and you just talked to him in your way, I'm sure he'd come through for me. The class came right before practice, see, and I didn't go enough. Would you talk to him? He'd like you, Pop. You know the way you could talk.
WILLY You're on. We'll drive right back.
BIFF Oh, Dad, good work! I'm sure he'll change it for you!
WILLY Go downstairs and tell the clerk I'm checkin' out. Go right down.
BIFF Yes, sir! See, the reason he hates me, Pop—one day he was late for class so I got up at the blackboard and imitated him. I crossed my eyes and talked with a lithp.
WILLY, *laughing* You did? The kids like it?
BIFF They nearly died laughing!
WILLY Yeah? What'd you do?
BIFF The thquare root of thixthy twee is . . . *Willy bursts out laughing; Biff joins him.* And in the middle of it he walked in!

Willy laughs and The Woman joins in offstage.

WILLY, *without hesitation* Hurry downstairs and—
BIFF Somebody in there?
WILLY No, that was next door.

The Woman laughs offstage.

BIFF Somebody got in your bathroom!
WILLY No, it's the next room, there's a party—
THE WOMAN, *enters laughing. She lisps this:* Can I come in? There's something in the bathtub, Willy, and it's moving!

Willy looks at Biff, who is staring open-mouthed and horrified at The Woman.

WILLY Ah—you better go back to your room. They must be finished painting by now. They're painting her room so I let her take a shower here. Go back, go back . . . *He pushes her.*
THE WOMAN, *resisting* But I've got to get dressed, Willy, I can't—
WILLY Get out of here! Go back, go back . . . *Suddenly striving for the ordinary:* This is Miss Francis, Biff, she's a buyer. They're painting her room. Go back, Miss Francis, go back . . .
THE WOMAN But my clothes, I can't go out naked in the hall!
WILLY, *pushing her offstage* Get outa here! Go back, go back!

Biff slowly sits down on his suitcase as the argument continues offstage.

THE WOMAN Where's my stockings? You promised me stockings, Willy!
WILLY I have no stockings here!
THE WOMAN You had two boxes of size nine sheers for me, and I want them!
WILLY Here, for God's sake, will you get outa here!
THE WOMAN, *enters holding a box of stockings* I just hope there's nobody in the hall. That's all I hope. *To Biff:* Are you football or baseball?
BIFF Football.
THE WOMAN, *angry, humiliated* That's me too. G'night.

She snatches her clothes from Willy, and walks out.

WILLY, *after a pause* Well, better get going. I want to get to the school first thing in the morning. Get my suits out of the closet. I'll get my valise. *Biff doesn't move.* What's the matter? *Biff remains motionless, tears falling.* She's a buyer. Buys for J. H. Simmons. She lives down the hall—they're painting. You don't imagine— *He breaks off. After a pause:* Now listen, pal, she's just a buyer. She sees merchandise in her room and they have to keep it looking just so . . . *Pause. Assuming command:* All right, get my suits. *Biff doesn't move.* Now stop crying and do as I say. I gave you an order. Biff, I gave you a order! Is that what you do when I give you an order? How dare you cry! *Putting his arm around Biff:* Now look, Biff, when you grow up you'll understand about these things. You mustn't—you mustn't overemphasize a thing like this. I'll see Birnbaum first thing in the morning.
BIFF Never mind.
WILLY, *getting down beside Biff* Never mind! He's going to give you those points. I'll see to it.
BIFF He wouldn't listen to you.
WILLY He certainly will listen to me. You need those points for the U. of Virginia.
BIFF I'm not going there.
WILLY Heh? If I can't get him to change that mark you'll make it up in summer school. You've got all summer to—
BIFF, *his weeping breaking from him* Dad . . .
WILLY, *infected by it* Oh, my boy . . .
BIFF Dad . . .
WILLY She's nothing to me, Biff. I was lonely, I was terribly lonely.
BIFF You—you gave her Mama's stockings! *His tears break through and he rises to go.*
WILLY, *grabbing for Biff* I gave you an order!
BIFF Don't touch me, you—liar!
WILLY Apologize for that!
BIFF You fake! You phony little fake! You fake! *Overcome, he turns quickly and weeping fully goes out with his suitcase. Willy is left on the floor on his knees.*
WILLY I gave you an order! Biff, come back here or I'll beat you! Come back here! I'll whip you!

Stanley comes quickly in from the right and stands in front of Willy.

WILLY, *shouts at Stanley* I gave you an order . . .

STANLEY Hey, let's pick it up, pick it up, Mr. Loman. *He helps Willy to his feet.* Your boys left with the chippies. They said they'll see you home.

A second waiter watches some distance away.

WILLY But we were supposed to have dinner together.

Music is heard, Willy's theme.

STANLEY Can you make it?

WILLY I'll—sure, I can make it. *Suddenly concerned about his clothes:* Do I—I look all right?

STANLEY Sure, you look all right. *He flicks a speck off Willy's lapel.*

WILLY Here—here's a dollar.

STANLEY Oh, your son paid me. It's all right.

WILLY, *putting it in Stanley's hand* No, take it. You're a good boy.

STANLEY Oh, no, you don't have to . . .

WILLY Here—here's some more, I don't need it any more. *After a slight pause:* Tell me—is there a seed store in the neighborhood?

STANLEY Seeds? You mean like to plant?

As Willy turns, Stanley slips the money back into his jacket pocket.

WILLY Yes. Carrots, peas . . .

STANLEY Well, there's hardware stores on Sixth Avenue, but it may be too late now.

WILLY, *anxiously* Oh, I'd better hurry. I've got to get some seeds. *He starts off to the right.* I've got to get some seeds, right away. Nothing's planted. I don't have a thing in the ground.

Willy hurries out as the light goes down. Stanley moves over to the right after him, watches him off. The other waiter has been staring at Willy.

STANLEY, *to the waiter* Well, whatta you looking at?

The Waiter picks up the chairs and moves off right. Stanley takes the table and follows him. The light fades on this area. There is a long pause, the sound of the flute coming over. The light gradually rises on the kitchen, which is empty. Happy appears at the door of the house, followed by Biff. Happy is carrying a large bunch of long-stemmed roses. He enters the kitchen, looks around for Linda. Not seeing her, he turns to Biff, who is just outside the house door, and makes a gesture with his hands, indicating "Not here, I guess." He looks into the living-room and freezes. Inside, Linda, unseen, is seated, Willy's coat on her lap. She rises ominously and quietly and moves toward Happy, who backs up into the kitchen, afraid.

HAPPY Hey, what're you doing up? *Linda says nothing but moves toward him implacably.* Where's Pop? *He keeps backing to the right, and now Linda is in full view in the doorway to the livingroom.* Is he sleeping?

LINDA Where were you?

HAPPY, *trying to laugh it off* We met two girls, Mom, very fine types. Here, we brought you some flowers. *Offering them to her:* Put them in your room, Ma.

She knocks them to the floor at Biff's feet. He has now come inside and closed the door behind him. She stares at Biff, silent.

HAPPY Now what'd you do that for? Mom, I want you to have some flowers—

LINDA, *cutting Happy off, violently to Biff* Don't you care whether he lives or dies?

HAPPY, *going to the stairs* Come upstairs, Biff.

BIFF, *with a flare of disgust, to Happy* Go away from me! *To Linda:* What do you mean, lives or dies? Nobody's dying around here, pal.

LINDA Get out of my sight! Get out of here!

BIFF I wanna see the boss.

LINDA You're not going near him!

BIFF Where is he? *He moves into the living-room and Linda follows.*

LINDA, *shouting after Biff* You invite him for dinner. He looks forward to it all day— *Biff appears in his parents' bedroom, looks around, and exits* —and then you desert him there. There's no stranger you'd do that to!

HAPPY Why? He had a swell time with us. Listen, when I— *Linda comes back into the kitchen—* desert him I hope I don't outlive the day!
LINDA Get out of here!
HAPPY Now look, Mom . . .
LINDA Did you have to go to women tonight? You and your lousy rotten whores!

Biff re-enters the kitchen.

HAPPY Mom, all we did was follow Biff around trying to cheer him up! *To Biff:* Boy, what a night you gave me!
LINDA Get out of here, both of you, and don't come back! I don't want you tormenting him any more. Go on now, get your things together! *To Biff:* You can sleep in his apartment. *She starts to pick up the flowers and stops herself.* Pick up this stuff, I'm not your maid any more. Pick it up, you bum, you!

Happy turns his back to her in refusal. Biff slowly moves over and gets down on his knees, picking up the flowers.

LINDA You're a pair of animals! Not one, not another living soul would have had the cruelty to walk out on that man in a restaurant!
BIFF, *not looking at her* Is that what he said?
LINDA He didn't have to say anything. He was so humiliated he nearly limped when he came in.
HAPPY But, Mom, he had a great time with us—
BIFF, *cutting him off violently* Shut up!

Without another word, Happy goes upstairs.

LINDA You! You didn't even go in to see if he was all right!
BIFF, *still on the floor in front of Linda, the flowers in his hand; with self-loathing* No. Didn't. Didn't do a damned thing. How do you like that, heh? Left him babbling in a toilet.
LINDA You louse. You . . .
BIFF Now you hit it on the nose! *He gets up, throws the flowers in the wastebasket.* The scum of the earth, and you're looking at him!
LINDA Get out of here!
BIFF I gotta talk to the boss, Mom. Where is he?
LINDA You're not going near him. Get out of this house!
BIFF, *with absolute assurance, determination* No. We're gonna have an abrupt conversation, him and me.
LINDA You're not talking to him!

Hammering is heard from outside the house, off right. Biff turns toward the noise.

LINDA, *suddenly pleading* Will you please leave him alone?
BIFF What's he doing out there?
LINDA He's planting the garden!
BIFF, *quietly* Now? Oh, my God!

Biff moves outside, Linda following. The light dies down on them and comes up on the center of the apron as Willy walks into it. He is carrying a flashlight, a hoe, and a handful of seed packets. He raps the top of the hoe sharply to fix it firmly, and then moves to the left, measuring off the distance with his foot. He holds the flashlight to look at the seed packets, reading off the instructions. He is in the blue of night.

WILLY Carrots . . . quarter-inch apart. Rows . . . one-foot rows. *He measures it off.* One foot. *He puts down a package and measures off.* Beets. *He puts down another package and measures again.* Lettuce. *He reads the package, puts it down.* One foot— *He breaks off as Ben appears at the right and moves slowly down to him.* What a proposition, ts, ts. Terrific, terrific. 'Cause she's suffered, Ben, the woman has suffered. You understand me? A man can't go out the way he came in, Ben, an man has got to add up to something. You can't, you can't— *Ben moves toward him as though to interrupt.* You gotta consider, now. Don't answer so quick. Remember, it's a guaranteed twenty-thousand-dollar proposition. Now look, Ben, I want you to go through the ins and outs of this thing with me. I've got nobody to talk to, Ben, and the woman has suffered, you hear me?

BEN, *standing still, considering* What's the proposition?

WILLY It's twenty thousand dollars on the barrel-head. Guaranteed, gilt-edged, you understand?

BEN You don't want to make a fool of yourself. They might not honor the policy.

WILLY How can they dare refuse? Didn't I work like a coolie to meet every premium on the nose? And now they don't pay off? Impossible!

BEN It's called a cowardly thing, William.

WILLY Why? Does it take more guts to stand here the rest of my life ringing up a zero?

BEN, *yielding* That's a point, William. *He moves, thinking, turns.* And twenty thousand—that *is* something one can feel with the hand, it is there.

WILLY, *now assured, with rising power* Oh, Ben, that's the whole beauty of it! I see it like a diamond, shining in the dark, hard and rough, that I can pick up and touch in my hand. Not like—like an appointment! This would not be another damned-fool appointment, Ben, and it changes all the aspects. Because he thinks I'm nothing, see, and so he spites me. But the funeral—*Straightening up:* Ben, that funeral will be massive! They'll come from Maine, Massachusetts, Vermont, New Hampshire! All the old-timers with the strange license plates—that boy will be thunder-struck, Ben, because he never realized—I am known! Rhode Island, New York, New Jersey—I am known, Ben, and he'll see it with his eyes once and for all. He'll see what I am. Ben! He's in for a shock, that boy!

BEN, *coming down to the edge of the garden* He'll call you a coward.

WILLY, *suddenly fearful* No, that would be terrible.

BEN Yes. And a damned fool.

WILLY No, no, he mustn't, I won't have that! *He is broken and desperate.*

BEN He'll hate you, William.

The gay music of the Boys is heard.

WILLY Oh, Ben, how do we get back to all the great times? Used to be so full of light, and comradeship, the sleigh-riding in winter, and the ruddiness on his cheeks. And always some kind of good news coming up, always something nice coming up ahead. And never even let me carry the valises in the house, and simonizing, simonizing that little red car! Why, why can't I give him something and not have him hate me?

BEN Let me think about it. *He glances at his watch.* I still have a little time. Remarkable proposition, but you've got to be sure you're not making a fool of yourself.

Ben drifts off upstage and goes out of sight. Biff comes down from the left.

WILLY, *suddenly conscious of Biff, turns and looks up at him, then begins picking up the packages of seeds in confusion* Where the hell is that seed? *Indignantly:* You can't see nothing out here! They boxed in the whole goddam neighborhood!

BIFF There are people all around here. Don't you realize that?

WILLY I'm busy. Don't bother me.

BIFF, *taking the hoe from Willy* I'm saying good-by to you, Pop. *Willy looks at him, silent, unable to move.* I'm not coming back any more.

WILLY You're not going to see Oliver tomorrow?

BIFF I've got no appointment, Dad.

WILLY He put his arm around you, and you've got no appointment?

BIFF Pop, get this now, will you? Everytime I've left it's been a fight that sent me out of here. Today I realized something about myself and I tried to explain it to you and I—I think I'm just not smart enough to make any sense of it for you. To hell with whose fault it is or anything like that. *He takes Willy's arm.* Let's just wrap it up, heh? Come on in, we'll tell Mom. *He gently tries to pull Willy to left.*

WILLY, *frozen, immobile, with guilt in his voice* No, I don't want to see her.

BIFF Come on! *He pulls again, and Willy tries to pull away.*

WILLY, *highly nervous* No, no, I don't want to see her.

BIFF, *tries to look into Willy's face, as if to find the answer there* Why don't you want to see her?
WILLY, *more harshly now* Don't bother me, will you?
BIFF What do you mean, you don't want to see her? You don't want them calling you yellow, do you? This isn't your fault; it's me, I'm a bum. Now come inside! *Willy strains to get away.* Did you hear what I said to you?

Willy pulls away and quickly goes by himself into the house. Biff follows.

LINDA, *to Willy* Did you plant, dear?
BIFF, *at the door, to Linda* All right, we had it out, I'm going and I'm not writing any more.
LINDA, *going to Willy in the kitchen* I think that's the best way, dear. 'Cause there's no use drawing it out, you'll just never get along.

Willy doesn't respond.

BIFF People ask where I am and what I'm doing, you don't know, and you don't care. That way it'll be off your mind and you can start brightening up again. All right? That clears it, doesn't it? *Willy is silent, and Biff goes to him.* You gonna wish me luck, scout? *He extends his hand.* What do you say?
LINDA Shake his hand, Willy.
WILLY, *turning to her, seething with hurt* There's no necessity to mention the pen at all, y'know.
BIFF, *gently* I've got no appointment, Dad.
WILLY, *erupting fiercely* He put his arm around . . . ?
BIFF Dad, you're never going to see what I am, so what's the use of arguing? If I strike oil I'll send you a check. Meantime forget I'm alive.
WILLY, *to Linda* Spite, see?
BIFF Shake hands, Dad.
WILLY Not my hand.
BIFF I was hoping not to go this way.
WILLY Well, this is the way you're going. Good-by.

Biff looks at him a moment, then turns sharply and goes to the stairs.

WILLY, *stops him with* May you rot in hell if you leave this house!
BIFF, *turning* Exactly what is it that you want from me?
WILLY I want you to know, on the train, in the mountains, in the valleys, wherever you go, that you cut down your life for spite!
BIFF No, no.
WILLY Spite, spite, is the word of your undoing! And when you're down and out, remember what did it. When you're rotting somewhere beside the railroad tracks, remember, and don't you dare blame it on me!
BIFF I'm not blaming it on you!
WILLY I won't take the rap for this, you hear?

Happy comes down the stairs and stands on the bottom step, watching.

BIFF That's just what I'm telling you!
WILLY, *sinking into a chair at the table, with full accusation* You're trying to put a knife in me—don't think I don't know what you're doing!
BIFF All right, phony! Then let's lay it on the line. *He whips the rubber tube out of his pocket and puts it on the table.*
HAPPY You crazy—
LINDA Biff! *She moves to grab the hose, but Biff holds it down with his hand.*
BIFF Leave it there! Don't move it!
WILLY, *not looking at it* What is that?
BIFF You know goddam well what that is.
WILLY, *caged, wanting to escape* I never saw that.
BIFF You saw it. The mice didn't bring it into the cellar! What is this supposed to do, make a hero out of you? This supposed to make me sorry for you?
WILLY Never heard of it.
BIFF There'll be no pity for you, you hear it? No pity!
WILLY, *to Linda* You hear the spite!
BIFF No, you're going to hear the truth—what you are and what I am!
LINDA Stop it!
WILLY Spite!
HAPPY, *coming down toward Biff* You cut it now!
BIFF, *to Happy* The man don't know who we are! The man is gonna know! *To Willy:*

We never told the truth for ten minutes in this house!

HAPPY We always told the truth!

BIFF, *turning on him* You big blow, are you the assistant buyer? You're one of the two assistants to the assistant, aren't you?

HAPPY Well, I'm practically—

BIFF You're practically full of it! We all are! And I'm through with it. *To Willy:* Now hear this, Willy, this is me.

WILLY I know you!

BIFF You know why I had no address for three months? I stole a suit in Kansas City and I was in jail. *To Linda, who is sobbing:* Stop crying. I'm through with it.

Linda turns away from them, her hands covering her face.

WILLY I suppose that's my fault!

BIFF I stole myself out of every good job since high school!

WILLY And whose fault is that?

BIFF And I never got anywhere because you blew me so full of hot air I could never stand taking orders from anybody! That's whose fault it is!

WILLY I hear that!

LINDA Don't, Biff!

BIFF It's goddam time you heard that! I had to be boss big shot in two weeks, and I'm through with it!

WILLY Then hang yourself! For spite, hang yourself!

BIFF No! Nobody's hanging himself, Willy! I ran down eleven flights with a pen in my hand today. And suddenly I stopped, you hear me? And in the middle of that office building, do you hear this? I stopped in the middle of that building and I saw—the sky. I saw the things that I love in this world. The work and the food and time to sit and smoke. And I looked at the pen and said to myself, what the hell am I grabbing this for? Why am I trying to become what I don't want to be? What am I doing in an office, making a contemptuous, begging fool of myself, when all I want is out there, waiting for me the minute I say I know who I am! Why can't I say that, Willy?

He tries to make Willy face him, but Willy pulls away and moves to the left.

WILLY, *with hatred, threateningly* The door of your life is wide open!

BIFF Pop! I'm a dime a dozen, and so are you!

WILLY, *turning on him now in an uncontrolled outburst* I am not a dime a dozen! I am Willy Loman, and you are Biff Loman!

Biff starts for Willy, but is blocked by Happy. In his fury, Biff seems on the verge of attacking his father.

BIFF I am not a leader of men, Willy, and neither are you. You were never anything but a hard-working drummer who landed in the ash can like all the rest of them! I'm one dollar an hour, Willy! I tried seven states and couldn't raise it. A buck an hour! Do you gather my meaning? I'm not bringing home any prizes any more, and you're going to stop waiting for me to bring them home!

WILLY, *directly to Biff* You vengeful, spiteful mut!

Biff breaks from Happy. Willy, in fright, starts up the stairs. Biff grabs him.

BIFF, *at the peak of his fury* Pop, I'm nothing! I'm nothing, Pop. Can't you understand that? There's no spite in it any more. I'm just what I am, that's all.

Biff's fury has spent itself, and he breaks down, sobbing, holding on to Willy, who dumbly fumbles for Biff's face.

WILLY, *astonished* What're you doing? What're you doing? *To Linda:* Why is he crying?

BIFF, *crying, broken* Will you let me go, for Christ's sake? Will you take that phony dream and burn it before something happens? *Struggling to contain himself, he pulls away and moves to the stairs.* I'll go in the morning. Put him—put him to bed. *Exhausted, Biff moves up the stairs to his room.*

WILLY, *after a long pause, astonished, elevated* Isn't that—isn't that remarkable? Biff—he likes me!

LINDA He loves you, Willy!

HAPPY, *deeply moved* Always did, Pop.

WILLY Oh, Biff! *Staring wildly*: He cried! Cried to me. *He is choking with his love, and now cries out his promise*: That boy—that boy is going to be magnificent!

Ben appears in the light just outside the kitchen.

BEN Yes, outstanding, with twenty thousand behind him.
LINDA, *sensing the racing of his mind, fearfully, carefully* Now come to bed, Willy. It's all settled now.
WILLY, *finding it difficult not to rush out of the house* Yes, we'll sleep. Come on. Go to sleep, Hap.
BEN And it does take a great kind of a man to crack the jungle.

In accents of dread, Ben's idyllic music starts up.

HAPPY, *his arm around Linda* I'm getting married, Pop, don't forget it. I'm changing everything. I'm gonna run that department before the year is up. You'll see, Mom. *He kisses her.*
BEN The jungle is dark but full of diamonds, Willy.

Willy turns, moves, listening to Ben.

LINDA Be good. You're both good boys, just act that way, that's all.
HAPPY 'Night, Pop. *He goes upstairs.*
LINDA, *to Willy* Come, dear.
BEN, *with greater force* One must go in to fetch a diamond out.
WILLY, *to Linda, as he moves slowly along the edge of the kitchen, toward the door* I just want to get settled down, Linda. Let me sit alone for a little.
LINDA, *almost uttering her fear* I want you upstairs.
WILLY, *taking her in his arms* In a few minutes, Linda. I couldn't sleep right now. Go on, you look awful tired. *He kisses her.*
BEN Not like an appointment at all. A diamond is rough and hard to the touch.
WILLY Go on now. I'll be right up.
LINDA I think this is the only way, Willy.
WILLY Sure, it's the best thing.
BEN Best thing!
WILLY The only way. Everything is gonna be—go on, kid, get to bed. You look so tired.
LINDA Come right up.
WILLY Two minutes.

Linda goes into the livingroom, then reappears in her bedroom. Willy moves just outside the kitchen door.

WILLY Loves me. *Wonderingly*: Always loved me. Isn't that a remarkable thing? Ben, he'll worship me for it!
BEN, *with promise* It's dark there, but full of diamonds.
WILLY Can you imagine that magnificence with twenty thousand dollars in his pocket?
LINDA, *calling from her room* Willy! Come up!
WILLY, *calling into the kitchen* Yes! Yes. Coming! It's very smart, you realize that, don't you, sweetheart? Even Ben sees it. I gotta go, baby. 'By! 'By! *Going over to Ben, almost dancing*: Imagine? When the mail comes, he'll be ahead of Bernard again!
BEN A perfect proposition all around.
WILLY Did you see how he cried to me? Oh, if I could kiss him, Ben!
BEN Time, William, time!
WILLY Oh, Ben, I always knew one way or another we were gonna make it, Biff and I!
BEN, *looking at his watch* The boat. We'll be late. *He moves slowly off into the darkness.*
WILLY, *elegiacally, turning to the house* Now when you kick off, boy, I want a seventy-yard boot, and get right down the field under the ball, and when you hit, hit low and hit hard, because it's important, boy. *He swings around and faces the audience.* There's all kind of important people in the stands, and the first thing you know . . . *Suddenly realizing he is alone*: Ben! Ben, where do I . . . ? *He makes a sudden movement of search.* Ben, how do I . . . ?
LINDA, *calling from within the house* Willy, you coming up?
WILLY, *uttering a gasp of fear, whirling about as if to quiet her* Sh! *He turns around as*

if to find his way; sounds, faces, voices, seem to be swarming in upon him and he flicks at them, crying, Sh! Sh! Suddenly music, faint and high, stops him. It rises in intensity, almost to an unbearable scream. He goes up and down on his toes, and rushes off around the house. Shhh!

LINDA Willy?

There is no answer. Linda waits. Biff gets up off his bed. He is still in his clothes. Happy sits up. Biff stands listening.

LINDA, *with real fear* Willy, answer me! Willy!

There is the sound of a car starting and moving away at full speed.

LINDA No!
BIFF, *rushing down the stairs* Pop!

As the car speeds off, the music crashes down in a frenzy of sound, which becomes the soft pulsation of a single cello string. Biff slowly returns to his bedroom. He and Happy gravely don their jackets. Linda slowly walks out of her room. The music has developed into a dead march. The leaves of day are appearing over everything. Charley and Bernard, somberly dressed, appear and knock on the kitchen door. Biff and Happy slowly descend the stairs to the kitchen as Charley and Bernard enter. All stop a moment when Linda, in clothes of mourning, bearing a little bunch of roses, comes through the draped doorway into the kitchen. She goes to Charley and takes his arm. Now all move toward the audience, through the wall-line of the kitchen. At the limit of the apron, Linda lays down the flowers, kneels, and sits back on her heels. All stare down at the grave.

REQUIEM

CHARLEY It's getting dark, Linda.

Linda doesn't react. She stares at the grave.

BIFF How about it, Mom? Better get some rest, heh? They'll be closing the gate soon.
Linda makes no move. Pause.

HAPPY, *deeply angered* He had no right to do that. There was no necessity for it. We would've helped him.
CHARLEY, *grunting* Hmmm.
BIFF Come along, Mom.
LINDA Why didn't anybody come?
CHARLEY It was a very nice funeral.
LINDA But where are all the people he knew? Maybe they blame him.
CHARLEY Naa. It's a rough world, Linda. They wouldn't blame him.
LINDA I can't understand it. At this time especially. First time in thirty-five years we were just about free and clear. He only needed a little salary. He was even finished with the dentist.
CHARLEY No man only needs a little salary.
LINDA I can't understand it.
BIFF There were a lot of nice days. When he'd come home from a trip; or on Sundays, making the stoop; finishing the cellar; putting on the new porch; when he built the extra bathroom; and put up the garage. You know something, Charley, there's more of him in that front stoop than in all the sales he ever made.
CHARLEY Yeah. He was a happy man with a batch of cement.
LINDA He was so wonderful with his hands.
BIFF He had the wrong dreams. All, all, wrong.
HAPPY, *almost ready to fight Biff* Don't say that!
BIFF He never knew who he was.
CHARLEY, *stopping Happy's movement and reply. To Biff* Nobody dast blame this man. You don't understand: Willy was a salesman. And for a salesman, there is no rock bottom to the life. He don't put a bolt to a nut, he don't tell you the law or give you medicine. He's a man way out there in the blue, riding on a smile and a shoeshine. And when they start not smiling back—that's an earthquake. And then you get yourself a couple of spots on your hat, and you're finished. Nobody dast blame this man. A salesman is got to dream, boy. It comes with the territory.
BIFF Charley, the man didn't know who he was.
HAPPY, *infuriated* Don't say that!

BIFF Why don't you come with me, Happy?

HAPPY I'm not licked that easily. I'm staying right in this city, and I'm gonna beat this racket! *He looks at Biff, his chin set.* The Loman Brothers!

BIFF I know who I am, kid.

HAPPY All right, boy. I'm gonna show you and everybody else that Willy Loman did not die in vain. He had a good dream. It's the only dream you can have—to come out number-one man. He fought it out here, and this is where I'm gonna win it for him.

BIFF, *with a hopeless glance at Happy, bends toward his mother* Let's go, Mom.

LINDA I'll be with you in a minute. Go on, Charley. *He hesitates.* I want to, just for a minute. I never had a chance to say good-by.

Charley moves away, followed by Happy. Biff remains a slight distance up and left of Linda. She sits there, summoning herself. The flute begins, not far away, playing behind her speech.

LINDA Forgive me, dear. I can't cry. I don't know what it is, but I can't cry. I don't understand it. Why did you ever do that? Help me, Willy, I can't cry. It seems to me that you're just on another trip. I keep expecting you. Willy, dear, I can't cry. Why did you do it? I search and search and I search, and I can't understand it, Willy. I made the last payment on the house today. Today, dear. And there'll be nobody home. *A sob rises in her throat.* We're free and clear. *Sobbing more fully, released:* We're free. *Biff comes slowly toward her.* We're free . . . We're free . . .

Biff lifts her to her feet and moves out up right with her in his arms. Linda sobs quietly. Bernard and Charley come together and follow them, followed by Happy. Only the music of the flute is left on the darkening stage as over the house the hard towers of the apartment buildings rise into sharp focus, and
                              Curtain.

Pullman Car Hiawatha*

by THORNTON WILDER

At the back of the stage is a balcony or bridge or runway leading out of sight in both directions. Two flights of stairs descend from it to the stage. There is no further scenery.

---

* Pullman Car Hiawatha" from *The Long Christmas Dinner and Other Plays in One Act* by Thornton Wilder. Copyright 1931 by Yale University Press and Coward-McCann, Inc.; Copyright © 1959 by Thornton Wilder. By permission of Harper & Row, Publishers, Incorporated.

Caution: *The Long Christmas Dinner and Other Plays in One Act* is the sole property of the author and is fully protected by copyright. The plays herein may not be acted by professionals or amateurs without formal permission and the payment of a royalty. All rights, including professional, amateur, stock, radio and television, broadcasting, motion picture, recitation, lecturing, public reading, and the rights of translation into foreign languages are reserved. All professional inquiries and all requests for amateur rights should be addressed to Samuel French, 25 West 45th Street, New York, New York 10019.

At the rise of the curtain the Stage Manager is making lines with a piece of chalk on the floor of the stage by the footlights.

THE STAGE MANAGER This is the plan of a Pullman car. Its name is Hiawatha and on December twenty-first it is on its way from New York to Chicago. Here at your left are three compartments. Here is the aisle and five lowers. The berths are all full, uppers and lowers, but for the purposes of this play we are limiting our interest to the people in the lower berths on the further side only.

The berths are already made up. It is half-past nine. Most of the passengers are in bed behind the green curtains. They are dropping their shoes on the floor, or wrestling with their trousers, or wondering whether they dare hide their valuables in the pillow-slips during the night.

All right! Come on, everybody!

The actors enter carrying chairs. Each improvises his berth by placing two chairs "facing one another" in his chalk-marked space. They then sit in one chair, profile to the audience, and rest their feet on the other. This must do for lying in bed.

The passengers in the compartments do the same.

Reading from left to right we have:

Compartment Three: *An insane woman with a male attendant and a trained nurse.*

Compartment Two: Philip *and*

Compartment One: Harriet, *his young wife.*

Lower One: *A maiden lady.*

Lower Five: *A stout, amiable woman of fifty.*

Lower Three: *A middle-aged doctor.*

Lower Seven: *An engineer going to California.*

Lower Nine: *Another engineer.*

LOWER ONE   Porter, be sure and wake me up at quarter of six.

PORTER   Yes, mam.

LOWER ONE   I know I shan't sleep a wink, but I want to be told when it's quarter of six.

PORTER   Yes, mam.

LOWER SEVEN   [*putting his head through the curtains*] Hsst! Porter! Hsst! How the hell do you turn on this other light?

PORTER   [*fussing with it*] I'm afraid it's outa order, suh. You'll have to use the other end.

THE STAGE MANAGER   [*falsetto, substituting for some woman in an upper berth*] May I ask if some one in this car will be kind enough to lend me some aspirin?

PORTER   [*rushing about*] Yes, mam.

LOWER NINE   [*one of these engineers, descending the aisle and falling into Lower Five*] Sorry, lady, sorry. Made a mistake.

LOWER FIVE   [*grumbling*] Never in all my born days!

LOWER ONE   [*in a shrill whisper*] Porter! Porter!

PORTER   Yes, mam.

LOWER ONE   My hot water bag's leaking. I guess you'll have to take it away. I'll have to do without it tonight. How awful!

LOWER FIVE   [*sharply to the passenger above her*] Young man, you mind your own business, or I'll report you to the conductor.

STAGE MANAGER   [*substituting for Upper Five*] Sorry, mam, I didn't mean to upset you. My suspenders fell down and I was trying to catch them.

LOWER FIVE   Well, here they are. Now go to sleep. Everybody seems to be rushing into my berth tonight.

She puts her head out.

Porter! Porter! Be a good soul and bring me a glass of water, will you? I'm parched.

LOWER NINE   Bill!

No answer.

Bill!

LOWER SEVEN   Ye'? Wha' d'y'a want?

LOWER NINE   Slip me one of those magazines, willya?

LOWER SEVEN   Which one d'y'a want?

LOWER NINE   Either one. "Detective Stories." Either one.

LOWER SEVEN   Aw, Fred. I'm just in the middle of one of'm in "Detective Stories."

LOWER NINE   That's all right. I'll take the "Western."—Thanks.

THE STAGE MANAGER   [*to the actors*] All right! —Sh! Sh! Sh!—.

To the audience.

Now I want you to hear them thinking.

There is a pause and then they all begin a murmuring-swishing noise, very soft. In turn each one of them can be heard above the others.

LOWER FIVE   [*the lady of fifty*] Let's see: I've got the doll for the baby. And the slip-on for Marietta. And the fountain pen for Herbert. And the subscription to *Time* for George . . .

LOWER SEVEN   [*Bill*] God! Lillian, if you don't turn out to be what I think you are, I don't know what I'll do.—I guess it's bad politics to let a woman know that you're going all the way to California to see her. I'll think up a song-and-dance about a business trip or something. Was I ever as hot and bothered about anyone like this before? Well, there was Martha. But that was different. I'd better try and read or I'll go cookoo. "How did you know it was ten o'clock when the visitor left the house?" asked the detective. "Because at ten o'clock," answered the girl, "I always turn out the lights in the conservatory and in the back hall. As I was coming down the stairs I heard the master talking to someone at the front door. I heard him say, 'Well, good night . . .' "—Gee, I don't feel like reading; I'll just think about Lillian. That yellow hair. Them eyes! . . .

LOWER THREE [*the doctor reads aloud to himself from a medical journal the most hair-raising material, every now and then punctuating his reading with an interrogative "So?"*].

LOWER ONE [*the maiden lady*] I know I'll be awake all night. I might just as well make up my mind to it now. I can't imagine what got hold of that hot water bag to leak on the train of all places. Well now, I'll lie on my right side and breathe deeply and think of beautiful things, and perhaps I can doze off a bit.

and lastly:

LOWER NINE [*Fred*] That was the craziest thing I ever did. It's set me back three whole years. I could have saved up thirty thousand dollars by now, if I'd only stayed over here. What business had I got to fool with contracts with the goddam Soviets. Hell, I thought it would be interesting. Interesting, what-the-hell! It's set me back three whole years. I don't even know if the company'll take me back. I'm green, that's all. I just don't grow up.

The Stage Manager *strides toward them with lifted hand crying "Hush," and their whispering ceases.*

THE STAGE MANAGER That'll do!—Just one minute. Porter!

THE PORTER [*appearing at the left*] Yessuh.

THE STAGE MANAGER It's your turn to think.

THE PORTER [*is very embarrassed*].

THE STAGE MANAGER Don't you want to? You have a right to.

THE PORTER [*torn between the desire to release his thoughts and his shyness*] Ah . . . ah . . . I'm only thinkin' about my home in Chicago and . . . and my life insurance.

THE STAGE MANAGER That's right.

THE PORTER . . . well, thank you. . . . Thank you.

He slips away, blushing violently, in an agony of self-consciousness and pleasure.

THE STAGE MANAGER [*to the audience*] He's a good fellow, Harrison is. Just shy.

To the actors again.

Now the compartments, please.

The berths fall into shadow.

Philip *is standing at the door connecting his compartment with his wife's.*

PHILIP Are you all right, angel?

HARRIET Yes. I don't know what was the matter with me during dinner.

PHILIP Shall I close the door?

HARRIET Do see whether you can't put a chair against it that will hold it half open without banging.

PHILIP There.—Good night, angel. If you can't sleep, call me and we'll sit up and play Russian Bank.

HARRIET You're thinking of that awful time when we sat up every night for a week. . . . But at least I know I shall sleep tonight. The noise of the wheels has become sort of nice and homely. What state are we in?

PHILIP We're tearing through Ohio. We'll be in Indiana soon.

HARRIET I know those little towns full of horse-blocks.

PHILIP Well, we'll reach Chicago very early. I'll call you. Sleep tight.

HARRIET Sleep tight, darling.

He returns to his own compartment. In Compartment Three, the male attendant tips his chair back against the wall and smokes a cigar. The trained nurse knits a stocking. The insane woman leans her forehead against the windowpane, that is: stares into the audience.

THE INSANE WOMAN [*her words have a dragging, complaining sound, but lack any conviction*] Don't take me there. Don't take me there.

THE FEMALE ATTENDANT Wouldn't you like to lie down, dearie?

THE INSANE WOMAN I want to get off the train. I want to go back to New York.

THE FEMALE ATTENDANT Wouldn't you like me to brush your hair again? It's such a nice feeling.

THE INSANE WOMAN [*going to the door*] I want to get off the train. I want to open the door.

THE FEMALE ATTENDANT [*taking one of her*

hands] Such a noise! You'll wake up all the nice people. Come and I'll tell you a story about the place we're going to.

THE INSANE WOMAN I don't want to go to that place.

THE FEMALE ATTENDANT Oh, it's lovely! There are lawns and gardens everywhere. I never saw such a lovely place. Just lovely.

THE INSANE WOMAN [*lies down on the bed*] Are there roses?

THE FEMALE ATTENDANT Roses! Red, yellow, white . . . just everywhere.

THE MALE ATTENDANT [*after a pause*] That musta been Cleveland.

THE FEMALE ATTENDANT I had a case in Cleveland once. Diabetes.

THE MALE ATTENDANT [*after another pause*] I wisht I had a radio here. Radios are good for *them*. I had a patient once that had to have the radio going every minute.

THE FEMALE ATTENDANT Radios are lovely. My married niece has one. It's always going. It's wonderful.

THE INSANE WOMAN [*half rising*] I'm not beautiful. I'm not beautiful as she was.

THE FEMALE ATTENDANT Oh, I think you're beautiful! Beautiful.—Mr. Morgan, don't you think Mrs. Churchill is beautiful?

THE MALE ATTENDANT Oh, fine lookin'! Regular movie star, Mrs. Churchill.

She looks inquiringly at them and subsides. Harriet *groans slightly. Smothers a cough. She gropes about with her hand and finds the bell.*

The Porter *knocks at her door.*

HARRIET [*whispering*] Come in. First, please close the door into my husband's room. Softly. Softly.

PORTER [*a plaintive porter*] Yes, mam.

HARRIET Porter, I'm not well. I'm sick. I must see a doctor.

PORTER Why, mam, they ain't no doctor . . .

HARRIET Yes, when I was coming out from dinner I saw a man in one of the seats on *that* side, reading medical papers. Go and wake him up.

PORTER [*flabbergasted*] Mam, I cain't wake anybody up.

HARRIET Yes, you can. Porter. Porter. Now don't argue with me. I'm very sick. It's my heart. Wake him up. Tell him it's my heart.

PORTER Yes, mam.

He goes into the aisle and starts pulling the shoulder of the man in Lower Three.

LOWER THREE Hello. Hello. What is it? Are we there?

The Porter *mumbles to him.*

I'll be right there.—Porter, is it a young woman or an old one?

PORTER I dono, suh. I guess she's kinda old, suh, but not so very old.

LOWER THREE Tell her I'll be there in a minute and to lie quietly.

The Porter *enters Harriet's compartment. She has turned her head away.*

PORTER He'll be here in a minute, mam. He says you lie quiet.

LOWER THREE *stumbles along the aisle muttering:* "Damn these shoes!"

SOMEONE'S VOICE Can't we have a little quiet in this car, please?

LOWER NINE [*Fred*] Oh, shut up!

The Doctor *passes the* Porter *and enters Harriet's compartment. He leans over her, concealing her by his stooping figure.*

LOWER THREE She's dead, porter. Is there anyone on the train traveling with her?

PORTER Yessuh. Dat's her husband in dere.

LOWER THREE Idiot! Why didn't you call him? I'll go in and speak to him.

The Stage Manager *comes forward.*

THE STAGE MANAGER All right. So much for the inside of the car. That'll be enough of that for the present. Now for its position geographically, meteorologically, astronomically, theologically considered.

Pullman Car Hiawatha, ten minutes of ten. December twenty-first, 1930. All ready.

Some figures begin to appear on the balcony.

No, no. It's not time for the planets yet. Nor the hours.

They retire.

The Stage Manager *claps his hands. A grinning boy in overalls enters from the left behind the berths.*

GROVER'S CORNERS, OHIO [*in a foolish voice as though he were reciting a piece at a Sunday*

School entertainment] I represent Grover's Corners, Ohio. 821 souls. "There's so much good in the worst of us and so much bad in the best of us, that it ill behooves any of us to criticize the rest of us." Robert Louis Stevenson. Thankya.

He grins and goes out right.

Enter from the same direction somebody in shirt sleeves. This is a field.

THE FIELD   I represent a field you are passing between Grover's Corners, Ohio, and Parkersburg, Ohio. In this field there are 51 gophers, 206 field mice, 6 snakes and millions of bugs, insects, ants, and spiders. All in their winter sleep. "What is so rare as a day in June? Then, if ever, come perfect days." *The Vision of Sir Launfal*, William Cullen—I mean James Russell Lowell. Thank you.

Exit.

Enter a tramp.

THE TRAMP   I just want to tell you that I'm a tramp that's been traveling under this car, Hiawatha, so I have a right to be in this play. I'm going from Rochester, New York, to Joliet, Illinois. It takes a lotta people to make a world. "On the road to Mandalay, where the flying fishes play and the sun comes up like thunder, over China cross the bay." Frank W. Service. It's bitter cold. Thank you.

Exit.

Enter a gentle old farmer's wife with three stringy young people.

PARKERSBURG, OHIO   I represent Parkersburg, Ohio. 2604 souls. I have seen all the dreadful havoc that alcohol has done and I hope no one here will ever touch a drop of the curse of this beautiful country.

She beats a measure and they all sing unsteadily:

"Throw out the lifeline! Throw out the lifeline! Someone is sinking today-ay . . ."

The Stage Manager *waves them away tactfully.*

Enter a workman.

THE WORKMAN   Ich bin der Arbeiter der hier sein Leben verlor. Bei der Sprengung für diese Brücke über die Sie in dem Moment fahren—

The engine whistles for a trestle crossing— erschlug mich ein Felsbock. Ich spiele jetzt als Geist in diesem Stuck mit. "Vor sieben und achtzig Jahren haben unsere Väter auf diesem Continent eine neue Nation hervorgebracht. . . ."

THE STAGE MANAGER   [*helpfully, to the audience*] I'm sorry; that's in German. He says that he's the ghost of a workman who was killed while they were building the trestle over which the car Hiawatha is now passing— *The engine whistles again—* and he wants to appear in this play. A chunk of rock hit him while they were dynamiting. —His motto you know: "Three score and seven years ago our fathers brought forth upon this continent a new nation dedicated," and so on. Thank you, Mr. Krüger.

Exit the ghost.

Enter another worker.

THIS WORKER   I'm a watchman in a tower near Parkersburg, Ohio. I just want to tell you that I'm not asleep and that the signals are all right for this train. I hope you all have a fine trip. "If you can keep your heads when all about you are losing theirs and blaming it on you. . . ." Rudyard Kipling. Thank you.

Exit.

The Stage Manager *comes forward.*

THE STAGE MANAGER   All right. That'll be enough of that. Now the weather.

Enter a mechanic.

A MECHANIC   It is eleven degrees above zero. The wind is north-northwest, velocity, 57. There is a field of low barometric pressure moving eastward from Saskatchewan to the Eastern Coast. Tomorrow it will be cold with some snow in the Middle Western States and Northern New York.

Exit.

THE STAGE MANAGER   All right. Now for the hours.

Helpfully to the audience:

The minutes are gossips; the hours are philosophers; the years are theologians. The hours are philosophers with the exception of Twelve O'clock who is also a theologian.— Ready Ten O'clock!

The hours are beautiful girls dressed like

Elihu Vedder's Pleiades. Each carries a great gold Roman numeral. They pass slowly across the balcony at the back moving from right to left.

What are you doing, Ten O'clock? Aristotle?

TEN O'CLOCK   No, Plato, Mr. Washburn.

THE STAGE MANAGER   Good.—"Are you not rather convinced that he who thus . . ."

TEN O'CLOCK   "Are you not rather convinced that he who sees Beauty as only it can be seen will be specially favored? And since he is in contact not with images but with realities. . . ."

She continues the passage in a murmur as Eleven O'clock *appears.*

ELEVEN O'CLOCK   "What else can I, Epictetus, do, a lame old man, but sing hymns to God? If then I were a nightingale, I would do the nightingale's part. If I were a swan I would do a swan's. But now I am a rational creature. . . ."

Her voice too subsides to a murmur. Twelve O'clock *appears.*

THE STAGE MANAGER   Good.—Twelve O'clock, what have you?

TWELVE O'CLOCK   Saint Augustine and his mother.

THE STAGE MANAGER   So.—"And we began to say: If to any the tumult of the flesh were hushed. . . ."

TWELVE O'CLOCK   "And we began to say: If to any the tumult of the flesh were hushed; hushed the images of earth; of waters and of air; . . ."

THE STAGE MANAGER   Faster.—"Hushed also the poles of Heaven."

TWELVE O'CLOCK   "Yea, were the very soul to be hushed to herself."

STAGE MANAGER   A little louder, Miss Foster.

TWELVE O'CLOCK [*a little louder*]   "Hushed all dreams and imaginary revelations. . . ."

THE STAGE MANAGER [*waving them back*]   All right. All right. Now the planets. December twenty-first, 1930, please.

The hours unwind and return to their dressing rooms at the right. The planets appear on the balcony. Some of them take their place halfway on the steps. These have no words, but each has a sound. One has a pulsating, zinging sound. Another has a thrum. One whistles ascending and descending scales. Saturn does a slow, obstinate:

$$\text{M—M—M—M—}$$

Louder, Saturn.—Venus, higher. Good. Now, Jupiter.—Now the earth.

He turns to the beds on the train.

Come, everybody. This is the earth's sound.

The towns, workmen, etc. appear at the edge of the stage. The passengers begin their "thinking" murmur.

Come, Grover's Corners. Parkersburg. You're in this.

Watchman. Tramp. This is the earth's sound.

He conducts it as the director of an orchestra would. Each of the towns and workmen does his motto.

The Insane Woman breaks into passionate weeping. She rises and stretches out her arms to the Stage Manager.

THE INSANE WOMAN   Use me. Give me something to do.

He goes to her quickly, whispers something in her ear, and leads her back to her guardians. She is unconsoled.

THE STAGE MANAGER   Now sh—sh—sh! Enter the archangels.

To the audience:

THE STAGE MANAGER   We have now reached the theological position of Pullman Car Hiawatha.

The towns and workmen have disappeared. The planets, off stage, continue a faint music. Two young men in blue serge suits enter along the balcony and descend the stairs at the right. As they pass each bed the passenger talks in his sleep.

Gabriel *points out* Bill *to* Michael *who smiles with raised eyebrows. They pause before* Lower Five *and* Michael *makes the sound of assent that can only be rendered "Hn-Hn." The remarks that the characters make in their sleep are not all intelligible, being lost in the sound of sigh or groan or whisper by which they are conveyed. But we seem to hear:*

LOWER NINE [*loud*] Some people are slower than others, that's all.

LOWER SEVEN [*Bill*] It's no fun, y'know. I'll try.

LOWER FIVE [*the lady of the Christmas presents, rapidly*] You know best, of course. I'm ready whenever you are. One year's like another.

LOWER ONE I can teach sewing. I can sew.

They approach Harriet's *compartment.*

The Insane Woman *sits up and speaks to them.*

THE INSANE WOMAN Me?

THE ARCHANGELS [*shake their heads*].

THE INSANE WOMAN What possible use can there be in my simply waiting?—Well, I'm grateful for anything. I'm grateful for being so much better than I was. The old story, the terrible story, doesn't haunt me as it used to. A great load seems to have been taken off my mind.—But no one understands me any more. At last I understand myself perfectly, but no one else understands a thing I say.—So I must wait?

THE ARCHANGELS [*nod, smiling*].

THE INSANE WOMAN [*resignedly, and with a smile that implies their complicity*] Well, you know best. I'll do whatever is best; but everyone is so childish, so absurd. They have no logic. These people are all so mad. . . . These people are like children; they have never suffered.

She returns to her bed and sleeps. The archangels *stand beside* Harriet. *The doctor has drawn* Philip *into the next compartment and is talking to him in earnest whispers.* Harriet's *face has been toward the wall; she turns it slightly and speaks toward the ceiling.*

HARRIET I wouldn't be happy there. Let me stay dead down here. I belong here. I shall be perfectly happy to roam about my house and be near Philip.—You know I wouldn't be happy there.

Gabriel *leans over and whispers into her ear. After a short pause she bursts into fierce tears.*

I'm ashamed to come with you. I haven't done anything. I haven't done anything with my life. Worse than that: I was angry and sullen. I never realized anything. I don't dare go a step in such a place.

They whisper to her again.

But it's not possible to forgive such things. I don't want to be forgiven so easily. I want to be punished for it all. I won't stir until I've been punished a long, long time. I want to be freed of all that—by punishment. I want to be all new.

They whisper to her. She puts her feet slowly on the ground.

But no one else could be punished for me. I'm willing to face it all myself. I don't ask anyone to be punished for me.

They whisper to her again. She sits long and brokenly looking at her shoes and thinking it over.

It wasn't fair. I'd have been willing to suffer for it myself,—if I could have endured such a mountain.

She smiles.

Oh, I'm ashamed! I'm just a stupid and you know it. I'm just another American.—But then what wonderful things must be beginning now. You really want me? You really want me?

They start leading her down the aisle of the car.

Let's take the whole train. There are some lovely faces on this train. Can't we all come? You'll never find anyone better than Philip. Please, please, let's all go.

They reach the steps. The archangels *interlock their arms as a support for her as she leans heavily on them, taking the steps slowly. Her words are half singing and half babbling.*

But look at how tremendously high and far it is. I've a weak heart. I'm not supposed to climb stairs. "I do not ask to see the distant scene: One step enough for me." It's like Switzerland. My tongue keeps saying things. I can't control it.—Do let me stop a minute: I want to say goodbye.

She turns in their arms.

Just a minute, I want to cry on your shoulder.

She leans her forehead against Gabriel's *shoulder and laughs long and softly.*

Goodbye, Philip.—I begged him not to marry me, but he would. He believed in me just as you do.—Goodbye, 1312 Ridgewood Avenue, Oaksbury, Illinois. I hope I remember all its steps and doors and wallpapers forever. Goodbye, Emerson Grammar School on the corner of Forbush Avenue and Wherry Street. Goodbye, Miss Walker and Miss Cramer who taught me English and Miss Matthewson, who taught me Biology. Goodbye, First Congregational Church on the corner of Meyerson Avenue and 6th Street and Dr. McReady and Mrs. McReady and Julia. Goodbye, Papa and Mama. . . .

She turns.

Now I'm tired of saying goodbye.—I never used to talk like this. I was so homely I never used to have the courage to talk. Until Philip came. I see now. I see now. I understand everything now.

The Stage Manager comes forward.

THE STAGE MANAGER [*to the actors*] All right. All right.—Now we'll have the whole world together, please. The whole solar system, please.

The complete cast begins to appear at the edges of the stage. He claps his hands.

The whole solar system, please. Where's the tramp?—Where's the moon?

He gives two raps on the floor, like the conductor of an orchestra attracting the attention of his forces, and slowly lifts his hand. The human beings murmur their thoughts; The hours discourse; the planets chant or hum. Harriet's voice finally rises above them all saying:

HARRIET "I was not ever thus, nor asked that Thou
Shouldst lead me on, and spite of fears,
Pride ruled my will: Remember not past years."

The Stage Manager *waves them away.*

THE STAGE MANAGER Very good. Now clear the stage, please. Now we're at Englewood Station, South Chicago. See the University's towers over there! The best of them all.

LOWER ONE [*the spinster*] Porter, you promised to wake me up at quarter of six.

PORTER Sorry, mam, but it's been an awful night on this car. A lady's been terrible sick.

LOWER ONE Oh! Is she better?

PORTER No'm. She ain't one jot better.

LOWER FIVE Young man, take your foot out of my face.

THE STAGE MANAGER [*again substituting for Upper Five*] Sorry, lady, I slipped—

LOWER FIVE [*grumbling not unamiably*] I declare, this trip's been one long series of insults.

THE STAGE MANAGER Just one minute, mam, and I'll be down and out of your way.

LOWER FIVE Haven't you got anybody to darn your socks for you? You ought to be ashamed to go about that way.

THE STAGE MANAGER Sorry, lady.

LOWER FIVE You're too stuck up to get married. That's the trouble with you.

LOWER NINE Bill!—Bill!

LOWER SEVEN Ye'? Wha' d'y'a want?

LOWER NINE Bill, how much d'y'a give the porter on a train like this? I've been outa the country so long . . .

LOWER SEVEN Hell, Fred, I don't know myself.

THE PORTER CHICAGO, CHICAGO. All out. This train don't go no further.

The passengers jostle their way out and an army of old women with mops and pails enter and prepare to clean up the car.

The curtain falls.

Six Characters in Search of an Author*

A Comedy in the Making

by LUIGI PIRANDELLO

(English Version by Edward Storer)

Characters of the Comedy in the Making

THE FATHER
THE MOTHER
THE STEP-DAUGHTER
THE SON
  THE BOY
  THE CHILD
(The last two do not speak.)
MADAME PACE

Actors of the Company

THE MANAGER
LEADING LADY
LEADING MAN
SECOND LADY
LEAD
L'INGENUE
JUVENILE LEAD
  OTHER ACTORS AND ACTRESSES
  PROPERTY MAN
  PROMPTER
  MACHINIST
  MANAGER'S SECRETARY
  DOOR-KEEPER
  SCENE-SHIFTERS

SCENE: *Daytime. The stage of a theater.*

N.B. *The Comedy is without acts or scenes. The performance is interrupted once, without the curtain being lowered, when the* MANAGER *and the chief characters withdraw to arrange a scenario. A second interruption of the action takes place when, by mistake, the stage hands let the curtain down.*

ACT I

(*The spectators will find the curtain raised and the stage as it usually is during the day time. It will be half dark, and empty, so that from the beginning the public may have the impression of an impromptu performance.*

PROMPTER'S *box and a small table and chair for the* MANAGER,

Two other small tables and several chairs scattered about as during rehearsals.

The ACTORS *and* ACTRESSES *of the company enter from the back of the stage: first one, then another, then two together; nine or ten in all. They are about to rehearse a Pirandello play: Mixing It Up.*[1] *Some of the company moves off towards their dressing rooms. The* PROMPTER, *who has the "book" under his arm, is waiting for the* MANAGER *in order to begin the rehearsal.*

The ACTORS *and* ACTRESSES, *some standing, some sitting, chat and smoke. One perhaps reads a paper; another cons his part.*

Finally the MANAGER *enters and goes to the table prepared for him. His* SECRETARY *brings him his mail, through which he glances. The* PROMPTER *takes his seat, turns on a light, and opens the "book."*)

THE MANAGER [*throwing a letter down on the table*] I can't see. [*To* PROPERTY MAN.] Let's have a little light, please!
PROPERTY MAN: Yes sir, yes, at once. [*A light comes down on to the stage.*]

---

* From the book *Naked Masks: Five Plays* by Luigi Pirandello, edited by Eric Bentley. Copyright, 1922, by E. P. Dutton & Co., Inc. Renewal, 1950, in the names of Stefano, Fausto, and Lietta Pirandello. Reprinted by permission of the publishers.

[1] *Il giuoco delle parti.*

THE MANAGER [*clapping his hands*] Come along! Come along! Second act of "Mixing It Up." [*Sits down.*]

[*The* ACTORS *and* ACTRESSES *go from the front of the stage to the wings, all except the three who are to begin the rehearsal.*]

THE PROMPTER [*reading the "book"*] "Leo Gala's house. A curious room serving as dining-room and study."

THE MANAGER [*to* PROPERTY MAN] Fix up the old red room.

PROPERTY MAN [*noting it down*] Red set. All right!

THE PROMPTER [*continuing to read from the "book"*] "Table already laid and writing desk with books and papers. Book-shelves. Exit rear to Leo's bedroom. Exit left to kitchen. Principal exit to right."

THE MANAGER [*energetically*] Well, you understand: The principal exit over there; here, the kitchen. [*Turning to actor who is to play the part of* SOCRATES.] You make your entrances and exits here. [*To* PROPERTY MAN.] The baize doors at the rear, and curtains.

PROPERTY MAN [*noting it down*] Right!

PROMPTER [*reading as before*] "When the curtain rises, Leo Gala, dressed in cook's cap and apron, is busy beating an egg in a cup. Philip, also dressed as a cook, is beating another egg. Guido Venanzi is seated and listening."

LEADING MAN [*to* MANAGER] Excuse me, but must I absolutely wear a cook's cap?

THE MANAGER [*annoyed*] I imagine so. It says so there anyway. [*Pointing to the "book."*]

LEADING MAN: But it's ridiculous!

THE MANAGER [*jumping up in a rage*] Ridiculous? Ridiculous? Is it my fault if France won't send us any more good comedies, and we are reduced to putting on Pirandello's works, where nobody understands anything, and where the author plays the fool with us all? [*The* ACTORS *grin. The* MANAGER *goes to* LEADING MAN *and shouts.*] Yes, sir, you put on the cook's cap and beat eggs. Do you suppose that with all this egg-beating business you are on an ordinary stage? Get that out of your head. You represent the shell of the eggs you are beating! [*Laughter and comments among the* ACTORS.] Silence! and listen to my explanations, please! [*To* LEADING MAN.] "The empty form of reason without the fullness of instinct, which is blind."—You stand for reason, your wife is instinct. It's a mixing up of the parts, according to which you who act your own part become the puppet of yourself. Do you understand?

LEADING MAN I'm hanged if I do.

THE MANAGER Neither do I. But let's get on with it. It's sure to be a glorious failure anyway. [*Confidentially.*] But I say, please face three-quarters. Otherwise, what with the abstruseness of the dialogue, and the public that won't be able to hear you, the whole thing will go to hell. Come on! come on!

PROMPTER Pardon sir, may I get into my box? There's a bit of a draught.

THE MANAGER Yes, yes, of course!

[*At this point, the* DOOR-KEEPER *has entered from the stage door and advances towards the* MANAGER'S *table, taking off his braided cap. During this manoeuvre, the* SIX CHARACTERS *enter, and stop by the door at back of stage, so that when the* DOOR-KEEPER *is about to announce their coming to the* MANAGER, *they are already on the stage. A tenuous light surrounds them, almost as if irradiated by them —the faint breath of their fantastic reality.*

This light will disappear when they come forward towards the actors. They preserve, however, something of the dream lightness in which they seem almost suspended; but this does not detract from the essential reality of their forms and expressions.

He who is known as THE FATHER *is a man of about 50: hair, reddish in color, thin at the temples; he is not bald, however; thick moustaches, falling over his still fresh mouth, which often opens in an empty and uncertain smile. He is fattish, pale; with an especially wide forehead. He has blue, oval-shaped eyes, very clear and piercing. Wears light trousers and a dark jacket. He is alternatively mellifluous and violent in his manner.*

THE MOTHER *seems crushed and terrified as if by an intolerable weight of shame and abasement. She is dressed in modest black and wears a thick widow's veil of crêpe. When she lifts this, she reveals a wax-like face. She always keeps her eyes downcast.*

THE STEP-DAUGHTER is dashing, almost impudent, beautiful. She wears mourning too, but with great elegance. She shows contempt for the timid half-frightened manner of the wretched BOY *(14 years old, and also dressed in black); on the other hand, she displays a lively tenderness for her little sister,* THE CHILD *(about four), who is dressed in white, with a black silk sash at the waist.*

THE SON (22) is tall, severe in his attitude of contempt for THE FATHER, *supercilious and indifferent to* THE MOTHER. *He looks as if he had come on the stage against his will.*]

DOOR-KEEPER [*cap in hand*] Excuse me, sir . . .

THE MANAGER [*rudely*] Eh? What is it?

DOOR-KEEPER [*timidly*] These people are asking for you, sir.

THE MANAGER [*furious*] I am rehearsing, and you know perfectly well no one's allowed to come in during rehearsals! [*Turning to the* CHARACTERS.] Who are you, please? What do you want?

THE FATHER [*coming forward a little, followed by the others who seem embarrassed*] As a matter of fact . . . we have come here in search of an author . . .

THE MANAGER [*half angry, half amazed*] An author? What author?

THE FATHER Any author, sir.

THE MANAGER But there's no author here. We are not rehearsing a new piece.

THE STEP-DAUGHTER [*vivaciously*] So much the better, so much the better! We can be your new piece.

AN ACTOR [*coming forward from the others*] Oh, do you hear that?

THE FATHER [*to* STEP-DAUGHTER] Yes, but if the author isn't here . . . [*To* MANAGER.] unless you would be willing . . .

THE MANAGER You are trying to be funny.

THE FATHER No, for Heaven's sake, what are you saying? We bring you a drama, sir.

THE STEP-DAUGHTER We may be your fortune.

THE MANAGER Will you oblige me by going away? We haven't time to waste with mad people.

THE FATHER [*mellifluously*] Oh sir, you know well that life is full of infinite absurdities, which, strangely enough, do not even need to appear plausible, since they are true.

THE MANAGER What the devil is he talking about?

THE FATHER I say that to reverse the ordinary process may well be considered a madness: that is, to create credible situations, in order that they may appear true. But permit me to observe that if this be madness, it is the sole *raison d'être* of your profession, gentlemen. [*The* ACTORS *look hurt and perplexed.*]

THE MANAGER [*getting up and looking at him*] So our profession seems to you one worthy of madmen then?

THE FATHER Well, to make seem true that which isn't true . . . without any need . . . for a joke as it were . . . Isn't that your mission, gentlemen: to give life to fantastic characters on the stage?

THE MANAGER [*interpreting the rising anger of the* COMPANY] But I would beg you to believe, my dear sir, that the profession of the comedian is a noble one. If today, as things go, the playwrights give us stupid comedies to play and puppets to represent instead of men, remember we are proud to have given life to immortal works here on these very boards! [*The* ACTORS, *satisfied, applaud their* MANAGER.]

THE FATHER [*interrupting furiously*] Exactly, perfectly, to living beings more alive than those who breathe and wear clothes: beings less real perhaps, but truer! I agree with you entirely. [*The* ACTORS *look at one another in amazement.*]

THE MANAGER But what do you mean? Before, you said . . .

THE FATHER No, excuse me, I meant it for you, sir, who were crying out that you had no time to lose with madmen, while no one better than yourself knows that nature uses the instrument of human fantasy in order to pursue her high creative purpose.

THE MANAGER Very well,—but where does all this take us?

THE FATHER Nowhere! It is merely to show you that one is born to life in many forms, in many shapes, as tree, or as stone, as water, as butterfly, or as woman. So one may also be born a character in a play.

THE MANAGER [*with feigned comic dismay*] So you and these other friends of yours have been born characters?

THE FATHER Exactly, and alive as you see! [MANAGER *and* ACTORS *burst out laughing.*]

THE FATHER [*hurt*] I am sorry you laugh, because we carry in us a drama, as you can guess from this woman here veiled in black.

THE MANAGER [*losing patience at last and almost indignant*] Oh, chuck it! Get away please! Clear out of here! [*To* PROPERTY MAN.] For Heaven's sake, turn them out!

THE FATHER [*resisting*] No, no, look here, we . . .

THE MANAGER [*roaring*] We come here to work, you know.

LEADING ACTOR One cannot let oneself be made such a fool of.

THE FATHER [*determined, coming forward*] I marvel at your incredulity, gentlemen. Are you not accustomed to see the characters created by an author spring to life in yourselves and face each other? Just because there is no "book" [*pointing to the* PROMPTER'*s box*] which contains us, you refuse to believe . . .

THE STEP-DAUGHTER [*advances toward* MANAGER, *smiling and coquettish*] Believe me, we are really six most interesting characters, sir; side-tracked however.

THE FATHER Yes, that is the word! [*To* MANAGER *all at once.*] In the sense, that is, that the author who created us alive no longer wished, or was no longer able, materially to put us into a work of art. And this was a real crime, sir; because he who has had the luck to be born a character can laugh even at death. He cannot die. The man, the writer, the instrument of the creation will die, but his creation does not die. And to live for ever, it does not need to have extraordinary gifts or to be able to work wonders. Who was Sancho Panza? Who was Don Abbondio? Yet they live eternally because—live germs as they were—they had the fortune to find a fecundating matrix, a fantasy which could raise and nourish them: make them live for ever!

THE MANAGER That is quite all right. But what do you want here, all of you?

THE FATHER We want to live.

THE MANAGER [*ironically*] For Eternity?

THE FATHER No, sir, only for a moment . . . in you.

AN ACTOR Just listen to him!

LEADING LADY They want to live, in us . . . !

JUVENILE LEAD [*pointing to the* STEP-DAUGHTER] I've no objection, as far as that one is concerned!

THE FATHER Look here! look here! The comedy has to be made. [*To the* MANAGER.] But if you and your actors are willing, we can soon concert it among ourselves.

THE MANAGER [*annoyed*] But what do you want to concert? We don't go in for concerts here. Here we play dramas and comedies!

THE FATHER Exactly! That is just why we have come to you.

THE MANAGER And where is the "book"?

THE FATHER It is in us! [*The* ACTORS *laugh.*] The drama is in us, and we are the drama. We are impatient to play it. Our inner passion drives us on to this.

THE STEP-DAUGHTER [*disdainful, alluring, treacherous, full of impudence*] My passion, sir! Ah, if you only knew! My passion for him! [*Points to the* FATHER *and makes a pretense of embracing him. Then she breaks out into a loud laugh.*]

THE FATHER [*angrily*] Behave yourself! And please don't laugh in that fashion.

THE STEP-DAUGHTER With your permission, gentlemen, I, who am a two months' orphan, will show you how I can dance and sing. [*Sings and then dances* Prenez garde à Tchou-Tchin-Tchou.]

    Les chinois sont un peuple malin,
    De Shangaï à Pékin,
    Ils ont mis des écriteaux partout:
    Prenez garde à Tchou-Tchin-Tchou.

ACTORS *and* ACTRESSES Bravo! Well done! Tip-top!

THE MANAGER Silence! This isn't a café concert, you know! [*Turning to the* FATHER *in consternation.*] Is she mad?

THE FATHER Mad? No, she's worse than mad.

THE STEP-DAUGHTER [*to* MANAGER] Worse? Worse? Listen! Stage this drama for us at once! Then you will see that at a certain moment I . . . when this little darling here. . . . [*Takes the* CHILD *by the hand and leads her to the* MANAGER.] Isn't she a dear? [*Takes her up and kisses her.*] Darling! Darling! [*Puts her down again and adds feelingly.*] Well, when God suddenly takes this dear little child away from that poor mother there; and this imbecile here [*seizing hold of the* BOY *roughly and pushing him forward*] does the stupidest things, like the fool he is, you will see me run away. Yes, gentlemen, I shall be off. But the moment hasn't arrived yet. After what has taken place between him and me [*indicates the* FATHER *with a horrible wink*] I can't remain any longer in this society, to have to witness the anguish of this mother here for that fool. . . . [*Indicates the* SON.] Look at him! Look at him! See how indifferent, how frigid he is, because he is the legitimate son. He despises me, despises him [*pointing to the* BOY], despises this baby here; because . . . we are bastards. [*Goes to the* MOTHER *and embraces her.*] And he doesn't want to recognize her as his mother—she who is the common mother of us all. He looks down upon her as if she were only the mother of us three bastards. Wretch! [*She says all this very rapidly, excitedly. At the word "bastards" she raises her voice, and almost spits out the final "Wretch!"*]

THE MOTHER [*to the* MANAGER, *in anguish*] In the name of these two little children, I beg you. . . . [*She grows faint and is about to fall.*] Oh God!

THE FATHER [*coming forward to support her as do some of the* ACTORS] Quick, a chair, a chair for this poor widow!

THE ACTORS Is it true? Has she really fainted?

THE MANAGER Quick, a chair! Here!

[*One of the* ACTORS *brings a chair, the* OTHERS *proffer assistance. The* MOTHER *tries to prevent the* FATHER *from lifting the veil which covers her face.*]

THE FATHER Look at her! Look at her!
THE MOTHER No, no; stop it please!
THE FATHER [*raising her veil*] Let them see you!

THE MOTHER [*rising and covering her face with her hands, in desperation*] I beg you, sir, to prevent this man from carrying out his plan which is loathsome to me.

THE MANAGER [*dumbfounded*] I don't understand at all. What is the situation? [*To the* FATHER.] Is this lady your wife?

THE FATHER Yes, gentlemen: my wife!

THE MANAGER But how can she be a widow if you are alive? [*The* ACTORS *find relief for their astonishment in a loud laugh.*]

THE FATHER Don't laugh! Don't laugh like that, for Heaven's sake. Her drama lies just here in this: she has had a lover, a man who ought to be here.

THE MOTHER [*with a cry*] No! No!

THE STEP-DAUGHTER Fortunately for her, he is dead. Two months ago as I said. We are in mourning, as you see.

THE FATHER He isn't here you see, not because he is dead. He isn't here—look at her a moment and you will understand—because her drama isn't a drama of the love of two men for whom she was incapable of feeling anything except possibly a little gratitude—gratitude not for me but for the other. She isn't a woman, she is a mother, and her drama—powerful sir, I assure you—lies, as a matter of fact, all in these four children she has had by two men.

THE MOTHER I had them? Have you got the courage to say that I wanted them? [*To the* COMPANY.] It was his doing. It was he who gave me that other man, who forced me to go away with him.

THE STEP-DAUGHTER It isn't true.

THE MOTHER [*startled*] Not true, isn't it?

THE STEP-DAUGHTER No, it isn't true, it just isn't true.

THE MOTHER And what can you know about it?

THE STEP-DAUGHTER It isn't true. Don't believe it. [*To* MANAGER.] Do you know why she says so? For that fellow there. [*Indicates the* SON.] She tortures herself, destroys herself on account of the neglect of that son there; and she wants him to believe that if she abandoned him when he was only two years old, it was because he [*indicates the* FATHER] made her do so.

THE MOTHER [*vigorously*] He forced me to it, and I call God to witness it. [*To the* MANAGER.] Ask him [*indicates* HUSBAND] if it isn't true. Let him speak. You [*to* DAUGHTER] are not in a position to know anything about it.

THE STEP-DAUGHTER I know you lived in peace and happiness with my father while he lived. Can you deny it?

THE MOTHER No, I don't deny it. . . .

THE STEP-DAUGHTER He was always full of affection and kindness for you. [*To the* BOY, *angrily*.] It's true, isn't it? Tell them! Why don't you speak, you little fool?

THE MOTHER Leave the poor boy alone. Why do you want to make me appear ungrateful, daughter? I don't want to offend your father. I have answered him that I didn't abandon my house and my son through any fault of mine, nor from any wilful passion.

THE FATHER It is true. It was my doing.

LEADING MAN [*to the* COMPANY] What a spectacle!

LEADING LADY We are the audience this time.

JUVENILE LEAD For once, in a way.

THE MANAGER [*beginning to get really interested*] Let's hear them out. Listen!

THE SON Oh yes, you're going to hear a fine bit now. He will talk to you of the Demon of Experiment.

THE FATHER You are a cynical imbecile. I've told you so already a hundred times. [*To the* MANAGER.] He tries to make fun of me on account of this expression which I have found to excuse myself with.

THE SON [*with disgust*] Yes, phrases! phrases!

THE FATHER Phrases! Isn't everyone consoled when faced with a trouble or fact he doesn't understand, by a word, some simple word, which tells us nothing and yet calms us?

THE STEP-DAUGHTER Even in the case of remorse. In fact, especially then.

THE FATHER Remorse? No, that isn't true. I've done more than use words to quieten the remorse in me.

THE STEP-DAUGHTER Yes, there was a bit of money too. Yes, yes, a bit of money. There were the hundred lire he was about to offer me in payment, gentlemen. . . . [*Sensation of horror among the* ACTORS.]

THE SON [*to the* STEP-DAUGHTER] This is vile.

THE STEP-DAUGHTER Vile? There they were in a pale blue envelope on a little mahogany table in the back of Madame Pace's shop. You know Madame Pace—one of those ladies who attract poor girls of good family into their ateliers, under the pretext of their selling *robes et manteaux*.

THE SON And he thinks he has bought the right to tyrannize over us all with those hundred lire he was going to pay; but which, fortunately—note this, gentlemen—he had no chance of paying.

THE STEP-DAUGHTER It was a near thing, though, you know! [*Laughs ironically*.]

THE MOTHER [*protesting*] Shame, my daughter, shame!

THE STEP-DAUGHTER Shame indeed! This is my revenge! I am dying to live that scene . . . The room . . . I see it . . . Here is the window with the mantles exposed, there the divan, the looking-glass, a screen, there in front of the window the little mahogany table with the blue envelope containing one hundred lire. I see it. I see it. I could take hold of it. . . . But you, gentlemen, you ought to turn your backs now: I am almost nude, you know. But I don't blush: I leave that to him. [*Indicating* FATHER.]

THE MANAGER I don't understand this at all.

THE FATHER Naturally enough. I would ask you, sir, to exercise your authority a little here, and let me speak before you believe all she is trying to blame me with. Let me explain.

THE STEP-DAUGHTER Ah yes, explain it in your own way.

THE FATHER But don't you see that the whole trouble lies here? In words, words. Each one of us has within him a whole world of things, each man of us his own special world. And how can we ever come to an understanding if I put in the words I utter the sense and value of things as I see them; while you who listen to me must inevitably translate them according to the conception of things each one of you has within himself. We think we understand each other, but we never really do. Look here! This woman [*indicating the* MOTHER] takes all my pity for her as a specially ferocious form of cruelty.

THE MOTHER But you drove me away.

THE FATHER Do you hear her? I drove her away! She believes I really sent her away.

THE MOTHER You know how to talk, and I don't; but, believe me, sir [*to* MANAGER], after he had married me . . . who knows why? . . . I was a poor insignificant woman. . . .

THE FATHER But, good Heavens! it was just for your humility that I married you. I loved this simplicity in you. [*He stops when he sees she makes signs to contradict him, opens his arms wide in sign of desperation, seeing how hopeless it is to make himself understood.*] You see she denies it. Her mental deafness, believe me, is phenomenal, the limit: [*touches his forehead*] deaf, deaf, mentally deaf! She has plenty of feeling. Oh yes, a good heart for the children; but the brain—deaf, to the point of desperation—!

THE STEP-DAUGHTER Yes, but ask him how his intelligence has helped us.

THE FATHER If we could see all the evil that may spring from good, what should we do? [*At this point the* LEADING LADY, *who is biting her lips with rage at seeing the* LEADING MAN *flirting with the* STEP-DAUGHTER, *comes forward and speaks to the* MANAGER.]

LEADING LADY Excuse me, but are we going to rehearse today?

MANAGER Of course, of course; but let's hear them out.

JUVENILE LEAD This is something quite new.

L'INGENUE Most interesting!

LEADING LADY Yes, for the people who like that kind of thing. [*Casts a glance at* LEADING MAN.]

THE MANAGER [*to* FATHER] You must please explain yourself quite clearly. [*Sits down.*]

THE FATHER Very well then: listen! I had in my service a poor man, a clerk, a secretary of mine, full of devotion, who became friends with her. [*Indicating the* MOTHER.] They understood one another, were kindred souls in fact, without, however, the least suspicion of any evil existing. They were incapable even of thinking of it.

THE STEP-DAUGHTER So he thought of it—for them!

THE FATHER That's not true. I meant to do good to them—and to myself, I confess, at the same time. Things had come to the point that I could not say a word to either of them without their making a mute appeal, one to the other, with their eyes. I could see them silently asking each other how I was to be kept in countenance, how I was to be kept quiet. And this, believe me, was just about enough of itself to keep me in a constant rage, to exasperate me beyond measure.

THE MANAGER And why didn't you send him away then—this secretary of yours?

THE FATHER Precisely what I did, sir. And then I had to watch this poor woman drifting forlornly about the house like an animal without a master, like an animal one has taken in out of pity.

THE MOTHER Ah yes . . . !

THE FATHER [*suddenly turning to the* MOTHER] It's true about the son anyway, isn't it?

THE MOTHER He took my son away from me first of all.

THE FATHER But not from cruelty. I did it so that he should grow up healthy and strong by living in the country.

THE STEP-DAUGHTER [*pointing to him ironically*] As one can see.

THE FATHER [*quickly*] Is it my fault if he has grown up like this? I sent him to a wet nurse in the country, a peasant, as *she* did not seem to me strong enough, though she is of humble origin. That was, anyway, the reason I married her. Unpleasant all this may be, but how can it be helped? My mistake possibly, but there we are! All my life I have had these confounded aspirations towards a certain moral sanity. [*At this point the* STEP-DAUGHTER *bursts into a noisy laugh.*] Oh, stop it! Stop it! I can't stand it.

THE MANAGER Yes, please stop it, for Heaven's sake.

THE STEP-DAUGHTER But imagine moral sanity from him, if you please—the client of certain ateliers like that of Madame Pace!

THE FATHER Fool! That is the proof that I am a man! This seeming contradiction, gentlemen, is the strongest proof that I stand here a live man before you. Why, it is just for this very incongruity in my nature that I have had to suffer what I have. I could not live by the side of that woman [*indicating the* MOTHER] any longer; but not so much for the boredom she inspired me with as for the pity I felt for her.

THE MOTHER   And so he turned me out—.

THE FATHER   —well provided for! Yes, I sent her to that man, gentlemen . . . to let her go free of me.

THE MOTHER   And to free himself.

THE FATHER   Yes, I admit it. It was also a liberation for me. But great evil has come of it. I meant well when I did it; and I did it more for her sake than mine. I swear it. [*Crosses his arms on his chest; then turns suddenly to the* MOTHER.] Did I ever lose sight of you until that other man carried you off to another town, like the angry fool he was? And on account of my pure interest in you . . . my pure interest, I repeat, that had no base motive in it . . . I watched with the tenderest concern the new family that grew up around her. She can bear witness to this. [*Points to the* STEP-DAUGHTER.]

THE STEP-DAUGHTER   Oh yes, that's true enough. When I was a kiddie, so so high, you know, with plaits over my shoulders and knickers longer than my skirts, I used to see him waiting outside the school for me to come out. He came to see how I was growing up.

THE FATHER   This is infamous, shameful!

THE STEP-DAUGHTER   No. Why?

THE FATHER   Infamous! infamous! [*Then excitedly to* MANAGER *explaining*.] After she [*indicating the* MOTHER] went away, my house seemed suddenly empty. She was my incubus, but she filled my house. I was like a dazed fly alone in the empty rooms. This boy here [*indicating the* SON] was educated away from home, and when he came back, he seemed to me to be no more mine. With no mother to stand between him and me, he grew up entirely for himself, on his own, apart, with no tie of intellect or affection binding him to me. And then—strange but true—I was driven, by curiosity at first and then by some tender sentiment, towards her family, which had come into being through my will. The thought of her began gradually to fill up the emptiness I felt all around me. I wanted to know if she were happy in living out the simple daily duties of life. I wanted to think of her as fortunate and happy because far away from the complicated torments of my spirit. And so, to have proof of this, I used to watch that child coming out of school.

THE STEP-DAUGHTER   Yes, yes. True. He used to follow me in the street and smiled at me, waved his hand, like this. I would look at him with interest, wondering who he might be. I told my mother, who guessed at once. [*The* MOTHER *agrees with a nod*.] Then she didn't want to send me to school for some days; and when I finally went back, there he was again—looking so ridiculous—with a paper parcel in his hands. He came close to me, caressed me, and drew out a fine straw hat from the parcel, with a bouquet of flowers —all for me!

THE MANAGER   A bit discursive this, you know!

THE SON [*contemptuously*]   Literature! Literature!

THE FATHER   Literature indeed! This is life, this is passion!

THE MANAGER   It may be, but it won't act.

THE FATHER   I agree. This is only the part leading up. I don't suggest this should be staged. She [*pointing to the* STEP-DAUGHTER], as you see, is no longer the flapper with plaits down her back—,

THE STEP-DAUGHTER   —and the knickers showing below the skirt!

THE FATHER   The drama is coming now, sir; something new, complex, most interesting.

THE STEP-DAUGHTER   As soon as my father died . . .

THE FATHER   —there was absolute misery for them. They came back here, unknown to me. Through her stupidity! [*Pointing to the* MOTHER.] It is true she can barely write her own name; but she could anyhow have got her daughter to write to me that they were in need . . .

THE MOTHER   And how was I to divine all this sentiment in him?

THE FATHER   That is exactly your mistake, never to have guessed any of my sentiments.

THE MOTHER   After so many years apart, and all that had happened . . .

THE FATHER   Was it my fault if that fellow carried you away? It happened quite suddenly; for after he had obtained some job or other, I could find no trace of them; and so, not unnaturally, my interest in them dwindled. But the drama culminated unforeseen and violent on their return, when I was impelled by my miserable flesh that still lives. . . . Ah! what misery, what wretchedness is that of the man who is alone and disdains debasing *liaisons!* Not old enough to do without women, and not young enough to go and look for one without shame. Misery? It's worse than misery; it's a horror; for no woman can any longer give him love; and when a man feels this. . . . One ought to do without, you say? Yes, yes, I know. Each of us when he appears before his fellows is clothed in a certain dignity. But every man knows what unconfessable things pass within the secrecy of his own heart. One gives way to the temptation, only to rise from it again, afterwards, with a great eagerness to re-establish one's dignity, as if it were a tombstone to place on the grave of one's shame, and a monument to hide and sign the memory of our weaknesses. Everybody's in the same case. Some folks haven't the courage to say certain things, that's all!

THE STEP-DAUGHTER   All appear to have the courage to do them though.

THE FATHER   Yes, but in secret. Therefore, you want more courage to say these things. Let a man but speak these things out, and folks at once label him a cynic. But it isn't true. He is like all the others, better indeed, because he isn't afraid to reveal with the light of the intelligence the red shame of human bestiality on which most men close their eyes so as not to see it.

Woman—for example, look at her case! She turns tantalizing inviting glances on you. You seize her. No sooner does she feel herself in your grasp than she closes her eyes. It is the sign of her mission, the sign by which she says to man: "Blind yourself, for I am blind."

THE STEP-DAUGHTER   Sometimes she can close them no more: when she no longer feels the need of hiding her shame to herself, but dry-eyed and dispassionately, sees only that of the man who has blinded himself without love. Oh, all these intellectual complications make me sick, disgust me—all this philosophy that uncovers the beast in man, and then seeks to save him, excuse him . . . I can't stand it, sir. When a man seeks to "simplify" life bestially, throwing aside every relic of humanity, every chaste aspiration, every pure feeling, all sense of ideality, duty, modesty, shame . . . then nothing is more revolting and nauseous than a certain kind of remorse—crocodiles' tears, that's what it is.

THE MANAGER   Let's come to the point. This is only discussion.

THE FATHER   Very good, sir! But a fact is like a sack which won't stand up when it's empty. In order that it may stand up, one has to put into it the reason and sentiment which have caused it to exist. I couldn't possibly know that after the death of that man, they had decided to return here, that they were in misery, and that she [*pointing to the* MOTHER] had gone to work as a modiste, and at a shop of the type of that of Madame Pace.

THE STEP-DAUGHTER   A real high-class modiste, you must know, gentlemen. In appearance, she works for the leaders of the best society; but she arranges matters so that these elegant ladies serve her purpose . . . without prejudice to other ladies who are . . . well . . . only so so.

THE MOTHER   You will believe me, gentlemen, that it never entered my mind that the old hag offered me work because she had her eye on my daughter.

THE STEP-DAUGHTER   Poor mamma! Do you know, sir, what that woman did when I brought her back the work my mother had finished? She would point out to me that I had torn one of my frocks, and she would give it back to my mother to mend. It was

I who paid for it, always I; while this poor creature here believed she was sacrificing herself for me and these two children here, sitting up at night sewing Madame Pace's robes.

THE MANAGER   And one day you met there . . .

THE STEP-DAUGHTER   Him, him. Yes sir, an old client. There's a scene for you to play! Superb!

THE FATHER   She, the Mother arrived just then . . .

THE STEP-DAUGHTER   [*treacherously*] Almost in time!

THE FATHER   [*crying out*] No, in time! in time! Fortunately I recognized her . . . in time. And I took them back home with me to my house. You can imagine now her position and mine; she, as you see her; and I who cannot look her in the face.

THE STEP-DAUGHTER   Absurd! How can I possibly be expected—after that—to be a modest young miss, a fit person to go with his confounded aspirations for "a solid moral sanity"?

THE FATHER   For the drama lies all in this—in the conscience that I have, that each one of us has. We believe this conscience to be a single thing, but it is many-sided. There is one for this person, and another for that. Diverse consciences. So we have this illusion of being one person for all, of having a personality that is unique in all our acts. But it isn't true. We perceive this when, tragically perhaps, in something we do, we are as it were, suspended, caught up in the air on a kind of hook. Then we perceive that all of us was not in that act, and that it would be an atrocious injustice to judge us by that action alone, as if all our existence were summed up in that one deed. Now do you understand the perfidy of this girl? She surprised me in a place, where she ought not to have known me, just as I could not exist for her; and she now seeks to attach to me a reality such as I could never suppose I should have to assume for her in a shameful and fleeting moment of my life. I feel this above all else. And the drama, you will see, acquires a tremendous value from this point. Then there is the position of the others . . . his. . . . [*Indicating the* SON.]

THE SON   [*shrugging his shoulders scornfully*] Leave me alone! I don't come into this.

THE FATHER   What? You don't come into this?

THE SON   I've got nothing to do with it, and don't want to have; because you know well enough I wasn't made to be mixed up in all this with the rest of you.

THE STEP-DAUGHTER   We are only vulgar folk! He is the fine gentleman. You may have noticed, Mr. Manager, that I fix him now and again with a look of scorn while he lowers his eyes—for he knows the evil he has done me.

THE SON   [*scarcely looking at her*] I?

THE STEP-DAUGHTER   You! you! I owe my life on the streets to you. Did you or did you not deny us, with your behavior, I won't say the intimacy of home, but even that mere hospitality which makes guests feel at their ease? We were intruders who had come to disturb the kingdom of your legitimacy. I should like to have you witness, Mr. Manager, certain scenes between him and me. He says I have tyrannized over everyone. But it was just his behavior which made me insist on the reason for which I had come into the house,—this reason he calls "vile"—into his house, with my mother who is his mother too. And I came as mistress of the house.

THE SON   It's easy for them to put me always in the wrong. But imagine, gentlemen, the position of a son, whose fate it is to see arrive one day at his home a young woman of impudent bearing, a young woman who inquires for his father, with whom who knows what business she has. This young man has then to witness her return bolder than ever, accompanied by that child there. He is obliged to watch her treat his father in an equivocal and confidential manner. She asks money of him in a way that lets one suppose he must give it to her, *must*, do you understand, because he has every obligation to do so.

THE FATHER   But I have, as a matter of fact, this obligation. I owe it to your mother.

THE SON   How should I know? When had I ever seen or heard of her? One day there arrive with her [*indicating* STEP-DAUGHTER] that lad and this baby here. I am told: "This is *your* mother too, you know." I divine from her manner [*indicating* STEP-DAUGHTER *again*] why it is they have come home. I had rather not say what I feel and think about it. I shouldn't even care to confess to myself. No action can therefore be hoped for from me in this affair. Believe me, Mr. Manager, I am an "unrealized" character, dramatically speaking; and I find myself not at all at ease in their company. Leave me out of it, I beg you.

THE FATHER   What? It is just because you are so that . . .

THE SON   How do you know what I am like? When did you ever bother your head about me?

THE FATHER   I admit it. I admit it. But isn't that a situation in itself? This aloofness of yours which is so cruel to me and to your mother, who returns home and sees you almost for the first time grown up, who doesn't recognize you but knows you are her son. . . . [*Pointing out the* MOTHER *to the* MANAGER.] See, she's crying!

THE STEP-DAUGHTER [*angrily, stamping her foot*] Like a fool!

THE FATHER [*indicating* STEP-DAUGHTER] She can't stand him, you know. [*Then referring again to the* SON.] He says he doesn't come into the affair, whereas he is really the hinge of the whole action. Look at that lad who is always clinging to his mother, frightened and humiliated. It is on account of this fellow here. Possibly his situation is the most painful of all. He feels himself a stranger more than the others. The poor little chap feels mortified, humiliated at being brought into a home out of charity as it were. [*In confidence.*] He is the image of his father. Hardly talks at all. Humble and quiet.

THE MANAGER   Oh, we'll cut him out. You've no notion what a nuisance boys are on the stage. . . .

THE FATHER   He disappears soon, you know. And the baby too. She is the first to vanish from the scene. The drama consists finally in this: when that mother re-enters my house, her family born outside of it, and shall we say superimposed on the original, ends with the death of the little girl, the tragedy of the boy and the flight of the elder daughter. It cannot go on, because it is foreign to its surroundings. So after much torment, we three remain: I, the mother, that son. Then, owing to the disappearance of that extraneous family, we too find ourselves strange to one another. We find we are living in an atmosphere of mortal desolation which is the revenge, as he [*indicating* SON] scornfully said of the Demon of Experiment, that unfortunately hides in me. Thus, sir, you see when faith is lacking, it becomes impossible to create certain states of happiness, for we lack the necessary humility. Vaingloriously, we try to substitute ourselves for this faith, creating thus for the rest of the world a reality which we believe after their fashion, while, actually, it doesn't exist. For each one of us has his own reality to be respected before God, even when it is harmful to one's very self.

THE MANAGER   There is something in what you say. I assure you all this interests me very much. I begin to think there's the stuff for a drama in all this, and not a bad drama either.

THE STEP-DAUGHTER [*coming forward*] When you've got a character like me . . .

THE FATHER [*shutting her up, all excited to learn the decision of the* MANAGER] You be quiet!

THE MANAGER [*reflecting, heedless of interruption*] It's new . . . hem . . . yes. . . .

THE FATHER   Absolutely new!

THE MANAGER   You've got a nerve though, I must say, to come here and fling it at me like this . . .

THE FATHER   You will understand, sir, born as we are for the stage . . .

THE MANAGER   Are you amateur actors then?

THE FATHER   No. I say born for the stage, because . . .

THE MANAGER   Oh, nonsense. You're an old hand, you know.

THE FATHER   No sir, no. We act that rôle for which we have been cast, that rôle which we are given in life. And in my own case, passion itself, as usually happens, becomes a trifle theatrical when it is exalted.

THE MANAGER   Well, well, that will do. But

you see, without an author.... I could give you the address of an author if you like ...
THE FATHER No, no. Look here! You must be the author.
THE MANAGER I? What are you talking about?
THE FATHER Yes, you, you! Why not?
THE MANAGER Because I have never been an author: that's why.
THE FATHER Then why not turn author now? Everybody does it. You don't want any special qualities. Your task is made much easier by the fact that we are all here alive before you....
THE MANAGER It won't do.
THE FATHER What? When you see us live our drama....
THE MANAGER Yes, that's all right. But you want someone to write it.
THE FATHER No, no. Someone to take it down, possibly, while we play it, scene by scene! It will be enough to sketch it out at first, and then try it over.
THE MANAGER Well ... I am almost tempted. It's a bit of an idea. One might have a shot at it.
THE FATHER Of course. You'll see what scenes will come out of it. I can give you one, at once ...
THE MANAGER By Jove, it tempts me. I'd like to have a go at it. Let's try it out. Come with me to my office. [*Turning to the* ACTORS.] You are at liberty for a bit, but don't step out of the theatre for long. In a quarter of an hour, twenty minutes, all back here again! [*To the* FATHER.] We'll see what can be done. Who knows if we don't get something really extraordinary out of it?
THE FATHER There's no doubt about it. They [*indicating the* CHARACTERS] had better come with us too, hadn't they?
THE MANAGER Yes, yes. Come on! come on! [*Moves away and then turning to the* ACTORS.] Be punctual, please! [MANAGER *and the* SIX CHARACTERS *cross the stage and go off. The other* ACTORS *remain, looking at one another in astonishment.*]
LEADING MAN Is he serious? What the devil does he want to do?
JUVENILE LEAD This is rank madness.

THIRD ACTOR Does he expect to knock up a drama in five minutes?
JUVENILE LEAD Like the improvisers!
LEADING LADY If he thinks I'm going to take part in a joke like this....
JUVENILE LEAD I'm out of it anyway.
FOURTH ACTOR I should like to know who they are. [*Alludes to* CHARACTERS.]
THIRD ACTOR What do you suppose? Madmen or rascals!
JUVENILE LEAD And he takes them seriously!
L'INGENUE Vanity! He fancies himself as an author now.
LEADING MAN It's absolutely unheard of. If the stage has come to this ... well I'm ...
FIFTH ACTOR It's rather a joke.
THIRD ACTOR Well, we'll see what's going to happen next.

[*Thus talking, the* ACTORS *leave the stage; some going out by the little door at the back; others retiring to their dressing-rooms.*

The curtain remains up.
The action of the play is suspended for twenty minutes.]

ACT II

[*The stage call-bells ring to warn the company that the play is about to begin again.*
The STEP-DAUGHTER *comes out of the* MANAGER'S *office along with the* CHILD *and the* BOY. *As she comes out of the office, she cries:*—

Nonsense! nonsense! Do it yourselves! I'm not going to mix myself up in this mess. [*Turning to the* CHILD *and coming quickly with her on to the stage.*] Come on, Rosetta, let's run!

The BOY *follows them slowly, remaining a little behind and seeming perplexed.*]

THE STEP-DAUGHTER [*stops, bends over the* CHILD *and takes the latter's face between her hands*] My little darling! You're frightened, aren't you? You don't know where we are, do you? [*Pretending to reply to a question* of the CHILD.] What is the stage? It's a place, baby, you know, where people play at being serious, a place where they act comedies. We've got to act a comedy now, dead serious, you know; and you're in it also, little one. [*Embraces her, pressing the little head to her breast, and rocking the* CHILD *for a moment.*] Oh darling, darling, what a horrid comedy you've got to play! What a wretched part they've found for you! A garden . . . a fountain . . . look . . . just suppose, kiddie, it's here. Where, you say? Why, right here in the middle. It's all pretense you know. That's the trouble, my pet: it's all make-believe here. It's better to imagine it though, because if they fix it up for you, it'll only be painted cardboard, painted cardboard for the rockery, the water, the plants. . . . Ah, but I think a baby like this one would sooner have a make-believe fountain than a real one, so she could play with it. What a joke it'll be for the others! But for you, alas! not quite such a joke: you who are real, baby dear, and really play by a real fountain that is big and green and beautiful, with ever so many bamboos around it that are reflected in the water, and a whole lot of little ducks swimming about. . . . No, Rosetta, no, your mother doesn't bother about you on account of that wretch of a son there. I'm in the devil of a temper, and as for that lad. . . . [*Seizes* BOY *by the arm to force him to take one of his hands out of his pockets.*] What have you got there? What are you hiding? [*Pulls his hand out of his pocket, looks into it and catches the glint of a revolver.*] Ah! where did you get this? [*The* BOY, *very pale in the face, looks at her, but does not answer.*] Idiot! If I'd been in your place, instead of killing myself, I'd have shot one of those two, or both of them: father and son.

[*The* FATHER *enters from the office, all excited from his work. The* MANAGER *follows him.*]

THE FATHER Come on, come on dear! Come here for a minute! We've arranged everything. It's all fixed up.

THE MANAGER [*also excited*] If you please, young lady, there are one or two points to settle still. Will you come along?

THE STEP-DAUGHTER [*following him towards the office*] Ouff! what's the good, if you've arranged everything.

[*The* FATHER, MANAGER *and* STEP-DAUGHTER *go back into the office again (off) for a moment. At the same time, the* SON, *followed by his* MOTHER, *comes out.*]

THE SON [*looking at the three entering office*] Oh this is fine, fine! And to think I can't even get away!

[*The* MOTHER *attempts to look at him, but lowers her eyes immediately when he turns away from her. She then sits down. The* BOY *and the* CHILD *approach her. She casts a glance again at the* SON, *and speaks with humble tones, trying to draw him into conversation.*]

THE MOTHER And isn't my punishment the worst of all? [*Then seeing from the* SON's *manner that he will not bother himself about her.*] My God! Why are you so cruel? Isn't it enough for one person to support all this torment? Must you then insist on others seeing it also?

THE SON [*half to himself, meaning the* MOTHER *to hear, however*] And they want to put it on the stage! If there was at least a reason for it! He thinks he has got the meaning of it all. Just as if each one of us in every circumstance of life couldn't find his own explanation of it! [*Pauses.*] He complains he was discovered in a place where he ought not to have been seen, in a moment of his life which ought to have remained hidden and kept out of the reach of that convention which he has to maintain for other people. And what about my case? Haven't I had to reveal what no one ought ever to reveal: how father and mother live and are man and wife for themselves quite apart from that idea of father and mother which we give them? When this idea is revealed, our life is then linked at one point only to that man and that woman; and as such it should shame them, shouldn't it?

[*The* MOTHER *hides her face in her hands. From the dressing-rooms and the little door at the back of the stage the* ACTORS *and* STAGE MANAGER *return, followed by the* PROPERTY MAN, *and the* PROMPTER. *At the same moment, the* MANAGER *comes out of his office, accompanied by the* FATHER *and the* STEP-DAUGHTER.]

THE MANAGER   Come on, come on, ladies and gentlemen! Heh! you there, machinist!

MACHINIST   Yes sir?

THE MANAGER   Fix up the white parlor with the floral decorations. Two wings and a drop with a door will do. Hurry up!

[*The* MACHINIST *runs off at once to prepare the scene, and arranges it while the* MANAGER *talks with the* STAGE MANAGER, *the* PROPERTY MAN, *and the* PROMPTER *on matters of detail.*]

THE MANAGER   [*to* PROPERTY MAN]   Just have a look, and see if there isn't a sofa or divan in the wardrobe . . .

PROPERTY MAN   There's the green one.

THE STEP-DAUGHTER   No no! Green won't do. It was yellow, ornamented with flowers—very large! and most comfortable!

PROPERTY MAN   There isn't one like that.

THE MANAGER   It doesn't matter. Use the one we've got.

THE STEP-DAUGHTER   Doesn't matter? It's most important!

THE MANAGER   We're only trying it now. Please don't interfere. [*To* PROPERTY MAN.] See if we've got a shop window—long and narrowish.

THE STEP-DAUGHTER   And the little table! The little mahogany table for the pale blue envelope!

PROPERTY MAN   [*to* MANAGER]   There's that little gilt one.

THE MANAGER   That'll do fine.

THE FATHER   A mirror.

THE STEP-DAUGHTER   And the screen! We must have a screen. Otherwise how can I manage?

PROPERTY MAN   That's all right, Miss. We've got any amount of them.

THE MANAGER   [*to the* STEP-DAUGHTER]   We want some clothes pegs too, don't we?

THE STEP-DAUGHTER   Yes, several, several!

THE MANAGER   See how many we've got and bring them all.

PROPERTY MAN   All right!

[*The* PROPERTY MAN *hurries off to obey his orders. While he is putting things in their places, the* MANAGER *talks to the* PROMPTER *and then with the* CHARACTERS *and the* ACTORS.]

THE MANAGER   [*to* PROMPTER]   Take your seat. Look here: this is the outline of the scenes, act by act. [*Hands him some sheets of paper.*] And now I'm going to ask you to do something out of the ordinary.

PROMPTER   Take it down in shorthand?

THE MANAGER   [*pleasantly surprised*]   Exactly! Can you do shorthand?

PROMPTER   Yes, a little.

THE MANAGER   Good! [*Turning to a* STAGE HAND.] Go and get some paper from my office, plenty, as much as you can find.

[*The* STAGE HAND *goes off, and soon returns with a handful of paper which he gives to the* PROMPTER.]

THE MANAGER   [*to* PROMPTER]   You follow the scenes as we play them, and try and get the points down, at any rate the most important ones. [*Then addressing the* ACTORS.] Clear the stage, ladies and gentlemen! Come over here [*pointing to the left*] and listen attentively.

LEADING LADY   But, excuse me, we . . .

THE MANAGER   [*guessing her thought*]   Don't worry! You won't have to improvise.

LEADING MAN   What have we to do then?

THE MANAGER   Nothing. For the moment you just watch and listen. Everybody will get his part written out afterwards. At present we're going to try the thing as best we can. They're going to act now.

THE FATHER   [*as if fallen from the clouds into the confusion of the stage*]   We? What do you mean, if you please, by a rehearsal?

THE MANAGER   A rehearsal for them. [*Points to the* ACTORS.]

THE FATHER But since we are the characters . . .

THE MANAGER All right: "characters" then, if you insist on calling yourselves such. But here, my dear sir, the characters don't act. Here the actors do the acting. The characters are there, in the "book" [pointing towards PROMPTER's box] —when there is a "book"!

THE FATHER I won't contradict you; but excuse me, the actors aren't the characters. They want to be, they pretend to be, don't they? Now if these gentlemen here are fortunate enough to have us alive before them . . .

THE MANAGER Oh this is grand! You want to come before the public yourselves then?

THE FATHER As we are. . . .

THE MANAGER I can assure you it would be a magnificent spectacle!

LEADING MAN What's the use of us here anyway then?

THE MANAGER You're not going to pretend that you can act? It makes me laugh! [The ACTORS laugh.] There, you see, they are laughing at the notion. But, by the way, I must cast the parts. That won't be difficult. They cast themselves. [To the SECOND LADY LEAD.] You play the Mother [To the FATHER.] We must find her a name.

THE FATHER Amalia, sir.

THE MANAGER But that is the real name of your wife. We don't want to call her by her real name.

THE FATHER Why ever not, if it is her name? . . . Still, perhaps, if that lady must . . . [Makes a slight motion of the hand to indicate the SECOND LADY LEAD.] I see this woman here [means the MOTHER] as Amalia. But do as you like. [Gets more and more confused.] I don't know what to say to you. Already, I begin to hear my own words ring false, as if they had another sound. . . .

THE MANAGER Don't you worry about it. It'll be our job to find the right tones. And as for her name, if you want her Amalia, Amalia it shall be; and if you don't like it, we'll find another! For the moment though, we'll call the characters in this way: [To JUVENILE LEAD.] You are the Son. [To the LEADING LADY.] You naturally are the Step-Daughter. . . .

THE STEP-DAUGHTER [excitedly] What? what? I, that woman there? [Bursts out laughing.]

THE MANAGER [angry] What is there to laugh at?

LEADING LADY [indignant] Nobody has ever dared to laugh at me. I insist on being treated with respect; otherwise I go away.

THE STEP-DAUGHTER No, no, excuse me . . . I am not laughing at you. . . .

THE MANAGER [to STEP-DAUGHTER] You ought to feel honored to be played by . . .

LEADING LADY [at once, contemptuously] "That woman there" . . .

THE STEP-DAUGHTER But I wasn't speaking of you, you know. I was speaking of myself—whom I can't see at all in you! That is all. I don't know . . . but . . . you . . . aren't in the least like me. . . .

THE FATHER True. Here's the point. Look here, sir, our temperaments, our souls. . . .

THE MANAGER Temperament, soul, be hanged! Do you suppose the spirit of the piece is in you? Nothing of the kind!

THE FATHER What, haven't we our own temperaments, our own souls?

THE MANAGER Not at all. Your soul or whatever you like to call it takes shape here. The actors give body and form to it, voice and gesture. And my actors—I may tell you—have given expression to much more lofty material than this little drama of yours, which may or may not hold up on the stage. But if it does, the merit of it, believe me, will be due to my actors.

THE FATHER I don't dare contradict you, sir; but, believe me, it is a terrible suffering for us who are as we are, with these bodies of ours, these features to see. . . .

THE MANAGER [cutting him short and out of patience] Good heavens! The make-up will remedy all that, man, the make-up. . . .

THE FATHER Maybe. But the voice, the gestures . . .

THE MANAGER Now, look here! On the stage, you as yourself, cannot exist. The actor here acts you, and that's an end to it!

THE FATHER I understand. And now I think I see why our author who conceived us as we are, all alive, didn't want to put us on the stage after all. I haven't the least desire to offend your actors. Far from it! But when I think that I am to be acted by . . . I don't know by whom. . . .

LEADING MAN [*on his dignity*] By me, if you've no objection!

THE FATHER [*humbly, mellifluously*] Honored, I assure you, sir. [*Bows.*] Still, I must say that try as this gentleman may, with all his good will and wonderful art, to absorb me into himself. . . .

LEADING MAN Oh chuck it! "Wonderful art!" Withdraw that, please!

THE FATHER The performance he will give, even doing his best with make-up to look like me. . . .

LEADING MAN It will certainly be a bit difficult! [*The* ACTORS *laugh.*]

THE FATHER Exactly! It will be difficult to act me as I really am. The effect will be rather—apart from the make-up—according as to how he supposes I am, as he senses me—if he does sense me—and not as I inside of myself feel myself to be. It seems to me then that account should be taken of this by everyone whose duty it may become to criticize us. . . .

THE MANAGER Heavens! The man's starting to think about the critics now! Let them say what they like. It's up to us to put on the play if we can. [*Looking around.*] Come on! come on! Is the stage set? [*To the* ACTORS *and* CHARACTERS.] Stand back—stand back! Let me see, and don't let's lose any more time! [*To the* STEP-DAUGHTER.] Is it all right as it is now?

THE STEP-DAUGHTER Well, to tell the truth, I don't recognize the scene.

THE MANAGER My dear lady, you can't possibly suppose that we can construct that shop of Madame Pace piece by piece here? [*To the* FATHER.] You said a white room with flowered wall paper, didn't you?

THE FATHER Yes.

THE MANAGER Well then. We've got the furniture right more or less. Bring that little table a bit further forward. [*The* STAGE HANDS *obey the order. To* PROPERTY MAN.] You go and find an envelope, if possible, a pale blue one; and give it to that gentleman. [*Indicates* FATHER.]

PROPERTY MAN An ordinary envelope?

MANAGER *and* FATHER Yes, yes, an ordinary envelope.

PROPERTY MAN At once, sir. [*Exit.*]

THE MANAGER Ready, everyone! First scene—the Young Lady. [*The* LEADING LADY *comes forward.*] No, no, you must wait. I meant her. [*Indicating the* STEP-DAUGHTER.] You just watch—

THE STEP-DAUGHTER [*adding at once*] How I shall play it, how I shall live it! . . .

LEADING LADY [*offended*] I shall live it also, you may be sure, as soon as I begin!

THE MANAGER [*with his hands to his head*] Ladies and gentlemen, if you please! No more useless discussions! Scene I: the Young Lady with Madame Pace: Oh! [*Looks around as if lost.*] And this Madame Pace, where is she?

THE FATHER She isn't with us, sir.

THE MANAGER Then what the devil's to be done?

THE FATHER But she is alive too.

THE MANAGER Yes, but where is she?

THE FATHER One minute: Let me speak! [*Turning to the* ACTRESSES.] If these ladies would be so good as to give me their hats for a moment. . . .

THE ACTRESSES [*half surprised, half laughing, in chorus*] What? Why? Our hats? What does he say?

THE MANAGER What are you going to do with the ladies' hats? [*The* ACTORS *laugh.*]

THE FATHER Oh nothing. I just want to put them on these pegs for a moment. And one of the ladies will be so kind as to take off her mantle. . . .

THE ACTORS Oh, what d'you think of that? Only the mantle? He must be mad.

SOME ACTRESSES But why? Mantles as well?

THE FATHER To hang them up here for a moment. Please be so kind, will you?

THE ACTRESSES [*taking off their hats, one or two also their cloaks, and going to hang them on the racks*] After all, why not? There you are! This is really funny. We've got to put them on show.

THE FATHER Exactly; just like that, on show.

THE MANAGER May we know why?

THE FATHER I'll tell you. Who knows if, by arranging the stage for her, she does not come here herself, attracted by the very articles of her trade? [*Inviting the* ACTORS *to look towards the exit at back of stage.*] Look! Look!

[*The door at the back of stage opens and* MADAME PACE *enters and takes a few steps forward. She is a fat, oldish woman with puffy oxygenated hair. She is rouged and powdered, dressed with a comical elegance in black silk. Round her waist is a long silver chain from which hangs a pair of scissors. The* STEP-DAUGHTER *runs over to her at once amid the stupor of the* ACTORS.]

THE STEP-DAUGHTER [*turning towards her*] There she is! There she is!
THE FATHER [*radiant*] It's she! I said so, didn't I? There she is!
THE MANAGER [*conquering his surprise, and then becoming indignant*] What sort of a trick is this?
LEADING MAN [*almost at the same time*] What's going to happen next?
JUVENILE LEAD Where does *she* come from?
L'INGENUE They've been holding her in reserve, I guess.
LEADING LADY A vulgar trick!
THE FATHER [*dominating the protests*] Excuse me, all of you! Why are you so anxious to destroy in the name of a vulgar, commonplace sense of truth, this reality which comes to birth attracted and formed by the magic of the stage itself, which has indeed more right to live here than you, since it is much truer than you—if you don't mind my saying so? Which is the actress among you who is to play Madame Pace? Well, here is Madame Pace herself. And you will allow, I fancy, that the actress who acts her will be less true than this woman here, who is herself in person. You see my daughter recognized her and went over to her at once. Now you're going to witness the scene!

[*But the scene between the* STEP-DAUGHTER *and* MADAME PACE *has already begun despite the protest of the* ACTORS *and the reply of the* FATHER. *It has begun quietly, naturally, in a manner impossible for the stage. So when the* ACTORS, *called to attention by the* FATHER, *turn round and see* MADAME PACE, *who has placed one hand under the* STEP-DAUGHTER'S *chin to raise her head, they observe her at first with great attention, but hearing her speak in an unintelligible manner their interest begins to wane.*]

THE MANAGER Well? well?
LEADING MAN What does she say?
LEADING LADY One can't hear a word.
JUVENILE LEAD Louder! Louder please!
THE STEP-DAUGHTER [*leaving* MADAME PACE, *who smiles a Sphinx-like smile, and advancing towards the* ACTORS] Louder? Louder? What are you talking about? These aren't matters which can be shouted at the top of one's voice. If I have spoken them out loud, it was to shame him and have my revenge. [*Indicates* FATHER.] But for Madame it's quite a different matter.
THE MANAGER Indeed? indeed? But here, you know, people have got to make themselves heard, my dear. Even we who are on the stage can't hear you. What will it be when the public's in the theatre? And anyway, you can very well speak up now among yourselves, since we shan't be present to listen to you as we are now. You've got to pretend to be alone in a room at the back of a shop where no one can hear you.

[*The* STEP-DAUGHTER *coquettishly and with a touch of malice makes a sign of disagreement two or three times with her finger.*]

THE MANAGER What do you mean by no?
THE STEP-DAUGHTER [*sotto voce, mysteriously*] There's someone who will hear us if she [*indicating* MADAME PACE] speaks out loud.
THE MANAGER [*in consternation*] What? Have you got someone else to spring on us now? [*The* ACTORS *burst out laughing.*]
THE FATHER No, no sir. She is alluding to me. I've got to be here—there behind that door, in waiting; and Madame Pace knows it. In fact, if you will allow me, I'll go there at once, so I can be quite ready. [*Moves away.*]
THE MANAGER [*stopping him*] No! Wait! wait! We must observe the conventions of the theatre. Before you are ready. . . .
THE STEP-DAUGHTER [*interrupting him*] No, get on with it at once! I'm just dying, I tell

you, to act this scene. If he's ready, I'm more than ready.

THE MANAGER [*shouting*] But, my dear young lady, first of all, we must have the scene between you and this lady.... [*Indicates* MADAME PACE.] Do you understand?...

THE STEP-DAUGHTER Good Heavens! She's been telling me what you know already: that mama's work is badly done again, that the material's ruined; and that if I want her to continue to help us in our misery I must be patient....

MADAME PACE [*coming forward with an air of great importance*] Yes indeed, sir, I no wanta take advantage of her, I no wanta be hard....

[*Note:* MADAME PACE *is supposed to talk in a jargon half Italian, half English.*]

THE MANAGER [*alarmed*] What? What? She talks like that? [*The* ACTORS *burst out laughing again.*]

THE STEP-DAUGHTER [*also laughing*] Yes yes, that's the way she talks, half English, half Italian! Most comical it is!

MADAME PACE Itta seem not verra polite gentlemen laugha atta me eeff I trya best speaka English.

THE MANAGER *Diamine!* Of course! Of course! Let her talk like that! Just what we want. Talk just like that, Madame, if you please! The effect will be certain. Exactly what was wanted to put a little comic relief into the crudity of the situation. Of course she talks like that! Magnificent!

THE STEP-DAUGHTER Magnificent? Certainly! When certain suggestions are made to one in language of that kind, the effect is certain, since it seems almost a joke. One feels inclined to laugh when one hears her talk about an "old signore" "who wanta talka nicely with you." Nice old signore, eh, Madame?

MADAME PACE Not so old my dear, not so old! And even if you no lika him, he won't make any scandal!

THE MOTHER [*jumping up amid the amazement and consternation of the* ACTORS, *who had not been noticing her. They move to restrain her.*] You old devil! You murderess!

THE STEP-DAUGHTER [*running over to calm her* MOTHER] Calm yourself, Mother, calm yourself! Please don't....

THE FATHER [*going to her also at the same time*] Calm yourself! Don't get excited! Sit down now!

THE MOTHER Well then, take that woman away out of my sight!

THE STEP-DAUGHTER [*to* MANAGER] It is impossible for my mother to remain here.

THE FATHER [*to* MANAGER] They can't be here together. And for this reason, you see: that woman there was not with us when we came. ... If they are on together, the whole thing is given away inevitably, as you see.

THE MANAGER It doesn't matter. This is only a first rough sketch—just to get an idea of the various points of the scene, even confusedly.... [*Turning to the* MOTHER *and leading her to her chair.*] Come along, my dear lady, sit down now, and let's get on with the scene....

[*Meanwhile, the* STEP-DAUGHTER, *coming forward again, turns to* MADAME PACE.]

THE STEP-DAUGHTER Come on, Madame, come on!

MADAME PACE [*offended*] No, no, *grazie*. I not do anything witha your mother present.

THE STEP-DAUGHTER Nonsense! Introduce this "old signore" who wants to talk nicely to me. [*Addressing the* COMPANY *imperiously.*] We've got to do this scene one way or another, haven't we? Come on! [*To* MADAME PACE.] You can go!

MADAME PACE Ah yes! I go'way! I go'way! Certainly! [*Exits furious.*]

THE STEP-DAUGHTER [*to the* FATHER] Now you make your entry. No, you needn't go over there. Come here. Let's suppose you've already come in. Like that, yes! I'm here with bowed head, modest like. Come on! Out with your voice! Say "Good morning, Miss" in that peculiar tone, that special tone....

THE MANAGER Excuse me, but are you the Manager, or am I? [*To the* FATHER, *who looks undecided and perplexed.*] Get on with it, man! Go down there to the back of the stage. You needn't go off. Then come right forward here.

[The FATHER *does as he is told, looking troubled and perplexed at first. But as soon as he begins to move, the reality of the action affects him, and he begins to smile and to be more natural. The* ACTORS *watch intently.*]

THE MANAGER [*sotto voce, quickly to the* PROMPTER *in his box*] Ready! ready? Get ready to write now.

THE FATHER [*coming forward and speaking in a different tone*] Good afternoon, Miss!

THE STEP-DAUGHTER [*head bowed down slightly, with restrained disgust*] Good afternoon!

THE FATHER [*looks under her hat which partly covers her face. Perceiving she is very young, he makes an exclamation, partly of surprise, partly of fear lest he compromise himself in a risky adventure*] Ah . . . but . . . ah . . . I say . . . this is not the first time that you have come here, is it?

THE STEP-DAUGHTER [*modestly*] No sir.

THE FATHER You've been here before, eh? [*Then seeing her nod agreement.*] More than once? [*Waits for her to answer, looks under her hat, smiles, and then says:*] Well then, there's no need to be so shy, is there? May I take off your hat?

THE STEP-DAUGHTER [*anticipating him and with veiled disgust*] No sir . . . I'll do it myself. [*Takes it off quickly.*]

[*The* MOTHER, *who watches the progress of the scene with the* SON *and the other two children who cling to her, is on thorns; and follows with varying expressions of sorrow, indignation, anxiety, and horror the words and actions of the other two. From time to time she hides her face in her hands and sobs.*]

THE MOTHER Oh, my God, my God!

THE FATHER [*playing his part with a touch of gallantry*] Give it to me! I'll put it down. [*Takes hat from her hands.*] But a dear little head like yours ought to have a smarter hat. Come and help me choose one from the stock, won't you?

L'INGENUE [*interrupting*] I say . . . those are our hats you know.

THE MANAGER [*furious*] Silence! silence! Don't try and be funny, if you please. . . . We're playing the scene now, I'd have you notice. [*To the* STEP-DAUGHTER.] Begin again, please!

THE STEP-DAUGHTER [*continuing*] No thank you, sir.

THE FATHER Oh, come now. Don't talk like that. You must take it. I shall be upset if you don't. There are some lovely little hats here; and then—Madame will be pleased. She expects it, anyway, you know.

THE STEP-DAUGHTER No, no! I couldn't wear it!

THE FATHER Oh, you're thinking about what they'd say at home if they saw you come in with a new hat? My dear girl, there's always a way round these little matters, you know.

THE STEP-DAUGHTER [*all keyed up*] No, it's not that. I couldn't wear it because I am . . . as you see . . . you might have noticed . . .

[*Showing her black dress.*]

THE FATHER . . . in mourning! Of course: I beg your pardon: I'm frightfully sorry. . . .

THE STEP-DAUGHTER [*forcing herself to conquer her indignation and nausea*] Stop! Stop! It's I who must thank you. There's no need for you to feel mortified or specially sorry. Don't think any more of what I've said. [*Tries to smile.*] I must forget that I am dressed so. . . .

THE MANAGER [*interrupting and turning to the* PROMPTER] Stop a minute! Stop! Don't write that down. Cut out that last bit. [*Then to the* FATHER *and* STEP-DAUGHTER.] Fine! it's going fine! [*To the* FATHER *only.*] And now you can go on as we arranged. [*To the* ACTORS.] Pretty good that scene, where he offers her the hat, eh?

THE STEP-DAUGHTER The best's coming now. Why can't we go on?

THE MANAGER Have a little patience! [*To the* ACTORS.] Of course, it must be treated rather lightly.

LEADING MAN Still, with a bit of go in it!

LEADING LADY Of course! It's easy enough! [*To* LEADING MAN.] Shall you and I try it now?

LEADING MAN Why, yes! I'll prepare my entrance. [*Exit in order to make his entrance.*]

THE MANAGER [*to* LEADING LADY] See here! The scene between you and Madame Pace is finished. I'll have it written out properly after. You remain here . . . oh, where are you going?

LEADING LADY   One minute. I want to put my hat on again. [*Goes over to hat-rack and puts her hat on her head.*]

THE MANAGER   Good! You stay here with your head bowed down a bit.

THE STEP-DAUGHTER   But she isn't dressed in black.

LEADING LADY   But I shall be, and much more effectively than you.

THE MANAGER [*to* STEP-DAUGHTER]   Be quiet please, and watch! You'll be able to learn something. [*Clapping his hands.*] Come on! come on! Entrance, please!

[*The door at rear of stage opens, and the* LEADING MAN *enters with the lively manner of an old gallant. The rendering of the scene by the* ACTORS *from the very first words is seen to be quite a different thing, though it has not in any way the air of a parody. Naturally, the* STEP-DAUGHTER *and the* FATHER, *not being able to recognize themselves in the* LEADING LADY *and the* LEADING MAN, *who deliver their words in different tones and with a different psychology, express, sometimes with smiles, sometimes with gestures, the impression they receive.*]

LEADING MAN   Good afternoon, Miss . . .
THE FATHER [*at once unable to contain himself*] No!

[*The* STEP-DAUGHTER, *noticing the way the* LEADING MAN *enters, bursts out laughing.*]

THE MANAGER [*furious*]   Silence! And you please just stop that laughing. If we go on like this, we shall never finish.

THE STEP-DAUGHTER   Forgive me, sir, but it's natural enough. This lady [*indicating* LEADING LADY] stands there still; but if she is supposed to be me, I can assure you that if I heard anyone say "Good afternoon" in that manner and in that tone, I should burst out laughing as I did.

THE FATHER   Yes, yes, the manner, the tone. . . .

THE MANAGER   Nonsense! Rubbish! Stand aside and let me see the action.

LEADING MAN   If I've got to represent an old fellow who's coming into a house of an equivocal character. . . .

THE MANAGER   Don't listen to them, for Heaven's sake! Do it again! It goes fine. [*Waiting for the* ACTORS *to begin again.*] Well?

LEADING MAN   Good afternoon, Miss.
LEADING LADY   Good afternoon.
LEADING MAN [*imitating the gesture of the* FATHER *when he looked under the hat, and then expressing quite clearly first satisfaction and then fear*]   Ah, but . . . I say . . . this is not the first time that you have come here, is it?

THE MANAGER   Good, but not quite so heavily. Like this. [*Acts himself.*] "This isn't the first time that you have come here" . . . [*To* LEADING LADY.] And you say: "No, sir."

LEADING LADY   No, sir.
LEADING MAN   You've been here before, more than once.

THE MANAGER   No, no, stop! Let her nod "yes" first. "You've been here before, eh?" [*The* LEADING LADY *lifts up her head slightly and closes her eyes as though in disgust. Then she inclines her head twice.*]

THE STEP-DAUGHTER [*unable to contain herself*] Oh my God! [*Puts a hand to her mouth to prevent herself from laughing.*]

THE MANAGER [*turning round*]   What's the matter?

THE STEP-DAUGHTER   Nothing, nothing!
THE MANAGER [*to* LEADING MAN]   Go on!
LEADING MAN   You've been here before, eh? Well then, there's no need to be so shy, is there? May I take off your hat?

[*The* LEADING MAN *says this last speech in such a tone and with such gestures that the* STEP-DAUGHTER, *though she has her hand to her mouth, cannot keep from laughing.*]

LEADING LADY [*indignant*]   I'm not going to stop here to be made a fool of by that woman there.

LEADING MAN   Neither am I! I'm through with it!

THE MANAGER [*shouting to* STEP-DAUGHTER] Silence! for once and all, I tell you!

THE STEP-DAUGHTER Forgive me! forgive me!

THE MANAGER You haven't any manners: that's what it is! You go too far.

THE FATHER [*endeavoring to intervene*] Yes, it's true, but excuse her. . . .

THE MANAGER Excuse what? It's absolutely disgusting.

THE FATHER Yes, sir, but believe me, it has such a strange effect when . . .

THE MANAGER Strange? Why strange? Where is it strange?

THE FATHER No, sir; I admire your actors—this gentleman here, this lady; but they are certainly not us!

THE MANAGER I should hope not. Evidently they cannot be you, if they are actors.

THE FATHER Just so: actors! Both of them act our parts exceedingly well. But, believe me, it produces quite a different effect on us. They want to be us, but they aren't, all the same.

THE MANAGER What is it then anyway?

THE FATHER Something that is . . . that is theirs—and no longer ours . . .

THE MANAGER But naturally, inevitably. I've told you so already.

THE FATHER Yes, I understand . . . I understand . . .

THE MANAGER Well then, let's have no more of it! [*Turning to the* ACTORS.] We'll have the rehearsals by ourselves, afterwards, in the ordinary way. I never could stand rehearsing with the author present. He's never satisfied! [*Turning to* FATHER *and* STEP-DAUGHTER.] Come on! Let's get on with it again; and try and see if you can't keep from laughing.

THE STEP-DAUGHTER Oh, I shan't laugh any more. There's a nice little bit coming for me now: you'll see.

THE MANAGER Well then: when she says "Don't think any more of what I've said, I must forget, etc.," you [*addressing the* FATHER] come in sharp with "I understand, I understand"; and then you ask her . . .

THE STEP-DAUGHTER [*interrupting*] What?

THE MANAGER Why she is in mourning.

THE STEP-DAUGHTER Not at all! See here: when I told him that it was useless for me to be thinking about my wearing mourning, do you know how he answered me? "Ah well," he said, "then let's take off this little frock."

THE MANAGER Great! Just what we want, to make a riot in the theatre!

THE STEP-DAUGHTER But it's the truth!

THE MANAGER What does that matter? Acting is our business here. Truth up to a certain point, but no further.

THE STEP-DAUGHTER What do you want to do then?

THE MANAGER You'll see, you'll see! Leave it to me.

THE STEP-DAUGHTER No sir! What you want to do is to piece together a little romantic sentimental scene out of my disgust, out of all the reasons, each more cruel and viler than the other, why I am what I am. He is to ask me why I'm mourning; and I'm to answer with tears in my eyes, that it is just two months since papa died. No sir, no! He's got to say to me, as he did say: "Well, let's take off this little dress at once." And I, with my two months' mourning in my heart, went there behind that screen, and with these fingers tingling with shame. . . .

THE MANAGER [*running his hands through his hair*] For Heaven's sake! What are you saying?

THE STEP-DAUGHTER [*crying out excitedly*] The truth! The truth!

THE MANAGER It may be. I don't deny it, and I can understand all your horror; but you must surely see that you can't have this kind of thing on the stage. It won't go.

THE STEP-DAUGHTER Not possible, eh? Very well! I'm much obliged to you—but I'm off!

THE MANAGER Now be reasonable! Don't lose your temper!

THE STEP-DAUGHTER I won't stop here! I won't! I can see you've fixed it all up with him in your office. All this talk about what is possible for the stage . . . I understand! He wants to get at his complicated "cerebral drama," to have his famous remorses and torments acted; but I want to act my part, *my part*!

THE MANAGER [*annoyed, shaking his shoulders*] Ah! Just *your* part! But, if you will pardon me, there are other parts than yours: His [indicating the FATHER] and hers [indicating the MOTHER]! On the stage you can't have a character becoming too prominent and overshadowing all the others. The thing is to pack them all into a neat little framework and then act what is actable. I am aware of the fact that everyone has his own interior life which he wants very much to put forward. But the difficulty lies in this fact: to set out just so much as is necessary for the stage, taking the other characters into consideration, and at the same time hint at the unrevealed interior life of each. I am willing to admit, my dear young lady, that from your point of view it would be a fine idea if each character could tell the public all his troubles in a nice monologue or a regular one hour lecture. [Good humoredly.] You must restrain yourself, my dear, and in your own interest, too; because this fury of yours, this exaggerated disgust you show, may make a bad impression, you know. After you have confessed to me that there were others before him at Madame Pace's and more than once . . .

THE STEP-DAUGHTER [bowing her head, impressed] It's true. But remember those others mean him for me all the same.

THE MANAGER [not understanding] What? The others? What do you mean?

THE STEP-DAUGHTER For one who has gone wrong, sir, he who was resopnsible for the first fault is responsible for all that follow. He is responsible for my faults, was, even before I was born. Look at him, and see if it isn't true!

THE MANAGER Well, well! And does the weight of so much responsibility seem nothing to you? Give him a chance to act it, to get it over!

THE STEP-DAUGHTER How? How can he act all his "noble remorses," all his "moral torments," if you want to spare him the horror of being discovered one day—after he had asked her what he did ask her—in the arms of her, that already fallen woman, that child, sir, that child he used to watch come out of school? [She is moved.]

[The MOTHER at this point is overcome with emotion, and breaks out into a fit of crying. All are touched. A long pause.]

THE STEP-DAUGHTER [as soon as the MOTHER becomes a little quieter, adds resolutely and gravely] At present, we are unknown to the public. Tomorrow, you will act us as you wish, treating us in your own manner. But do you really want to see drama, do you want to see it flash out as it really did?

THE MANAGER Of course! That's just what I do want, so I can use as much of it as is possible.

THE STEP-DAUGHTER Well then, ask that Mother there to leave us.

THE MOTHER [changing her low plaint into a sharp cry] No! No! Don't permit it, sir, don't permit it!

THE MANAGER But it's only to try it.

THE MOTHER I can't bear it. I can't.

THE MANAGER But since it has happened already . . . I don't understand!

THE MOTHER It's taking place now. It happens all the time. My torment isn't a pretended one. I live and feel every minute of my torture. Those two children there—have you heard them speak? They can't speak any more. They cling to me to keep up my torment actual and vivid for me. But for themselves, they do not exist, they aren't any more. And she [indicating the STEP-DAUGHTER] has run away, she has left me, and is lost. If I now see her here before me, it is only to renew for me the tortures I have suffered for her too.

THE FATHER The eternal moment! She [indicating the STEP-DAUGHTER] is here to catch me, fix me, and hold me eternally in the stocks for that one fleeting and shameful moment of my life. She can't give it up! And you, sir, cannot either fairly spare me it.

THE MANAGER I never said I didn't want to act it. It will form, as a matter of fact, the nucleus of the whole first act right up to her surprise. [Indicates the MOTHER.]

THE FATHER Just so! This is my punishment: the passion in all of us that must culminate in her final cry.

THE STEP-DAUGHTER I can hear it still in my ears. It's driven me mad, that cry!—You can put me on as you like; it doesn't matter. Fully dressed, if you like—provided I have at least the arm bare; because, standing like this [*she goes close to the* FATHER *and leans her head on his breast*] with my head so, and my arms round his neck, I saw a vein pulsing in my arm here; and then, as if that live vein had awakened disgust in me, I closed my eyes like this, and let my head sink on his breast. [*Turning to the* MOTHER.] Cry out, mother! Cry out! [*Buries head in* FATHER'S *breast, and with her shoulders raised as if to prevent her hearing the cry, adds in tones of intense emotion:*] Cry out as you did then!
THE MOTHER [*coming forward to separate them*] No! My daughter, my daughter! [*And after having pulled her away from him.*] You brute! you brute! She is my daughter! Don't you see she's my daughter?
THE MANAGER [*walking backwards towards footlights*] Fine! fine! Damned good! And then, of course—curtain!
THE FATHER [*going towards him excitedly*] Yes, of course, because that's the way it really happened.
THE MANAGER [*convinced and pleased*] Oh, yes, no doubt about it. Curtain here, curtain!

[*At the reiterated cry of the* MANAGER, *the* MACHINIST *lets the curtain down, leaving the* MANAGER *and the* FATHER *in front of it before the footlights.*]

THE MANAGER The darned idiot! I said "curtain" to show the act should end there, and he goes and lets it down in earnest. [*To the* FATHER, *while he pulls the curtain back to go on to the stage again.*] Yes, yes, it's all right. Effect certain! That's the right ending. I'll guarantee the first act at any rate.

ACT III

[*When the curtain goes up again, it is seen that the* STAGE HANDS *have shifted the bit of scenery used in the last part, and have rigged up instead at the back of the stage a drop, with some trees, and one or two wings. A portion of a fountain basin is visible. The* MOTHER *is sitting on the right with the two children by her side. The* SON *is on the same side, but away from the others. He seems bored, angry, and full of shame. The* FATHER *and the* STEP-DAUGHTER *are also seated towards the right front. On the other side (left) are the* ACTORS, *much in the positions they occupied before the curtain was lowered. Only the* MANAGER *is standing up in the middle of the stage, with his hand closed over his mouth in the act of meditating.*]

THE MANAGER [*shaking his shoulders after a brief pause*] Ah yes: the second act! Leave it to me, leave it all to me as we arranged, and you'll see! It'll go fine!
THE STEP-DAUGHTER Our entry into his house [*indicates* FATHER] in spite of him . . . [*indicates the* SON].
THE MANAGER [*out of patience*] Leave it to me, I tell you!
THE STEP-DAUGHTER Do let it be clear, at any rate, that it is in spite of my wishes.
THE MOTHER [*from her corner, shaking her head*] For all the good that's come of it. . . .
THE STEP-DAUGHTER [*turning towards her quickly*] It doesn't matter. The more harm done us, the more remorse for him.
THE MANAGER [*impatiently*] I understand! Good Heavens! I understand! I'm taking it into account.
THE MOTHER [*supplicating*] I beg you, sir, to let it appear quite plain that for conscience' sake I did try in every way. . . .
THE STEP-DAUGHTER [*interrupting indignantly and continuing for the* MOTHER] . . . to pacify me, to dissuade me from spiting him. [*To* MANAGER.] Do as she wants: satisfy her, because it is true! I enjoy it immensely. Anyhow, as you can see, the meeker she is, the more she tries to get at his heart, the more distant and aloof does he become.
THE MANAGER Are we going to begin this second act or not?
THE STEP-DAUGHTER I'm not going to talk any more. But I must tell you this: you can't have the whole action take place in the garden, as you suggest. It isn't possible!

THE MANAGER Why not?

THE STEP-DAUGHTER Because he [*indicates the* SON *again*] is always shut up alone in his room. And then there's all the part of that poor dazed-looking boy there which takes place indoors.

THE MANAGER Maybe! On the other hand, you will understand—we can't change scenes three or four times in one act.

THE LEADING MAN They used to once.

THE MANAGER Yes, when the public was up to the level of that child there.

THE LEADING LADY It makes the illusion easier.

THE FATHER [*irritated*] The illusion! For Heaven's sake, don't say illusion. Please don't use that word, which is particularly painful for us.

THE MANAGER [*astounded*] And why, if you please?

THE FATHER It's painful, cruel, really cruel; and you ought to understand that.

THE MANAGER But why? What ought we to say then? The illusion, I tell you, sir, which we've got to create for the audience. . . .

THE LEADING MAN With our acting.

THE MANAGER The illusion of a reality.

THE FATHER I understand; but you, perhaps, do not understand us. Forgive me! You see . . . here for you and your actors, the thing is only—and rightly so . . . a kind of game. . . .

THE LEADING LADY [*interrupting indignantly*] A game! We're not children here, if you please! We are serious actors.

THE FATHER I don't deny it. What I mean is the game, or play, of your art, which has to give, as the gentleman says, a perfect illusion of reality.

THE MANAGER Precisely—!

THE FATHER Now, if you consider the fact that we [*indicates himself and the other five* CHARACTERS], as we are, have no other reality outside of this illusion. . . .

THE MANAGER [*astonished, looking at his* ACTORS, *who are also amazed*] And what does that mean?

THE FATHER [*after watching them for a moment with a wan smile*] As I say, sir, that which is a game of art for you is our sole reality. [*Brief pause. He goes a step or two nearer the* MANAGER *and adds:*] But not only for us, you know, by the way. Just you think it over well. [*Looks him in the eyes.*] Can you tell me who you are?

THE MANAGER [*perplexed, half smiling*] What? Who am I? I am myself.

THE FATHER And if I were to tell you that that isn't true, because you and I . . . ?

THE MANAGER I should say you were mad—! [*The* ACTORS *laugh.*]

THE FATHER You're quite right to laugh: because we are all making believe here. [*To* MANAGER.] And you can therefore object that it's only for a joke that that gentleman there [*indicates the* LEADING MAN], who naturally is himself, has to be me, who am on the contrary myself—this thing you see here. You see I've caught you in a trap! [*The* ACTORS *laugh.*]

THE MANAGER [*annoyed*] But we've had all this over once before. Do you want to begin again?

THE FATHER No, no! That wasn't my meaning! In fact, I should like to request you to abandon this game of art [*looking at the* LEADING LADY *as if anticipating her*] which you are accustomed to play here with your actors, and to ask you seriously once again: who are you?

THE MANAGER [*astonished and irritated, turning to his* ACTORS] If this fellow here hasn't got a nerve! A man who calls himself a character comes and asks me who I am!

THE FATHER [*with dignity, but not offended*] A character, sir, may always ask a man who he is. Because a character has really a life of his own, marked with his especial characteristics; for which reason he is always "somebody." But a man—I'm not speaking of you now—may very well be "nobody."

THE MANAGER Yes, but you are asking these questions of me, the boss, the manager! Do you understand?

THE FATHER But only in order to know if you, as you really are now, see yourself as you once were with all the illusions that were yours then, with all the things both inside and outside of you as they seemed to you—as they were then indeed for you. Well, sir, if you think of all those illusions that mean nothing to you now, of all those things which don't even *seem* to you to exist any more, while once they *were* for you, don't you feel that—I won't say these boards—but the very earth under your feet is sinking away from you when you reflect that in the same way this *you* as you feel it today—all this present reality of yours—is fated to seem a mere illusion to you tomorrow?

THE MANAGER [*without having understood much, but astonished by the specious argument*] Well, well! And where does all this take us anyway?

THE FATHER Oh, nowhere! It's only to show you that if we [*indicating the* CHARACTERS] have no other reality beyond the illusion, you too must not count overmuch on your reality as you feel it today, since, like that of yesterday, it may prove an illusion for you tomorrow.

THE MANAGER [*determining to make fun of him*] Ah, excellent! Then you'll be saying next that you, with this comedy of yours that you brought here to act, are truer and more real than I am.

THE FATHER [*with the greatest seriousness*] But of course; without doubt!

THE MANAGER Ah, really?

THE FATHER Why, I thought you'd understand that from the beginning.

THE MANAGER More real than I?

THE FATHER If your reality can change from one day to another. . . .

THE MANAGER But everyone knows it can change. It is always changing, the same as anyone else's.

THE FATHER [*with a cry*] No, sir, not ours! Look here! That is the very difference! Our reality doesn't change: it can't change! It can't be other than what it is, because it is already fixed for ever. It's terrible. Ours is an immutable reality which should make you shudder when you approach us if you are really conscious of the fact that your reality is a mere transitory and fleeting illusion, taking this form today and that tomorrow, according to the conditions, according to your will, your sentiments, which in turn are controlled by an intellect that shows them to you today in one manner and tomorrow . . . who knows how? . . . Illusions of reality represented in this fatuous comedy of life that never ends, nor can ever end! Because if tomorrow it were to end . . . then why, all would be finished.

THE MANAGER Oh for God's sake, will you *at least* finish with this philosophizing and let us try and shape this comedy which you yourself have brought me here? You argue and philosophize a bit too much, my dear sir. You know you seem to me almost, almost . . . [*Stops and looks him over from head to foot.*] Ah, by the way, I think you introduced yourself to me as a—what shall . . . we say—a "character," created by an author who did not afterward care to make a drama of his own creations.

THE FATHER It is the simple truth, sir.

THE MANAGER Nonsense! Cut that out, please! None of us believes it, because it isn't a thing, as you must recognize yourself, which one can believe seriously. If you want to know, it seems to me you are trying to imitate the manner of a certain author whom I heartily detest—I warn you—although I have unfortunately bound myself to put on one of his works. As a matter of fact, I was just starting to rehearse it, when you arrived. [*Turning to the* ACTORS.] And this is what we've gained—out of the frying-pan into the fire!

THE FATHER I don't know to what author you may be alluding, but believe me I feel what I think; and I seem to be philosophizing only for those who do not think what they feel, because they blind themselves with their own sentiment. I know that for many people this self-blinding seems much more "human"; but the contrary is really true. For man never reasons so much and becomes so introspective as when he suffers; since he is anxious to get at the cause of his sufferings, to learn who has produced them, and whether it is just or unjust that he should have to bear them. On the other hand, when he is happy, he takes his happiness as it comes and doesn't analyze it, just as if happiness were his right. The animals suffer without reasoning about their sufferings. But take the case of a man who suffers and begins to reason about it. Oh no! it can't be allowed! Let him suffer like an animal, and then—ah yet, he is "human"!

THE MANAGER Look here! Look here! You're off again, philosophizing worse than ever.

THE FATHER Because I suffer, sir! I'm not philosophizing: I'm crying aloud the reason of my sufferings.

THE MANAGER [*makes brusque movement as he is taken with a new idea*] I should like to know if anyone has ever heard of a character who gets right out of his part and perorates and speechifies as you do. Have you ever heard of a case? I haven't.

THE FATHER You have never met such a case, sir, because authors, as a rule, hide the labor of their creations. When the characters are really alive before their author, the latter does nothing but follow them in their action, in other words, in the situations which they suggest to him; and he has to will them the way they will themselves—for there's trouble if he doesn't. When a character is born, he acquires at once such an independence, even of his own author, that he can be imagined by everybody even in many other situations where the author never dreamed of placing him; and so he acquires for himself a meaning which the author never thought of giving him.

THE MANAGER Yes, yes, I know this.

THE FATHER What is there then to marvel at in us? Imagine such a misfortune for characters as I have described to you: to be born of an author's fantasy, and be denied life by him; and then answer me if these characters left alive, and yet without life, weren't right in doing what they did do and are doing now, after they have attempted everything in their power to persuade him to give them their stage life. We've all tried him in turn, I, she [*indicating the* STEP-DAUGHTER] and she [*indicating the* MOTHER].

THE STEP-DAUGHTER It's true. I too have sought to tempt him, many, many times, when he has been sitting at his writing table, feeling a bit melancholy, at the twilight hour. He would sit in his armchair too lazy to switch on the light, and all the shadows that crept into his room were full of our presence coming to tempt him. [*As if she saw herself still there by the writing table, and was annoyed by the presence of the* ACTORS.] Oh, if you would only go away, go away and leave us alone—mother here with that son of hers—I with that Child—that Boy there always alone—and then I with him [*just hints at the* FATHER]—and then I alone, alone . . . in those shadows! [*Makes a sudden movement as if in the vision she has of herself illuminating those shadows she wanted to seize hold of herself.*] Ah! my life! my life! Oh, what scenes we proposed to him—and I tempted him more than any of the others!

THE FATHER Maybe. But perhaps it was your fault that he refused to give us life: because you were too insistent, too troublesome.

THE STEP-DAUGHTER Nonsense! Didn't he make me so himself? [*Goes close to the* MANAGER *to tell him as if in confidence.*] In my opinion he abandoned us in a fit of depression, of disgust for the ordinary theatre as the public knows it and likes it.

THE SON Exactly what it was, sir; exactly that!

THE FATHER Not at all! Don't believe it for a minute. Listen to me! You'll be doing quite right to modify, as you suggest, the excesses both of this girl here, who wants to do too much, and of this young man, who won't do anything at all.

THE SON No, nothing!

THE MANAGER You too get over the mark occasionally, my dear sir, if I may say so.

THE FATHER I? When? Where?

THE MANAGER Always! Continuously! Then there's this insistence of yours in trying to make us believe you are a character. And then too, you must really argue and philosophize less, you know, much less.

THE FATHER Well, if you want to take away from me the possibility of representing the torment of my spirit which never gives me peace, you will be suppressing me: that's all. Every true man, sir, who is a little above the level of the beasts and plants does not live for the sake of living, without knowing how to live; but he lives so as to give a meaning and a value of his own to life. For me this is *everything*. I cannot give up this, just to represent a mere fact as she [*indicating the* STEP-DAUGHTER] wants. It's all very well for her, since her "vendetta" lies in the "fact." I'm not going to do it. It destroys my *raison d'être.*

THE MANAGER   Your *raison d'être!* Oh, we're going ahead fine! First she starts off, and then you jump in. At this rate, we'll never finish.

THE FATHER   Now, don't be offended! Have it your own way—provided, however, that within the limits of the parts you assign us each one's sacrifice isn't too great.

THE MANAGER   You've got to understand that you can't go on arguing at your own pleasure. Drama is action, sir, action and not confounded philosophy.

THE FATHER   All right. I'll do just as much arguing and philosophizing as everybody does when he is considering his own torments.

THE MANAGER   If the drama permits! But for Heaven's sake, man, let's get along and come to the scene.

THE STEP-DAUGHTER   It seems to me we've got too much action with our coming into his house. [*Indicating* FATHER.] You said, before, you couldn't change the scene every five minutes.

THE MANAGER   Of course not. What we've got to do is to combine and group up all the facts in one simultaneous, close-knit action. We can't have it as you want, with your little brother wandering like a ghost from room to room, hiding behind doors and meditating a project which—what did you say it did to him?

THE STEP-DAUGHTER   Consumes him, sir, wastes him away!

THE MANAGER   Well, it may be. And then at the same time, you want the little girl there to be playing in the garden . . . one in the house, and the other in the garden: isn't that it?

THE STEP-DAUGHTER   Yes, in the sun, in the sun! That is my only pleasure: to see her happy and careless in the garden after the misery and squalor of the horrible room where we all four slept together. And I had to sleep with her—I, do you understand?—with my vile contaminated body next to hers; with her folding me fast in her loving little arms. In the garden, whenever she spied me, she would run to take me by the hand. She didn't care for the big flowers, only the little ones; and she loved to show me them and pet me.

THE MANAGER   Well then, we'll have it in the garden. Everything shall happen in the garden; and we'll group the other scenes there. [*Calls a* STAGE HAND.] Here, a backcloth with trees and something to do as a fountain basin. [*Turning round to look at the back of the stage.*] Ah, you've fixed it up. Good! [*To* STEP-DAUGHTER.] This is just to give an idea, of course. The Boy, instead of hiding behind the doors, will wander about here in the garden, hiding behind the trees. But it's going to be rather difficult to find a child to do that scene with you where she shows you the flowers. [*Turning to the* BOY.] Come forward a little, will you please? Let's try it now! Come along! come along! [*Then seeing him come shyly forward, full of fear and looking lost.*] It's a nice business, this lad here. What's the matter with him? We'll have to give him a word or two to say. [*Goes close to him, puts a hand on his shoulders, and leads him behind one of the trees.*] Come on! come on! Let me see you a little! Hide here . . . yes, like that. Try and show your head just a little as if you were looking for someone. . . . [*Goes back to observe the effect, when the* BOY *at once goes through the action.*] Excellent! fine! [*Turning to* STEP-DAUGHTER.] Suppose the little girl there were to surprise him as he looks round, and run over to him, so we could give him a word or two to say?

THE STEP-DAUGHTER   It's useless to hope he will speak, as long as that fellow there is here. . . . [*Indicates the* SON.] You must send him away first.

THE SON [*jumping up*]   Delighted! Delighted! I don't ask for anything better. [*Begins to move away.*]

THE MANAGER [*at once stopping him*]   No! No! Where are you going? Wait a bit!

[*The* MOTHER *gets up alarmed and terrified at the thought that he is really about to go away. Instinctively she lifts her arms to prevent him, without, however, leaving her seat.*]

THE SON [*to* MANAGER, *who stops him*] I've got nothing to do with this affair. Let me go, please! Let me go!

THE MANAGER What do you mean by saying you've got nothing to do with this?

THE STEP-DAUGHTER [*calmly, with irony*] Don't bother to stop him: he won't go away.

THE FATHER He has to act the terrible scene in the garden with his mother.

THE SON [*suddenly resolute and with dignity*] I shall act nothing at all. I've said so from the very beginning. [*To the* MANAGER.] Let me go!

THE STEP-DAUGHTER [*going over to the* MANAGER] Allow me? [*Puts down the* MANAGER'S *arm which is restraining the* SON.] Well, go away then, if you want to! [*The* SON *looks at her with contempt and hatred. She laughs and says:*] You see, he can't, he can't go away! He is obliged to stay here, indissolubly bound to the chain. If I, who fly off when that happens which has to happen, because I can't bear him—if I am still here and support that face and expression of his, you can well imagine that he is unable to move. He has to remain here, has to stop with that nice father of his, and that mother whose only son he is. [*Turning to the* MOTHER.] Come on, mother, come along! [*Turning to* MANAGER *to indicate her.*] You see, she was getting up to keep him back. [*To the* MOTHER, *beckoning her with her hand.*] Come on! come on! [*Then to* MANAGER.] You can imagine how little she wants to show these actors of yours what she really feels; but so eager is she to get near him that. . . . There, you see? She is willing to act her part. [*And in fact, the* MOTHER *approaches him; and as soon as the* STEP-DAUGHTER *has finished speaking, opens her arms to signify that she consents.*]

THE SON [*suddenly*] No! no! If I can't go away, then I'll stop here; but I repeat: I act nothing!

THE FATHER [*to* MANAGER *excitedly*] You can force him, sir.

THE SON Nobody can force me.

THE FATHER I can.

THE STEP-DAUGHTER Wait a minute, wait . . . First of all, the baby has to go to the fountain. . . . [*Runs to take the* CHILD *and leads her to the fountain.*]

THE MANAGER Yes, yes of course; that's it. Both at the same time.

[*The* SECOND LADY LEAD *and the* JUVENILE LEAD *at this point separate themselves from the group of* ACTORS. *One watches the* MOTHER *attentively; the other moves about studying the movements and manner of the* SON *whom he will have to act.*]

THE SON [*to* MANAGER] What do you mean by both at the same time? It isn't right. There was no scene between me and her. [*Indicates the* MOTHER.] Ask her how it was!

THE MOTHER Yes, it's true. I had come into his room. . . .

THE SON Into my room, do you understand? Nothing to do with the garden.

THE MANAGER It doesn't matter. Haven't I told you we've got to group the action?

THE SON [*observing the* JUVENILE LEAD *studying him*] What do you want?

THE JUVENILE LEAD Nothing! I was just looking at you.

THE SON [*turning towards the* SECOND LADY LEAD] Ah! she's at it too: to react her part! [*Indicating the* MOTHER.]

THE MANAGER Exactly! And it seems to me that you ought to be grateful to them for their interest.

THE SON Yes, but haven't you yet perceived that it isn't possible to live in front of a mirror which not only freezes us with the image of ourselves, but throws our likeness back at us with a horrible grimace?

THE FATHER That is true, absolutely true. You must see that.

THE MANAGER [*to* SECOND LADY LEAD *and* JUVENILE LEAD] He's right! Move away from them!

THE SON Do as you like. I'm out of this!

THE MANAGER Be quiet, you, will you? And let me hear your mother! [*To* MOTHER.] You were saying you had entered. . . .

THE MOTHER Yes, into his room, because I couldn't stand it any longer. I went to empty my heart to him of all the anguish that tortures me. . . . But as soon as he saw me come in. . . .

THE SON Nothing happened! There was no scene. I went away, that's all! I don't care for scenes!

THE MOTHER It's true, true. That's how it was.

THE MANAGER Well now, we've got to do this bit between you and him. It's indispensable.

THE MOTHER I'm ready . . . when you are ready. If you could only find a chance for me to tell him what I feel here in my heart.

THE FATHER [*going to* SON *in a great rage*] You'll do this for your mother, for your mother, do you understand?

THE SON [*quite determined*] I do nothing!

THE FATHER [*taking hold of him and shaking him*] For God's sake, do as I tell you! Don't you hear your mother asking you for a favor? Haven't you even got the guts to be a son?

THE SON [*taking hold of the* FATHER] No! No! And for God's sake stop it, or else. . . . [*General agitation. The* MOTHER, *frightened, tries to separate them.*]

THE MOTHER [*pleading*] Please! please!

THE FATHER [*not leaving hold of the* SON] You've got to obey, do you hear?

THE SON [*almost crying from rage*] What does it mean, this madness you've got? [*They separate.*] Have you no decency, that you insist on showing everyone our shame? I won't do it! I won't! And I stand for the will of our author in this. He didn't want to put us on the stage, after all!

THE MANAGER Man alive! You came here . . .

THE SON [*indicating* FATHER] He did! I didn't!

THE MANAGER Aren't you here now?

THE SON It was his wish, and he dragged us along with him. He's told you not only the things that did happen, but also things that have never happened at all.

THE MANAGER Well, tell me then what did happen. You went out of your room without saying a word?

THE SON Without a word, so as to avoid a scene!

THE MANAGER And then what did you do?

THE SON Nothing . . . walking in the garden. . . . [*Hesitates for a moment with expression of gloom.*]

THE MANAGER [*coming closer to him, interested by his extraordinary reserve*] Well, well . . . walking in the garden. . . .

THE SON [*exasperated*] Why on earth do you insist? It's horrible!

[*The* MOTHER *trembles, sobs, and looks towards the fountain.*]

THE MANAGER [*slowly observing the glance and turning towards the* SON *with increasing apprehension*] The baby?

THE SON There in the fountain. . . .

THE FATHER [*pointing with tender pity to the* MOTHER] She was following him at the moment. . . .

THE MANAGER [*to the* SON *anxiously*] And then you. . . .

THE SON I ran over to her; I was jumping in to drag her out when I saw something that froze my blood . . . the boy standing stock still, with eyes like a madman's, watching his little drowned sister, in the fountain! [*The* STEP-DAUGHTER *bends over the fountain to hide the* CHILD. *She sobs.*] Then. . . . [*A revolver shot rings out behind the trees where the* BOY *is hidden.*]

THE MOTHER [*with a cry of terror runs over in that direction together with several of the* ACTORS *amid general confusion*] My son! My son! [*Then amid the cries and exclamations one hears her voice.*] Help! Help!

THE MANAGER [*pushing the* ACTORS *aside while they lift up the* BOY *and carry him off*] Is he really wounded?

SOME ACTORS He's dead! dead!

OTHER ACTORS No, no, it's only make believe, it's only pretense!

THE FATHER [*with a terrible cry*] Pretense? Reality, sir, reality!

THE MANAGER Pretense? Reality? To hell with it all! Never in my life has such a thing happened to me. I've lost a whole day over these people, a whole day!

The American Dream*

by EDWARD ALBEE

The Players

MOMMY
DADDY
GRANDMA
MRS. BARKER
YOUNG MAN

THE SCENE *A living room. Two armchairs, one toward either side of the stage, facing each other diagonally out toward the audience. Against the rear wall, a sofa. A door, leading out from the apartment, in the rear wall, far stage-right. An archway, leading to other rooms, in the side wall, stage-left.*

At the beginning, MOMMY *and* DADDY *are seated in the armchairs,* DADDY *in the armchair stage-left,* MOMMY *in the other.*

Curtain up. A silence. Then:

MOMMY I don't know what can be keeping them.

DADDY They're late, naturally.

MOMMY Of course, they're late; it never fails.

DADDY That's the way things are today, and there's nothing you can do about it.

MOMMY You're quite right.

DADDY When we took this apartment, they were quick enough to have me sign the lease; they were quick enough to take my check for two months' rent in advance . . .

---

* *The American Dream* by Edward Albee reprinted by permission of Coward-McCann, Inc. Copyright © 1960, 1961 by Edward Albee. *The American Dream* is the sole property of the author and is fully protected by copyright. It may not be acted either by professionals or amateurs without written consent. Public readings, radio and television broadcasts likewise are forbidden. All inquiries concerning these rights should be addressed to the agent, The William Morris Agency, 1350 Avenue of the Americas, New York, New York 10019.

MOMMY And one month's security . . .

DADDY . . . and one month's security. They were quick enough to check my references; they were quick enough about all that. But now! But now, try to get the icebox fixed, try to get the doorbell fixed, try to get the leak in the johnny fixed! Just try it . . . they aren't so quick about that.

MOMMY Of course not; it never fails. People think they can get away with anything these days . . . and, of course they can. I went to buy a new hat yesterday.
  (*Pause*)
I said, I went to buy a new hat yesterday.

DADDY Oh! Yes . . . yes.

MOMMY Pay attention.

DADDY I *am* paying attention, Mommy.

MOMMY Well, be sure you do.

DADDY Oh, I am.

MOMMY All right, Daddy; now listen.

DADDY I'm listening, Mommy.

MOMMY You're sure!

DADDY Yes . . . yes, I'm sure, I'm all ears.

MOMMY (*Giggles at the thought; then*) All right, now. I went to buy a new hat yesterday and I said, "I'd like a new hat, please." And so, they showed me a few hats, green ones and blue ones, and I didn't like any of them, not one bit. What did I say? What did I just say?

DADDY You didn't like any of them, not one bit.

MOMMY That's right; you just keep paying attention. And then they showed me one that I like. It was a lovely little hat, and I said, "Oh, this is a lovely little hat; I'll take this hat; oh my, it's lovely. What color is it?" And they said, "Why, this is beige; isn't it a lovely little beige hat?" And I said, "Oh, it's just lovely." And so, I bought it.
  (*Stops, looks at* DADDY)

DADDY (*To show he is paying attention*) And so you bought it.

MOMMY And so I bought it, and I walked out of the store with the hat right on my head, and I ran spang into the chairman of our woman's club, and she said, "Oh, my dear, isn't that a lovely little hat? Where did you get that lovely little hat? It's the loveliest little hat; I've always wanted a wheat-colored hat *myself*." And, I said, "Why, no, my dear; this hat is beige; beige." And she laughed and said, "Why no, my dear, that's a wheat-colored hat . . . wheat. I know beige from wheat." And I said, "Well, my dear, I know beige from wheat, too." What did I say? What did I just say?

DADDY (*Tonelessly*) Well, my dear, I know beige from wheat, too.

MOMMY That's right. And she laughed, and she said, "Well, my dear, they certainly put one over on you. That's wheat if I ever saw wheat. But it's lovely, just the same." And then she walked off. She's a dreadful woman, you don't know her; she has dreadful taste, two dreadful children, a dreadful house, and an absolutely adorable husband who sits in a wheel chair all the time. You don't know him. You don't know anybody, do you? She's just a dreadful woman, but she *is* chairman of our woman's club, so naturally I'm terribly fond of her. So, I went right back into the hat shop, and I said, "Look here; what do you mean selling me a hat that you say is beige, when it's wheat all the time . . . wheat! I can tell beige from wheat any day in the week, but not in this artificial light of yours." They have artificial light, Daddy.

DADDY Have they!

MOMMY And I said, "The minute I got outside I could tell that it wasn't a beige hat at all; it was a wheat hat." And they said to me, "How could you tell that when you had the hat on the top of your head?" Well, that made me angry, and so I made a scene right there; I screamed as hard as I could; I took my hat off and I threw it down on the counter, and oh, I made a terrible scene. I said, I made a terrible scene.

DADDY (*Snapping to*) Yes . . . yes . . . good for you!

MOMMY And I made an absolutely terrible scene; and they became frightened, and they said, "Oh, madam; oh, madam." But I kept right on, and finally they admitted that they might have made a mistake; so they took my hat into the back, and then they came out again with a hat that looked exactly like it. I took one look at it, and I said, "This hat is wheat-colored; wheat." Well, of course, they said, "Oh, no, madam, this hat is beige; you go outside and see." So, I went outside, and lo and behold, it *was* beige. So I bought it.

DADDY (*Clearing his throat*) I would imagine that it was the same hat they tried to sell you before.

MOMMY (*With a little laugh*) Well, of course it was!

DADDY That's the way things are today; you just can't get satisfaction; you just try.

MOMMY Well, *I* got satisfaction.

DADDY That's right, Mommy. *You did* get satisfaction, didn't you?

MOMMY Why are they so late? I don't know what can be keeping them.

DADDY I've been trying for two weeks to have the leak in the johnny fixed.

MOMMY You can't get satisfaction; just try. *I* can get satisfaction, but you can't.

DADDY I've been trying for two weeks and it isn't so much for my sake; I can always go to the club.

MOMMY It isn't so much for my sake, either; I can always go shopping.

DADDY It's really for Grandma's sake.

MOMMY Of course it's for Grandma's sake. Grandma cries every time she goes to the johnny as it is; but now that it doesn't work it's even worse, it makes Grandma think she's getting feeble-headed.

DADDY Grandma *is* getting feeble-headed.

MOMMY Of course Grandma is getting feeble-headed, but not about her johnny-do's.

DADDY No; that's true. I must have it fixed.

MOMMY WHY are they so late? I don't know what can be keeping them.

DADDY When they came here the first time, they were ten minutes early; they were quick enough about it then.

(*Enter* GRANDMA *from the archway, stage left. She is loaded down with boxes, large and small, neatly wrapped and tied.*)

MOMMY Why Grandma, look at you! What *is* all that you're carrying?

GRANDMA They're boxes. What do they look like?

MOMMY Daddy! Look at Grandma; look at all the boxes she's carrying!

DADDY My goodness, Grandma; look at all those boxes.

GRANDMA Where'll I put them?

MOMMY Heavens! I don't know. Whatever are they for?

GRANDMA That's nobody's damn business.

MOMMY Well, in that case, put them down next to Daddy; there.

GRANDMA (*Dumping the boxes down, on and around* DADDY's *feet*) I sure wish you'd get the john fixed.

DADDY Oh, I do wish they'd come and fix it. We hear you . . . for hours . . . whimpering away. . . .

MOMMY Daddy! What a terrible thing to say to Grandma!

GRANDMA Yeah. For shame, talking to me that way.

DADDY I'm sorry, Grandma.

MOMMY Daddy's sorry, Grandma.

GRANDMA Well, all right. In that case I'll go get the rest of the boxes. I suppose I deserve being talked to that way. I've gotten so old. Most people think that when you get so old, you either freeze to death, or you burn up. But you don't. When you get so old, all that happens is that people talk to you that way.

DADDY (*Contrite*) I said I'm sorry, Grandma.

MOMMY Daddy said he was sorry.

GRANDMA Well, that's all that counts. People being sorry. Makes you feel better; gives you a sense of dignity, and that's all that's important . . . a sense of dignity. And it doesn't matter if you don't care, or not, either. You got to have a sense of dignity, even if you don't care, 'cause, if you don't have that, civilization's doomed.

MOMMY You've been reading my book club selections again!

DADDY How dare you read Mommy's book club selections, Grandma!

GRANDMA Because I'm old! When you're old you gotta do something. When you get old, you can't talk to people because people snap at you. When you get so old, people talk to you that way. That's why you become deaf, so you won't be able to hear people talking to you that way. And that's why you go and hide under the covers in the big soft bed, so you won't feel the house shaking from people talking to you that way. That's why old people die, eventually. People talk to them that way. I've got to go and get the rest of the boxes.

(GRANDMA *exits*)

DADDY Poor Grandma, I didn't mean to hurt her.

MOMMY Don't you worry about it; Grandma doesn't know what she means.

DADDY She knows what she says, though.

MOMMY Don't you worry about it; she won't know that soon. I love Grandma.

DADDY I love her, too. Look how nicely she wrapped these boxes.

MOMMY Grandma has always wrapped boxes nicely. When I was a little girl, I was very poor, and Grandma was very poor, too, because Grandpa was in heaven. And every day, when I went to school, Grandma used to wrap a box for me, and I used to take it with me to school; and when it was lunchtime, all the little boys and girls used to take out their boxes of lunch, and they weren't wrapped nicely at all, and they used to open them and eat their chicken legs and chocolate cakes; and I used to say, "Oh, look at my lovely lunch box; it's so nicely wrapped it would break my heart to open it." And so, I wouldn't open it.

DADDY Because it was empty.

MOMMY Oh no. Grandma always filled it up, because she never ate the dinner she cooked the evening before; she gave me all her food for my lunch box the next day. After school, I'd take the box back to Grandma, and she'd open it and eat the chicken legs and chocolate cake that was inside. Grandma used to say, "I love day-old cake." That's where the expression day-old cake came from. Grandma always ate everything a day late. I used to eat all the other little boys' and girls' food at school, because they thought my lunch box was empty. They thought my lunch box was empty, and that's why I wouldn't open it. They thought I suffered from the sin of pride, and since that made them better than me, they were very generous.

DADDY You were a very deceitful little girl.

MOMMY We were very poor! But then I married you, Daddy, and now we're very rich.

DADDY Grandma isn't rich.

MOMMY No, but you've been so good to Grandma she feels rich. She doesn't know you'd like to put her in a nursing home.

DADDY I wouldn't!

MOMMY Well, heaven knows, *I* would! I can't stand it, watching her do the cooking and the housework, polishing the silver, moving the furniture. . . .

DADDY She likes to do that. She says it's the least she can do to earn her keep.

MOMMY Well, she's right. You can't live off people. I can live off you, because I married you. And aren't you lucky all I brought with me was Grandma. A lot of women I know would have brought their whole families to live off you. All I brought was Grandma. Grandma is all the family I have.

DADDY I feel very fortunate.

MOMMY You should. I have a right to live off you because I married you, and because I used to let you get on top of me and bump your uglies; and I have a right to all your money when you die. And when you do, Grandma and I can live by ourselves . . . if she's still here. Unless you have her put away in a nursing home.

DADDY I have no intention of putting her in a nursing home.

MOMMY Well, I wish somebody would do something with her!

DADDY At any rate, you're very well provided for.

MOMMY You're my sweet Daddy; that's very nice.

DADDY I love my Mommy.

(*Enter* GRANDMA *again, laden with more boxes*)

GRANDMA (*Dumping the boxes on and around* DADDY's *feet*) There; that's the lot of them.

DADDY They're wrapped so nicely.

GRANDMA (*To* DADDY) You won't get on my sweet side that way . . .

MOMMY Grandma!

GRANDMA . . . telling me how nicely I wrap boxes. Not after what you said: how I whimpered for hours. . . .

MOMMY Grandma!

GRANDMA (*To* MOMMY) Shut up!

(*To* DADDY) You don't have any feelings, that's what's wrong with you. Old people make all sorts of noises, half of them they can't help. Old people whimper, and cry, and belch, and make great hollow rumbling sounds at the table; old people wake up in the middle of the night screaming, and find out they haven't even been asleep; and when old people *are* asleep, they try to wake up, and they can't . . . not for the longest time.

MOMMY Homilies, homilies!

GRANDMA And there's more, too.

DADDY I'm really very sorry, Grandma.

GRANDMA I know you are, Daddy; it's Mommy over there makes all the trouble. If you'd listened to me, you wouldn't have married her in the first place. She was a tramp and a trollop and a trull to boot, and she's no better now.

MOMMY Grandma!

GRANDMA (*To* MOMMY) Shut up!

(*To* DADDY) When she was no more than eight years old she used to climb up on my lap and say, in a sickening little voice, "When I gwo up, I'm going to mahwy a wich old man; I'm going to set my wittle were end right down in a tub o' butter, that's what I'm going to do." And I warned you, Daddy; I told you to stay away from her type. I told you to. I did.

MOMMY You stop that! You're my mother, not his!

GRANDMA I am?

DADDY That's right, Grandma. Mommy's right.

GRANDMA Well, how would you expect somebody as old as I am to remember a thing like that? You don't make allowances for people. I want an allowance. I want an allowance!

DADDY All right, Grandma; I'll see to it.

MOMMY Grandma! I'm ashamed of you.

GRANDMA Humf! It's a fine time to say that. You should have gotten rid of me a long time ago if that's the way you feel. You should have had Daddy set me up in business somewhere . . . I could have gone into the fur business, or I could have been a singer. But no; not you. You wanted me around so you could sleep in my room when Daddy got fresh. But now it isn't important, because Daddy doesn't want to get fresh with you any more, and I don't blame him. You'd rather sleep with me, wouldn't you, Daddy?

MOMMY Daddy doesn't want to sleep with anyone. Daddy's been sick.
DADDY I've been sick. I don't want to sleep in the apartment.
MOMMY You see? I told you.
DADDY I just want to get everything over with.
MOMMY That's right. Why are they so late? Why can't they get here on time?
GRANDMA (*An owl*) Who? Who? ... Who? Who?
MOMMY You know, Grandma.
GRANDMA No, I don't.
MOMMY Well, it doesn't really matter whether you do or not.
DADDY Is that true?
MOMMY Oh, more or less. Look how pretty Grandma wrapped these boxes.
GRANDMA I didn't really like wrapping them; it hurt my fingers, and it frightened me. But it had to be done.
MOMMY Why, Grandma?
GRANDMA None of your damn business.
MOMMY Go to bed.
GRANDMA I don't want to go to bed. I just got up. I want to stay here and watch. Besides . . .
MOMMY Go to bed.
DADDY Let her stay up, Mommy; it isn't noon yet.
GRANDMA I want to watch; besides . . .
DADDY Let her watch, Mommy.
MOMMY Well all right, you can watch; but don't you dare say a word.
GRANDMA Old people are very good at listening; old people don't like to talk; old people have colitis and lavender perfume. Now I'm going to be quiet.
DADDY She never mentioned she wanted to be a singer.
MOMMY Oh, I forgot to tell you, but it was ages ago.
    (*The doorbell rings*)
Oh, goodness! Here they are!
GRANDMA Who? Who?
MOMMY Oh, just some people.
GRANDMA The van people? Is it the van people? Have you finally done it? Have you called the van people to come and take me away?
DADDY Of course not, Grandma!
GRANDMA Oh, don't be too sure. She'd have you carted off too, if she thought she could get away with it.
MOMMY Pay no attention to her, Daddy.
    (*An aside to* GRANDMA)
My God, you're ungrateful!
    (*The doorbell rings again*)
DADDY (*Wringing his hands*) Oh dear; oh dear.
MOMMY (*Still to* GRANDMA) Just you wait; I'll fix your wagon.
(*Now to* DADDY) Well, go let them in Daddy. What are you waiting for?
DADDY I think we should talk about it some more. Maybe we've been hasty . . . a little hasty, perhaps.
    (*Doorbell rings again*)
I'd like to talk about it some more.
MOMMY There's no need. You made up your mind; you were firm; you were masculine and decisive.
DADDY We might consider the pros and the . . .
MOMMY I won't argue with you; it has to be done; you were right. Open the door.
DADDY But I'm not sure that . . .
MOMMY Open the door.
DADDY Was I firm about it?
MOMMY Oh, so firm; so firm.
DADDY And was I decisive?
MOMMY SO decisive! Oh, I shivered.
DADDY And masculine? Was I really masculine?
MOMMY Oh, Daddy, you were so masculine; I shivered and fainted.
GRANDMA Shivered and fainted, did she? Humf!
MOMMY You be quiet.
GRANDMA Old people have a right to talk to themselves; it doesn't hurt the gums, and it's comforting.
    (*Doorbell rings again*)
DADDY I shall now open the door.
MOMMY WHAT a masculine Daddy! Isn't he a masculine Daddy?
GRANDMA Don't expect me to say anything. Old people are obscene.
MOMMY Some of your opinions aren't so bad. You know that?
DADDY (*Backing off from the door*) Maybe we can send them away.

MOMMY Oh, look at you! You're turning into jelly; you're indecisive; you're a woman.
DADDY All right. Watch me now; I'm going to open the door. Watch. Watch!
MOMMY We're watching; we're watching.
GRANDMA *I'm* not.
DADDY Watch now; it's opening.
   (*He opens the door*)
   It's open!
   (MRS. BARKER *steps into the room*)
   Here they are!
MOMMY Here they are!
GRANDMA Where?
DADDY Come in. You're late. But, of course, we expected you to be late; we were saying that we expected you to be late.
MOMMY Daddy, don't be rude! We were saying that you just can't get satisfaction these days, and we were talking about you, of course. Won't you come in?
MRS. BARKER Thank you. I don't mind if I do.
MOMMY We're very glad that you're here, late as you are. You do remember us, don't you? You were here once before. I'm Mommy, and this is Daddy, and that's Grandma, doddering there in the corner.
MRS. BARKER Hello, Mommy, hello, Daddy; and hello there, Grandma.
DADDY Now that you're here, I don't suppose you could go away and maybe come back some other time.
MRS. BARKER Oh no; we're much too efficient for that. I said, hello there, Grandma.
MOMMY Speak to them, Grandma.
GRANDMA I don't see them.
DADDY For shame, Grandma; they're here.
MRS. BARKER Yes, we're here, Grandma. I'm Mrs. Barker. I remember you; don't you remember me?
GRANDMA I don't recall. Maybe you were younger, or something.
MOMMY Grandma! What a terrible thing to say!
MRS. BARKER Oh now, don't scold her, Mommy; for all she knows she may be right.
DADDY Uh . . . Mrs. Barker, is it? Won't you sit down?
MRS. BARKER I don't mind if I do.
MOMMY Would you like a cigarette, and a drink, and would you like to cross your legs?
MRS. BARKER You forget yourself, Mommy; I'm a professional woman. But I will cross my legs.
DADDY Yes, make yourself comfortable.
MRS. BARKER I don't mind if I do.
GRANDMA Are they still here?
MOMMY Be quiet, Grandma.
MRS. BARKER Oh, we're still here. My, what an unattractive apartment you have!
MOMMY Yes, but you don't know what a trouble it is. Let me tell you . . .
DADDY I was saying to Mommy . . .
MRS. BARKER Yes, I know. I was listening outside.
DADDY About the icebox, and . . . the doorbell . . . and the . . .
MRS. BARKER . . . and the johnny. Yes, we're very efficient; we have to know everything in our work.
DADDY Exactly what do you do?
MOMMY Yes, what is your work?
MRS. BARKER Well, my dear, for one thing, I'm chairman of your woman's club.
MOMMY Don't be ridiculous. I was talking to the chairman of my woman's club just yester— Why, so you are. You remember, Daddy, the lady I was telling you about? The lady with the husband who sits in the *swing*? Don't you remember?
DADDY No . . . no. . . .
MOMMY Of course you do. I'm so sorry, Mrs. Barker. I would have known you anywhere, except in this artificial light. And look! You have a hat just like the one I bought yesterday.
MRS. BARKER (*With a little laugh*) No, not really; this hat is cream.
MOMMY Well, my dear, that may look like a cream hat to you, but I can . . .
MRS. BARKER Now, now; you seem to forget who I am.
MOMMY Yes, I do, don't I? Are you sure you're comfortable? Won't you take off your dress?
MRS. BARKER I don't mind if I do.
   (*She removes her dress*)
MOMMY There. You must feel a great deal more comfortable.
MRS. BARKER Well, I certainly *look* a great deal more comfortable.

DADDY I'm going to blush and giggle.

MOMMY Daddy's going to blush and giggle.

MRS. BARKER (*Pulling the hem of her slip above her knees*) You're lucky to have such a man for a husband.

MOMMY Oh, don't I know it!

DADDY I just blushed and giggled and went sticky wet.

MOMMY Isn't Daddy a caution, Mrs. Barker?

MRS. BARKER Maybe if I smoked . . . ?

MOMMY Oh, that isn't necessary.

MRS. BARKER I don't mind if I do.

MOMMY No; no, don't. Really.

MRS. BARKER I don't mind . . .

MOMMY I won't have you smoking in my house, and that's that! You're a professional woman.

DADDY Grandma drinks AND smokes; don't you, Grandma?

GRANDMA No.

MOMMY Well, now, Mrs. Barker; suppose you tell us why you're here.

GRANDMA (*As* MOMMY *walks through the boxes*) The boxes . . . the boxes . . .

MOMMY Be quiet, Grandma.

DADDY What did you say, Grandma?

GRANDMA (*As* MOMMY *steps on several of the boxes*) The boxes, damn it!

MRS. BARKER Boxes; she said boxes. She mentioned the boxes.

DADDY What about the boxes, Grandma? Maybe Mrs. Barker is here because of the boxes. Is that what you meant, Grandma?

GRANDMA I don't know if that's what I meant or not. It's certainly not what I *thought* I meant.

DADDY Grandma is of the opinion that . . .

MRS. BARKER Can we assume that the boxes are for us? I mean, can we assume that you had us come here for the boxes?

MOMMY Are you in the habit of receiving boxes?

DADDY A very good question.

MRS. BARKER Well, that would depend on the reason we're here. I've got my fingers in so many little pies, you know. Now, I can think of one of my little activities in which we are in the habit of receiving *baskets*; but more in a literary sense than really. We *might* receive boxes, though, under very special circumstances. I'm afraid that's the best answer I can give you.

DADDY It's a very interesting answer.

MRS. BARKER I thought so. But, does it help?

MOMMY No; I'm afraid not.

DADDY I wonder if it might help us any if I said I feel misgivings, that I have definite qualms.

MOMMY Where, Daddy?

DADDY Well, mostly right here, right around where the stitches were.

MOMMY Daddy had an operation, you know.

MRS. BARKER Oh, you poor Daddy! I didn't know; but then, how could I?

GRANDMA You might have asked; it wouldn't have hurt you.

MOMMY Dry up, Grandma.

GRANDMA There you go. Letting your true feelings come out. Old people aren't dry enough, I suppose. My sacks are empty, the fluid in my eyeballs is all caked on the inside edges, my spine is made of sugar candy, I breathe ice; but you don't hear me complain. Nobody hears old people complain because people think that's all old people do. And *that's* because old people are gnarled and sagged and twisted into the shape of a complaint.

(*Signs off*)

That's all.

MRS. BARKER What was wrong, Daddy?

DADDY Well, you know how it is: the doctors took out something that was there and put in something that wasn't there. An operation.

MRS. BARKER You're very fortunate, I should say.

MOMMY Oh, he is; he is. All his life, Daddy has wanted to be a United States Senator; but now . . . why now he's changed his mind, and for the rest of his life he's going to want to be Governor . . . it would be nearer the apartment, you know.

MRS. BARKER You *are* fortunate, Daddy.

DADDY Yes, indeed; except that I get these qualms now and then, definite ones.

MRS. BARKER Well, it's just a matter of things settling; you're like an old house.

MOMMY Why Daddy, thank Mrs. Barker.

DADDY Thank you.

MRS. BARKER Ambition! That's the ticket. I

have a brother who's very much like you, Daddy . . . ambitious. Of course, he's a great deal younger than you; he's even younger than I am . . . if such a thing is possible. He runs a little newspaper. Just a little newspaper . . . but he runs it. He's chief cook and bottle washer of that little newspaper, which he calls *The Village Idiot*. He has such a sense of humor; he's so self-deprecating, so modest. And he'd never admit it himself, but he *is* the Village Idiot.

MOMMY   Oh, I think that's grand. Don't you think so, Daddy?

DADDY   Yes, just grand.

MRS. BARKER   My brother's a dear man, and he has a dear little wife, whom he loves, dearly. He loves her so much he just can't get a sentence out without mentioning her. He wants everybody to know he's married. He's really a stickler on that point; he can't be introduced to anybody and say hello without adding, "Of course, I'm married." As far as I'm concerned, he's the chief exponent of Woman Love in this whole country; he's even been written up in psychiatric journals because of it.

DADDY   Indeed!

MOMMY   Isn't that lovely.

MRS. BARKER   Oh, I think so. There's too much woman hatred in this country, and that's a fact.

GRANDMA   Oh, I don't know.

MOMMY   Oh, I think that's just grand. Don't you think so, Daddy?

DADDY   Yes, just grand.

GRANDMA   In case anybody's interested . . .

MOMMY   Be quiet, Grandma.

GRANDMA   Nuts!

MOMMY   Oh, Mrs. Barker, you *must* forgive Grandma. She's rural.

MRS. BARKER   I don't mind if I do.

DADDY   Maybe Grandma has something to say.

MOMMY   Nonsense. Old people have nothing to say; and if old people *did* have something to say, nobody would listen to them. (*To* GRANDMA) You see? I can pull that stuff just as easy as you can.

GRANDMA   Well, you got the rhythm, but you don't really have the quality. Besides, you're middle-aged.

MOMMY   I'm proud of it!

GRANDMA   Look. I'll show you how it's really done. Middle-aged people think they can do anything, but the truth is that middle-aged people can't do most things as well as they used to. Middle-aged people think they're special because they're like everybody else. We live in the age of deformity. You see? Rhythm *and* content. You'll learn.

DADDY   I do wish I weren't surrounded by women; I'd like some men around here.

MRS. BARKER   You can say that again!

GRANDMA   I don't hardly count as a woman, so can I say my piece?

MOMMY   Go on. Jabber away.

GRANDMA   It's very simple; the fact is, these boxes don't have anything to do with why this good lady is come to call. Now, if you're interested in knowing why these boxes *are* here . . .

DADDY   I'm sure that must be all very true, Grandma, but what does it have to do with why . . . pardon me, what is that name again?

MRS. BARKER   Mrs. Barker.

DADDY   Exactly. What does it have to do with why . . . that name again?

MRS. BARKER   Mrs. Barker.

DADDY   Precisely. What does it have to do with why what's-her-name is here?

MOMMY   They're here because we asked them.

MRS. BARKER   Yes. That's why.

GRANDMA   Now if you're interested in knowing why these boxes *are* here . . .

MOMMY   Well, nobody *is* interested!

GRANDMA   You can be as snippety as you like for all the good it'll do you.

DADDY   You two will have to stop arguing.

MOMMY   I don't argue with her.

DADDY   It will just have to stop.

MOMMY   Well, why don't you call a van and have her taken away?

GRANDMA   Don't bother; there's no need.

DADDY   No, now, perhaps I can go away myself. . .

MOMMY   Well, one or the other; the way things are now it's impossible. In the first place, it's too crowded in this apartment. (*To* GRANDMA) And it's you that takes up all the space, with your enema bottles, and your Pekinese, and God-only-knows-what-else . . . and now all these boxes. . . .

GRANDMA   These boxes are . . .
MRS. BARKER   I've never heard of enema *bottles.* . . .
GRANDMA   She means enema bags, but she doesn't know the difference. Mommy comes from extremely bad stock. And besides, when Mommy was born . . . well, it was a difficult delivery, and she had a head shaped like a banana.
MOMMY   You ungrateful— Daddy? Daddy, you see how ungrateful she is after all these years, after all the things we've done for her? (*To* GRANDMA) One of these days you're going away in a van; that's what's going to happen to you!
GRANDMA   Do tell!
MRS. BARKER   Like a banana?
GRANDMA   Yup, just like a banana.
MRS. BARKER   My word!
MOMMY   You stop listening to her; she'll say anything. Just the other night she called Daddy a hedgehog.
MRS. BARKER   She didn't!
GRANDMA   That's right, baby; you stick up for me.
MOMMY   I don't know where she gets the words; on the television, maybe.
MRS. BARKER   Did you really call him a hedgehog?
GRANDMA   Oh, look; what difference does it make whether I did or not?
DADDY   Grandma's right. Leave Grandma alone.
MOMMY   (*To* DADDY) How dare you!
GRANDMA   Oh, leave her alone, Daddy; the kid's all mixed up.
MOMMY   You see? I told you. It's all those television shows. Daddy, you go right into Grandma's room and take her television and shake all the tubes loose.
DADDY   Don't mention tubes to me.
MOMMY   Oh! Mommy forgot! (*To* MRS. BARKER) Daddy has tubes now, where he used to have tracts.
MRS. BARKER   Is that a fact!
GRANDMA   I know why this dear lady is here.
MOMMY   You be still.
MRS. BARKER   Oh, I do wish you'd tell me.
MOMMY   No! No! That wouldn't be fair at all.
DADDY   Besides, she knows why she's here; she's here because we called them.
MRS. BARKER   La! But that still leaves me puzzled. I know I'm here because you called us, but I'm such a busy girl, with this committee and that committee, and the Responsible Citizens Activities I indulge in.
MOMMY   Oh my; busy, busy.
MRS. BARKER   Yes, indeed. So I'm afraid you'll have to give me some help.
MOMMY   Oh, no. No, you must be mistaken. I can't believe we asked you here to give you any help. With the way taxes are these days, and the way you can't get satisfaction in ANYTHING . . . no, I don't believe so.
DADDY   And if you need help . . . why, I should think you'd apply for a Fulbright Scholarship. . . .
MOMMY   And if not that . . . why, then a Guggenheim Fellowship. . . .
GRANDMA   Oh, come on; why not shoot the works and try for the Prix de Rome. (*Under her breath to* MOMMY *and* DADDY) Beasts!
MRS. BARKER   Oh, what a jolly family. But let me think. I'm knee-deep in work these days; there's the Ladies' Auxiliary Air Raid Committee, for one thing; how do you feel about air raids?
MOMMY   Oh, I'd say we're hostile.
DADDY   Yes, definitely; we're hostile.
MRS. BARKER   Then, you'll be no help there. There's too much hostility in the world these days as it is; but I'll not badger you! There's a surfeit of badgers as well.
GRANDMA   While we're at it, there's been a run on old people, too. The Department of Agriculture, or maybe it wasn't the Department of Agriculture—anyway, it was some department that's run by a girl—put out figures showing that ninety per cent of the adult population of the country is over eighty years old . . . or eighty per cent is over ninety years old . . .
MOMMY   You're such a liar! You just finished saying that everyone is middle-aged.
GRANDMA   I'm just telling you what the government says . . . that doesn't have anything to do with what . . .
MOMMY   It's that television! Daddy, go break her television.
GRANDMA   You won't find it.

DADDY (*Wearily getting up*) If I must . . . I must.
MOMMY And don't step on the Pekinese; it's blind.
DADDY It may be blind, but Daddy isn't.
(*He exits, through the archway, stage left*)
GRANDMA You won't find *it*, either.
MOMMY Oh, I'm so fortunate to have such a husband. Just think; I could have a husband who was poor, or argumentative, or a husband who sat in a wheel chair all day . . . OOOOHHHH! *What* have I said? What *have* I said?
GRANDMA You said you could have a husband who sat in a wheel . . .
MOMMY I'm mortified! I could die! I could cut my tongue out! I could . . .
MRS. BARKER (*Forcing a smile*) Oh, now . . . now . . . don't think about it . . .
MOMMY I could . . . why, I could . . .
MRS. BARKER . . . don't think about it . . . really. . . .
MOMMY You're quite right. I won't think about it, and that way I'll forget that I ever said it, and that way it will be all right.
(*Pause*)
There . . . I've forgotten. Well, now, now that Daddy is out of the room we can have some girl talk.
MRS. BARKER I'm not sure that I . . .
MOMMY You *do* want to have some girl talk, don't you?
MRS. BARKER I was going to say I'm not sure that I wouldn't care for a glass of water. I feel a little faint.
MOMMY Grandma, go get Mrs. Barker a glass of water.
GRANDMA Go get it yourself. I quit.
MOMMY Grandma loves to do little things around the house; it gives her a false sense of security.
GRANDMA I quit! I'm through!
MOMMY Now, you be a good Grandma, or you know what will happen to you. You'll be taken away in a van.
GRANDMA You don't frighten me. I'm too old to be frightened. Besides . . .
MOMMY WELL! I'll tend to you later. I'll hide your teeth . . . I'll . . .
GRANDMA Everything's hidden.
MRS. BARKER I *am* going to faint. I *am*.

MOMMY Good heavens! I'll go myself.
(*As she exits, through the archway, stage-left*)
I'll fix you, Grandma. I'll take care of you later.
(*She exits*)
GRANDMA Oh, go soak your head.
(To MRS. BARKER) Well, dearie, how do you feel?
MRS. BARKER A little better, I think. Yes, much better, thank you, Grandma.
GRANDMA That's good.
MRS. BARKER But . . . I feel so lost . . . not knowing why I'm here . . . and, on top of it, they say I was here before.
GRANDMA Well, you were. You weren't *here*, exactly, because we've moved around a lot, from one apartment to another, up and down the social ladder like mice, if you like similes.
MRS. BARKER I don't . . . particularly.
GRANDMA Well, then, I'm sorry.
MRS. BARKER (*Suddenly*) Grandma, I feel I can trust you.
GRANDMA Don't be too sure; it's every man for himself around this place. . . .
MRS. BARKER Oh . . . is it? Nonetheless, I really do feel that I can trust you. *Please* tell me why they called and asked us to come. I implore you!
GRANDMA Oh my; that feels good. It's been so long since anybody implored me. Do it again. Implore me some more.
MRS. BARKER You're your daughter's mother, all right!
GRANDMA Oh, I don't mean to be hard. If you won't implore me, then beg me, or ask me, or entreat me . . . just anything like that.
MRS. BARKER You're a dreadful old woman!
GRANDMA You'll understand some day. Please!
MRS. BARKER Oh, for heaven's sake! . . . I implore you . . . I beg you . . . I beseech you!
GRANDMA Beseech! Oh, that's the nicest word I've heard in ages. You're a dear, sweet woman. . . . You . . . beseech . . . me. I can't resist that.
MRS. BARKER Well, then . . . please tell me why they asked us to come.
GRANDMA Well, I'll give you a hint. That's the best I can do, because I'm a muddle-headed old woman. Now listen, because it's important. Once upon a time, not too very

long ago, but a long enough time ago . . . oh, about twenty years ago . . . there was a man very much like Daddy, and a woman very much like Mommy, who were married to each other, very much like Mommy and Daddy are married to each other; and they lived in an apartment very much like one that's very much like this one, and they lived there with an old woman who was very much like yours truly, only younger, because it was some time ago; in fact, they were all somewhat younger.

MRS. BARKER How fascinating!

GRANDMA Now, at the same time, there was a dear lady very much like you, only younger then, who did all sorts of Good Works. . . . And one of the Good Works this dear lady did was in something very much like a volunteer capacity for an organization very much like the Bye-Bye Adoption Service, which is nearby and which was run by a terribly deaf old lady very much like the Miss Bye-Bye who runs the Bye-Bye Adoption Service nearby.

MRS. BARKER How enthralling!

GRANDMA Well, be that as it may. Nonetheless, one afternoon this man, who was very much like Daddy, and this woman who was very much like Mommy came to see this dear lady who did all the Good Works, who was very much like you, dear, and they were very sad and very hopeful, and they cried and smiled and bit their fingers, and they said all the most intimate things.

MRS. BARKER How spellbinding! What did they say?

GRANDMA Well, it was very sweet. The woman, who was very much like Mommy, said that she and the man who was very much like Daddy had never been blessed with anything very much like a bumble of joy.

MRS. BARKER A what?

GRANDMA A bumble; a bumble of joy.

MRS. BARKER Oh, like bundle.

GRANDMA Well, yes; very much like it. Bundle, bumble; who cares? At any rate, the woman, who was very much like Mommy, said that they wanted a bumble of their own, but that the man, who was very much like Daddy, couldn't have a bumble; and the man, who was very much like Daddy, said that yes, they had wanted a bumble of their own, but that the woman, who was very much like Mommy, couldn't have one, and that now they wanted to buy something very much like a bumble.

MRS. BARKER How engrossing!

GRANDMA Yes. And the dear lady, who was very much like you, said something that was very much like, "Oh, what a shame; but take heart . . . I think we have just the bumble *for* you." And, well, the lady, who was very much like Mommy, and the man, who was very much like Daddy, cried and smiled and bit their fingers, and said some more intimate things, which were totally irrelevant but which were pretty hot stuff, and so the dear lady, who was very much like you, and who had something very much like a penchant for pornography, listened with something very much like enthusiasm. "Whee," she said. "Whooooo-peeeeee!" But that's beside the point.

MRS. BARKER I suppose *so*. But how gripping!

GRANDMA Anyway . . . they *bought* something very much like a bumble, and they took it away with them. But . . . things didn't work out very well.

MRS. BARKER You mean there was trouble?

GRANDMA You got it.

(*With a glance through the archway*) But, I'm going to have to speed up now because I think I'm leaving soon.

MRS. BARKER Oh. Are you really?

GRANDMA Yup.

MRS. BARKER But old people don't go any where; they're either taken places, or put places.

GRANDMA Well, this old person is different. Anyway . . . things started going badly.

MRS. BARKER Oh yes. Yes.

GRANDMA Weeeeellll . . . in the first place, it turned out the bumble didn't look like either one of its parents. That was enough of a blow, but things got worse. One night, it cried its heart out, if you can imagine such a thing.

MRS. BARKER Cried its heart out! Well!

GRANDMA But that was only the beginning. Then it turned out it only had eyes for its Daddy.

MRS. BARKER For its Daddy! Why, any self-respecting woman would have gouged those eyes right out of its head.

GRANDMA Well, she did. That's exactly what

she did. But then, it kept its nose up in the air.

MRS. BARKER Ufggh! How disgusting!

GRANDMA That's what they thought. But *then*, it began to develop an interest in its you-know-what.

MRS. BARKER In its you-know-what! Well! I hope they cut its hands off at the wrists!

GRANDMA Well, yes, they did that eventually. But first, they cut off its you-know-what.

MRS. BARKER A much better idea!

GRANDMA That's what they thought. But after they cut off its you-know-what, it *still* put its hands under the covers, *looking* for its you-know-what. So, finally, they *had* to cut off its hands at the wrists.

MRS. BARKER Naturally!

GRANDMA And it was such a resentful bumble. Why, one day it called its Mommy a dirty name.

MRS. BARKER Well, I hope they cut its tongue out!

GRANDMA Of course. And then, as it got bigger, they found out all sorts of terrible things about it, like: it didn't have a head on its shoulders, it had no guts, it was spineless, its feet were made of clay . . . just dreadful things.

MRS. BARKER Dreadful!

GRANDMA So you can understand how they became discouraged.

MRS. BARKER I certainly can! And what did they do?

GRANDMA What did they do? Well, for the last straw, it finally up and died; and you can imagine how *that* made them feel, their having paid for it, and all. So, they called up the lady who sold them the bumble in the first place and told her to come right over to their apartment. They wanted satisfaction; they wanted their money back. That's what they wanted.

MRS. BARKER My, my, my.

GRANDMA How do you like *them* apples?

MRS. BARKER My, my, my.

DADDY (*Off stage*) Mommy! I can't find Grandma's television, and I can't find the Pekinese, either.

MOMMY (*Off stage*) Isn't that funny! And I can't find the water.

GRANDMA Heh, heh, heh. I told them everything was hidden.

MRS. BARKER Did you hide the water, too?

GRANDMA (*Puzzled*) No. No, I didn't do *that*.

DADDY (*Off stage*) The truth of the matter is, I can't even find Grandma's room.

GRANDMA Heh, heh, heh.

MRS. BARKER My! You certainly did hide things, didn't you?

GRANDMA Sure, kid, sure.

MOMMY (*Sticking her head in the room*) Did you ever hear of such a thing, Grandma? Daddy can't find your television, and he can't find the Pekinese, and the truth of the matter is he can't even find your room.

GRANDMA I told you. I hid everything.

MOMMY Nonsense, Grandma! Just wait until I get my hands on you. You're a troublemaker . . . that's what you are.

GRANDMA Well, I'll be out of here pretty soon, baby.

MOMMY Oh, you don't know how right you are! Daddy's been wanting to send you away for a long time now, but I've been restraining him. I'll tell you one thing, though . . . I'm getting sick and tired of this fighting, and I might just let him have his way. Then you'll see what'll happen. Away you'll go; in a van, too. I'll let Daddy call the van man.

GRANDMA I'm way ahead of you.

MOMMY How can you be so old and so smug at the same time? You have no sense of proportion.

GRANDMA You just answered your own question.

MOMMY Mrs. Barker, I'd much rather you came into the kitchen for that glass of water, what with Grandma out here, and all.

MRS. BARKER I don't see what Grandma has to do with it; and besides, I don't think you're very polite.

MOMMY You seem to forget that you're a guest in this house . . .

GRANDMA Apartment!

MOMMY Apartment! And that you're a professional woman. So, if you'll be so good as to come into the kitchen, I'll be more than happy to show you where the water is, and where the glass is, and then you can put two and two together, if you're clever enough.

(*She vanishes*)

MRS. BARKER (*After a moment's consideration*) I suppose she's right.

GRANDMA Well, that's how it is when people call you up and ask you over to do something for them.

MRS. BARKER I suppose you're right too. Well, Grandma, it's been very nice talking to you.

GRANDMA And I've enjoyed listening. Say, don't tell Mommy or Daddy that I gave you that hint, will you?

MRS. BARKER Oh, dear me, the hint! I'd forgotten about it, if you can imagine such a thing. No, I won't breathe a word of it to them.

GRANDMA I don't know if it helped you any . . .

MRS. BARKER I can't tell, yet. I'll have to . . . what *is* the word I want? . . . I'll have to relate it . . . that's it . . . I'll have to relate it to certain things that I *know*, and . . . draw . . . conclusions. . . . What I'll really have to do is to see if it applies to anything. I mean, after all, I *do* do volunteer work for an adoption service, but it isn't very much *like* the Bye-Bye Adoption Service . . . it *is* the Bye-Bye Adoption Service . . . and while I can remember Mommy and Daddy coming to see me, oh, about twenty years ago, about buying a bumble, I can't quite remember anyone very much *like* Mommy and Daddy coming to see me about buying a bumble. Don't you see? It really presents quite a problem. . . . I'll have to think about it . . . mull it . . . but at any rate, it was truly first-class of you to try to help me. Oh, will you still be here after I've had my drink of water?

GRANDMA Probably . . . I'm not as spry as I used to be.

MRS. BARKER Oh. Well, I won't say good-by then.

GRANDMA No. Don't.

(MRS. BARKER *exits through the archway*)

People don't say good-by to old people because they think they'll frighten them. Lordy! If they only knew how awful "hello" and "my, you're looking chipper" sounded, they wouldn't say those things either. The truth is, there isn't much you *can* say to old people that doesn't sound just terrible.

(*The doorbell rings*)

Come on in!

(*The* YOUNG MAN *enters.* GRANDMA *looks him over*)

Well, now, aren't you a breath of fresh air!

YOUNG MAN Hello there.

GRANDMA My, my, my. Are you the van man?

YOUNG MAN The what?

GRANDMA The van man. The van man. Are you come to take me away?

YOUNG MAN I don't know what you're talking about.

GRANDMA Oh.

(*Pause*)

Well.

(*Pause*)

My, my, aren't you something!

YOUNG MAN Hm?

GRANDMA I said, my, my, aren't you something.

YOUNG MAN Oh. Thank you.

GRANDMA You don't sound very enthusiastic.

YOUNG MAN Oh, I'm . . . I'm used to it.

GRANDMA Yup . . . yup. You know, if I were about a hundred and fifty years younger I could go for you.

YOUNG MAN Yes, I imagine so.

GRANDMA Unh-hunh . . . will you look at those muscles!

YOUNG MAN (*Flexing his muscles*) Yes, they're quite good, aren't they?

GRANDMA Boy, they sure are. They natural?

YOUNG MAN Well the basic structure was there, but I've done some work, too . . . you know, in a gym.

GRANDMA I'll bet you have. You ought to be in the movies, boy.

YOUNG MAN I know.

GRANDMA Yup! Right up there on the old silver screen. But I suppose you've heard that before.

YOUNG MAN Yes, I have.

GRANDMA You ought to try out for them . . . the movies.

YOUNG MAN Well, actually, I may have a career there yet. I've lived out on the West

Coast almost all my life . . . and I've met a few people who . . . might be able to help me. I'm not in too much of a hurry, though. I'm almost as young as I look.

GRANDMA Oh, that's nice. And will you look at that face!

YOUNG MAN Yes, it's quite good, isn't it? Clean-cut, midwest farm boy type, almost insultingly good-looking in a typically American way. Good profile, straight nose, honest eyes, wonderful smile . . .

GRANDMA Yup. Boy, you know what you are, don't you? You're the American Dream, that's what you are. All those other people, they don't know what they're talking about. You . . . *you* are the American Dream.

YOUNG MAN Thanks.

MOMMY (*Off stage*) Who rang the doorbell?

GRANDMA (*Shouting off-stage*) The American Dream!

MOMMY (*Off stage*) What? What was that, Grandma?

GRANDMA (*Shouting*) The American Dream! The American Dream! Damn it!

DADDY (*Off stage*) How's that, Mommy?

MOMMY (*Off stage*) Oh, some gibberish; pay no attention. Did you find Grandma's room?

DADDY (*Off stage*) No. I can't even find Mrs. Barker.

YOUNG MAN What was all that?

GRANDMA Oh, that was just the folks, but let's not talk about them, honey; let's talk about you.

YOUNG MAN All right.

GRANDMA Well, let's see. If you're not the van man, what are you doing here?

YOUNG MAN I'm looking for work.

GRANDMA Are you! Well, what kind of work?

YOUNG MAN Oh, almost anything . . . almost anything that pays. I'll do almost anything for money.

GRANDMA Will you . . . will you? Hmmmm. I wonder if there's anything you could do around here?

YOUNG MAN There might be. It looked to be a likely building.

GRANDMA It's always looked to be a rather unlikely building to me, but I suppose you'd know better than I.

YOUNG MAN I can sense these things.

GRANDMA There *might* be something you could do around here. Stay there! Don't come any closer.

YOUNG MAN Sorry.

GRANDMA I don't mean I'd *mind*. I don't know whether I'd mind, or not. . . . But it wouldn't look well; it would look just *awful*.

YOUNG MAN Yes; I suppose so.

GRANDMA Now, stay there, let me concentrate. What could you do? The folks have been in something of a quandary around here today, sort of a dilemma, and I wonder if you mightn't be some help.

YOUNG MAN I hope so . . . if there's money in it. Do you have any money?

GRANDMA Money! Oh, there's more money around here than you'd know what to do with.

YOUNG MAN I'm not so sure.

GRANDMA Well, maybe not. Besides, I've got money of my own.

YOUNG MAN You have?

GRANDMA Sure. Old people quite often have lots of money; more often than most people expect. Come here, so I can whisper to you . . . not too close. I might faint.

YOUNG MAN Oh, I'm sorry.

GRANDMA It's all right, dear. Anyway . . . have you ever heard of that big baking contest they run? The one where all the ladies get together in a big barn and bake away?

YOUNG MAN I'm . . . not . . . sure. . .

GRANDMA Not so close. Well, it doesn't matter whether you've heard of it or not. The important thing is—and I don't want anybody to hear this . . . the folks think I haven't been out of the house in eight years—the important thing is that I won first prize in that baking contest this year. Oh, it was in all the papers; not under my own name, though. I used a *nom de boulangère*; I called myself Uncle Henry.

YOUNG MAN Did you?

GRANDMA Why not? I didn't see any reason

not to. I look just as much like an old man as I do like an old woman. And you know what I called it . . . what I won for?

YOUNG MAN   No. What did you call it?

GRANDMA   I called it Uncle Henry's Day-Old Cake.

YOUNG MAN   That's a very nice name.

GRANDMA   And it wasn't any trouble, either. All I did was go out and get a store-bought cake, and keep it around for a while, and then slip it in, unbeknownst to anybody. Simple.

YOUNG MAN   You're a very resourceful person.

GRANDMA   Pioneer stock.

YOUNG MAN   Is all this true? Do you want me to believe all this?

GRANDMA   Well, you can believe it or not . . . it doesn't make any difference to me. All *I* know is, Uncle Henry's Day-Old Cake won me twenty-five thousand smackerolas.

YOUNG MAN   Twenty-five thou—

GRANDMA   Right on the old loggerhead. Now . . . how do you like them apples?

YOUNG MAN   Love 'em.

GRANDMA   I thought you'd be impressed.

YOUNG MAN   Money talks.

GRANDMA   Hey! You look familiar.

YOUNG MAN   Hm? Pardon?

GRANDMA   I said, you look familiar.

YOUNG MAN   Well, I've done some modeling.

GRANDMA   No . . . no. I don't mean that. You look familiar.

YOUNG MAN   Well, I'm a type.

GRANDMA   Yup; you sure are. Why do you say you'd do anything for money . . . if you don't mind my being nosy?

YOUNG MAN   No, no. It's part of the interviews. I'll be happy to tell you. It's that I have no talents at all, except what you see . . . my person; my body, my face. In every other way I am incomplete, and I must therefore . . . compensate.

GRANDMA   What do you mean, incomplete? You look pretty complete to me.

YOUNG MAN   I think I can explain it to you, partially because you're very old, and very old people have perceptions they keep to themselves, because if they expose them to other people . . . well, you know what ridicule and neglect are.

GRANDMA   I do, child, I do.

YOUNG MAN   Then listen. My mother died the night that I was born, and I never knew my father; I doubt my mother did. But, I wasn't alone, because lying with me . . . in the placenta . . . there was someone else . . . my brother . . . my twin.

GRANDMA   Oh, my child.

YOUNG MAN   We were identical twins . . . he and I . . . not fraternal . . . identical; we were derived from the same ovum; and in *this*, in that we were twins not from separate ova but from the same one, we had a kinship such as you cannot imagine. We . . . we felt each other breathe . . . his heartbeats thundered in my temples . . . mine in his . . . our stomachs ached and we cried for feeding at the same time . . . are you old enough to understand?

GRANDMA   I think so, child; I think I'm nearly old enough.

YOUNG MAN   I hope so. But we were separated when we were still very young, my brother, my twin and I . . . inasmuch as you can separate one being. We were torn apart . . . thrown to opposite ends of the continent. I don't know what became of my brother . . . to the rest of myself . . . except that, from time to time, in the years that have passed, I have suffered losses . . . that I can't explain. A fall from grace . . . a departure of innocence . . . loss . . . loss. How can I put it to you? All right; like this: Once . . . it was as if all at once my heart . . . became numb . . . almost as though I . . . almost as though . . . just like that . . . it had been wrenched from my body . . . and from that time I have been unable to love. Once . . . I was asleep at the time . . . I awoke, and my eyes were burning. And since that time I have been unable to see anything, *anything*, with pity, with affection . . . with anything but . . . cool disinterest. And my groin . . . even there . . . since one time . . . one specific agony . . . since then I have not been able to *love* anyone with my body. And even my hands . . . I cannot touch another person and feel love. And there is more . . . there are more losses, but it all comes down to this: I no longer have the capacity to feel anything. I have no emotions. I have been drained, torn asunder . . . disemboweled. I have, now, only my person . . . my body, my face. I use what I have . . . I let people love me . . . I accept the syntax around me, for while I know I cannot relate . . . I know I must be related *to*. I let people love me . . . I let people touch me . . . I let them draw pleasure from my groin . . . from my presence . . . from the fact of me . . . but, that is all it comes to. As I told you, I am incomplete . . . I can feel nothing. I can feel nothing. And so . . . here I am . . . as you see me. I am . . . but this . . . what you see. And it will always be thus.

GRANDMA   Oh, my child; my child.
 (*Long pause; then*)
I was mistaken . . . before. I don't know you from somewhere, but I knew . . . once . . . someone very much like you . . . or, very much as perhaps you were.

YOUNG MAN   Be careful; be very careful. What I have told you may not be true. In my profession . . .

GRANDMA   Shhhhhh.
 (*The* YOUNG MAN *bows his head, in acquiescence*)
Someone . . . to be more precise . . . who might have turned out to be very much like you might have turned out to be. And . . . unless I'm terribly mistaken . . . you've found yourself a job.

YOUNG MAN   What are my duties?

MRS. BARKER   (*Off stage*) Yoo-hoo! Yoo-hoo!

GRANDMA   Oh-oh. You'll . . . have to play it by ear, my dear . . . unless I get a chance to talk to you again. I've got to go into my act, now.

YOUNG MAN   But, I . . .

GRANDMA   Yoo-hoo!

MRS. BARKER   (*Coming through archway*) Yoo-hoo . . . . oh, there you are, Grandma. I'm glad to see somebody. I can't find Mommy or Daddy.
 (*Double takes*)
Well . . . who's this?

GRANDMA   This? Well . . . un . . . oh, this is the . . . uh . . . the van man. That's who it is . . . the van man.

MRS. BARKER   So! It's true! They *did* call the van man. They *are* having you carted away.

GRANDMA   (*Shrugging*) Well, you know. It figures.

MRS. BARKER   (*To* YOUNG MAN), How dare you cart this poor old woman away!

YOUNG MAN   (*After a quick look at* GRANDMA, *who nods*) I do what I'm paid to do. I don't ask any questions.

MRS. BARKER   (*After a brief pause*) Oh.
 (*Pause*)
Well, you're quite right, of course, and I shouldn't meddle.

GRANDMA   (*To* YOUNG MAN) Dear, will you take my things out to the van?
 (*She points to the boxes*)

YOUNG MAN   (*After only the briefest hesitation*) Why certainly.

GRANDMA   (*As the* YOUNG MAN *takes up half the boxes, exits by the front door*) Isn't that a nice young van man?

MRS. BARKER   (*Shaking her head in disbelief, watching the* YOUNG MAN *exit*) Unh-hunh . . . some things have changed for the better. I remember when I had *my* mother carted off . . . the van man who came for her wasn't anything near as nice as this one.

GRANDMA   Oh, did you have your mother carted off, too?

MRS. BARKER   (*Cheerfully*) Why certainly! Didn't you?

GRANDMA   (*Puzzling*) No . . . no, I didn't. At least, I can't remember. Listen dear; I got to talk to you for a second.

MRS. BARKER   Why certainly, Grandma.

GRANDMA   Now, listen.

MRS. BARKER   Yes, Grandma. Yes.

GRANDMA   Now listen carefully. You got this dilemma here with Mommy and Daddy . . .

MRS. BARKER   Yes! I wonder where they've gone to?

GRANDMA   They'll be back in. Now, LISTEN!

MRS. BARKER   Oh, I'm sorry.

GRANDMA   Now, you got this dilemma here with Mommy and Daddy, and I think I got the way out for you.
 (*The* YOUNG MAN *re-enters through the front door*)
Will you take the rest of my things out now, dear?

(*To* MRS. BARKER, *while the* YOUNG MAN *takes the rest of the boxes, exits again by the front door*)
Fine. Now listen, dear.
(*She begins to whisper in* MRS. BARKER'*s ear*)
MRS. BARKER   Oh! Oh! Oh! I don't think I could . . . do you really think I could? Well, why not? What a wonderful idea . . . what an absolutely wonderful idea!
GRANDMA   Well, yes, I thought it was.
MRS. BARKER   And you so old!
GRANDMA   Heh, heh, heh.
MRS. BARKER   Well, I think it's absolutely marvelous, anyway. I'm going to find Mommy and Daddy right now.
GRANDMA   Good. You do that.
MRS. BARKER   Well, now. I think I will say good-by. I can't thank you enough.
(*She starts to exit through the archway*)
GRANDMA   You're welcome. Say it!
MRS. BARKER   Huh? What?
GRANDMA   Say good-by.
MRS. BARKER   Oh. Good-by.
(*She exits*)
Mommy! I say, Mommy! Daddy!
GRANDMA   Good-by.
(*By herself now, she looks about*)
Ah me.
(*Shakes her head*)
Ah me.
(*Takes in the room*)
Good-by.
(*The* YOUNG MAN *re-enters*)
GRANDMA   Oh, hello, there.
YOUNG MAN   All the boxes are outside.
GRANDMA   (*A little sadly*)   I don't know why I bother to take them with me. They don't have much in them . . . some old letters, a couple of regrets . . . Pekinese . . . blind at that . . . the television . . . my Sunday teeth . . . eighty-six years of living . . . some sounds . . . a few images, a little garbled by now . . . and, well . . .
(*She shrugs*)
. . . you know . . . the things one accumulates.
YOUNG MAN   Can I get you . . . a cab, or something?
GRANDMA   Oh no, dear . . . thank you just the same. I'll take it from here.

YOUNG MAN   And what shall I do now?
GRANDMA   Oh, you stay here, dear. It will all become clear to you. It will be explained. You'll understand.
YOUNG MAN   Very well.
GRANDMA   (*After one more look about*) Well . . .
YOUNG MAN   Let me see you to the elevator.
GRANDMA   Oh . . . that *would* be nice, dear.
(*They both exit by the front door, slowly*)

(*Enter* MRS. BARKER, *followed by* MOMMY *and* DADDY)
MRS. BARKER   . . . and I'm happy to tell you that the whole thing's settled. Just like that.
MOMMY   Oh, we're so glad. We were afraid there might be a problem, what with delays, and all.
DADDY   Yes, we're very relieved.
MRS. BARKER   Well, now; that's what professional women are for.
MOMMY   Why . . . where's Grandma? Grandma's not here! Where's Grandma? And look! The boxes are gone, too. Grandma's gone, and so are the boxes. She's taken off, and she's stolen something! Daddy!
MRS. BARKER   Why, Mommy, the van man was here.
MOMMY   (*Startled*)   The what?
MRS. BARKER   The van man. The van man was here.
(*The lights might dim a little, suddenly*)
MOMMY   (*Shakes her head*)   No, that's impossible.
MRS. BARKER   Why, I saw him with my own two eyes.
MOMMY   (*Near tears*)   No, no, that's impossible. No. There's no such thing as the van man. There is no van man. We . . . we made him up. Grandma? Grandma?
DADDY   (*Moving to* MOMMY)   There, there, now.
MOMMY   Oh Daddy . . . where's Grandma?
DADDY   There, there, now.
(*While* DADDY *is comforting* MOMMY, GRANDMA *comes out, stage right, near the footlights*)
GRANDMA   (*To the audience*)   Shhhhhh I want to watch this.
(*She motions to* MRS. BARKER *who, with*

a secret smile, tiptoes to the front door and opens it. The YOUNG MAN *is framed therein. Lights up full again as he steps into the room*)

MRS. BARKER   Surprise! Surprise! Here we are!
MOMMY   What? What?
DADDY   Hm? What?
MOMMY   (*Her tears merely sniffles now*) What surprise?
MRS. BARKER   Why, I told you. The surprise I told you about.
DADDY   You . . . you know, Mommy.
MOMMY   Sur . . . prise?
DADDY   (*Urging her to cheerfulness*) You remember, Mommy; why we asked . . . uh . . . what's-her-name to come here?
MRS. BARKER   Mrs. Barker, if you don't mind.
DADDY   Yes. Mommy? You remember now? About the bumble . . . about wanting satisfaction?
MOMMY   (*Her sorrow turning into delight*) Yes. Why yes! Of course! Yes! Oh, how wonderful!
MRS. BARKER   (*To the* YOUNG MAN) This is Mommy.
YOUNG MAN   How . . . how do you do?
MRS. BARKER   (*Stage whisper*) Her name's Mommy.
YOUNG MAN   How . . . how do you do, Mommy?
MOMMY   Well! Hello there!
MRS. BARKER   (*To the* YOUNG MAN) And that is Daddy.
YOUNG MAN   How do you do, sir?
DADDY   How do you do?
MOMMY   (*Herself again, circling the* YOUNG MAN, *feeling his arm, poking him*) Yes, sir! Yes, sirree! Now this is more like it. Now this is a great deal more like it! Daddy! Come see. Come see if this isn't a great deal more like it.
DADDY   I . . . I can see from here, Mommy. It does look a great deal more like it.
MOMMY   Yes, sir. Yes sirree! Mrs. Barker, I don't know *how* to thank you.
MRS. BARKER   Oh, don't worry about that. I'll send you a bill in the mail.
MOMMY   What this really calls for is a celebration. It calls for a drink.
MRS. BARKER   Oh, what a nice idea.
MOMMY   There's some sauterne in the kitchen.
YOUNG MAN   I'll go.
MOMMY   Will you? Oh, how nice. The kitchen's through the archway there.
   (*As the* YOUNG MAN *exits: to* MRS. BARKER)
He's very nice. Really top notch; much better than the other one.
MRS. BARKER   I'm glad you're pleased. And I'm glad everything's all straightened out.
MOMMY   Well, at least we know why we sent for you. We're glad that's cleared up. By the way, what's his name?
MRS. BARKER   Ha! Call him whatever you like. He's yours. Call him what you called the other one.
MOMMY   Daddy? What did we call the other one?
DADDY   (*Puzzles*) Why . . .
YOUNG MAN   (*Re-entering with a tray on which are a bottle of sauterne and five glasses*) Here we are!
MOMMY   Hooray! Hooray!
MRS. BARKER   Oh, good!
MOMMY   (*Moving to the tray*) So, let's— Five glasses? Why five? There are only four of us. Why five?
YOUNG MAN   (*Catches* GRANDMA'S *eye;* GRANDMA *indicates she is not there*) Oh, I'm sorry.
MOMMY   You must learn to count. We're a wealthy family, and you must learn to count.
YOUNG MAN   I will.
MOMMY   Well, everybody take a glass.
   (*They do*)
And we'll drink to celebrate. To satisfaction! Who says you can't get satisfaction these days!
MRS. BARKER   What dreadful sauterne!
MOMMY   Yes, isn't it?
   (*To* YOUNG MAN, *her voice already a little fuzzy from the wine*)
You don't know how happy I am to see you! Yes sirree. Listen, that time we had with . . . with the other one. I'll tell you about it some time.
   (*Indicates* MRS. BARKER)
After she's gone. She was responsible for all the trouble in the first place. I'll tell you all about it.

(*Sidles up to him a little*) Maybe . . . maybe later tonight.

YOUNG MAN (*Not moving away*) Why yes. That would be very nice.

MOMMY (*Puzzles*) Something familiar about you . . . you know that? I can't quite place it. . . .

GRANDMA (*Interrupting . . . to audience*) Well, I guess that just about wraps it up. I mean, for better or worse, this is a comedy, and I don't think we'd better go any further. No, definitely not. So, let's leave things as they are right now . . . while everybody's happy . . . while everybody's got what he wants . . . or everybody's got what he thinks he wants. Good night, dears.

CURTAIN

Unit 6

HUMOR AND SATIRE

ON HUMOR AND SATIRE

Certain fundamental abilities—to think and to choose freely—set man apart and distinguish him from the world in which he lives. From these fundamentals there follow other abilities which are equally distinctive of man. Laughter is one of them. It is a notorious fact that animals simply never see a joke. Man's sense of the laughable is another sign of his rationality; it is rooted in his ability to see the incongruous in people and situations. Without a sense of what is normal or abnormal humanly, socially, politically, or morally, man would never find anything funny. That is why nothing ever is funny to animals; they don't know the normal but sense only the momentary and the sensibly convenient.

The world of the laughable runs through the full spectrum, from mere *humor* through *satire* to *ridicule*. Humor is the gayest and most irresponsible of the three. The purpose of mere humor, when it is intentional, is to provide the pleasure of a laugh at the incongruity of character or situation; it has fulfilled its purpose when it has done so. It does not make its subject the butt of criticism, but merely the source of the laugh. At the other end of the spectrum is *ridicule*, in which the laughter evoked at the incongruous person or situation implies a bitter condemnation of the irrational aberration from the normal. Here the abnormal person or situation is definitely made the bitter butt of the laugh, and is implicitly criticized as foolish or irrational. If this attitude is exaggerated, it becomes mere personal invective and awakens, not laughter at all, but resentment.

Midway between these two extremes and participating in the nature of each is *satire*. It has been defined as a literary manner which points up the fundamental incongruity of an action or situation and makes it appear laughable and ridiculous. Mere humor is content with the laughter that the incongruity evokes; satire provokes the laugh for the purpose of correcting the aberration. As Professor M. H. Abrams puts it, satire "uses laughter as a weapon, and against a butt existing outside the work itself." It is the difference between a joke in which we merely laugh at the incongruity involved in the story itself and a political cartoon in which we are really laughing at an incongruous situation in the political world. Implicit in our laugh at the cartoon is a criticism of the irrationality of the particular abuse pictured there.

Even mere humor implies that we know what is normal; otherwise we would not recognize the very incongruity of the situation that evokes the laugh. The baby laughs instinctively at the grimaces of its mother only when it has become sufficiently accustomed to her normal appearance to recognize in a flash the incongruity of the grimace. But satire most especially implies a clear knowledge of the norm on the part of both the writer and his audience. Satire is at its best when there is some common agreement between the author and his public about what is normal, right, and rational for man. It loses much of its punch when we suspect that the satirist himself is confused or uncertain about the normal itself. That is one of the reasons for the thinness and ineffectiveness of a great deal of modern satire. There is a lack of certitude about what is right and normal for man at its very core.

There is, then, a tremendous difference in tone among works as they are predominantly humorous, satirical, or productive of ridicule. But even among works that are all clearly satiric there is a tremendous difference in tone. Two of the most fundamentally different kinds of satire have been labeled Horatian and Juvenalian after the great Roman writers who worked these different veins. *Horatian* satire never gets terribly excited about the evils it is ridiculing. It is more playful and amused than violently disturbed about the follies of men, and induces an urbane kind of laughter at them. *Juvenalian satire,* on the contrary, is possessed of what Juvenal himself called a *saeva ignatio,* a savage indignation at the sheer irrationality of man's actions; it puts them in their most ridiculous light and invites indignant, critical laughter at the irrationality of it all. This can, of course, easily push on into invective if the laughter is made too personal. Good satire is always a nice balance between hate and love—a hate for the sin but a love for the sinner. When the indignation is aimed directly at the person and not at his aberration, it can become invective rather than satire.

There are, in the prose and poetic selections that follow, examples of all these different shades of humor and satire. Steinbeck's "My War With the Ospreys" and Edward Lear's "The Jumblies," for instance, are almost purely humorous, whereas the rest of the prose and poetic selections range through all sorts and degrees of satiric tone. It is part of the pleasure of reading any satirical work to determine what its precise tone is and how it achieves it.

Among the many devices that the satirist uses to achieve his purpose of making aberrations from the normal look ridiculous, the chief one is *irony*—both *irony of statement* and *irony of situation.* We have discussed the meaning of irony as it is employed by the dramatist in the introduction to the drama section, but it has even a greater pertinence here.

Since *irony* in general is the contrast between the appearances and the reality of a statement or situation, and since the purpose of satire is to point up the ridiculousness of an aberration from some norm, it should be apparent why irony is such a good weapon of the satirist. By having his characters say or do certain things when all the circumstances and context into which they have been placed make it apparent to the reader that they should be saying or doing quite the opposite, the satirist makes brilliantly apparent both the norm from which they have strayed and the ridiculousness of their particular aberration. Thus, for instance, when Pope in "The Rape of the Lock" says of Hampton Court,

> Hither the heroes and the nymphs resort,
> To taste a while the pleasures of a Court;
> In various talk th' instructive hours they past,
> Who gave the ball, or paid the visit last;
> One speaks the glory of the British Queen,
> And one describes a charming Indian screen;
> A third interprets motions, looks, and eyes;
> Snuff or the fan, supply each pause of chat,
> With singing, laughing, ogling, *and all that.*

the very use of the words "heroes" and "nymphs" to describe the courtiers summons up images from epic and even pastoral poetry, where the characters have much more serious business in hand than gossiping and flirting. This immediately sets up a contrast in our minds, that continues as we read, between what a serious court should be and what this one, where only idle pleasures are sought for, actually is. In contrast to the weighty matters of state that might conceivably concern courtiers in a serious court, these courtiers spend the hours in such "instructive" conversation as who gave the last ball, and they can, in their chatter, put the whole dignity of the British throne on the same level as an Indian curio. In this context, the fan and snuff become symbols of the idleness, frivolity, chitchat, and utter consciencelessness that is ready to slay a reputation with a witty word for the sake of a laugh, in contrast to the serious dedication to duty and truth that might be expected of people in high places at court. Except in relation to the ideal or norm that should prevail at court, neither the irony of situation nor the rich irony of statement that suffuse this passage would be apparent. In reading ironic passages, one must habituate himself to seeing what is explicitly said and done in relation to what should be said and done in the circumstances. This the good satiric writer always manages to imply.

In poetry the *heroic couplet* (two rhymed verses of iambic pentameter) has been found a particularly suitable frame for ironic statement. Frequently in the heroic couplet there is a strong *caesura* (thought pause) in the middle of each line, and a thought pause at the end of the first line; while the end of the second line frequently coincides with the end of the clause or sentence. This division makes an ideal framework for *antithesis*, which is a perfect medium for suggesting the kinds of contrasts between the actual and the ideal, between the apparent and the real upon which irony is built. This couplet from "The Rape of the Lock" will illustrate the point:

> Not louder shrieks to pitying Heaven are cast,
> When husbands, or when lap dogs breathe their last.

The ironic antithesis, in the second verse, between husbands and lap dogs is emphasized by their position in the two parts of the line separated by the thought pause after husbands. Sometimes the antithesis is between the thoughts expressed in the two successive lines of the couplet as in the first couplet of the following passage:

> Whether the nymph shall break Diana's law,
> Or some frail China jar receive a flaw;
> Or stain her honour, or her new brocade;
> Forget her prayers, or miss a masquerade;
> Or lose her heart, or necklace, at a ball;
> Or whether Heaven has doomed that Shock must fall.

Notice again the added emphasis given the antithesis between honour and brocade, prayers and masquerade, heart and necklace, by their position in these balanced and parallel verses. Numberless other examples of such expert use of the heroic couplet for ironic purposes can be found in "The Rape of the Lock" and in other satiric poems that use the form.

We might remind ourselves again that satire is not a type of literature but a reflection of an attitude toward one's subject matter in the manner of its handling that may be found in any type. Sometimes it is so pervasive that the whole work is satiric; in other instances it pervades only sections of a work. Satire has been present in many of the short stories, novels, plays, and poems already studied; but we have gathered together in this unit some outstanding examples of satiric literature in both prose and poetry.

Prose

Animal Stories*
by ELLEN DOUGLASS LEYBURN

"prettie Allegories stealing under the formall Tales of beastes, makes many more beastly then beastes: begin to heare the sound of vertue from these dumb speakers." —
SIR PHILIP SIDNEY

Brute creation seems sometimes to exist as a satire on mankind. All that the allegorist needs to do is to point the parallel. Moralists have used man's likeness to the animals for instruction in a variety of ways ranging from the strange edification of the medieval bestiary to the reproof of the newspaper political cartoon. There has never been a time when men were not trying to teach each other the lessons to be learned from the creatures. The Bible is full of such teaching; and the stories spread under the name of Aesop are probably more widely known than any other classical literature. The Orient is as rich as the Occident in this lore; and the African folk tales, many of which reappear with a new set of animal characters in the Uncle Remus stories, attest the vitality of the genre without dependence on a written language.

Sometimes the teaching is so explicit that the resulting work cannot be called allegory. This is true of many of the fables of Aesop and his successors; but it is a significant proof of the value of indirection in art, even the art of pedagogy, that the best and best known of the Aesopic fables label the moral and leave it as something distinct and outside the story instead of making it explicit within the narrative. The ones that do point the lesson within the tale are the least effective of the group. When the mother of the wayward thrush explains to her son, who wants to make a companion of the swallow, that friendship between those who cannot bear the same climate is folly, we have the feeling that the bird would have learned more by making the experiment and we by watching its outcome. In this fable, the moral is at least dramatized to the extent of being explained to a character within the action. The reader is even more dismayed when the point is simply explained directly to him, as in the fable of Jupiter's not granting horns to the camel because the prayer was for some-

---

* Reprinted by permission of Yale University Press from *Satiric Allegory: Mirror of Man*, by Ellen Douglass Leyburn. Copyright © 1956 by Yale University Press.

thing nature had not intended. The more artistic fables tell the story and stop like true allegories, allowing the reader the pleasure of drawing his own conclusion before he reaches the labeled moral, which remains outside the story.

When the cock tells the fox who has been preaching a general peace among the animals in order to make the cock come down out of the tree, that the dogs are coming, the story is complete with the dramatic ending of the fox's running off. When the fox who has refused to visit the sick lion says that he notices tracks of other animals going to the lion's palace, but none coming away, we know what to think without having the moral further pointed. The moral is left suspended within the tale in all the most familiar of Aesop's fables: The Fox and the Grapes, The Dog in the Manger, The Hare and the Tortoise, The Fox and the Stork, The Dog and His Shadow, and The Country Mouse and the City Mouse. And when any of these reappear in the writings of sophisticated artists, as when Horace retells the last named story, the same rule holds. The artist respects the integrity of the story and the intelligence of the reader and lets the tale make its own point. Perhaps L'Estrange is right in the preface to his edition of the Fables when he says that we are all like children and prefer the pill of moral teaching sweetened with the pleasure of the tale.[1] Nor do we want the pleasure of the allegory spoiled by being told that it is really moral medicine after all. The moral labeled and separated from the tale as is customary in Aesop's stories, we accept without protest because no disguise is presented, and there is therefore no violation of conception; but having the moral stated within the story, where we expect to get it only through the images, destroys the imaginative effect which it has been the whole object of the story to produce. The case is somewhat altered in a work like Swift's "Beasts' Confession," where the application is longer than the tale, and the animal allegory serves just as introduction to the classes of mankind who mistake their talents. But even here Swift announces the pointing of the moral as distinct from the tale.

A different sort of problem is created by the animal story which is instruction about man observed from the point of view of the animals. A highly effective example of this use of the beasts is Johnson's *Idler*, 22[2] in which the old vulture gives instruction to her young about the order of the universe in which man is created as the "natural food of a vulture." The mother bird, in response to the puzzled inquiry as to how man is to be killed if he is so much bigger and stronger than the vulture, replies:

> "We have not the strength of man . . . and I am sometimes in doubt whether we have the subtilty; and the vultures would seldom feast upon his flesh, had not nature, that devoted him to our uses, infused into him a strange ferocity, which I have never observed in any other being that feeds upon the earth. Two herds of men will often meet and shake the earth with noise, and fill the air with fire. When you hear noise, and see fire, with flashes along the ground, hasten to the place with your swiftest wing, for men are surely destroying one another; you will then find the ground smoking with blood, and covered with carcasses, of which many are dismembered, and mangled for the convenience of the vulture."—"But when men have killed their prey," said the pupil, "Why do they not eat it?" "When the wolf has killed a sheep, he suffers not the vulture to touch it till he has satisfied himself. Is not man another kind of wolf?"—"Man," said the mother, "is the only beast who kills that which he does not devour, and this quality makes him so much a benefactor to our species."

In the effort to explain the mystery of human behavior, the mother quotes a wise old vulture of the Carpathian rocks:

---

[1] *Fables of Aesop and Other Eminent Mythologists: with Morals and Reflexions by Sir Roger L'Estrange* (London, 1692), A₂.

[2] Johnson omitted this essay from collected editions of the *Idler*; but it is reprinted at the end of Chalmers's edition. The quotations are from *British Essayists*, ed. A. Chalmers (Boston, 1864), 27, 400–2.

"His opinion was, that man had only the appearance of animal life, being really vegetables with a power of motion; and that as the boughs of an oak are dashed together by the storm, that swine may fatten upon the falling acorns, so men are, by some unaccountable power, driven one against another, till they lose their motion, that vultures may be fed. Others think they have observed something of contrivance and policy among these mischievous beings; and those that hover more closely round them, pretend, that there is, in every herd, one that gives directions to the rest, and seems to be more eminently delighted with a wide carnage. What it is that entitles him to such preëminence we know not; he is seldom the biggest or the swiftest, but he shows by his eagerness and diligence that he is, more than any of the others, a friend to vultures."

The impact of the satire here comes from the ironic point of view. At first the essay seems not allegorical at all since the animals are not acting in a way that parallels man's actions. But it turns out that the point of view itself is an allegory of man's assumption that he is the center of the universe, with all other beings created for his benefit. This attitude of the vultures, which is perfectly sustained once Johnson leaves the awkward introduction of the shepherd for the story itself, contributes an extra level to the irony of the analysis of the reasons why men kill each other for the "convenience of the vulture."

In addition to the large body of assorted kinds of fables, there are a great many more strictly allegorical satires with animal characters. The very universality and obviousness of the relation of animals to man makes at once the appeal of this sort of satiric story and its special difficulty. Both sides of the parallel are so familiar that it is hard to keep them in proper balance, and every reader feels himself competent from his own observation to judge what the writer is doing with the material. But beyond this recognition of the familiar, there are certain criteria by which to judge success in the form.

One gift essential to the teller of satiric animal tales is the power to keep his reader conscious simultaneously of the human traits satirized and of the animals as animals. The moment he loses hold on resemblance and lets his protagonists becomes merely animals or merely people, his instrument has slipped in his hands and deflected his material away from satiric allegory into something like *Black Beauty* or *The Three Bears*. But if the writer of animal allegory can successfully sustain and play upon two levels of perception, making us feel that his animals are really animals and yet as human as ourselves, he can control the imaginative response. This doubleness of effect is the central power of great animal stories as different as the *Nun's Priest's Tale* and *The Tar Baby*. We delight in Chaunticleer and Pertelote and Brer Rabbit because they are at once real as people and real as animals. The climax of the Tar Baby story, "Bred en bawn in a brier-patch, Brer Fox—bred en bawn in a brier-patch!" reminds us inescapably that this creature is a rabbit exactly while it reminds us of his resemblance to the human being who by his wit can extricate himself from any difficulty. Uncle Remus concludes, "en wid dat he skip out des ez lively ez a cricket in de embers," and we find his liveliness irresistible because we see a real rabbit skipping off in a mood that we know as human. So with Chaucer's masterpiece: Pertelote's "Pekke hem up right as they growe and ete hem yn" is often cited as one of Chaucer's wittiest reductions to the animal level in all his mock-heroic scheme. Yet this remark, which reminds the reader with humorous felicity that a hen is speaking, conveys also the quintessence of Pertelote's wifely solicitude. It seems that when she is most a chicken, she is most full of the particular sort of femininity that Chaucer is placing beside masculine roosterishness for amused scrutiny.

Indeed, it is belief in these creatures as animals that accentuates and isolates the human trait singled out for laughing observation. The animal make-up from which the human characteristic emerges throws it into high light and sharpens perception, acting as a proper vehicle for the tenor. Thus the true animal allegory fulfills I. A. Richards' requirement: "the vehicle is not . . . a mere embellishment of a tenor which is otherwise unchanged but the vehicle and tenor in co-operation give a meaning of more varied powers than can be ascribed to either."[3]

Since the whole point of animal satire is to show up humanity by revealing human traits in nonhuman characters, it follows that the few human beings who appear must not be characterized at all lest they break into the allegorical scheme. At the end of the Uncle Remus stories we know no more about "Miss Meadows en de gals" than does the little boy when he first asks, "Who was Miss Meadows, Uncle Remus?" and gets the unenlightening response: "Don't ax me, honey. She wuz in de tale, Miss Meadows en de gals wuz, en de tale I give you like hi't wer' gun ter me." The characterization of Mr. Man is if possible even vaguer: "Des a man, honey. Dat's all."[4] In George Orwell's *Animal Farm*, where the notion of man as tyrannical master is necessary to the imaginative plan, the only human character who really figures after the ousting of Mr. Jones is Whymper, who as his name suggests has no personality at all, and he is never seen by the nonporcine animals from whose point of view the story is told. The *Nun's Priest's Tale* may seem an exception to this rule, for there is a good deal of circumstantial detail in the depicting of the widow who owns the fowls. But when we come to examine the treatment of her "sooty bower" and her "attempree diete," we find that all the attention is given to externals. As a person, the widow has no more identity than do the peasants who own Chaunticleer in Chaucer's sources. The realistic detail of her few possessions and her meager life is all used to sharpen the humor of the elaborate mock-heroic treatment of the cock and his lady. It seems safe to say that there does not exist anywhere a successful animal allegory which includes a vivid human character.

Another outgrowth of the choice of animal characters to throw human traits into bold relief is the concentration upon isolated human characteristics. The successful writer of animal allegory rarely gives his characters more than one human trait at a time. This concentrated singleness of attack might almost be laid down as a second law of the genre, as binding as the first that the animals shall stay both animal and human. It removes the possibility of very complex characterization. The complexity comes from the double consciousness of animal and human attributes; and the force of the tale is almost in proportion to the singleness and simplicity on the human level. This is true even of a fairly sustained piece such as Munro Leaf's *Ferdinand*. The increasingly funny repetition of the comment that Ferdinand just sat down quietly and smelled the flowers whenever he was expected to fight not only endears the bull to us in our belligerent world, but leaves the essence of his character indelibly fixed in our minds. This is all we know of him and all we need to know except that "He is very happy."

The same practice holds in aggregations of stories centered around one character such as in the medieval beast epic of *Reynard the Fox*, where Reynard is always cruelly taking advantage of his neighbors, and the Uncle Remus stories, where Brer Rabbit always mischievously turns the tables on his stronger enemies. As Uncle Remus puts it, "Eve'y time I run over in my min' 'bout the pranks er Brer Rabbit . . . hit make me laugh mo' en mo'. He mos' allers come out on top, yit dey wuz times w'en he hatter be mighty spry."[5] His invention is boundless, but he is always himself.

> I 'speck dat 'uz de reas'n w'at make ole Brer Rabbit git 'long so well, kaze he aint copy atter none er de yuther creeturs. . . . W'en he make his disappearance 'fo' um, hit 'uz allers in some bran new place. Dey aint know wharbouts fer ter watch out fer 'im. He wuz de funniest creetur er de whole gang. Some folks moughter call him lucky, en yit, w'en he git in bad luck,

---

[3] *The Philosophy of Rhetoric* (New York, 1936), p. 100.
[4] Joel Chandler Harris, *Uncle Remus, His Songs and His Sayings* (New York, 1921), pp. 25, and 143.
[5] Joel Chandler Harris, *Nights with Uncle Remus* (Boston, 1911), p. 311. All further quotations from *Uncle Remus* are from this edition.

hit look lak he mos' allers come out on top. Hit look mighty kuse now, but 't wa'n't kuse in dem days, kaze hit 'uz done gun up dat, strike 'im w'en you might en whar you would, Brer Rabbit wuz de soopless creetur gwine.

The essence of his character revealed in story after story Uncle Remus summarizes: "dey wa'n't no man 'mungs de creeturs w'at kin stan' right flat-footed en wuk he min' quick lak Brer Rabbit." What most stimulates his intelligence is being in a tight place: "Brer Rabbit 'gun ter git skeer'd, en w'en dat creetur git skeer'd, he min' wuk lak one er deze yer flutter-mills."

A corollary of the focus upon single human traits in animal tales is brevity. The swiftness with which the narrative reaches its climax sharpens the concentrated effect of the flashing out of the human motive. Uncle Remus's comment on his hero's character gives the clue to the simple plot of most of his stories, which without ever seeming monotonous repeatedly show Brer Rabbit "monst'us busy . . . sailin' 'roun' fixin' up his tricks" to outdo the other animals who have it in for him: "dem t'er creeturs. Dey wuz allers a-layin' traps fer Brer Rabbit en gittin' cotch in um deyse'f." Though he is usually extricating himself from a difficulty, he sometimes initiates pranks from sheer love of mischief. He is always alert for fun. "Brer Rabbit, he one er deze yer kinder mens w'at sleep wid der eye wide open." The illustrations of his ingenuity as it makes the plots for the tales are endless: he gets Mr. Fox, who has come to fetch him for revenge to serve as his "ridin' hoss" by pretending to be too ill to accompany Brer Fox on foot; he gets Miss Cow stuck fast by the horns in the persimmon tree so that he and all his family can milk her by promising her a feast of persimmons that she is to shake down by butting the tree; he scalds Mr. Wolf, who runs into his chest for protection from the dogs; he gets the bag after Mr. Fox's hunt by playing dead and tempting Brer Fox to add the rabbit to his game; on two occasions he nibbles up the butter and manages to let the 'possum and the weasel have the blame; he saves the meat of his own cow, takes Mr. Man's cow from Brer Fox, and steals Mr. Man's meat and money by a series of ruses; he often persuades other animals to take his place in traps by appealing to their greed; he escapes from the hawk by begging to be allowed to grow big enough to make a full meal and from the embrace of the wildcat by offering to tell him how to get turkey meat; he turns the tables on other enemies by appealing to their perversity in many variations on the Tar Baby story. Always Brer Rabbit is equal to the emergency. His own ruses succeed and those to outwit him fail. Only the Terrapin and the Crow ever best him, never any of the stronger animals like the Fox, the Bear, and the Lion. After the account of his exploits, Uncle Remus's judgment seems a model of understatement: "Bless yo' soul, honey, Brer Rabbit mought er bin kinder fibble in de legs, but he wa'n't no ways cripple und' de hat."

Just as the hero of these stories represents always mischievous fooling, so he confronts only one trait in his antagonist in each story. The singleness of impression, which enforces the sharpness, is never violated. But one source of variety from story to story is the range of human traits singled out in the other creatures for Brer Rabbit's laughter. To be sure, laughter is the quality of his prankish intelligence. "Well . . . you know w'at kinder man Brer Rabbit is. He des went off some 'ers by he own-alone se'f en tuck a big laugh." Uncle Remus's adjective for him is "sassy." But the very story of his Laughing Place is another illustration that the weaknesses of the other creatures give him ample scope to exercise his ingenuity in besting them for his own amusement. Here it is Brer Fox's curiosity that makes him the victim. The stories already mentioned show Brer Rabbit playing upon greed, vanity, eagerness for revenge, or sheer cruelty in his more imposing neighbors. The stories of his frightening the other and bigger animals, even the Lion, by playing upon their natural timorousness are especially striking in view of his own physical helplessness. The Lion lets Brer Rabbit tie him to a tree to save him from being blown away by a nonexistent wind; the animals all run from Brer Rabbit when he appears bedecked in leaves;

he scares them from the house they have built by saying that the cannon is his sneeze and the pail of water his spit; he sets a stampede in motion by simply running past and saying he has heard a big noise; and he outdoes himself in frightening the others by the clatter he makes dressed up in the tin plates they are waiting to steal from him:

> Brer Rabbit got right on um 'fo dey kin git away. He holler out, he did:
> "Gimme room! Tu'n me loose! I'm ole man Spewter-Splutter wid long claws, en scales on my back! I'm snaggle-toofed en double-jinted! Gimme room!"
> Eve'y time he'd fetch a whoop, he'd rattle de cups en slap de platters tergedder —*rickety, rackety, slambang!* En I let you know w'en dem creeturs got dey lim's tergedder dey split de win', dey did dat. Ole Brer B'ar, he struck a stump w'at stan' in de way, en I ain't gwine tell you how he to' it up 'kaze you won't b'leeve me, but de nex' mawnin' Brer Rabbit en his chilluns went back dar, dey did, en dey got nuff splinters fer ter make um kin'lin' wood all de winter.

The human bully is probably the character most roundly mocked by Brer Rabbit.

In Caxton's version of the medieval stories of Reynard, on the other hand, the hero is the bully. Surely from the folklorist's viewpoint one of the most interesting aspects of animal stories is the relationships among the various groups. The story of Brer Rabbit's rising from the well by getting the fox to leap into the other well bucket, for instance, is identical with the story that Erswynd, wife of Isegrim the Wulf, tells of her being tricked into the well bucket by Reynard. A plot that is repeated with different characters in both sets of stories is that of the creature delivered and turning on his deliverer, only to be re-imprisoned by the judgment of a third party. Rukenaw tells in Caxton the story of the man's freeing the serpent, who then turns on the man, with Reynard as the judge who refuses advice until he sees the contestants in their original positions. In the Uncle Remus version, the creature under the rock is the wolf, who is freed by Brer Rabbit, and the judge is Brer Tarrypin (aways Brer Rabbit's ally except when he outruns his speedier friend in the Uncle Remus variant of the story of the Tortoise and the Hare) who says: "I hates might'ly fer ter put you all gents ter so much trouble; yit, dey aint no two ways, I'll hatter see des how Brer Wolf was kotch, en des how de rock wuz layin' 'pun top un 'im." Then of course the wolf is left pinned under the rock just as is the snake in the other story.

The intricate ramifications of interrelations of sources for both sets of stories lie beyond the scope of this study, which is concerned with the artistry of the telling. But the subject of the representation of the heroes is an aesthetic problem which is curiously linked with the larger anthropological relation. It is hard to resist the impression that somewhere in the course of the development of the two groups of tales, one hero was set up in deliberate response to the other. Both are extremely clever; and both triumph over the other animals by deceits. But the feeling created by the two is totally different. When Uncle Remus says, "dat seetful Brer Rabbit done fool ole Brer Fox," we laugh with the rabbit. When Erswynd says, "Ache felle reynart / noman can kepe hym self fro the[e] / thou canst so wel vttre thy wordes and thy falsenes and reson sette forth,"[6] our sympathy is all with the duped she-wolf. Instead of rejoicing at Reynard's triumphs, the reader shudders at the cruelty of his tricks, which grow in evil from his making Bruin lose "his scalp, ears, and forepaws," in his bloody escape "nearly dead" from the cloven tree, through his preparing for his false pilgrimage by securing a square foot of Bruin's hide for his scrip and two shoes from each by ripping off the pawskins of Isegrim and Erswynd, through his cold-blooded devouring of Cuwart, the Hare, to the horrors of the final fight in which he slips his shaved and oiled body always out of Isegrim's grasp while he blinds the wolf by slapping his face with the tail befouled according to Rukenaw's suggestion, kicking sand into Isegrim's eyes, and

---

[6] Quotations are from *The History of Reynard the Fox, translated and printed by William Caxton*, ed. Edward Arber (London, 1880), pp. 96 and 71.

treating him with every sort of indignity until he wins with his ugly stratagem leaving Isegrim mutilated and half dead. Parallel to the mounting cruelty of his deeds is the increasing baseness of his false speeches. His deceits instead of tickling the fancy like those of Brer Rabbit make their treachery abhorrent. There is serious hatred of Reynard and serious reason for it:

> Alle the beestis both poure and riche were alle stylle when the foxe spak so stoutly / the cony laprel and the roek were so sore aferde that they durst not speke but pyked and stryked them out of the court bothe two. and whan they were a room fer in the playne they said. god graunte that this felle murderare may fare euyl. he can bywrappe and couere his falshede. that his wordes seme as trewe as the gospel herof knoweth noman than we. how shold we brynge wytnesse. it is better that we wyke and departe. than we sholde holde a felde and fyghte with hym. he is so shrewde. ye[a] thaugh ther of vs were fuye we coude not defende vs. but he shold sle vs alle.

While the narrative management in *Reynard the Fox*, as in other groups of animal stories is episodic, Caxton's version of the epic has decided organization toward a climax. The increasing tension is craftily arranged. Reynard's first false defense is filled with consummate treachery; but his villainy is greater in his second hoodwinking of the king. When honors are finally heaped upon him after his foul play to Isegrim, perfidy is left triumphant. If we turn from such a spectacle of evil to the merry pranks of Brer Rabbit, we are bound to feel some slight restoring of poetic justice in the fact that Brer Fox is always defeated in his efforts to outwit Brer Rabbit. Nothing can bring to life the hens and pigeons and other helpless creatures, even Cuwart the Hare himself, whom Reynard has foully murdered; but it is hard to resist the feeling that the sly Brer Fox is suffering some retribution for the sins of Reynard.

The strong difference in response to the two protagonists suggests a third criterion by which to judge the satirist using animal tales for his allegory. The kinds of smartness displayed by Reynard and Brer Rabbit are, of course, different; but much of the difference in the feeling about them is determined by the attitude toward them displayed in the stories. The establishing of a clear point of view toward the animal characters seems as important a requisite for the successful animal tale as does the focusing on a single dominant trait in the animal. The rejoicing of Uncle Remus and his various hearers in the exploits of Brer Rabbit is an incalculable aid to Harris in communicating the same attitude to the reader; but as he repeatedly says in the introductions to his various volumes, he did not create Uncle Remus's point of view. Brer Rabbit is the hero, in the full admiring sense of the word, of the stories as Harris heard them told by Negro after Negro. To be sure, he is a hero that can be laughed at; but the gay satire is directed at the human foibles of the other animals which lead them into Brer Rabbit's traps. In the stories of Reynard, on the other hand, while there is some mockery of the animals who are Reynard's dupes, the appalling comment on human character comes in Reynard himself. Modern experience of the rise of tyrants through cruelty and lies must intensify response to the revelation of iniquity in Reynard; but there can be no doubt that Caxton intends Reynard to be regarded as a villain. We see that Isegrim is as simple-minded as Brer Wolf; but instead of feeling that his stupidity is mocked, we resent the violence done him. We are conscious of the greed of Bruin and Tybert which helps make them prey to Reynard's wiles; Bellin's desire for importance is directly responsible for his being killed as Cuwart's murderer; and Nobel seems a very unsuspecting monarch indeed to be taken in by Reynard's flattery. But many of the fox's victims have no other weakness than physical helplessness. The revealing light of the allegorical satire is turned most searchingly upon the villainous hero himself; and when he is allowed to go off triumphant in the end, the feeling is that the wicked ways of the world have been convincingly displayed.

There is obviously a good deal of social satire, especially of abuses in the church, in *Reynard the Fox*. This would be in a measure true of any group of stories presenting a number of animals together. The mere assembling of individuals suggests some comment on social structure. Even the fables of La Fontaine display the classes of society, as does the assembly of birds alone in *The Parlement of Foules*. But in some animal stories, the central purpose is clearly comment on society rather than on individual human traits. In such stories the same artistic criteria hold. The sustaining of the animal disguise is still the first requisite; the absence of strong human characters and the presence of sharply individualized animal characters with a single dominant human trait seem as important for the social satire couched in animal terms as for the story whose object is simply laughter at a human foible; a clear viewpoint again must control the response. The failure to meet these tests of the successful writer of animal allegory explains the ineptitudes of so great an allegorist as Spenser when he tries to tell an animal story.

Mother Hubberd's Tale, for all its vivid picture of abuses in church and court, is not a successful animal satire. The Fox and the Ape are specious rogues indeed, but we never believe in them as animals except possibly for the moment of their stealing the Lion's skin. Many similarities have been shown between Spenser's material and that of the medieval stories of Reynard, including the basic one of alliance in trickery of these two animals.[7] But Spenser never succeeds in giving them the life of their prototypes. Part of his difficulty in giving his characters reality as animals may come from his being unable to transmute the images of real men. It seems clear that the animals stand for actual individuals at Elizabeth's court, though scholars dispute about the identification of the Ape. The result of their not becoming convincing animal characters is that the poem affords none of the pleasure of using the imagination at two levels, which is the chief reason for being of allegory. When Spenser's protagonists trick the husbandman into hiring them as shepherd and dog, they are simply thieves who enjoy stealing and slaying the sheep. They do eat the flock; but there is no distinction between the eating done by Ape and Fox, for they are both all the while simply deceitful men. In the final episode when they come to rule, with the Ape in the stolen skin of the Lion, we forget altogether that it is a lion's throne they have usurped and are given almost a lecture on the abuses of false human courtiers and the pitiful plight of suitors at court, with the lesson pointed by the contrasting picture of the man who truly loves honor. Spenser is writing here with too much passion of personal disillusion to achieve artistic detachment and the indirection of allegory. Animals are forgotten in lines like these:

> Most miserable man, whom wicked fate
> Hath brought to Court, to sue for had ywist,
> That few haue found, and manie one hath mist;
> Full little knowest thou that hast not tride,
> What hell it is, in suing long to bide:
> To loose good dayes, that might be better spent;
> To wast long nights in pensiue discontent;
> To speed to day, to be put back to morrow;
> To feed on hope, to pine with feare and sorrow;
> To haue thy Princes grace, yet want her Peeres;
> To haue thy asking, yet waite manie yeeres;
> To fret thy soule with crosses and with cares;
> To eate thy heart through comfortlesse dispaires;
> To fawne, to crowche, to waite, to ride, to ronne,
> To spend, to giue, to want, to be vndonne.
> Vnhappie wight, borne to desastrous end,
> That does his life in so long tendance spend.
>   (ll. 892–908, Variorum ed.)

It is, in fact, startling to return to the story of the sleeping Lion by the awkward device of having Jove send Mercury to awaken him and spur him back to his kingdom to drive out the usurpers. The encounter with the priest whom the Fox and the Ape meet between

---

[7] Cf. Edwin Greenlaw, "The Sources of Spenser's 'Mother Hubberd's Tale,'" *Modern Philology*, 2 (1905), 411–32.

their tricks as shepherds and as courtiers is a sharply ironic indictment of the worldly practices of churchmen. But the account of the proper way to make a priest's life a soft one is put into the mouth of a real priest, who is all too convincingly human. Consequently, we almost nowhere feel that we are in an animal world; and when Sir Mule or the sheep whose lamb the wolf has killed does appear as an actual animal, we are startled and jarred. *Mother Hubberd's Tale* is almost as far from being true animal allegory as is *The Hind and the Panther*. The force of Spenser's satiric feeling and the variety of his poetic power carry us along; but the poem does not succeed as a work of art.

George Orwell, a writer of much less stature than Spenser, has written in *Animal Farm* a more effective social satire than *Mother Hubberd's Tale*. His animals are absolutely real as animals from the first meeting in the big barn to hear Old Major's dream of a world in which the animals are equal and free of their human masters to their frightened approach to the farmhouse window at the end of the book when only those animals who are tall enough can peep in. The horses are always horses who pull loads; the cows are cows who must be milked, however awkwardly, by the pigs, "their trotters being well adapted to this task";[8] the hens are hens who lay eggs and want to keep them; even the bureaucratic pigs remain pigs, hard as they try to be human—which gives its overwhelming force to the denouement of the story when the terrified subject animals creep back to the window of the farmhouse and look "from pig to man, and from man to pig, and from pig to man again; but already it [is] impossible to say which [is] which."

The point of view is always that of the animals who are being duped. Their plight is deepened for the reader by his being allowed to discover the successive machinations of the pigs only as they are borne in upon the stupider animals. Orwell never forgets and lets us inside the consciousness of Napoleon and Squealer. We simply see the one strutting and lording it over his victims and hear the other giving specious explanations of why the pigs must live in luxury. We see and hear what the subject animals see and hear.

While they are consistently animals, each reveals a predominant human trait. Clover is a "stout motherly mare" from the time when at the opening meeting she makes a protecting wall around the motherless ducklings with her great foreleg, through the time after the purge when the desolate survivors huddle around her, and through her efforts to keep Boxer from overworking and then to rescue him from the knacker, until she leads her fearful fellow creatures up to the farmhouse at the end, to witness the full extent of their betrayal.

Boxer "was not of first-rate intelligence, but he was universally respected for his steadiness of character and tremendous powers of work." His inability to learn the alphabet is linked with his unswerving devotion to his two mottoes: "I will work harder" and "Comrade Napoleon is always right," for there is something stupid in his letting his great strength be used up to serve the interests of the oppressors in the totalitarian state. Yet his loyalty is intensely moving, especially as his strength fails and he still works harder than ever: "Sometimes on the slope leading to the top of the quarry, when he braced his muscles against the weight of some vast boulder, it seemed that nothing kept him on his feet except the will to continue. At such times his lips were seen to form the words, 'I will work harder'; he had no voice left." And when in the knacker's van the drumming of his hoofs grows fainter and dies away, we feel all the force of human goodness traduced so that after the faithful horse has been made into glue and dog meat, there is all the greater sense of outrage at Squealer's fraudulent speech to the Comrades distorting all the circumstances of Boxer's life and death (for which he makes up a sentimental deathbed scene in a beautifully tended hospital instead of the actual slaughter house one) to make the other animals more servile slaves than ever.

The delineation of a single human trait is just as vivid in the other animals: the boar Snowball, the impetuous, inventive leader who is ousted; the other boar Napoleon the dic-

---

[8] George Orwell, *Animal Farm* (New York, 1946), p. 22. All quotations are from this edition.

tator, who starts out by taking the milk and apples for the pigs and goes on to the creating of a slave state; Squealer, the pig propagandist, who shifts the commandments to suit the leaders' actions and explains all their oppressions as to the advantage of the comrades; the donkey Benjamin, who is a cynic; Mollie, the pretty white mare who loves ribbons more than principle; and all the others. Even the animals who are not named and appear in groups show up human crowds in single moods. The silly sheep always bleat at the pigs' command, whether their tune is "Four legs good, two legs bad" or "Four legs good, two legs better." The terrible dogs trained as Napoleon's bodyguard are always the ferocious, bloodthirsty instruments of terror. They are the police of the police state.

Since Orwell has succeeded in his underlining of separate human characteristics in his individual animals, his comment on society is convincing. It is because the imaginative scheme of the animal allegory is sustained that the revelation of the ease with which well-meaning citizens can be duped into serving the masters of a totalitarian state achieves its power. Orwell's keeping the point of view consistently that of the helpless animals and letting us make only the discoveries that they make forces us to interpret for ourselves not just the misfortunes of the renamed Manor Farm, but also those of our own world. We are compelled to participate imaginatively. *Animal Farm* is successful social satire because it is successful allegory.

My War with the Ospreys*

by JOHN STEINBECK

My war with the ospreys,[1] like most wars, was largely accidental and had a tendency to spread in unforeseen directions. It is not over yet. The coming of winter caused an uneasy truce. I had to go into New York while the ospreys migrated to wherever they go in the winter. Spring may open new hostilities, although I can find it in my heart to wish for peace and even friendship. I hope the ospreys, wherever they may be, will read this.

I shall go back to the beginning and set down my side of the affair, trying to be as fair as I possibly can, placing Truth above either propaganda or self-justification. I am confident that until near the end of the association my motives were kind to the point of being sloppy.

Two years and a half ago I bought a little place near Sag Harbor which is quite near to the tip of Long Island. The outer end of Long Island is like the open jaws of an alligator and, deep in the mouth, about where the soft palate would be, is Sag Harbor, a wonderful village inhabited by people who have been here for a long time. It is a fishing town, a local town which has resisted the inroads of tourists by building no motor courts and putting up no hotels.

Sag Harbor was once one of the two great whaling ports of the world and was, according to local accounts, not at all second to Nantucket Island. At that time no fewer than one hundred and fifty whaling bottoms roved the great seas and brought back their riches in oil. Sag Harbor and Nantucket lighted the lamps of the world until kerosene was developed and the whaling industry languished.

With the wealth brought back by the whalers, beautiful houses were built in the village during the early 1800's, houses of neo-Greek architecture with fluted columns, Greek key decorations, with fanlights and Adam doors and mantels. Some of these magnificent old houses have widow's walks, those high balconies on which the women kept watch for the return of their men from their year-long voyages. Some of these old houses are being rediscovered and restored. Many of the streets of Sag Harbor are named after old whaling men.

---

* Copyright © 1957 by John Steinbeck. Reprinted by permission of McIntosh and Otis, Inc.
[1] *osprey* a fish hawk.

My own place is near Jesse Halsey Lane and he is still locally known as Old Cap'n Jesse. I have a picture of his rough and whiskered face.

The place I bought is not one of the great old houses but a beautiful little point of land on the inland waters, a place called Bluff Point, with its own little bay—incidentally a bay which is considered hurricane-proof. Ordinarily only two boats are moored there, mine and one other, but during hurricane warnings as many as thirty craft come in for anchorage until the all-clear is broadcast.

My point, just under two acres, is shaded by great oak trees of four varieties and there are many bushes and pines to edge it on the water side. I myself have planted a thousand Japanese black pines, furnished by the State of New York to edge my point, to hold the soil with their roots and eventually to curve beautifully inward, urged by the wind which blows every day of the year—sometimes a zephyr and sometimes a fierce and strident gale.

Greensward grows on my place. On the highest point I have a small, snug cottage and in front of it a pier going out to nine feet at low water so that a fairly large boat can dock. My own boat, the *Lillymaid*, with Astolat as her port of registry, is named for my wife. She, the boat, is a utility craft twenty feet long, a clinker-built[2] Jersey sea skiff. Her eight-foot beam makes her highly dependable and seaworthy. Many of these specifications could also describe my wife. She is not clinker-built, however. The *Lillymaid* has a Navy top to put up when the weather gets too rough and she has a hundred-horsepower engine so that we can run for it if a storm approaches. She is a lovely, efficient and seaworthy craft and all we need for the fishing and coastal exploring which is our pleasure.

Our house, while very small, is double-walled and winterized so that we can drive out during cold weather when the not-so-quiet desperation of New York gets us down.

My young sons, ten and twelve, but eight and ten when the osprey war began, adore the place and spend most of their summers here, exploring about in their skiffs or quarreling happily on the pier or on the lawn under the oak trees. My wife, who I believe was realistically skeptical when I bought the place, has become its stanchest defender.

Our association with the village people of Sag Harbor is, I think, pleasant to all of us. I come originally from a small town on the West Coast, a fishing town where my people have lived for a long time. And I find that what applies in my home country is equally acceptable in Sag Harbor. If you pay your bills, trade locally as much as possible, mind your own business and are reasonably pleasant, pretty soon they forget that you are an outlander. I feel that I belong in Sag Harbor and I truly believe that the people of the village have accepted us as citizens. I do not sense the resentment from them which is reserved for tourists and summer people.

But I must get back to the ospreys, because with them I have not only failed to make friends but have, on the contrary, been insulted, have thrown down the gauntlet and had it accepted.

On the West Coast, in California's Monterey County where I was born, I learned from childhood the grasses and flowers, the insects and the fishes, the animals from gopher and ground squirrel to bobcat and coyote, deer and mountain lion, and of course the birds, the common ones at least. These are things a child absorbs as he is growing up.

When I first came to Long Island I knew none of these things. Trees, grasses, animals and birds were all strange to me; they had to be learned. And sometimes the natives could not help me much because they knew the things so well and deeply that they could not bring them to the surface.

Thus with books and by asking questions I have begun to learn the names of trees and bushes, of berries and flowers. With a telescope, a birthday present from my wife, I have watched muskrats and a pair of otters swimming in our bay. I have tried to identify the migrating ducks and geese when they sit down in our bay to rest from their journey.

The mallards mate and nest in the reeds along our waterline and bring their ducklings for the bread we throw to them from the pier. I have watched my boys sitting quietly on the

---

[2] *clinker-built* built of overlapping pieces of wood held together by clinker nails.

lawn with the wild ducks crawling over their legs to get pieces of doughnut from their fingers.

The baby rabbits skitter through my vegetable garden and, since I like the rabbits better than my scrawny vegetables, I permit them not only to live but to pursue happiness on my land.

Our house has a glassed-in sun porch and outside its windows I have built a feeding station for birds. Sitting inside I do my best to identify the different visitors with the help of an Audubon, and I have not always, I confess, been successful. There is one common blackish bird which looks to be of the grackle persuasion but his bill is the wrong color and I don't know what he is.

In the upper branches of a half-dead oak tree on the very tip of our point, there was, when I took possession, a tattered lump of trash which looked like an unmade bed in a motor court. In my first early spring a native named Ray Bassenden, our contractor and builder, told me, "That's an osprey's nest. They come back every year. I remember that nest since I was a little boy."

"They build a messy nest," I said.

"Messy, yes," he said professionally, "but I doubt if I could design something the winds wouldn't blow out. It isn't pretty but it's darned good architecture from a staying point of view."

Toward the end of May, to my delight, the ospreys came back from wherever they had been, and from the beginning they fascinated me. They are about the best fishermen in the world and I am about the worst. I watched them by the hour. They would coast along hanging on the breeze perhaps fifty feet above the water, then suddenly their wings raised like the fins of a bomb and they arrowed down and nearly always came up with a fish. Then they would turn the fish in their talons so that its head was into the wind and fly to some high dead branch to eat their catch. I became a habitual osprey watcher.

In time, two of my ospreys were nudged by love and began to install new equipment in the great nest on my point. They brought unusual material—pieces of wood, rake handles, strips of cloth, reeds, swatches of seaweed. One of them, so help me, brought a piece of two-by-four pine three feet long to put into the structure. They weren't very careful builders. The ground under the tree was strewn with the excess stuff that fell out.

I mounted my telescope permanently on the sun porch and even trimmed some branches from intervening trees, and from then on, those lovedriven ospreys didn't have a moment of privacy.

Then June came and school was out and my boys trooped happily out to Sag Harbor. I warned them not to go too near the point for fear of offending the nest builders, and they promised they would not.

And then one morning the ospreys were gone and the nest abandoned. When it became apparent that they weren't coming back I walked out to the point and saw, sticking halfway out of the nest, the shaft and feathers of an arrow.

Now Catbird, my youngest son, is the archer of the family. I ran him down and gave him whatfor in spite of his plaintive protests that he had not shot at the nest.

For a week I waited for the birds to come back, but they did not. They were across the bay. I could see them through the telescope building an uneasy nest on top of a transformer on a telephone pole where they were definitely not wanted.

I got a ladder and climbed up to the nest on our point and when I came down I apologized to Catbird for my unjust suspicions. For in the nest I had found not only the arrow, but my bamboo garden rake, three T shirts belonging to my boys and a Plaza Hotel bath towel. Apparently nothing was too unusual for the ospreys to steal for their nest building. But our birds were definitely gone and showed no intention of returning. I went back to my Audubon and it told me the following:

"Osprey (fish hawk) *Pandion haliaëtus*, length 23 inches, wingspread about 6½ feet, weight 3½ pounds.

"Identification—in flight the wings appear long and the outer half has a characteristic backward sweep.

"Habits—(age 21 years) Provided they are not molested, ospreys will nest wherever there is a reasonably extensive body of clear water and some sort of elevated nest sites exist. The birds have little fear of man and are excellent watchdogs, cheeping loudly at intruders and driving off crows and other birds of prey. For this reason platforms on tall poles are often erected to encourage them to nest about homes and farmyards. Their food consists entirely of fish. These they spot from heights of thirty to one hundred feet, then, after hovering for a moment, they half close their wings and plunge into the water. The fish is seized in their talons, the toes of which are used in pairs, two to a side. This and the rough surface of the foot gives them a firm grip on the most slippery prey. After a catch, they rise quickly . . . and arrange the fish head first."

There followed a list of the kinds of fish they eat and their range and habits. Those were our boys, all right.

I must admit I had been pleased and a little proud to have my own osprey nest, apart from being able to watch them fish. I had planned to observe the nestlings when they arrived. The empty nest on the point was a matter of sorrow and perplexity to me. The summer was a little darkened by the empty nest, and later the winter winds ripped at its half-completed messiness.

It was in February of 1956 that the answer came to me. If people put up platforms on poles, why could I not build a nest so attractive as to be irresistible to any passing osprey with procreation on his mind? Why could I not win back my own birds from the uncomfortable nest which the power company had meanwhile torn off the transformer? I had been to Denmark and had seen what the country people there did for storks. And the storks loved them for it and had their young on the roof tops and year by year brought luck to their benefactors.

In the late winter I went to work. Climbing the oak tree on the point, I cleaned away the old debris of the nest. Then I mounted and firmly wired in place horizontally a large wagon wheel. I cut dry pampas grass stalks and bound them in long faggots. Then with the freezing blasts of winter tearing at my clothes, I reascended the tree and wove the reeds into the spokes of the wheel until I had a nest which, if I had any oviparous[3] impulses, I should have found irresistible.

My wife, dressed in warm clothing, stood dutifully on the ground under the trees and hooked bundles of reeds on the line I threw down to her. She has a highly developed satiric sense which on other occasions I have found charming. She shouted up against the howling wind: "If anybody sees you, a middle-aged man, up a tree in midwinter, building a nest, I will have trouble explaining it to a sanity commission."

Misplaced humor can, under some circumstances, almost amount to bad taste. Silently and doggedly I completed what I believe was the handsomest nest in the Western Hemisphere. Then I went back to my sun porch to await eventualities.

I did have some difficulty explaining the project to my boys. To my oldest son Thom's question, "Why do you build nests for birds?" I could only jocularly reply, "Well, I can build a better nest than they can, but I can't lay eggs, so you see we have to get together."

The winter was long and cold and there was hardly any spring at all. Summer came without warning about June first. I had trouble with the novel I was writing since I had to rush constantly to the telescope to see whether the ospreys, my prospective tenants, had returned.

Then school was out and my boys moved to Sag Harbor and I put them on watch.

One morning Catbird charged into my study, which is a corner of the garage.

"Ospreys!" he shouted. "Come running—ospreys!"

"Sh!" I shouted back. "Keep your voice down. You'll disturb them."

I rushed for my telescope, bowling Catbird over in my rush and tripping over Thom's feet.

There were the ospreys all right. But they weren't settling into my beautiful nest. They were dismantling it, tearing it to pieces, lifting out the carefully bound reed pads and carrying them across the bay and propping them clumsily on top of the same transformer.

Of course my feelings were hurt. Why

---

[3] *oviparous* egg producing.

should I deny it? And on top of all my work. But on the heels of injury came anger. Those lousy, slipshod, larcenous birds, those ingrates, those—those ospreys. My eyes strayed to the shotgun that hangs over my fireplace, but before I could reach for it a Machiavellian[4] thought came to me.

I wanted to hurt the ospreys, yes. I wanted revenge on them, but with number-four shot? No. I ached to hurt them as they had hurt me—in their feelings, psychologically.

I am an adept at psychological warfare. I know well how to sink the knife into sensibilities. I was coldly quiet, even deadly in my approach and manner, so that my boys walked about under a cloud and Thom asked, "What's the matter, Father, did you lose some money playing poker?"

"You stay out of the garage," I said quietly.

I had made my plan. I declared the garage off limits to everyone. My novel came to a dead stop. Daily I worked in the garage using pieces of chicken wire and a great deal of plaster of Paris.

Then I paid a call on my neighbor, Jack Ramsey, a very good painter, and asked him to come to my work shop and to bring his palette and brushes. At the end of two days we emerged with our product—a lifesize perfect replica of a nesting whooping crane. It is my belief that there are only thirty-seven of these rare and wonderful birds in the world. Well, this was the thirty-eighth.

Chuckling evilly I hoisted the plaster bird up in the tree and wired her firmly in the nest where her blinding white body, black tail and brilliant red mask stood out magnificently against the sky. I had even made her bill a little overlarge to take care of foreshortening.

Finally I went back to the sun porch and turned my telescope on the ospreys who pretended to go about their nest building on the transformer as though nothing had happened. But I knew what must be going on over there, although they kept up their façade of listlessness, and I must say they were building an even messier nest than usual.

---

[4] *Machiavellian* scheming, diabolically politic.

Mrs. Osprey was saying, "Lord almighty, George! Look who has moved into the apartment *you* didn't want. Why did I listen to you?"

To which he was replying, "*I* didn't want —what do you mean *I* didn't want? It was you who said the neighborhood wasn't good enough. Don't you put words in my mouth, Mildred."

"Everybody knows you have no taste or background," she was replying. "Your Uncle Harry built his nest over a slaughterhouse."

And I laughed to myself. These are the wounds that never heal. This is psychological warfare as it should be fought.

Two days later, Thom came running into my study in the garage.

"The nest," he cried. "Look at the nest."

I bolted for the door. The ospreys in jealous rage were dive-bombing my whooping crane, but all they could accomplish was the breaking of their talons on the hard surface of the plaster. Finally they gave up and flew away, followed by my shouts of derision.

I did hear my oldest boy say to his brother, "Father has been working too hard. He has gone nuts."

Catbird replied, "His id has been ruptured. Sometimes one broods too much on a subject and throws the whole psychic pattern into an uproar."

That isn't quite where it rests.

It is true that the ospreys have not attacked any more, but we have had other visitors, human visitors.

One morning I looked out the window to see a rather stout lady in khaki trousers and a turtle-neck sweater creeping across my lawn on her hands and knees. Field glasses dangled from her neck and she held a camera in front of her. When I went out to question her, she angrily waved me away.

"Go back," she whispered hoarsely. "Do you want her to fly away?"

"But you don't understand—" I began.

"*Will* you keep your voice down," she said hoarsely. "Do you know what that is? The club will never believe me. If I don't get a picture of her I'll kill you."

Yes, we have had bird watchers—lots of

them. You see, our whooping crane can be sighted from a long way off. After a time they discovered the nature of the thing, but they would not listen to my explanation of the ruse. In fact, they became angry; not at the ospreys, where the blame rests—but at me.

As I write, it is autumn of 1956 and from the coldness and the growing winds, an early winter and a cold one is indicated. I have taken my whooping crane down and restored the nest to its old beauty. When the spring comes again—we shall see what we shall see. No one can say that I am unforgiving. The nest is ready and waiting. Let us see whether the ospreys are big enough to let bygones be bygones.

My wife says that if she has to go through another year like this she will—no, I won't tell you what she says. Sometimes her sense of humor seems a little strained.

Walden*

by E. B. WHITE

Miss Nims, take a letter to Henry David Thoreau. Dear Henry: I thought of you the other afternoon as I was approaching Concord doing fifty on Route 62. That is a high speed at which to hold a philosopher in one's mind, but in this century we are a nimble bunch.

On one of the lawns in the outskirts of the village a woman was cutting the grass with a motorized lawn mower. What made me think of you was that the machine had rather got away from her, although she was game enough, and in the brief glimpse I had of the scene it appeared to me that the lawn was mowing the lady. She kept a tight grip on the handles, which throbbed violently with every explosion of the one-cylinder motor, and as she sheered around bushes and lurched along at a reluctant trot behind her impetuous servant, she looked like a puppy who had grabbed something that was too much for him. Concord hasn't changed much, Henry; the farm implements and the animals still have the upper hand.

I may as well admit that I was journeying to Concord with the deliberate intention of visiting your woods; for although I have never knelt at the grave of a philosopher nor placed wreaths on moldy poets, and have often gone a mile out of my way to avoid some place of historical interest, I have always wanted to see Walden Pond. The account that you left of your sojourn there is, you will be amused to learn, a document of increasing pertinence; each year it seems to gain a little headway, as the world loses ground. We may all be transcendental yet, whether we like it or not. As our common complexities increase, any tale of individual simplicity (and yours is the best written and the cockiest) acquires a new fascination; as our goods accumulate, but not our well-being, your report of an existence without material adornment takes on a certain awkward credibility.

My purpose in going to Walden Pond, like yours, was not to live cheaply or to live dearly there, but to transact some private business with the fewest obstacles. Approaching Concord, doing forty, doing forty-five, doing fifty, the steering wheel held snug in my palms, the highway held grimly in my vision, the crown of the road now serving me (on the righthand curves), now defeating me (on the lefthand curves), I began to rouse myself from the stupefaction that a day's motor journey induces. It was a delicious evening, Henry, when the whole body is one sense, and imbibes delight through every pore, if I may coin a phrase. Fields were richly brown where the harrow, drawn by the stripped Ford, had lately sunk its teeth; pastures were green; and overhead the sky had that same everlasting great look which

---

* "Walden"—June 1939—in *One Man's Meat* by E. B. White. Copyright 1939 by E. B. White. Reprinted by permission of Harper & Row, Publishers, Incorporated.

you will find on Page 144 of the Oxford pocket edition. I could feel the road entering me, through tire, wheel, spring, and cushion; shall I not have intelligence with earth too? Am I not partly leaves and vegetable mold myself?—a man of infinite horsepower, yet partly leaves.

Stay with me on 62 and it will take you into Concord. As I say, it was a delicious evening. The snake had come forth to die in a bloody S on the highway, the wheel upon its head, its bowels flat now and exposed. The turtle had come up too to cross the road and die in the attempt, its hard shell smashed under the rubber blow, its intestinal yearning (for the other side of the road) forever squashed. There was a sign by the wayside which announced that the road had a "cotton surface." You wouldn't know what that is, but neither, for that matter, did I. There is a cryptic ingredient in many of our modern improvements—we are awed and pleased without knowing quite what we are enjoying. It is something to be traveling on a road with a cotton surface.

The civilization round Concord today is an odd distillation of city, village, farm, and manor. The houses, yards, fields look not quite suburban, not quite rural. Under the bronze beech and the blue spruce of the departed baron grazes the milch goat of the heirs. Under the porte-cochère stands the reconditioned station wagon; under the grape arbor sit the puppies for sale. (But why do men degenerate ever? What makes families run out?)

It was June and everywhere June was publishing her immemorial stanza; in the lilacs, in the syringa, in the freshly edged paths and the sweetness of moist beloved gardens, and the little wire wickets that preserve the tulips' front. Farmers were already moving the fruits of their toil into their yards, arranging the rhubarb, the asparagus, the strictly fresh eggs on the painted stands under the little shed roofs with the patent shingles. And though it was almost a hundred years since you had taken your ax and started cutting out your home on Walden Pond, I was interested to observe that the philosophical spirit was still alive in Massachusetts: in the center of a vacant lot some boys were assembling the framework of the rude shelter, their whole mind and skill concentrated in the rather inauspicious helter-skeleton of studs and rafters. They too were escaping from town, to live naturally, in a rich blend of savagery and philosophy.

That evening, after supper at the inn, I strolled out into the twilight to dream my shapeless transcendental dreams and see that the car was locked up for the night (first open the right front door, then reach over, straining, and pull up the handles of the left rear and the left front till you hear the click, then the handle of the right rear, then shut the right front but open it again, remembering that the key is still in the ignition switch, remove the key, shut the right front again with a bang, push the tiny keyhole cover to one side, insert key, turn, and withdraw). It is what we all do, Henry. It is called locking the car. It is said to confuse thieves and keep them from making off with the laprobe. Four doors to lock behind one robe. The driver himself never uses a laprobe, the free movement of his legs being vital to the operation of the vehicle; so that when he locks the car it is a pure and unselfish act. I have in my life gained very little essential heat from laprobes, yet I have ever been at pains to lock them up.

The evening was full of sounds, some of which would have stirred your memory. The robins still love the elms of New England villages at sundown. There is enough of the thrush in them to make song inevitable at the end of day, and enough of the tramp to make them hang round the dwellings of men. A robin, like many another American, dearly loves a white house with green blinds. Concord is still full of them.

Your fellow-townsmen were stirring abroad—not many afoot, most of them in their cars; and the sound that they made in Concord at evening was a rustling and a whispering. The sound lacks steadfastness and is wholly unlike that of a train. A train, as you know who lived so near the Fitchburg line, whistles once or twice sadly and is gone, trailing a memory in smoke, soothing to ear and mind. Automobiles, skirting a village green, are like flies that have gained the inner ear—they buzz, cease, pause, start, shift, stop, halt, brake, and the whole effect is a nervous polytone curiously disturbing.

As I wandered along, the toc toc of ping pong balls drifted from an attic window. In front of the Reuben Brown house a Buick was drawn up. At the wheel, motionless, his hat upon his head, a man sat, listening to Amos and Andy on the radio (it is a drama of many scenes and without an end). The deep voice of Andrew Brown, emerging from the car, although it originated more than two hundred miles away, was unstrained by distance. When you used to sit on the shore of your pond on Sunday morning, listening to the church bells of Acton and Concord, you were aware of the excellent filter of the intervening atmosphere. Science has attended to that, and sound now maintains its intensity without regard for distance. Properly sponsored, it goes on forever.

A fire engine, out for a trial spin, roared past Emerson's house, hot with readiness for public duty. Over the barn roofs the martins dipped and chittered. A swarthy daughter of an asparagus grower, in culottes, shirt, and bandanna, pedalled past on her bicycle. It was indeed a delicious evening, and I returned to the inn (I believe it was your house once) to rock with the old ladies on the concrete veranda.

Next morning early I started afoot for Walden, out Main Street and down Thoreau, past the depot and the Minuteman Chevrolet Company. The morning was fresh, and in a bean field along the way I flushed an agriculturalist, quietly studying his beans. Thoreau Street soon joined Number 126, an artery of the State. We number our highways nowadays, our speed being so great we can remember little of their quality or character and are lucky to remember their number. (Men have an indistinct notion that if they keep up this activity long enough all will at length ride somewhere, in next to no time.) Your pond is on 126.

I knew I must be nearing your woodland retreat when the Golden Pheasant lunchroom came into view—Sealtest ice cream, toasted sandwiches, hot frankfurters, waffles, tonics, and lunches. Were I the proprietor, I should add rice, Indian meal, and molasses—just for old time's sake. The Pheasant, incidentally, is for sale: a chance for some nature lover who wishes to set himself up beside a pond in the Concord atmosphere and live deliberately, fronting only the essential facts of life on Number 126. Beyond the Pheasant was a place called Walden Breezes, an oasis whose porch pillars were made of old green shutters sawed into lengths. On the porch was a distorting mirror, to give the traveler a comical image of himself, who had miraculously learned to gaze in an ordinary glass without smiling. Behind the Breezes, in a sun-parched clearing, dwelt your philosophical descendants in their trailers, each trailer the size of your hut, but all grouped together for the sake of congeniality. Trailer people leave the city, as you did, to discover solitude and in any weather, at any hour of the day or night, to improve the nick of time; but they soon collect in villages and get bogged deeper in the mud than ever. The camp behind Walden Breezes was just rousing itself to the morning. The ground was packed hard under the heel, and the sun came through the clearing to bake the soil and enlarge the wry smell of cramped housekeeping. Cushman's bakery truck had stopped to deliver an early basket of rolls. A camp dog, seeing me in the road, barked petulantly. A man emerged from one of the trailers and set forth with a bucket to draw water from some forest tap.

Leaving the highway I turned off into the woods toward the pond, which was apparent through the foliage. The floor of the forest was strewn with dried old oak leaves and *Transcripts*. From beneath the flattened popcorn wrapper (*granum explosum*) peeped the frail violet. I followed a footpath and descended to the water's edge. The pond lay clear and blue in the morning light, as you have seen it so many times. In the shallows a man's waterlogged shirt undulated gently. A few flies came out to greet me and convoy me to your cove, past the No Bathing signs on which the fellows and the girls had scrawled their names. I felt strangely excited suddenly to be snooping around your premises, tiptoeing along watchfully, as though not to tread by mistake upon the intervening century. Before I got to the cove I heard something that seemed to me quite wonderful: I heard your frog, a full, clear *troonk*, guiding me, still hoarse and solemn, bridging the years as the robins had bridged them in the sweetness of the village evening. But he soon quit, and I came on a couple of young boys throwing stones at him.

Your front yard is marked by a bronze tablet set in a stone. Four small granite posts, a few feet away, show where the house was. On top of the tablet was a pair of faded blue bathing trunks with a white stripe. Back of it is a pile of stones, a sort of cairn, left by your visitors as a tribute I suppose. It is a rather ugly little heap of stones, Henry. In fact the hillside itself seems faded, browbeaten; a few tall skinny pines, bare of lower limbs, a smattering of young maples in suitable green, some birches and oaks, and a number of trees felled by the last big wind. It was from the bole of one of these fallen pines, torn up by the roots, that I extracted the stone that I added to the cairn—a sentimental act in which I was interrupted by a small terrier from a nearby picnic group, who confronted me and wanted to know about the stone.

I sat down for a while on one of the posts of your house to listen to the bluebottles and the dragonflies. The invaded glade sprawled shabby and mean at my feet, but the flies were tuned to the old vibration. There were the remains of a fire in your ruins, but I doubt that it was yours; also two beer bottles trodden into the soil and become part of earth. A young oak had taken root in your house, and two or three ferns, unrolling like the ticklers at a banquet. The only other furnishings were a DuBarry pattern sheet, a page torn from a picture magazine, and some crusts in wax paper.

Before I quit I walked clear round the pond and found the place where you used to sit on the northeast side to get the sun in the fall, and the beach where you got sand for scrubbing your floor. On the eastern side of the pond, where the highway borders it, the State has built dressing rooms for swimmers, a float with diving towers, drinking fountains of porcelain, and rowboats for hire. The pond is in fact a State Preserve, and carries a twenty-dollar fine for picking wild flowers, a decree signed in all solemnity by your fellow-citizens Walter C. Wardwell, Erson B. Barlow, and Nathaniel I. Bowditch. There was a smell of creosote where they had been building a wide wooden stairway to the road and the parking area. Swimmers and boaters were arriving; bodies plunged vigorously into the water and emerged wet and beautiful in the bright air. As I left, a boatload of town boys were splashing about in mid-pond, kidding and fooling, the young fellows singing at the tops of their lungs in a wild chorus:

Amer-ica, Amer-ica, God shed his grace on thee,
And crown thy good with brotherhood—
From sea to shi-ning sea!

I walked back to town along the railroad, following your custom. The rails were expanding noisily in the hot sun, and on the slope of the roadbed the wild grape and the blackberry sent up their creepers to the track.

The expense of my brief sojourn in Concord was:

Canvas shoes	$1.95
Baseball bat	.25 } gifts to take back
Left-handed	to a boy
fielder's glove	1.25
Hotel and meals	4.25
In all	$7.70

As you see, this amount was almost what you spent for food for eight months. I cannot defend the shoes or the expenditure for shelter and food: they reveal a meanness and grossness in my nature which you would find contemptible. The baseball equipment, however, is the kind of impediment with which you were never on even terms. You must remember that the house where you practiced the sort of economy that I respect was haunted only by mice and squirrels. You never had to cope with a shortstop.

New York, C'est Formidable!*

by ART BUCHWALD

Monsieur François De Paul,
235 Rue Faubourg St. Honoré,
Paris, France.

Dear François,

And so I have arrived in New York and am writing to you as you requested. My dear friend, New York is formidable. It is much larger than either one of us expected and the movies do not do it justice. I have had many adventures but I do not know where to begin. When I first arrived at Idlewild Airport I changed my francs into dollars at the official rate as I feared to get involved in the black market so early on my arrival.

Then I took a taxi into New York City making sure to check the meter as you advised me to do. The driver was very talkative and as soon as we started moving he said to me:

"What do you think the Dodgers will do this year?"

I told him I knew of no dodgers and he was very surprised. I explained I lived in France and he said, "Okay, we'll talk about France."

He knew everything about France. He said France had too many political parties and he was getting sick of having his money poured down the sewers of Europe, whatever that means. He said the trouble with the French is that they are always making love and sitting at sidewalk cafés and they never get down to work. He also told me his brother-in-law was in France for three months during the war, and his brother-in-law told him the French weren't serious people.

When we arrived at my hotel he told me that everyone gives him a dollar tip from the airport. I gave it to him but he did not say thank you. I discovered later that it is forbidden for a taxi driver in New York City to say thank you to his customers.

My hotel is located in the province of Manhattan. New York is divided into five provinces. There is the Bronx, Brooklyn, Queens, Staten Island, and Manhattan, where the seat of the government is. Most of the people in New York take the *métro* from the other provinces to go to work in Manhattan, where the Bourse is located.

But there is no *métro* connection with Staten Island and these people have to take a boat every morning and every evening. I understand that Staten Island is very primitive and has a Wild West atmosphere. I plan to go there if I can find a reliable guide.

New Yorkers have so many strange habits. You will be amused to hear that they eat enormous breakfasts including thick oats, strange wheat kernels, eggs, ham, bacon, large crepes called pancakes, and they put a thick sweet syrup on them. The coffee is just terrible and I would give anything for a good café filtre. I have also been unsuccessful in getting a brioche, but I was surprised to find things named after France that we do not have there. To name a few, French crullers, French toast, French dressing, and French bread (which has no resemblance to our bread at all).

Although they eat grand breakfasts they have hardly any lunch at all and the people eat in pharmacies. I don't think they take more than thirty minutes for lunch and it is criminal to see them shove the food in their mouths. It was only after I ate some pharmacy foods that I understood why they eat that way. It's better that you don't taste the food. You may not believe this, François, but I saw people drinking milk with their entrée. The first time I saw it I became sick, but now I am getting used to it.

The buildings in New York are almost as high as the Eiffel Tower but except for Central Park there are no trees or grass to be seen anywhere. The elevators work both ways and you don't have to walk downstairs as you do in Paris.

---

* This article first appeared in the *Saturday Review* of April 17, 1954; copyright 1954 by The Saturday Review Associates, Inc. Reprinted by permission of Art Buchwald and *Saturday Review*.

There are, unfortunately, no sidewalk cafés in New York and everyone must sit in dark drab bars if they wish to drink. The bars are very busy around 5:30 in the afternoon and people drink very fast and very much. Dinner is at 6:30, if that is not a laugh, but by then everyone is so drunk they do not know what they are eating anyway.

The theater is very good in New York and I saw two plays. One is called *Tea and Sympathy* and it is about a boy who is trying to prove he is not a homosexual. The other based on Gide is called *The Immoralist* and is about a man who is trying to prove he is one. So you see Broadway gives you both sides of every story.

A funny thing happened—someone, a lady, called me up one day and asked me to come on her television program and tell her all about France.

I went on like she wanted me to. The first question she asked me was "Will the French fight?" I do not remember what I answered but it made no difference because her second question was "Why are all you Frenchmen Communists?" I said we weren't all Communists and she said that is not what she read in the papers. Then she said, "Why are prices so high in Paris?" but before I could answer she said, "And now let's hear from the sponsor." But there was no sponsor so she had to make the publicity herself. She was making publicity for a seasoning and she said it was the best seasoning you could buy anywhere. Then she asked me if the French used this seasoning and I said they did not, and so she said, "Well, if they did their food would taste much better." This is the truth, François, I swear it.

After the publicity she asked me what I thought of American women and I said they had very nice legs but they all looked alike. She did not like this and said American women are very beautiful, particularly those that used a certain kind of soap which she held up in her hand. She promised all the women in the audience that if they used the soap twice a day they would be loved by men. This is the truth, François. Then she asked me what I thought of American men and I said they were very nice. And she said the reason they were nice is because they drank fruit juice in the morning, and she held up a can of a certain kind of fruit juice and said that angry men become happy men when they drink this certain kind of fruit juice. She gave me a can of it and said, "And even Frenchmen like fruit juice, don't they?" I had to say yes.

Before the program was over I admitted that French floors would look better if they had a certain kind of house wax, that a certain California wine was as good as wines we have in France, that French couturiers received their inspiration from American fabrics, and that the French had no refrigerators to compare with one the lady commentator showed me. The program was over and they asked me to leave the studio immediately as they had to prepare for another show. I guess I did not leave fast enough because as I was looking for my coat two guards grabbed me by the arms and showed me to the door. I never found out the lady's name.

That is all, François. I wish I could tell you more about New York, but I'm sure you would not believe me anyway.

      My affectionate sentiments,
           PIERRE

A Wonderful Time*

by SUSAN LARDNER

We were on an escalator last Wednesday afternoon, riding from the fourth floor of Stern's department store to the fifth floor, when a bright-eyed lady in a long fur coat turned to us and said, "Don't you think I look like a mature woman who's trying to reenter the business world? The sign on the main floor said there was going to be a symposium here today for the mature woman who wants to reenter the business world. Actually, I'm *passing* as a mature woman. And can you reenter something if you've never been in it?"

As we stepped off the escalator right behind her, trying to remember what we were there for, she handed us an orange-paper package. "Here, will you please hold this for a minute? It's a Bloomingdale's bag. I don't know whether I should be seen with it here. Maybe that man over there can tell me where the symposium is." Crying "Hey, sir," she sprang toward a small salesman, who ducked gracefully behind a television console. Undaunted, she tracked down a larger salesman and obtained directions to the Special Events Center, on the sixth floor. Though ordinarily we are not easily distracted from our purpose (whatever it *was*), we followed the lady across the floor and up a flight of stairs that led to the Credit Department. "Oh, my God!" she exclaimed. "Why do I always end up here?" She raced past the row of credit adjusters to the entrance of the meeting hall. We did, too. Each symposiast was being handed an envelope filled with pamphlets and press releases concerning the topic to be discussed—like "Do's and Don'ts for Mature Job Seekers" ("Do hold yourself erect" and "Don't keep stressing your need for a job")—and a program of the afternoon's events. Marching through a crowd of three or four men and hundreds of women, most of whom appeared to be in their forties or fifties, our companion led us to the first two rows of chairs, which were decked with "Reserved" signs. She removed two of the signs and her coat, sat down, and beckoned to us to join her. We sat down. She reached into the envelope and pulled out a thin paperback book called "Women! Business Needs You! A Back-to-Business Guide for Modern Women," by Sabatino A. Russo, Jr., with William Laas.

"Can you tell how old I am?" she asked.

"Oh, about thirty-five," we said, since we couldn't tell.

"By the way, my name is Janet," she said. "Business needs me."

The stage, which was a few feet in front of the chairs we were occupying, was furnished with a wooden lectern, a table set for three panelists, and several colorful freestanding doors, labelled with the names of fictional business concerns. According to the program, the symposium was the third annual "Business Needs You" gathering, and was sponsored by Stern Brothers and the American Girl Division of AGS Services Corporation, a temporary-office-work agency, whose president, Sabatino A. Russo, Jr., was listed as moderator of the symposium.

Janet scanned the program and remarked that the only speaker she really wanted to hear was Dr. Rose Franzblau, the well-known psychologist, who was scheduled to be the final speaker and offer advice on "How to Weather the Emotional Crisis of Returning to Work." "I think she knows my Aunt Clara," Janet said, and she proceeded to pick up an earlier train of thought. "As a matter of fact, I *have* been in the business world. I worked at Bloomingdale's for a week before Christmas. I made ten dollars a day and spent thirty. See this?"

We looked, and she pointed to the heading of Chapter 4 in Mr. Russo's book: "The One Crucial Skill—Typing." "I can't type," she said, growing glum. "But I once took dictation from Orson Welles."

Just at that moment, Miss Mildred Collins appeared on the stage. She is a vice-president of Stern Brothers and a rare exception,

---

* Reprinted by permission; © 1969 The New Yorker Magazine, Inc. From *The New Yorker*, February 8, 1969.

we later learned, to the general absence of women from executive positions in business. Miss Collins welcomed the audience, addressing them as "ladies like you," by which she meant, we figured out, ladies over forty who had been without jobs for the last ten or twenty years, and who were now interested in finding jobs but fearful of being turned away for being too old or for possessing rusty secretarial skills.

Janet glanced up at Miss Collins and then back at the book in her lap. "'Ask yourself these questions,'" Janet murmured. "'What is my education? How is my health? Physical needs?' Nobody's ever asked me that before. 'What are my present interests?' My present interests are my physical needs. 'Favorite recreation?' I think that taking a bath is my favorite recreation."

Meanwhile, Miss Collins was introducing Mr. Russo: "A young man . . . He is married, unfortunately . . . Brilliant . . . Dynamic leadership . . ."

Janet continued reading. "'What are my natural aptitudes?' Do you have a pencil?" We handed her a pencil, and she used it to check "Car driving," "Dancing," "Handling people," and "Travel."

Mr. Russo, a fine-looking young man and a dynamic moderator, introduced Miss Dorothy Pendergast, a Regional Director of the Women's Bureau of the United States Department of Labor, who said that the concept of the meaning of femininity is expanding, that the average woman worker today is forty-one and married, that many states have laws banning discrimination by employers on the basis of age and sex, and that "older workers" are frequently steadier and more reliable than younger ones. Mr. Russo then returned to the lectern to explain the difference between permanent work, part-time work, temporary work, and home work. Before comparing the business world to an oyster, he advised the ladies to brush up their skills, and warned them not to forget to find out whether their husbands or teen-age children might have objections to their plans to reenter the business world.

"Nobody objects to my working except me," muttered Janet. She nudged us and pointed to the book again—to a questionnaire designed to indicate whether temporary work would be the most suitable form of employment for a particular mature job seeker. "Does your husband travel a great deal, leaving you alone for extended periods of time?" one question went. Janet looked thoughtful. "Is eight years considered an extended period of time?" she asked us.

While Mrs. Kathryn Kozlowski, from Personnel Services of the Allied Chemical Corporation, was saying that "realism is a mandatory characteristic of the mature woman," Janet was making a perfect score on a sample vocabulary quiz.

". . . as certain of her shortcomings as of her abilities," said Mrs. Kozlowski.

"I'm certain of my shortcomings," Janet said.

". . . room at the top, even if you start at the bottom," said Mrs. Kozlowski.

"I want to start at the top," Janet said.

Mrs. Evelyn Cunningham, Director of the Women's Unit of the Office of the Governor, urged the members of the audience to consider the expense of going back to work—the cost of lunches, subway fares, taxes, proper garments, and visits to the beauty parlor. This, Janet told us, reminded her of her week at Bloomingdale's.

Mrs. Mary D. Keyserling, a mature woman who said she had just lost her job as Director of the Women's Bureau of the United States Department of Labor, owing to the change of Administrations, was presented with the first annual Woman Behind the Woman Award, for encouraging large numbers of her fellow-women to return to work. Mrs. Lyndon Johnson was quoted more than once as having said, "This is a wonderful time to be a woman."

Janet reached into her coat pocket and pulled out a crumpled scrap torn from the help-wanted page of the *Times*. She stood up abruptly. "I've got to go brush up my skills," she said. In spite of the prospect of hearing Dr. Franzblau, she grabbed her coat and her package and ran.

Later in the week, when we read in the *Times* that the Forty-second Street branch of Stern's would be closed down forever before summer, we were still trying to remember what we went there to buy the day we met Janet.

The Spectator Club
by RICHARD STEELE

The Spectator, No. 2: Friday, March 2, 1711.

The first of our society is a gentleman of Worcestershire, of ancient descent, a baronet; his name Sir Roger de Coverley. His great-grandfather was inventor of that famous country-dance which is called after him. All who know that shire are very well acquainted with the parts and merits of Sir Roger. He is a gentleman that is very singular in his behavior, but his singularities proceed from his good sense, and are contradictions to the manners of the world only as he thinks the world is in the wrong. However, this humor creates him no enemies, for he does nothing with sourness of obstinacy; and his being unconfined to modes and forms makes him but the readier and more capable to please and oblige all who know him. When he is in town, he lives in Soho Square.[1] It is said he keeps himself a bachelor by reason he was crossed in love by a perverse, beautiful widow of the next county to him. Before this disappointment, Sir Roger was what you call a fine gentleman, had often supped with my Lord Rochester[2] and Sir George Etherege,[3] fought a duel upon his first coming to town, and kicked Bully Dawson[4] in a public coffee-house for calling him "youngster." But being ill-used by the above-mentioned widow, he was very serious for a year and a half; and though, his temper being naturally jovial, he at last got over it, he grew careless of himself, and never dressed afterward. He continues to wear a coat and doublet of the same cut that were in fashion at the time of his repulse, which, in his merry humors, he tells us, has been in and out twelve times since he first wore it. 'Tis said Sir Roger grew humble in his desires after he had forgot this cruel beauty; but this is looked upon by his friends rather as matter of raillery than truth. He is now in his fifty-sixth year, cheerful, gay, and hearty; keeps a good house in both town and country; a great lover of mankind; but there is such a mirthful cast in his behavior that he is rather beloved than esteemed. His tenants grow rich, his servants look satisfied, all the young women profess love to him, and the young men are glad of his company; when he comes into a house he calls the servants by their names, and talks all the way upstairs to a visit. I must not omit that Sir Roger is a justice of the quorum;[5] that he fills the chair at a quarter-session with great abilities; and, three months ago, gained universal applause by explaining a passage in the Game Act. The gentleman next in esteem and authority among us is another bachelor, who is a member of the Inner Temple;[6] a man of great probity, wit, and understanding; but he has chosen his place of residence rather to obey the direction of an old humorsome father, than in pursuit of his own inclinations. He was placed there to study the laws of the land, and is the most learned of any of the house in those of the stage. Aristotle and Longinus[7] are much better understood by him than Littleton or Coke.[8] The father sends up, every post, questions relating to marriage-articles, leases, and tenures, in the neighborhood; all which questions he agrees with an attorney to answer and takes care of in the lump. He is studying the passions themselves, when he should be inquiring into the debates among men which arise from them. He knows the argument of each of the orations

---

[1] *Soho Square* at the time the most fashionable part of London.
[2] *Lord Rochester* a notorious rake of Charles II's court.
[3] *Sir George Etherege* a Restoration dramatist, author of *The Man of Mode.*
[4] *Bully Dawson* a clever double-crosser.

[5] *justice of the quorum* justice of peace.
[6] *Inner Temple* one of the centers of the study and practice of law in London.
[7] *Aristotle and Longinus* Greek critics.
[8] *Littleton or Coke* authorities on the law.

of Demosthenes and Tully,[9] but not one case in the reports of our own courts. No one ever took him for a fool, but none, except his intimate friends, know he has a great deal of wit. This turn[10] makes him at once both disinterested and agreeable; as few of his thoughts are drawn from business, they are most of them fit for conversation. His taste of books is a little too just[11] for the age he lives in; he has read all, but approves of very few. His familiarity with the customs, manners, actions, and writings of the ancients makes him a very delicate observer of what occurs to him in the present world. He is an excellent critic, and the time of the play is his hour of business; exactly at five he passes through New Inn,[12] crosses through Russell Court, and takes a turn at Will's[13] till the play begins; he has his shoes rubbed and his periwig powdered at the barber's as you go into the Rose. It is for the good of the audience when he is at a play, for the actors have an ambition to please him.

The person of next consideration is Sir Andrew Freeport, a merchant of great eminence in the city of London, a person of indefatigable industry, strong reason, and great experience. His notions of trade are noble and generous, and (as every rich man has usually some sly way of jesting which would make no great figure were he not a rich man) he calls the sea the British Common.[14] He is acquainted with commerce in all its parts, and will tell you that it is a stupid and barbarous way to extend dominion by arms; for true power is to be got by arts and industry. He will often argue that if this part of our trade were well cultivated, we should gain from one nation; and if another, from another. I have heard him prove that diligence makes more lasting acquisitions than valor, and that sloth has ruined more nations than the sword. He abounds in several frugal maxims, among which the greatest favorite is, "A penny saved is a penny got." A general trader of good sense is pleasanter company than a general scholar; and Sir Andrew having a natural unaffected eloquence, the perspicuity of his discourse gives the same pleasure that wit would in another man. He has made his fortunes himself, and says that England may be richer than other kingdoms by as plain methods as he himself is richer than other men; though at the same time I can say this of him, that there is not a point in the compass but blows home a ship in which he is an owner.

Next to Sir Andrew in the club-room sits Captain Sentry, a gentleman of great courage, good understanding, but invincible modesty. He is one of those that deserve very well, but are very awkward at putting their talents within the observation of such as should take notice of them. He was some years a captain, and behaved himself with great gallantry in several engagements and at several sieges; but having a small estate of his own, and being next heir to Sir Roger, he has quitted a way of life in which no man can rise suitably to his merit who is not something of a courtier as well as a soldier. I have heard him often lament that in a profession where merit is placed in so conspicuous a view, impudence should get the better of modesty. When he has talked to this purpose I never heard him make a sour expression, but frankly confess that he left the world because he was not fit for it. A strict honesty and an even, regular behavior are in themselves obstacles to him that must press through crowds who endeavor at the same end with himself—the favor of a commander. He will, however, in this way of talk, excuse generals for not disposing according to men's desert, or inquiring into it, "For," says he, "that great man who has a mind to help me, has as many to break through to come at me as I have to come at him"; therefore he will conclude that the man who would make a figure, especially in a military way, must get over all false modesty, and assist his patron against the importunity of other pretenders by a proper assurance in his own vindication. He says it is a civil cowardice to be backward in asserting what you

---

[9] *Demosthenes and Tully* (Cicero) A Greek and a Roman orator.
[10] *turn* characteristic.
[11] *too just* critical or severe.
[12] *New Inn* one of the inns of Court in London.
[13] *Will's* a coffee house.
[14] *British Common* like the commons—property open to all for grazing or cultivation.

ought to expect, as it is a military fear to be slow in attacking when it is your duty. With this candor does the gentleman speak of himself and others. The same frankness runs through all his conversation. The military part of his life has furnished him with many adventures, in the relation of which he is very agreeable to the company; for he is never overbearing, though accustomed to command men in the utmost degree below him; nor ever too obsequious from an habit of obeying men highly above him.

But that our society may not appear a set of humorists unacquainted with the gallantries and pleasures of the age, we have among us the gallant Will Honeycomb,[15] a gentleman who, according to his years, should be in the decline of his life, but having ever been very careful of his person, and always had a very easy fortune, time has made but very little impression either by wrinkles on his forehead or traces in his brain. His person is well turned and of a good height. He is very ready at that sort of discourse with which men usually entertain women. He has all his life dressed very well, and remembers habits as others do men. He can smile when one speaks to him, and laughs easily. He knows the history of every mode, and can inform you from which of the French King's wenches our wives and daughters had this manner of curling their hair, that way of placing their hoods; whose frailty was covered by such a sort of petticoat, and whose vanity to show her foot made that part of the dress so short in such a year. In a word, all his conversation and knowledge has been in the female world. As other men of his age will take notice to you what such a minister said upon such and such an occasion, he will tell when the Duke of Monmouth danced at court such a woman was then smitten, another was taken with him at the head of his troop in the Park. In all these important relations, he has ever about the same time received a kind glance or a blow of a fan from some celebrated beauty, mother of the present Lord Such-a-one. If you speak of a young commoner that said a lively thing in the House, he starts up: "He has good blood in his veins; Tom Mirabell, the rogue, cheated me in that affair; that young fellow's mother used me more like a dog than any woman I ever made advances to." This way of talking of his very much enlivens the conversation among us of a more sedate turn; and I find there is not one of the company but myself, who rarely speak at all, but speaks of him as of that sort of man who is usually called a well-bred, fine gentleman. To conclude his character, where women are not concerned, he is an honest, worthy man.

I cannot tell whether I am to account him whom I am next to speak of as one of our company, for he visits us but seldom; but when he does, it adds to every man else a new enjoyment of himself. He is a clergyman, a very philosophic man, of general learning, great sanctity of life, and the most exact good breeding. He has the misfortune to be of a very weak constitution, and consequently cannot accept of such cares and business as preferments in his function would oblige him to; he is therefore among divines what a chamber-counselor is among lawyers. The probity of his mind and the integrity of his life create him followers, as being eloquent or loud advances others. He seldom introduces the subject he speaks upon; but we are so far gone in years that he observes, when he is among us, an earnestness to have him fall on some divine topic, which he always treats with much authority, as one who has no interest in this world, as one who is hastening to the object of all his wishes and conceives hope from his decays and infirmities. These are my ordinary companions.

---

[15] *Will Honeycomb* cf. this portrait with Addison's *Beau* and Sir Plume in *The Rape of the Lock*.

Sir Roger at Church

by JOSEPH ADDISON

The Spectator, No. 112: Monday, July 9, 1711.

I am always very well pleased with a country Sunday, and think, if keeping holy the seventh day were only a human institution, it would be the best method that could have been thought of for the polishing and civilizing of mankind. It is certain the country people would soon degenerate into a kind of savages and barbarians were there not such frequent returns of a stated time in which the whole village meet together with their best faces, and in their cleanliest habits, to converse with one another upon indifferent subjects, hear their duties explained to them, and join together in adoration of the Supreme Being. Sunday clears away the rust of the whole week, not only as it refreshes in their minds the notions of religion, but as it puts both the sexes upon appearing in their most agreeable forms, and exerting all such qualities as are apt to give them a figure in the eye of the village. A country fellow distinguishes himself as much in the churchyard as a citizen does upon the 'Change,[1] the whole parish politics being generally discussed in that place either after sermon or before the bell rings.

My friend Sir Roger, being a good churchman, has beautified the inside of his church with several texts of his own choosing; he has likewise given a handsome pulpit-cloth, and railed in the communion-table at his own expense. He has often told me that, at his coming to his estate, he found his parishioners very irregular; and that, in order to make them kneel and join in the responses, he gave every one of them a hassock[2] and a common-prayer-book, and at the same time employed an itinerant singing-master, who goes about the country for that purpose, to instruct them rightly in the tunes of the Psalms; upon which they now very much value themselves, and indeed outdo most of the country churches that I have ever heard.

As Sir Roger is landlord to the whole congregation, he keeps them in very good order, and will suffer nobody to sleep in it besides himself; for, if by chance he has been surprised into a short nap at sermon, upon recovering out of it he stands up and looks about him, and if he sees anybody else nodding, either wakes them himself, or sends his servant to them. Several other of the old knight's particularities break out upon these occasions; sometimes he will be lengthening out a verse in the Singing-Psalms half a minute after the rest of the congregation have done with it; sometimes, when he is pleased with the matter of his devotion, he pronounces "Amen" three or four times to the same prayer; and sometimes stands up when everybody else is upon their knees, to count the congregation, or see if any of his tenants are missing.

I was yesterday very much surprised to hear my old friend, in the midst of the service, calling out to one John Matthews to mind what he was about, and not disturb the congregation. This John Matthews, it seems, is remarkable for being an idle fellow, and at that time was kicking his heels for his diversion. This authority of the knight, though exerted in that odd manner which accompanies him in all circumstances of life, has a very good effect upon the parish, who are not polite enough to see anything ridiculous in his behavior; besides that the general good sense and worthiness of his character makes his friends observe these little singularities as foils that rather set off than blemish his good qualities.

As soon as the sermon is finished, nobody presumes to stir till Sir Roger is gone out of the church. The knight walks down from his seat in the chancel between a double row of his tenants, that stand bowing to him on each

---

[1] *'Change* the Exchange; the Stock Exchange in London.
[2] *hassock* kneeler.

side, and every now and then inquires how such an one's wife, or mother, or son, or father do, whom he does not see at church—which is understood as a secret reprimand to the person that is absent.

The chaplain has often told me that, upon a catechizing day, when Sir Roger had been pleased with a boy that answers well, he has ordered a Bible to be given him next day for his encouragement, and sometimes accompanies it with a flitch of bacon to his mother. Sir Roger has likewise added five pounds a year to the clerk's place; and, that he may encourage the young fellows to make themselves perfect in the church service, has promised, upon the death of the present incumbent, who is very old, to bestow it according to merit.

The fair understanding between Sir Roger and his chaplain, and their mutual concurrence in doing good, is the more remarkable because the very next village is famous for the differences and contentions that rise between the parson and the squire, who live in a perpetual state of war. The parson is always preaching at the squire, and the squire, to be revenged on the parson, never comes to church. The squire has made all his tenants atheists and tithestealers, while the parson instructs them every Sunday in the dignity of his order, and insinuates to them in almost every sermon that he is a better man than his patron. In short, matters are come to such an extremity that the squire has not said his prayers either in public or in private this half year; and that the parson threatens him, if he does not mend his manners, to pray for him in the face of the whole congregation.

Feuds of this nature, though too frequent in the country, are very fatal to the ordinary people, who are so used to be dazzled with riches that they pay as much deference to the understanding of a man of an estate as of a man of learning; and are very hardly brought to regard any truth, how important soever it may be, that is preached to them, when they know there are several men of five hundred a year who do not believe it.

A Modest Proposal
by JONATHAN SWIFT

For preventing the children of poor people from being a burthen to their parents or country, and for making them beneficial to the public.

It is a melancholy object to those, who walk through this great town,[1] or travel in the country, when they see the streets, the roads, and cabin-doors, crowded with beggars of the female sex, followed by three, four, or six children, *all in rags*, and importuning every passenger for an alms. These mothers instead of being able to work for their honest livelihood, are forced to employ all their time in strolling, to beg sustenance for their helpless infants, who, as they grow up, either turn thieves for want of work, or leave their dear Native Country to fight for the Pretender in Spain,[2] or sell themselves to the Barbadoes.

I think it is agreed by all parties, that this

---

[1] *this great town* Dublin. Swift wrote this ironic proposal to express his indignation at the way the Irish were treated by their English masters. He had written several previous treatises on the problem of poverty in Ireland to which no heed had been paid in England. The purpose of this treatise was to expose the English selfishness that excused itself by saying that the Irish were poor because they were lazy.

[2] *Pretender in Spain* James Stuart, son of the deposed King James II, who made several attempts to get the British throne.

prodigious number of children, in the arms, or on the backs, or at the heels of their mothers, and frequently of their fathers, is in the present deplorable state of the kingdom, a very great additional grievance; and therefore whoever could find out a fair, cheap and easy method of making these children sound useful members of the commonwealth would deserve so well of the public, as to have his statue set up for a preserver of the nation.

But my intention is very far from being confined to provide only for the children of professed beggars, it is of a much greater extent, and shall take in the whole number of infants at a certain age, who are born of parents in effect as little able to support them, as those who demand our charity in the streets.

As to my own part, having turned my thoughts, for many years, upon this important subject, and maturely weighed the several schemes of other projectors, I have always found them grossly mistaken in their computation. It is true a child, just dropped from its dam, may be supported by her milk for a solar year with little other nourishment, at most not above the value of two shillings, which the mother may certainly get, or the value in scraps, by her lawful occupation of begging, and it is exactly at one year old that I propose to provide for them, in such a manner, as, instead of being a charge upon their parents, or the parish, or wanting food and raiment for the rest of their lives, they shall, on the contrary, contribute to the feeding and partly to the clothing of many thousands.

There is likewise another great advantage in my scheme, that it will prevent those voluntary abortions, and the horrid practice of women murdering their bastard children, alas, too frequent among us, sacrificing the poor innocent babes, I doubt, more to avoid the expense, than the shame, which would move tears and pity in the most savage and inhuman breast.

The number of souls in this kingdom being usually reckoned one million and a half, of these I calculate there may be about two hundred thousand couple whose wives are breeders, from which number I subtract thirty thousand couples, who are able to maintain their own children, although I apprehend there cannot be so many under the present distresses of the kingdom, but this being granted, there will remain an hundred and seventy thousand breeders. I again subtract fifty thousand for those women who miscarry, or whose children die by accident, or disease within the year. There only remain an hundred and twenty thousand children of poor parents annually born: The question therefore is, how this number shall be reared, and provided for, which, as I have already said, under the present situation of affairs, is utterly impossible by all the methods hitherto proposed, for we can neither employ them in handicraft, or agriculture; we neither build houses, (I mean in the country) nor cultivate land: they can very seldom pick up a livelihood by stealing till they arrive at six years old, except where they are of towardly parts,[3] although, I confess they learn the rudiments much earlier, during which time, they can however be properly looked upon only as *probationers*, as I have been informed by a principal gentleman in the County of Cavan, who protested to me, that he never knew above one or two instances under the age of six, even in a part of the kingdom so renowned for the quickest proficiency in that art.

I am assured by our merchants, that a boy or a girl, before twelve years old, is no saleable commodity, and even when they come to this age, they will not yield above three pounds, or three pounds and a half-a-crown at most on the Exchange, which cannot turn to account either to the parents or the kingdom, the charge of nutriment and rags having been at least four times that value.

I shall now therefore humbly propose my own thoughts, which I hope will not be liable to the least objection.

I have been assured by a very knowing American[4] of my acquaintance in London, that a young healthy child well nursed is at a year old a most delicious, nourishing, and wholesome food, whether stewed, roasted, baked,

---

[3] *towardly parts* of unusual talents.

[4] *knowing American* the American Indian.

or boiled, and I make no doubt that it will equally serve in a fricassee, or a ragout.

I do therefore humbly offer it to public consideration, that of the hundred and twenty thousand children, already computed, twenty thousand may be reserved for breed, whereof only one fourth part to be males, which is more than we allow to sheep, black-cattle, or swine, and my reason is that these children are seldom the fruits of marriage, a circumstance not much regarded by our savages, therefore one male will be sufficient to serve four females. That the remaining hundred thousand may at a year old be offered in a sale to the persons of quality, and fortune, through the kingdom, always advising the mother to let them suck plentifully in the last month, so as to render them plump, and fat for a good table. A child will make two dishes at an entertainment for friends, and when the family dines alone, the fore or hind quarter will make a reasonable dish, and seasoned with a little pepper or salt will be very good boiled on the fourth day, especially in winter.

I have reckoned upon a medium,[5] that a child just born will weigh 12 pounds, and in a solar year if tolerably nursed increaseth to 28 pounds.

I grant this food will be somewhat dear, and therefore very proper for landlords, who, as they have already devoured most of the parents, seem to have the best title to the children.

Infants' flesh will be in season throughout the year, but more plentiful in March, and a little before and after, for we are told by a grave author, an eminent French physician,[6] that fish being a prolific diet, there are more children born in Roman Catholic countries about nine months after Lent, than at any other season; therefore reckoning a year after Lent, the markets will be more glutted than usual, because the number of Popish infants, is at least three to one in this kingdom, and therefore it will have one other collateral advantage by lessening the number of Papists among us.

---

[5] *upon a medium*   on an average.
[6] *French physician*   Rabelais.

I have already computed the charge of nursing a beggar's child (in which list I reckon all cottagers, labourers, and four-fifths of the farmers) to be about two shillings *per annum*, rags included, and I believe no gentleman would repine to give ten shillings for the carcass of a good fat child, which, as I have said will make four dishes of excellent nutritive meat, when he hath only some particular friend, or his own family to dine with him. Thus the Squire will learn to be a good landlord, and grow popular among his tenants, the mother will have eight shillings net profit, and be fit for work till she produces another child.

Those who are more thrifty (as I must confess the times require) may flay the carcass; the skin of which, artificially dressed, will make admirable gloves for ladies, and summer boots for fine gentlemen.

As to our City of Dublin, shambles may be appointed for this purpose, in the most convenient parts of it, and butchers we may be assured will not be wanting, although I rather recommend buying the children alive, and dressing them hot from the knife, as we do roasting pigs.

A very worthy person, a true lover of his country, and whose virtues I highly esteem, was lately pleased, in discoursing on this matter, to offer a refinement upon my scheme. He said, that many gentlemen of this kingdom having of late destroyed their deer, he conceived that the want of venison might be well supplied by the bodies of young lads and maidens, not exceeding fourteen years of age, nor under twelve, so great a number of both sexes in every country being now ready to starve for want of work and service: and these to be disposed of by their parents if alive, or otherwise by their nearest relations. But with due deference to so excellent a friend, and so deserving a patriot, I cannot be altogether in his sentiments; for as to the males, my American acquaintance assured me from frequent experience, that their flesh was generally tough and lean, like that of our schoolboys, by continual exercise, and their taste disagreeable, and to fatten them would not answer the charge. Then as to the females, it would, I think with humble submission, be a loss to the public, because they soon would become breeders themselves: And besides, it is not improbable that some scrupulous people might be apt to censure such a practice, (although indeed very unjustly) as a little bordering upon cruelty, which, I confess, hath always been with me the strongest objection against any project, however so well intended.

But in order to justify my friend, he confessed that this expedient was put into his head by the famous Psalmanazar,[7] a native of the island Formosa, who came from thence to London, above twenty years ago, and in conversation told my friend, that in his country when any young person happened to be put to death, the executioner sold the carcass to persons of quality, as a prime dainty, and that, in his time, the body of a plump girl of fifteen, who was crucified for an attempt to poison the emperor, was sold to his Imperial Majesty's Prime Minister of State, and other great Mandarins of the Court, in joints from the gibbet, at four hundred crowns. Neither indeed can I deny, that if the same use were made of several plump young girls in this town, who, without one single groat to their fortunes, cannot stir abroad without a chair,[8] and appear at the playhouse, and assemblies in foreign fineries, which they never will pay for, the kingdom would not be the worse.

Some persons of a desponding spirit are in great concern about that vast number of poor people, who are aged, diseased, or maimed, and I have been desired to employ my thoughts what course may be taken, to ease the nation of so grievous an encumbrance. But I am not in the least pain upon that matter, because it is very well known, that they are every day dying, and rotting, by cold, and famine, and filth, and vermin, as fast as can be reasonably expected. And as to the younger labourers they are now in almost as hopeful a condition. They cannot get work, and consequently pine away for want of nourishment, to a degree, that if at any time they are accidentally hired to common labour, they have not strength to perform it; and thus the country and themselves are happily delivered from the evils to come.

I have too long digressed, and therefore shall return to my subject. I think the advantages by the proposal which I have made are obvious and many, as well as of the highest importance.

For first, as I have already observed, it would greatly lessen the number of Papists, with whom we are yearly over-run, being the principal breeders of the nation, as well as our most dangerous enemies, and who stay at home on purpose with a design to deliver the kingdom to the Pretender, hoping to take their advantage by the absence of so many good Protestants,[9] who have chosen rather to leave their country, than stay at home, and pay tithes against their conscience, to an Episcopal curate.

Secondly, The poorer tenants will have something valuable of their own, which by law may be made liable to distress, and help to pay their landlord's rent, their corn and cattle being already seized, and *money a thing unknown*.

Thirdly, Whereas the maintenance of an hundred thousand children, from two years old, and upwards, cannot be computed at less than ten shillings a piece *per annum*, the nation's stock will be thereby increased fifty thousand pounds *per annum*, besides the profit of a new dish, introduced to the tables of all gentlemen of fortune in the kingdom, who have any refinement in taste, and the money will circulate among ourselves, the goods being entirely of our own growth and manufacture.

Fourthly, The constant breeders, besides the gain of eight shillings sterling *per annum*, by the sale of their children, will be rid of the charge of maintaining them after the first year.

Fifthly, This food would likewise bring great custom to taverns, where the vinters[10]

---

[7] *Psalmanazar* actually a Frenchman who published an imaginary *Description of Formosa*.
[8] *chair* a sedan chair.
[9] *Protestants* a jibe at the dissenters who refused to pay tithes for the support of an Anglican clergyman.
[10] *vintners* wine sellers or tavern keepers.

will certainly be so prudent as to procure the best receipts for dressing it to perfection, and consequently have their houses frequented by all the fine gentlemen, who justly value themselves upon their knowledge in good eating; and a skilful cook, who understands how to oblige his guests will contrive to make it as expensive as they please.

Sixthly, This would be a great inducement to marriage, which all wise nations have either encouraged by rewards, or enforced by laws and penalties. It would increase the care and tenderness of mothers toward their children, when they were sure of a settlement for life, to the poor babes, provided in some sort by the public to their annual profit instead of expense. We should see an honest emulation among the married women, which of them could bring the fattest child to the market; men would become as fond of their wives, during the time of their pregnancy, as they are now of their mares in foal, their cows in calf, or sows when they are ready to farrow, nor offer to beat or kick them (as it is too frequent a practice) for fear of a miscarriage.

Many other advantages might be enumerated: For instance, the addition of some thousand carcasses in our exportation of barrelled beef, the propagation of swine's flesh, and improvement in the art of making good bacon, so much wanted among us by the great destruction of pigs, too frequent at our tables, which are no way comparable in taste, or magnificence to a well-grown, fat yearling child, which roasted whole will make a considerable figure at a Lord Mayor's feast, or any other public entertainment. But this, and many others I omit being studious of brevity.

Supposing that one thousand families in this city, would be constant customers for infants' flesh, besides others who might have it at merry-meetings, particularly weddings and christenings, I compute that Dublin would take off annually about twenty thousand carcasses, and the rest of the kingdom (where probably they will be sold somewhat cheaper) the remaining eighty thousand.

I can think of no one objection, that will possibly be raised against this proposal, unless it should be urged that the number of people will be thereby much lessened in the kingdom. This I freely own, and was indeed one principal design in offering it to the world. I desire the reader will observe, that I calculate my remedy *for this one individual Kingdom of Ireland, and for no other that ever was, is, or, I think, ever can be upon earth.* Therefore let no man talk to me of other expedients:[11] *Of taxing our absentees at five shillings a pound: Of using neither clothes, nor household furniture, except what is of our own growth and manufacture: Of utterly rejecting the materials and instruments that promote foreign luxury: Of curing the expensiveness of pride, vanity, idleness, and gaming in our women: Of introducing a vein of parsimony, prudence and temperance: Of learning to love our Country, wherein we differ even from* LAPLANDERS, *and the inhabitants of* TOPINAMBOO:[12] *Of quitting our animosities and factions, nor act any longer like the Jews, who were murdering one another at the very moment their city was taken: Of being a little cautious not to sell our country and consciences for nothing: Of teaching landlords to have at least one degree of mercy toward their tenants. Lastly of putting a spirit of honesty, industry and skill into our shopkeepers, who, if a resolution could now be taken to buy our native goods, would immediately unite to cheat and exact upon us in the price, the measure, and the goodness, nor could ever yet be brought to make one fair proposal of just dealing, though often and earnestly invited to it.*

Therefore I repeat, let no man talk to me of these and the like expedients, till he hath at least some glimpse of hope that there will ever be some hearty and sincere attempt to put them in practice.

But as to myself, having been wearied out for many years with offering vain, idle, visionary thoughts, and at length utterly despairing

---

[11] *other expedients* many of these things Swift himself had advocated to no avail in previous pamphlets.
[12] *Topinamboo* a section of Brazil, supposed to be inhabited by savages.

of success, I fortunately fell upon this proposal, which as it is wholly new, so it hath something solid and real, of no expense and little trouble, full in our own power, and whereby we can incur no danger in *disobliging* ENGLAND. For this kind of commodity will not bear exportation, the flesh being of too tender a consistence, to admit a long continuance in salt, *although perhaps I could name a country, which would be glad to eat up our whole nation without it.*

After all I am not so violently bent upon my own opinion, as to reject any offer, proposed by wise men, which shall be found equally innocent, cheap, easy and effectual. But before something of that kind shall be advanced in contradiction to my scheme, and offering a better, I desire the author, or authors will be pleased maturely to consider two points. First, as things now stand, how they will be able to find food and raiment for an hundred thousand useless mouths and backs. And secondly, there being a round million of creatures in human figure, throughout this kingdom, whose whole subsistence put into a common stock, would leave them in debt two millions of pounds sterling adding those, who are beggars by profession, to the bulk of farmers, cottagers and labourers with their wives and children, who are beggars in effect. I desire those politicians, who dislike my overture,[13] and may perhaps be so bold to attempt an answer, that they will first ask the parents of these mortals, whether they would not at this day think it a great happiness to have been sold for food at a year old, in the manner I prescribe, and thereby have avoided such a perpetual scene of misfortunes, as they have since gone through, by the oppression of landlords, the impossibility of paying rent without money or trade, the want of common sustenance, with neither house nor clothes to cover them from the inclemencies of the weather, and the most inevitable prospect of entailing the like, or greater miseries upon their breed for ever.

I profess in the sincerity of my heart that I have not the least personal interest in endeavouring to promote this necessary work, having no other motive than the *public good of my country, by advancing our trade, providing for infants, relieving the poor, and giving some pleasure to the rich.* I have no children, by which I can propose to get a single penny; the youngest being nine years old, and my wife past child-bearing.

---

[13] *overture*   proposition or suggestion.

Poetry

The Jumblies

by EDWARD LEAR

I

They went to sea in a sieve, they did;
   In a sieve they went to sea:
In spite of all their friends could say,
   On a winter's morn, on a stormy day,
   In a sieve they went to sea.   5
And when the sieve turned round and round,
And every one cried, "You'll all be drowned!"
They called aloud, "Our sieve ain't big;
But we don't care a button, we don't care a fig:
   In a sieve we'll go to sea!"   10
     Far and few, far and few,
       Are the lands where the Jumblies live:

  Their heads are green, and their
   hands are blue;
   And they went to sea in a sieve.

II

They sailed away in a sieve, they did,
 In a sieve they sailed so fast,
With only a beautiful pea-green veil
Tied with a ribbon, by way of a sail,
 To a small tobacco-pipe mast.
And every one said who saw them go,
"Oh! won't they be soon upset, you know?
For the sky is dark, and the voyage is long;
And, happen what may, it's extremely wrong
 In a sieve to sail so fast."
  Far and few, far and few,
   Are the lands where the Jumblies live:
   Their heads are green, and their hands are blue;
   And they went to sea in a sieve.

III

The water it soon came in, it did;
 The water it soon came in;
So, to keep them dry, they wrapped their feet
In a pinky paper all folded neat;
 And they fastened it down with a pin.
And they passed the night in a crockery-jar;
And each of them said, "How wise we are!
Though the sky be dark, and the voyage be long,
Yet we never can think we were rash or wrong,
 While round in our sieve we spin."
  Far and few, far and few,
   Are the lands where the Jumblies live:
   Their heads are green, and their hands are blue;
   And they went to sea in a sieve.

IV

And all night long they sailed away;
 And when the sun went down,
They whistled and warbled a moony song
To the echoing sound of a coppery gong,
 In the shade of the mountains brown.
"O Timballoo! How happy we are
When we live in a sieve and a crockery-jar!
And all night long, in the moonlight pale,
We sail away with a pea-green sail
 In the shade of the mountains brown."
  Far and few, far and few,
   Are the lands where the Jumblies live:
   Their heads are green, and their hands are blue;
   And they went to sea in a sieve.

V

They sailed to the Western Sea, they did,
 To a land all covered with trees:
And they bought an owl, and a useful cart,
And a pound of rice, and a cranberry-tart,
 And a hive of silvery bees;
And they bought a pig and some green jackdaws,
And a lovely monkey with lollipop paws,
And forty bottles of ring-bo-ree,
 And no end of Stilton cheese.
  Far and few, far and few,
   Are the lands where the Jumblies live:
   Their heads are green, and their hands are blue;
   And they went to sea in a sieve.

VI

And in twenty years they all came back,—
 In twenty years or more;
And every one said, "How tall they've grown!
For they've been to the Lakes, and the Torrible Zone,
 And the hills of the Chankly Bore."
And they drank their health, and gave them a feast
Of dumplings made of beautiful yeast;
And every said, "If we only live,
We, too, will go to sea in a sieve,
 To the hills of the Chankly Bore."

Far and few, far and few, 80
   Are the lands where the Jumblies live:
Their heads are green, and their hands are blue;
   And they went to sea in a sieve.

Kind of an Ode to Duty*
by OGDEN NASH

O Duty,
Why hast thou not the visage of a sweetie or a cutie?
Why displayest thou the countenance of the kind of conscientious organizing spinster
That the minute you see her you are aginster?
Why glitter thy spectacles so ominously? 5
Why art thou clad so abominously?
Why art thou so different from Venus
And why do thou and I have so few interests mutually in common between us?
Why art thou fifty per cent. martyr
And fifty-one per cent. Tartar? 10
Why is it thy unfortunate wont
To try to attract people by calling on them either to leave undone the deeds they like, or to do the deeds they don't?
Why art thou so like an April post mortem
Or something that died in the ortumn?
Above all, why dost thou continue to hound me? 15
Why art thou always albatrossly hanging around me?
Thou so ubiquitous,
And I so iniquitous.
I seem to be the one person in the world thou art perpetually preaching at who or to who;
Whatever looks like fun, there art thou standing between me and it, calling yoo-hoo. 20
O Duty, Duty!
How noble a man should I be hadst thou the visage of a sweetie or a cutie!
Wert thou but houri instead of hag
Then would my halo indeed be in the bag!
But as it is thou art so much forbiddinger than a Wodehouse hero's forbiddingest aunt 25
That in the words of the poet, When Duty whispers low, Thou must, this erstwhile youth replies, I just can't.

*From *I'm a Stranger Here Myself*, by Ogden Nash. Copyright 1938, by Ogden Nash. By permission of Little, Brown & Co.

Two Butterflies Went Out at Noon*
by EMILY DICKINSON

Two butterflies went out at noon
And waltzed upon a farm,
And then espied circumference
And caught a ride with him;
Then lost themselves and found themselves 5
In eddies of the sun,
Till rapture missed her footing
And both were wrecked in noon.

To all surviving butterflies
Be this biography, 10
Example, and monition
To entomology.

* Reprinted by permission of the publishers and the Trustees of Amherst College from Thomas H. Johnson, Editor, *The Poems of Emily Dickinson*, Cambridge, Mass.: The Belknap Press of Harvard University Press. Copyright, 1951, 1955, by The President and Fellows of Harvard College.

Little Trotty Wagtail
by JOHN CLARE

Little trotty wagtail, he went in the rain,
And tittering, tottering sideways he ne'er got straight again,
He stooped to get a worm, and looked up to get a fly,
And then he flew away ere his feathers they were dry.
Little trotty wagtail, he waddled in the mud,   5
And left his little footmarks, trample where he would.
He waddled in the water-pudge, and waggle went his tail,
And chirrupt up his wings to dry upon the garden rail.
Little trotty wagtail, you nimble all about,
And in the dimpling water-pudge you waddle in and out;   10
Your home is nigh at hand, and in the warm pigsty,
So, little Master Wagtail, I'll bid you a good-bye.

The Singletrack Mind*
by ARTHUR GUITERMAN

Upon the reef that guards the palm-fringed sands
The heron stands.
Around him sweeps the azure Caribbean
Where cities Atlantean
Lie buried; through that strait, to lasting fame,   5
Columbus came,
And thousands on those shores where lizards glide
Have fought and died.
But nothing for such great and vast affairs
The heron cares.   10
Oblivious alike of Ocean's mystery
And Man's dark history,
He scans the waves that round him seethe,—and swish!——
He gets his fish!

*From *Lyric Laughter*, by Arthur Guiterman. Copyright 1939 by E. P. Dutton & Co., Inc.; renewal 1967 by Vida Lindo Guiterman. Reprinted by permission of Vida Lindo Guiterman.

Strictly Germ-proof*
by ARTHUR GUITERMAN

The Antiseptic Baby and the Prophylactic Pup
Were playing in the garden when the Bunny gamboled up;
They looked upon the Creature with a loathing undisguised;—
It wasn't Disinfected and it wasn't Sterilized.
They said it was a Microbe and a Hotbed of Disease;   5
They steamed it in a vapor of a thousand-odd degrees;

*From *Lyric Laughter*, by Arthur Guiterman. Copyright 1939 by E. P. Dutton & Co., Inc.; renewal 1967 by Vida Lindo Guiterman. Reprinted by permission of Vida Lindo Guiterman.

They froze it in a freezer that was cold as Banished Hope
And washed it in permanganate with carbolated soap.

In sulphureted hydrogen they steeped its wiggly ears,
They trimmed its frisky whiskers with a pair of hard-boiled shears;
They donned their rubber mittens and they took it by the hand

And 'lected it a member of the Fumigated Band.

There's not a Micrococcus in the garden where they play,
They bathe in pure iodoform a dozen times a day,
And each imbibes his rations from a Hygienic Cup,—
The Bunny and the Baby and the Prophylactic Pup.

Departmental*
by ROBERT FROST

An ant on the tablecloth
Ran into a dormant moth
Of many times his size.
He showed not the least surprise.
His business wasn't with such.
He gave it scarcely a touch,
And was off on his duty run.
Yet if he encountered one
Of the hive's enquiry squad
Whose work is to find out God
And the nature of time and space,
He would put him onto the case.
Ants are a curious race;
One crossing with hurried tread
The body of one of their dead
Isn't given a moment's arrest—
Seems not even impressed.
But he no doubt reports to any
With whom he crosses antennae,
And they no doubt report
To the higher up at court.
Then word goes forth in Formic:
'Death's come to Jerry McCormic,
Our selfless forager Jerry.
Will the special Janizary
Whose office it is to bury
The dead of the commissary
Go bring him home to his people.
Lay him in state on a sepal.
Wrap him for shroud in a petal.
Embalm him with ichor of nettle.
This is the word of your Queen.'
And presently on the scene
Appears a solemn mortician;
And taking formal position
With feelers calmly atwiddle,
Seizes the dead by the middle,
And heaving him high in air,
Carries him out of there.
No one stands round to stare.
It is nobody else's affair.
It couldn't be called ungentle.
But how thoroughly departmental.

* From *Complete Poems of Robert Frost*. Copyright 1916, 1923, 1930, 1939 by Holt, Rinehart and Winston, Inc. Copyright 1936, 1942, 1944, 1951, © 1958 by Robert Frost. Copyright © 1964, 1967 by Lesley Frost Ballantine. Reprinted by permission of Holt, Rinehart and Winston, Inc.

Portraits from the Prologue to the Canterbury Tales*

by GEOFFREY CHAUCER

PORTRAIT OF THE PRIORESS

Ther was also a Nonne, a Prioresse,
That of hir smiling was ful simple and coy.
Hir gretteste ooth was but by sainte Loy!
And she was cleped Madame Eglantine.
Ful wel she soong the service divine, 5
Entuned in hir nose ful semely;
And Frenssh she spake ful faire and fetisly,
After the scole of Stratford at the Bowe—
For Frenssh of Paris was to hire unknowe.
At mete wel ytaught was she withalle: 10
She leet no morsel from hir lippes falle,
Ne wette hir fingres in hir sauce deepe;
Wel coude she carye a morsel, and wel keepe
That no drope ne fille upon hir brest.
In curteisye was set ful muchel hir lest. 15
Hir over-lippe wiped she so clene
That in hir coppe ther was no ferthing seene
Of grece, whan she dronken hadde hir draughte;
Ful semely after hir mete she raughte.
And sikerly she was a greet disport, 20
And ful plesant, and amiable of port,
And pained hire to countrefete cheere
Of court, and to been estatlich of manere,
And to been holden digne of reverence.
But, for to speken of hir conscience, 25
She was so charitable and so pitous
She wolde weepe if that she saw a mous
Caught in a trappe, if it were deed or bledde.
Of smale houndes hadde she that she fedde

There was also a nun, a prioress, whose smiles were very innocent and demure. Her strongest oath was no more than "by St. Elegius" [this handsome and charming saint was a goldsmith, a courtier, and finally a bishop]. Her name was My Lady Eglantine [Sweetbriar]. She sang the divine office very well, chanting it in a very proper nasal tone. And she spoke very beautiful and elegant French—with the accent of Stratford at the Bowe—since Parisian French was unknown to her. At meals, too, she was very well-bred: she never allowed a morsel to fall from her lips nor did she wet her fingers by dipping them deep in her sauce. She could handle a bit of food very well and took great care that no drop should fall upon her breast. She was very much concerned about good manners. She wiped her upper lip so clean that not a speck of grease could be seen on her cup after she had taken a drink. She reached for her food with great propriety, and certainly she was quite entertaining and very pleasant and amiable in her behavior and tried painstakingly to imitate the manners of the court and to have a dignified bearing and to be considered worthy of respect. But, to speak of her conscience [this word may also mean "sensibility"] she was so charitable and pious ["pitous" may also mean "tender-hearted"] that she would weep if she saw a mouse caught in a trap, if it were dead or bleeding. She had some small dogs that she fed with roasted meat, or milk and fine bread. But she wept bitterly if one of them died or if someone whipped it smartly with a switch. She was all sensibility and tender-heartedness. Her wimple was pleated very properly. Her nose was well-proportioned, her eyes as gray as glass [that is, they were sparkling and "smoky" green or blue, like some Venetian glass], her mouth

---

* From *Chaucer's Poetry: An Anthology for the Modern Reader*, selected and edited by E. T. Donaldson. Copyright © 1958 The Ronald Press Company, New York.

With rosted flessh, or milk and wastel-
 breed;
But sore wepte she if oon of hem were
 deed,
Or if men smoot it with a yerde smerte;
And al was conscience and tendre herte.
Ful semely hir wimpel pinched was,
Hir nose tretis, hir yën greye as glas,
Hir mouthful smal, and thereto softe and
 reed—
But sikerly she hadde a fair forheed:
It was almost a spanne brood, I trowe,
For hardily, she was nat undergrowe.
Ful fetis was hir cloke, as I was war;
Of smal coral aboute hir arm she bar
A paire of bedes, gauded al with greene,
And theron heeng a brooch of gold ful
 sheene,
On which ther was first writen a crowned
 A,
And after, *Amor vincit omnia*.

quite small, and also soft and red. But certainly she had a *beautiful* forehead: it was almost a handslength broad, I believe, for assuredly she was not undersized. Her cloak was very elegant, as it seemed to me; around her arm she carried a rosary with small coral beads, decorated with green beads [for the "Our Father's" between the decades of "Hail Mary's"]; and on it hung a brooch made of very bright gold, on which was written first an "A" ornamented with a crown and after it was written *Amor vincit omnia* [Love conquers all things].

PORTRAIT OF THE MONK

A Monk ther was, a fair for the
 maistrye,
An outridere that loved venerye,
A manly man, to been an abbot able.
Ful many a daintee hors hadde he in
 stable,
And when he rood, men mighte his bridel
 heere
Ginglen in a whistling wind as clere
And eek as loude as dooth the chapel belle
Ther as this lord was kepere of the celle.
The rule of Saint Maure or of Saint
 Beneit,
By cause that it was old and somdeel
 strait—
This ilke Monk leet olde thinges pace,
And heeld after the newe world the space.
He yaf nought of that text a pulled hen
That saith that hunteres been nought
 holy men,
Ne that a monk, whan he is recchelees,
Is likned til a fissh that is waterlees—
This is to sayn, a monk out of his cloistre;
But thilke text heeld he nat worth an
 oystre.
And I saide his opinion was good:

A monk there was, an extremely fine one, an "out-rider" [a monk who rides out to supervise outlying property of the monastery] who loved hunting, a manly man, competent to be an abbot. Many an excellent horse he had in the stable, and when he rode one could hear his bridle jingle in the whistling wind as clearly and also as loudly as does the bell of the chapel where this lord was Keeper of the Cell [Head of a subordinate monastery]. The monastic rule of St. Maurus or of St. Benedict, because it was old and somewhat strict—this same monk let old things pass away and set his course according to the modern world. He didn't give a plucked hen for that text which says that hunters are not holy men or for the one which says that a monk, when he is neglectful of his duty, is comparable to a fish out of water—that is to say, a monk out of his cloister—but that text he considered not worth an oyster. And I said that his opinion was a good one: why should he study, and drive himself crazy by always poring over a book in a cloister, or work with his hands and labor as [St.] Augustine commands? How shall the world be served? Let

What sholde he studye and make him-
    selven wood
Upon a book in cloistre alway to poure,   20
Or swinke with his handes and laboure,
As Austin bit? How shal the world be
    served?
Lat Austin have his swink to him
    reserved!
Therfore he was a prikasour aright.   25
Grehoundes he hadde as swift as fowl in
    flight.
Of priking and of hunting for the hare
Was al his lust, for no cost wolde he
    spare.
I sawgh his sleeves purfiled at the hand
With gris, and that the fineste of a land;   30
And for to festne his hood under his chin
He hadde of gold wrought a ful curious
    pin:
A love-knotte in the grettere ende ther
    was.
His heed was balled, that shoon as any
    glas,
And eek his face, as he hadde been
    anoint:
He was a lord ful fat and in good point;   35
His yën steepe, and rolling in his heed,
That stemed as a furnais of a leed,
His bootes souple, his hors in greet estat—
Now certainly he was a fair prelat.   40
He was nat pale as a forpined gost:
A fat swan loved he best of any rost.
His palfrey was as brown as is a berye.

PORTRAIT OF THE FRIAR

    A Frere ther was, a wantoune and a
        merye,
A limitour, a ful solempne man.
In alle the ordres foure is noon that can
So muche of daliaunce and fair langage:
He hadde maad ful many a mariage   5
Of yonge wommen at his owene cost;
Unto his ordre he was a noble post.
Ful wel biloved and familier was he
With frankelains over al in his contree,
And with worthy wommen of the town—   10
For he hadde power of confessioun
As saide himself, more than a curat,
For of his ordre he was licenciat.

Augustine have his work reserved to himself [bishops (like St. Augustine) are said to "reserve" to themselves certain decisions or cases for absolution]! Hence he was a hard-riding hunter *par excellence*. He had greyhounds as swift as a bird in flight. His heart was set on tracking and hunting the hare; no matter how expensive it was he would not give it up. I saw his sleeves lined at the wrist with gray fur, and that the finest in the land. To fasten his hood under his chin he had a very well-wrought pin, made of gold. At the larger end of it there was a love-knot [either a bow-knot or two loops intertwined]. His head was bald and shone like glass; so did his face, as if it had been anointed. He was a lord, quite plump with *embonpoint*. His eyes, prominent and rolling in his head, gleamed like a furnace with a pot in it. His boots were supple; his horse [or horses] in excellent condition—now certainly he was a fine prelate. He was not pale like a withered ghost. He loved a fat swan better than any other roast. His palfrey was as brown as a berry.

A friar there was, a gay ["wantoun" can also mean "wanton, licentious"] and merry one, a limiter [a friar who paid a fee, the "ferme," for the exclusive right to beg in a certain area], a very festive man. In all the four orders [Franciscans, Dominicans, Carmelites, and Augustinians] there is no one so well versed in sweet talk and flowery language. He had arranged for the marriage of very many young women at his own expense. He was a noble pillar of his order. He was well-beloved and on familiar terms with franklins [wealthy landowners] everywhere in his district and with respectable townswomen—for he had larger

Ful swetely herde he confessioun,
And plesant was his absolucioun.
He was an esy man to yive penaunce
Ther as he wiste to have a good pitaunce;
For unto a poore ordre for to yive
Is signe that man is wel yshrive;
For if he yaf, he dorste make avaunt
He wiste that a man was repentaunt;
For many a man so hard is of his herte
He may nat weepe though him sore smerte:
Therfore, in stede of weeping and prayeres,
Men mote yive silver to the poore freres.
    His tipet was ay farsed ful of knives
And pinnes, for to yiven faire wives;
And certainly he hadde a merry note;
Wel coude he singe and playen on a rote;
Of yeddinges he bar outrely the pris.
His nekke whit was as the flowr-de-lis;
Therto he strong was as a champioun.
He knew the tavernes wel in every town,
And every hostiler and tappestere,
Bet than a lazar or a beggestere.
For unto swich a worthy man as he
Accorded nat, as by his facultee,
To have with sike lazars acquaintance:
It is nat honeste, it may nought avaunce,
For to delen with no switch poraile,
But al with riche, and selleres of vitaile;
And over al ther as profit sholde arise,
Curteis he was, and lowely of servise.
Ther was no man nowher so vertuous:
He was the beste beggere in his hous.
And yaf a certain ferme for the graunt:
Noon of his brethren cam ther in his haunt.
For though a widwe hadde nought a sho,
So plesant was his *In principio*
Yit wolde he have a ferthing er he wente;
His purchas was wel bettre than his rente.
And rage he coude as it were right a whelpe;
In love-dayes ther coude he muchel helpe,
For ther he was nat like a cloisterer,
With a thredbare cope, as is a poore scoler,
But he was lik a maister or a pope.
Of double worstede was his semicope,
And rounded as a belle out of the presse.

15
20
25
30
35
40
45
50
55

powers of confession, as he himself said, than a parish priest, since he was licensed by his order [to absolve more serious sins]. He heard confession very sweetly, and his absolution was pleasant. He was a lenient man in giving penance, whenever he knew he would receive a good donation; for to give to a poor order is a sign that a person is well absolved. For if he gave, he [the friar] dared to assert that he knew the man was penitent. For many a man has such a hard heart that he cannot weep even though he is sorely grieved. Therefore, instead of weeping and saying prayers, one may give silver to the poor friars. His tippet [a long scarf fastened to his hood or sleeve] was always stuffed full of knives and pins to give to pretty wives. And certainly he sang a merry tune. Well could he sing and play on a fiddle. He absolutely took the prize for ballads. His neck was as white as a lily. Moreover, he was as strong as a champion. He knew the taverns well in every town, and every innkeeper and bar-maid, better than a leper or a beggar woman. For it was not fitting because of his profession, that such a worthy man as he should have any acquaintance with sick lepers. It is not respectable, it does not help one get ahead, to have any dealings with such paupers, but rather exclusively with rich persons and wholesale grocers. And wherever there was any profit to be made, he was courteous and humbly helpful. Nowhere was there such an efficient ["vertuous" may also have its modern meaning] man: he was the best beggar in his monastery. He paid a fixed fee for the privilege of begging; none of his brethren came there into his territory. For even though a widow didn't even have a shoe, his *In principio* ["In the beginning," Genesis 1:1 and John 1:1, also the opening words of the last gospel in the Mass, sung by the friar as he goes from house to house as a cry announcing his arrival and a superstitious blessing or greeting to his clientele] was so pleasant that he would still get a farthing [about a nickel or perhaps a dime] before he left. His [illegal] gains were more than his regular income [from begging]. He could flirt as wantonly as if he were a puppy. On lovedays [days appointed for settling disputes out of court] he was a great help,

Somwhat he lipsed for his wantounesse
To make his Englissh sweete upon his tonge;
And in his harping, whan that he hadde songe,
His yën twinkled in his heed aright
As doon the sterres in the frosty night.
This worthy limitour was cleped Huberd.

for at these meetings he was not like a cloistered monk with a threadbare cloak such as a poor student would have, but rather like a distinguished professor or a pope. His half-length cape was of double worsted and rounded like a bell fresh from the mold. In his affectation he lisped somewhat to make his English sweet on his tongue. When he played the harp after he had sung, his eyes twinkled away in his head just the way the stars do on a frosty night. The name of this worthy limiter was Hubert.

PORTRAIT OF THE CLERK

A Clerk ther was of Oxenforde also
That unto logik hadde longe ygo.
As lene was his hors as is a rake,
And he was nought right fat, I undertake,
But looked holwe, and therto sobrely.
Ful thredbare was his overeste courtepy
For he hadde geten him yit no benefice,
Ne was so worldly for to have office.
For him was levere have at his beddes heed
Twenty bookes, clad in blak or reed,
Of Aristotle and his philosophye,
Than robes riche, or fithele, or gay sautrye.
But al be that he was a philosophre
Yit hadde he but litel gold in cofre;
But al that he mighte of his freendes hente,
On bookes and on lerning he it spente,
And bisily gan for the soules praye
Of hem that yaf him wherwith to scoleye.
Of studye took he most cure and most heede.
Nought oo word spak he more than was neede,
And that was said in forme and reverence,
And short and quik, and ful of heigh sentence:
Souning in moral vertu was his speeche,
And gladly wolde he lerne, and gladly teche.

There was also a seminarian from Oxford [the "clerk" or clerical student has received minor, and possibly major, orders] who had long since proceeded to logic. [To begin studying logic would be roughly equivalent to entering college or a major seminary nowadays. The clerk is probably doing what we would call post-graduate work for a master's degree, perhaps in philosophy.] His horse was as lean as a rake and *he* [the clerk] was not very fat, I assure you, but had a hollow and also sober gaze. His outer jacket was quite threadbare, for he had not yet obtained a benefice [an ecclesiastical assignment with a fixed income] nor was he worldly enough to accept secular employment [for example, as a secretary or administrative assistant to the king or a powerful noble]. He would rather have at the head of his bed, twenty books of Aristotle's philosophy, bound in black or red, than rich robes or a fiddle or a gay harp. [Twenty handwritten books would have cost the equivalent of several thousands of dollars.] Although he was a philosopher [this word could also mean "alchemist"; one of the primary aims of the alchemists was to change base metals into gold] he had little enough gold in his chest. But all the money he could get from his friends he spent on books and learning, and he assiduously undertook to pray for the souls of those who gave [perhaps "bequeathed"] him the wherewithal to study. He devoted more care and attention to his studies than to anything else. He spoke not one word more than was necessary, and what he did say was spoken with decorum and due respect, brief and to the point and full of elevated thought. He tended to speak mostly about moral excellence; and gladly would he learn and gladly teach.

PORTRAIT OF THE PARSON

A good man was ther of religioun
And was a poore Person of a town,
But riche he was of holy thought and werk.
He was also a lerned man, a clerk,
That Cristes gospel trewely wolde preche; 5
His parisshens devoutly wolde he teche.
Benigne he was, and wonder diligent,
And in adversitee ful pacient,
And switch he was preved ofte sithes.
Ful loth were him to cursen for his tithes, 10
But rather wolde he yiven, out of doute,
Unto his poore parisshens aboute
Of his offring and eek of his substaunce:
He coude in litel thing have suffisaunce.
Wid was his parissh, and houses fer asonder,
But he ne lafte nought for rain ne thonder, 15
In siknesse nor in meschief, to visite
The ferreste in his parrissh, muche and lite,
Upon his feet, and in his hand a staf.
This noble ensample to his sheep he yaf 20
That first he wroughte, and afterward he taughte.
Out of the Gospel he tho wordes caughte,
And this figure he added eek therto:
That if gold ruste, what shal iren do?
For if a preest be foul, on whom we truste,
No wonder is a lewed man to ruste. 25
And shame it is, if a preest take keep,
A shiten shepherde and a clene sheep.
Wel oughte a preest ensample for to yive
By his clennesse how that his sheep sholde live. 30
He sette nought his benefice to hire
And leet his sheep encombred in the mire
And ran to London, unto Sainte Poules,
To seeken him a chaunterye for soules,

There was a good religious man: he was a poor parson in a village, but he was rich in holy thought and deeds. He was also a learned man, a scholar, who would preach Christ's gospel truly. He would teach his parishioners devoutly. He was kind and wonderfully diligent, and very patient in adversity—he was proved to be such many times. He would be most reluctant to invoke excommunication in order to collect his tithes; rather he would give, no doubt, some of his offerings and also of his property to his poor parishioners round about. He could be satisfied with very little. His parish was large and the houses far apart, but he never ceased, in spite of rain and thunder, in sickness or misfortune, to visit the most distant persons in his parish, both great persons and ordinary folk, traveling by foot and with a staff in his hand. This noble example he gave to his sheep; first he practised and then he preached. He took those words out of the gospel [Matthew, 5:19] and he also added this comparison to them: if gold should rust, what must iron do? For if a priest, whom we trust, should be degenerate, there is no wonder that an uneducated man should rust. And shameful it is, if a priest would pay attention to it, [that there should be] a dirty shepherd and clean sheep. Certainly a priest ought, by the purity of his life, to give an example of how his sheep should live. He did not farm out his benefice and leave his sheep encumbered in the mud; nor did he run to London, to St. Paul's [Cathedral] to find himself a steady income from chanting masses for the souls [of certain dead persons] or to be employed [as a chaplain] by a guild. Rather he remained at home and took care of his sheepfold, so that the wolf could not bring it to ruin. He was a shepherd and not a mercenary. And even though he was holy and virtuous, he was not scornful of sinful men, nor was he standoffish or haughty in his

Or with a bretherhede to been withholde, 35
But dwelte at hoom and kepte wel his folde,
So that the wolf ne made it nought miscarye:
He was a shepherde and nought a mercenarye.
And though he holy were and vertuous,
He was to sinful men nought despitous, 40
Ne of his speech daungerous ne digne,
But in his teching discreet and benigne,
To drawen folk to hevene by fairnesse
By good ensample—this was his bisinesse.
But it were any persone obstinat, 45
What so he were, of heigh or lowe estat,
Him wolde he snibben sharply for the nones:
A bettre preest I trowe ther nowher noon is.
He waited after no pompe and reverence,
Ne marked him a spiced conscience, 50
But Cristes lore and his Apostles twelve
He taughte, but first he folwed it himselve.

speech; rather in his teaching he was tactful and kind. To draw people to heaven by beauty, by good example—to this he devoted himself eagerly. Unless some person were obstinate—in that case he would scold him sharply, no matter who he might be, of high or low rank. A better priest, I think, is nowhere to be found. He expected no ceremony and reverence, nor did he cultivate an overfastidious conscience. Rather he taught the message of Christ and His twelve apostles, but first he followed it himself.

PORTRAIT OF THE PARDONER

With him ther rood a gentil Pardoner
Of Rouncival, his freend and his compeer,
That straight was comen fro the Court of Rome.
Ful loude he soong, "Com hider, love, to me."
This Somnour bar to him a stif burdoun: 5
Was nevere trompe of half so greet a soun.
This Pardoner hadde heer as yelow as wex,
But smoothe it heeng as dooth a strike of flex;
By ounces heenge his lokkes that he hadde,
And therwith he his shuldres overspradde, 10
But thinne it lay, by colpons, oon by oon;
But hood for jolitee wered he noon,
For it was trussed up in his walet:
Him thoughte he rood al of the newe jet.
Dischevelee save his cappe he rood al bare. 15
Swiche glaring yën hadde he as an hare.

With him, [the Summoner, one of the pilgrims, a vicious bailiff of a diocesan court] there rode a noble Pardoner of Rouncivalle, his friend and comrade. [Properly speaking a pardoner was the traveling agent of a church, religious house, or charitable institution which had received from the Pope or a member of the hierarchy the right to grant an indulgence to those who made contributions and confessed and repented their sins. Since many pardoners were as corrupt as Chaucer's, the word came to mean "seller of indulgences." The Pardoner here is an agent of the Hospital of Blessed Mary of Rouncivalle, a London branch of a famous hospital at Roncesvalles in Spain.] He sang quite loudly "Come hither, love, to me." The Summoner sang a strong bass part along with him; no trumpet was ever half so loud. This Pardoner had hair as yellow as wax; but it hung as smooth as a hank of flax. What locks he had hung down in little bits, and he spread it over his shoulders.

A vernicle hadde he sowed upon his
  cappe,
His walet biforn him in his lappe,
Bretful of pardon, comen from Rome al
  hoot.
A vois he hadde as smal as hath a goot; 20
No beerd hadde he, ne nevere sholde
  have;
As smoothe it was as it were late yshave:
I trowe he were a gelding or a mare.
But of his craft, fro Berwik into Ware,
Ne was ther switch another pardoner; 25
For in his male he hadde a pilwe-beer
Which that he saide was Oure Lady veil;
He saide he hadde a gobet of the sail
That Sainte Peter hadde whan that he
  wente
Upon the see, til Jesu Crist him hente. 30
He hadde a crois of laton, ful of stones,
And in a glas he hadde pigges bones,
But with thise relikes whan that he foond
A poore person dwelling upon lond,
Upon a day he gat him more moneye 35
Than that the person gat in monthes
  twaye;
And thus with feined flaterye and japes
He made the person and the peple his
  apes.
But trewely to tellen at the laste,
He was in chirche a noble ecclesiaste; 40
Wel coude he rede a lesson and a storye,
But alderbest he soong an offertorye,
For wel he wiste whan that song was
  songe,
He moste preche and wel affile his tonge
To winne silver, as he ful wel coude— 45
Therfore he soong the merierly and loude.

But it lay there thin, in fine strands, one by one. In order to be nonchalant he wore no hood, for it was packed up in his knapsack. It seemed to him he was riding in the latest fashion. He rode with his hair loose and uncovered except for his cap. He had glaring eyes like a hare. He had a Veronica [a small replica of the cloth with which Veronica wiped Christ's face and on which His portrait was impressed] sewn on his cap. In front of him on his lap [he had] his knapsack, brimful of indulgences that had come all steaming fresh from Rome. His voice was as thin as a goat's. He had no beard, nor would he ever have one. His face was as smooth as if it were freshly shaven. I believe he was a gelding or a mare. But for cunning there was not another pardoner like him from Berwick to Ware [that is, in all England]. For in his bag he had a pillowcase which he said was Our Lady's veil. He said he had a piece of the sail that St. Peter had when he sailed on the sea, before Christ took him. He had a cross of cheap brass, with [imitation] jewels set all over it, and in a glass [reliquary] he had pig's bones. Still, when he found a poor parson living in the country, he got more money with these relics than the parson got in two month's time. And so, with his false flattery and tricks, he played the parson and the people for suckers.

But finally to admit the truth about him, he was a noble ecclesiastic in church. He could read a *lectio* and an *historia* [selections from the epistles and gospels read at Mass just before offertory] well. But he sang an offertory [of the mass] best of all, for he was well aware that after that song was sung he would have to preach and sharpen up his tongue to gain silver—as he was able to do very well. Therefore he sang more merrily and loudly.

The Nun's Priest's Tale*
by GEOFFREY CHAUCER

Once, long ago, there dwelt a poor old widow
In a small cottage by a little meadow
Beside a grove and standing in a dale.
This widow-woman of whom I tell my tale
Since the sad day when last she was a wife 5
Had led a very patient, simple life.
Little she had in capital or rent,
But still by making do with what God sent
She kept herself and her two daughters going.
Three hefty sows—no more—were all her showing, 10
Three cows as well; there was a sheep called Molly.
    Sooty her hall, her kitchen melancholy,
And there she ate full many a slender meal;
There was no *sauce piquante* to spice her veal,
No dainty morsel ever passed her throat, 15
According to her cloth she cut her coat.
Repletion never left her in disquiet
And all her physic was a temperate diet,
Hard work for exercise and heart's content.
And rich man's gout did nothing to prevent 20
Her dancing, apoplexy struck her not;
She drank no wine, nor white nor red had got.
Her board was mostly served with white and black,
Milk and brown bread, in which she found no lack;
Broiled bacon or an egg or two were common, 25
She was in fact a sort of dairy-woman.

She had a yard that was enclosed about
By a stockade and a dry ditch without,
In which she kept a cock called Chanticleer.
In all the land for crowing he'd no peer; 30
His voice was jollier than the organ blowing
In church on Sundays, he was great at crowing.
Far, far more regular than any clock
Or abbey bell the crowing of this cock.
The equinoctial wheel and its position 35
At each ascent he knew by intuition;
At every hour—fifteen degrees of movement—
He crowed so well there could be no improvement.
His comb was redder than fine coral, tall
And battlemented like a castle wall, 40
His bill was black and shone as bright as jet,
Like azure were his leg and they were set
On azure toes with nails of lily white,
Like burnished gold his feathers, flaming bright.
    This gentlecock was master in some measure 45
Of seven hens, all there to do his pleasure.
They were his sisters and his paramours,
Colored like him in all particulars;
She with the loveliest dyes upon her throat
Was known as gracious Lady Pertelote. 50
Courteous she was, discreet and debonair,
Companionable too, and took such care
In her deportment, since she was seven days old
She held the heart of Chanticleer controlled,
Locked up securely in her every limb; 55
O such a happiness his love to him!
And such a joy it was to hear them sing,
As when the glorious sun began to spring,
In sweet accord *My Love is far from land*

---

*From *The Canterbury Tales*, translated by Nevill Coghill. Reprinted by permission of Penguin Books Ltd.

—For in those far off days I understand
All birds and animals could speak and sing.
    Now it befell, as dawn began to spring,
When Chanticleer and Pertelote and all
His wives were perched in this poor widow's hall
(Fair Pertelote was next him on the perch), 65
This Chanticleer began to groan and lurch
Like someone sorely troubled by a dream,
And Pertelote who heard him roar and scream
Was quite aghast and said, "O dearest heart,
What's ailing you? Why do you groan and start? 70
Fie, what a sleeper! What a noise to make."
"Madam," he said, "I beg you not to take
Offense, but by the Lord I had a dream
So terrible just now I had to scream;
I still can feel my heart racing from fear. 75
God turn my dream to good and guard all here,
And keep my body out of durance vile!
I dreamt that roaming up and down a while
Within our yard I saw a kind of beast,
A sort of hound that tried or seemed at least
To try and seize me—would have killed me dead! 80
His color was a blend of yellow and red,
His ears and tail were tipped with sable fur
Unlike the rest; he was a russet cur.
Small was his snout, his eyes were glowing bright.
It was enough to make one die of fright. 85
That was no doubt what made me groan and swoon."
    "For shame," she said, "you timorous poltroon!
Alas, what cowardice! By God above,
You've forfeited my heart and lost my love.
I cannot love a coward, come what may. 90

For certainly, whatever we may say,
All women long—and O that it might be!—
For husbands tough, dependable and free,
Secret, discreet, no niggard, not a fool 95
That boasts and then will find his courage cool
At every trifling thing! By God above,
How dare you say for shame, and to your love,
That anything at all was to be feared?
Have you no manly heart to match your beard? 100
And can a dream reduce you to such terror?
Dreams are a vanity, God knows, pure error.
Dreams are engendered in the too-replete
From vapors in the belly, which compete
With others, too abundant, swollen tight. 105
    "No doubt the redness in your dream to-night
Comes from the superfluity and force
Of the red choler in your blood. Of course;
That is what puts a dreamer in the dread
Of crimsoned arrows, fires flaming red, 110
Of great red monsters making as to fight him,
And big red whelps and little ones to bite him;
Just so the black and melancholy vapors
Will set a sleeper shrieking, cutting capers
And swearing that black bears, black bulls as well, 115
Or blackest fiends are haling him to Hell.
And there are other vapors that I know
That on a sleeping man will work their woe,
But I'll pass on as lightly as I can.
    "Take Cato now, that was so wise a man, 120
Did he not say, 'Take no account of dreams'?
Now, sir," she said, "on flying from these beams,
For love of God do take some laxative;
Upon my soul that's the advice to give

For melancholy choler; let me urge
You free yourself from vapors with a
    purge.
And that you may have no excuse to tarry
By saying this town has no apothecary,
I shall myself instruct you and prescribe
Herbs that will cure all vapors of that
    tribe,
Herbs from our very farmyard! You will
    find
Their natural property is to unbind
And purge you well beneath and well
    above.
Now don't forget it, dear, for God's own
    love!
Your face is choleric and shows
    distension;
Be careful lest the sun in his ascension
Should catch you full of humors, hot and
    many.
And if he does, my dear, I'll lay a penny
It means a bout of fever or a breath
Of tertian ague. You may catch your
    death,
    "Worms for a day or two I'll have to
        give
As a digestive, then your laxative.
Centaury, fumitory, caper-spurge
And hellebore will make a splendid purge;
And then there's laurel on the blackthorn
    berry,
Ground-ivy too that makes our yard so
    merry;
Peck them right up, my dear, and swallow
    whole.
Be happy, husband, by your father's soul!
Don't be afraid of dreams. I'll say no
    more."
    "Madam," he said, "I thank you for
        your lore,
But with regard to Cato all the same,
His wisdom has, no doubt, a certain fame,
But though he said that we should take
    no heed
Of dreams, by God in ancient books I
    read
Of many a man of more authority
Than ever Cato was, believe you me,
Who say the very opposite is true
And prove their theories by experience
    too.

125

130

135

140

145

150

155

Dreams have quite often been
    significations
As well of triumphs as of tribulations
That people undergo in this our life.
This needs no argument at all, dear wife,
The proof is all too manifest indeed.
    "One of the greatest authors one can
        read
Says thus: there were two comrades once
    who went
On pilgrimage, sincere in their intent.
And as it happened they had reached a
    town
Where such a throng was milling up and
    down,
And yet so scanty the accommodation,
They could not find themselves a
    habitation,
No, not a cottage that could lodge them
    both;
And so they separated, very loath,
Under constraint of this necessity
And each went off to find some hostelry,
And lodge whatever way his luck might
    fall.
    "The first of them found refuge in a
        stall
Down in a yard, with oxen and a plow.
His friend found lodging for himself
    somehow
Elsewhere, by accident or destiny
Which governs all of us and equally.
    "Now it so happened, long ere it was
        day,
This fellow had a dream, and as he lay
In bed it seemed he heard his comrade
    call,
'Help! I am lying in an ox's stall
And shall to-night be murdered as I lie.
Help me, dear brother, help or I shall die!
Come in all haste!' Such were the words
    he spoke;
The dreamer, lost in terror, then awoke.
But once awake he paid it no attention,
Turned over and dismissed it as
    invention,
It was a dream, he thought, a fantasy.
And twice he dreamt this dream
    successively.
    "Yet a third time his comrade came
        again,

160

165

170

175

180

185

190

Or seemed to come, and said, 'I have been slain.
Look, look! my wounds are bleeding wide and deep. 195
Rise early in the morning, break your sleep
And go to the west gate. You there shall see
A cart all loaded up with dung,' said he,
'And in that dung my body has been hidden.
Boldly arrest that cart as you are bidden. 200
It was my money that they killed me for.'
    "He told him every detail, sighing sore,
And pitiful in feature, pale of hue.
This dream, believe me, Madam, turned out true;
For in the dawn as soon as it was light, 205
He went to where his friend had spent the night;
And when he came up the cattle-stall
He looked about him and began to call.
    "The innkeeper, appearing thereupon,
Quickly gave answer, 'Sir, your friend has gone. 210
He left the town a little after dawn.'
The man began to feel suspicious, drawn
By memories of his dream—the western gate,
The dung-cart—off he went, he would not wait,
Towards the western entry. There he found, 215
Seemingly on its way to dung some ground,
A dung-cart loaded on the very plan
Described so closely by the murdered man.
So he began to shout courageously
For right and vengeance on the felony, 220
'My friend's been killed! There's been a foul attack,
He's in that cart and gaping on his back!
Fetch the authorities, get the sheriff down
—Whosever job it is to run the town—
Help! My companion's murdered, sent to glory!' 225
    "What need I add to finish off the story?
People ran out and cast the cart to ground,
And in the middle of the dung they found
The murdered man. The corpse was fresh and new.
    "O blessed God, that art so just and true, 230
Thus thou revealest murder! As we say,
'Murder will out.' We see it day by day.
Murder's a foul, abominable treason,
So loathsome to God's justice, to God's reason,
He will not suffer its concealment. True, 235
Things may lie hidden for a year or two,
But still 'Murder will out,' that's my conclusion.
    "All the town officers in great confusion
Seized on the carter and they gave him hell,
And then they racked the innkeeper as well, 240
And both confessed. And then they took the wrecks
And there and then they hanged them by their necks.
    "By this we see that dreams are to be dreaded.
And in the self-same book I find embedded,
Right in the very chapter after this 245
(I'm not inventing, as I hope for bliss)
The story of two men who started out
To cross the sea—for merchandise no doubt—
But as the winds were contrary they waited.
It was a pleasant town, I should have stated, 250
Merrily grouped about the haven-side.
A few days later with the evening tide
The wind veered round so as to suit them best;
They were delighted and they went to rest
Meaning to sail next morning early. Well, 255
To one of them a miracle befell.
    "This man as he lay sleeping, it would seem,

Just before dawn, had an astonishing dream.
He thought a man was standing by his bed
Commanding him to wait, and thus he said: 260
'If you set sail to-morrow as you intend,
You will be drowned. My tale is at an end.'
    "He woke and told his friend what had occurred
And begged him that the journey be deferred
At least a day, implored him not to start. 265
But his companion, lying there apart,
Began to laugh and treat him to derision.
'I'm not afraid,' he said, 'of any vision,
To let it interfere with my affairs;
A straw for all your dreamings and your scares. 270
Dreams are just empty nonsense, merest japes;
Why people dream all day of owls and apes,
All sorts of trash that can't be understood,
Things that have never happened and never could.
But as I see you mean to stay behind 275
And miss the tide for willful sloth of mind
God knows I'm sorry for it, but good day!'
And so he took his leave and went his way.
    "And yet, before they'd covered half the trip
—I don't know what went wrong—there was a rip 280
And by some accident the ship went down,
Her bottom rent, all hands aboard to drown
In sight of all the vessels at her side
That had put out upon the self-same tide.
    "So, my dear Pertelote, if you discern 285
The force of these examples you may learn
One never should be careless about dreams,
For undeniably I say it seems
That many are a sign of trouble breeding.
    "Now, take St Kenelm's life which I've been reading; 290
He was Kenulphus' son, the noble King
Of Mercia. Now, St Kenelm dreamt a thing
Shortly before they murdered him one day.
He saw his murder in a dream, I say.
His nurse expounded it and gave her reason 295
On every point and warned him against treason.
But as the saint was only seven years old
All that she said about it left him cold.
He was so holy, how could visions hurt?
    "By God, I willingly would give my shirt 300
To have you read his legend as I've read it;
And, Madam Pertelote, upon my credit,
Macrobius wrote of dreams and can explain us
The vision of young Scipio Africanus,
And he affirms that dreams can give a due 305
Warning of things that later on come true.
    "And then there's the Old Testament—a manual
Well worth your study; see the *Book of Daniel*.
Did Daniel think a dream was vanity?
Read about Joseph too and you will see 310
That many dreams—I do not say that all—
Give cognizance of what is to befall.
    "Look at Lord Pharaoh, king of Egypt! Look
At what befell his butler and his cook.
Did not their visions have a certain force? 315
But those who study history of course
Meet many dreams that set them wondering.
    "What about Croesus too, the Lydian king,
Who dreamt that he was sitting in a tree,
Meaning he would be hanged? It had to be. 320

"Or take Andromache, great Hector's wife;
The day on which he was to lose his life
She dreamt about, the very night before,
And realized that if Hector went to war
He would be lost that very day in battle. 325
She warned him; he dismissed it all as prattle
And sallied forth to fight, being self-willed,
And there he met Achilles and was killed.
The tale is long and somewhat overdrawn,
And anyhow it's very nearly dawn, 330
So let me say in very brief conclusion
My dream undoubtedly fortells confusion,
It bodes me ill, I say. And, furthermore,
Upon your laxatives I set no store,
For they are venomous. I've suffered by them 335
Often enough before and I defy them.
  "And now, let's talk of fun and stop all this.
Dear Madam, as I hope for Heaven's bliss,
Of one thing God has sent me plenteous grace,
For when I see the beauty of your face, 340
That scarlet loveliness about your eyes,
All thought of terror and confusion dies.
For it's as certain as the Creed, I know,
Mulier est hominis confusio
(A Latin tag, dear Madam, meaning this: 345
'Woman is man's delight and all his bliss'),
For when at night I feel your feathery side,
Although perforce I cannot take a ride,
Because, alas, our perch was made too narrow,
Delight and solace fill me to the marrow 350
And I defy all visions and all dreams!"
  And with that word he flew down from the beams,
For it was day, and down his hens flew all,
And with a chuck he gave the troupe a call
For he had found a seed upon the floor. 355
Royal he was, he was afraid no more.
He feathered Pertelote in wanton play
And trod her twenty times ere prime of day.
Grim as a lion's was his manly frown
As on his toes he sauntered up and down; 360

He scarcely deigned to set his foot to ground
And every time a seed of corn was found
He gave a chuck, and up his wives ran all.
Thus royal as a prince who strides his hall
Leave we this Chanticleer engaged on feeding 365
And pass to the adventure that was breeding.
  Now when the month in which the world began,
March, the first month, when God created man,
Was over, and the thirty-second day
Thereafter ended, on the third of May, 370
It happened that Chanticleer in all his pride,
His seven wives attendant at his side,
Cast his eyes upward to the blazing sun,
Which in the sign of *Taurus* then had run
His twenty-one degrees and somewhat more, 375
And knew by nature and no other lore
That it was nine o'clock. With blissful voice
He crew triumphantly and said, "Rejoice,
Behold the sun! The sun is up, my seven.
Look, it has climbed forty degrees in heaven, 380
Forty degrees and one in fact, by this.
Dear Madam Pertelote, my earthly bliss,
Hark to those blissful birds and how they sing!
Look at those pretty flowers, how they spring!
Solace and revel fill my heart!" He laughed. 385
  But in that moment Fate let fly her shaft;
Ever the latter end of joy is woe,
God knows that worldly joy is swift to go.
A rhetorician with a flair for style
Could chronicle this maxim in his file 390
Of Notable Remarks with safe conviction.
Then let the wise give ear; this is no fiction.
My story is as true, I undertake,
As that of good Sir Lancelot du Lake
Who held all women in such high esteem. 395

Let me return full circle to my theme.
    A coal-tipped fox of sly iniquity
That had been lurking round the grove for three
Long years, that very night burst through and passed
Stockade and hedge, as Providence forecast, 400
Into the yard where Chanticleer the Fair
Was wont, with all his ladies, to repair.
Still in a bed of cabbages he lay
Until about the middle of the day
Watching the cock and waiting for his cue, 405
As all these homicides so gladly do
That lie about in wait to murder men.
O false assassin, lurking in thy den!
O new Iscariot, new Ganelon!
And O Greek Sinon, thou whose treachery won 410
Troy town and brought it utterly to sorrow!
O Chanticleer, accursed be that morrow
That brought thee to the yard from thy high beams!
Thou hadst been warned, and truly, by thy dreams
That this would be a perilous day for thee. 415
    But that which God's foreknowledge can foresee
Must needs occur, as certain men of learning
Have said. Ask any scholar of discerning;
He'll say the Schools are filled with altercation
On this vexed matter of predestination, 420
Long bandied by a hundred thousand men.
How can I sift it to the bottom then?
The Holy Doctor St Augustine shines
In this, and there is Bishop Bradwardine's
Authority, Boethius' too, decreeing 425
Whether the fact of God's divine foreseeing
Constrains me to perform a certain act
—And by "constraint" I mean the simple fact
Of mere compulsion by necessity—
Or whether a free choice is granted me 430
To do a given act or not to do it,
Though, ere it was accomplished, God foreknew it,
Or whether Providence is not so stringent
And merely makes necessity contingent.
    But I decline discussion of the matter; 435
My tale is of a cock and of the clatter
That came of following his wife's advice
To walk about his yard on the precise
Morning after the dream of which I told.
    O women's counsel is so often cold! 440
A woman's counsel brought us first to woe,
Made Adam out of Paradise to go,
Where he had been so merry, so well at ease.
But, for I know not whom it may displease
If I suggest that women are to blame, 445
Pass over that; I only speak in game.
Read the authorities to know about
What has been said of women; you'll find out.
These are the cock's words, and not mine, I'm giving;
I think no harm of any woman living. 450
    Merrily in her dust-bath in the sand
Lay Pertelote. Her sisters were at hand
Basking in sunlight. Chanticleer sang free,
More merrily than a mermaid in the sea
(For *Physiologus* reports the thing 455
And says how well and merrily they sing).
And so it happened as he cast his eye
Towards the cabbage at a butterfly
It fell upon the fox there, lying low.
Gone was all inclination then to crow. 460
"Cok cok," he cried, giving a sudden start,
As one who feels a terror at his heart,
For natural instinct teaches beasts to flee
The moment they perceive an enemy,
Though they had never met with it before. 465
    This Chanticleer was shaken to the core
And would have fled. The fox was quick to say
However, "Sir! Whither so fast away?

Are you afraid of me that am your friend?
It would be worse than fiendish to intend 470
Some violence or villainy upon you;
Dear sir, I was not even spying on you!
Truly I came to do no other thing
Than just to lie and listen to you sing.
You have as merry a voice as God has given 475
To any angel in the courts of Heaven;
To that you add a musical sense as strong
As had Boethius who was skilled in song.
My Lord your Father (God receive his soul!),
Your mother too—how courtly, what control!— 480
Have honored my poor house, to my great ease;
And you, sir, too, I should be glad to please.
For, when it comes to singing, I'll say this
(Else may these eyes of mine be barred from bliss),
There never was a singer I would rather 485
Have heard at dawn than your respected father.
All that he sang came welling from his soul
And how he put his voice under control!
The pains he took to keep his eyes tight shut
In concentration—then the tip-toe strut, 490
The slender neck stretched out, the delicate beak!
No singer could approach him in technique
Or rival him in song, still less surpass.
I've read the story in *Burnel the Ass*,
Among some other verses, of a cock 495
Whose leg in youth was broken by a knock
A clergyman's son had given him, and for this
He made the father lose his benefice.
But certainly there's no comparison
Between the subtlety of such an one 500
And the discretion of your father's art
And wisdom. Oh, for charity of heart,
Can you not emulate your sire and sing?"
   This Chanticleer began to beat a wing
As one incapable of smelling treason, 505
So wholly had this flattery ravished reason.
Alas, my lords! there's many a sycophant
And flatterer that fill your courts with cant
And give more pleasure with their zeal forsooth
Than he who speaks in soberness and truth. 510
Read what *Ecclesiasticus* records
Of flatterers. 'Ware treachery, my lords!
   This Chanticleer stood high upon his toes,
He stretched his neck, his eyes began to close,
His beak to open; with his eyes shut tight 515
He then began to sing with all his might.
   Sir Russel Fox then leapt to the attack,
Grabbing his gorge he flung him o'er his back
And off he bore him to the woods, the brute,
And for the moment there was no pursuit. 520
   O Destiny that may not be evaded!
Alas that Chanticleer had so paraded!
Alas that he had flown down from the beams!
O that his wife took no account of dreams!
And on a Friday, too, to risk their necks! 525
O Venus, goddess of the joys of sex,
Since Chanticleer thy mysteries professed
And in thy service always did his best,
And more for pleasure than to multiply
His kind, on thine own day is he to die? 530
   O Geoffrey, thou my dear and sovereign master
Who, when they brought King Richard to disaster
And shot him dead, lamented so his death,
Would that I had thy skill, thy gracious breath,
To chide a Friday half so well as you! 535
(For he was killed upon a Friday too.)
Then I could fashion you a rhapsody
For Chanticleer in dread and agony.
   Sure never such a cry or lamentation
Was made by ladies of high Trojan station, 540

When Ilium fell and Pyrrhus with his sword
Grabbed Priam by the beard, their king and lord,
And slew him there as the *Aeneid* tells,
As what was uttered by those hens. Their yells
Surpassed them all in palpitating fear 545
When they beheld the rape of Chanticleer.
Dame Pertelote emitted sovereign shrieks
That echoed up in anguish to the peaks
Louder than those extorted from the wife
Of Hasdrubal when he had lost his life 550
And Carthage all in flame and ashes lay.
She was so full of torment and dismay
That in the very flames she chose her part
And burnt to ashes with a steadfast heart.
O woeful hens, louder your shrieks and higher 555
Than those of Roman matrons when the fire
Consumed their husbands, senators of Rome,
When Nero burnt their city and their home,
Beyond a doubt that Nero was their bale!
    Now let me turn again to tell my tale; 560
This blessed widow and her daughters two
Heard all these hens in clamor and halloo
And, rushing to the door at all this shrieking,
They saw the fox towards the covert streaking
And, on his shoulder, Chanticleer stretched flat.
"Look, look!" they cried. "O mercy, look at that!
Ha! Ha! the fox!" and after him they ran,
And stick in hand ran many a serving man,
Ran Coll our dog, ran Talbot, Bran and Shaggy,
And with a distaff in her hand ran Maggie,
Ran cow and calf and ran the very hogs 570
In terror at the barking of the dogs;
The men and women shouted, ran and cursed,
They ran so hard they thought their hearts would burst
They yelled like fiends in Hell, ducks left the water 575
Quacking and flapping as on point of slaughter,
Up flew the geese in terror over the trees,
Out of the hive came forth the swarm of bees;
So hideous was the noise—God bless us all,
Jack Straw and all his followers in their brawl 580
Were never half so shrill, for all their noise,
When they were murdering those Flemish boys,
As that day's hue and cry upon the fox.
They grabbed up trumpets made of brass and box,
Of horn and bone, on which they blew and pooped, 585
And therewithal they shouted and they whooped
So that it seemed the very heavens would fall.
    And now, good people, pay attention all.
See how Dame Fortune quickly changes side
And robs her enemy of hope and pride! 590
This cock that lay upon the fox's back
In all his dread contrived to give a quack
And said, "Sir Fox, if I were you, as God's
My witness, I would round upon these clods
And shout, 'Turn back, you saucy bumpkins all! 595
A very pestilence upon you fall!
Now that I have in safety reached the wood
Do what you like, the cock is mine for good;
I'll eat him there in spite of every one.'
    The fox replying, "Faith, it shall be done!" 600

Opened his mouth and spoke. The nimble bird,
Breaking away upon the uttered word,
Flew high into the tree-tops on the spot.
And when the fox perceived where he had got,
"Alas," he cried, "alas my Chanticleer, 605
I've done you grievous wrong, indeed I fear
I must have frightened you; I grabbed too hard
When I caught hold and took you from the yard.
But, sir, I meant no harm, don't be offended,
Come down and I'll explain what I intended; 610
So help me God I'll tell the truth—on oath!"
"No," said the cock, "and curses on us both,
And first on me if I were such a dunce
As let you fool me oftener than once.
Never again, for all your flattering lies, 615
You'll coax a song to make me blink my eyes;
And as for those who blink when they should look,
God blot them from his Everlasting Book!"
"Nay, rather," said the fox, "his plagues be flung
On all who clatter that should hold their tongue." 620

Character of Atticus—Joseph Addison
by ALEXANDER POPE

from The Epistle to Dr. Arbuthnot

Peace to all such! but were there one whose fires
True Genius kindles, and fair Fame inspires,
Bless'd with each talent and each art to please,
And born to write, converse, and live with ease;
Should such a man, too fond to rule alone, 5
Bear, like the Turk, no brother near the throne;
View him with scornful, yet with jealous eyes,
And hate for arts that caus'd himself to rise;
Damn with faint praise, assent with civil leer,
And without sneering teach the rest to sneer; 10
Willing to wound, and yet afraid to strike,
Just hint a fault, and hesitate dislike;
Alike reserv'd to blame or to commend,
A tim'rous foe, and a suspicious friend;
Dreading ev'n fools; by flatterers besieged, 15
And so obliging that he ne'er obliged;
Like Cato, give his little Senate laws,
And sit attentive to his own applause;
While Wits and Templars ev'ry sentence raise,
And wonder with a foolish face of praise— 20
Who but must laugh if such a man there be?
Who would not weep, if Atticus were he?

---

like the Turk Turkish tyrants were said to protect their position on the throne by murdering all their nearest kinsmen.

Like Cato Addison wrote a play on *Cato*, and to guarantee a favorable reception for it, was supposed to have hired friends to applaud it on its first presentation. *Atticus* Addison; Pope thought he was not forthright and courageous enough in his satire in the *Spectator Papers*.

Character of Sporus—Lord Hervey

by ALEXANDER POPE

from *The Epistle to Dr. Arbuthnot*

Let Sporus tremble—A. What? that thing of silk,
Sporus, that mere white curd of Ass's milk?
Satire or sense, alas! can Sporus feel?
Who breaks a butterfly upon a wheel?
    P. Yet let me flap this bug with gilded wings, 5
This painted child of dirt, that stinks and stings;
Whose buzz the witty and the fair annoys,
Yet Wit ne'er tastes, and Beauty ne'er enjoys;
So well-bred spaniels civilly delight
In mumbling of the game they dare not bite. 10
Eternal smiles his emptiness betray,
As shallow streams run dimpling all the way;
Whether in florid impotence he speaks,
And, as the prompter breathes, the puppet squeaks, 15
Or at the ear of Eve, familiar toad,
Half froth, half venom, spits himself abroad,
In puns, or politics, or tales, or lies,
Or spite, or smut, or rhymes, or blasphemies;
His wit all see-saw between *that* and *this*, 20
Now high, now low, now master up, now miss,
And he himself one vile Antithesis.
Amphibious thing! that acting either part,
The trifling head, or the corrupted heart;
Fop at the toilet, flatt'rer at the board, 25
Now trips a lady, and now struts a lord.
Eve's tempter thus the Rabbins have exprest,
A cherub's face, a reptile all the rest;
Beauty that shocks you, Parts that none will trust,
Wit that can creep, and Pride that licks the dust. 30

Sporus Lord Hervey who had insulted Pope and who was a rather disreputable person. *mumbling* mouthing without injuring a bird. *at the ear of Eve* like Satan in the garden. *now master up, now miss* acting now like a man, now like a woman. *vile Antithesis* a living contradiction. *Amphibious thing* having the vices of both sexes. *Rabbins have exprest* Rabbinical commentators on Scripture; artists (Lucas Cranach and Michelangelo are good examples) have also so represented Eve's tempter.

The Rape of the Lock

by ALEXANDER POPE

To Mrs. Arabella Fermor

Madam,

    It will be in vain to deny that I have some regard for this piece, since I dedicate it to you. Yet you may bear me witness it was intended only to divert a few young ladies, who have good sense and good humor enough to laugh not only at their sex's little unguarded follies, but at their own. But as it was communicated with the air of a secret, it soon found its way into the world. An imperfect copy having been offer'd to a bookseller, you had the good-nature for my sake, to consent to the publication of one more correct: this I was forced to, before I had executed half my design, for the Machinery was entirely wanting to complete it.

The Machinery, Madam, is a term invented by the critics, to signify that part which the Deities, Angels or Demons, are made to act in a poem; for the ancient poets are in one respect like many modern ladies; let an action be never so trivial in itself, they always make it appear of the utmost importance. These Machines I determined to raise on a very new and odd foundation, the Rosicrucian doctrine of Spirits.

I know how disagreeable it is to make use of hard words before a lady; but it is so much the concern of a poet to have his works understood, and particularly by your sex, that you must give me leave to explain two or three difficult terms. The Rosicrucians are a people I must bring you acquainted with. The best account I know of them is in a French book called *La Comte de Gabalis*, which, both in its title and size, is so like a novel, that many of the fair sex have read it for one by mistake. According to these gentlemen, the four elements are inhabited by Spirits, which they call Sylphs, Gnomes, Nymphs, and Salamanders. The Gnomes, or Demons of earth, delight in mischief; but the Sylphs, whose habitation is in the air, are the best-conditioned creatures imaginable; for, they say, any mortal may enjoy the most intimate familiarities with these gentle spirits, upon a condition very easy to all true adepts—an inviolate preservation of chastity.

As to the following cantos, all the passages of them are as fabulous as the Vision at the beginning, or the Transformation at the end (except the loss of your hair, which I always mention with reverence). The human persons are as fictitious as the airy ones; and the character of Belinda, as it is now managed, resembles you in nothing but in beauty.

If this poem had as many graces as there are in your person or in your mind, yet I could never hope it should pass thro' the world half so uncensured as you have done. But let its fortune be what it will, mine is happy enough, to have given me this occasion of assuring you that I am, with the truest esteem, Madam,

Your most obedient, humble servant,

A. POPE

CANTO I

What dire offense from am'rous causes springs,
What mighty contests rise from trivial things.
I sing—This verse to *Caryll*, muse! is due:
This, ev'n Belinda may vouchsafe to view:
Slight is the subject, but not so the praise,   5
If she inspire, and he approve my lays.
    Say what strange motive, Goddess! could compel
A well-bred Lord t' assault a gentle Belle?
O say what stranger cause, yet unexplor'd
Could make a gentle Belle reject a Lord?   10
In tasks so bold can little men engage,
And in soft bosoms dwells such mighty rage?
    Sol thro' white curtains shot a tim'rous ray,
And oped those eyes that must eclipse the day.
Now lapdogs give themselves the rousing shake   15
And sleepless lovers just at twelve awake;
Thrice rung the bell, the slipper knock'd the ground,
And the press'd watch return'd a silver sound.
Belinda still her downy pillow prest,
Her guardian Sylph prolong'd the balmy rest.   20
'T was he had summon'd to her silent bed
The morning-dream that hover'd o'er her head;
A youth more glitt'ring than a Birthnight Beau

Caryll John Caryll, who suggested that Pope write the poem to heal a breach between the families of Lord Petre and Miss Arabella Fermor occasioned by Lord Petre's having cut off a lock of Miss Fermor's hair. The poem is a mock-heroic in which the conventions of the serious epic are used to point up the triviality of the life of high society at the time. *slipper knock'd* to call the maid. *press'd watch* a watch that strikes the last hour again when its stem is pressed. *guardian Sylph* the heavenly creatures in charge of chastity. Pope at first planned only the first canto; when he added the later cantoes he also inserted this heavenly machinery. See his introductory letter to Mrs. Fermor.

(That ev'n in slumber caus'd her cheek
    to glow)
Seem'd to her ear his winning lips to lay,   25
And thus in whispers said, or seem'd to
    say:
    "Fairest of mortals, thou
        distinguish'd care
Of thousand bright Inhabitants of Air!
If e'er one vision touch'd thy infant
    thought,
Of all the nurse and all the priest have
    taught—   30
Of airy elves by moonlight shadows seen,
The silver token, and the circled green,
Or virgins visited by Angel-powers,
With golden crowns and wreaths of
    heav'nly flowers;
Hear and believe! thy own importance
    know,   35
Nor bound thy narrow views to things
    below.
Some secret truths, from learned pride
    conceal'd,
To maids alone and children are reveal'd:
What tho' no credit doubting Wits may
    give?
The fair and innocent shall still believe.   40
Know, then, unnumber'd Spirits round
    thee fly,
The light militia of the lower sky:
These, tho' unseen, are ever on the wing,
Hang o'er the Box, and hover around the
    Ring.
Think what an equipage thou hast in air,   45
And view with scorn two pages and a
    chair.
As now your own, our beings were of old,
And once inclosed in woman's beauteous
    mold;
Thence, by a soft transition, we repair
From earthly vehicles to these of air.   50
Think not, when woman's transient breath
    is fled,
That all her vanities at once are dead;
Succeeding vanities she still regards,
And, tho' she plays no more, o'erlooks
    the cards.
Her joy in gilded chariots, when alive,   55
And love of Ombre, after death survive.
For when the Fair in all their pride
    expire,
To their first elements their souls retire.
The sprites of fiery termagants in flame
Mount up, and take a Salamander's name.   60
Soft yielding minds to water glide away,
And sip, with Nymphs, their elemental
    tea.
The graver prude sinks downward to a
    Gnome
In search of mischief still on earth to
    roam.
The light coquettes in Sylphs aloft repair,   65
And sport and flutter in the fields of air.
    "Know further yet: whoever fair and
        chaste
Rejects mankind, is by some Sylph
    embraced;
For spirits, freed from mortal laws, with
    ease
Assume what sexes and what shapes they
    please.   70
What guards the purity of melting maids,
In courtly balls, and midnight
    masquerades,
Safe from the treach'rous friend, the
    daring spark,
The glance by day, the whisper in the
    dark;

Box a box in the theater where the fair go to be seen rather than to see. *Ring* a circular promenade in Hyde Park, London. *chair* a sedan chair in which ladies were carried about the streets.

Ombre a fashionable card game. *termagants* originally, a violent Mohammedan deity; it ultimately came to mean any brawling person, but particularly a shrewish woman. *Salamander* associated with the element of fire because the salamander was a lizard that was supposed to be able to endure fire without harm. *Nymphs* associated with the element of water because Nymphs, in ancient mythology, were water deities who inhabited fountains and rivers. *Gnome* associated with the element of earth because the gnomes were dwarfs who lived in the bowels of the earth and were guardians of mines and quarries. According to Paracelsus, they could pass through their element, the earth, as a fish passes through water. *Sylph* associated with the element of air because, according to Paracelsus, they were immortal but soulless beings that inhabited the air. *Rejects mankind* with the typical scorn of the coquette. See Addison's essay on the *Dissecting of a Coquette's Heart*.

When kind occasion prompts their warm
    desires, 75
When music softens, and when dancing
    fires?
'Tis but their Sylph, the wise Celestials
    know,
Tho' Honor is the word with men below.
    "Some nymphs there are, too
        conscious of their face,
For life predestin'd to the Gnome's
    embrace. 80
These swell their prospects and exalt their
    pride,
When offers are disdain'd, and love
    denied;
Then gay ideas crowd the vacant brain,
While peers, and dukes, and all their
    sweeping train,
And garters, stars, and coronets appear, 85
And in soft sounds, 'Your Grace' salutes
    their ear.
'Tis these that early taint the female
    soul,
Instruct the eyes of young coquettes to
    roll,
Teach infant cheeks a bidden blush to
    know,
And little hearts to flutter at a Beau. 90
    "Oft, when the world imagine
        women stray,
The Sylphs thro' mystic mazes guide their
    way,
Thro' all the giddy circle they pursue,
And old impertinence expel by new.
What tender maid but must a victim fall 95
To one man's treat, but for another's ball?
When Florio speaks, what virgin could
    withstand,
If gentle Damon did not squeeze her
    hand?
With varying vanities, from every part,
They shift the moving toyshop of their
    heart; 100
Where wigs with wigs, with sword-knots
    sword-knots strive,
Beaux banish beaux, and coaches coaches
    drive.
This erring mortals levity may call;
Oh blind to truth! the Sylphs contrive
    it all.
    "Of these am I, who thy protection
        claim, 105
A watchful sprite, and Ariel is my name.
Late, as I ranged the crystal wilds of air,
In the clear mirror of thy ruling star
I saw, alas! some dread event impend,
Ere to the main this morning sun
    descend, 110
But Heav'n reveals not what, or how or
    where.
Warn'd by the Sylph, O pious maid,
    beware!
This to disclose is all thy guardian can:
Beware of all, but most beware of Man!"
    He said; when Shock, who thought
        she slept too long, 115
Leap'd up, and waked his mistress with
    his tongue.
'Twas then, Belinda, if report say true,
Thy eyes first open'd on a billet-doux;
Wounds, charms, and ardors were no
    sooner read,
But all the vision vanish'd from thy head. 120
    And now, unveil'd, the toilet stands
        display'd,
Each silver vase in mystic order laid.
First, robed in white, the nymph intent
    adores,
With head uncover'd the cosmetic
    powers.
A heav'nly image in the glass appears; 125
To that she bends, to that her eyes she
    rears.
Th' inferior priestess, at her altar's side,
Trembling begins the sacred rites of Pride.
Unnumber'd treasures ope at once, and
    here
The various off'rings of the world
    appear; 130

Florio . . . Damon names, taken from Pastoral literature, and assumed by the eighteenth-century aristocracy in their toy pastoral.

Ariel probably an allusion to the Ariel of Shakespeare's *Tempest*, the tricky sprite that served Prospero. *Shock* Belinda's lap dog. *billet-doux* a tender note, a love letter. *inferior priestess* her maid, Betty. Belinda herself is the chief priestess, adoring her own image in the mirror.

From each she nicely culls with curious toil,
And decks the Goddess with the glitt'ring spoil.
This casket India's glowing gems unlocks,
And all Arabia breathes from yonder box.
The tortoise here and elephant unite, 135
Transform'd to combs, the speckled, and the white.
Here files of pins extend their shining rows,
Puffs, powders, patches, bibles, billet-doux.
Now awful beauty puts on all its arms;
The Fair each moment rises in her charms, 140
Repairs her smiles, awakens every grace,
And calls forth all the wonders of her face;
Sees by degrees a purer blush arise,
And keener lightnings quicken in her eyes.
The busy Sylphs surround their darling care, 145
These set the head, and those divide the hair,
Some fold the sleeve, whilst others plait the gown;
And Betty's prais'd for labors not her own.

CANTO II

Not with more glories, in th' ethereal plain,
The sun first rises o'er the purpled main,
Than, issuing forth, the rival of his beams
Launch'd on the bosom of the silver Thames.
Fair nymphs, and well-dress'd youths around her shone, 5
But every eye was fix'd on her alone.
On her white breast a sparkling cross she wore,
Which Jews might kiss, and infidels adore.
Her lively looks a sprightly mind disclose,
Quick as her eyes and as unfix'd as those; 10
Favors to none, to all she smiles extends;
Oft she rejects, but never once offends.
Bright as the sun, her eyes the gazers strike,
And, like the sun, they shine on all alike.
Yet graceful ease, and sweetness void of pride, 15
Might hide her faults, if belles had faults to hide;
If to her share some female errors fall,
Look on her face, and you'll forget 'em all.
    This nymph, to the destruction of mankind,
Nourish'd two locks, which graceful hung behind 20
In equal curls, and well conspired to deck
With shining ringlets the smooth iv'ry neck.
Love in these labyrinths his slaves detains,
And mighty hearts are held in slender chains.
With hairy springes we the birds betray, 25
Slight lines of hair surprise the finny prey,
Fair tresses man's imperial race ensnare,
And beauty draws us with a single hair.
    Th' adventurous Baron the bright locks admired;
He saw, he wish'd, and to the prize aspired. 30
Resolv'd to win, he meditates the way,
By force to ravish, or by fraud betray;
For when success a lover's toil attends,
Few ask if fraud or force attain'd his ends.
    For this, ere Phoebus rose, he had implor'd 35
Propitious Heav'n, and every Power ador'd,
But chiefly Love—to Love an altar built
Of twelve vast French romances, neatly gilt.
There lay three garters, half a pair of gloves,
And all the trophies of his former loves; 40
With tender billet-doux he lights the pyre,
And breathes three am'rous sighs to raise the fire.

---

patches beauty marks applied to the face to call attention to striking details of one's features. *Thames* she is embarking on the Thames for Hampton Court, one of the royal palaces.

Phoebus the sun.

Then prostrate falls, and begs with ardent
    eyes
Soon to obtain, and long possess the
    prize:
The Powers gave ear, and granted half
    his prayer, 45
The rest the winds dispers'd in empty air
    But now secure the painted vessel
        glides,
The sunbeams trembling on the floating
    tides;
While melting music steals upon the sky,
And soften'd sounds along the waters
    die; 50
Smooth flow the waves, the zephyrs gently
    play,
Belinda smil'd, and all the world was
    gay.
All but the Sylph—with careful thoughts
    opprest
Th' impending woe sat heavy on his
    breast.
He summons straight his denizens of air; 55
The lucid squadrons round the sails repair;
Soft o'er the shrouds aërial whispers
    breathe
That seem'd but zephyrs to the train
    beneath.
Some to the sun their insect-wings unfold,
Waft on the breeze, or sink in clouds of
    gold; 60
Transparent forms too fine for mortal
    sight,
Their fluid bodies half dissolv'd in light,
Loose to the wind their airy garments
    flew,
Thin glitt'ring textures of the filmy dew,
Dipt in the richest tincture of the skies, 65
Where light disports in ever-mingling
    dyes,
While ev'ry beam new transient colors
    flings,
Colors that change whene'er they wave
    their wings.
Amid the circle, on the gilded mast,
Superior by the head was Ariel placed; 70
His purple pinions opening to the sun,
He raised his azure wand, and thus begun:
    "Ye Sylphs and Sylphids, to your
        chief gave ear.

Fayes, Fairies, Genii, Elves, and Demons,
    hear!
Ye know the spheres and various tasks
    assign'd 75
By laws eternal to th' aërial kind.
Some in the fields of purest ether play,
And bask and whiten in the blaze of day;
Some guide the course of wand'ring orbs
    on high,
Or roll the planets thro' the boundless
    sky; 80
Some, less refin'd, beneath the moon's
    pale light
Pursue the stars that shoot athwart the
    night,
Or suck the mists in grosser air below,
Or dip their pinions in the painted bow,
Or brew fierce tempests on the wintry
    main, 85
Or o'er the glebe distill the kindly rain.
Others, on earth, o'er human race preside,
Watch all their ways, and all their actions
    guide:
Of these the chief the care of nations
    own,
And guard with arms divine the British
    Throne. 90
    "Our humbler province is to tend the
        Fair,
Not a less pleasing, tho' less glorious care;
To save the Powder from too rude a gale;
Nor let th' imprison'd Essences exhale;
To draw fresh colors from the vernal
    flowers; 95
To steal from rainbows ere they drop in
    showers
A brighter Wash; to curl their waving
    hairs,
Assist their blushes and inspire their airs;
Nay oft, in dreams invention we bestow,
To change a Flounce, or add a Furbelow. 100
    "This day black omens threat the
        brightest Fair
That e'er deserv'd a watchful spirit's care;
Some dire disaster, or by force or slight;
But what, or where, the Fates have wrapt
    in night.

---

glebe the earth.   *Furbelow* frill or ruffle.

Whether the nymph shall break Diana's law, 105
Or some frail China jar receive a flaw;
Or stain her honor, or her new brocade,
Forget her prayers, or miss a masquerade,
Or lose her heart, or necklace, at a ball;
Or whether Heav'n has doom'd that Shock must fall. 110
Haste, then, ye Spirits! to your charge repair:
The flutt'ring fan be Zephyretta's care;
The drops to thee, Brilliante, we consign;
And, Momentilla, let the watch be thine;
Do thou, Crispissa, tend her fav'rite Lock; 115
Ariel himself shall be the guard of Shock.
 "To fifty chosen sylphs, of special note,
We trust th' important charge, the petticoat;
Oft have we known that sev'n-fold fence to fail,
Tho' stiff with hoops, and arm'd with ribs of whale; 120
Form a strong line about the silver bound,
And guard the wide circumference around.
 "Whatever spirit, careless of his charge,
His post neglects, or leaves the Fair at large,
Shall feel sharp vengeance soon o'ertake his sins: 125
Be stopp'd in vials, or transfix'd with pins,
Or plunged in lakes of bitter washes lie,
Or wedg'd whole ages in a bodkin's eye;
Gums and pomatums shall his flight restrain,
While clogg'd he beats his silken wings in vain, 130
Or alum styptics with contracting power
Shrink his thin essence like a rivel'd flower;
Or, as Ixion fix'd, the wretch shall feel
The giddy motion of whirling mill,
In fumes of burning chocolate shall glow, 135
And tremble at the sea that froths below!"
 He spoke; the spirits from the sails descend;
Some, orb in orb, around the nymph extend;
Some thread the mazy ringlets of her hair;
Some hang upon the pendants of her ear; 140
With beating hearts the dire event they wait,
Anxious, and trembling for the birth of Fate.

CANTO III

Close by those meads, for ever crown'd with flowers,
Where Thames with pride surveys his rising towers,
There stands a structure of majestic frame,
Which from the neighb'ring Hampton takes its name.
Here Britain's statesmen oft the fall foredoom 5
Of foreign tyrants, and of nymphs at home;
Here, thou, great ANNA! whom three realms obey,
Dost sometimes counsel take—and sometimes tea.
 Hither the Heroes and the Nymphs resort,
To taste awhile the pleasures of a court; 10
In various talk th' instructive hours they past,
Who gave the ball, or paid the visit last;
One speaks the glory of the British Queen,
And one describes a charming Indian screen;
A third interprets motions, looks, and eyes; 15
At every word a reputation dies.

Diana's law the law of chastity. Diana was goddess of maidenhood. *bodkin* a large needle. *Gums and pomatums* perfumed ointments. *rivel'd* shriveled. *Ixion* fixed to an endlessly turning wheel in Hades in punishment for having made love to Jupiter's wife, Juno.

Hampton The palace described here is the famous Hampton Court built by Cardinal Wolsey and taken over by Henry VIII. It was remodeled by Sir Christopher Wren for William and Mary, and, in Pope's time, was the scene of much court frivolity. ANNA Anne, Queen of England, 1702–1714. *three realms* England, Scotland, and Wales.

Snuff, or the fan, supply each pause of chat,
With singing, laughing, ogling, *and all that.*
    Meanwhile, declining from the noon of day,
The sun obliquely shoots his burning ray;   20
The hungry judges soon the sentence sign,
And wretches hang that jurymen may dine;
The merchant from th' Exchange returns in peace,
And the long labors of the toilet cease.
Belinda now, whom thirst of fame invites,   25
Burns to encounter two adventurous knights,
At Ombre singly to decide their doom,
And swells her breast with conquests yet to come.
Straight the three bands prepare in arms to join,
Each band the number of the sacred Nine.   30
Soon as she spreads her hand, th' aërial guard
Descend, and sit on each important card:
First Ariel perch'd upon a Matadore,
Then each according to the rank they bore;
For Sylphs, yet mindful of their ancient race,   35
Are, as when women, wondrous fond of place.
    Behold four Kings in majesty revered,
With hoary whiskers and a forky beard;
And four fair Queens, whose hands sustain a flower,
Th' expressive emblem of their softer power;   40
Four Knaves, in garbs succinct, a trusty band,
Caps on their heads, and halberts in their hand;
And party-color'd troops, a shining train,
Draw forth to combat on the velvet plain.
    The skillful nymph reviews her force with care;   45
"Let Spades be trumps!" she said, and trumps they were.
    Now move to war her sable Matadores,
In show like leaders of the swarthy Moors.
Spadillio first, unconquerable lord!
Led off two captive trumps, and swept the board.   50
As many more Manillio forced to yield,
And march'd a victor from the verdant field.
Him Basto follow'd, but his fate more hard
Gain'd but one trump and one plebeian card.
With his broad saber next, a chief in years,   55
The hoary Majesty of Spades appears,
Puts forth one manly leg, to sight reveal'd;
The rest his many color'd robe conceal'd.
The rebel Knave, who dares his prince engage,
Proves the just victim of his royal rage.   60
Ev'n mighty Pam, that kings and queens o'erthrew,
And mow'd down armies in the fights of Loo,
Sad chance of war! now destitute of aid,
Falls undistinguish'd by the victor Spade.
    Thus far both armies to Belinda yield;   65
Now to the Baron Fate inclines the field.
His warlike amazon her host invades,
Th' imperial consort of the crown of Spades.
The Club's black tyrant first her victim died,
Spite of his haughty mien and barb'rous pride: 70
What boots the regal circle on his head,

---

ogling See Addison's *Dissection of a Coquette's Heart* for a humorous discussion of the art of ogling.   *three bands* Ombre was ordinarily played by three people; each player held nine cards.   *Matadore* name for three principal trumps in ombre; the three are named later in this passage: *Spadillo*—ace of spades; *Manillio*—the deuce of trumps when black, the seven of trumps when red; and *Basto*—the ace of clubs.

velvet plain the velvet table cover.   *Loo* a card game in which Pam (the knave or jack of Clubs) is the highest card.

His giant limbs, in state unwieldy spread;
That long behind he trails his pompous robe,
And of all monarchs only grasps the globe?
The Baron now his Diamonds pours apace; 75
Th' embroider'd King who shows but half his face,
And his refulgent Queen, with powers combin'd,
Of broken troops an easy conquest find.
Clubs, Diamonds, Hearts, in wild disorder seen,
With throngs promiscuous strew the level green. 80
Thus when dispers'd a routed army runs,
Of Asia's troops, and Afric's sable sons,
With like confusion diff'rent nations fly,
Of various habit, and of various dye;
The pierced battalions disunited fall 85
In heaps on heaps; one fate o'erwhelms them all.
    The Knave of Diamonds tries his wily arts,
And wins (oh shameful chance!) the Queen of Hearts.
At this, the blood the virgin's cheek forsook,
A livid paleness spreads o'er all her look; 90
She sees, and trembles at th' approaching ill,
Just in the jaws of ruin, and Codille.
And now (as oft in some distemper'd state)
On one nice trick depends the gen'ral fate!
An Ace of Hearts steps forth; the King unseen 95
Lurk'd in her hand, and mourn'd his captive Queen.
He springs to vengeance with an eager pace,
And falls like thunder on the prostrate Ace.
The nymph, exulting, fills with shouts the sky;
The walls, the woods, and long canals reply. 100
    Oh thoughtless mortals! ever blind to fate,
Too soon dejected, and too soon elate;
Sudden these honors shall be snatch'd away,
And curs'd forever this victorious day.
    For lo! the board with cups and spoons is crown'd, 105
The berries crackle, and the mill turns round;
On shining altars of japan they raise
The silver lamp; the fiery spirits blaze:
From silver spouts the grateful liquors glide,
While China's earth receives the smoking tide. 110
At once they gratify their scent and taste,
And frequent cups prolong the rich repast.
Straight hover round the Fair her airy band;
Some, as she sipp'd, the fuming liquor fann'd,
Some o'er her lap their careful plumes display'd, 115
Trembling, and conscious of the rich brocade.
Coffee (which makes the politician wise,
And see thro' all things with his half-shut eyes)
Sent up in vapors to the Baron's brain
New stratagems, the radiant Lock to gain. 120
Ah, cease, rash youth! desist ere 'tis too late,
Fear the just Gods, and think of Scylla's fate!
Changed to a bird, and sent to flit in air,
She dearly pays for Nisus' injured hair!
    But when to mischief mortals bend their will, 125

Codille a term used in ombre when the challenger loses the game.

berries coffee-berries. *mill* a hand mill in which the coffee was ground at the table. *shining altars of japan* Japanese lacquered tables. *Scylla's fate* not the sea-monster but the daughter of King Nisus of Megara. She gave a lock of her father's hair, on which his life depended, to his enemy, Minos, in punishment for which she was changed into a bird.

How soon they find fit instruments of ill!
Just then, Clarissa drew with tempting
   grace
A two-edg'd weapon from her shining
   case:
So ladies in romance assist their knight,
Present the spear, and arm him for the
   fight.   130
He takes the gift with rev'rence, and
   extends
The little engine on his fingers' ends;
This just behind Belinda's neck he spread,
As o'er the fragrant steams she bends her
   head.
Swift to the Lock a thousand sprites
   repair;   135
A thousand wings, by turns, blow back
   the hair;
And thrice they twitch'd the diamond in
   her ear;
Thrice she look'd back, and thrice the foe
   drew near.
Just in that instant, anxious Ariel sought
The close recesses of the virgin's thought;   140
As on the nosegay in her breast reclin'd,
He watch'd th' ideas rising in her mind,
Sudden he view'd, in spite of all her art,
An earthly Lover lurking at her heart.
Amazed, confused, he found his power
   expired,   145
Resign'd to fate, and with a sigh retired.
   The Peer now spreads the glitt'ring
   forfex wide,
T'inclose the Lock; now joins it, to divide.
Ev'n then, before the fatal engine closed,
A wretched Sylph too fondly interposed;   150
Fate urged the shears, and cut the Sylph
   in twain,
(But airy substance soon unites again).
The meeting points the sacred hair
   dissever
From the fair head, forever, and forever!
   Then flash'd the living lightning from
   her eyes,   155
And screams of horror rend th' affrighted
   skies.
Not louder shrieks to pitying Heav'n are
   cast,
When husbands, or when lapdogs
   breathe their last;
Or when rich China vessels, fall'n from
   high,
In glitt'ring dust and painted fragments
   lie!   160
"Let wreaths of triumph now my temples
   twine,"
The Victor cried, "the glorious prize is
   mine!
While fish in streams, or birds delight in
   air,
Or in a coach and six the British Fair,
As long as Atalantis shall be read,   165
Or the small pillow grace a lady's bed,
While visits shall be paid on solemn days,
When numerous wax-lights in bright
   order blaze,
While nymphs take treats, or assignations
   give,
So long my honor, name, and praise shall
   live!   170
What Time would spare, from Steel
   receives its date,
And monuments, like men, submit to
   Fate!
Steel could the labor of the Gods destroy,
And strike to dust th' imperial towers
   of Troy;
Steel could the works of mortal pride
   confound,   175
And hew triumphal arches to the ground.
What wonder, then, fair Nymph! thy
   hairs should feel
The conquering force of unresisted steel?"

CANTO IV

But anxious cares the pensive nymph
   opprest,
And secret passions labor'd in her breast.
Not youthful kings in battle seiz'd alive,

An earthly Lover The sylph sees that Belinda has yielded up her chastity in her heart at the very moment that she is going to raise a storm about the rape of the lock. As guardian of her chastity, this makes the sylph helpless, and he retires. *forfex* scissors.

Atalantis *The New Atalantis* (1709) by Mrs. Mary Manley, a book of contemporary gossip and scandal.

Not scornful virgins who their charms
    survive,
Not ardent lovers robb'd of all their
    bliss, 5
Not ancient ladies when refused a kiss,
Not tyrants fierce that unrepenting die,
Not Cynthia when her mantua's pinn'd
    awry,
E'er felt such rage, resentment, and
    despair,
As thou, sad Virgin! for thy ravish'd hair. 10
    For, that sad moment, when the
        Sylphs withdrew,
And Ariel weeping from Belinda flew,
Umbriel, a dusky, melancholy sprite
As ever sullied the fair face of light,
Down to the central earth, his proper
    scene, 15
Repair'd to search the gloomy cave of
    Spleen.
    Swift on his sooty pinions flits the
        Gnome,
And in a vapor reach'd the dismal dome.
No cheerful breeze this sullen region
    knows,
The dreaded East is all the wind that
    blows. 20
Here in a grotto shelter'd close from air,
And screen'd in shades from day's
    detested glare,
She sighs forever on her pensive bed,
Pain at her side, and Megrim at her head.
Two handmaids wait the throne; alike
    in place, 25
But diff'ring far in figure and in face.
Here stood Ill-nature, like an ancient
    maid,
Her wrinkled form in black and white
    array'd!
With store of prayers for mornings,
    nights, and noons,
Her hand is fill'd; her bosom with
    lampoons. 30
There Affectation, with a sickly mien,
Shows in her cheek the roses of eighteen,
Practic'd to lisp, and hang the head aside,
Faints into airs, and languishes with
    pride;
On the rich quilt sinks with becoming
    woe, 35
Wrapt in a gown for sickness and for
    show.
The fair ones feel such maladies as these,
When each new night-dress gives a new
    disease.
    A constant vapor o'er the palace flies;
Strange phantoms rising as the mists
    arise; 40
Dreadful as hermits' dreams in haunted
    shades,
Or bright as visions of expiring maids:
Now glaring fiends, and snakes on rolling
    spires,
Pale specters, gaping tombs, and purple
    fires;
Now lakes of liquid gold, Elysian scenes, 45
And crystal domes, and angels in
    machines.
    Unnumber'd throngs on ev'ry side
        are seen,
Of bodies changed to various forms by
    Spleen.
Here living Teapots stand, one arm held
    out,
One bent; the handle this, and that the
    spout; 50
A Pipkin there, like Homer's Tripod
    walks;
Here sighs a Jar, and there a Goose-pie
    talks;
Men prove with child, as powerful fancy
    works,

Cynthia Diana, goddess of chastity. *mantua* mantle. *Umbriel* Notice that a gnome, an earth spirit, takes over now that Belinda has yielded up her chastity in her heart and lost the protection of Ariel and the other sylphs. The gnomes are the controlling spirits for the rest of the poem. *Spleen* bad temper: a cave in the gnomish earth is the proper place for the abode of spleen. *Megrim* melancholy, migraine, depression.

constant vapor The vapor was a fashionable disease in Pope's day, somewhat akin to the "Melancholy" of Elizabethan times. It was supposed to induce all kinds of morbid hallucinations. *Pipkin* a small jar. *Homer's Tripod* Homer's tripod was self-moving: it occurs in the *Iliad*, XVIII. *a Goose-pie talks* Pope's own note: "Alludes to a real fact; a lady of distinction imagined herself in this condition."

And maids turn'd bottles call aloud for corks.
    Safe pass'd the Gnome thro' this fantastic band, 55
A branch of healing spleenwort in his hand.
Then thus address'd the Power—"Hail, wayward Queen!
Who rule the sex to fifty from fifteen:
Parent of Vapors and of female wit,
Who give th' hysteric or poetic fit, 60
On various tempers act by various ways,
Make some take physic, others scribble plays;
Who cause the proud their visits to delay,
And send the godly in a pet to pray.
A nymph there is that all your power disdains, 65
And thousands more in equal mirth maintains.
But oh! if e'er thy Gnome could spoil a grace,
Or raise a pimple on a beauteous face,
Like citron-waters matrons' cheeks inflame,
Or change complexions at a losing game; 70
If e'er with airy horns I planted heads,
Or rumpled petticoats, or tumbled beds,
Or caused suspicion when no soul was rude,
Or discomposed the head-dress of a prude,
Or e'er to costive lapdog gave disease, 75
Which not the tears of brightest eyes could ease,
Hear me, and touch Belinda with chagrin;
That single act gives half the world the spleen."
    The Goddess, with a discontented air,
Seems to reject him tho' she grants his prayer. 80
A wondrous Bag with both her hands she binds,
Like that where once Ulysses held the winds;

---

spleenwort a fern used as a remedy for the spleen. *Ulysses* an allusion to the episode in the *Odyssey* in which Ulysses visited Aeolus, god of the winds, and was given the unruly winds tied up in a bag.

There she collects the force of female lungs
Sighs, sobs, and passions, and the war of tongues.
A Vial next she fills with fainting fears, 85
Soft sorrows, melting griefs, and flowing tears.
The Gnome rejoicing bears her gifts away,
Spreads his black wings, and slowly mounts to day.
    Sunk in Thalestris' arms the nymph he found,
Her eyes dejected, and her hair unbound. 90
Full o'er their heads the swelling Bag he rent,
And all the Furies issued at the vent.
Belinda burns with more than mortal ire,
And fierce Thalestris fans the rising fire.
"O wretched maid!" she spread her hands, and cried 95
(While Hampton's echoes, "Wretched maid!" replied),
"Was it for this you took such constant care
The bodkin, comb, and essence to prepare?
For this your locks in paper durance bound?
For this with torturing irons wreathed around? 100
For this with fillets strain'd your tender head,
And bravely bore the double loads of lead?
Gods! shall the ravisher display your hair,
While the fops envy, and the ladies stare!
Honor forbid! at whose unrival'd shrine 105
Ease, Pleasure, Virtue, all, our sex resign.
Methinks already I your tears survey,
Already hear the horrid things they say,
Already see you a degraded toast.
And all your honor in a whisper lost! 110
How shall I, then, your hapless fame defend?
'Twill then be infamy to seem your friend!

Thalestris' probably Mrs. Morley, a friend of the Fermors.

And shall this prize, th' inestimable prize,
Exposed thro' crystal to the gazing eyes,
And heighten'd by the diamond's circling rays, 115
On that rapacious hand forever blaze?
Sooner shall grass in Hyde Park Circus grow,
And Wits take lodgings in the sound of Bow;
Sooner let earth, air, sea, to chaos fall,
Men, monkeys, lapdogs, parrots, perish all!" 120
    She said; then raging to Sir Plume repairs,
And bids her beau demand the precious hairs
(Sir Plume, of amber snuff-box justly vain,
And the nice conduct of a clouded cane):
With earnest eyes, and round unthinking face, 125
He first the snuff-box open'd, then the case,
And thus broke out—"My lord, why, what the devil!
Z——ds! damn the Lock! 'fore Gad, you must be civil!
Plague on 't! 'tis past a jest—nay, prithee, pox!
Give her the hair."—He spoke, and rapp'd his box. 130
    "It grieves me much," replied the Peer again,
"Who speaks so well should ever speak in vain;
But by this Lock, this sacred Lock, I swear
(Which never more shall join its parted hair;
Which never more its honor shall renew, 135
Clipp'd from the lovely head where late it grew),
That, while my nostrils draw the vital air,
This hand, which won it, shall forever wear."
He spoke, and speaking, in proud triumph spread
The long-contended honors of her head. 140
    But Umbriel, hateful Gnome, forbears not so;
He breaks the Vial whence the sorrows flow.
Then see! the nymph in beauteous grief appears,
Her eyes half-languishing, half drown'd in tears;
On her heav'd bosom hung her drooping head, 145
Which with a sigh she rais'd, and thus she said:
    "Forever curs'd be this detested day,
Which snatch'd my best, my fav'rite curl away!
Happy! ah, ten times happy had I been,
If Hampton Court these eyes had never seen! 150
Yet am not I the first mistaken maid,
By love of courts to numerous ills betray'd.
O had I rather unadmired remain'd
In some lone isle, or distant northern land;
Where the gilt chariot never marks the way, 155
Where none learn Ombre, none e'er taste Bohea!
There kept my charms conceal'd from mortal eye,
Like roses, that in deserts bloom and die.
What mov'd my mind with youthful lords to roam?
O had I stay'd, and said my prayers at home; 160
'Twas this the morning omens seem'd to tell,
Thrice from my trembling hand the patchbox fell;
The tott'ring china shook without a wind;

Hyde Park Circus the circular drive in Hyde Park, promenade for the fashionable. *Bow* church of St. Mary le Bow, famous for its bells, but in an unfashionable district of London, where the fashionable wits would not be likely to live. *beau* read Addison's *Dissection of a Beau's Head* as background for this passage on Sir Plume.

Bohea an exotic kind of black tea. *patchbox* a box for the beauty patches worn on the face.

Nay, Poll sat mute, and Shock was most unkind!
A Sylph, too, warn'd me of the threats of fate, 165
In mystic visions, now believ'd too late!
See the poor remnants of these slighted hairs!
My hands shall rend what ev'n thy rapine spares.
These, in two sable ringlets taught to break,
Once gave new beauties to the snowy neck; 170
The sister-lock now sits uncouth alone,
And in its fellow's fate foresees its own;
Uncurl'd it hangs, the fatal shears demands,
And tempts once more thy sacrilegious hands.
O hadst thou, cruel! been content to seize 175
Hairs less in sight, or any hairs but these!"

CANTO V

She said; the pitying audience melt in tears;
But Fate and Jove had stopp'd the Baron's ears.
In vain Thalestris with reproach assails,
For who can move when fair Belinda fails?
Not half so fix'd the Trojan could remain, 5
While Anna begg'd and Dido raged in vain.
Then grave Clarissa graceful waved her fan;
Silence ensued, and thus the nymph began:
    "Say, why are beauties prais'd and honor'd most,
The wise man's passion, and the vain man's toast? 10
Why deck'd with all that land and sea afford,
Why angels call'd, and angel-like ador'd?
Why round our coaches crowd the white-glov'd beaux?
Why bows the side-box from its inmost rows?
How vain are all these glories, all our pains, 15
Unless Good Sense preserve what Beauty gains;
That men may say when we the front-box grace,
'Behold the first in virtue as in face!'
Oh! if to dance all night, and dress all day,
Charm'd the smallpox, or chased old age away; 20
Who would not scorn what housewife's cares produce,
Or who would learn one earthly thing of use?
To patch, nay, ogle, might become a saint,
Nor could it sure be such a sin to paint.
But since, alas! frail beauty must decay, 25
Curl'd or uncurl'd, since locks will turn to gray;
Since painted, or not painted, all shall fade,
And she who scorns a man must die a maid;
What then remains, but well our power to use,
And keep good humor still whate'er we lose? 30
And trust me, dear, good humor can prevail,
When airs, and flights, and screams, and scolding fail.
Beauties in vain their pretty eyes may roll;
Charms strike the sight, but merit wins the soul."
    So spoke the dame, but no applause ensued; 35
Belinda frown'd, Thalestris call'd her prude.
"To arms, to arms!" the fierce virago cries,
And swift as lightning to the combat flies.

---

the Trojan Aeneas—who was unmoved by the pleas of Dido and her sister Anna. *Clarissa* The name means "most clear"; she is the voice of common sense or reason in this passage.

All side in parties, and begin th' attack;
Fans clap, silks rustle, and tough whale-
   bones crack;   40
Heroes' and heroines' shouts confusedly
   rise,
And bass and treble voices strike the skies.
No common weapons in their hands are
   found,
Like Gods they fight nor dread a mortal
   wound.
   So when bold Homer makes the
      Gods engage,   45
And heav'nly breasts with human passions
   rage;
'Gainst Pallas, Mars; Latona, Hermes
   arms;
And all Olympus rings with loud alarms;
Jove's thunder roars, Heav'n trembles all
   around,
Blue Neptune storms, the bell'wing deeps
   resound;   50
Earth shakes her nodding towers, the
   ground gives way,
And the pale ghosts start at the flash of
   day!
   Triumphant Umbriel, on a sconce's
      height,
Clapp'd his glad wings, and sat to view
   the fight;
Propp'd on their bodkin-spears, the
   sprites survey   55
The growing combat, or assist the fray.
   While thro' the press enraged
      Thalestris flies,
And scatters death around from both her
   eyes,
A Beau and Witling perish'd in the
   throng,
One died in metaphor, and one in song: 60
"O cruel Nymph! a living death I bear,"
Cried Dapperwit, and sunk beside his
   chair

A mournful glance Sir Fopling upwards
   cast,
"Those eyes are made so killing"—was his
   last.
Thus on Maeander's flowery margin lies   65
Th' expiring swan, and as he sings he dies.
   When bold Sir Plume had drawn
      Clarissa down,
Chloe stepp'd in, and kill'd him with a
   frown;
She smiled to see the doughty hero slain,
But, at her smile, the beau revived again. 70
Now Jove suspends his golden scales in air,
Weighs the men's wits against the lady's
   hair;
The doubtful beam long nods from side
   to side;
At length the wits mounts up, the hairs
   subside.
   See fierce Belinda on the Baron flies, 75
With more than usual lightning in her
   eyes;
Nor fear'd the chief th' unequal fight to
   try,
Who sought no more than on his foe to
   die.
But this bold lord, with manly strength
   endued,
She with one finger and a thumb subdued: 80
Just where the breath of life his nostrils
   drew,
A charge of snuff the wily virgin threw;
The Gnomes direct, to every atom just,
The pungent grains of titillating dust.
Sudden, with starting tears each eye
   o'erflows,   85
And the high dome re-echoes to his nose.
   "Now meet thy fate," incens'd
      Belinda cried,
And drew a deadly bodkin from her side.
(The same, his ancient personage to deck,
Her great-great-grandsire wore about his
   neck,   90

Pallas Pallas Athena, goddess of Wisdom and War. *Mars* god of War. *Latona* mother of Apollo and goddess of night. *Hermes* messenger of the gods. *Olympus* mountain home of the gods. *Neptune* god of the sea. *sconce's* a bracket for a torch or candle. *Dapperwit* an allusion to a fop in William Wycherley's *Love in a Wood*.

Sir Fopling an allusion to Sir Fopling Flutter, a character in Sir George Etherege's *The Man of Mode*. *Maeander's flowery margin* a river in Asia Minor, noted for its winding course. *bodkin* here a pin for fastening the hair. Compare this passage with that describing the progress of Agamemnon's sceptre in the *Iliad*, II.

In three seal-rings; which after, melted
    down,
Form'd a vast buckle for his widow's
    gown;
Her infant grandame's whistle next it
    grew,
The bells she jingled, and the whistle
    blew;
Then in a bodkin graced her mother's
    hairs,   95
Which long she wore and now Belinda
    wears.)
    "Boast not my fall," he cried,
        "insulting foe!
Thou by some other shalt be laid as low;
Nor think to die dejects my lofty mind:
All that I dread is leaving you behind!   100
Rather than so, ah, let me still survive,
And burn in Cupid's flames—but burn
    alive."
"Restore the Lock!" she cries; and all
    around
"Restore the Lock!" the vaulted roofs
    rebound.
Not fierce Othello in so loud a strain   105
Roar'd for the handkerchief that caus'd
    his pain.
But see how oft ambitious aims are
    cross'd,
And chiefs contend till all the prize is lost!
The lock, obtain'd with guilt, and kept
    with pain,
In ev'ry place is sought, but sought in
    vain;   110
With such a prize no mortal must be
    blest.
So Heav'n decrees! with Heav'n who can
    contest?
    Some thought it mounted to the
        lunar sphere,
Since all things lost on earth are treasured
    there.
There heroes' wits are kept in pond'rous
    vases,   115
And beaux' in snuffboxes and tweezer-
    cases.

There broken vows, and deathbed alms
    are found,
And lovers' hearts with end of riband
    bound,
The courtier's promises, and sick man's
    prayers,
The smiles of harlots, and the tears of
    heirs,   120
Cages for gnats, and chains to yoke a flea,
Dried butterflies, and tomes of casuistry.
    But trust the Muse—she saw it
        upward rise,
Tho' marked by none but quick poetic
    eyes
(So Rome's great founder to the heav'ns
    withdrew,   125
To Proculus alone confess'd in view):
A sudden star, it shot thro' liquid air,
And drew behind a radiant trail of hair.
Not Berenice's locks first rose so bright,
The heav'ns bespangling with dishevel'd
    light.   130
The Sylphs behold it kindling as it flies,
And pleas'd pursue its progress thro' the
    skies.
    This the beau monde shall from the
        Mall survey,
And hail with music its propitious ray;
This the blest lover shall for Venus take,   135
And send up vows from Rosamonda's lake;
This Partridge soon shall view in cloudless
    skies,
When next he looks thro' Galileo's eyes;
And hence th' egregious wizard shall fore-
    doom

Othello Shakespeare's Othello falls into a rage when he finds Desdemona's handkerchief in the possession of Cassio.

tomes of casuistry large volumes of very subtle arguments about moral problems.   *Rome's great founder* Romulus, who, after being translated to the heavens, appeared only to Proculus with a message for the Roman people.   *Berenice's locks* an Egyptian Queen; she pledged a lock of her hair to Venus for the safe return of her husband. The lock was transported to heaven by the goddess and transformed into a constellation—Berenice's Locks (*Coma Berenicis*).   *beau monde* the fashionable world.   *the Mall* a fashionable walk in St. James' Park, London.   *Rosamonda's lake* a lake in St. James' Park, London.   *Partridge* John Partridge, an astrologer and maker of almanacs; he was forever predicting the fall of the king of France (the fate of Louis) and of the Pope (the fall of Rome).   *Galileo's eyes* the telescope.

The fate of Louis, and the fall of Rome. 140
    Then cease, bright Nymph! to mourn
        they ravish'd hair,
Which adds new glory to the shining
    sphere!
Not all the tresses that fair head can boast
Shall draw such envy at the Lock you lost.
For after all the murders of your eye, 145
When, after millions slain, yourself shall die;
When those fair suns shall set, as set they
    must,
And all those tresses shall be laid in dust,
This Lock the Muse shall consecrate to
    fame,
And 'midst the stars inscribe Belinda's
    name. 150

A Satirical Elegy on the Death of a Late Famous General
by JONATHAN SWIFT

    His Grace! impossible! what dead!
Of old age too, and in his bed!
And could that Mighty Warrior fall?
And so inglorious, after all!
Well, since he's gone, no matter how, 5
The last loud trump must wake him now:
And, trust me, as the noise grows
    stronger,
He'd wish to sleep a little longer.
And could he be indeed so old
As by the news-papers we're told? 10
Threescore, I think, is pretty high;
'Twas time in conscience he should die.
This world he cumber'd long enough;
He burnt his candle to the snuff;
And that's the reason, some folks think, 15
He left behind *so great a s . . . k.*
Behold his funeral appears,
Nor widow's sighs, nor orphan's tears,
Wont at such times each heart to pierce,
Attend the progress of his herse. 20
But what of that, his friends may say,
He had those honours in his day.
True to his profit and his pride,
He made them weep before he dy'd.
    Come hither, all ye empty things, 25
Ye bubbles rais'd by breath of Kings;
Who float upon the tide of state,
Come hither, and behold your fate.
Let pride be taught by this rebuke,
How very mean a thing's a Duke; 30
From all his ill-got honours flung,
Turn'd to that dirt from whence he
    sprung.

"Ah, Are You Digging On My Grave?"*
by THOMAS HARDY

"Ah, are you digging on my grave
    My loved one? planting rue?"
—"No: yesterday he went to wed
One of the brightest wealth has bred.
'It cannot hurt her now,' he said, 5
    'That I should not be true.' "

"Then who is digging on my grave?
    My nearest dearest kin?"
—"Ah, no: they sit and think, 'What
    use!
What good will planting flowers produce? 10
No tendance of her mound can loose
    Her spirit from Death's gin.' "

---

* Reprinted with permission of The Macmillan Company, the Hardy Estate, Macmillan & Co. Ltd., London, and The Macmillan Company of Canada Limited from *Collected Poems of Thomas Hardy.* Copyright 1925 by The Macmillan Company.

rue a plant associated with sorrow or grief.

---

gin snare.

"But some one digs upon my grave?
  My enemy?—prodding sly?"
—"Nay: when she heard you had passed
  the Gate
That shuts on all flesh soon or late,
She thought you no more worth her hate,
  And cares not where you lie."

"Then, who is digging on my grave?
  Say—since I have not guessed!"
—"O it is I, my mistress dear,
Your little dog, who still lives near,
And much I hope my movements here
  Have not disturbed your rest?"

"Ah, yes! *You* dig upon my grave . . .
  Why flashed it not on me
That one true heart was left behind!
What feeling do we ever find
To equal among human kind
  A dog's fidelity!"

"Mistress, I dug upon your grave
  To bury a bone, in case
I should be hungry near this spot
When passing on my daily trot.
I am sorry, but I quite forgot
  It was your resting-place."

Hell Gate*

by A. E. HOUSMAN

Onward led the road again
Through the sad uncoloured plain
Under twilight brooding dim,
And along the utmost rim
Wall and rampart risen to sight
Cast a shadow not of night,
And beyond them seemed to glow
Bonfires lighted long ago.
And my dark conductor broke
Silence at my side and spoke,
Saying, 'You conjecture well:
Yonder is the gate of hell.'

Ill as yet the eye could see
The eternal masonry,
But beneath it on the dark
To and fro there stirred a spark.
And again the sombre guide
Knew my question, and replied:
'At hell gate the damned in turn
Pace for sentinel and burn.'

Dully at the leaden sky
Staring, and with idle eye
Measuring the listless plain,
I began to think again.
Many things I thought of then,
Battle, and the loves of men,
Cities entered, oceans crossed,
Knowledge gained and virtue lost,
Cureless folly done and said,
And the lovely way that led
To the slimepit and the mire
And the everlasting fire.
And against a smoulder dun
And a dawn without a sun
Did the nearing bastion loom,
And across the gate of gloom
Still one saw the sentry go,
Trim and burning, to and fro,
One for women to admire
In his finery of fire.
Something, as I watched him pace,
Minded me of time and place,
Soldiers of another corps
And a sentry known before.

Ever darker hell on high
Reared its strength upon the sky,
And our footfall on the track
Fetched the daunting echo back.
But the soldier pacing still
The insuperable sill,

---

* From *The Collected Poems of A. E. Housman*. Copyright 1922 by Holt, Rinehart and Winston, Inc. Copyright 1950 by Barclays Bank Limited. Reprinted by permission of Holt, Rinehart and Winston, Inc., and The Society of Authors as the literary representatives of the Estate of A. E. Housman, and Jonathan Cape Ltd., publishers of A. E. Housman's *Collected Poems*.

---

dun dark brown.   *sill* timber or stone at the foot of door or window.

Nursing his tormented pride,
Turned his head to neither side,
Sunk into himself apart
And the hell-fire of his heart.
But against our entering in   55
From the drawbridge Death and Sin
Rose to render key and sword
To their father and their lord.
And the portress foul to see
Lifted up her eyes on me   60
Smiling, and I made reply:
'Met again, my lass,' said I.
Then the sentry turned his head,
Looked, and knew me, and was Ned.

    Once he looked, and halted straight,   65
Set his back against the gate,
Caught his musket to his chin,
While the hive of hell within
Sent abroad a seething hum
As of towns whose king is come   70
Leading conquest home from far
And the captives of his war,
And the car of triumph waits,
And they open wide the gates.
But across the entry barred   75
Straddled the revolted guard,
Weaponed and accoutred well
From the arsenals of hell;

And beside him, sick and white,
Sin to left and Death to right   80
Turned a countenance of fear
On the flaming mutineer.
Over us the darkness bowed,
And the anger in the cloud
Clenched the lightning for the stroke;   85
But the traitor musket spoke.

    And the hollowness of hell
Sounded as its master fell,
And the mourning echo rolled
Ruin through his kingdom old.   90
Tyranny and terror flown
Left a pair of friends alone,
And beneath the nether sky
All that stirred was he and I.

    Silent, nothing found to say,   95
We began the backward way;
And the ebbing lustre died
From the soldier at my side,
As in all his spruce attire
Failed the everlasting fire.   100
Midmost of the homeward track
Once we listened and looked back;
But the city, dusk and mute,
Slept, and there was no pursuit.

In Schrafft's*

by W. H. AUDEN

Having finished the Blue-plate Special
And reached the coffee stage,
Stirring her cup she sat,
A somewhat shapeless figure
Of indeterminate age   5
In an undistinguished hat.

When she lifted her eyes it was plain
That our globular furore,
Our international rout
Of sin and apparatus   10
And dying men galore,
Was not being bothered about.

Which of the seven heavens
Was responsible her smile
Wouldn't be sure but attested   15
That, whoever it was, a god
Worth kneeling-to for a while
Had tabernacled and rested.

---

* Copyright 1949 by W. H. Auden. Reprinted from *Collected Shorter Poems 1927–1957*, by W. H. Auden, by permission of Random House, Inc.
Schrafft's a chain of restaurants.

The Unknown Citizen*
by W. H. AUDEN

*To JS/07/M/378
This Marble Monument Is Erected by the State*

He was found by the Bureau of Statistics to be
One against whom there was no official complaint,
And all the reports on his conduct agree
That, in the modern sense of an old-fashioned word, he was a saint,
For in everything he did he served the Greater Community. 5
Except for the War till the day he retired
He worked in a factory and never got fired,
But satisfied his employers, Fudge Motors Inc.
Yet he wasn't a scab or odd in his views,
For his Union reports that he paid his dues, 10
(Our report on his Union shows it was sound)
And our Social Psychology workers found
That he was popular with his mates and liked a drink.
The Press are convinced that he bought a paper every day
And that his reactions to advertisements were normal in every way.
Policies taken out in his name prove that he was fully insured, 15
And his Health-card shows he was once in hospital but left it cured.
Both Producers Research and High-Grade Living declare
He was fully sensible to the advantages of the Installment Plan
And had everything necessary to the Modern Man,
A gramophone, a radio, a car and a frigidaire. 20
Our researchers into Public Opinion are content
That he held the proper opinions for the time of year;
When there was peace, he was for peace; when there was war, he went.
He was married and added five children to the population,
Which our Eugenist says was the right number for a parent of his generation, 25
And our teachers report that he never interfered with their education.
Was he free? Was he happy? The question is absurd:
Had anything been wrong, we should certainly have heard.

---

* Copyright 1940 and renewed 1968 by W. H. Auden. Reprinted from *Collected Shorter Poems 1927–1957*, by W. H. Auden, by permission of Random House, Inc., and Faber and Faber Ltd.

In Westminster Abbey

by JOHN BETJEMAN

Let me take this other glove off
   As the *vox humana* swells,
And the beauteous fields of Eden
   Bask beneath the Abbey bells.
Here, where England's statesmen lie,   5
Listen to a lady's cry.

Gracious Lord, oh bomb the Germans.
   Spare their women for Thy Sake,
And if that is not too easy
   We will pardon Thy Mistake.   10
But, gracious Lord, whate'er shall be,
Don't let anyone bomb me.

Keep our Empire undismembered
   Guide our Forces by Thy Hand,
Gallant blacks from far Jamaica,   15
   Honduras and Togoland;
Protect them Lord in all their fights,
And, even more, protect the whites.

Think of what our Nation stands for,
   Books from Boots' and country lanes,   20
Free speech, free passes, class distinction,
   Democracy and proper drains.
Lord, put beneath Thy special care
One-eighty-nine Cadogan Square.

Although dear Lord I am a sinner,   25
   I have done no major crime;
Now I'll come to Evening Service
   Whensoever I have time.
So, Lord, reserve for me a crown,
And do not let my shares go down.   30

I will labour for Thy Kingdom,
   Help our lads to win the war,
Send white feathers to the cowards
   Join the Women's Army Corps,
Then wash the Steps around Thy Throne   35
In the Eternal Safety Zone.

Now I feel a little better,
   What a treat to hear Thy Word,
Where the bones of leading statesmen,
   Have so often been interr'd.   40
And now, dear Lord, I cannot wait
Because I have a luncheon date.

---

* From John Betjeman, *Collected Poems*, John Murray (Publishers), Ltd., and Houghton Mifflin Company. Reprinted by permission of John Murray Ltd.

vox humana the human voice. *Honduras* British Honduras in Central America. *Togoland* a British mandate in South Africa. *Boots'* a chain of drugstores. *Cadogan Square* the London address of the lady.

Portrait

by KENNETH FEARING

The clear brown eyes, kindly and alert, with 12–20 vision, give confident regard
   to the passing world through R. K. Lampert & Company lenses framed in gold;
His soul, however, is all his own;
Arndt Brothers necktie and hat (with feather) supply a touch of youth.

With his soul his own, he drives, drives, chats and drives,
   The first and second bicuspids, lower right, replaced by bridgework, while two
     incisors have porcelain crowns;   5

---

* From *New and Selected Poems* by Kenneth Fearing. Copyright © 1956 by the author. Reprinted by permission of Indiana University Press.

(Render unto Federal, state, and city Caesar, but not unto time;
Render nothing unto time until Amalgamated Death serves final notice, in
  proper form:

The vault is ready;
The will has been drawn by Clagget, Clagget, Clagget & Brown;
The policies are adequate, Confidential's best, reimbursing for disability, partial
  or complete, with double indemnity should the end be a pure and simple
  accident)
Nothing unto time,
Nothing unto change, nothing unto fate,
Nothing unto you, and nothing unto me, or to any other known or unknown
  party or parties, living or deceased;

But Mercury shoes, with special arch supports, take much of the wear and tear;
On the course, a custombuilt driver corrects a tendency to slice;
Love's ravages have been repaired (it was a textbook case) by Drs. Schultz,
  Lightner, Mannheim, and Goode,
While all of it is enclosed in excellent tweed, with Mr. Baumer's personal
  attention to the shoulders and the waist;
And all of it now roving, chatting amiably through space in a Plymouth 6,
With his soul (his own) at peace, soothed by Walter Lippmann, and sustained
  by Haig & Haig.

Confession Overheard in a Subway*
by KENNETH FEARING

You will ask how I came to be eavesdropping, in the first place.
The answer is, I was not.
The man who confessed to these several crimes (call him John Doe) spoke
  into my right ear on a crowded subway train, while the man whom he
  addressed (call him Richard Roe) stood at my left.
Thus, I stood between them, and they talked, or sometimes shouted, quite
  literally straight through me.
How could I help but overhear?
Perhaps I might have moved away to some other strap. But the aisles were full.
Besides, I felt, for some reason, curious.

"I do not deny my guilt," said John Doe. "My own, first, and after that my
  guilty knowledge of still further guilt.
I have counterfeited often, and successfully.
I have been guilty of ignorance, and talking with conviction. Of intolerable
  wisdom, and keeping silent.
Through carelessness, or cowardice, I have shortened the lives of better men.
  And the name for that is murder.
All my life I have been a receiver of stolen goods."

---
* From *Afternoon of a Pawnbroker* by Kenneth Fearing, copyright 1943, by Kenneth Fearing.
Reprinted by permission of Harcourt Brace Jovanovich, Inc.

"Personally, I always mind my own business," said Richard Roe. "Sensible people don't get into those scrapes."

I was not the only one who overheard this confession.
Several businessmen, bound for home, and housewives and mechanics, were within easy earshot.
A policeman sitting in front of us did not lift his eyes, at the mention of murder, from his paper.
Why should I be the one to report these crimes?
You will understand why this letter to your paper is anonymous. I will sign it: Public-Spirited Citizen, and hope that it cannot be traced.
But all the evidence, if there is any clamor for it, can be substantiated.
I have heard the same confession many times since, in different places.
And now that I come to think of it, I had heard it many times before.

"Guilt," said John, "is always and everywhere nothing less than guilt.
I have always, at all times, been a willing accomplice of the crass and the crude.
I have overheard, daily, the smallest details of conspiracies against the human race, vast in their ultimate scope, and conspired daily, to launch my own.
You have heard of innocent men who died in the chair. It was my greed that threw the switch.
I helped, and I do not deny it, to nail that guy to the cross, and shall continue to help.
Look into my eyes, you can see the guilt.
Look at my face, my hair, my very clothing, you will see guilt written plainly everywhere.
Guilt of the flesh. Of the soul. Of laughing, when others do not. Of breathing and eating and sleeping.
I am guilty of what? Of guilt. Guilty of guilt, that is all, and enough."

Richard Roe looked at his wristwatch and said: "We'll be twenty minutes late. After dinner we might take in a show."

Now, who will bring John Doe to justice for his measureless crimes?
I do not, personally, wish to be involved.
Such nakedness of the soul belongs in some other province, probably the executioner's.
And who will bring the blunt and upright Richard Roe to the accuser's stand, where he belongs?
Or will he deny and deny his partnership?

I have done my duty, as a public-spirited citizen, in any case.

A Glass of Beer*
by JAMES STEPHENS

The lanky hank of a she in the inn over there
Nearly killed me for asking the loan of a glass of beer;
May the devil grip the whey-faced slut by the hair,
And beat bad manners out of her skin for a year.

That parboiled ape, with the toughest jaw you will see
On virtue's path, and a voice that would rasp the dead,
Came roaring and raging the minute she looked at me,
And threw me out of the house on the back of my head!

If I asked her master he'd give me a cask a day;
But she, with the beer at hand, not a gill would arrange!
May she marry a ghost and bear him a kitten, and may
The High King of Glory permit her to get the mange.

---

* Reprinted with permission of The Macmillan Company, Mrs. Iris Wise, Macmillan & Co. Ltd., London, and The Macmillan Company of Canada Limited, from Collected Poems of James Stephens. Copyright 1925, 1926 by The Macmillan Company, renewed 1953, 1954 by James Stephens.

Haircut*
by KARL SHAPIRO

O wonderful nonsense of lotions of Lucky Tiger,
Of savory soaps and oils of bottle-bright green,
The gold of liqueurs, the unguents of Newark and Niger,
Powders and balms and waters washing me clean;

In mirrors of marble and silver I see us forever
Increasing, decreasing the puzzles of luminous spaces
As I turn, am resolved and am pumped in the air on a lever,
With the backs of my heads in chorus with all of my faces.

Scissors and comb are mowing my hair into neatness,
Now pruning my ears, now smoothing my neck like a plain;
In the harvest of hair and the chaff of powdery sweetness
My snow-covered slopes grow dark with the wooly rain.

And the little boy cries, for it hurts to sever the curl,
And we too are quietly bleating to part with our coat.
Does the barber want blood in a dish? I am weak as a girl,
I desire my pendants, the fatherly chin of a goat.

I desire the pants of a bear, the nap of a monkey
Which trousers of friction have blighted down to my skin.
I am bare as a tusk, as jacketed up as a flunkey,
With the chest of a moth-eaten camel growing within.

---

* Copyright 1942 by Karl Shapiro. Reprinted from Selected Poems, by Karl Shapiro, by permission of Random House, Inc.

But in death we shall flourish, you
    summer-dark leaves of my head,
While the flesh of the jaw ebbs away
    from the shores of my teeth;

You shall cover my sockets and soften
    the boards of my bed
And lie on the flat of my temples as
    proud as a wreath.

Boom!*
by HOWARD NEMEROV

Sees Boom in Religion, Too

Atlantic City, June 23, 1957 (AP). — President Eisenhower's pastor said tonight that Americans are living in a period of "unprecedented religious activity" caused partially by paid vacations, the eight-hour day and modern conveniences.

    "These fruits of material progress," said the Rev. Edward L. R. Elson of the National Presbyterian Church, Washington, "have provided the leisure, the energy, and the means for a level of human and spiritual values never before reached."

Here at the Vespasian-Carlton, it's just
    one
religious activity after another; the sky
is constantly being crossed by cruciform
airplanes, in which nobody disbelieves
for a second, and the tide, the tide   5
of spiritual progress and prosperity
miraculously keeps rising, to a level
never before attained. The churches are
    full,
the beaches are full, and the filling-
    stations
are full, God's great ocean is full   10
of paid vacationers praying an eight-
    hour day
to the human and spiritual values, the
    fruits,
the leisure, the energy, and the means,
    Lord,
the means for the level, the unprece-
    dented level,

and the modern conveniences, which also
    are full.   15
Never before, O Lord, have the prayers
    and praises
from belfry and phonebooth, from ball-
    park and barbecue
the sacrifices, so endlessly ascended.

It was not thus when Job in Palestine
sat in the dust and cried, cried bitterly;   20
when Damien kissed the lepers on their
    wounds
it was not thus; it was not thus
when Francis worked a fourteen-hour day
strictly for the birds; when Dante took
a week's vacation without pay and it
    rained   25
part of the time, O Lord, it was not thus.

But now the gears mesh and the tires
    burn
and the ice chatters in the shaker and
    the priest
in the pulpit, and Thy Name, O Lord,
is kept before the public, while the fruits   30
ripen and religion booms and the level
    rises

---

* From *New and Selected Poems* by Howard Nemerov; copyright © 1960 by the University of Chicago. Reprinted by permission of the Margot Johnson Agency.

and every modern convenience runneth
   over,
that it may never be with us as it hath
   been
with Athens and Karnak and Nagasaki,
nor Thy sun for one instant refrain from
   shining 35
on the rainbow Buick by the breezeway
or the Chris Craft with the uplift life raft;
that we may continue to be the just folks
   we are,
plain people with ordinary superliners and
disposable diaperliners, people of the
   stop'n'shop 40
'n'pray as you go, of hotel, motel, boatel,
the humble pilgrims of no deposit no
   return
and please adjust thy clothing, who will
   give to Thee,
if Thee will keep us going, our annual
Miss Universe, for Thy Name's Sake,
   Amen. 45

Unit 7

POETRY:
CRITICAL ESSAYS

The Nature of Poetry*
by DONALD A. STAUFFER

Few people have ever been brave enough to define poetry. Not many among those few have felt happy with their definitions. Yet most of us have experienced poetry, and many of us believe that we can recognize it when we see it, just as we can recognize life when we see it, although we cannot satisfactorily define it. Like life, poetry exists in so many forms and on so many levels that it triumphantly defies description. Keats has written of poetry as the realms of gold, and has noted its many goodly states and kingdoms, its many islands held in fealty to Apollo. The metaphor is a good one, though it hardly goes far enough. There are more poems than there are islands in the Caribbean, or the Mediterranean; and they vary more in shape, size, color, contour, and human habitability.

Furthermore, any individual poem, as Keats wrote of Homer's *Iliad*, may in itself be a complete domain, illimitable as the Pacific, ruled by its own king and creator, a wide expanse arched over by a pure and serene air. Or—and here is the rub—it may not be like that at all. It may be as small and limited as an epigram by Martial, as precipitous and rocky as a lyric by Donne, as barely above sea level as a poem by Edgar Guest. And it might be quite different from any now known. Surely there is good reason to avoid a definition of poetry. The clearer and more concise the definition is, the more poems it leaves out.

If we are to understand the nature of poetry, we must view the realms of gold from many points of vantage. We must travel on various single quests across many islands. At the start we must take certain bearings and ask certain questions. Are we to consider the *medium* of words in which poetry is composed? Or the *subjects* which poetry treats? Or the *purposes* for which the subjects are being used? Or the *forms* created in that verbal medium in order to give expression to certain subjects and purposes? The first of these possibilities will occupy us in later paragraphs. The second need not detain us, for the answer, if we judge by actual practice, is that any subject matter may furnish raw materials for poets, from Chaucer, who used warts and running sores, to T. S. Eliot, who uses statistics. The last two possibilities present the further question: Are we to consider poetry or poems? Poetry, of course, may serve as a generic name for a group of poems or for all poems taken together. Often, however, the word is used to describe the spirit or mood which may find expression in a poem but may also find expression in, say, a painting or a piece of music. Many critical battles and misunderstandings have arisen because one man was viewing the qualities of the *poetic spirit* and his opponent was seeing only the qualities of a *poem*. We might at this point decide on a procedure: to consider first those elements which most usually combine in the poetic spirit; and then, more narrowly, the technical and formal elements which shape words into a poem.

Poetry labors under the further handicap of being the most misunderstood of all the arts. And yet of all the arts, poetry should afford to the greatest number of people the most delight. Actually it does nothing of the kind. Instead, the average adolescent or adult (for children know what poetry is) feels uncomfortable or irritated or bored when he confronts a poem. Partly this defect in sympathy may be attributed to the many easy substitutes that now satisfy everyone's natural craving for esthetic experience—the comic strips and the movies, the detective stories and the weekly magazines, the soap opera on the radio and the trip in the car. A debased currency will always drive out the genuine article, and there are plenty of ways today to get others to do our thinking and our feeling for us. Partly the

---

* Reprinted from *The Nature of Poetry* by Donald A. Stauffer. By permission of W. W. Norton & Company, Inc. Copyright 1946 by W. W. Norton & Company, Inc.

misunderstanding springs from the amount of rapid reading we do, skimming newspapers and billboards and novels, so that we are impatient when anything demands close scrutiny. We have also had little practice in taking in through the ear esthetically ordered words. The eye has displaced the ear as the instrument for literary communication, although it is quite possible that the radio, some day in the future, may help to restore the enjoyment of poetry as a verbal pattern of meaningful *sounds*.

But the main cause of the popular uneasiness before poetry lies in the very medium which this art uses—the medium of words. We are accustomed to using words almost solely for the practical purposes of living. We cannot understand without an effort—or better still, without long experience—that in poetry words are used in a different way and serve different purposes. Poetry alone among the arts suffers this serious handicap. We understand that almost all the other arts are not aiming at the practical. No one supposes that ballet dancers are building up their muscles for military service or are running to the store to buy a loaf of bread. A painting and a symphony concert cannot readily be considered to be of immediate practical usefulness, and there is little likelihood of approaching them with dangerously wrong expectations. But let us imagine for a moment that from childhood we had constantly used square or rectangular surfaces solely as dining tables, writing tables, or checkerboards. A painting might then fill us with contempt because it would be so poorly designed to satisfy what we felt to be its natural functions. Or suppose from the cradle up we had sipped our milk and drunk our coffee from receptacles resembling saxophones. Would it not then seem to us ludicrous to see a man blowing into his cup in order to make it produce inedible and therefore unedifying saxophonic sounds?

We need not resort to such far-fetched parables when we turn to poetry. We are already in the midst of a comedy, or tragedy, of errors. Continually we use words to say: "Please pass the butter," or "I think free trade is obviously the solution," or "I hear Marjorie has given up Steve for Dick." And when the words of poetry fail to say similar things satisfying similar purposes, we are irked or bewildered. Or worse, we try to force them into our ordinary modes of practical or logical thought. We are constantly coming out with the wrong answers. We call poetry a means of escape—as if we actually lived all the time, or even most of the time, in the practical and active world, and never among dreams, aspirations, values, and the sheer sensations of being alive. Even when we know that there are other ways of life than the business of the world, we fail to look for them in poetry, for the barrier of words is still there, and words in our experience are used for immediate utilitarian purposes. And therefore we collect a small handful of commonplace notions and facts from the rich mines of poetry. We feel that we have settled Hardy's business when we label him pessimistic and fatalistic, we consider *Macbeth* simply as a tract to show that too much ambition is a bad thing, we read *Childe Harold's Pilgrimage* because it deals with travels through Europe and an actual battle of Waterloo, or we abstain from *Paradise Lost* because Milton was a Puritan who took the story of Adam and Eve literally. Poetry, we feel, contains some history and some facts, but the *World Almanac* organizes them more efficiently.

Another of our misapprehensions is that reason is the prime distinction of man and that poetry is inferior intellectually to mathematics or philosophy. One of America's most notable critics, John Crowe Ransom, finds the distinguishing mark of poetry to lie in the logical irrelevancy of its local details; to most readers this would immediately appear a flaw in poetry resulting from the ignorance or perversity of poets. That there are other modes of thought and of knowledge than the logical and the practical is not one of our habitual assumptions. My purpose here is to present an approach to poetry as poetry. I am trying to show how poets use words. The notion is difficult to express and to grasp, but it is also, I think inevitably, the basic assumption for any further profitable discussion. Stated in its simplest terms, my position rests on the assumption that a poem is like a person. We can classify persons as Vermonters or Italians, just as we can classify poems as elegies, ballads, and the rest; but perhaps such categories do little to help us understand either personality or poetry. The first safe generalization to make about persons is that each one of them is individual, unmistakable, unduplicable, and that if he were not—if there were any identical substitute for him—he would not be a person. The same is true of a poem, of any poem. I have tried to express this notion in the statement: "Poetry is exact." The phrase is not good enough: its very failure proves the point I am attempting to establish. A poem, through its overtones, its suggestions, the relations between its words and motifs, and its other complexities, may express with complete adequacy a definite and unique experience. But the limited language of analysis, in such a phrase as "Poetry is exact," does not satisfactorily "cover" its subject. Even in this first sketching of the idea, without amplification or illustration or qualification, I must at least point out that the exactness of poetic language is not the logical invariability of a mathematical proposition; rather, it is the unmistakability by which we recognize one person as different from another, depending upon a multiplicity of traits, features, and qualities, material and immaterial, which defy complete analysis. The mere fact that the words of a poem can *not* be analyzed and described exhaustively does not make it less exact: instead, it constitutes the peculiar "exactness," the particularity, the uniqueness, of that poem. Wherever we find poetry, we find also this pleasure in recognizing the unique.

The same voice is not speaking in

The curfew tolls the knell of parting day

that speaks in

For God's sake, hold your tongue and let me love,

and there is no good in trying to make them sound alike. Even when the same poet speaks, he may speak in various moods. We should not bring the temper of the "Elegy in a Country Churchyard" to a reading of

Ruin seize thee, ruthless King!
Confusion on thy banners wait!

All of this is only a way of saying that the first enjoyment we may get from poetry comes from accepting it for what it is and not for something else. We do not enjoy a friend by reducing him to a set of categories: age, 30; hair, dark brown; nationality, U.S.; religion, Methodist. And the better we know the friend, the less we are satisfied to ticket him as 30% justice; 30% cantankerousness; 20% amiability; 15% laziness; and 5% hot temper. Instead, we take pleasure in recognizing that

I must confess it could not choose but be
Profane to think thee anything but thee.

A poem, just as clearly, is a fusion of innumerable elements, large and small, in many fields of experience, obvious or subtle or even not consciously noticed or describable. Experienced fully as a poem, it is not made up of separable or interchangeable parts, and its exactness lies in this unique wholeness.

We may grasp completely the meaning of a scientific law such as "For every action there is an equal and opposite reaction" when that law is stated in other words. But we have lost something when we take the last line of Dante's *Divine Comedy*,

L'amor che move il sole e l'altre stelle,

and translate it literally as

The love which moves the sun and the other stars.

Furthermore, in the Italian, that line gains its full illumination, its precision of meaning, only in its relation to all the rest of the poem with its great weight and glory of details.

The poetic world is the world seen through the eyes of an individual and expressed in his words. Even when that world appears most abstracted and generalized, the poetic view is still unique, and cannot be changed or added to or translated into other terms, as can the propositions in the communal and rational world of science. A poem is an individual imaginative experience recorded as faithfully as possible by an individual poet.

Suppose we accept as the necessary first approach to poetry this recognition that poetic exactness consists in the unique individuality of each complete poetic expression. Does it follow, then, that any further observations on the nature of poetry are rendered impossible because each separate poem is a law unto itself? Does anarchy or multiplicity crowd out order? By no means. But the order cannot be mechanical, for a poem is comparable to a living organism. I have no desire to set up shop as Procrustes and reduce all poems to a long or short bed. On the contrary I am aware that the art of poetry is not the exclusive possession of any century or school or age or race or nation. The range of poetry is immense, and good poems are inexhaustible in number and in variety.

Everything that I have to say here amounts to a single argument regarding the nature of poetry—that a poem is like a person. Now a person does not lose his personality because he is subject to certain general laws: of gravity, of chemistry, of heredity, or of Nemesis. If one considers the laws governing poetry not as grim fiats, but as descriptions of what usually happens in a poem, as generalizations based on experience, they need not seem stern and inflexible and forbidding. The nature of poetry is fluid, so that the laws of poetry, like the laws of nature, may be deduced as great guiding principles within which individual entities move easily, in accordance with their own particular natures, and with no sense of let or hindrance. The biological laws of intussusception and of senescence apply equally to an Anopheles mosquito, an oak tree, and an elephant, but they do not compel the mosquito to be the elephant. Similarly, the qualities of poetry which I am proposing here are found as constants in all poetry, yet are uniquely embodied in each particular poem. No one law of poetry reveals all its secrets; and only open, comprehensive, tolerant minds will save us from clamping poetry in too narrow a cage.

Secondly, I maintain that poetry is intense. To create any work of art requires strenuous effort; only an experience of more than average intensity is strong enough to compel an artist to reproduce that experience as exactly as poetry requires. The more traditional way of stating the fact of poetic intensity would be to say that poetry is emotional or passionate. Calling poetry emotional, however, suggests to some people that poetry gushes and sentimentalizes. So it does, when it wishes, and still it remains poetry: far too many modern critics and readers assume that sentiment and even sentimentality are no fit parts of human experience. But romantic sentiment is not the only way of expressing feeling; restraint and understatement can produce equally powerful emotional effects. Profound thought, no less than smiles and tears, may stamp passion upon a poem; and following the convolutions of a controlled argument may produce an exhilaration and an awareness which cannot be distinguished from emotion. Nevertheless, to avoid the popular limitations set upon the word "emotion," I have chosen to speak of the *intensity* of poetry. Even the idea of intensity must be considered closely to prevent misunderstanding. It might imply that the sensation of poetry is comparable to an electric shock or an exploding firecracker; and much of the discussion, in consequence, is devoted to showing how intensity may be secured through diffusion as well as through compression, through simple serious statement as well as through distortion and hyperbole, through repetition as well as through epigram. For again, though the goal of intensity is single for all poems, it may be reached by various individual paths.

A man does not write a poem in a typhoon or on the bier of his child. He must be at least detached enough from any intense experience to express satisfactorily its meaning for him. Poetry is significant. The care to put exact words in right places, the intensity evoked by the poet and felt by the reader—these could not exist if the poet did not believe that he was being exact and intense about *something*. In part, then, I am attacking the idea of art as an end in itself, an ivory tower walled off from and raised beyond the world of common sense. In part also, since poetry presents one man's consciousness as he regards his material, and since his material is usually human life, I maintain that poetry almost inescapably contains judgments on human values. The discussion, therefore, again argues the venerable case, now somewhat unfashionable, that the end of art is to teach, and that the significance of poetry is primarily a moral significance. Poetry may even be considered as the most effective of moral agents, since it presents not bloodless propositions, but one man's answer to particular situations. In other words, it affords useful examples, for each of us must reach his own moral decisions under similar circumstances of particularity. Such a position demands that many warning signs be set up to show that moral beliefs need not be expressed directly; that poetry is not narrow, rigid, and crude in dogmatism; and that a poem, though it strives toward meaning as intently as a sermon, a legal brief, or a scientific journal, possesses a significance different in kind and different in expression.

In developing this argument, a fourth conclusion naturally follows: "Poetry is concrete." Its significance is embodied in the symbols of all the senses; and moral statements, abstract speculations, convictions, hopes, and tenuous emotions, are all set forth to walk in images and actions. Like the ordinary man, the poet naturally grasps an idea in terms of an example. He "sees" his thought. His pictures and vivid instances convey his sense of the immediacy, the tangibility, the actuality, of the world and of his own existence. The gorgeous galleries of poetry afford ample illustrations that the typical poet thinks in images. Even philosophical or reflective or didactic poetry possesses, to a remarkable degree, this quality of concreteness.

"But poetry is also complex." The earlier principles are, I think, applicable to all poetry; each is quite able to get along independently; each differs from the others; yet how are they to subsist simultaneously in the same poem? Words must be set down in a satisfying and inevitable order; figures and panoramas and symbols must be summoned up before the mind's eye; the dance of the words and figures must not be meaningless, but must rouse in the reader a sense of significance; and thought, words, images, must not clog each other, nor interfere with the sense of heightened experience, of intensity, which gives to art its life and joyousness. The various modes of living—in sensation, in intellect, in emotion, in desire, in conscience—must be allowed full and harmonious interplay. This is the miracle of poetry. This is the mystery of unity-achieved-through-variety which again makes inevitable the comparison: a poem is like a person. The four first statements express merely a few of the great guiding general principles in poetry; there are innumerable smaller laws and local ordinances and temporary edicts and proclamations in time of emergency. Fortunately the immense domains of poetry can never be reduced to mathematical or legal order; and this fifth statement is not so much a law as a description, a recognition, of the complexity of poetry. In art, and perhaps only in art, are the full possibilities of man's existence imaginatively realized, so that life may be apprehended, for a moment, at its highest and its most complete.

Poetry is also rhythmic. A poem maintains its life by walking the knife-edge between rhythmical formlessness on one side and mechanical meter on the other.

And finally, "Poetry is formal." The word is forbidding in its stiffness, but here we are dealing with the most purely esthetic aspects of our subject, the most strictly poetic. And we are finding that poetry is not only a way of looking at the world, but a way of speaking about it. No one can enjoy a poem to the full who does not take it on its own incomparable terms, not only in its unique words and images and rhythms, but also in its form. The structures of poems are as beautiful in themselves as the structures of music or architecture. That poems may appeal to us on so many additional levels is no adequate reason for neglecting or minimizing the delight they afford through the sheer beauty of their forms. We may agree with Plato and with Spenser that

> Soule is forme, and doth the bodie make.

But conversely, we arrive at the highest and purest pleasures of poetry by observing the control, the shape, the harmony which the artist's activity has brought into being.

The nature of poetry is not mechanical. Its laws are not edicts, but observations; they are not forced upon poetry, but derived from it. In all fairness, I should offer here, in very brief compass, an illustration. Let us take a short poem by Housman:

> Into my heart an air that kills
>   From yon far country blows:
> What are those blue remembered hills,
>   What spires, what farms are those?
>
> That is the land of lost content,
>   I see it shining plain,
> The happy highways where I went
>   And cannot come again.*

The voice is unmistakably Housman's: even a parody of it, though it might catch salient traits, would destroy some of the nuances that give it *exactness*. No word can be changed without changing the effect of the whole. If we substitute "distant countries" for "yon far country," we not only destroy Housman's characteristic sense of the past underlying the present, which he manages to suggest through the use of the slightly archaic word "yon," but we also lose the almost concrete action of pointing which "yon" gives, and we weaken the unity of the stanza by canceling the echoing "far" and "farms." We might say also that literally the air is not "killing" anything; the image would be closer to possible sensations if we substituted "an air that chills." But "kills" is the more exact word, for it can suggest the emotional *intensity* of Housman's intuition, which he has made even more poignant by the statement, meaningless in the actual world of matter, that the killing air blows into his heart. This intensity he makes specific by speaking of the content, the shining happiness, which now is lost. Few of us would miss his *significance*—that youth is irrecoverable, or the ecstasy, once past, cannot be recaptured; many of us would feel that judgments of value are also implicit: that content and happiness are good, and that if we cannot have them, it is good at least to see clearly what we have lost, and to recognize time as evil, truth and self-control as good. Any such values are not stated in abstract propositions, but with *concreteness*, in controlled and harmonized images, so that we are made to feel the air, the country, the hills, the spires, the farms, the land, and the highways of Shropshire, perhaps even the plains. *Complexity* is evident enough in the working together of these disparate elements. "Far," for instance, conveys in the thought the years between past and present; in the emotion, regret; in the image, the distant panorama; in the sound, a link with "farms" and other words. Complexity arises from those ambiguities which, to a greater or less degree, all readers find in a poem. If they heard it read orally, many readers might sense as the prime meaning of the sixth line, "I see *its* shining *plain*"; and is this panoramic overtone lacking even when we see that it is not grammatically permissible in the printed version? "Spires," for me at least, is better than "towers" because it makes me think of "aspiring" and "suspiration." Such complexities are not controlled, but will vary from reader to reader; so long as they remain relevant to the whole, they enrich the poem.

We respond to the complex nature of poetry, our imaginations becoming eager and alert, because of the formal qualities of the poem itself. *Rhythm* has a powerful emotional effect, rousing and quieting at the same time, so that we take delight, usually an unconscious delight, in points in the pattern—the alternate rhymes, and the alternating line lengths which compel a pause after each even-numbered line to fill it up to the rhythmical length of its odd-numbered predecessor. Variations from the rhythmical pattern are here not only pleasing in themselves but aid in successful expression: the two inverted first feet—"Ínto my heart" and "Whát are those blue"—suggest spontaneous emotion, and the extra accented syllables—"yón fár coúntry," "Whát spíres,

---

* From "A Shropshire Lad"—Authorised Edition—from *The Collected Poems of A. E. Housman.* Copyright 1939, 1940, © 1959 by Holt, Rinehart and Winston, Inc. Copyright © 1967, 1968 by Robert E. Symons. Reprinted by permission of Holt, Rinehart and Winston, Inc. Also by permission of The Society of Authors as the literary representative of the Estate of A. E. Housman, and Jonathan Cape Ltd., publishers of A. E. Housman's *Collected Poems.*

whát fárms"—add power to the thought and emotion, extension to the landscape. And finally, the perfect *form* of the whole, the echoes, repetitions, and balances, the contrast between the question of the first stanza and the answer of the second, make all these materials into a poem. And the poem, as distinct from its poetic qualities and potentialities, consists precisely in *these* words, *this* rhythm, *this* form. Therein lies its esthetic delight, so that we would not trade the eight lines themselves for eight bushel baskets of such analyses as this. Nevertheless, developing one's power to analyze increases one's capacity to enjoy.

Robert Frost: The Way to the Poem*
by JOHN CIARDI

Stopping by Woods on a
Snowy Evening†

Whose woods these are I think I know.
His house is in the village though;
He will not see me stopping here
To watch his woods fill up with snow.

My little horse must think it queer
To stop without a farmhouse near
Between the wood and frozen lake
The darkest evening of the year.

He gives his harness bells a shake
To ask if there is some mistake.
The only other sound's the sweep
Of easy wind and downy flake.

The woods are lovely, dark and deep.
But I have promises to keep,
And miles to go before I sleep,
And miles to go before I sleep.
                    ROBERT FROST

The School System has much to say these days of the virtue of reading widely, and not enough about the virtues of reading less but in depth. There are any number of reading lists for poetry, but there is not enough talk about individual poems. Poetry, finally, is one poem at a time. To read any one poem carefully is the ideal preparation for reading another. Only a poem can illustrate how poetry works.

Above, therefore, is a poem—one of the master lyrics of the English language, and almost certainly the best-known poem by an American poet. What happens in it?—which is to say, not *what* does it mean, but *how* does it mean? How does it go about being a human reenactment of a human experience? The author—perhaps the thousandth reader would need to be told—is Robert Frost.

Even the TV audience can see that this poem begins as a seemingly-simple narration of a seemingly-simple incident but ends by suggesting meanings far beyond anything specifically referred to in the narrative. And even readers with only the most casual interest in poetry might be made to note the additional fact that, though the poem suggests those larger meanings, it is very careful never to abandon its pretense to being simple narration. There is duplicity at work. The poet pretends to be talking about one thing, and all the while he is talking about many others.

Many readers are forever unable to accept the poet's essential duplicity. It is almost safe to say that a poem is never about what it seems to be about. As much could be said of the proverb. The bird in the hand, the rolling stone, the stitch in time never (except by an artful double-deception) intend any sort of statement about birds, stones, or sewing. The

---

* From the *Saturday Review*, April 12, 1958. Reprinted by permission of the author and of the *Saturday Review*.
† From *Complete Poems of Robert Frost*. Copyright 1916, 1923, 1930, 1939 by Holt, Rinehart and Winston, Inc. Copyright 1936, 1942, 1944, 1951, © 1958 by Robert Frost. Copyright © 1964, 1967 by Lesley Frost Ballantine. Reprinted by permission of Holt, Rinehart and Winston, Inc.

incident of this poem, one must conclude, is at root a metaphor.

Duplicity aside, this poem's movement from the specific to the general illustrates one of the basic formulas of all poetry. Such a grand poem as Arnold's "Dover Beach" and such lesser, though unfortunately better known, poems as Longfellow's "The Village Blacksmith" and Holmes's "The Chambered Nautilus" are built on the same progression. In these three poems, however, the generalization is markedly set apart from the specific narration, and even seems additional to the telling rather than intrinsic to it. It is this sense of division one has in mind in speaking of "a tacked-on moral."

There is nothing wrong-in-itself with a tacked-on moral. Frost, in fact, makes excellent use of the device at times. In this poem, however, Frost is careful to let the whatever-the-moral-is grow out of the poem itself. When the action ends the poem ends. There is no epilogue and no explanation. Everything pretends to be about the narrated incident. And that pretense sets the basic tone of the poem's performance of itself.

The dramatic force of that performance is best observable, I believe, as a progression in three scenes.

In scene one, which coincides with stanza one, a man—a New England man—is driving his sleigh somewhere at night. It is snowing, and as the man passes a dark patch of woods he stops to watch the snow descend into the darkness. We know, moreover, that the man is familiar with these parts (he knows who owns the woods and where the owner lives), and we know that no one has seen him stop. As scene one forms itself in the theatre of the mind's-eye, therefore, it serves to establish some as yet unspecified relation between the man and the woods.

It is necessary, however, to stop here for a long parenthesis: Even so simple an opening statement raises any number of questions. It is impossible to address all the questions that rise from the poem stanza by stanza, but two that arise from stanza one illustrate the sort of thing one might well ask of the poem detail by detail.

Why, for example, does the man not say what errand he is on? What is the force of leaving the errand generalized? He might just as well have told us that he was going to the general store, or returning from it with a jug of molasses he had promised to bring Aunt Harriet and two suits of long underwear he had promised to bring the hired man. Frost, moreover, can handle homely detail to great effect. He preferred to leave his motive generalized. Why?

And why, on the other hand, does he say so much about knowing the absent owner of the woods and where he lives? Is it simply that one set of details happened-in whereas another did not? To speak of things "happening-in" is to assault the integrity of a poem. Poetry cannot be discussed meaningfully unless one can assume that everything in the poem— every last comma and variant spelling—is in it by the poet's specific act of choice. Only bad poets allow into their poems what is haphazard or cheaply chosen.

The errand, I will venture a bit brashly for lack of space, is left generalized in order the more aptly to suggest *any* errand in life and, therefore, life itself. The owner is there because he is one of the forces of the poem. Let it do to say that the force he represents is the village of mankind (that village at the edge of winter) from which the poet finds himself separated (has separated himself?) in his moment by the woods (and to which, he recalls finally, he has promises to keep). The owner is he-who-lives-in-his-village-house, thereby locked away from the poet's awareness of the-time-the-snow-tells as it engulfs and obliterates the world the village man allows himself to believe he "owns." Thus, the owner is a representative of an order of reality from which the poet has divided himself for the moment, though to a certain extent he ends by reuniting with it. Scene one, therefore, establishes not only a relation between the man and the woods, but the fact that the man's relation begins with his separation (though momentarily) from mankind.

End parenthesis one, begin parenthesis two.

Still considering the first scene as a kind of

dramatic performance of forces, one must note that the poet has meticulously matched the simplicity of his language to the pretended simplicity of the narrative. Clearly, the man stopped because the beauty of the scene moved him, but he neither tells us that the scene is beautiful nor that he is moved. A bad writer, always ready to overdo, might have written: "The vastness gripped me, filling my spirit with the slow steady sinking of the snow's crystalline perfection into the glimmerless profundities of the hushed primeval wood." Frost's avoidance of such a spate illustrates two principles of good writing. The first, he has stated himself in "The Mowing": "Anything *more* than the truth would have seemed too weak" (italics mine). Understatement is one of the basic sources of power in English poetry. The second principle is to let the action speak for itself. A good novelist does not tell us that a given character is good or bad (at least not since the passing of the Dickens tradition): he shows us the character in action and then, watching him, we know. Poetry, too, has fictional obligations: even when the characters are ideas and metaphors rather than people, they must be *characterized in action*. A poem does not *talk about* ideas; it *enacts* them. The force of the poem's performance, in fact, is precisely to act out (and thereby to make us act out emphatically, that is, to *feel out*, that is, *to identify with*) the speaker and why he stopped. The man is the principle actor in this little "drama of why" and in scene one he is the only character, though as noted, he is somehow related to the absent owner.

End second parenthesis.

In scene two (stanzas two and three) a *foil* is introduced. In fiction and drama, a foil is a character who "plays against" a more important character. By presenting a different point of view or an opposed set of motives, the foil moves the more important character to react in ways that might not have found expression without such opposition. The more important character is thus more fully revealed —to the reader and to himself. The foil here is the horse.

The horse forces the question. Why did the man stop? Until it occurs to him that his "little horse must think it queer" he had not asked himself for reasons. He had simply stopped. But the man finds himself faced with the question he imagines the horse to be asking: what *is* there to stop for out there in the cold, away from bin and stall (house and village and mankind?) and all that any self-respecting beast could value on such a night? In sensing that other view, the man is forced to examine his own more deeply.

In stanza two the question arises only as a feeling within the man. In stanza three, however (still scene two), the horse acts. He gives his harness bells a shake. "What's wrong?" he seems to say. "What are we waiting for?"

By now, obviously, the horse—without losing its identity as horse—has also become a symbol. A symbol is something that stands for something else. Whatever that something else may be, it certainly begins as that order of life that does not understand why a man stops in the wintry middle of nowhere to watch the snow come down. (Can one fail to sense by now that the dark and the snowfall symbolize a death-wish, however momentary, *i.e.*, that hunger for final rest and surrender that a man may feel, but not a beast?)

So by the end of scene two the performance has given dramatic force to three elements that work upon the man. There is his relation to the world of the owner. There is his relation to the brute world of the horse. And there is that third presence of the unknowable world, the movement of the all-engulfing snow across all the orders of life, the man's, the owner's, and the horse's—with the difference that the man knows of that second dark-within-the-dark of which the horse cannot, and the owner will not, know.

The man ends scene two with all these forces working upon him simultaneously. He feels himself moved to a decision. And he feels a last call from the darkness: "the sweep / Of easy wind and downy flake." It would be so easy and so downy to go into the woods and let himself be covered over.

But scene three (stanza four) produces a fourth force. This fourth force can be given many names. It is certainly better, in fact, to give it many names than to attempt to limit it to one. It is social obligation, or personal commitment, or duty, or just the realization that a man cannot indulge a mood forever. All of these and more. But, finally, he has a simple decision to make. He may go into the woods and let the darkness and the snow swallow him from the world of beast and man. Or he must move on. And unless he is going to stop here forever, it is time to remember that he has a long way to go and that he had best be getting there. (So there is something to be said for the horse, too.)

Then and only then, his question driven more and more deeply into himself by these cross-forces, does the man venture a comment on what attracted him "The woods are lovely, dark and deep." His mood lingers over the thought of that lovely dark-and-deep (as do the very syllables in which he phrases the thought), but the final decision is to put off the mood and move on. He has his man's way to go and his man's obligations to tend to before he can yield. He has miles to go before his sleep. He repeats that thought and the performance ends.

But why the repetition? The first time Frost says "And miles to go before I sleep," there can be little doubt that the primary meaning is: "I have a long way to go before I get to bed tonight." The second time he says it, however, "miles to go" and "sleep" are suddenly transformed into symbols. What are those "something-elses" the symbols stand for? Hundreds of people have tried to ask Mr. Frost that question and he has always turned it away. He has turned it away *because he cannot answer it*. He could answer some part of it. But some part is not enough.

For a symbol is like a rock dropped into a pool: it sends out ripples in all directions, and the ripples are in motion. Who can say where the last ripple disappears? One may have a sense that he knows the approximate center point of the ripples, the point at which the stone struck the water. Yet even then he has trouble marking it surely. How does one make a mark on water? Oh very well—the center point of that second "miles to go" is probably approximately in the neighborhood of being close to meaning, perhaps, "the road of life"; and the second "before I sleep" is maybe that close to meaning "before I take my final rest," the rest in darkness that seemed so temptingly dark-and-deep for the moment of the mood. But the ripples continue to move and the light to change on the water, and the longer one watches the more changes he sees. Such shifting-and-being-at-the-same-instant is of the very sparkle and life of poetry. One experiences it as one experiences life, for every time he looks at an experience he sees something new, and he sees it change as he watches it. And that sense of continuity in fluidity is one of the primary kinds of knowledge, one of man's basic ways of knowing, and one that only the arts can teach, poetry foremost among them.

Frost himself certainly did not ask what that repeated last line meant. It came to him and he received it. He "felt right" about it. And what he "felt right" about was in no sense a "meaning" that, say, an essay could apprehend, but an act of experience that could be fully presented only by the dramatic enactment of forces which is the performance of the poem.

Now look at the poem in another way. Did Frost know what he was going to do when he began? Considering the poem simply as an act of skill, as a piece of juggling, one cannot fail to respond to the magnificent turn at the end where, with one flip, seven of the simplest words in the language suddenly dazzle full of never-ending waves of thought and feeling. Or, more precisely, of felt-thought. Certainly an equivalent stunt by a juggler—could there be an equivalent—would bring the house down. Was it to cap his performance with that grand stunt that Frost wrote the poem?

Far from it. The obvious fact is that *Frost could not have known he was going to write those lines until he wrote them.* Then a second fact must be registered: *he wrote them because, for the fun of it, he had got himself into trouble.*

Frost, like every good poet, began by playing a game with himself. The most usual way of writing a four line stanza with four feet to the line is to rhyme the third line with the first, and the fourth line with the second. Even that much rhyme is so difficult in English that many poets and almost all of the anonymous ballad makers do not bother to rhyme the first and third lines at all, settling for two rhymes in four lines as good enough. For English is a rhyme-poor language. In Italian and in French, for example, so many words end with the same sounds that rhyming is relatively easy—so easy that many modern French and Italian poets do not bother to rhyme at all. English, being a more agglomerate language, has far more final sounds, hence fewer of them rhyme. When an Italian poet writes a line ending with "vita" (life) he has literally hundreds of rhyme choices available. When an English poet writes "life" at the end of a line he can summon "strife, wife, knife, fife, rife," and then he is in trouble. Now "life-strife" and "life-rife" and "life-wife" seem to offer a combination of possible ideas that can be related by more than just the rhyme. Inevitably, therefore, the poets have had to work and rework these combinations until the sparkle has gone out of them. The reader is normally tired of such rhyme-led associations. When he encounters "life-strife" he is certainly entitled to suspect that the poet did not really want to say "strife"—that had there been in English such a word as, say, "hife," meaning "infinite peace and harmony," the poet would as gladly have used that word instead of "strife." Thus, the reader feels that the writing is haphazard, that the rhyme is making the poet say things he does not really feel, and which, therefore, the reader does not feel except as boredom. One likes to see the rhymes fall into place, but he must end with the belief that it is the poet who is deciding what is said and not the rhyme scheme that is forcing the saying.

So rhyme is a kind of game, and an especially difficult one in English. As in every game, the fun of the rhyme is to set one's difficulties high and then to meet them skilfully. As Frost himself once defined freedom, it consists of "moving easy in harness."

In "Stopping by Woods on a Snowy Evening" Frost took a long chance. He decided to rhyme not two lines in each stanza, but three. Not even Frost could have sustained that much rhyme in a long poem (as Dante, for example, with the advantage of writing in Italian, sustained triple rhyme for thousands of lines in "The Divine Comedy"). Frost would have known instantly, therefore, when he took the original chance, that he was going to write a short poem. He would have had that much foretaste of it.

So the first stanza emerged rhymed a-a-b-a. And with the sure sense that this was to be a short poem, Frost decided to take an additional chance and to redouble: in English three rhymes in four lines is more than enough; there is no need to rhyme the fourth line. For the fun of it, however, Frost set himself to pick up that loose rhyme and to weave it into the pattern, thereby accepting the all but impossible burden of quadruple rhyme.

The miracle is that it worked. Despite the enormous freight of rhyme, the poem not only came out as a neat pattern, but managed to do so with no sense of strain. Every word and every rhyme falls into place as naturally and as inevitably as if there were no rhyme restricting the poet's choices.

That ease-in-difficulty is certainly inseparable from the success of the poem's performance. One watches the skill-man juggle three balls, then four, then five, and every addition makes the trick more wonderful. But unless he makes the hard trick seem as easy as an easy trick, then all is lost.

The real point, however, is not only that Frost took on a hard rhyme-trick and made it seem easy. It is rather as if the juggler, carried away, had tossed up one more ball than he could really handle, and then amazed himself by actually handling it. So with the real triumph of this poem. Frost could not have known what a stunning effect his repetition of the last line was going to produce. He could not even know he was going to repeat the line. He simply found himself up against a difficulty he almost certainly had not foreseen and he had to improvise to meet it. For in picking up the rhyme from the third line of stanza one and carrying it over into stanza two, he had created an endless chain-link form within which each stanza left a hook sticking out for the next stanza to hang on. So by stanza four, feeling the poem rounding to its end, Frost had to do something about that extra rhyme.

He might have tucked it back into a third line rhyming with the *know-though-snow* of stanza one. He could thus have rounded the poem out to the mathematical symmetry of using each rhyme four times. But though such a device might be defensible in theory, a rhyme repeated after eleven lines is so far from its original rhyme sound that its feeling as rhyme must certainly be lost. And what good is theory if the reader is not moved by the writing?

It must have been in some such quandary that the final repetition suggested itself—a suggestion born of the very difficulties the poet had let himself in for. So there is that point beyond mere ease in handling a hard thing, the point at which the very difficulty offers the poet the opportunity to do better than he knew he could. What, aside from having that happen to oneself, could be more self-delighting than to participate in its happening by one's reader-identification with the poem?

And by now a further point will have suggested itself: that the human-insight of the poem and the technicalities of its poetic artifice are inseparable. Each feeds the other. That interplay is the poem's meaning, a matter not of WHAT DOES IT MEAN, for no one can ever say entirely what a good poem means, but of HOW DOES IT MEAN, a process one can come much closer to discussing.

There is a necessary epilogue. Mr. Frost has often discussed this poem on the platform, or more usually in the course of a long-evening-after a talk. Time and again I have heard him say that he just wrote it off, that it just came to him, and that he set it down as it came.

Once at Bread Loaf, however, I heard him add one very essential piece to the discussion of how it "just came." One night, he said, he had sat down after supper to work at a long piece of blank verse. The piece never worked out, but Mr. Frost found himself so absorbed in it that, when next he looked up, dawn was at his window. He rose, crossed to the window, stood looking out for a few minutes, and *then* it was that "Stopping by Woods" suddenly "just came," so that all he had to do was cross the room and write it down.

Robert Frost is the sort of artist who hides his traces. I know of no Frost worksheets anywhere. If someone has raided his wastebasket in secret, it is possible that such worksheets exist somewhere, but Frost would not willingly allow anything but the finished product to leave him. Almost certainly, therefore, no one will ever know what was in that piece of unsuccessful blank verse he had been working at with such concentration, but I for one would stake my life that could that worksheet be uncovered, it would be found to contain the germinal stuff of "Stopping by Woods"; that what was a-simmer in him all night without finding its proper form, suddenly, when he let his still-occupied mind look away, came at him from a different direction, offered itself in a different form, and that finding that form exactly right the impulse proceeded to marry itself to the new shape in one of the most miraculous performances of English lyricism.

And that, too—whether or not one can accept so hypothetical a discussion—is part of *HOW* the poem means. It means that marriage to the perfect form, the poem's shapen declaration of itself, its moment's monument fixed beyond all possibility of change. And thus, finally, in every truly good poem, "How does it mean?" must always be answered "Triumphantly." Whatever the poem "is about," *how* it means is always how Genesis means: the word become a form, and the form become a thing, and—when the becoming is true—the thing become a part of the knowledge and experience of the race forever.

Notes on the Art of Poetry*
by DYLAN THOMAS

You want to know why and how I just began to write poetry, and which poets or kinds of poetry I was first moved and influenced by.

To answer the first part of this question, I should say I wanted to write poetry in the beginning because I had fallen in love with words. The first poems I knew were nursery rhymes, and before I could read them for myself I had come to love just the words of them, the words alone. What the words stood for, symbolised, or meant, was of very secondary importance. What mattered was the *sound* of them as I heard them for the first time on the lips of the remote and incomprehensible grown-ups who seemed, for some reason, to be living in my world. And these words were, to me, as the notes of bells, the sounds of musical instruments, the noises of wind, sea, and rain, the rattle of milkcarts, the clopping of hooves on cobbles, the fingering of branches on a window pane, might be to someone, deaf from birth, who has miraculously found his hearing. I did not care what the words said, overmuch, nor what happened to Jack and Jill and the Mother Goose rest of them; I cared for the shapes of sound that their names, and the words describing their actions, made in my ears; I cared for the colours the words cast on my eyes. I realise that I may be, as I think back all that way, romanticising my reactions to the simple and beautiful words of those pure poems; but that is all I can honestly remember, however much time might have falsified my memory. I fell in love—that is the only expression I can think of—at once, and am still at the mercy of words, though sometimes now, knowing a little of their behaviour very well, I think I can influence them slightly and have even learned to beat them now and then, which they appear to enjoy. I tumbled for words at once. And, when I began to read the nursery rhymes for myself, and, later, to read other verses and ballads, I knew that I had discovered the most important things, to me, that could be ever. There they were, seemingly lifeless, made only of black and white, but out of them, out of their own being, came love and terror and pity and pain and wonder and all the other vague abstractions that make our ephemeral lives dangerous, great, and bearable. Out of them came the gusts and grunts and hiccups and heehaws of the common fun of the earth; and though what the words meant was, in its own way, often deliciously funny enough, so much funnier seemed to me, at that almost forgotten time, the shape and shade and size and noise of the words as they hummed, strummed, jugged and galloped along. That was the time of innocence; words burst upon me, unencumbered by trivial or portentous association; words were their spring-like selves, fresh with Eden's dew, as they flew out of the air. They made their own original associations as they sprang and shone. The words, "Ride a cock-horse to Banbury Cross," were as haunting to me, who did not know then what a cock-horse was nor cared a damn where Banbury Cross might be, as, much later, were such lines as John Donne's, "Go and catch a falling star, Get with child a mandrake root," which also I could not understand when I first read them. And as I read more and more, and it was not all verse, by any means, my love for the real life of words increased until I knew that I must live *with* them and *in* them always. I knew, in fact, that I must be a writer of words, and nothing else. The first thing was to feel and know their sound and substance; what I was going to do with those words, what use I was going to make of them, what I was going to *say* through them, would come later. I knew I had to know them most intimately in all their forms and moods, their ups and downs, their chops and changes, their needs and demands. (Here, I am afraid, I am beginning to talk too vaguely. I do not like

---

* Reprinted by permission of Harold Ober Associates Incorporated. Copyright © 1961 by Trustees of the Copyrights of Dylan Thomas.

writing *about* words, because then I often use bad and wrong and stale and wooly words. What I like to do is to treat words as a craftsman does his wood or stone or what-have-you, to hew, carve, mould, coil, polish and plane them into patterns, sequences, sculptures, fugues of sound expressing some lyrical impulse, some spiritual doubt or conviction, some dimly-realised truth I must try to reach and realise.) It was when I was very young, and just at school, that, in my father's study, before homework that was never done, I began to know one kind of writing from another, one kind of goodness, one kind of badness. My first, and greatest, liberty was that of being able to read everything and anything I cared to. I read indiscriminately, and with my eyes hanging out. I could never have dreamt that there were such goings-on in the world between the covers of books, such sand-storms and ice-blasts of words, such slashing of humbug, and humbug too, such staggering peace, such enormous laughter, such and so many blinding bright lights breaking across the just-awaking wits and splashing all over the pages in a million bits and pieces all of which were words, words, words, and each of which was alive forever in its own delight and glory and oddity and light. (I must try not to make these supposedly helpful notes as confusing as my poems themselves.) I wrote endless imitations, though I never thought them to be imitations but, rather, wonderfully original things, like eggs laid by tigers. They were imitations of anything I happened to be reading at the time: Sir Thomas Browne, de Quincey, Henry Newbolt, the Ballads, Blake, Baroness Orczy, Marlowe, Chums, the Imagists, the Bible, Poe, Keats, Lawrence, Anon., and Shakespeare. A mixed lot, as you see, and randomly remembered. I tried my callow hand at almost every poetical form. How could I learn the tricks of a trade unless I tried to do them myself? I learned that the bad tricks come easily; and the good ones, which help you to say what you think you wish to say in the most meaningful, moving way, I am still learning. (But in earnest company you must call these tricks by other names, such as technical devices, prosodic experiments, etc.)

The writers, then, who influenced my earliest poems and stories were, quite simply and truthfully, all the writers I was reading at the time, and, as you see from a specimen list higher up the page, they ranged from writers of schoolboy adventure yarns to incomparable and inimitable masters like Blake. That is, when I began, bad writing had as much influence on my stuff as good. The bad influences I tried to remove and renounce bit by bit, shadow by shadow, echo by echo, through trial and error, through delight and disgust and misgiving, as I came to love words more and to hate the heavy hands that knocked them about, the thick tongues that [had] no feel for their multitudinous tastes, the dull and blotching hacks who flattened them out into a colourless and insipid paste, the pedants who made them moribund and pompous as themselves. Let me say that the things that first made me love language and want to work *in* it and *for* it were nursery rhymes and folk tales, the Scottish Ballads, a few lines of hymns, the most famous Bible stories and the rhythms of the Bible, Blake's "Songs of Innocence," and the quite incomprehensible magical majesty and nonsense of Shakespeare heard, read, and near-murdered in the first forms of my school.

You ask me, next, if it is true that three of the dominant influences on my published prose and poetry are Joyce, the Bible, and Freud. (I purposely say my "published" prose and poetry, as in the preceding pages I have been talking about the primary influences upon my very first and forever unpublishable juvenilia.) I cannot say that I have been "influenced" by Joyce, whom I enormously admire and whose "Ulysses," and earlier stories I have read a great deal. I think this Joyce question arose because somebody once, in print, remarked on the closeness of the title of my book of short stories, "Portrait of the Artist As a Young Dog" to Joyce's title, "Portrait of the Artist as a Young Man." As you know, the name given to innumerable portrait paintings by their artists is, "Portrait of the Artist as a Young Man"—a perfectly straightforward title. Joyce used the painting-title for the first time as the title of a literary work. I myself made a bit of doggish fun of the *painting*-title and, of course, intended no possible reference to Joyce. I do not think that Joyce has had any hand at all in my writing; certainly, his "Ulysses" has not. On the other hand, I cannot deny that the shaping of some of my "Portrait" stories might owe something to Joyce's stories in the volume "Dubliners." But then, "Dubliners" was a pioneering work in the world of the short story, and no good storywriter since can have failed, in some way, however little, to have benefited by it.

The Bible, I have referred to in attempting to answer your first question. Its great stories, of Noah, Jonah, Lot, Moses, Jacob, David, Solomon and a thousand more, I had, of course, known from very early youth; the great rhythms had rolled over me from the Welsh pulpits; and I read, for myself, from Job and Ecclesiastes; and the story of the New Testament is part of my life. But I have never sat down and studied the Bible, never consciously echoed its language, and am, in reality, as ignorant of it as most brought-up Christians. All of the Bible that I use in my work is remembered from childhood, and is the common property of all who were brought up in English-speaking communities. Nowhere, indeed, in all my writing, do I use any knowledge which is not commonplace to any literate person. I *have* used a few difficult words in early poems, but they are easily looked-up and were, in any case, thrown into the poems in a kind of adolescent showing-off which I hope I have now discarded.

And that leads me to the third "dominant influence": Sigmund Freud. My only acquaintance with the theories and discoveries of Dr. Freud has been through the work of novelists who have been excited by his case-book histories, of popular newspaper scientific-potboilers who have, I imagine, vulgarised his work beyond recognition, and of a few modern poets, including Auden, who have attempted to use psychoanalytical phraseology and theory in some of their poems. I have read only one book of Freud's, "The Interpretation of Dreams," and do not recall having been influenced by it in any way. Again, no honest writer today can possibly avoid being influenced by Freud through his pioneering work into the Unconscious and by the influence of those discoveries on the scientific, philosophic, and artistic work of his contemporaries: but not, by any means, necessarily through Freud's own writing.

To your third question—Do I deliberately utilise devices of rhyme, rhythm, and word-formation in my writing—I must, of course, answer with an immediate Yes. I am a painstaking, conscientious, involved, and devious craftsman in words, however unsuccessful the result so often appears, and to whatever wrong uses I may apply my technical paraphernalia. I use everything and anything to make my poems work and move in the direction I want them to: old tricks, new tricks, puns, portmanteau-words, paradox, allusion, paronomasia, paragram, catachresis, slang, assonantal rhymes, vowel rhymes, sprung rhythm. Every device there is in language is there to be used if you will. Poets have got to enjoy themselves sometimes, and the twisting and convolutions of words, the inventions and contrivances, are all part of the joy that is part of the painful, voluntary work.

Your next question asks whether my use of combinations of words to create something new, "in the Surrealist way," is according to a set formula or is spontaneous.

There is a confusion here, for the Surrealists' set formula *was* to juxtapose the unpremeditated.

Let me make it clearer if I can. The Surrealists—(that is, super-realists, or those who work *above* realism)—were a coterie of painters and writers in Paris, in the nineteen twenties, who did not believe in the conscious selection of images. To put it in another way: They were artists who were dissatisfied with both the realists—(roughly speaking, those who tried to put down in paint and words an actual representation of what they imagined to be the real world in which they lived)—and the impressionists who, roughly speaking again, were those who tried to give an impression of what they imagined to be the real world. The Surrealists wanted to dive into the subconscious mind, the mind below the conscious surface, and dig up their images from there without the aid of logic of reason, and put them down, illogically and unreasonably, in paint and words. The Surrealists affirmed that, as three quarters of the mind was submerged, it was the function of the artist to gather his material from the greatest, submerged mass of the mind rather than from that quarter of the mind which, like the tip of an iceberg, protruded from the subconscious sea. One method the Surrealists used in their poetry was to juxtapose words and images that had no rational relationship; and out of this they hoped to achieve a kind of subconscious, or dream, poetry that would be truer to the real, imaginative world of the mind, mostly submerged, than is the poetry of the conscious mind that relies upon the rational and logical relationship of ideas, objects, and images.

This is, very crudely, the credo of the Surrealists, and one with which I profoundly disagree. I do not mind from where the images of a poem are dragged up; drag them up, if you like, from the nethermost sea of the hidden self; but, before they reach paper, they must go through all the rational processes of the intellect. The Surrealists, on the other hand, put their words down together on paper exactly as they emerge from chaos; they do not shape these words or put them in order; to them, chaos is the shape and order. This seems to me to be exceedingly presumptuous; the Surrealists imagine that whatever they dredge from their subconscious selves and put down in paint or in words must essentially be of some interest or value. I deny this. One of the arts of the poet is to make comprehensible and articulate what might emerge from subconscious sources; one of the great main uses of the intellect is to *select*, from the amorphous mass of subconscious images those that will best further his imaginative purpose, which is to write the best poem he can.

And question five is, God help us, what is my definition of Poetry?

I myself, do not read poetry for anything but pleasure. I read only the poems I like. This means, of course, that I have to read a lot of poems I don't like before I find the ones I do, but, when I *do* find the ones I do, then all I can say is "Here they are," and read them to myself for pleasure.

Read the poems you like reading. Don't bother whether they're important, or if they'll live. What does it matter what poetry *is*, after all? If you want a definition of poetry, say: "Poetry's what makes me laugh or cry or yawn, what makes my toenails twinkle, what makes me want to do this or that or nothing," and let it go at that. All that matters about poetry is the enjoyment of it, however tragic it may be. All that matters is the eternal movement behind it, the vast undercurrent of human grief, folly, pretension, exaltation, or ignorance, however unlofty the intention of the poem.

You can tear a poem apart to see what makes it technically tick, and say to yourself, when the works are laid out before you, the vowels, the consonants, the rhymes and rhythms. "Yes, this is *it*. This is why the poem moves me so. It is because of the craftsmanship." But you're back again where you began. You're back with the mystery of having been moved by words. The best craftsmanship always leaves holes and gaps in the works of the poem so that something that is *not* in the poem can creep, crawl, flash, or thunder in.

The joy and function of poetry is, and was, the celebration of man, which is also the celebration of God.

Unit 8

**BALLADS,
AND OTHER FORMS OF
NARRATIVE POETRY**

ON THE BALLAD

There is a fundamental reason for the fact that the most ancient and perennially popular of literary types is the narrative. Young or old, simple or sophisticated, man has always loved a story. It satisfies his curiosity about the actions and motivations of his fellow human beings. At every age of the individual and of society, there have always been stories to satisfy that curiosity. Whether nursery tale or epic, beast fable or romance, short story or novel—every age has had its literary vehicles in which to frame some of the dramatic moments in the lives of men.

Who are these people? What have they done? Why did they do it? These are the questions that entice us to keep on reading any story.

DEFINITION

One of the oldest, simplest, and most popular of narrative forms is the ballad. It is a literary type that is easy to recognize but almost too simple to define. Many critics are content to define it as a very brief folk story meant to be sung. But perhaps that is a little too simple. It is not really a complete story, but usually only the climactic episode of a highly dramatic action. Most of the action of the story has already happened before the ballad begins. In the ballad "Edward," for instance, the father has already been murdered by his son; the ballad merely concerns itself with a climactic dialogue between mother and son which faintly hints at the motivation of the murder. Reading or listening to a ballad, many critics have pointed out, is like happening in on the last act of a play. We are provided with little or no character development, with no gradually built-up plot, and with only minimal hints at the motivation in the final episode of the action with which the ballad deals.

ORIGINS

The characteristic subject matter, structure, and style of ballads arise for the most part from the circumstances of their origin and life history. The English and Scottish folk ballads date back only to the Middle Ages; even "Judas," the oldest of them, was composed sometime in the thirteenth century. The ballads owe their origin not to communal composition by a group of the folk, as was formerly held by many scholars, but to a single composer of fairly well-developed poetic abilities, who gave to the folk who sang the ballads an essentially finished poem. It was this song that the folk made their own and handed on orally from generation to generation, imposing on it the slight and gradual changes in content and form to which anything handed down orally is subject. The ballads, however, were most often sung by a skilled ballad singer who, like his kind in every age, changed their wording slightly to suit his own and his audience's interests. Unessential stanzas were dropped, new names were substituted for old ones, local references were inserted. This process continued for centuries in the Old World and was carried into the hill country of the Atlantic Coast and the Midwest of the New World, where the ballads of tradition are still sung. This gradual modification of the ballad in its travels in time and space accounts for the several versions of many ballads that exist in Child's collection of Scottish and English ballads and for the literally dozens of versions of the same ballads that are still being sung in the hill country of certain sections of the United States.

SUBJECT MATTER

Much of the subject matter of the medieval ballads was determined by the fact that they were composed for a medieval folk audience. But this audience was not a group of completely illiterate, barefooted peasants padding around a backwoods, but rather a lower middle-class group of tavern keepers, craftsmen, and guildsmen in a highly stratified society. "The evidence from numerous records as far back as the Middle Ages," says MacEdward Leach in his introduction to *The Ballad Book*, "points rather to the middle class; small farmers, shoemakers, village schoolteachers, nursemaids, tinkers, wives of small tradesmen, innkeepers, drovers. Among these too are the itinerant singers of songs who go from village to village plying a small trade but concerning themselves largely with singing their stores of songs." The fact that their audiences learned the ballads from the itinerant singers and joined in the singing itself accounts for much of the subject matter and tone of many of the traditional ballads.

It at first seems strange that very great numbers of these "folk" songs are not concerned with the life and activities of the peasant, nor even those of this lower middle class. More often than not it is the nobility that figure in the stories of the medieval ballad. It is *Lord* Randals and *Lady* Margarets, *King* Henrys and *Queen* Ellinors about whom a great many of these stories are told—even Robin Hood was a nobleman in disguise. But this fact need not be too surprising, because the subject matter of most of these ballads is unflattering domestic intrigue.

Even in our much less stratified society a scandal seems to be more scandalous and better news when it involves the upper reaches of society than when it concerns the denizens of the slums and the underworld, where no better conduct is expected. There definitely is something of the flavor of the gossip column and the scandal sheet about some of these old ballads in which the members of this lower middle class narrate, in a very cold and unsympathetic tone, the "goings-on" of their "betters"—wives arranging for the murder of their husbands, sweethearts poisoning their lovers, a jealous young girl drowning her sister without compunction, infidelities, family feuds, murders, suicides, that would match the headlines in any modern tabloid. The taste in middle-class gossip does not change much from age to age. The stark, cold, unsympathetic way in which these stories of upper-class domestic intrigue are narrated in the ballad almost suggests that the middle-class narrators are half gloating over this evidence that their social superiors were no better, or perhaps worse, than themselves.

The completely unsympathetic tone of these narratives of domestic tragedy in high places becomes all the more impressive when it is contrasted with the few instances in these traditional ballads where the tragedy involves members of the lower middle class itself. "The Wife of Usher's Well" is a good instance; here the tragic loss of all her sons by the fisherman's wife is treated quite warmly and with a great deal of delicate human sympathy and understanding. Some of the same kind of sympathy is extended toward "Sir Patrick Spens," a self-made man who had earned his "Sir" by courageous adventures at sea. Sir Patrick was a man whom the ballad singers could respect as someone closer to themselves than the cork-heeled Scots lords who drowned with him, for whom they had neither respect nor sympathy.

The habitual treatment of women in these ballads about upper-class intrigue is worth noting. For the most part, they are a rather cold-hearted, cruel, and calculating lot, with none of the warmth of ordinary human kindness about them, to say nothing of feminine tenderness and love. Witness the unimpassioned discussion of Edward's mother with her son about the murder of her husband. On the other hand, the rejected or wronged young lady in these love triangles is often given an unreal, Ophelia-like, pathetic quality that is hauntingly touching. Margaret in "Sweet William's Ghost" and the younger sister in "The Twa Sisters" are good examples of these pathetic, lovelorn lasses.

But there is one human quality which the ballad singers honor in whatever class they find it—the quality of physical courage. It is the central virtue of the heroes of the ballads that came out of the border warfare between the Scotch and the English and of all those that have to do with adventures in battle at sea and on land. Loyalty to country or to king or lord is another virtue that commands the respect of the ballad singers. It is the main virtue, for instance, of Sir Patrick Spens. As a matter of fact, the ballad singers respect all the virtues associated with kingship and nobility in an ideal feudal society—courage, unselfishness, and a sense of social duty to one's inferiors. Since they found these virtues so seldom exemplified in the kings and nobility of history, they gave many of them to a hero of their own making, one Robin Hood, and sang about him to their heart's content.

We might expect that, since the ballads were composed in the heart of the Catholic Middle Ages, they would frequently deal with religious subject matter. But, as a matter of fact, in the ballads that have come down to us there is little if any trace of religious dogma. There are superficial references to the Church Calendar, such as "the Martinmas time," etc., but practically none of the solid religious content that does appear in the medieval drama and sometimes even in the medieval romance. On the other hand, what continually reoccur in the ballad are such superstitious beliefs as the evil influences of the moon and the return of ghosts of the dead from the grave and their departing again at the crow of the cock. Ghosts are almost universally identified with the body in the grave; it is the physical body that somehow leaves the grave, is fed, put to bed, and vanishes to the grave again at cockcrow. The ballad singers seem incapable of thinking of a ghost as a spirit. All of this is only what might be expected, however, when we remind ourselves again of the group in society that sang these songs—a lower, semi-illiterate, middle class. The minds of this class in any age are much more apt to be possessed of superstitions of all kinds than of any very clear notions of religious dogma. "Sweet William's Ghost" illustrates many of the superstitions, magical practices, and faery lore that characterize a great number of the ballads.

Some songs or carols in the Middle Ages were, however, concerned with episodes in the life of Our Lord and His Blessed Mother and in the lives of the Saints which have many of the characteristics of the ballad. "The Cherry Tree Carol" in our selection is an example.

The vast majority of the surviving medieval ballads deal with serious, somber, and even tragic subject matter. But there are some few cast in a lighter and more humorous vein. Some of the Robin Hood ballads are quite jaunty in spirit, and

"Get Up and Bar the Door" is almost slapstick and rowdy in its humor. It is all of a piece with the kind of broad humor that we encounter in the middle-class medieval fabliaux, and in the sheep-stealing Mak episode of *The Second Shepherd's Play*.

NARRATIVE STRUCTURE

If most of the subject matter of the ballads of tradition is explained by their lower middle-class origins, a great deal of their narrative structure is explained by the fact that they were stories meant to be sung. They are full of the *repetition* of phrase and clause and *parallel construction* that characterize all simple song and folk narrative meant for oral delivery. The fact, too, that the story is frequently developed in *dramatic dialogue* makes for even more repetition. And the dialogue is very often framed in a question and answer formula, which contributes even further to a formal repetitious pattern.

In many ballads this element of repetition is further manifested in the occurrence of a burden or refrain. The refrain is a line (sometimes a mere nonsense rhyme, sometimes a line related in content to the narrative verses of the ballad) which is repeated after every one or two narrative lines of the poem. The burden, on the other hand, is a full stanza which is repeated, like a chorus, after each narrative stanza. The ballad "Edward" combines the use of the refrains "Mither, Mither," and "Edward, Edward" with the parallel question and answer technique.

Another device that is frequently combined in the ballad narrative is *incremental repetition*—a repetition of phrase, clause, verse, or whole refrain or burden with a substitution (sometimes of only one word), which either builds to a climax or substantially advances the story. The successive substitution of "reid-roan steid," and "fadir," for "hauke," in stanzas 2 and 3 of "Edward" is a good example of such incremental repetition. Here the substitution creates a climactic effect in degrees of kinship from a negligible hawk, to a horse—much closer to and necessary for the well-being of a young nobleman such as Edward—to the closest kinship of fatherhood. It is also this mere substitution of a word that suddenly reveals the whole nature of the tragic act of patricide around which the story revolves. The device of incremental repetition frequently makes possible the unbelievable condensation and quick narrative movement of the typical ballad.

Along with these repetitive devices there frequently go two others—the climax of *relations* and the *testament*. Both are also exemplified in "Edward." In the first device a whole series of relationships or relatives is mustered to help build a climax and advance the narrative. In "Edward" the muster consists of "towirs and ha," "bairns and wife," and "ain mither deir." With them are combined examples of the testament device, when the main character is asked to whom he will leave what. "What wul ye leive to your bairns and your wife?" "What wul ye leive to your ain mither deir?" are indications of the use of this narrative device in "Edward."

This all makes for a quick-moving narrative which has no time for gradual transitions from one moment of a story to another. In fact, one of the most characteristic features of the ballad narrative is the *leaps* it takes from one moment to another of the highly compressed story, leaving the reader free to supply the transitions. A ballad is apt to be made up of separate stanzas which frame separate dramatic moments in the story; between stanzas there may be great lapses in time, space, and action. This makes for what has been called the *leaping-lingering* narrative technique of the ballad. The imagination lingers for a moment over the picture that is being suggested by the action and dialogue of one stanza and then leaps on to the picture suggested in the next one.

DICTION

As would be expected in a literary form which had its origin and oral life among the lower middle-class folk, the ballad is simple and straightforward in diction, free of complicated figures of speech and detailed descriptive phrases. It is much more often content with conventional descriptive phrases. It is the "red, red cock" that crows, and wine is more often than not apt to be "blude-red," hair "golden," and hands "lily white."

Very little individuality is given the characters of the ballad in verbal description. As in all dramatic forms we learn what we know about them by what they say and do.

BALLAD METER AND STANZA FORM

In approaching these elements of the ballad form, we must remember that ballads are meant to be sung. What sometimes appears as a rather unreadable stanza may sound acceptable when sung. Ballad tunes as folk music are rather simple, as is the metrical pattern of the verse which supports the tunes. The meter for the most part is iambic, and frequently the lines are organized into what has come to be called "the ballad stanza"—a four-verse stanza of alternating iambic tetrametric and trimetric verses rhyming *a b c b*. The music that has come down to us for many ballads rather suggests that these ballads were originally written as a rhyming couplet of heptametric verse. They were probably arranged in the present "ballad stanza" form when the words were first written down and the long seven-foot verses were too clumsy to handle. Be that as it may, the fact that they were so written down has given rise to the stanza which has often been imitated in literary ballads. A good many other stanza forms occur in the traditional ballads, but this pattern occurs frequently enough to give it some right to be called the "ballad stanza."

Edward

1. "Why dois your brand sae drap wi bluid,
    Edward, Edward,
Why dois your brand sae drap wi bluid,
And why sae sad gang yee O?"
"O I hae killed my hauke sae guid, 5
    Mither, Mither

O I hae killed my hauke sae guid,
And I had nae mair bot hee O."

2. "Your haukis bluid was nevir sae reid,
    Edward, Edward, 10
Your haukis bluid was nevir sae reid,
My deir son I tell thee O."

---
brand sword.

bot but.

"O I hae killed my reid-roan steid,
    Mither, Mither
O I hae killed my reid-roan steid,   15
  That erst was sae fair and frie O."

3. "Your steid was auld, and ye hae gat
    mair
    Edward, Edward,
Your steid was auld, and ye hae gat
    mair,
  Sum other dule ye drie O."   20
"O I hae killed my fadir deir,
    Mither, Mither
O I hae killed my fadir deir,
  Alas, and wae is mee O!"

4. "And whatten penance wul ye drie,   25
    for that,
    Edward, Edward?
And whatten penance will ye drie
    for that?
My deir son, now tell me O."
"I'le set my feit in yonder boat,
    Mither, Mither   30
"I'le set my feit in yonder boat,
  And I'le fare ovir the sea O."

5. "And what wul ye doe wi your towirs
    and your ha,
    Edward, Edward?
And what wul ye doe wi your towirs
    and your ha,   35
  That were sae fair to see O?"

"I'le let thame stand tul they doun
    fa,
    Mither, Mither
I'le let thame stand tul they down fa,
  For here nevir mair maun I
    bee O."   40

6. "And what wul ye leive to your
    bairns and your wife,
    Edward, Edward?
And what wul ye leive to your bairns
    and your wife,
Whan ye gang ovir the sea O?"
"The warldis room, late them beg
    thrae life,   45
    Mither, Mither
The warldis room, late them beg
    thrae life,   45
  For thame nevir mair wul I
    see O."

7. "And what wul ye leive to your ain
    mither deir,
    Edward, Edward?   50
And what wul ye leave to your ain
    mither deir?
My deir son, now tell me O."
"The curse of hell frae me sall ye
    beir,
    Mither, Mither
The curse of hell frae me sall ye
    beir,   55
  Sic counseils ye gave to me O."

---

erst once.   *dule* grief.   *drie* suffer.   *ha* hall.   *maun* must.   *bairns* children.   *thrae* through.

The Twa Corbies

1. As I was walking all alane,
  I heard twa corbies making a mane;
  The tane unto the t'other say,
  "Where sall we gang and dine
    to-day?"

2. "In behint yon auld fail dyke,   5
  I wot there lies a new slain knight;

And naebody kens that he lies there,
But his hawk, his hound, and lady
    fair.

3. "His hound is to the hunting gane,
His hawk to fetch the wild-fowl hame,   10
His lady's ta'en another mate,
So we may mak our dinner sweet.

---

corbies ravens.   *mane* moan, lament.   *tane* the one.   *fail dyke* turf wall.   *kens* knows.

4. "Ye'll sit on his white hause-bane,
    And I'll pike out his bonny blue een;
    Wi ae lock o his gowden hair   15
    We'll theek our nest when it grows
        bare.

5. "Mony a one for him makes mane,
    But nane sall ken where he is gane;
    O'er his white banes, when they are
        bare,
    The wind sall blaw for evermair."   20

---

hause-bane neck bone. *een* eyes. *gowden* golden. *theek* thatch.

The Twa Sisters

1. There was twa sisters in a bowr,
        Edinburgh, Edinburgh,
    There was twa sisters in a bowr,
        Stirling for ay,
    There was twa sisters in a bowr,   5
    There came a knight to be their
            wooer.
        Bonny Saint Johnson stands upon
            Tay.

2. He courted the eldest wi glove an
            ring,
    But he lovd the youngest above a'
            thing.

3. He courted the eldest wi brotch an
            knife,   10
    But lovd the youngest as his life.

4. The eldest she was vexed sair,
    An much envi'd her sister fair.

5. Into her bowr she could not rest,
    Wi grief an spite she almos brast.   15

6. Upon a morning fair an clear,
    She cried upon her sister dear,

7. "O sister, come to yon sea stran,
    An see our father's ships come to
            lan."

8. She's taen her by the milk-white han,   20
    And led her down to yon sea stran.

9. The youngest stood upon a stane,
    The eldest came an threw her in.

10. She tooke her by the middle sma,
    And dashd her bonny back to the
            jaw.   25

11. "O sister, sister, take my han,
    An Ise mack you heir to a' my lan.

12. "O sister, sister, tak my middle,
    An yes get my goud and my gouden
            girdle.

13. "O sister, sister, save my life,   30
    An I swear Ise never be nae man's
            wife."

14. "Foul fa the han that I should tacke,
    It twin'd me an my wardles make.

15. "Your cherry cheeks an yallow hair
    Gars me gae maiden for evermair."   35

16. Sometimes she sank, an sometimes
            she swam,
    Till she came down yon bonny mill-
            dam.

17. O out it came the miller's son,
    And saw the fair maid swimming in.

18. "O father, father, draw your dam,   40
    Here's either a mermaid or a swan."

19. The miller quickly drew the dam,
    An there he found a drownd woman.

---

bowr lady's boudoir. *brast* burst. *stran* shore. *jaw* wave. *Ise* I will. *goud* gold. *twin'd* enshared. *wardles make* worldly mate. *gars* makes.

20. You coudna see her yallow hair
    For gold and pearle that were so rare. 45

21. You coudna see her middle sma
    For gouden girdle that was sae braw.

22. You couldna see her fingers white,
    For gouden rings that was sae gryte.

23. An by there came a harper fine, 50
    That harped to the king at dine.

24. When he did look that lady upon,
    He sighd and made a heavy moan.

25. He's taen three locks o her yallow hair,
    And wi them strung his harp sae fair. 55

26. The first tune he did play and sing,
    Was, "Farewell to my father the king."

27. The nextin tune that he playd syne,
    Was, "Farewell, to my mother the queen."

28. The lasten tune that he playd then, 60
    Was, "Wae to my sister, fair Ellen."

braw broad. *gryte* large. *dine* dinner. *syne* afterwards.

Lord Randal

1. "O where ha you been, Lord Randal, my son?
   And where ha you been, my handsome young man?"
   "I ha been at the greenwood, mother, mak my bed soon,
   For I'm wearied wi hunting and fain wad lie down."

2. "And wha met ye there, Lord Randal, my son? 5
   And wha met you there my handsome young man?"
   "O I met wi my true-love, mother, mak my bed soon,
   For I'm wearied wi hunting and fain wad lie down."

3. "And what did she give you, Lord Randal, my son?
   And what did she give you, my handsome young man?" 10
   "Eels fried in a pan, mother, mak my bed soon,
   For I'm wearied wi huntin, and fain wad lie down."

4. "And wha gat your leavins, Lord Randal, my son?
   And wha gat your leavins, my handsome young man?"
   "My hawks and my hounds, mother, mak my bed soon, 15
   For I'm wearied wi hunting and fain wad lie down."

5. "And what becam of them, Lord Randal, my son?
   And what becam of them, my handsome young man?"
   "They stretched their legs out an died, mother, mak my bed soon,
   For I'm wearied wi hunting and fain wad lie down." 20

6. "O I fear you are poisoned, Lord Randal, my son.
   I fear you are poisoned, my handsome young man."
   "O yes, I am poisoned, mother, mak my bed soon,
   For I'm sick at the heart and I fain wad lie down."

7. "What d' ye leave to your mother, Lord Randal, my son? 25
   What d'ye leave to your mother, my handsome young man?"

wha gat your leavins who got your leavings.

"Four and twenty milk kye, mother,
   mak my bed soon,
For I'm sick at the heart, an I fain
   wad lie down."

8. "What d' ye leave to your sister,
   Lord Randal, my son?
What d' ye leave to your sister, my
   handsome young man?"   30
"My gold and my silver, mother, mak
   my bed soon,
For I'm sick at the heart, an I fain
   wad lie down."

9. "What d' ye leave to your brother,
   Lord Randal, my son?
What d' ye leave to your brother,
   my handsome young man?"
"My houses and my lands, mother,
   mak my bed soon,   35
For I'm sick at the heart, and I fain
   wad lie down."

10. "What d' ye leave to your true-love,
   Lord Randal, my son?
What d' ye leave to your true-love,
   my handsome young man?"
"I leave her hell and fire, mother,
   mak my bed soon,
For I'm sick at the heart and I fain
   wad lie down."   40

Sweet William's Ghost

1. There came a ghost to Margret's
   door,
   With many a grievous groan,
And ay he tirled at the pin,
   But answer made she none.

2. "Is that my father Philip,   5
   Or is't my brother John?
Or is't my true-love, Willy,
   From Scotland new come home?"

3. " 'T is not thy father Philip,
   Nor yet thy brother John;   10
But 't is thy true-love, Willy,
   From Scotland new come home.

4. "O Sweet Margret, O dear
   Margret,
I pray thee speak to me;
Give me my faith and troth,
   Margret,   15
   As I gave it to thee."

5. "Thy faith and troth thou's never
   get,
Nor yet will I thee lend,
Till that thou come within my
   bower,
   And kiss my cheek and chin."   20

6. "If I shoud come within thy bower,
   I am no earthly man;
And shoud I kiss thy rosy lips,
   Thy days will not be lang.

7. "O sweet Margret, O dear Margret,   25
   I pray thee speak to me;
Give me my faith and troth,
   Margret,
   As I gave it to thee."

8. "Thy faith and troth thou's never
   get,
Nor yet will I thee lend,   30
Till you take me to yon kirk,
   And wed me with a ring."

9. "My bones are buried in yon kirk-
   yard,
   Afar beyond the sea,
And it is but my spirit, Margret,   35
   That's now speaking to thee."

10. She stretched out her lilly-white
    hand,
    And, for to do her best,
"Hae, there's your faith and troth,
    Willy,
    God send your soul good rest."   40

11. Now she has kilted her robes of
    green

---

tirled twirled.   *lend* help.

      A piece below her knee,
  And a' the live-lang winter night
      The dead corp followed she.

12. "Is there any room at your head,
      Willy?   45
  Or any room at your feet?
  Or any room at your side, Willy,
      Wherein that I may creep?"

13. "There's no room at my head,
      Margret,
  There's no room at my feet;   50
  There's no room at my side, Margret,
      My coffin's made so meet."

14. Then up and crew the red, red cock,
      And up then crew the gray:
  "Tis time, tis time, my dear Margret,   55
      That you were going away."

15. No more the ghost to Margret said,
      But, with a grievous groan,
  Evanishd in a cloud of mist,
      And left her all alone.   60

16. "O stay, my only true-love, stay,"
      The constant Margret cry'd;
  Wan grew her cheeks, she closd
      her een,
  Stretched her soft limbs, and dy'd.

Sir Patrick Spens

1. The king sits in Dumferling toune,
      Drinking the blude-reid wine:
  "O whar will I get guid sailor,
      To sail this schip of mine?"

2. Up and spak an eldern knicht,   5
      Sat at the kings richt kne:
  "Sir Patrick Spens is the best sailor
      That sails upon the se."

3. The king has written a braid letter,
      And signd it wi his hand,
  And sent it to Sir Patrick Spens,   10
      Was walking on the sand.

4. The first line that Sir Patrick red,
      A loud lauch lauched he;
  The next line that Sir Patrick red,
      The teir blinded his ee.   15

5. "O wha is this has don this deid,
      This ill deid don to me,
  To send me out this time o' the yeir,
      To sail upon the se!

6. "Mak hast, mak haste, my mirry
      men all,   20
  Our guid schip sails the morn."

  "O say na sae, my master deir,
      For I feir a deadlie storme.

7. "Late, late yestreen I saw the new
      moone,
  Wi the auld moone in hir arme,   25
  And I feir, I feir, my deir master,
      That we will cum to harme."

8. O our Scots nobles wer richt laith
      To weet their cork-heild schoone;
  Bot lang owre a' the play wer playd,   30
      Thair hats they swam aboone.

9. O lang, lang may their ladies sit,
      Wi thair fans into their hand,
  Or eir they se Sir Patrick Spens
      Cum sailing to the land.   35

10. O lang, lang may the ladies stand,
      Wi thair gold kems in their hair,
  Waiting for thair ain deir lords,
      For they'll se thame na mair.

11. Haf owre, haf owre to Aberdour,   40
      It's fiftie fadom deip,
  And thair lies guid Sir Patrick Spens,
      Wi the Scots lords at his feit.

---

braid broad.

richt laith right loath.   *cork-heild schoone* cork-heeled shoes.   *aboone* above.

The Wife of Usher's Well

1. There lived a wife at Usher's Well,
    And a wealthy wife was she;
   She had three stout and stalwart sons,
    And sent them o'er the sea.

2. They hadna been a week from her, 5
    A week but barely ane,
   Whan word came to the carlin wife
    That her three sons were gane.

3. They hadna been a week from her,
    A week but barely three, 10
   Whan word came to the carlin wife
    That her sons she'd never see.

4. "I wish the wind may never cease,
    Nor fashes in the flood,
   Till my three sons come hame to me, 15
    In earthly flesh and blood."

5. It fell about the Martinmass,
    When nights are lang and mirk,
   The carlin wife's three sons came hame,
    And their hats were o the birk. 20

6. It neither grew in syke nor ditch,
    Nor yet in ony sheugh;
   But at the gates o Paradise,
    That birk grew fair eneugh.

7. "Blow up the fire, my maidens, 25
    Bring water from the well;
   For a' my house shall feast this night,
    Since my three sons are well."

8. And she has made to them a bed,
    She's made it large and wide, 30
   And she's taen her mantle her about,
    Sat down at the bed-side.

9. Up then crew the red, red cock,
    And up and crew the gray;
   The eldest to the youngest said, 35
    " 'T is time we were away."

10. The cock he hadna crawd but once,
     And clapped his wings at a',
    When the youngest to the eldest said,
     "Brother, we must awa. 40

11. "The cock doth craw, the day doth daw,
     The channerin worm doth chide;
    Gin we be mist out o our place,
     A sair pain we maun bide.

12. "Fare ye weel, my mother dear. 45
     Farewell to barn and byre.
    And fare ye weel, the bonny lass
     That kindles my mother's fire."

---

carlin peasant. *fashes* storms. *o the birk* of the birch. *syke* trench. *sheugh* furrow. *channerin* impatient. *Gin* if. *sair* sore. *maun* must. *byre* stable.

Robin Hood and Little John

1. When Robin Hood was about twenty years old,
    With a hey down down and a down
   He happened to meet Little John,
   A jolly brisk blade, right fit for the trade,
    For he was a lusty young man. 5

2. Tho he was calld Little, his limbs they were large,
    And his stature was seven foot high;
   Where-ever he came, they quak'd at his name,
    For soon he would make them to fly.

3. How came they acquainted, I'll tell
    you in brief,
  If you will but listen a while;
  For this very jest, amongst all the
      rest,
  I think it may cause you to smile.

4. Bold Robin Hood said to his jolly
      bowmen,
  Pray tarry you here in this grove;
  And see that you all observe well
      my call,
  While through the forest I rove.

5. We have had no sport for these
      fourteen long days,
  Therefore now abroad will I go;
  Now should I be beat, and cannot
      retreat,
  My horn I will presently blow.

6. Then did he shake hands with his
      merry men all,
  And bid them at present good
      b'w'ye;
  Then, as near a brook his journey
      he took,
  A stranger he chancd to espy.

7. They happened to meet on a long
      narrow bridge,
  And neither of them would give
      way;
  Quoth bold Robin Hood, and
      sturdily stood,
  "I'll show you right Nottingham
      play."

8. With that from his quiver an arrow
      he drew,
  A broad arrow with a goose-wing.
  The stranger reply'd "I'll liquor thy
      hide,
  If thou offerst to touch the
      string."

9. Quoth bold Robin Hood, "Thou
      dost prate like an ass,
  For were I to bend but my bow,
  I could send a dart quite thro thy
      proud heart,
  Before thou couldst strike me one
      blow."

10. "Thou talkst like a coward," the
      stranger reply'd,
  "Well armd with a long bow you
      stand,
  To shoot at my breast, while I,
      I protest,
  Have nought but a staff in my
      hand."

11. "The name of a coward," quoth
      Robin, "I scorn,
  Wherefore my long bow I'll lay by;
  And now, for thy sake, a staff will
      I take;
  The truth of thy manhood to try."

12. Then Robin Hood stept to a thicket
      of trees,
  And chose him a staff of ground-
      oak;
  Now this being done, away he did
      run
  To the stranger, and merrily
      spoke:

13. "Lo! see my staff, it is lusty and
      tough,
  And here on the bridge we will
      play;
  Whoever falls in, the other shall win
  The battel, and so we'll away."

14. "With all my whole heart," the
      stranger reply'd;
  "I scorn in the least to give out."
  This said, they fell to't without
      more dispute,
  And their staffs they did flourish
      about.

15. And first Robin he gave the stranger
      a bang,
  So hard that it made his bones
      ring;
  The stranger he said, "This must be
      repaid,
  I'll give you as good as you bring.

16. "So long as I'm able to handle my
      staff,
  To die in your debt, friend,
      I scorn."

Then to it each goes, and followed their blows,
   As if they had been threshing of corn.

17. The stranger gave Robin a crack on the crown, 65
   Which caused the blood to appear;
Then Robin, enrag'd, more fiercely engag'd,
   And followed his blows more severe.

18. So thick and so fast did he lay it on him, 70
   With a passionate fury and ire,
At every stroke, he made him to smoke,
   As if he had been all on fire.

19. O then into fury the stranger he grew,
   And gave him a damnable look, 75
And with it a blow that laid him full low,
   And tumbld him into the brook.

20. "I prithee, good fellow, O where art thou now?"
   The stranger, in laughter, he cry'd.
Quoth bold Robin Hood, "Good faith, in the flood, 80
   And floating along with the tide.

21. "I needs must acknowledge thou art a brave soul;
   With thee I'll no longer contend;
For needs must I say, thou hast got the day,
   Our battel shall be at an end." 85

22. Then unto the bank he did presently wade,
   And pulld himself out by a thorn;
Which done, at the last, he blowd a loud blast
   Straitway on his fine bugle-horn.

23. The eccho of which through the vallies did fly, 90
   At which his stout bowmen appeard;
All cloathed in green, most gay to be seen;
   So up to their master they steerd.

24. "O what's the matter?" quoth William Stutely;
   "Good master, you are wet to the skin." 95
"No matter," quoth he; "The lad which you see,
   In fighting, hath tumbld me in."

25. "He shall not go scot-free," the others reply'd;
   So strait they were seizing him there,
To duck him like wise, but Robin Hood cries,
   "He is a stout fellow, forbear. 100

26. "There's no one shall wrong thee, friend, be not afraid;
   These bowmen upon me do wait;
There's threescore and nine; if thou wilt be mine,
   Thou shalt have my livery strait. 105

27. "And other accoutrements fit for a man;
   Speak up, jolly blade, never fear;
I'll teach you also the use of the bow,
   To shoot at the fat fallow-deer."

28. "O here is my hand," the stranger reply'd, 110
   "I'll serve you with all my whole heart;
My name is John Little, a man of good mettle;
   Nere doubt me, for I'll play my part."

29. "His name shall be alterd," quoth William Stutely,
   "And I will his godfather be; 115
Prepare then a feast, and none of the least,
   For we will be merry," quoth he.

30. They presently fetchd in a brace of fat does,
   With humming strong liquor likewise;

They loved what was good; so, in
    the greenwood, 120
  This pretty sweet babe they
    baptize.

31. He was, I must tell you, but seven
    foot high,
  And, may be, an ell in the waste;
  A pretty sweet lad; much feasting
    they had;
  Bold Robin the christning grac'd. 125

32. With all his bowmen, which stood
    in a ring,
  And were of the Nottingham
    breed;
  Brave Stutely comes then, with
    seven yeomen,
  And did in this manner proceed.

33. "This infant was called John Little,"
    quoth he. 130
  "Which name shall be changed
    anon;
  The words we'll transpose, so where-
    ever he goes,
  His name shall be calld Little
    John."

34. They all with a shout made the
    elements ring,
  So soon as the office was ore; 135
  To feasting they went, with true
    merriment,
  And tippld strong liquor gillore.

35. Then Robin he took the pretty
    sweet babe,
  And cloathed him from top to the
    toe.
  In garments of green, most gay to
    be seen, 140
  And gave him a curious long bow.

36. "Thou shalt be an archer as well as
    the best,
  And range in the greenwood with
    us;
  Where we'll not want gold nor silver,
    behold,
  While bishops have ought in their
    purse. 145

37. "We live here like squires, or lords
    of renown,
  Without ere a foot of free land;
  We feast on good cheer, with wine,
    ale, and beer,
  And everything at our command."

38. Then musick and dancing did finish
    the day 150
  At length, when the sun waxed
    low,
  Then all the whole train the grove
    did refrain,
  And unto their caves they did go.

39. And so ever after, as long as he livd,
  Altho he was proper and tall, 155
  Yet nevertheless, the truth to
    express,
  Still Little John they did him call.

Get Up and Bar the Door

1. It fell about the Martinmas time,
  And a gay time it was then,
  When our goodwife got puddings
    to make,
  And she's boild them in the pan.

2. The wind sae cauld blew south and
    north, 5
  And blew into the floor;
  Quoth our goodman to our goodwife,
  "Gae out and bar the door."

3. "My hand is in my hussyfskap,
  Goodman, as ye may see; 10
  An it should nae be barrd this
    hundred year,
  It's no be barrd for me."

---
hussyfskap kneading-trough.

4. They made a paction tween them twa,
    They made it firm and sure,
   That the first word whaeer shoud speak,
    Should rise and bar the door.

5. Then by there came two gentlemen,
    At twelve o clock at night,
   And they could neither see house nor hall,
    Nor coal nor candle-light.

6. "Now whether is this a rich man's house,
    Or whether it is a poor?"
   But neer a word ane o them speak,
    For barring of the door.

7. And first they ate the white puddings,
    And then they ate the black;
   Tho muckle thought the goodwife to hersel,
    Yet neer a word she spake.

8. Then said the one unto the other,
    "Here, man, tak ye my knife;
   Do ye tak aff the auld man's beard,
    And I'll kiss the goodwife."

9. "But there's nae water in the house,
    And what shall we do than?"
   "What ails ye at the pudding-broo,
    That boils into the pan?"

10. O up then started our goodman,
     An angry man was he:
    "Will ye kiss my wife before my een,
     And scad me wi pudding-bree?"

11. Then up and started our goodwife,
     Gied three skips on the floor:
    "Goodman, you've spoken the foremost word,
     Get up and bar the door."

---
paction agreement.

muckle much.

The Cherry-Tree Carol

1. Joseph was an old man,
    and an old man was he,
   When he wedded Mary,
    in the land of Galilee.

2. Joseph and Mary walked
    through an orchard good,
   Where was cherries and berries,
    so red as any blood.

3. Joseph and Mary walked
    through an orchard green,
   Where was berries and cherries,
    as thick as might be seen.

4. O then bespoke Mary,
    so meek and so mild:
   "Pluck me one cherry, Joseph,
    for I am with child."

5. O then bespoke Joseph,
    with words most unkind:
   "Let him pluck thee a cherry
    that brought thee with child."

6. O then bespoke the babe,
    within his mother's womb:
   "Bow down then the tallest tree,
    for my mother to have some."

7. Then bowed down the highest tree
    unto his mother's hand;
   Then she cried, "See Joseph,
    I have cherries at command."

8. O then bespake Joseph:
    "I have done Mary wrong;
   But cheer up, my dearest,
    and be not cast down."

9. Then Mary plucked a cherry,
    as red as the blood,
   Then Mary went home
    with her heavy load.

10. Then Mary took her babe,
     and sat him on her knee,
    Saying, My dear son, tell me
     what this world will be.

11. "O I shall be as dead, mother,
    as the stones in the wall;
  O the stones in the streets, mother,
    shall mourn for me all.

12. "Upon Easter-day, mother,
    my uprising shall be:
  O the sun and the moon, mother,
    shall both rise with me."

45

ON THE ROMANCE

Although the ballad of tradition did frequently concern itself with the "goings-on" of the nobility, in tone and style it bore the marks of its origin and oral development among the lower middle class. But there was a form of story-song in the Middle Ages, the *metrical romance*, which in every respect—subject matter, tone, and style—was related to the upper class. Like the ballad, it was meant to be sung, but not by a folk singer or a communal group; it required an accomplished minstrel who had perfected his poetic style to suit the sophisticated tastes of a leisured, upper-class, aristocratic audience. It was not a group of ale-drinking tavern haunters that listened to the romances but, more often than not, velvet- and silk-clad lords and ladies seated about a banquet table in a torchlit hall of a medieval castle. Its appeal to this aristocratic audience explains almost everything about the metrical romance. One might define it, in fact, as a long story of love, adventure, and the preternatural, composed by a court minstrel, devised in every way to suit the tastes of a sophisticated court audience.

SUBJECT MATTER

One of the perennial demands of that audience in their court entertainment was for the unusual, the startling, and even the fantastic. The romances abundantly satisfied that taste with their large measure of *faery lore*. The procession of faeries and werewolves, with their spells, curses, and packs of black and white magic, that pervades the romances creates an atmosphere of the wild, the mysterious, and the fantastic sufficient to pique the wilted interest of the most blasé upper-class audience in the Middle Ages, and sufficient too, to satisfy the hunger for the mysterious and the unreal that is part of human make-up in every age.

Interwoven almost always with this element of strange and unreal faery lore were strands of *history* and *pseudo-history*. It was not events, however, of the tangible present and the immediate past that interested this audience, but events distant in time and place—Aeneas and his adventures, Charlemagne and his paladins, but most of all Arthur and the Knights of his Round Table.

The exploits of these romance heroes are very different from those of the ancient epic heroes. The greatest motivation of the romance hero is *love*. Mysterious quests are undertaken, great battles and single combats are fought, strange compacts with preternatural beings of all kinds are entered into by the heroes of these stories, all in the interest of proving their superior prowess and chivalry to their lady-loves. Conventional love is sometimes operative in these romances, but more often than not it is *courtly love* that prevails. This is a literary convention developed toward the end of the Middle Ages in which a lady (generally married) is coldly aloof and disdainful of her lover (not her husband), and he in turn pines away in alternating fits of fever and chills at her cruel scorn but is abject in his devotion and service to her. He deifies her and transfers to her all the adulation of a votary to a goddess; she is his lord and master and he her abject vassal. The relationship is carried on in utmost secrecy and according to a strict code of etiquette; but ultimately the cold-hearted lady yields to the importunings of her lover, and the whole story becomes a glorification of adultery. It was, indeed, a strange by-product of the chivalrous feudal ages, and one which was never enthusiastically accepted in England. English romances, for the most part, turn out to be ironic treatments of this strange literary convention that flowered in southern France. *Sir Gawain and the Green Knight* is an especially good example of the ironic treatment of the convention. English poets, from the author of *Sir Gawain* through Chaucer, Spenser, and Shakespeare, are more often heard singing the glories of married love than the adulterous unions of the courtly love tradition.

Another prominent element in the romances was sheer *adventure*, almost for adventure's sake. Action is never as carefully motivated in the romance as in the epic. Knights wander off into weird lands on strange quests to relieve ladies in distress or to slay dragons and, in general, display their knightly virtues. In the best of the romances there is a cluster of these virtues—loyalty, courage, fidelity to oaths, unselfish service of others, the most delicate courtesy, and—when the courtly love theme was not operative—chastity as well. All of these virtues enter substantially into the action and motivation of *Sir Gawain and the Green Knight*.

FORM AND STYLE

Since the chief interest of the courtly audience for which the romances were sung was love, adventure, and chivalrous deeds, it is not surprising that there is little of the careful characterization that we find in epics and the drama. The romance heroes are types; much more attention is lavished on detailed description of their rich costume and castle furniture, and on their rich armor and battle accoutrements, than on their own individual personalities. There is much more detailed description in general in the romance than in the more rhythmic ballad. However, most of this detail was employed to build up, not a realistic impression, but the strange, preternatural, and faerylike atmosphere that is most characteristic of the romance.

The greater length of the romance gave the poet more room than the ballad singer in which to work details of plot and action, but a great many plot patterns became conventional. Examples of these are the *challenge* (or the *beheading game*), the *temptation*, and the *quest*, all of which are intertwined in the structure of *Sir Gawain and the Green Knight*.

Sir Gawain and the Green Knight*

Translated by JAMES L. ROSENBERG

A NOTE BY THE TRANSLATOR

John Ciardi, in the introduction to his translation of *The Inferno*, stated it aptly, it seems to me, when he likened verse translation to taking a tune written for the piano and playing it on the violin. The melody is the same, but the texture of the music is significantly different. Actually, I am not enough of a musician to know whether the analogy is really a valid one, but it sounds good to me, for it was my feeling in the course of translating *Sir Gawain and the Green Knight* that this is what my endeavors consisted of: taking the melody composed by an unknown author in the fourteenth century and transcribing it as best I could for my own instrument—Modern English. The notes are identical—or as nearly so as I could make them—but the music is necessarily different. Where the original author draws his bow across the strings and plays "Ther hales in at the halle dor an aghlich mayster," (l. 136), I blow into my twentieth-century kazoo and out comes "When suddenly came crashing in a frightening great creature." It is not adequate, but how else am I to reproduce the delightful melody of "aghlich mayster"? "Terrible" or "frightening" is about the best I can do with "aghlich," while neither "master" nor "mister" will do for "mayster," since their modern connotations are distinctly inappropriate. It is a little like hearing a stirring symphonic theme in the concert hall, then going home and picking it out with one finger on the piano. The notes may be all there, but, as Wordsworth once lamented, "Oh, the difference to me!"

With these prefatory apologies and disclaimers, let me now try to suggest briefly what I have sought to accomplish in the following pages—and why I have not always succeeded in accomplishing it.

I began with what seems to me a truism so painfully self-evident as scarcely to require argument (although I am aware that it sometimes still *does!*): i.e., that a poem, if it is to make any sense, must be translated into poetry, not prose. This also provided me with one of my excuses for attempting the translation in the first place, since two of the most widely anthologized earlier "translations" were prose retellings of the plot and seemed to me to be no more adequate renderings of the original *Sir Gawain* than a rather blurry pen-and-ink copying of an El Greco. Surely the rhyme and music and rhythmic movement of any piece of poetry is as much a part of the meaning as is the prosaic interpretation of the words themselves, and any "translation" which ignores or seriously distorts these factors (another version of *Sir Gawain* is in hexametric couplets!) is nothing more than a prose "pony" of the argument, or perhaps an author's freehand variations on the original theme. Translation is a matter, not merely of the letter, but of the spirit; a competent translator will strive to reproduce not only the meaning but the music, not only the shadow but the substance.

What all this means, then, is that, in taking up my task of translation, I was committed to as accurate an imitation of the exact rhythmic and stanzaic patterns of the original as I could manage—in other words, stanzas of varying length and in regularly alliterative lines, each stanza concluding with a five-line, cross-rhyming "bob and wheel." May I say, in passing, that the obvious fact that this was a flat impossibility deterred me not a whit. Idiots, poets, and translators (the terms are roughly synonymous) have never been discouraged by impossibility since Lucifer, their spiritual progenitor, first defied omnipotence. I was perhaps ten lines into the poem when my cheerfulness be-

---

* From *Sir Gawain and the Green Knight* translated by James L. Rosenberg. Introduction by James R. Kreuzer. Translation copyright © 1959 by James L. Rosenberg. Reprinted by permission of Holt, Rinehart and Winston, Inc.

came somewhat dampened, and it was not long after when I decided that I would have to settle for a *few* imperfect lines. I have not been able to bring myself to count the exact number of imperfect lines in my translation; suffice it to say, there are enough. I can rationalize their existence on two counts: there are a number of imperfect lines in the original (although not as many as in my version); the scheme of alliterative verse, like any poetic scheme, is intended as a pattern, not a strait jacket, and a mathematically perfect adherence to it would be intolerably monotonous. There is no such thing as a perfect iambic pentameter poem, and the composition of such a work would be, it seems to me, a triumph of technology over poetry. Much of the beauty and music of some of Shakespeare's most famous soliloquies comes from the deftly irregular variations he is able to weave against the basic pattern of his verse.

The scheme or format of alliterative verse is roughly this: each line must contain four heavy beats or stresses; the number of light stresses is infinitely variable. There must be, in every line, a caesura, or pause. Three of the four main stresses must alliterate, two on one side of the caesura, one on the other. (In my alliteration, incidentally, I have followed the principle—generally observed by the original author, too—that the alliterative accents should fall, not necessarily on the initial syllables of words, but on the stressed syllables. Thus, "far," "field" and "defense" might alliterate. In actual practice, and since an alliterative poet needs all the help he can get, you will find both the original author and me playing both ends against the middle and employing a word like "defense" to alliterate either with "d" or "f" as suits our purpose in the given line. This, I have discovered, is one of the medieval equivalents of what today we call "poetic license.")

My irregular lines seem to fall into several distinct groups, or types, of which the following are the most numerous and noteworthy:

a. Lines containing fewer than the requisite three alliterators:

"I never flinched nor fled when you struck at me" (l. 2274)

When one is required to come up with, not just a couple of rhyming words every two or three lines, but three alliterative words in *every* line, demand very quickly exceeds supply, once in a while to the point where the translator has to throw up his hands in despair and alliteration disappears completely:

"She who dwells within my house and knows many arts" (l. 2447)

b. Lines containing more than three alliterators:

Once in a while, for reasons which are by no means clear to me, I developed a line in which the alliterations seemed to fall like a shower of grace notes all over the page:

"A brave bushy beard hung before his breast" (l. 182)

I suppose my feeling was that, since alliterators were not easy to come by at best, I could scarcely afford to be so prodigal as to throw any away that happened to fall into my lap!

c. Lines in which the alliterators are all on one side of the caesura:

"And the whanging clamor rang from the rocks around" (l. 2220)

d. Lines containing what I have come to think of as "slant-alliteration"—that is, not quite perfect alliteration, in the same way that "slant-rhyme" is not quite perfect rhyme:

"Thus Arthur was granted this green New Year's gift" (l. 491)

The alliterative "gr" sound of "granted" and "green" fades to the plain generalized "g" of "gift."

A variant of this is the following:

"Now shall we see skill in courtly courtesy" (l. 916)

Here the "k" sound in "courtly" and "courtesy" alliterates with the "k" in "(s)k."

I remind the reader, too, that alliteration is determined by the ear, not the eye; it is a question of phonetics, not of spelling. Thus, a word like "one" alliterates with "w" sounds, and a word like "queen" ("kw*i*n") alliterates with "k" sounds.

e. Lines which are imperfect in that one of the alliterators is actually an unstressed syllable:

"The lord placed beside her upon the broad benches" (l. 1002)

No matter how you read it, the "b" in "beside" is in an unstressed syllable, although it is supposed to alliterate with "broad benches." This, I suppose, is the most awkward type of irregularity, and I can only plead expediency, plus the fact that I have tried to keep lines of this type at an absolute minimum.

f. Lines in which the alliteration is technically imperfect but is compensated for by a pattern of assonance or what the Welsh poets call "consonant chime" or some other type of internal music. This is difficult to describe, but can best be exemplified, I think, by the following:

"In lavish revelry and reckless frolic mirth"
(l. 40)

The alliteration is actually imperfect here, but the rather complex tissue of "l," "v," "r," and "k" sounds gives—to my ear, at any rate—the sound and *feel* of a richly alliterative line. Indeed, this is one of the few lines in the whole poem with which I feel satisfied, for it seems to me that here I have actually come very near to reproducing some of the music of the original ("With rych reuel oryght and rechles merthes").

In addition to adhering to a cruelly demanding pattern of alliterative lines, I had also, as I mentioned a few paragraphs back, to find rhyming words for the refrainlike "bob and wheel" at the end of each stanza, and here too I frequently had to settle for imperfection and employ one of the "slant-rhymes" which were delightful and startling irregularities when Emily Dickinson used them, but which have now almost become one of the clichés of modern poetry. A pair of examples will suffice:

In truth.
Then Michaelmas morn
Is come in bitter sooth;
Gawain in his turn
Bethinks him of his oath.
(ll. 531–535)

"Hold fast!
One stroke was due unto me,
According to our pact;
My turn again is due me—
Defend yourself. Stand back!"
(ll. 2326–2330)

Elsewhere I have rhymed "merriment" and "kettledrums" and "brothers" and "suppers," which may set the teeth of traditionalists on edge, but will not, I trust, be received too unsympathetically by readers (and writers) of modern poetry. And one of my aims in this translation has been to present to my readers a fresh and enjoyable modern poem rather than an exhumed medieval fossil.

This brings me to another and perhaps even more important matter—the problem of diction.

The besetting sin of most translations of more or less ancient literature—particularly of the medieval period, it would seem—is that the translator all too readily yields to a rush of coyness to his vocabulary and comes up with a pastiche of "prithees" and "God wots" and "yea verilies" and "gramercies" which make his translation not only overpoweringly "quaint" but, in the final analysis, very nearly as impenetrable as the original. The author of *Sir Gawain and the Green Knight*, though he lived and wrote around 1375, was a modern writing for moderns in language they could understand and appreciate. There is, as a matter of fact, no such thing as an ancient author; every author who ever wrote (and who was worth his salt) wrote modern literature, and to translate him in rags and patches of old-fashioned, archaic language is simply an injustice and a sin in the sight of Heaven. "Prithee" sounded no more "quaint" or "archaic" to men of the fourteenth century than "please" does to us, and it should probably be translated as such in most instances. The "forsooth" and "gadzooks" school of writing is, it seems to me, a parody of a parody—and not a very good one, at that.

There are, on the other hand, certain definite limits to "modernization," limits imposed, for the most part, by sheer common sense. What these are, I think, can be suggested by stating that it is one thing to write about archaic times and customs, and another to write about them in an archaic manner. The *Gawain* poet, as I have already tried to point out, was an extremely "modern" poet, but he was writing about events which had presumably taken place hundreds of years before his own day. So he had to "modernize" his version of the story, just as I have had to "modernize" my translation. But please note that by "modernization" I do not mean I have wantonly violated the spirit of the original; I have not, for example, turned Gawain into an eager young Madison Avenue junior executive embowered in a Manhattan penthouse with an importunate married woman whose husband is off hunting the bulls and bears of Wall Street! To say that this would be a ridiculous distortion of the original would be to put it as mildly as possible. It is my feeling that, while many earlier translators may have erred in being too consciously quaint and old-fashioned, modern translators of the post-Pound era are too often inclined to stray in the other direction and strive so hard to be "modern" that the original is again badly distorted. *Sir Gawain and the Green Knight* does, after all, take place in a dim, legendary past—probably around the sixth century—when the customs, dress, and manners were quite strikingly different from those of today. This historical context is part of the poem's flavor, is, indeed, as much a part of its very meaning, again, as are the rhythm and alliteration. There are, for example, a number of words in the original poem—technical terms, referring to the hunting field or to armor—which simply have no convenient and appropriate equivalent in Modern English, and striving to find one, or to force one upon the language, can often, I fear, lead to disaster. Modern warriors do not, for example, wear "greaves," or even anything very similar to them, and the translator who, in a brisk attempt to be "modern" if it kills him (and his readers), translates "greaves" as, let us say, "iron pants" is trembling drunkenly on the ragged edge of unintentional humor. 'Twere invidious to name names, but I have read some modern translations in which the authors' evident attempts to be "modern" at all costs have led to lapses almost as bad, lapses which are surely as unfortunate as the cumbersome and coy "archaic" locutions of some nineteenth-century translators.

There remains, finally, the problem of "inversions," one of the more glaring stigmata of many older translations—particularly from the medieval period—and I can only say that I have approached not only "inversions" but "archaisms" and "poeticisms" generally as a modern St. Patrick might approach a nest of rattlesnakes—although with not quite, I trust, the intransigence of that militant cleric. My test for "inversions" as well as for "archaisms" has been, in the final analysis, my ear, not any convenient book of rules. If it sounded right, I left it in; if it sounded awkward or pretentious or phony, I cut it out. I do not think that an inversion is an evil per se, as some modern critics and writers would seem to maintain; the language recognizes and allows for occasional inverted constructions, which sometimes have a musical value, sometimes actually determine meaning—as in questions. This was generally my touchstone, then: if the inversion contributed something of value to the line, by way of verbal music or heightening of meaning through throwing stress on a certain word, I left it in; if it seemed to be merely a nonfunctional decoration, perhaps even an awkward attempt to escape the exigencies of syntax or meter or rhyme, I removed it.

To sum up, then, my aim has been to present to my readers, not a disinterred, moss-covered, medieval relic, but a fresh, exciting, readable modern poem, for this is what the original was above all. A translation is at best only a pale shadow of the real thing; it is like reading a one-page prose summary of the plot of *Hamlet*, as compared to spending an evening in the theater watching the play burst into life on the living stage. I can at least hope, though, that the shadow of my translation falls steady on the page.

Not only have I learned more from this translation than I have ever learned before in the years since I have been studying the fine art of linking and coupling words into units of meaningful music, but this has been from the very first a labor of love if there ever was one. As Dylan Thomas said of his poems, I have done it "for the love of Man, and in praise of God," and I'd be a damned fool if I hadn't. If even a little of that love and praise shines through the dull and intractable words, my time will not have been wasted. Nor, I trust, will yours.

PART ONE

1

After the siege and assault had ceased at Troy,
And the city was blasted and burned to brands and ashes,
The traitor who there devised the treasonous stratagems
Won hatred for his treachery and his deep betrayal.
Then came the kingly Aeneas with kith and kindred,   5
Who, claiming and conquering provinces, patrons became
Of well-nigh all the wealth of the Western Isles.
And, after the regal Romulus gets him to Rome
(With pompous strength that state he establishes,
Giving his own name to it, as now it is known),   10
Ticius turns him to Tuscany, there begins building,
Longbeard in Lombardy lays down his firm foundations,
And over the English Channel Felix Brutus
Brave on banks and braes founds and fathers Britain
             In splendor,   15
        Where, mixed in the misty air,
        War and woe and wonder
        Of times have dwelt, and where
        Is mingled rain and thunder.

2

And when this Britain was founded by this brave baron,   20
Bold were the warriors bred there, battles they joyed in,
Many the wonders they worked in that wild long-ago.
Greater the glories they wrought in their gallant domain
Than in any state in the sun men now sing of.
But of the brave British kings who built here   25
Arthur was ever the strongest in story and song.
Whereof a valiant adventure I plan to reveal,
A miracle some men will call it and some men a marvel,
A strange, surprising adventure from King Arthur's story.
Listen a little, oh, friend, to this lay,   30
And I shall tell it you truly and quickly, with tongue,

The traitor   Critics are not agreed upon who the traitor is. Some suggest that it was Aeneas himself as he had come to be treated in medieval lore rather than in Vergil's *Aeneid*. In the former, he concealed Polyxena from Achilles, who was ultimately slain by Paris in attempting to find and wed her. It was Achilles' death that started the Trojan War again, and thus brought on the final destruction of Troy. Because Aeneas, in hiding Polyxena, had occasioned the renewal of hostilities, he was tried by the Greeks and exiled. Hence he might be called "the traitor." Other critics, however, claim that it is Antenor and not Aeneas that is meant. The wording of our translation would seem to suggest Antenor or someone other than Aeneas as "the traitor." *Ticius* and *Longbeard*   fictitious descendants of Aeneas.   *Felix Brutus*   according to tradition, the grandson of Aeneas, and founder of Britain.   *Arthur*   mythical king of Britain, served by Knights of the Round Table. He had in the British tradition the honored position that Aeneas had in the story of Rome.

>   As it's sung
> In mead-hall and mansion,
> With linked letters strong,
> In accord with tradition
> Of tight-knit song.

3

This king at Camelot once lay on Christmastide,
And many a lithesome lord, lads of the best,
Brothers bright of the Table Round, boys bravely rich,
In lavish revelry and reckless frolic mirth.
There champions tilted and tourneyed many a time,
And these gentle knights jousted there full jolly,
Paraded then to the court to caper and make carols.
For there was song and feasting full fifteen days,
With all the mirth and meat and drink that men could devise;
Such gaiety and glee glorious to hear,
Delightful din by day, dancing by night.
All was sprightly and happy in high halls and chambers
With gay lords and ladies, lightsome and tripping.
Full of courtly fun they bode in fellowship,
The worthiest of warrior-knights under Christ's welkin,
And the lovesomest ladies ever life beheld,
And the comeliest king ever in keep or castle;
For all this was a fair folk in their first free age,
>   In grove and holt,
> The happiest known to fame,
> The king the purest of heart;
> Hard it were to name
> A merrier, gayer court.

4

Then came the keen New Year, icy-crisp and sharp;
That day double portions were doled to the throng
After the king had come to his knightly court
And the holy chanting had ceased in the chapel.
Loud was the crying then of Christ's goodly clerics,
Noel proclaimed anew, Christ named full often;
And after, the gallants, giving season's gifts,
Hollaed their wares aloud, held them high in hand,
Busily debated about those gifts;
Ladies laughed full loud, though they had lost,
And he that won was merry, that much you may guess.
All this rare mirth they made till the meat-time.

Camelot King Arthur's mythical capital, associated with various actual English cities—but especially with Winchester, where to this day what is supposed to be his Round Table is still displayed.   *carols* dances accompanied by song.   *welkin* the vault of heaven.

When they had worthily washed, forth they went to sit,
The greatest man above, as best befits his grace,
Queen Guinevere full blithe throned in their midst,
Regal on the dais and dearly adorned, 75
Backed by beauteous silk beneath a canopy
Of truest Toulouse and cloth of Turkestan
That was embroidered and bound with the brightest gems
That pounds or pence could buy at any rare price.
          She seemed 80
          The fairest, comeliest queen,
          Her gray eyes gleaming,
          That men had ever seen,
          Waking or dreaming.

5

But Arthur would not eat till all around were served, 85
So jolly was he and joyous and boyish in his jesting;
Lissome and light-hearted, he loved the less
Either long to lie or long to sit and listen,
So busied him his blood, and his brain was leaping.
And too another matter moved him in this manner, 90
That nobly had he sworn, nay, nevermore to eat
On such a dear day till someone had devised him
Some strange story of mystery or adventure,
Some miraculous marvel he might well believe
Of arms and of armies, of great and desperate deeds; 95
Or else some man besought him of some noble knight
To join with him in jousting, in jeopardy to lie,
To risk life for life, allowing one another,
As fortune would help them, to have the fairer chance.
Thus was the king's behavior when he came to court 100
At these fair feasts among the free ménage.
          And thus,
          With face bright and clear,
          He stands at his place
          Making merry cheer 105
          And full of goodly grace.

6

So there stands at his place the strong and sturdy king,
Talking of trifles before the royal table.
There was the good Gawain, Guinevere beside him,
And Agravain, the hard of hand, opposite to her, 110
Both the king's nephews and full noble knights;
Bishop Baldwin next, beginning the board,
And Ywain, Urin's son, eating beside him:

Toulouse a city in southern France famous for its textiles.   *Turkestan* source of very rich materials such as cloth of gold.

These were grouped upon the dais and graciously were greeted,
And many trusty servitors sat at the sideboards. 115
Then the first course came with cracking of trumpets,
With many bright banners hanging high nearby,
Rumbling music of drums and the mellow noble pipes,
With wild sweet warbling wakening the lute,
And many a merry heart leaped at their music. 120
Dishes full of delicacies, rare meats and dainties,
Plenteous provisioning on steaming plates and platters
That fill the board to overflow so no place is found
To set the silver dishes rich with sparkling sauces:
          Thus they dined. 125
      The servants, they were lissome;
      The fare was rich and fine;
      Twelve dishes for each twosome,
      And good beer and bright wine.

7

Now will I of their merry-making no more describe, 130
For each of you may guess no guest went hungry.
A new blast of music was boldly blown forth,
Signal to the banqueteers the banquet was begun,
But merely had the music melted into echoes
And the opening course had been commanded and carved, 135
When suddenly came crashing in a frightening great creature,
Terrible to look upon, tall as a forest tree;
From his throat to his thigh so sturdy and so thick,
And his loins and limbs so powerful and long,
Half legendary giant I jest not to name him, 140
But nonetheless a man I must believe him to be,
And that the likeliest and mightiest ever lanced or galloped,
For, back and breast, full-muscled was his body,
But his sides and waist were worthily slim,
And all his facial features likewise were fair, 145
          Cheery and clean.
      But wonder of his color!
      The like I've never seen.
      The strange and ominous fellow
      Was a vivid green. 150

8

And everything was green, all this creature with his weeds:
A close, clipped jacket that clung to his sides,
Over that a mantle made and masked within

---

upon the dais—at the sideboards Tolkien has pointed out that the graded seating arrangement here reinstates the class gradation according to rank which the Round Table was designed to avoid.   *green* Green was the color of faeryland; it was suitable for this strange knight of the Green Chapel. The Green Chapel was actually a faery mound. (See the description of it in the last episode of the poem.)

With featly trimmed fur fair for to see,
A white ermine hem handsome on the hood, 155
That loosely from his locks lay upon his shoulders;
Neat, tight hose, green like hood and habit,
That clung to his calves, and golden, clanking spurs,
Joined to silken straps and richly gemmed and jeweled,
And long pointed slippers both proper and neat; 160
Forth this rider fares clad all in forest green,
Even the bars of his belt and the other bright stones
Richly arrayed about his verdant robe,
About his suit and saddle and all his silk belongings;
Too tedious it were to tell half the bonny trifles 165
That were embroidered there, birds and butterflies,
In gay gaudy green studded round with gold.
His beast's breast-trappings, the studs of its bit,
All his gear and rigging, were greenly enameled;
The stirrups that he stood in, they were stained the same, 170
And all his sparkling tackle from saddle-bows to spurs
Gleamed and glittered grandly with green, glinting stones;
The steed that he straddled, stoutest of stallions,
  Green was beside him,
  A steed strong and thick, 175
  Straining at the bridle,
  Mettlesome and quick,
  Well-suited to his rider.

9

And this giant was full gay, geared all in green,
The hair of his head matching his horse, 180
Fair fanning flax falling round his shoulders;
A brave bushy beard hung before his breast,
Which, like the hair hanging from his head,
Was clipped all about just above his elbows,
So half his arms thereunder were hidden as it were 185
Beneath a king's cape enclosing his neck;
That mane of his mount in much the same fashion,
Well crisped and combed in many curious knots
And plaited with gold throughout the goodly green:
Here a strand of green, there a gleam of gold; 190
His tail and his forelock likewise framed and fitted
And bound with a band of bright glittering green
And studded to the tip with the starriest of stones,
Then twisted with a thong and tied into a knot,
Where many bright bells of burnished gold rang. 195
Such a rare horse, such a rarer rider
Had never before been seen at one of Arthur's banquets.
  His gaze
  Was blinding, bold and bright,
  Dazzling to his foes. 200

It seemed no mortal wight
Might stand beneath his blows.

10

However, he wore no helmet, neither any halberd,
No gorgeret nor greaves, grim plates of battle,
No shaft nor shield wherewith to shear and smite,　　　　　　205
But he held in one hand a giant branch of holly
That waxes and grows great when the green groves are bare,
And in his other an ax, horrible and huge,
A deadly weapon to describe or deal with in words.
The ax head measured long as an ell in length,　　　　　　　210
The spike of green steel beat with goodly gold,
The bit burnished bright with a biting edge,
As shaped to split or shear as the sharpest razor.
And this grim knight gripped and grasped it tight
By a stout shaft spun and wound with iron,　　　　　　　　　215
All engraved in green in grave and curious fashion;
A thong tied around that was twisted at the head
And along the handle's length was looped round about,
With tassels tied thereto and tightly attached
On bosses of bright green, rich with splendid braid.　　　　220
Boldly then this burly fellow bursts into the hall,
Fares forward to the very dais, fearless and free;
Never once he spoke, but coolly looked about.
The first sound that he uttered: "Show me," he said,
"The governor of this gathering. Gladly I would　　　　　　225
See and speak with him, whosoe'er he be."
　　　　　　　Silent and strong,
　　　　　He rode before the dais
　　　　　And seemed to study long,
　　　　　Searching that still place　　　　　　　　　　　　　230
　　　　　For the leader of the throng.

11

Great was the goggling and gaping at that creature,
And each man in his heart thought what it might mean,
This stranger and his steed stained so rich and strangely,
As green as growing grass and seeming even greener　　　　235
Than enamel on a golden ground, glowing even brighter.
All stood still about him, staring curiously,
Full of fear and wonder, what work he planned there.
For many marvels had they seen, but never such a monster,
Wherefore they deemed him phantom, troll or fay,　　　　　240
And full of goodly fear all this folk were then;

---

halberd shoulder and neck armor.　　*gorgeret* throat armor.　　*an ell* a unit of measurement (45 inches.)

And all, astonished at his voice, sat stone-still;
And a breathing silence settled on the scene;
All, as though enchanted, ceased their cheery chatter.
>(See, 245
>>Some are hushed with fear,
>>Some out of courtesy,
>>But every person there
>>Leans forward, tensed to see.)

12

Then Arthur, standing on the dais, gazed upon the scene 250
And he smiled and nodded freely; fear he never felt.
Cheerily he cried: "Good friend, greetings from this group.
Men call me Arthur, master of this manor.
Leap lightly down and linger, I pray you,
And whatsoever be your will, well let it be answered." 255
"Nay," the creature cried, "as He is my creator,
I have no longing long to linger here.
But your kingly fame, my lord, is known far and fair,
Your city and your knights said to be most excellent,
Mightiest of men in armor, masters in the lists, 260
Most modest and most manly in all this merry world,
Cheeriest of champions at chevying or tilting,
And here are care and courtesy, kindliness and honor,
And that has drawn me hither upon this dear day;
But know you by this holly which here I hold on high 265
That I pass in peace, seeking no plunder,
For, had I fared forth fiercely and thirsting for to fight,
I have a halberd home and a goodly helmet
And a sharp spear, shining, long and bright,
And other direful weapons, warlike and wieldy. 270
But as I seek no war, see, my gear is softer.
However, if you are as bold as bards and ballads tell,
You will goodly grant me the gift that I demand
>By right."
>>Arthur moved to answer 275
>>And said, "Sir courteous knight,
>>If battle is your pleasure,
>>Here will fail no fight."

13

"Nay, I crave no contest," cheerily he called.
"Here about this bench I see but beardless boys. 280
If I were strapped in steel and on a stirring charger,
Here are no men to match me or measure with my might.
But I crave within this court a bit of Christmas sport,

---

chevying hunting on horseback.

For it is Yule and New Year, and here are limber youths;
If any on the dais deems himself so daring, 285
So bold in his blood and fiery in his brain,
He fears not to strike against me stroke for stroke,
I shall give him as my gift this great green ax,
Heavy enough it is to test a hero's handling,
And I shall bide the first blow, bare as you see me. 290
If any fellow be so fearless thus to test my fettle,
Let him now leap forward and lift up this weapon;
I quit-claim it forever, let him keep it as his own.
And I shall stand upon his stroke here upon this station.
But render me the right to deal him in return 295
        A year and a day
     From this holy hour.
     Dare any man now say,
     'I dare the green knight's power'?
     Let him walk this way." 300

14

If first he had astonished them, ah, stiller were they then,
All the courtiers in that castle, both great and common.
The man on his mount slowly moved about
And boldly his boring eyes burned into their souls;
He knotted his bristling brows, bushy-broad and green, 305
And his great wild beard waved as in the wind.
When none would rise to face him, rudely he roared
And, swelling out his mighty breast, boldly then he bellowed:
"What, is this King Arthur's court?" laughingly he cried,
"Whose fame is forever and as far as men can travel? 310
Where is now your pride, your pomp and your posturing,
Your fierceness in fight and your chivalry and fame?
Now all the glory of your noble knights
Is sullied by mere words from a weaponless wanderer.
Cowering like cravens, all fear to taste my ax!" 315
With this he laughed so loud that his eyes flamed like lightning
And the blood shot into Arthur's face, and he blushed in bitter shame,
        Then
     Waxed as wroth as wind
     And so did all his men. 320
     Solemnly he raised his hand
     And spoke to the man again.

15

"Knight," he said, "by heaven, never name another!
I am your man, sweet sir; cease your merry mocking.
No lord here fears your lewd laughter; 325
Hand me the ax, and, as heaven is my hope,
I shall greatly grant you that grim blow you long for."

Lightly he leaped unto him, laying forth his hand;
Then swiftly the green man slid from his saddle,
And Arthur grasped the ax, gripping the great handle, 330
And wielded it from side to side, wondering at its weight.
The mocking intruder, intrepid as a tree,
Imperiously proud, expressionlessly stood there,
Then, stroking his beard, he blithely bared his breast,
Casting off his cloak with a smile of cool contempt, 335
No more dismayed by his deadly danger
Than had a goodly page given him a goblet
          Of wine.
      Gawain, beside the queen,
      Then called out fair and fine: 340
      "My lord, I beg a boon.
      Let this feat be mine."

16

"I pray you, mighty master," said Gawain to the monarch,
"Bid me from this bench to stand there beside you,
So that in courtesy I might come from my queen 345
And that my liege lady shall not mislike it.
Let me come and counsel you here before this court;
I think it not seemly nor suitable nor wise,
When such a loutish challenge affronts our chivalry,
Though you yourself be anxious and yearning to answer it, 350
To seize the ax so boldly when all these broad benches
Are bursting with brave men burning for battle;
There are no stancher fellows where the fight is fiercest.
I know I am the weakest both in wit and warfare
And little would the loss of my life be felt; 355
Only do I owe to fame that Arthur is my uncle;
Proudly my body bears your royal blood.
And since this silly business somewhat is beneath you
And I have first bespoke it, pass me this privilege.
And if I strike not sternly a good stout blow, 360
          Mine be the blame."
      The nobles whispered round
      And all agreed the same;
      The king should step down
      And let Gawain have the game. 365

Gawain Gawain's mother was Arthur's half-sister. The oldest Gawain tradition made him the noblest of Arthur's followers, famous for both his physical prowess and courtesy. This is the concept of Gawain that is presented in this poem. This is in contrast to the character of Gawain as it developed in some of the French romances where he was downgraded, retaining his courtesy but ceasing to be a model of chastity. English romances that are based on the French also reduce the status and virtue of Gawain; he appears in this reduced status, for instance, in Malory's *Morte d'Arthur*. Tennyson follows the Malory tradition rather than *Sir Gawain and the Green Knight*.

17

Then the king commanded Gawain to come forward,
And he left his meat and came before his master.
Kneeling before the king, he caught up the ax,
And gracious Arthur greeted him and granted him the weapon
And gave him God's blessing, bidding him in gladness 370
That his heart and his hand both should be hardy.
"May Christ," said the king, "grant you fruitful cutting,
And if you strike him strongly then stoutly I believe
You shall stand the stroke he shall serve you after."
Gawain then advances with his awful ax. 375
The Green Man awaits him, unworried but watchful,
And presently he halts him, holding up his hand:
"Let us reaffirm our terms before we fare further.
First must I know, knight, how do men name you?
See you tell me truly in words that I may trust." 380
"As God is my good, men call me Gawain;
He it is who serves you with this stern and stunning stroke,
And twelve months from this time will take from you another
With whatever weapon be your goodly will,
    By my faith." 385
   The Green Knight then spoke:
   "Gawain, be not loth
   To deal me this stroke.
   I have no fear of death."

18

"By God," the Green Knight cried, "Sir Gawain, I am glad 390
That it shall be a blow of yours my bare neck shall bear.
And you have well accepted the careful conditions,
The covenant of honor I called for from the king,
But see that you swear me one further sentence,
That you yourself shall seek me, in sickness or sorrow, 395
In pleasure or peril, that I may recompense you
Those wages that you pay me within these worthy walls."
"Where might I come unto your castle or court?"
Said Gawain, "for plainly I know no place or palace
That you call home. Where is the high hall 400
That you call your castle? I will come unto it
Through the wildest weathers to the ending of the world;
By all the saints and sureties, I swear this unto you."
"No more is needful upon the New Year,"
The Green Man replied readily and rightly, 405
"I will tell you truly after you have struck me
And smartly have smitten me with the smooth steel;
Then I will most freely name my house and myself
So fairly you may find me and finish out our bargain.

But if I do not speak you are spared your obligation 410
And lightly you may linger at home as you like.
        So—good luck!
     Take up your grim tool
     And deal me now a knock!"
     Gawain said: "I will!" 415
     And stroked the shining ax.

19

The Green Knight, stalwart and stanch, boldly takes his stand,
Bows his brave neck, uncovering it to the bone;
His long lovely locks he lays over his crown,
Leaving the naked neck bare at the nape. 420
Gawain braced his feet and brandished the bright ax,
The left foot forward upon the firm floor,
Then smote down smartly upon the smooth skin
So that the shining steel sundered the neck bones
And, slicing through the sheer flesh, severed it in twain, 425
And the ax's bright edge bit deep into the boards.
The fair head fell from the neck and bounced over the floor
And the folk there with their feet thrust at it like a ball;
The blood burst from the body, brilliant red on green;
And neither faltered nor fell the fearful headless trunk, 430
But stiffly started forth upon unstaggering legs
And violently rushed to where they stood around in ranks,
Caught up his bonny head, and boldly he brandished it;
And, turning then to his beast, seized the blazoned bridle,
Stepped into the stirrups and grandly strode aloft, 435
Holding by the long hair his head in his hands.
And the stranger settled himself as firmly in the saddle
As though no harm had happened to him, headless though he be.
        And worse.
     He turned his bleeding body 440
     Around atop his horse
     And many a man felt fear
     That the head might now discourse.

20

For the head indeed in his hand now he held on high;
Toward Gawain, the fearless, he fixed the blank face, 445
And it lifted its lids and looked at him clearly
And spoke in spectral tones this solemn speech:
"Gawain, be brisk in binding up our bargain;
Look long throughout the land until, lord, you find me;
As you have promised here within these heroes' hearing, 450
At the chosen Green Chapel I charge you to claim
Such a dint as you have dealt—well have you deserved it—
To merrily be meted you upon the New Year's morn.

The Knight of the Green Chapel—all men know my name;
Seek and you shall find me, most certain and most sure. 455
Therefore, come unto me, or coward be called."
With a rough roar he whipped the reins about
And galloped from the hall, his head in his hand,
And the fiery flint flew from the horse's hooves.
To what faery land he fared forth from thither, 460
No man knew, nor from where he'd come.
        What then?
      The king and Gawain there
      Laughed like merry men
      At a sight so rare, 465
      The strangest ever seen.

21

Though Arthur the fair felt fear in his heart,
He let no semblance there be seen, but he said full jolly
To the comely queen with most courteous speech:
"Dear dame, this day be you undismayed; 470
Such a faery feat well befits our feasting,
Playing of interludes, laughter and lute song,
Lilting of carols among the lords and ladies.
Nevertheless, to my meat I may now address me,
For I have seen a miracle, a merry one to marvel at." 475
He smiled at Sir Gawain and softly he said:
"Now, sir, hang up the ax, it has hewed enough."
And it was done above the dais; duly there it hung,
So all men for marvel might look upon it,
And by a true description testify to the wonder. 480
Then they turned to the tables, these goodly knights together,
The monarch and his men, and the minions served them
Double all the delicacies as suited their deserts,
With all manner of meat and minstrelsy as well;
With joy they celebrated until the sun had set 485
      Like a dying beacon.
      Now, Gawain, go with God;
      Fear not to be forsaken.
      But heavy is the load
      That you have undertaken. 490

PART TWO

22

Thus Arthur was granted this green New Year's gift
In the young year as he had yearned for.
Though he was tight-lipped returning to the table.
The dire deed he had witnessed was dark within his thoughts.
Gawain was cheerful to have undergone that game, 495

But wondered in his heart how heavy it might hang.
For though men be merry when the wine is in their midst,
A year speeds as swift as the skimming swallow's shadow,
And the gay beginnings seldom match the goal.
And so this Yuletide yielded to the rushing year, 500
And season after season swiftly ensued:
After the Christmastide there crept the crabbed Lent,
To try the flesh with fish and bare simple food;
But then the world's weathers contend with the winter,
The cold shrinks down, and the clouds lift and clear; 505
Fair falls the rain in warm, gentle floods,
Sowing on the merry mead marigolds and lilies;
All the glades and groves gladden and grow green,
Birds briskly build and boisterously warble
For sweetness of the summer that gently ensues 510
   On every side;
  And the green world sings
  Like a bonny bride,
  And cheery birdsong rings
  From glen and glade. 515

23

Afterward, the season of summer, with the soft winds,
When Zephyrus sweetly sighs over the seeds and grasses;
Then all the gay plants grow graceful in greenery
And the fresh dewdrops drip from the drinking leaves
And sparkle like diamonds in the dazzling sun. 520
But the hoary harvest hies him over the fields,
Warning seeds to wax ripe before the coming of winter;
He drives with drought the dry, swirling dust
Across the earth's face in whirling, clinging clouds;
Wild, whistling winds wrestle in the welkin, 525
The leaves lance from the lime tree and light upon the ground,
And gray is the grass that yesterday grew green;
Ripening and rotting reign over the rich earth.
Thus the year dies and the days diminish,
And winter turns again as the world wishes, 530
   In truth.
  Then Michaelmas morn
  Is come in bitter sooth;
  Gawain in his turn
  Bethinks him of his oath. 535

24

Yet till All Saints' Day he stayed at Arthur's side,
And there were feasts and games for Gawain's good sake,
With revelry and richness of the Table Round.

Michaelmas Feast of St. Michael, September 29.   *All Saints' Day* November 1.

Goodly courteous knights and fair comely ladies,
All were heavyhearted for love of their hero, 540
But never a word was mentioned save of merriment and mirth,
Though many joyless in their hearts jested there and joked.
Gawain after the banquet goes to greet his uncle
And speaking of his peril plainly he said:
"Lord of my life, I come to take my leave; 545
You know the law that binds me, I cannot linger longer,
Nor come I to complain of my deadly compact;
Faithful I have pledged me on the morrow morning
To seek the Green Chapel as God is my guide."
Then those noble knights knelt there together, 550
Aywan and Eric, and with them all the others,
Sir Dodinal the Direful and the Duke of Clarence,
Lancelot and Lionel and Lucan the good,
Sir Bors and Sir Bedivere, bold warriors both,
And many other mighty men, with Madoc de la Port. 555
All this company of court came near the king
To counsel their comrade with care at their hearts.
Woeful was the wailing by that worthy throng
That so goodly as Gawain should go on that grim errand
To face so fell a stroke, without hope or defense, 560
    But aye
    Gawain made good cheer.
    "Why," he said, "should I
    Wonder now or fear?
    What may man do but try?" 565

25

He dwells there all that day and dresses on the morn,
Early asks his arms, and they were all brought to him.
First a flowered cloth flat upon the flooring,
And much was the golden gear gleaming thereon;
The warrior stepped forward and coolly weighed his weapons, 570
Slipping on a doublet of the softest silk,
And after that a colored cape caught around the neck
And finely trimmed and lined with the fairest fur.
Then they set the steel shoes and strapped them to his feet.
They geared his legs in steel, with bright goodly greaves, 575
With knee-plates thereto, polished to perfection,
And boldly buckled there with bolts of purest gold;
Quaint cuisses then that cunningly enclosed
His thick sturdy thighs, with stout thongs attached;
And then the mighty mail-shirt made all of steel 580
Enveloped that fellow, both front and back,
And well-burnished braces upon both his arms,
With gay goodly elbows and great gloves of plate,
And all in good gear, splendid and gleaming,

Aywan and Eric, etc. all Knights of the Round Table.   *Cuisses* armor for the thighs.

    Stood this lord,   585
  With rich trappings and rare,
  Girt with a gleaming sword,
  Armored full fair,
  And ready for his reward.

26

When he was hasped in arms, his harness it was rich;   590
The least loop or latchet, goldenly it gleamed.
So, harnessed as he was, he went to hear the mass
Offered and honored at the high holy altar.
Then he comes to the king and to his court-companions,
And lovingly takes his leave from these lords and ladies.   595
And they cheered and kissed him, commending him to Christ.
Then Gringolet was readied and girded with a saddle
That gleamed and glittered gaily with many golden fringes,
Bravely ornamented with newly polished nails;
The bridle barred about with bright gold bindings,   600
The peitrel's apparel and the proud skirts,
The crupper and the coverlet according with the saddle-bows,
And all arrayed in red with rich golden nails
That glittered there and glinted like the gleaming sun.
Then he caught up his helmet and clasped it and kissed it;   605
Boldly it was bolted and bound and lined within;
High on his head it was hasped and fastened,
With a silken streamer bound above the beaver,
Embroidered and studded with the best and brightest gems
On the broad silken border, and birds on the seams,   610
And pretty preening butterflies depicted between,
Turtledoves and mourning doves, as richly bedight
As it were seven maidens had woven seven winters
    Thereon.
    The circlet or diadem   615
    That circled his crown
    Was dazzling with diamonds,
    Fair to look upon.

27

Then they showed him the shield which was of shining red
With the pentagon depicted in pure golden hues.   620

Gringolet. name of Sir Gawain's horse. In French it is *Guingalet* and may be derived from the Welsh *gwen*, meaning white. A white horse would be a suitable mount for Gawain as he leaves to meet the challenge of the Green Knight on his green charger. *peitrel's apparel* Peitrel is an old French word for breastplate trappings. *Turtledoves* symbols of love. *pentagon* The pentangle is the word ordinarily used here. A pentangle (pentagon) is a five-pointed star. It was traditionally the symbol of perfection or integrity. (In color symbolism, gold had the same meaning.) Solomon's seal consisted of a five-pointed star surrounded by a circle.

He catches up the baldric, casts it about his neck,
And sweetly it suited him, seemly and most meet.
And why the pentagon pertains to that noble prince
I am intent to tell you, though it tarry me:
It is a sign that Solomon set once on a time   625
In tokening of truth by the symbol it contains,
For it is a figure featured with five points,
And each line interlocks and overlaps another
And everywhere is endless, so that the English call it,
As neatly I've heard named, the Endless Knot.   630
Thus it befits this knight and his fair fittings,
For fivefold faithful and five times in each way
Was this goodly Gawain and pure as purest gold,
Devoid of villainy and all adorned with virtue
               Untold.   635
     So, proudly he bore
     The pentagon on his shield,
     The stoutest in war,
     The fairest in the fold.

28

First he was found faultless in his five senses,   640
And, second, never failed with his five fingers,
And all his firm faith was in the five wounds
Of Christ on the cross, according to the creed;
And wheresoever this wight was stationed in warfare
His most steadfast thought, through all other things,   645
Was that all his courage came from the clear five joys
That Heaven's holy queen had of her child;
Wherefore the knight fittingly had fixed
On the inside of his shield her shining painted image,
So that when he cast his eyes thereto his courage never cooled.   650
The fifth five that I find this knight was favored with
Were frankness and fellowship before all other things;
His cleanliness and courtesy were never called in question,
And pity, that surpasses all—these five points
Were deeper bound within his breast than in any other warrior.   655
Now all these five fives were firm within this knight
And all looped together, endlessly and lightly,
And fixed upon five points, nowhere incomplete or faulty,
Nevermore the same, yet never sundered neither,
Without an end at any notch or any nook or corner,   660
Where'er the web began or wove to an ending.
Thus upon this shining shield the Endless Knot was shaped,

Endless Knot   The pentangle gets this name because its interlacing lines are combined so as to be continuous, and, if followed, always bring one back to the point of origin.   *five joys*   the five joyful mysteries in the life of the Blessed Virgin: The Annunciation, Visitation, Nativity, Assumption, and Coronation.

Royally with red gold upon a red ground,
And which the learned people call the pure pentagon.
              Wherefore 665
       Armored and gay,
       And girt with goodly gear,
       He gives them all good day
       And farewell forevermore.

29

He struck the steed with his spurs and sprang on his way, 670
So sternly that the stone-fire spurted out thereafter.
All that saw that sight then sickened at heart,
And all said the same, assembled there together,
Pitying Gawain's plight: "By Heaven, 'tis a pity
That you, lord, shall be lost, in life the noblest one. 675
To find your equal on earth, in faith, would not be easy.
More cautious then you should have been, of cool consideration,
And should have grown to greatness and a gracious dukedom;
A brilliant master of men you well may have become
And so had better been than blasted to nothing, 680
Cut down by an elfish creature because of pride and custom.
Who ever knew a king such cruel counsel to take
As courtiers in their quarreling at their Christmas games!"
Oh, many were the warm tears that welled in their eyes
When that seemly sire passed from their sight 685
              That day.
       He hesitated not
       But swiftly went his way
       From that beloved spot
       As the book does say. 690

30

Now this royal knight is riding through the realm of Logres,
Sir Gawain, on God's behalf, not for game or pleasure.
Often cold and companionless, he makes camp at night
Where there are neither friends nor the free fare that he liked,
His horse his only faithful fellow over friths and downs, 695
And no one save God to guide him as he goes
Till finally he nears full nigh unto the north of Wales.
All the isles of Anglesey he holds on his left
And fares over the fords by the forelands
Over across the Holy Head, and soon he was hid 700
In the wilderness of Wirral, where darkly there wended
Few who greeted graciously either God or man,

Longres a Welsh name for England south of the Humber River.   *Anglesey* an island off the coast of Wales.   *Holy Head* a Welsh seaport.   *Wirral* a forest in Cheshire, near the present city of Liverpool. Sir Gawain is traveling north. The Green Knight's castle would probably be in the neighborhood of Carlisle in Cumberland, not far from the Scottish border.

And always he asked as anxiously he wandered
If any there had heard or known a neighboring Green Knight
Or any church or chantry called the Green Chapel, 705
And all denied and said him nay, that never in their lives
Had they seen such a sight, a knight and his steed
              All of green.
          Gawain took strange ways
          Through many a dreary scene, 710
          Through many dreary days,
          But never a knight of green.

31

Many cliffs he clambers over in strange, cold countries.
Far from friendly skies, forsaken now he rides.
At each shore or ford where he fared or foundered, 715
He found a foe before him, monstrous and fearful,
So foul and so fell that to fight he was beholden.
So many marvels mongst those hills the good man encountered
It were too tedious to tell of the tenth portion.
Sometimes he wars with snakes and with wild wolves, 720
Sometimes with satyrs, secret in their rocks,
Then with bulls and bears, and sometimes with boars,
And giants who pursued him, gesturing and jumping;
Had he not been doughty, as dearly God directs,
Doubtless he had been dead and utterly destroyed. 725
Yet warfare vexed him not so much, but winter was worse,
When the cold clear water fell from the clouds
And froze before it fell upon the faded earth;
Nearly slain with the freezing sleet, he slept in his irons
More nights than needful upon the naked rocks, 730
Where clattering from the crest the cold current plashed
Or sometimes hung above his head in hard icicles.
Thus in peril and in pain and full grievous plight
This knight wends his way to the weary Christmastide
              All alone. 735
          Then the faithful knight
          To Mary made his moan
          To lend him some light
          And lead him gently home.

32

By a mountain next morning merrily he rides 740
Into a full deep forest, fierce and wondrous wild,
High hills on every hand and holts beneath
Full of huge hoar-oaks, a hundred together;
Here the hazel and hawthorne were hasped and tangled,

So many marvels Most romances are made up of sequences of the kind of wild adventures that are concentrated here in this one stanza.

With rough ragged moss all arrayed about, 745
And many an unblithe bird upon the bare twigs
That piteously there piped for pain of the cold.
This gallant upon Gringolet glides then thereunder,
Through many a bog and mire, one man alone,
Concerned and full of care that he could not 750
Attend the mass that morning for the son of Mary,
He who was born in Bethlehem to be our help.
And therefore with a sigh he said, "I beseech thee, Lord,
And Mary, that is mildest, Mother so dear,
Show me some shelter where I may worship 755
And sing thy matins on the morrow, meekly I ask,
And thereto priestly pray my *pater* and *ave*
                And *credo*."
        He rode, alone and holy,
        Through his dreary day 760
        And crossed himself slowly
        With: "Christ's Cross speed my way!"

33

But thrice had he crossed himself, carefully and Christianly,
When he was aware in the woods of a dwelling set in a moat,
Above a lawn on a knoll laced about with branches 765
Of many a strong tree planted around the trenches:
A castle, the comeliest that ever a knight commanded,
Pitched on a green peak, a park all about,
With a spiked palisade pointedly enfolding it
Which rounded that royal place two miles around. 770
That stronghold Gawain there beheld, hushed in admiration,
As it shone and shimmered through the shining oaks;
Then meekly he removed his helmet, murmuring full soft
Thanks to Jesus and Saint Julian, both good and gentle,
Who lovingly had led him and heard his lamentations. 775
"Now harbor and hostel grant me," he cried,
Then gladly spurred Gringolet with his gilt heels
And charged by chance up to the chief gate
And bravely arrived at the broad bridge's end
                In good heart. 780
        The bridge was drawn tight,
        The gates were barred short,
        The walls bannered bright;
        No winds could shake that fort.

34

The stalwart on horseback stood on the steep bank 785
Of the deep double ditch drawn around that place;

Saint Julian   the patron and protector of travelers.

The wall stood in the water wonderfully deep,
And a full huge height it upreared into the heavens,
Of hard hewn stone even to the high cornices,
Fettled under the battlements in the fairest fashion; 790
And there were many turrets stationed between
With many a wedged window sternly geared for warfare;
A grimmer barbican Sir Gawain never gazed upon.
And further in he beheld that hall full high,
Turrets studded tightly, pinnacled full thick, 795
Fair fitted spires, fabulously high,
With carven ornamental tops, craftily constructed.
And there he cheerily perceived many a chalk-white chimney
Upon the domed roof-towers that dazzled dearly white;
So many painted pinnacles peppered here and there 800
Among the castle cornices clambering so thick
That like a paper pattern prettily it seemed.
The noble night on his steed thought it fair enough
If he could manage to come within that enclosure,
To harbor in that hostel while the holy day lasted 805
            In good order.
        He called, and soon there came
        A pure pleasant porter
        Who asked to know his name
        Across the still water. 810

35

"Good sir," said Gawain, "would you go my errand
To the high lord of this house, harborage to crave?"
"Yea, Peter," said the porter, "and plainly I swear
That you be welcome, wight, to dwell as you wish."
Then that churl came down cheerfully to greet him 815
And many wights were with him, to welcome the knight.
They let lightly down the great log drawbridge
And knelt nobly there upon the naked earth
To welcome this wight in a worthy manner;
They granted him the broad gate, gaping free and wide, 820
And he raised them royally and rode over the bridge.
Many seized his saddle and set him gently down
And stoutly and freely then stabled his steed.
Numerous knights and squires nobly then descended
To bring this high stranger with honor into the hall. 825
When he hove up his helmet, they hastened unto him
To seize it from his hand and stand at his service;
His sword and his shield he cheerly there surrendered.
Then he hailed full courteously each high attendant,
And many a proud man pressed there to honor this prince. 830
All in his golden gear, to the hall they guided him,

---

barbican   outer fortified walls and towers of a castle.

Where the fire upon the hearth fiercely flamed and burned.
Then the lord of the castle came from his chamber
To greet his noble guest with honor and thanksgiving;
He said, "You are welcome to dwell with us here;   835
All you see is yours to have at your will
              And desire."
        "I thank you," said Gawain,
        "May Christ requite you, sire."
        They spoke, these twain,   840
        As men of honor fair.

36

Gawain glanced at this lord who greeted him so goodly
And thought him a fine fellow, possessor of this fortress,
A big burly host, broad as he was tall;
Long and luxuriant was his loose reddish beard;   845
Firm in his stance, stalwart and strong,
A face as bright as fire, and fair in his speech;
And well he seemed, forsooth, or so Gawain thought,
To live in goodly lordship within this fair land.
He conducted him to a chamber and cheerily commanded   850
To fetch forth a fellow to serve him and attend him;
And there came at his command churls and carls aplenty
Who brought him to a bright bower where noble was the bedding,
Curtains of clean silk with clear golden hems,
And covertures full curious with broad comely panels   855
Of white fur above, embossed and embroidered,
Curtains running on ropes, red golden rings,
Tapestries on the wall of tulle and Tharsian silk,
And underfoot the same, rugs of silks and satins.
There he was disrobed, with dear jests and dalliance,   860
Of his mighty mail-shirt and his bright metallic gear.
Rich red robes were brought to him by runners
To change and to charge and to choose of the best.
As soon as he reached for one and wrapped it round about him,
Fitting and seemly, with wide sailing skirts,   865
It seemed to each servant there that spring had descended,
Fresh and free and merry, with its colors and flowers;
Glowing and lovely were his limbs beneath
And a comelier courtier, sure, never Christ made,
            So fair and bright.   870
        From wherever in the world he were,
        It seemed as if he might
        Be a prince without a peer
        In the field where brave men fight.

---

tulle a thin silk material.   *Tharsian silk* a costly textile made in Tharsia (Turkestan).

37

A chair before the chimney, where the charcoal burned, 875
Was pleasantly prepared for the princely guest,
Cushions on quilted coverings, curiously wrought;
And then a merry mantle was cast upon that man,
Of a brownish velvet, and broadly embroidered
And fairly furred within with fells of the best— 880
All adorned in ermine, and also his hood.
And he sat upon that seat, both seemly and rich,
And warmed himself merrily and so his mood amended.
Soon was trundled up a table on trestles full fair,
Clad with a clean cloth that showed clear white, 885
Covering-cloth and saltcellar and gleaming silver spoons.
The wight washed at his will and went to his meat.
Servants there served him seemly enough
With many savory soups seasoned of the best,
With full double portions, and with many a fine fish, 890
Some baked in bread, some broiled above the embers,
Some boiled, some in broth, and all spiced full briskly,
And sauces so splendid Gawain could but sigh.
Oh, he called it a fair feast freely and often,
Full cheerily when all the court encouraged him at once: 895
      "Good friend,
    This penance now you take,
    But soon it shall amend."
    Such mirth do gay men make
    When they have wined and dined. 900

38

Then tactfully there were asked questions concerning
The lord to whom Gawain pledged his allegiance,
And calmly he responded to their kind queries
That the lordly Arthur was his lord and liege,
He who was the royal king of the rich Round Table, 905
And that it was Gawain who goodly there greeted them,
Having come to them that Christmastide as chance him befell.
When the lord had learned his beloved guest's identity,
He laughed loud thereat, so delightful it seemed to him,
And all the men there in his midst made much joy 910
To appear in the presence, priestly and shining,
Of one whose praise and prowess and pure holy conduct
Were famed in song and story far and forever;
Of all fearless knights, his fame was the fairest.
Each man murmured merrily to his mate: 915

---

penance On Christmas eve, a day of fast and abstinence, fish was being served, but it was so well prepared that it was slight penance—actually as Sir Gawain himself says, a "fair feast." But his entertainers promised a far better feast on the morrow.

"Now shall we see skill in courtly courtesy
And the delicate devices of chivalrous discourse;
Spaciousness in speech now splendidly we'll learn,
Since we have found and welcomed the captain of courtliness;
God has given us grace, in goodly truth, 920
That such a guest as Gawain he grants us to have,
He whom the merry minstrels tell of his marvels
    And sing.
   News of courtly fashions
   This gentle knight shall bring, 925
   Of manners and of passions
   And all the newest things."

39

When the dinner was done and the dear guest arisen,
The time was near to night and nigh to the darkness;
Chaplains to the chapels took then their ways, 930
Rang the bells full richly and full righteously,
Summoning God's servants to the evensong.
The lord wended his way and his lady with him;
Into a carved and comely pew with courtly grace he entered.
Gawain glided gaily, going thither with them; 935
And the lord then took him by the lapel and led him to sit,
Fairly and in friendship, calling him by name,
And saying he was the welcomest wight in all the world;
And he thanked him truly and they embraced together
And sat together soberly throughout the service. 940
Then the lady liked to look on the knight,
Coming from her enclosed pew with many cheery ladies.
She was the fairest in the field in flesh and in feature,
In compass and in color and in all other qualities
And goodlier than Guinevere, or so Gawain thought. 945
He moved through the multitude to meet that sweet lady;
Another lady led her by the left hand,
More aged than she, an ancient it seemed,
But held in high honor, with handmaidens waiting.
But unlike in looks those two ladies were, 950
For if the young was soft and sweet, that other was sallow;
Rich rosy blushes played around the one,
Rough wry cheeks and wrinkles on the other;
Kerchiefs on the one, with cool clear pearls;
Her breast and her bright throat, bravely displayed, 955
Shone sheerer than the snow that sleeps upon the hills;
That other with a gorget was geared around the gullet,
Muffled under her hairy chin with chalk-white veils,

---

courtly courtesy Gawain had the reputation of being the most courteous of all knights, a quality which he displays throughout the castle episode.

Her front in silk enfolded and fast bundled up,
Turreted and tricked out with trifles round about, 960
So that naught was bare except her black brows,
Her two eyes and nose, and her naked lips,
And those were sour to see and wondrously beslubbered;
A worshipful old woman well might men call her,
    Before God! 965
  She was thick around the waist;
  Her buttocks round and broad.
  Ah, more to Gawain's taste
  Was the one she walked beside.

40

When Gawain glanced at that fair one, so gracious and gay, 970
With the lord's light permission he approached those ladies;
He bowed before the older, as was befitting,
The fairer he enfolded freely in his arms,
Kissing her in comely fashion and courteously speaking;
She begged to know him better and blithely then he asked 975
To stand at her service in sweet, sober chivalry.
They took him between them, and with talking they led him
To chamber, to chimney-corner; chiefly they commanded
Spices, and unsparingly men sped to bring them,
And the winsome wine therewith each time. 980
Lightly the lord leaped up full often,
Commanding that mirth and merriment be general,
Hove off his hood and hung it on a spear
And waved it, challenging champions to chase it,
Urging most merriness that Christenmas feast— 985
"And I shall endeavor to strive among the brave ones
Ere I lose my garment to my gay, goodly friends."
Thus with laughter and jesting the lord decreed levity
To entertain Gawain with gladness and games
    That night. 990
  The wine bubbled blithe,
  The torches burned bright,
  Until Gawain took his leave
  And bade them all good night.

41

On the morn, as each man remembers that time 995
The Savior was sent to be our salvation,
Joy waxes in each heart for his holy sake;
So did it there on that day through dainties and delights;
At midday and mealtime marvelous dishes
Servingmen upon the dais dearly displayed. 1000
The hairy old hag sits in the highest,

The lord placed beside her upon the broad benches;
Gawain and the gay lady, they sat together
In the middle of the table when the meal meetly came,
And thence through the hall, as fitting it seemed to them,   1005
Each groom by degree graciously was served.
There was meat, there was mirth, there was much joy,
That to tell thereof tedious would prove,
Even if perchance I took pains to depict it.
Yet a little Gawain and the lovely lady   1010
Comfort of their company caught there together
Through their dear dalliance and their dulcet words
With clean, courteous converse free from all cunning;
And their sport surpassed each princely game
          That day.   1015
     Trumpets and kettledrums
     Made music loud and gay;
     All found much merriment,
     But none so much as they.

42

Much deep delight was there that day and the next,   1020
And a third as purely packed with frolic and pleasure;
The joy of St. John's Day was gentle to hear
And was the end of the holiday in hall and on high.
Guests prepared to go upon the gray morning,
So wondrously they waked all night and drank the red wine,   1025
Danced ceaselessly and sweetly with pleasant songs and carols;
At last when it was late they gently took their leave,
Each one to wend his long way home.
Gawain gave them good day; the good man seized him,
Led him to his own chamber cheerly by the chimney,   1030
There drew him gently down and dearly then thanked him
For the sweet service that he had shown him
To honor his house on that holy day
And adorn his dining hall with his gay grace.
"Faith, while I live my fame will be the fairer   1035
That Gawain has been my guest at God's own feast."
"Grant mercy, sir," cried Gawain, "but in good faith it is yours,
All the honor is your own, forever and always,
And I am at your will to work as you wish,
As I am holy holden to, in high and in low,   1040
          By right."
     The lord pleads and tries
     To longer hold the knight,
     But Gawain replies
     That nowise he might.   1045

St. John's Day   December 27.

43

Then the lord sought to know in sober solicitude
What dark deed had driven him at that dear season
So keenly from the king's court to campaign alone
Ere the holiday's holly were haggard and brown.
"Forsooth, sir," said Gawain, "you have guessed the game, 1050
A high, hasty errand has called me from my home,
For I am summoned by myself to seek out a place,
I know not where nor whither in all the wide world;
I only know I must draw nigh on the New Year's morning
To a place within the land of Logres, may the Lord help me! 1055
Thereof let me beg you, sir, soberly to say to me
And tell me in truth if you have heard a tale
Of a Green Chapel or the ground where it grows
Or the Green Knight who keeps it, a rough, grim gallant.
There was arranged by ritual a rendezvous between us 1060
That I would meet that man if I might survive,
And namely on New Year, now nearing apace;
Oh, I would look upon that lord, if Heaven would let me,
More gladly, by God, than to have gold or riches!
Therefore, in sooth, I swiftly must bestir me; 1065
I have now for the business but three brief days
Before I fall and falter, a failure and faithless!"
Then the lord said, laughing: "Long is your lease,
For I shall guide you to your goal, all in good time!
The Green Chapel's ground, let it grieve you no more; 1070
But you shall bide in bed at your bliss and your ease
While New Year's morning mellows and mount at your leisure
And come by mid-morning to that appointed mark.
     Amen!
    Dwell here New Year's Day 1075
    And rise and travel thence.
    I shall set you on the way;
    It is not two miles hence."

44

Then Gawain was full glad and gaily he laughed—
"Now truly I thank you through all other things; 1080
I have gained my goal, now goodly I shall
Dwell here and do whatever you deem."
Then the sire seized him and sat down beside him,
Called for the ladies, the lissome and light ones;
There was sweet solace and comfort from sorrow. 1085
The lord laughed so merry, so wildly and loudly,
As though he were a wight gone in his wits.
Then he called to the knight, crying full cannily,
"You have sworn to do the deed that I bid;

Will you hold this behest here as behooves you?" 1090
"Yea, sir, for sooth," said the true knight,
"While I bide in your court I am bound to your bidding."
"Since you have wandered widely and wearily
And caroled and capered here, you are not recovered
In sustenance or sleep, surely I know. 1095
You shall linger in your loft, then, and lie at your ease
Tomorrow at mass-time and wend to your meat
When you wish, with my wife, who shall sit beside you
And comfort you with company till I return to court
            In the evening. 1100
       And I shall early rise
       And spend the day in hunting."
       Gawain grants all this,
       Scarce knowing what he's granting.

45

"Yet further," said the fair host, "a fast pact we make: 1105
Whatsoever I win in the woods, it will be yours,
And what chance you achieve, change it with me.
Then sweetly we'll swap, swear now in truth,
In winning, in wasting, for better, for worse."
"By God," said Gawain, "I grant all this, 1110
And gentle and jolly seems to me this jest."
"Let us drink boldly, this bargain is bound!"—
So said the lord; and they lightly laughed.
They drank then and dallied in dearest abandon,
These lords and ladies, while the mood liked them; 1115
Then with purest politeness and most polished pleasantries
They stood a while together, and softly they spoke,
Kissed then full comely and called their good nights.
With servants to show them and bright, shining torches,
Each to his bed was blithely brought at last 1120
            For resting.
       And so to bed and sleep,
       And later comes the testing.
       The old lord of that castle-keep
       Was skilled in curious jesting. 1125

PART THREE

46

Full fair and early all the folk uprose;
Guests who homeward longed to go called forth their grooms
And swiftly they sped to saddle the steeds,
Made ready their tackle, trussed up their trunks,
Prepared them with richness to ride in fine array, 1130

Lightly leaped to saddles in joy and in laughter,
Each wight to wend his way where his heart yearned.
The liege lord of the land, he was not the last
Arrayed for the riding with servants ranked about him;
He ate a morsel hastily after the morning mass,   1135
Then, with bugles growling, forth to the grassy ground.
Before the dimmest daylight had dawned upon the earth
He with his merry men was mounted and riding.
Then the crafty kennel-keepers coupled their hounds,
Opened the kennels and called to them keenly,   1140
Blew upon the bugle three blaring notes;
There was braying and bellowing of hounds and of bugles,
Courtiers and captains in brilliant confusion,
Full a hundred hunters, as I have heard tell,
    There stood: 1145
      Huntsmen and hounds,
      Stalwart and good;
      Merry were the sounds
      Within that wild wood.

47

At the first bugle blast all the beasts trembled;   1150
Deer fled from the dales, desperate with fear,
Hastened to the the heights, but harshly they were
Turned back by the beaters who held there the bounds.
They let pass the harts, with high, horny antlers,
Likewise the brave bucks with their broad horns,   1155
For the lord had stated in the close season
That no man should molest any male deer.
The hinds were haled in with "Heigh!" and with "Ho!"
And the does were driven to the deep valleys.
There as they sheered forth showered the shafts,   1160
Raining of arrows in the shadowy retreats,
Biting into the brown skins with their bright heads—
What! they brayed and bled, by green banks they died.
And ever hurtling hounds swiftly harassed them,
Hunters with silver horns hastened thereafter   1165
With such a cracking cry as though a cliff had burst;
Those that fled by the bowmen and buglers
Were struck down and slain at the receiving stations.
Harassed on the heights, they were harried to the waters.
The servants at the stations were swift and so skillful,   1170
The greyhounds so goodly in tracking and chasing,
That they brought them down as fast as falling leaves or feathers
    In man's sight.
      The lord in very joy
      Laughed in wild delight   1175
      And so that fiery day
      Drove to the dark night.

48

Thus this lord delights himself in linden-woods and thickets
And Gawain, the good man, in gay bed lodges,
Lies there in lurk until the first light gleams, 1180
Under clean covertures and curtained all about.
And as in slumbering he slept slightly he heard
A wee din at his door, delicate and light;
And he heaved up his head out of the clothes,
A corner of the curtain he caught up a little 1185
And then awaited warily whatever it might be.
It was the lady, loveliest in the land,
That shut the door behind her full secretly and still
And glided toward the bed, and Gawain half-guiltily
Laid him down lightly and looked as though he slept. 1190
And she stepped stealthily and stole to his bed,
Cast up the curtain and sweetly crept within
And set her full softly on the bed-side,
And long lingered there looking lovingly upon him.
Gawain lay in lodgment then a full long while, 1195
Casting in his conscience as to what this case might mean,
For it moved him to mystery and to marvel and wonder.
But yet he said silently: "More seemly it would be
Coolly to question her concerning her company."
Then he wakened and stretched as though sleepily disturbed 1200
And unlocked his eyelids and looked upon her, wondering,
And calmly he crossed himself (as though for safe conduct,
    I suppose).
    Her cheeks rounded sweetly
    And as pink as is the rose, 1205
    She greeted him full meetly
    With laughing lips and eyes.

49

"Good morrow, Sir Gawain," said that gay lady.
"You are a slothful sleeper, sir, that one may slip in thus;
Now truly are you trapped, but let us shape a truce, 1210
And I shall bind you in your bed, the better to speak with you."
Laughingly the lady uttered these light words.
"Good morrow, gay one," said Gawain the blithe,
"I shall work at your will, and that suits me well,
For I yield me promptly and yearn for your grace, 1215
And that is the best of fates, so blithely to be bound."
Thus he jested with the lady with much lightsome laughter.
"But would you, lovely lady, sweetly grant me leave,
Let spring your prisoner and pray him to rise;
I would climb from this couch and array me in clothing, 1120
The more cheerfully and cosily to chat with you here."
"Nay, forsooth, beau sir," said then that sweet one,

"You shall not rise from bed; I shall bid you better;
I shall hold you here hasped within my arms
And chat with my knight whom I have neatly netted; 1225
For I am well aware you are the noted Gawain
Whom all the world worships wheresoever he rides;
Your honor, your courtliness hardily is hymned,
With lords and with ladies and with all who bear life.
And now you lie here, and we lodge alone. 1230
My lord and his fellows are far in the forest,
The others sleep soundly, my servants as well,
The door is drawn and bolted with a broad bolt;
And since I have here in my house him the world loves,
I shall spend my time shrewdly and sweetly, 1235
        In style.
        You are welcome to my arms
        To work your sweet will.
        Tender are my charms;
        Lie with me a while." 1240

50

"In good faith," said Gawain, "glorious would that be,
Though I am not the man that you seem to think me;
To hope for such honor as you here propose,
I am an unworthy one, this I know full well.
By God, I would be glad, and goodly you bethought you, 1245
If I might perform proudly for your pleasure
Some simple service—sweet would that be."
"In good faith, Sir Gawain," said the gay lady,
"The practice and the prowess that pleases all others,
If I set it at naught, that would not be nice; 1250
But there are ladies enough who liefer would lie
With you in their hold, as I have you here,
Dearly to dally with your fresh dainty words,
Sweetly to rest them, assuaging their sorrows,
Than to gambol and gladden them with gold and with treasure. 1255
Although I honor that Lord who upholds the heavens,
I have here wholly in my hand he whom all maids love,
        Through grace."
        She spoke with goodly cheer
        And sweet she was of face. 1260
        Gawain's heart was pure,
        But his thoughts were in a race.

51

"Madam," said the modest man, "may Mary requite you,
For I have found, in faith, your frankness becomes you;
Folk are fain to follow wildfires and fancies, 1265
But the honor they deal me is widely overdone;

The glory you would grant me springs mainly from your goodness."
"By Mary," cried the merry lady, "methinks it is otherwise;
For were I worth the host of women on earth,
And all the world's weal were here in my hand, 1270
And I could bicker and bargain to obtain a lord,
From the moods and the manners that you have here maintained
Of sweetness and suavity and swiftness in speech,
And from what heretofore I've heard of your honor,
No fellow in the field would I choose before you." 1275
"Fairest one," said Gawain, "a better fate befits you,
But I am proud of the price that you put upon me,
And, soberly your servant, my sovereign I hold you,
And your knight I become, as Christ is my king."
Thus they chatted of nothings till the noontime was nigh, 1280
And the lady let it seem that she loved him truly;
Gawain sparred cautiously, but coolly and courteously;
Though she were the loveliest in all the lovely land,
Love was light upon his mind; he thought of the long road
                    Ahead: 1285
        The blow he'd soon be taking,
        Living or dead.
        She spoke of leave-taking,
        And he nodded his head.

52

Then she gave him good day and with a glance laughed, 1290
And, as she stood, astonished him with these stern words:
"Now he that speeds each speech repay you for your sport!
But, that you are the dashing Gawain, this I deeply doubt."
"Wherefore?" he said, in simple surprise,
Afraid that he had failed in the forms of chivalry. 1295
But the lady blessed him and said to him full blithely:
"One so good as Gawain is greatly said to be,
One in whom all courtesy cleanly is enclosed,
Could not have lingered lightly so long with a lady
But he had craved a kiss by his courtesy, 1300
By some light allusion let fall from his lips."
Then Gawain said lightly: "Let it be as you like;
I shall kiss at your commandment, as is right and comely;
Let my reply now please you and plead it no more."
She draws near with that and softly she seizes him, 1305
Bends blithely down, and boldly she kisses him.
Then comely they commend one another to Christ,
And she slips from the room without rustle or ripple,
And he hastens to rise in a high hurry,
Calls to his chamberlain, chooses his clothing, 1310
And goes forth modestly to the morning mass;
Then he moved to his meat, did this goodly man,
And made merry all the day till the moon was risen,

> In pleasure.
> Was never knight so blithe and spry, 1315
> With pleasantest of leisure,
> Between two ladies, one old and dry,
> One fair as fairest treasure.

53

And still the lord of the land lingers in the forest
To hunt the fawnless does through holt and heath. 1320
He slew such a sum by the time the sun had set,
Of does and of other deer, men scarcely could dream it.
Then fiercely they flocked forward, all that fiery folk,
And quickly of the quelled deer a quarry they made.
The best men among them, with their merry servants, 1325
Gathered the fullest portions of the fat and flesh
And cunningly undid them as the custom requires.
They searched them at the assay, those that were there;
Two finger-breadths of fat they found in the feeblest of the lot.
Then they slit the slot and they seized the erber, 1330
Shaved it wtih a sharp knife and sewed up the flesh;
They lopped off the legs and skinned off the leather pelt,
Then they broke the belly and removed the bowels,
And neatly then they nipped out the flesh of the knot;
They gripped at the gullet and goodly then removed 1335
The wesaunt and the windpipe and wrenched out the guts.
Then they sheered off the shoulders with their sharp knives,
Held them by a little hole to have whole sides;
Then they broke up the breast and split it in two,
And again at the gullet they deftly began, 1340
Ripped it up readily right to the bight,
Voided out the avanters and verily thereafter
All the membranes near the ribs rapidly they cut;
So cleanly they cleared away around the clipped bones
Straight down to the haunch, hanging handily at last, 1345
And heaved it all up whole and hewed it off there,
Leaving that at last as numbles neatly, by name,
> And by kind;
> By the bight of all the thighs
> They cut the flaps behind 1350
> And carved it in this wise,
> The backbone to unbind.

---

a quarry collection of slain deer. *The best men* It was expected that even the noblest of huntsmen be expert at dressing the fruits of the hunt. *the assay* the examination. The deer was cut down from the front quarters towards the belly to test the quality of the flesh. *slot* the hollow depression running down the middle of the breast. *erber* the first stomach of ruminants. It was plucked out, emptied, cleaned, then filled with blood and fat, and tied or sewn together again to form a sort of blood sausage. *flesh of the knot* The knot is the name for two special pieces of flesh in the neck of an animal. *wesaunt* the esophagus. *bight* curved section. *avanters* entrails near the neck of a deer. *numbles* certain edible entrails.

54

Both the head and the neck they handily hewed off
And sundered then the sides swiftly from the backbone
And the corbies' fee they cast into a clearing;   1355
Then they thurled each thick side through by the ribs
And hanged them on high by the hocks of the legs;
Each fellow claimed his fee as it befell him.
Upon a fell of the fair beast, they fed then the hounds
With the liver and the lights, the leather of the paunches,   1360
And bread soaked in blood blended thereamongst.
Boldly they blew praise and their hounds bayed;
Then they took their meat and turned them toward home,
Blasting bravely on the horns many blaring notes.
By the time day was done they had all drawn   1365
Back to the castle, where Gawain coolly kept
        His peace.
    With bliss the torches burn
    And music fills the place
    As the lord returns   1370
    With sounds of joy and praise.

55

Then the lord commanded to call all the company,
Summoned down the ladies with their dainty damsels;
Before all the folk he bids his fellows
Fairly and freely to fetch in the venison.   1375
Then mirthfully and merrily he commanded Gawain,
Displayed to him the tallies of the nimble dead deer,
Showed him all the sheer flesh shorn from the ribs:
"How pay you this price? Have I won the prize?
Have I richly deserved through my subtle skill?"   1280
"By Mary," cried Gawain, "here is the mightiest meat
That I have seen this seven years in the winter's season."
"I give you all, Gawain," said the lord gaily,
"For by accord of covenant you claim it as your own."
"This is true," said the knight, "and I turn the same to you: 1385
What I have won, here within these walls,
Truly and in trust I return it to you."
Then he neatly clasped his arms about his noble neck
And kissed him as comely as he could devise:
"Take you this treasure I have obtained;   1390
Fair and free I swear there was nothing further."
"It is good," said the good man; "glory be to God.

---

corbies' fee   the gristle on the breastbone that was tossed out to crows or ravens.   *claimed his fee*   claimed the part of the deer which by custom was his depending upon his rank and function in the hunt.   *blew praise*   the call blown when the deer had been taken. (The Old French word is *prise*—a taking or capture.)   *Blasting bravely*   Special tunes were blown on the trumpets all the way home from the hunt.

It may be so, it would be better if you would declare me
Where you won this bounty? By your own wit?"
"That was not in our compact. Question me no more. 1395
You have taken what befits you, you will find nothing further
    Here."
    They laughed then like brothers
    In joy and good cheer,
    And turned to their suppers 1400
    With heart and conscience clear.

56

And after by the chimney they sat in the chamber;
Servants brought the choice wine cheerfully unto them.
And soon in their jollity, their jesting and joking,
They planned to repeat their pact upon the morrow: 1405
Each to give the other whatever goods he gained
Swiftly and nimbly at night when next they met.
They agreed to the covenant before the gathered group;
The beverage was brought forth blithely and with laughter,
Then lightly they took their leave in merriment and love; 1410
Each lord and lady hurried to his lodging.
By the time the cock had crowed and cackled but thrice,
The lord had leaped up from his bed, and all his merry lads;
The meat and the mass were meetly delivered,
And all the court clad for the chase before the dawn came, 1415
    And ho!
    With holloing and horns
    To the deep woods they go;
    Through thickets, through thorns,
    A brave and noisy show. 1420

57

Soon they called for a search beneath a bankside;
The huntsman hailed those hounds who had first howled;
Wild words he shouted there, with a warlike sound:
All the hounds who heard him hastened thither swiftly
And forty sprang upon the spoor like growling despoilers. 1425
Then such a baying and bellowing, such howling and barking
Rose, that the rocks rang all about,
And the hunters heartened them with horn and with voice.
Then all rushed together in a thrashing throng
Between a still pool and a steep, stark cliff. 1430
In a rocky copse beneath a knobby crag
Where the rough rocks ruggedly had fallen
They fell upon the scent, with all those fellows following;
They broke down the bushes, rushed through the underbrush,

---

spoor track or trail.

And those wights well knew that within there was 1435
A bold goodly beast; and the bloodhounds richly bayed.
So they beat upon the bushes and bade him uprise
And suddenly he rushed out, roaring and rampaging,
The hugest of boars, a bold and a burly one;
Long from the herd had he wandered alone, 1440
And now he was tough and old, with strong teeth and tusks,
Full grim when he grunted, and many there grieved,
For three at the first thrust he thrashed to the earth
And snorting sped him forth to spy out more sport.
Then they holloed: "Heigh!" and "Hay! Hay!" they cried, 1445
Sounded on the horns the high hunting cry;
And many were the mingled sounds of men and of hounds
Pursuing this boar with bellowing and blaring
    To the kill.
    Full oft he turns and stands 1450
    And drives them back at will;
    He gores the baying hounds
    And loud they yowl and yell.

58

Bowmen to shoot the boar were bidden forth then,
Showered their sharp arrows on him, struck him full often; 1455
But the trenchant points were turned by the toughness of his thews
And no barb could bite his hard, bristled brow;
All the spearing shafts splintered into pieces,
And the barbs rebounded as though from off a boulder.
But, as the dints are dealt him of their dire strokes, 1460
Thus, frenzied in the fight, he rushes at his foe,
Goring those who goaded him; grievously he hurt them.
And many then felt fear and fell back before him.
But the lord upon a light horse launched in full pursuit;
Like a boldened warrior he blew upon his bugle. 1465
Blaringly he blew, rushing through the deep brush,
Pursuing this wild swine until the sun set.
Thus the hours flew within the fierce forest,
While our hardy hero harbored him in bed,
Gawain, the good, in raiment and gear 1470
    Full bright.
    The lady was not late
    In coming to his side,
    Nor long he had to wait
    Her lovely face to greet. 1475

59

She came to the curtain and peeped coyly in,
And Gawain, he greeted her with most goodly gallantry
And she replied to him prettily and pertly,

Set her softly by his side, and sweetly she laughed
And with a lovely look she delivered these words: 1480
"Sir, if you are Gawain, strange it seems to me
That one so well disposed always to do good
Cannot in lady's company comprehend the code,
And if one craves to know you you coolly discard her;
You have forgotten utterly what yesterday I taught you 1485
By the truest of tokens in the talk that I know best."
"What is that?" said Gawain. "By God, I cannot guess.
Though if what you say is true, then truly I'm to blame."
"I instructed you in kissing," cried that gay lady,
"That which a Christian knight is always quick to claim, 1490
As beauteously becomes his manners and behavior."
"No more," he said, "my dear, of such sweet merriment,
For that I dare not do, lest I be denied;
Were I refused, I were wrong to have proffered."
"My faith," cried the merry wife, "how may one refuse you? 1495
You are strong enough stoutly to constrain me
If I were so foolish as to refuse or flout you."
Said Gawain, "Before God, goodly is your speaking,
But force is not thought fitting in the land where I fare from
And worthless that gift not given with goodwill. 1500
I am at your commandment to kiss at your content,
You may start as you will and cease when you think seemly,
    In peace."
   The lady drops down
   And kisses his face, 1505
   And long then they expound
   Upon love's subtle grace.

60

"I would know of you, knight," that lady said neatly,
"If you would not resent it rudely, what is the riddle
Of one so young and yearning as you seem at this season, 1510
So free and so fair as your fame declares you?
For of all princely chivalry the principle most praised
Is the lore of love, the liberty of arms;
When the deeds of noble kinghts are loudly sung and named,
It is the truest title and text of their works, 1515
How heroes for their ladies' love have ventured their lives,
Endured for their dear ones dire, doleful trials,
Avenged them with valor, verily, in contest,
And brought bliss to the bower with bounty and virtue—
And you are the comeliest of the king's courtiers, 1520
Your grace and your fairness are famed wide and far,
And I have sat beside you two separate times,
Yet never have I heard the slightest hint of love,
The smallest hint of gallantry, greatly or lightly;
Oh, you who are so quaint and careful in your conduct 1525

Ought to yield and yearn to show unto a young thing
Some traits and some tokens of true love's craft.
What! are you a fool, who possesses this false fame?
Or do you deem me too dull to hark unto your dalliance?
     For shame!   1530
    I come here and sit,
    To learn from you some game.
    Come, teach me of your wit,
    While my lord is far from home."

61

"In good faith," said Gawain, "may God reward you!   1535
Great is my gladness and goodly my pleasure;
That so worthy as you would wend her way hither
And play with so poor a man as plainly I am
With any dint of pleasure, it drowns me in delight;
But to take the task upon myself true love to expound   1540
And touch upon romantic themes and tell tales of arms
To you who, well I know, are wiser by far
In that awesome art a hundred times again
Than I am, or ever shall aspire to attain to,
That would be a foolish folly, by my goodly faith.   1545
I will do your desires, as dearly as I may,
For thus I am beholden and bound to obey—
To serve you and succor you, as God is my savior."
Thus that lovely lady, lovingly she tempted him
To win him to sin and to serve her desire,   1550
But he defended him so fair no fault there seemed,
Nothing on either side, nor naught did they know
     But bliss.
    They laughed and lingered long;
    She took a second kiss;   1555
    He smiled, but held strong,
    And she went her way with this.

62

Then the man rises and goes to morning mass
And after, food was fixed and fetched unto the tables.
This knight with the ladies thus lingered long that day,   1560
But the lord over the land launched his furious chase,
Pursuing his ferocious pig, which turned upon the pack
And bit the backs in sunder of the best dogs
As he stood at bay, till the bowmen broke upon him
And forced him to fight or flee to the open plain,   1565
Where the flying arrows fell fiercely about him.
Still he made the stoutest-hearted stop and step back,
Till at last he was so weak he could walk or run no more,
But hastily as he might he hied him to a hole

In a bank beneath a rock where a brook bubbled. 1570
He got the bank at his back and began to snort and blow;
The froth foamed at his mouth foul around his whiskers,
And he whetted his white tusks; oh, loth were those warriors,
Heavy with their hurts, to draw nearer to him;
They dallied at a distance, avoiding the danger 1575
          Like fire.
         He had hurt them so much
         That none had a desire
         To feel again his tearing tusks
         Or face his savage ire. 1580

63

Till the lord sprang among them, spurring on his steed,
Saw the boar at bay, bloody but unchastened;
He leaped lightly down, leaving the reins a-dangle,
Snatched from the scabbard his long, shining sword,
Fared swashing through the ford to where the fell brute lurked. 1585
The wild beast was wary of the man with the weapon;
All his bristles stiffened, and he stamped and blew and snorted,
So all the fellows in the field feared for their lord.
Then the boar charged savagely straight for the waiting knight,
And down they crashed together, thrashing and struggling, 1590
In the deepest part of the water. But woe for the wild beast!
For the man caught him keenly as they clashed head-on,
Set the sharp sword-blade in the slot beneath the throat,
Drove it direly in to the hilt, and the heart burst,
And, snarling bloody bubbles, the boar grimly yielded 1595
          And died.
         A hundred hounds then leapt
         To tear at him and bite,
         For now no keepers kept
         Their dogs from his side. 1600

64

Then they blew triumphantly their brave silver bugles,
And there was hallooing on the heights by all those hearty hunters;
And the bloodhounds bayed while their masters cheered beside them,
They who were the chiefest in that charging chase;
Then an ancient woodsman, wise in the ways of woodcraft, 1605
Began in careful fashion to butcher this great boar.
First he hewed off the head and set it on high,
Then roughly he ripped down the ridged backbone,
Carved out the bowels and cast them on the coals,
And the brachs he rewarded with the baked bowels and bread. 1610
Then he slices up the flesh in fat sleek slabs
And portions out the pieces as is fitting and proper;
And then he loops and harnesses the halves of the boar together

And stoutly he hangs them upon a strong stick.
So then with this swine they swing toward the castle; 1615
The boar's head, it was borne aloft before the lord,
He who in the swirling ford had felled the fierce beast
        In man's view.
      And when the lord saw Gawain
      He called him forward, too, 1620
      To trade once more their day's gain,
      As they had sworn to do.

65

The lord with merry jest then laughed loud and long
When he saw Sir Gawain and joyously he spoke;
The good ladies were gotten, and the company gathered; 1625
He showed for them the sheared meat and shaped for them the tale
Of the largeness and length, the litheness and savagery
Of that wild snarling swine in woodlands where he fled.
Gawain in full comeliness courteously commended him
And praised the wondrous prize that he had proved and won. 1630
For such a brawny beast, the bold Gawain said,
Or such a splendid boar he had never seen.
Then they handled the horrible head and praised the high prowess
Of that noble warrior who worthily had won it.
"Now, Gawain," said the good man, "this gain is your own, 1635
According to our covenant, on which we clasped hands."
"It is true," said the knight, "and as surely true,
All my gains I give to you, as goodly we compacted."
He hasped the lord about the neck and heartily he kissed him,
And likewise once again he served him in that fashion. 1640
"Now we're even," said the knight, "upon this sweet evening,
Of all the covenants we claimed since I came hither."
        Then
      The lord cried, "By Saint Giles,
      You are the best of men! 1645
      Sure, in a little while
      You'll be as rich as ten!"

66

Then the tables were set atop the neat trestles,
Cloths were cast upon them; clear light then
From the waxen torches whispered on the walls. 1650
Servants came and went, serving in the hall;
Much din and merriment mingled gaily there
About the friendly fire, and many fair times,
At the supper and after, many artful songs,

Saint Giles a hermit saint whose only companion in his forest retreat near Nîmes, France, was a hind.

Old Christmas carols and carefree roundelays, 1655
With all the mannerly mirth men may devise,
And ever our lovely knight beside the fair lady.
Such sweetness she showed to that stalwart knight
With sly secret looks and with silent smiling,
That all bewildered was that man and angry with himself, 1660
But it proved against his nature for him to deny her,
So daintily he dealt with her, dearly he dallied there,
    Come what may.
   As long as she pleased,
   He agreed to play. 1665
   Then the tables were upraised
   And they moved away.

67

In the chimney corner then they drank, deeply and daintily,
And agreed once more to grant their gains on the New Year's Eve;
But Gawain craved leave to go the next morning, 1670
For it drew near the term when he was sworn to travel.
The lord objected then, bade him linger longer,
And said, "As I have honor, I here highly swear
You shall find the Green Chapel to fare as fate directs,
Lad, by New Year's light, long before prime. 1675
Therefore, lie in your loft and take your lovely ease,
And I shall hunt in the holt and hold to our terms,
Swap you my winnings when I return from the woods;
For twice have I tested you and faithful I find you.
Now let the third time be the charm; think of the morrow! 1680
Let's make merry while we may; morning is near.
For man may laugh at sorrow, so his heart be merry."
This graciously was granted, with no thought of regret.
Drink was blithely brought and soon they went to bed
    That night. 1685
   Sir Gawain lay and slept
   Full soft and still all night,
   But the lord leapt
   From bed before the light.

68

After mass, a morsel he takes with his men; 1690
Oh, merry was the morning! His horse then he commanded.
All his fair followers, waiting to fare after him,
Were ready to ride, arrayed before the gates.
Fairy-fleece were the bushes for the frost clung upon them;
Red upon the cloud-rack the royal sun arose 1695
And coasted calmly through the white clouds in the heavens.
Hunters loosed the hounds by a holt-side,
Rocks rang like silver when the great horns roared.

Some fell upon the trail of a fleeing fox
And craftily they crissed and crossed, for the fox is cunning; 1700
Sharply then a cur cried and called the hunt unto him;
And swift his fellows followed him, sniffing in confusion,
Running forth in a rabble, pursuing the rich scent,
And he frisked along before them; but soon enough they found him,
And when they came in sight of him, swiftly they pursued, 1705
Baying and bellowing with a noise like bugles,
And he turned and doubled through many a tangled thicket,
Lay low and listened, lurking under hedges.
At last by a little ditch he leaped across a spinney
And subtly; stole him forth at a still edge of a grove 1710
And, wily as he was, was half-escaped from the woods
When soft he stumbled on one of the hunting stations
Where three howling hounds hurled themselves upon him,
    And hey!
   He swerved swiftly off 1715
   And lightly danced away.
   For the fox who runs when woods are rough
   Will run another day.

69

Then there was merry sport! hounds sprang to the spoor,
All the pack commingled, bellowing their wild music; 1720
Such uproar at the sight of him raucously uprose
As though the clambering cliffs around had clattered down in heaps.
Here he was hallooed when a huntsman stumbled on him,
And goodly was he greeted with grievous yelps and snarls;
There he was threatened, and "Thief!" they shouted after him, 1725
And still the hot hounds tickled his tail: oh, he dare not tarry!
Often he was rushed upon as he made for the open ways
And often he redoubled neatly, for Reynard, he is wily,
And light he dappled through the puddles, splashing his pursuers,
Merrily tormenting them, and midday came and went; 1730
While home, the handsome knight wholesomely is sleeping
Within comely curtains upon this cold morning.
But the lady for love lingered not in sleep,
Nor weakened in the purpose that was pitched within her heart,
But up she rose in readiness and rushed to his chamber 1735
In a merry mantle that almost reached the floor
And was finely furred with many a trimmed fell,
No colors on her head, but the clear stones
Were twined about her tresses in clusters of twenty;
Her fair face and throat shone white and fine 1740
And her shoulders showed sheer as whitest snow.
She comes within the chamber door and softly shuts it after,

---

spinney a thorny clump of bushes.

Throws open a window and sweetly calls that sleeper,
And readily she rallies him with these rich words,
            And with cheer: 1745
              "Ah, man! How can you sleep
              When the morning is so clear?"
              His dreams were dark and deep,
              But he could sense her near.

70

In dire dark dreams the good knight drifted,   1750
Like a man thickly troubled with many grievous thoughts—
How destiny was due that day to deal him his fate
At the Green Chapel, where a green knight waited,
And he was bound there to abide that knight's stern buffet;
But when the comely lady came he concealed his thoughts,   1755
Drove up from dreams, and deftly then answered her.
The lovely lady came, smiling, laughing sweetly,
Leaned above his fair face, and so featly kissed him;
Worthily he welcomed her with a cheery will.
And seeing her so glorious, so gaily attired,   1760
So faultless in her features and of such lovely hues,
Warm, worthy joy welled in his heart.
With smooth merry smiling they melted into mirth,
And all was purest pleasantry that was there spoken
              In delight.   1765
              In sweetest sunniest pleasure
              They laughed loud and bright,
              But they might have stood in danger,
              Had not Mary guided her knight.

71

For that proud princess pressed him so warmly,   1770
Urged him so near the edge at last it behoved him
Either yield him to her charms or churlishly repel her.
He cared for his courtesy lest he be considered boorish,
But more he feared the mischief if he committed sin   1775
And thus became a traitor to the keeper of that castle.
"God grant," said the knight, "that shall not befall."
With loving laughs and levity, lightly he parried
All the fair sentences that fell from her lips.
That beauteous lady said: Sir, you be blameworthy
If you love not the lady that you lie beside   1780
Before all other fair ones, freely and frankly,
Except that you have a lady now, a lover you like better,
And your faith have plighted so firmly unto her
You may not buy release—and that I scarce believe;
Now tell me that truly, this much I pray you;   1785
For all the loves there are, do not belie me

With guile."
The knight said, "By Saint John,"
And smoothly can he smile,
"I am sworn to none, 1790
Nor will be for some while."

72

"There is a word," the woman cried, "that is worst of all,
But well have you answered now, the worse woe for me.
Kiss me then comely, give me this much consolation,
And I will go mourning, like many a lovelorn maid." 1795
Sighing, she swayed lightly down, and sweetly she kissed him,
And then she stepped back and said there as she stood,
"Now, dear, at this departing, do me this ease,
Give me some trifling gift, your kerchief or glove,
That I may think upon you, man, and lessen my mourning." 1800
"Now, by Heaven," said the knight, "I would I had here
The purest and most prized of all my bright possessions,
For sure and most certain, my lady, you deserve
More rich reward than my estate comprises;
Whatever prize I give you now little would profit you 1805
And small would be the honor to have at this time
A glove or a trinket as a gift from Gawain,
And I a strolling wanderer on strange and foreign strands,
And alas, I have no serving-train with trunks crammed with trifles;
Sorely I regret it for your sake at this season. 1810
But each must do as fate demands and as chance moves
            By design."
      "Nay, lovely lord,"
      Said that lady free and fine,
      "Though I had none of your reward, 1815
      Yet you shall take of mine."

73

She handed him a rich ring, worked in reddish gold,
With one bright stone, standing alone,
That blazed and sparkled, brilliant as the burning sun;
Oh, I warrant it was worth a rich man's wealth. 1820
But the knight refused it and fair and free he spoke:
"I want no gracious gifts, lady, at this time;
I have none to tender you, and none will I take."
Still she urged insistently, and still he refused her
And swore by his sooth that he would not accept it. 1825
Then, grieved that he denied her, she sighed and declared:
"Though you refuse my ring because it seems too rich,
You would not be beholden so highly unto me
If I gave you my girdle; that would obligate you less."
She lightly loosed a lace that was looped around her waist, 1830

Knit upon her kirtle beneath the clear mantle—
This girdle was of green silk, trimmed in goodly gold,
Fairly braided round about by fine and cunning fingers;
And that she gave to Gawain and goodly she besought him
To take and accept it, unworthy though it be.   1835
But still he was steadfast and swore he could never
Accept gold or gifts before God sent him grace
Boldly to achieve the chance he had chosen there.
"And therefore I pray you, do not be displeased,
But peace to your pleadings and your importunings   1840
      True and free.
    I am beholden to you,
    And ever will be;
    What service I can do you,
    Demand it of me."   1845

74

"Now you forsake this silk," said the lady slyly,
"Because it's simple in itself, as indeed it seems;
Lo! it is so little, and even less its worth,
But he who knows the virtues woven deep within it,
He would, perhaps, put a higher price upon it,   1850
For whosoever girds himself with this green girdle,
While he has it neatly hasped around his waist
Nothing under Heaven can hew him down or harm him,
For not by any force or sleight may he be hurt or slain."
Then the knight considered, and it came into his heart   1855
That this might stand him in good stead when he stood his stroke
At the wild chapel where his foe awaited;
Might he escape unslain, the sleight would be worthy.
Then he listened silently and suffered her to speak,
And she pressed it upon him and urged him to accept,   1860
And he granted, and she gave it with a good will
And begged and besought him never to betray her,
But to hide it from her husband, and he agreed
That none would ever know of it but those two alone,
      For any price.   1865
    He thanked her, and then
    She who had kissed him twice
    Embraced him once again,
    And now has kissed him thrice.

75

Then she takes her leave and leaves him there alone,   1870
For further satisfaction she might nowise get.
When she was gone Gawain quickly geared him,
Rose and arrayed him in his noblest robes,
Took up that girdle that the gay lady gave him,

Wound it well about his waist and then went his way; 1875
To the castle chapel he neatly chose his path,
Privately approached a priest and prayed to him there
To hear his confession and freely to teach him
How his soul might be saved when he should go from there.
Then he shrived him surely, confessing his sins, 1880
The greater and the smaller, and he besought God's mercy,
And for absolution he sighed to the holy man;
The priest assoiled him certainly and sent him off so clean
Doomsday might have dawned next day with nothing to fear.
And then he made merry among the fair ladies, 1885
With clear comely carols and all kinds of joy
(As never before that day he'd done) until the dark night,
   With bliss.
    All men wondered there
    To see his joyousness, 1890
    And they said, "How fair
    And free a knight is this."

76

Now let him linger in that lea, and love be his comfort!—
The lord is still abroad in the land, leading his men,
And he has slain the fox which fiercely he had followed: 1895
As he had sped through a spinney to spy out the rascal,
There he had heard the hounds hastening unto him,
And Reynard came a-running through a ragged grove,
All the rabble in a rush right on his heels.
Wary and wily was the lord then, 1900
Drew out his shining sword and hurled it like a spear;
The fox flinched and sprang aside, whirling to flee,
But a hound pounced upon him, pinning him in pain,
And full before the horse's feet the pack fell upon him
And worried me this wily fellow with a yapping tumult. 1905
The lord leapt down and lightly caught up
The fallen fox there out of those fierce jaws,
Held him high above his head and mightily hallooed
And all the howling hounds bayed response unto him.
Hunters hied them thither with many merry horns 1910
Answering from glade to glade till they saw their master.
Quickly there assembled all his company,
All who bore bugles blaring forth together
And all who had no horns whooping and hallooing.
Oh, it was the merriest music ever men did hear, 1915
That uproar that they raised over Reynard's doom.
   And, gay,
    The hounds they goodly praised
    For their work that day
    And Reynard then they seized 1920
    And stripped his pelt away.

77

And then they headed homeward, for it was near night,
Blaring full boldly upon their great bright horns.
The lord alights at last at his beloved home,
Finds a fire upon the hearth and the knight before it,   1925
Gawain the good, who was glad and merry,
For among the lovely ladies lively was his lot.
He wore a fair blue mantle that fell to the floor
And well his surcoat suited him, softly it was furred,
While his hood of that same stuff lay soft upon his shoulders,   1930
And all worked with white fur were both these garments.
He met with the good man in the middle of the hall
And greeted him with graciousness; then gravely did he say,
"I shall be the first this time to fulfill our pact
Which we swore together when the wine was free."   1935
Then he clasped the lord and three times he kissed him
As soberly and seriously as the deed suited.
"By Christ!" cried the lord, "now you are a lucky rascal,
And powerfully you ply your trade if such be your profits!"
"Cheap are my charges," Gawain said cheerily,   1940
"And purely now have I repaid the profits that I gained."
"By Mary," said the merry lord, "in this I am remiss,
For I have hunted all the day and I have gotten nothing
But this foul fox fell (the Devil take such fortune!),
And that is poor indeed to repay such precious goods   1945
As you have thrust upon me here through three such kisses
        So good."
     "Enough," said Sir Gawain,
     "I thank you, by the rood."
     Then how the fox was slain   1950
     They talked of as they stood.

78

With mirth and with minstrelsy, with good meat and wine,
They made as merry there as any men might,
With laughing of ladies and lighthearted jests—
Gawain and the good man, so glad were they both,   1955
And the company caroused there in wild, half-drunken capers.
Both the good man and his followers made many jokes
Till the time of severance drew swiftly upon them.
Each baron finally betook him to his bed;
Then the goodly Gawain goes to take his leave   1960
From the fair lord of the castle, and freely he thanks him:
"For the sweet sojourning that I have had here,
The high King yield you honor at this holy day!
I am still your servant, if so it pleases you,
But now I must, as well you know, move on the morrow,   1965
And beg you to lend me some skillful servant

To show me the way to the wild Green Chapel
Where I will suffer on New Year's Day what Fate has willed me."
"In good faith," said the good man, "with a good will;
All I ever vowed to you, faithful I'll fulfill." 1970
Then he assigned a servant to set him in the way
And conduct him by the downs along the dearest path,
To fare through the ford and through fair groves,
            The green way.
           Gawain thanks the lord 1975
           For his services that day,
           Then goes to say a word
           To those ladies sweet and gay.

79

With care and with kissing, he clasps them unto him
And graciously and greatly he thanks them there. 1980
And they reply unto him in the self-same fashion,
Commending him to Christ with full careworn sighings.
Then from their midst he manfully departs;
Each man that he met, he made him many thanks
For his service and his solace and his great concern 1985
That he had had in serving and assisting him;
And every servant was as sad to sever with him there
As though they'd wended worthily with him all their lives.
Then with lights and good men he was led to his chamber
And blithely brought to bed to be at his rest. 1990
If there he slept soundly, I dare not say,
For he had much to mind him of on the morrow morning
           In his thought.
           Now let him lie there still,
           He is near to what he sought, 1995
           And I will tell you, if you will,
           How and what he wrought.

PART FOUR

80

Now the New Year nears and the night passes,
The day drives to the dark as God directs;
But wild weathers of the world awake about, 2000
Clouds keenly cast the cold to the earth
With ice enough of the north to chill the naked beasts;
The sleet spits down, and the stinging snow;
The wild whistling wind whirls from the heights,
Driving each dale full of the billowy drifts. 2005
The knight listened well as he lay in his bed,

And, though he locked his lids, little he slept;
By every cock that crew he counted the hours.
Before the day had dawned he rose and dressed
By the little light of a lamp that gleamed in his chamber; 2010
He called to his chamberlain, who quickly answered,
And bade him bring him his armor and his broad saddle.
The fellow fared forth to fetch him his tackle
And helped to gear him then in goodly garments.
First he clad him in clothes to ward off the cold, 2015
And then his other harness, handsome and splendid,
All the gleaming plates polished and clean,
The rust rubbed from the rings of his rich armor;
And all was fresh as at first, and freely Gawain thanked
     The man. 2020
   Each piece of armor showed
   Bright and clear and clean;
   Fair as a god he strode
   Upon that winter's scene.

81

While he arrayed himself in the richest robes— 2025
His coat with its badge and its shield of bravery
Adorning the plushy velvet, virtuous stones
Beaten about and bound, embroidered seams,
All fairly furred within with the finest pelts—
He forgot not the girdle, the lady's green gift; 2030
That he was sure to wear for his safety's sake!
After he'd strapped the sword on his sinewy thigh,
Then he bound the girdle about him twice.
Quickly that worthy knight enswathed his waist
With the lovely lady's gift, the green love token, 2035
And richly it shone against his deep red robes.
But Gawain wore the girdle, not for goodly show,
For pride of its pendants, though they were brightly polished,
And though the goodly gold gleamed at their ends,
But to save himself when it behoved him to suffer, 2040
To abide without debate a deadly blow from a knife
     Or a sword.
   And then the goodly man
   Freely fared forward,
   And all that jolly band 2045
   He thanked with a cheery word.

82

Then Gringolet was saddled and made ready to go,
He who had sojourned safely meanwhile in the stables;
Eager to gallop forth was that great steed then.
The knight drew near and gazed on his glossy coat 2050

And softly said to himself as he swore by his faith:
"The men within this moat are servants of honor;
The lord who is their liege, joy be his lot!
And his lightsome lady, may love betide her!
They who thus in charity cherish a guest 2055
And hold honor in their hands, may He repay
Who holds the heavens on high, and all within this hall!
And if I should chance to live longer in the land,
I shall reward you all richly as befits you."
Then he stepped in the stirrups and lightly strode aloft; 2060
His man gave him his shield, and he laid it on his shoulder,
And Gringolet he spurred with his gilt heels,
And the sturdy steed across the stark stones
    Started to prance.
    His squire was mounted last, 2065
    Bearing his spear and lance.
    "This castle I commend to Christ
    And his dear maintenance."

83

The bridge was buckled and lowered, and the broad gates
Unbarred and laid open on either side. 2070
The knight blessed himself and crossed over the planks—
Praised the goodly porter, who knelt to that prince
And gave him good day, praying God protect him—
And Gawain went his way with his one attendant
Who would guide and direct him to the dire place 2075
Where his rueful course would reach an unknown end.
They wandered past banks where the boughs were bare,
They clambered over cliffs where the cold clung.
The sky was updrawn, but ugly thereunder,
Mist moved on the moors, melted over the mountains, 2080
And every hill was hooded in a huge cloud of fog.
Brooks boiled and bubbled between bare banks,
Shattering on the rocky shelves where they sheered sharp down.
Oh, weary was their way within a darkening wood,
Till soon it was the season of the sun's arising, 2085
    Far and wide.
    Upon a high hill,
    Where the white snow lay beside,
    They paused and were still,
    The good knight and his guide. 2090

84

"Lord, I have led you hither," the squire said then,
"And now you are not far from that noted place
That you have long sought and sorely searched after.

But I shall tell you truly, since you know me and trust me,
And you are such a lord that a man may serve and love, 2095
If you follow my advice, you will fare forward better.
The place that you press toward full perilous is rumored.
There dwells a wight within that place, the worst upon earth,
For he is stout and stern and dearly loves to strike,
And huger than any man upon middle-earth, 2100
His body broader and bigger than the best four
That are in Arthur's house, be they second Hectors!
He plies his dire trade at the Green Chapel.
No man passes by that place so proud in his arms,
But he dings him to death with fearful blows and dints; 2105
For he is cruel and murderous; mercy is unknown to him.
And be it churl or chaplain who rides beside the Chapel,
Hooded monk or mass-priest or any other man,
He is as quick to kill him as he'd be to crack a knuckle.
So I tell you as surely as you sit upon your saddle, 2110
Come there and be killed, neatly and quickly—
Trust me, I speak the truth—though you had twenty lives
          To spend.
          Long has he lived upon that lea,
          With never a guest or friend; 2115
          Against his savage cruelty
          No man may defend."

85

"Therefore, good Sir Gawain, let this game alone
And go away from this grim place by an easier path!
Go out by another gate, and God speed you well, 2120
And I shall hie me home again, and on my highest honor
I swear before the sovereign of Heaven and all his goodly saints,
So may He help and guide me here and hereafter,
That I shall keep your secret and never speak or whisper
Account of how you feared or failed to face your deadly foe." 2125
"Thanks, good sir," said Gawain, but grudgingly and curtly.
"May God requite and serve him who wishes me thus well,
And that you'd keep your bargain I can well believe.
But, though you kept your silence, were I here to fail
And flee in craven fear, according to your counsel, 2130
Then would I be a coward knight and could not be excused.
No, I will fare to the Chapel, whatever chance befalls,
And boldly speak to that great man you grimly have described,
Be it for weal or woe, as destiny decides
          And ordains. 2135
          Though he be even worse
          Than your account maintains,
          God directs my course,
          My losses and my gains."

86

"By Mary!" cried that other man, "you have said so much, 2140
Now let your doom, how great it be, be on your own head,
For if you long to lose your life I will not here delay you.
Clap your helmet on your head, take your spear in hand,
And ride you down this same road by yonder rock wall
Till you be brought to the bottom of that broad valley; 2145
Then look a little over the fields upon your left side
And you shall spy within that dale the dire Green Chapel,
And the turbulent brook that guards it round about.
Now fare thee well on God's behalf, good and noble Gawain!
For all the gold within the ground I would not go with you, 2150
Nor bear you fellow through these woods one foot further."
With that the honest servant tugged at his horse's head,
Hit him with his heels as hard as he was able,
And galloped away across the lawn, leaving Gawain there
            Alone. 2155
      "By God's dear self," said Gawain,
      "I will neither sigh nor groan.
      Though this road bring me pain,
      I will follow to my goal."

87

Then he spurred Gringolet and, picking up the path, 2160
Pressed forward along the bank beside a little wood,
Riding through the rough bankside right to the dale;
He reined in and waited within that wild place,
And he saw no sign of shelter anywhere about,
Only bleak and broken cliffs rising on both sides 2165
And gnarled and knuckled boulders and twisted, knotted stones;
And the crags grazed the clouds, or so at least it looked.
So he stayed his steed and warily and stealthily
He turned round about, searching for that Chapel,
But there was nothing to be seen, and strange it seemed to him, 2170
Until he spied upon a lawn a low green mound—
A green bulge by a bank beside the brimming stream,
By a ford of the river which forked at that place,
And where the bubbling waters boiled and burbled whitely.
The knight turned his horse and rode toward that spot, 2175
Lightly leapt down and tied to a linden branch
The reins of his steed tightly and securely.
Then he turned to the mound and slowly moved around it,
Debating with himself what manner of thing it was.
It had a hole in the end and one on either side, 2180
All overgrown with greenish weeds in shaggy, grassy clumps,
And all within was hollow, just an empty cave,
Or a crevice of an old crag, but he could not be sure

     Or tell.
  "Good Lord!" cried the knight,   2185
  "Is this the Green Chapel?
  The Devil here in the middle of the night
  Might weave his evil spell."

88

"Now, indeed," said Gawain, "here is a wizardly waste,
And this an ugly oratory, all overgrown with weeds;   2190
Well it befits that wight, warped and wrapped in green,
To hold his dark devotions here in the Devil's service!
Now, sure in my five wits I fear it is the foul fiend
Who here has led me far astray, the better to destroy me.
This is a Chapel of Mischance, ill luck betide it!   2195
A more accursed church, in truth, I never chanced upon!"
With his high helmet on his head, his lance in his hand,
He drew near the roof of that rough, rocky dwelling.
Then he heard from a high hill, out of the hard rock,
Beyond the brook upon a bank, a wondrous battering noise. 2200
What! it clattered against the cliff as though to cleave and crack it;
It seemed someone were sharpening a scythe against a grindstone.
What! it whined and whirred like water through a mill.
What! it rushed and rang, terrible to hear.
Then "By God," said Gawain, "that gear, I do believe, 2205
Is being duly honed for me by that horrible creature
    Who lives here.
   Let God work as he might;
   There is no succor near.
   Though I forego my life,   2210
   I will not yield to fear."

89

Then the knight called out clear and bold and true:
"What man stands upon this post to hold a tryst with me?
For here now is Gawain, come to seek him out.
Let any man who wants to see me wend his way forward, 2215
Either now or never; I will strive to fit his needs."
"Abide!" a voice upon the bank cried above his head,
"And you shall richly reap all I promised to repay you."
But yet for another little while he went on with his whetting,
And the whanging clamor rang from the rocks around;   2220
And finally from under a crag he sprang forth out of a cave,
Leaping out of the living rock, whirling his fell weapon,
A new and shiny Danish ax with which to deal the dint,
With a bright bit bound unto the handle,
And it was fitly honed and filed; four feet long—   2225
It was no less in length—all wrapped in brightest lace;

And the Man in Green was geared as at first
From his face to his feet, his hair, his flowing beard,
Except that this time free on foot he fared over the earth,
Holding the stern steel stiff against his side. 2230
When he reached the water, he did not wade through it,
But hopped across it on his ax and actively he strode
Across the wide and open field, all smooth and white
    With snow.
   Sir Gawain met him there 2235
   Without a word of greeting.
   The other cried: "Sweet sir,
   You're prompt for our fell meeting."

90

"Gawain," said the Green Knight, "God grant you grace!
Fellow, you are welcome to this unworthy place, 2240
And you have timed your travel as a true man should.
Now you recall the covenant we have cast between us:
Twelve months past at this time you took your share,
And now on this New Year I must needs repay you.
And verily alone we are met within this valley, 2245
No servants to second us, we meet man to man.
Off with your helmet now! here is your repayment.
And give me no more argument than that I gave to you
When you whacked my head off with one fell blow."
"Nay, by God," said Gawain, "who granted me my soul, 2250
I shall bear no grudge, whatever bane befalls me.
But deal me your one stroke and I shall stand still
And offer no resistance; and you may sternly strike
    As you will."
   He bent his fair neck 2255
   Under the sharp steel.
   No word did he speak,
   No fear did he seem to feel.

91

Then the Man in Green gathered his strength,
Grasping his grim tool greatly to smite; 2260
With all the brawn in his body he bore it aloft,
Aiming it as direly as though to destroy the man;
Had he driven it down as deadly as he threatened,
That doughtiest of knights would sure have died of the dint.
But Gawain glanced aslant at the descending ax 2265
As it came gliding grimly down where he knelt upon the ground
And with a shrugging motion shrank from the sharp iron.
The other, with a slight start, drew back the blade
And then reproved that prince with these proud and stinging words:
"Why, you're not Gawain, man!" he jeered, "of such high fame, 2270

He who never quaked or quailed in the clash of battle,
For now you flinch in craven fear before you feel my steel!
I never heard such cowardice ascribed to that great knight!
I never flinched nor fled when you struck at me,
Nor offered an objection there in Arthur's hall. 2275
My head fell bouncing at my feet but still I stood fast.
But you, before my ax has fallen, quail within your heart.
Let me now be known by men as the better man,
          Therefore."
       Said Gawain: "I flinched once, 2280
       And I will no more;
       But if *my* head falls on the stones,
       God knows I have no more!"

92

"But to it, man, and quick! and bring me to the point.
Deal me now my destiny, and do it as it suits you. 2285
For I shall stand your stroke and never start again
Till your ax has hit and hewn me: here is my oath."
"Have at you, then!" yelled the other and heaved the ax aloft,
Rolling his eyes as rashly as one who'd run amuck.
He feinted at him fiercely but then deferred the blow 2290
Just at the last blink above the bare neck.
Gawain held fast and never a nerve quivered,
But stood as still upon that spot as a stone or stump,
One that's bedded in the rocks with a hundred roots.
Then merrily he mocked, that monstrous Man in Green: 2295
"Now that your heart is whole, I'll hold back no longer.
Hold now the high hood that Arthur gave you
And, after this whacking blow, let's see you wet your windpipe!"
Gawain growled wrathfully and said then in anger:
"Thrash away, then, man, and cease these hollow threats. 2300
I half suspect you quake and fear within your secret heart."
"Well, then," cried the other fellow, "since you speak so fiercely,
I'll defer no further the fees you've come to claim
          From me."
       He raised his ax to strike, 2305
       Grimacingly savagely;
       But nothing now could daunt the knight,
       For void of hope was he.

93

The Green Man lifted his ax and lightly let it down
With the bright blade against the bare neck. 2310
But though he struck straight he harmed him not at all,
Except upon the one side where he sliced the skin.
The blade slashed through the skin, through the sheer flesh,
So that the bubbling blood bathed the broad shoulders.

And when the knight espied his blood, crimson on the snow, 2315
He sprawled aside and sprang away, more than a spear's length,
Seized up his goodly helmet and hove it onto his head,
Caught up his shining shield and threw it over his shoulders,
Drew out his deadly sword and direly then he spoke
(Oh, never since the day he was delivered of his mother 2320
Had he felt so glad and grand, walking the green earth!):
"Hold your hand, man, and give no more commands!
I have stood your stroke without dispute or flinching,
And if you touch me once again, I'm ready to requite you
And give you back as good as that you gave me. 2325
    Hold fast!
   One stroke was due unto me,
   According to our pact;
   My turn again is due me—
   Defend yourself. Stand back!" 2330

94

The Green Knight drew back and rested on his ax,
Setting the shaft upon the ground and leaning on the blade,
And he gazed upon Gawain, who stood his ground before him,
Noting how that fearless fellow stood fast, unflinching,
Armed and unawed. (And he smiled within his heart.) 2335
Then he grumbled gruffly and with a great voice,
And in a rough rumbling tone bluntly he roared:
"Bold sir, be not so fierce upon this free field.
No man has met you here with unfitting manners,
Nor will, save as cast at court in our firm covenant. 2340
I owed a dint, I dealt it; regard yourself repaid.
Now I release you from all remnant rights.
If I had been rougher, more rudely to have rapped you,
I might have hurt you heavily, and with a hearty will.
First I feinted at you merrily with a mighty swing, 2345
But hurt you never a single hair. That, I'll have you know,
Was for the pact we pledged together that first pure night,
When you swore on your honor, and highly you upheld it,
That you would give me all your gains, as a good man should.
The second stroke I offered you was for the second morning 2350
When you kissed my comely wife, then paid the kiss to me.
For these two kisses, then, I feigned two fell blows,
    Without hurt.
   A true man deals true,
   Nor lies within his heart. 2355
   The third time, though, you played untrue;
   And I made your red blood start."

95

"For that's my girdle that you wear wound about your waist;
My own wife wove its strands; this I remember well.

So, you see, I know a little of you, both bad and good! 2360
And, Lord, the wooing of my wife! Why, man, I willed it all.
I sent her to seduce you, and freely I must say
You are one of the worthiest knights who ever walked the earth.
As a pearl is to a white pea, for purity, for praise,
So Gawain is, in good faith, to other gay knights! 2365
And though you lacked a little, sir, in loyalty and honor,
It was not for lustful love nor low villainy,
But simply that you loved your life, the less be your blame."
Gawain stood pondering a great and goodly while,
So aggrieved and angered, his spirit groaned within. 2370
All his body's blood burned into his cheeks
And, oh, he shrank for very shame the while the Green Knight talked.
At last in faltering fashion he started to speak:
"Cursed now be cowardice and covetousness, too!
In them are villainy and vice instead of pure virtue!" 2375
With that he caught the knot and loosed the bright lace,
Fiercely flung the girdle across to his foeman:
"Lo! take the false thing and foul fate befall it!
Fear of your fell ax taught me fright and cowardice,
Allied me with covetousness, divorced me from my nature, 2380
That largeness and that loyalty which should belong to knighthood.
Now I am false and faulty and fear has stained my honor.
Oh, treachery and truthlessness, both bring distraction
         And woe!
         Man, I confess it free: 2385
         I played you false, and so
         Come, take your will of me—
         Then let me go."

96

Then the Green Man laughed and lightly he said:
"Whatever harm I had is wholly healed and restored. 2390
Your small misdeeds are known and you are clean confessed
And well have borne the penance of my ax's purging point.
I highly hold you here absolved and purified as clean
As though you'd never slipped or strayed since the day you were born.
And I give you, sir, the girdle, hemmed all in gold, 2395
Green as is my gown, you see. Look on it, Gawain,
And think upon this meeting as you thrive over the land
Among princes of praise: preserve this as a token
Of the wild Green Chapel in ways where you wander.
Now you shall upon this New Year return to my castle 2400
And we shall revel through the remainder of this rich feast
         Tonight."
         The lord clasped him close
         And said: "With my wife,
         Who lately was your foe, 2405
         You shall dance in delight!"

97

"No, indeed," said the knight, seizing his helmet,
And he heaved it off and thanked his green opponent.
"Too long have I lingered. Good luck be your lot.
May he reward you richly who ordains all honor. 2410
Commend me to that courteous lady, your sweet and comely wife,
Both she and that elder other, worthy women both,
Who thus beguiled a callow knight curiously and quaintly.
But yet it is no rare fault to be made a fool
And through the wiles of women to be won to sorrow, 2415
For thus was Adam on this earth early beguiled,
And Solomon with more than one, and Samson in his season—
Delilah dealt him his fate—and David thereafter
Suffered sorely from Bathsheba's sweetness and softness.
All these worthy men were snared by women's subtle wiles; 2420
All laud therefore unto that man who loves without believing!
For these were the mightiest men ever God made,
In excellence and honor they outstripped all others.
    What then?
    Still they were beguiled 2425
    By cunning, subtle women.
    Though I have been betrayed,
    I am not the first of men."

98

"But for your girdle," Gawain said, "may God the gift repay you!
And I will wear it with good will, not for the worthy gold, 2430
Nor the samite nor the silk nor the soft pendants,
Not out of pride or pomp, nor for love of the pure works,
But as a sign of my sin I shall see it ever
When I ride in renown, a reproach to my soul
For the fault and frailty of the warped flesh, 2435
How weak and willing it is to yield to evil's workings;
And when I feel the prick of pride in prowess of arms
I'll look a little upon this lace, and my heart will grow less.
But one point would I pray of you, may it not displease you:
Since you are lord of yonder land where I lay awhile 2440
With you in honor—and may He ever reward you
Who upholds the heavens and sits in the high places!—
How do men name you? Tell me this, and no more."
"Why, that I'll tell you truly," the other said at this.
"Bercilak de Hautdesert they call me in this country, 2445

---

samite a heavy silk fabric.   *Bercilak de Hautdesert* The name "Bercilak" is the same as "Bertelak," a name which occurs in several Old French and Middle English romances. "Hautdesert" refers to the Green Chapel and means "high hermitage" or high desert or "solitary wasteland." A *desert* in Celtic meant a solitary place where anchorites had their abode.

And through the might of Morgan le Fay I am maintained,
She who dwells within my house and knows many arts,
The mistress of Merlin—many a one she's tricked!
Oh, she has had dark dealings on many a deep evening
With that crafty clerk, he who is well acquainted 2450
      With Arthur's hall.
    And Morgan, the goddess,
    Or so she is called,
    Takes pride in her prowess
    And her subtle skill." 2455

99

"She it was who sent me to Arthur's high hall
To test your pompous pride and see if they were true,
Those reports of renown about the Round Table.
She contrived me this trick for to crack your wits
And Guinevere to grieve, to goad her unto death 2460
Through fear of that spectre who spoke in spooky fashion
Holding his head within his hand before the high table.
That is she who is at home, the ancient, wrinkled lady;
She is even your own aunt, Arthur's half-sister,
Born of Tintagel's duchess, she whom Uther after 2465
Begat Arthur upon, he who now is king.
So I entreat you, man, come and meet your aunt.
Make merry in my house. All my company loves you.
And I wish you as well, fellow, by my faith,
As any lord within the land for your tested loyalty." 2470
But Gawain firm refused him, he would hear no further.
So they clasped and kissed, commending one another
To the Prince of Paradise, and they parted there
      On the white hill.
    Gawain on his steed 2475
    Fares forward still;
    And the knight in green—
    Wheresoever he will.

100

Wild ways in the world Gawain now wanders,
Having gotten after his test the grace of his life. 2480
Sometimes he harbored in a house, sometimes in the weather,

Morgan le Fay sister of King Arthur. She was banished from Arthur's court because of a love affair with a knight of the court which Queen Guinevere discovered and revealed; hence her jealousy and hatred of Guinevere. In her banishment she took up with the magician Merlin and became herself something of an ugly enchantress.   *crafty clerk* Merlin.   *Tintagel's duchess* King Arthur was the illegitimate son of Uther Pendragon and Igern, Duchess of Tintagel—the wife of Gorlois. When Gorlois was slain, through the magic of Merlin, Uther took on the appearance of Gorlois and fathered Arthur.

And many a venture chanced upon and vanquished many a foe,
Tales that now at this place I have not time to tell.
The wound in his neck was healed now and whole
And the bright belt of green he wore wound about him, 2485
Twisted like a baldric, bound at his side,
Underneath his left arm, knotted by the lace,
As a token of his sin and his secret sorrow.
And so he came at last to court, Gawain the good.
Oh, joy awakened in those walls when it was known 2490
That Gawain was returned, he whom they had grieved for.
The king clasped and kissed him, and the queen as well,
And many proud and noble knights pressed forward to greet him,
And keenly they questioned him, how he had come to them,
And truly he told them there of all his toil and care, 2495
The meeting at the Chapel, the mystery of the Green Man,
The love of the lady, the girdle at the last.
Then he bared his naked neck and showed them the nick
That he'd been dealt in the snowy dale for his dishonor
              And blame. 2500
     He suffered, telling his disgrace,
     He groaned for his soiled fame;
     The hot blood mounted to his face
     In anguish and shame.

101

"Lo, lord!" he cried, handling the lace, 2505
"Here is the brand of that blame I bear upon my neck;
This is the dishonor and the death of my fame,
The cowardice and covetousness I was caught in there.
This is the token of untruth that I was trapped within,
And now I must wear this lace while life lasts. 2510
For none may hide his guilt, nor may it be undone;
Once a man is trapped and taken, the trap is not unsprung!"
Then Arthur cheered the knight, and all the court joined him,
Laughing loudly at the tale, and lightly they agreed,
All those lords and ladies, belonging to the Table, 2515
Each fellow the Brotherhood should bear as a baldric
A band bound about his waist, a badge of brightest green,
To wear ever after in honor of that knight.
With one accord they swore together, those true knights,
That he who wore a green girdle won greater honor, 2520
As it is rhymed and written in the best book of Romance.
So in Arthur's time this adventure happened,

---

fellow of the Brotherhood Some have seen in the decision to wear the green badges an allusion to the Order of the Garter, but there is no evidence that the author had this in mind, even though the legend at the end of the poem (*Hony Soyt Qui Mal Pence*) is the motto of the Order of the Garter. In a later romance, *The Green Knight*, based on *Sir Gawain*, the lace worn is white, and this is associated with the collar worn by the Knights of the Bath.

And the books of Brutus bear witness unto it.
And since Brutus the bold first bent his way here
After the siege and assault had ceased at Troy, 2525
      I say:
      There have been more
      Adventures such as this.
      May Jesus Christ forevermore
      Bring us to his bliss! 2530
         AMEN.

Hony Soyt Qui Mal Pence

---

books of Brutus Early chronicles of England were called *Bruts,* or stories of Brutus, the legendary founder of Britain, even when they did not contain the story of Brutus.

ON OTHER TYPES OF MEDIEVAL NARRATIVE POETRY

The romance and the ballad were perhaps the most popular forms of narrative poetry in the Middle Ages, but there were other forms of almost equal popularity. Most of them were in some way related to the dominant didactic purpose of medieval literature and art. The *exemplum,* or tale told to illustrate a moral, found frequent place in the medieval sermon and devotional work. Chaucer's *The Pardoner's Tale* of the three thieves who contrive one another's deaths out of greed for a heap of gold, told by the Pardoner to exemplify the text that greed is the root of all evil, is a classic example of the type. The *beast fable,* in which animals were given human qualities related to their animal characteristics and made to impersonate human virtues and vices, was another favorite type of didactic story; Chaucer's *The Nun's Priest's Tale* of Chanticleer, Pertelote, and Sir Reynard the Fox is a typical example. The *fabliaux* was a kind of tavern story, a bit vulgar and frequently satirical of the vices of the clergy, which appealed to the tastes of the lower middle class. The rather coarse miller and some of his companions tell this kind of story in *The Canterbury Tales.*

In fact, it is strongly suggested that this unit on narrative poetry be supplemented by a first-hand experience of the wide variety of story types in Chaucer's *Canterbury Tales.* This can be done conveniently in Nevill Coghill's very readable translation in *The Penguin Classics*—the volume from which *The Nun's Priest's Tale* in this anthology is reprinted.

ON NARRATIVE POETRY

One of the most moneyed of modern businesses is built on our inveterate curiosity about the doings of our fellow human beings, but, for the most part, news stories supply only the surface facts of human events. If the stories told in the poems of this unit were capsuled in newspaper columns, the headlines would read something like this: *Boy Dies as Result of Accident on Jackson's Farm; Farm of Michael Hinsley Sold at Public Auction.* Such headlines as these occur in almost every morning paper and are followed by a run down of the essential surface facts of the stories they report.

But the poems on these subjects begin where a news story leaves off. What the narrative poet is interested in is not the surface facts of the story, but the insights those facts reveal of human life. It is not the mere fact of the boy's accidental loss of an arm in a buzz saw and his subsequent death in the hospital that is the real center of attention in "Out, Out," but the flashes of insight that the accident reveals about the boy's relationship to his too practical and money-minded elders and the bond of understanding between him and his little sister. No news story could ever begin to reveal Michael's dramatic conflict between love of the land and love of his son, resolved in the tragic decision which ended in the loss of both, as does Wordsworth's poem.

Thus, the superiority of a good narrative poem over a mere news story is perhaps best appreciated when we consciously advert to the insights into human relationships and deep human feelings provided by the poem which we would not expect to find even in the most expert news story. It is the business of the newsman to give us the story; the narrative poet strives to communicate his insights into the meaning of the story and his own feelings about it. To achieve this he has to use every means at his disposal—dramatic irony, symbolism, associations, metaphor, concrete and connotative language, and the emotional overtones of rhythm.

"Out, Out—"*
by ROBERT FROST

The buzz saw snarled and rattled in the yard
And made dust and dropped stove-length sticks of wood,
Sweet-scented stuff when the breeze drew across it.
And from there those that lifted eyes could count
Five mountain ranges one behind the other   5
Under the sunset far into Vermont.
And the saw snarled and rattled, snarled and rattled,
As it ran light, or had to bear a load.
And nothing happened: day was all but done.
Call it a day, I wish they might have said   10
To please the boy by giving him the half hour
That a boy counts so much when saved from work.
His sister stood beside them in her apron
To tell them "Supper." At the word, the saw,
As if to prove saws knew what supper meant,   15
Leaped out at the boy's hand, or seemed to leap—

"*Out, Out—*" the title is an allusion to the famous soliloquy of Macbeth on the brevity of life when all life has become meaningless to him.
"Out, out, brief candle,
Life's but a walking shadow, a poor player
That struts and frets his hour on the stage
And then is heard no more." (V, 5, 23-26)

* From *Complete Poems of Robert Frost*. Copyright 1916, 1923, 1930, 1939 by Holt, Rinehart and Winston, Inc. Copyright 1936, 1942, 1944, 1951, © 1958 by Robert Frost. Copyright © 1964, 1967 by Lesley Frost Ballantine. Reprinted by permission of Holt, Rinehart and Winston, Inc.

He must have given the hand. However it was,
Neither refused the meeting. But the hand!
The boy's first outcry was a rueful laugh,
As he swung toward them holding up the hand
Half in appeal, but half as if to keep
The life from spilling. Then the boy saw all—
Since he was old enough to know, big boy
Doing a man's work, though a child at heart—
He saw all spoiled. "Don't let him cut my hand off— 25
The doctor, when he comes. Don't let him, sister!"
So. But the hand was gone already.
The doctor put him in the dark of ether.
He lay and puffed his lips out with his breath.
And then—the watcher at his pulse took fright. 30
No one believed. They listened at his heart.
Little—less—nothing!—and that ended it.
No more to build on there. And they, since they
Were not the one dead, turned to their affairs.

Michael

A Pastoral Poem

by WILLIAM WORDSWORTH

If from the public way you turn your steps
Up the tumultuous brook of Greenhead Ghyll,
You will suppose that with an upright path
Your feet must struggle; in such bold ascent
The pastoral mountains front you, face to face. 5
But, courage! for around that boisterous brook
The mountains have all opened out themselves,
And made a hidden valley of their own.
No habitation can be seen; but they
Who journey thither find themselves alone 10
With a few sheep, with rocks and stones, and kites
That overhead are sailing in the sky.
It is in truth an utter solitude;
Nor should I have made mention of this Dell
But for one object which you might pass by, 15
Might see and notice not. Beside the brook
Appears a straggling heap of unhewn stones!
And to that simple object appertains
A story—unenriched with strange events,
Yet not unfit, I deem, for the fireside, 20
Or for the summer shade. It was the first
Of those domestic tales that spake to me
Of shepherds, dwellers in the valleys, men
Whom I already loved; not verily
For their own sakes, but for the fields and hills 25
Where was their occupation and abode.
And hence this Tale, while I was yet a Boy

---

a straggling heap of unhewn stones "The sheepfold on which so much of the poem turns, remains, or rather the ruins of it. The character and circumstances of Luke were taken from a family to whom had belonged, many years before, the house we lived in at Town-end." A note by Wordsworth himself.

Careless of books, yet having felt the power
Of Nature, by the gentle agency
Of natural objects, led me on to feel 30
For passions that were not my own, and think
(At random and imperfectly indeed)
On man, the heart of man, and human life.
Therefore, although it be a history
Homely and rude, I will relate the same 35
For the delight of a few natural hearts:
And, with yet fonder feeling, for the sake
Of youthful Poets, who among these hills
Will be my second self when I am gone.

    Upon the forest-side in Grasmere Vale 40
There dwelt a Shepherd, Michael was his name;
An old man, stout of heart, and strong of limb.
His bodily frame had been from youth to age
Of an unusual strength: his mind was keen,
Intense, and frugal, apt for all affairs, 45
And in his shepherd's calling he was prompt
And watchful more than ordinary men.
Hence had he learned the meaning of all winds,
Of blasts of every tone; and, oftentimes,
When others heeded not, He heard the South 50
Make subterraneous music, like the noise
Of bagpipers on distant Highland hills.
The Shepherd, at such warning, of his flock
Bethought him, and he to himself would say,
"The winds are now devising work for me!" 55
And, truly, at all times, the storm, that drives
The traveler to a shelter, summoned him

Grasmere Vale a valley in the Lake District near Grasmere Lake.

Up to the mountains: he had been alone
Amid the heart of many thousand mists,
That came to him, and left him, on the heights. 60
So lived he till his eightieth year was past.
And grossly that man errs, who should suppose
That the green valleys, and the streams and rocks,
Were things indifferent to the Shepherd's thoughts.
Fields, where with cheerful spirits he had breathed 65
The common air; hills, which with vigorous step
He had so often climbed; which had impressed
So many incidents upon his mind
Of hardship, skill or courage, joy or fear;
Which, like a book, preserved the memory 70
Of the dumb animals, whom he had saved,
Had fed or sheltered, linking to such acts
The certainty of honorable gain;
Those fields, those hills—what could they less? had laid
Strong hold on his affections, were to him 75
A pleasurable feeling of blind love,
The pleasure which there is in life itself.

    His days had not been passed in singleness.
His Helpmate was a comely matron, old—
Though younger than himself full twenty years. 80
She was a woman of a stirring life,
Whose heart was in her house: two wheels she had
Of antique form; this large, for spinning wool;
That small, for flax; and if one wheel had rest
It was because the other was at work. 85
The Pair had but one inmate in their house,
An only Child, who had been born to them

When Michael, telling o'er his years, began
To deem that he was old,—in shepherd's phrase,
With one foot in the grave. This only Son, 90
With two brave sheep-dogs tried in many a storm,
The one of an inestimable worth,
Made all their household. I may truly say,
That they were as a proverb in the vale
For endless industry. When day was gone, 95
And from their occupations out of doors
The Son and Father were come home, even then,
Their labor did not cease; unless when all
Turned to the cleanly supper-board, and there,
Each with a mess of pottage and skimmed milk, 100
Sat round the basket piled with oaten cakes,
And their plain home-made cheese. Yet when the meal
Was ended, Luke (for so the Son was named)
And his old Father both betook themselves
To such convenient work as might employ
Their hands by the fireside; perhaps to card 105
Wool for the Housewife's spindle, or repair
Some injury done to sickle, flail, or scythe,
Or other implement of house or field.

    Down from the ceiling, by the chimney's edge,
That in our ancient uncouth country style 110
With huge and black projection over-browed
Large space beneath, as duly as the light
Of day grew dim the Housewife hung a lamp;
An aged utensil, which had performed 115
Service beyond all others of its kind.
Early at evening did it burn—and late,
Surviving comrade of uncounted hours,
Which, going by from year to year, had found,
And left, the couple neither gay perhaps 120
Nor cheerful, yet with objects and with hopes,
Living a life of eager industry.
And now, when Luke had reached his eighteenth year,
There by the light of this old lamp they sate,
Father and Son, while far into the night 125
The Housewife plied her own peculiar work,
Making the cottage through the silent hours
Murmur as with the sound of summer flies.
This light was famous in its neighborhood,
And was a public symbol of the life 130
That thrifty Pair had lived. For, as it chanced,
Their cottage on a plot of rising ground
Stood single, with large prospect, north and south,
High into Easedale, up to Dunmail-Raise,
And westward to the village near the lake; 135
And from this constant light, so regular
And so far seen, the House itself, by all
Who dwelt within the limits of the vale,
Both old and young, was named
The Evening Star.

    Thus living on through such a length of years, 140
The Shepherd, if he loved himself, must needs
Have loved his Helpmate; but to Michael's heart
This son of his old age was yet more dear—
Less from instinctive tenderness, the same
Fond spirit that blindly works in the blood of all— 145
Than that a child, more than all other gifts
That earth can offer to declining man,

Brings hope with it, and forward-looking
    thoughts,
And stirrings of inquietude, when they
By tendency of nature needs must fail. 150
Exceeding was the love he bare to him,
His heart and his heart's joy! For
    oftentimes
Old Michael, while he was a babe in
    arms,
Had done him female service, not alone
For pastime and delight, as is the use 155
Of fathers, but with patient mind
    enforced
To acts of tenderness; and he had rocked
His cradle, as with a woman's gentle hand.

    And, in a later time, ere yet the Boy
Had put on boy's attire, did Michael
    love, 160
Albeit of a stern unbending mind,
To have the Young-one in his sight,
    when he
Wrought in the field, or on his
    shepherd's stool
Sate with a fettered sheep before him
    stretched
Under the large old oak, that near his
    door 165
Stood single, and, from matchless depth
    of shade,
Chosen for the Shearer's covert from the
    sun,
Thence in our rustic dialect was called
The *Clipping Tree,* a name which yet it
    bears.
There, while they two were sitting in the
    shade, 170
With others round them, earnest all and
    blithe,
Would Michael exercise his heart with
    looks
Of fond correction and reproof bestowed
Upon the Child, if he disturbed the sheep
By catching at their legs, or with his
    shouts 175
Scared them, while they lay still beneath
    the shears.

    And when by Heaven's good grace
    the boy grew up
A healthy Lad, and carried in his cheek
Two steady roses that were five years old;
Then Michael from winter coppice cut 180
With his own hand a sapling, which he
    hooped
With iron, making it throughout in all
Due requisites a perfect shepherd's staff,
And gave it to the Boy; wherewith equipt
He as a watchman oftentimes was placed 185
At gate or gap, to stem or turn the flock;
And, to his office prematurely called,
There stood the urchin, as you will divine,
Something between a hindrance and a
    help;
And for this cause not always, I believe, 190
Receiving from his Father hire of praise;
Though nought was left undone which
    staff, or voice,
Or looks, or threatening gestures, could
    perform.

    But soon as Luke, full ten years old,
    could stand
Against the mountain blasts; and to the
    heights, 195
Not fearing toil, nor length of weary
    ways,
He with his Father daily went, and they
Were as companions, why should I relate
That objects which the Shepherd loved
    before
Were dearer now? that from the Boy
    there came 200
Feelings and emanations—things which
    were
Light to the sun and music to the wind;
And that the old Man's heart seemed
    born again?
    Thus in his Father's sight the Boy
    grew up:
And now, when he had reached his
    eighteenth year, 205
He was his comfort and his daily hope.

    While in this sort the simple
    household lived
From day to day, to Michael's ear there
    came
Distressful tidings. Long before the time
Of which I speak, the Shepherd had been
    bound 210
In surety for his brother's son, a man

Of an industrious life, and ample means;
But unforeseen misfortunes suddenly
Had prest upon him; and old Michael now
Was summoned to discharge the forfeiture, 215
A grievous penalty, but little less
Than half his substance. This unlooked-for claim,
At the first hearing, for a moment took
More hope out of his life than he supposed
That any old man ever could have lost. 220
As soon as he had armed himself with strength
To look his trouble in the face, it seemed
The Shepherd's sole resource to sell at once
A portion of his patrimonial fields.
Such was his first resolve; he thought again, 225
And his heart failed him. "Isabel," said he,
Two evenings after he had heard the news,
"I have been toiling more than seventy years,
And in the open sunshine of God's love
Have we all lived; yet if these fields of ours 230
Should pass into a stranger's hand, I think
That I could not lie quiet in my grave.
Our lot is a hard lot; the sun himself
Had scarcely been more diligent than I;
And I have lived to be a fool at last 235
To my own family. An evil man
That was, and made an evil choice, if he
Were false to us; and if he were not false,
There are ten thousand to whom loss like this
Had been no sorrow. I forgive him;—but 240
'Twere better to be dumb than to talk thus.
  When I began, my purpose was to speak
Of remedies and of a cheerful hope.
Our Luke shall leave us, Isabel; the land
Shall not go from us, and it shall be free; 245
He shall possess it, free as is the wind
That passes over it. We have, thou know'st,
Another kinsman—he will be our friend
In this distress. He is a prosperous man,
Thriving in trade—and Luke to him shall go, 250
And with his kinsman's help and his own thrift
He quickly will repair this loss, and then
He may return to us. If here he stay,
What can be done? Where everyone is poor,
What can be gained?"
  At this the old Man paused, 255
And Isabel sat silent, for her mind
Was busy, looking back into past times.
There's Richard Bateman, thought she to herself,
He was a parish-boy—at the church-door
They made a gathering for him, shillings, pence 260
And halfpennies, wherewith the neighbors brought
A basket, which they filled with pedlar's wares;
And, with this basket on his arm, the lad
Went up to London, found a master there,
Who, out of many, chose the trusty boy 265
To go and overlook his merchandise
Beyond the seas; where he grew wondrous rich,
And left estates and monies to the poor.
And, at his birth-place, built a chapel, floored
With marble which he sent from foreign lands. 270
These thoughts, and many others of like sort,
Passed quickly through the mind of Isabel,
And her face brightened. The old Man was glad,
And thus resumed: "Well, Isabel! this scheme
These two days, has been meat and drink to me. 275
Far more than we have lost is left us yet.
—We have enough—I wish indeed that I
Were younger;—but this hope is a good hope.
—Make ready Luke's best garments, of the best

Buy for him more, and let us send him forth
Tomorrow, or the next day, or tonight:
—If he *could* go, the Boy should go tonight." 280

  Here Michael ceased, and to the fields went forth
With a light heart. The Housewife for five days
Was restless morn and night, and all day long
Wrought on with her best fingers to prepare 285
Things needful for the journey of her son.
But Isabel was glad when Sunday came
To stop her in her work: for, when she lay
By Michael's side, she through the last two nights
Heard him, how he was troubled in his sleep: 290
And when they rose at morning she could see
That all his hopes were gone. That day at noon
She said to Luke, while they two by themselves
Were sitting at the door, "Thou must not go: 295
We have no other Child but thee to lose—
None to remember—do not go away,
For if thou leave thy Father he will die."
The Youth made answer with a jocund voice;
And Isabel, when she had told her fears, 300
Recovered heart. That evening her best fare
Did she bring forth, and all together sat
Like happy people round a Christmas fire.

  With daylight Isabel resumed her work;
And all the ensuing week the house appeared 305
As cheerful as a grove in Spring: at length
The expected letter from their kinsman came,
With kind assurances that he would do
His utmost for the welfare of the Boy;
To which, requests were added, that forthwith 310
He might be sent to him. Ten times or more
The letter was read over; Isabel
Went forth to show it to the neighbors round;
Nor was there at that time on English land
A prouder heart than Luke's. When Isabel 315
Had to her house returned, the old Man said,
"He shall depart tomorrow." To this word
The Housewife answered, talking much of things
Which, if at such short notice he should go,
Would surely be forgotten. But at length 320
She gave consent, and Michael was at ease.

  Near the tumultuous brook of Greenhead Ghyll,
In that deep valley, Michael had designed
To build a Sheepfold; and, before he heard
The tidings of his melancholy loss, 325
For this same purpose he had gathered up
A heap of stones, which by the streamlet's edge
Lay thrown together, ready for the work.
With Luke that evening thitherward he walked:
And soon as they had reached the place he stopped, 330
And thus the old Man spake to him: "My Son,
Tomorrow thou wilt leave me: with full heart
I look upon thee, for thou art the same
That wert a promise to me ere thy birth,
And all thy life hast been my daily joy. 335
I will relate to thee some little part
Of our two histories; 'twill do thee good
When thou art from me, even if I should touch

On things thou canst not know of.——
   After thou
First cam'st into the world—as oft
   befalls 340
To new-born infants—thou didst sleep
   away
Two days, and blessings from thy Father's
   tongue
Then fell upon thee. Day by day passed
   on,
And still I loved thee with increasing love.
Never to living ear came sweeter sounds 345
Than when I heard thee by our own
   fireside
First uttering, without words, a natural
   tune;
While thou, a feeding babe, didst in thy
   joy
Sing at thy Mother's breast. Month
   followed month,
And in the open fields my life was
   passed 350
And on the mountains; else I think that
   thou
Hadst been brought up upon thy Father's
   knees.
But we were playmates, Luke: among
   these hills,
As well thou knowest, in us the old and
   young
Have played together, nor with me didst
   thou 355
Lack any pleasure which a boy can
   know."
Luke had a manly heart; but at these
   words
He sobbed aloud. The old Man grasped
   his hand,
And said, "Nay, do not take it so—I see
That these are things of which I need
   not speak. 360
—Even to the utmost I have been to
   thee
A kind and a good Father: and herein
I but repay a gift which I myself
Received at others' hands; for, though
   now old
Beyond the common life of man, I still
Remember them who loved me in my
   youth. 365

Both of them sleep together: here they
   lived,
As all their Forefathers had done; and
   when
At length their time was come, they were
   not loth
To give their bodies to the family mold. 370
I wished that thou should'st live the life
   they lived:
But, 'tis a long time to look back, my Son,
And see so little gain from threescore
   years.
These fields were burdened when they
   came to me;
Till I was forty years of age, not more 375
Than half of my inheritance was mine.
I toiled and toiled; God blessed me in
   my work,
And till these three weeks past the land
   was free.
—It looks as if it never could endure
Another Master. Heaven forgive me,
   Luke, 380
If I judge ill for thee, but it seems good
That thou should'st go."
                    At this the old Man paused;
Then, pointing to the stones near which
   they stood,
Thus, after a short silence, he resumed:
"This was a work for us; and now, my
   Son, 385
It is a work for me. But, lay one stone—
Here, lay it for me, Luke, with thine
   own hands.
Nay, Boy, be of good hope;—we both
   may live
To see a better day. At eighty-four
I still am strong and hale;—do thou thy
   part; 390
I will do mine.—I will begin again
With many tasks that were resigned
   to thee:
Up to the heights, and in among the
   storms,
Will I without thee go again, and do
All works which I was wont to do alone, 395
Before I knew thy face.—Heaven bless
   thee, Boy!
Thy heart these two weeks has been
   beating fast

With many hopes; it should be so—yes—yes—
I knew that thou could'st never have a wish
To leave me, Luke: thou hast been bound to me 400
Only by links of love: when thou art gone,
What will be left to us!—But, I forget
My purposes. Lay now the corner-stone,
As I requested; and hereafter, Luke,
When thou art gone away, should evil men 405
Be thy companions, think of me, my Son,
And of this moment; hither turn thy thoughts,
And God will strengthen thee: amid all fear
And all temptation, Luke, I pray that thou
May'st bear in mind the life thy Fathers lived, 410
Who, being innocent, did for that cause
Bestir them in good deeds. Now, fare thee well—
When thou return'st, thou in this place wilt see
A work which is not here: a covenant
'Twill be between us; but, whatever fate 415
Befall thee, I shall love thee to the last,
And bear thy memory with me to the grave."

    The Shepherd ended here; and Luke stooped down,
And, as his Father had requested, laid
The first stone of the Sheepfold. At the sight 420
The old Man's grief broke from him; to his heart
He pressed his Son, he kissed him and wept;
And to the house together they returned.
—Hushed was that House in peace, or seeming peace,
Ere the night fell:—with morrow's dawn the Boy
Began his journey, and when he had reached 425
The public way, he put on a bold face;
And all the neighbors, as he passed their doors,
Came forth with wishes and with farewell prayers,
That followed him till he was out of sight. 430

    A good report did from their Kinsman come,
Of Luke and his well-doing; and the Boy
Wrote loving letters, full of wondrous news,
Which, as the Housewife phrased it, were throughout
"The prettiest letters that were ever seen." 435
Both parents read them with rejoicing hearts.
So, many months passed on: and once again
The Shepherd went about his daily work
With confident and cheerful thoughts; and now
Sometimes when he could find a leisure hour 440
He to that valley took his way, and there
Wrought at the Sheepfold. Meantime Luke began
To slacken in his duty; and, at length,
He in the dissolute city gave himself
To evil courses: ignominy and shame 445
Fell on him, so that he was driven at last
To seek a hiding-place beyond the seas.

    There is a comfort in the strength of love;
'Twill make a thing endurable, which else
Would overset the brain, or break the heart: 450
I have conversed with more than one who well
Remember the old Man, and what he was
Years after he had heard this heavy news.
His bodily frame had been from youth to age
Of an unusual strength. Among the rocks 455
He went, and still looked up to sun and cloud,

And listened to the wind; and, as before,
Performed all kinds of labor for his sheep,
And for the land, his small inheritance.
And to that hollow dell from time to time   460
Did he repair, to build the Fold of which
His flock had need. 'Tis not forgotten yet
The pity which was then in every heart
For the old Man—and 'tis believed by all
That many and many a day he thither went,   465
And never lifted up a single stone.

    There, by the Sheepfold, sometimes was he seen
Sitting alone, or with his faithful Dog,
Then old, beside him, lying at his feet.
The length of full seven years, from time to time,   470
He at the building of this Sheepfold wrought,
And left the work unfinished when he died.
Three years, or little more, did Isabel
Survive her Husband: at her death the estate
Was sold, and went into a stranger's hand.   475
The Cottage which was named the *Evening Star*
Is gone—the plowshare has been through the ground
On which it stood; great changes have been wrought
In all the neighborhood:—yet the oak is left
That grew beside their door; and the remains   480
Of the unfinished Sheepfold may be seen
Beside the boisterous brook of Greenhead Ghyll.

Unit 9

LYRIC POEMS ARRANGED BY TYPE

ON LYRIC POETRY

Lyric poetry is like narrative poetry in that it is *verse*, but it lacks the story element that holds the narrative together. We have seen that narrative poetry differs from the news story in being interested in the significance and emotional implication of the events and the characters involved in the story—rather than in the bare events themselves. But the narrative poem, like the news story, does focus on characters and events distinct from the poet. No poet, of course, can hide, nor does he entirely wish to hide, his personality and emotional attitude in telling a story; but expressing his personal feelings is not his primary purpose in writing. He rather tries to be faithful to the emotional demands of the characters and situation involved in the narrative itself. That is one way in which the narrative poem differs fundamentally from the lyric. The primary purpose of the lyric poet is to build a little patterned world of words that will suggest to the reader some of the thoughts and feelings of the *author himself*; it is not the subject matter that is his primary concern, but rather what he personally thinks and feels about it.

The lyric poet's concern is to create a pattern, a small unified world, distinct from the confused and confusing multiplicity that surrounds us all—an ordered world that will reveal something of himself, both of the way he thinks and of the way he feels about the world in which he lives, or at least about the small facet of that world with which the poem is concerned. We can find truth about God, man, and the universe in which man lives, more systematically treated and more deeply explored in philosophy; science provides more accurately tested knowledge of the universe and of certain aspects of man himself; but in lyric poetry we learn what experiencing the world has personally meant to other individuals. Lyric poetry is, therefore, as diversified in subject matter as is reality itself, and as distinctive and individualized in inner tone and external pattern as are individual persons. Lyric poetry has an interest for all of us, because people and their experiences have an interest for all of us.

How does the lyric poet go about creating his little unified world of words? Conversation with poets, or the analysis of one's own attempts to write a poem or create any kind of artistic pattern, reveals that there is no one way in which it is done. The sensitive and thoughtful soul—and the artist must be both—has had hundreds of thoughtful reactions to hundreds of experiences and sensations. If he is a painter, he has probably tried to put some of his reactions on canvas—or into words, if he is a poet—and probably without much success. Then some day a new insight dawns. Some new experience or a repetition of an old one suddenly makes him see the significance of what was only an interesting *separate* event before. If he is a poet, simply a happy phrase or line may occur to him—one which he knows expresses exactly some part of a new insight that is dawning in him. This one phrase, verse, or image, may and often does act like a seed from which the whole poem grows and proliferates. Such an intuitional flash is like a magnet suddenly passed over a confused field of steel filings; it provides a unifying center for what previously had been merely haphazard experience. The significance of these newly discovered relationships grows and evolves as the poet works; but it is this primal glimpse of the possible unified pattern that enables him to go on with his work, rejecting this word and selecting that, choosing one image or eliminating another, preferring one rhythmic movement to another, until he is satisfied that the completed poem is a harmoniously wrought pattern of words revealing some of the insights and relationships that were involved in his own experience, and expressing its subtle emotional tone. He knows that it cannot express all the nuances of his own experience and that it will never reveal quite the same thing to every reader; but, when he signs his name to the poem, he is at least indicating that he is satisfied that there is nothing in the poem that positively works counter to the impression he wants the whole to create.

The poet certainly does not always start with, nor perhaps does he work at all from, a clearly defined idea of what the whole poem means; but, if he is an artist at all, he must, before he is finished, make a judgment that the verbal world he has created is a consistent one, that there is in it an internal unity and harmony of thought and tone, that the words he has chosen and the images and rhythm he has employed work together to create a unified and harmonious impression. Unless he takes this responsibility, he really is not working as an artist at all. It is precisely the business of a poet as artist to create a harmonious verbal pattern that will reveal to the reader some of the insight into the meaning of things and some of the emotional tone that were the source and root of that harmonious pattern as the poet himself first experienced it. If this is what the poet is trying to do in writing a poem, what we should do in reading his poem is clear; we should look for the verbal cues that will reveal the pattern.

Perhaps following through the clues that one poet has provided in one poem will make the point clearer. The poem is Gerard Manley Hopkins' "Pied Beauty."

Pied Beauty

Glory be to God for dappled things—
  For skies of couple-colour as a brinded cow;
    For rose-moles all in stipple upon trout that swim;
Fresh-firecoal chestnut-falls; finches' wings;
  Landscape plotted and pieced—fold, fallow, and plough;
    And áll trádes, their gear and tackle and trim.

All things counter, original, spare, strange;
  Whatever is fickle, freckled (who knows how?)
    With swift, slow; sweet, sour; adazzle, dim;
He fathers-forth whose beauty is past change:
    Praise him.

The beauty of the physical world all about us has been the subject of poems by dozens of poets. Hopkins, like any sensitive soul, had often been impressed with that beauty but the stuff out of which poems are made is not any such general impression. Nor is the idea that God is reflected in all the beauty of creation the real soul of this poem. It is rather the notion that this revelation is made through the individual, distinctive, and utterly unique beauty of each particular beautiful thing; and that the more distinctive the beauty of each thing, the more striking a revelation of God it makes. Each beautiful object in the universe gives a unique reflection of some facet of the beauty and excellence of God. Any excellence seen and experienced invites recognition or acknowledgment; it elicits praise, honor, glory for the one who possesses the excellence. Hopkins reminds us of that by beginning and ending his poem with a statement of that idea: "Glory be to God for dappled things" and "He fathers-forth whose beauty is past change:/Praise him."

But a poem is not a collection of statements; the poet is interested in creating a pattern that will so effectively embody an insight that statements about its meaning may be and often are superfluous. Here Hopkins is not so much interested in the invitation to acknowledge God manifested in the beauty of all creation as he is in the fact that it is the *individual, particular,* and *distinctive* beautiful object which most irresistibly issues that invitation.

We get our first cue that this is the central interest of the poem from its very title—"Pied Beauty." "Pied" is an unusual word, meaning variegated or motley in color. So we are warned by its very title that the poem is not about beauty in general but about beautiful things that are distinctive for their varied color. The notion is pressed home in the first line of the poem by the word "dappled." "Dappled" is almost synonymous with "pied." It also means variegated in color, but in a special configuration. In dappled things dots or rings of deeper color splash across a lighter background. Some apples are dappled with deep red spots; some light gray horses are dappled with darker gray rings. The very use of these almost synonymous but unusual words describing an unusual kind of beauty suggests that it takes the distinctive, the unique, and the highly individualized beautiful object to catch our attention and remind us that all beauty is a manifestation of God's beauty and invites our recognition—our praise and glory: "Glory be to God for *dappled* things." It is this world of dappled things particularly, the poet seems to be saying, that God "fathers-forth."

This is Hopkins' insight here, but as a poet he is not content to talk about it; he rather attempts to embody some of the variegated, distinctive beauty of God's universe in the *structure* of the poem itself. He wants me—as a reader—to experience that variegated beauty in a more condensed and intense way than I have perhaps ever experienced it in nature itself. To achieve this he has given his expression shape and structure, partly internal and partly external.

Internally the thought structure of the poem from lines 2 through 9 is really a series of concrete examples of the variegated, dappled beauty of God's universe presented for our contemplation. The external stanzaic pattern merely frames this inner thought structure and helps to create a repetitive rhythmic pattern appropriate to the enumeration. The first six lines, which we shall see frame completely parallel enumerations of concrete individual examples of dappled beauty, are also related to one another by the external frame of the rhyme scheme *a b c, a b c*. When the thought changes in line 7 to a more generic statement of all beauty of contrast, the rhyme scheme also changes to *d b c d c*, but the repetition of the *b c* rhymes links this last part of the poem to the previous part. The external structure links the two parts just as does the internal thought.

Also contributing to this sense of the parade or formal display of these concrete objects of variegated beauty is the parallel grammatical structure in which they are presented. Glory be to God—"*for* dappled things"; "*For* skies of couple-colour"; "*For* rose-moles . . . upon trout"; and then, in quick succession, objects without their prepositions: "chestnut-falls; finches' wings; Landscape . . . And áll trádes." A further formality is given the enumeration by the alliterative pattern that occurs in almost every verse:

> For skies of *couple*-*c*olour as a brinded *c*ow;
> For rose-moles all in *s*tipple upon trout that *s*wim;
> *F*resh-*f*irecoal chestnut-*f*alls; *f*inches' wings;
> Landscape *p*lotted and *p*ierced—*f*old, *f*allow, and *p*lough;
> And áll *t*rádes, their gear and *t*ackle and *t*rim.

All of this structure, both internal and external, sets off the experience of the poem from the experience of real life and gives it a shape and form of its own. The external stanzaic pattern is something like a frame on a picture. The internal structure of thought and mood is like the visual pattern of the painting itself.

But a poet is not content with verbal patterns or patterns of thought. He wants the poem to sensitize the reader in a very special way. Hopkins, for instance, does not want us to think abstractly about variegated beauty but to sense it, to see it. To achieve this he avoids colorless abstract terms and builds his poem with *concrete* terms and *imagery* which enable us to experience vividly the parade of variegated sensible beauty. It is not just any kind of sky he wants us to see but dappled skies—"skies of couple-colour"—and not just any color but the "couple-colour" of random shape, such as we are familiar with on a spotted ("brinded") cow.

From the broad expanse of a very particular sky he directs our attention to a placid stream in which we catch a glimpse of the mottled pattern on the side of the fish. It is not just any fish, however, but a particular kind, a speckled trout darting in a quick motion which reveals the variegated colored pattern on its side. And whether we have ever seen a speckled trout or not, Hopkins makes us see it here in the imagery of his line . . . "rose-moles all in stipple upon trout that swim"; it is the fish in motion that we are looking at. At rest in the stream, its brown mottled back would camouflage it against the mottled pattern of the bed of the stream. But when it moves we catch for a moment a glimpse of its bright side dappled with rosy spots—"stipple" Hopkins says, in a word that is just right to describe the random pattern of the side of the fish. We are familiar with walls painted in stipple; we are familiar with the exact shape of moles on a face. But these are *rose*-moles that are *stippled* on the side of the trout. By the use of these homely familiar associations Hopkins has enabled us to see for a moment the very special and distinctive beauty of this lively creature of the stream.

From the dappled beauty of sky and fish, which we might associate with a bright summer's day, our attention is suddenly switched to the pied beauty of autumn—but again to a particular and individuated aspect of that beauty—to "Fresh-firecoal chestnut-falls." We may never have been in England in autumn and seen the real chestnuts nesting in their burs on the ground when they have fallen from the tree ("chestnut-falls") or may never even have seen the horse chestnuts freshly fallen from the tree in our own country; but whether we have or not, Hopkins has again made it possible for us to see them precisely as they look with the kind of contrast in color that makes them also an example of pied beauty. We have all seen the glowing red of a fresh coal that has just fallen on its bed of gray ashes. That's what the fresh-fallen chestnut looks like—its red waxy surface glows like a coal against the dull gray of the newly cracked hull: "Fresh-firecoal chestnut-falls."

And then from the static chestnut we are back again to a world of life and movement—but a world still of bright contrasts. It is only the *finches' wings* that are mentioned; but that is all we need to see the mottled fan of the delicate wings looking even more variegated against the red breast of the bird. (Hopkins is thinking, of course, of the English chaffinch or bullfinch and not of the American goldfinch. These birds are both more "pied" and "dappled" than is our more pure-colored goldfinch.) Hopkins' single phrase, "finches' wings," suggests the particular pied beauty of the finches as vividly as the dappled pattern on the side of the trout.

And then, in an image that is completely right, we are given a glimpse of a rural landscape seen from a height—a landscape that is a particularly good example of the random pattern of pied beauty. It looks like the haphazard design of a crazy quilt: "Landscape plotted and pieced—fold, fallow, and plough." It is stitched together of blocks (or fields) of random size, shape, and color—some used as sheep *fold*, green and nibbled smooth; some lying *fallow*, rougher and gone to rank growth; and still others brown and ribbed with the furrows of the *plough*. We have all seen such a scene from a hilltop or from an airplane, but there is a special pleasure of recognition in seeing this variegated pattern, through the eyes of the poet here, as nature's crazy quilt— *"plotted and pieced—fold, fallow, and plough."*

Thus far the enumeration of distinctively beautiful things has been vaguely associated with the agricultural scene: "skies of couple-colour as a *brinded cow*"; "*chestnut*-falls"; "*finches*' wings"; and "Landscape plotted and pieced—*fold, fallow,* and *plough.*" But the poet wants to include all the variegated, the "pied beauty" that is experienced in the distinctive features of "áll trádes, their gear and tackle and trim." He chooses words that push our imaginations into the world of three of the most primitive, natural, and least artificial of man's trades—hunting ("gear"), fishing ("tackle"), and sailing ("trim").

In the second part of the poem, beginning with line 7, the poet pushes the generalization even further. He includes pied beauty wherever and whenever found— anything that is remarkable for its sharp contrasts ("counter") or striking because of its originality, rarity, or strangeness: "All things counter, original, spare, strange." But he is particularly interested in the quick flashes of sensory experience that are changing and unpredictable: "Whatever is fickle, freckled," pied or dappled, with contrasts in motion ("swift, slow"), in taste ("sweet, sour"), or in sight ("adazzle, dim"). All of this variegated pageant of "pied beauty" God "fathers-forth." The bold use of the word "fathers-forth" suggests that Hopkins is not thinking of any mere cold manifestation of God as creator revealed in His creation. The procession of material beauty is a manifestation of the providential provision of a father for his child.

Interested as the poet is in presenting as vividly as possible in his verse the sense experiences of the variegated beauty of God's universe, he would not be a poet at all if he were not interested in affecting our attitude toward it. In other words, he gives his material a definite emotional tone. It is interesting to see how Hopkins achieves this from the opening line of the poem. The tone is suggested by the very rhetorical structure of the line itself: "Glory be to God for dappled things." It is couched in the formal phraseology of the doxological prayer, "Glory be to the Father, and to the Son, and to the Holy Spirit," and has some of that incantatory flavor. It also echoes the tone of the "laudate" psalms (Numbers 146, 147, and 148) in which the whole cosmos from sky to sod is invited to give praise to God. This tone set by the opening invocation pervades the whole catalogue of "pied beauty" and raises it from the level of a simple vivid catalogue to that of an actual psalm of praise. It is worth noting that the tone of prayerful invocation introduced in the first verse and sustained through the catalogue of pied beauty in the rest of the poem shifts to the imperative in the last verse—"Glory be to God" becomes "Praise him." When we have experienced the fresh vision of God's beauty provided for us in the body of the poem, we are emotionally conditioned to accept the tone of command assumed in "Praise him." We would not have been ready to accept it at the beginning of the poem.

Perhaps this analysis of some of the cues provided by Hopkins in this poem makes clearer some of the methods which the poet employs to give structure, pattern, and tone to the little world of words he creates to embody some of his insights into the meaning of life.

ON THE SONNET

The sonnet is one of the shortest but most formal of lyric types. Since the Renaissance period its restricted fourteen-line form has challenged many a poet to test his powers of concentrated expression.

The sonnet originally developed in Italy, where its multiple identical rhymes were much easier than they are in English; among other factors, for example, there are fewer noun endings in Italian than in English. Francis Petrarch especially made the sonnet a popular medium for love poetry in his sonnet sequence to Laura and gave it a form which has come to bear his name—the *Petrarchan sonnet*. This is a poem of fourteen lines made up of an octave (eight lines) of iambic pentametric lines rhyming *a b b a, a b b a*, followed by a sestet (six lines) rhyming variously, but often *c d e, c d e*. There is a break in the thought after the octave, which usually states a problem or raises a question which is answered or brought to a resolution in the sestet. The sonnet, therefore, provides a definite opportunity for observing the connection between the external stanzaic structure of a poem and its inner thought structure. The stanzaic pattern is like the frame on a picture; it frames the inner thought units of the poem.

When the sonnet form was brought to England, the difficulty of finding the multiple identical rhymes for the octave soon led to a change in its form. Shakespeare used the changed form so often that it has come to bear his name, the *Shakespearean sonnet*; or sometimes it is merely called the *English sonnet*. It is made up of three successive quatrains, usually of separate rhyme schemes, followed by a couplet; that is, *a b a b, c d c d, e f e f, g g*. Hence in this form there is very frequently no thought pause after the first eight lines, but rather the thought moves on continuously through the three quatrains to the couplet, which quite often gives a summary statement of the thought or theme of the whole sonnet. Sonnet 73 of Shakespeare is a particularly good example of the use of this form; the poet has framed three parallel images in the three successive quatrains and then given expression to his thematic idea in the final couplet.

Edmund Spenser developed a special kind of linked rhyming in his sonnet, which he partly borrowed from the Italian *terza rima* stanza; the second rhyme of the first quatrain becomes the first rhyme of the second, thus, *a b a b, b c b c, c d c d, e e*. This creates a forward-moving rhythm that is baroque in effect, in contrast to the more segmented division between the octave and sestet of the Petrarchan sonnet, and it corresponds to the continuous movement of the thought from the beginning of the sonnet to the end. This continuous thought movement frequently occurs, of course, in the Shakespearean sonnet as well.

Thousands of English sonnets were written in the sixteenth and seventeenth centuries, generally on the subject of love—expressed in the somewhat artificial language of the courtly and Petrarchan love conventions. Shakespeare frequently pokes gentle fun at these conventions, as he does, for instance, in Sonnet 130. Very often the poets arranged their love sonnets in long sequences, after the pattern of Petrarch's *Sonnets to Laura*. Sir Philip Sidney's *Astrophel and Stella* and Edmund Spenser's *Amoretti* were two of the most famous Elizabethan sonnet sequences, but the most famous of all was Shakespeare's, which he directed partly to a mysterious "dark lady" and partly to a male friend. Shakespeare's Sonnet 146 is unusual for the period in that it has a theme other than love, but Milton was the poet to disassociate the sonnet from the love theme by writing some of the best sonnets in the language on such varied subjects as Cromwell, Puritan battles, and his own blindness. The sonnet was not popular in the eighteenth century, but it flourished again in the nineteenth century in the hands of such poets as Wordsworth, Keats, Elizabeth Barrett Browning, Bridges, and Hopkins.

Some of the best of these sonnets are gathered together in this unit, and others are scattered through some of the later topical units.

Nuns Fret Not at Their Convent's Narrow Room
by WILLIAM WORDSWORTH

Nuns fret not at their convent's narrow room;
And hermits are contented with their cells;
And students with their pensive citadels;
Maids at the wheel, the weaver at his loom,
Sit blithe and happy; bees that soar for bloom,
High as the highest Peak of Furness-fells,
Will murmur by the hour in foxglove bells:
In truth the prison, into which we doom
Ourselves, no prison is: and hence for me,
In sundry moods, 'twas pastime to be bound   10
Within the Sonnet's scanty plot of ground;
Pleased if some Souls (for such there needs must be)
Who have felt the weight of too much liberty,
Should find brief solace there, as I have found.

Furness-fells hills in northern Lancashire.

I Swore to Stab the Sonnet with My Pen*

by KARL SHAPIRO

I swore to stab the sonnet with my pen
Squash the black widow in a grandstand
    play
By gunning down the sonnet form—and
    then
I heard you quote my schoolboy love
    Millay.
I went to find out what she used to say   5
About her tribulations and her men
And loved her poetry though I now am
    gray
And found out love of love poems once
    again.
Now I'm the one that's stabbed—son
    of a bitch!—
With my own poisoned ballpoint pen of
    love   10
And write in *sonnet* form to make my
    pitch,
Words I no longer know the meaning of.
If I could write one honest sentence now
I'd say I love you but I don't know how.

---

* Copyright © 1967 by Karl Shapiro. Reprinted from *White-Haired Lover*, by Karl Shapiro, by permission of Random House, Inc.

Sonnets

by WILLIAM SHAKESPEARE

33

Full many a glorious morning have I seen
Flatter the mountain tops with sovereign
    eye,
Kissing with golden face the meadows
    green,
Gilding pale streams with heavenly
    alchemy;
Anon permit the basest clouds to ride   5
With ugly rack on his celestial face,
And from the forlorn world his visage
    hide,
Stealing unseen to west with this disgrace:
Even so my sun one early morn did shine
With all-triumphant splendour on my
    brow;   10
But out, alack! he was but one hour mine,
The region-cloud hath mask'd him
    from me now
        Yet him for this my love no whit
            disdaineth;
Suns of the world may stain when
    heaven's sun staineth.

65

Since brass, nor stone, nor earth, nor
    boundless sea,
But sad mortality o'er-sways their power,
How with this rage shall beauty hold a
    plea,
Whose action is no stronger than a
    flower?
O, how shall summer's honey breath hold
    out   5
Against the wreckful siege of batt'ring
    days,
When rocks impregnable are not so stout,
Nor gates of steel so strong, but Time
    decays?
O fearful meditation! Where, alack,
Shall Time's best jewel from Time's chest
    lie hid?   10

---

rack broken mass of clouds.   *region-cloud* of the upper air.

stain be stained or obscured.   *plea* legal petition in court.   *action* legal action.   *Time's best jewel* beauty.

Or what strong hand can hold his swift foot back?
Or who his spoil [of] beauty can forbid?
   Oh, none, unless this miracle have might,
     That in black ink my love may still shine bright.

73

That time of year thou mayst in me behold
When yellow leaves, or none, or few, do hang
Upon those boughs which shake against the cold,
Bare ruined choirs where late the sweet birds sang.
In me thou seest the twilight of such day   5
As after sunset fadeth in the west,
Which by and by black night doth take away,
Death's second self that seals up all in rest.
In me thou seest the glowing of such fire
That on the ashes of his youth doth lie,   10
As the deathbed whereon it must expire,
Consumed with that which it was nourished by.
   This thou perceiv'st, which makes thy love more strong,
     To love that well which thou must leave ere long.

ruined choirs the part of the church where the monks formerly sang the Divine office. The ruins look like the bare branches of the trees where the birds formerly sang.

129

Th' expense of spirit in a waste of shame
Is lust in action; and, till action, lust
Is perjured, murd'rous, bloody, full of blame,
Savage, extreme, rude, cruel, not to trust;
Enjoyed no sooner but despisèd straight;   5
Past reason hunted, and no sooner had,
Past reason hated as a swallowed bait
On purpose laid to make the taker mad:
Mad in pursuit, and in possession so;
Had, having, and in quest to have, extreme;   10
A bliss in proof, and proved, a very woe;
Before, a joy proposed; behind, a dream.
   All this the world well knows; yet none knows well
     To shun the heaven that leads men to this hell.

Batter My Heart
by JOHN DONNE

Batter my heart, three-personed God; for You
As yet but knock, breathe, shine, and seek to mend;
That I may rise, and stand, o'erthrow me, and bend
Your force, to break, blow, burn, and make me new.
I, like an usurped town to another due,   5
Labor to admit You, but oh! to no end;
Reason, Your viceroy in me, me should defend,
But is captived and proves weak or untrue.
Yet dearly I love You, and would be loved fain,
But am betrothed unto Your enemy.   10
Divorce me, untie, or break that knot again,
Take me to You, imprison me, for I
Except You enthrall me, never shall be free;
Nor ever chaste, except You ravish me.

At the Round Earth's Imagined Corners
by JOHN DONNE

At the round earth's imagined corners, blow
Your trumpets, angels; and arise, arise
From death, you numberless infinities
Of souls, and to your scattered bodies go;
All whom the flood did, and fire shall, o'erthrow,   5
All whom war, dearth, age, agues, tyrannies,
Despair, law, chance hath slain, and you whose eyes
Shall behold God, and never taste death's woe.
But let them sleep, Lord, and me mourn a space;
For, if above all these, my sins abound,   10
'Tis late to ask abundance of Thy grace
When we are there. Here on this lowly ground,
Teach me how to repent; for that's as good
As if Thou hadst sealed my pardon with Thy blood.

When I Consider How My Light Is Spent
by JOHN MILTON

When I consider how my light is spent
Ere half my days in this dark world and wide,
And that one talent which is death to hide
Lodged with me useless, though my soul more bent
To serve therewith my Maker, and present   5
My true account, lest he returning chide;
"Doth God exact day-labour, light denied?"
I fondly ask. But Patience, to prevent
That murmur, soon replies, "God doth not need
Either man's work or his own gifts. Who best
Bear his mild yoke, they serve him best. His state   10
Is kingly: thousands at his bidding speed,
And post o'er land and ocean without rest;
They also serve who only stand and wait."

---

one talent An allusion to the parable of the talents in which one servant buried his talent and was punished for doing so (Matthew 25:15-30). The one talent of the poem is probably Milton's poetic power apparently made useless now because of his blindness.

Composed upon Westminster Bridge
by WILLIAM WORDSWORTH

Earth has not anything to show more fair;
Dull would he be of soul who could pass by
A sight so touching in its majesty:
This City now doth like a garment wear
The beauty of the morning; silent, bare,   5
Ships, towers, domes, theaters, and temples lie
Open unto the fields, and to the sky;
All bright and glittering in the smokeless air.

Never did sun more beautifully steep
In his first splendor valley, rock, or hill;   10
Ne'er saw I, never felt, a calm so deep!
The river glideth at his own sweet will:
Dear God! the very houses seem asleep;
And all that mighty heart is lying still!

The World Is Too Much with Us
by WILLIAM WORDSWORTH

The world is too much with us; late and
   soon,
Getting and spending, we lay waste our
   powers:
Little we see in Nature that is ours;
We have given our hearts away, a sordid
   boon!
The sea that bares her bosom to the
   moon;
The winds that will be howling at all   5
   hours,
And are up-gathered now like sleeping
   flowers;
For this, for everything, we are out of
   tune;
It moves us not.—Great God! I'd rather
   be
A Pagan suckled in a creed outworn;   10
So might I, standing on this pleasant lea,
Have glimpses that would make me less
   forlorn;
Have sight of Proteus rising from the sea;
Or hear old Triton blow his wreathéd
   horn.

Proteus a sea god who had the power of changing his appearance at will. *Triton* a sea god, son of Poseidon, the god of the sea, with head and upper body of a man and a tail of a fish; he carried a conch shell trumpet.

Ozymandias
by PERCY BYSSHE SHELLEY

I met a traveler from an antique land
Who said: "Two vast and trunkless legs
   of stone
Stand in the desert. Near them, on the
   sand,
Half sunk, a shattered visage lies,
   whose frown,
And wrinkled lip, and sneer of cold
   command,   5
Tell that its sculptor well those passions
   read
Which yet survive, stamped on these
   lifeless things,
The hand that mocked them, and the
   heart that fed:
And on the pedestal these words appear:
'My name is Ozymandias, king of kings: 10
Look on my works, ye Mighty, and
   despair!'
Nothing beside remains. Round the
   decay
Of that colossal wreck, boundless and
   bare
The lone and level sands stretch far
   away."

Ozymandias The statue of the Egyptian king, Ozymandias, supposed to have been the largest in Egypt, bore this inscription: "I am Ozymandias, the King of Kings, if any man wishes to know what I am and where I am buried, let him surpass me in some of my achievements."

On First Looking into Chapman's Homer
by JOHN KEATS

Much have I traveled in the realms of
    gold,
And many goodly states and kingdoms
    seen;
Round many western islands have I been
Which bards in fealty to Apollo hold.
Oft of one wide expanse had I been told   5
That deep-browed Homer ruled as his
    demesne;
Yet did I never breathe its pure serene
Till I heard Chapman speak out loud
    and bold:
Then felt I like some watcher of the
    skies
When a new planet swims into his ken;   10
Or like stout Cortez when with eagle
    eyes
He stared at the Pacific—and all his
    men
Looked at each other with a wild
    surmise—
Silent, upon a peak in Darien.

Apollo god of poetry and music   *Chapman* a sixteenth-century translator of Homer. Keats wrote this sonnet after spending a night reading Chapman's translation with his friend, Charles Cowden Clarke.

Cortez It was not Cortez but Balboa who discovered the Pacific in 1513.   *Darien* a section of the eastern part of the Isthmus of Panama.

Lucifer in Starlight
by GEORGE MEREDITH

On a starred night Prince Lucifer uprose.
Tired of his dark dominion, swung the
    fiend
Above the rolling ball, in cloud part
    screened,
Where sinners hugged their specter of
    repose.
Poor prey to his hot fit of pride were
    those.
And now upon his western wing he   5
    leaned,
Now his huge bulk o'er Afric's sands
    careened,
Now the black planet shadowed Arctic
    snows.
Soaring through wider zones that pricked
    his scars
With memory of the old revolt from
    Awe,   10
He reached a middle height, and at the
    stars,
Which are the brain of heaven, he looked,
    and sank.
Around the ancient track marched, rank
    on rank,
The army of unalterable law.

Spring
by GERARD MANLEY HOPKINS

Nothing is so beautiful as spring—
    When weeds, in wheels, shoot long
    and lovely and lush;
    Thrush's eggs look little low heavens,
    and thrush
Through the echoing timber does so
    rinse and wring

The ear, it strikes like lightnings to hear
    him sing;
  The glassy peartree leaves and blooms,
    they brush
  The descending blue; that blue is all
    in a rush
With richness; the racing lambs too have
    fair their fling.

What is all this juice and all this joy?
  A strain of the earth's sweet being in
    the beginning
In Eden garden.—Have, get, before it
    cloy,
  Before it cloud, Christ, lord, and sour
    with sinning,
Innocent mind and Mayday in girl and boy,
  Most, O maid's child, thy choice and
    worthy the winning.

Hurrahing in Harvest
by GERARD MANLEY HOPKINS

Summer ends now; now, barbarous in
    beauty, the stooks arise
  Around; up above, what wind-walks!
    what lovely behaviour
  Of silk-sack clouds! has wilder, wilful-
    wavier
Meal-drift moulded ever and melted
    across skies?

I walk, I lift up, I lift up heart, eyes,
  Down all that glory in the heavens to
    glean our Saviour;

And, éyes, heárt, what looks, what lips
    yet gave you a
Rapturous love's greeting of realer, of
    rounder replies?

And the azurous hung hills are his world-
    wielding shoulder
  Majestic—as a stallion stalwart, very-
    violet-sweet!—
These things, these things were here and
    but the beholder
  Wanting; which two when they once
    meet,
The heart réars wíngs bold and bolder
  And hurls for him, O half hurls earth
    for him off under his feet.

stooks shocks of grain. *silk-sack* a flowing silk cape; here clouds that have the flowing shape, color, and texture of such a cape. *meal-drift moulded* clouds that are sifted across the sky like soft, powdery meal.

The Caged Skylark
by GERARD MANLEY HOPKINS

As a dare-gale skylark scanted in a dull
    cage
  Man's mounting spirit in his bone-
    house, mean house, dwells—
  That bird beyond the remembering his
    free fells;
This in drudgery, day-labouring-out life's
    age.

Though aloft on turf or perch or poor
    low stage,
  Both sing sometímes the sweetest,
    sweetest spells,
  Yet both droop deadly sómetimes in
    their cells
Or wring their barriers in bursts of fear
    or rage.

scanted confined, restricted. *fells* hills.

Not that the sweet-fowl, song-fowl, needs
    no rest—
Why, hear him, hear him babble and
    drop down to his nest,   10
  But his own nest, wild nest, no prison.

Man's spirit will be flesh-bound when
    found at best,
But uncumbered: meadow-down is not
    distressed
  For a rainbow footing it nor he for
    his bónes rísen.

The Windhover

by GERARD MANLEY HOPKINS

To Christ Our Lord

I caught this morning morning's minion,
    kingdom of daylight's dauphin,
    dapple-dawn-drawn Falcon, in his
    riding
Of the rolling level underneath him
    steady air, and striding
High there, how he rung upon the rein
    of a wimpling wing
In his ecstasy! then off, off forth on swing,
  As a skate's heel sweeps smooth on a
    bow-bend: the hurl and gliding   5
    Rebuffed the big wind. My heart in
    hiding
Stirred for a bird,—the achieve of, the
    mastery of the thing!

Brute beauty and valour and act, oh, air,
    pride, plume here
  Buckle! *and* the fire that breaks from
    thee then, a billion
Times told lovelier, more dangerous,
    O my chevalier!   10

  No wonder of it: shéer plód makes
    plough down sillion
Shine, and blue-bleak embers, ah my dear,
    Fall, gall themselves, and gash gold-
    vermilion.

---

minion darling or favorite.   *dauphin* crowned prince.   *rung* a term from falconry, meaning to rise in a spiral flight.   *act* in the philosophical sense of realization of potentiality, fulfillment. *here Buckle* both these words have been variously interpreted: *here* as still applying to the bird or to the poet; *buckle* as meaning to combine, work together; or to buckle on as of armor; or to crumple. The whole meaning of the poem is dependent upon how one interprets these words, and the "thee" and "my chevalier" of lines 9 and 10. Is the poet still addressing merely the bird and saying that its greatest beauty and mastery are manifest at the very moment when all its achievement seems to collapse at the end of its flight or is he rather addressing himself and saying that when the equivalent of *air, pride, plume* combine in him in the supernatural order, a fire a billion times lovelier flashes off his exploits than any that can ever flash off the achievement of a mere bird no matter how masterful? If the latter is something like what the poet means, it is clear why this supernatural venture is more beautiful but also more *dangerous* than that of the bird because there is so much more at stake if it fails. *sillion* furrow.

The End of the World*
by ARCHIBALD MacLEISH

Quite unexpectedly as Vasserot
The armless ambidextrian was lighting
A match between his great and second toe
And Ralph the lion was engaged in biting
The neck of Madame Sossman while
  the drum   5
Pointed, and Teeny was about to cough
In waltz-time swinging Jocko by the
  thumb—

Quite unexpectedly the top blew off:
And there, there overhead, there, there,
  hung over
Those thousands of white faces, those
  dazed eyes,   10
There in the starless dark the poise, the
  hover,
There with vast wings across the canceled
  skies,
There in the sudden blackness the black
  pall
Of nothing, nothing, nothing—nothing
  at all.

---

* From *Collected Poems*. Copyright, 1952, by Archibald MacLeish. Reprinted by permission of the publisher, Houghton Mifflin Company.

The Silken Tent*
by ROBERT FROST

She is as in a field a silken tent
At midday when a sunny summer breeze
Has dried the dew and all its ropes relent,
So that in guys it gently sways at ease,
And its supporting central cedar pole,   5
That is its pinnacle to heavenward
And signifies the sureness of the soul,
Seems to owe naught to any single cord,
But strictly held by none, is loosely bound
By countless silken ties of love and
  thought   10
To everything on earth the compass
  round,
And only by one's going slightly taut
In the capriciousness of summer air
Is of the slightest bondage made aware.

---

guys ropes attached to stakes to steady the tent.

* From *Complete Poems of Robert Frost*. Copyright 1916, 1923, 1930, 1939 by Holt, Rinehart and Winston, Inc. Copyright 1936, 1942, 1944, 1951, © 1958 by Robert Frost. Copyright © 1964, 1967 by Lesley Frost Ballantine. Reprinted by permission of Holt, Rinehart and Winston, Inc.

ON THE ODE

The term "ode" is not used in English to describe a very clearly defined type of poetry. It simply refers to a long lyric poem that is fairly serious in subject matter, formal in style, and usually written in a rather complex stanza pattern.

In the eighteenth century a good many odes were written in partial imitation of the Greek Pindaric ode, which was built up of three types of stanzas corresponding to the three movements of a dramatic chorus—the *strophe*, sung while the chorus moved to the left, the *antistrophe*, sung while it moved to the right, and the *epode*, sung while the chorus was standing still. This complete form was seldom imitated completely in English. It was soon modified to an irregular form in which the stanzas vary in length and rhyme pattern quite unpredictably.

All of the odes included here represent this more irregular form, except Keats' "Ode to the Nightingale" and Shelley's "Ode to the West Wind," which are written in a monostrophic form in which the whole poem is built up by a repetition of the same stanzaic pattern.

From the time of Pindar the ode was used to celebrate a formal occasion such as the Olympic games. Dryden's ode, "A Song for St. Cecelia's Day," is an example of such an occasional piece. Most English odes, especially of the nineteenth and twentieth centuries, however, are not pinned to any such specific occasion. They are apt to be serious pieces meditating on some more general aspect of human experience.

Corinna's Going A-Maying*

by ROBERT HERRICK

Get up! get up for shame! the blooming
    morn
Upon her wings presents the god unshorn.
    See how Aurora throws her fair
    Fresh-quilted colors through the air:
    Get up, sweet slug-a-bed, and see   5
    The dew bespangling herb and tree.
Each flower has wept and bowed toward
    the east
Above an hour since, yet you not dressed;
    Nay, not so much as out of bed?
    When all the birds have matins said,   10
    And sung their thankful hymns, 'tis sin,
    Nay, profanation to keep in,
Whenas a thousand virgins on this day
Spring, sooner than the lark, to fetch in
    May.

Rise and put on your foliage, and be seen   15
To come forth, like the springtime, fresh
    and green,
And sweet as Flora. Take no care
    For jewels for your gown or hair;
    Fear not, the leaves will strew
    Gems in abundance upon you;   20
Besides, the childhood of the day has
    kept,
Against you come, some orient pearls
    unwept;
    Come and receive them while the light
    Hangs on the dew-locks of the night,
    And Titan on the eastern hill   25
    Retires himself, or else stands still
Till you come forth. Wash, dress, be brief
    in praying:
Few beads are best when once we go
    a-Maying.

Come, my Corinna, come; and, coming,
    mark
How each field turns a street, each street
    a park   30
    Made green and trimmed with trees;
    see how
    Devotion gives each house a bough
    Or branch: each porch, each door ere
    this,
    An ark, a tabernacle is,

A-Maying the practice of going out to the fields early on the morning of the first of May and gathering spring greens and flowers for decking the Maypole, the May-queen, and the doorways of houses. *god unshorn* Apollo, the sun god, appearing early in the dawn without rays surrounding it. *Aurora* the goddess of dawn. *matins* morning prayers, part of the liturgical Divine office. *May* blossom of the hawthorne (white or red thorn) or other similar blossoming trees or shrubs.

Flora goddess of flowers. *Titan* the sun god. *Few beads* a few prayers of the rosary beads (each bead marks a prayer of the rosary). *turns a street* is full of people.

Made up of white-thorn neatly interwove, 35
As if here were those cooler shades of love.
  Can such delights be in the street
  And open fields, and we not see't?
  Come, we'll abroad; and let's obey
  The proclamation made for May, 40
And sin no more, as we have done, by staying;
But, my Corinna, come, let's go a-Maying.

There's not a budding boy or girl this day
But is got up and gone to bring in May;
  A deal of youth, ere this, is come 45
  Back, and with white-thorn laden home.
  Some have dispatched their cakes and cream
  Before that we have left to dream;
And some have wept, and wooed, and plighted troth,
And chose their priest, ere we can cast off sloth. 50
  Many a green-gown has been given,
  Many a kiss, both odd and even;
  Many a glance, too, has been sent
  From out the eye, love's firmament;
Many a jest told of the keys betraying 55
This night, and locks picked; yet we're not a-Maying.

Come, let us go while we are in our prime,
And take the harmless folly of the time.
  We shall grow old apace, and die
  Before we know our liberty. 60
  Our life is short, and our days run
  As fast away as does the sun;
And, as a vapor or a drop of rain
Once lost, can ne'er be found again;
  So when or you or I are made 65
  A fable, song, or fleeting shade,
  All love, all liking, all delight
  Lies drowned with us in endless night.
Then while time serves, and we are but decaying,
Come, my Corinna, come, let's go a-Maying. 70

---

green-gown . . . given gowns stained by grass because their wearers have been thrown down.

A Song for St. Cecelia's Day*

by JOHN DRYDEN

From harmony, from heavenly harmony,
  This universal frame began:
    When Nature underneath a heap
    Of jarring atoms lay,
    And could not heave her head, 5
The tuneful voice was heard from high:
    "Arise, ye more than dead."

Then cold and hot and moist and dry
  In order to their stations leap,
    And Music's power obey. 10
From harmony, from heavenly harmony,
  This universal frame began:
  From harmony to harmony
Through all the compass of the notes it ran,
The diapason closing full in Man. 15

What passion cannot Music raise and quell!
  When Jubal struck the chorded shell,
  His listening brethren stood around,
  And wondering, on their faces fell
To worship that celestial sound. 20

St. Cecelia's Day This poem was written for a London musical society in honor of its patron, St. Cecelia, Her feast is celebrated on November 22. She is the patron of music.

Jubal inventor of the harp and organ (Genesis 4:-21). It was Mercury, however, who invented a musical instrument by fastening strings across a turtle shell (*The chorded shell*).

Less than a god they thought there could
    not dwell
    Within the hollow of that shell
    That spoke so sweetly and so well.
What passion cannot Music raise and
    quell!

    The trumpet's loud clangor   25
      Excites us to arms
      With shrill notes of anger
        And mortal alarms.
    The double, double, double beat
      Of the thundering drum   30
      Cries: "Hark! the foes come;
Charge, charge, 'tis too late to retreat!"

The soft complaining flute
    In dying notes discovers
      The woes of hopeless lovers,   35
Whose dirge is whispered by the warbling
    lute.
    Sharp violins proclaim
Their jealous pangs and desperation,
Fury, frantic indignation,
Depth of pains, and height of passion,   40
    For the fair, disdainful dame.

But oh! what art can teach,
What human voice can reach
    The sacred organ's praise?
    Notes inspiring holy love,   45
Notes that wing their heavenly ways
    To mend the choirs above.
Orpheus could lead the savage race;
And trees unrooted left their place,
    Sequacious of the lyre;   50
But bright Cecelia raised the wonder
    higher:
When to her organ vocal breath was
    given,
An angel heard, and straight appeared,
    Mistaking earth for heaven.

GRAND CHORUS

As from the power of sacred lays   55
    The spheres began to move,
And sung the great Creator's praise
    To all the blessed above;
So when the last and dreadful hour
This crumbling pageant shall devour,   60
The trumpet shall be heard on high,
The dead shall live, the living die,
And Music shall untune the sky.

Orpheus a Greek legendary figure to whose music even the animals and trees responded. *Cecelia* a martyr of the second century. An angel from heaven was supposed to have come down from heaven to hear her sing. She was frequently represented in art as playing an organ.

Ode to the Nightingale
by JOHN KEATS

My heart aches, and a drowsy numbness
    pains
    My sense, as though of hemlock I had
    drunk,
Or emptied some dull opiate to the drains
One minute past, and Lethe-wards had
    sunk:
'Tis not through envy of thy happy lot,   5
    But being too happy in thine
    happiness—
      That thou, light-wingéd Dryad of
      the trees,
        In some melodious plot
Of beechen green, and shadows numberless,
    Singest of summer in full-throated ease.   10

Nightingale a prefatory note of Lord Houghton to the poem: "In the spring of 1819 a nightingale built her nest next to Mr. Bevan's house. Keats took great pleasure in her song, and one morning took his chair from the breakfast table to the grass plot under a plum tree, where he remained between two and three hours. He then reached the house with some scraps of paper in his hand, which he soon put together in the form of this ode."

Lethe river of forgetfulness in Hades. *Dryad* a tree nymph.

John Keats • Ode to the Nightingale

O, for a draught of vintage! that hath been
    Cooled a long age in the deep-delvéd earth,
Tasting of Flora and the country green,
    Dance, and Provençal song, and sun-burnt mirth!
O for a beaker full of the warm South,   15
    Full of the true, the blushful Hippocrene,
        With beaded bubbles winking at the brim,
            And purple stainéd mouth;
That I might drink, and leave the world unseen,
    And with thee fade away into the forest dim: 20

Fade far away, dissolve, and quite forget
What thou among the leaves hast never known,
    The weariness, the fever, and the fret
    Here, where men sit and hear each other groan;
Where palsy shakes a few, sad, last gray hairs,   25
Where youth grows pale, and specter-thin, and dies;
        Where but to think is to be full of sorrow
            And leaden-eyed despairs,
    Where Beauty cannot keep her lustrous eyes,
Or new Love pine at them beyond tomorrow.   30

Away! away! for I will fly to thee,
    Not charioted by Bacchus and his pards,
But on the viewless wings of Poesy,
    Though the dull brain perplexes and retards:
Already with thee! tender is the night,   35
    And haply the Queen-Moon is on her throne,
        Clustered around by all her starry Fays;
            But here there is no light,
Save what from heaven is with the breezes blown
    Through verdurous glooms and winding mossy ways.   40

I cannot see what flowers are at my feet,
    Nor what soft incense hangs upon the boughs,
But, in embalméd darkness, guess each sweet
    Wherewith the seasonable month endows
The grass, the thicket, and the fruit-tree wild;   45
    White hawthorn, and the pastoral eglantine;
        Fast fading violets covered up in leaves;
            And mid-May's eldest child,
The coming musk-rose, full of dewy wine,
    The murmurous haunt of flies on summer eves.   50

Darkling I listen; and, for many a time,
    I have been half in love with easeful Death,
Called him soft names in many a muséd rime,
    To take into the air my quiet breath;
Now more than ever seems it rich to die,   55
    To cease upon the midnight with no pain,
        While thou art pouring forth thy soul abroad
            In such an ecstasy!
Still wouldst thou sing, and I have ears in vain—
    To thy high requiem become a sod.   60

Flora goddess of flowers. *Provençal song* southern France, home of medieval troubadours; a real locale of lyric poetry in contrast to *Hippocrene,* the Greek legendary fountain on Mount Helicon sacred to the Muses. *Where youth grows pale,* etc. Keats' brother had died of consumption in December of 1818, and this poem was written early in the spring of 1819. *Bacchus* god of wine, whose chariot is frequently represented as being drawn by leopards (pards).

Fays faeries. *embalméd* laden with fragrance. *eglantine* wild rose.

Thou wast not born for death, immortal
    Bird!
  No hungry generations tread thee
    down;
The voice I hear this passing night was
    heard
In ancient days by emperor and clown:
Perhaps the self-same song that found a
    path   65
  Through the sad heart of Ruth, when,
    sick for home,
    She stood in tears amid the alien
      corn;
      The same that oft-times hath

Charmed magic easements, opening on
    the foam
Of perilous seas, in faery lands forlorn.   70

Forlorn! the very word is like a bell
  To toll me back from thee to my sole
    self,
Adieu! the fancy cannot cheat so well
  As she is famed to do, deceiving elf.
Adieu! adieu! thy plaintive anthem fades   75
  Past the near meadows, over the still
    stream,
    Up the hillside; and now 'tis buried
      deep
        In the next valley glades:
Was it a vision, or a waking dream?
  Fled is that music—Do I wake or
    sleep?   80

clown peasant. *Ruth* The Biblical story of Ruth's sadness in a strange land is in Ruth 2. *corn* Wheat. Corn is used in England as a generic term for small grain on any kind.

The Leaden Echo and the Golden Echo

by GERARD MANLEY HOPKINS

Maidens' Song from
St. Winefred's Well

THE LEADEN ECHO

How to kéep—is there ány any, is there
  none such, nowhere known some, bow
  or brooch or braid or brace, láce
  latch or catch or key to keep
Back beauty, keep it, beauty, beauty,
  beauty, . . . from vanishing away?
O is there no frowning of these wrinkles,
  rankèd wrinkles deep,
Dówn? no waving off of these most

mournful messengers, still messengers,
  sad and stealing messengers of grey?
No there's none, there's none, O no
  there's none,   5
Nor can you long be, what you now are,
  called fair,
Do what you may do, what, do what you
  may,
And wisdom is early to despair:
Be beginning; since, no, nothing can be
  done
To keep at bay   10
Age and age's evils, hoar hair,
Ruck and wrinkle, drooping, dying,
  death's worst, winding sheets, tombs
  and worms and tumbling to decay;
So be beginning, be beginning to despair.
O there's none, no no no there's none:
Be beginning to despair, to despair,   15
Despair, despair, despair, despair.

St. Winefred's Well this poem was written as a chorus for a play on St. Winefred. The legend was that St. Winefred fled the suit of Carodoc, who pursued her and beheaded her. A miraculous well sprang up where her head landed (Holywell, Wales). She was restored to life by her uncle St. Beuno, and she became abbess of a convent in Holywell where she lived in almost constant ecstasy. Hopkins wrote this poem at St. Beuno's in Wales not far from Holywell. The legend of St. Winefred suggests the subject matter and much of the diction of the poem—a young girl's dedicating her beauty and whole being to God.

Ruck crease or wrinkle.

THE GOLDEN ECHO

    Spare!
There ís one, yes I have one (Hush there!);
Only not within seeing of the sun,
Not within the singeing of the strong sun,
Tall sun's tingeing, or treacherous the tainting of the earth's air,
Somewhere elsewhere there is ah well where! one,
One. Yes I cán tell such a key, I dó know such a place,
Where whatever's prized and passes of us, everything that's fresh and fast flying of us, seems to us sweet of us and swiftly away with, done away with, undone,
Undone, done with, soon done with, and yet dearly and dangerously sweet
Of us, the wimpled-water-dimpled, not-by-morning-matchèd face,
The flower of beauty, fleece of beauty, too too apt to, ah! to fleet,
Never fleets móre, fastened with the tenderest truth
To its own best being and its loveliness of youth: it is an everlastingness of, O it is an all youth!
Come, then, your ways and airs and looks, locks, maiden gear, gallantry and gaiety and grace,
Winning ways, airs innocent, maiden manners, sweet looks, loose locks, long locks, lovelocks, gaygear, going gallant, girlgrace—
Resign them, sign them, seal them, send them, motion them with breath,
And with sighs soaring, soaring sighs deliver
Them; beauty-in-the-ghost, deliver it, early now, long before death
Give beauty back, beauty, beauty, beauty, back to God, beauty's self and beauty's giver.
See; not a hair is, not an eyelash, not the least lash lost; every hair
Is, hair of the head, numbered.
Nay, what we had lighthanded left in surly the mere mould
Will have waked and have waxed and have walked with the wind what while we slept,
This side, that side hurling a heavyheaded hundred-fold
What while we, while we slumbered.
O then, weary then why should we tread? O why are we so haggard at the heart, so care-coiled, care-killed, so fagged, so fashed, so cogged, so cumbered,
When the thing we freely fórfeit is kept with fonder a care,
Fonder a care kept than we could have kept it, kept
Far with fonder a care (and we, we should have lost it) finer, fonder
A care kept.—Where kept? Do but tell us where kept, where.—
Yonder.—What high as that! We follow, now we follow.—
    Yonder, yes yonder, yonder,
Yonder.

---

fleet to glide or hasten away.

surly hard to manage; intractable; therefore in surly the mere mould—means in a downright intractable or unpromising soil. *fashed* weary, troubled. *cogged* deceived, cheated.

Ode to the West Wind
by PERCY BYSSHE SHELLEY

1

O wild West Wind, thou breath of Autumn's being,
Thou, from whose unseen presence the leaves dead
Are driven, like ghosts from an enchanter fleeing,
Yellow, and black, and pale, and hectic red,
Pestilence-stricken multitudes: O thou, 5
Who chariotest to their dark wintry bed
The wingéd seeds, where they lie cold and low,
Each like a corpse within its grave, until
Thine azure sister of the Spring shall blow
Her clarion o'er the dreaming earth, and fill 10
(Driving sweet buds like flocks to feed in air)
With living hues and odors plain and hill:
Wild Spirit, which art moving everywhere;
Destroyer and preserver; hear, oh, hear!

2

Thou on whose stream, mid the steep sky's commotion, 15
Loose clouds like earth's decaying leaves are shed,
Shook from the tangled boughs of Heaven and Ocean,
Angels of rain and lightning: there are spread
On the blue surface of thine aëry surge,
Like the bright hair uplifted from the head 20
Of some fierce Maenad, even from the dim verge
Of the horizon to the zenith's height,
The locks of the approaching storm. Thou dirge
Of the dying year, to which this closing night
Will be the dome of a vast sepulcher, 25
Vaulted with all thy congregated might
Of vapors, from whose solid atmosphere
Black rain, and fire, and hail will burst: oh, hear!

3

Thou who didst waken from his summer dreams
The blue Mediterranean, where he lay, 30
Lulled by the coil of his crystalline streams,
Beside a pumice isle in Baiae's bay,
And saw in sleep old palaces and towers
Quivering within the wave's intenser day,
All overgrown with azure moss and flowers 35
So sweet, the sense faints picturing them! Thou
For whose path the Atlantic's level powers
Cleave themselves into chasms, while far below
The sea-blooms and the oozy woods which wear
The sapless foliage of the ocean, know 40
Thy voice, and suddenly grow gray with fear,

West Wind The poet's own note: "This poem was conceived and chiefly written in a wood that skirts the Arno, near Florence, and on a day when that tempestuous wind, whose temperature is at once mild and animating, was collecting the vapors which pour down the autumnal rains. They began as I foresaw, at sunset with a violent tempest of hail and rain, attended by that magnificent thunder and lightning peculiar to the Cisalpine regions." *sister of the Spring* the south wind.

Maenad a female priestess of Bacchus, the god of wine. *pumice* a light volcanic rock. *Baiae's* a seaport near Naples. *The sea-blooms*, etc. Shelley's own note: "The vegetation at the bottom of the sea, of rivers, and of lakes, sympathizes with that of the land in the change of seasons, and is consequently influenced by the winds which announce it."

And tremble and despoil themselves: oh, hear!

4

If I were a dead leaf thou mightest bear,
If I were a swift cloud to fly with thee;
A wave to pant beneath thy power, and share
The impulse of thy strength, only less free
Than thou, O uncontrollable! If even
I were as in my boyhood, and could be
The comrade of thy wanderings over Heaven,
As then, when to outstrip thy skyey speed 50
Scarce seemed a vision; I would ne'er have striven
As thus with thee in prayer in my sore need.
Oh, lift me as a wave, a leaf, a cloud!
I fall upon the thorns of life! I bleed!
A heavy weight of hours has chained and bowed 55

One too like thee: tameless, and swift, and proud.

5

Make me thy lyre, even as the forest is:
What if my leaves are falling like its own!
The tumult of thy mighty harmonies
Will take from both a deep, autumnal tone, 60
Sweet though in sadness. Be thou, Spirit fierce,
My Spirit! Be thou me, impetuous one!
Drive my dead thoughts over the universe
Like withered leaves to quicken a new birth!
And, by the incantation of this verse, 65
Scatter, as from an unextinguished hearth
Ashes and sparks, my words among mankind!
Be through my lips to unawakened earth
The trumpet of a prophecy! O Wind,
If Winter comes, can Spring be far behind?

45

Out of the Cradle Endlessly Rocking
by WALT WHITMAN

Out of the cradle endlessly rocking,
Out of the mocking-bird's throat, the musical shuttle,
Out of the Ninth-month midnight,
Over the sterile sands and the fields beyond, where the child leaving his bed
    wander'd alone, bareheaded, barefoot,
Down from the shower'd halo, 5
Up from the mystic play of shadows twining and twisting as if they were alive,
Out from the patches of briers and blackberries,
From the memories of the bird that chanted to me,
From your memories sad brother, from the fitful risings and fallings I heard,
From under that yellow half-moon late-risen and swollen as if with tears, 10
From those beginning notes of yearning and love there in the mist,
From the thousand responses of my heart never to cease,
From the myriad thence-arous'd words,
From the word stronger and more delicious than any,
From such as now they start the scene revisiting, 15
As a flock, twittering, rising, or overhead passing,
Borne hither, ere all eludes me, hurriedly,
A man, yet by these tears a little boy again,

Throwing myself on the sand, confronting the waves,
I, chanter of pains and joys, uniter of here and hereafter, 20
Taking all hints to use them, but swiftly leaping beyond them,
A reminiscence sing.

Once Paumanok,
When the lilac-scent was in the air and Fifth-month grass was growing,
Up this seashore in some briers, 25
Two feather'd guests from Alabama, two together,
And their nest, and four light-green eggs spotted with brown,
And every day the he-bird to and fro near at hand,
And every day the she-bird crouch'd on her nest, silent, with bright eyes,
And every day I, a curious boy, never too close, never disturbing them, 30
Cautiously peering, absorbing, translating.

Shine! shine! shine!
Pour down your warmth, great sun!
While we bask, we two together,

Two together! 35
Winds blow south, or winds blow north,
Day come white, or night come black,
Home, or rivers and mountains from home,
Singing all time, minding no time,
While we two keep together. 40

Till of a sudden,
May-be kill'd, unknown to her mate,
One forenoon the she-bird crouch'd not on the nest,
Nor return'd that afternoon, nor the next,
Nor ever appear'd again. 45

And thenceforward all summer in the sound of the sea,
And at night under the full of the moon in calmer weather,
Over the hoarse surging of the sea,
Or flitting from brier to brier by day,
I saw, I heard at intervals the remaining one, the he-bird, 50
The solitary guest from Alabama.

Blow! blow! blow!
Blow up sea-winds along Paumanok's shore;
I wait and I wait till you blow my mate to me.

Yes, when the stars glisten'd, 55
All night long on the prong of a moss-scallop'd stake,
Down almost amid the slapping waves,
Sat the lone singer wonderful causing tears.

Paumanok   Long Island.

He call'd on his mate,
He pour'd forth the meanings which I of all men know.

Yes my brother I know,
The rest might not, but I have treasur'd every note,
For more than once dimly down to the beach gliding,
Silent, avoiding the moonbeams, blending myself with the shadows,
Recalling now the obscure shapes, the echoes, the sounds and sights after their sorts,
The white arms out in the breakers tirelessly tossing,
I, with bare feet, a child, the wind wafting my hair,
Listen'd long and long.

Listen'd to keep, to sing, now translating the notes,
Following you my brother.

Soothe! soothe! soothe!
Close on its wave soothes the wave behind,
And again another behind embracing and lapping, every one close,
But my love soothes not me, not me.
Low hangs the moon, it rose late,
It is lagging—O I think it is heavy with love, with love.

O madly the sea pushes upon the land,
With love, with love.

O night! do I not see my love fluttering out among the breakers?
What is that little black thing I see there in the white?

Loud! loud! loud!
Loud I call to you, my love!
High and clear I shoot my voice over the waves,
Surely you must know who is here, is here,
You must know who I am, my love.

Low-hanging moon!
What is that dusky spot in your brown yellow?
O it is the shape, the shape of my mate!
O moon do not keep her from me any longer.

Land! land! O land!
Whichever way I turn, O I think you could give me my mate back again if you only would,
For I am almost sure I see her dimly whichever way I look.

O rising stars!
Perhaps the one I want so much will rise, will rise with some of you.

O throat! O trembling throat!
Sound clearer through the atmosphere!

Pierce the woods, the earth,
Somewhere listening to catch you must be the one I want.

Shake out carols!
Solitary here, the night's carols! 100

Carols of lonesome love! death's carols!
Carols under that lagging, yellow, waning moon!
O under the moon where she droops almost down into the sea!
O reckless despairing carols.

But soft! sink low! 105
Soft! let me just murmur,
And do you wait a moment you husky-nois'd sea,
For somewhere I believe I heard my mate responding to me,
So faint, I must be still, be still to listen,
But not altogether still, for then she might not come immediately to me. 110

Hither my love!
Here I am! here!
With this just-sustain'd note I announce myself to you.
This gentle call is for you my love, for you.
Do not be decoy'd elsewhere, 115
That is the whistle of the wind, it is not my voice,
That is the fluttering, the fluttering of the spray,
Those are the shadows of leaves.

O darkness! O in vain!
O I am very sick and sorrowful. 120

O brown halo in the sky near the moon, drooping upon the sea!
O troubled reflection in the sea!
O throat! O throbbing heart!
And I singing uselessly, uselessly all the night.

O past! O happy life! O songs of joy! 125
In the air, in the woods, over fields,
Loved! loved! loved! loved! loved!
But my mate no more, no more with me!
We two together no more.

The aria sinking, 130
All else continuing, the stars shining,
The winds blowing, the notes of the bird continuous echoing,
With angry moans the fierce old mother incessantly moaning,
On the sands of Paumanok's shore gray and rustling,
The yellow half-moon enlarged, sagging down, drooping, the face of the sea
    almost touching, 135
The boy ecstatic, with his bare feet the waves, with his hair the atmosphere dallying,
The love in the heart long pent, now loose, now at last tumultuously bursting,

The aria's meaning, the ears, the soul, swiftly depositing,
The strange tears down the cheeks coursing,
The colloquy there, the trio, each uttering, 140
The undertone, the savage old mother incessantly crying,
To the boy's soul's questions sullenly timing, some drown'd secret hissing,
To the outsetting bard.

Demon or bird! (said the boy's soul,)
Is it indeed toward your mate you sing? or is it really to me? 145
For I, that was a child, my tongue's use sleeping, now I have heard you,
Now in a moment I know what I am for, I awake,
And already a thousand singers, a thousand songs, clearer, louder and more
    sorrowful than yours,
A thousand warbling echoes have started to life within me, never to die.

O you singer, solitary, singing by yourself, projecting me, 150
O solitary me listening, never more shall I cease perpetuating you,
Never more shall I escape, never more the reverberations,
Never more the cries of unsatisfied love be absent from me,
Never again leave me to be the peaceful child I was before what there in the night,
By the sea under the yellow and sagging moon, 155
The messenger there arous'd, the fire, the sweet hell within,
The unknown want, the destiny of me.

O give me the clew! (it lurks in the night here somewhere,)
O if I am to have so much, let me have more!

A word then, (for I will conquer it,) 160
The word final, superior to all,
Subtle, sent up—what is it? I listen;
Are you whispering it, and have been all the time, you sea waves?
Is that it from your liquid rims and wet sands?

Whereto answering, the sea, 165
Delaying not, hurrying not,
Whisper'd me through the night, and very plainly before daybreak,
Lisp'd to me the low and delicious word death,
And again death, death, death, death,
Hissing melodious, neither like the bird nor like my arous'd child's heart, 170
But edging near as privately for me rustling at my feet,
Creeping thence steadily up to my ears and laving me softly all over,
Death, death, death, death, death.

Which I do not forget,
But fuse the song of my dusky demon and brother, 175
That he sang to me in the moonlight on Paumanok's gray beach,
With the thousand responsive songs at random,
My own songs awaked from that hour,
And with them the key, the word up from the waves,
The word of the sweetest song and all songs, 180

That strong and delicious word which, creeping to my feet,
(Or like some old crone rocking the cradle, swathed in sweet garments,
   bending aside,)
The sea whisper'd me.

from Howl*
by ALLEN GINSBERG

(PART 1)

I saw the best minds of my generation destroyed by madness, starving hysterical
   naked,
dragging themselves through the negro streets at dawn looking for an angry fix,
angelheaded hipsters burning for the ancient heavenly connection to the starry
   dynamo in the machinery of night,
who poverty and tatters and hollow-eyed and high sat up smoking in the
   supernatural darkness of cold-water flats floating across the tops of cities
   contemplating jazz,
who bared their brains to Heaven under the El and saw Mohammedan angels
   staggering on tenement roofs illuminated,
who passed through universities with radiant cool eyes hallucinating Arkansas
   and Blake-light tragedy among the scholars of war,
who were expelled from the academies for crazy & publishing obscene odes on
   the windows of the skull,
who cowered in unshaven rooms in underwear, burning their money in waste-
   baskets and listening to the Terror through the wall,
who got busted in their public beards returning through Laredo with a belt of
   marijuana for New York,
who ate fire in paint hotels or drank turpentine in Paradise Alley, death, or
   purgatoried their torsos night after night
with dreams, with drugs, with waking nightmares, alcohol and cock and endless
   balls,
incomparable blind streets and shuddering cloud and lightning in the mind
   leaping toward poles of Canada & Paterson, illuminating all the motionless
   world of Time between,
Peyote solidities of halls, backyard green tree cemetery dawns, wine drunkenness
   over the roof tops, storefront boroughs of teahead joyride neon blinking traffic light, sun and moon and tree vibrations in the roaring winter dusks of
   Brooklyn, ashcan rantings and kind king light of mind,
who chained themselves to subways for the endless ride from Battery to holy
   Bronx on benzedrine until the noise of wheels and children brought them
   down shuddering mouthwracked and battered bleak of brain all drained of
   brilliance in the drear light of Zoo,
who sank all night in submarine light of Bickford's floated out and sat through
   the stale beer afternoon in desolate Fugazzi's, listening to the crack of doom
   on the hydrogen jukebox,

---

* Copyright © 1956, 1959 by Allen Ginsberg. Reprinted by permission of City Lights Books.

who talked continuously seventy hours from park to pad to bar to Bellevue to museum to the Brooklyn Bridge,
a lost battalion of platonic conversationalists jumping down the stoops off fire escapes off windowsills off Empire State out of the moon.
yacketayakking screaming vomiting whispering facts and memories and anecdotes and eyeball kicks and shocks of hospitals and jails and wars,
whole intellects disgorged in total recall for seven days and nights with brillant eyes, meat for the Synagogue cast on the pavement,
who vanished into nowhere Zen New Jersey leaving a trail of ambiguous picture postcards of Atlantic City Hall,
suffering Eastern sweats and Tangerian bone-grindings and migraines of China under junk-withdrawal in Newark's bleak furnished room,
who wandered around and around at midnight in the railroad yard wondering where to go, and went, leaving no broken hearts,
who lit cigarettes in boxcars boxcars boxcars racketing through snow toward lonesome farms in grandfather night,
who studied Plotinus Poe St. John of the Cross telepathy and bop kaballa because the cosmos instinctively vibrated at their feet in Kansas,
who loned it through the streets of Idaho seeking visionary indian angels who were visionary indian angels,
who thought they were only mad when Baltimore gleamed in supernatural ecstasy,
who jumped in limousines with the Chinaman of Oklahoma on the impulse of winter midnight streetlight smalltown rain,
who lounged hungry and lonesome through Houston seeking jazz or sex or soup, and followed the brilliant Spaniard to converse about America and Eternity, a hopeless task, and so took ship to Africa,
who disappeared into the volcanoes of Mexico leaving behind nothing but the shadow of dungarees and the lava and ash of poetry scattered in fireplace Chicago,
who reappeared on the West Coast investigating the F.B.I. in beards and shorts with big pacifist eyes sexy in their dark skin passing out incomprehensible leaflets,
who burned cigarette holes in their arms protesting the narcotic tobacco haze of Capitalism,
who distributed Supercommunist pamphlets in Union Square weeping and undressing while the sirens of Los Alamos wailed them down, and wailed down Wall, and the Staten Island ferry also wailed,
who broke down crying in white gymnasiums naked and trembling before the machinery of other skeletons,

* * * * *

who faded out in vast sordid movies, were shifted in dreams, woke on a sudden Manhattan, and picked themselves up out of basements hungover with heartless Tokay and horrors of Third Avenue iron dreams & stumbled to unemployment offices,
who walked all night with their shoes full of blood on the snowbank docks waiting for a door in the East River to open to a room full of steamheat and opium,

who created great suicidal dramas on the apartment cliff-banks of the Hudson under the wartime blue floodlight of the moon & their heads shall be crowned with laurel in oblivion,

who ate the lamb stew of the imagination or digested the crab at the muddy bottom of the rivers of Bowery,

who wept at the romance of the streets with their pushcarts full of onions and bad music,

who sat in boxes breathing in the darkness under the bridge, and rose up to build harpsichords in their lofts,

who coughed on the six floor of Harlem crowned with flame under the tubercular sky surrounded by orange crates of theology,

who scribbled all night rocking and rolling over lofty incantations which in the yellow morning were stanzas of gibberish,

who cooked rotten animals lung heart feet tail borsht & tortillas dreaming of the pure vegetable kingdom,

who plunged themselves under meat trucks looking for an egg,

who threw their watches off the roof to cast their ballot for Eternity outside of Time, & alarm clocks fell on their heads every day for the next decade,

who cut their wrists three times successively unsuccessfully, gave up and were forced to open antique stores where they thought they were growing old and cried,

who were burned alive in their innocent flannel suits on Madison Avenue amid blasts of leaden verse & the tanked-up clatter of the iron regiments of fashion & the nitroglycerine shrieks of the fairies of advertising & the mustard gas of sinister intelligent editors, or were run down by the drunken taxicabs of Absolute Reality,

who jumped off the Brooklyn Bridge this actually happened and walked away unknown and forgotten into the ghostly daze of Chinatown soup alleyways & firetrucks, not even one free beer,

who sang out of their windows in despair, fell out of the subway window, jumped in the filthy Passaic, leaped on negroes, cried all over the street, danced on broken wineglasses barefoot smashed phonograph records of nostalgic European 1930's German jazz finished the whiskey and threw up groaning into the bloody toilet, moans in their ears and the blast of colossal steamwhistles,

who barreled down the highways of the past journeying to each other's hotrod Golgotha jail-solitude watch or Birmingham jazz incarnation,

who drove crosscountry seventy-two hours to find out if I had a vision or you had a vision or he had a vision to find out Eternity,

who journeyed to Denver, who died in Denver, who came back to Denver & waited in vain, who watched over Denver & brooded & loned in Denver and finally went away to find out the Time, & now Denver is lonesome for her heroes,

who fell on their knees in hopeless cathedrals praying for each other's salvation and light and breasts, until the soul illuminated its hair for a second,

who crashed through their minds in jail waiting for impossible criminals with golden heads and the charm of reality in their hearts who sang sweet blues to Alcatraz,

who retired to Mexico to cultivate a habit, or Rocky Mount to tender Buddha or Tangiers to boys or Southern Pacific to the black locomotive or Harvard to Narcissus to Woodlawn to the daisychain or grave,

who demanded sanity trials accusing the radio of hypnotism & were left with their insanity & their hands & a hung jury, 55
who threw potato salad at CCNY lecturers on Dadaism and subsequently presented themselves on the granite steps of the madhouse with shaven heads and harlequin speech of suicide, demanding instantaneous lobotomy,
and who were given instead the concrete void of insulin metrasol electricity hydrotherapy psychotherapy occupational therapy pingpong & amnesia,
who in humorless protest overturned only one symbolic pingpong table, resting briefly in catatonia,
returning years later truly bald except for a wig of blood, and tears and fingers, to the visible madman doom of the wards of the madtowns of the East,
Pilgrim State's Rockland's and Greystone's foetid halls, bickering with the echoes of the soul, rocking and rolling in the midnight solitude-bench dolmen--realms of love, dream of life a nightmare, bodies turned to stone as heavy as the moon, 60
with mother finally . . . . . , and the last fantastic book flung out of the tenement window, and the last door closed at 4 AM and the last telephone slammed at the wall in reply and the last furnished room emptied down to the last piece of mental furniture, a yellow paper rose twisted on a wire hanger in the closet, and even that imaginary, nothing but a hopeful little bit of hallucination—
ah, Carl, while you are not safe I am not safe, and now you're really in the total animal soup of time—
and who therefore ran through the icy streets obsessed with a sudden flash of the alchemy of the use of the ellipse the catalog the meter & the vibrating plane,
who dreamt and made incarnate gaps in Time & Space through images juxtaposed, and trapped the archangel of the soul between 2 visual images and joined the elemental verbs and set the noun and dash of consciousness together jumping with sensation of Pater Omnipotens Aeterna Deus
to recreate the syntax and measure of poor human prose and stand before you speechless and intelligent and shaking with shame, rejected yet confessing out the soul to conform to the rhythm of thought in his naked and endless head, 65
the madman bum and angel beat in Time, unknown, yet putting down here what might be left to say in time come after death,
and rose reincarnate in the ghostly clothes of jazz in the gold-horn shadow of the band and blew the suffering of America's naked mind for love into an eli eli lamma lamma sabacthani saxophone cry that shivered the cities down to the last radio
with the absolute heart of the poem of life butchered out of their own bodies good to eat a thousand years.

ON THE ELEGY

The *elegy* is a special type of lyric poetry expressing grief at the death of a friend or some other individual. Today it tends to be rather brief and intense, but in the past it was frequently quite long. Tennyson's *In Memoriam*—which he wrote in honor of his friend, Arthur Hugh Clough—for instance, embraces over a hundred separate poems.

English elegies in the past have frequently taken the form of the pastoral elegy which is governed by rather strict conventions. Milton's "Lycidas," included in the elegiac selections here, is a classic example of the type. It begins with a statement of purpose and a formal invocation to the muse. This is followed by an expression of grief at the loss of the friend, and then a procession of mourners. At this point a digression is usually inserted (in "Lycidas" on the conditions of the church and the clergy); then there is a passage in which flowers are brought to deck the hearse; and finally there is the consolation in which the tone shifts from grief to peace and resignation. The whole poem is developed with shepherds as the *dramatis personae*. "Lycidas," like other poems following these pastoral conventions, is highly stylized.

The several other more modern elegiac poems included here are much more natural expressions of grief ranging from the sophisticated and symbolic tone of Whitman's poem on the dead Lincoln to the very unsophisticated and personal tone of "Bringing Mother Home."

Lycidas

by JOHN MILTON

Yet once more, O ye laurels, and once more,
Ye myrtles brown, with ivy never sear,
I come to pluck your berries harsh and crude,
And with forced fingers rude
Shatter your leaves before the mellowing year. 5
Bitter constraint and sad occasion dear
Compels me to disturb your season due;
For Lycidas is dead, dead ere his prime,
Young Lycidas, and hath not left his peer.
Who would not sing for Lycidas? He knew 10
Himself to sing, and build the lofty rime.
He must not float upon his watery bier
Unwept, and welter to the parching wind,
Without the meed of some melodious tear.
     Begin, then, Sisters of the sacred well, 15
That from beneath the seat of Jove doth spring;
Begin, and somewhat loudly sweep the string.
Hence with denial vain and coy excuse;
So may some gentle muse
With lucky words favor my destined urn, 20
And as he passes turn
And bid fair peace be to my sable shroud!
     For we were nursed upon the self-same hill,
Fed the same flock, by fountain, shade, and rill;
Together both, ere the high lawns appeared 25
Under the opening eyelids of the Morn,
We drove afield, and both together heard

Lycidas a shepherd in the 9th Eclogue of Virgil. Milton used a good many of the names and conventions of pastoral poetry throughout the poem. The poem is an elegy written in memory of Edward King, a fellow student of Milton's at Cambridge, who was drowned in the Irish sea. It is not a very personalized dirge on King; Milton is really more concerned with himself and his own poetic problems than with King. He begins the poem with doubts about his own poetic powers but ends confident that he is ready to launch more serious literary projects. *Yet once more* Milton had written his *Comus* four years before. *laurels, myrtle, ivy* all plants associated in ancient literature with literary accomplishments; poets were crowned with leaves from these evergreens.

meed tribute. ***Sisters of the sacred well*** the muses who were associated with Aganippe, the fountain of poetic inspiration on Mount Helicon. ***high lawns*** grass covered hills.

What time the gray-fly winds her sultry horn,
Battening our flocks with the fresh dews of night,
Oft till the star that rose at evening, bright, 30
Toward heaven's descent had sloped his westering wheel.
Meanwhile the rural ditties were not mute,
Tempered to the oaten flute;
Rough Satyrs danced, and Fauns with cloven heel
From the glad sound would not be absent long; 35
And old Damoetas loved to hear our song.
    But, oh! the heavy change, now thou art gone,
Now thou art gone, and never must return!
Thee, Shepherd, thee the woods and desert caves,
With wild thyme and the gadding vine o'ergrown, 40
And all their echoes, mourn.
The willows, and the hazel copses green,
Shall now no more be seen
Fanning their joyous leaves to thy soft lays.
As killing as the canker to the rose, 45
Or taint-worm to the weanling herds that graze,
Or frost to flowers, that their gay wardrobe wear,
When first the white-thorn blows—
Such, Lycidas, thy loss to shepherd's ear.
    Where were ye, Nymphs, when the remorseless deep 50
Closed o'er the head of your loved Lycidas?
For neither were ye playing on the steep
Where your old bards, the famous Druids, lie,
Nor on the shaggy top of Mona high,
Nor yet where Deva spreads her wizard stream. 55
Aye me! I fondly dream
"Had ye been there"—for what could that have done?
What could the Muse herself that Orpheus bore,
The Muse herself, for her enchanting son,
Whom universal nature did lament, 60
When, by the rout that made the hideous roar,
His gory visage down the stream was sent,
Down the swift Hebrus to the Lesbian shore?
    Alas! what boots it with uncessant care
To tend the homely, slighted shepherd's trade, 65
And strictly meditate the thankless Muse?
Were it not better done as others use,
To sport with Amaryllis in the shade,
Or with the tangles of Neaera's hair?
Fame is the spur that the clear spirit doth raise 70
(That last infirmity of noble mind)
To scorn delights, and laborious days;
But, the fair guerdon when we hope to find,
And think to burst out into sudden blaze,
Comes the blind Fury with the abhorréd shears, 75
And slits the thin-spun life. "But not the praise,"
Phoebus replied, and touched my trembling ears;
"Fame is no plant that grows on mortal soil,
Nor in the glistering foil

---

winds sounds. *battening* fattening. *rural ditties* simple pastoral poetry written by King and Milton. *Damoetas* pastoral name for one of their Cambridge tutors. *taint-worm* a destructive parasitic worm; it was thought to be poisonous to cattle. *white-thorn* hawthorn. *Nymphs* sea maidens identified here with the muses. *Druids* the priests of the ancient Celts of Britain.

Mona Isle of Man. *Deva spreads her wizard stream* the river Dee, between England and Wales, whose various movements were supposed to forecast the fortune of the two countries. *Orpheus* son of Calliope, muse of epic poetry; he was torn apart by the women of Thrace, who threw his head in the river Hebrus. *Amaryllis . . . Neaera* shepherd maidens from pastoral poetry. *Fury* Atropos, one of the three fates, who cuts the thread of life with her scissors. *Phoebus* Apollo, god of poetic inspiration. *glistering foil* the metal leaf put under gems to set them off more brilliantly.

Set off to the world, nor in broad rumor
   lies, 80
But lives and spreads aloft by those pure
   eyes
And perfect witness of all-judging Jove;
As he pronounces lastly on each deed,
Of so much fame in heaven expect thy
   meed."
      O fountain Arethuse, and thou
         honored flood, 85
Smooth-sliding Mincius, crowned with
   vocal reeds,
That strain I heard was of a higher
   mood.
But now my oat proceeds,
And listens to the Herald of the Sea
That came in Neptune's plea. 90
He asked the waves, and asked the felon
   winds,
What hard mishaps hath doomed this
   gentle swain!
And questioned every gust of rugged
   wings
That blows from off each beakéd pro-
   montory.
They knew not of his story; 95
And sage Hippotades their answer brings,
That not a blast was from his dungeon
   strayed;
The air was calm, and on the level brine
Sleek Panope with all her sisters played.
It was that fatal and perfidious bark, 100
Built in the eclipse, and rigged with
   curses dark,
That sunk so low that sacred head of
   thine.
      Next, Camus, reverend sire, went
         footing slow,
His mantle hairy, and his bonnet sedge,
Inwrought with figures dim, and on the
   edge 105
Like to that sanguine flower inscribed
   with woe.
"Ah! who hath reft," quoth he, "my
   dearest pledge?"
Last came, and last did go,
The Pilot of the Galilean Lake;
Two massy keys he bore of metals twain 110
(The golden opes, the iron shuts amain).
He shook his mitered locks, and stern
   bespake:
"How well could I have spared for thee,
   young swain,
Enow of such as, for their bellies' sake,
Creep, and intrude, and climb into the
   fold! 115
Of other care they little reckoning make
Than how to scramble at the shearers'
   feast,
And shove away the worthy bidden guest.
Blind mouths! that scarce themselves
   know how to hold
A sheep-hook, or have learned aught else
   the least 120
That to the faithful herdman's art
   belongs!
What recks it them? What need they?
   They are sped;
And, when they list, their lean and flashy
   songs
Grate on their scrannel pipes of wretched
   straw;
The hungry sheep look up, and are not
   fed, 125
But, swoln with wind and the rank mist
   they draw,
Rot inwardly, and foul contagion spread;
Besides what the grim wolf with privy
   paw
Daily devours apace, and nothing said.
But that two-handed engine at the door 130

Arethuse a fountain in Sicily associated with Theocritus, a Greek pastoral poet.   *Mincius* a river near the home of Virgil, a Roman pastoral poet.   *Herald of the Sea* the herald of the sea god Neptune.   *Hippotades* Aeolus (son of Hippotes), god of winds.   *Panope* a sea nymph.   *in the eclipse* always an omen of ill fortune.   *Camus* spirit of the river Cam at Cambridge.   *sanguine flower* the purple hyacinth, symbol of woe, because of its association with Hyacinthus slain by Apollo. It was supposed to bear the marks *ai, ai* (woe! woe!).   *Pilot* St. Peter, keeper of keys of heaven.   *mitered* wearing a miter (as the first bishop).   *recks it them* matter to them.   *sped* successful.   *scrannel* thin, feeble.   *grim wolf* variously interpreted as the Catholic Church, Laudian reforms, or Satan.   *two-handed engine* heavy sword or axe of God's justice.

Stands ready to smite once, and smite no more."
    Return, Alpheus, the dread voice is past
That shrunk thy streams; return, Sicilian Muse,
And call the vales, and bid them hither cast
Their bells and flowerets of a thousand hues.   135
Ye valleys low, where the mild whispers use
Of shades, and wanton winds, and gushing brooks,
On whose fresh lap the swart star sparely looks,
Throw hither all your quaint enameled eyes,
That on the green turf suck the honeyed showers,   140
And purple all the ground with vernal flowers.
Bring the rathe primrose that forsaken dies,
The tufted crow-toe, and pale jessamine,
The white pink, and the pansy freaked with jet,
The glowing violet,   145
The musk-rose, and the well-attired woodbine,
With cowslips wan that hang the pensive head,
And every flower that sad embroidery wears;
Bid amaranthus all his beauty shed,
And daffodillies fill their cups with tears,   150
To strew the laureate hearse where Lycid lies.
For so, to interpose a little ease,
Let our frail thoughts dally with false surmise.
Aye me! Whilst thee the shores and sounding seas
Wash far away, where'er thy bones are hurled,   155
Whether beyond the stormy Hebrides,
Where thou perhaps under the whelming tide
Visit'st the bottom of the monstrous world;
Or whether thou, to our moist vows denied,
Sleep'st by the fable of Bellerus old,   160
Where the great Vision of the guarded mount
Looks toward Namancos and Bayona's hold.
Look homeward, Angel, now, and melt with ruth;
And, O ye dolphins, waft the hapless youth.
    Weep no more, woeful shepherds, weep no more.   165
For Lycidas, your sorrow, is not dead,
Sunk though he be beneath the watery floor;
So sinks the day-star in the ocean bed,
And yet anon repairs his drooping head,
And tricks his beams, and with new-spangled ore   170
Flames in the forehead of the morning sky.
So Lycidas sunk low, but mounted high,
Through the dear might of Him that walked the waves,
Where, other groves and other streams along,   174
With nectar pure his oozy locks he laves,

Alpheus a river whose god was the lover of Arethusa, goddess of the Sicilian pastoral fountain. *Sicilian Muse* muse of pastoral poetry; invoked by Milton upon his return to the pastoral vein after the digression on the clergy. *swart star* the Dog Star, Sirius, associated with the hottest days of summer. *quaint enameled eyes* strange vari-colored flowers. *rathe* early. *freaked* speckled. *amaranthus* an unfading flower, symbol of immortality. *hearse* bier.

Hebrides islands off West coast of Scotland. *monstrous* full of monsters. *Bellerus* the land of the giant Bellerus, Land's End in Cornwall. *Vision of the guarded mount* the mount off the coast of Cornwall supposed to be guarded by St. Michael the Archangel. *Namancos and Bayona's hold* strongholds in Spain. *Look homeward, Angel* St. Michael is asked to turn his attention from Spain to England itself. *dolphins* they were supposed to bring dead men to shore. *day-star* sun sets to rise again. *tricks* decorates. *ore* gold. *Him that walked* Christ.

And hears the unexpressive nuptial song,
In the blest kingdoms meek of joy and love.
There entertain him all the Saints above,
In solemn troops, and sweet societies,
That sing, and singing in their glory move, 180
And wipe the tears forever from his eyes.
Now, Lycidas, the shepherds weep no more;
Henceforth thou art the Genius of the shore,
In thy large recompense, and shalt be good
To all that wander in that perilous flood. 185

    Thus sang the uncouth swain to the oaks and rills,
While the still morn went out with sandals gray;
He touched the tender stops of various quills,
With eager thought warbling his Doric lay. 190
And now the sun had stretched out all the hills,
And now was dropped into the western bay.
At last he rose, and twitched his mantle blue;
Tomorrow to fresh woods and pastures new.

---

unexpressive inexpressible. *nuptial song* the song sung at the marriage feast of the Lamb (see The Apocalypse 19:9). *Genius* Lycidas, besides being in heaven, as part of his large recompense has also become guardian spirit of the Irish Sea.

uncouth swain unskilled or rustic shepherd (Milton is thus referring to himself). *Doric* the dialect of the Sicilian pastoral poets. *pastures new* new fields of poetic endeavor to which Milton will turn.

Memorial to D. C.*

by EDNA ST. VINCENT MILLAY

Let them bury your big eyes
In the secret earth securely,
Your thin fingers, and your fair,
Soft, indefinite-coloured hair,—
All of these in some way, surely, 5
From the secret earth shall rise;
Not for these I sit and stare,
Broken and bereft completely:
Your young flesh that sat so neatly
On your little bones will sweetly 10
Blossom in the air.

But your voice . . . never the rushing
Of a river underground,
Not the rising of the wind
In the trees before the rain, 15
Not the woodcock's watery call,
Not the note the white-throat utters,

Not the feet of children pushing
Yellow leaves along the gutters
In the blue and bitter fall, 20
Shall content my musing mind
For the beauty of that sound
That in no new way at all
Ever will be heard again.

Sweetly through the sappy stalk 25
Of the vigourous weed,
Holding all it held before,
Cherished by the faithful sun,
On and on eternally
Shall your altered fluid run, 30
Bud and bloom and go to seed:
But your singing days are done;
But the music of your talk
Never shall the chemistry
Of the secret earth restore. 35
All your lovely words are spoken.
Once the ivory box is broken,
Beats the golden bird no more.

---

* "Elegy" from "Memorial to D. C." *Collected Poems,* Harper & Row. Copyright 1921, 1948 by Edna St. Vincent Millay.

Song of a Second April*
by EDNA ST. VINCENT MILLAY

April this year, not otherwise
   Than April of a year ago,
Is full of whispers, full of sighs,
   Of dazzling mud and dingy snow;
Hepaticas that pleased you so 5
Are here again, and butterflies.

There rings a hammering all day,
   And shingles lie about the doors;
In orchards near and far away
   The grey wood-pecker taps and bores; 10
   And men are merry at their chores,
And children earnest at their play.

The larger streams run still and deep,
   Noisy and swift the small brooks run;
Among the mullein stalks the sheep 15
   Go up the hillside in the sun,
   Pensively,—only you are gone,
You that alone I cared to keep.

* From *Collected Poems*, Harper & Row. Copyright 1921, 1948 by Edna St. Vincent Millay.

When Lilacs Last in the Dooryard Bloom'd
by WALT WHITMAN

I

When lilacs last in the dooryard bloom'd,
And the great star early droop'd in the western sky in the night,
I mourn'd, and yet shall mourn with ever-returning spring.
Ever-returning spring, trinity sure to me you bring,
Lilac blooming perennial and drooping star in the west, 5
And thought of him I love.

II

O powerful western fallen star!
O shades of night—O moody, tearful night!
O great star disappear'd—O the black murk that hides the star!
O cruel hands that hold me powerless—O helpless soul of me! 10
O harsh surrounding cloud that will not free my soul.

III

In the dooryard fronting an old farm-house near the white-wash'd palings,
Stands the lilac-bush tall-growing with heart-shaped leaves of rich green,

---

I mourn'd This is an elegy on President Lincoln. It is written in a form completely independent of the pastoral elegy of which Milton's *Lycidas* is an example. The poem is built up around three experiences accidentally associated with the death and funeral procession of Lincoln: the scent of the lilac, the night song of the thrush, and the falling star. The poem is remarkable for creating the impression of the universal grief of the whole nation for the dead Lincoln as the coffin moves westward through town and countryside.

With many a pointed blossom rising delicate, with the perfume strong I love,
With every leaf a miracle—and from this bush in the dooryard,
With delicate-color'd blossoms and heart-shaped leaves of rich green,
A sprig with its flower I break.

IV

In the swamp in secluded recesses,
A shy and hidden bird is warbling a song.

Solitary the thrush,
The hermit withdrawn to himself, avoiding the settlements,
Sings by himself a song.

Song of the bleeding throat,
Death's outlet song of life, (for well dear brother I know,
If thou wast not granted to sing thou would'st surely die.)

V

Over the breast of the spring, the land, amid cities,
Amid lanes and through old woods, where lately the violets peep'd from the ground, spotting the gray debris,
Amid the grass in the fields each side of the lanes, passing the endless grass,
Passing the yellow-spear'd wheat, every grain from its shroud in the dark-brown fields uprisen,
Passing the apple-tree blows of white and pink in the orchards,
Carrying a corpse to where it shall rest in the grave,
Night and day journeys a coffin.

VI

Coffin that passes through lanes and streets,
Through day and night with the great cloud darkening the land,
With the pomp of the inloop'd flags with the cities draped in black,
With the show of the States themselves as of crape-veil'd women standing,
With processions long and winding and the flambeaus of the night,
With the countless torches lit, with the silent sea of faces and the unbared heads,
With the waiting depot, the arriving coffin, and the sombre faces,
With dirges through the night, with the thousand voices rising strong and solemn,
With all the mournful voices of the dirges pour'd around the coffin,
The dim-lit churches and the shuddering organs—where amid these you journey,
With the tolling tolling bell's perpetual clang,
Here, coffin that slowly passes,
I give you my sprig of lilac.

VII

(Nor for you, for one alone,
Blossoms and branches green to coffins all I bring,

For fresh as the morning, thus would I chant a song for you O sane and sacred death.

All over bouquets of roses,
O death, I cover you over with roses and early lilies, 50
But mostly and now the lilac that blooms the first,
Copious I break, I break the sprigs from the bushes,
With loaded arms I come, pouring for you,
For you and the coffins all of you O death.)

VIII

O western orb sailing the heaven, 55
Now I know what you must have meant as a month since I walk'd,
As I walk'd in silence the transparent shadowy night,
As I saw you had something to tell as you bent to me night after night,
As you droop'd from the sky low down as if to my side, (while the other stars all look'd on,)
As we wander'd together the solemn night, (for something I know not what kept me from sleep,) 60
As the night advanced, and I saw on the rim of the west how full you were of woe,
As I stood on the rising ground in the breeze in the cool transparent night,
As I watch'd where you pass'd and was lost in the netherward black of the night,
As my soul in its trouble dissatisfied sank, as where you sad orb,
Concluded, dropt in the night, and was gone. 65

IX

Sing on there in the swamp,
O singer bashful and tender, I hear your notes, I hear your call,
I hear, I come presently, I understand you,
But a moment I linger, for the lustrous star has detain'd me,
The star my departing comrade holds and detains me. 70

X

O how shall I warble myself for the dead one there I love?
And how shall I deck my song for the large sweet soul that has gone?
And what shall my perfume be for the grave of him I love?

Sea-winds blown from east and west,
Blown from the Eastern sea and blown from the Western sea, till there on the prairies meeting, 75
These and with these and the breath of my chant,
I'll perfume the grave of him I love.

XI

O what shall I hang on the chamber walls?
And what shall the pictures be that I hang on the walls,

To adorn the burial-house of him I love?
Pictures of growing spring and farms and homes,
With the Fourth-month eve at sundown, and the gray smoke lucid and bright,
With floods of the yellow gold of the gorgeous, indolent, sinking sun, burning, expanding the air,
With the fresh sweet herbage under foot, and the pale green leaves of the trees prolific,
In the distance the flowing glaze, the breast of the river, with a wind-dapple here and there,
With ranging hills on the banks, with many a line against the sky, and shadows,
And the city at hand with dwellings so dense, and stacks of chimneys,
And all the scenes of life and the workshops, and the workmen homeward returning.

XII

Lo, body and soul—this land,
My own Manhattan with spires, and the sparkling and hurrying tides, and the ships,
The varied and ample land, the South and the North in the light, Ohio's shores and flashing Missouri,
And ever the far-spreading prairies cover'd with grass and corn.

Lo, the most excellent sun so calm and haughty,
The violet and purple morn with just-felt breezes,
The gentle soft-born measureless light,
The miracle spreading bathing all, the fulfill'd noon,
The coming eve delicious, the welcome night and the stars,
Over my cities shining all, enveloping man and land.

XIII

Sing on, sing on you gray-brown bird,
Sing from the swamps, the recesses, pour your chant from the bushes,
Limitless out of the dusk, out of the cedars and pines.

Sing on dearest brother, warble your reedy song,
Loud human song, with voice of uttermost woe.

O liquid and free and tender!
O wild and loose to my soul—O wondrous singer!
You only I hear—yet the star holds me, (but will soon depart,)
Yet the lilac with mastering odor holds me.

XIV

Now while I sat in the day and look'd forth,
In the close of the day with its light and the fields of spring, and the farmers preparing their crops,
In the large unconscious scenery of my land with its lakes and forests,
In the heavenly aerial beauty, (after the perturb'd winds and the storms,)

Under the arching heavens of the afternoon swift passing, and the voices of
    children and women,
The many-moving sea-tides, and I saw the ships how they sail'd,
And the summer approaching with richness, and the fields all busy with labor,
And the infinite separate houses, how they all went on, each with its meals and
    minutia of daily usages,
And the streets how their throbbings throbb'd, and the cities pent—lo, then
    and there,
Falling upon them all and among them all, enveloping me with the rest,
Appear'd the cloud, appear'd the long black trail,
And I knew death, its thought, and the sacred knowledge of death.

Then with the knowledge of death as walking one side of me,
And the thought of death close-walking the other side of me,
And I in the middle as with companions, and as holding the hands of
    companions,
I fled forth to the hiding receiving night that talks not,
Down to the shores of the water, the path by the swamp in the dimness,
To the solemn shadowy cedars and ghostly pines so still.

And the singer so shy to the rest receiv'd me,
The gray-brown bird I know receiv'd us comrades three,
And he sang the carol of death, and a verse for him I love.
From deep secluded recesses,
From the fragrant cedars and the ghostly pines so still,
Came the carol of the bird.

And the charm of the carol rapt me,
As I held as if by their hands my comrades in the night,
And the voice of my spirit tallied the song of the bird.

Come lovely and soothing death,
Undulating round the world, serenely arriving, arriving,
In the day, in the night, to all, to each,
Sooner or later delicate death.

Prais'd be the fathomless universe,
For life and joy, and for objects and knowledge curious,
And for love, sweet love—but praise! praise! praise!
For the sure-enwinding arms of cool-enfolding death.

Dark mother always gliding near with soft feet,
Have none chanted for thee a chant of fullest welcome?
Then I chant it for thee, I glorify thee above all,
I bring thee a song that when thou must indeed come, come unfalteringly.

Approach strong deliveress,
When it is so, when thou hast taken them I joyously sing the dead,
Lost in the loving floating ocean of thee,
Laved in the flood of thy bliss O death.

From me to thee glad serenades,
Dances for thee I propose saluting thee, adornments and feastings for thee,
And the sights of the open landscape and the high-spread sky are fitting,
And life and the fields, and the huge and thoughtful night.

The night in silence under many a star,
The ocean shore and the husky whispering wave whose voice I know,
And the soul turning to thee O vast and well-veil'd death,
And the body gratefully nestling close to thee.

Over the treetops I float thee a song,
Over the rising and sinking waves, over the myriad fields and the prairies wide,
Over the dense-pack'd cities all and the teeming wharves and ways,
I float this carol with joy, with joy to thee O death.

XV

To the tally of my soul,
Loud and strong kept up the gray-brown bird,
With pure deliberate notes spreading filling the night.

Loud in the pines and cedars dim,
Clear in the freshness moist and the swamp-perfume,
And I with my comrades there in the night.

While my sight that was bound in my eyes unclosed,
As to long panoramas of visions.

And I saw askant the armies,
I saw as in noiseless dreams hundreds of battle-flags,
Borne through the smoke of the battles and pierc'd with missiles I saw them,
And carried hither and yon through the smoke, and torn and bloody,
And at last but a few shreds left on the staffs, (and all in silence,)
And the staffs all splinter'd and broken.
I saw battle-corpses, myriads of them,
And the white skeletons of young men, I saw them,
I saw the debris and debris of all the slain soldiers of the war,
But I saw they were not as was thought,
They themselves were fully at rest, they suffer'd not,
The living remain'd and suffer'd, the mother suffer'd,
And the wife and the child and the musing comrade suffer'd,
And the armies that remain'd suffer'd.

XVI

Passing the visions, passing the night,
Passing, unloosing the hold of my comrades' hands,
Passing the song of the hermit bird and the tallying song of my soul,
Victorious song, death's outlet song, yet varying ever-altering song,
As low and wailing, yet clear the notes, rising and falling, flooding the night,

Sadly sinking and fainting, as warning and warning, and yet again bursting with joy, 190
Covering the earth and filling the spread of the heaven,
As that powerful psalm in the night I heard from recesses,
Passing, I leave thee lilac with heart-shaped leaves,
I leave thee there in the door-yard, blooming, returning with spring.

I cease from my song for thee, 195
From my gaze on thee in the west, fronting the west, communing with thee,
O comrade lustrous with silver face in the night.

Yet each to keep and all, retrievements out of the night,
The song, the wondrous chant of the gray brown bird,
And the tallying chant, the echo arous'd in my soul, 200
With the lustrous and drooping star with the countenance full of woe,
With the holders holding my hand nearing the call of the bird,
Comrades mine and I in the midst, and their memory ever to keep, for the dead I loved so well,
For the sweetest, wisest soul of all my days and lands—and this for his dear sake,
Lilac and star and bird twined with the chant of my soul, 205
There in the fragrant pines and the cedars dusk and dim.

Felix Randal

by GERARD MANLEY HOPKINS

Felix Randal the farrier, O he is dead then? my duty all ended,
Who have watched his mould of man, big-boned and hardy-handsome
Pining, pining, till time when reason rambled in it and some
Fatal four disorders, fleshed there, all contended?

Sickness broke him. Impatient he cursed at first, but mended 5
Being anointed and all; though a heavenlier heart began some
Months earlier, since I had our sweet reprieve and ransom
Tendered to him. Ah well, God rest him all road ever he offended!

This seeing the sick endears them to us, us too it endears.
My tongue had taught thee comfort, touch had quenched thy tears, 10
Thy tears that touched my heart, child, Felix, poor Felix Randal;

How far from then forethought of, all thy more boisterous years,
When thou at the random grim forge, powerful amidst peers,
Didst fettle for the great grey drayhorse his bright and battering sandal!

---

the farrier blacksmith.   *anointed* having received *Extreme Unction,* the Last Anointing. *sweet reprieve and ransom* the last Sacraments—confession, Extreme Unction, and Viaticum. *Felix* probably a play on the Latin meaning of the name—*happy,* in spite of grief and death. *fettle* prepare.

Bells for John Whiteside's Daughter*

by JOHN CROWE RANSOM

There was such speed in her little body,
And such lightness in her footfall,
It is no wonder her brown study
Astonishes us all.

Her wars were bruited in our high window.   5
We looked among orchard trees and
  beyond,
Where she took arms against her shadow,
Or harried unto the pond

---
brown study serious expression on face of the dead child.   *bruited* announced.
* Copyright 1924 by Alfred A. Knopf, Inc., and renewed 1952 by John Crowe Ransom. Reprinted from *Selected Poems*, by John Crowe Ransom, by permission of the publisher.

The lazy geese, like a snow cloud
Dripping their snow on the green grass,   10
Tricking and stopping, sleepy and proud,
Who cried in goose, Alas,

For the tireless heart within the little
Lady with rod that made them rise
From their noon-apple dreams, and
  scuttle   15
Goose-fashion under the skies!

But now go the bells, and we are ready;
In one house we are sternly stopped
To say we are vexed at her brown study,
Lying so primly propped.

Dead Boy*

by JOHN CROWE RANSOM

The little cousin is dead, by foul
  subtraction,
A green bough from Virginia's aged tree,
And none of the county kin like the
  transaction
Nor some of the world of outer dark, like
  me.

A boy not beautiful, nor good, nor clever,   5
A black cloud full of storms too hot for
  keeping,
A sword beneath his mother's heart—yet
  never
Woman bewept her babe as this is
  weeping.

A pig with a pasty face, so I had said.
Squealing for cookies, kinned by pure
  pretense   10

---
* Copyright 1927 by Alfred A. Knopf, Inc., and renewed 1955 by John Crowe Ransom. Reprinted from *Selected Poems*, by John Crowe Ransom, by permission of the publisher.

With a noble house. But the little man
  quite dead,
I can see the forebears' antique
  lineaments.

The elder men have strode by the box of
  death
To the wide flag porch, and muttering
  low send round
The bruit of the day. O friendly waste of
  breath!   15
Their hearts are hurt with a deep dynastic
  wound.

He was pale and little, the foolish
  neighbors say;
The first-fruits, saith the Preacher, the
  Lord hath taken;
But this was the old tree's late branch
  wrenched away,
Grieving the sapless limbs, the shorn and
  shaken.

Dirge*
by KENNETH FEARING

1-2-3 was the number he played but today the number came 3-2-1;
Bought his Carbide at 30 and it went to 29; had the favorite at Bowie but the track was slow—

O executive type, would you like to drive a floating-power, knee-action, silk-upholstered six? Wed a Hollywood star? Shoot the course in 58? Draw to the ace, king, jack?
O fellow with a will who won't take no, watch out for three cigarettes on the same, single match; O democratic voter born in August under Mars, beware of liquidated rails—

Denouement to denouement, he took a personal pride in the certain, certain way he lived his own, private life,
But nevertheless, they shut off his gas; nevertheless, the bank foreclosed; nevertheless, the landlord called; nevertheless, the radio broke,

And twelve o'clock arrived just once too often,
Just the same he wore one gray tweed suit, bought one straw hat, drank one straight Scotch, walked one short step, took one long look, drew one deep breath,
Just one too many,

And wow he died as wow he lived,
Going whop to the office and blooie home to sleep and biff got married and bam had children and oof got fired,
Zowie did he live and zowie did he die,

With who the hell are you at the corner of his casket, and where the hell're we going on the right-hand silver knob, and who the hell cares walking second from the end with an American Beauty wreath from why the hell not,

Very much missed by the circulation staff of the New York Evening Post; deeply, deeply mourned by the B.M.T.
Wham, Mr. Roosevelt; pow, Sears Roebuck; awk, big dipper; bop, summer rain;
Bong, Mr., bong, Mr., bong, Mr., bong.

Carbide Union Carbon and Carbide Company. *Bowie* a race track in Maryland.
B.M.T. Brooklyn-Manhattan Transit, a subway line. *Bong* imitation of a call bell in a department store.

* From *New and Selected Poems* by Kenneth Fearing. Copyright © 1956 by the author. Reprinted by permission of Indiana University Press.

Elegy for Jane

by THEODORE ROETHKE

(My Student, Thrown by a Horse)

I remember the neckcurls, limp and damp as tendrils;
And her quick look, a sidelong pickerel smile;
And how, once startled into talk, the light syllables leaped for her,
And she balanced in the delight of her thought,
A wren, happy, tail into the wind,   5
Her song trembling the twigs and small branches.
The shade sang with her;
The leaves, their whispers turned to kissing;
And the mould sang in the bleached valleys under the rose.

Oh, when she was sad, she cast herself down into such a pure depth,   10
Even a father could not find her:
Scraping her cheek against straw;
Stirring the clearest water.

My sparrow, you are not here,
Waiting like a fern, making a spiney shadow.   15
The sides of wet stones cannot console me,
Nor the moss, wound with the last light.

If only I could nudge you from this sleep,
My maimed darling, my skittery pigeon.
Over this damp grave I speak the words of my love: 20
I, with no rights in this matter,
Neither father nor lover.

---

* "Elegy for Jane," copyright 1950 by Theodore Roethke, from *The Collected Poems of Theodore Roethke*. Reprinted by permission of Doubleday & Company, Inc.

Elegy

by WENDELL BERRY

Pryor Thomas Berry
March 4, 1864–February 23, 1946

1

All day our eyes could find no resting place.
Over a flood of snow sight came back
Empty to the mind. The sun
In a shutter of clouds, light
Staggered down the fall of snow.   5
All circling surfaces of earth were white.
No shape or shadow moved the flight
Of winter birds. Snow held the earth its silence.
We could pick no birdsong from the wind.
At nightfall our father turned his eyes away.   10
It was this storm of silence shook out his ghost.

---

* © 1964 by Wendell Berry. Reprinted from his volume, *The Broken Ground*, by permission of Harcourt Brace Jovanovich, Inc.

2

We sleep; he only wakes
Who is unshapen in a night of snow.
His shadow in the shadow of the earth
Moves the dark to wholeness.
We watch beside his body here, his image
Shape of silence in the room.

3

           Sifting
Down the wind, the winter rain
Spirals about the town
And the church hill's jut of stones.
Under the mounds, below
The weather's moving, the numb dead
   know
No fitfulness of wind.

On the road that in his knowledge ends
We bear our father to the earth.
We have adorned the shuck of him
With flowers as for a bridal, burned
Lamps about him, held death apart
Until the grave should mound it whole.

Behind us rain breaks the corners
Of our father's house, quickens
On the downslope to noise.
                  Our steps
Clamor in his silence, who tracked
The sun to autumn in the dust.
                  Below the hill
The rivers bear the rain away, that cut
His fields their shape and stood them dry.

Water wearing the earth
Is the shape of the earth,
The river flattening in its bends.
Their mingling held
Ponderable in his words—
Knowledge polished on a stone.

4

River and earth and sun and wind
   disjoint,
Over his silence flow apart. His words
Are sharp to memory as cold rain
But are not ours.
              We stare dumb
Upon the fulcrum dust, across which
   death
Lifts up our love. There is no more to
   add
To this perfection. We turn away
Into the shadow of his death.

Time in blossom and fruit and seed,
Time in the dust huddles in his darkness.
The world, spun in its shadow, holds all.
Until the morning comes his death is
   ours.

Until morning comes say of the blind
   bird:
His feet are netted with darkness, or he
   flies
His heart's distance into the darkness of
   his eyes.
A season's sun will light him no tree
   green.

5

Spring tangles shadow and light,
Branches of trees
Knit vision and wind.
The shape of the wind is a tree
Bending, spilling its birds.
From the cloud to the stone
The rain stands tall,
Columned into his darkness.
Water over blanched bones
Jangles in a forest of roots.
The church hill heals our father in.
Our remembering moves from a different
   place.

Bringing Mother Home*

by DOROTHY ROSENBERG

The narrator of "Bringing Mother Home" is an old woman, half-Indian and half-Negro. She is literate to the extent of being able to sign her own name but for reasons of her own she has wished to sign only "Martha." Miss Rosenberg writes us that she not only set down the words exactly as they were told, but that when Martha repeated the story after a long interval the details and the wording of the retelling were almost identical with those of the version here set down. I am not sure that what follows is a poem in the most formal sense. Certainly, however, it is a rare example of a kind of folk-telling so charged and so self-formed in the telling as to suggest the very roots of poetry. We at SR have found Martha's story unforgettable. We think many readers will share our sense that Martha is an authentic and moving voice speaking the native matter of poetry. — J. C.

I went to Louisiana to get my mother
   (that's where she was at)
The twenty-third of December.
(That was my borned state. I left there
   when I was seventeen.)
And when I got there she didn't know me.
She had to look at me a long time.   5
But she come to remember; she finally
   come to:
She said, "This is *Martha*.
Martha?" she says, "Is this you?"
So my brother he come from New York.
He got there on the twenty-fourth of
   December.   10
(He has two children and a wife),
And so they said, "We come after you
   mama,
That's what we come for."
But she didn't want to go with them,
And I didn't want her to, because   15
They had little children and his wife
   couldn't—you know—

---

* From "Bringing Mother Home," by Martha as told to Dorothy Rosenberg, *The Saturday Review,* December 15, 1956.

Take care of all.
So we carried her to a doctor—Dr. King,
And he gives her some examines
And he said she was a mentality case.   20
He told me, "Don't leave her. Stay with
   her."
I stayed with her 'til February,
Just me alone.

She would go out of the house and
   walk
In the rain and I would follow close
   behind—   25
To see would she know the way back.
A lot of times she wouldn't know where
   she was going.
I would come up beside her and she
   would look at me
And say, "Martha, *where* we going?"
"Where *you* going?" "I do'know."
"Then le's go home."   30

Then she agreed to come back to
   California with me.
She agreed to. So, on the seventeenth of
   February,

We left in a car. But we got to the place
    where she wouldn't
Stay in the car no more. She would ask
    for the key until
We had to give it to her (Can't drive no
    more without the key).
Then she would get out and walk; so
I would walk too, until she was tired.
I couldn't get her to eat, not anything.
So, come to El Paso, Texas, I put her in
    the hospital
For five days. I asked the doctor there,
Could she take a plane or a train to
    California,
Or could she make it in a car. He said,
    "She can."

We got as far as Fresno, and rainin'!
It rained so hard the windshield wiper
Couldn't make it. Mama was laughin'
    and
Talkin', so I said "Mama's better. I'm
    glad
I had her in the hospital."
Then we went into a gas station
And all of a sudden Mama said to me,
"Martha, look at me. I'm as *white*. I'm
    as white as that white man standing
    over there."
So then I knew she was very sick.
We carried her to the hospital.
The lady there, she said "This is a payin'
    hospital."
I said, "That's all right, if you can do her
    some good."
The doctor, he gave her a injection, and
    then,
Just like that, she died.

Well, I mean
I would'uv stayed there in El Paso with
    her.
I asked the doctor "Can she make it?"
And he said, "She can."
I told them all, "I kin keep my mother.
    I kin keep her."
I wasn't thinking of no money. I didn't
    care.
I was thinking how to keep my mother.

Unit **10**

LYRIC POEMS
ARRANGED BY TOPIC

A Selection of Poems about Poetry

The poems in this first group express very different notions about the process of poetic creation itself.

To R. B.
by GERARD MANLEY HOPKINS

The fine delight that fathers thought; the strong
Spur, live and lancing like the blowpipe flame,
Breathes once and, quenchèd faster than it came,
Leaves yet the mind a mother of immortal song.
Nine months she then, nay years, nine years she long   5
Within her wears, bears, cares and combs the same:
The widow of an insight lost she lives, with aim
Now known and hand at work now never wrong.
    Sweet fire the sire of muse, my soul needs this;
I want the one rapture of an inspiration.   10
O then if in my lagging lines you miss
The roll, the rise, the carol, the creation,
My winter world, that scarcely breathes that bliss
Now, yields you, with some sighs, our explanation.

R. B. Robert Bridges, poet laureate, a great personal friend of Hopkins.   *combs* put into order.

Poetry*
by MARIANNE MOORE

I, too, dislike it: there are things that are
    important beyond all this fiddle.
  Reading it, however, with a perfect contempt for it, one discovers in
  it after all, a place for the genuine.
    Hands that can grasp, eyes
    that can dilate, hair that can rise   5
      if it must, these things are important not because a

high-sounding interpretation can be put
    upon them but because they are
useful. When they become so derivative as to become unintelligible,
the same thing may be said for all of us, that we
  do not admire what   10
  we cannot understand: the bat
    holding on upside down or in quest of something to

eat, elephants pushing, a wild horse taking a roll, a tireless wolf under

---
* Reprinted with permission of The Macmillan Company from *Collected Poems of Marianne Moore*. Copyright 1935 by Marianne Moore, renewed 1963 by Marianne Moore and T. S. Eliot.

a tree, the immovable critic twitching
    his skin like a horse that feels
    a flea, the base-
ball fan, the statistician—
    nor is it valid
    to discriminate against "business
        documents and

schoolbooks"; all these phenomena are
    important. One must make
    a distinction
however: when dragged into promi-
    nence by half poets, the
    result is not poetry,
nor till the poets among us can be

"literalists of
    the imagination"—above
    insolence and triviality and can
        present

for inspection, "imaginary gardens with
    real toads in them," shall we
    have
it. In the meantime, if you demand on
    the one hand
    the raw material of poetry in
    all its rawness and
    that which is on the other hand
        genuine, you are interested in
        poetry.

Ars Poetica[*]

by ARCHIBALD MacLEISH

A poem should be palpable and mute
As a globed fruit,

Dumb
As old medallions to the thumb,

Silent as the sleeve-worn stone
Of casement ledges where the moss has
    grown—

A poem should be wordless
As the flight of birds.

A poem should be motionless in time
As the moon climbs,

Leaving, as the moon releases
Twig by twig the night-entangled trees,

Leaving, as the moon behind the winter
    leaves,
Memory by memory the mind—

A poem should be motionless in time
As the moon climbs.

A poem should be equal to:
Not true.

For all the history of grief
An empty doorway and a maple leaf.

For love
The leaning grasses and two lights above
    the sea—

A poem should not mean
But be.

---

[*] From *Collected Poems.* Copyright, 1952, by Archibald MacLeish. Reprinted by permission of the publisher, Houghton Mifflin Company.

In Memory of W. B. Yeats*
by W. H. AUDEN

(d. Jan. 1939)

1

He disappeared in the dead of winter:
The brooks were frozen, the air-ports almost deserted,
And snow disfigured the public statues;
The mercury sank in the mouth of the dying day.
O all the instruments agree
The day of his death was a dark cold day.

Far from his illness
The wolves ran on through the evergreen forests,
The peasant river was untempted by the fashionable quays;
By mourning tongues
The death of the poet was kept from his poems.

But for him it was his last afternoon as himself,
An afternoon of nurses and rumours;
The provinces of his body revolted,
The squares of his mind were empty,
Silence invaded the suburbs,
The current of his feeling failed: he became his admirers.

Now he is scattered among a hundred cities
And wholly given over to unfamiliar affections;
To find his happiness in another kind of wood
And be punished under a foreign code of conscience.
The words of a dead man
Are modified in the guts of the living.

But in the importance and noise of to-morrow
When the brokers are roaring like beasts on the floor of the Bourse,
And the poor have the sufferings to which they are fairly accustomed,
And each in the cell of himself is almost convinced of his freedom;
A few thousand will think of this day
As one thinks of a day when one did something slightly unusual.

O all the instruments agree
The day of his death was a dark cold day.

2

You were silly like us: your gift survived it all;
The parish of rich women, physical decay,
Yourself; mad Ireland hurt you into poetry.
Now Ireland has her madness and her weather still,
For poetry makes nothing happen: it survives
In the valley of its saying where executives
Would never want to tamper; it flows south
From ranches of isolation and the busy griefs,
Raw towns that we believe and die in; it survives,
A way of happening, a mouth.

3

Earth, receive an honoured guest;
William Yeats is laid to rest:
Let the Irish vessel lie
Emptied of its poetry.

---

* Copyright 1940 and renewed 1968 by W. H. Auden. Reprinted from *Collected Shorter Poems 1927–1957*, by W. H. Auden, by permission of Random House, Inc., and Faber and Faber Ltd.

Bourse stock exchange of Paris.

Time that is intolerant
Of the brave and innocent,
And indifferent in a week
To a beautiful physique,

Worships language and forgives 50
Everyone by whom it lives;
Pardons cowardice, conceit,
Lays its honours at their feet.

Time that with this strange excuse
Pardoned Kipling and his views, 55
And will pardon Paul Claudel,
Pardons him for writing well.

In the nightmare of the dark
All the dogs of Europe bark,

And the living nations wait, 60
Each sequestered in its hate;

Intellectual disgrace
Stares from every human face,
And the seas of pity lie
Locked and frozen in each eye. 65

Follow, poet, follow right
To the bottom of the night,
With your unconstraining voice
Still persuade us to rejoice;

With the farming of a verse 70
Make a vineyard of the curse,
Sing of human unsuccess
In a rapture of distress;

In the deserts of the heart
Let the healing fountain start, 75
In the prison of his days
Teach the free man how to praise.

Kipling nineteenth-century English poet and fiction writer, who was very critical of the government. *Paul Claudel* modern French poet and dramatist.

Nature

Certainly one of the most perennial topics of lyric poems is nature—the world of daffodils and skylarks, of forests, mountains, and seas. But the significance of external nature has shifted tremendously from epoch to epoch and from poet to poet. Read chronologically, nature poems reveal some of these shifts of attitude. The selections included here range from the seventeenth-century poet George Herbert to such contemporary poets as Donald Finkel and Galway Kinnell, and express the shifting attitudes toward external nature that resulted from fundamental shifts in the world view in successive centuries.

The Pulley
by GEORGE HERBERT

When God at first made man,
Having a glass of blessings standing by,
  "Let us," said He, "pour on him all
    we can.

Let the world's riches, which dispersed
  lie,
  Contract into a span." 5

The Pulley an emblem for the indirect way in which God draws man to Himself through creatures. *glass* a laboratory beaker.

span a unit of measurement; the distance between the tip of the thumb and little finger when the fingers are spread wide.

So strength first made a way;
Then beauty flowed, then wisdom, honor,
    pleasure.
  When almost all was out, God made
    a stay,
Perceiving that, alone of all His treasure,
  Rest in the bottom lay.   10

"For if I should," said He,
"Bestow this jewel also on my creature,

He would adore my gifts instead of me
And rest in nature, not the God of nature;
  So both should losers be.   15

"Yet let him keep the rest,
But keep them with repining restlessness.
  Let him be rich and weary, that at least,
If goodness lead him not, yet weariness
  May toss him to my breast."   20

To Daffodils
by ROBERT HERRICK

Fair daffodils, we weep to see
  You haste away so soon;
As yet the early-rising sun
  Has not attained his noon.
    Stay, stay   5
    Until the hasting day
      Has run
    But to the evensong;
And, having prayed together, we
  Will go with you along.   10

We have short time to stay, as you,
  We have as short a spring;
As quick a growth to meet decay,
  As you, or anything.
    We die   15
    As your hours do, and dry
      Away
    Like to the summer's rain;
Or as the pearls of morning's dew,
  Ne'er to be found again.   20

To a Mouse
by ROBERT BURNS

*On Turning Up Her Nest
with the Plow, November, 1785*

Wee, sleekit, cowrin, tim'rous beastie,
O, what a panic's in thy breastie!
Thou need na start awa sae hasty
    Wi' bickering brattle!
I wad be laith to rin an' chase thee,   5
    Wi' murdering pattle!

I'm truly sorry man's dominion
Has broken Nature's social union,
An' justifies that ill opinion

    Which makes thee startle   10
At me, thy poor, earth-born companion
    An' fellow-mortal!

I doubt na, whyles, but thou may thieve;
What then? poor beastie, thou maun live:
A daimen icker in a thrave   15
    'S a sma' request;
I'll get a blessin wi' the lave,
    An' never miss 't!

---

sleekit sleek.   *bickering brattle* quick scamper.
pattle paddle, stick for cleaning the plough.

whyles at times.   *maun* must.   *daimen icker
in a thrave* an occasional head of grain in a whole
shock.   *lave* the remainder.

Thy weebit housie, too, in ruin!
Its silly wa's the win's are strewin! 20
An' naething, now, to big a new ane,
    O' foggage green!
An' bleak December's win's ensuin,
    Baith snell an' keen!

Thou saw the fields laid bare an' waste, 25
An' weary winter comin' fast,
An' cozie here, beneath the blast,
    Thou thought to dwell,
Till, crash! the cruel coulter passed
    Out through thy cell. 30

That wee bit heap o' leaves an' stibble,
Has cost thee monie a weary nibble!
Now thou's turned out, for a' thy trouble,
But house or hald,
To thole the winter's sleety dribble, 35
    An' cranreuch cauld!

But Mousie, thou art no thy lane,
In proving foresight may be vain:
The best-laid schemes o' mice an' men
    Gang aft agley, 40
An' lea'e us naught but grief an' pain,
    For promised joy!

Still thou art blest, compared wi' me!
The present only toucheth thee:
But och! I backward cast my e'e, 45
    On prospects drear!
An' forward, though I canna see,
    I guess an' fear!

---

silly poor, feeble, pitiable. *big* build. *foggage* rough grass. *snell* bitter. *coulter* a blade or disk on a plough for making vertical cuts in the soil.

But without. *hald* shelter. *thole* suffer or endure. *cranreuch* hoar frost. *no thy lane* not alone. *Gang aft agley* go often awry.

To Autumn

by JOHN KEATS

Season of mists and mellow fruitfulness,
  Close bosom-friend of the maturing
    sun;
Conspiring with him how to load and
    bless
  With fruit the vines that round the
    thatched-eaves run;
To bend with apples the mossed cottage-
    trees,
  And fill all fruit with ripeness to the
    core; 5
  To swell the gourd, and plump the
    hazel shells
With a sweet kernel; to set budding more,
  And still more, later flowers for the bees,
  Until they think warm days will never
    cease, 10
    For Summer has o'er-brimmed their
    clammy cells.

Who hath not seen thee oft amid thy
    store?
  Sometimes whoever seeks abroad may
    find
Thee sitting careless on a granary floor,
  Thy hair soft-lifted by the winnowing
    wind; 15
Or on a half-reaped furrow sound asleep,
  Drowsed with the fume of poppies,
    while thy hook
  Spares the next swath and all its
    twinéd flowers:
And sometime like a gleaner thou dost
    keep

Season Autumn always had a fascination for Keats. On September 22, 1819, he wrote to his friend Reynolds: "How beautiful the season is now—How fine the air. A temperate sharpness about it. Really, without joking, chaste weather—Dian skies—I never liked stubble-fields so much as now—Aye better than the chilly green of the spring. Somehow, a stubble-field looks warm—in the same way that some pictures look warm. This struck me so much in my Sunday's walk that I composed upon it." *To Autumn* is the result. This note is particularly relevant to the last stanza.

Steady thy laden head across a brook;
Or by a cider-press, with patient look,
   Thou watchest the last oozings,
      hours by hours.

Where are the songs of Spring? Ay, where
      are they?
   Think not of them, thou hast thy
      music too—
While barréd clouds bloom the soft-dying
      day,
   And touch the stubble-plains with rosy
      hue;
Then in a wailful choir the small gnats
      mourn

Among the river sallows, borne aloft
   Or sinking as the light wind lives or
      dies;
And full-grown lambs loud bleat from
      hilly bourn;
   Hedge-crickets sing; and now with
      treble soft
The redbreast whistles from a garden-
      croft,
   And gathering swallows twitter in the
      skies.

---

sallows willows.   *bourn* domain, place.   *garden-croft* small enclosed garden.

I Wandered Lonely as a Cloud

by WILLIAM WORDSWORTH

I wandered lonely as a cloud
That floats on high o'er vales and hills,
When all at once I saw a crowd,
A host, of golden daffodils;
Beside the lake, beneath the trees,
Fluttering and dancing in the breeze.

Continuous as the stars that shine
And twinkle on the Milky Way,
They stretched in never-ending line
Along the margin of a bay:
Ten thousand saw I at a glance,
Tossing their heads in sprightly dance.

The waves beside them danced; but they
Outdid the sparkling waves in glee:
A poet could not but be gay,
In such a jocund company:
I gazed—and gazed—but little thought
What wealth the show to me had brought:

For oft, when on my couch I lie
In vacant or in pensive mood,
They flash upon that inward eye
Which is the bliss of solitude;
And then my heart with pleasure fills,
And dances with the daffodils.

Lines

by WILLIAM WORDSWORTH

*Composed a Few Miles
above Tintern Abbey*

Five years have past, five summers, with
   the length
Of five long winters! and again I hear

These waters, rolling from their moun-
   tain-springs
With a soft inland murmur.—Once again

Tintern Abbey a beautiful ruin in Monmouthshire, on the river Wye. Wordsworth says of the composition of this poem: "No poem of mine was composed under circumstances more pleasant for me to remember than this. I began it upon leaving Tintern, after crossing the Wye, and concluded it just as I was entering Bristol, in the evening, after a ramble of four or five days, with my sister. Not a line of it was altered, and not any part of it written down till I reached Bristol."

Do I behold these steep and lofty cliffs,
That on a wild secluded scene impress
Thoughts of more deep seclusion; and connect
The landscape with the quiet of the sky.
The day is come when I again repose 10
Here, under this dark sycamore, and view
These plots of cottage-ground, these orchard-tufts,
Which at this season, with their unripe fruits,
Are clad in one green hue, and lose themselves
Mid groves and copses. Once again I see
These hedgerows, hardly hedgerows, little lines 15
Of sportive wood run wild: these pastoral farms,
Green to the very door; and wreaths of smoke
Sent up, in silence, from among the trees!
With some uncertain notice, as might seem
Of vagrant dwellers in the houseless woods, 20
Or of some hermit's cave, where by his fire
The Hermit sits alone.
                These beauteous forms,
Through a long absence, have not been to me
As is a landscape to a blind man's eye:
But oft, in lonely rooms, and 'mid the din 25
Of towns and cities, I have owed to them,
In hours of weariness, sensations sweet,
Felt in the blood, and felt along the heart;
And passing even into my purer mind,
With tranquil restoration—feelings too 30
Of unremembered pleasure: such, perhaps,
As have no slight or trivial influence
On that best portion of a good man's life,
His little, nameless, unremembered acts
Of kindness and of love. Nor less, I trust, 35
To them I may have owed another gift,
Of aspect more sublime; that blesséd mood,
In which the burthen of the mystery,
In which the heavy and the weary weight
Of all this unintelligible world, 40
Is lightened—that serene and blesséd mood, 5
In which the affections gently lead us on—
Until, the breath of this corporeal frame
And even the motion of our human blood
Almost suspended, we are laid asleep 45
In body, and become a living soul:
While with an eye made quiet by the power
Of harmony, and the deep power of joy,
We see into the life of things.
                        If this
Be but a vain belief, yet, oh! how oft— 50
In darkness and amid the many shapes
Of joyless daylight; when the fretful stir
Unprofitable, and the fever of the world,
Have hung upon the beatings of my heart—
How oft, in spirit, have I turned to thee, 55
O sylvan Wye! thou wanderer through the woods.
How often has my spirit turned to thee!
    And now, with gleams of half-extinguished thought,
With many recognitions dim and faint,
And somewhat of a sad perplexity, 60
The picture of the mind revives again:
While here I stand, not only with the sense
Of present pleasure, but with pleasing thoughts
That in this moment there is life and food
For future years. And so I dare to hope, 65
Though changed, no doubt, from what I was when first
I came among these hills; when like a roe
I bounded o'er the mountains, by the sides
Of the deep rivers, and the lonely streams,
Wherever nature led: more like a man 70
Flying from something that he dreads than one
Who sought the thing he loved. For nature then
(The coarser pleasures of my boyish days,
And their glad animal movements all gone by) 75
To me was all in all.—I cannot paint
What then I was. The sounding cataract

Haunted me like a passion: the tall rock,
The mountain, and the deep and gloomy wood,
Their colors and their forms, were then to me   80
An appetite; a feeling and a love,
That had no need of a remoter charm,
By thought supplied, nor any interest
Unborrowed from the eye.—That time is past,
And all its aching joys are now no more,   85
And all its dizzy raptures. Nor for this
Faint I, nor mourn nor murmur; other gifts
Have followed; for such loss, I would believe,
Abundant recompense. For I have learned
To look on nature, not as in the hour   90
Of thoughtless youth; but hearing oftentimes
The still, sad music of humanity,
Nor harsh nor grating, though of ample power
To chasten and subdue. And I have felt
A presence that disturbs me with the joy   95
Of elevated thoughts; a sense sublime
Of something far more deeply interfused,
Whose dwelling is the light of setting suns,
And the round ocean and the living air,
And the blue sky, and in the mind of man: 100
A motion and a spirit, that impels
All thinking things, all objects of all thought,
And rolls through all things. Therefore am I still
A lover of the meadows and the woods,
And mountains; and of all that we behold   105
From this green earth; of all the mighty world
Of eye, and ear—both what they half create,
And what perceive; well pleased to recognize
In nature and the language of the sense
The anchor of my purest thoughts, the nurse,   110
The guide, the guardian of my heart, and soul
Of all my moral being.
                         Nor perchance,
If I were not thus taught, should I the more
Suffer my genial spirits to decay:
For thou art with me here upon the banks
Of this fair river; thou my dearest Friend,   115
My dear, dear Friend; and in thy voice I catch
The language of my former heart, and read
My former pleasures in the shooting lights
Of thy wild eyes. Oh! yet a little while
May I behold in thee what I was once,   120
My dear, dear Sister! and this prayer I make,
Knowing that Nature never did betray
The heart that loved her; 'tis her privilege,
Through all the years of this our life, to lead
From joy to joy: for she can so inform   125
The mind that is within us, so impress
With quietness and beauty, and so feed
With lofty thoughts, that neither evil tongues,
Rash judgments, nor the sneers of selfish men,
Nor greetings where no kindness is, nor all   130
The dreary intercourse of daily life,
Shall e'er prevail against us, or disturb
Our cheerful faith, that all which we behold
Is full of blessings. Therefore let the moon
Shine on thee in thy solitary walk;   135
And let the misty mountain-winds be free
To blow against thee: and, in after years,
When these wild ecstasies shall be matured
Into a sober pleasure; when thy mind
Shall be a mansion for all lovely forms,   140
Thy memory be as a dwelling-place
For all sweet sounds and harmonies; oh! then,
If solitude, or fear, or pain, or grief,
Should be thy portion, with what healing thoughts   145

---

dear Friend his sister Dorothy.

Of tender joy wilt thou remember me,
And these my exhortations! Nor, perchance—
If I should be where I no more can hear
Thy voice, nor catch from thy wild eyes these gleams
Of past existence—wilt thou then forget
That on the banks of this delightful stream 150
We stood together; and that I, so long
A worshiper of Nature, hither came
Unwearied in that service: rather say
With warmer love—oh! with far deeper zeal
Of holier love. Nor wilt thou then forget 155
That after mnay wanderings, many years
Of absence, these steep woods and lofty cliffs,
And this green pastoral landscape, were to me
More dear, both for themselves and for thy sake!

The Lotos Eaters

by ALFRED, LORD TENNYSON

"Courage!" he said, and pointed toward the land,
"This mounting wave will roll us shoreward soon."
In the afternoon they came unto a land
In which it seeméd always afternoon.
All round the coast the languid air did swoon, 5
Breathing like one that hath a weary dream.
Full-faced above the valley stood the moon;
And, like a downward smoke, the slender stream
Along the cliff to fall and pause and fall did seem.

A land of streams! some, like a downward smoke, 10
Slow-dropping veils of thinnest lawn, did go;
And some through wavering lights and shadows broke,
Rolling a slumbrous sheet of foam below.
They saw the gleaming river seaward flow
From the inner land; far off, three mountain-tops, 15
Three silent pinnacles of aged snow,
Stood sunset-flushed; and, dewed with showery drops,
Up-clomb the shadowy pine above the woven copse.

The charméd sunset lingered low adown
In the red West; through mountain clefts the dale 20
Was seen far inland, and the yellow down
Bordered with palm, and many a winding vale
And meadow, set with slender galingale;
A land where all things always seemed the same!
And round about the keel with faces pale, 25
Dark faces pale against that rosy flame,
The mild-eyed melancholy Lotos-eaters came.

Branches they bore of that enchanted stem,
Laden with flower and fruit, whereof they gave
To each, but whoso did receive of them 30
And taste, to him the gushing of the wave

Lotos Eaters The poem is based on the passage in Book IX of the *Odyssey* about the land of the lotus. The sailors who ate of its fruit wished to stay with the lotus-eaters and never go home. *he* Ulysses *lawn* a fine sheer cloth of cotton or linen.

galingale sedge plant with pungent root, of the ginger family.

Far far away did seem to mourn and rave
On alien shores; and if his fellow spake,
His voice was thin, as voices from the grave;
And deep-asleep he seemed, yet all awake, 35
And music in his ears his beating heart did make.

They sat them down upon the yellow sand
Between the sun and moon upon the shore;
And sweet it was to dream of Fatherland,
Of child, and wife, and slave; but evermore 40
Most weary seemed the sea, weary the oar,
Weary the wandering fields of barren foam.
Then someone said, "We will return no more";
And all at once they sang, "Our island home
Is far beyond the wave; we will no longer roam." 45

CHORIC SONG

There is sweet music here that softer falls
Than petals from blown roses on the grass,
Or night-dews on still waters between walls
Of shadowy granite, in a gleaming pass;
Music that gentlier on the spirit lies, 50
Than tired eyelids upon tired eyes;
Music that brings sweet sleep down from the blissful skies.
Here are cool mosses deep,
And through the moss the ivies creep,
And in the stream the long-leaved flowers weep, 55
And from the craggy ledge the poppy hangs in sleep.

Why are we weighed upon with heaviness,
And utterly consumed with sharp distress,
While all things else have rest from weariness?
All things have rest; why should we toil alone, 60
We only toil, who are the first of things,
And make perpetual moan,
Still from one sorrow to another thrown;
Nor ever fold our wings,
And cease from wanderings, 65
Nor steep our brows in slumber's holy balm;
Nor harken what the inner spirit sings,
"There is no joy but calm!"—
Why should we only toil, the roof and crown of things?

Lo! in the middle of the wood, 70
The folded leaf is wooed from out the bud
With winds upon the branch, and there
Grows green and broad, and takes no care,
Sun-steeped at noon, and in the moon
Nightly dew-fed; and turning yellow 75
Falls, and floats adown the air.
Lo! sweetened with the summer light,
The full-juiced apple, waxing over-mellow,
Drops in a silent autumn night.
All its allotted length of days 80
The flower ripens in its place,
Ripens and fades, and falls, and hath no toil,
Fast-rooted in the fruitful soil.

Hateful is the dark-blue sky,
Vaulted o'er the dark-blue sea. 85
Death is the end of life; ah, why
Should life all labor be?
Let us alone. Time driveth onward fast,
And in a little while our lips are dumb.
Let us alone. What is it that will last? 90
All things are taken from us, and become
Portions and parcels of the dreadful past.
Let us alone. What pleasure can we have
To war with evil? Is there any peace
In ever climbing up the climbing wave? 95
All things have rest, and ripen toward the grave
In silence—ripen, fall, and cease;
Give us long rest or death, dark death, or dreamful ease.
How sweet it were, hearing the downward stream

With half-shut eyes ever to seem
Falling asleep in a half-dream!
To dream and dream, like yonder amber
    light,
Which will not leave the myrrh-bush on
    the height;
To hear each other's whispered speech;
Eating the Lotos day by day,   105
To watch the crisping ripples on the
    beach,
And tender curving lines of creamy spray;
To lend our hearts and spirits wholly
To the influence of mild-minded melan-
    choly;
To muse and brood and live again in
    memory,   110
With those old faces of our infancy
Heaped over with a mound of grass,
Two handfuls of white dust, shut in an
    urn of brass!

Dear is the memory of our wedded lives,
And dear the last embraces of our wives   115
And their warm tears; but all hath
    suffered change;
For surely now our household hearths
    are cold,
Our sons inherit us, our looks are strange,
And we should come like ghosts to trouble
    joy.
Or else the island princes over-bold   120
Have eat our substance, and the minstrel
    sings
Before them of the ten years' war in Troy,
And our great deeds, as half-forgotten
    things.
Is there confusion in the little isle?
Let what is broken so remain.   125
The gods are hard to reconcile;
'Tis hard to settle order once again.
There *is* confusion worse than death,
Trouble on trouble, pain on pain,
Long labor unto aged breath,   130
Sore task to hearts worn out by many
    wars
And eyes grown dim with gazing on the
    pilot-stars.

---

little isle Ithaca, the little island home of Ulysses.

But, propped on beds of amaranth and
    moly,
How sweet—while warm airs lull us,
    blowing lowly—
With half-dropped eyelid still,   135
Beneath a heaven dark and holy,
To watch the long bright river drawing
    slowly
His waters from the purple hill—
To hear the dewy echoes calling
From cave to cave through the thick-
    twined vine—   140
To watch the emerald-colored water
    falling
Through many a woven acanthus-wreath
    divine!
Only to hear and see the far-off sparkling
    brine,
Only to hear were sweet, stretched out
    beneath the pine.

The Lotos blooms below the barren
    peak,   145
The Lotos blows by every winding creek;
All day the wind breathes low with
    mellower tone;
Through every hollow cave and alley
    lone
Round and round the spicy downs the
    yellow Lotos-dust is blown.
We have had enough of action, and of
    motion we,   150
Rolled to starboard, rolled to larboard,
    when the surge was seething free,
Where the wallowing monster spouted
    his foam-fountains in the sea.
Let us swear an oath, and keep it with an
    equal mind,
In the hollow Lotos-land to live and lie
    reclined
On the hills like gods together, careless
    of mankind.   155

---

amaranth an imaginary flower that never fades or dies. *moly* mythical herb of magic powers (in the *Odyssey*, given to Odysseus by Hermes to protect his men against Circe). *acanthus-wreath* a plant of the Mediterranean area, the curled leaves of which were used as patterns for architectural capitals.

For they lie beside their nectar, and the
    bolts are hurled
Far below them in the valleys, and the
    clouds are lightly curled
Round their golden houses, girdled with
    the gleaming world;
Where they smile in secret, looking over
    wasted lands,
Blight and famine, plague and earthquake,
    roaring deeps and fiery sands,   160
Clanging fights, and flaming towns, and
    sinking ships, and praying hands
But they smile, they find a music centered
    in a doleful song
Steaming up, a lamentation and an
    ancient tale of wrong,
Like a tale of little meaning though the
    words are strong;
Chanted from an ill-used race of men that
    cleave the soil,   165

Sow the seed, and reap the harvest with
    enduring toil,
Storing yearly little dues of wheat, and
    wine and oil;
Till they perish and they suffer—some,
    'tis whispered—down in hell
Suffer endless anguish, others in Elysian
    valleys dwell,
Resting weary limbs at last on beds of
    asphodel.   170
Surely, surely, slumber is more sweet than
    toil, the shore
Than labor in the deep mid-ocean, wind
    and wave and oar;
O rest ye, brother mariners, we will not
    wander more.

Elysian paradisaic, happy.   *asphodel* a plant of the lily family, probably the Narcissus or daffodil.

Loveliest of Trees*

by A. E. HOUSMAN

Loveliest of trees, the cherry now
Is hung with bloom along the bough,
And stands about the woodland ride
Wearing white for Eastertide.

Now, of my threescore years and ten,   5
Twenty will not come again,
And take from seventy springs a score,
It only leaves me fifty more.

And since to look at things in bloom
Fifty springs are little room,   10
About the woodlands I will go
To see the cherry hung with snow.

---

* From "A Shropshire Lad"—Authorised Edition—from *The Collected Poems of A. E. Housman.* Copyright 1939, 1940, © 1959 by Holt, Rinehart and Winston, Inc. Copyright © 1967, 1968 by Robert E. Symons. Reprinted by permission of Holt, Rinehart and Winston, Inc., and The Society of Authors as the literary representative of the Estate of A. E. Housman, and Jonathan Cape Ltd., publishers of A. E. Housman's *Collected Poems.*

White in the Moon the Long Road Lies

by A. E. HOUSMAN

White in the moon the long road lies,
   The moon stands blank above;
White in the moon the long road lies
   That leads me from my love.

Still hangs the hedge without a gust,   5
   Still, still the shadows stay:
My feet upon the moonlit dust
   Pursue the ceaseless way.

The world is round, so travellers tell,
   And straight though reach the track,   10
Trudge on, trudge on, 'twill all be well,
   The way will guide one back.

But ere the circle homeward hies
   Far, far must it remove:
White in the moon the long road lies   15
   That leads me from my love.

---

* From "A Shropshire Lad"—Authorised Edition—from *The Collected Poems of A. E. Housman*. Copyright 1939, 1940, © 1959 by Holt, Rinehart and Winston, Inc. Copyright © 1967, 1968 by Robert E. Symons. Reprinted by permission of Holt, Rinehart and Winston, Inc., and The Society of Authors as the literary representative of the Estate of A. E. Housman, and Jonathan Cape Ltd., publishers of A. E. Housman's *Collected Poems*.

The Darkling Thrush

by THOMAS HARDY

I leant upon a coppice gate
   When Frost was spectre-gray
And Winter's dregs made desolate
   The weakening eye of day.
The tangled bine-stems scored the sky   5
   Like strings of broken lyres,
And all mankind that haunted nigh
   Had sought their household fires.

The land's sharp features seemed to be
   The Century's corpse outleant,   10
His crypt the cloudy canopy,
   The wind his death-lament.
The ancient pulse of germ and birth
   Was shrunken hard and dry,
And every spirit upon earth   15
   Seemed fervourless as I.

At once a voice arose among
   The bleak twigs overhead
In a full-hearted evensong
   Of joy illimited;   20
An aged thrush, frail, gaunt, and small,
   In blast-beruffled plume,
Had chosen thus to fling his soul
   Upon the growing gloom.

So little cause for carolings   25
   Of such ecstatic sound
Was written on terrestrial things
   Afar or nigh around,
That I could think there trembled
   through
   His happy good-night air   30
Some blessed Hope, whereof he knew
   And I was unaware.

---

coppice a grove of trees or shrubs.

* Reprinted with permission of The Macmillan Company, the Hardy Estate, Macmillan & Co. Ltd., London, and The Macmillan Company of Canada Limited from *Collected Poems of Thomas Hardy*. Copyright 1925 by The Macmillan Company.

In Harmony with Nature
by MATTHEW ARNOLD

"In harmony with Nature?" Restless fool,
Who with such heat dost preach what were to thee,
When true, the last impossibility—
To be like Nature strong, like Nature cool!
Know, man hath all which Nature hath, but more,   5
And in that *more* lie all his hopes of good.
Nature is cruel, man is sick of blood;
Nature is stubborn, man would fain adore;
Nature is fickle, man hath need of rest;
Nature forgives no debt, and fears no grave;   10
Man would be mild, and with safe conscience blest.
Man must begin, know this, where Nature ends;
Nature and man can never be fast friends.
Fool, if thou canst not pass her, rest her slave!

Home-Thoughts, from Abroad
by ROBERT BROWNING

Oh, to be in England
Now that April's there,
And whoever wakes in England
Sees, some morning, unaware,
That the lowest boughs and the brush-wood sheaf   5
Round the elm-tree bole are in tiny leaf,
While the chaffinch sings on the orchard bough
In England—now!

And after April, when May follows,
And the whitethroat builds, and all the swallows!   10
Hark, where my blossomed pear-tree in the hedge
Leans to the field and scatters on the clover
Blossoms and dewdrops—at the bent spray's edge—
That's the wise thrush; he sings each song twice over,
Lest you should think he never could recapture   15
The first fine careless rapture!
And though the fields look rough with hoary dew,
All will be gay when noontide wakes anew
The buttercups, the little children's dower—
Far brighter than this gaudy melon-flower!   20

Abroad Browning lived for some time in Italy. *bole* tree trunk. *chaffinch* one of the most common small English song birds, often kept in a cage as a pet. *whitethroat* a warbler.

God's Grandeur

by GERARD MANLEY HOPKINS

The world is charged with the grandeur
   of God.
  It will flame out, like shining from
   shook foil;
  It gathers to a greatness, like the ooze
   of oil
Crushed. Why do mén then nów not
   reck his rod?
Generations have trod, have trod, have
   trod;   5
  And all is seared with trade; bleared,
   smeared with toil;
And wears man's smudge and shares
   man's smell: the soil
Is bare now, nor can foot feel, being shod.

And for all this, nature is never spent,
  There lives the dearest freshness deep
   down things;   10
And though the last lights off the black
   West went
  Oh, morning, at the brown brink
   eastward, springs—
Because the Holy Ghost over the bent
   World broods with warm breast and
   with ah! bright wings.

---

charged as with an electric current. *like the ooze of oil crushed* like the ooze of oil from crushed olives that gathers drop by drop to a mass (a greatness) until it flows; it is flowing oil that symbolizes divine operation and more specifically the action of the Holy Spirit. *reck his rod* recognize his authority.

being shod Hopkins knew the wood-soled miner's shoes with steel cleats that look almost like horse shoes; it is a particularly good image for the insulation of man from God's nature through mining and other trades. *bent* bent low and out of shape by man's abuses. *broods* as a dove on its nest, symbol of the Holy Ghost as a fosterer of New life.

To a Snowflake

by FRANCIS THOMPSON

What heart could have thought you?—
Past our devisal
(O filigree petal!)
Fashioned so purely,
Fragiley, surely,   5
From what Paradisal
Imagineless metal,
Too costly for cost?
Who hammered you, wrought you,
From argentine vapour?—   10
'God was my shaper.
Passing surmisal,
He hammered, He wrought me,
From curled silver vapour,
To lust of His mind:—   15
Thou could'st not have thought me!
So purely, so palely,
Tinily, surely,
Mightily, frailly,
Insculped and embossed,   20
With His hammer of wind,
And His graver of frost.'

---

filigree delicate, lacelike ornament woven of metal wire. *argentine* silver.

lust desire.

Sea-Fever*

by JOHN MASEFIELD

I must go down to the seas again, to the
 lonely sea and the sky,
And all I ask is a tall ship and a star to
 steer her by,
And the wheel's kick and the wind's song
 and the white sail's shaking,
And a grey mist on the sea's face and a
 grey dawn breaking.

I must go down to the seas again, for the
 call of the running tide   5
Is a wild call and a clear call that may
 not be denied;
And all I ask is a windy day with the
 white clouds flying,
And the flung spray and the blown spume,
 and the sea-gulls crying.

I must go down to the seas again to the
 vagrant gypsy life,
To the gull's way and the whale's way
 where the wind's like a whetted knife;   10
And all I ask is a merry yarn from a
 laughing fellow-rover,
And quiet sleep and a sweet dream when
 the long trick's over.

* Reprinted with the permission of The Macmillan Company from *Poems of John Masefield*. Copyright 1912 by The Macmillan Company, renewed 1940 by John Masefield.

The Landscape near an Aerodrome*

by STEPHEN SPENDER

More beautiful and soft than any moth
With burring furred antennae feeling
 its huge path
Through dusk, the air liner with shut-off
 engines
Glides over suburbs and the sleeves set
 trailing tall
To point the wind. Gently, broadly, she
 falls,   5
Scarcely disturbing charted currents of air.

Lulled by descent, the travellers across sea
And across feminine land indulging its
 easy limbs
In miles of softness, now let their eyes
 trained by watching
Penetrate through dusk the outskirts of
 this town   10
Here where industry shows a fraying edge.
Here they may see what is being done.

Beyond the winking masthead light
And the landing ground, they observe the
 outposts
Of work: chimneys like lank black fingers   15
Or figures, frightening and mad: and
 squat buildings
With their strange air behind trees, like
 women's faces
Shattered by grief. Here where few houses
Moan with faint light behind their blinds,
They remark the unhomely sense of
 complaint, like a dog   20
Shut out, and shivering at the foreign
 moon.

* Copyright 1934 and renewed 1962 by Stephen Spender. Reprinted from *Selected Poems*, by Stephen Spender, by permission of Random House, Inc., and from *Collected Poems 1928–1953* by Stephen Spender, by permission of Faber and Faber Ltd.

In the last sweep of love, they pass over
   fields
Behind the aerodrome, where boys play
   all day
Hacking dead grass: whose cries, like wild
   birds,
Settle upon the nearest roofs   25
But soon are hid under the loud city.

Then, as they land, they hear the tolling
   bell
Reaching across the landscape of hysteria,
To where, louder than all those batteries
And charcoaled towers against that dying
   sky,   30
Religion stands, the Church blocking
   the sun.

Fern Hill*

by DYLAN THOMAS

Now as I was young and easy under the
      apple boughs
About the lilting house and happy as the
      grass was green,
   The night above the dingle starry,
   Time let me hail and climb
   Golden in the heydays of his eyes,   5
And honoured among wagons I was
      prince of the apple towns
And once below a time I lordly had the
      trees and leaves
   Trail with daisies and barley
   Down the rivers of the windfall light.

And as I was green and carefree, famous
      among the barns   10
About the happy yard and singing as the
      farm was home,
   In the sun that is young once only,
   Time let me play and be
   Golden in the mercy of his means,
And green and golden I was huntsman
      and herdsman, the calves   15
Sang to my horn, the foxes on the hills
      barked clear and cold.
   And the sabbath rang slowly
   In the pebbles of the holy streams.
All the sun long it was running, it was
      lovely, the hay

Fields high as the house, the tunes from
      the chimneys, it was air   20
   And playing, lovely and watery
   And fire green as grass.
   And nightly under the simple stars
As I rode to sleep the owls were bearing
      the farm away,
All the moon long I heard, blessed among
      stables, the nightjars   25
   Flying with the ricks, and the horses
   Flashing into the dark.

And then to awake, and the farm, like
      a wanderer white
With the dew, come back, the cock on his
      shoulder: it was all
   Shining, it was Adam and maiden,   30
   The sky gathered again
   And the sun grew round that very day.
So it must have been after the birth of
      the simple light
In the first, spinning place, the spell-
      bound horses walking warm   35
   Out of the whinnying green stable
   On to the fields of praise.

And honoured among foxes and pheasants
      by the gay house
Under the new made clouds and happy
      as the heart was long,
   In the sun born over and over,
   I ran my heedless ways,   40
   My wishes raced through the house
      high hay

---
dingle small wooded valley.
* Dylan Thomas, *Collected Poems.* Copyright 1946 by New Directions Publishing Corporation. Reprinted by permission of New Directions Publishing Corporation, J. M. Dent & Sons Ltd., and the Trustees for the Copyrights of the late Dylan Thomas.

---
nightjars nighthawk, called *jar* from the whirring noise of its flight.   *ricks* hay stacks.

And nothing I cared, at my sky blue
    trades, that time allows
In all his tuneful turning so few and
    such morning songs
    Before the children green and golden
       Follow him out of grace,   45

Nothing I cared, in the lamb white days,
    that time would take me
Up to the swallow thronged loft by the
    shadow of my hand,

In the moon that is always rising,
    Nor that riding to sleep
I should hear him fly with the high
    fields   50
And wake to the farm forever fled from
    the childless land.
Oh as I was young and easy in the mercy
    of his means,
    Time held me green and dying
    Though I sang in my chains like the
        sea.

Pastoral*

by WILLIAM CARLOS WILLIAMS

The little sparrows
hop ingenuously
about the pavement
quarreling
with sharp voices   5
over those things
that interest them.
But we who are wiser
shut ourselves in
on either hand   10

and no one knows
whether we think good
or evil.
            Meanwhile,
the old man who goes about
gathering dog-lime   15
walks in the gutter
without looking up
and his tread
is more majestic than
that of the Episcopal minister   20
approaching the pulpit
of a Sunday.
        These things
astonish me beyond words.

---

* From William Carlos Williams, *Collected Earlier Poems*. Copyright 1938 by William Carlos Williams. Reprinted by permission of New Directions Publishing Corporation.

when serpents bargain for the right to squirm*

by e. e. cummings

when serpents bargain for the right to squirm
and the sun strikes to gain a living wage—
when thorns regard their roses with alarm
and rainbows are insured against old age

when every thrush may sing no new moon in
if all screech-owls have not okayed his voice
—and any wave signs on the dotted line
or else an ocean is compelled to close

when the oak begs permission of the birch
to make an acorn—valleys accuse their
mountains of having altitude—and march
denounces april as a saboteur

then we'll believe in that incredible
unanimal mankind (and not until)

---

* Copyright, 1950, by E. E. Cummings. Reprinted from his volume, *Poems 1923–1954*, by permission of Harcourt Brace Jovanovich, Inc.

Reason for Not Writing Orthodox Nature Poetry*
by JOHN WAIN

The January sky is deep and calm.
The mountain sprawls in comfort, and
   the sea
Sleeps in the crook of that enormous arm.

And Nature from a simple recipe—
Rocks, water, mist, a sunlit winter's day—   5
Has brewed a cup whose strength has
   dizzied me.

So little beauty is enough to pay;
The heart so soon yields up its store of
   love,
And where you love you cannot break
   away.

So sages never found it hard to prove   10
Nor prophets to declare in metaphor
That God and Nature must be hand in
   glove.

And this became the basis of their lore.
Then later poets found it easy going
To give the public what they bargained
   for,   15

And like a spectacled curator showing
The wares of his museum to the crowd,
They yearly waxed more eloquent and
   knowing

More slick, more photographic, and more
   proud:
From Tennyson with notebook in his
   hand   20
(His truth to Nature fits him like a
   shroud)

To moderns who devoutly hymn the land.
So be it: each is welcome to his voice;
They are a gentle, if a useless, band.

But leave me free to make a sterner
   choice;   25
Content, without embellishment, to note
How little beauty bids the heart rejoice,

How little beauty catches at the throat,
Simply, I love this mountain and this bay
With love that I can never speak by rote,   30
And where you love you cannot break
   away.

---

* From *A Word Carved on a Sill* by John Wain. Reprinted by permission of St. Martin's Press, Inc., and Routledge & Kegan Paul Ltd.

Black Rook in Rainy Weather*
by SYLVIA PLATH

On the stiff twig up there
Hunches a wet black rook
Arranging and rearranging its feathers
   in the rain.
I do not expect miracle
Or an accident   5

To set the sight on fire
In my eye, nor seek
Any more in the desultory weather
   some design,
But let spotted leaves fall as they fall,
Without ceremony, or portent.   10

Although, I admit, I desire,
Occasionally, some backtalk

---

* From *The Colossus and Other Poems* by Sylvia Plath. Reprinted by permission of Olwyn Hughes, representing the Estate of Sylvia Plath.

From the mute sky, I can't honestly complain:
A certain minor light may still
Leap incandescent　　　　　　　　　　　　15

Out of a kitchen table or chair
As if a celestial burning took
Possession of the most obtuse objects now and then—
Thus hallowing an interval
Otherwise inconsequent　　　　　　　　　20

By bestowing largesse, honour,
One might say love. At any rate, I now walk
Wary (for it could happen
Even in this dull, ruinous landscape); sceptical,
Yet politic; ignorant　　　　　　　　　　　25

Of whatever angel may choose to flare
Suddenly at my elbow. I only know that a rook
Ordering its black feathers can so shine
As to seize my senses, haul
My eyelids up, and grant　　　　　　　　30

A brief respite from fear
Of total neutrality. With luck,
Trekking stubborn through this season
Of fatigue, I shall
Patch together a content　　　　　　　　35

Of sorts. Miracles occur,
If you care to call those spasmodic
Tricks of radiance miracles. The wait's begun again,
The long wait for the angel,
For that rare, random descent.　　　　　40

Dust of Snow*
by ROBERT FROST

The way a crow
Shook down on me
The dust of snow
From a hemlock tree

Has given my heart　　　　　　　　　　　5
A change of mood
And saved some part
Of a day I had rued.

---

* From *Complete Poems of Robert Frost*. Copyright 1916, 1923, 1930, 1939 by Holt, Rinehart and Winston, Inc. Copyright 1936, 1942, 1944, 1951, © 1958 by Robert Frost. Copyright © 1964, 1967 by Lesley Frost Ballantine. Reprinted by permission of Holt, Rinehart and Winston, Inc.

The Eye*
by ROBINSON JEFFERS

The Atlantic is a stormy moat; and the Mediterranean,
The blue pool in the old garden,

More than five thousand years has drunk sacrifice
Of ships and blood, and shines in the sun; but here the Pacific—
Our ships, planes, wars are perfectly irrelevant.　　　　　　　　　　　　　　5
Neither our present blood-feud with the brave dwarfs

---

* Copyright 1941 by Yardstick Press. Copyright 1944 by Oscar Williams. Reprinted from *Selected Poems*, by Robinson Jeffers, by permission of Random House, Inc.

Nor any future world-quarrel of westering
And eastering man, the bloody migrations,
   greed of power, clash of faiths—
Is a speck of dust on the great scale-pan.
Here from this mountain shore, headland
   beyond stormy headland plunging like
   dolphins through the blue sea-smoke 10
Into pale sea—look west at the hill of
water: it is half the planet: this dome,
   this half-globe, this bulging
Eyeball of water, arched over to Asia,
Australia and white Antarctica: those are
   the eyelids that never close; this is the
   staring unsleeping
Eye of the earth; and what it watches is
   not our wars.

Bone Thoughts on a Dry Day*
by GEORGE STARBUCK

Walking to the museum
over the Outer Drive,
I think, before I see them
dead, of the bones alive.

How perfectly the snake smooths over
   the fact 5
he strings sharp beads around that
   charmer's neck.

Bird bone may be breakable, but
have you ever held a cat's jaw shut?
Brittle as ice.

Take mice: 10
the mouse is a berry, his bones mere
   seeds:
step on him once and see.

You mustn't think that the fish
choke on those bones, or that chickens
   wish.

The wise old bat 15
hangs his bones in a bag.

Two chicks ride a bike,
unlike
that legless swinger of crutches, the
   ostrich.

Only the skull of a man is much of an
   ashtray. 20

Each owl
turns on a dowel.

When all the other tents are struck, an
   old
elephant pitches himself on his own poles.

But as for my bones— 25
tug of a toe, blunt-bowed barge of a
   thighbone,
gondola-squadron of ribs, and the jaw
   scow—
they weather the swing and storm of the
   flesh they plow,
out of conjecture of shore, one jolt from
   land.

I climb the museum steps like a beach. 30
There, on squared stone, some cast-up
   keels bleach.
Here, a dark sea speaks with white hands.

---

museum the Museum of Natural History in Chicago, which houses a spectacular collection of skeletal and stuffed animals.

* From *Bone Thoughts* by George Starbuck. Reprinted by permission of the Yale University Press. This poem first appeared in *The New Yorker*.

Surprised by Evening*
by ROBERT BLY

There is unknown dust that is near us,
Waves breaking on shores just over the
    hill,
Trees full of birds that we have never
    seen,
Nets drawn down with dark fish.

The evening arrives; we look up and it
    is there,   5
It has come through the nets of the stars,
Through the tissues of the grass,
Walking quietly over the asylums of the
    waters.

The day shall never end, we think:
We have hair that seems born for the
    daylight;   10
But, at last, the quiet waters of the night
    will rise,
And our skin shall see far off, as it does
    under water.

---

* Reprinted from *Silence in the Snowy Fields* by Robert Bly, Wesleyan University Press, 1962; copyright © 1962 by Robert Bly, and reprinted by permission of the author.

Spring Song*
by DONALD FINKEL

For a toad enjoys a finer prospect than another creature to compensate his lack . . . for there are stones, whose constituent particles are toads.—Christopher Smart.

B'york! but it's lovely under the leaf,
cool, green, slimy, sleeping,
quietly breathing at all my pores,
a jade toad in a rainy garden.

Down here, ceiling zero,   5
pulse steady, breathing slow,
heart smiling under his harness,
brain grinning behind the bone;

down here in the dead of winter
nothing happens, honey of time   10
slowly, sweetly melts and oozes
in the vein.

Tall in the saddle, hulking stranger,
looking for trouble, blind with anger,
you who think to stand between   15
the sun and me: think again.

Ten feet up you cannot see
further than your bleeding fist,
blows leap out from every tree,
the night is your antagonist.   20

Sad Goliath, gloomy champion,
lost in an unfriendly wood,
riding high, riding handsome,
ten feet up from where my gleaming
stones can do you any good: 25

far away your love is sleeping,
far away your king is dead,
your eye is almost shut with weeping,
your foot is bruised against my head.

---

* From the book *A Joyful Noise* by Donald Finkel, published by Atheneum. Copyright © 1965, 1966 by Donald Finkel. Reprinted by permission of Atheneum. This poem originally appeared in *The New Yorker*.

Cells Breathe in the Emptiness*

by GALWAY KINNELL

1

When the flowers turn to husks
And the great trees suddenly die
And rocks and old weasel bones lose
The little life they suddenly had
And the air quells and goes so still 5
It gives the ears something like the bends,
It is an errie thing to keep vigil,
The senses racing in the emptiness.

2

From the compost heap
Now arises the sound of the teeth 10
Of one of those sloppy green cabbage-
  worms
Eating his route through a cabbage,
Now snarling like a petite chainsaw,
  now droning on . . .

A butterfly blooms on a buttercup,
From the junkpile flames up a junco. 15

3

How many plants are really very quiet
  animals?
How many inert molecules are ready to
  break into life?

---

* From *Flower Herding on Mount Monodnock.* Copyright © 1964 by Galway Kinnell. Reprinted by permission of the publisher, Houghton Mifflin Company.

---

junco a type of American finch sometimes called a snowbird.

On War

War has been a constant subject of literature, in both poetry and prose, in all epochs and in all languages. A great portion of all epic poetry is concerned with honor won by clash of arms on the battlefield. But as we approach modern times, there is less and less glorification of war as such. War is, with increasing frequency, treated ironically. The soldier is more pitied than admired, and, even if some admiration is retained for the self-sacrifice of the individual soldier, the subject of war itself is handled rather cynically. These varying attitudes of admiration and pity for the soldier, and of exaltation and cynical deflation of achievement on the battlefield, are revealed in the tone of the poems in this unit.

To Lucasta, Going to the Wars
by RICHARD LOVELACE

Tell me not, sweet, I am unkind,
    That from the nunnery
Of thy chaste breast and quiet mind
    To war and arms I fly.

True, a new mistress now I chase,   5
    The first foe in the field;
And with a stronger faith embrace
    A sword, a horse, a shield.

Yet this inconstancy is such
    As thou too shalt adore;   10
I could not love thee, dear, so much,
    Loved I not honor more.

---
adore honor, praise.

The Destruction of Sennacherib
by GEORGE GORDON, LORD BYRON

The Assyrian came down like the wolf on the fold,
And his cohorts were gleaming in purple and gold;
And the sheen of their spears was like stars on the sea,
When the blue wave rolls nightly on deep Galilee.

Like the leaves of the forest when Summer is green,   5
That host with their banners at sunset were seen:
Like the leaves of the forest when Autumn hath blown,
That host on the marrow lay withered and strown.

For the Angel of Death spread his wings on the blast,
And breathed in the face of the foe as he passed;   10
And the eyes of the sleepers waxed deadly and chill,
And their hearts but once heaved, and forever grew still!

And there lay the steed with his nostril all wide,
But through it there rolled not the breath of his pride;
And the foam of his gaspings lay white on the turf,   15
And cold as the spray of the rock-beating surf.

And there lay the rider distorted and pale,
With dew on his brow, and the rust on his mail:
And the tents were all silent—the banners alone—
The lances uplifted—the trumpet unblown.   20

And the widows of Ashur are loud in their wail,
And the idols are broken in the temple of Baal;
And the might of the Gentile, unsmote by the sword,
Hath melted like snow in the glance of the Lord!

Sennacherib an Assyrian King (705-681 B.C.), whose forces were almost destroyed by plague at Jerusalem.

Ashur Assyria.   *Baal* an Assyrian deity.

Channel Firing

by THOMAS HARDY

That night your great guns, unawares,
Shook all our coffins as we lay,
And broke the chancel window-squares,
We thought it was the Judgment-day

And sat upright. While drearisome   5
Arose the howl of wakened hounds:
The mouse let fall the altar-crumb,
The worms drew back into the mounds,

The glebe cow drooled. Till God called,
    "No;
It's gunnery practice out at sea   10
Just as before you went below;
The world is as it used to be:

"All nations striving strong to make
Red war yet redder. Mad as hatters
They do no more for Christès sake   15
Than you who are helpless in such
    matters.

"That this is not the judgment-hour
For some of them's a blessed thing,
For if it were they'd have to scour
Hell's floor for so much threatening. . . .   20

"Ha, ha. It will be warmer when
I blow the trumpet (if indeed
I ever do; for you are men,
And rest eternal sorely need)."

So down we lay again. "I wonder,   25
Will the world ever saner be,"
Said one, "than when He sent us under
In our indifferent century!"

And many a skeleton shook his head.
"Instead of preaching forty year,"   30
My neighbour Parson Thirdly said,
"I wish I had stuck to pipes and beer."

Again the guns disturbed the hour,
Roaring their readiness to avenge,
As far inland as Stourton Tower,   35
And Camelot, and starlit Stonehenge.

---

chancel sanctuary.   *glebe* land belonging to church.

* Reprinted with permission of The Macmillan Company, the Hardy Estate, Macmillan & Co. Ltd., London, and The Macmillan Company of Canada Limited from *Collected Poems of Thomas Hardy.* Copyright 1925 by The Macmillan Company.

Stourton Tower Stourton in Staffordshire, England. *Camelot* in West of England, and legendary capital of Arthur's kingdom.   *Stonehenge* ancient Druidical center near Salisbury.

The Man He Killed

by THOMAS HARDY

"Had he and I but met
    By some old ancient inn,
We should have sat us down to wet
    Right many a nipperkin!

"But ranged as infantry,   5
    And staring face to face,
I shot at him as he at me,
    And killed him in his place.

"I shot him dead because—
    Because he was my foe,   10
Just so: my foe of course he was;
    That's clear enough; although

---

nipperkin a measure of liquor, less than half a pint.

* Reprinted with permission of The Macmillan Company, the Hardy Estate, Macmillan & Co. Ltd., London, and The Macmillan Company of Canada Limited from *Collected Poems of Thomas Hardy.* Copyright 1925 by The Macmillan Company.

"He thought he'd 'list, perhaps,
  Off-hand like—just as I—
Was out of work—had sold his traps— 15
  No other reason why.

"Yes; quaint and curious war is!
  You shoot a fellow down
You'd treat if met where any bar is,
  Or help to half-a-crown." 20

The Soldier

by GERARD MANLEY HOPKINS

Yes. Why do we all, seeing of a soldier, bless him? bless
Our redcoats, our tars? Both these being, the greater part,
But frail clay, nay but foul clay. Here it is: the heart,
Since, proud, it calls the calling manly, gives a guess
That, hopes that, makesbelieve, the men must be no less; 5
It fancies, feigns, deems, dears the artist after his art;
And fain will find as sterling all as all is smart,
And scarlet wear the spirit of war there express.

Mark Christ our King. He knows war, served this soldiering through;
He of all can reeve a rope best. There he bides in bliss 10
Now, and seeing somewhere some man do all that man can do,
For love he leans forth, needs his neck must fall on, kiss,
And cry 'O Christ-done deed! So God-made flesh does too:
Were I come o'er again, cries Christ 'it should be this.'

---

tars sailors.   *dears* considers dear, endears.

reeve pass a rope through holes.

1887*

by A. E. HOUSMAN

From Clee to heaven the beacon burns,
  The shires have seen it plain,
From north and south the sign returns
  And beacons burn again.

Look left, look right, the hills are bright, 5
  The dales are light between,
Because 'tis fifty years to-night
  That God has saved the Queen.

Now, when the flame they watch not towers
  About the soil they trod; 10
Lads, we'll remember friends of ours
  Who shared the work with God.

To skies that knit their heartstrings right,
  To fields that bred them brave,
The saviours come not home to-night: 15
  Themselves they could not save.

1887 golden jubilee year of Queen Victoria. *Clee* a town in Shropshire, England.

* From "A Shropshire Lad"—Authorised Edition—from *The Collected Poems of A. E. Housman.* Copyright 1939, 1940, © 1959 by Holt, Rinehart and Winston, Inc. Copyright © 1967, 1968 by Robert E. Symons. Reprinted by permission of Holt, Rinehart and Winston, Inc., and The Society of Authors as the literary representative of the Estate of A. E. Housman, and Jonathan Cape Ltd., publishers of A. E. Housman's *Collected Poems.*

It dawns in Asia, tombstones show
   And Shropshire names are read;
And the Nile spills his overflow
   Beside the Severn's dead.

We pledge in peace by farm and town   20
   The Queen they served in war,
And fire the beacons up and down
   The land they perished for.

'God save the Queen' we living sing,
   From height to height 'tis heard;   25
And with the rest your voices ring,
   Lads of the Fifty-third.

Oh, God will save her, fear you not:
   Be you the men you've been,
Get you the sons your fathers got,
   And God will save the Queen.

Asia eastern locale of foreign engagements. *Shropshire* western shire in England from which the dead soldiers came. *Nile* in Egypt, scene of other foreign wars. *Severn* river in western England.

Arms and the Boy*
by WILFRED OWEN

Let the boy try along this bayonet-blade
How cold steel is, and keen with hunger
   of blood;
Blue with all malice, like a madman's
   flash;
And thinly drawn with famishing for
   flesh.

Lend him to stroke these blind, blunt
   bullet-heads   5
Which long to nuzzle in the hearts of
   lads,
Or give him cartridges of fine zinc teeth,
Sharp with the sharpness of grief and
   death.

For his teeth seem for laughing round
   an apple.
There lurk no claws behind his fingers
   supple;   10
And God will grow no talons at his heels,
Nor antlers through the thickness of his
   curls.

Arms, etc. an ironic play on the opening words of Virgil's heroic poem *Arma virumque cano*, arms and the man I sing.

* From *The Collected Poems of Wilfred Owen*. Copyright © 1963 by Chatto & Windus, Ltd. Reprinted by permission of New Directions Publishing Corporation, Mr. Harold Owen, and Chatto and Windus Ltd.

Anthem for Doomed Youth*
by WILFRED OWEN

What passing-bells for these who die as
   cattle?
   Only the monstrous anger of the guns.
   Only the stuttering rifles' rapid rattle

Can patter out their hasty orisons.
No mockeries for them from prayers or
   bells,   5
   Nor any voice of mourning save the
      choirs,—
The shrill, demented choirs of wailing
   shells;
   And bugles calling for them from sad
      shires.

---

* From *The Collected Poems of Wilfred Owen*. Copyright © 1963 by Chatto & Windus, Ltd. Reprinted by permission of New Directions Publishing Corporation, Mr. Harold Owen, and Chatto and Windus Ltd.

What candles may be held to speed them
    all?
  Not in the hands of boys, but in their
    eyes
Shall shine the holy glimmers of good-
    byes.

The pallor of girls' brows shall be their
    pall;
Their flowers the tenderness of silent
    minds,
And each slow dusk a drawing-down of
    blinds.

Ultima Ratio Regum*
by STEPHEN SPENDER

The guns spell money's ultimate reason
In letters of lead on the Spring hillside.
But the boy lying dead under the olive
    trees
Was too young and too silly
To have been notable to their important
    eye.
He was a better target for a kiss.

When he lived, tall factory hooters never
    summoned him
Nor did restaurant plate-glass doors
    revolve to wave him in
His name never appeared in the papers.
The world maintained its traditional wall
Round the dead with their gold sunk
    deep as a well,
Whilst his life, intangible as a Stock
    Exchange rumour, drifted outside.

O too lightly he threw down his cap
One day when the breeze threw petals
    from the trees.
The unflowering wall sprouted with guns,
Machine-gun anger quickly scythed the
    grasses;
Flags and leaves fell from hands and
    branches;
The tweed cap rotted in the nettles.

Consider his life which was valueless
In terms of employment, hotel ledgers,
    news files.
Consider. One bullet in ten thousand
    kills a man.
Ask. Was so much expenditure justified
On the death of one so young, and so
    silly
Lying under the olive trees, O world,
    O death?

Ultima, etc. the last justification of kings.   *silly* helpless, weak.

* Copyright 1942 by Stephen Spender. Reprinted from *Selected Poems*, by Stephen Spender, by permission of Random House, Inc., and from *Collected Poems 1928–1953* by *Stephen Spender* by permission of Faber and Faber Ltd.

The Death of the Ball Turret Gunner*
by RANDALL JARRELL

From my mother's sleep I fell into the
    State,
And I hunched in its belly till my wet
    fur froze.
Six miles from earth, loosed from its
    dream of life,
I woke to black flak and the nightmare
    fighters.
When I died they washed me out of the
    turret with a hose.

---

* Reprinted with the permission of Farrar, Straus & Giroux, Inc., from *Complete Poems* by Randall Jarrell. Copyright © 1945, 1951, 1955 by Randall Jarrell, copyright © 1969 by Mrs. Randall Jarrell.

Losses*

by RANDALL JARRELL

It was not dying: everybody died.
It was not dying: we had died before
In the routine crashes—and our fields
Called up the papers, wrote home to our
    folks,
And the rates rose, all because of us.   5
We died on the wrong page of the
    almanac,
Scattered on mountains fifty miles away;
Diving on haystacks, fighting with a
    friend,
We blazed up on the lines we never saw.
We died like ants or pets or foreigners.   10
(When he left high school nothing else
    had died
For us to figure we had died like.)

In our new planes, with our new crews,
    we bombed
The ranges by the desert or the shore,
Fired at towed targets, waited for our
    scores—   15
And turned into replacements and woke
    up
One morning, over England, operational.
It wasn't different: but if we died
It was not an accident but a mistake
(But an easy one for anyone to make).   20
We read our mail and counted up our
    missions—
In bombers named for girls, we burned
The cities we had learned about in
    school—
Till our lives wore out; our bodies lay
    among
The people we had killed and never seen.   25
When we lasted long enough they gave
    us medals;
When we died they said, "Our casualties
    were low."
They said, "Here are the maps"; we
    burned the cities.

It was not dying—no, not ever dying;
But the night I died I dreamed that I
    was dead,   30
And the cities said to me: "Why are you
    dying?
We are satisfied, if you are; but why did
    I die?"

---

* Reprinted with the permission of Farrar, Straus & Giroux, Inc., from *Complete Poems* by Randall Jarrell. Copyright © 1945, 1951, 1955 by Randall Jarrell, copyright © 1969 by Mrs. Randall Jarrell.

The Fury of Aerial Bombardment*

by RICHARD EBERHART

You would think the fury of aerial
    bombardment
Would rouse God to relent; the infinite
    spaces
Are still silent. He looks on shock-pried
    faces.
History, even, does not know what is
    meant.
You would feel that after so many
    centuries   5
God would give man to repent; yet he
    can kill

---

* From *Collected Poms 1930–1960* by Richard Eberhart. Reprinted by permission of Oxford University Press, Inc., the author, and Chatto and Windus Ltd.

As Cain could, but with multitudinous
    will,
No farther advanced than in his ancient
    furies.

Was man made stupid to see his own
    stupidity?
Is God by definition indifferent, beyond
    us all?   10
Is the eternal truth man's fighting soul
Wherein the Beast ravens in its own
    avidity?

Of Van Wettering I speak, and Averill,
Names on a list, whose faces I do not
    recall
But they are gone to early death, who
    late in school   15
Distinguished the belt feed lever from the
    belt holding pawl.

---

pawl a device preventing movement of a wheel except in one direction.

the season 'tis, my lovely lambs*

by e. e. cummings

the season 'tis, my lovely lambs
of Sumner Volstead Christ and Co.
the epoch of Mann's righteousness
the age of dollars and no sense.
Which being quite beyond dispute   5

as prove from Troy (N. Y.) to Cairo
(Egypt) the luminous dithyrambs
of large immaculate unmute
antibolshevistic gents
(each manufacturing word by word   10
his own unrivalled brand of pyro
-technic blurb anent the (hic)
hero dead that gladly (sic)
in far lands perished of unheard
of maladies including flu)   15

my little darlings, let us now
passionately remember how—

braving the worst, of peril heedless,
each braver than the other, each
(a typewriter within his reach)   20
upon his fearless derrière
sturdily seated—Colonel Needless
To Name and General You know who
a string of pretty medals drew

(while messrs jack james john and jim   25
in token of their country's love
received my dears the order of
The Artificial Arm and Limb)

—or, since bloodshed and kindred questions
inhibit unprepared digestions,   30
come: let us mildly contemplate
beginning with his wellfilled pants
earth's biggest grafter, nothing less;
the Honorable Mr. (guess)
who, breathing on the ear of fate,   35
landed a seat in the legislat-
ure whereas tommy so and so
(an erring child of circumstance
whom the bulls nabbed at 33rd)

pulled six months for selling snow   40

Sumner Volstead Christ and Co. perhaps John S. Sumner is alluded to—a well-known Methodist lobbyist for censorship; the Volstead Act had to do with prohibition, the puritanical defenders of which, of course, identified themselves with Christ. *Mann's* the Mann Act, the White-slave-traffic act.

* Copyright, 1926, by Horace Liveright; renewed, 1954 by E. E. Cummings. Reprinted from his volume, *Poems 1923–1954*, by permission of Harcourt Brace Jovanovich, Inc.

---

bulls police.   *snow* dope.

next to of course god america i*
by e. e. cummings

"next to of course god america i
love you land of the pilgrims and so forth oh
say can you see by the dawn's early my
country 'tis of centuries come and go
and are no more what of it we should worry

in every language even deafanddumb
thy sons acclaim your glorious name by gorry
by jingo by gee by gosh by gum
why talk of beauty what could be more beautiful than these heroic happy dead
who rushed like lions to the roaring slaughter
they did not stop to think they died instead
then shall the voice of liberty be mute?"

He spoke. And drank rapidly a glass of water

---

* Copyright, 1926, by Horace Liveright; renewed, 1954, by E. E. Cummings. Reprinted from his volume, *Poems 1923–1954*, by permission of Harcourt Brace Jovanovich, Inc.

Watching the Jet Planes Dive*
by WILLIAM STAFFORD

We must go back and find a trail on the
    ground
back of the forest and mountain on the
    slow land;
we must begin to circle on the intricate
    sod.
By such wild beginnings without help we
    may find
the small trail on through the buffalo-
    bean vines.   5

We must go back with noses and palms
    of our hands,
and climb over the map in far places,
    everywhere,
and lie down whenever there is doubt
    and sleep there.
If roads are unconnected we must make
    a path,
no matter how far it is, or how lowly we
    arrive.   10

We must find something forgotten by
    everyone alive,
and make some fabulous gesture when
    the sun goes down
as they do by custom in little Mexico
    towns
where they crawl for some ritual up a
    rocky steep.
The jet planes dive; we must travel on
    our knees.   15

---

* Copyright © 1960 by William Stafford; reprinted by permission of the author. This poem first appeared in *West of Your City* by William Stafford, published by Talisman Press.

The Hometown Hero Comes Home*
by DAVID ETTER

This train, two Illinois counties late,
slips through jungles of corn and hot
    leaves,
and the blazing helmets of huge barns.

My head spins with too much beer and
    sun
and the mixed feelings of going home.   5

The coach window has melted my face.
I itch where a birthmark darkens my skin.

The Jewish woman who sits next to me
sheds tears for a son, dead in Viet Nam.
Her full lips are the color of crushed
    plums.   10
I want to go off with her to some lost
fishing village on the Mississippi
and be quiet among stones and small
    boats.

My fever breaks in the Galena hills.

It's too humid: no one will meet me.   15
And there are no brass bands in Dubuque.

---

* Copyright 1965 by the Massachusetts Review Inc., reprinted from Dave Etter: *Go Read The River,* Copyright 1966, The University of Nebraska Press, and used by permission of the publisher.

Love

    Love has so long and so frequently been the theme of lyric poetry that today "lyric" has almost become synonymous with "love song." Sometimes it is the emotion of love itself that poets have made the subject of their song, but more often it is the person of the beloved. The sincere, tested love of husband and wife, the love of friend for friend, of father for a child or a child for a father, have at times invited mementos in song; but by far the greatest number of love songs have given voice to the young romantic love of sweethearts. Each of these loves has found expression in one or the other of the poems in this unit. And love has been handled by the poets with every conceivable emotional tone—sincerely and simply, artificially and with elaborate convention and conceit, ironically and with tongue in cheek. These and other tones and poetic textures will be discovered in even this brief a selection of love poetry from several centuries.

My Love Is Like to Ice
by EDMUND SPENSER

My love is like to ice and I to fire;
How comes it then that this her cold so great
Is not dissolved through my so hot desire,
But harder grows the more I her entreat?
Or how comes it that my exceeding heat   5
Is not delayed by her heart frozen cold,
But that I burn much more in boiling sweat
And feel my flames augmented manifold?
What more miraculous thing may be told,
That fire, which all things melts, should harden ice,   10
And ice, which is congealed with senseless cold,
Should kindle fire by wonderful device?
Such is the power of love in gentle mind,
That it can alter all the course of kind.

---
love his lover.
kind nature.

Sonnets
by WILLIAM SHAKESPEARE

116

Let me not to the marriage of true minds
Admit impediments. Love is not love
Which alters when it alteration finds,
Or bends with the remover to remove.
O, no! it is an ever-fixed mark   5
That looks on tempests and is never shaken;
It is the star to every wand'ring bark,
Whose worth's unknown, although his height be taken.
Love's not Time's fool, though rosy lips and cheeks
Within his bending sickle's compass come;   10
Love alters not with his brief hours and weeks,
But bears it out even to the edge of doom.
    If this be error and upon me proved,
    I never writ, nor no man ever loved.

130

My mistress' eyes are nothing like the sun;
Coral is far more red than her lips' red;
If snow be white, why then her breasts are dun;
If hairs be wires, black wires grow on her head.
I have seen roses damask'd, red and white,   5
But no such roses see I in her cheeks;
And in some perfumes is there more delight
Than in the breath that from my mistress reeks.
I love to hear her speak, yet well I know
That music hath a far more pleasing sound;   10
I grant I never saw a goddess go;
My mistress, when she walks, treads on the ground:
    And yet, by heaven, I think my love as rare
    As any she beli'd with false compare.

---
dun a dull brown.

A Litany

by SIR PHILIP SIDNEY

Ring out your bells, let mourning shows
    be spread;
For Love is dead.
    All Love is dead, infected
With plague of deep disdain;
    Worth, as nought worth, rejected,   5
And Faith fair scorn doth gain.
    From so ungrateful fancy,
    From such a female franzy,
      From them that use men thus,
      Good Lord, deliver us!   10

Weep, neighbors, weep! do you not hear
    it said
That Love is dead?
    His death-bed, peacock's folly;
His winding-sheet is shame;
    His will, false-seeming holy;   15
His sole executor, blame.
    From so ungrateful fancy,
    From such a female franzy,
      From them that use men thus,
      Good Lord, deliver us!   20

Let dirge be sung and trentals rightly
    read,
For Love is dead.
    Sir Wrong his tomb ordaineth
My mistress Marble-heart,
    Which epitaph containeth,   25
"Her eyes were once his dart."
    From so ungrateful fancy,
    From such a female franzy,
      From them that use men thus,
      Good Lord, deliver us!   30

Alas! I lie, rage hath this error bred;
Love is not dead.
    Love is not dead, but sleepeth
In her unmatchèd mind,
    Where she his counsel keepeth,   35
Till due desert she find.
    Therefore from so vile fancy,
    To call such wit a franzy,
      Who Love can temper thus,
      Good Lord, deliver us!   40

---

disdain This whole poem is a playful handling of the courtly love situation in which the lady was scornful of her lover. *franzy* frenzy, madness. *trentals* a series of thirty Masses offered for the dead. *wit* intellgience.

A Valediction: Forbidding Mourning

by JOHN DONNE

As virtuous men pass mildly away,
    And whisper to their souls, to go,
Whilst some of their sad friends do say,
    The breath goes now, and some say, no:

So let us melt, and make no noise,   5
    No tear-floods nor sigh-tempests move,
T'were profanation of our joys
    To tell the laity our love.

Moving of th' earth brings harms and fears,
    Men reckon what it did and meant,   10

But trepidation of the spheres,
    Though greater far, is innocent.

Dull sublunary lovers' love
    (Whose soul is sense) cannot admit
Absence, because it does remove   15
    Those things which elemented it.

But we by a love, so much refined
    That our selves know not what it is,
Inter-assurèd of the mind,
    Care less, eyes, lips, and hands to miss.   20

Our two souls therefore, which are one,
   Though I must go, endure not yet
A breach, but an expansion,
   Like gold to airy thinness beat.

If they be two, they are two so   25
   As stiff twin compasses are two,
Thy soul, the fixt foot, makes no show
   To move, but doth, if th' other do.

And though it in the center sit,
   Yet when the other far doth roam,   30
It leans, and hearkens after it,
   And grows erect as that comes home.

Such wilt thou be to me, who must,
   Like the other foot, obliquely run;
Thy firmness makes my circle just,
   And makes me end where I begun.

Love's Diet

by JOHN DONNE

To what a cumbersome unwieldiness
And burdenous corpulence my love had
     grown,
   But that I did, to make it less,
   And keep it in proportion,
Give it a diet, made it feed upon   5
That which love worst endures, discretion.

Above one sigh a day I allowed him not,
Of which my fortune, and my faults had
     part;
   And if sometimes by stealth he got
   A she sigh from my mistress' heart,   10
And thought to feast on that, I let him see
'Twas neither very sound, nor meant to
     me.

If he wrung from me a tear, I brined it so
With scorn or shame, that him it
     nourished not;
   If he sucked hers, I let him know   15
   'Twas not a tear, which he had got;

His drink was counterfeit, as was his meat;
For, eyes which roll towards all, weep not,
     but sweat.

Whatever he would dictate, I writ that,
But burnt my letters; when she writ to me,   20
   And that that favour made him fat,
   I said, if any title be
Conveyed by this, Ah, what doth it avail,
To be the fortieth name in an entail?

Thus I reclaimed my buzzard love, to fly   25
At what, and when, and how, and where
     I choose;
   Now negligent of sport I lie,
   And now as other falconers use,
I spring a mistress, swear, write, sigh and
     weep;
And the game killed, or lost, go talk, and
     sleep.

---

entail   a legal document settling and estate.

Love

by GEORGE HERBERT

Love bade me welcome: yet my soul drew
     back,
          Guiltie of dust and sinne.
But quick-ey'd Love observing me grow
     slack
          From my first entrance in,
Drew nearer to me, sweetly questioning,   5
          If I lack'd any thing.

A guest, I answer'd, worthy to be here:
          Love said, you shall be he.
I the unkinde, ungratefull? Ah my deare,
          I cannot look on thee.   10
Love took my hand, and smiling did
     reply,
          Who made the eyes but I?

Truth Lord, but I have marr'd them: let
   my shame
          Go where it does deserve.
And know you not, sayes Love, who bore
   the blame?   15

        My deare, then I will serve.
You must sit down, sayes Love, and taste
   my meat:
          So I did sit and eat.

On a Girdle
by EDMUND WALLER

That which her slender waist confined
Shall now my joyful temples bind;
No monarch but would give his crown,
His arms might do what this has done.

   It was my heaven's extremest sphere,   5
The pale which held that lovely deer;

My joy, my grief, my hope, my love,
Did all within this circle move.

   A narrow compass, and yet there
Dwelt all that's good and all that's fair;   10
Give me but what this ribband bound,
Take all the rest the sun goes round!

---
pale enclosure.

John Anderson, My Jo
by ROBERT BURNS

John Anderson my jo, John,
   When we were first acquent,
Your locks were like the raven,
   Your bonie brow was brent;
But now your brow is beld, John,   5
   Your locks are like the snaw,
But blessings on your frosty pow,
   John Anderson my jo!

John Anderson my jo, John,
   We clamb the hill thegither,   10
And monie a cantie day, John,
   We've had wi' ane anither;
Now we maun totter down, John,
   And hand in hand we'll go,
And sleep thegither at the foot,   15
   John Anderson my jo!

Jo sweetheart.   *brent* smooth.   *beld* bald.
pow head.

cantie happy.   *maun* must.

A Red, Red Rose
by ROBERT BURNS

O, my luve is like a red, red rose,
   That's newly sprung in June.
O, my luve is like the melodie,
   That's sweetly played in tune.

As fair art thou, my bonie lass,   5
   So deep in luve am I,
And I will luve thee still, my dear,
   Till a' the seas gang dry.

Till a' the seas gang dry, my dear,
   And the rocks melt wi' the sun!   10
And I will luve thee still, my dear,
   While the sands o' life shall run.

And fare thee weel, my only luve,
   And fare thee weel a while!
And I will come again, my luve,   15
   Tho' it were ten thousand mile!

She Dwelt among the Untrodden Ways
by WILLIAM WORDSWORTH

She dwelt among the untrodden ways
   Beside the springs of Dove,
A Maid whom there were none to praise
   And very few to love:

A violet by a mossy stone   5
   Half hidden from the eye!

—Fair as a star, when only one
   Is shining in the sky.

She lived unknown, and few could know
   When Lucy ceased to be;   10
But she is in her grave, and, oh,
   The difference to me!

Dove there are several rivers by that name known to Wordsworth.

Lucy it isn't known who Lucy was; the value of the poem in no way depends on her identity.

How Do I Love Thee?
by ELIZABETH BARRETT BROWNING

How do I love thee? Let me count the ways.
I love thee to the depth and breadth and height
My soul can reach, when feeling out of sight
For the ends of Being and ideal Grace.
I love thee to the level of everyday's   5
Most quiet need, by sun and candle-light.
I love thee freely, as men strive for Right;
I love thee purely, as they turn from Praise.
I love thee with the passion put to use
In my old griefs, and with my childhood's faith.   10
I love thee with a love I seemed to lose
With my lost saints—I love thee with the breath,
Smiles, tears, of all my life!—and, if God choose,
I shall but love thee better after death.

A Prayer for My Daughter*
by WILLIAM BUTLER YEATS

Once more the storm is howling, and half hid
Under this cradle-hood and coverlid
My child sleeps on. There is no obstacle
But Gregory's wood and one bare hill
Whereby the haystack-and-roof-leveling wind,   5
Bred on the Atlantic, can be stayed;
And for an hour I have walked and prayed
Because of the great gloom that is in my mind.

I have walked and prayed for this young child an hour

---

* Reprinted with permission of The Macmillan Company, Mr. Michael Butler Yeats, A. P. Watt & Son, Macmillan & Co. Ltd., London, and The Macmillan Company of Canada Limited, from *Collected Poems of William Butler Yeats.* Copyright 1924 by The Macmillan Company, renewed 1952 by Bertha Georgie Yeats.

And heard the sea-wind scream upon the tower,
And under the arches of the bridge, and scream
In the elms above the flooded stream;
Imagining in excited reverie
That the future years had come,
Dancing to a frenzied drum,
Out of the murderous innocence of the sea.

May she be granted beauty and yet not
Beauty to make a stranger's eye distraught,
Or hers before a looking-glass, for such,
Being made beautiful overmuch,
Consider beauty a sufficient end,
Lose natural kindness and may be
The heart-revealing intimacy
That chooses right, and never find a friend.

Helen being chosen found life flat and dull
And later had much trouble from a fool,
While that great Queen, that rose out of the spray,
Being fatherless could have her way,
Yet chose a bandy-leggèd smith for man.
It's certain that fine women eat
A crazy salad with their meat,
Whereby the Horn of Plenty is undone.

In courtesy I'd have her chiefly learned;
Hearts are not had as a gift, but hearts are earned
By those that are not entirely beautiful;
Yet many, that have played the fool
For beauty's very self, has charm made wise,
And many a poor man that has roved,
Loved and thought himself beloved,
From a glad kindness cannot take his eyes.

May she become a flourishing hidden tree
That all her thoughts may like the linnet be,
And have no business but dispensing round
Their magnanimities of sound,
Nor but in merriment begin a chase,
Nor but in merriment a quarrel.
Oh, may she live like some green laurel
Rooted in one dear perpetual place.

My mind, because the minds that I have loved,
The sort of beauty that I have approved,
Prosper but little, has dried up of late,
Yet knows that to be choked with hate
May well be of all evil chances chief.
If there's no hatred in a mind
Assault and battery of the wind
Can never tear the linnet from the leaf.

An intellectual hatred is the worst,
So let her think opinions are accursed.
Have I not seen the loveliest woman born
Out of the month of Plenty's horn,
Because of her opinionated mind
Barter that horn and every good
By quiet natures understood
For an old bellows full of angry wind?

Considering that, all hatred driven hence,
The soul recovers radical innocence
And learns at last that it is self-delighting,
Self-appeasing, self-affrighting,
And that its own sweet will is heaven's will;
She can, though every face should scowl
And every windy quarter howl
Or every bellows burst, be happy still.

And may her bridegroom bring her to a house
Where all's accustomed, ceremonious;
For arrogance and hatred are the wares
Peddled in the thoroughfares.
How but in custom and in ceremony
Are innocence and beauty born?
Ceremony's a name for the rich horn,
And custom for the spreading laurel tree.

Helen of Troy, chosen and stolen from Menelaus by Paris. *Queen* Greek goddess, Aphrodite, the foam-born, because she was supposed to have come from the sea. She was identified with Venus by the Romans. *bandy-leggèd smith* Vulcan, the smithy.

Down by the Salley Garden*
by WILLIAM BUTLER YEATS

Down by the salley gardens my love and
    I did meet;
She passed the salley gardens with little
    snow-white feet.
She bid me take love easy, as the leaves
    grow on the tree;

But I, being young and foolish, with her
    would not agree.

In a field by the river my love and I did
    stand,   5
And on my leaning shoulder she laid her
    snow-white hand.
She bid me take life easy, as the grass
    grows on the weirs;
But I was young and foolish, and now
    am full of tears.

Salley willow.
* Reprinted with permission of The Macmillan Company, Mr. Michael Butler Yeats, A. P. Watt & Son, Macmillan & Co. Ltd., London, and The Macmillan Company of Canada Limited, from *Collected Poems of William Butler Yeats.* Copyright 1906 by The Macmillan Company, renewed 1934 by William Butler Yeats.

weirs milldams.

Love Is Not All*
by EDNA ST. VINCENT MILLAY

Love is not all: it is not meat nor drink
Nor slumber nor a roof against the rain;
Nor yet a floating spar to men that sink
And rise and sink and rise and sink again;
Love can not fill the thickened lung with
    breath,   5
Nor clean the blood, nor set the fractured
    bone;

Yet many a man is making friends with
    death
Even as I speak, for lack of love alone.
It well may be that in a difficult hour,
Pinned down by pain and moaning for
    release,   10
Or nagged by want past resolution's
    power,
I might be driven to sell your love for
    peace,
Or trade the memory of this night for food.
It well may be. I do not think I would.

---
* From *Collected Poems,* Harper & Row. Copyright 1931, 1958 by Edna St. Vincent Millay and Norma Millay Ellis.

if everything happens that can't be done*
by e. e. cummings

if everything happens that can't be done
(and anything's righter
than books

could plan)
the stupidest teacher will almost guess   5
(with a run
skip
around we go yes)
there's nothing as something as one

---
* Copyright, 1944, by E. E. Cummings. Reprinted from his volume, *Poems 1923–1954,* by permission of Harcourt Brace Jovanovich, Inc.

one hasn't a why or because or although 10
(and buds know better
than books
don't grow)
one's anything old being everything new
(with a what 15
which
around we come who)
one's everyanything so

so world is a leaf so tree is a bough
(and birds sing sweeter 20
than books
tell how)
so here is away and so your is a my
(with a down
up 25
around again fly)
forever was never till now

now i love you and you love me
(and books are shuter
than books 30
can be)
and deep in the high that does nothing but fall
(with a shout
each
around we go all) 35
there's somebody calling who's we

we're anything brighter than even the sun
(we're everything greater
than books
might mean) 40
we're everyanything more than believe
(with a spin
leap
alive we're alive)
we're wonderful one times one 45

Love Calls Us to the Things of This World*
by RICHARD WILBUR

The eyes open to a cry of pulleys,
And spirited from sleep, the astounded
    soul
Hangs for a moment bodiless and simple
As false dawn.
                  Outside the open window
The morning air is all awash with angels. 5

  Some are in bed-sheets, some are in
    blouses,
Some are in smocks: but truly there they
    are.
Now they are rising together in calm
    swells
Of halcyon feeling, filling whatever they
    wear
With the deep joy of their impersonal
    breathing; 10

Now they are flying in place, conveying
The terrible speed of their omnipresence,
    moving
And staying like white water; and now
    of a sudden
They swoon down into so rapt a quiet
That nobody seems to be there.
                  The soul shrinks 15

  From all that it is about to
    remember,
From the punctual rape of every blessèd
    day,
And cries,
        "Oh, let there be nothing on
        earth but laundry,
Nothing but rosy hands in the rising
    steam
And clear dances done in the sight of
    heaven." 20

  Yet, as the sun acknowledges
With a warm look the world's hunks
    and colors,

halcyon   the halcyon, a kingfisher, was, according to legend, supposed to nest on the surface of the sea at certain very calm seasons.

* From *Things of This World* © 1956, by Richard Wilbur. Reprinted by permission of Harcourt Brace Jovanovich, Inc.

The soul descends once more in bitter
    love
To accept the waking body, saying
    now
In a changed voice as the man yawns
    and rises,   25

    "Bring them down from their ruddy
        gallows;

Let there be clean linen for the backs
    of thieves;
Let lovers go fresh and sweet to be
    undone,
And the heaviest nuns walk in a pure
    floating
Of dark habits,
        keeping their difficult
        balance."   30

Love, It Is Time I Memorized Your Phone*
by KARL SHAPIRO

Love, it is time I memorized your phone
Number and made it part of what I keep
Not in a black book but in living bone
Of fingertips that dial you in my sleep.
Time that the Roman wires of my heart   5
Lead all to you like artery or vein
Or tourist roadmap or a fever chart,

Since you are central now to my love's
    brain.
Teri, I have your number in my blood,
Your name is red and racing in my pulse   10
And all my nerves are ringing as they
    should
Through the night's black and sweet
    umbilicus
Connecting our two lives with strings
    of words
That you send back this spring like flights
    of birds.

---

* Copyright © 1967 by Karl Shapiro. Reprinted from *White-Haired Lover*, by Karl Shapiro, by permission of Random House, Inc.

I Knew a Woman*
by THEODORE ROETHKE

I knew a woman, lovely in her bones,
When small birds sighed, she would
    sigh back at them;
Ah, when she moved, she moved more
    ways than one:
The shapes a bright container can
    contain!
Of her choice virtues only gods should
    speak,   5
Or English poets who grew up on Greek
(I'd have them sing in chorus, cheek to
    cheek).

How well her wishes went! She stroked
    my chin,
She taught me Turn, and Counter-turn,
    and Stand;
She taught me Touch, that undulant
    white skin;   10
I nibbled meekly from her proffered
    hand;
She was the sickle; I, poor I, the rake,
Coming behind her for her pretty sake
(But what prodigious mowing we did
    make).

---

* "I Knew a Woman" by Theodore Roethke, copyright 1954 by Theodore Roethke. From *The Collected Poems of Theodore Roethke*. Reprinted by permission of Doubleday & Company, Inc.

Loves like a gander, and adores a goose: 15
Her full lips pursed, the errant note to
    seize;

She played it quick, she played it light
   and loose;
My eyes, they dazzled at her flowing
   knees;
Her several parts could keep a pure repose,
Or one hip quiver with a mobile nose   20
(She moved in circles, and those circles
   moved).

Let seed be grass, and grass turn into hay:
I'm martyr to a motion not my own;
What's freedom for? To know eternity.
I swear she cast a shadow white as stone.   25
But who would count eternity in days?
These old bones live to learn her wanton
   ways:
(I measure time by how a body sways).

Defense Rests*
by VASSAR MILLER

I want
a love to hold
in my hand because love
is too much for the heart to bear
alone.   5

Then stop
mouthing to me
"Faith and Sacraments" when
the Host feather-heavy weighs down
my soul.   10

So I
blaspheme! My Lord,
John's head on your breast or
Mary's lips on your feet, would you
agree?   15

If this
is not enough—
upon Your sweat, Your thirst,
Your nails, and nakedness I rest
my case.   20

---

* Copyright © 1960 by Vassar Miller. Reprinted from *Wage War on Silence*, by Vassar Miller, by permission of Wesleyan University Press.

Notes from a Suburban Heart*
by MONA VAN DUYN

*Freud says that ideas are libidinal cathexes, that is
to say, acts of love.—Norman O. Brown*

It's time to put fertilizer on the grass again.
The last time I bought it, the stuff was smelly and black,
and said "made from Philadelphia sewage" on the sack.
It's true that the grass shot up in a violent green,
but my grass-roots patriotism tells me to stick   5
to St. Louis sewage, and if the Mississippi isn't thick
enough to put in a bag and spread on a lawn,
I'll sprinkle 5-10-5 from nobody's home,
that is to say . . .

---

cathexes Cathexis is the concentration of desire upon some object or idea.
* From *A Time of Bees*, by Mona Van Duyn. Reprinted by permission of The University of North Carolina Press.

it's been a long winter. The new feeder scared off the birds 10
for the first month it was up. Those stupid starvelings,
puffed up like popcorn against the cold, thought the thing
was a death-trap. The seeds and suet on its boards
go down their gullets now, and come out song,
but scot-free bugs slit up the garden. It is spring. 15
I've "made bums out of the birdies," in my next-door neighbor's words,
that is to say . . .

your life is as much a mystery to me as ever.
The dog pretends to bite fleas out of sheer boredom,
and not even the daffodils know if it's safe to come 20
up for air in this crazy, hot-and-cold weather.
Recognitions are shy, the faintest tint of skin
that says we are coming up, is it the same
as it was last year? Who can remember that either?
That is to say, 25

I love you, in my dim-witted way.

Death

Strangely enough, death has been almost as universal and persistent a subject of lyric poetry as love. Its inescapability and the mystery of what lies beyond it may account for its haunting interest to the lyric poet. But the fact that so many poets have written on the subject provides another opportunity of studying again the varied poetic tone that different personalities, talents, and attitudes can give to quite similar subject matter.

Sonnet

by WILLIAM SHAKESPEARE

146

Poor soul, the center of my sinful earth,
Thrall to these rebel powers that thee array,
Why dost thou pine within and suffer dearth,
Painting thy outward walls so costly gay?
Why so large cost, having so short a lease, 5
Dost thou upon thy fading mansion spend?
Shall worms, inheritors of this excess,
Eat up thy charge? Is this thy body's end?
Then, soul, live thou upon they servant's loss,
And let that pine to aggravate thy store. 10
Buy terms divine in selling hours of dross,
Within be fed, without be rich no more.
   So shalt thou feed on Death, that feeds on men,
   And Death once dead, there's no more dying then.

---

array oppose in battle.   *dearth* loss.   *aggravate* increase.

On the Tombs in Westminster Abbey
by FRANCIS BEAUMONT

Mortality, behold and fear!
What a change of flesh is here!
Think how many royal bones
Sleep within this heap of stones:
Here they lie had realms and lands, 5
Who now want strength to stir their hands:
Where from their pulpits seal'd with dust
They preach, 'In greatness is no trust.'
Here's an acre sown indeed
With the richest, royall'st seed 10
That the earth did e'er suck in
Since the first man died for sin:
Here the bones of birth have cried—
'Though gods they were, as men they died.'
Here are sands, ignoble things, 15
Dropt from the ruin'd sides of kings;
Here's a world of pomp and state,
Buried in dust, once dead by fate.

Death
by JOHN DONNE

Death, be not proud, though some have callèd thee
Mighty and dreadful, for thou art not so;
For those whom thou think'st thou dost overthrow
Die not, poor Death; nor yet canst thou kill me.
From rest and sleep, which but thy picture be, 5
Much pleasure; then from thee much more must flow;
And soonest our best men with thee do go—
Rest of their bones and souls' delivery!
Thou 'rt slave to fate, chance, kings, and desperate men,
And dost with poison, war, and sickness dwell; 10
And poppy or charms can make us sleep as well
And better than thy stroke. Why swell'st thou then?
One short sleep past, we wake eternally,
And Death shall be no more: Death, thou shalt die!

Prospice
by ROBERT BROWNING

Fear death?—to feel the fog in my throat,
　The mist in my face,
When the snows begin, and the blasts denote
　I am nearing the place,
The power of the night, the press of the storm, 5
　The post of the foe;
Where he stands, the Arch Fear in a visible form,
　Yet the strong man must go.
For the journey is done and the summit attained,

Prospice look forward. This sets the tone of the whole poem, a courageous acceptance of the challenge of death. The poem was written shortly after the death of Mrs. Browning.

Arch Fear death, the thing most feared.

And the barriers fall, 10
Though a battle's to fight ere the guerdon
   be gained,
   The reward of it all.
I was ever a fighter, so—one fight more,
   The best and the last!
I would hate that death bandaged my
   eyes, and forebore, 15
   And bade me creep past.
No! let me taste the whole of it, fare like
   my peers,
   The heroes of old,
Bear the brunt, in a minute pay glad life's
   arrears

Of pain, darkness, and cold. 20
For sudden the worst turns the best to
   the brave,
   The black minute's at end,
And the elements' rage, the fiend-voices
   that rave,
   Shall dwindle, shall blend.
Shall change, shall become first a peace
   out of pain, 25
   Then a light, then thy breast,
O thou soul of my soul! I shall clasp thee
   again,
   And with God be the rest!

---

guerdon prize, reward.

soul of my soul his wife, Elizabeth.

Crossing the Bar
by ALFRED, LORD TENNYSON

Sunset and evening star,
   And one clear call for me!
And may there be no moaning of the bar,
   When I put out to sea,

But such a tide as moving seems asleep, 5
   Too full for sound and foam,

When that which drew from out the
   boundless deep
   Turns again home.

Twilight and evening bell,
   And after that the dark! 10
And may there be no sadness of farewell,
   When I embark;

For though from out our bourne of Time
   and Place
   The flood may bear me far,
I hope to see my Pilot face to face 15
   When I have crossed the bar.

---

bar The poem was suggested to Tennyson by his experience of crossing the sandbar on the ferry between the mainland and the Isle of Wight, where his home was. The poem expresses the poet's final assertion of his belief in immorality. Just before his death he asked that this poem be placed at the end of all editions of his poetry.

After Apple-Picking*
by ROBERT FROST

My long two-pointed ladder's sticking
   through a tree
Toward heaven still,

And there's a barrel that I didn't fill
Beside it, and there may be two or three
Apples I didn't pick upon some bough. 5
But I am done with apple-picking now.
Essence of winter sleep is on the night,
The scent of apples: I am drowsing off.
I cannot rub the strangeness from my
   sight
I got from looking through a pane of glass 10

---

*From *Complete Poems of Robert Frost*. Copyright 1916, 1923, 1930, 1939 by Holt, Rinehart and Winston, Inc. Copyright 1936, 1942, 1944, 1951, © 1958 by Robert Frost. Copyright © 1964, 1967 by Lesley Frost Ballantine. Reprinted by permission of Holt, Rinehart and Winston, Inc.

I skimmed this morning from the drink-
  ing trough
And held against the world of hoary grass.
It melted, and I let it fall and break.
But I was well
Upon my way to sleep before it fell,   15
And I could tell
What form my dreaming was about to
  take.
Magnified apples appear and disappear,
Stem end and blossom end,
And every fleck of russet showing clear.   20
My instep arch not only keeps the ache,
It keeps the pressure of a ladder-round.
I feel the ladder sway as the boughs bend.
And I keep hearing from the cellar bin
The rumbling sound   25
Of load on load of apples coming in.
For I have had too much
Of apple-picking: I am overtired
Of the great harvest I myself desired.
There were ten thousand thousand fruit
  to touch,   30
Cherish in hand, lift down, and not let
  fall.
For all
That struck the earth,
No matter if not bruised or spiked with
  stubble,
Went surely to the cider-apple heap   35
As of no worth.
One can see what will trouble
This sleep of mine, whatever sleep it is.
Were he not gone,
The woodchuck could say whether it's
  like his   40
Long sleep, as I describe its coming on,
Or just some human sleep.

Because I Could Not Stop for Death[*]

by EMILY DICKINSON

Because I could not stop for Death—
He kindly stopped for me—
The Carriage held but just Ourselves—
And Immortality.

We slowly drove—He knew no haste   5
And I had put away
My labor and my leisure too,
For His Civility—

We passed the School, where Children
  strove
At Recess—in the Ring—   10

We passed the Fields of Gazing Grain—
We passed the Setting Sun—

Or rather—He passed Us—
The Dews drew quivering and chill—
For only Gossamer, my Gown—   15
My Tippet—only Tulle—

We paused before a House that seemed
A Swelling of the Ground—
The Roof was scarcely visible—
The Cornice—in the Ground—   20

Since then—'tis Centuries—and yet
Feels shorter than the Day
I first surmised the Horses Heads
Were toward Eternity—

---

[*] Reprinted by permission of the publishers and the Trustees of Amherst College from Thomas H. Johnson, Editor, *The Poems of Emily Dickinson*, Cambridge, Mass.: The Belknap Press of Harvard University Press. Copyright, 1951, 1955, by The President and Fellows of Harvard College.

Tippet hood or scarf. *Tulle* thin, fine netting of silk.

I Heard a Fly Buzz When I Died*
by EMILY DICKINSON

I heard a Fly buzz—when I died—
The Stillness in the Room
Was like the Stillness in the Air—
Between the Heaves of Storm—

The Eyes around—had wrung them
    dry—   5
And Breaths were gathering firm
For that last Onset—when the King
Be witnessed—in the Room—

I willed my Keepsakes—Signed away
What portion of me be   10
Assignable—and then it was
There interposed a Fly—

With Blue-uncertain stumbling Buzz—
Between the light—and me—
And then the Windows failed—and then   15
I could not see to see—

---

*Reprinted by permission of the publishers and the Trustees of Amherst College from Thomas H. Johnson, Editor, *The Poems of Emily Dickinson*, Cambridge, Mass.: The Belknap Press of Harvard University Press. Copyright, 1951, 1955, by The President and Fellows of Harvard College.

Sailing to Byzantium*
by WILLIAM BUTLER YEATS

[1]

That is no country for old men. The
    young
In one another's arms, birds in the trees
—Those dying generations—at their
    song,
The salmon-falls, the mackerel-crowded
    seas,
Fish, flesh, or fowl, commend all summer
    long   5
Whatever is begotten, born, and dies.
Caught in that sensual music all neglect
Monuments of unaging intellect.

[2]

An aged man is but a paltry thing,
A tattered coat upon a stick, unless   10
Soul clap its hands and sing, and louder
    sing
For every tatter in its mortal dress,
Nor is there singing school but studying
Monuments of its own magnificence;
And therefore I have sailed the seas and
    come   15
To the holy city of Byzantium.

[3]

O sages standing in God's holy fire
As in the gold mosaic of a wall,
Come from the holy fire, perne in a gyre,
And be the singing-masters of my soul.   20
Consume my heart away; sick with desire
And fastened to a dying animal
It knows not what it is; and gather me
Into the artifice of eternity.

[4]

Once out of nature I shall never take   25
My bodily form from any natural thing,

---

*Reprinted with permission of The Macmillan Company, Mr. Michael Butler Yeats, A. P. Watt & Son, Macmillan & Co. Ltd., London, and The Macmillan Company of Canada Limited, from *Collected Poems of William Butler Yeats*. Copyright 1928 by The Macmillan Company, renewed 1956 by Georgie Yeats.

perne spin or turn.   *gyre* circular motion.

But such a form as Grecian goldsmiths make
Of hammered gold and gold enameling
To keep a drowsy Emperor awake;
Or set upon a golden bough to sing
To lords and ladies of Byzantium
Of what is past, or passing, or to come.

Auto Wreck
by KARL SHAPIRO

Its quick soft silver bell beating, beating,
And down the dark one ruby flare
Pulsing out red light like an artery,
The ambulance at top speed floating down
Past beacons and illuminated clocks
Wings in a heavy curve, dips down,
And brakes speed, entering the crowd.
The doors leap open, emptying light;
Stretchers are laid out, the mangled lifted
And stowed into the little hospital.
Then the bell, breaking the hush, tolls once,
And the ambulance with its terrible cargo
Rocking, slightly rocking, moves away,
As the doors, an afterthought, are closed.

We are deranged, walking among the cops
Who sweep glass and are large and composed.
One is still making notes under the light.

One with a bucket douches ponds of blood
Into the street and gutter.
One hangs lanterns on the wrecks that cling,
Empty husks of locusts, to iron poles.

Our throats were tight as tourniquets,
Our feet were bound with splints, but now,
Like convalescents intimate and gauche,
We speak through sickly smiles and warn
With the stubborn saw of common sense,
The grim joke and the banal resolution.
The traffic moves around with care,
But we remain, touching a wound
That opens to our richest horror.
Already old, the question Who shall die?
Becomes unspoken Who is innocent?

For death in war is done by hands;
Suicide has cause and stillbirth, logic;
And cancer, simple as a flower, blooms.
But this invites the occult mind,
Cancels our physics with a sneer,
And splatters all we knew of denouement
Across the expedient and wicked stones.

* Copyright 1941 by Karl Shapiro. Reprinted from *Selected Poems*, by Karl Shapiro, by permission of Random House, Inc.

Tract
by WILLIAM CARLOS WILLIAMS

I will teach you my townspeople
how to perform a funeral—
for you have it over a troop
of artists—
unless one should scour the world—
you have the ground sense necessary.

See! the hearse leads.
I begin with a design for a hearse.
For Christ's sake not black—
nor white either—and not polished!
Let it be weathered—like a farm wagon—

* From William Carlos Williams, *Collected Earlier Poems*. Copyright 1938 by William Carlos Williams. Reprinted by permission of New Directions Publishing Corporation.

with gilt wheels (this could be
applied fresh at small expense)
or no wheels at all:
a rough dray to drag over the ground.

Knock the glass out!
My God—glass, my townspeople!
For what purpose? Is it for the dead
to look out or for us to see
how well he is housed or to see
the flowers or the lack of them—
or what?
To keep the rain and snow from him?
He will have a heavier rain soon:
pebbles and dirt and what not.
Let there be no glass—
and no upholstery phew!
and no little brass rollers
and small easy wheels on the bottom—
my townspeople what are you thinking
of?

A rough plain hearse then
with gilt wheels and no top at all.
On this the coffin lies
by its own weight.

    No wreaths please—
especially no hot house flowers.
Some common memento is better,
something he prized and is known by:
his old clothes—a few books perhaps—
God knows what! You realize
how we are about these things

my townspeople—
something will be found—anything
even flowers if he had come to that.
So much for the hearse.

For heaven's sake though see to the
 driver!
Take off the silk hat! In fact
that's no place at all for him—
up there unceremoniously
dragging our friend out to his own
 dignity!
Bring him down—bring him down!
Low and inconspicuous! I'd not have him
 ride
on the wagon at all—damn him—
the undertaker's understrapper!
Let him hold the reins
and walk at the side
and inconspicuously too!

Then briefly as to yourselves:
Walk behind—as they do in France,
seventh class, or if you ride
Hell take curtains! Go with some show
of inconvenience; sit openly—
to the weather as to grief.
Or do you think you can shut grief in?
What—from us? We who have perhaps
nothing to lose? Share with us
share with us—it will be money
in your pockets.
    Go now
I think you are ready.

Sled Burial, Dream Ceremony*
by JAMES DICKEY

While the south rains, the north
Is snowing, and the dead southerner
Is taken there. He lies with the top of his casket
Open, his hair combed, the particles in the air
Changing to other things. The train stops

In a small furry village, and men in flap-eared caps
And others with women's scarves tied around their heads
And business hats over those, unload him,

---

* Copyright © 1965 by James Dickey. Reprinted from *Poems 1957–1967*, by James Dickey, by permission of Wesleyan University Press.

And one of them reaches inside the coffin and places
The southerner's hand at the center   10

Of his dead breast. They load him onto a sled,
An old-fashioned sled with high-curled runners,
Drawn by horses with bells, and begin
To walk out of town, past dull red barns
Inching closer to the road as it snows   15

Harder, past an army of gunny-sacked bushes,
Past horses with flakes in the hollows of their sway-backs,
Past round faces drawn by children
On kitchen windows, all shedding basic-shaped tears.
The coffin top still is wide open;   20

His dead eyes stare through his lids,
Not fooled that the snow is cotton. The woods fall
Slowly off all of them, until they are walking
Between rigid little houses of ice-fishers
On a plain which is a great plain of water   25

Until the last rabbit track fails, and they are
At the center. They take axes, shovels, mattocks,
Dig the snow away, and saw the ice in the form
Of his coffin, lifting the slab like a door
Without hinges. The snow creaks under the sled   30

As they unload him like hay, holding his weight by ropes.
Sensing an unwanted freedom, a fish
Slides by, under the hole leading up through the snow
To nothing, and is gone. The coffin's shadow
Is white, and they stand there, gunny-sacked bushes,   35

Summoned from village sleep into someone else's dream
Of death, and let him down, still seeing the flakes in the air
At the place they are born of pure shadow
Like his dead eyelids, rocking for a moment like a boat
On utter foreignness, before he fills and sails down.

Old Age Compensation*
by JAMES WRIGHT

There are no roads but the frost,
And the pumpkins look haggard.
The ants have gone down to the grave,
   crying
God spare them one green blade.
Failing the grass, they have abandoned
   the grass.   5
All creatures who have died today of old
   age
Have gone more than ten miles already.
All day I have slogged behind
And dreamed of them praying for one
   candle,

---

* Copyright © 1968 by James Wright. Reprinted from *Shall We Gather at the River*, by James Wright, by permission of Wesleyan University Press. This poem was first published in *Poetry*.

Only one.
Fair enough. Only, from where I stand,
I can see one last night nurse shining in
  one last window
In the Home for Senior Citizens.
The white uniform flickers, the town is
  gone.
What do I do now? I have one candle,
But what's the use?
If only they can catch up with twilight,
They'll be safe enough.
Their boats are moored there, among the
  cattails
And the night-herons' nests.
All they have to do now
Is to get one of those lazy birds awake
  long enough
To guide them across the river.
Herons fly low, too.
All it will take is one old man trawling
  one oar.
Anybody can follow a blue wing,
They don't need my candle.
But I do.

Anxiety

Since the mid-nineteenth century, personal anxiety has increasingly been the subject of lyric poetry. The source of this feeling is the apparent isolation of man in an indifferent cosmos, in social estrangement, and in personal psychological crisis. The poems in this section express either the anxiety itself or an attempt to resolve it.

Dover Beach

by MATTHEW ARNOLD

The sea is calm tonight,
The tide is full, the moon lies fair
Upon the straits;—on the French coast
  the light
Gleams and is gone; the cliffs of England
  stand,
Glimmering and vast, out in the tranquil
  bay.
Come to the window, sweet is the night-
  air!

Only, from the long line of spray
Where the sea meets the moon-blanched
  land,
Listen! you hear the grating roar
Of pebbles which the waves draw back,
  and fling,
At their return, up the high strand,
Begin, and cease, and then again begin,
With tremendous cadence slow, and bring
The eternal note of sadness in.

Sophocles long ago
Heard it on the Aegean, and it brought
Into his mind the turbid ebb and flow
Of human misery; we
Find also in the sound a thought,
Hearing it by this distant northern sea.

The Sea of Faith
Was once, too, at the full, and round
  earth's shore
Lay like the folds of a bright girdle
  furled.
But now I only hear

Sophocles a Greek tragedian who, in his *Antigone*, has a famous passage occasioned by the sound of the sea, on the misery of life.

Its melancholy, long, withdrawing roar,
Retreating, to the breath
Of the night-wind, down the vast edges drear
And naked shingles of the world.

Ah, love, let us be true
To one another! for the world, which seems
To lie before us like a land of dreams,
So various, so beautiful, so new,
Hath really neither joy, nor love, nor light,
Nor certitude, nor peace, nor help for pain;

And we are here as on a darkling plain
Swept with confused alarms of struggle and flight,
Where ignorant armies clash by night.

---

shingles limestone beach, shingle-like in its formation.

I Wake and Feel the Fell of Dark, Not Day
by GERARD MANLEY HOPKINS

I wake and feel the fell of dark, not day.
What hours, O what black hoürs we have spent
This night! what sights you, heart, saw; ways you went!
And more must, in yet longer light's delay.
   With witness I speak this. But where I say
Hours I mean years, mean life. And my lament
Is cries countless, cries like dead letters sent
To dearest him that lives alas! away.

I am gall, I am heartburn. God's most deep decree
Bitter would have me taste: my taste was me;
Bones built in me, flesh filled, blood brimmed the curse.
   Selfyeast of spirit a dull dough sours. I see
The lost are like this, and their scourge to be
As I am mine, their sweating selves; but worse.

---

fell bitterness.

Carrion Comfort
by GERARD MANLEY HOPKINS

Not, I'll not, carrion comfort, Despair, not feast on thee;
Not untwist—slack they may be—these last strands of man
In me ór, most weary, cry *I can no more.* I can;
Can something, hope, wish day come, not choose not to be.
But ah, but O thou terrible, why wouldst thou rude on me
Thy wring-world right foot rock? lay a lionlimb against me? scan
With darksome devouring eyes my bruisèd bones? and fan,
O in turns of tempest, me heaped there; me frantic to avoid thee and flee?

---

carrion of a dead body; the poet means he will not seek out comfort and ease, as a vulture seeks dead bodies, to escape the struggle against anxiety and despair; he will confront them head-on.

Why? That my chaff might fly; my grain
   lie, sheer and clear.
Nay in all that toil, that coil, since
   (seems) I kissed the rod,   10
Hand rather, my heart lo! lapped strength,
   stole joy, would laugh, chéer.

Cheer whom though? the hero whose
   heaven-handling flung me, fóot tród
Me? or me that fought him? O which
   one? is it each one? That night, that
   year
Of now done darkness I wretch lay
   wrestling with (my God!) my God.

Preludes*
by T. S. ELIOT

I

The winter evening settles down
With smell of steaks in passageways.
Six o'clock.
The burnt-out ends of smoky days.
And now a gusty shower wraps   5
The grimy scraps
Of withered leaves about your feet
And newspapers from vacant lots;
The showers beat
On broken blinds and chimney-pots,   10
And at the corner of the street
A lonely cab-horse steams and stamps.
And then the lighting of the lamps.

II

The morning comes to consciousness
Of faint stale smells of beer   15
From the sawdust-trampled street
With all its muddy feet that press
To early coffee-stands.
With the other masquerades
That time resumes,   20
One thinks of all the hands
That are raising dingy shades
In a thousand furnished rooms.

III

You tossed a blanket from the bed,
You lay upon your back, and waited; 25

You dozed, and watched the night
   revealing
The thousand sordid images
Of which your soul was constituted;
They flickered against the ceiling.
And when all the world came back   30
And the light crept up between the
   shutters
And you heard the sparrows in the
   gutters,
You had such a vision of the street
As the street hardly understands;
Sitting along the bed's edge, where   35
You curled the papers from your hair,
Or clasped the yellow soles of feet
In the palms of both soiled hands.

IV

His soul stretched tight across the skies
That fade behind a city block,   40
Or trampled by insistent feet
At four and five and six o'clock;
And short square fingers stuffing pipes,
And evening newspapers, and eyes
Assured of certain certainties,   45
The conscience of a blackened street
Impatient to assume the world.

I am moved by fancies that are curled
Around these images, and cling:
The notion of some infinitely gentle 50
Infinitely suffering thing.

Wipe your hand across your mouth, and
   laugh;
The worlds revolve like ancient women
Gathering fuel in vacant lots.

---

* From *Collected Poems* 1909–1962 by T. S. Eliot, copyright, 1936, by Harcourt, Brace & World, Inc.; copyright, © 1963, 1964, by T. S. Eliot. Reprinted by permission of Harcourt Brace Jovanovich, Inc., and Faber and Faber Limited.

About Money*
by DAVID IGNATOW

The wonder of cherries
has gone into the wonder of money.

My mind is green with anxiety
about money.

---
* Copyright © 1963 by David Ignatow. Reprinted from *Figures of the Human*, by David Ignatow, by permission of Wesleyan University Press.

Song on the Dread of a Chill Spring*
by JOHN LOGAN

I thought (and before it was too late)
my heart had begun to turn, that was
shut to love, for I was adamant
as saints, and tough as the martyr's heart
as a wooden statue of a god,   5
where my father sat in the straight pew,
my mother bowed to the stone, bearing
flowers she had cut out of the earth
of my life. Ah the candles bloom cold
in the earthen air of early Mass,   10
like the tops of wan hepatica
that lift their light cups in the first time.
So shy we touch at these Ides of March!

Winter was too long and cold. The spring
is brief. These tulips offer up their gold   15
and the purple plum our grief.

---
* From *Spring of the Thief*, by John Logan. Copyright © 1963 by John Logan. Reprinted by permission of Alfred A. Knopf, Inc.

North on one-eleven*
by JOHN KNOEPFLE

The swamp alongside the road
fed a world so dark
I could not see it
when I drove there each night
due north for home.   5
Sometimes a thin moon in the east
dropped shafts of light
on the steel rails that crossed the road.
I learned to watch for this light
gliding for the crossing   10
at precisely the speed of the car.
I would argue with myself,
the moonlight is without substance,
then feel it slam my stomach
and splinter in my nerves   15
when I hit the rails.

Later I remembered that light,
thinking of Augustine,
raw meat on the hooks of time
when Vandals were breaking the gates   20
at Hippo, and I told myself
it is the Vandals who are dead,
but the mouth of the old saint
gleams with foxfire.
Now tonight   25
the swamp fevers my road
and the moon is put out
and my headlights pierce the dark
with beams riven into banks of fog,
and I raise my arm   30
warding a blow.

---
* From *Rivers into Islands* by John Knoepfle. Copyright 1965 by University of Chicago. Reprinted by permission of The University of Chicago Press.

Augustine   St. Augustine, Bishop of Hippo in North Africa when it was invaded by the Vandals, a Germanic tribe.

The Heavy Bear Who Goes with Me*

by DELMORE SCHWARTZ

"the withness of the body"—Whitehead

The heavy bear who goes with me,
A manifold honey to smear his face,
Clumsy and lumbering here and there,
The central ton of every place,
The hungry beating brutish one   5
In love with candy, anger, and sleep,
Crazy factotum, dishevelling all,
Climbs the building, kicks the football,
Boxes his brother in the hate-ridden city.
Breathing at my side, that heavy animal,   10
That heavy bear who sleeps with me,
Howls in his sleep for a world of sugar,
A sweetness intimate as the water's clasp,
Howls in his sleep because the tight-rope
Trembles and shows the darkness
    beneath.   15
—The strutting show-off is terrified,
Dressed in his dress-suit, bulging his
    pants,
Trembles to think that his quivering meat
Must finally wince to nothing at all.
That inescapable animal walks with me,   20
Has followed me since the black womb
    held,
Moves where I move, distorting my
    gesture,
A caricature, a swollen shadow,
A stupid clown of the spirit's motive,
Perplexes and affronts with his own
    darkness,   25
The secret life of belly and bone,
Opaque, too near, my private, yet
    unknown,
Stretches to embrace the very dear
With whom I would walk without him
    near,
Touches her grossly, although a word   30
Would bare my heart and make me clear,
Stumbles, flounders, and strives to be fed
Dragging me with him in his mouthing
    care,
Amid the hundred million of his kind,
The scrimmage of appetite everywhere.   35

---

* From Delmore Schwartz, *Selected Poems: Summer Knowledge*. Copyright 1938 by New Directions Publishing Corporation. Reprinted by permission of New Directions Publishing Corporation.

Incident*

by COUNTEE CULLEN

Once riding in old Baltimore,
Heart-filled, head-filled with glee,
I saw a Baltimorean
Keep looking straight at me.

Now I was eight and very small,   5
And he was no whit bigger,
And so I smiled, but he poked out
His tongue, and called me, "Nigger."

I saw the whole of Baltimore
From May until December;   10
Of all the things that happened there
That's all that I remember.

---

* "Incident" from *On These I Stand* by Countee Cullen. Copyright 1925 by Harper & Brothers; renewed 1953 by Ida M. Cullen.

At the Slackening of the Tide*
by JAMES WRIGHT

Today I saw a woman wrapped in rags
Leaping along the beach to curse the sea.
Her child lay floating in the oil, away
From oarlock, gunwale, and the blades
    of oars.
The skinny lifeguard, raging at the sky,   5
Vomited sea, and fainted on the sand.

The cold simplicity of evening falls
Dead on my mind.
And underneath the piles the water
Leaps up, leaps up, and sags down slowly,   10
    farther
Than seagulls disembodied in the drag
Of oil and foam.

Plucking among the oyster shells a man
Stares at the sea, that stretches on its
    side.
Now far along the beach, a hungry dog   15
Announces everything I knew before:
Obliterate naiads weeping underground,
Where Homer's tongue thickens with
    human howls.

I would do anything to drag myself
Out of this place: 20
Root up a seaweed from the water,
To stuff it in my mouth, or deafen me,
Free me from all the force of human
    speech;
Go drown, almost.

Warm in the pleasure of the dawn I
    came   25
To sing my song
And look for mollusks in the shallows,
The whorl and coil that pretty up the
    earth,
While far below us, flaring in the dark,
The stars go out.   30

What did I do to kill my time today,
After the woman ranted in the cold,
The mellow sea, the sound blown dark
    as wine?
After the lifeguard rose up from the
    waves
Like a sea-lizard with the scales washed
    off?   35
Sit there, admiring sunlight on a shell?

Abstract with terror of the shell, I stared
Over the waters where
God brooded for the living all one day.
Lonely for weeping, starved for a sound
    of mourning,   40
I bowed my head, and heard the sea far
    off
Washing its hands.

---

* Reprinted from *Saint Judas*, by James Wright, by permission of Wesleyan University Press.

In Quest of Meaning

    The world has never become so confused that men have not continued to try to find some meaning in it. The poems in this unit are related, in one way or another, to the perennial human endeavor to reconcile the reach for the ideal and the limitations of the real.

Lapis Lazuli

by WILLIAM BUTLER YEATS

I have heard that hysterical women say
They are sick of the palette and fiddle bow,
Of poets that are always gay,
For everybody knows or else should know
That if nothing drastic is done 5
Aeroplane and zeppelin will come out,
Pitch like King Billy bomb-balls in
Until the town lie beaten flat.

All perform their tragic play,
There struts Hamlet, there is Lear, 10
That's Ophelia, that Cordelia;
Yet they, should the last scene be there,
The great stage curtain about to drop,
If worthy their prominent part in the play,
Do not break up their lines to weep. 15
They know that Hamlet and Lear are gay;
Gaiety transfiguring all that dread.
All men have aimed at, found and lost;
Black out; Heaven blazing into the head:
Tragedy wrought to its uttermost. 20
Though Hamlet rambles and Lear rages,
And all the drop-scenes drop at once
Upon a hundred thousand stages,
It cannot grow by an inch or an ounce.

On their own feet they came, or on shipboard, 25
Camel-back, horse-back, ass-back, mule-back,
Old civilizations put to the sword.
Then they and their wisdom went to rack:
No handiwork of Callimachus,
Who handled marble as if it were bronze, 30
Made draperies that seemed to rise
When sea wind swept the corner, stands;
His long lamp chimney shaped like the stem
Of a slender palm, stood but a day;
All things fall and are built again, 35
And those that build them again are gay.

Two Chinamen, behind them a third,
Are carved in lapis lazuli,
Over them flies a long-legged bird,
A symbol of longevity; 40
The third, doubtless a servingman,
Carries a musical instrument.

Every discoloration of the stone,
Every accidental crack or dent,
Seems a watercourse or an avalanche, 45
Or lofty slope where it still snows
Though doubtless plum or cherry branch
Sweetens the little half-way house
Those Chinamen climb towards, and I
Delight to imagine them seated there; 50
There, on the mountain and the sky,
On all the tragic scene they stare.
One asks for mournful melodies;
Accomplished fingers begin to play.
Their eyes mid many wrinkles, their eyes, 55
Their ancient, glittering eyes, are gay.

King Billy King William III of England, who put down an Irish rebellion early in his reign.

* Reprinted with permission of The Macmillan Company, Mr. Michael Butler Yeats, A. P. Watt & Son, Macmillan & Co. Ltd., London, and The Macmillan Company of Canada Limited, from *Collected Poems of William Butler Yeats.* Copyright 1940 by Georgie Yeats, renewed 1968 by Bertha Georgie Yeats, Michael Butler Yeats, and Anne Yeats.

Callimachus a Greek sculptor of the fifth century B.C.

Birches*

by ROBERT FROST

When I see birches bend to left and right
Across the lines of straighter darker trees,
I like to think some boy's been swinging them.
But swinging doesn't bend them down to stay
As ice-storms do. Often you must have seen them
Loaded with ice a sunny winter morning
After a rain. They click upon themselves
As the breeze rises, and turn many-colored
As the stir cracks and crazes their enamel.
Soon the sun's warmth makes them shed crystal shells
Shattering and avalanching on the snow-crust—
Such heaps of broken glass to sweep away
You'd think the inner dome of heaven had fallen.
They are dragged to the withered bracken by the load,
And they seem not to break; though once they are bowed
So low for long, they never right themselves:
You may see their trunks arching in the woods
Years afterwards, trailing their leaves on the ground
Like girls on hands and knees that throw their hair
Before them over their heads to dry in the sun.
But I was going to say when Truth broke in
With all her matter-of-fact about the ice-storm
I should prefer to have some boy bend them
As he went out and in to fetch the cows—
Some boy too far from town to learn baseball,
Whose only play was what he found himself,
Summer or winter, and could play alone.
One by one he subdued his father's trees
By riding them down over and over again
Until he took the stiffness out of them,
And not one but hung limp, not one was left
For him to conquer. He learned all there was
To learn about not launching out too soon
And so not carrying the tree away
Clear to the ground. He always kept his poise
To the top branches, climbing carefully
With the same pains you use to fill a cup
Up to the brim, and even above the brim.
Then he flung outward, feet first, with a swish,
Kicking his way down through the air to the ground.
So was I once myself a swinger of birches.
And so I dream of going back to be.
It's when I'm weary of considerations,
And life is too much like a pathless wood
Where your face burns and tickles with the cobwebs
Broken across it, and one eye is weeping
From a twig's having lashed across it open.
I'd like to get away from earth awhile
And then come back to it and begin over.
May no fate willfully misunderstand me
And half grant what I wish and snatch me away
Not to return. Earth's the right place for love:

---

* From *Complete Poems of Robert Frost*. Copyright 1916, 1923, 1930, 1939 by Holt, Rinehart and Winston, Inc. Copyright 1936, 1942, 1944, 1951, © 1958 by Robert Frost. Copyright © 1964, 1967 by Lesley Frost Ballantine. Reprinted by permission of Holt, Rinehart and Winston, Inc.

I don't know where it's likely to go better.
I'd like to go by climbing a birch tree,
And climb black branches up a snow-
    white trunk   55
Toward heaven, till the tree could bear
    no more,

But dipped its top and set me down
    again.
That would be good both going and
    coming back.
One could do worse than be a swinger
    of birches.

To a Dog Injured in the Street*

by WILLIAM CARLOS WILLIAMS

IT IS MYSELF,
    not the poor beast lying there
        yelping with pain
that brings me to myself with a start—
    as at the explosion   5
        of a bomb, a bomb that has laid
all the world waste.
    I can do nothing
        but sing about it
and so I am assuaged   10
    from my pain.
A DROWSY NUMBNESS drowns my sense
    as if of hemlock
        I had drunk, I think
of the poetry   15
    of René Char
        and all he must have seen
and suffered
    that has brought him
        to speak only of   20
sedgy rivers,
    of daffodils and tulips
        whose roots they water,
even to the freeflowing river
    that laves the rootlets   25
        of those sweet scented flowers
that people the
    milky
        way.
I REMEMBER *Norma*   30
    our English setter of my childhood
        her silky ears

and expressive eyes.
    She had a litter
        of pups one night   35
in our pantry and I kicked
    one of them
        thinking, in my alarm,
that they
    were biting her breasts   40
        to destroy her.
I REMEMBER also
    a dead rabbit
        lying harmlessly
on the outspread palm   45
    of a hunter's hand.
        As I stood by
watching
    he took a hunting knife
        and with a laugh   50
thrust it
    up into the animal's private parts.
    I almost fainted.
WHY SHOULD I think of that now?
    the cries of a dying dog   55
        are to be blotted out
as best I can.
    René Char
        You are a poet who believes
in the power of beauty   60
    to right all wrongs.
        I believe it also.
With invention and courage
    we shall surpass
        the pitiful dumb beasts,   65
let all men believe it,
    as you have taught me also
        to believe it.

* From William Carlos Williams, *Pictures from Brueghel and Other Poems.* Copyright 1953 by William Carlos Williams. Reprinted by permission of New Directions Publishing Corporation.

The Steeple-Jack*
by MARIANNE MOORE

Dürer would have seen a reason for living
   in a town like this, with eight stranded
     whales
to look at; with the sweet sea air coming
   into your house
on a fine day, from water etched
   with waves as formal as the scales
on a fish.

One by one, in two's, in three's, the
   seagulls keep
flying back and forth over the town
   clock,
or sailing around the lighthouse without
   moving their wings—
rising steadily with a slight
   quiver of the body—or flock
mewing where

a sea the purple of the peacock's neck is
   paled to greenish azure as Dürer
     changed
the pine green of the Tyrol to peacock
   blue and guinea
grey. You can see a twenty-five-
   pound lobster and fishnets arranged
to dry. The

whirlwind fife-and-drum of the storm
   bends the salt
     marsh grass, disturbs stars in the sky
   and the

star on the steeple; it is a privilege to see so
much confusion.

      A steeple-jack in red, has let
   a rope down as a spider spins a thread;
he might be part of a novel, but on the
   sidewalk a
sign says C. J. Poole, Steeple-Jack,
   in black and white; and one in red
and white says

Danger. The church portico has four
   fluted
     columns, each a single piece of stone,
     made
modester by white-wash. This would be
   a fit haven for
waifs, children, animals, prisoners,
   and presidents who have repaid
sin-driven

senators by not thinking about them.
   One
     sees a school-house, a post-office in a
store, fish-houses, hen-houses, a three-
   masted schooner on
the stocks. The hero, the student,
   the steeple-jack, each in his way,
is at home.

It scarcely could be dangerous to be living
   in a town like this, of simple people
who have a steeple-jack placing danger-
   signs by the church
when he is gilding the solid-
   pointed star, which on a steeple
stands for hope.

Dürer a sixteenth-century German painter.
* Reprinted with permission of The Macmillan Company from *Collected Poems of Marianne Moore.* Copyright 1951 by Marianne Moore.

Heaven*
by RUPERT BROOKE

Fish (fly-replete, in depth of June,
Dawdling away their wat'ry noon)
Ponder deep wisdom, dark or clear,
Each secret fishy hope or fear.
Fish say, they have their Stream and
   Pond;   5
But is there anything Beyond?
This life cannot be All, they swear,
For how unpleasant, if it were!
One may not doubt that, somehow, Good
Shall come of Water and of Mud;   10
And, sure, the reverent eye must see
A purpose in Liquidity.
We darkly know, by Faith we cry,
The future is not Wholly Dry.
Mud unto mud!—Death eddies near— 15
Not here the appointed End, not here!
But somewhere, beyond Space and Time,
Is wetter water, slimier slime!
And there (they trust) there swimmeth
   One
Who swam ere rivers were begun,   20
Immense, of fishy form and mind,
Squamous, omnipotent, and kind;
And under that Almighty Fin,
The littlest fish may enter in.
Oh! never fly conceals a hook,   25
Fish say, in the Eternal Brook,
But more than mundane weeds are there,
And mud, celestially fair;
Fat caterpillars drift around,
And Paradisal grubs are found;   30
Unfading moths, immortal flies,
And the worm that never dies.
And in that Heaven of all their wish,
There shall be no more land, say fish.

---

* Reprinted by permission of Dodd, Mead & Company, Inc., and The Canadian Publishers, McClelland and Stewart Limited, from *The Collected Poems of Rupert Brooke*. Copyright 1915 by Dodd, Mead & Company, Inc. Copyright 1943 by Edward Marsh.

squamous scaly.

A Baroque Wall-Fountain in the Villa Sciarra*
by RICHARD WILBUR

   Under the bronze crown
Too big for the head of the stone cherub
     whose feet
   A serpent has begun to eat,
Sweet water brims a cockle and braids
   down

   Past spattered mosses, breaks   5
On the tipped edge of a second shell, and
   fills
   The massive third below. It spills
In threads then from the scalloped rim,
   and makes

   A scrim or summery tent
For a faun-ménage and their familiar
   goose.   10
   Happy in all that ragged, loose
Collapse of water, its effortless descent

   And flatteries of spray,
The stocky god upholds the shell with
   ease,
   Watching, about his shaggy knees, 15
The goatish innocence of his babes at
   play;

---

* From *Things of This World* © 1956, by Richard Wilbur. Reprinted by permission of Harcourt Brace Jovanovich, Inc.,

scrim a transparent screen of thin textile used in stage settings.

His fauness all the while
Leans forward, slightly, into a clambering
    mesh
Of water-lights, her sparkling flesh
In a saecular ecstasy, her blinded smile   20

    Bent on the sand floor
Of the trefoil pool, where ripple-shadows
    come
    And go in swift reticulum,
More addling to the eye than wine, and
    more

    Interminable to thought   25
Than pleasure's calculus. Yet since this all
    Is pleasure, flash, and waterfall,
Must it not be too simple? Are we not

    More intricately expressed
In the plain fountains that Maderna set   30
    Before St. Peter's—the main jet
Struggling aloft until it seems at rest

    In the act of rising, until
The very wish of water is reversed,
    That heaviness borne up to burst   35
In a clear, high, cavorting head, to fill

    With blaze, and then in gauze
Delays, in a gnatlike shimmering, in a
    fine

---

trefoil three-leaved shape. *reticulum* in the pattern of a net. *Maderna* the architect who designed the façade of St. Peter's and the fountains in the piazza in front of it.

    Illumined version of itself, decline,
And patter on the stones its own
    applause?   40

    If that is what men are
Or should be, if those water-saints display
    The pattern of our areté,
What of these showered fauns in their
    bizarre,

    Spangled, and plunging house?   45
They are at rest in fulness of desire
    For what is given, they do not tire
Of the smart of the sun, the pleasant
    water-douse

    And riddled pool below,
Reproving our disgust and our ennui   50
    With humble insatiety.
    Francis, perhaps, who lay in sister snow

    Before the wealthy gate
Freezing and praising, might have seen
    in this
    No trifle, but a shade of bliss—   55
That land of tolerable flowers, that state

    As near and far as grass
Where eyes become the sunlight, and
    the hand
    Is worthy of water: the dreamt land
Toward which all hungers leap, all
    pleasures pass.   60

---

areté a Greek word meaning virtue. *Francis* St. Francis of Assisi.

Journey of the Magi*
by T. S. ELIOT

"A cold coming we had of it,
Just the worst time of the year
For a journey, and such a long journey;
The ways deep and the weather sharp,
The very dead of winter."   5
And the camels galled, sore-footed,
    refractory,
Lying down in the melting snow.
There were times we regretted
The summer palaces on slopes, the
    terraces,

---

* From *Collected Poems 1909–1962* by T. S. Eliot, copyright, 1936, by Harcourt Brace Jovanovich, Inc.; copyright, © 1963, 1964, by T. S. Eliot. Reprinted by permission of Harcourt Brace Jovanovich, Inc., and Faber and Faber Limited.

And the silken girls bringing sherbet.
Then the camel men cursing and
   grumbling
And running away, and wanting their
   liquor and women,
And the night-fires going out, and the
   lack of shelters,
And the cities hostile and the towns
   unfriendly
And the villages dirty and charging high
   prices:
A hard time we had of it.
At the end we preferred to travel all
   night,
Sleeping in snatches,
With the voices singing in our ears, saying
That this was all folly.

Then at dawn we came down to a
   temperate valley,
Wet, below the snow line, smelling of
   vegetation;
With a running stream and a water-mill
   beating the darkness,
And three trees on the low sky,
And an old white horse galloped away
   in the meadow.
Then we came to a tavern with vine-
   leaves over the lintel,

Six hands at an open door dicing for
   pieces of silver,
And feet kicking the empty wine-skins.
But there was no information, and so we
   continued
And arrived at evening, not a moment too
   soon
Finding the place; it was (you may say)
   satisfactory.

All this was a long time ago, I remember,
And I would do it again, but set down
This set down
This: were we led all that way for
Birth or Death? There was a Birth,
   certainly,
We had evidence and no doubt. I had
   seen birth and death,
But had thought they were different; this
   Birth was
Hard and bitter agony for us, like Death,
   our death.
We returned to our places, these
   Kingdoms,
But no longer at ease here, in the old
   dispensation,
With an alien people clutching their
   gods.
I should be glad of another death.

The Jet and Urban Setting

   Although over eighty percent of our population is urban, it is surprising how little of our modern poetry is urban inspired. Hence the poems of this section represent the exception rather than the rule. The city and our modern industrial world have been treated much more often by modern painters and sculptors than by modern poets.

To a Locomotive in Winter
by WALT WHITMAN

Thee for my recitative,
Thee in the driving storm even as now, the snow, the winter-day declining,
Thee in thy panoply, thy measur'd dual throbbing and thy beat convulsive,
Thy black cylindric body, golden brass and silvery steel,

Thy ponderous side-bars, parallel and connecting rods, gyrating, shuttling at thy sides,
Thy metrical, now swelling pant and roar, now tapering in the distance,
Thy great protruding head-light fix'd in front,
Thy long, pale, floating vapor-pennants, tinged with delicate purple,
The dense and murky clouds out-belching from thy smoke-stack,
Thy knitted frame, thy springs and valves, the tremulous twinkle of thy wheels,
Thy train of cars behind, obedient, merrily following,
Through gale or calm, now swift, now slack, yet steadily careering;
Type of the modern—emblem of motion and power—pulse of the continent,
For once come serve the Muse and merge in verse, even as here I see thee,
With storm and buffeting gusts of wind and falling snow,
By day thy warning ringing bell to sound its notes,
By night thy silent signal lamps to swing.

Fierce-throated beauty!
Roll through my chant with all thy lawless music, thy swinging lamps at night,
Thy madly-whistled laughter, echoing, rumbling like an earthquake, rousing all,
Law of thyself complete thine own track firmly holding,
(No sweetness debonair of tearful harp or glib piano thine,)
Thy trills of shrieks by rocks and hills return'd,
Launch'd o'er the prairies wide, across the lakes,
To the free skies unpent and glad and strong.

A Supermarket in California*

by ALLEN GINSBERG

What thoughts I have of you tonight, Walt Whitman, for I walked down the sidestreets under the trees with a headache self-conscious looking at the full moon.

In my hungry fatigue, and shopping for images, I went into the neon fruit supermarket, dreaming of your enumerations!

What peaches and what penumbras! Whole families shopping at night! Aisles full of husbands! Wives in the avocados, babies in the tomatoes!—and you, Garcia Lorca, what were you doing down by the watermelons?

I saw you, Walt Whitman, childless, lonely old grubber, poking among the meats in the refrigerator and eyeing the grocery boys.

I heard you asking questions of each: Who killed the pork chops? What price bananas? Are you my Angel?

I wandered in and out of the brilliant stacks of cans following you, and followed in my imagination by the store detective.

We strode down the open corridors together in our solitary fancy tasting artichokes, possessing every frozen delicacy, and never passing the cashier.

---

* Copyright © 1956, 1959 by Allen Ginsberg. Reprinted by permission of City Lights Books.

Where are we going, Walt Whitman? The doors close in an hour. Which way does your beard point tonight?
    (I touch your book and dream of our odyssey in the supermarket and feel absurd.)
    Will we walk all night through solitary streets? The trees add shade to shade, lights out in the houses, we'll both be lonely.   10

    Will we stroll dreaming of the lost America of love past blue automobiles in driveways, home to our silent cottage?
    Ah, dear father, graybeard, lonely old courage-teacher, what America did you have when Charon quit poling his ferry and you got out on a smoking bank and stood watching the boat disappear on the black waters of Lethe?

Morning Sun*
by LOUIS MacNEICE

Shuttles of trains going north, going south, drawing threads of blue,
The shining of the lines of trams like swords,
Thousands of posters asserting a monopoly of the good, the beautiful, the true,
Crowds of people all in the vocative, you and you,
The haze of the morning shot with words.   5

Yellow sun comes white off the wet streets but bright
Chromium yellows in the gay sun's light,
Filleted sun streaks the purple mist,
Everything is kissed and reticulated with sun
Scooped-up and cupped in the open fronts of shops   10
And bouncing on the traffic which never stops.

And the street fountain blown across the square
Rainbow-trellises the air and sunlight blazons
The red butcher's and scrolls of fish on marble slabs,
Whistled bars of music crossing silver sprays   15
And horns of cars touché, touché, rapiers' retort, a moving cage,
A turning page of shine and sound, the day's maze.

But when the sun goes out, the streets go cold, the hanging meat
And tiers of fish are colourless and merely dead,
And the hoots of cars neurotically repeat and the tiptoed feet   20
Of women hurry and falter whose faces are dead;
And I see in the air but not belonging there
The blown grey powder of the fountain grey as the ash
That forming on a cigarette covers the red.

---

* From *The Collected Poems of Louis MacNeice*, edited by E. R. Dodds. Copyright © The Estate of Louis MacNeice 1966. Reprinted by permission of Oxford University Press, Inc., and Faber and Faber Ltd.

Merritt Parkway*
by DENISE LEVERTOV

As if it were
forever that they move, that we
  keep moving—

    Under a wan sky where
    as the lights went on a star   5
      pierced the haze & now
    follows steadily
               a constant
    above our six lanes
    the dreamlike continuum . . .   10

And the people—ourselves!
  the humans from inside the
cars, apparent
only at gasoline stops
              unsure,   15
  eyeing each other

---

*From Denise Levertov, *The Jacob's Ladder*. Copyright © 1958 by Denise Levertov Goodman. Reprinted by permission of New Directions Publishing Corporation.

drink coffee hastily at the
  slot machines & hurry
back to the cars
    vanish   20
    into them forever, to
  keep moving—

Houses now & then beyond the
sealed road, the trees / trees, bushes
passing by, passing   25
  the cars that
    keep moving ahead of
  us, past us, pressing behind us
                and
    over left, those that come   30
    toward us shining too brightly
moving relentlessly

    in six lanes, gliding
north & south, speeding with
a slurred sound—   35

At the San Francisco Airport*
by YVOR WINTERS

This is the terminal: the light
Gives perfect vision, false and hard;
The metal glitters, deep and bright.
Great planes are waiting in the yard—
They are already in the night.   5

And you are here beside me, small,
Contained and fragile, and intent
On things that I but half recall—
Yet going whither you are bent.
I am the past, and that is all.   10

But you and I in part are one:
The frightened brain, the nervous will,

The knowledge of what must be done,
The passion to acquire the skill
To face that which you dare not shun.   15

The rain of matter upon sense
Destroys me momently. The score:
There comes what will come. The expense
Is what one thought, and something
  more—
One's being and intelligence.   20

This is the terminal, the break.
Beyond this point, on lines of air,
You take the way that you must take;
And I remain in light and stare—
In light, and nothing else, awake.   25

---

*Yvor Winters, "At the San Francisco Airport," *Collected Poems*: Swallow Press, Chicago; Copyright 1960.

Storm on Fifth Avenue*
by SIEGFRIED SASSOON

A sallow waiter brings me six huge oysters . . .
Gloom shutters up the sunset with a plague
Of unpropitious twilight jagged asunder
By flashlight demonstrations. *Gee, what a peach
Of a climate!* (Pardon slang: these sultry storms   5
Afflict me with neurosis: rumbling thunder
Shakes my belief in academic forms.)

An oyster-coloured atmospheric rumpus
Beats up to blot the sunken daylight's gildings.
Against the looming cloud-bank, ivory-pale,   10
Stand twenty-storied blocks of office-buildings.
Snatched upward on a gust, lost news-sheets sail
Forlorn in lone arena of mid-air;
Flapping like melancholy kites, they scare
My gaze, a note of wildness in the scene.   15

Out on the pattering side-walk, people hurry
For shelter, while the tempest swoops to scurry
Across to Brooklyn. Bellying figures clutch
At wide-brimmed hats and bend to meet the weather,
Alarmed for fresh-worn silks and flurried feather.   20

Then hissing deluge splashes down to beat
The darkly glistening flatness of the street.
Only the cars nose on through rain-lashed twilight:
Only the Sherman Statue, angel-guided,
Maintains its mock-heroic martial gesture.   25

A sallow waiter brings me beans and pork . . .
Outside there's fury in the firmament.
Ice-cream, of course, will follow; and I'm content.
O Babylon! O Carthage! O New York!

---
* From *Collected Poems, 1908–1956*, of Siegfried Sassoon. Reprinted by permission of George Sassoon.

Hot Night on Water Street*
by LOUIS SIMPSON

A hot midsummer night on Water Street—
The boys in jeans were combing their blond hair,
Watching the girls go by on tired feet;
And an old woman with a witch's stare

Cried "Praise the Lord!" She vanished on a bus   5
With hissing air brakes, like an incubus.

Three hardware stores, a barbershop, a bar,
A movie playing Westerns—where I went
To see a dream of horses called *The Star*. . . .

---
* Copyright © 1957 by Louis Simpson. Reprinted from *A Dream of Governors*, by Louis Simpson, by permission of Wesleyan University Press.

Some day, when this uncertain continent
Is marble, and men ask what was the
    good
We lived by, dust may whisper
    "Hollywood."

Then back along the river bank on foot
By moonlight . . . . On the West
    Virginia side
An owlish train began to huff and hoot;
It seemed to know of something that had
    died.

I didn't linger—sometimes when I travel
I think I'm being followed by the Devil.

At the newsstand in the lobby, a cigar
Was talkative: "Since I've been in this
    town
I've seen one likely woman, and a car
As she was crossing Main Street, knocked
    her down."
I was a stranger here myself, I said,
And bought the *New York Times*, and
    went to bed.

The Day I Schooled Myself in Stone*
by SAMUEL HAZO

Agreed—that God created just so many
    stones
to be until the end of things, letting them
    spread
by splitting under lightning and the
    avalanche
of sledging rain or simply lasting in a
    world
of all that multiplies and serves its term
    and dies.

Boarding the airport bus behind the
    U. S. Mint,
I found a stone no rounder than a run-
    down dime
and thumbed it warm against the pocket
    of my palm.
It still was stone when men on mountains
    spoke to God
or when I last took off from Truman's
    Washington
by DC-6 and never thought of coming
    back.
A similar, different man on similar, dif-
    ferent streets,
I did return to find what turned all clocks
    to toys.

_____
* Reprinted from *My Sons in God*, by Samuel
Hazo, University of Pittsburgh Press, © 1965.

Knowing in part within the always known
    to God,
I tried to probe my more-than-animal
    but less-
than-angel past before I heard my flight
    announced.
Ten years had given me less willingness
    to die,
more lustfire in the chest, more singular
    a need
to leave mementos more than bones to
    stoke my grave.
Simple in its perfect death, the stone I
    gripped defied
those years that made me die a little to
    survive
to new departures from an older terminal.
Later, at fourteen thousand feet above
    the rocks
of Maryland, I dreamed of death again
    and fought
to think of something else by watching
    clouds as bare

and beautiful as untouched snow or
    studying
the adequate backside of either
    stewardess.

Nothing would work, and there was
    nothing I could say
to still that timebomb-stone created to
    outlast
the turbo-jet that battled gravity to
    climb   30
on schedule over Arlington—the ring of
    roads

around the target-town of presidents,
    parades,
hoteling clans, continuous burlesque and
    cabs—
the self I had to save from trying stonily
    to spite
what cramped my hand and heart until
    I let it go.

The skyscrapers of the financial district dance with Gasman*
by MARGE PIERCY

The skyscrapers are dancing by the river,
they are leaping over their reflections
their lightning bright zigzag and beady
    reflections
jagged and shattered on East River.
With voices shrill as children's whistles
    they hop   5
while the safes pop open like corn
and the files come whizzing through the
    air
to snow on the streets that lie throbbing,
eels copulating in heaps.

Ticker tape hangs in garlands from the
    wagging streetlamps.   10
Standard Oil and General Foods have
    amalgamated
and duPont, Schenley and AT&T lie
    down together.
It does not matter, don't hope, it does
    not matter.
In the morning the buildings stand
    smooth and shaven and straight
and all goes on whirring and ticking.   15
Money is reticulated and stronger than
    steel or stone or vision,
though sometimes at night
the skyscrapers bow and lean and leap
    under no moon.

---

* Copyright © 1967 by Marge Piercy. Reprinted from *Breaking Camp*, by Marge Piercy, by permission of Wesleyan University Press.

Committee*
by DAVID RAY

Men have through all ages sat in council
And sometimes around tables, Homeric
Men, and standing men, Indians, and these
Men in their dark ties. We are in a circle
And talking in a circle and making the   5
Choice of our lives:

---

* © 1968 by David Ray. Reprinted from *Dragging the Main*, by David Ray. Reprinted by permission of the author.

backache,
the green blackboard,
the pipe to be chewed,
the cough drop,   10
the bitter lemon,
the coil of red cellophane around the finger,
Paper Topics,
sad doodles of cages and zigzags,
the Regional Report,   15
sinus carrying Nile sludge,
all the windows closed,
backache,
courtyard brick,
a report from the other committee,   20
the sun moving away as if appalled,
All afternoon on the ship where there is no leader
and the garrulous lap at us like endless ocean
waves, insignificant and tireless.
Sometimes around this magnificent table   25
Men who have always been dull and defeated
Seem to take on life as they say "It seems to me . . ."
Or "I should think . . ." or "If you ask me. . . ."
Often we get up as if we'd decided where
To send our frogmen or how to scale the wall.   30
But no one can find a wall or name a sea.

For the First Manned Moon Orbit*

by JAMES DICKEY

So long
So long as the void
Is hysterical, bolted out, you float on nothing

But procedure alone,

Eating, sleeping like a man   5
Deprived of the weight of his own
And all humanity in the name

Of a new life
            and through this, making new
Time slowly, the moon comes.

---

* From *The Eye Beater, Blood, Victory, Madness, Buckhead & Mercy* by James Dickey. Copyright © 1968, 1969, 1970 by James Dickey. Reprinted by permission of Doubleday & Company, Inc., and the author.

        Its mountains bulge 10
     They crack they hold together
  Closer spreading smashed crust
Of uncanny rock ash-glowing alchemicalizing the sun
    With peace: with the peace of a country
Bombed-out by the universe. 15
        You lean back from the great light-
   shattered face the pale blaze
     Of God-stone coming

    Close too close, and the dead seas turn
     The craters hover turn 20
      Their dark side to kill
     The radio, and the one voice
Of earth.
      You and your computers have brought out
     The silence of mountains the animal 25
    Eye has not seen since the earth split,
     Since God first found geometry
      Would move move
     In mysterious ways. You hang

  Mysteriously, pulling the moon-dark pulling, 30
     And solitude breaks down
   Like an electrical system: it is something

    Else: nothing is something
     Something I am trying

     To say O God 35
Almighty! To come back! To complete the curve to come back
   Singing with procedure back through the last dark
     Of the moon, past the dim ritual
   Random stones of oblivion, and through the blinding edge
     Of moonlight into the sun 40

     And behold

The blue planet steeped in its dream

  Of reality, its calculated vision shaking with
     The only love.

Unit **11**

IMPRESSIONISTIC AND DESCRIPTIVE POETRY

ON IMPRESSIONISTIC AND DESCRIPTIVE POETRY

Since lyric poets are so largely concerned with the expression of their individual insights, one of the very best ways of discovering these insights and feelings is to study together poems on comparable subjects by different poets. By doing so we begin to appreciate how almost infinite the reactions to the same subject can be. We apprehend more of the significance and distinctive tone of each poem when it is read in relation to others than we do when we read it entirely in isolation. For that reason this unit groups poems on similar subjects together to facilitate comparative study. But the poems are not only grouped in topical clusters; they are also arranged to progress from poems that are almost entirely impressionistic or imagistic to those which, through these impressions, attempt to suggest meanings and attitudes that go quite beyond mere sense impressions. The difference between the impressionistic or imagistic poem, which is content to communicate as exactly and vividly as possible a set of sense impressions, and the descriptive poem, which functions as a symbol of something beyond the sense impressions it conveys, is well exemplified by a contrast between such poems as James Stephens' "The Main-Deep" and Roy Campbell's "To a Pet Cobra." Stephens has fulfilled his purpose by an adept selection and arrangement of words that by association and rhythm subtly convey to us the sight, sound, and movement of a wave of the sea. Campbell's "To a Pet Cobra" similarly gives us an impression of the cobra, but, at the same time, the situation and action of the cobra become a peculiarly appropriate symbol of the position and action of the satirist in society. A similar contrast could be made between Tennyson's "The Eagle" and Walt Whitman's "A Noiseless Patient Spider," and between Robert Farren's "The Cyclist" and John Gillespie Magee's "High Flight."

Fog*
by CARL SANDBURG

The fog comes
on little cat feet.

It sits looking
over harbor and city
on silent haunches
and then moves on.

---

* From *Chicago Poems* by Carl Sandburg. Copyright 1916 by Holt, Rinehart and Winston, Inc. Copyright 1944 by Carl Sandburg. Reprinted by permission of Holt, Rinehart and Winston, Inc.

The Harbor

by CARL SANDBURG

Passing through huddled and ugly walls
By doorways where women
Looked from their hunger-deep eyes,
Haunted with shadows of hunger-hands,

Out from the huddled and ugly walls, 5
I came sudden, at the city's edge,
On a blue burst of lake,
Long lake waves breaking under the sun
On a spray-flung curve of shore;
And a fluttering storm of gulls, 10
Masses of great gray wings
And flying white bellies
Veering and wheeling free in the open.

---

* From *Chicago Poems* by Carl Sandburg. Copyright 1916 by Holt, Rinehart and Winston, Inc. Copyright 1944 by Carl Sandburg. Reprinted by permission of Holt, Rinehart and Winston, Inc.

The Main-Deep

by JAMES STEPHENS

The long-rólling,
Steady-póuring,
Deep-trenchéd
Green billów:

The wide-topped, 5
Unbróken,
Green-glacid,
Snow-sliding,

Cold-flushing,
—On—on—on— 10
Chill-rushing,
Hush—hushing,

. . . Hush—hushing . . .

---

* Reprinted with permission of The Macmillan Company, Mrs. Iris Wise, Macmillan & Co. Ltd., London, and The Macmillan Company of Canada Limited from *Collected Poems of James Stephens*. Copyright 1925, 1926 by The Macmillan Company, renewed 1953, 1954 by James Stephens.

Oread

by H. D.

Whirl up, sea—
whirl your pointed pines,
splash your great pines
on our rocks,
hurl your green over us,
cover us with your pools of fir.

Oread One of the Greek nymphs of mountains and hills; sometimes, as here, also a water nymph.

* From *Selected Poems of H.D.* (New York: Grove Press, Inc., 1957).

Heat
by H. D.

O wind, rend open the heat,
cut apart the heat,
rend it to tatters.

Fruit cannot drop
through this thick air—   5
fruit cannot fall into heat
that presses up and blunts
the points of pears
and rounds the grapes.

Cut the heat—   10
plow through it,
turning it on either side
of your path.

---
*From *Selected Poems of H.D.* (New York: Grove Press, Inc., 1957).

Pear Tree
by H. D.

Silver dust,
lifted from the earth,
higher than my arms reach,
you have mounted,
O, silver,   5
higher than my arms reach,
you front us with great mass;

no flower ever opened
so staunch a white leaf,
no flower ever parted silver   10
from such rare silver;

O, white pear,
your flower-tufts
thick on the branch
bring summer and ripe fruits   15
in their purple hearts.

---
*From *Selected Poems of H.D.* (New York: Grove Press, Inc., 1957).

Night Clouds
by AMY LOWELL

The white mares of the moon rush along
    the sky
Beating their golden hoofs upon the glass
    Heavens;
The white mares of the moon are all
    standing on their hind legs
Pawing at the green porcelain doors of
    the remote Heavens.
Fly, Mares!   5
Strain your utmost,
Scatter the milky dust of stars,
Or the tiger sun will leap upon you and
    destroy you
With one lick of his vermilion tongue.

---
*From *The Complete Poetical Works of Amy Lowell*, 1955; reprinted by permission of Houghton Mifflin Company, the authorized publishers.

A Tulip Garden

by AMY LOWELL

Guarded within the old red wall's
    embrace,
    Marshalled like soldiers in gay company,
    The tulips stand arrayed. Here infantry
Wheels out into the sunlight. What bold
    grace
Sets off their tunics, white with crimson
    lace!   5
    Here are platoons of gold-frocked
        cavalry,
    With scarlet sabres tossing in the eye
Of purple batteries, every gun in place.
    Forward they come, with flaunting
        colours spread,
With torches burning, stepping out in
    time   10
    To some quick, unheard march. Our
        ears are dead,
We cannot catch the tune. In pantomime
    Parades that army. With our utmost
        powers
We hear the wind stream through a
    bed of flowers.

* From *The Complete Poetical Works of Amy Lowell*, 1955; reprinted by permission of Houghton Mifflin Company, the authorized publishers.

Silver

by WALTER DE LA MARE

Slowly, silently, now the moon
Walks the night in her silver shoon;
This way, and that, she peers, and sees
Silver fruit upon silver trees;
One by one the casements catch   5
Her beams beneath the silvery thatch;
Couched in his kennel, like a log,
With paws of silver sleeps the dog;
From their shadowy cote the white
    breasts peep
Of doves in a silver-feathered sleep;   10
A harvest mouse goes scampering by,
With silver claws, and silver eye;
And moveless fish in the water gleam,
By silver reeds in a silver stream.

* From *Collected Poems, 1901–1918*, vol. II (New York: Holt, Rinehart and Winston, Inc., 1920). Reprinted by permission of The Literary Trustees of Walter de la Mare and The Society of Authors as their representative.

The Train*
by EMILY DICKINSON

I like to see it lap the Miles—
And lick the Valleys up—
And stop to feed itself at Tanks—
And then—prodigious step

Around a Pile of Mountains—　　　　　5
And supercilious peer
In Shanties—by the sides of Roads—
And then a Quarry pare

To fit its sides
And crawl between　　　　　10
Complaining all the while
In horrid—hooting stanza—
Then chase itself down Hill—

And neigh like Boanerges—
Then—prompter than a Star　　　　　15
Stop—docile and omnipotent
At its own stable door—

---

* Reprinted by permission of the publishers and the Trustees of Amherst College from Thomas H. Johnson, Editor, *The Poems of Emily Dickinson*, Cambridge, Mass.: The Belknap Press of Harvard University Press. Copyright, 1951, 1955, by The President and Fellows of Harvard College.

Boanerges an appellation given by Christ to James and John; it meant "sons of thunder." Here—as impressive as the sons of thunder.

The Express*
by STEPHEN SPENDER

After the first powerful, plain manifesto
The black statement of pistons, without more fuss
But gliding like a queen, she leaves the station.
Without bowing and with restrained unconcern
She passes the houses which humbly crowd outside,　　　　　5
The gasworks, and at last the heavy page
Of death, printed by gravestones in the cemetery.
Beyond the town, there lies the open country
Where, gathering speed, she acquires mystery,
The luminous self-possession of ships on ocean.　　　　　10
It is now she begins to sing—at first quite low
Then loud, and at last with a jazzy madness—
The song of her whistle screaming at curves,
Of deafening tunnels, brakes, innumerable bolts.
And always light, aerial, underneath,　　　　　15
Retreats the elate metre of her wheels.
Steaming through metal landscape on her lines,
She plunges new eras of white happiness,
Where speed throws up strange shapes, broad curves
And parallels clean like trajectories from guns.　　　　　20
At last, further than Edinburgh or Rome,
Beyond the crest of the world, she reaches night
Where only a low stream-line brightness
Of phosphorus on the tossing hills is light.
Ah, like a comet through flame, she moves entranced,　　　　　25
Wrapt in her music no bird song, no, nor bough
Breaking with honey buds, shall ever equal.

---

* Copyright 1934 and renewed 1962 by Stephen Spender. Reprinted from *Collected Poems, 1928–1953*, by Stephen Spender, by permission of Random House, Inc., and Faber and Faber Ltd.

The Eagle
by ALFRED, LORD TENNYSON

He clasps the crag with crooked hands;
Close to the sun in lonely lands,
Ringed with the azure world, he stands.

The wrinkled sea beneath him crawls;
He watches from his mountain walls,
And like a thunderbolt he falls.

A Bird Came Down the Walk*
by EMILY DICKINSON

A Bird came down the Walk—
He did not know I saw—
He bit an Angleworm in halves
And ate the fellow, raw,

And then he drank a Dew   5
From a convenient Grass—
And then hopped sidewise to the Wall
To let a Beetle pass—

He glanced with rapid eyes
That hurried all around—   10
They looked like frightened Beads,
   I thought—
He stirred his Velvet Head

Like one in danger, Cautious,
I offered him a Crumb
And he unrolled his feathers   15
And rowed him softer home—

Than Oars divide the Ocean,
Too silver for a seam—
Or Butterflies, off Banks of Noon
Leap, plashless as they swim.   20

---
* Reprinted by permission of the publishers and the Trustees of Amherst College from Thomas H. Johnson, Editor, *The Poems of Emily Dickinson*, Cambridge, Mass.: The Belknap Press of Harvard University Press. Copyright, 1951, 1955, by The President and Fellows of Harvard College.

A Noiseless Patient Spider
by WALT WHITMAN

A noiseless patient spider,
I mark'd where on a little promontory it
   stood isolated,
Mark'd how to explore the vacant vast
   surrounding,
It launch'd forth filament, filament,
   filament, out of itself,
Ever unreeling them, ever tirelessly
   speeding them.   5

And you O my soul where you stand,
Surrounded, detached, in measureless
   oceans of space,
Ceaselessly musing, venturing, throwing,
   seeking the spheres to connect them,
Till the bridge you will need be form'd,
   till the ductile anchor hold
Till the gossamer thread you fling catch
   somewhere, O my soul.   10

The Snake*
by EMILY DICKINSON

A narrow Fellow in the Grass
Occasionally rides—
You may have met Him—did you not
His notice sudden is—
The Grass divides as with a Comb—
A spotted shaft is seen—
And then it closes at your feet
And opens further on—

He likes a Boggy Acre
A Floor too cool for Corn—　　　　　10
Yet when a Boy, and Barefoot—
I more than once at Noon
Have passed, I thought, a Whip lash

Unbraiding in the Sun
When stooping to secure it　　　　　15
It wrinkled, and was gone—

Several of Nature's People
I know, and they know me—
I feel for them a transport
Of cordiality—　　　　　　　　　　20
But never met this Fellow
Attended, or alone
Without a tighter breathing
And Zero at the Bone—　　　　　　25

Sweet is the swamp with its secrets,
Until we meet a snake;
'Tis then we sigh for houses,
And our departure take
At that enthralling gallop　　　　　30
That only childhood knows.
A snake is summer's treason,
And guile is where it goes.

---

* Reprinted by permission of the publishers and the Trustees of Amherst College from Thomas H. Johnson, Editor, *The Poems of Emily Dickinson*, Cambridge, Mass.: The Belknap Press of Harvard University Press. Copyright, 1951, 1955, by The President and Fellows of Harvard College.

To a Pet Cobra*
by ROY CAMPBELL

With breath indrawn and every nerve alert,
As at the brink of some profound abyss,
I love on my bare arm, capricious flirt,
To feel the chilly and incisive kiss
Of your lithe tongue that forks its swift
　　caress　　　　　　　　　　　　　　5
Between the folded slumber of your fangs,
And half reveals the nacreous recess
Where death upon those dainty hinges
　　hangs.

Our lonely lives in every chance agreeing,
It is no common friendship that you
　　bring,　　　　　　　　　　　　　10

It was the desert starved us into being,
The hate of men that sharpened us to
　　sting:
Sired by starvation, suckled by neglect,
Hate was the surly tutor of our youth:
I too can hiss the hair of men erect　　15
Because my lips are venomous with truth.

Where the hard rock is barren, scorched
　　the spring,
Shrivelled the grass, and the hot wind
　　of death
Hornets the crag with whirred metallic
　　wing—

---

nacreous irridescent or pearl-like.
* From *Adamastor, Poems by Roy Campbell* (London: Faber and Faber Ltd., 1930). Reprinted by permission of Curtis Brown Ltd.

Hate was the surly tutor of our youth Roy Campbell was raised in South Africa and was exiled from the country for criticizing the government and talking out plainly against race discrimination.

We drew the fatal secret of our breath: 20
By whirlwinds bugled forth, whose
   funneled suction
Scrolls the spun sand into a golden spire,
Our spirits leaped, hosannas of
   destruction,
Like desert lilies forked with tongues of
   fire.

Dainty one, deadly one, whose folds are
   panthered 25
With stars, my slender Kalihari flower,
Whose lips with fangs are delicately
   anthered,
Whose coils are volted with electric
   power,
I love to think how men of my dull
   nation
Might spurn your sleep with inadvertent
   heel 30
To kindle up the lithe retaliation
And caper to the slash of sudden steel.

There is no sea so wide, no waste so
   sterile
But holds a rapture for the sons of strife:
There shines upon the topmost peak of
   peril 35
A throne for spirits that abound in life:
There is no joy like theirs who fight
   alone,
Whom lust or gluttony has never tied,
Who in their purity have built a throne,
And in their solitude a tower of pride. 40

I wish my life, O suave and silent sphinx,
Might flow like yours in some such
   strenuous line,
My days the scales, my years the bony
   links
That chain the length of its resilient
   spine:
And when at last the moment comes to
   strike, 45
Such venom give my hilted fangs the
   power,
Like drilling roots the dirty soil that
   spike,
To sting these rotted wastes into a flower.

---

panthered spotted (like the panther). *Kalihari flower* a native South African flower. *my dull nation* the Union of South Africa.

Snake*

by D. H. LAWRENCE

A snake came to my water-trough
On a hot, hot day, and I in pyjamas for
   the heat,
To drink there.

In the deep, strange-scented shade of the
   great dark carobtree
I came down the steps with my pitcher 5
And must wait, must stand and wait, for
   there he was at the trough before me.

He reached down from a fissure in the
   earth-wall in the gloom
And trailed his yellow-brown slackness
   soft-bellied down, over the edge of the
   stone trough
And rested his throat upon the stone
   bottom,
And where the water had dripped from
   the tap, in a small clearness, 10
He sipped with his straight mouth,
Softly drank through his straight gums,
   into his slack long body,
Silently.

Someone was before me at my water-
   trough,
And I, like a second comer, waiting. 15

---

carobtree an evergreen tree of Mediterranean area.
* From *The Complete Poems of D. H. Lawrence,* Volume I, edited by Vivian de Sola Pinto and F. Warren Roberts. Copyright 1923, renewed 1951 by Frieda Lawrence. Reprinted by permission of The Viking Press, Inc.

He lifted his head from his drinking, as cattle do,
And looked at me vaguely, as drinking cattle do,
And flickered his two-forked tongue from his lips, and mused a moment,
And stooped and drank a little more,
Being earth-brown, earth-golden from the burning bowels of the earth   20
On the day of Sicilian July, with Etna smoking.

The voice of my education said to me
He must be killed,
For in Sicily the black, black snakes are innocent, the gold are venomous.

And voices in me said, If you were a man   25
You would take a stick and break him now, and finish him off.

But must I confess how I liked him,
How glad I was he had come like a guest in quiet, to drink at my water-trough
And depart peaceful, pacified, and thankless,
Into the burning bowels of this earth?   30

Was it cowardice, that I dared not kill him?
Was it perversity, that I longed to talk to him?
Was it humility, to feel so honoured?
I felt so honoured.

And yet those voices: 35
If you were not afraid, you would kill him!

And truly I was afraid, I was most afraid,
But even so, honoured still more
That he should seek my hospitality
From out the dark door of the secret earth.

He drank enough   40
And lifted his head, dreamily, as one who has drunken,
And flickered his tongue like a forked night on the air, so black,
Seeming to lick his lips,
And looked around like a god, unseeing, into the air,   45
And slowly turned his head,
And slowly, very slowly, as if thrice adream,
Proceeded to draw his slow length curving round
And climb again the broken bank of my wall-face.

And as he put his head into that dreadful hole,   50
And as he slowly drew up, snake-easing his shoulders, and entered farther,
A sort of horror, a sort of protest against his withdrawing into that horrid black hole,
Deliberately going into the blackness, and slowly drawing himself after,
Overcame me now his back was turned.

I looked round, I put down my pitcher,   55
I picked up a clumsy log
And threw it at the water-trough with a clatter.

I think it did not hit him,
But suddenly that part of him that was left behind convulsed in undignified haste,
Writhed like lightning, and was gone   60
Into the black hole, the earth-lipped fissure in the wall-front,
At which, in the intense still noon, I stared with fascination.

And immediately I regretted it.
I thought how paltry, how vulgar, what a mean act!
I despised myself and the voices of my accursed human education.   65

And I thought of the albatross,
And I wished he would come back, my snake.

---
albatross the bird shot by the Ancient Mariner, which he wore about his neck in penance for the deed. See Coleridge's *The Rime of the Ancient Mariner*, Part I, lines 71–82.

The Dive*
by TED ROBINS

Like a strong bow bent forcefully,
His body curves; then, like the bow released,
His body straightens and becomes the shaft
Which plugs the center of the amber targe,
The eye from which the rapid wavelets spread   5
In silver rings. Under their largening,
Under their lacy froth, their bubbling spume,
His body melts into the liquid mass,
Foreshortens, gleams with an unnatural light—
Half, green-and-amber water, half, smooth flesh.   10
Each hair gives up its tiny crystal globe,
Which buoyant rises. Other bubbles join
To weave together in the fretted plan,
The elusive pattern of the growing wake.
Urged by an otter twist, up the incline   15
Of the translucency his body glides,
The muscles rippling. Soon the surface breaks.
Dark as sleek seal the shining head appears;
The strong, tanned shoulders, glistening, arise.
And from the phantom plane, the phantom being,   20
Fabulous merman, issues now the man.

---
targe   target.
* From *Forms and Fragments* (Claremont, Calif.: Saunders Studio Press, 1934).

The Cyclist*
by ROBERT FARREN

Back bent; hands gripped; breath coming heavily;
face flushed; brow damp; feet driving steadily;
teeth clenched; lips wide; chain grinding rustily.
Lord! what a hill! Breeze blowing gustily.

Now for the top! Just-a-few-yards away.   5
Drive-down-the-pedals—hard! hard!—
We're up! hooray!

Poised here an instant—downhill before us—
now hear the wheels sing crescendo in chorus,

down, down the long, falling roadway flushed and radiant-
ly fast-and-faster, fast-and-faster whining down the gradient   10
with tyres a-slur-and-slither and the spokes like organs droning
to the long, smooth, straight, spread road slow homing.

---
* Three stanzas from "The Cyclist," by Robert Farren, from *How to Enjoy Poetry*. Copyright 1948, Sheed and Ward, Inc., New York.

High Flight*
by Pilot-Officer JOHN GILLESPIE MAGEE, JR., R.C.A.F.

Oh! I have slipped the surly bonds of
    Earth
      And danced the skies on laughter-
        silvered wings;
Sunward I've climbed, and joined the
    tumbling mirth
      Of sun-split clouds,—and done a hun-
        dred things
You have not dreamed of—wheeled and
    soared and swung   5
      High in the sunlit silence. Hov'ring
        there,
I've chased the shouting wind along, and
    flung
      My eager craft through footless halls
        of air. . . .

Up, up the long, delirious, burning blue
    I've topped the wind-swept heights
      with easy grace,   10
Where never lark, or even eagle flew—
    And, while with silent, lifting mind
      I've trod
The high untrespassed sanctity of
    space,
Put out my hand and touched the face
    of God.

---

* From *Sunward I've Climbed, Story of John Magee, Poet & Soldier, 1922–1941*, by Herman Hagedorn (New York: The Macmillan Company, 1942). Reprinted by permission of Mrs. John G. Magee.

Cargoes*
by JOHN MASEFIELD

Quinquireme of Nineveh from Distant
    Ophir,
Rowing home to haven in sunny
    Palestine,
With a cargo of ivory,
And apes and peacocks;
Sandalwood, cedarwood, and sweet, white
    wine.   5

Stately Spanish galleon coming from the
    Isthmus,

Dipping through the Tropics by the palm-
    green shores,
With a cargo of diamonds,
Emeralds, amethysts,
Topazes, and cinnamon, and gold
    moidores.   10

Dirty British coaster with a salt-caked
    smoke stack,
Butting through the Channel in the mad
    March days,
With a cargo of Tyne coal,
Road-rails, pig-lead,
Firewood, iron-ware, and cheap tin trays.

Quinquireme a galley ship with five banks of oars. *Nineveh* a city in ancient Assyria, on the Tigris river. *Ophir* a Biblical land, rich in gold. *galleon* a heavy Spanish ship with several decks. *Isthmus* The Isthmus of Panama.

* Reprinted with permission of The Macmillan Company from *Poems by John Masefield*. Copyright 1912 by The Macmillan Company, renewed 1940 by John Masefield.

moidores a seventeenth-century gold Portuguese coin. *Tyne* mining district in Northumberland.

Brooklyn Bridge at Dawn*
by RICHARD LeGALLIENNE

Out of the cleansing night of stars and tides,
Building itself anew in the slow dawn,
The long sea-city rises: night is gone,
Day is not yet; still merciful, she hides
Her summoning brow, and still the night-car glides   5
Empty of faces; the night-watchmen yawn
One to the other, and shiver and pass on,
Nor yet a soul over the great bridge rides.
Frail as a gossamer, a thing of air,
A bow of shadow o'er the river flung,   10
Its sleepy masts and lonely lapping flood;
Who, seeing thus the bridge a-slumber there,
Would dream such softness, like a picture hung,
Is wrought of human thunder, iron and blood?

---

*From *New Poems* by Richard LeGallienne. Reprinted by permission of Dodd, Mead & Company, and The Society of Authors as the literary representative of the Estate of Richard LeGallienne.

Chicago*
by CARL SANDBURG

Hog Butcher for the World,
Tool Maker, Stacker of Wheat,
Player with Railroads and the Nation's Freight Handler;
Stormy, husky, brawling,
City of the Big Shoulders: 5
They tell me you are wicked and I believe them, for I have seen your painted women under the gas lamps luring the farm boys.
And they tell me you are crooked and I answer: Yes, it is true I have seen the gunman kill and go free to kill again.
And they tell me you are brutal and my reply is: On the faces of women and children I have seen the marks of wanton hunger.
And having answered so I turn once more to those who sneer at this my city, and I give them back the sneer and say to them:
Come and show me another city with lifted head singing so proud to be alive and coarse and strong and cunning.   10
Flinging magnetic curses amid the toil of piling job on job, here is a tall bold slugger set vivid against the little soft cities;
Fierce as a dog with tongue lapping for action, cunning as a savage pitted against the wilderness,
    Bareheaded,
    Shoveling,
    Wrecking,   15

---

*From *Chicago Poems* by Carl Sandburg. Copyright 1916 by Holt, Rinehart and Winston, Inc. Copyright, 1944, by Carl Sandburg. Reprinted by permission of Holt, Rinehart and Winston, Inc.

Planning,
    Building, breaking, rebuilding,
Under the smoke, dust all over his mouth, laughing with white teeth,
Under the terrible burden of destiny laughing as a young man laughs,
Laughing even as an ignorant fighter laughs who has never lost a battle,   20
Bragging and laughing that under his wrist is the pulse, and under his ribs the heart of the people,
    Laughing!
Laughing the stormy, husky, brawling laughter of Youth, half-naked, sweating, proud to be Hog Butcher, Tool Maker, Stacker of Wheat, Player with Railroads and Freight Handler to the Nation.

Hollywood*

by KARL SHAPIRO

Farthest from any war, unique in time
Like Athens or Baghdad, this city lies
Between dry purple mountains and the
    sea.
The air is clear and famous, every day
Bright as a postcard, bringing bungalows   5
    And sights. The broad nights advertise
For love and music and astronomy.

Heart of a continent, the hearts converge
On open boulevards where palms are
    nursed
With flare-pots like a grove, on villa
    roads   10
Where castles cultivated like a style
Breed fabulous metaphors in foreign
    stone,
    And on enormous movie lots
Where history repeats its vivid blunders.

Alice and Cinderella are most real.   15
Here may the tourist, quite sincere at last,
Rest from his dream of travels. All is new.
No ruins claim his awe, and permanence,
Despised like customs, fails at every turn

Here where the eccentric thrives,   20
Laughter and love are leading industries.

Luck is another. Here the bodyguard,
The parasite, the scholar are well paid,
The quack erects his alabaster office,
The moron and the genius are enshrined,   25
And the mystic makes a fortune quietly;
    Here all superlatives come true
And beauty is marketed like a basic food.

O can we understand it? Is it ours,
A crude whim of a beginning people,   30
A private orgy in a secluded spot?
Or alien like the word *harem*, or true
Like hideous Pittsburgh or depraved
    Atlanta?
    Is adolescence just as vile
As this its architecture and its talk?   35

Or are they parvenus, like boys and girls?
Or ours and happy, cleverest of all?
Yes. Yes. Though glamorous to the
    ignorant
This is the simplest city, a new school.
What is more nearly ours? If soul can
    mean   40
    The civilization of the brain,
This is a soul, a possible proud Florence.

Athens the political and artistic capital of Ancient Greece.   *Baghdad* center of the caliphate of Baghdad, symbol of oriental culture.

* Copyright 1941 by Karl Shapiro. Reprinted from *Selected Poems*, by Karl Shapiro, by permission of Random House, Inc.

---

parvenus upstarts.   *Florence* the great center of art in Renaissance Italy.

Unit **12**

DRAMATIC POETRY

ON DRAMATIC POETRY

Drama, a literary type in which a story is told and character is revealed by the dialogue and action of actors on a stage, has a very ancient history, but the independent short *dramatic monologue* is a comparative newcomer. Its antecedents may, however, be found in the *soliloquy* of the Elizabethan play. We are familiar, for instance, with the soliloquies of Hamlet in which he is alone on the stage and seems to be thinking aloud about the meaning or meaninglessness of life. The dramatic convention which allowed the actor to talk to himself was devised to reveal aspects of the inner motives and conflicts of the main characters in a play, but the situation was always rather artificial. Laurence Olivier overcame some of this artificiality in his screen delivery of Richard III's famous soliloquy by speaking it directly to the audience.

THE DRAMATIC MONOLOGUE

In its most developed form, the *dramatic monologue* is a short poem in which a single person—other than the poet himself—at some critical moment of his life, reveals a great deal of his own character and the characters of the person or persons he is addressing in the poem, merely by what he says. Robert Browning made the best use of this form in such famous dramatic monologues as "My Last Duchess" and "Andrea del Sarto." The reader is usually kept conscious throughout the poem of the person Browning's speaker is addressing, and he learns almost as much about this second person as he does about the speaker. Tennyson developed a form resembling the dramatic monologue in "Ulysses"; the Greek hero, speaking at a crucial moment of his career, reveals much of his character in the process, but it is not until almost the end of the poem that we are conscious of the comrades he is addressing, and even then we learn very little about them.

Someone has said that a dramatic monologue is like listening to one end of a telephone conversation. We hear only the speaker on our end of the line, but what he says and how he says it can tell us a great deal about the party on the other end. In the best of dramatic monologues we are also made conscious, by concrete references in the monologue itself, of the setting in which the talk takes place.

Drama in general is noteworthy for its concentration and emotional intensity. In contrast to the novel, it dispenses with all but the most essential episodes of a story and develops them with great emotional intensity. The dramatic monologue is even more concentrated and intense than the stage play. It is perhaps for that reason that this literary type has been very popular, in modified form, with such modern poets as Robinson, Frost, and Eliot. They have increased its economy of expression and intensity of feeling by employing a good deal of symbolism in its development. Frost's "Death of the Hired Man," although not strictly a monologue, and T. S. Eliot's "The Love Song of J. Alfred Prufrock" are particularly good examples of the use of symbolism to give an added dimension to the character revelations of the dramatic poem.

Soliloquies
by WILLIAM SHAKESPEARE

HAMLET

O, that this too too solid flesh would melt,
Thaw, and resolve itself into a dew!
Or that the Everlasting had not fix'd
His canon 'gainst self-slaughter! O God! God!
How weary, stale, flat, and unprofitable,   5
Seems to me all the uses of this world!
Fie on't! oh fie, fie! 'Tis an unweeded garden,
That grows to seed; things rank and gross in nature
Possess it merely. That it should come to this!
But two months dead! Nay, not so much, not two.   10
So excellent a king; that was, to this,
Hyperion to a satyr; so loving to my mother
That he might not beteem the winds of heaven
Visit her face too roughly. Heaven and earth!
Must I remember? Why, she would hang on him   15
As if increase of appetite had grown
By what it fed on; and yet, within a month,—
Let me not think on't!—Frailty, thy name is woman!—
A little month, or e'er those shoes were old
With which she followed my poor father's body,   20
Like Niobe, all tears,—why she, even she—
O [God]! a beast, that wants discourse of reason,
Would have mourn'd longer—married with mine uncle,
My father's brother, but no more like my father
Than I to Hercules; within a month,   25
Ere yet the salt of most unrighteous tears
Had left the flushing of her galled eyes,
She married. O, most wicked speed, to post
With such dexterity to incestuous sheets!
It is not, nor it cannot come to good.—   30
But break my heart, for I must hold my tongue.

Hamlet: Act I, 2, 129–158

Hyperion Apollo, god of manly beauty. *satyr* a sylvan deity with tail and ears of a horse, associated with lasciviousness and sensuality. *Niobe* wife of King of Thebes. She boasted to Leto that she had many children, while he had only two. But her children were all slain by the jealous Apollo and Artemis, the children of Leto. Niobe spent herself in tears for her children and was turned into a weeping marble statue. *Hercules* the god of violent, powerful action—the exact opposite of the indecisive Hamlet.

HAMLET

To be, or not to be: that is the question.
Whether 'tis nobler in the mind to suffer
The slings and arrows of outrageous fortune,
Or to take arms against a sea of troubles,
And by opposing end them. To die; to sleep;   5
No more; and by a sleep to say we end
The heart-ache and the thousand natural shocks
That flesh is heir to. 'Tis a consummation
Devoutly to be wish'd. To die; to sleep;—
To sleep? Perchance to dream! Ay, there's the rub;   10
For in that sleep of death what dreams may come,
When we have shuffl'd off this mortal coil,
Must give us pause. There's the respect
That makes calamity of so long life.
For who would bear the whips and scorns of time,   15
The oppressor's wrong, the [proud] man's contumely,

The pangs of dispriz'd love, the law's delay,
The insolence of office, and the spurns
That patient merit of the unworthy takes,
When he himself might his quietus make 20
With a bare bodkin? Who would fardels bear,
To grunt and sweat under a weary life,
But that the dread of something after death,
The undiscover'd country from whose bourn
No traveller returns, puzzles the will 25
And makes us rather bear those ills we have
Than fly to others that we know not of?
Thus conscience does make cowards of us all;
And thus the native hue of resolution
Is sicklied o'er with the pale cast of thought, 30
And enterprises of great pith and moment
With this regard their currents turn [awry],
And lose the name of action.
    Hamlet: Act III, 1, 56–88

---

fardels burdens.

HAMLET

How all occasions do inform against me,
And spur my dull revenge! What is a man,
If his chief good and market of his time
Be but to sleep and feed? A beast, no more.
Sure, He that made us with such large discourse, 5
Looking before and after, gave us not
That capability and god-like reason
To fust in us unus'd. Now, whether it be
Bestial oblivion, or some craven scruple
Of thinking too precisely on th' event,— 10
A thought which, quarter'd, hath but one part wisdom
And ever three parts coward,—I do not know

---

fust to become mouldy.

Why yet I live to say, "This thing's to do,"
Sith I have cause and will and strength and means
To do't. Examples gross as earth exhort me; 15
Witness this army of such mass and charge
Led by a delicate and tender prince,
Whose spirit with divine ambition puff'd
Makes mouths at the invisible event,
Exposing what is mortal and unsure 20
To all that fortune, death, and danger dare,
Even for an egg-shell. Rightly to be great
Is not to stir without great argument,
But greatly to find quarrel in a straw
When honour's at the stake. How stand I then, 25
That have a father kill'd, a mother stain'd,
Excitements of my reason and my blood,
And let all sleep, while to my shame I see
The imminent death of twenty thousand men,
That for a fantasy and trick of fame 30
Go to their graves like beds, fight for a plot
Whereon the numbers cannot try the cause,
Which is not tomb enough and continent
To hide the slain? O, from this time forth,
My thoughts be bloody, or be nothing worth! 35
    Hamlet: Act IV, 4, 32–66

GLOUCESTER

Now is the winter of our discontent
Made glorious summer by this sun of York;
And all the clouds that lour'd upon our house

Gloucester later Richard III   *sun of York* Edward IV, of the House of York, King of England, under whom there is momentary peace. Richard hopes to put himself close to the throne by stirring up trouble between Edward "the sun of York" and his brother George, Duke of Clarence—the "G of Edward's heirs."

In the deep bosom of the ocean buried.
Now are our brows bound with victorious wreaths, 5
Our bruised arms hung up for monuments;
Our stern alarums chang'd to merry meetings,
Our dreadful marches to delightful measures.
Grim-visag'd War hath smooth'd his wrinkled front;
And now, instead of mounting barbed steeds 10
To fright the souls of fearful adversaries,
He capers nimbly in a lady's chamber
To the lascivious pleasing of a lute.
But I, that am not shap'd for sportive tricks,
Nor made to court an amorous looking-glass; 15
I, that am rudely stamp'd, and want love's majesty
To strut before a wanton ambling nymph;
I, that am curtail'd of this fair proportion,
Cheated of feature by dissembling nature,
Deform'd, unfinish'd, sent before my time 20
Into this breathing world, scarce half made up,
And that so lamely and unfashionable
That dogs bark at me as I halt by them;
Why, I, in this weak piping time of peace,
Have no delight to pass away the time, 25
Unless to see my shadow in the sun
And descant on mine own deformity.
And therefore, since I cannot prove a lover
To entertain these fair well-spoken days,
I am determined to prove a villain 30
And hate the idle pleasures of these days.
Plots have I laid, inductions dangerous,
By drunken prophecies, libels, and dreams,
To set my brother Clarence and the King
In deadly hate the one against the other; 35
And if King Edward be as true and just
As I am subtle, false, and treacherous,
This day should Clarence closely be mew'd up
About a prophecy, which says that G
Of Edward's heirs the murderer shall be. 40
Dive, thoughts, down to my soul! Here Clarence comes.

Richard III: Act I, 1, 1–141

Ulysses

by ALFRED, LORD TENNYSON

It little profits that an idle king,
By this still hearth, among these barren crags,
Matched with an agèd wife, I mete and dole
Unequal laws unto a savage race,
That hoard, and sleep, and feed, and know not me. 5
I cannot rest from travel: I will drink
Life to the lees: all times I have enjoyed
Greatly, have suffered greatly, both with those
That loved me, and alone; on shore, and when
Through scudding drifts the rainy Hyades 10
Vext the dim sea: I am become a name;

Ulysses the poem is partly based on the prophecy by the ghost of Tiresias that Ulysses will be discontent to remain quietly at home in Ithaca after his adventures (*Odyssey*, XI); but it also owes something to Dante's treatment of Ulysses in the *Inferno* (XXVI, 90 ff.) Dante puts Ulysses in the eighth ring of hell because of his presumption in counseling men to inquire into the mysteries of nature and the heavens. Tennyson accepts this evaluation of Ulysses by Dante but makes him a symbol of the whole 19th Century notion that the very perfection of man consists in his following knowledge "like a sinking star, Beyond the utmost bound of human thought." In this view, it is not the achievement of the goal but the striving toward it that is the ideal.

---

agèd wife Penelope.   *rainy Hyades* a group of stars associated with the rainy season.

For always roaming with a hungry heart.
Much have I seen and known; cities of men
And manners, climates, councils, governments,
Myself not least, but honoured of them all; 15
And drunk delight of battle with my peers,
Far on the ringing plains of windy Troy.
I am a part of all that I have met;
Yet all experience is an arch wherethrough
Gleams that untravelled world, whose margin fades 20
For ever and for ever when I move.
How dull it is to pause, to make an end,
To rust unburnished, not to shine in use!
As though to breathe were life. Life piled on life
Were all too little, and of one to me 25
Little remains: but every hour is saved
From that eternal silence, something more,
A bringer of new things; and vile it were
For some three suns to store and hoard myself,
And this gray spirit yearning in desire 30
To follow knowledge like a sinking star,
Beyond the utmost bound of human thought.
      This is my son, mine own Telemachus,
To whom I leave the sceptre and the isle—
Well-loved of me, discerning to fulfil 35
This labour, by slow prudence to make mild
A rugged people, and through soft degrees
Subdue them to the useful and the good.
Most blameless is he, centred in the sphere
Of common duties, decent not to fail 40
In offices of tenderness, and pay
Meet adoration to my household gods,
When I am gone. He works his work, I mine.
      There lies the port; the vessel puffs her sail:
There gloom the dark broad seas. My mariners, 45
Souls that have toiled, and wrought, and thought with me—
That ever with a frolic welcome took
The thunder and the sunshine, and opposed
Free hearts, free foreheads,—you and I are old;
Old age hath yet his honour and his toil; 50
Death closes all; but something ere the end,
Some work of noble note, may yet be done,
Not unbecoming men that strove with Gods.
The lights begin to twinkle from the rocks:
The long day wanes: the slow moon climbs: the deep 55
Moans round with many voices. Come, my friends,
'Tis not too late to seek a newer world.
Push off, and sitting well in order smite
The sounding furrows; for my purpose holds
To sail beyond the sunset, and the baths 60
Of all the western stars, until I die.
It may be that the gulfs will wash us down:
It may be we shall touch the Happy Isles,
And see the great Achilles, whom we knew.
Though much is taken, much abides: and though 65
We are not now that strength which in old days
Moved earth and heaven; that which we are, we are;
One equal temper of heroic hearts,
Made weak by time and fate, but strong in will
To strive, to seek, to find, and not to yield. 70

Happy Isles Elysia, the home of departed heroes. It was supposed to exist somewhere beyond the Gates of Hercules or Gibraltar. *Achilles* the great Greek hero of *The Iliad* and the Trojan War.

My Last Duchess
by ROBERT BROWNING

That's my last Duchess painted on the wall,
Looking as if she were alive. I call
That piece a wonder, now: Frà Pandolf's hands
Worked busily a day, and there she stands.
Will't please you sit and look at her? I said   5
"Frà Pandolf" by design, for never read
Strangers like you that pictured countenance,
The depth and passion of its earnest glance,
But to myself they turned (since none puts by
The curtain I have drawn for you, but I)   10
And seemed as they would ask me, if they durst,
How such a glance came there; so, not the first
Are you to turn and ask thus. Sir, 'twas not
Her husband's presence only, called that spot
Of joy into the Duchess' cheek: perhaps   15
Frà Pandolf chanced to say, "Her mantle laps
Over my lady's wrist too much," or "Paint
Must never hope to reproduce the faint
Half-flush that dies along her throat": such stuff
Was courtesy, she thought, and cause enough   20
For calling up that spot of joy. She had
A heart—how shall I say?—too soon made glad,
Too easily impressed: she liked whate'er
She looked on, and her looks went everywhere.
Sir, 'twas all one! My favour at her breast,   25
The dropping of the daylight in the West,
The bough of cherries some officious fool
Broke in the orchard for her, the white mule
She rode with round the terrace—all and each
Would draw from her alike the approving speech,   30
Or blush, at least. She thanked men,—good! but thanked
Somehow—I know not how—as if she ranked
My gift of a nine-hundred-years-old name
With anybody's gift. Who'd stoop to blame
This sort of trifling? Even had you skill   35
In speech—(which I have not)—to make your will
Quite clear to such an one, and say, "Just this
Or that in you disgusts me; here you miss,
Or there exceed the mark"—and if she let
Herself be lessoned so, nor plainly set   40
Her wits to yours, forsooth, and made excuse,
—E'en then would be some stooping; and I choose
Never to stoop. Oh sir, she smiled, no doubt,
Whene'er I passed her; but who passed without
Much the same smile? This grew; I gave commands;   45
Then all smiles stopped together. There she stands
As if alive. Will't please you rise? We'll meet
The company below, then. I repeat,

---

my last Duchess The Duke (probably Alonso II of Ferrara) is showing a portrait of his first wife to an envoy of a count whose daughter he is arranging to take as his second wife.   *Frà Pandolph* Both this painter and the sculptor, Claus of Innsbruck, in the last line, are fictitious artists.

---

commands that she be killed.

The Count your master's known munificence
Is ample warrant that no just pretence 50
Of mine for dowry will be disallowed;
Though his fair daughter's self, as I avowed
At starting, is my object. Nay, we'll go
Together down, sir. Notice Neptune, though,
Taming a sea-horse, thought a rarity, 55
Which Claus of Innsbruck cast in broze for me!

Neptune a statue of the sea-god.

The Death of the Hired Man*
by ROBERT FROST

Mary sat musing on the lamp-flame at the table
Waiting for Warren. When she heard his step,
She ran on tip toe down the darkened passage
To meet him in the doorway with the news
And put him on his guard. "Silas is back." 5
She pushed him outward with her through the door
And shut it after her. "Be kind," she said.
She took the market things from Warren's arms
And set them on the porch, then drew him down
To sit beside her on the wooden steps. 10

"When was I ever anything but kind to him?
But I'll not have the fellow back," he said.
"I told him so last haying, didn't I?
'If he left then,' I said, 'that ended it.'
What good is he? Who else will harbor him 15
At his age for the little he can do?
What help he is there's no depending on.
Off he goes always when I need him most.
'He thinks he ought to earn a little pay,
Enough at least to buy tobacco with, 20
So he won't have to beg and be beholden.'
'All right,' I say, 'I can't afford to pay
Any fixed wages, though I wish I could.'
'Someone else can.' 'Then someone else will have to.'
I shouldn't mind his bettering himself 25
If that was what it was. You can be certain,
When he begins like that, there's someone at him
Trying to coax him off with pocket-money,—
In haying time, when any help is scarce.
In winter he comes back to us. I'm done." 30

"Sh! not so loud: he'll hear you," Mary said.

"I want him to: he'll have to soon or late."

"He's worn out. He's asleep beside the stove.
When I came up from Rowe's I found him here,
Huddled against the barn-door fast asleep, 35
A miserable sight, and frightening, too—
You needn't smile—I didn't recognize him—
I wasn't looking for him—and he's changed.
Wait till you see."

---

* From *Complete Poems of Robert Frost*. Copyright, 1916, 1923, 1930, 1939 by Holt, Rinehart and Winston, Inc. Copyright 1936, 1942, 1944, 1951, © 1958 by Robert Frost. Copyright © 1964, 1967 by Lesley Frost Ballantine. Reprinted by permission of Holt, Rinehart and Winston, Inc.

"Where did you say he'd been?"

"He didn't say. I dragged him to the house,
And gave him tea and tried to make him smoke.
I tried to make him talk about his travels.
Nothing would do: he just kept nodding off." 40

"What did he say? Did he say anything?"

"But little." 45

           "Anything? Mary, confess
He said he'd come to ditch the meadow for me."

"Warren!"

           "But did he? I just want to know."

"Of course he did. What would you have him say?
Surely you wouldn't grudge the poor old man 50
Some humble way to save his self-respect.
He added, if you really care to know,
He meant to clear the upper pasture, too.
That sounds like something you have heard before?
Warren, I wish you could have heard the way 55
He jumbled everything. I stopped to look
Two or three times—he made me feel so queer—
To see if he was talking in his sleep.
He ran on Harold Wilson—you remember—
The boy you had in haying four years since. 60
He's finished school, and teaching in his college.
Silas declares you'll have to get him back.
He says they two will make a team for work:
Between them they will lay this farm as smooth!" 65
The way he mixed that in with other things.
He thinks young Wilson a likely lad, though daft 40
On education—you know how they fought
All through July under the blazing sun,
Silas up on the cart to build the load, 70
Harold along beside to pitch it on."

"Yes, I took care to keep well out of earshot."

"Well, those days trouble Silas like a dream. 45
You wouldn't think they would. How some things linger!
Harold's young college boy's assurance piqued him. 75
After so many years he still keeps finding
Good arguments he sees he might have used.
I sympathize. I know just how it feels
To think of the right thing to say too late.
Harold's associated in his mind with Latin. 80
He asked me what I thought of Harold's saying
He studied Latin like the violin
Because he liked it—that an argument!
He said he couldn't make the boy believe
He could find water with a hazel prong— 85
Which showed how much good school had ever done him.
He wanted to go over that. But most of all
He thinks if he could have another chance
To teach him how to build a load of hay—"

"I know, that's Silas' one accomplishment. 90
He bundles every forkful in its place,
And tags and numbers it for future reference,
So he can find and easily dislodge it
In the unloading. Silas does that well.
He takes it out in bunches like big birds' nests. 95

You never see him standing on the hay
He's trying to lift, straining to lift
   himself."

"He thinks if he could teach him that,
   he'd be
Some good perhaps to someone in the
   world.
He hates to see a boy the fool of books.   100
Poor Silas, so concerned for other folk,
And nothing to look backward to with
   pride,
And nothing to look forward to with
   hope,
So now and never any different."

Part of a moon was falling down the
   west,   105
Dragging the whole sky with it to the
   hills.
Its light poured softly in her lap. She
   saw it
And spread her apron to it. She put out
   her hand
Among the harp-like morning-glory
   strings,
Taut with the dew from garden bed to
   eaves,   110
As if she played unheard some tenderness
That wrought on him beside her in the
   night.
"Warren," she said, "he has come home
   to die:
You needn't be afraid he'll leave you
   this time."

"Home," he mocked gently.   115

        "Yes, what else but home?
It all depends on what you mean by home.
Of course he's nothing to us, any more
Than was the hound that came a stranger
   to us
Out of the woods, worn out upon the
   trail."   120

"Home is the place where, when you
   have to go there,
They have to take you in."

        "I should have called it
Something you somehow haven't to
   deserve."

Warren leaned out and took a step or
   two,   125
Picked up a little stick, and brought it
   back
And broke it in his hand and tossed it by.
"Silas has better claim on us you think
Than on his brother? Thirteen little
   miles
As the road winds would bring him to his
   door.   130
Silas has walked that far no doubt today.
Why doesn't he go there? His brother's
   rich,
A somebody—director in the bank."

"He never told us that."

        "We know it though."   135

"I think his brother ought to help, of
   course.
I'll see to that if there is need. He ought
   of right
To take him in, and might be willing to—
He may be better than appearances.
But have some pity on Silas. Do you
   think   140
If he had any pride in claiming kin
Or anything he looked for from his
   brother,
He'd keep so still about him all this
   time?"

"I wonder what's between them."

        "I can tell you.   145
Silas is what he is—we wouldn't mind
   him—
But just the kind that kinsfolk can't
   abide.
He never did a thing so very bad.
He don't know why he isn't quite as good
As anybody. Worthless though he is,   150
He won't be made ashamed to please his
   brother."

"I can't think Si ever hurt anyone."

"No, but he hurt my heart the way he lay
And rolled his old head on that sharp-edged chairback.
He wouldn't let me put him on the lounge.
You must go in and see what you can do.
I made the bed up for him there tonight.
You'll be surprised at him—how much he's broken.
His working days are done; I'm sure of it."

I'd not be in a hurry to say that."

"I haven't been. Go, look, see for yourself.
But, Warren, please remember how it is:
He's come to help you ditch the meadow.
He has a plan. You mustn't laugh at him.
He may not speak of it, and then he may.
I'll sit and see if that small sailing cloud
Will hit or miss the moon."

         It hit the moon.
Then there were three there, making a dim row,
The moon, the little silver cloud, and she.

Warren returned—too soon, it seemed to her,
Slipped to her side, caught up her hand and waited.

"Warren?" she questioned.

         "Dead," was all he answered.

Mr. Flood's Party*

by EDWIN ARLINGTON ROBINSON

Old Eben Flood, climbing alone one night
Over the hill between the town below
And the forsaken upland hermitage
That held as much as he should ever know
On earth again of home, paused warily.
The road was his with not a native near;
And Eben, having leisure, said aloud,
For no man else in Tilbury Town to hear:

"Well, Mr. Flood, we have the harvest moon
Again, and we may not have many more;
The bird is on the wing, the poet says,
And you and I have said it here before.
Drink to the bird." He raised up to the light
The jug that he had gone so far to fill,
And answered huskily: "Well, Mr. Flood,
Since you propose it, I believe I will."

Alone, as if enduring to the end
A valiant armor of scarred hopes outworn,
He stood there in the middle of the road
Like Roland's ghost winding a silent horn.
Below him, in the town among the trees,
Where friends of other days had honored him,
A phantom salutation of the dead
Rang thinly till old Eben's eyes were dim.

Then, as a mother lays her sleeping child
Down tenderly, fearing it may awake,
He set the jug down slowly at his feet

Roland's ghost Roland was the most famous follower of Charlemagne. According to legend, he sounded his horn too late in a pass in the Pyrenees to summon the help that might have saved him and his followers from death at the hands of the Saracens.

---

* Reprinted with the permission of The Macmillan Company from *Collected Poems of Edwin Arlington Robinson.* Copyright 1921 by Edwin Arlington Robinson, renewed 1949 by Ruth Nivison.

With trembling care, knowing that most
    things break;
And only when assured that on firm earth
It stood, as the uncertain lives of men   30
Assuredly did not, he paced away,
And with his hand extended paused again:

"Well, Mr. Flood, we have not met like
    this
In a long time; and many a change has
    come
To both of us, I fear, since last it was   35
We had a drop together. Welcome
    home!"
Convivially returning with himself,
Again he raised the jug up to the light;
And with an acquiescent quaver said:
"Well, Mr. Flood, if you insist, I might.   40

"Only a very little, Mr. Flood—
For auld lang syne. No more, sir; that will
    do."

So, for the time, apparently it did,
And Eben evidently thought so too;
For soon amid the silver loneliness   45
Of night he lifted up his voice and sang,
Secure, with only two moons listening,
Until the whole harmonious landscape
    rang—

"For auld lang syne." The weary throat
    gave out,
The last word wavered, and the song was
    done.   50
He raised again the jug regretfully
And shook his head, and was again alone.
There was not much that was ahead of
    him,
And there was nothing in the town
    below—
Where strangers would have shut the
    many doors   55
That many friends had opened long ago.

The Love Song of J. Alfred Prufrock*
by T. S. ELIOT

Let us go then, you and I,
When the evening is spread out against
    the sky
Like a patient etherised upon a table;
Let us go, through certain half-deserted
    streets,
The muttering retreats   5
Of restless nights in one-night cheap
    hotels
And sawdust restaurants with oyster-
    shells:

Streets that follow like a tedious
    argument
Of insidious intent
To lead you to an overwhelming
    question . . .   10
Oh, do not ask, "What is it?"
Let us go and make our visit.

In the room the women come and go
Talking of Michelangelo.

The yellow fog that rubs its back upon
    the window-panes,   15
The yellow smoke that rubs its muzzle
    on the window-panes
Licked its tongue into the corners of the
    evening,

Alfred Prufrock a name which Eliot may have remembered from St. Louis. It is meant to suggest a bourgeois, middle-class background, which is out of place in the world of teacups and gossip in which Prufrock finds himself.

* From *Collected Poems 1909–1962* by T. S. Eliot, copyright, 1936, by Harcourt Brace Jovanovich, Inc.; copyright, © 1963, 1964, by T. S. Eliot. Reprinted by permission of Harcourt Brace Jovanovich, Inc., and Faber and Faber Limited.

Michelangelo the most dynamic and virile genius among Renaissance artists—worlds removed from the comprehension of the women of the poem.

Lingered upon the pools that stand in drains,
Let fall upon its back the soot that falls from chimneys,
Slipped by the terrace, made a sudden leap, 20
And seeing that it was a soft October night,
Curled once about the house, and fell asleep.

And indeed there will be time
For the yellow smoke that slides along the street,
Rubbing its back upon the window-panes; 25
There will be time, there will be time
To prepare a face to meet the faces that you meet;
There will be time to murder and create,
And time for all the works and days of hands
That lift and drop a question on your plate; 30
Time for you and time for me,
And time yet for a hundred indecisions,
And for a hundred visions and revisions,
Before the taking of a toast and tea.

In the room the women come and go 35
Talking of Michelangelo.

And indeed there will be time
To wonder, "Do I dare?" and, "Do I dare?"
Time to turn back and descend the stair,
With a bald spot in the middle of my hair— 40
[They will say: "How his hair is growing thin!"]
My morning coat, my collar mounting firmly to the chin,
My necktie rich and modest, but asserted by a simple pin—
[They will say: "But how his arms and legs are thin!"]
Do I dare 45

Disturb the universe?
In a minute there is time
For decisions and revisions which a minute will reverse.

For I have known them all already, known them all:—
Have known the evenings, mornings, afternoons, 50
I have measured out my life with coffee spoons;
I know the voices dying with a dying fall
Beneath the music from a farther room.
     So how should I presume?

And I have known the eyes already, known them all— 55
The eyes that fix you in a formulated phrase,
And when I am formulated, sprawling on a pin,
When I am pinned and wriggling on the wall,
Then how should I begin
To spit out all the butt-ends of my days and ways?
     And how should I presume? 60

And I have known the arms already, known them all—
Arms that are braceleted and white and bare
[But in the lamplight, downed with light brown hair!]
Is it perfume from a dress
That makes me so digress? 65
Arms that lie along a table, or wrap about a shawl.
     And should I then presume?
     And how should I begin?

          .   .   .   .   .

Shall I say, I have gone at dusk through narrow streets
And watched the smoke that rises from the pipes 70
Of lonely men in shirt-sleeves, leaning out of windows? . . .

---

works and days an allusion to Hesiod's (8th Century B.C.) *Works and Days*, a serious discussion of farming, marriage, and so on.

I should have been a pair of ragged claws
Scuttling across the floors of silent seas.

     . . . . .

And the afternoon, the evening, sleeps so
    peacefully!
Smoothed by long fingers, 75
Asleep . . . tired . . . or it malingers,
Stretched on the floor, here beside you
    and me.
Should I, after tea and cakes and ices,
Have the strength to force the moment
    to its crisis?
But though I have wept and fasted, wept
    and prayed, 80
Though I have seen my head [grown
    slightly bald] brought it upon a platter,
I am no prophet—and here's no great
    matter;
I have seen the moment of my greatness
    flicker,
And I have seen the eternal Footman
    hold my coat, and snicker, 85
And in short, I was afraid.
And would it have been worth it, after
    all,
After the cups, the marmalade, the tea,
Among the porcelain, among some talk
    of you and me,
Would it have been worth while, 90
To have bitten off the matter with a
    smile,
To have squeezed the universe into a ball
To roll it toward some overwhelming
    question,
To say: "I am Lazarus, come from the
    dead,
Come back to tell you all, I shall tell
    you all"— 95

If one, settling a pillow by her head,
    Should say: "That is not what I
        meant at all.
    That is not it, at all."

And would it have been worth it, after all,
Would it have been worth while,
After the sunsets and the dooryards and
    the sprinkled streets, 100
After the novels, after the teacups, after
    the skirts that trail along the floor—
And this, and so much more?—
It is impossible to say just what I mean!
But as if a magic lantern threw the
    nerves in patterns on a screen:
Would it have been worth while 105
If one, settling a pillow by her head or
    throwing off a shawl,
And turning toward the window, should
    say:
    "That is not it at all,
    That is not what I meant, at all."

     . . . . .

No! I am not Prince Hamlet, nor was
    meant to be; 110
Am an attendant lord, one that will do
To swell a progress, start a scene or two,
Advise the prince; no doubt, an easy tool,
Deferential, glad to be of use,
Politic, cautious, and meticulous; 115
Full of high sentence, but a bit obtuse;
At times, indeed, almost ridiculous—
Almost, at times, the Fool.

I grow old . . . I grow old . . .
I shall wear the bottoms of my trousers
    rolled. 120

Shall I part my hair behind? Do I dare
    to eat a peach?
I shall wear white flannel trousers, and
    walk upon the beach.
I have heard the mermaids singing, each
    to each.

I do not think that they will sing to me.

---

head . . . upon a platter an illusion to St. John the Baptist, who was beheaded by Herod at the request of the dancer Salome, and whose head was brought into the banquet hall on a platter. *eternal Footman* probably death. *into a ball* an allusion to a passage in Marvell's *To His Coy Mistress*— "Let us roll all our strength and all/ Our sweetness up into a ball,/ And tear our pleasures with rough strife/ Through the iron gates of life."

I have seen them riding seaward on the waves
Combing the white hair of the waves blown back
When the wind blows the water white and black.

We have lingered in the chambers of the sea
By sea-girls wreathed with seaweed red and brown
Till human voices wake us, and we drown.

# APPENDIXES

Appendix One
SAMPLE ANALYSES OF SHORT STORIES

The Peasant Marey
by FYODOR DOSTOEVSKY

The short story of yesteryear depended strongly upon graphic, external action. The wagon train halted thirty miles east of Fort Laramie because smoke signals had appeared above the ridges ahead and an Indian attack was feared. Some of the settlers were in favor of returning to Dodge City, but the lead scout persuaded the settlers to try a bold stratagem. The migrants drew their train up on high ground into an impregnable fortress by day, and moved only by night in the shadow of a long escarpment leading toward Laramie. They easily repelled the half-hearted attacks of the Indians, who were disconcerted by such unorthodox tactics; without losing a man or a wagon, they pulled safely into the fort on the third night.

Incontestably, such a narrative has all the ingredients necessary for a short story: setting, a problem, characterization, suspense, etc. Above all, it has action, a sequence of events, one growing out of the other. The situation at the end of the story is different from the situation at the beginning: the pioneers have traversed the danger-filled thirty miles and are safely in Fort Laramie.

"The Peasant Marey," like the tale just outlined, is the story of a progression from one condition to another. The situation at the end of the story differs from that which obtained at its beginning, but the movement is internal.[1] Externally, there is no change whatsoever. The central figure is in a Siberian prison at the tale's outset; he is there at the end. Withal, his condition is drastically different. His viewpoint, and therefore his perspective, shift markedly; in the course of the story he traverses a distance far greater than the thirty miles to Fort Laramie. From his new viewpoint he sees the world and his fellow men in a startlingly different light.

At the outset of the story Dostoevsky is plunged in gloom. He is filled with revulsion at the coarse, animal-like behavior of his fellow-prisoners, most of whom are of the peasant class. At length the grossness of his fellow-convicts becomes intolerable, "blind fury blazed up" in his heart, and he flees from the sight of the "common people." The emotional, the internal point—and we must remember that the internal is the major dimension in this story—is fixed by the remark of another prisoner, a Pole who, like Dostoevsky, is not of peasant origin. Sensing Dostoevsky's disgust, the Pole hisses in an undertone, "I hate these brigands."

This remark is still echoing in Dostoevsky's mind when he retires to his bunk and pretends to be asleep. Gradually, however, he loses the awareness of his whereabouts and is borne on a tide of recollection to a scene of his boyhood, to the time of glad acceptance of the mysterious and lovely world around him. He remembers the hazel and the birch twigs, the beetles, the insects, the lizards, "the wood with its mushrooms and wild berries, its beetles and its birds, its hedgehogs and squirrels, and its damp smell of rotted leaves."

Above these impressions of the good earth, however, looms the memory of a good man. While at play amid the pleasant realities of the fields, the boy had an hallucination; he imagined that he heard the cry, "Wolf!" Terrified, he fled to a peasant ploughing nearby. Gently, lovingly, the illiterate serf calmed the boy, touching his quivering lips with his thick finger stained with earth—with the good earth—and murmuring, "There now! Christ be with you, cross yourself, there's a good lad!"

---

[1] Someone has wisely said that the story of modern literature has been the story of the discovery and colonization of inwardness.

Reliving the incident years later in his prison reverie, Dostoevsky finds it both vivid and significant.

> . . . I suddenly remembered this meeting so distinctly that not a single detail of it was lost. . . . I remembered the tender, motherly smile of the serf, the way he made the sign of the cross over me and crossed himself . . . the thick finger of his, smeared with earth, with which he touched my twitching lips so gently and with such shy tenderness . . . if I had been his own son, he could not have looked at me with eyes shining with brighter love.

When Dostoevsky arises from his bunk and goes out again among his fellow-prisoners, he finds that he "could look at these unhappy creatures with quite different eyes, and that suddenly by some miracle all hatred and anger had vanished . . ." Now he goes about the enclosure, not avoiding, but "peering into the faces" of, the prisoners. He perceives that that

> peasant with his shaven head and branded face, yelling his hoarse drunken song at the top of his voice—why, he, too, may be the same sort of peasant as Marey . . .

And behind Marey's unrefined appearance, Dostoevsky well knows, lay a whole world of gentleness, warmth, and love. Within his new purview he sees the scornful Polish prisoner, also, in a new light. Although the bitter Pole retains at the end of the story the harsh opinion ("I hate these brigands") that he expressed at the story's beginning, Dostoevsky has no word of reproof for him. Instead he sees him as a man twice imprisoned, first within the palings of a Siberian jail but even more closely enclosed within the cage of his own hate—a predicament Dostoevsky views with compassion:

> Yes, it was much harder for those Poles than for us.

The story of this prison "escape" is, therefore, the story of a traverse from one point of view to another, and it is interesting to note some of the clues that the author has left us to mark the journey. Note, first of all, the time that he has chosen for opening his narrative; from among the fifty-five or sixty days of the year on which the convicts do not work he has selected Easter Monday, the second day of the principal Christian feast, the feast celebrating Christ's triumph over death. Although the day is a lovely one ("the air was warm, the sky blue, the sun high, warm, and bright . . .") the writer is unresponsive to its beauty because he is "plunged in gloom." He is filled with revulsion at the behavior of the convicts (note the plural at the beginning of the story as he groups the convicts; at the end he will shift to the singular and the particular). His revulsion is also felt by a Pole named Miretski.[2] Each flees, as well as he can, from the prison society—and from each other. Dostoevsky takes refuge in memories of his past life, especially of his boyhood. He describes at surprising length for so short a story his rambles through a summer-touched countryside. Where a sentence or two would suffice to localize the incident he is going to describe, he expands upon the beauties and joys of the fields; almost in litany form he recounts his happiness in the look of frogs, beetles, and lizards, the taste of wild berries and mushrooms, the song of birds, the feel of brittle hazel twigs, and the fragrance of birch wood. Working quite deliberately, the writer leads us through the whole canon of sense—seeing, tasting, hearing, feeling, and smelling; he sounds a paean of affirmation, of glad acceptance of the good earth. Against these chords he will presently vibrate another note linking Marey, the good man, with the good earth.

> . . . He quietly stretched out his thick finger with its black nail, smeared with earth, and gently touched my trembling lips. . . . And particularly I remembered that thick finger of his, smeared with earth, with which he touched my twitching lips so gently and with such tenderness.

---

[2] Note that the two men cannot be said to "share" their hatred; hatred is divisive, as is implied in the sentence "'*Je hais ces brigands!* he hissed at me in an undertone and walked past me.'" Presumably the two intellectuals could not endure each other any better than they could tolerate their rougher fellow-prisoners.

Somewhat in the manner of a symphony the story surges towards its end, lifting and bearing both writer and reader to a point far beyond the glum and hate-filled outlook of the tale's beginning. This wave of affirmation carries us forward to a glad acceptance of the world and of man, past negation, past the hasty rejection of any human being, however unrefined, to the vantage point from which we see each man as a creature "fearfully and wonderfully made."

And when we speak of a "creature fearfully and wonderfully made," we are, of course, in the main stream of the Judaeo-Christian tradition, which presents to us one of the two basic ways of looking at man. Within this framework the universe is seen as more than a mechanism and man as more than a fragment of this mechanism. The curt dismissal by an American sociologist of a group of slump-shouldered convicts (similar, no doubt, to those in the Siberian prison) as "poor protoplasm poorly put together" is not allowable to the Christian. As an honest observer the Christian must admit that there is some external evidence for such a view, but the point—and, indeed, this is the major point of the story—is that there is more to be said.

Exploring human nature in the concrete, specific example of the peasant Marey, Dostoevsky finds in it a complexity, a depth, a dimension untouched by the poor-protoplasm-poorly-put-together hypothesis. This dimension becomes explicable only within the Christian context in which the touch of God is seen even in the meanest of His creatures. This affirmation, this locus, is the point toward which the story progresses and at which its elements converge. Now we can see why Dostoevsky chose Easter Monday for the opening of the story, why his form shifts from plural to singular, why he lingers over boyhood's glad acceptance of the good earth with its frogs, its lizards, its beetles, its hedgehogs, its birch wood, its fragrant leaves,[3] why the "wolf" that intruded upon his enjoyment was, like the hatred that possessed him at the story's beginning, something that existed only within his own mind. Now we can understand why the peasant comforts the frightened child in religious terms ("Come, come, there; Christ be with you! Cross yourself") and why the author is at pains to show that Marey's kindness was not prompted by hope of reward (". . . only God, perhaps, may have seen from above . . .").

Perhaps, too, we can glimpse at the story's surging close at least part of the reason why Dostoevsky is regarded as a Christian Realist.

---

[3] The lines in the story recounting the marvelous variety on the good earth are kindred to those of another Christian Realist who celebrated this variety in a poem beginning "Glory be to God for dappled things"—see Gerard Manley Hopkins, "Pied Beauty" at the beginning of Unit 9.

Pericles on 31st Street
by HARRY MARK PETRAKIS

This story, deceptively simple on first reading, deals for the most part with ordinary people. Certainly Dan Ryan, Olaf Johnson, Sol Reidman, and Bernard Klioris are ordinary enough and, not incidentally, represent the American melting pot—a kind of League of Nations. The protagonist, Nick Simonakis, is a peanut vender, an object of ridicule to the other characters, ordinary as they are. The story presents a slight twist to the proposition in the introduction to this volume that the average man is capable of heroism. Simonakis at first alone supports the idea. He is dignified, ceremonious, even poetic, blessed with self-respect, dignity, and an indomitable heart. Most of all, he is a man with a code of ethics, and he lives by that code. Not only does he refuse to be put down himself; he will not abide watching those whom he regards as the oppressed humiliated. Given his rugged leadership, the weak rise to the stature of real men. We have a deftly presented example of the way in which a man (or perhaps a nation) willing to take a stand for what is right and just can unite the little world of the saloon (or possibly a bigger world) to action that will drive out the tyrant. This is not to say that the story is at all points, or even at any point, an allegory, but the parallel is there for those who choose to think so.

Stated in a slightly different fashion, the theme is the role of courage in opposing oppression or tyranny. The action, however, is the attempt of a mean-spirited slum landlord to squeeze a few extra dollars out of his storekeeping tenants, men to whom an additional fifteen percent rent increase is a serious matter. It is the Greek, with his memories of the heroic days of Greece, with his references to Leonidas, Themistocles, the "men like lions," with his one-man attack on the landlord, and finally his appeal to Pericles, who at last gives unity and courage to the tenants and unites them in rebellion. Thus, very gradually as the story progresses, the grubby little action grows to fit the stature of the theme. Petrakis is not concerned with such things as the nature of time or "the dark recesses of the soul." He is repeating what he says in so many other of his fine stories: that existence is not always the tangled, tortuous, defeating jungle that the naturalists present; courage is the key to life.

Technically, the story offers no real problems. It is told in a simple, economical, straightforward fashion. In form it is close to drama and, with few changes, it could be staged as a one-act play with protagonist, antagonist, and commentator. Petrakis, preoccupied in most of his writing with Greek characters, may have had some such idea in the back of his mind as he wrote. You might note that the bartender speaks of the businessmen as a "chorus."

The point of view is that of the first-person, dispassionate narrator, George. Why "George" rather than "Roger" or "Alfred"? Although it is scarcely necessary, Petrakis takes time out to have George explain his neutral stance, in which he is the prototype of almost every bartender in the world.

A careful reader may detect a slight weakness of craftsmanship in the drawing of this character. Although George acts like a bartender, he does not talk like one (granting that an occasional bartender may be a college graduate). A typical bartender would be unlikely to speak of the attempt to "mediate an argument," or to use such quasi-literary words as "episode," "indignantly," "berated," "beamed," "fumed," "huskily," or to say, "He wore a stern and studied look on his face," especially when he will elsewhere say such things as, "Barsevick stood there like rocks were being bounced off his head . . ." All that needs to be noted here is that it is difficult for a writer to say precisely what he has in mind without using precise, literary words. Even though such words do not fit a character the writer may, of course, use them at the risk of criticism from the sophisticated reader. The better the craftsman, the more able he is to avoid such a pitfall. An instance in which Joyce was more successful in handling this problem can be found in his use of a different point of view in "Clay."

The characters are in no degree complicated, nor is there any necessity for their being so. One might note that the author uses here a common literary device: for the purpose of promoting realism and making his dialogue more interesting and easy to handle, he has split the single necessary character (the downtrodden storekeeper) into four characters. Only in names and some slight attempt to give each a single characteristic do they differ much from one another: one is stolid, one is belligerent, one rather stupid, etc. Otherwise they bow their shoulders together under oppression and they rise as one to manhood.

It may be worthwhile to point out the use which the author makes of beer and wine as contrasting symbols.

Students would enjoy reading a collection of Petrakis' short stories entitled *Pericles on 31st Street*, or his novel *A Dream of Kings*.

Appendix Two
SAMPLE ANALYSIS OF A SHORT NOVEL

The Dead
by JAMES JOYCE

This massive story by one of the literary giants of the age, generally considered one of the finest stories of the past fifty years, is less likely to impress the inexperienced reader than are some of the more exciting, action-filled, or anecdotal stories of the collection. However, the ever-growing body of approval for it and its companion stories in *Dubliners* strongly suggests that if you do not find its greatness in a first reading then you owe it a second, a third, or even a fourth reading. It is a story to grow up to; more than most it requires the application to it of a rather formal reading technique.

As you will have observed, "The Dead" has no plot, or at least no obvious plot. Almost all the action seems to be sequential rather than consequential although, as a matter of fact, the story is strongly based on consequence. It is a revelation of a truth about life (and death) presented in the space of one evening in several major scenes. In the first and longest scene, Gabriel moves gradually to the fore. At first the story is seen through the eyes of the author in what is sometimes called the "effaced narrator" point of view: it is as though the author were standing in the hall, on the stairs, in the pantry—invisible—noting and recording all that is to be seen or heard. He makes little attempt to get inside the characters' minds to tell us what they are thinking. Notice, for an example of the technique, what happens when Gabriel, attempting a pleasantry with Lily, elicits the bitter reply, "The men that is now is only all palaver and what they can get out of you." The author continues, "Gabriel coloured, *as if he felt* he had made a mistake . . ." The author is judging Gabriel's reaction, not from what he sees going on inside Gabriel's head, but simply from what an acute observer could see by looking at him. A few paragraphs later the author does move inside Gabriel's mind as the latter fingers his notes and worries about his speech, and we read, "He was undecided about the lines from Robert Browning, for he feared they would be above the heads of his listeners." This point of view is known as *omniscient* and, more specifically, *central intelligence*: omniscient because the author is now arrogating to himself the privilege of seeing everything inside and outside the characters' heads; central intelligence because he confines himself principally to seeing the story and interpreting the action through the eyes of the centrally placed character who is the most perceptive member of the group. The remainder of the story holds to the omniscient point of view, with much of it central intelligence. The final section is all central intelligence: we know Gretta's heart and mind only through what her husband sees and hears in the privacy of their hotel room. Although it is not always recognized as such, the central intelligence point of view is a strong factor in giving structural as well as psychological unity to a story. However end-to-end the incidents might seem to be, there is a certain oneness given to the account because it is an evening experienced by one man who, falling asleep at the conclusion, brings a natural end to the observation.

There is, however, a much stronger structural element in the use of what Frank O'Connor calls the "muted symbol." The two following paragraphs quoted from O'Connor's essay "And It's a Lonely, Personal Art" (see pages 9–10) carry their own explanation:

> The device of the muted symbol is superbly used in "The Dead." The events of the story have already long taken place, and were never very significant. A tubercular young man who sang a song called "The Lass of Aughrin" fell in love with

a West of Ireland girl called Gretta. One night, she found him outside her window, wet and shivering, and soon after, he died. The story proper opens years later with the arrival of Gretta and her husband at a musical party given by two old music teachers in Dublin. As Gabriel Conroy, the husband, enters, he scrapes snow from his galoshes and cracks a joke with the maid about getting married. She retorts bitterly that "the men that is now is only all palaver and what they can get out of you." These two things—the snow and the maid's retort—form the theme of the story, and they are repeated in varied and more menacing forms until the climax.

"The men that is now" cannot be great lovers; it is only the dead who can be perfect. The young Gaelic League girl with whom Gabriel chats about the West of Ireland—the subject, like the dead themselves, rising—may be charming, but she cannot have the courtesy and grace of the old music teachers who are passing into the shadow; Caruso—a subtle touch, this—may, for all we know, be a good singer, but he cannot be as great as Parkinson, the obscure English tenor, whom one of the old ladies once heard. And in the tremendous cadenza we realize that Gabriel, good husband though he may be, can never mean to his wife what the dead boy who once stood shivering beneath her window means—till he too has been buried under the snow which is Death's symbol.

Of course "The Dead" is considerably more than the working out of a thesis in skeletal form. The story is alive with brilliantly portrayed settings and people. As Harry Levin has pointed out in his critical work, *James Joyce*, "An unconscionable amount of talking and singing and drinking goes on in *Dubliners*," and that is particularly true here. As Levin further observes, "This promotes style and poetry and fantasy—all peculiarly Irish qualities, and talents of Joyce." You might ask yourself why Joyce goes to all the trouble to bring the old maids' dance party so vividly before us, why it is necessary for us to see the party wit, Mr. Browne, and the forty-year-old youth, Freddy, and all the others so clearly. Part of the answer is that Joyce simply had that wonderful evocative power, and part is that in making the people and scenes surrounding Gabriel so vivid he makes Gabriel all the more believable too.

Gabriel is a young man at the height of his powers, but he is conscious, as Joyce was, of the decadence and decay that is part of Dublin, and of the sense of sadness and isolation that is part of every human being. Gabriel, surrounded by the gaiety of the party, looks out the window, taps the cold pane with his fingers, and envisions the snow lying out along the riverbanks and in the park, and wishes he could walk out in it alone. A little later, rising nervously to his feet to deliver his annual speech, he again sees the same scene and again wishes to be out there where "the Wellington Monument wore a gleaming cap of snow that flashed westward over the white field of Fifteen Acres."

In his speech Gabriel anticipated his own full realization of this sense of loneliness of the soul. In composing it he had felt no interest in or intention of being either truthful or sincere. He felt himself to be, and perhaps was, the most intelligent person present. He wished out of a certain genuine affection to make his two rather ignorant and silly old aunts happy by saying a few "nice things." The chief quality of the speech, thinly concealed, was condescension. By introducing what he regarded as being a few trite bits of sentimentalism he expected to bring the easy tears to his aunts' eyes and to replace the tears with smiles by a deft turn of phrase. The deep irony of the speech lay in the fact that he was telling the truth without meaning to, and this truth was to rise up and almost destroy him within a few hours: "Thoughts of the past, of youth, of changes, of absent faces that we miss here tonight. Our path through life is strewn with many such sad memories: and were we to brood upon them always we could not find the heart to go on bravely with our work among the living."

No doubt it was this train of thought which helped stir in Gretta's mind the memory of Michael Furey, the lost dead boy who loved her. Standing at the head of the stairs listening to Bartell D'Arcy sing "The Lass of Aughrim" was the second and reinforcing incident which brought about the somber climax of the story.

Appendix Three
SOME NOTES ON POETRY

THE WORDS OF POETRY

Diction in Poetry

By *diction* in poetry is meant the choice by the poet of the exactly right words to express the idea and mood he is attempting to communicate. The real artistry of the poet is revealed here. His selection of precisely the right words to suit the context of the whole poem is comparable to the painter's ability to select the exactly right color and line to create the impression he is trying to convey to us on the canvas. (Contrast, for instance, the colors and lines in Van Gogh's *Potato Eaters* with those in his *Starry Night*.)

To achieve this the poet must know and savor the exact *denotation* (the most precise possible meaning) of the words he uses. He must know words as a painter knows colors and lines. But even more important for his purposes is the *connotation* of words. This is one of the poet's chief tools through which he achieves much of the concentration and rich emotional appeal of his poetry. We might compare the *denotation* of a word to the central axial point created by dropping a pebble in the water. Like that point the denotation of a word remains permanent and fixed. The connotations of words, on the other hand, are multiple and expanding like the rings that spread out on the surface of a pond from the point where the pebble was dropped. There are some rings of connotation that are immediate and almost universal. The word "tulip," for instance, *denotes* a precise kind of chalice-like flower that grows from a bulb. But the mere mention of the word almost immediately *connotes* Holland to any listener. This is the first ring of connotation. Other rings are almost sure to follow, including dikes, windmills, wooden shoes, and Old Dutch Cleanser. These rings of connotation move farther and farther away from the central point of the denotation of a word, and the remote meanings are almost sure to be different for each person reacting to the word.

It is the ability of words to stimulate the imagination in this way that the poet relies on for much of the expressiveness of his poetry. As an artist he has to choose words that will connote much more than they denote and that will set up a train of associations appropriate to the whole spirit and feeling of his poem. The poet, of course, if he is serious about communicating with his reader, must be fair and not rely on a connotation of a word that is so personal to himself that no reader could possibly be expected to catch it. And the reader of the poem, on the other hand, must be willing to cooperate with the poet and not insist on a personal connotation of a word that does violence to the whole context of the poem. A nice interplay is demanded here between poet and reader. As readers we must be as diligent in getting at the exact denotation of words as the poet was in choosing them; and we have also to allow them to work on our imagination and select the *connotation* that best suits both the immediate and remote context of the poem in which they occur.

The connotation of one word, moreover, can create an atmosphere or context in a poem that will suggest other words and images to the poet as he writes, and a single evocative word can, in turn, give direction to the mind and imagination of the reader for interpreting many other words and images in the poem. The word *dauphin* in Hopkins' "Windhover" (in Unit Nine) is such a word. It literally means "crowned prince"; but its connotation of plumed chivalry or horsemanship gives added meaning to a whole series of other words in the rest of the poem, such as *falcon* and *chevalier*, and to the image of the windhover itself riding the cloud like a horseman on a mettlesome mount. Re-read that poem and notice how the connotations of *dauphin* reach out and interpenetrate the whole poem.

Besides a professional attitude toward the

exact *denotation* of words and an ability to choose the word with the right connotation for his purpose, the poet must be aware of the imaginative appeal of *concrete* words rather than abstractions. And this for a very good reason. If he wants his reader to see and sense what he is talking about, he must use concrete words because it is only *concrete things* that any of us have ever seen. *Birds* exist only in the mind. What we have seen are robins, eagles, hummingbirds, crows, owls, and sparrows. Any one of these concrete words will summon up in our imagination images in full color. The abstract "bird" is apt to revoke only a blur of feathers and wings. Because our actual experiences have been of concrete examples of the species, the concrete word is apt to be much more connotative, much richer in imaginative associations, and ordinarily, therefore, serves the purposes of the poet better.

This does not mean, however, that the abstract word has no place in poetry. The purpose and intention of the poet in a precise line of a precise poem is the only thing that determines whether a word is poetically effective or ineffective. There are times when the abstract word is the only right word; but for evoking the imaginative and emotionally connotative picture, the concrete is the better word. Note, for instance, the increasing pictorial and associative evocativeness of the following series of words: *thing, building, house, cottage, thatched cottage, bungalow, brownstone mansion, rambling ranch house.*

In general, then, it is the specific, the concrete, and connotative word that is the stock in trade of the poet.

Imagery in Poetry

In its broadest sense, *imagery* refers to the use of any word or group of words that has a strong sense appeal but especially an appeal to the sense of sight. This appeal is made chiefly to the imagination by means of concrete and connotative words. "Golden daffodils," "pastoral farms, green to the very door," "the gaunt crag," are examples of word groups that make an appeal to the sense of sight; "rolling from their mountain springs with a soft inland murmur," "in a wailful choir the small gnats mourn," and "crickets sing" all appeal to the sense of hearing; "and plump the hazel shells with a sweet kernel" appeals to the sense of taste; "drowsed with the fume of poppies," to the sense of smell; and "the mossed cottage trees," to the sense of touch. In a real-life experience all our senses are likely to be appealed to at once. A poet often attempts to approximate that experience by the varied sense appeal of his diction, as Keats does, for instance, in his ode "To Autumn" (in Unit Ten) from which several of the examples above are taken.

But the term *imagery* is sometimes used in a more restricted sense as synonymous with *figurative* language. Figurative language, in general, is language which departs from the ordinary meaning of words to achieve special effects. The two most usual figures of speech are the *simile* and the *metaphor*.

The *simile* consists in an explicit comparison of two objects which are essentially unlike but which are strikingly alike in one or more respects. The simile relies on the familiar to clarify the unknown. Greater clarity and precision of understanding is the result. But the two things compared must be essentially unlike; it is not a simile, for instance, to compare John to James or one lion to another—these are simple comparisons. But when we say that John is like a lion, that is a simile. The fact that the things compared are essentially different makes the points in which they are alike all the more striking (in this instance, their strength, courage, and fierce action). In similes the two things compared may be alike either in *qualities* that the two things have in common or in *actions* that the two things perform. Thus, in the simile "John entered like a lion," John and the lion are represented as alike in the quality of their wrath and in the action of their fierce stride. The comparison in a simile is always explicit and indicated by such words as "like" or "as." This keeps the two things compared distinct from one another in our minds but focuses on the points that they have in common.

The *metaphor*, on the other hand, is an *identification* of two things that are essentially different with such completeness that qualities and actions proper to one are predicated of the other. In a metaphor we do not say that one thing is like another, but rather we identify it with the other and go on talking about it as if it were that other. In a metaphorical expression we would not say that John entered the room like a lion, but that "a lion entered, tearing the crowd to tatters." In this case we have identified John with the lion and given him all the prerogatives of a lion. The effect of a metaphor is not increased clarity but rather a kind of obscurity; through this very obscurity, however, a richer connotation and emotional suggestiveness is obtained. John, without ceasing to be a man, takes on the qualities and actions of a lion and continues to function in both natures. Frequently one or two words can give a metaphorical cast to a whole sentence or passage. For example: "He growled out his complaints, but whined for sympathy when some criticism was aimed at him." The words "growled" and "whined" imply the identification of the person described with a dog and invite the kind of emotional response that an unpleasant cur would evoke. Such a response would not be invited nearly as effectively by a straightforward statement, as for instance: "He gave his answers reluctantly, and then asked for sympathy when he was criticized." Metaphor is the device most used by the poet for obtaining condensation and emotional intensity in his poetry. It is also through metaphor that the poet succeeds in expressing his freshest and most personal insights.

Allegory is an extended metaphor.

A *parable*, on the other hand, is an extended simile. Whereas the simile is generally content with one or another explicit point of comparison, the parable extends the comparison point by point into a full-fledged story. Study, for instance, the parable of the Prodigal Son, in which the point-by-point details of the story represent the condition of the sinner in relation to God.

The *symbol* is a sign of some kind (a word or thing) that suggests something outside and beyond itself. Smoke is a symbol of fire; a flag is a symbol of a country. Thus, in Frost's "The Death of the Hired Man" in Unit Twelve, it is clear from the context that the wife's playing on the harp-like morning-glory strings is a symbol of her playing on the heart of her husband. And, in Wordsworth's "Michael" in Unit Eight, the heap of stones from the unfinished sheepfold is a symbol of the tragic frustration of Michael's whole life. Symbols add a great deal to the expressiveness and suggestiveness of a great many poems.

Personification is really a kind of metaphor in which some abstract thing or inanimate object is given a human nature and personality. Thus Keats gives autumn the personality of a human being and then of a thresher, a reaper, and a gleaner, by turns, in the ode "To Autumn" in Unit Ten. Personification enables objects and abstractions to act like persons and therefore to take on some of the emotional associations of persons.

Synecdoche is a metaphor in which a part of something is used to signify the whole. Thus we speak of "ten sails" on the lake, when we mean ten boats; or of all "hands on deck," when we mean all the men in the crew.

Metonymy is a metaphor in which the name of one thing is used for another with which it is closely associated. Thus we speak of "allegiance to the flag," when we mean allegiance to country, or of "studying Shakespeare," when we mean studying his plays.

Figures of speech, in general, provide the pleasure of surprise in the recognition of hidden resemblances between things that we ourselves may not have noticed, and the pleasure of recognition when we see the appropriateness of the comparison or identification of the two things. They also make concrete and richly connotative what may, without them, remain cold, colorless, and lifeless abstractions.

THE SOUNDS OF POETRY

Rhythm in Life

Rhythm is a very important part of the expressiveness of any poem. In general, rhythm may be defined as *the regular repetition of anything.*

There is nothing more universal in our experience than this regular repetition. The cycle of the seasons, night following day, the ebb and flow of the tides, the regular turning of the earth on its axis, the waxing and waning of the moon—these constitute the rhythm of the physical world in which we live. And our own physical makeup is a complex of rhythms, the regularity of which contributes largely to the health of our bodies. The circulatory system, the respiratory system, the nervous system, the digestive system are the major rhythms of our bodies.

Rhythm in general is of two kinds—*static* and *mobile*—depending on whether the pattern of repetition is made up of static units or units in motion. The regular repetition of leaves on either side of the stem of a fern frond and the symmetrical balance of part with part on either side of the central axis of the human body are examples of static rhythm or symmetry. The regular surge of waves on the shore, the regularity of the heartbeat, and the repeated pattern of a dance exemplify mobile rhythm.

But, generally, for rhythm of any kind to be pleasing to us it must not only set up a pattern of repeat but must also introduce a subtle variation in the repetition. Rhythmic patterns that we find in nature generally follow that law. If we study a fern frond, for instance, we notice that the pairs of leaves are not all of the same size, nor are they exactly aligned with one another on either side of the stem. This combination of variety and repetition provides the double pleasure that we experience in every good pattern. The repetition gives the *pleasure of recognition*. Once we have grasped the fundamental unit of the design, whatever it is, an expectation is set up for its repetition; and when we catch the repeat, we have the pleasure of recognizing an old friend. The artist observes this same law in creating his artistic pattern. In a symphony, for instance, a sound pattern or dominant theme is established early in the composition, and it is repeated over and over in the course of the development of the symphony, providing the listener, each time it recurs, with the pleasure of recognition. But if the theme were repeated each time without variation, the experience, far from being pleasurable, would be monotonous (literally, one-toned) and boring. Much of the pleasure of listening to a symphony comes from the subtle variations that are rung on the fundamental theme or countertheme. It may be played in a variant key, or by different choirs of instruments, or be so varied and developed itself that its original pattern is hardly recognizable; but, however it is achieved, the *pleasure of surprise* is provided the listener by the variations on the fundamental theme.

Our reaction to rhythm, especially to mobile rhythm, is immediate and instinctive. The almost unconscious foot tapping in response to music is perhaps the best proof of this. And the instinct for rhythm serves a very important function in our lives. It enables us to put unity into the confusing multiplicity of sense experience and therefore facilitates our grasp and ultimately our understanding of the universe in which we live. We are definitely limited in our capacities of apprehension; unless regular, repeated sense experiences are grouped for us, they are apt to melt into an indistinguishable blur. So true is this that we subconsciously tend to group identically repeated sounds into sound groups that we can cope with. The regular, monotonous, *tick, tick, tick, tick* of the clock becomes, *tick, tock; tick, tock* to our ear; and the *click, click, click, click* of train wheels on the track intersections becomes *clickity, click; clickity, click*.

But there is another very important effect of rhythm that makes it indispensable to the purposes of the poet: its almost immediate influence on the emotions. And this is not at all surprising because the emotions themselves are inextricably mixed up with the rhythmic processes of our bodies. The difference between a simple feeling of like or dislike and a real emotion of love or hate is largely a matter of a simple feeling that has been so prolonged or intensified that it has begun to register in the rhythmic processes of the body. Why does an angry man flush, for instance, and a frightened man blanch? Because, in the first instance, he has been insulted and instinctively inclines to do physical violence to the aggressor. This inclination has reacted on the rhythm of his whole physical makeup. A shot of adrenalin has been released directly into the blood, speeding up the heart, which in turn pumps more blood to every organ of the body in preparation for the expected physical exertion; as a result, the face flushes and advertises the man's anger. By contrast, when a man meets with something that is really terrifying, he instinctively recognizes that it is a situation beyond his physical powers to cope with and, rather than preparing for physical violence, his heart is momentarily paralyzed. The blood is drained from his face and other extremities and he turns white with fear. These biological facts are emphasized only to call attention to the close relationship between emotion and the rhythmic processes of our bodies.

Because of this close connection and because of our instinctive reaction to the experience of rhythm, a repeated rhythmic pattern can induce an emotion in us, as the writers of mood music for the movies know so well. This is true, of course, of all the arts. Very much of the contrasted emotional effects, for instance, between a painting of classical and one of highly baroque feeling is a matter of the poised and symmetrical patterns of the classical painting (a Raphael Madonna, for instance) and the broken and asymmetric patterns of the baroque (Rubens' *Descent from the Cross*, for example). An effect something akin to mood music in cinema is what the poet achieves through the rhythm of his poem. That is why we can sometimes feel the mood of a poem before we have entirely grasped what the poem is all about. This is true, at least, of good poems, where the sound does echo the sense and actually becomes part of the sense.

Nonmetrical Rhythm in Poetry

There is a great deal of rhythm in any artistic literary expression, prose or poetry, which is made up of the regular repetition of *single words*, *phrases*, or *clauses*; of *similar* or *balanced grammatical* clauses and whole sentences; of similar sounding vowels (*assonance*); or of identical consonants (*alliteration*). Much poetry adds the further rhythmic elements of *rhyme*, a *stanza pattern*, and the *refrain*. It will be helpful here to discuss and illustrate each of these types of nonmetrical rhythm.

REPETITION OF ONE WORD

A rhythm created by the repetition of one word is well exemplified by the repetition of "charity" in Saint Paul's famous discourse on charity in Corinthians I, 13. It is a device frequently employed in impassioned oratory. Note, for instance, the repetition of "honor" in the oration of Mark Antony over the dead body of Caesar (Shakespeare's *Julius Caesar*, III, ii, 78-257). The repetition of "silver" in the following poem by Walter de la Mare is a good example of this device creating much of the rhythmic texture of a poem.

Silver

Slowly, silently, now the moon
Walks the night in her *silver* shoon;
This way, and that, she peers, and sees
Silver fruit upon *silver* trees;
One by one the casements catch
Her beams beneath the *silvery* thatch;
Couched in his kennel, like a log,
With paws of *silver* sleeps the dog;
From their shadowy cote the white breasts peep
Of doves in a *silver*-feathered sleep;
A harvest mouse goes scampering by,
With *silver* claws and a *silver* eye;
And moveless fish in the water gleam,
By *silver* reeds in a *silver* stream.

REPETITION OF PHRASES AND CLAUSES

This is a device of emphasis very characteristic of impassioned prose, but it is frequently employed for rhythmic effects in poetry as well. Sometimes it consists in exact word for word repetition; but more often it consists in rhetorical balance and parallelism in phrase, clause, and sentence structure. Both kinds of repetition are exemplified in the following stanza from Thompson's "The Hound of Heaven." This stanza contains several examples of word repetition as well.

The Hound of Heaven

I FLED HIM, *down* the nights and *down* the days;
I FLED HIM, *down* the arches of the years;

I FLED HIM, *down* the labyrinthine ways
  Of my own mind; and *in* the mist of
    tears
I HID FROM HIM, and *under* running
    laughter.
  Up vistaed hopes I SPED;
  And shot, precipitated,
A*down* Titanic glooms of chasmed fears,
  From those strong Feet that followed,
    followed after.
    But with unhurrying chase,
    And unperturbed pace,
Deliberate speed, majestic instancy,
  THEY BEAT—and a VOICE BEAT
    More instant than the Feet—
  "All things betray thee, who betrayest
    Me."

This repetitive device is the most distinguishing feature of the rhythmic movement of some poets, notably of Walt Whitman. Notice, for instance, its use in the following excerpt from his "Out of the Cradle Endlessly Rocking."

  Out of the cradle endlessly rocking,
  Out of the mocking-bird's throat, the musical shuttle.
  Out of the Ninth-month midnight,
  Over the sterile sands and the fields beyond, where the child leaving his bed wandered alone, bareheaded, barefoot,
  Down from the showered halo,
  Up from the mystic play of shadows twining and twisting as if they were alive,
  Out from the patches of briers and blackberries,
  From the memories of the bird that chanted to me,
  From your memories, sad brother, from the fitful risings and fallings I heard,
  From under that yellow half-moon late-risen and swollen as if with tears,
  From those beginning notes of yearning and love there in the mist,
  From the thousand responses of my heart never to cease,
  From the myriad thence-aroused words,
  From the word stronger and more delicious than any,
  From such as now they start the scene revisiting,
  As a flock, *twittering, rising,* or overhead *passing*
  Borne hither, ere all eludes me, hurriedly,
  A man, yet by these tears a little boy again
  Throwing myself on the sand, *confronting* the waves,
  I, chanter of pains and joys, uniter of here and hereafter,
  Taking all hints to use them, *but swiftly* leaping beyond them,
  A reminiscence sing.

ALLITERATION

The repetition of like-sounding consonants at the beginning of words coming in close succession to one another is *alliteration*. If overused in prose, as it was, for instance, in the euphuistic style, it is apt to appear affected and artificial; but it frequently is used to very good effect in poetry. For one thing, identical initial sounds in words occurring in close succession tend to associate them more closely with one another. The little patterns of like sound enshrining patterns of thought in a poem have much the same unifying effect as do repeated touches of the same color in a painting. This rhythmic device, unlike end rhyme, tends to call attention to the interior of the verses, rather than to the end of them. Some poets have used the device of alliteration so profusely that it becomes one of the most characteristic features of their style. This is particularly true of Spenser and Hopkins. The following quotation from Spenser's description of Error in the *Faerie Queene* and a line from Hopkins' "The Leaden Echo and The Golden Echo" (Unit Nine) well illustrate alliterative patterns.

  But FULL of FIRE and greedy hardiment,
  The youthful knight could not for ought be staide,
  But forth unto the darksome hole he went,
  And looked in: his GListring armor made
  A little GLooming light, much like a shade,
  By which he saw the ugly monster plaine,
  Halfe like a serpent Horribly displaide,
  But th' other Halfe did womans shape retaine,
  Most lothsom, Filthie, Foule, and Full of vile disdaine.

  O why are we so Haggard at the Heart, so care-coiled, care-Killed, so Fagged, so Fashed, so cogged, so cumbered?

CONSONANCE

The repetition of a pattern of consonants, with changes in the intervening vowels, is called *consonance*. It is not nearly as much used as alliteration. "Leaves—lives," "hell—hall" are examples. W. H. Auden has used this device extensively in his poem, " 'O where are you going?' said *reader* to *rider*."

ASSONANCE

The repetition of identical or closely related vowel sounds in close proximity to one another is *assonance*. The following lines from Hopkins' "The Wreck of the Deutschland" illustrate it.

> Wiry and and white-fiery and whirl-wind-swivelled snow
> Spins to widows-making, unchilding, unfathering deeps.

PITCH

The real sustained music of a line or longer passage of poetry is largely owing to the predominance of one or other kind of vowel sound creating a definite *pitch*. The vowels have been arranged by James H. Smith (*Reading of Poety*, Houghton Mifflin, 1939) in the following scale, moving from high to low pitch:

1) rite, mete, date, hit, due;
2) hat, set;
3) dot, tar, foot, boil, hut;
4) nor, food, brow, urn
5) tall, note.

As this scale is vocalized, there is a general relaxation of the speech organs as the point of sound release shifts from the tip of the tongue placed high in the front of the mouth (high pitch) to deep in the rear of the mouth with the back of the tongue raised and the front retracted (low pitch). Read aloud the quotation from Hopkins' "Wreck" (under *Assonance*) with this in mind, and notice how the pitch moves from high to low. Do the same for the following passage from his "The Blessed Virgin Compared to the Air We Breathe."

> Or if there does some soft,
> On things aloof, aloft,
> Bloom breathe, that one breath more
> Earth is the fairer for.
> Whereas did air not make
> This bath of blue and slake
> His fire, the sun would shake,
> A blear and binding ball
> With blackness bound, and all
> The thick stars round him roll
> Flashing like flecks of coal,
> Quartz-fret, or sparks of salt,
> In grimy vasty vault.

ONOMATOPOEIA

Onomatopoeia is the attempt to recreate the exact sound effect being described by a combination of vowel and consonantal sounds. The following lines from Tennyson are a classic example.

> The moan of doves in immemorial elms,
> And murmur of innumerable bees.

Or these from his *The Brook*.

> I bubble into eddying bays
> I babble on the pebbles.

CONSONANTAL PATTERN

Very much of the sound pattern of poetry is created by the predominance of one kind or another of consonant sound. But, unlike vowels, consonants are articulated with a certain stricture in the breath stream. The most vowel-like of the consonants are "l," "m," "n," and "r." According to the manner of articulation, consonants are divided into (1) *stops* or *plosives* (p, b, t, d, k, g); (2) *nasals* (m, n, ng); (3) *fricatives* (roughly all remaining consonants). Those in the first group are formed by blocking completely the breath stream, and then releasing it in a "puff"; in the second group, by a gradual release of the breath stream with air passing out through the nose; and in the third, by an incomplete obstruction to the breath emerging from the mouth. The quality of each consonant sound depends upon the degree and place of obstruction, and the vibration or nonvibration of the vocal chords while the consonant is being sounded. By choosing words in which one or the other kind of consonantal or vowel sound predominates the poet can create a sound tone in his poem that is appropriate to the mood and idea he is attempting to communicate. Notice, for instance, what the predominance of plosives and fricatives does to create a feeling of being torn and worn to pieces by worry and work in the lines on page 598 from "The Leaden Echo and the Golden Echo" by Hopkins. Or note the babbling and bubbling impression created by the procession of plosive "b's" in the following lines from Tennyson's *The Brook*:

> I **b**u**bb**le into eddying **b**ays
> I **b**a**bb**le on the pe**bb**les.

Or note the fragile effect partly created by the liquid and delicate fricative consonants in these lines from Thompson's "To a Snowflake" (Unit Ten):

> **f**ashioned *s*o pure*l*y,
> **f**ragi*l*e*l*y, sure*l*y,
> **f**rom what Paradisa*l*
> Imagine*l*ess meta*l*
> Too costly for cost.

Or in these lines from Hopkins:

> . . . goes home betwixt
> The **f**leeciest, **f**railest-**f**li*x*ed
> Snow**f**lake.

RHYME

Rhyme is a sound pattern in which the last accented vowel and all the sounds following it are identical, but in which the consonantal and vowel sounds preceding the last accented syllable are different, *Sing-ring*; *defender-pretender*; *partake-mistake* are examples of rhyming words. Every good rhyme, or what is sometimes called *perfect rhyme*, illustrates the double law of every pleasing pattern: the identically repeated element provides the pleasure of recognition and the varied element, in turn, the pleasure of surprise because we never know from rhyme to rhyme what the variation will be. When the repeated element is accented on the final syllable of the word as in *partake-mistake* or when the rhymed words are monosyllabic as in *sing-ring*, the rhyme is called *masculine*; when the final syllable is unaccented as in *defender-pretender*, it is called *feminine*. *Defender-pretender* is also an example of a *double rhyme* because there are two identical final syllables. Rhymes which occur at the end of lines are called *end-rhymes* while those occurring within the lines are called *internal-rhymes*. The following stanza from Coleridge's *The Rime of the Ancient Mariner* exemplifies both end and internal rhyme.

> The fair breeze *blew*, the white foam *flew*,
>   The furrow followed FREE;
> We were the *first* that ever *burst*
>   Into that silent SEA.

In a *perfect rhyme* the repeated sound is identical in both rhyming words, but in imperfect or *slant rhyme* the repeated elements only approximate one another. Emily Dickinson frequently used *slant rhyme* in her poetry. It is exemplified in the following stanzas (from Unit Eleven).

> He glanced with rapid eyes
> That hurried all *abroad*,—
> They looked like frightened beads, I
>   thought
> He stirred his velvet *head*

> Like one in danger; cautious,
> I offered him a *crumb*,
> And he unrolled his feathers
> And rowed him softer *home*

> Than oars divide the sea.

Rhyme is employed by good poets as a part of the meaning of the poem. Key rhymed words can emphasize a point, as they do frequently in the heroic couplets of Pope. For example:

> One speaks the glory of the British *Queen*,
> And one describes a charming Indian
>   *screen*.

Strong masculine rhymes give force and finality to the movement of the verse, while grace and delicacy tend to be the effect of feminine rhymes. Note the difference in feeling, for instance, between the effect achieved by the rhymes in the following verses.

> Generations have *trod*, have *trod*, have
>   *trod*;
> And all is *seared* with trade; *bleared*,
>   *smeared* with TOIL;

And *wears* man's smudge and *shares*
   man's smell; the SOIL
Is bare now, nor can foot feel, being *shod*.

What heart could have *thought you?*	a
Past our *devisal*	b
(O filigree *petal*.)	c
Fashioned so PURELY,	d
Fragilely, SURELY	d
From what *Paradisal*	b
Imagineless *metal*,	c
Too costly for *cost?*	e
Who hammered you, *wrought you?*	a
From argentine *vapour?*	f
'God was my *shaper*.	f
He hammered, He *wrought me*	g
From curled silver *vapour*,	f
To lust of his *mind*.	h
Thou couldst not have *thought me*.	g
So purely, so PALELY,	i
Tinily, SURELY,	d
Mightily, FRAILY,	i
Insculped and *embossed*	e
With His hammer of *wind*,	h
And His graver of *frost*.'	e

Both the end and internal masculine rhymes of the first selection plod along in the monotonous humdrum of the factory labor being described; while the predominantly feminine rhymes of Thompson's poem have some of the lightness and delicacy of the snowflake itself. The intricate interweaving of the end rhymes also resembles the intricate filigree of the delicate snowflake. The rhyme scheme in the margin gives some indication of the complexity of the pattern.

Sometimes exaggerated or enforced rhyme, especially when it is *multiple* and *feminine*, helps give a comic or mock tone to a poem, as it does, for instance, in the following lines from Ogden Nash's "Kind of an Ode to Duty" (Unit Six).

> O *Duty*,
> Why hast thou not the visage of a sweetie
>   or a *cutie?*
> Why displayest thou the countenance of a
>   kind of conscientious organizing *spinster*
> That the minute you see her you are
>   *aginster?*

And, of course, one of the chief functions of rhyme is the building of the stanzaic patterns that are the structural framework in the sound pattern of much traditional poetry.

STANZA PATTERNS

A stanza is a sound pattern in a poem made up of a specified number of lines of definite length and metrical pattern and usually bound together by uniform rhyme scheme. The most usual English stanza patterns are the *couplet*, the *tercet*, *terza rima*, the *quatrain*, *rhyme royal*, the *ottava rima*, and the *Spenserian stanza*.

The *couplet* is a pair of rhymed lines of any length, but the most usual form is the *heroic couplet*—two rhyming lines of iambic pentameter. Ordinarily, too, the lines of a heroic couplet are end-stopped. Much satiric poetry employs the heroic couplet. (See the introduction to Satire in the text for a discussion of the propriety of the heroic couplet to satire.)

The *tercet* is a three-verse stanza made up of lines of any length, ordinarily, of identical rhymes. *Terza rima* is made up of tercets rhyming *a b a*. In a poem written in *terza rima* the middle rhyme of the first tercet becomes the first rhyme of the second one, thus: *a b a, b c b,* etc. This creates a continuous linked progression from one stanza to the next. Dante's *Divine Comedy* is written in this stanza form as, in a loose way, is "Ode to the West Wind" by Shelley (Unit Nine).

The *quatrain*, a stanza of four verses, rhyming variously and of various metrical patterns, is perhaps the most frequently used stanza pattern in English poetry. The *ballad stanza* is a quatrain of alternating tetrametric and trimetric verses rhyming *a b c b*. Many of the ballads of tradition are written in this stanza form. See "Sir Patrick Spens" (Unit Eight), for instance. Other popular forms of the quatrain are the *heroic quatrain*—four verses of iambic pentameter rhyming *a b a b*, and the *In Memoriam* stanza—four verses of iambic tetrameter rhyming *a b b a*.

Rhyme royal is a seven line stanza of iambic pentametric verses rhyming *a b a b b c c*. Chaucer introduced this form into English.

Ottava rima, adopted from the Italian, is a stanza of eight verses of iambic pentameter rhyming *a b a b a b c c*. Byron used it throughout his long poem, *Don Juan*.

The *Spenserian stanza*, the stanza pattern of Spenser's *Faerie Queene* and Keats's "Eve of St. Agnes," and many other poems in English, is a nine-line stanza, the first eight of which are in iambic pentameter, and the ninth of which (called an *Alexandrine*) is in iambic hexameter. The rhyme scheme is *a b a b b c b c c*. It, like the Spenserian sonnet, has the progressive linkage system of the Italian *terza rima*.

The *refrain* is either a line or a part of a line or a whole stanza that is repeated, either word for word or with only slight variations, several times in the course of the poem. It is an integral part of many ballads, and of some longer narrative poems where it sometimes marks off divisions in the action of the poem. Study, for instance, this use of the refrain in such poems as "The Love Song of J. Alfred Prufrock" (Unit Twelve).

Blank verse is unrhymed iambic pentameter. It is the verse form used in *Paradise Lost*, Wordsworth's "Michael," and dozens of other poems in the English language.

Free verse is more rhythmic than prose, but it lacks even the regular metrical pattern of blank verse, and more often than not rhyme as well. It has a great deal of ryhthm, however, but not of the conventional and predictable kind familiar to us in traditional poetry. It shifts its rhythm without forewarning, and frequently gets its effects through highly artistic nonmetrical use of sound devices. Many of the poems in this anthology by modern poets are written in free verse.

Metrical Rhythm in Poetry

There remains one kind of poetic rhythm to discuss, the rhythm which, in poetry antecedent to free verse, is the most specifically poetic, namely *meter*. The word itself means a measure, and what is measured in metrical rhythm is the regular repetition of accent. Meter is not a sound pattern arbitrarily imposed on expression like a cookie cutter on a mass of raw dough. In a successful poem, at least, it is an intimate part of the expression and is closely wed to the thought and mood of the poem. What is being measured in the metrical analysis of a poem is the *word accent* and *thought accent*, and, therefore, the metrical analysis presupposes a knowledge of the correct pronunciation of every word in the poem and of the thought and mood of the poem. Otherwise we have no way of recognizing the word and thought accents we are actually measuring.

Since this is true, we should not begin analyzing the meter of a poem by deciding that it is written in iambic pentameter, for instance, and by imposing the five iambic feet on the lines irrespective of what is going on in the actual thought the line expresses. Since we are measuring *word* and *thought* accents, a sensible way to scan a poem is to proceed in the following two steps.

First: Put an accent mark on all polysyllables in the line, both primary and secondary accents if the words have them, since we know that polysyllables have to receive their accents to be pronounced at all.

Second: Put an accent on all the monosyllables which demand an accent by reason of the thought of the line. This is sometimes called a *rhetorical accent*. This accent is impossible to detect unless you know the whole meaning of the line, because it is the thought of the line that determines what monosyllables will be stressed in an oral reading.

With these accents determined, it is possible to go back and see how they are actually distributed in the line in relationship to one another and to the unaccented syllables which intervene. In this way we get at the actual accentual movement of the line as it exists rather than impose accents where they do not belong because a predetermined metrical pattern seems to demand them.

We might exemplify this by a scansion of Shakespeare's "Sonnet 146."

/ / × / × × / ×
Poor soul,//the cen/ter / of / my sin/ful
/
earth,
/ × × / × / × ×
Thrall // to / these reb/el pow/ers that
/ × /
thee / array,

Why dost / thou pine / within / and
   suf/fer dearth,
Painting / thy out/ward wal/ls so cos/tly
   gay?
Why so l/arge cost,//having / so shor/t
   a lease,
Dost thou / upon / thy fad/ing man/sion
   spend?
Shall worms,//inhe/ritors / of this /
   excess,
Eat up / thy charge?//Is this / thy
   bod/y's end?
Then,//soul,//live thou / upon / thy
   ser/vant's loss,
And let / that pine / to ag/gravate / thy
   store.
Buy terms / divine / in sel/ling hou/rs of
   dross,
Within / be fed,//without / be rich /
   no more.
So shalt / thou feed / on Death, that
   fee/ds on men,
And Death / once dead,//there's no /
   more dy/ing then.

Poor soul, the center of my sinful earth. We know that, as polysyllables, "center" and "sinful" must have accents on their first syllables. Of the remaining monosyllabic words the thought demands an accent on both "Poor"

and "soul" of "Poor soul." Whether you put one on "my" will be determined by whether you want to emphasize in interpreting the line that it is *my* sinful earth in contrast to anybody else's or whether you want the emphasis to go on *sinful* earth (body) as opposed to the soul. In the first instance *my* would get an accent; in the last one it would

not. "Earth" certainly demands a thought accent. So looking back at the whole line we see that its accents are distributed in this fashion:

Poor soul,//the center of / my sin/ful
   earth,

If we were proceeding with the idea of this being an iambic pentametric line, we might be tempted to put an accent on "of" to create an iambus where none exists if we follow the strict word and thought accent in an oral vocalization of the meaning of the line.

Take another line:

Shall worms, inheritors of this excess,

Following the same procedure as above, one would first put the primary and secondary accents on "inheritors" and the accent on the second syllable of "excess." The thought would seem to demand accents on the following monosyllables: "Shall worms" and "this." "This" demands an accent because it is a strong demonstrative pronoun pointing back to all the excess enumerated in the previous lines of the poem. The whole line, then, reads metrically as follows:

Shall worms, inher/itors / of this /
   excess,

A good example of how completely a correct scansion of a line depends on full knowledge of the meaning and context of the whole poem is illustrated in line ten of this poem.

And let / that pine / to ag/gravate / thy
   store.

"Aggravate," as a polysyllable, has to have its primary and secondary accents. It is perfectly obvious that the thought demands accents on "let," "pine," and "store." But it is only from the context of the whole poem that one knows that "that" and "thy" demand accents, too.

All of this shows how closely the metrical pattern is woven into the whole meaning and tone of a poem. If they are approached in this way, metrics will be seen to be part of the very life of a poem and not a meaningless pattern imposed on it.

THE CHIEF METRICAL PATTERNS

If the above procedure is followed, the actual metrical pattern of the lines of a poem will be discovered. The chief metrical patterns in English (determined by the alternation of accented and unaccented syllables) are the following:

Iambic. An unaccented syllable followed by an accented one: re×bo´und

Anapestic. Two unaccented syllables followed by an accented one: in××ter´cede

Trochaic. An accented syllable followed by an unaccented one: bo´l×der

Dactylic. An accented syllable followed by two unaccented ones: da´s××tardly

Spondaic. Two accented syllables in succession: spe´ll´bound. This is more often made up of two monosyllabic words such as *Po´or so´ul* in the Shakespeare sonnet above, and occurs as a variant foot rather than as a fundamental meter.

A verse of poetry or a whole poem may be composed in predominantly one or the other of these metrical patterns. Each of them gives a very distinctive tone and mood to a poem or a part of it in which it occurs.

Lines of poetry are described metrically by the kind of metrical pattern that predominates in them and by the number of such patterns in the line. A line composed of *iambic pentameter*, for instance, would be a line of five iambuses. The other numerical terms employed are as follows: *monometer (1 foot), dimeter (2 feet), trimeter (3 feet), tetrameter (4 feet), hexameter (6 feet), heptameter (7 feet).*

NONMETRICAL VARIATIONS IN THE METRICAL PATTERN

A too regular repetition of any pattern soon becomes monotonous. But there are many ways in which variety of sound is introduced into a poem even without variations in the metrical pattern itself. Two lines which are identical in the fundamental metrical pattern will sound quite different if the words carrying the pattern in one line are *predominantly monosyllabic* and in the other, *polysyllabic*. Notice, for instance, the difference in sound between the following two lines from Tennyson's "The Brook" which are metrically identical.

× /   ×   /   ×   /   ×   /
I come / from haunts / of coot / and hern.

and

×   /   × /   ×   /   × /
I chat/ter o/ver sto/ny ways.

Another source of variant sound in metrically identical verses is the *presence* or *lack* of caesurae (thought pauses) in the lines. Note, for example, the difference in sound and movement between these two lines from the same poem.

×   /   ×   /   ×   /   ×   /
I slip,//I slide,//I gloom,//I glance.

and

×   /   ×   /   ×   /   ×   /
I make / the net/ted sun/beam dance.

A *variation in pitch* will also give a very different sound to lines identical in their metrical pattern, as in the following two sets of lines from Hopkins.

× /   ×   /   ×   /
Or if / there does / some soft
×   /   × /   × /
On things / aloof, / aloft.
 /   /
Bloom breathe.

and

 /   /   ×   /   ×   /
A blear / and bli/nding ball.
× / ×   /   × /
In gri/my vas/ty vault

A *change in the predominant consonantal quality* of verses will also result in quite different sound effects in spite of identical metrical patterns. Note, for instance, the difference in sound between the two sets of lines from Hopkins just quoted, owing not merely to the high pitch of the first and the lower pitch of the second lines but also to the shift from the sibilant "s's" and sharp "t's" of the first to the plosive "b's" and harsh "g" of the second lines. A *run-on line* as opposed to an *end-stopped line* will also introduce a variation in the sound and movement of metrically identical pairs of lines.

These devices taken singly or combined are sources of limitless variety in the sound of lines unvaried in their fundamental metrical pattern. Two lines varied only by one or the other of these devices may sound as different as the same melody played first by violins and then by the bass viols in a symphony orchestra.

METRICAL VARIATIONS

But this is not the only way in which variation is achieved. In a symphony the fundamental theme is itself developed and varied internally as it is repeated—so much so that there is sometimes only a ghost of the original pattern left. The same is true of the metrical pattern in poetry. It is frequently altered by substitution of one foot for another as the thought and mood of the poem demand. It is these variations, in fact, that frequently constitute the most interesting moments in the poem metrically. Of course a reader does not sense these variations in the metrical pattern itself until he has read enough of the poem to know what the fundamental metrical pattern is. For instance, in the sonnet of Shakespeare, one has to know that the poem is moving in iambic pentameter to feel the effect of the substitution of the spondees in the following lines:

/ / × / × × × / ×
Poor soul, / the cen/ter of / my sinf/ul
/
earth.
/ /   / / × /   ×
Why dost / thou pine / within / and
/ × /
suf/fer dearth
/ /   / /   ×   ×
Then, soul,// live thou / upon / thy
/ × /
serv/ant's loss.

× / / / × / × /   /
And let /that pine / to ag/gravate / thy
/
store.

But when one does have a feeling of the regular movement of the iambic pentametric line, an expectation for its continuation is set up; and, when the spondees occur, they call attention to that part of the line. In each instance here they reinforce the mood and thought which the lines at that juncture are actually expressing. This is the way a skillful poet employs variations in his metrical pattern, in general, not merely to relieve the monotony but actually to add to the forcefulness, propriety, and expressiveness of his verse.

The following are the most usual internal metrical variations employed by poets writing in the traditional metrical patterns:

1) *Substitution*. In this instance an iamb ($×/$) and anapest ($××/$) or a trochee ($/×$) and dactyl ($/××$) are interchanged. A spondee ($//$) is also a frequent substitution for an iamb ($×/$), and less frequently a pyrrhic foot ($××$) substitutes for an iamb. Some examples:

/ / × × / × /
Then pu/nctual as / a star.
× / × ×/   × /   ×   /
I hur/ry amai/n to reach / the plain.
× ×   /   × / × ×
And the / smooth stream / in smoo/ther
/ × /
num/bers flows.
/ × ×   / × × /
Mine be a / handful of / ashes.

2) *Inversion*. In the case of inversion an iamb is interchanged with a trochee and a dactyl with an anapest. An example:

/ × × / × / × / ×
Painting / thy out/ward wall/s so cos/tly
/
gay

3) *Hypermeter*. This consists in the addition of an unstressed syllable at the beginning of a trochaic line or at the end of an iambic line. An example:

× / × / × / ×
Around / a pair of mou/ntains

The names of these variations are relatively unimportant. The variations themselves are easily detected, if the system of scansion outlined above is followed.

Appendix Four
SAMPLE ANALYSES OF POEMS

Since Brass, nor Stone, nor Earth
by WILLIAM SHAKESPEARE

Since brass,//nor stone,//nor earth,//nor
   bound/less sea,
But sad / mortal/ity / o'er-sways / their
   pow/er,
How with / this rage / shall beau/ty hold
   / a plea,
Whose act/ion is / no stro/nger than / a
   flow/er?
O,//how / shall sum/mer's hon/ey breath
   / hold out
Against / the wrac/kful sieg/e of
   batt/'ring days,
When rock/s impre/gnable / are not / so
   stout,
Nor gates / of steel / so strong,//but
   Time / decays?
O fear/ful med/itation!//where,//alack,
Shall Time's / best jew/el from / Time's
   chest / lie hid?
Or what / strong hand / can hold / his
   swift / foot back?
Or who / his spoil / of bea/uty can /
   forbid?
O, none,//unless / this mir/acle / have
   might,
That in / black ink / my love / may still
   / shine bright.

The fleeting nature of all earthly things is a perennial subject with lyric poets. It is not subject matter alone, of course, but rather the ideas and attitudes that the poet builds into a self-sufficient structure of words, imagery, and rhythm that is the poem. Here Shakespeare takes this almost hackneyed theme of the short-lived nature of everything in time and gives it a new twist. After an overwhelming catalogue of the depredations of destructive mortality on even earth's sturdiest creatures from long-lived brass to impregnable gates of steel, he makes the delicate frailty and impermanency of human beauty seem all the more inevitable. And then he suddenly reverses the situation in the "miracle" of the final couplet where the beauty of his beloved is made to shine on permanently in the black ink of his verse.

This, in baldest prose, is the large idea of his poem; but the interest of this sonnet lies not so much in this idea as in the shape, texture, and tone that Shakespeare gives these few lines by exploiting almost every language device at his disposal. In the first place, he makes an interesting use of the external structure of the English sonnet form to frame the inner thought progression. This form progresses through three successive quatrains (each with its independent rhyme scheme) to a final couplet. The structure of the three opening quatrains is ideally suited to frame three parallel thought units which create a problem or raise a question that comes to some kind of resolution or conclusion in the final couplet. This method is exactly what Shakespeare uses here. The futility of hoping for any permanence for human beauty is developed in three successive images in the opening quatrains: the futility of an orderly legal action against time's destructive rage in stanza one; the futility of the gentle breath of summer holding out against time's battering ram in stanza two; and, finally, in stanza three, the futility of trying to protect human beauty (Time's best jewel) from thieving Time. To reinforce this parallelism and intensify the problematic tone of these first stanzas, they are cast entirely in the form of questions. This clearly helps to create the skeptical tone of this first part of the poem, but also prepares us for the forthright yet unexpected answer to the series of questions formulated in the final couplet.

The more specific texture and tone of the poem, however, is created not so much by this over-all external and internal structure, as by the quality of the diction, imagery, and rhythm. Since the apparent futility of hoping for any permanence for frail human beauty, when time makes such ravages on nature's strongest creatures, is part of the poet's theme, he is at pains to make this contrast as vivid as possible in the parallel quatrains.

In the first quatrain, he selects two things which for their hardness are almost synonymous with perdurance—brass and stone. When memorials are constructed to preserve the memory of men for posterity, they are made of brass and granite. And because of their immensity, if nothing else, the perdurance and power of the earth itself and of the mighty sea seem boundless. And yet, the poet tells us, their power of survival is only imaginary because "sad mortality," grief-bringing death, eats away voraciously at all of them. There is a suggestion in the "o'er-sway" coupled with "rage" of the next line of an inexorable monster devouring even the strongest and most measureless things of the earth. Since this is the fact, the efforts of frail human beauty to hold out against the rage of this monster can be expected to be just about as effective, the poet says, as making a legal plea of mercy or even of justice to this outrageous destroyer. Even the plea of the strongest (of brass and stone, earth and boundless sea) goes unheeded when legal action is brought against the rage of "sad mortality"; and, compared to the actions of such powerful contenders for permanence, any legal action that human beauty could take against this despoiler would be about as strong and effective as a flower. The image of the flower brings out both the delicate attractiveness of human beauty and also its frailty and inability to do anything at all to contend with the outrageous depredations of time. There is no better symbol of the fleeting nature of human beauty than a flower which is in full-blown loveliness today and will tomorrow be withered and faded. Shakespeare suggests some of the strength and perdurance associated with brass and stone in the very regular monosyllabic march of the first line, which is punctuated by multiple thought pauses:

$$\overset{\times}{\text{Since}} \overset{/}{brass,}/\!/\overset{\times}{\text{nor}} \overset{/}{stone,}/\!/\overset{\times}{\text{nor}} \overset{/}{earth,}/\!/\overset{\times}{\text{nor}}$$
$$\overset{/}{bound}/\overset{\times}{\text{less}} \overset{/}{sea,}$$

The one polysyllabic word in the line, "boundless," sets the sea apart from the other things enumerated in the verse and gives it an additional climactic quality, which is also enhanced by the fuller open vowel quality of the accented syllable of "bóundless"—the longest vowel sound in the line.

In the second quatrain the contrast is between the sweet gentle breeze of summer and the destructive force of a battering ram. To identify human beauty, especially feminine beauty, with "summer's honey breath" is to give it at the same time a sweetness that is attractive but also a softness that makes it utterly incapable of standing up against the "battering siege" of time. Battering rams are successfully directed even against "*rocks* impregnable" and "gates of *steel*," so what chance has soft, sweet "summer's honey breath" of withstanding the siege of time?

The answer to the questions posed so far by the poet seems so inevitable—the utter inescapableness of death for frail human beauty—that, at the beginning of the third quatrain, he shifts from interrogation to exclamation about the melancholy fact of ubiquitous mortality. "O fearful meditation!" This exclamation suggests the tone of the first part of the poem—the lugubrious meditation on the certainties of death. But to reinforce what seems to be this melancholy fact, Shakespeare returns to a last question involving a third vivid image casting time in the role of a thief against whom there is no protection. In this image human beauty becomes a precious jewel, the object of Time's covetous eye, "Time's best jewel." And Time is so set on having it stored away in his chest and he is so swift to suit the action to the thought, that there is no arm strong enough to resist him and no authority capable of commanding him to desist from the theft. In this quatrain, a sense of the irresistibleness and inevitableness of the situation of human beauty in the face of indomitable time is partly achieved by the spondaic movement interjected into the second and third stanzas. Notice how much emphasis falls on "Time's best jewel," "Time's chest," "strong hand" and "swift foot back" by reason of the spondaic substitutions in those lines.

    Shall Time's / best jew/el from / Time's
        chest / lie hid?
    Or what / strong hand / can hold / his
        swift / foot back?

The effect of all this accumulation of parallel questions, contrasts, and images is that we are in the mood to accept the conclusion of this "fearful meditation." There simply is no way for human beauty to escape the rage, the siege, and the thievery of Time. And in the first words of the couplet, the poet says so too—"O, none." Then he reverses his and our whole position by introducing what does look like a miracle in the light of the inexorable law of death that the quatrains have been developing. There is a miraculous way—outside the laws that govern everything else—that can give immortality to the beauty of the poet's human lover,

    That in / Black ink / my love / may still /
        shine Bright.

The miracle is that the memory of human beauty may be perpetuated in verse. The poem amounts in the end, then, to a reworking of Horace's old theme—*Exegi monumentum aere perennius*—I have built a monument more lasting than bronze. Shakespeare expresses that theme freshly and wittily in his final line, and the rhythm of the last line helps to underscore the statement of the theme. The spondaic substitutions call attention to "black ink" and "shine bright," and the fact that "*b*lack" and "*b*right" are alliterated relate those two words more closely. And it is these words that point up the conceit of the miracle. "Black" has the connotation of darkness and the complete absence of light. Yet it is through the black ink of the poet's verse that the beauty of his beloved and of his own love for her will shine out for posterity. Thus "sad mortality," in this instance, will be "o'er-swayed." This, Shakespeare is suggesting, is the miracle of poetry.

At the Round Earth's Imagined Corners by JOHN DONNE

At the round earth's imagined corners,
    blow
Your trumpets, angels, and arise, arise
From death, you numberless infinities
Of souls, and to your scattered bodies go;
All whom the flood did, and fire shall
    o'erthrow;
All whom war, dearth, age, agues,
    tyrannies,
Despair, law, chance, hath slain, and you
    whose eyes
Shall behold God, and never taste death's
    woe.
But let them sleep, Lord, and me mourn
    a space,
For, if above all these, my sins abound,
'Tis late to ask abundance of Thy grace,
When we are there; here on this lowly
    ground,
Teach me how to repent; for that's as
    good
As if Thou hadst sealed my pardon with
    Thy blood.

One of the most fascinating things about poetry is the ability of mere words to communicate a tone which may be as individual and personal to the poet as are his shadow and his own handwriting. This sonnet by John Donne is a particularly good example of the verbal creation of a tone which shifts subtly but radically from one part of the poem to the other.

Donne here exploits the structure of the Petrarchan sonnet as skilfully as Shakespeare did that of the English form in the previous sonnet. He makes use of the octet (rhyming *a b b a a b b a*) as a frame for the first unit of his thought and mood in which he creates a tone of eager but bold confident command. Both the thought and mood, however, shift sharply in the sestet (rhyming *c d, c d, e e*) to a tone of gentle imprecation. In the first part, the poet, eager for the last assizes, boldly commands the angels to blow their trumpets and hasten the day of the Last Judgment when all men will be summoned before God to receive their final reward. But on second thought, when he thinks of his own unpreparedness for this final judgment, he becomes less eager for hastening the day of doom, and settles down, in part two, to a humble prayer to the Lord that He delay the day of final reckoning to give him time to make a better preparation by proper repentance for his sins. It is interesting to study closely how the language structures of the poem combine to create these shifting moods.

Part one is really all one long imperative addressed to the angels of the last judgment and to the infinities of souls: "*blow* your trumpets angels," and "*arise*, you numberless infinities of souls," "and to your scattered bodies *go*." It is not only the imperative voice, however, that gives this section of the poem a tone of command. The poet so manages the word order of the first four lines that the words of command are the strong rhyme words at the end of the lines: *blow, arise, go*.

The universality of the invitation to resurrection is suggested in various interesting ways. The angel's trumpet is to be blown not throughout the whole world but "at the round earth's imagined corners." Here Donne, the seventeenth-century poet, is showing his awareness of the new knowledge of the earth's actual roundness, but, at the same time, of men's habit of talking as if the world were flat and had corners. His image of the angels blowing their trumpets at the earth's imagined corners almost summons up a picture of one of those antique maps of a flat earth with puff-cheeked winds blowing from each corner. And the infinities of souls which receive the command to arise are suggested in many ways besides the overt statement that they are numberless. We are given a vision of the countless souls separated from their bodies in the whole sweep of human history, from the Old Testament flood down to the destructive fire preceding the end of the world. "All whom the flood did, and fire shall o'erthrow." And then in a kind of cumulative *danse macabre*, we are given a picture of all the souls who will have fallen victim to every conceivable kind of death down to the end of time. The massed crowd of these souls is suggested in the very accumulation that flows over from one line to the next.

> All whom war, dearth, age, agues, tyrannies,
> Despair, law, chance, hath slain.

Every kind of death is here: war, the wholesale slayer; poverty (dearth), the next most fatal killer; age and agues; tyranny, which cannot abide a rival near the throne; suicide and despair; and finally predictable law and unpredictable chance. And to leave no one unnamed who will stand at the last judgment, the poet includes those whom a long tradition would free from the necessity of passing through death:

> —and you whose eyes
> Shall behold God, and never taste death's woe.

And then suddenly all this tone of command and eager anticipation is halted by the "But" that ushers in the sestet in which all tone of command vanishes and is replaced by a tone of simple, humble entreaty. "Let them sleep, Lord, and me mourn a space." The feeling of a self-reliance sufficient even to command the angels of heaven is suddenly replaced by this humble prayer addressed directly to the Lord. A sudden realization of his own *abound-*

ing sinfulness makes the poet realize that his eternity is dependent upon the *abundance* of God's grace; and he needs time to ask for it and use it. There is deliberate verbal play upon sin *abounding* and the great *abundance* of God's grace *in time,* in order to suggest the folly of the overconfident demand in part one that the angels push the clock ahead. This contrast between time and eternity is further emphasized by the "there" and "here" of line 12. It is only *here* in time "on this lowly ground" that the grace of repentance can be fruitful; *there* in eternity it will be too late to repent—which again points up the folly of his arrogant command to the angels to blow their trumpets to end the *here* of time and usher in the *there* of eternity. And in the final reversal of the poem, the poet is admitting that he is no longer eager for the judgment but is rather humbly asking for a prolongation of time in which he can guarantee his own repentence

> —for that's as good
> As if Thou hadst sealed my pardon with
>   Thy blood.

The tone of arrogant and eager command of part one has all vanished here and has been supplanted entirely by a simple supplication of a servant to his master, "Teach me how to repent."

Pilgrimage by EILEEN DUGGAN*

```
  /  x    x  /   x  / x   /
Now are / the bells / unlim/bered from
      x    /
    / their spires
  x  /  x    /  x  /  x   /  x
In ev/ery stee/ple-loft / from pole / to
     /
   pole:
  x   /      /       /     x   /   x x
The four / winds wheel / and blow / into
        /  /
      / this gate,
   x    /  x    /   x  /   x
And ev/ery wind / is wet / with
       / x   /
     car/rillons.
   x   /   x  /   /x  / x   /x    /
The two / Amer/icas / at eag/le height,
   x   /   x /    x    /    / x /x
The pure,//abstra/cted Him/alay/an
          /
        chimes,
    x      /   x  /  x   x    x
Great ghosts / of clap/pers from / the
     /   x   /
   Rus/sian fries,
   x   /   /   /  x   /   x
And sweet,//wind-sex/toned tremb/lers
       x   /  /
     from / Cathay;
   x   /  x  /   x    /    / x / x
The bells / of Ire/land, // jesting all / the
       /
     way,
```

* From *Poems* by Eileen Duggan (London: George Allen and Unwin Ltd., 1937).

```
      x    /   x    /    / /   x   x
The Engl/ish bells,//slowboso/med as /
    x    /
  a swan,
   x    /    /    /x  /    x  /  x
The queen/ly,//weary din / of No/tre
       /
     Dame,
  x  x   /    /  x    /   x   /
And the Low Coun/tries ring/ing back /
      x   /
    the sea.
   x    /    x   /    /    / x
Then Spain,//the Moor / still moaning
      /    x    /
    through / the saint,
   x    /    /    /x  /     x   / x /
The fros/ty,//fie/ry bells / of Ger/many,
   x   /   x  /    x     /   x
And on / before / them,//bay/ing,//
         /  x   /
       sweep/ing down,
   x    /    x  /   x    /   x   /   x
The hea/vy,//joyful pack / of thun/der-
       /
     jowls
      x  /   x   x     x    /
That tong/ue hosan/nas from / the leas/h
      x   /
    of Rome—
   /  /    x  /  x    / x  /  x /
All float / untet/hered ov/er Jaf/fa Gate
   x   /    x  /     x  /   x  /
To fling / one peal / when ang/els cheat /
      x    /
    the stone.
   x   /    /    /x  /    x  /   x    /
But if / one lit/tle gap/ping coun/try bell,
```

    Blown from / its wea/ther-boar/ding in /
       the south,
    Should be / too lost / to keep / its
       cov/enant,
    Or lift / its hear/t and reins / up to / the
       hour,
    Know that / its dumb/ness ri/ots more /
       than sound.

Eileen Duggan is a New Zealand poet. The tiny segment of Christendom in her faraway island home seems to her simple, and humble indeed when she compares it to the antiquity and immensity of the Catholic Church. It is the oneness of faith binding nations and peoples together—dissimilar in almost everything else—that is her subject matter in this poem. But a poem, if it deals in such assertions at all, is not made up of them. As a poet Miss Duggan has caught a new vision of this old truth and embodied her vision in fresh imagery and rhythm that enable us to share her vision.

The new image in which she captures this old theme of the universality of the Church is that of bells from steeples all over the world on an Easter pilgrimage to the sepulchre of Christ. We have all been struck by the sound of bells flinging their very distinctive voices far out over a city or country landscape from some church spire. If the belfry was an open one, we may have been fascinated by the bells tossing on their bows as if they were about to detach themselves and float off in pursuit of their clangorous voices, blown on the winds. It may have been such an experience that suggested to Miss Duggan the fundamental image of her poem. For her the bells do take off "unlimbered from their spires / In every steeple-loft from pole to pole." From the four winds they blow into the Jaffa Gate of Jerusalem to join their diverse voices in one hosanna at the tomb of the Risen Savior.

    All float untethered over Jaffa Gate
    To fling one peal when angels cheat the
       stone.

This is certainly a fresh image in which to capture the diversity of nationality yet unity of faith that together constitute the universality of the Church. This unity amidst diversity is emphasized and reiterated poetically in lines 1–4 and 18–19.

But the body of the poem is given over to a procession of images, framed in a shifting rhythm, that by sound and association evoke the bells from "every steeple-loft from pole to pole" and almost make us hear the carillons in the winds. The procession starts with the bells from the Americas "at eagle height." The eagle association is just right to suggest the self-confidence and sense of power that we associate with the Americas as countries and with American Christianity. Besides the fact that the eagle is a symbol of the United States and Mexico, its strong bold flight into the face of the sun suggests the bold, self-assured activities of the two brash American continents. The high pitch of the line is perfectly suited to the high flight it suggests. As a matter of fact, this poem was chosen for analysis here because, in a small compass, it so well illustrates the shift of rhythm to suit a shifting subject matter.

In contrast to the line on the Americas marching along in an unbroken rhythm, without caesuras, and as clipped in its short vowels and sharp consonants as the go-getting Americans themselves, is the next line which enshrines the Himalayan chimes in a movement as dreamy and contemplative as an Indian mystic. These two lines are scanned exactly alike, but in sound and movement they are as different as day and night. To achieve the slow tempo appropriate to the associations that cling to a picture of an oriental monastery in the Himalayas, the poet has dropped the pitch slightly from the high level of the previous line and has employed much more long-voweled words such as "*pu*re," "*a*bstracted," "Hima*la*yan," and words with more plosive ("*p*ure,") and fricative ("*ch*imes") consonants which take longer to pronounce and which slow down the movement of the line to a dreamy, contemplative pace. The strong thought pause after "pure" works to the same effect.

Next to join the pilgrimage are the bells from Russia, and both the imagery and the rhythm of the line in which they appear do much to evoke whole epochs of Russian culture and history. "Fries" is enough to summon up a picture of those fantastic Russian churches with their dozens of strawberry shaped domes and belfries that are familiar to us from pictures of St. Basil's in the Kremlin. But the Russian contingent on this pilgrimage of bells are only "ghosts of clappers" because their tongues have been silenced by the Communist regime. Something of the roughness and harshness of the whole Russian character has crept into the very sound of this line with its opening double accent (spondee) and its harsh grating consonants ("Gréat ghósts/ of cláppers").

In utter contrast to these harsh clappers of Russia are the "sweet, wind-sextoned tremblers from Cathay." This pilgrimage is becoming far more motley than that which Chaucer sent on its way to a tomb in Canterbury. The variety that goes into the unity of faith is being beautifully imaged for us line by line by the poet. There is something quintessentially Oriental about the sweet tinkling sound of little brass bells or glass tremblers blown (sextoned) by the wind in an open-walled Chinese temple. It has all the charm and delicacy about it of one of the most ancient cultures of the Orient. And some of that sweetness and delicacy the poet embodies within the thin-vowelled, sharp-consonanted, high-pitched, and slow movement of the verse. We can almost catch the tinkle in the repeated "t's" of the "sweeт, wind-sexтoned тremblers."

Bells from the newest and the oldest of worlds, from the West and the East, are in this clangorous pilgrimage; and now they are joined (lines 9–17) by pilgrim bells from Europe— what for centuries was the very heart of Christendom. Most distant from Jaffa Gate in space but most loyal to the faith are the jesting bells of Ireland. It is only half of the Irish character that the poet has caught here but a real half. The other half is the haunting sadness that lurks in even the most joyous Irish songs.

But Miss Duggan has probably chosen this jesting trait of the Irish, caught in the very bouncing movement of the line, to serve as a contrast with the dignity and reserve of the English bells of the next line "slowbosomed as a swan." It would be hard to think of an image that better evokes the poise, reserve, and dignity of the English than the graceful, "slowbosomed," movement of the swan. The spondee on "slów-bósomed" and the long-vowelled quality of that word as opposed to "jesting" also create a pace suitable to the unboisterous character of the Englishman.

Then from the Seine come the bells of Notre Dame. Theirs is a stately sound with all the queenly dignity of France, the eldest daughter of the Church, but weary from all the wars and revolutions that have surged about the walls of Notre Dame. Both the dignity and the weariness breathe through the slow moving line embroidered with nasals.

The queéNly, weary diN of NoTre Daḿe.

In the wake of the bells of Paris come those of the Low Countries "ringing back the sea." They echo the struggle of the Low Countries to fight back the sea from behind their dikes.

And the bells of Spain, like everything else Spanish, are a strange mixture of the Christian and the Moorish. No other Western country lived so long nor so intimately with this Eastern culture as did Spain. As a result the Moors left their mark on the Spanish character, features, thought, and art; and colored even Spanish religion. That subtle admixture Miss Duggan suggests in her happy phrase, "the Moore still moaning through the saint." There is something of a moan in the phrase itself, as if the Christian bells on pilgrimage to Christ's sepulchre were voicing their faith in the strange, Oriental, moaning tone of a muezzin from the tower of a Moorish mosque. And this is not so far-fetched because the bells of Seville Cathedral, for instance, are actually hung in the beautiful tower of an ancient mosque.

From the frosty North come the bells of Germany voicing some of the fiery nature of the German people that has made them from the beginning a warlike folk. The fricative "f's" and the short vowels in "frosty, fiery" give the line a harsh but quick, energetic movement that contrasts markedly with the nasal moan of the Moor in the previous line.

Then, in the place of climax, and given

two whole lines in which to revel, come the bells of Rome. When you have stood in the piazza of St. Peter's at a canonization ceremony and heard the mighty bells booming from the great open belfry and then heard them joined by the hundreds of bells from all over Rome, you are sure of the propriety of Miss Duggan's image for the bells of the Eternal City. They do sound like a confused and excited pack of hounds on the leash—"the heavy, joyful pack of thunder-jowls / That tongue hosannas from the leash of Rome." There is a weight and force to these lines, created by the long vowels and plosive and fricative consonants, that give appropriate voice to the thunderous chorus of the Roman bells.

All these clamorous pilgrim bells, from far and near, from East and West, and North and South, and everyone with a different voice—

> All float untethered over Jaffa Gate
> To fling one peal when angels cheat the stone.

Understandably, in this ancient and august company, the poor "little gaping country bell" blown from its clapboard steeple in New Zealand is awed into silence. It wheels along in the rear of the procession, and the poet has deliberately pushed it off into the last lines of her poem. But simple and dumb in the midst of all the splendor and varied clamor of Christendom, its heart is a riot of mixed emotions that it is too awed to express. But its very presence amidst the vocal and demonstrative bells all about it is a profession of faith in and a song of praise to the Risen Savior. It too adds to the variety that is harmonized in the unity of faith.

Miss Duggan has not told us anything new in this poem (that is not the concern of poets); and, unless we are of her faith, we may not even feel that what she says is true; but she has handled her theme with a concreteness, a freshness, and in a rhythm that give it new meaning and interest.

INDEX OF AUTHORS, TITLES, TOPICS, AND FIRST LINES

ON THE INDEX

The dates of the author's lives appear in parentheses following the names of the authors. Entries in CAPITAL LETTERS are introductory sections by the editors. *Italic numbers* refer to an analysis or discussion of the work, and *italic lines* refer to titles of selections.

A bird came down the walk, 710
"A cold coming we had of it, 693
A hot midsummer night on Water Street, 698
A narrow Fellow in the Grass, 711
A noiseless patient spider, 710
A poem should be palpable and mute, 632
A sallow waiter brings me huge oysters . . ., 698
A snake came to my water-trough, 712
About Money, 685
Addison, Joseph (1672–1719), 409
After Apple-Picking, 676
After the first powerful, plain manifesto, 709
After You, My Dear Alphonse, 65
Agreed—that God created just so many stones, 699
Ah, Are You Digging on My Grave?, 454
"Ah, are you digging on my grave?, 454
Albee, Edward (1928–), 360
All day our eyes could find no resting place, 624
American Dream, The, 360
An ant on the tablecloth, 419
And It's a Lonely, Personal Art, 8
Animal Stories, 384
Anthem for Doomed Youth, 658
ANXIETY, 682
April this year, not otherwise, 615
Arms and the Boy, 658
Arnold, Matthew (1822–1888), 645, 682
Ars Poetica, 632
As a dare-gale skylark scanted in a dull cage, 591
As I was walking all alane, 490
As if it were forever that they move, that we keep moving—, 697
As virtuous men pass mildly away, 665
At Mrs. Farrelly's, 99
At the Heart of the Story Is Man, 6
At the Round Earth's Imagined Corners, 588, 758
At the round earth's imagined corners, blow, 588
At the San Francisco Airport, 697
At the Slackening of the Tide, 687
Auden, W. H. (1907–), 456, 457, 633
Auto Wreck, 679

Babylon Revisited, 37
Back bent; hands gripped; breath coming heavily, 714
BALLAD, ON THE, 485
Baroque Fountain in the Villa Sciarra, A, 692
Batter My Heart, 587
Batter my heart, three-personed God; for You, 587

Bear, The, 89
Beaumont, Francis (1584–1616), 675
Because I Could Not Stop for Death, 677
Because I could not stop for Death—, 677
Bells for John Whiteside's Daughter, 622
Berry, Wendell (1934–), 624
Betjeman, John (1906–), 458
Between Absurdity and the Playwright, 228
BEYOND CATEGORIES, 153
Birches, 689
Bird Came Down the Walk, A, 710
Black Rook in Rainy Weather, 650
Bly, Robert, 653
Bone Thoughts on a Dry Day, 652
Boom! Sees Boom in Religion, Too, 462
Bradbury, Ray (1920—), 154
Breakfast, 97
Bredvold, Louis I. (1888—), 219
Bringing Mother Home, 626
Brooke, Rupert (1887–1915), 692
Brooklyn Bridge at Dawn, 716
Browning, Elizabeth Barrett (1806–1861), 668
Browning, Robert (1812–1889), 645, 675, 726
Buchwald, Art, (1925—), 402
Burns, Robert (1759–1796), 635, 667
B'york! but it's lovely under the leaf, 653
Byron, Lord (George Gordon) (1788–1824), 655

Caged Skylark, The, 591
Campbell, Roy (1902–1957), 711
Cargoes, 715
Carrion Comfort, 683
Carroll, Joseph (1911—), 99
Cather, Willa (1873–1947), 20
Cells Breathe in the Emptiness, 654
Channel Firing, 656
Character of Atticus—Joseph Addison (from *The Epistle to Dr. Arbuthnot*), 437
Character of Sporus—Lord Hervey (from *The Epistle to Dr. Arbuthnot*), 438
Chaucer, Geoffrey (1340?–1400), 420, 428
Chekhov, Anton (1860–1904), 113
Cherry-Tree Carol, The, 499
Chicago, 716
Ciardi, John (1916—), 473
Clare, John (1793–1864), 418
Clay, 116
Committee, 700
COMPLEXITY OF LIFE, THE, 65

Composed upon Westminster Bridge, 588
Confession Overheard in a Subway, 461
Corrina's Going A-Maying, 594
COURAGE, 48
"Courage!" he said, and pointed toward the land, 640
Crossing the Bar, 676
Cullen, Countee (1903–1946), 686
cummings, e. e. (1894–1962), 649, 661, 662, 670
Cyclist, The, 714

Darkling Thrush, The, 644
Davis, Robert Gorham (1908—), 6
Day I Schooled Myself in Stone, The, 699
Dead Boy, 622
Dead, The, 184, 741
DEATH, 674
Death, 676
Death, be not proud, though some have called thee, 675
Death of a Salesman, 274
Death of the Ball Turret Gunner, The, 659
Death of the Hired Man, The, 727
Defense Rests, 673
de la Mare, Walter (1873–1956), 708
Departmental, 419
DEPRIVED, THE, 112
Destruction of Sennacherib, The, 655
Destructors, The, 72
Dickey, James (1923—), 680, 701
Dickinson, Emily (1830–1886), 417, 677, 678, 709, 710, 711
Dirge, 623
Dive, The, 714
Donne, John (1572–1631), 587, 588, 665, 666, 677, 758
Dostoevsky, Fyodor (1821–1881), 17, 174, 737
Down by the Salley Garden, 670
Down by the salley garden my love and I did meet, 670
Dover Beach, 682
DRAMA, ON, 209
DRAMATIC POETRY, ON, 721
Dream of a Ridiculous Man, The, 174
Dryden, John (1631–1700), 595
Duggan, Eileen (No date given, MA in 1918), 760
Dürer would have seen a reason for living in a town like this, with eight stranded whales, 691
Dust of Snow, 651

Eagle, The, 710
Earth has not anything to show more fair, 588
Eberhart, Richard (1904—), 660
Edward, 491
1887, 657
ELEGY, ON THE, 609
Elegy, 624
Elegy for Jane: My Student Thrown by a Horse, 624
Eliot, T. S. (1888–1965), 684, 693, 731
End of the World, The, 593

Etter, David (1928—), 663
Expense of Spirit in a Waste of Shame, Th' (Sonnet No. 129), 587
Express, The, 709
Eye, The, 651

Fair daffodils, we weep to see, 635
Farren, Robert (1909—), 714
Farthest from any war, unique in time, 717
Faulkner, William (1897–1962), 89
Fear death?—to feel the fog in my throat, 675
Fearing, Kenneth (1902—), 458, 459, 623
Felix Randal, 621
Felix the farrier, O he is dead then? my duty all ended, 621
Fern Hill, 648
FICTION, ON, 3
Finkel, Donald (1929—), 653
Fish (fly-replete, in depth of June), 692
Fitzgerald, F. Scott (1896–1940), 37
Five years have past, five summers, with the length, 637
Fog, 705
For the First Manned Moon Orbit, 701
From Clee to heaven the beacon burns, 657
From harmony, from heavenly harmony, 595
From *Howl, Part I,* 606
From my mother's sleep I fell into the State, 659
From *The Canterbury Tales;* Portrait of the Prioress, Portrait of the Monk, Portrait of the Friar, Portrait of the Clerk, Portrait of the Parson, Portrait of the Pardoner, The Nun's Priest's Tale, 420–437
Frost, Robert (1874–1963), 419, 473, 566, 593, 651, 676, 689, 727
Full Many a Glorious Morning Have I Seen (Sonnet No. 33), 586
Full many a glorious morning have I seen, 586
Fury of Aerial Bombardment, The, 660

Gaines, Ernest J. (1933—), 130
Garden Party, The, 105
Get up! get up for shame! the blooming morn, 594
Get Up and Bar the Door, 498
Ginsberg, Allen (1926—), 606, 695
Glass Menagerie, The, 238
Glass of Beer, A, 461
Glory be to God for dappled things, 581
God's Grandeur, 646
Good Man Is Hard to Find, A, 80
Gordon, Caroline (1895—), 157
Greene, Graham (1904—), 72
Guarded within the old red wall's embrace, 708
Guiterman, Arthur (1871–1943), 418

H. D. (1886–1961), 706, 707
"Had he and I but met, 656
Haircut, 461
Harbor, The, 706
Hardy, Thomas (1840–1928), 454, 644, 656
Having finished the Blue-plate Special, 456

Index of Authors, Titles, Topics, and First Lines   769

Hazo, Samuel (1928—), 699
He clasps the crag with crooked hands, 710
He disappeared in the dead of winter, 633
He was found by the Bureau of Statistics to be, 457
Heat, 706
Heaven, 692
Heavy Bear That Goes with Me, The, 686
Hell Gate, 455
Hemingway, Ernest (1899–1961), 53
Herbert, George (1593–1633), 634, 666
Here at the Vespasian-Carlton, it's just one, 462
Herrick, Robert (1591–1674), 594, 635
High Flight, 715
His Grace! impossible! what dead!, 454
Hog Butcher for the World, 716
Hollywood, 717
Home-Thoughts, from Abroad, 645
Hometown Hero Comes Home, The, 663
Hopkins, Gerard Manley (1844–1889), 580, 590, 591, 592, 598, 621, 631, 646, 657, 683
Hot Night on Water Street, 698
Housman, A. E., (1859–1936), 455, 643, 644, 657
How Beautiful with Shoes, 119
How Do I Love Thee?, 668
How do I love thee? Let me count the ways, 668
How to keep—is there any any, is there none such, nowhere known, some, bow or brooch or braid or brace, lace latch or catch or key to keep, 598
Howl, Part I, from, 606
HUMOR AND SATIRE, ON, 381
Hurrahing in Harvest, 591

I caught this morning morning's minion, 592
I have heard that hysterical women say, 688
I Heard a Fly Buzz When I Died, 678
I heard a Fly buzz—when I died—, 678
I Knew a Woman Lovely in Her Bones, 672
I knew a woman, lovely in her bones, 672
I leant upon a coppice gate, 644
I like see it lap the Miles—, 709
I met a traveler from an antique land, 589
I must go down to the seas again, to the lonely sea and the sky, 647
I remember the neckcurls, limp and damp as tendrils, 624
I saw the best minds of my generation destroyed by madness, starving hysterical naked, 606
I Swore to Stab the Sonnet with My Pen, 586
I swore to stab the sonnet with my pen, 586
I thought (and before it was too late, 685
I, too, dislike it: there are things that are important beyond all this fiddle, 631
I Wake and Feel the Fell of Dark, Not Day, 683
I wake and feel the fell of dark, not day, 683
I Wandered Lonely as a Cloud, 637
I wandered lonely as a cloud, 637
I want a love to hold in my hand because love is too much for the heart to bear alone, 673
I went to Louisiana to get my mother (that's where she was at), 626
I will teach you my townspeople, 679

if everything happens that can't be done, 670
if everything happens that can't be done, 670
If from the public way you turn your steps, 567
Ignatow, David (1914—), 685
IMPRESSIONISTIC AND DESCRIPTIVE POETRY, ON, 705
Incident, 686
In Harmony with Nature, 645
"In harmony with Nature?" Restless fool, 645
In Memory of W. B. Yeats, 633
In Schrafft's, 456
In Westminster Abbey, 458
It fell about the Martinmas time, 498
It is myself, not the poor beast lying there yelping with pain, 690
It little profits that an idle king, 724
It was not dying: everybody died, 660
Its quick soft silver bell beating, beating, 679
It's time to put fertilizer on the grass again, 673

Jackson, Shirley (1919–1965), 65
Jarrell, Randall (1914—), 559, 660
Jeffers, Robinson (1887–1962), 651
JET AND URBAN SETTING, THE, 694
Jilting of Granny Weatherall, The, 48
John Anderson, My Jo, 667
Joseph was an old man, 499
Journey of the Magi, 693
Joyce, James (1882–1941), 116, 184, 741
Jumblies, The, 415

Kafka, Franz (1883–1924), 153
Keats, John (1795–1821), 590, 596, 636
Killers, The, 53
Kind of An Ode To Duty, 417
Kinnell, Galway (1927—), 654
Knoepfle, John (1923—), 685

Lament, The, 113
Landscape Near an Aerodrome, The, 647
Lapis Lazuli, 688
Lardner, Susan, 404
Lawrence, D. H. (1885–1930), 145, 712
Leaden Echo and the Golden Echo, The, 598
Lear, Edward (1812–1888), 415
LeGallienne, Richard (1866–1947), 716
Let Me Not to the Marriage of True Minds (Sonnet No. 116), 664
Let me not to the marriage of true minds, 664
Let me take this other glove off, 458
Let Sporus tremble—A. What? that thing of silk, 438
Let the boy try along this bayonet-blade, 658
Let them bury your big eyes, 614
Let us go then, you and I, 731
Levertov, Denise (1923—), 697
Leyburn, Ellen Douglas (1907—), 384
Like a strong bow bent forcefully, 714
Lines Composed a Few Miles above Tintern Abbey, 637
Litany, A, 665
Little Trotty Wagtail, 418

Little trotty wagtail, he went in the rain, 418
Logan, John (1923—), 685
Lord Randal, 492
Losses, 660
Lotos Eaters, The, 640
LOVE, 16, 663
Love, 666
Love bade me welcome: yet my soul drew back, 666
Love Calls Me to the Things of This World, 671
Love Is Not All, 670
Love is not all: it is not meat nor drink, 670
Love, It Is Time I Memorized Your Phone, 672
Love, it is time I memorized your phone, 672
Love Song of J. Alfred Prufrock, The, 731
Lovelace, Richard (1618–1658), 655
Loveliest of Trees, 643
Loveliest of trees, the cherry now, 643
Love's Diet, 666
Lowell, Amy (1874–1925), 707, 708
Lucifer in Starlight, 590
Lycidas, 610
LYRIC POETRY, ON, 579

MacLeish, Archibald (1892—), 594, 632
MacNeice, Louis (1907–1963), 696
Magee, John Gillespie, Jr. (1922–1941), 715
Main Deep, The, 706
Majesty of the Law, The, 67
Man He Killed, The, 656
Mansfield, Katherine (1888–1923), 105
Mary sat musing on the lamp-flame at the table, 727
Masefield, John (1878–1967), 647, 715
Memorial to D. C., 614
Men have through all ages sat in council, 700
Meredith, George (1828–1909), 590
Merrit Parkway, 697
Michael, 567
Millay, Edna St. Vincent (1892–1950), 614, 615, 670
Miller, Arthur (1915—), 274
Miller, Vassar (1924—), 673
Milton, John (1608–1674), 588, 610
Modern Temper and Tragic Drama, The, 219
Modest Proposal, A, 410
Moore, Marianne (1887—), 631, 691
More beautiful and soft than any moth, 647
Morning Sun, 696
Mr. Flood's Party, 730
Much have I traveled in the realms of gold, 590
My heart aches, and a drowsy numbness pains, 596
My Last Duchess, 726
My long two-pointed ladder's sticking through a tree, 676
My Love Is Like to Ice, 664
My love is like to ice and I to fire, 664
My Mistress' Eyes Are Nothing Like the Sun (Sonnet No. 130), 664
My mistress' eyes are nothing like the sun, 664
My War with the Ospreys, 393
Myers, Henry Alonzo (1906–1955), 212

NARRATIVE POETRY, ON, 565
Nash, Ogden (1902—), 417
NATURE, 634
Nature of Poetry, The, 467
Neighbour Rosicky, 20
Nemerov, Howard (1920—), 462
next to of course america i, 662
"next to of course america i, 662
New York, C'Est Formidable!, 402
Night Clouds, 707
Noiseless Patient Spider, A, 710
North on one-eleven, 685
Not, I'll not, carrion comfort, Despair, not feast on thee, 685
Notes on the Art of Poetry, 479
Notes from a Suburban Heart, 673
Nothing is so beautiful as spring—, 590
Now are the bells unlimbered from their spires, 760
Now as I was young and easy under the apple boughs, 648
Nuns Fret Not at Their Convent's Narrow Room, 585
Nuns fret not at their convent's narrow room, 585
Nun's Priest's Tale, The, 428

O Duty, 417
O, My luve is like a red, red rose, 667
O, that this too too solid flesh would melt, 722
"O where ha you been, Lord Randal, my son?, 492
O wild West Wind, thou breath of Autumn's being, 600
O wind, rend upon the heat, 707
O wonderful nonsense of lotions of Lucky Tiger, 461
O'Connor, Flannery (1925–1964), 80
O'Connor, Frank (1903—), 8, 67
ODE, ON THE, 593
Ode to the Nightingale, 596
Ode to the West Wind, 600
Oh! I have slipped the surly bonds of Earth, 715
Oh, to be in England, 645
Old Age Compensation, 681
Old Eben Flood, climbing alone one night, 730
Old Manuscript, An, 153
Old Red, 157
Oliver, William I. (1926—), 229
On a Girdle, 667
On a starred night Prince Lucifer uprose, 590
On First Looking Into Chapman's Homer, 590
On the stiff twig up there, 650
On the Tombs in Westminster Abbey, 675
Once more the storm is howling, and half hid, 668
Once riding in old Baltimore, 686
1-2-3 was the number he played but today the number came 3-2-1, 623
Onward led the road again, 455
Oread, 706
OTHER TYPES OF MEDIEVAL NARRATIVE POETRY, ON, 565
Out of the cleansing night of stars and tides, 716
Out of the Cradle Endlessly Rocking, 601
Out of the cradle endlessly rocking, 601

Index of Authors, Titles, Topics, and First Lines   771

'Out, Out—', 566
Owen, Wilfred, (1893–1918), 658
Ozymandias, 589

Passing through huddled and ugly walls, 706
Pastoral, 649
Peace to all such! but were there one whose fires, 437
Pear Tree, 707
Peasant Marey, The, 17, 737
Pericles on 31st Street, 58, 739
Petrakis, Harry Mark (1923—), 58
Pied Beauty, 581
Piercy, Marge, 700
Pilgrimage, 760
Pirandello, Luigi (1867–1936), 330
Platform and a Passion or Two, A, 224
Plath, Sylvia (1932–1963), 650
Poetry, 631
Poor Soul, the Center of My Sinful Earth (Sonnet No. 146), 674, 752
Poor soul, the center of my sinful earth, 674
Pope, Alexander (1688–1744), 437, 438
Porter, Katherine Ann (1890—), 48
Portrait, 458
Portraits from the prologue to the Canterbury Tales, 420
  Portrait of the Clerk, 424
  Portrait of the Friar, 422
  Portrait of the Monk, 421
  Portrait of the Pardoner, 426
  Portrait of the Parson, 425
  Portrait of the Prioress, 420
Prayer for My Daughter, A, 668
Preludes, 684
Prospice, 675
Pulley, The, 634
Pullman Car Hiawatha, 323

QUEST FOR MEANING, THE, 89
QUEST OF MEANING, IN, 687
Quinquireme of Nineveh from Distant Ophir, 715
Quite unexpectedly as Vasserot, 593

Ransom, John Crowe (1888—), 622
Rape of the Lock, The, 438
Ray, David (1932—), 700
Reason for Not Writing Orthodox Nature Poetry, 650
Red, Red Rose, A, 667
Ring out your bells, let mourning shows be spread, 665
Robert Frost: The Way to the Poem, 473
Robin Hood and Little John, 495
Robins, Ted, 714
Robinson, Edwin Arlington (1869–1935), 730
Rocking-Horse Winner, The, 145
Roethke, Theodore (1908–1963), 624, 672
ROMANCE, ON THE, 500
Romeo and Juliet, and A Midsummer Night's Dream: Tragedy and Comedy, 212
Rosenberg, Dorothy, 626

Sailing to Byzantium, 678
SAMPLE ANALYSES OF SHORT STORIES, 737
SAMPLE ANALYSIS OF A SHORT NOVEL, 741
Sandburg, Carl (1878–1967), 705, 706, 716
Sassoon, Siegfried (1886–1967), 698
Satirical Elegy on the Death of a Late Famous General, A, 454
Schwartz, Delmore (1913–1966), 686
Sea-Fever, 647
Season of mists and mellow fruitfulness, 636
season 'tis, my lovely lambs, the, 661
SELECTION OF PLAYS, ON THIS, 238
SELECTION OF POEMS ABOUT POETRY, A, 631
Shakespeare, William (1564–1616), 586, 587, 664, 674, 722, 752, 756
Shapiro, Karl (1913—), 461, 586, 672, 679, 717
She Dwelt among the Untrodden Ways, 668
She dwelt among the untrodden ways, 668
She is as in a field a silken tent, 593
Shelley, Percy Bysshe (1792–1822), 589, 600
SHORT NOVEL, ON THE, 173
SHORT STORY, ON THE, 13
Shuttles of trains going north, going south, drawing threads of blue, 696
Sidney, Sir Philip (1554–1586), 665
Silken Tent, The, 593
Silver, 708
Silver dust, 707
Simpson, Louis (1923—), 698
Since Brass, Nor Stone, Nor Earth, Nor Boundless Sea (Sonnet No. 65), 586, 756
Singletrack Mind, The, 418
Sir Gawain and the Green Knight, 502
Sir Patrick Spens, 494
Sir Roger at Church (*Spectator*, No. 112), 409
Six Characters in Search of an Author, 331
Sky Is Gray, The, 130
Skyscrapers of the financial district dance with Gasman, The, 700
Sled Burial, Dream Ceremony, 680
Slowly, silently, now the moon, 708
Snake, 712
Snake, The, 711
So long, 701
Soldier, The, 657
Soliloquies from Hamlet, 722, 723
Soliloquy from Richard III, 723
SOME NOTES ON POETRY, 743
Song for St. Cecilia's Day, A, 595
Song of a Second April, 615
Song on the Dread of a Chill Spring, 685
SONNET, ON THE, 584
Sonnets, 586, 664, 674
Sounds of Poetry, 746
Spectator Club, The (*Spectator*, No. 2), 406
Spender, Stephen (1909—), 647, 659, 709
Spenser, Edmund (1552–1599), 664
Spring, 590
Spring Song, 653
Stafford, William (1914—), 662
Starbuck, George (1931—), 652

Stauffer, Donald (1902–1952), 467
Steele, Richard (1672–1729), 406
Steele, Wilbur Daniel (1886—), 119
Steeple-Jack, The, 691
Steinbeck, John (1902–1968), 97, 393
Stephens, James (1882–1950), 461, 706
Stopping by Woods on a Snowy Evening, 473
Storm on Fifth Avenue, 698
Strictly Germproof, 418
Summer ends now; now barbarous in beauty, the stooks arise, 591
Sunset and evening star, 676
Supermarket in California, A, 695
Surprised by Evening, 653
Sweet William's Ghost, 493
Swift, Jonathan (1667–1745), 411, 454

Tell me not, sweet, I am unkind, 654
Tennyson, Alfred Lord (1809–1892), 640, 676, 710, 724
Th' expense of spirit in a waste of shame, 587
That is no country for old men. The young, 678
That night your great guns, unawares, 656
That Time of Year Thou Mayst in Me Behold (Sonnet No. 73), 587
That which her slender waist confined, 667
That's my last Duchess painted on the wall, 726
The Antiseptic Baby and the Prophylactic Pup, 418
The Assyrian came down like the wolf on the fold, 655
The Atlantic is a stormy moat; and the Mediterranean, 651
The buzz saw snarled and rattled in the yard, 566
The clear brown eyes, kindly and alert, with 12-20 vision, gave confident regard to the passing world through R. K. Lampert & Company lenses framed in gold, 459
The eyes open to a cry of pulleys, 671
The fine delight that fathers thought; the strong, 631
The fog comes on little cat feet, 705
The guns spell money's ultimate reason, 659
The heavy bear who goes with me, 686
The January sky is deep and calm, 650
The king sits in Dumferling toune, 494
The lanky hank of a she in the inn over there, 461
The little cousin is dead, by foul subtraction, 622
The little sparrows, 649
The long-rolling, 706
The sea is calm tonight, 682
the season 'tis my lovely lambs, 661
The skyscrapers are dancing by the river, 700
The swamp alongside the road, 685
The way a crow, 651
The white mares of the moon rush along the sky, 707
The winter evening settles down, 684
The wonder of cherries, 685
The world is charged with the grandeur of God, 646
The world is too much with us; late and soon, 589

Thee for my recitative, 694
There are no roads but the frost, 681
There came a ghost to Margaret's door, 493
There is unknown dust that is near us, 653
There lived a wife at Usher's Well, 495
There was such speed in her little body, 622
There was twa sisters in a bowr, 491
There Will Come Soft Rains, 154
They went to sea in a sieve, they did, 415
This is the terminal: the light, 697
This train, two Illinois counties late, 663
Thomas, Dylan (1914–1953), 479, 648
Thompson, Francis (1859–1907), 646, 751
To a Dog Injured in the Street, 690
To a Locomotive in Winter, 694
To a Mouse, 635
To a Pet Cobra, 711
To a Snowflake, 646, 751
To Autumn, 636
To Daffodils, 635
To Lucasta, Going to the Wars, 654
To R. B., 631
To what a cumbersome unwieldiness, 666
Today I saw a woman wrapped in rags, 687
Tract, 679
Train, The, 709
Tulip Garden, A, 708
Twa Corbies, The, 490
Twa Sisters, The, 491
Two Butterflies Went Out at Noon, 417
Two butterflies went out at noon, 417

Ultima Ratio Regum, 659
Ulysses, 724
Under the bronze crown, 692
Unknown Citizen, The, 457
Upon the reef that guards the palm-fringed sands, 418

Valediction: Forbidding Mourning, A, 665
Van Duyn, Mona, 673
Visit of Charity, A, 167

Wain, John (1925—), 650
Walden, 398
Walking to the museum, 652
Waller, Edmund (1606–1687), 667
WAR, ON, 654
Watching the Jet Planes Dive, 663
We must go back and find a trail on the ground, 662
Wee, sleekit, cowrin, tim'rous beastie, 635
Welty, Eudora (1909—), 167
What dire offense from am'rous causes, 438
What heart could have thought you?— 646, 751
What passing-bells for these who die as cattle?, 658
What thoughts I have of you tonight, Walt Whitman, for I walked down the sidestreets under the trees with a headache self-conscious looking at the full moon, 695
When God at first made man, 634

When I Consider How My Light Is Spent, 587
When I consider how my light is spent, 587
When I see birches bend to left and right, 689
When Lilacs Last in the Dooryard Bloom'd, 615
When lilacs last in the dooryard bloom'd, 615
When Robin Hood was about twenty years old, 495
when serpents bargain for the right to squirm, 649
when serpents bargain for the right to squirm, 649
When the flowers turn to husks, 654
While the south rains, the north, 680
Whirl up, sea— 706
White, E. B. (1899—), 399
White in the Moon the Long Road Lies, 644
White in the moon the long road lies, 644
Whitman, Walt (1819–1892), 601, 615, 694, 710
Whose woods these are I think you know, 473
"Why dois your brand sae drop wi bluid, Edward, Edward, 489
Wife of Usher's Well, The, 495
Wilbur, Richard (1921—), 671, 692
Wilder, Thornton, (1897—), 224, 322
Williams, Tennessee (1914—), 238

Williams, William Carlos (1883–1963), 649, 679, 690
Windhover, The, 592
Winters, Yvor (1900–1968), 697
With breath indrawn and every nerve alert, 711
Wonderful Time, A, 404
Words of Poetry, 744
Wordsworth, William (1770–1850), 567, 585, 588, 589, 637, 668
World Is Too Much with Us, The, 589
Wright, James (1927—), 681, 687

Yeats, William Butler (1865–1939), 668, 670, 678, 688
Yes. Why do we all, seeing of a soldier, bless him? bless, 657
Yet once more, O ye laurels, and once more, 610
You will ask how I came to be eavesdropping, in the first place, 459
You would think the fury of aerial bombardment, 660